D0939242

Pro VB 2005 and the .NET 2.0 Platform

Second Edition

Andrew Troelsen

Apress®

Pro VB 2005 and the .NET 2.0 Platform

Copyright © 2006 by Andrew Troelsen

ISBN-13 (pbk): 978-1-59059-578-7

ISBN-10 (pbk): 1-59059-578-5

Printed and bound in the United States of America 9 8 7 6 5 4 3 2

Lead Editor: Ewan Buckingham
Technical Reviewer: Don Reamey
Editorial Board: Steve Anglin, Ewan Buckingham, Gary Cornell, Jason Gilmore, Jonathan Gennick, Jonathan Hassell, James Huddleston, Chris Mills, Matthew Moodie, Dominic Shakeshaft, Jim Sumser, Kier Thomas, Matt Wade
Production Director and Project Manager: Grace Wong
Copy Edit Manager: Nicole LeClerc
Senior Copy Editor: Ami Knox
Assistant Production Director: Kari Brooks-Copony
Production Editor: Kelly Winquist
Compositor and Artist: Kinetic Publishing Services, LLC
Proofreaders: April Eddy, Lori Bring, Nancy Sixsmith
Indexer: Broccoli Information Management
Cover Designer: Kurt Krames
Manufacturing Director: Tom Debolski

Distributed to the book trade worldwide by Springer-Verlag New York, Inc., 233 Spring Street, 6th Floor, New York, NY 10013. Phone 1-800-SPRINGER, fax 201-348-4505, e-mail orders-ny@springer-sbm.com, or visit http://www.springeronline.com.

For information on translations, please contact Apress directly at 2560 Ninth Street, Suite 219, Berkeley, CA 94710. Phone 510-549-5930, fax 510-549-5939, e-mail info@apress.com, or visit http://www.apress.com.

The source code for this book is available to readers at http://www.apress.com in the Source Code section. You will need to answer questions pertaining to this book in order to successfully download the code.

To my wife Mandy.
Thank you babes for supporting me in yet another book.
I love you.

Contents at a Glance

PART 1 ■ ■ ■ Introducing Visual Basic 2005 and the .NET Platform

PART 2 ■ ■ ■ Visual Basic 2005 Language Fundamentals

PART 3 ■ ■ ■ Core Object-Oriented Programming Techniques

PART 4 ■ ■ ■ Advanced Object-Oriented Programming Techniques

PART 5 ■■■ Programming with .NET Assemblies

PART 6 ■■■ Exploring the .NET Base Class Libraries

PART 7 ■■■ Web Applications and XML Web Services

Contents

PART 1 ■■■ Introducing Visual Basic 2005 and the .NET Platform

PART 2 ■ ■ ■ Visual Basic 2005 Language Fundamentals

PART 3 ■ ■ ■ Core Object-Oriented Programming Techniques

PART 4 ■■■ Advanced Object-Oriented Programming Techniques

PART 5 ■ ■ ■ Programming with .NET Assemblies

PART 6 ■ ■ ■ Exploring the .NET Base Class Libraries

PART 7 ■■■ Web Applications and XML Web Services

About the Author

ANDREW TROELSEN is a Microsoft MVP (Visual C#) and a partner, trainer, and consultant with Intertech Training (http://www.IntertechTraining.com), a .NET and J2EE developer education center. He is the author of numerous books, including *Developer's Workshop to COM and ATL 3.0* (Wordware Publishing, 2000), *COM and .NET Interoperability* (Apress, 2002), *Visual Basic .NET and the .NET Platform: An Advanced Guide* (Apress, 2001), and the award-winning *Pro C# 2005 and the .NET 2.0 Platform, Third Edition* (Apress, 2006). Andrew has also authored numerous articles on .NET for MSDN online and MacTech (where he explored the platform-independent aspects of the .NET platform), and he is a frequent speaker at various .NET conferences and user groups.

Andrew currently lives in Minneapolis, Minnesota, with his wife, Amanda. He spends his free time waiting for the Wild to win the Stanley Cup, the Vikings to win the Super Bowl (before he retires would be nice), and the Timberwolves to grab numerous NBA championship titles.

About the Technical Reviewer

DON REAMEY is a software development engineer at Microsoft Corporation, where he works in the Office Business Applications division.

Acknowledgments

I have to admit that I love writing books for Apress. Reason? Each and every individual I have worked with is a consummate professional. Thanks to all of you for taking my raw manuscripts and dotting the i's and crossing the t's (especially Grace Wong for having mercy on me, despite too many late submissions). Special thanks to my technical reviewer Don Reamey, who did a wonderful job pouring over the text looking for technical typos (any remaining errors are my responsibility alone). Last but not least, thanks once again to my friends and coworkers at Intertech Training. Everyone but Tom Salonek and Dave Brenner has been wonderful to work with ("Son of a...").

Introduction

The initial release of the .NET platform (circa 2001) caused quite a stir within the Visual Basic programming community. One the one hand, many die-hard VB 6.0 developers were up in arms at the *major* differences between VB 6.0 and Visual Basic .NET. Individuals in this group were a bit stunned to see that VB .NET was not in fact "VB 7.0" (i.e., the same syntax and programming constructs as VB 6.0 with some new features thrown in for good measure), but something altogether different.

The truth of the matter is that VB .NET has little to do with VB 6.0, and might best be regarded as a new language in the BASIC family. This cold hard fact caused some individuals to recoil to such a degree that they coined terms such as "VB .NOT" or "Visual Fred" to express their displeasures. In fact, there are even web sites (http://vb.mvps.org/vfred/Trust.asp) and petitions dedicated to criticizing Microsoft's decision to abandon VB 6.0 in favor of this new creature termed VB .NET.

Beyond the major syntactical changes introduced with VB .NET, several VB 6.0–isms have been deprecated or entirely removed under the .NET platform, which only added to the confusion. As well, the core object models (data access, web and desktop application development) used for application development are entirely different from their COM-based counterparts. To be sure, Microsoft could have done a better job letting developers know up front that VB .NET had very little to do with the much beloved VB 6.0 programming language (to this end, the term "Visual Fred" is not too far off).

On the other end of the spectrum, there were many VB 6.0 developers who were excited by the myriad new language features and openly embraced the necessary learning curve. Members of this group were ready to dive into the details of object-oriented programming (OOP), multithreaded application development, and the wealth of types found within the .NET base class libraries. These individuals quickly realized that in many (if not a majority of) cases, existing VB 6.0 code could remain VB 6.0 code, while new development could take place using the .NET platform and Visual Basic .NET.

Strangely enough, there is also a *third* group of individuals, formed with the release of Visual Basic .NET. Given that VB .NET is indeed a brand new OOP language, many developers who would have never considered learning a BASIC-centric language (typically C++, Java, C# programmers) were now much more open to the idea of exploring a language devoid of semicolons and curly brackets.

With the release of .NET 2.0, the Visual Basic .NET programming language has been officially renamed as Visual Basic 2005—perhaps in an attempt to highlight the fact that the BASIC language used with the .NET platform has nothing to do with the COM-centric VB 6.0. As you would guess, VB 2005 adds even more language features to a developer's tool chest such as operator overloading, custom conversion routines, and generics. For all practical purposes, there really is no difference between VB 2005, C#, or any other .NET programming language. Now more than ever, an individual's language of choice is based on personal preferences rather than the language's overall feature set.

In any case, regardless of which group you identify with, I do welcome you to this book. The overall approach I will be taking is to treat VB 2005 as a unique member of the BASIC family. As you read over the many chapters that follow, you will be exposed to the syntax and semantics of VB 2005, dive into each of the major .NET code libraries (Windows Forms, ASP.NET, ADO.NET, XML web services, etc.), and have a thorough grounding in object-oriented development.

We're a Team, You and I

Technology authors write for a demanding group of people (I should know—I'm one of them). You know that building software solutions using any platform is extremely detailed and is very specific to your department, company, client base, and subject matter. Perhaps you work in the electronic publishing industry, develop systems for the state or local government, or work at NASA or a branch of the military. Speaking for myself, I have developed children's educational software, various n-tier systems, and numerous projects within the medical and legal industries. The chances are almost 100 percent that the code you write at your place of employment has little to do with the code I write at mine (unless we happened to work together previously!).

Therefore, in this book, I have deliberately chosen to avoid creating examples that tie the example code to a specific industry or vein of programming. Given this, I choose to explain VB 2005, OOP, the CLR, and the .NET 2.0 base class libraries using industry-agnostic examples. Rather than having every blessed example fill a grid with data, calculate payroll, or whatnot, I'll stick to subject matter we can all relate to: automobiles (with some geometric structures and employees thrown in for good measure). And that's where you come in.

My job is to explain the VB 2005 programming language and the core aspects of the .NET platform the best I possibly can. To this end, I will do everything I can to equip you with the tools and strategies you need to continue your studies at this book's conclusion.

Your job is to take this information and apply it to your specific programming assignments. I obviously understand that your projects most likely don't revolve around automobiles with pet names, but that's what applied knowledge is all about! Rest assured, once you understand the concepts presented within this text, you will be in a perfect position to build .NET solutions that map to your own unique programming environment.

Who Should Read This Book?

I do not expect that you have any current experience with BASIC-centric languages or the .NET platform (however, if this is the case, all the better). I am assuming that you are either a professional software engineer or a student of computer science. Given this, please know that this book may not be a tight fit for individuals who are brand-spanking new to software development, as we will be exploring many lower-level/advanced topics and will *not* be spending all of our time binding data to grids (at least not until Chapter 24) or spending twenty pages looking at every option of the Visual Studio 2005 menu system.

An Overview of This Book

Pro VB 2005 and the .NET 2.0 Platform, Second Edition is logically divided into seven distinct sections, each of which contains some number of chapters that are focused on a given technology set and/or specific task. To set the stage, here is a part-by-part and chapter-by-chapter breakdown of the book you are holding in your hands.

Part 1: Introducing Visual Basic 2005 and the .NET Platform

The purpose of Part 1 is to acclimate you to the core aspects of the .NET platform, the .NET type system, and various development tools (many of which are open source) used during the construction of .NET applications. Along the way, you will also check out some basic details of the VB 2005 programming language.

Chapter 1: The Philosophy of .NET

This first chapter functions as the backbone for the remainder of the text. We begin by examining the world of traditional Windows development and uncover the shortcomings with the previous state of affairs. The primary goal of this chapter, however, is to acquaint you with a number of .NET-centric building blocks, such as the common language runtime (CLR), Common Type System (CTS), Common Language Specification (CLS), and the base class libraries. Also, you will take an initial look at the VB 2005 programming language and the .NET assembly format, and you'll examine the platform-independent nature of the .NET platform and the role of the Common Language Infrastructure (CLI).

Chapter 2: Building Visual Basic 2005 Applications

The goal of this chapter is to introduce you to the process of compiling and debugging VB 2005 source code files using various tools and techniques. First, you will learn how to make use of the command-line compiler (vbc.exe) and VB 2005 response files. Over the remainder of the chapter, you will examine numerous IDEs, including TextPad, SharpDevelop, Visual Basic 2005 Express, and (of course) Visual Studio 2005. As well, you will be exposed to a number of open source tools (NAnt, NDoc, etc.) that any .NET developer should have in their back pocket.

Part 2: Visual Basic 2005 Language Fundamentals

This part explores the core aspects of the VB 2005 programming language such as intrinsic data types, decision and iteration constructs, constructing (and overloading) methods, as well as manipulating arrays, strings, enumerations, and modules. Don't worry; this section is not as dry as you may fear, given that you will be exposed to numerous types of the .NET base class libraries along the way.

Chapter 3: VB 2005 Programming Constructs, Part I

This chapter begins by examining the role of the VB 2005 `Module` type and the related topic of an executable's entry point—the `Main()` method. You will also come to understand the intrinsic data types of VB 2005 (and their CLR equivalents), implicit and explicit casting operations, iteration and decision constructs, and the construction of valid code statements.

Chapter 4: VB 2005 Programming Constructs, Part II

Here you will complete your examination of basic coding constructs. The major thrust of this chapter is to dive into the details of building subroutines and functions using the syntax of VB 2005. Along the way you will get to know the roles of the `ByVal`, `ByRef`, and `ParamArray` keywords and understand the topic of method overloading. This chapter also examines how to build and manipulate strings, arrays, enums, and structures and the underlying classes that lurk in the background (`System.String`, `System.Array`, `System.Enum`, and `System.ValueType`).

Part 3: Core Object-Oriented Programming Techniques

This part explores how VB 2005 supports the core principals of object-oriented programming, namely encapsulation, inheritance, and polymorphism. In addition, this section explores the role of structured exception handling and a detailed look at the .NET garbage collection process.

Chapter 5: Defining Encapsulated Class Types

This chapter will dive into all the details of encapsulation services. Not only will you learn the basics of class construction (constructors, shared members, and property syntax), but you will also investigate several new constructs brought about with .NET 2.0. For example, you will learn about the role of the Partial keyword and the new XML code documentation syntax.

Chapter 6: Understanding Inheritance and Polymorphism

The role of Chapter 6 is to examine the details of how VB 2005 2.0 accounts for the remaining "pillars" of OOP: inheritance and polymorphism. Here you will learn how to build families of related classes using inheritance, virtual methods, abstract methods (and classes!), as well various casting operations. This chapter will also explain the role of the ultimate base class in the .NET libraries: System.Object.

Chapter 7: Understanding Structured Exception Handling

The point of this chapter is to discuss how to handle runtime anomalies in your code base through the use of structured exception handling. Not only will you learn about the VB 2005 keywords that allow you to handle such problems (Try, Catch, Throw, and Finally), but you will also come to understand the distinction between application-level and system-level exceptions. In addition, this chapter examines various tools within Visual Studio 2005 that allow you to debug the exceptions that have escaped your view.

Chapter 8: Understanding Object Lifetime

This chapter examines how the CLR manages memory using the .NET garbage collector. Here you will come to understand the role of application roots, object generations, and the System.GC type. Once you understand the basics, the remainder of this chapter covers the topics of building "disposable objects" (via the IDisposable interface) and how to interact with the finalization process (via the System.Object.Finalize() method).

Part 4: Advanced Object-Oriented Programming Techniques

This section furthers your understanding of OOP using VB 2005. Here you will learn the role of interface types, delegates, and events, and several advanced topics such as operator overloading and custom type conversions. As well, this section dives into the details of a major CTS enhancement brought about with .NET 2.0–generics.

Chapter 9: Working with Interfaces and Collections

The material in this chapter builds upon your understanding of object-based development by covering the topic of interface-based programming. Here you will learn how to define types that support multiple behaviors, how to discover these behaviors at runtime, and how to selectively hide particular behaviors from an object level. To showcase the usefulness of interface types, the remainder of this chapter examines the System.Collections namespace.

Chapter 10: Callback Interfaces, Delegates, and Events

The purpose of Chapter 10 is to demystify the delegate type. Simply put, a .NET *delegate* is an object that "points" to other methods in your application. Using this pattern, you are able to build systems that allow multiple objects to engage in a two-way conversation. After you have examined the use of .NET delegates, you will then be introduced to the VB 2005 Event, RaiseEvent, Handles, and Custom keywords, which are used to simplify the manipulation of programming with delegates in the raw.

Chapter 11: Advanced VB 2005 Programming Constructs

This chapter deepens your understanding of the VB 2005 programming language by introducing a number of advanced programming techniques. We begin with a detailed examination of *value types* and *reference types*. Next, you will learn how to overload operators and create custom conversion routines (both implicit and explicit). We wrap up by contrasting the use of CType(), DirectCast(), and TryCast() for explicit casting operations.

Chapter 12: Understanding Generics and Nullable Data Types

As of .NET 2.0, the VB 2005 programming language has been enhanced to support a new feature of the CTS termed *generics*. As you will see, generic programming greatly enhances application performance and type safety. Not only will you explore various generic types within the System.Collections.Generic namespace, but you will also learn how to build your own generic methods and types (with and without constraints).

Part 5: Programming with .NET Assemblies

Part 5 dives into the details of the .NET assembly format. Not only will you learn how to deploy and configure .NET code libraries, you will understand the internal composition of a .NET binary image. This section of the text also explains the role of .NET attributes and the construction of multithreaded applications as well as accessing legacy COM applications using *interop assemblies*.

Chapter 13: Introducing .NET Assemblies

From a very high level, *assembly* is the term used to describe a managed *.dll or *.exe file. However, the true story of .NET assemblies is far richer than that. Here you will learn the distinction between single-file and multifile assemblies, and how to build and deploy each entity. You'll examine how private and shared assemblies may be configured using XML-based *.config files and publisher policy assemblies. You will also investigate the internal structure of the global assembly cache (GAC) and the role of the .NET Framework 2.0 configuration utility.

Chapter 14: Type Reflection, Late Binding, and Attribute-based Programming

Chapter 14 continues our examination of .NET assemblies by checking out the process of runtime type discovery via the System.Reflection namespace. Using these types, you are able to build applications that can read an assembly's metadata on the fly. You will learn how to dynamically activate and manipulate types at runtime using *late binding*. The final topic of this chapter explores the role of .NET attributes (both standard and custom). To illustrate the usefulness of each of these topics, the chapter concludes with the construction of an extendable Windows Forms application.

Chapter 15: Processes, AppDomains, Contexts, and CLR Hosts

Now that you have a solid understanding of assemblies, this chapter dives much deeper into the composition of a loaded .NET executable. The first goal is to illustrate the relationship between processes, application domains, and contextual boundaries. Once these terms have been qualified, you will then understand exactly how the CLR itself is hosted by the Windows operating system and deepen your understanding of mscoree.dll. The information presented here is a perfect lead-in to Chapter 16.

Chapter 16: Building Multithreaded Applications

This chapter examines how to build multithreaded applications and illustrates a number of techniques you can use to author thread-safe code. The chapter opens by revisiting the .NET delegate type in order to understand a delegate's intrinsic support for asynchronous method invocations. Next, you will investigate the types within the System.Threading namespace. You will look at numerous types (Thread, ThreadStart, etc.) that allow you to easily create additional threads of execution.

Chapter 17: COM and .NET Interoperability

The last chapter in the part will examine a unique type of .NET assembly termed an *interop assembly*. These binary images are used to allow .NET applications to make use of classic COM types. Once you dive into the details of how .NET applications can consume COM servers, you will then learn the functional opposite: COM applications consuming .NET objects. Once you have completed this chapter, you will have a solid understanding of the interoperability layer.

Part 6: Exploring the .NET Base Class Libraries

By this point in the text, you have a very solid handle of the VB 2005 language and the details of the .NET assembly format. Part 6 leverages your newfound knowledge by exploring a number of namespaces within the base class libraries including file I/O, the .NET remoting layer, Windows Forms development, and database access using ADO.NET.

Chapter 18: The System.IO Namespace

As you can gather from its name, the System.IO namespace allows you to interact with a machine's file and directory structure. Over the course of this chapter, you will learn how to programmatically create (and destroy) a directory system as well as move data into and out of various streams (file based, string based, memory based, etc.).

Chapter 19: Understanding Object Serialization

This chapter examines the object serialization services of the .NET platform. Simply put, *serialization* allows you to persist the state of an object (or a set of related objects) into a stream for later use. *Deserialization* (as you might expect) is the process of plucking an object from the stream into memory for consumption by your application. Once you understand the basics, you will then learn how to customize the serialization process via the ISerializable interface and a set of new attributes introduced with .NET 2.0.

Chapter 20: The .NET Remoting Layer

Contrary to popular belief, XML web services are not the only way to build distributed applications under the .NET platform. Here you will learn about the .NET remoting layer. As you will see, the CLR supports the ability to easily pass objects between application and machine boundaries using marshal-by-value (MBV) and marshal-by-reference (MBR) semantics. As well, you will learn how to alter the runtime behavior of a distributed .NET application in a declarative manner using XML configuration files.

Chapter 21: Building a Better Window with System.Windows.Forms

This chapter begins your examination of the System.Windows.Forms namespace. Here you will learn the details of building traditional desktop GUI applications that support menu systems, toolbars, and status bars. As you would hope, various design-time aspects of Visual Studio 2005 will be examined, as well as a number of .NET 2.0 Windows Forms types (MenuStrip, ToolStrip, etc.).

Chapter 22: Rendering Graphical Data with GDI+

This chapter covers how to dynamically render graphical data in the Windows Forms environment. In addition to discussing how to manipulate fonts, colors, geometric images, and image files, this chapter examines hit testing and GUI-based drag-and-drop techniques. You will learn about the new .NET resource format, which as you may suspect by this point in the text is based on XML data representation.

Chapter 23: Programming with Windows Forms Controls

This final Windows-centric chapter will examine numerous GUI widgets that ship with the .NET Framework 2.0. Not only will you learn how to program against various Windows Forms controls, but you will also learn about dialog box development and Form inheritance. As well, this chapter examines how to build *custom* Windows Forms controls that integrate into the IDE.

Chapter 24: Database Access with ADO.NET

ADO.NET is the data access API of the .NET platform. As you will see, you are able to interact with the types of ADO.NET using a connected and disconnected layer. Over the course of this chapter, you will have the chance to work with both modes of ADO.NET, and you'll learn about several new .NET 2.0 ADO.NET topics, including the data provider factory model, connection string builders, and asynchronous database access.

Part 7: Web Applications and XML Web Services

Part 7 is devoted to the construction of ASP.NET web applications and XML web services. As you will see in the first three chapters of this section, ASP.NET 2.0 is a major upgrade from ASP.NET 1.*x* and includes numerous new bells and whistles.

Chapter 25: Building ASP.NET 2.0 Web Pages

This chapter begins your study of web technologies supported under the .NET platform using ASP.NET. As you will see, server-side scripting code is now replaced with "real" object-oriented languages (such as VB 2005, C#, and the like). This chapter will introduce you to key ASP.NET topics such as working with (or without) code-behind files, the ASP.NET 2.0 directory structure, and the role of the web.config file.

Chapter 26: ASP.NET 2.0 Web Controls, Themes, and Master Pages

This chapter will dive into the details of the ASP.NET web controls. Once you understand the basic functionality of these web widgets, you will then build a simple but illustrative web site making use of various .NET 2.0 features (master pages, *.sitemap files, themes, and skins). As well, this chapter will examine the use of the validator controls and the enhanced data binding engine.

Chapter 27: ASP.NET State Management Techniques

This chapter extends your current understanding of ASP.NET by examining various ways to handle state management under .NET. Like classic ASP, ASP.NET allows you to easily create cookies, as well as application-level and session-level variables. Once you have looked at the numerous ways to handle state with ASP.NET, you will then come to learn the role of the System.HttpApplication base class (lurking within the Global.asax file) and how to dynamically alter the runtime behavior of your web application using the Web.config file. We wrap up with an examination of the new ASP.NET 2.0 profile management API.

Chapter 28: Understanding XML Web Services

In this final chapter of this book, you will examine the role of .NET XML web services. Simply put, a *web service* is an assembly that is activated using standard HTTP requests. The beauty of this approach is the fact that HTTP is the one wire protocol almost universal in its acceptance, and it is therefore an excellent choice for building platform- and language-neutral distributed systems. You will also check out numerous surrounding technologies (WSDL, SOAP, and UDDI) that enable a web service and external client to communicate in harmony.

Obtaining This Book's Source Code

All of the code examples contained within this book (minus small code snippets here and there) are available for free and immediate download from the Source Code area of the Apress website. Simply navigate to http://www.apress.com, select the Source Code link, and look up this title by name. Once you are on the "homepage" for *Pro VB 2005 and the .NET 2.0 Platform, Second Edition*, you may download a self-extracting *.zip file. After you unzip the contents, you will find that the code has been logically divided by chapter.

Do be aware that Source Code notes like the following in the chapters are your cue that the example under discussion may be loaded into Visual Studio 2005 for further examination and modification:

■Source Code This is a source code note referring you to a specific directory!

To do so, simply open the *.sln file found in the correct subdirectory.

Obtaining Updates for This Book

As you read through this text, you may find an occasional grammatical or code error (although I sure hope not). If this is the case, my apologies. Being human, I am sure that a glitch or two may be present, despite my best efforts. If this is the case, you can obtain the current errata list from the Apress website (located once again on the "homepage" for this book) as well as information on how to notify me of any errors you might find.

Contacting Me

If you have any questions regarding this book's source code, are in need of clarification for a given example, or simply wish to offer your thoughts regarding the .NET platform, feel free to drop me a line at the following e-mail address (to ensure your messages don't end up in my junk mail folder, please include "VB 2005 SE" in the Subject line somewhere): atroelsen@IntertechTraining.com.

Please understand that I will do my best to get back to you in a timely fashion; however, like yourself, I get busy from time to time. If I don't respond within a week or two, do know I am not trying to be a jerk or don't care to talk to you. I'm just busy (or, if I'm lucky, on vacation somewhere).

So, then! Thanks for buying this text (or at least looking at it in the bookstore while you try to decide if you will buy it). I hope you enjoy reading this book and putting your newfound knowledge to good use.

Take care,
Andrew Troelsen

PART 1

■■■

Introducing Visual Basic 2005 and the .NET Platform

■■■

## CHAPTER 1

The Philosophy of .NET

Every few years or so, the modern-day programmer must be willing to perform a self-inflicted knowledge transplant to stay current with the new technologies of the day. The languages (Visual Basic 6.0, Java, C++) and frameworks (COM, J2EE, CORBA) that were touted as the silver bullets of software development eventually become overshadowed by something better or at the very least something new. Regardless of the frustration you can feel when upgrading your internal knowledge base, it is frankly unavoidable. The .NET 2.0 platform is Microsoft's current offering within the landscape of software engineering.

The point of this chapter is to lay the conceptual groundwork for the remainder of the book. It begins with a high-level discussion of a number of .NET-related topics such as assemblies, the common intermediate language (CIL), and just-in-time (JIT) compilation. In addition to previewing some key features of the Visual Basic 2005 programming language, you will also come to understand the relationship between various aspects of the .NET Framework, such as the common language runtime (CLR), the Common Type System (CTS), and the Common Language Specification (CLS). As you would hope, all of these topics are explored in much more detail throughout the remainder of this text.

This chapter also provides you with an overview of the functionality supplied by the .NET base class libraries, sometimes abbreviated as the "BCL" or alternatively as the "FCL" (being the Framework class libraries). Finally, this chapter investigates the language-agnostic and platform-independent nature of the .NET platform (yes it's true! .NET is not confined to the Windows family of operating systems).

Understanding the Previous State of Affairs

Before examining the specifics of the .NET universe, it's helpful to consider some of the issues that motivated the genesis of Microsoft's current platform. To get in the proper mind-set, let's begin this chapter with a brief and painless history lesson to remember our roots and understand the limitations of the previous state of affairs. After completing this quick tour of life as we knew it, we turn our attention to the numerous benefits provided by Visual Basic 2005 and the .NET platform.

Life As a C/Win32 API Programmer

Traditionally speaking, developing software for the Windows family of operating systems involved using the C programming language in conjunction with the Windows application programming interface (API). While it is true that numerous applications have been successfully created using this time-honored approach, few of us would disagree that building applications using the raw API is a complex undertaking.

The first obvious problem is that C is a very terse language. C developers are forced to contend with manual memory management, ugly pointer arithmetic, and ugly syntactical constructs. Furthermore, given that C is a structured language, it lacks the benefits provided by the object-oriented approach. When you combine the thousands of global functions and data types defined by the Win32 API to an already formidable language, it is little wonder that there are so many buggy applications floating around today.

Life As a C++/MFC Programmer

One vast improvement over raw C/API development is the use of the C++ programming language. In many ways, C++ can be thought of as an object-oriented *layer* on top of C. Thus, even though C++ programmers benefit from the famed "pillars of OOP" (encapsulation, inheritance, and polymorphism), they are still at the mercy of the painful aspects of the C language (e.g., manual memory management, ugly pointer arithmetic, and ugly syntactical constructs).

Despite its complexity, many C++ frameworks exist today. For example, the Microsoft Foundation Classes (MFC) provides the developer with a set of C++ classes that simplifies the construction of Win32 applications. The main role of MFC is to wrap a "sane subset" of the raw Win32 API behind a number of classes and numerous code-generation tools (aka *wizards*). Regardless of the helpful assistance offered by the MFC framework (as well as many other C++-based toolkits), the fact of the matter is that C++ programming remains a difficult and error-prone experience, given its historical roots in C.

Life As a Visual Basic 6.0 Programmer

Due to a heartfelt desire to enjoy a simpler lifestyle, many programmers avoided the world of C(++)-based frameworks altogether in favor of kinder, gentler languages such as Visual Basic 6.0 (VB6). VB6 is popular due to its ability to build sophisticated user interfaces, code libraries (e.g., ActiveX servers), and data access logic with minimal fuss and bother. Much more than MFC, VB6 hides the complexities of the raw Win32 API from view using a number of integrated programming wizards, intrinsic data types, classes, and VB6-specific functions.

The major limitation of VB6 (which has been rectified given the advent of the .NET platform) is that it is not a fully object-oriented language; rather, it is "object aware." For example, VB6 does not allow the programmer to establish "is-a" relationships between types (i.e., no classical inheritance) and has no intrinsic support for parameterized class construction. Moreover, VB6 doesn't provide the ability to build multithreaded applications unless you are willing to drop down to low-level Win32 API calls (which is complex at best and dangerous at worst).

Life As a Java/J2EE Programmer

Enter Java. The Java programming language is (almost) completely object-oriented and has its syntactic roots in C++. As many of you are aware, Java's strengths are far greater than its support for platform independence. Java (as a language) cleans up many unsavory syntactical aspects of C++. Java (as a platform) provides programmers with a large number of predefined "packages" that contain various type definitions. Using these types, Java programmers are able to build "100% Pure Java" applications complete with database connectivity, messaging support, web-enabled front ends, and a rich user interface.

Although Java is a very elegant language, one potential problem is that using Java typically means that you must use Java front-to-back during the development cycle. In effect, Java offers little hope of language integration, as this goes against the grain of Java's primary goal (a single programming language for every need). In reality, however, there are millions of lines of existing code out there in the world that would ideally like to commingle with newer Java code. Sadly, Java makes this task problematic.

Pure Java is simply not appropriate for many graphically or numerically intensive applications (in these cases, you may find Java's execution speed leaves something to be desired). A better approach for such programs would be to use a lower-level language (such as C++) where appropriate. Alas, while Java does provide a limited ability to access non-Java APIs, there is little support for true cross-language integration.

Life As a COM Programmer

The Component Object Model (COM) was Microsoft's previous component framework. COM is an architecture that says in effect, "If you build your classes in accordance with the rules of COM, you end up with a block of *reusable binary code.*"

The beauty of a binary COM server is that it can be accessed in a language-independent manner. Thus, VB6 programmers can build COM classes that can be used by C++ programs. Delphi programmers can use COM classes built using C, and so forth. However, as you may be aware, COM's language independence is somewhat limited. For example, there is no way to derive a new COM class using an existing COM class (as COM has no support for classical inheritance).

Another benefit of COM is its location-transparent nature. Using constructs such as application identifiers (AppIDs), stubs, proxies, and the COM runtime environment, programmers can avoid the need to work with raw sockets, RPC calls, and other low-level details. For example, consider the following VB6 COM client code:

```
' This block of VB6 code can activate a COM class written in
' any COM-aware language, which may be located anywhere
' on the network (including the local machine).
Dim myObj As MyCOMClass
Set myObj = New MyCOMClass     ' Location resolved using AppID.
c.DoSomeWork
```

Although COM can be considered a very successful object model, it is extremely complex under the hood. To help simplify the development of COM binaries, numerous COM-aware frameworks have come into existence (most notably VB6). However, framework support alone is not enough to hide the complexity of COM. Even when you choose a relatively simply COM-aware language such as VB6, you are still forced to contend with fragile registration entries and numerous deployment-related issues (collectively termed *DLL hell*).

Life As a Windows DNA Programmer

To further complicate matters, there is a little thing called the Internet. Over the last several years, Microsoft has been adding more Internet-aware features into its family of operating systems and products. Sadly, building a web application using COM-based Windows Distributed interNet Applications Architecture (DNA) is also quite complex.

Some of this complexity is due to the simple fact that Windows DNA requires the use of numerous technologies and languages (ASP, HTML, XML, JavaScript, VBScript, COM(+), as well as a data access API such as ADO). One problem is that many of these technologies are completely unrelated from a syntactic point of view. For example, JavaScript has a syntax much like C, while VBScript is a subset of VB6. The COM servers that are created to run under the COM+ runtime have an entirely different look and feel from the ASP pages that invoke them. The result is a highly confused mishmash of technologies.

Furthermore, and perhaps more important, each language and/or technology has its own type system (that may look nothing like another's type system). An "int" in JavaScript is not quite the same as an "Integer" in VB6.

The .NET Solution

So much for the brief history lesson. The bottom line is that life as a Windows programmer has been less than perfect. The .NET Framework is a rather radical and brute-force approach to streamlining the application development process. The solution proposed by .NET is "Change everything" (sorry, you can't blame the messenger for the message). As you will see during the remainder of this book, the .NET Framework is a completely new model for building systems on the Windows family of operating systems, as well as on numerous non-Microsoft operating systems such as Mac OS X and various Unix/Linux distributions. To set the stage, here is a quick rundown of some core features provided courtesy of .NET:

- *Full interoperability with existing code*: This is (of course) a good thing. Existing ActiveX components can commingle (i.e., interop) with newer .NET applications and vice versa. Also, Platform Invocation Services (PInvoke) allows you to call C-based libraries (including the underlying API of the operating system) from .NET code.

- *Complete and total language integration*: .NET supports cross-language inheritance, cross-language error handling, and cross-language debugging.

- *A common runtime engine shared by all .NET-aware languages*: One aspect of this engine is a well-defined set of types that each .NET-aware language "understands."

- *A common base class library*: This library provides shelter from the complexities of raw API calls and offers a consistent object model used by all .NET-aware languages.

- *No more COM plumbing*: Legacy COM interfaces (such as IUnknown and IDispatch), COM type libraries, and the COM-centric Variant data type have no place in a native .NET binary.

- *A truly simplified deployment model*: Under .NET, there is no need to register a binary unit into the system registry. Furthermore, .NET allows multiple versions of the same *.dll to exist in harmony on a single machine.

As you can most likely gather from the previous bullet points, the .NET platform has nothing to do with COM (beyond the fact that both frameworks originated from Microsoft). In fact, the only way .NET and COM types can interact with each other is using the interoperability layer (a topic you'll explore in Chapter 17).

Introducing the Building Blocks of the .NET Platform (the CLR, CTS, and CLS)

Now that you know some of the benefits provided by .NET, let's preview three key (and interrelated) entities that make it all possible: the CLR, CTS, and CLS. From a programmer's point of view, .NET can be understood as a new runtime environment and a comprehensive base class library. The runtime layer is properly referred to as the *common language runtime*, or CLR. The primary role of the CLR is to locate, load, and manage .NET types on your behalf. The CLR also takes care of a number of low-level details such as memory management and performing security checks.

Another building block of the .NET platform is the *Common Type System*, or CTS. The CTS specification fully describes the underlying type system and programming constructs supported by the runtime, specifies how these entities can interact with each other, and details how they are represented in the .NET metadata format (more information on metadata later in this chapter).

Understand that a given .NET-aware language might not support each and every feature defined by the CTS. The *Common Language Specification* (CLS) is a related specification that defines a subset of common types and programming constructs that all .NET programming languages can agree on. Thus, if you build .NET types that only expose CLS-compliant features, you can rest assured that all .NET-aware languages can consume them. Conversely, if you make use of a data type or programming construct that is outside of the bounds of the CLS, you cannot guarantee that every .NET programming language can interact with your .NET code library.

The Role of the Base Class Libraries

available to all .Net pgming languages

In addition to the CLR and CTS/CLS specifications, the .NET platform provides a base class library that is available to all .NET programming languages. Not only does this base class library encapsulate various primitives such as threads, file input/output (I/O), graphical rendering, and interaction with various external hardware devices, but it also provides support for a number of services required by most real-world applications.

For example, the base class libraries define types that facilitate database access, XML manipulation, programmatic security, and the construction of web-enabled (as well as traditional desktop and console-based) front ends. From a high level, you can visualize the relationship between the CLR, CTS, CLS, and the base class library, as shown in Figure 1-1.

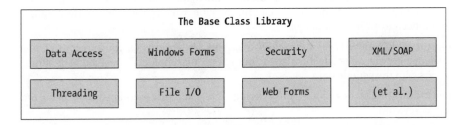

Figure 1-1 content:

```
                    The Base Class Library

  ┌──────────────┐  ┌──────────────┐  ┌──────────────┐  ┌──────────────┐
  │ Data Access  │  │ Windows Forms│  │   Security   │  │   XML/SOAP   │
  └──────────────┘  └──────────────┘  └──────────────┘  └──────────────┘

  ┌──────────────┐  ┌──────────────┐  ┌──────────────┐  ┌──────────────┐
  │  Threading   │  │   File I/O   │  │  Web Forms   │  │   (et al.)   │
  └──────────────┘  └──────────────┘  └──────────────┘  └──────────────┘


                 The Common Language Runtime

  ┌───────────────────────────────────────────────────────────┐
  │ Common Type System                                          │
  │   ┌───────────────────────────────────────────────────┐   │
  │   │ Common Language Specification                       │   │
  │   └───────────────────────────────────────────────────┘   │
  └───────────────────────────────────────────────────────────┘
```

Figure 1-1. *The CLR, CTS, CLS, and base class library relationship*

What Visual Basic 2005 Brings to the Table

Because .NET is such a radical departure from previous Microsoft technologies, it should be clear that legacy COM-based languages such as VB6 are unable to directly integrate with the .NET platform. Given this fact, Microsoft introduced a brand-new programming language, Visual Basic .NET (VB .NET), with the release of .NET 1.0. As developers quickly learned, although VB .NET had a similar look and feel to VB6, it introduced such a large number of new keywords and constructs that many programmers (including myself) eventually regarded VB .NET as a new member of the BASIC family rather than "Visual Basic 7.0."

For example, unlike VB6, VB .NET provided developers with a full-blown object-oriented language that is just about as powerful as languages such as C++, Java, or C#. Using VB .NET, developers are able to build multithreaded desktop applications, websites, and XML web services; define custom class construction subroutines; overload members; and define callback functions (via delegates). In a nutshell, here are some of the core features provided courtesy of VB .NET:

- Full support for classical inheritance and classical polymorphism.

- Strongly typed keywords to define classes, structures, enumerations, delegates, and interfaces. Given these new keywords, VB .NET code is always contained within a `*.vb` file (in contrast to the VB6-centric `*.cls`, `*.bas`, and `*.frm` files).

- Full support for interface-based programming techniques.

- Full support for attribute-based programming. This brand of development allows you to annotate types and their members to further qualify their behavior.

With the release of .NET 2.0, the VB .NET programming language is now properly referred to as *Visual Basic 2005* (VB 2005). While VB 2005 is fully backward-compatible with VB .NET, it adds numerous new additional bells and whistles, most notability the following:

- The ability to redefine how intrinsic operators of the language (such as the + symbol) can be interpreted by your custom classes or structures. Formally speaking, this feature is termed *operator overloading*.

- The introduction of the `My` namespace. The introduction of the `My` namespace, which provides instant access to machine- and project-specific information (which greatly reduces the amount of code you need to author manually).

- The ability to build generic types and generic members. Using generics, you are able to build very efficient and type-safe code that defines numerous "placeholders" specified at the time you interact with the generic item.

- The ability to customize the process of registering, unregistering, or sending events using the new `Custom` keyword.

- Support for signed data types (`SByte`, `ULong`, etc.).

- The ability to define a single type across multiple code files using the `Partial` keyword.

Perhaps the most important point to understand about Visual Basic 2005 is that it can only produce code that can execute within the .NET runtime (therefore, you could never use VB 2005 to build a native ActiveX COM server). Officially speaking, the term used to describe the code targeting the .NET runtime is *managed code*. The binary unit that contains the managed code is termed an *assembly* (more details on assemblies in just a bit). Conversely, code that cannot be directly hosted by the .NET runtime is termed *unmanaged code*.

Additional .NET-Aware Programming Languages

Understand that Visual Basic 2005 is not the only language that can be used to build .NET applications. When the .NET platform was first revealed to the general public during the 2000 Microsoft Professional Developers Conference (PDC), several vendors announced they were busy building .NET-aware versions of their respective compilers.

At the time of this writing, dozens of different languages have undergone .NET enlightenment. In addition to the five languages that ship with Visual Studio 2005 (Visual Basic 2005, C#, J#, Managed Extensions for C++, and JScript .NET), there are .NET compilers for Smalltalk, COBOL, and Pascal (to name a few). Although this book focuses (almost) exclusively on Visual Basic 2005, be aware of the following website (please note that this URL is subject to change):

http://www.dotnetlanguages.net

Here you will find a list of numerous .NET programming languages and related links where you are able to download various compilers (see Figure 1-2).

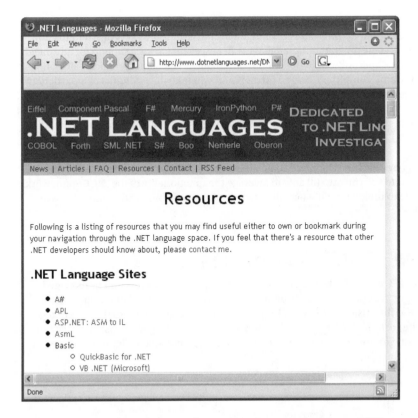

Figure 1-2. *.NET Languages is one of many sites documenting known .NET programming languages.*

While I assume you are primarily interested in building .NET programs using the syntax of VB 2005, I encourage you to visit this site, as you are sure to find many .NET languages worth investigating at your leisure (LISP .NET, anyone?).

Life in a Multilanguage World

As developers first come to understand the language-agnostic nature of .NET, numerous questions arise. The most prevalent of these questions would have to be, "If all .NET languages compile down to 'managed code,' why do we need more than one compiler?" There are a number of ways to answer this question. First, we programmers are a *very* particular lot when it comes to our choice of programming language (myself included). Some prefer languages full of semicolons and curly brackets, with as few keywords as possible (such as C#, C++, and J#). Others enjoy a language that offers more "human-readable" syntax (such as Visual Basic 2005). Still others may want to leverage their mainframe skills while moving to the .NET platform (via COBOL .NET).

Now, be honest. If Microsoft were to build a single "official" .NET language that was derived from the C family of languages, can you really say all programmers would be happy with this choice? Or, if the only "official" .NET language was based on Fortran syntax, imagine all the folks out there who would ignore .NET altogether. Because the .NET runtime couldn't care less which language was used to build an assembly, .NET programmers can stay true to their syntactic preferences, and share the compiled code among teammates, departments, and external organizations (regardless of which .NET language others choose to use).

Another excellent by-product of integrating various .NET languages into a single unified software solution is the simple fact that all programming languages have their own sets of strengths and weaknesses. For example, some programming languages offer excellent intrinsic support for advanced mathematical processing. Others offer superior support for financial calculations, logical calculations, interaction with mainframe computers, and so forth. When you take the strengths of a particular programming language and then incorporate the benefits provided by the .NET platform, everybody wins.

Of course, in reality the chances are quite good that you will spend much of your time building software using your .NET language of choice. However, once you learn the syntax of one .NET language, it is very easy to master another. This is also quite beneficial, especially to the consultants of the world. If your language of choice happens to be Visual Basic 2005, but you are placed at a client site that has committed to C#, you are still able to leverage the functionality of the .NET Framework, and you should be able to understand the overall structure of the code base with minimal fuss and bother. Enough said.

An Overview of .NET Assemblies

Despite the fact that .NET binaries take the same file extension as COM servers and unmanaged Win32 binaries (*.dll or *.exe), they have absolutely no internal similarities. For example, .NET assemblies are not described using COM type libraries and are not registered into the system registry. Perhaps most important, .NET binaries do not contain platform-specific instructions, but rather platform-agnostic *intermediate language* (*IL*) as well as type metadata. Figure 1-3 shows the big picture of the story thus far.

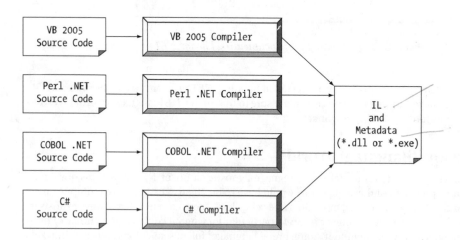

Figure 1-3. *All .NET-aware compilers emit IL instructions and metadata.*

*.net compiler produces intermediate lang. code (IL)
which is not platform specific.*

Note There is one point to be made regarding the abbreviation "IL." During the development of .NET, the official term for IL was Microsoft intermediate language (MSIL). However with the final release of .NET 1.0, the term was changed to common intermediate language (CIL). Thus, as you read the .NET literature, understand that IL, MSIL, and CIL are all describing the same exact entity. In keeping with the current terminology, I will use the abbreviation "CIL" throughout this text.

When a `*.dll` or `*.exe` has been created using a .NET-aware compiler, the resulting module is bundled into an *assembly*. You will examine numerous details of .NET assemblies in Chapter 13. However, to facilitate the discussion of the .NET runtime environment, you do need to understand some basic properties of this new file format.

As mentioned, an assembly contains CIL code, which is conceptually similar to Java bytecode in that it is not compiled to platform-specific instructions until absolutely necessary. Typically, "absolutely necessary" is the point at which a block of CIL instructions (such as a method implementation) is referenced for use by the .NET runtime.

In addition to CIL instructions, assemblies also contain *metadata* that describes in vivid detail the characteristics of every "type" living within the binary. For example, if you have a class named SportsCar, the type metadata describes details such as SportsCar's base class, which interfaces are implemented by SportsCar (if any), as well as a full description of each member supported by the SportsCar type.

.NET metadata is a dramatic improvement to COM type metadata. As you may already know, COM binaries are typically described using an associated type library (which is little more than a binary version of Interface Definition Language [IDL] code). The problems with COM type information are that it is not guaranteed to be present and the fact that IDL code has no way to document the externally referenced servers that are required for the correct operation of the current COM server. In contrast, .NET metadata is always present and is automatically generated by a given .NET-aware compiler.

Finally, in addition to CIL and type metadata, assemblies themselves are also described using metadata, which is officially termed a *manifest*. The manifest contains information about the current version of the assembly, culture information (used for localizing string and image resources), and a list of all externally referenced assemblies that are required for proper execution. You'll examine various tools that can be used to examine an assembly's types, metadata, and manifest information over the course of the next few chapters.

Single-File and Multifile Assemblies

In a great number of cases, there is a simple one-to-one correspondence between a .NET assembly and the binary file (`*.dll` or `*.exe`). Thus, if you are building a .NET `*.dll`, it is safe to consider that the binary and the assembly are one and the same. Likewise, if you are building an executable desktop application, the `*.exe` can simply be referred to as the assembly itself. As you'll see in Chapter 13, however, this is not completely accurate. Technically speaking, if an assembly is composed of a single `*.dll` or `*.exe` module, you have a *single-file assembly*. Single-file assemblies contain all the necessary CIL, metadata, and associated manifest in an autonomous, single, well-defined package.

Multifile assemblies, on the other hand, are composed of numerous .NET binaries, each of which is termed a *module*. When building a multifile assembly, one of these modules (termed the *primary module*) must contain the assembly manifest (and possibly CIL instructions and metadata for various types). The other related modules contain a module level manifest, CIL, and type metadata. As you might suspect, the primary module documents the set of required secondary modules within the assembly manifest.

So, why would you choose to create a multifile assembly? When you partition an assembly into discrete modules, you end up with a more flexible deployment option. For example, if a user is referencing a remote assembly that needs to be downloaded onto his or her machine, the runtime will only download the required modules. Therefore, you are free to construct your assembly in such a way that less frequently required types (such as a type named HardDriveReformatter) are kept in a separate stand-alone module.

In contrast, if all your types were placed in a single-file assembly, the end user may end up downloading a large chunk of data that is not really needed (which is obviously a waste of time). Thus, as you can see, an assembly is really a *logical grouping* of one or more related modules that are intended to be initially deployed and versioned as a single unit.

The Role of the Common Intermediate Language

Now that you have a better feel for .NET assemblies, let's examine the role of the common intermediate language (CIL) in a bit more detail. CIL is a language that sits above any particular platform-specific instruction set. Regardless of which .NET-aware language you choose, the associated compiler emits CIL instructions. For example, the following Visual Basic 2005 code models a trivial calculator. Don't concern yourself with the exact syntax for now, but do notice the format of the Add() function in the Calc class:

```
' Calc.vb
Imports System

Namespace CalculatorExample
  ' Defines the program's entry point
  Module CalcApp
    Sub Main()
      Dim ans As Integer
      Dim c As New Calc()
      ans = c.Add(10, 84)
      Console.WriteLine("10 + 84 is {0}.", ans)
      Console.ReadLine()
    End Sub
  End Module

  ' The VB 2005 calculator.
  Class Calc
    Public Function Add(ByVal x As Integer, ByVal y As Integer) As Integer
      Return x + y
    End Function
  End Class
End Namespace
```

Once the VB 2005 compiler (vbc.exe) compiles this source code file, you end up with a single-file executable assembly that contains a manifest, CIL instructions, and metadata describing each aspect of the Calc and CalcApp classes. For example, if you were to open this assembly using the ildasm.exe utility (examined a little later in this chapter), you would find that the Add() method is represented using CIL such as the following:

```
.method public instance int32 Add(int32 x, int32 y) cil managed
{
  // Code size 9 (0x9)
  .maxstack  2
  .locals init ([0] int32 Add)
  IL_0000:  nop
  IL_0001:  ldarg.1
```

```
IL_0002:  ldarg.2
IL_0003:  add.ovf
IL_0004:  stloc.0
IL_0005:  br.s  IL_0007
IL_0007:  ldloc.0
IL_0008:  ret
}  // end of method Calc::Add
```

Don't worry if you are unable to make heads or tails of the resulting CIL code for this method. In reality, a vast majority of .NET developers could care less about the details of the CIL programming language. Simply understand that the Visual Basic 2005 compiler translates your code statements into terms of CIL.

Now, recall that this is true of all .NET-aware compilers. To illustrate, assume you created this same application using C#, rather than VB 2005 (again, don't sweat the syntax, but do note the similarities in the code bases):

```csharp
// Calc.cs
using System;

namespace CalculatorExample
{
  // Defines the program's entry point.
  public class CalcApp
  {
    static void Main()
    {
      Calc c = new Calc();
      int ans = c.Add(10, 84);
      Console.WriteLine("10 + 84 is {0}.", ans);
      Console.ReadLine();
    }
  }

  // The C# calculator.
  public class Calc
  {
    public int Add(int x, int y)
    { return x + y; }
  }
}
```

If you examine the CIL for the Add() method, you find similar instructions (slightly tweaked by the C# compiler):

```
.method public hidebysig instance int32 Add(int32 x, int32 y) cil managed
{
  // Code size   8 (0x8)
  .maxstack  2
  .locals init ([0] int32 CS$1$0000)
  IL_0000:  ldarg.1
  IL_0001:  ldarg.2
  IL_0002:  add
  IL_0003:  stloc.0
  IL_0004:  br.s        IL_0006
  IL_0006:  ldloc.0
  IL_0007:  ret
}   // end of method Calc::Add
```

Source Code The `Calc.vb` and `Calc.cs` code files are included under the Chapter 1 subdirectory.

Benefits of CIL

At this point, you might be wondering exactly what is gained by compiling source code into CIL rather than directly to a specific instruction set. One benefit is language integration. As you have already seen, each .NET-aware compiler produces nearly identical CIL instructions. Therefore, all languages are resolved to a well-defined binary arena that makes use of the same identical type system.

Furthermore, given that CIL is platform-agnostic, the .NET Framework itself is platform-agnostic, providing the same benefits Java developers have grown accustomed to (i.e., a single code base running on numerous operating systems). In fact, .NET distributions already exist for many non-Windows operating systems (more details at the conclusion of this chapter). In contrast to the J2EE platform, however, .NET allows you to build applications using your language of choice.

Compiling CIL to Platform-Specific Instructions

Due to the fact that assemblies contain CIL instructions, rather than platform-specific instructions, CIL code must be compiled on the fly before use. The entity that compiles CIL code into meaningful CPU instructions is termed a *just-in-time (JIT) compiler*, which sometimes goes by the friendly name of *Jitter.* The .NET runtime environment leverages a JIT compiler for each CPU targeting the runtime, each optimized for the underlying platform.

For example, if you are building a .NET application that is to be deployed to a handheld device (such as a Pocket PC or .NET-enabled cell phone), the corresponding Jitter is well equipped to run within a low-memory environment. On the other hand, if you are deploying your assembly to a back-end server (where memory is seldom an issue), the Jitter will be optimized to function in a high-memory environment. In this way, developers can write a single body of code that can be efficiently JIT-compiled and executed on machines with different architectures.

Furthermore, as a given Jitter compiles CIL instructions into corresponding machine code, it will cache the results in memory in a manner suited to the target operating system. In this way, if a call is made to a method named `PrintDocument()`, the CIL instructions are compiled into platform-specific instructions on the first invocation and retained in memory for later use. Therefore, the next time `PrintDocument()` is called, there is no need to recompile the CIL.

The Role of .NET Type Metadata

In addition to CIL instructions, a .NET assembly contains full, complete, and accurate metadata, which describes each and every type (class, structure, enumeration, and so forth) defined in the binary, as well as the members of each type (properties, methods, events, and so on). Thankfully, it is always the job of the compiler (not the programmer) to emit the latest and greatest type metadata. Because .NET metadata is so wickedly meticulous, assemblies are completely self-describing entities— so much so, in fact, that .NET binaries have no need to be registered into the system registry.

To illustrate the format of .NET type metadata, let's take a look at the metadata that has been generated for the `Add()` method of the `Calc` class you examined previously (the metadata generated for the C# version of the `Add()` method is similar):

```
TypeDef #2 (02000003)
--------------------------------------------------------
  TypDefName: CalculatorExample.Calc  (02000003)
  Flags     : [Public] [AutoLayout] [Class]
  [AnsiClass] [BeforeFieldInit]  (00100001)
  Extends   : 01000001 [TypeRef] System.Object
  Method #1 (06000003)
--------------------------------------------------------
  MethodName: Add (06000003)
  Flags     : [Public] [HideBySig] [ReuseSlot]  (00000086)
  RVA       : 0x00002090
  ImplFlags : [IL] [Managed]  (00000000)
  CallCnvntn: [DEFAULT]
  hasThis
  ReturnType: I4
    2 Arguments
    Argument #1:  I4
    Argument #2:  I4
    2 Parameters
    (1) ParamToken : (08000001) Name : x flags: [none] (00000000)
    (2) ParamToken : (08000002) Name : y flags: [none] (00000000)
```

Despite what you may be thinking, metadata is a very useful entity (rather than an academic detail) consumed by numerous aspects of the .NET runtime environment, as well as by various development tools. For example, the IntelliSense feature provided by Visual Studio 2005 is made possible by reading an assembly's metadata at design time. Metadata is also used by various object-browsing utilities, debugging tools, and the Visual Basic 2005 compiler itself. To be sure, metadata is the backbone of numerous .NET technologies including the remoting layer, reflection services, late binding facilities, XML web services, and the object serialization process. Chapter 14 will formalize the role of .NET metadata.

The Role of the Assembly Manifest

Last but not least, remember that a .NET assembly also contains metadata that describes the assembly itself (technically termed a *manifest*). Among other details, the manifest documents all external assemblies required by the current assembly to function correctly, the assembly's version number, copyright information, and so forth. Like type metadata, it is always the job of the compiler to generate the assembly's manifest. Here are some relevant details of the manifest defined by the VB 2005 calculator example shown earlier:

```
.assembly extern mscorlib
{
  .publickeytoken = (B7 7A 5C 56 19 34 E0 89 )
  .ver 2:0:0:0
}
...
.assembly VbNetCalculator
{
...
  .ver 0:0:0:0
}
.module VbNetCalculator.exe
.imagebase 0x00400000
.subsystem 0x00000003
.file alignment 512
.corflags 0x00000001
```

In a nutshell, this manifest documents the list of external assemblies required by VbNetCalculator.exe (via the .assembly extern directive) as well as various characteristics of the assembly itself (version number, module name, etc.).

Understanding the Common Type System

A given assembly may contain any number of distinct "types." In the world of .NET, "type" is simply a generic term used to refer to a member from the set {class, structure, interface, enumeration, delegate}. When you build solutions using a .NET-aware language, you will most likely interact with each of these types. For example, your assembly may define a single class that implements some number of interfaces. Perhaps one of the interface methods takes an enumeration type as an input parameter and returns a structure to the caller.

Recall that the Common Type System (CTS) is a formal specification that documents how types must be defined in order to be hosted by the CLR. Typically, the only individuals who are deeply concerned with the inner workings of the CTS are those building tools and/or compilers that target the .NET platform. It is important, however, for all .NET programmers to learn about how to work with the five types defined by the CTS in their language of choice. Here is a brief overview.

CTS Class Types

Every .NET-aware language supports, at the very least, the notion of a *class type*, which is the cornerstone of object-oriented programming (OOP). A class may be composed of any number of members (such as properties, methods, and events) and data points (field data, otherwise known as *member variables*). In Visual Basic 2005, classes are declared using the Class keyword:

```
' A class type.
Public Class Calc
  Public Function Add(ByVal x As Integer, ByVal y As Integer) As Integer
    Return x + y
  End Function
End Class
```

If you have a background in VB6 class development, be aware that class types are no longer defined within a *.cls file, given the fact that we now have a specific keyword for defining class types. Chapters 5 and 6 will examine the full details of building class types with Visual Basic 2005.

CTS Structure Types

The concept of a structure is also formalized under the CTS. If you have a background in C or C++, you may recall that *structures* can be thought of as a lightweight alternative to class types, which have value-based semantics (see Chapter 11 for full details). Typically, structures are best suited for modeling geometric and mathematical data and are created in VB 2005 using the Structure keyword:

```
' A structure type.
Structure Point
  Public xPos As Integer
  Public yPos As Integer

  Public Sub New(ByVal x As Integer, ByVal y As Integer)
    xPos = x
    yPos = y
  End Sub
  Public Sub Display()
    Console.WriteLine("({0}, {1}", xPos, yPos)
  End Sub
End Structure
```

CTS Interface Types

Interfaces are nothing more than a named collection of members definitions, which may be supported (i.e., implemented) by a given class or structure. Unlike COM, .NET interfaces do *not* derive a common base interface such as IUnknown. In VB 2005, interface types are defined using the Interface keyword, for example:

```
' Classes or structures which implement this interface
' know how to render themselves.
Public Interface IDraw
  Sub Draw()
End Interface
```

On their own, interfaces are of little use. However, when a class or structure implements a given interface in its unique way, you are able to request access to the supplied functionality using an interface reference in a "polymorphic manner." Interface-based programming will be fully explored in Chapter 9.

CTS Enumeration Types

Enumerations are a handy programming construct that allows you to group name/value pairs. For example, assume you are creating a video game application that allows the player to select one of three character categories (Wizard, Fighter, or Thief). Rather than keeping track of raw numerical values to represent each possibility, you could build a custom enumeration using the VB 2005 Enum keyword:

```
' An enumeration type.
Public Enum CharacterType
  Wizard = 100
  Fighter = 200
  Thief = 300
End Enum
```

The CTS demands that enumerated types derive from a common base class, System.Enum. As you will see in Chapter 4, this base class defines a number of interesting members that allow you to extract, manipulate, and transform the underlying name/value pairs programmatically.

CTS Delegate Types

Delegates are the .NET equivalent of a type-safe C-style function pointer. Again, based on your programming background, you may know that C and C++ programmers make use of function pointers to allow distinct aspects of a program to engage in a two-way conversation. The key difference is that a .NET delegate is a *class* that derives from System.MulticastDelegate, rather than a simple pointer to a raw memory address. In Visual Basic 2005, delegates are declared using the Delegate keyword:

```
' This delegate type can 'point to' any method
' returning an integer and taking two integers as input.
Public Delegate Function BinaryOp(ByVal x As Integer, _
  ByVal y As Integer) As Integer
```

Delegates are useful when you wish to provide a way for one entity to forward a call to another entity, and provide the foundation for the .NET event architecture. As you will see in Chapters 10 and 16, delegates have intrinsic support for multicasting (i.e., forwarding a request to multiple recipients) and asynchronous (i.e., nonblocking) method invocations.

■**Note** VB 2005 provides numerous keywords that remove the need to manually define delegate types. However, you are able to define delegates directly when you wish to build more intricate and powerful solutions.

CTS Type Members

Now that you have previewed each of the types formalized by the CTS, realize that most types take any number of *members*. Formally speaking, a *type member* is constrained by the set {constructor, finalizer, shared constructor, nested type, operator, method, property, indexer, field, read-only field, constant, event}.

The CTS defines various "adornments" that may be associated with a given member. For example, each member has a given visibility trait (e.g., public, private, protected, etc.). Some members may be declared as abstract to enforce a polymorphic behavior on derived types as well as virtual to define a canned (but overridable) implementation. Also, most members may be configured as shared (bound at the class level) or instance (bound at the object level). The construction of type members is examined over the course of the next several chapters.

■**Note** As described in Chapter 12, .NET 2.0 supports the construction of generic types and generic members.

Intrinsic CTS Data Types

The final aspect of the CTS to be aware of for the time being is that it establishes a well-defined set of core data types. Although a given language typically has a unique keyword used to declare an intrinsic CTS data type, all language keywords ultimately resolve to the same type defined in an assembly named mscorlib.dll. Consider Table 1-1, which documents how key CTS data types are expressed in various .NET languages.

■**Note** With the release of .NET 2.0, Visual Basic 2005 now provides keywords for signed data types (SByte, UShort, UInteger, and ULong).

Table 1-1. *The Intrinsic CTS Data Types*

CTS Data Type	VB 2005 Keyword	C# Keyword	Managed Extensions for C++ Keyword
System.Byte	Byte	byte	unsigned char
System.SByte	SByte	sbyte	signed char
System.Int16	Short	short	short
System.Int32	Integer	int	int or long
System.Int64	Long	long	__int64
System.UInt16	UShort	ushort	unsigned short
System.UInt32	UInteger	uint	unsigned int or unsigned long
System.UInt64	ULong	ulong	unsigned __int64
System.Single	Single	float	float
System.Double	Double	double	double
System.Object	Object	object	Object^

CTS Data Type	VB 2005 Keyword	C# Keyword	Managed Extensions for C++ Keyword
System.Char	Char	char	wchar_t
System.String	String	string	String^
System.Decimal	Decimal	decimal	Decimal
System.Boolean	Boolean	bool	bool

Understanding the Common Language Specification

As you are aware, different languages express the same programming constructs in unique, language-specific terms. For example, in VB 2005 you typically denote string concatenation using the ampersand operator (&), while in C# you always make use of the plus sign (+). Even when two distinct languages express the same programmatic idiom (e.g., a method with no return value), the chances are very good that the syntax will appear quite different on the surface:

```
' A VB 2005 subroutine.
Public Sub MyMethod()
  ' Some interesting code...
End Sub

// A C# method returning nothing.
public void MyMethod()
{
  // Some interesting code...
}
```

As you have already seen, these minor syntactic variations are inconsequential in the eyes of the .NET runtime, given that the respective compilers (vbc.exe or csc.exe, in this case) emit a similar set of CIL instructions. However, languages can also differ with regard to their overall level of functionality. For example, a .NET language may or may not have a keyword to represent unsigned data, and may or may not support pointer types. Given these possible variations, it would be ideal to have a baseline to which all .NET-aware languages are expected to conform.

The Common Language Specification (CLS) is a set of rules that describe in vivid detail the minimal and complete set of features a given .NET-aware compiler must support to produce code that can be hosted by the CLR, while at the same time be accessed in a uniform manner by all languages that target the .NET platform. In many ways, the CLS can be viewed as a *subset* of the full functionality defined by the CTS.

The CLS is ultimately a set of rules that compiler builders must conform to, if they intend their products to function seamlessly within the .NET universe. Each rule is assigned a simple name (e.g., "CLS Rule 6") and describes how this rule affects those who build the compilers as well as those who (in some way) interact with them. The crème de la crème of the CLS is the mighty Rule 1:

- *Rule 1*: CLS rules apply only to those parts of a type that are exposed outside the defining assembly.

Given this rule, you can (correctly) infer that the remaining rules of the CLS do not apply to the logic used to build the inner workings of a .NET type. The only aspects of a type that must conform to the CLS are the member definitions themselves (i.e., naming conventions, parameters, and return types). The implementation logic for a member may use any number of non-CLS techniques, as the outside world won't know the difference.

To illustrate, the following Add() method is not CLS-compliant, as the parameters and return values make use of unsigned data (which is not a requirement of the CLS):

```
Public Class Calc
  ' Exposed unsigned data is not CLS compliant!
  Public Function Add(ByVal x As ULong, ByVal y As ULong) As ULong
    Return x + y
  End Function
End Class
```

However, if you were to simply make use of unsigned data internally as follows:

```
Public Class Calc
  Public Function Add(ByVal x As Integer, ByVal y As Integer) As Integer
    ' As this ULong variable is only used internally,
    ' we are still CLS compliant.
    Dim temp As ULong
    ...
    Return x + y
  End Function
End Class
```

you have still conformed to the rules of the CLS, and can rest assured that all .NET languages are able to invoke the Add() method.

Of course, in addition to Rule 1, the CLS defines numerous other rules. For example, the CLS describes how a given language must represent text strings, how enumerations should be represented internally (the base type used for storage), how to define shared members, and so forth. Luckily, you don't have to commit these rules to memory to be a proficient .NET developer. Again, by and large, an intimate understanding of the CTS and CLS specifications is only of interest to tool/compiler builders.

Ensuring CLS Compliance

As you will see over the course of this book, VB 2005 does define a few programming constructs that are *not* CLS-compliant. The good news, however, is that you can instruct the VB 2005 compiler to check your code for CLS compliance using a single .NET attribute:

```
' Tell the compiler to check for CLS compliance.
<Assembly: System.CLSCompliant(True)>
```

Chapter 14 dives into the details of attribute-based programming. Until then, simply understand that the <CLSCompliant> attribute will instruct the VB 2005 compiler to check each and every line of code against the rules of the CLS. If any CLS violations are discovered, you receive a compiler error and a description of the offending code.

Understanding the Common Language Runtime

In addition to the CTS and CLS specifications, the next TLA (three letter abbreviation) to contend with at the moment is the CLR. Programmatically speaking, the term *runtime* can be understood as a collection of external services that are required to execute a given compiled unit of code. For example, when developers make use of the Microsoft Foundation Classes (MFC) to create a new application, they are aware that their program requires the MFC runtime library (i.e., mfc42.dll). Other popular languages also have a corresponding runtime. VB6 programmers are also tied to a runtime module or two (e.g., msvbvm60.dll). Java developers are tied to the Java Virtual Machine (JVM) and so forth.

The .NET platform offers yet another runtime system. The key difference between the .NET runtime and the various other runtimes I just mentioned is the fact that the .NET runtime provides a single well-defined runtime layer that is shared by *all* languages and platforms that are .NET-aware.

The crux of the CLR is physically represented by a library named `mscoree.dll` (aka the Common Object Runtime Execution Engine). When an assembly is referenced for use, `mscoree.dll` is loaded automatically, which in turn loads the required assembly into memory. The runtime engine is responsible for a number of tasks. First and foremost, it is the entity in charge of resolving the location of an assembly and finding the requested type within the binary by reading the contained metadata. The CLR then lays out the type in memory, compiles the associated CIL into platform-specific instructions, performs any necessary security checks, and then executes the code in question.

In addition to loading your custom assemblies and creating your custom types, the CLR will also interact with the types contained within the .NET base class libraries when required. Although the entire base class library has been broken into a number of discrete assemblies, the key assembly is `mscorlib.dll`. `mscorlib.dll` contains a large number of core types that encapsulate a wide variety of common programming tasks as well as the core data types used by all .NET languages. When you build .NET solutions, you automatically have access to this particular assembly.

Figure 1-4 illustrates the workflow that takes place between your source code (which is making use of base class library types), a given .NET compiler, and the .NET execution engine.

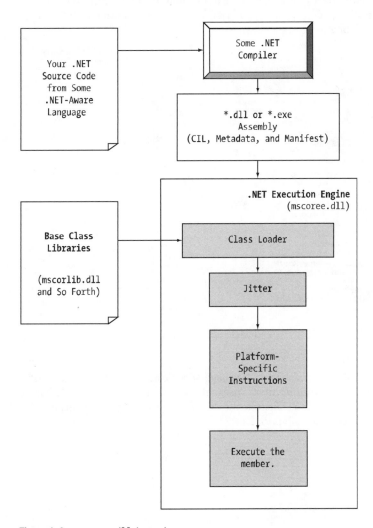

Figure 1-4. `mscoree.dll` *in action*

The Assembly/Namespace/Type Distinction

Each of us understands the importance of code libraries. The point of libraries found within VB6, J2EE, or MFC is to give developers a well-defined set of existing code to leverage in their applications. However, the VB 2005 language does not come with a language-specific code library. Rather, VB 2005 developers leverage the language-neutral .NET libraries. To keep all the types within the base class libraries well organized, the .NET platform makes extensive use of the *namespace* concept.

Simply put, a namespace is a grouping of related types contained in an assembly. For example, the System.IO namespace contains file I/O related types, the System.Data namespace defines core database access types, the System.Windows.Forms namespace defines GUI elements, and so on. It is very important to point out that a single assembly (such as mscorlib.dll) can contain any number of namespaces, each of which can contain any number of types (classes, interfaces, structures, enumerations, or delegates).

To clarify, Figure 1-5 shows a screen shot of the Visual Studio 2005 Object Brower utility (you'll learn more about this tool in Chapter 2). This tool allows you to examine the assemblies referenced by your current solution, the namespaces within a particular assembly, the types within a given namespace, and the members of a specific type. Note that mscorlib.dll contains many different namespaces, each with its own semantically related types.

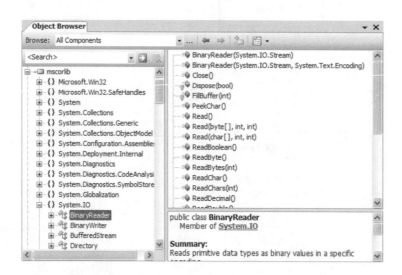

Figure 1-5. *A single assembly can have any number of namespaces.*

The key difference between this approach and a language-specific library such as the Java API is that any language targeting the .NET runtime makes use of the *same* namespaces and *same* types. For example, the following three programs all illustrate the ubiquitous "Hello World" application, written in VB 2005, C#, and Managed Extensions for C++:

```
' Hello world in VB 2005
Imports System

Public Module MyApp
  Sub Main()
    Console.WriteLine("Hi from VB 2005")
  End Sub
End Module
```

```
// Hello world in C#
using System;

public class MyApp
{
  static void Main()
  {
    Console.WriteLine("Hi from C#");
  }
}
```

```
// Hello world in Managed Extensions for C++
#include "stdafx.h"
using namespace System;

int main(array<System::String ^> ^args)
{
  Console::WriteLine(L"Hi from managed C++");
  return 0;
}
```

Notice that each language is making use of the Console class defined in the System namespace. Beyond minor syntactic variations, these three applications look and feel very much alike, both physically and logically.

Clearly, your primary goal as a .NET developer is to get to know the wealth of types defined in the (numerous) .NET namespaces. The most fundamental namespace to get your hands around is named System. This namespace provides a core body of types that you will need to leverage time and again as a .NET developer. In fact, you cannot build any sort of functional .NET application without at least making a reference to the System namespace. Table 1-2 offers a rundown of some (but certainly not all) of the .NET namespaces.

Table 1-2. *A Sampling of .NET Namespaces*

.NET Namespace	Meaning in Life
System	Within System you find numerous useful types dealing with intrinsic data, mathematical computations, random number generation, environment variables, and garbage collection, as well as a number of commonly used exceptions and attributes.
System.Collections System.Collections.Generic	These namespaces define a number of stock container objects (ArrayList, Queue, and so forth), as well as base types and interfaces that allow you to build customized collections. As of .NET 2.0, the collection types have been extended with generic capabilities.
System.Data System.Data.Odbc System.Data.OracleClient System.Data.OleDb System.Data.SqlClient	These namespaces are used for interacting with databases using ADO.NET.
System.Diagnostics	Here, you find numerous types that can be used to programmatically debug and trace your source code.
System.Drawing System.Drawing.Drawing2D System.Drawing.Printing	Here, you find numerous types wrapping graphical primitives such as bitmaps, fonts, and icons, as well as printing capabilities.

Continued

Table 1-2. *Continued*

.NET Namespace	Meaning in Life
System.IO System.IO.Compression System.IO.Ports	These namespaces define numerous types for I/O operations. As of .NET 2.0, the IO namespaces now include support compression and port manipulation.
System.Net	This namespace (as well as other related namespaces) contains types related to network programming (requests/responses, sockets, end points, and so on).
System.Reflection System.Reflection.Emit	These namespaces define types that support runtime type discovery as well as dynamic creation of types.
System.Runtime.InteropServices	This namespace provides facilities to allow .NET types to interact with "unmanaged code" (e.g., C-based DLLs and COM servers) and vice versa.
System.Runtime.Remoting	This namespace (among others) defines types used to build solutions that incorporate the .NET remoting layer.
System.Security	Security is an integrated aspect of the .NET universe. In the security-centric namespaces you find numerous types dealing with permissions, cryptography, and so on.
System.Threading	This namespace defines types used to build multithreaded applications.
System.Web	A number of namespaces are specifically geared toward the development of .NET web applications, including ASP.NET and XML web services.
System.Windows.Forms	This namespace contains types that facilitate the construction of traditional desktop GUI applications.
System.Xml	The XML-centric namespaces contain numerous types used to interact with XML data.

Accessing a Namespace Programmatically

It is worth reiterating that a namespace is nothing more than a convenient way for us mere humans to logically understand and organize related types. Consider again the System namespace. From your perspective, you can assume that System.Console represents a class named *Console* that is contained within a namespace called *System*. However, in the eyes of the .NET runtime, this is not so. The runtime engine only sees a single entity named *System.Console*.

In Visual Basic 2005, the Imports keyword simplifies the process of referencing types defined in a particular namespace. Here is how it works. Let's say you are interested in building a traditional desktop application. The main window renders a bar chart based on some information obtained from a back-end database and displays your company logo. While learning the types each namespace contains takes study and experimentation, here are some obvious candidates to reference in your program:

```
' Here are all the namespaces used to build this application.
Imports System              ' General base class library types.
Imports System.Drawing      ' Graphical rendering types.
Imports System.Windows.Forms ' GUI widget types.
Imports System.Data         ' General data-centric types.
Imports System.Data.SqlClient ' MS SQL Server data access types.
```

Once you have specified some number of namespaces (and set a reference to the assemblies that define them, which is explained in Chapter 2), you are free to create instances of the types they contain. For example, if you are interested in creating an instance of the Bitmap class (defined in the System.Drawing namespace), you can write the following:

```
' Explicitly list the namespaces used by this file.
Imports System
Imports System.Drawing

Class MyApp
  Public Sub DisplayLogo()
    ' Create a 20 x 20 pixel bitmap.
    Dim companyLogo As Bitmap = New Bitmap(20, 20)
    ...
  End Sub
End Class
```

Because your application is referencing System.Drawing, the compiler is able to resolve the Bitmap class as a member of this namespace. If you did not specify the System.Drawing namespace, you would be issued a compiler error. However, you are free to declare variables using a *fully quali-fied name* as well:

```
' Not listing System.Drawing namespace!
Imports System

Class MyApp
  Public Sub DisplayLogo()
    ' Create a 20 x 20 pixel bitmap.
    Dim companyLogo As System.Drawing.Bitmap = _
      New System.Drawing.Bitmap(20, 20)
    ...
  End Sub
End Class
```

While defining a type using the fully qualified name provides greater readability, I think you'd agree that the VB 2005 Imports keyword reduces keystrokes. In this text, I will avoid the use of fully qualified names (unless there is a definite ambiguity to be resolved) and opt for the simplified approach of the Imports keyword.

However, always remember that this technique is simply a shorthand notation for specifying a type's fully qualified name, and each approach results in the exact same underlying CIL (given the fact that CIL code always makes use of fully qualified names) and has no effect on performance or the size of the generated assembly.

Referencing External Assemblies

In addition to specifying a namespace via the VB 2005 Imports keyword, you also need to tell the VB 2005 compiler the name of the assembly containing the actual CIL definition for the referenced type. As mentioned, many core .NET namespaces live within mscorlib.dll. However, the System.Drawing.Bitmap type is contained within a separate assembly named System.Drawing.dll. A vast majority of the .NET Framework assemblies are located under a specific directory termed the *global assembly cache* (GAC). On a Windows machine, this can be located under C:\WINDOWS\assembly, as shown in Figure 1-6.

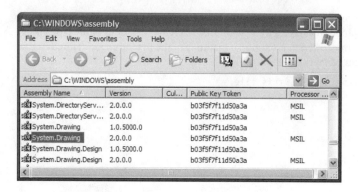

Figure 1-6. *The base class libraries reside in the GAC.*

Depending on the development tool you are using to build your .NET applications, you will have various ways to inform the compiler which assemblies you wish to include during the compilation cycle. You'll examine how to do so in the next chapter, so I'll hold off on the details for now.

Using ildasm.exe

If you are beginning to feel a tad overwhelmed at the thought of gaining mastery over every namespace in the .NET platform, just remember that what makes a namespace unique is that it contains types that are somehow *semantically related*. Therefore, if you have no need for a user interface beyond a simple console application, you can forget all about the System.Windows.Forms and System.Web namespaces (among others). If you are building a painting application, the database namespaces are most likely of little concern. Like any new set of prefabricated code, you learn as you go. (Sorry, there is no shortcut to "magically" know all the assemblies, namespaces. and types at your disposal; then again, that is why you are reading this book!)

The Intermediate Language Disassembler utility (ildasm.exe) allows you to load up any .NET assembly and investigate its contents, including the associated manifest, CIL code, and type metadata. By default, ildasm.exe should be installed under C:\Program Files\Microsoft Visual Studio 8\SDK\v2.0\Bin (if you cannot find ildasm.exe in this location, simply search your machine for an application named "ildasm.exe").

Once you locate and run this tool, proceed to the File ➤ Open menu command and navigate to an assembly you wish to explore. By way of illustration, Figure 1-7 shows the VbNetCalculator.exe assembly built using the code seen earlier in this chapter. As you can see, ildasm.exe presents the structure of an assembly using a familiar tree-view format.

Viewing CIL Code

In addition to showing the namespaces, types, and members contained in a given assembly, ildasm.exe also allows you to view the CIL instructions for a given member. For example, if you were to double-click the Main() method of the CalcApp class, a separate window would display the underlying CIL (see Figure 1-8).

C:\Documents and Settings\Andrew Troelse...
File View Help
C:\Documents and Settings\Andrew Troelsen\My Documents\MyBooks
MANIFEST
CalculatorExample
CalculatorExample.Calc
.class public auto ansi
.ctor : void()
Add : int32(int32,int32)
CalculatorExample.CalcApp
My
MySettings
.assembly VbNetCalculator
{

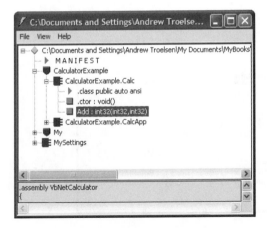

Figure 1-7. *Your new best friend,* `ildasm.exe`

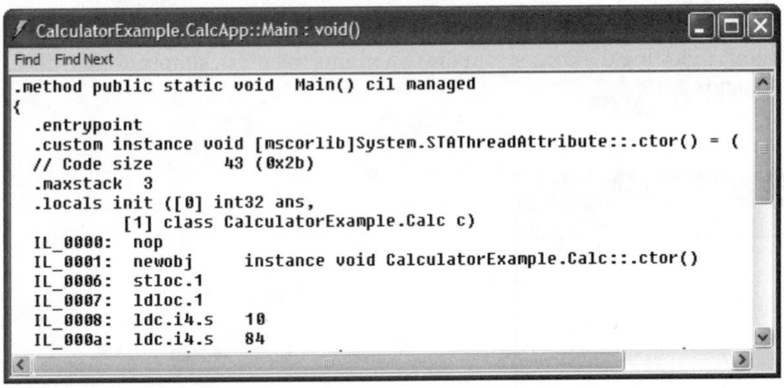

CalculatorExample.CalcApp::Main : void()
Find Find Next
.method public static void Main() cil managed
{
.entrypoint
.custom instance void [mscorlib]System.STAThreadAttribute::.ctor() = (
// Code size 43 (0x2b)
.maxstack 3
.locals init ([0] int32 ans,
[1] class CalculatorExample.Calc c)
IL_0000: nop
IL_0001: newobj instance void CalculatorExample.Calc::.ctor()
IL_0006: stloc.1
IL_0007: ldloc.1
IL_0008: ldc.i4.s 10
IL_000a: ldc.i4.s 84

Figure 1-8. *Viewing the underlying CIL*

Viewing Type Metadata

If you wish to view the type metadata for the currently loaded assembly, press Ctrl+M. Figure 1-9 shows the metadata for the `Calc.Add()` method.

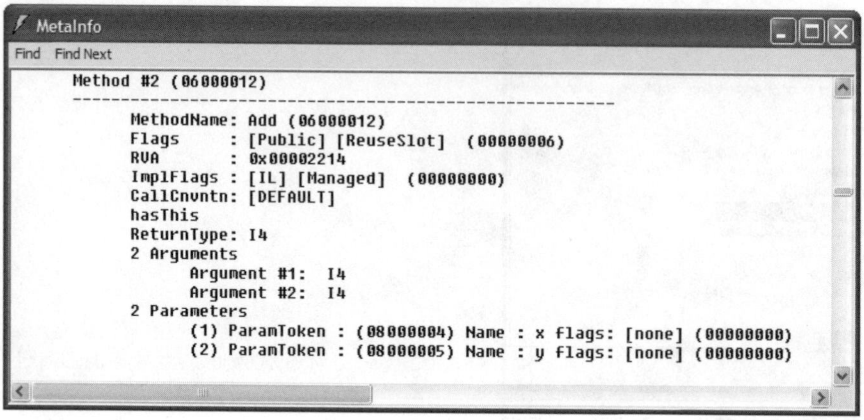

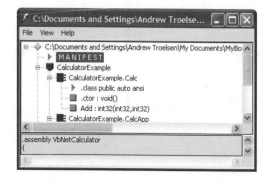

Figure 1-9. *Viewing type metadata via* ildasm.exe

Viewing Assembly Metadata

Finally, if you are interested in viewing the contents of the assembly's manifest, simply double-click the MANIFEST icon (see Figure 1-10).

Figure 1-10. *Double-click here to view the assembly manifest.*

To be sure, ildasm.exe has more options than shown here, and I will illustrate additional features of the tool where appropriate in the text. As you read through this book, I strongly encourage you to open your assemblies using ildasm.exe to see how your VB 2005 code is processed into platform-agnostic CIL code. Although you do *not* need to become an expert in CIL code to be a VB 2005 superstar, understanding the syntax of CIL will only strengthen your programming muscle.

Deploying the .NET Runtime

It should come as no surprise that .NET assemblies can be executed only on a machine that has the .NET Framework installed. As an individual who builds .NET software, this should never be an issue, as your development machine will be properly configured at the time you install the freely available

.NET Framework 2.0 SDK (as well as commercial .NET development environments such as Visual Studio 2005).

However, if you deploy an assembly to a computer that does not have .NET installed, it will fail to run. For this reason, Microsoft provides a setup package named `dotnetfx.exe` that can be freely shipped and installed along with your custom software. This installation program is included with the .NET Framework 2.0 SDK, and it is also freely downloadable from Microsoft (in fact, it is suggested by Windows Update when necessary).

Once `dotnetfx.exe` is installed, the target machine will now contain the .NET base class libraries, .NET runtime (`mscoree.dll`), and additional .NET infrastructure (such as the GAC).

■**Note** Do be aware that if you are building a .NET web application, the end user's machine does not need to be configured with the .NET Framework, as the browser will simply receive generic HTML and possibly client-side JavaScript.

The Platform-Independent Nature of .NET

To close this chapter, allow me to briefly comment on the platform-independent nature of the .NET platform. To the surprise of most developers, .NET assemblies can be developed and executed on non-Microsoft operating systems (Mac OS X, numerous Linux distributions, and FreeBSD, to name a few). To understand how this is possible, you need to come to terms with yet another abbreviation in the .NET universe: CLI (Common Language Infrastructure).

When Microsoft released the .NET platform, it also crafted a set of formal documents that described the syntax and semantics of the C# and CIL languages, the .NET assembly format, core .NET namespaces, and the mechanics of a hypothetical .NET runtime engine (known as the Virtual Execution System, or VES). Better yet, these documents have been submitted to Ecma International as official international standards (`http://www.ecma-international.org`). The specifications of interest are

- ECMA-334: The C# Language Specification
- ECMA-335: The Common Language Infrastructure (CLI)

■**Note** Microsoft has not defined a formal specification regarding the Visual Basic 2005 programming language. The good news, however, is that the major open-source .NET distributions ship with a compatible BASIC compiler.

The importance of these documents becomes clear when you understand that they enable third parties to build distributions of the .NET platform for any number of operating systems and/or processors. ECMA-335 is perhaps the more "meaty" of the two specifications, so much so that is has been broken into five partitions, as shown in Table 1-3.

Table 1-3. *Partitions of the CLI*

Partitions of ECMA-335	Meaning in Life
Partition I: Architecture	Describes the overall architecture of the CLI, including the rules of the CTS and CLS, and the mechanics of the .NET runtime engine
Partition II: Metadata	Describes the details of .NET metadata
Partition III: CIL	Describes the syntax and semantics of CIL code
Partition IV: Libraries	Gives a high-level overview of the minimal and complete class libraries that must be supported by a .NET distribution
Partition V: Annexes	A collection of "odds and ends" details such as class library design guidelines and the implementation details of a CIL compiler

Be aware that Partition IV (Libraries) defines only a *minimal* set of namespaces that represent the core services expected by a CLI distribution (collections, console I/O, file I/O, threading, reflection, network access, core security needs, XML manipulation, and so forth). The CLI does *not* define namespaces that facilitate web development (ASP.NET), database access (ADO.NET), or desktop graphical user interface (GUI) application development (Windows Forms).

The good news, however, is that the mainstream .NET distributions extend the CLI libraries with Microsoft-compatible equivalents of ASP.NET, ADO.NET, and Windows Forms in order to provide full-featured, production-level development platforms. To date, there are two major implementations of the CLI (beyond Microsoft's Windows-specific offering). Although this text focuses on the creation of .NET applications using Microsoft's .NET distribution, Table 1-4 provides information regarding the Mono and Portable .NET projects.

Table 1-4. *Open Source .NET Distributions*

Distribution	Meaning in Life
http://www.mono-project.com	The Mono project is an open source distribution of the CLI that targets various Linux distributions (e.g., SuSE, Fedora, and so on) as well as Win32 and Mac OS X.
http://www.dotgnu.org	Portable.NET is another open source distribution of the CLI that runs on numerous operating systems. Portable.NET aims to target as many operating systems as possible (Win32, AIX, BeOS, Mac OS X, Solaris, all major Linux distributions, and so on).

Both Mono and Portable.NET provide an ECMA-compliant C# compiler, .NET runtime engine, code samples, documentation, as well as numerous development tools that are functionally equivalent to the tools that ship with Microsoft's .NET Framework 2.0 SDK. Furthermore, Mono and Portable.NET collectively ship with a Visual Basic 2005, Java, and C complier.

■**Note** If you wish to learn more about Mono or Portable.NET, check out *Cross-Platform .NET Development: Using Mono, Portable.NET, and Microsoft .NET* by M. J. Easton and Jason King (Apress, 2004).

Summary

The point of this chapter was to lay out the conceptual framework necessary for the remainder of this book. I began by examining a number of limitations and complexities found within the technologies prior to .NET, and followed up with an overview of how .NET and Visual Basic 2005 attempt to streamline the current state of affairs.

.NET basically boils down to a runtime execution engine (mscoree.dll) and base class library (mscorlib.dll and associates). The common language runtime (CLR) is able to host any .NET binary (aka assembly) that abides by the rules of managed code. As you have seen, assemblies contain CIL instructions (in addition to type metadata and the assembly manifest) that are compiled to platform-specific instructions using a just-in-time (JIT) compiler. In addition, you explored the role of the Common Language Specification (CLS) and Common Type System (CTS).

This was followed by an examination of the ildasm.exe utility, as well as coverage of how to configure a machine to host .NET applications using dotnetfx.exe. I wrapped up by briefly addressing the platform-independent nature of the .NET platform and the Mono and Portable.NET CLI distributions.

CHAPTER 2

■■■

Building Visual Basic 2005 Applications

As a VB 2005 programmer, you may choose among numerous tools to build your .NET applications. This approach is quite different from the world of VB6, where we had only a single IDE to contend with: Microsoft Visual Basic 6.0. That being said, the point of this chapter is to provide a tour of various .NET development options, including, of course, Visual Studio 2005. The chapter opens, however, with an examination of working with the VB 2005 command-line compiler, vbc.exe, and the simplest of all text editors, Notepad (notepad.exe). Once you become comfortable compiling code "IDE-free," you will then examine how the TextPad application allows you to edit and compile VB 2005 source code files in a (slightly) more sophisticated manner.

While you could work through this entire text using nothing other than vbc.exe and Notepad/TextPad, I'd bet you are also interested in working with feature-rich integrated development environments (IDEs). To this end, you will be introduced to an open source IDE named SharpDevelop. This IDE rivals the functionality of many commercial .NET development environments (and it's free!). After briefly examining the Visual Basic 2005 Express IDE, you will turn your attention to Visual Studio 2005. This chapter also provides a quick tour of a number of complementary .NET development tools that every .NET developer should be aware of, and wraps up with a brief discussion regarding the role of the Microsoft.VisualBasic.dll assembly.

Installing the .NET Framework 2.0 SDK

Before you are able to build .NET applications using the VB 2005 programming language and the .NET Framework, the first step is to install the freely downloadable .NET Framework 2.0 Software Development Kit (SDK).

■**Note** Be aware that the .NET Framework 2.0 SDK is automatically installed with Visual Studio 2005 as well as Visual Basic 2005 Express; therefore, if you plan to use either of these IDEs, there is no need to manually download or install this software package.

If you are not developing with Visual Studio 2005/Visual Basic 2005 Express, navigate to http://msdn.microsoft.com/netframework and search for ".NET Framework 2.0 SDK". Once you have located the appropriate page, download the setup program (setup.exe) and save it to a convenient location on your hard drive. At this point, double-click the executable to install the software.

After the installation process has completed, not only will your development machine be configured with the necessary .NET infrastructure, but it also now contains numerous development tools (a majority of which are command-line utilities), a very robust local help system (the MSDN Library), sample code, tutorials, and various white papers.

By default, the .NET Framework 2.0 SDK is installed under C:\Program Files\Microsoft Visual Studio 8\SDK\v2.0. Here you will find StartHere.htm, which (as the name suggests) serves as an entry point to other related documentation. Table 2-1 describes the details behind some of the core subdirectories off the installation root.

Table 2-1. *Select Subdirectories of the .NET Framework 2.0 SDK Installation Root*

Subdirectory	Meaning in Life
\Bin	Contains a majority of the .NET development tools. Check out StartTools.htm for a description of each utility.
\BootStrapper	Although you can ignore most of the content in the directory, be aware that dotnetfx.exe (see Chapter 1) resides under the \Packages\dotnetfx subdirectory.
\CompactFramework	Contains the installer program for the .NET Compact Framework 2.0.
\Samples	Provides the setup program (and core content) for the .NET Framework 2.0 SDK samples. To learn how to install the samples, consult StartSamples.htm.

In addition to the content installed under C:\Program Files\Microsoft Visual Studio 8\SDK\v2.0, the setup program also creates the Microsoft.NET\Framework subdirectory under your Windows directory. Here you will find a subdirectory for each version of the .NET Framework installed on your machine. Within a version-specific subdirectory, you will find command-line compilers for each language that ships with the Microsoft .NET Framework (CIL, VB 2005, C#, J#, and JScript .NET), as well as additional command-line development utilities and .NET assemblies.

The VB 2005 Command-Line Compiler (vbc.exe)

There are a number of techniques you may use to compile VB 2005 source code. In addition to Visual Studio 2005 (as well as various third-party .NET IDEs), you are able to create .NET assemblies using the VB 2005 command-line compiler, vbc.exe (where vbc stands for the Visual Basic Compiler). This tool is included with the .NET Framework 2.0 SDK. While it is true that you may never decide to build a large-scale application using the command-line compiler, it is important to understand the basics of how to compile your *.vb files by hand. I can think of a few reasons you should get a grip on the process:

- The most obvious reason is the simple fact that you might not have a copy of Visual Studio 2005.

- You plan to make use of automated .NET build tools such as MSBuild or NAnt.

- You want to deepen your understanding of VB 2005. When you use graphical IDEs to build applications, you are ultimately instructing vbc.exe how to manipulate your VB 2005 input files. In this light, it's edifying to see what takes place behind the scenes.

Another nice by-product of working with vbc.exe in the raw is that you become that much more comfortable manipulating other command-line tools included with the .NET Framework 2.0 SDK. As you will see throughout this book, a number of important utilities are accessible only from the command line.

Configuring the VB 2005 Command-Line Compiler

Before you can begin to make use of the VB 2005 command-line compiler, you need to ensure that your development machine recognizes the existence of vbc.exe. If your machine is not configured correctly, you are forced to specify the full path to the directory containing vbc.exe before you can compile your VB 2005 code (which can be a pain in the neck).

To equip your development machine to compile *.vb files from any directory, follow these steps (which assume a Windows XP installation; Windows NT/2000 steps will differ slightly):

1. Right-click the My Computer icon and select Properties from the pop-up menu.

2. Select the Advanced tab and click the Environment Variables button.

3. Double-click the Path variable from the System Variables list box.

4. Add the following line to the end of the current Path value (note each value in the Path variable is separated by a semicolon):

```
C:\Windows\Microsoft.NET\Framework\v2.0.50727
```

Of course, your entry may need to be adjusted based on your current version and location of the .NET Framework 2.0 SDK (so be sure to do a sanity check using Windows Explorer). Once you have updated the Path variable, you may take a test run by closing any command windows open in the background (to commit the settings), and then open a new command window and enter the following command:

```
vbc /?
```

If you set things up correctly, you should see a list of options supported by the VB 2005 compiler.

■**Note** When specifying command-line arguments for a given .NET development tool, you may use either – or / (i.e., vbc -? or vbc /?).

Configuring Additional .NET Command-Line Tools

Before you begin to investigate vbc.exe, add the following additional Path variable to the System Variables list box using the steps outlined previously (again, perform a sanity check to ensure a valid path):

```
C:\Program Files\Microsoft Visual Studio 8\SDK\v2.0\Bin
```

Recall that this directory contains additional command-line tools that are commonly used during .NET development. With these two paths established, you should now be able to run any .NET utility from any command window. If you wish to confirm this new setting, close any open command windows, open a new command window, and enter the following command to view the options of the Global Assembly Cache (GAC) utility, gacutil.exe:

```
gacutil /?
```

■**Tip** Now that you have seen how to manually configure your machine, I'll let you in on a shortcut. The .NET Framework 2.0 SDK provides a preconfigured command window that recognizes all .NET command-line utilities out of the box. Click the Start button, and then activate the SDK Command Prompt located under the All Programs ➤ Microsoft .NET Framework SDK v2.0 menu selection.

Building VB 2005 Applications Using vbc.exe

Now that your development machine recognizes vbc.exe, the next goal is to build a simple single-file assembly named TestApp.exe using the VB 2005 command-line compiler and Notepad. First, you need some source code. Open Notepad and enter the following:

```
' A simple VB 2005 application.
Imports System

Module TestApp
  Sub Main()
    Console.WriteLine("Testing! 1, 2, 3")
  End Sub
End Module
```

Once you have finished, save the file in a convenient location (e.g., C:\VbcExample) as TestApp.vb. Now, let's get to know the core options of the VB 2005 compiler. The first point of interest is to understand how to specify the name and type of assembly to create (e.g., a console application named MyShell.exe, a code library named MathLib.dll, a Windows Forms application named MyWinApp.exe, etc.). Each possibility is represented by a specific flag passed into vbc.exe as a command-line parameter (see Table 2-2).

Table 2-2. *Output-centric Options of the VB 2005 Compiler*

Option	Meaning in Life
/out	This option is used to specify the name of the assembly to be created. By default, the assembly name is the same as the name of the initial input *.vb file.
/target:exe	This option builds an executable console application. This is the default target, and thus may be omitted when building console applications.
/target:library	This option builds a single-file *.dll assembly.
/target:module	This option builds a *module*. Modules are elements of multifile assemblies (fully described in Chapter 13).
/target:winexe	This option builds an executable Windows application. Although you are free to build Windows-based applications using the /target:exe flag, the /target:winexe flag prevents a console window from appearing in the background.

To compile TestApp.vb into a console application named TextApp.exe, open a command prompt and change to the directory containing your source code file using the cd command:

```
cd c:\VbcExample
```

Next, enter the following command set (note that command-line flags must come before the name of the input files, not after):

```
vbc /target:exe TestApp.vb
```

Here I did not explicitly specify an /out flag, therefore the executable will be named TestApp.exe, given the name of the initial input file. However, if you wish to specify a unique name for your assembly, you could enter the following command:

```
vbc /target:exe /out:MyFirstApp.exe TestApp.vb
```

Also be aware that most of the VB 2005 compiler flags support an abbreviated version, such as /t rather than /target (you can view all abbreviations by entering vbc /? at the command prompt). For example, you can save yourself a few keystrokes by specifying the following:

```
vbc /t:exe TestApp.vb
```

Furthermore, given that the /t:exe flag is the default output used by the VB 2005 compiler, you could also compile TestApp.vb simply by typing

```
vbc TestApp.vb
```

TestApp.exe can now be run from the command line by typing the name of the executable. If all is well, you should see the message "Testing! 1, 2, 3" print out to the command window (see Figure 2-1).

Figure 2-1. *TestApp in action*

Referencing External Assemblies Using vbc.exe

Next up, let's examine how to compile an application that makes use of types defined in an external .NET assembly. Speaking of which, just in case you are wondering how the VB 2005 compiler understood your reference to the System.Console type, recall from Chapter 1 that mscorlib.dll is automatically referenced during the compilation process.

To illustrate the process of referencing external assemblies, let's update the TestApp application to display a Windows Forms message box. Open your TestApp.vb file and modify it as follows:

```
' A simple VB 2005 application.
Imports System

' Add this!
Imports System.Windows.Forms

Module TestApp
  Sub Main()
    Console.WriteLine("Testing! 1, 2, 3")

    ' Add this!
    MessageBox.Show("Hello!")
  End Sub
End Module
```

Notice the reference to the System.Windows.Forms namespace via the VB 2005 Imports keyword (introduced in Chapter 1). Recall that when you explicitly list the namespaces used within a given *.vb file, you avoid the need to make use of fully qualified names (which can lead to hand cramps).

At the command line, you must inform vbc.exe which assembly contains the imported namespaces. Given that you have made use of the MessageBox class, you must specify the System.Windows.Forms.dll assembly using the /reference flag (which can be abbreviated to /r):

```
vbc /r:System.Windows.Forms.dll testapp.vb
```

If you now rerun your application, you should see what appears in Figure 2-2 in addition to the console output.

Figure 2-2. *Your first Windows Forms application*

Compiling Multiple Source Files Using vbc.exe

The current incarnation of the TestApp.exe application was created using a single *.vb source code file. While it is perfectly permissible to have all of your .NET types defined in a single *.vb file, most projects are composed of multiple *.vb files to keep your code base a bit more flexible. Assume you have authored an additional class (again, using Notepad) contained in a new file named HelloMsg.vb:

```
' The HelloMessage class
Imports System
Imports System.Windows.Forms

Class HelloMessage
  Sub Speak()
    MessageBox.Show("Hello Again")
  End Sub
End Class
```

Assuming you have saved this new file in the same location as your first file (e.g., C:\VbcExample), update your TestApp class to make use of this new type, and comment out the previous Windows Forms logic. Here is the complete update:

```
' A simple VB 2005 application.
Imports System

' Don't need this anymore.
' Imports System.Windows.Forms

Module TestApp
  Sub Main()
    Console.WriteLine("Testing! 1, 2, 3")

    ' Don't need this anymore either.
    ' MessageBox.Show("Hello!")

    ' Exercise the HelloMessage class!
    Dim h As New HelloMessage()
    h.Speak()
  End Sub
End Module
```

You can compile your VB 2005 files by listing each input file explicitly:

```
vbc /r:System.Windows.Forms.dll testapp.vb hellomsg.vb
```

As an alternative, the VB 2005 compiler allows you to make use of the wildcard character (*) to inform vbc.exe to include all *.vb files contained in the project directory as part of the current build:

```
vbc /r:System.Windows.Forms.dll *.vb
```

When you run the program again, the output is identical. The only difference between the two applications is the fact that the current logic has been split among multiple files.

Referencing Multiple External Assemblies Using vbc.exe

On a related note, what if you need to reference numerous external assemblies using vbc.exe? Simply list each assembly using a comma-delimited list. You don't need to specify multiple external assemblies for the current example, but some sample usage follows:

```
vbc /r:System.Windows.Forms.dll,System.Drawing.dll *.vb
```

Working with vbc.exe Response Files

As you might guess, if you were to build a complex VB 2005 application at the command prompt, your life would be full of pain as you type in the flags that specify numerous referenced assemblies and *.vb input files. To help lessen your typing burden, the VB 2005 compiler honors the use of *response files*.

VB 2005 response files contain all the instructions to be used during the compilation of your current build. By convention, these files end in an *.rsp (response) extension. Assume that you have created a response file named TestApp.rsp that contains the following arguments (as you can see, comments are denoted with the # character):

```
# This is the response file
# for the TestApp.exe app
# of Chapter 2.

# External assembly references.
/r:System.Windows.Forms.dll

# output and files to compile (using wildcard syntax).
/target:exe /out:TestApp.exe *.vb
```

Now, assuming this file is saved in the same directory as the VB 2005 source code files to be compiled, you are able to build your entire application as follows (note the use of the @ symbol):

```
vbc @TestApp.rsp
```

If the need should arise, you are also able to specify multiple *.rsp files as input (e.g., vbc @FirstFile.rsp @SecondFile.rsp @ThirdFile.rsp). If you take this approach, do be aware that the compiler processes the command options as they are encountered! Therefore, command-line arguments in a later *.rsp file can override options in a previous response file.

Also note that flags listed explicitly on the command line before a response file will be overridden by the specified *.rsp file. Thus, if you were to enter

```
vbc /out:MyCoolApp.exe @TestApp.rsp
```

the name of the assembly would still be `TestApp.exe` (rather than `MyCoolApp.exe`), given the `/out:TestApp.exe` flag listed in the `TestApp.rsp` response file. However, if you list flags after a response file, the flag will override settings in the response file. Thus, in the following command set, your assembly is indeed named `MyCoolApp.exe`.

```
vbc @TestApp.rsp /out:MyCoolApp.exe
```

Note The `/reference` flag is cumulative. Regardless of where you specify external assemblies (before, after, or within a response file) the end result is a summation of each reference assembly.

The Default Response File (vbc.rsp)

The final point to be made regarding response files is that the VB 2005 compiler has an associated default response file (`vbc.rsp`), which is located in the same directory as `vbc.exe` itself (e.g., C:\Windows\Microsoft.NET\Framework\v2.0.50727). If you were to open this file using Notepad, you will find that numerous .NET assemblies have already been specified using the `/r:` flag. As you would expect, you will come to understand the role of each of these .NET libraries over the course of the text. However, to set the stage, here is a look within `vbc.rsp`:

```
# This file contains command-line options that the VB
# command-line compiler (VBC) will process as part
# of every compilation, unless the "/noconfig" option
# is specified.

# Reference the common Framework libraries
/r:Accessibility.dll
/r:Microsoft.Vsa.dll
/r:System.Configuration.dll
/r:System.Configuration.Install.dll
/r:System.Data.dll
/r:System.Data.OracleClient.dll
/r:System.Data.SqlXml.dll
/r:System.Deployment.dll
/r:System.Design.dll
/r:System.DirectoryServices.dll
/r:System.dll
/r:System.Drawing.Design.dll
/r:System.Drawing.dll
/r:System.EnterpriseServices.dll
/r:System.Management.dll
/r:System.Messaging.dll
/r:System.Runtime.Remoting.dll
/r:System.Runtime.Serialization.Formatters.Soap.dll
/r:System.Security.dll
/r:System.ServiceProcess.dll
/r:System.Transactions.dll
/r:System.Web.dll
/r:System.Web.Mobile.dll
/r:System.Web.RegularExpressions.dll
/r:System.Web.Services.dll
/r:System.Windows.Forms.dll
/r:System.XML.dll
```

```
# Import System and Microsoft.VisualBasic
/imports:System
/imports:Microsoft.VisualBasic
```

■**Note** Understand that the default response file is only referenced when working with the command-line compiler.
The Visual Basic 2005 Express and Visual Studio 2005 IDEs do not automatically set references to these libraries.

When you are building your VB 2005 programs using vbc.exe, this file will be automatically referenced, even when you supply a custom *.rsp file. Given the presence of the default response file, the current TestApp.exe application could be successfully compiled using the following command set (as System.Windows.Forms.dll is referenced within vbc.rsp):

```
vbc /out:TestApp.exe *.vb
```

In the event that you wish to disable the automatic reading of vbc.rsp, you can specify the /noconfig option:

```
vbc @TestApp.rsp /noconfig
```

Obviously, the VB 2005 command-line compiler has many other options that can be used to control how the resulting .NET assembly is to be generated. At this point, however, you should have a handle on the basics. If you wish to learn more details regarding the functionality of vbc.exe, search the .NET Framework 2.0 documentation for the term "vbc.exe".

■**Source Code** The VbcExample project is included under the Chapter 2 subdirectory.

Building .NET Applications Using TextPad

While Notepad is fine for creating simple .NET programs, it offers nothing in the way of developer productivity. It would be ideal to author *.vb files using an editor that supports (at a minimum) keyword coloring, font settings, and integration with the VB 2005 compiler. As luck would have it, such a tool does exist: TextPad.

TextPad is an editor you can use to author and compile code for numerous programming languages, including VB 2005. The chief advantage of this product is the fact that it is very simple to use and provides just enough bells and whistles to enhance your coding efforts.

To obtain TextPad, navigate to http://www.textpad.com and download the current version (4.7.3 at the time of this writing). Once you have installed the product, you will have a feature-complete version of TextPad; however, this tool is not freeware. Until you purchase a single-user license (for around US$30.00 at the time of this writing), you will be presented with a "friendly reminder" each time you run the application.

Enabling VB 2005 Keyword Coloring

TextPad is not equipped to understand VB 2005 keywords or work with vbc.exe out of the box. To do so, you will need to install an additional free add-on. Navigate to http://www.textpad.com/add-ons/syna2g.html and locate and download vbdotnet8.zip using the "VB.NET(6)" link option. This add-on takes into account the new keywords introduced with VB 2005 (in contrast to the older "VB.NET" links, which are limited to keywords of Visual Basic .NET 1.1).

Once you have unzipped `vbdotnet8.zip`, place a copy of the extracted `vbdotnet8.syn` file in the Samples subdirectory of the TextPad installation (e.g., C:\Program Files\TextPad 4\Samples). Next, launch TextPad and perform the following tasks using the New Document Wizard.

1. Activate the Configure ➤ New Document Class menu option.

2. Enter the name **VB 2005** in the "Document class name" edit box.

3. In the next step, enter ***.vb** in the "Class members" edit box.

4. Finally, enable syntax highlighting, choose `vbdotnet8.syn` from the drop-down list box, and finish the wizard.

You can now tweak TextPad's VB 2005 support using the Document Classes node accessible from the Configure ➤ Preferences menu (see Figure 2-3).

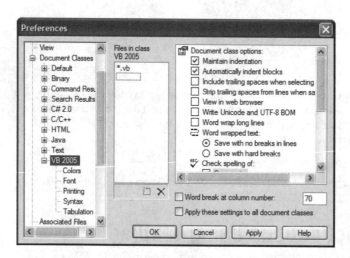

Figure 2-3. *Setting TextPad's VB 2005 preferences*

Configuring the *.vb File Filter

The next configuration detail is to create a filter for VB 2005 source code files displayed by the Open and Save dialog boxes:

1. Activate the Configure ➤ Preferences menu option and select File Name Filters from the tree-view control.

2. Click the New button, and enter **VB 2005** into the Description field and ***.vb** into the Wild cards text box.

3. Move your new filter to the top of the list using the Move Up button, and click OK.

Create a new file (using File ➤ New) and save it in a convenient location (such as C:\TextPadTestApp) as `TestPadTest.vb`. Next, enter a trivial class definition (see Figure 2-4).

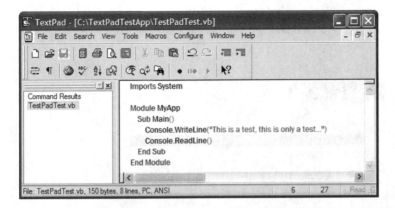

Figure 2-4. `TestPadTest.vb`

Hooking Into vbc.exe

The last major configuration detail to contend with is to associate `vbc.exe` with TextPad so you can compile your `*.vb` files. The first way to do so is using the Tools ➤ Run menu option. Here you are presented with a dialog box that allows you to specify the name of the tool to run and any necessary command-line flags. To compile `TestPadTest.vb` into a .NET console-based executable, follow these steps:

1. Enter the full path to `vbc.exe` into the Command text box (e.g., C:\Windows\Microsoft.NET\ Framework\v2.0.50727\vbc.exe).

2. Enter the command-line options you wish to specify within the Parameters text box (e.g., `/out:myApp.exe *.vb`). Recall that you can specify a custom response file to simplify matters (e.g., `@myInput.rsp`).

3. Enter the directory containing the input files via the Initial folder text box (C:\TextPadTestApp in this example).

4. If you wish TextPad to capture the compiler output directly (rather than within a separate command window), select the Capture Output check box.

Figure 2-5 shows the complete compilation settings.

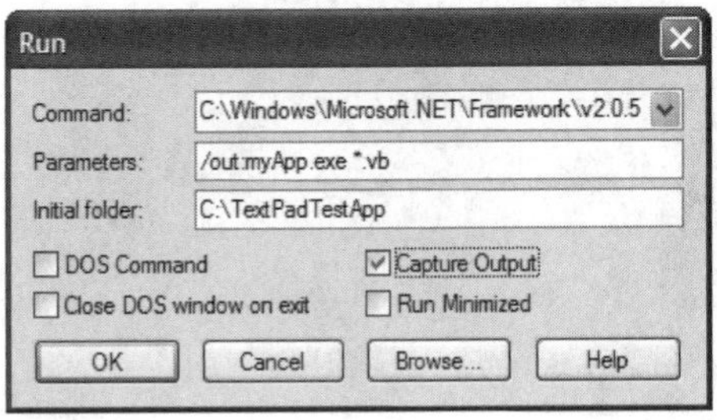

Figure 2-5. *Specifying a custom run command*

At this point, you can either run your program by double-clicking the executable using Windows Explorer or leverage the Tools ➤ Run menu option to specify myApp.exe as the current command (see Figure 2-6).

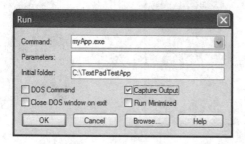

Figure 2-6. *Instructing TextPad to run* myApp.exe

When you click OK, you should see the program's output ("This is a test, this is only a test . . .") displayed in the Command Results document.

Associating Run Commands with Menu Items

TextPad also allows you to create custom menu items that represent predefined run commands. Let's create a custom item under the Tools menu named "Compile VB 2005 Code" that will compile all VB 2005 files in the current directory into a console application:

1. Activate the Configure ➤ Preferences menu option and select Tools from the tree-view control.

2. Using the Add button, select Program and specify the full path to vbc.exe.

3. If you wish, rename vbc.exe to a more descriptive label (Compile VB 2005 Code) by clicking the tool name and then clicking OK.

4. Finally, activate the Configure ➤ Preferences menu option once again, but this time select Compile VB 2005 from the Tools node, and specify ***.vb** as the sole value in the Parameters field (see Figure 2-7).

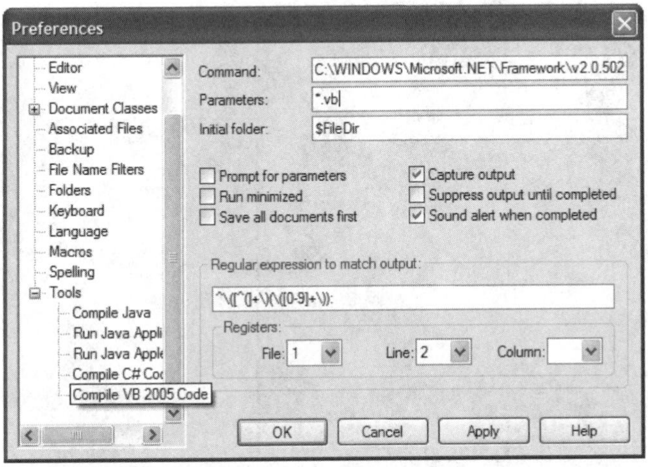

Figure 2-7. *Creating a Tools menu item*

With this, you can now compile all VB 2005 files in the current directory using your custom Tools menu item. Of course, you can repeat this process to add any number of custom menu items, which will compile your code and execute your assemblies.

As you may agree, TextPad is a step in the right direction when contrasted to Notepad and the command prompt. However, TextPad does not (currently) provide IntelliSense capabilities for VB 2005 code, GUI designer tools, project templates, or database manipulation wizards. To address such needs, allow me to introduce the next .NET development tool: SharpDevelop.

Building .NET Applications Using SharpDevelop

SharpDevelop is an open source and feature-rich IDE that you can use to build .NET assemblies using Visual Basic .NET, C#, Managed Extensions for C++, or CIL. Beyond the fact that this IDE is completely free, it is interesting to note that it was written entirely in C#. In fact, you have the choice to download and compile the *.cs files manually or run a setup.exe program to install SharpDevelop on your development machine. Both distributions can be obtained from http://www.icsharpcode. net/OpenSource/SD/Download.

Once you have installed SharpDevelop, the File ➤ New ➤ Combine menu option allows you to pick which type of project you wish to generate (and in which .NET language). In the lingo of SharpDevelop, a *combine* is a collection of individual projects (analogous to a Visual Studio *solution*). Assume you wish to create a VB 2005 Windows application named MySDWinApp (see Figure 2-8).

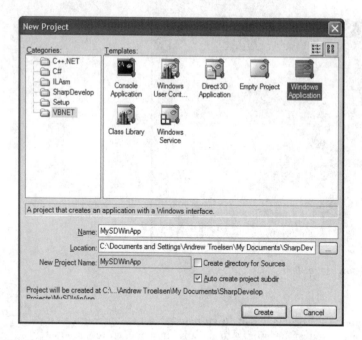

Figure 2-8. *The SharpDevelop New Project dialog box*

■Note Be aware that version 1.1 of SharpDevelop is configured to make use of the VB .NET 1.1 compiler. At the time of this writing, SharpDevelop 2.0 is in beta 2 and has full support for all .NET 2.0 language features. In this overview, the menu options and screen shots are all specific to SharpDevelop 1.1.

Learning the Lay of the Land: SharpDevelop

SharpDevelop provides numerous productivity enhancements and in many cases is as feature-rich as Visual Studio .NET 2003 (but not currently as powerful as Visual Studio 2005). Here is a hit list of some of the major benefits:

- Support for the Microsoft and Mono (see Chapter 1) compilers
- IntelliSense and code expansion capabilities
- An Add Reference dialog box to reference external assemblies, including assemblies deployed to the Global Assembly Cache (GAC)
- A visual Windows Forms designer
- Various project perspective windows (termed *scouts*) to view your projects
- An integrated object browser utility (the Assembly Scout)
- Database manipulation utilities
- A VB .NET to C# (and vice versa) code conversion utility
- Integration with the NUnit (a .NET unit test utility), NDoc (a .NET code documentation utility), and NAnt (a .NET build utility)
- Integration with the .NET Framework SDK documentation (e.g., the MSDN Library)

Impressive for a free IDE, is it not? Although this chapter doesn't cover each of these points in detail, let's walk through a few items of interest. If you require further details of SharpDevelop, be aware that it ships with very thorough documentation accessible from the Help ➤ Help Topics menu option.

The Project and Classes Scouts

When you create a new combine, you can make use of the Project Scout (accessed via the View ➤ Project menu option) to view the set of files, referenced assemblies, and resource files of each project (see Figure 2-9).

Figure 2-9. *The Project Scout*

When you wish to reference an external assembly for your current project, simply right-click the References icon within the Project Scout and select the Add Reference context menu. Once you do, you may select assemblies directly from the GAC as well as custom assemblies via the .NET Assembly Browser tab (see Figure 2-10).

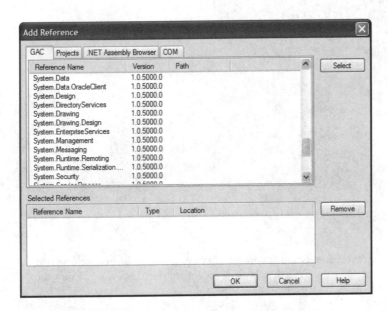

Figure 2-10. *The SharpDevelop Add Reference dialog box*

The Classes Scout (accessed via the View ➤ Classes menu option) provides a more object-oriented view of your combine in that it displays the namespaces, types, and members within each project (see Figure 2-11).

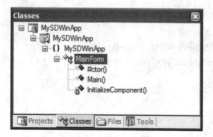

Figure 2-11. *The Classes Scout*

If you double-click any item, SharpDevelop responds by opening the corresponding file and placing your mouse cursor at the item's definition.

The Assembly Scout

The Assembly Scout utility (accessible from the View menu) allows you to graphically browse the assemblies referenced within your project. This tool is split into two panes. On the left is a tree-view control that allows you to drill into an assembly and view its namespaces and the contained types (see Figure 2-12).

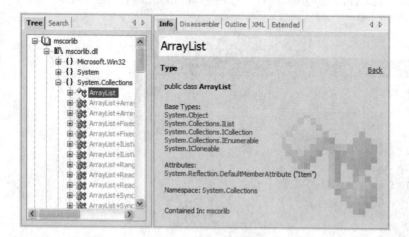

Figure 2-12. *Viewing referenced assemblies using the Assembly Scout*

The right side of the Assembly Scout utility allows you to view details of the item selected on the left pane. Not only can you view the basic details using the Info tab, but also you can view the underlying CIL code of the item and save its definition to an XML file.

Windows Forms Designers

As you will learn later in this book, *Windows Forms* is a toolkit used to build desktop applications with the .NET platform. To continue tinkering with SharpDevelop, click the Design tab located at the bottom of the MainForm.vb code window. Once you do, you will open the integrated Windows Forms designer.

Using the Windows Forms section of your Tools window, you can create a GUI for the Form you are designing. To demonstrate this, place a single Button type on your main Form by activating the Tools Scout (via the View menu), selecting the Button icon, and clicking the designer. To update the look and feel of any GUI item, you can make use of the Properties window (see Figure 2-13), which you activate from the View ➤ Properties menu selection. Select the Button from the drop-down list and change various aspects of the Button type (e.g., BackColor and Text).

Figure 2-13. *The Properties window*

Using this same window, you can handle events for a given GUI item. To do so, click the lightning bolt icon at the top of the Properties window. Next, select the GUI item you wish to interact with from the drop-down list (your Button in this case). Finally, handle the Click event by typing in the name of the method to be called when the user clicks the button (see Figure 2-14).

Figure 2-14. *Handing events via the Properties window*

Once you press the Enter key, SharpDevelop responds by generating stub code for your new method. To complete the example, enter the following statement within the scope of your event handler:

```
Private Sub ButtonClicked(sender As System.Object, _
  e As System.EventArgs)
  ' Update the Form's caption with a custom message.
  Me.Text = "Stop clicking my button!"
End Sub
```

At this point, you can run your program (using the Debug ➤ Run menu item). Sure enough, when you click your Button, you should see the Form's caption update as expected.

That should be enough information to get you up and running using the SharpDevelop IDE. I do hope you now have a good understanding of the basics, though obviously there is much more to this tool than presented here.

Building .NET Applications Using Visual Basic 2005 Express

During the summer of 2004, Microsoft introduced a brand-new line of IDEs that fall under the designation of "Express" products (http://msdn.microsoft.com/vstudio/express). To date, there are six members of the Express family:

- *Visual Web Developer 2005 Express*: A lightweight tool for building dynamic websites and XML web services using ASP.NET 2.0

- *Visual Basic 2005 Express*: A streamlined programming tool ideal for .NET programmers who want to learn how to build applications using the user-friendly syntax of Visual Basic

- *C# Express, Visual C++ 2005 Express, and Visual J# 2005 Express*: Targeted IDEs for students and enthusiasts who wish to learn the fundamentals of computer science in their syntax of choice

- *SQL Server 2005 Express*: An entry-level database management system geared toward hobbyists, enthusiasts, and student developers

---

■**Note** At the time of this writing, the Express family products are available free of charge for one calendar year. After that term of use has expired, you may purchase a given Express IDE for around US$49.00.

By and large, Express products are slimmed-down versions of their Visual Studio 2005 counterparts and are primarily targeted at .NET hobbyists and students. Like SharpDevelop, Visual Basic 2005 Express provides various object browsing tools, a Windows Forms designer, the Add References dialog box, IntelliSense capabilities, and code expansion templates. As well, Visual Basic 2005 Express offers a few (important) features currently not available in SharpDevelop, including

- An integrated graphical debugger

- Tools to simplify access to XML web services

Because the look and feel of Visual Basic 2005 Express is so similar to that of Visual Studio 2005 (and, to some degree, SharpDevelop) I will not provide a full walk-through of this particular IDE here. However, once you have installed this product, you may create a new Visual Basic 2005 project via the File ➤ New Project menu option. Notice in Figure 2-15 that not only are you able to define Windows, console, and code library–based projects, but also you can create a new "starter kit" application. Simply put, *starter kits* are complete VB 2005 applications that can be dissected and extended to your liking.

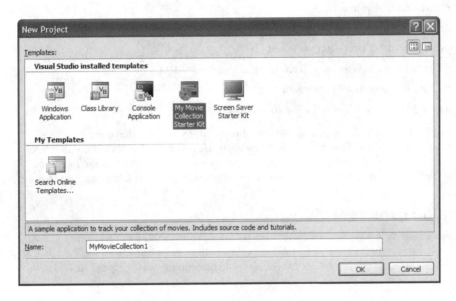

Figure 2-15. *Creating a new Visual Basic 2005 Express project*

The Big Kahuna: Building .NET Applications Using Visual Studio 2005

If you are a professional .NET software engineer, the chances are extremely good that your employer has purchased Microsoft's premier IDE, Visual Studio 2005, for your development endeavors (http://msdn.microsoft.com/vstudio/products). This tool is far and away the most feature-rich and enterprise-ready IDE examined in this chapter. Of course, this power comes at a price, which will vary based on the version of Visual Studio 2005 you purchase. As you might suspect, each version supplies a unique set of features.

My assumption during the remainder of this text is that you have chosen to make use of Visual Studio 2005 as your IDE of choice. Do understand that owning a copy of Visual Studio 2005 is not required for you to use this edition of the text. In the worst case, I may examine an option that is not provided by your IDE. However, rest assured that all of this book's sample code will compile just fine when processed by your tool of choice.

■**Note** Once you download the source code for this book from the Downloads area of the Apress website (http://www.apress.com), you may load the current example into Visual Studio 2005 by double-clicking the example's *.sln file. If you are not using Visual Studio 2005, you will need to manually configure your IDE to compile the provided *.vb files.

Learning the Lay of the Land: Visual Studio 2005

Visual Studio 2005 ships with the expected GUI designers, database manipulation tools, object and file browsing utilities, and an integrated help system. Unlike the IDEs we have already examined, Visual Studio 2005 provides numerous additions. Here is a partial list:

- Visual XML editors/designers
- Support for mobile device development (such as Smartphones and Pocket PC devices)
- Support for Microsoft Office development
- The ability to track changes for a given source document and view revisions
- Support for XML-based code expansions
- Visual tools to construct ASP.NET 2.0 web applications

To be completely honest, Visual Studio 2005 provides so many features that it would take an entire book (and a large book at that) to fully describe every aspect of the IDE. This is not that book. However, I do want to point out some of the major enhancements in the pages that follow. As you progress through the text, you'll learn more about the Visual Studio 2005 IDE where appropriate.

The Solution Explorer Utility

If you are following along, create a new VB 2005 console application (named Vs2005Example) using the File ➤ New ➤ Project menu item. The Solution Explorer utility (accessible from the View menu) allows you to view the set of all content files and referenced assemblies that comprise the current project (see Figure 2-16).

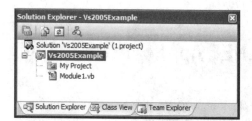

Figure 2-16. *Visual Studio 2005 Solution Explorer*

Similar to SharpDevelop, when you need to reference additional assemblies, right-click the Project icon and select Add Reference. At this point, you can select your assembly from the resulting dialog box (console projects reference System.dll, System.Data.dll, System.Deployment.dll, and System.Xml.dll by default).

Note If you wish to view the set of all assemblies referenced by your current project, one way to do so is to click the Show All Files button at the top of Solution Explorer and open the References folder. Once you do, you will see an icon for each assembly currently referenced.

The My Project Perspective

Next, notice an icon named My Project within Solution Explorer. When you double-click this item, you are presented with an enhanced project configuration editor (see Figure 2-17).

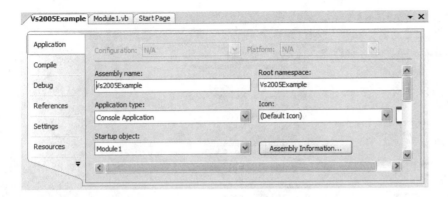

Figure 2-17. *The MyProject window*

You will see various aspects of the Project Properties window as you progress through this text. However, if you take some time to poke around, you will see that you can establish various security settings, "strongly name" your assembly, insert string resources, and configure pre- and postbuild events.

The Class View Utility

The next tool to examine is the Class View utility, which you can load from the View menu. Like SharpDevelop, the purpose of this utility is to show all of the types in your current project from an object-oriented perspective. The top pane displays the set of namespaces and their types, while the bottom pane displays the currently selected type's members (see Figure 2-18).

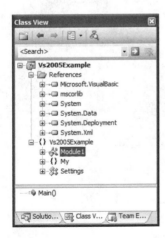

Figure 2-18. *The Class View utility*

The Object Browser Utility

As you may recall from Chapter 1, Visual Studio 2005 also provides a utility to investigate the set of referenced assemblies within your current project. Activate the Object Browser using the View ➤ Other Windows menu, and then select the assembly you wish to investigate (see Figure 2-19).

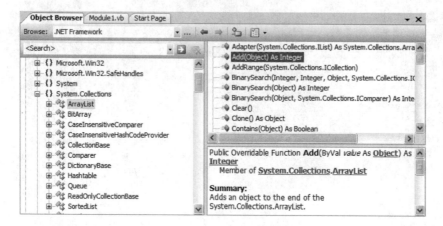

Figure 2-19. *The Visual Studio 2005 Object Browser utility*

Visual Studio 2005 Code Snippet Technology

Visual Studio 2005 (as well as Visual Basic 2005 Express) also has the capability to insert complex blocks of VB 2005 code using menu selections, context-sensitive mouse clicks, and/or keyboard shortcuts using *code snippets*. Simply put, a code snippet is a predefined block of Visual Basic 2005 code that will expand within the active code file. As you would guess, code snippets can greatly help increase productivity given that the tool will generate the necessary code statements (rather than us!).

To see this functionality firsthand, right-click a blank line within your Main() method and activate the Insert Snippet menu. From here, you will see that related code snippets are grouped under a specific category (Collections, Math, Security, XML, etc.). For this example, select the Math category and then activate the Calculate a Monthly Payment on a Loan snippet (see Figure 2-20).

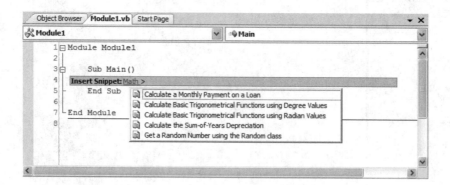

Figure 2-20. *Inserting VB 2005 code snippets*

Once you select a given snippet, you will find the related code is expanded automatically (press the Esc key to dismiss the pop-up menu). Many predefined code snippets identify specific "placeholders" for custom content. For example, once you activate the Calculate a Monthly Payment on a Loan snippet, you will find three regions are highlighted within the code window. Using the Tab key, you are able to cycle through each selection to modify the code as you see fit (see Figure 2-21).

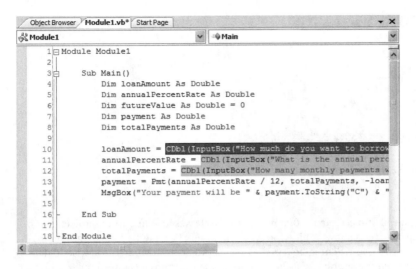

Figure 2-21. *The inserted snippet*

As you can see, Visual Studio 2005 defines a good number of code snippets. To be sure, the best way to learn about each possibility is simply through experimentation. Under the hood, each code snippet is defined within an XML document (taking a *.snippet extension by default) located under the C:\Program Files\Microsoft Visual Studio 8\Vb\Snippets\1033 directory. In fact, given that each snippet is simply an XML description of the code to be inserted within the IDE, it is very simple to build custom code snippets.

■Note Details of how to build custom snippets can be found in my article "Investigating Code Snippet Technology" at http://msdn.microsoft.com. While the article illustrates building C# code snippets, you can very easily build VB 2005 snippets by authoring VB 2005 code (rather than C# code) within the snippet's CDATA section.

The Visual Class Designer

Visual Studio 2005 gives us the ability to design classes visually (but this capability is not included in Visual Basic 2005 Express). The Class Designer utility allows you to view and modify the relationships of the types (classes, interfaces, structures, enumerations, and delegates) in your project. Using this tool, you are able to visually add (or remove) members to (or from) a type and have your modifications reflected in the corresponding *.vb file. As well, as you modify a given VB 2005 file, changes are reflected in the class diagram.

To work with this aspect of Visual Studio 2005, the first step is to insert a new class diagram file. There are many ways to do so, one of which is to click the View Class Diagram button located on Solution Explorer's right side (see Figure 2-22).

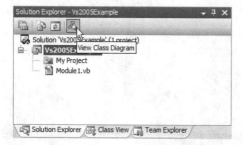

Figure 2-22. *Inserting a class diagram file*

Once you do, you will find class icons that represent the classes in your current project. If you click the arrow image, you can show or hide the type's members (see Figure 2-23). Do note that Visual Studio 2005 will show you *all* members in the current project by default. If you wish to delete a given item from the diagram, simply right-click and select Delete from the context menu (this will *not* delete the related code file).

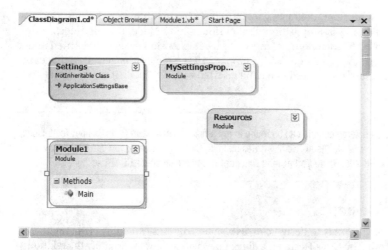

Figure 2-23. *The Class Diagram viewer*

This utility works in conjunction with two other aspects of Visual Studio 2005: the Class Details window (activated using the View ➤ Other Windows menu) and the Class Designer Toolbox (activated using the View ➤ Toolbox menu item). The Class Details window not only shows you the details of the currently selected item in the diagram, but also allows you to modify existing members and insert new members on the fly (see Figure 2-24).

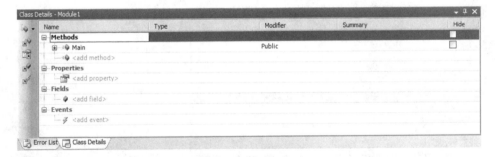

Figure 2-24. *The Class Details window*

The Class Designer Toolbox (see Figure 2-25) allows you to insert new types into your project (and create relationships between these types) visually. (Be aware that you must have a class diagram as the active window to view this toolbox.) As you do so, the IDE automatically creates new VB 2005 type definitions in the background.

Figure 2-25. *The Class Designer Toolbox*

By way of example, drag a new class from the Class Designer Toolbox onto your Class Designer. Name this class Car in the resulting dialog box. Now, using the Class Details window, add a public String field named petName (see Figure 2-26).

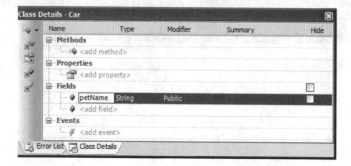

Figure 2-26. *Adding a field with the Class Details window*

If you now look at the VB 2005 definition of the Car class (within the newly generated Car.vb file), you will see it has been updated accordingly:

```
Public Class Car
  ' Public data is typically a bad idea,
  ' however it will simplify this example.
  Public petName As String
End Class
```

Now, add another new class to the designer named SportsCar. Next, select the Inheritance icon from the Class Designer Toolbox and click the SportsCar icon. Without releasing the mouse button, move the mouse cursor on top of the Car class icon and release the mouse button. If you performed these steps correctly, you have just derived the SportsCar class from Car (see Figure 2-27).

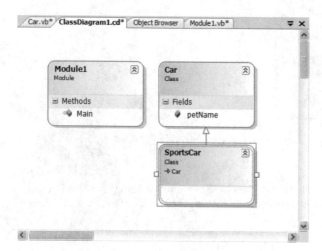

Figure 2-27. *Visually deriving from an existing class*

To complete this example, update the generated SportsCar class with a public method named PrintPetName() as follows (don't concern yourself with the syntax at this point; you'll dig into the details of class design beginning in the next chapter):

```
Public Class SportsCar
  Inherits Car
  Public Sub PrintPetName()
    petName = "Fred"
    Console.WriteLine("Name of this car is: {0}", petName)
  End Sub
End Class
```

Object Test Bench

Another nice visual tool provided by Visual Studio 2005 is Object Test Bench (OTB). This aspect of the IDE allows you to quickly create an instance of a class and invoke its members without the need to compile and run the entire application. This can be extremely helpful when you wish to test a specific method, but would rather not step through dozens of lines of code to do so.

To work with OTB, right-click the type you wish to create using the Class Designer. For example, right-click the SportsCar type, and from the resulting context menu select Create Instance ➤ SportsCar(). This will display a dialog box that allows you to name your temporary object variable (and supply any constructor arguments if required). Once the process is complete, you will find your object hosted within the IDE. Right-click the object icon and invoke the PrintPetName() method (see Figure 2-28).

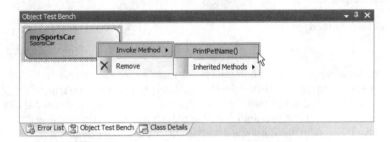

Figure 2-28. *The Visual Studio 2005 Object Test Bench*

You will see the message "Name of this car is: Fred" appear within the Visual Studio 2005 Quick Console.

The Integrated Help System

The final aspect of Visual Studio 2005 you must be comfortable with from the outset is the fully integrated help system. The .NET Framework 2.0 SDK documentation (aka, the MSDN Library) is extremely good, very readable, and full of useful information. Given the huge number of predefined .NET types (which number well into the thousands), you must be willing to roll up your sleeves and dig into the provided documentation. If you resist, you are doomed to a long, frustrating, and painful existence as a .NET developer.

Visual Studio 2005 provides the Dynamic Help window (accessed via the Help ➤ Dynamic Help menu selection), which changes its contents (dynamically!) based on what item (window, menu, source code keyword, etc.) is currently selected. For example, if you place the cursor on the Console class, the Dynamic Help window displays a set of links regarding the System.Console type.

You should also be aware of a very important subdirectory of the .NET Framework 2.0 SDK documentation. Under the .NET Development ➤ .NET Framework SDK ➤ Class Library Reference node of the documentation, you will find complete documentation of each and every namespace in the .NET base class libraries (see Figure 2-29).

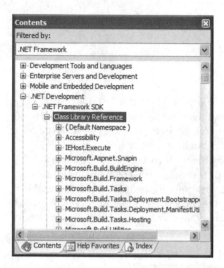

Figure 2-29. *The .NET base class library reference*

Each "book" defines the set of types in a given namespace, the members of a given type, and the parameters of a given member. Furthermore, when you view the help page for a given type, you will be told the name of the assembly and namespace that contains the type in question (located at the top of said page). As you read through the remainder of this book, I assume that you will dive into this very, very critical node to read up on additional details of the entity under examination.

■**Note** I'd like to stress again the importance of working with the supplied .NET Framework 2.0 documentation. When you are learning a brand-new framework and programming language, you will need to roll up your sleeves and dig into the details. No book, regardless of its size, can cover every detail of building applications with Visual Basic 2005. Thus, if you encounter a type or member that you would like more information about as you work through this text, be sure to leverage your help system!

The Role of the Visual Basic 6.0 Compatibility Assembly

As you will most certainly come to realize over the course of this book, Visual Basic 2005 is such as major overhaul of VB6 that it is often best to simply regard VB 2005 as a brand-new language in the BASIC family, rather than as "Visual Basic 7.0." To this end, many familiar VB6 functions, enumerations, user-defined types, and intrinsic objects are nowhere to be found directly within the .NET base class libraries.

While this is technically true, every Visual Basic 2005 project created with Visual Studio 2005 (as well as Visual Basic 2005 Express Edition) automatically references a particular .NET assembly named Microsoft.VisualBasic.dll, which defines types that provide the same functionality of the legacy VB6 constructs. As you would expect, the Microsoft.VisualBasic.dll assembly is composed of numerous namespaces that group together likeminded types (see Figure 2-30).

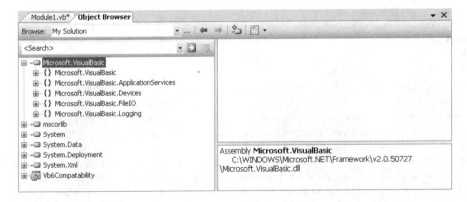

Figure 2-30. *The* `Microsoft.VisualBasic.dll` *VB6 compatibility assembly*

Furthermore, each of these namespaces are automatically available to each *.vb file in your project. Given this point, you do not need to explicitly add a set of Imports statements to gain access to their types. Thus, if you wished to do so, you could still make use of various VB6-isms, such as the MsgBox() call to display a simple message box:

```
' The Microsoft.VisualBasic namespaces
' are automatically referenced by a
' Visual Studio 2005 VB project.

Module Module1
  Sub Main()
    MsgBox("Hello, old friend...")
  End Sub
End Module
```

Notice how it appears that you are calling a global method named MsgBox() directly within Main(). In reality, the MsgBox() method is a member of a VB 2005 Module type named Interaction that is defined within the Microsoft.VisualBasic namespace (see Figure 2-31).

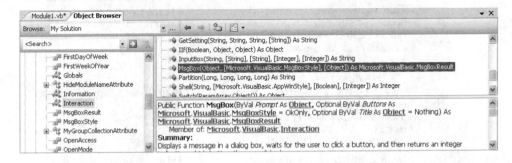

Figure 2-31. *The* `Microsoft.VisualBasic.Interaction.MsgBox()` *method*

As you will see in Chapter 3, a VB 2005 Module is similar to a VB6 *.bas file, in that members defined within a Module can be directly called without the need to prefix the name of the defining Module. However, if you were to prefix the Interaction Module to the MsgBox() function, the program would function identically:

```
Module Module1
  Sub Main()
    Interaction.MsgBox("Everything old is new again!")
  End Sub
End Module
```

Now although it may feel a bit reassuring to know that the functionality of VB6 can still be accessed from new Visual Basic 2005 projects, I recommend that you *avoid* using these types where possible. First of all, the writing seems to be on the wall regarding the lifetime of VB6, in that Microsoft itself plans to phase out support for VB6 over time, and given this, you cannot guarantee that this compatibility assembly will be supported in the future.

As well, the base class libraries provide numerous managed types that offer much more functionality than the (soon-to-be) legacy VB6 programming language. Given these points, this text will not make use of the VB6 compatibility layer. Rather, you will focus on learning the .NET base class libraries and how to interact with these types using the syntax of Visual Basic 2005.

A Partial Catalogue of Additional .NET Development Tools

Given the release of the .NET platform, Microsoft-centric programmers are now able to dive into the world of *open source* programming. As you may know, the Java and Unix/Linux communities have made use of this model for years. Simply put, open source development allows programmers to download free software tools with the underlying source code in order to extend or change the tool's functionality. (SharpDevelop is one example of such an open source application.)

To close this chapter, I would like to point out a number of .NET development tools that complement the functionality provided by your IDE of choice. While I don't have the space to cover the details of these utilities, Table 2-3 lists a number of the tools I have found to be extremely helpful as well as URLs you can visit to find more information about them (of course, the URLs are subject to change).

Table 2-3. *Select .NET Development Tools*

Tool	Meaning in Life	URL
FxCop	This is a must-have for any .NET developer interested in .NET best practices. FxCop will test any .NET assembly against the official Microsoft .NET best-practice coding guidelines.	http://www.gotdotnet.com/team/fxcop
Lutz Roeder's Reflector for .NET	This advanced .NET decompiler/object browser allows you to view the .NET implementation of any .NET type using CIL, VB 2005, Object Pascal .NET (Delphi), and Visual Basic .NET.	http://www.aisto.com/roeder/dotnet
NAnt	NAnt is the .NET equivalent of Ant, the popular Java automated build tool. NAnt allows you to define and execute detailed build scripts using an XML-based syntax.	http://sourceforge.net/projects/nant

Tool	Meaning in Life	URL
NDoc	NDoc is a tool that will generate code documentation files for VB 2005 code (or a compiled .NET assembly) in a variety of popular formats (MSDN's *.chm, XML, HTML, Javadoc, and LaTeX).	http://sourceforge.net/ projects/ndoc
NUnit	NUnit is the .NET equivalent of the Java-centric JUnit unit testing tool. Using NUnit, you are able to facilitate the testing of your managed code.	http://www.nunit.org
Refactor!	To the disappointment of many, Microsoft has chosen *not* to integrate refactoring capabilities for Visual Basic 2005 projects. The good news is that this freely downloadable plug-in allows Visual Basic 2005 developers to apply dozens of code refactorings using Visual Studio 2005.	http://msdn.microsoft.com/ vbasic/downloads/2005/tools/ refactor/
Vil	Think of Vil as a friendly "big brother" for .NET developers. This tool will analyze your .NET code and offer various opinions as to how to improve your code via refactoring, structured exception handling, and so forth.	http://www.1bot.com

Summary

So as you can see, you have many new toys at your disposal! The point of this chapter was to provide you with a tour of the major programming tools a VB 2005 programmer may leverage during the development process. You began the journey by learning how to generate .NET assemblies using nothing other than the free VB 2005 compiler and Notepad. Next, you were introduced to the TextPad application and walked through the process of enabling this tool to edit and compile *.vb code files.

You also examined three feature-rich IDEs, starting with the open source SharpDevelop, followed by Microsoft's Visual Basic 2005 Express and Visual Studio 2005. While this chapter only scratched the surface of each tool's functionality, you should be in a good position to explore your chosen IDE at your leisure. The chapter wrapped up by describing the role of Microsoft.VisualBasic.dll and examined a number of open source .NET development tools that extend the functionality of your IDE of choice.

■ ■ ■

## PART 2

Visual Basic 2005 Language Fundamentals

CHAPTER 3

■■■

VB 2005 Programming Constructs, Part I

This chapter begins your formal investigation of the Visual Basic 2005 programming language. Do be aware this chapter and the next will present a number of bite-sized stand-alone topics you must be comfortable with as you explore the .NET Framework. Unlike the remaining chapters in this text, there is no overriding theme in this part beyond examining the core syntactical features of VB 2005.

This being said, the first order of business is to understand the role of the `Module` type as well as the format of a program's entry point: the `Main()` method. Next, you will investigate the intrinsic VB 2005 data types (and their equivalent types in the `System` namespace) as well as various data type conversion routines. We wrap up by examining the set of operators, iteration constructs, and decision constructs used to build valid code statements.

The Role of the Module Type

Visual Basic 2005 supports a specific programming construct termed a *Module*. For example, when you create a console application using Visual Studio 2005, you automatically receive a *.vb file that contains the following code:

```
Module Module1
  Sub Main()
  End Sub
End Module
```

Under the hood, a `Module` is actually nothing more than a class type, with a few notable exceptions. First and foremost, any public function, subroutine, or member variable defined within the scope of a module is exposed as a "shared member" that is directly accessible throughout an application. Simply put, *shared members* allow us to simulate a global scope within your application that is roughly analogous to the functionality of a VB 6.0 *.bas file (full details on shared members can be found in Chapter 5).

Given that members in a `Module` type are directly accessible, you are not required to prefix the module's name when accessing its contents. To illustrate working with modules, create a new console application project (named FunWithModules) and update your initial `Module` type as follows:

```
Module Module1
  Sub Main()
    ' Show banner.
    DisplayBanner()
```

```
  ' Get user name and say howdy.
  GreetUser()
End Sub

Sub DisplayBanner()
  ' Pick your color of choice for the console text.
  Console.ForegroundColor = ConsoleColor.Yellow
  Console.WriteLine("******* Welcome to FunWithModules *******")
  Console.WriteLine("This simple program illustrates the role")
  Console.WriteLine("of the VB 2005 Module type.")
  Console.WriteLine("***************************************")
  ' Reset to previous color of your console text.
  Console.ForegroundColor = ConsoleColor.Green
  Console.WriteLine()
End Sub

Sub GreetUser()
  Dim userName As String
  Console.Write("Please enter your name: ")
  userName = Console.ReadLine()
  Console.WriteLine("Hello there {0}. Nice to meet ya.", userName)
End Sub
End Module
```

Figure 3-1 shows one possible output.

Figure 3-1. *Modules at work*

Projects with Multiple Modules

In our current example, notice that the Main() method is able to directly call the DisplayBanner()
and GreetUser() methods. Because these methods are defined within the same module as Main(),
we are not required to prefix the name of our module (Module1) to the member name. However, if
you wish to do so, you could retrofit Main() as follows:

```
Sub Main()
  ' Show banner.
  Module1.DisplayBanner()
  ' Get user name and say howdy.
  Module1.GreetUser()
End Sub
```

In this case, this is a completely optional bit of syntax (there is no difference in terms of per-
formance or the size of the compiled assembly). However, assume you were to define a new module
(MyModule) in your project (within the same *.vb file, for example), which defines an identically formed
GreetUser() method:

```
Module MyModule
  Public Sub GreetUser()
    Console.WriteLine("Hello user...")
  End Sub
End Module
```

If you wish to call MyModule.GreetUser() from within the Main() method, you would now need to *explicitly* prefix the module name. If you do not specify the name of the module, the Main() method automatically calls the Module1.GreetUser() method, as it is in the same scope as Main():

```
Sub Main()
  ' Show banner.
  DisplayBanner()

  ' Call the GreetUser() method in MyModule.
  MyModule.GreetUser()
End Sub
```

Again, do understand that when a single project defines multiple modules, you are not required to prefix the module name unless the methods are ambiguous. Thus, if your current project were to define yet another module named MyMathModule:

```
Module MyMathModule
  Function Add(ByVal x As Integer, ByVal y As Integer) As Integer
    Return x + y
  End Function
  Function Subtract(ByVal x As Integer, ByVal y As Integer) As Integer
    Return x - y
  End Function
End Module
```

you could directly invoke the Add() and Subtract() functions anywhere within your application (or optionally prefix the module's name):

```
Sub Main()
...
  ' Add some numbers.
  Console.WriteLine("10 + 10 is {0}.", Add(10, 10))

  ' Subtract some numbers
  ' (module prefix optional)
  Console.WriteLine("10 - 10 is {0}.", MyMathModule.Subtract(10, 10))
End Sub
```

■**Note** If you are new to the syntax of BASIC languages, rest assured that Chapter 4 will cover the details of building functions and subroutines using VB 2005.

Modules Are Not Creatable

Another trait of the Module type is that it cannot be directly created using the VB 2005 New keyword (any attempt to do so will result in a compiler error). Therefore the following code is illegal:

```
' Nope! Error, can't allocated modules!
Dim m as New Module1()
```

Rather, a Module type simply exposes shared members.

Note If you already have a background in object-oriented programming, be aware that Module types cannot be used to build class hierarchies as they are implicitly *sealed*. As well, unlike "normal" classes, modules cannot implement interfaces.

Renaming Your Initial Module

By default, Visual Studio 2005 names the initial Module type with the rather nondescript Module1. If you were to change the name of the module defining your Main() method to a more fitting name (Program, for example), the compiler will generate an error such as the following:

```
'Sub Main' was not found in 'FunWithModules.Module1'.
```

In order to inform Visual Studio 2005 of the new module name, you are required to reset the "startup object" using the Application tab of the My Project dialog box, as you see in Figure 3-2.

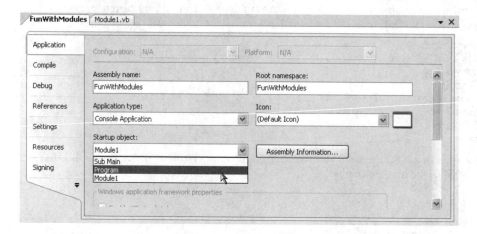

Figure 3-2. *Resetting the module name*

Once you do so, you will be able to compile your application without error.

Note As a shortcut, if you double-click this specific compiler error within the VS 2005 Error List window, you will be presented with a dialog box that allows you to select the new name of your project's entry point.

Members of Modules

To wrap up our investigation of Module types, do know that modules can have additional members beyond subroutines and functions. If you wish to define field data (as well as other members, such as properties or events), you are free to do so. For example, assume you wish to update MyModule to contain a single piece of public string data. Note that the GreetUser() method will now print out this value when invoked:

```
Module MyModule
  Public userName As String
```

```
  Sub GreetUser()
    Console.WriteLine("Hello, {0}.", userName)
  End Sub
End Module
```

Like any Module member, the userName field can be directly accessed by any part of your application. For example:

```
Sub Main()
...
  ' Set userName and call second form of GreetUser().
  userName = "Fred"
  MyModule.GreetUser()
...
End Sub
```

■ **Source Code** The FunWithModules project is located under the Chapter 3 subdirectory.

The Role of the Main Method

Every VB 2005 executable application (such as a console program, Windows service, or Windows
Forms application) must contain a type defining a Main() method, which represents the entry point
of the application. As you have just seen, the Main() method is typically placed within a Module type,
which as you recall implicitly defines Main() as a shared method.

Strictly speaking, however, Main() can also be defined within the scope of a Class type or Structure
type as well. If you do define your Main() method within either of these types, you must explicitly
make use of the Shared keyword. To illustrate, create a new console application named FunWithMain.
Delete the code within the initial *.vb file and replace it with the following:

```
Class Program
  ' Unlike Modules, members in a Class are not
  ' automatically shared.
  Shared Sub Main()
  End Sub
End Class
```

If you attempt to compile your program, you will again receive a compiler error informing you
that the Main() method cannot be located. Using the Application tab of the My Project dialog box,
you can now specify Sub Main() as the entry point to the program (as previously shown in Figure 3-2).

Processing Command-line Arguments Using System.Environment

One common task Main() will undertake is to process any incoming command-line arguments. For
example, consider the VB 2005 command-line compiler, vbc.exe (see Chapter 2). As you recall, we
specified various options (such as /target, /out, and so forth) when compiling our code files. The
vbc.exe compiler processed these input flags in order to compile the output assembly. When you
wish to build a Main() method that can process incoming command-line arguments for your custom applications, you have a few possible ways to do so.

Your first approach is to make use of the shared GetCommandLineArgs() method defined by the
System.Environment type. This method returns you an array of String data types. The first item in
the array represents the path to the executable program, while any remaining items in the array
represent the command-line arguments themselves. To illustrate, update your current Main() method
as follows:

```
Class Program
  Shared Sub Main()
    Console.WriteLine("***** Fun with Main() *****")
    ' Get command-line args.
    Dim args As String() = Environment.GetCommandLineArgs()
    Dim s As String
    For Each s In args
      Console.WriteLine("Arg: {0}", s)
    Next
  End Sub
End Class
```

If you were to now run your application at the command prompt, you can feed in your arguments in an identical manner as you did when working with vbc.exe (see Figure 3-3).

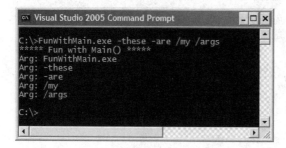

Figure 3-3. *Processing command-line arguments*

Of course, it is up to you to determine which command-line arguments your program will respond to and how they must be formatted (such as with a - or / prefix). Here we simply passed in a series of options that were printed to the command prompt. Assume however you were creating a new video game using Visual Basic 2005 and programmed your application to process an option named -godmode. If the user starts your application with the flag, you know the user is in fact a *cheater*, and can take an appropriate course of action.

Processing Command-line Arguments with Main()

If you would rather not make use of the System.Environment type to process command-line arguments, you can define your Main() method to take an incoming array of strings. To illustrate, update your code base as follows:

```
Shared Sub Main(ByVal args As String())
  Console.WriteLine("***** Fun with Main() *****")
  ' Get command-line args.
  Dim s As String
  For Each s In args
    Console.WriteLine("Arg: {0}", s)
  Next
End Sub
```

When you take this approach, the first item in the incoming array is indeed the first command-line argument (rather than the path to the executable). If you were to run your application once again, you will find each command-line option is printed to the console.

Main() As a Function (not a Subroutine)

It is also possible to define Main() as a function returning an Integer, rather than a subroutine (which never has a return value). This approach to building a Main() method has its roots in C-based languages, where returning the value 0 indicates the program has terminated without error. You will seldom (if ever) need to build your Main() method in this manner; however, for the sake of completion, here is one example:

```
Shared Function Main(ByVal args As String()) As Integer
  Console.WriteLine("***** Fun with Main() *****")
  Dim s As String
  For Each s In args
    Console.WriteLine("Arg: {0}", s)
  Next
  ' Return a value to the OS.
  Return 0
End Function
```

Regardless of how you define your Main() method, the purpose remains the same: interact with the types that carry out the functionality of your application. Once the final statement within the Main() method has executed, Main() exits and your application terminates.

Simulating Command-line Arguments Using Visual Studio 2005

Finally, let me point out that Visual Studio 2005 does allow you to simulate incoming command-line arguments. Rather than having to run your application at a command line to feed in arguments, you can explicitly specify arguments using the Debug tab of the My Project dialog box, shown in Figure 3-4 (note the Command line arguments text area).

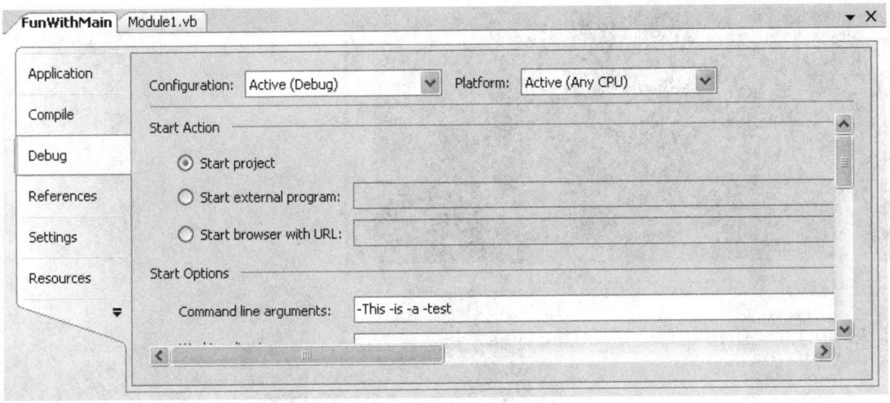

Figure 3-4. *Simulating command-line arguments*

When you compile and run your application under Debug mode, the specified arguments are passed to your Main() method automatically. Do know that when you compile and run a Release build of your application (which can be established using the Compile tab of the My Project dialog box), this is no longer the case.

An Interesting Aside: Some Additional Members of the System.Environment Class

The Environment type exposes a number of extremely helpful methods beyond GetCommandLineArgs(). This class allows you to obtain a number of details regarding the operating system currently hosting your .NET application using various shared members. To illustrate the usefulness of System.Environment, update your Main() method with the following logic:

```
Shared Function Main(ByVal args As String()) As Integer
...
  ' OS running this app?
  Console.WriteLine("Current OS: {0}", Environment.OSVersion)

  ' List the drives on this machine.
  Dim drives As String() = Environment.GetLogicalDrives()
  Dim d As String
  For Each d In drives
    Console.WriteLine("You have a drive named {0}.", d)
  Next

  ' Which version of the .NET platform is running this app?
  Console.WriteLine("Executing version of .NET: {0}", _
    Environment.Version)
  Return 0
End Function
```

Figure 3-5 shows a possible test run.

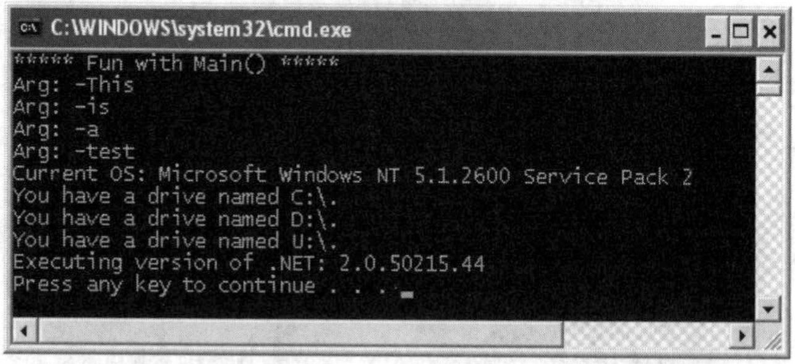

Figure 3-5. *Displaying system environment variables*

The Environment type defines members other than those seen in the previous example. Table 3-1 documents some additional properties of interest; however, be sure to check out the .NET Framework 2.0 SDK documentation for full details.

Table 3-1. *Select Properties of* System.Environment

Property	Meaning in Life
CurrentDirectory	Gets the full path to the current application
MachineName	Gets the name of the current machine
NewLine	Gets the newline symbol for the current environment
ProcessorCount	Returns the number of processors on the current machine
SystemDirectory	Returns the full path to the system directory
UserName	Returns the name of the user that started this application

■**Source Code** The FunWithMain project is located under the Chapter 3 subdirectory.

The System.Console Class

Almost all of the example applications created over the course of the initial chapters of this text make extensive use of the System.Console class. While it is true that a console user interface (CUI) is not as enticing as a graphical user interface (GUI) or web-based front end, restricting the early examples to console applications will allow us to keep focused on the syntax of Visual Basic 2005 and the core aspects of the .NET platform, rather than dealing with the complexities of building GUIs.

As its name implies, the Console class encapsulates input, output, and error stream manipulations for console-based applications. While System.Console has been a part of the .NET Framework since its inception, with the release of .NET 2.0, the Console type has been enhanced with additional functionality. Table 3-2 lists some (but definitely not all) of the new members of interest.

Table 3-2. *Select .NET 2.0–Specific Members of* System.Console

Member	Meaning in Life
Beep()	Forces the console to emit a beep of a specified frequency and duration.
BackgroundColor ForegroundColor	These properties set the background/foreground colors for the current output. They may be assigned any member of the ConsoleColor enumeration.
BufferHeight BufferWidth	These properties control the height/width of the console's buffer area.
Title	This property sets the title of the current console.
WindowHeight WindowWidth WindowTop WindowLeft	These properties control the dimensions of the console in relation to the established buffer.
Clear()	This method clears the established buffer and console display area.

Basic Input and Output with the Console Class

In addition to the members in Table 3-2, the Console type defines a set of methods to capture input and output, all of which are shared and are therefore called by prefixing the name of the class (Console) to the method name. As you have seen, WriteLine() pumps a text string (including a carriage return) to the output stream. The Write() method pumps text to the output stream without a carriage return. ReadLine() allows you to receive information from the input stream up until the carriage return, while Read() is used to capture a single character from the input stream.

To illustrate basic I/O using the Console class, create a new console application named BasicConsoleIO and update your Main() method with logic that prompts the user for some bits of information and echoes each item to the standard output stream.

```
Sub Main()
  Console.WriteLine("***** Fun with Console IO *****")
  ' Echo some information to the console.
  Console.Write("Enter your name: ")
  Dim s As String = Console.ReadLine()
  Console.WriteLine("Hello, {0}", s)
  Console.Write("Enter your age: ")
  s = Console.ReadLine()
  Console.WriteLine("You are {0} years old", s)
End Sub
```

Formatting Console Output

During these first few chapters, you have certainly noticed numerous occurrences of the tokens {0}, {1}, and the like embedded within a string literal. The .NET platform introduces a new style of string formatting, which can be used by any .NET programming language (including VB 2005). Simply put, when you are defining a string literal that contains segments of data whose value is not known until runtime, you are able to specify a placeholder within the literal using this curly-bracket syntax. At runtime, the value(s) passed into Console.WriteLine() are substituted for each placeholder. To illustrate, update your current Main() method as follows:

```
Sub Main()
...
  ' Specify string placeholders and values to use at
  ' runtime.
  Dim theInt As Integer = 90
  Dim theDouble As Double = 9.99
  Dim theBool As Boolean = True
  Console.WriteLine("Value of theInt: {0}", theInt)
  Console.WriteLine("theDouble is {0} and theBool is {1}.", _
    theDouble, theBool)
End Sub
```

The first parameter to WriteLine() represents a string literal that contains optional placeholders designated by {0}, {1}, {2}, and so forth. Be very aware that the first ordinal number of a curly-bracket placeholder always begins with 0. The remaining parameters to WriteLine() are simply the values to be inserted into the respective placeholders (in this case, an Integer, a Double, and a Boolean).

Note If you have a mismatch between the number of uniquely numbered curly-bracket placeholders and fill arguments, you will receive a FormatException exception at runtime.

It is also permissible for a given placeholder to repeat within a given string. For example, if you are a Beatles fan and want to build the string "9, Number 9, Number 9" you would write

```
' John says...
Console.WriteLine("{0}, Number {0}, Number {0}", 9)
```

Also know, that it is possible to position each placeholder in any location within a string literal, and need not follow an increasing sequence. For example, consider the following code snippet:

```
' Prints: 20, 10, 30
Console.WriteLine("{1}, {0}, {2}", 10, 20, 30)
```

.NET String Formatting Flags

If you require more elaborate formatting, each placeholder can optionally contain various format characters. Each format character can be typed in either uppercase or lowercase with little or no consequence. Table 3-3 shows your core formatting options.

Table 3-3. *.NET String Format Characters*

String Format Character	Meaning in Life
C or c	Used to format currency. By default, the flag will prefix the local cultural symbol (a dollar sign [$] for U.S. English).
D or d	Used to format decimal numbers. This flag may also specify the minimum number of digits used to pad the value.
E or e	Used for exponential notation.
F or f	Used for fixed-point formatting.
G or g	Stands for *general*. This character can be used to format a number to fixed or exponential format.
N or n	Used for basic numerical formatting (with commas).
X or x	Used for hexadecimal formatting. If you use an uppercase X, your hex format will also contain uppercase characters.

These format characters are suffixed to a given placeholder value using the colon token (e.g., {0:C}, {1:d}, {2:X}, and so on). Now, update the Main() method with the following logic:

```
' Now make use of some format tags.
Sub Main()
...
  Console.WriteLine("C format: {0:C}", 99989.987)
  Console.WriteLine("D9 format: {0:D9}", 99999)
  Console.WriteLine("E format: {0:E}", 99999.76543)
  Console.WriteLine("F3 format: {0:F3}", 99999.9999)
  Console.WriteLine("N format: {0:N}", 99999)
  Console.WriteLine("X format: {0:X}", 99999)
  Console.WriteLine("x format: {0:x}", 99999)
End Sub
```

Here we are defining numerous string literals, each of which has a segment not known until runtime. At runtime, the format character will be used internally by the Console type to print out the entire string in the desired format.

Be aware that the use of the .NET string formatting characters are not limited to console applications! These same flags can be used when calling the shared String.Format() method. This can be helpful when you need to build a string containing numerical values in memory for use in any application type (Windows Forms, ASP.NET, XML web services, and so on). To illustrate, update Main() with the following final code:

```
' Now make use of some format tags.
Sub Main()
...
  ' Use the shared String.Format() method to build a new string.
  Dim formatStr As String
  formatStr = _
    String.Format("Don't you wish you had {0:C} in your account?", 99989.987)
  Console.WriteLine(formatStr)
End Sub
```

Figure 3-6 shows a test run of our application.

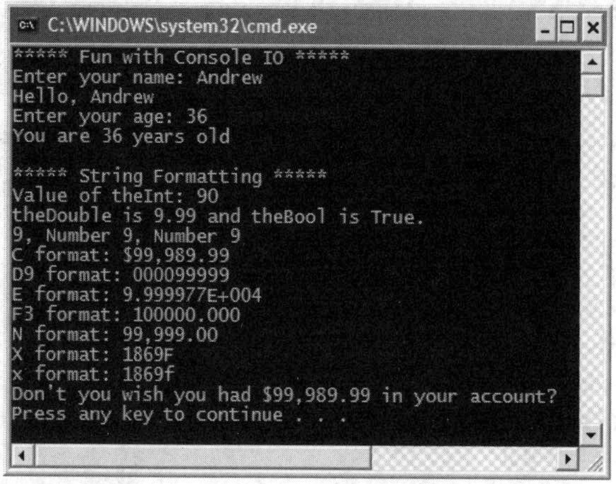

Figure 3-6. *The* System.Console *type in action*

■Source Code The BasicConsoleIO project is located under the Chapter 3 subdirectory.

The System Data Types and VB 2005 Shorthand Notation

Like any programming language, VB 2005 defines an intrinsic set of data types, which are used to represent local variables, member variables, and member parameters. Although many of the VB 2005 data types are named identically to data types found under VB 6.0, be aware that there is *not* a direct mapping (especially in terms of a data type's maximum and minimum range). Furthermore, VB 2005 defines a set of brand new data types not supported by previous versions of the language (UInteger, ULong, SByte) that account for signed and unsigned data.

■Note The UInteger, ULong, and SByte data types are *not* CLS compliant (see Chapters 1 and 14 for details on CLS compliance). Therefore, if you expose these data types from an assembly, you cannot guarantee that every .NET programming language will be able to process this data.

The most significant change from VB 6.0 is that the data type keywords of Visual Basic 2005 are actually shorthand notations for full-blown types in the System namespace. Table 3-4 documents the data types of VB 2005 (with the size of storage allocation), the System data type equivalents, and the range of each type.

Table 3-4. *The Intrinsic Data Types of VB 2005*

VB 2005 Data Type	System Data Type	Range
Boolean (platform dependent)	System.Boolean	True or False.
Byte (1 byte)	System.Byte	0 to 255 (unsigned).
Char (2 bytes)	System.Char	0 to 65535 (unsigned).
Date (8 bytes)	System.DateTime	January 1, 0001 to December 31, 9999.
Decimal (16 bytes)	System.Decimal	+/–79,228,162,514,264,337,593,543,950,335 with no decimal point. +/–7.9228162514264337593543950335 with 28 places to the right of the decimal; smallest nonzero number is +/–0.0000000000000000000000000001.
Double (8 bytes)	System.Double	–1.79769313486231E+308 to –4.94065645841247E–324 for negative values. 4.94065645841247E–324 to 1.79769313486231E+308 for positive values.
Integer (4 bytes)	System.Int32	–2,147,483,648 to 2,147,483,647.
Long (8 bytes)	System.Int64	–9,223,372,036,854,775,808 to 9,223,372,036,854,775,807.
Object (4 bytes)	System.Object	Any type can be stored in a variable of type Object.
SByte (1 byte)	System.SByte	–128 through 127 (signed).
Short (2 bytes)	System.Int16	–32,768 to 32,767.
Single (4 bytes)	System.Single	This single-precision floating-point value can take the range of –3.402823E+38 to –1.401298E–45 for negative values; 1.401298E–45 to 3.402823E+38 for positive values.
String (platform dependent)	System.String	A string of Unicode characters between 0 to approximately 2 billion characters.
UInteger (4 bytes)	System.UInt32	0 through 4,294,967,295 (unsigned).
ULong (8 bytes)	System.UInt64	0 through 18,446,744,073,709,551,615 (unsigned).
SByte (2 bytes)	System.UInt16	0 through 65,535 (unsigned).

Each of the numerical types (Short, Integer, and so forth) as well as the Date type map to a corresponding *structure* in the System namespace. In a nutshell, structures are "value types" allocated on the stack rather than on the garbage-collected heap. On the other hand, String and Object are "reference types," meaning the variable is allocated on the managed heap. You examine full details of value and reference types in Chapter 11.

Variable Declaration and Initialization

When you are declaring a data type as a local variable (e.g., within a member scope), you do so using the Dim and As keywords. By way of a few examples:

```
Sub MyMethod()
  ' Dim variableName As dataType
  Dim age As Integer
  Dim firstName As String
  Dim isUserOnline As Boolean
End Sub
```

One helpful syntactic change that has occurred with the release of the .NET platform is the ability to declare a sequence of variables on a single line of code. Of course, VB 6.0 also supported this ability, but the semantics were a bit nonintuitive and a source of subtle bugs. For example, under VB 6.0, if you do not explicitly set the data types of each variable, the unqualified variables were set to the VB 6.0 Variant data type:

```
' In this line of VB 6.0 code, varOne
' is implicitly defined to be of type Variant!
Dim varOne, varTwo As Integer
```

This behavior is a bit cumbersome, given that the only way you are able to define multiple variables of the same type under VB 6.0 is to write the following slightly redundant code:

```
Dim varOne As Integer, varTwo As Integer
```

or worse yet, on multiple lines of code:

```
Dim varOne As Integer
Dim varTwo As Integer
```

Although these approaches are still valid using VB 2005, when you declare multiple variables on a single line, they *all* are defined in terms of the specified data type. Thus, in the following VB 2005 code, you have created two variables of type Integer.

```
Sub MyMethod()
  ' In this line of VB 2005 code, varOne
  ' and varTwo are both of type Integer!
  Dim varOne, varTwo As Integer
End Sub
```

On a final note, VB 2005 now supports the ability to assign a value to a type directly at the point of declaration. To understand the significance of this new bit of syntax, consider the fact that under VB 6.0, you were forced to write the following:

```
' VB 6.0 code.
Dim i As Integer
i = 99
```

While this is in no way a major showstopper, VB 2005 allows you to streamline variable assignment using the following notation:

```
Sub MyMethod()
  ' Dim variableName As dataType = initialValue
  Dim age As Integer = 36
  Dim firstName As String = "Sid"
  Dim isUserOnline As Boolean = True
End Sub
```

Default Values of Data Types

All VB 2005 data types have a default value that will automatically be assigned to the variable. The default values are very predictable, and can be summarized as follows:

- Boolean types are set to False.
- Numeric data is set to 0 (or 0.0 in the case of floating-point data types).
- String types are set to empty strings.
- Char types are set to a single empty character.
- Date types are set to 1/1/0001 12:00:00 AM.
- Initialized object references are set to Nothing.

Given these rules, ponder the following code:

```
' Fields of a class or Module receive automatic default assignments.
Module Program
  Public myInt As Integer       ' Set to 0.
  Public myString As String     ' Set to empty String.
  Public myBool As Boolean      ' Set to False.
  Public myObj As Object        ' Set to Nothing.
End Module
```

In Visual Basic 2005, the same rules of default values hold true for local variables defined within a given scope. Given this, the following method would return the value 0, given that each local Integer has been automatically assigned the value 0:

```
Function Add() As Integer
  Dim a, b As Integer
  Return a + b     ' Returns zero.
End Function
```

The Data Type Class Hierarchy

It is very interesting to note that even the primitive .NET data types are arranged in a "class hierarchy." If you are new to the world of inheritance, you will discover the full details in Chapter 6. Until then, just understand that types at the top of a class hierarchy provide some default behaviors that are granted to the derived types. The relationship between these core system types can be understood as shown in Figure 3-7.

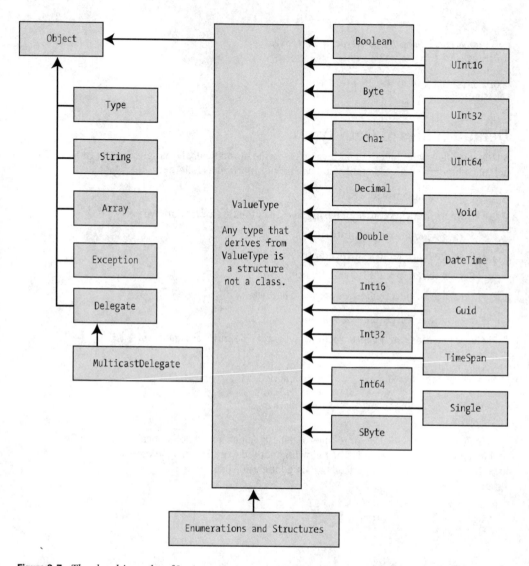

Figure 3-7. *The class hierarchy of* System *types*

Notice that each of these types ultimately derives from System.Object, which defines a set of methods (ToString(), Equals(), GetHashCode(), and so forth) common to all types in the .NET base class libraries (these methods are fully detailed in Chapter 6).

Also note that many numerical data types derive from a class named System.ValueType. Descendents of ValueType are automatically allocated on the stack and therefore have a very predictable lifetime and are quite efficient. On the other hand, types that do not have System.ValueType in their inheritance chain (such as System.Type, System.String, System.Array, System.Exception, and System.Delegate) are not allocated on the stack, but on the garbage-collected heap.

Without getting too hung up on the details of System.Object and System.ValueType for the time being (again, more details in Chapter 11), simply know that because a VB 2005 keyword (such as Integer) is simply shorthand notation for the corresponding system type (in this case, System.Int32), the following is perfectly legal syntax, given that System.Int32 (the VB 2005 Integer) eventually derives from System.Object, and therefore can invoke any of its public members:

```
Sub Main()
    ' A VB 2005 Integer is really a shorthand for System.Int32.
    ' which inherits the following members from System.Object.
    Console.WriteLine(12.GetHashCode())    ' Prints the type's hash code value.
    Console.WriteLine(12.Equals(23))       ' Prints False
    Console.WriteLine(12.ToString())       ' Returns the value "12"
    Console.WriteLine(12.GetType())        ' Prints System.Int32
End Sub
```

■**Note** By default, Visual Studio 2005 does not show these "advanced" methods from IntelliSense. To disable this behavior (which I recommend you do), activate the Tools ➤ Options menu, select Basic from the Text Editor node, and uncheck Hide Advanced members.

"New-ing" Intrinsic Data Types

All intrinsic data types support what is known as a *default constructor* (see Chapter 5). In a nutshell, this feature allows you to create a variable using the New keyword, which automatically sets the variable to its default value. Although it is more cumbersome to use the New keyword when creating a basic data type variable, the following is syntactically well-formed VB 2005 code:

```
' When you create a basic data type with New,
' it is automatically set to its default value.
Dim b1 As New Boolean()    ' b1 automatically set to False.
```

On a related note, you could also declare an intrinsic data type variable using the full type name through either of these approaches:

```
' These statements are also functionally identical.
Dim b2 As System.Boolean = New System.Boolean()
Dim b3 As System.Boolean
```

Of course, the chances that you will define a simple Boolean using the full type name or the New keyword in your code is slim to none. It is important, however, to always remember that the VB 2005 keywords for simple data types are little more than a shorthand notation for real types in the System namespace.

Experimenting with Numerical Data Types

To experiment with the intrinsic VB 2005 data types, create a new console application named BasicDataTypes. First up, understand that the numerical types of .NET support MaxValue and MinValue properties that provide information regarding the range a given type can store. For example:

```
Sub Main()
    Console.WriteLine("***** Fun with Data Types *****")
    Console.WriteLine("Max of Integer: {0}", Integer.MaxValue)
    Console.WriteLine("Min of Integer: {0}", Integer.MinValue)
    Console.WriteLine("Max of Double: {0}", Double.MaxValue)
    Console.WriteLine("Min of Double: {0}", Double.MinValue)
End Sub
```

In addition to the MinValue/MaxValue properties, a given numerical system type may define further useful members. For example, the System.Double type allows you to obtain the values for epsilon and infinity (which may be of interest to those of you with a mathematical flare):

```
Console.WriteLine("Double.Epsilon: {0}", Double.Epsilon)
Console.WriteLine("Double.PositiveInfinity: {0}", _
```

```
    Double.PositiveInfinity)
Console.WriteLine("Double.NegativeInfinity: {0}", _
    Double.NegativeInfinity)
```

Members of System.Boolean

Next, consider the System.Boolean data type. The only valid assignment a VB 2005 Boolean can take is from the set {True | False}. Given this point, it should be clear that System.Boolean does not support a MinValue/MaxValue property set, but rather TrueString/FalseString (which yields the string "True" or "False" respectively):

```
Console.WriteLine("Boolean.FalseString: {0}", Boolean.FalseString)
Console.WriteLine("Boolean.TrueString: {0}", Boolean.TrueString)
```

Members of System.Char

VB 2005 textual data is represented by the intrinsic String and Char keywords, which are simple shorthand notations for System.String and System.Char, both of which are Unicode under the hood. As you most certainly already know, a string is a contiguous set of characters (e.g., "Hello"). As of the .NET platform, VB now has a data type (Char) that can represent a single slot in a String type (e.g, 'H').

By default, when you define textual data within double quotes, the VB 2005 compiler assumes you are defining a full-blown String type. However, to build a single character string literal that should be typed as a Char, place the character between double quotes and tack on a single *c* after the closing quote. Doing so ensures that the double-quoted text literal is indeed represented as a System.Char, rather than a System.String:

```
Dim myChar As Char = "a"c
```

■**Note** When you enable Option Strict (described in just a moment) for your project, the VB 2005 compiler demands that you tack on the c suffix to a Char data type when assigning a value.

The System.Char type provides you with a great deal of functionality beyond the ability to hold a single point of character data. Using the shared methods of System.Char, you are able to determine whether a given character is numerical, alphabetical, a point of punctuation, or whatnot. To illustrate, update Main() with the following statements:

```
' Fun with System.Char.
Dim myChar As Char = "a"c
Console.WriteLine("Char.IsDigit('a'): {0}", Char.IsDigit(myChar))
Console.WriteLine("Char.IsLetter('a'): {0}", Char.IsLetter(myChar))
Console.WriteLine("Char.IsWhiteSpace('Hello There', 5): {0}", _
    Char.IsWhiteSpace("Hello There", 5))
Console.WriteLine("Char.IsWhiteSpace('Hello There', 6): {0}", _
    Char.IsWhiteSpace("Hello There", 6))
Console.WriteLine("Char.IsPunctuation('?'): {0}", _
    Char.IsPunctuation("?"c))
```

As illustrated in the previous code snippet, the members of System.Char have two calling conventions: a single character or a string with a numerical index that specifies the position of the character to test.

Parsing Values from String Data

The .NET data types provide the ability to generate a variable of their underlying type given a textual equivalent (e.g., parsing). This technique can be extremely helpful when you wish to convert a bit of user input data (such as a selection from a GUI-based drop-down list box) into a numerical value. Consider the following parsing logic:

```
' Fun with parsing
Dim b As Boolean = Boolean.Parse("True")
Console.WriteLine("Value of myBool: {0}", b)
Dim d As Double = Double.Parse("99.884")
Console.WriteLine("Value of myDbl: {0}", d)
Dim i As Integer = Integer.Parse("8")
Console.WriteLine("Value of myInt: {0}", i)
Dim c As Char = Char.Parse("w")
Console.WriteLine("Value of myChar: {0}", c)
```

■**Source Code** The BasicDataTypes project is located under the Chapter 3 subdirectory.

Understanding the System.String Type

As mentioned, String is a native data type in VB 2005. Like all intrinsic types, the VB 2005 String keyword actually is a shorthand notation for a true type in the .NET base class library, which in this case is System.String. Therefore, you are able to declare a String variable using either of these notations (in addition to using the New keyword as shown previously):

```
' These two string declarations are functionally equivalent.
Dim firstName As String
Dim lastName As System.String
```

System.String provides a number of methods you would expect from such a utility class, including methods that return the length of the character data, find substrings within the current string, convert to and from uppercase/lowercase, and so forth. Table 3-5 lists some (but by no means all) of the interesting members.

Table 3-5. *Select Members of* System.String

Member of String Class	Meaning in Life
Chars	This property returns a specific character within the current string.
Length	This property returns the length of the current string.
Compare()	Compares two strings.
Contains()	Determines whether a string contain a specific substring.
Equals()	Tests whether two string objects contain identical character data.
Format()	Formats a string using other primitives (i.e., numerical data, other strings) and the {0} notation examined earlier in this chapter.
Insert()	Inserts a string within a given string.
PadLeft() PadRight()	These methods are used to pad a string with some character.
Remove() Replace()	Use these methods to receive a copy of a string, with modifications (characters removed or replaced).

Continued

Table 3-5. *Continued*

Member of String Class	Meaning in Life
Split()	Returns a String array containing the substrings in this instance that are delimited by elements of a specified Char or String array.
Trim()	Removes all occurrences of a set of specified characters from the beginning and end of the current string.
ToUpper() ToLower()	Creates a copy of the current string in uppercase or lowercase format.

Basic String Manipulation

Working with the members of System.String is as you would expect. Simply create a String data type and make use of the provided functionality via the dot operator. Do be aware that a few of the members of System.String are shared members, and are therefore called at the class (rather than the object) level. Assume you have created a new console application named FunWithStrings, and updated Main() as follows:

```
Module Program
  Sub Main()
    Console.WriteLine("***** Fun with Strings *****")
    Dim firstName As String = "June"
    Console.WriteLine("Value of firstName: {0}", firstName)
    Console.WriteLine("firstName has {0} characters.", firstName.Length)
    Console.WriteLine("firstName in uppercase: {0}", firstName.ToUpper())
    Console.WriteLine("firstName in lowercase: {0}", firstName.ToLower())

    Dim myValue As Integer = 3456787
    Console.WriteLine("Hex vaule of myValue is: {0}", _
      String.Format("{0:X}", myValue))
    Console.WriteLine("Currency vaule of myValue is: {0}", _
      String.Format("{0:C}", myValue))
  End Sub
End Module
```

Notice how the shared Format() method supports the same formatting tokens as the Console.WriteLine() method examined earlier in the chapter. Also notice that unlike String.Format(), the ToUpper() and ToLower() methods have not implemented as shared members and are therefore called directly from the String object.

String Concatenation (and the "Newline" Constant)

String variables can be connected together to build a larger String via the VB 2005 ampersand operator (&). As you may know, this technique is formally termed *string concatenation*:

```
Module Program
  Sub Main()
    Console.WriteLine("***** Fun with Strings *****")
...
    Dim s1 As String = "Programming the "
    Dim s2 As String = "PsychoDrill (PTP)"
    Dim s3 As String = s1 & s2
    Console.WriteLine(s3)
  End Sub
End Module
```

■**Note** VB 2005 also allows you to concatenate String objects using the plus sign (+). However, given that the + symbol can be applied to numerous data types, there is a possibility that your String object cannot be "added" to one of the operands. The ampersand, on the other hand, can only apply to Strings, and therefore is the recommend approach.

You may be interested to know that the VB 2005 & symbol is processed by the compiler to emit a call to the shared String.Concat() method. In fact, if you were to compile the previous code and open the assembly within ildasm.exe (see Chapter 1), you would find the CIL code shown in Figure 3-8.

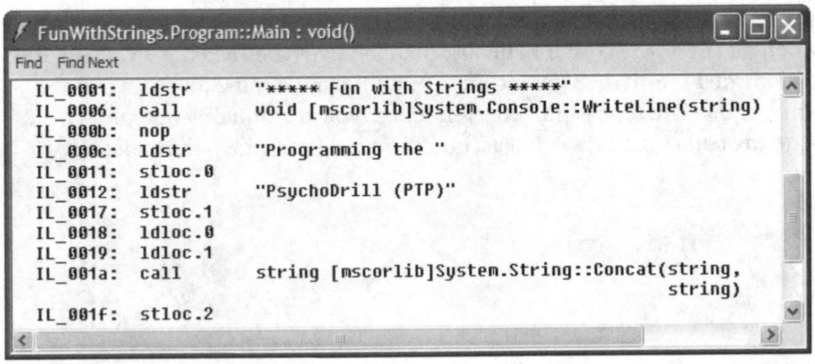

Figure 3-8. *The VB 2005 & operator results in a call to* String.Concat().

Given this, it is possible to perform string concatenation by calling String.Concat() directly (although you really have not gained anything by doing so, in fact you have incurred additional keystrokes!):

```
Module Program
  Sub Main()
    Console.WriteLine("***** Fun with Strings *****")
...
    Dim s1 As String = "Programming the "
    Dim s2 As String = "PsychoDrill (PTP)"
    Dim s3 As String = String.Concat(s1, s2)
    Console.WriteLine(s3)
  End Sub
End Module
```

On a related note, do know that the VB 6.0–style string constants (such as vbLf, vbCrLf, and vbCr) are still exposed through the Microsoft.VisualBasic.dll assembly (see Chapter 2). Therefore, if you wish to concatenate a string that contains various newline characters (for display purposes), you may do so as follows:

```
Module Program
  Sub Main()
    Console.WriteLine("***** Fun with Strings *****")
...
    Dim s1 As String = "Programming the "
    Dim s2 As String = "PsychoDrill (PTP)"
```

```
      Dim s3 As String = String.Concat(s1, s2)
      s3 += vbLf & "was a great industrial project."
      Console.WriteLine(s3)
    End Sub
End Module
```

■**Note** If you have a background in C-based languages, understand that the vbLf constant is functionally equivalent to the newline escape character (\n).

Strings and Equality

As fully explained in Chapter 11, a *reference type* is an object allocated on the garbage-collected managed heap. By default, when you perform a test for equality on reference types (via the VB 2005 = and <> operators), you will be returned True if the references are pointing to the same object in memory. However, even though the String data type is indeed a reference type, the equality operators have been redefined to compare the *values* of String objects, not the memory to which they refer:

```
Module Program
  Sub Main()
    Console.WriteLine("***** Fun with Strings *****")
...
    Dim strA As String = "Hello!"
    Dim strB As String = "Yo!"
    ' False!
    Console.WriteLine("strA = strB?: {0}", strA = strB)
    strB = "HELLO!"
    ' False!
    Console.WriteLine("strA = strB?: {0}", strA = strB)
    strB = "Hello!"
    ' True!
    Console.WriteLine("strA = strB?: {0}", strA = strB)
  End Sub
End Module
```

Notice that the VB 2005 equality operators perform a case-sensitive, character-by-character equality test. Therefore, "Hello!" is not equal to "HELLO!", which is different from "hello!".

Strings Are Immutable

One of the interesting aspects of System.String is that once you assign a String object with its initial value, the character data *cannot be changed*. At first glance, this might seem like a flat-out lie, given that we are always reassigning strings to new values and due to the fact that the System.String type defines a number of methods that appear to modify the character data in one way or another (uppercase, lowercase, etc.). However, if you look closer at what is happening behind the scenes, you will notice the methods of the String type are in fact returning you a brand new String object in a modified format:

```
Module Program
  Sub Main()
    Console.WriteLine("***** Fun with Strings *****")
...
    ' Set initial string value
    Dim initialString As String = "This is my string."
    Console.WriteLine("Initial value: {0}", initialString)
```

```
    ' Uppercase the initialString?
    Dim upperString As String = initialString.ToUpper()
    Console.WriteLine("Upper case copy: {0}", upperString)

    ' Nope!  initialString is in the same format!
    Console.WriteLine("Initial value: {0}", initialString)
  End Sub
End Module
```

If you examine the output in Figure 3-9, you can verify that the original String object (initialString) is not uppercased when calling ToUpper(), rather you are returned a copy of the string in a modified format.

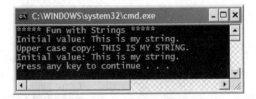

Figure 3-9. *Strings are immutable!*

The same law of immutability holds true when you use the VB 2005 assignment operator. To illustrate, comment out any existing code within Main() (to decrease the amount of generated CIL code) and add the following logic:

```
Module Program
  Sub Main()
    Dim strObjA As String = "String A reporting."
    strObjA = "This is a new string"
  End Sub
End Module
```

Now, compile your application and load the assembly into ildasm.exe (again, see Chapter 1). If you were to double-click the Main() method, you would find the CIL code shown in Figure 3-10.

```
FunWithStrings.Program::Main : void()
Find  Find Next
.method public static void  Main() cil managed
{
  .entrypoint
  .custom instance void [mscorlib]System.STAThreadAttribute::.ctor() = ( 01
  // Code size       26 (0x1a)
  .maxstack  1
  .locals init ([0] string strObjA)
  IL_0000:  nop
  IL_0001:  ldstr      "***** Fun with Strings *****"
  IL_0006:  call       void [mscorlib]System.Console::WriteLine(string)
  IL_000b:  nop
  IL_000c:  ldstr      "String A reporting."
  IL_0011:  stloc.0
  IL_0012:  ldstr      "This is a new string"
  IL_0017:  stloc.0
  IL_0018:  nop
  IL_0019:  ret
} // end of method Program::Main
```

Figure 3-10. *Assigning a value to a* String *object results in a new* String *object.*

Although I don't imagine you are too interested in the low-level details of the Common Intermediate Language (CIL), do note that the Main() method makes numerous calls to the ldstr (load string) opcode. Simply put, the ldstr opcode of CIL will always create a new String object on the managed heap. The previous String object that contained the value "String A reporting." is no longer being used by the program, and will eventually be garbage collected.

So, what exactly are we to gather from this insight? In a nutshell, the String type can be inefficient and result in bloated code if misused. If you need to represent basic character data such as a US Social Security number, first or last names, or simple string literals used within your application, the String data type is the perfect choice.

However, if you are building an application that makes heavy use of textual data (such as a word processing program), it would be a very bad idea to represent the word processing data using String types, as you will most certainly (and often indirectly) end up making unnecessary copies of string data. So what is a programmer to do? Glad you asked.

The System.Text.StringBuilder Type

Given that the String type can be quite inefficient when used with reckless abandon, the .NET base class libraries provide the System.Text namespace. Within this (relatively small) namespace lives a class named StringBuilder. Like the System.String class, StringBuilder defines methods that allow you to replace or format segments and so forth.

What is unique about the StringBuilder is that when you call members of the StringBuilder, you are directly modifying the object's internal character data, not obtaining a copy of the data in a modified format (and is thus more efficient). When you create an instance of the StringBuilder, you will supply the object's initial startup values via one of many *constructors*. Chapter 5 dives into the details of class constructors; however, if you are new to the topic, simply understand that constructors allow you to create an object with an initial state when you apply the New keyword. Consider the following usage of StringBuilder:

```
Imports System.Text    ' StringBuilder lives here!

Module Program
  Sub Main()
    ...
    ' Use the StringBuilder.
    Dim sb As New StringBuilder("**** Fantastic Games ****")
    sb.Append(vbLf)
    sb.AppendLine("Half Life 2")
    sb.AppendLine("Beyond Good and Evil")
    sb.AppendLine("Deus Ex 1 and 2")
    sb.Append("System Shock")
    sb.Replace("2", "Deus Ex: Invisible War")
    Console.WriteLine(sb)
    Console.WriteLine("sb as {0} chars.", sb.Length)
  End Sub
End Module
```

Here we see constructed a StringBuilder set to the initial value "**** Fantastic Games ****". As you can see, we are appending to the internal buffer, and are able to replace (or remove) characters at will. By default, a StringBuilder is only able to hold a string of 16 characters or less; however, this initial value can be changed via a constructor argument:

```
' Make a StringBuilder with an initial size of 256.
Dim sb As New StringBuilder("**** Fantastic Games ****", 256)
```

If you append more characters than the specified limit, the StringBuilder object will copy its data into a new instance and grow the buffer by the specified limit.

■Source Code The FunWithStrings project is located under the Chapter 3 subdirectory.

Final Commentary of VB 2005 Data Types

To wrap up the discussion of intrinsic data types, there are a few points of interest, especially when it comes to changes between VB 6.0 and VB 2005. As you have already seen in Table 3-4, the maximum and minimum bounds of many types have been retrofitted to be consistent with the rules of the .NET-specific Common Type System (CTS). In addition to this fact, also be aware of the following updates:

- VB 2005 does not support a Currency data type. The Decimal type supports far greater precision (and functionality) than the VB 6.0 Currency type.

- The Variant data type is no longer supported under the .NET platform. However, if you are using a legacy COM type returning a VB 6.0 Variant, it is still possible to process the data.

At this point, I hope you understand that each data type keyword of VB 2005 has a corresponding type in the .NET base class libraries, each of which exposes a fixed functionality. While I have not detailed each member of these core types, you are in a great position to dig into the details as you see fit. Be sure to consult the .NET Framework 2.0 SDK documentation for full details regarding the intrinsic .NET data types.

Narrowing (Explicit) and Widening (Implicit) Data Type Conversions

Now that you understand how to interact with intrinsic data types, let's examine the related topic of *data type conversion*. Assume you have a new console application (named TypeConversions) that defines the following module:

```
Module Program
  Sub Main()
    Console.WriteLine("***** The Amazing Addition Program *****")
    Dim a As Short = 9
    Dim b As Short = 10
    Console.WriteLine("a + b = {0}", Add(a, b))
  End Sub

  Function Add(ByVal x As Integer, ByVal y As Integer) As Integer
    Return x + y
  End Function
End Module
```

Notice that the Add() method expects to be sent two Integer parameters. However, note that the Main() method is in fact sending in two Short variables. While this might seem like a complete and total mismatch of data types, the program compiles and executes without error, returning the expected result of 19.

The reason that the compiler treats this code as syntactically sound is due to the fact that there is no possibility for loss of data. Given that the maximum value of a Short (32,767) is well within the range of an Integer (2,147,483,647), the compiler automatically *widens* each Short to an Integer. Technically speaking, *widening* is the term used to define a safe "upward cast" that does not result in a loss of data.

■**Note** In other languages (especially C-based languages such as C#, C++, and Java) "widening" is termed an *implicit cast.*

Table 3-6 illustrates which data types can be safely widened to a specific data types.

Table 3-6. *Safe Widening Conversions*

VB 2005 Type	Safely Widens to...
Byte	SByte, UInteger, Integer, ULong, Long, Single, Double, Decimal
SByte	SByte, Integer, Long, Single, Double, Decimal
Short	Integer, Long, Single, Double, Decimal
SByte	UInteger, Integer, ULong, Long, Single, Double, Decimal
Char	SByte, UInteger, Integer, ULong, Long, Single, Double, Decimal
Integer	Long, Double, Decimal
UInteger	Long, Double, Decimal
Long	Decimal
ULong	Decimal
Single	Double

Although this automatic widening worked in our favor for the previous example, other times this "automatic type conversion" can be the source of subtle and difficult-to-debug runtime errors. For example, assume that you have modified the values assigned to the a and b variables within Main() to values that (when added together) overflow the maximum value of a Short. Furthermore, assume you are storing the return value of the Add() method within a new local Short variable, rather than directly printing the result to the console:

```
Module Program
  Sub Main()
    Console.WriteLine("***** The Amazing Addition Program *****")
    Dim a As Short = 30000
    Dim b As Short = 30000
    Dim answer As Short = Add(a, b)
    Console.WriteLine("a + b = {0}", answer)
  End Sub

  Function Add(ByVal x As Integer, ByVal y As Integer) As Integer
    Return x + y
  End Function
End Module
```

In this case, although your application compiles just fine, when you run the application you will find the CLR throws a runtime error; specifically a System.OverflowException, as shown in Figure 3-11.

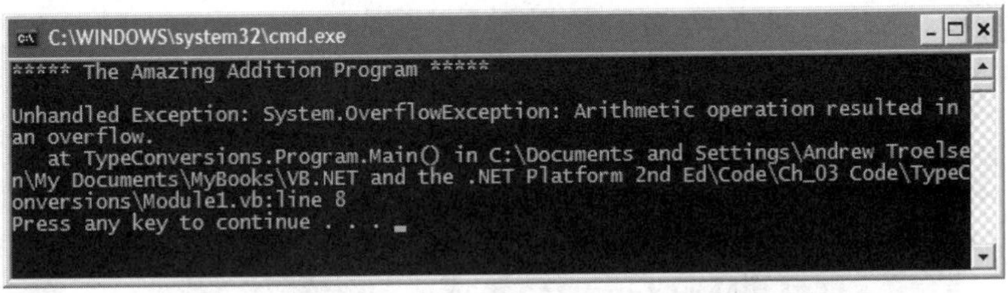

Figure 3-11. *Oops! The value returned from* Add() *was greater than the maximum value of a* Short!

The problem is that although the Add() method can return an Integer with the value 60,000 (as this fits within the range of an Integer), the value cannot be stored in a Short (as it overflows the bounds of this data type). In this case, the CLR attempts to apply a *narrowing operation*, which resulted in a runtime error. As you can guess, narrowing is the logical opposite of widening, in that a larger value is stored within a smaller variable.

■**Note** In other languages (especially C-based languages such as C#, C++, and Java) "narrowing" is termed an *explicit cast.*

Not all narrowing conversions result in a System.OverflowException of course. For example, consider the following code:

```
' This narrowing conversion is a-OK.
Dim myByte As Byte
Dim myInt As Integer = 200
myByte = myInt
Console.WriteLine("Value of myByte: {0}", myByte)
```

Here, the value contained within the Integer variable myInt is safely within the range of a Byte, therefore the narrowing operation does not result in a runtime error. Although it is true that many narrowing conversions are safe and nondramatic in nature, you may agree that it would be ideal to trap narrowing conversions at *compile time* rather than *runtime*. Thankfully there is such a way, using the VB 2005 Option Strict directive.

Understanding Option Strict

Option Strict ensures compile-time (rather than runtime) notification of any narrowing conversion so it can be corrected in a timely fashion. If we are able to identify these narrowing conversions upfront, we can take a corrective course of action and decrease the possibility of nasty runtime errors.

A Visual Basic 2005 project, as well as specific *.vb files within a given project, can elect to enable or disable implicit narrowing via the Option Strict directive. When turning this option On, you are informing the compiler to check for such possibilities during the compilation process. Thus, if you were to add the following to the very top of your current file:

```
' Option directives must be the very first code statements in a *.vb file!
Option Strict On
```

you would now find a compile-time error for each implicit narrowing conversion, as shown in Figure 3-12.

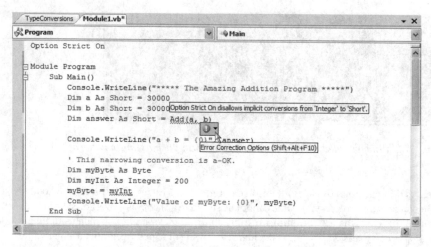

Figure 3-12. Option Strict *disables automatic narrowing of data*

Here, we have enabled Option Strict on a single file within our project. This approach can be useful when you wish to selectively allow narrowing conversions within specific *.vb files. However, if you wish to enable Option Strict for each and every file in your project, you can do so using the Compile tab of the My Project dialog box, as shown in Figure 3-13.

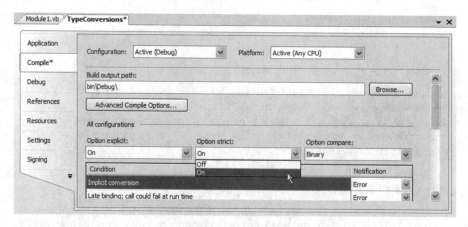

Figure 3-13. *Enabling* Option Strict *on the project level*

■**Note** Under Visual Studio 2005, Option Strict is disabled for new Visual Basic 2005 projects. I would recommend, however, that you always enable this setting for each application you are creating, given that it is far better to resolve problems at compile time than runtime!

Now that we have some compile-time checking, we are able to resolve the error using one of two approaches. The most direct (and often more favorable) choice is to simply redefine the variable to a data type that will safely hold the result. For example:

```
Sub Main()
  Console.WriteLine("***** The Amazing Addition Program *****")
  Dim a As Short = 30000
  Dim b As Short = 30000

  ' Nope...Dim answer As Short = Add(a, b)
  Dim answer As Integer = Add(a, b)
  Console.WriteLine("a + b = {0}", answer)
...
End Sub
```

Another approach is to make use of an explicit Visual Basic 2005 type conversion function, such as CByte() for this example:

```
Sub Main()
...
  Dim myByte As Byte
  Dim myInt As Integer = 200
  ' myByte = myInt
  myByte = CByte(myInt)
  Console.WriteLine("Value of myByte: {0}", myByte)
End Sub
```

■**Note** Another useful Option statement is Option Explicit. When enabled, the compiler demands that all variables are defined using a proper As clause (e.g., Dim a As Integer rather than Dim A). I would recommend you always enable Option Explicit, as this can pinpoint many otherwise unseen programming errors.

Explicit Conversion Functions

Visual Basic 2005 provides a number of conversion functions in addition to CByte() that enable you to explicitly allow a narrowing cast when Option Strict is enabled. Table 3-7 documents the core VB 2005 conversion functions.

Table 3-7. *VB 2005 Conversion Functions*

Conversion Function	Meaning in Life
CBool	Converts a Boolean expression into a Boolean value
CByte	Makes an expression a Byte
CChar	Makes the first character of a string into a Char
CDate	Makes a string containing a data expression into a Date
CDbl	Makes a numeric expression double precision
CDec	Makes a numeric expression of the Decimal type
CInt	Makes a numeric expression an Integer by rounding
CLng	Makes a numeric expression a long integer by rounding
CObj	Makes any item into an Object
CSByte	Makes a numeric expression into an SByte by rounding
CShort	Makes a numeric expression into a Short by rounding
CSng	Makes a numeric expression into a Single
CStr	Returns a string representation of the expression
CUInt	Makes a numeric expression into a UInteger by rounding
CULng	Makes a numeric expression into a ULong
CUShort	Makes a numeric expression into a UShort

In addition to these data type–specific conversion functions, with the release of the .NET platform, the Visual Basic language also supports the CType function. CType takes two arguments, the first is the "thing you have," while the second is the "thing you want." For example, the following conversions are functionally equivalent:

```
Sub Main()
...
  Dim myByte As Byte
  Dim myInt As Integer = 200
  myByte = CByte(myInt)
  myByte = CType(myInt, Byte)
  Console.WriteLine("Value of myByte: {0}", myByte)
End Sub
```

One benefit of the CType function is that it handles all the conversions of the (primarily VB 6.0-centric) conversion functions shown in Table 3-7. Furthermore, as you will see later in this text, CType allows you to convert between base and derived classes, as well as objects and their implemented interfaces.

Note As you will see in Chapter 11, VB 2005 provides two new alternatives to CType—DirectCast and TryCast. However, they can only be used if the arguments are related by inheritance or interface implementation.

The Role of System.Convert

To wrap up the topic of data type conversions, I'd like to point out the fact that the System namespace defines a class named Convert that can also be used to widen or narrow a data assignment:

```
Sub Main()
...
  Dim myByte As Byte
  Dim myInt As Integer = 200
  myByte = CByte(myInt)
  myByte = CType(myInt, Byte)
  myByte = Convert.ToByte(myInt)
  Console.WriteLine("Value of myByte: {0}", myByte)
End Sub
```

One benefit of using System.Convert is that it provides a language-neutral manner to convert between data types. However, given that Visual Basic 2005 provides numerous built-in conversion functions (CBool, CByte, and the like), using the Convert type to do your data type conversions is usually nothing more than a matter of personal preference.

Source Code The TypeConversions project is located under the Chapter 3 subdirectory.

Building Visual Basic 2005 Code Statements

As a software developer, you are no doubt aware that a *statement* is simply a line of code that can be processed by the compiler (without error, of course). For example, you have already seen how to craft a local variable declaration statement over the course of this chapter:

```
' VB 2005 variable declaration statements.
Dim i As Integer = 10
Dim j As System.Int32 = 20
Dim k As New Integer()
```

On a related note, you have also previewed the correct syntax to declare a Function using the syntax of VB 2005:

```
Function Add(ByVal x As Integer, ByVal y As Integer) As Integer
  Return x + y
End Function
```

While it is true that when you are comfortable with the syntax of your language of choice, you tend to intuitively know what constitutes a valid statement, there are two idioms of VB 2005 code statements that deserve special mention to the uninitiated.

The Statement Continuation Character

White space (meaning blank lines of code) are ignored by the VB 2005 compiler unless you attempt to define a single code statement over multiple lines of code. This is quite different from C-based languages, where white space never matters, given that languages in the C family explicitly mark the end of a statement with a semicolon and scope with curly brackets.

In this light, the following two C# functions are functionally identical (although the second version is hardly readable and very bad style!):

```
// C# Add() method take one.
public int Add(int x, int y)
{ return x + y; }
```

```
// C# Add() method take two.
public int Add(
int x, int y) { return x
  +
y;       }
```

Under Visual Basic 2005, if you wish to define a statement or member over multiple lines of code, you must split each line using the under bar (_) token, formally termed the *statement continuation character*. Furthermore, there *must* be a blank space on each side of the statement continuation character. Thus:

```
' VB 2005 Add() method take one.
Function Add(ByVal x As Integer, _
  ByVal y As Integer) As Integer
    Return x + y
End Function
```

```
' VB 2005 Add() method take two.
Function Add(ByVal x As Integer, _
  ByVal y As Integer) _
  As Integer
    Return x + y
End Function
```

```
' VB 2005 Add() method take three.
Function Add(ByVal x As Integer, _
  ByVal y As Integer) _
  As Integer
    Return x + y
End _
Function
```

Of course, you would never use the statement continuation character as shown in the last iteration of the Add() method, as the code is less than readable. In the real world, this feature is most helpful when defining a member that takes a great number of arguments, to space them out in such a way that you can view them within your editor of choice (rather than scrolling the horizontal scroll bar to see the full prototype!).

Defining Multiple Statements on a Single Line

Sometimes it is convenient to define multiple code statements on a single line of code within the editor. For example, assume you have a set of local variables that need to be assigned to initial values. While you could assign a value to each variable on discrete lines of code:

```
Sub MyMethod()
  Dim s As String
  Dim i As Integer
  s = "Fred"
  i = 10
End Sub
```

you can compact the scope of this subroutine using the colon character:

```
Sub MyMethod()
  Dim s As String
  Dim i As Integer
  s = "Fred" : i = 10
End Sub
```

Understand that misuse of the colon can easily result in hard-to-read code. As well, when combined with the statement continuation character, you can end up with nasty statements such as the following:

```
Sub MyMethod()
  Dim s As String : Dim i As Integer
  s = "Fred" _
  : i = 10
End Sub
```

To be sure, defining multiple statements on a single line using the colon character should be used sparingly. For the most part, this language feature is most useful when you need to make simple assignments to multiple variables.

VB 2005 Flow-control Constructs

Now that you can define a single simple code statement, let's examine the flow-control keywords that allow you to alter the flow of your program and several keywords that allow you to build complex code statements using the And, Or, and Not operators.

Like other programming languages, VB 2005 defines several ways to make runtime decisions regarding how your application should function. In a nutshell, we are offered the following flow-control constructs:

- The If/Then/Else statement
- The Select/Case statement

The If/Then/Else Statement

First up, you have your good friend, the If/Then/Else statement. In the simplest form, the If construct does not have a corresponding Else. Within the If statement, you will construct an expression that can resolve to a Boolean value. For example:

```
Sub Main()
  Dim userDone As Boolean
```

```
' Gather user input to assign
' Boolean value...

If userDone = True Then
   Console.WriteLine("Thanks for running this app")
End If
End Sub
```

A slightly more complex If statement can involve any number of Else statements to account for a range of values set to the expression being tested against:

```
Sub Main()
  Dim userOption As String

  ' Read user option from command line.
  userOption = Console.ReadLine()

  If userOption = "GodMode" Then
     Console.WriteLine("You will never die...cheater!")
  ElseIf userOption = "FullLife" Then
     Console.WriteLine("At the end, heh?")
  ElseIf userOption = "AllAmmo" Then
     Console.WriteLine("Now we can rock and roll!")
  Else
     Console.WriteLine("Unknown option...")
  End If
End Sub
```

Note that any secondary "else" condition is marked with the ElseIf keyword, while the final condition is simply Else.

Building Complex Expressions

The expression tested against within a flow-control construct need not be a simple assignment. If required, you are able to leverage the VB 2005 equality/relational operators listed in Table 3-8.

Table 3-8. *VB 2005 Relational and Equality Operators*

VB 2005 Equality/Relational Operator	Example Usage	Meaning in Life
=	If age = 30 Then	Returns true only if each expression is the same
<>	If "Foo" <> myStr Then	Returns true only if each expression is different

<
>
<=
>=
	If bonus < 2000 Then
	If bonus > 2000 Then
	If bonus <= 2000 Then
	If bonus >= 2000 Then
		Returns true if expression A is less than, greater than, less than or equal to, or greater than or equal to expression B, respectively

■**Note** Unlike C-based languages, the VB 2005 = token is used to denote both assignment and equality semantics (therefore VB 2005 does not supply a == operator).

In addition, you may build a complex expression to test within a flow-control construct using the code conditional operators (also known as the logical operators) listed in Table 3-9. This table outlines the most common conditional operators of the language.

Table 3-9. *VB 2005 Conditional Operators*

VB 2005 Conditional Operator	Example	Meaning in Life
And	If age = 30 And name = "Fred" Then	Conditional AND operator, where both conditions must be True for the condition to be True
AndAlso	If age = 30 AndAlso name = "Fred" Then	A conditional AND operator that supports *short-circuiting*, meaning if the first expression is False, the second expression is not evaluated
Or	If age = 30 Or name = "Fred" Then	Conditional OR operator
OrElse	If age = 30 OrElse name = "Fred" Then	Conditional OR operator that supports *short-circuiting*, meaning if either expression is True, True is returned
Not	If Not myBool Then	Conditional NOT operator

As I am assuming you have prior experience in BASIC or C-based languages, I won't belabor the use of these operators. If you require additional details beyond the following code snippet, I will assume you will consult the .NET Framework SDK documentation. However, here is a simple example:

```
Sub Main()
  Dim userOption As String
  Dim userAge As Integer

  ' Read user option from command line.
  userOption = Console.ReadLine()
  userAge = Console.ReadLine()

  If userOption = "AdultMode" And userAge >= 21 Then
    Console.WriteLine("We call this Hot Coffee Mode...")
  ElseIf userOption = "AllAmmo" Then
    Console.WriteLine("Now we can rock and roll!")
  Else
    Console.WriteLine("Unknown option...")
  End If
End Sub
```

The Select/Case Statement

The other selection construct offered by VB 2005 is the Select statement. This can be a more compact alternative to the If/Then/Else statement when you wish to handle program flow based on a known set of choices. For example, the following Main() method prompts the user for one of three known values. If the user enters an unknown value, you can account for this using the Case Else statement:

```
Sub Main()
  ' Prompt user with choices.
  Console.WriteLine("Welcome to the world of .NET")
  Console.WriteLine("1 = C#  2 = Managed C++ (MC++) 3 = VB 2005")
  Console.Write("Please select your implementation language: ")

  ' Get choice.
  Dim s As String = Console.ReadLine()
  Dim n As Integer = Integer.Parse(s)

  ' Based on input, act accordingly...
  Select Case n
    Case Is = 1
      Console.WriteLine("C# is all about managed code.")
    Case Is = 2
      Console.WriteLine("Maintaining a legacy system, are we?")
    Case Is = 3
      Console.WriteLine("VB 2005: Full OO capabilities...")
    Case Else
      Console.WriteLine("Well...good luck with that!")
  End Select
End Sub
```

VB 2005 Iteration Constructs

All programming languages provide ways to repeat blocks of code until a terminating condition has been met. Regardless of which language you are coming from, the VB 2005 iteration statements should cause no raised eyebrows and require little explanation. In a nutshell, VB 2005 provides the following iteration constructs:

- For/Next loop
- For/Each loop
- Do/While loop
- Do/Until loop
- With loop

Let's quickly examine each looping construct in turn. Do know that I will only concentrate on the core features of each construct. I'll assume that you will consult the .NET Framework 2.0 SDK documentation if you require further details.

For/Next Loop

When you need to iterate over a block of code statements a fixed number of times, the For statement is the looping construct of champions. In essence, you are able to specify how many times a block of code repeats itself, using an expression that will evaluate to a Boolean:

```
Sub Main()
  ' Prints out the numbers 5 - 25, inclusive.
  Dim i As Integer
  For i = 5 To 25
    Console.WriteLine("Number is: {0}", i)
  Next
End Sub
```

One nice improvement to the For looping construct is we are now able declare the counter variable directly within the For statement itself (rather than in a separate code statement). Therefore, the previous code sample could be slightly streamlined as the following:

```
Sub Main()
  ' A slightly simplified For loop.
  For i As Integer = 5 To 25
    Console.WriteLine("Number is: {0}", i)
  Next
End Sub
```

The For loop can also make use of the Step keyword to offset the value of the counter. For example, if you wish to increment the counter variable by five with each iteration, you would do so with the following:

```
Sub Main()
  ' Increment i by 5 with each pass.
  For i As Integer = 5 To 25 Step 5
    Console.WriteLine("Number is: {0}", i)
  Next
End Sub
```

For/Each Loop

The For/Each construct is a variation of the standard For loop, where you are able to iterate over the contents of an array without the need to explicitly monitor the container's upper limit (as in the case of a traditional For/Next loop). Assume you have defined an array of String types and wish to print each item to the command window (VB 2005 array syntax will be fully examined in the next chapter). In the following code snippet, note that the For Each statement can define the type of item iterated over directly within the statement:

```
Sub Main()
  Dim myStrings() As String = _
    {"Fun", "with", "VB 2005"}

  For Each str As String In myStrings
    Console.WriteLine(str)
  Next
End Sub
```

or on discrete lines of code:

```
Sub Main()
  Dim myStrings() As String = _
    {"Fun", "with", "VB 2005"}

  Dim item As String
  For Each item In myStrings
    Console.WriteLine(item)
  Next
End Sub
```

In these examples, our counter was explicitly defined as a String data type, given that our array is full of strings as well. However, if you wish to iterate over an array of Integers (or any other type), you would simply define the counter in the terms of the items in the array. For example:

```
Sub Main()
  ' Looping over an array of Integers.
  Dim myInts() As Integer = _
  {10, 20, 30, 40}

  For Each int As Integer In myInts
    Console.WriteLine(int)
  Next
End Sub
```

■**Note** The For Each construct can iterate over any types that support the correct infrastructure. I'll hold off on the details until Chapter 9, as this aspect of the For Each loop entails an understanding of interface-based programming and the system-supplied IEnumerator and IEnumerable interfaces.

Do/While and Do/Until Looping Constructs

You have already seen that the For/Next statement is typically used when you have some foreknowledge of the number of iterations you want to perform (e.g., *j* > 20). The Do statements, on the other hand, are useful for those times when you are uncertain how long it might take for a terminating condition to be met (such as when gathering user input).

Do/While and Do/Until are (in many ways) interchangeable. Do/While keeps looping until the terminating condition is *false*. On the other hand, Do/Until keeps looping until the terminating condition is *true*. For example:

```
' Keep looping until X is not equal to an empty string.
Do
   ' Some code statements to loop over.
Loop Until X <> ""

' Keep looping as long as X is equal to an empty string.
Do
   ' Some code statements to loop over.
Loop While X = ""
```

Note that in these last two examples, the test for the terminating condition was placed at the end of the Loop keyword. Using this syntax, you can rest assured that the code within the loop will be executed at least once (given that the test to exit the loop occurs after the first iteration). If you prefer to allow for the possibility that the code within the loop may never be executed, move the Until or While clause to the beginning of the loop:

```
' Keep looping until X is not equal to an empty string.
Do Until X <> ""
   ' Some code to loop over.
Loop

' Keep looping as long as X is not equal to an empty string.
Do While X = ""
   ' Some code to loop over.
Loop
```

Finally, understand that VB 2005 still supports the raw While loop. However, the Wend keyword has been replaced with a more fitting End While:

```
Dim j As Integer
While j < 20
  Console.Write(j & ", ")
  j += 1
End While
```

The With Construct

To wrap this chapter up, allow me to say that the VB 6.0 With construct is still supported under VB 2005. In a nutshell, the With keyword allows you to invoke members of a type within a predefined scope. Do know that the With keyword is nothing more than a typing time saver.

For example, the System.Collections namespace has a type named ArrayList, which like any type has a number of members. You are free to manipulate the ArrayList on a statement by statement basis as follows:

```
Sub Main()
  Dim myStuff As New ArrayList()
  myStuff.Add(100)
  myStuff.Add("Hello")
  Console.WriteLine("Size is: {0}", myStuff.Count)
End Sub
```

or use the VB 2005 With keyword:

```
Sub Main()
  Dim myStuff As New ArrayList()
  With myStuff
    .Add(100)
    .Add("Hello")
    Console.WriteLine("Size is: {0}", .Count)
  End With
End Sub
```

Summary

Recall that the goal of this chapter was to expose you to numerous core aspects of the VB 2005 programming language. Here, we examined the constructs that will be commonplace in any application you may be interested in building. After examining the Module type, you learned that every VB 2005 executable program must have a type defining a Main() method, which serves as the program's entry point. Within the scope of Main(), you typically create any number of objects that work together to breathe life into your application.

Next, we dove into the details of the built-in data types of VB 2005, and came to understand that each data type keyword (e.g., Integer) is really a shorthand notation for a full-blown type in the System namespace (System.Int32 in this case). Given this, each VB 2005 data type has a number of built-in members. Along the same vein, you also learned about the role of *widening* and *narrowing* as well as the role of Option Strict.

We wrapped up by checking out the various iteration and decision constructs supported by VB 2005. Now that you have some of the basic nuts-and-bolts in your mind, the next chapter completes our examination of core language features.

CHAPTER 4

■■■

VB 2005 Programming Constructs, Part II

This chapter picks up where the previous chapter left off, and completes your investigation of the core aspects of the Visual Basic 2005 programming language. We begin by examining various details regarding the construction of VB 2005 subroutines and functions, learning about the Optional, ByRef, ByVal, and ParamArray keywords along the way.

Once you examine the topic of *method overloading,* the next task is to investigate the details behind manipulating array types using the syntax of VB 2005 and get to know the functionality contained within the related System.Array class type. We wrap things up with a discussion regarding the construction of enumeration and structure types. Once you have completed this chapter, you will be well prepared for the next section where we dive into the world of object-oriented development using Visual Basic 2005.

Defining Subroutines and Functions

To begin this chapter, let's examine the details of defining subroutines and functions using Visual Basic 2005. As you know, a method exists to allow the type to perform a unit of work. Methods may or may not take parameters and may or may not return values. Visual Basic has long distinguished between a "subroutine" and "function." While you can collectively refer to each syntactic variation as a "method," the distinction is that subroutines do not return a value once the method has completed, whereas functions do.

When you define a subroutine, simply use the Sub keyword and list any necessary arguments. If you wish to define a function, use the Function keyword and establish the return value via the As keyword. To illustrate, create a new console application named FunWithMethods. Insert a new module into your current project named HelperFunctions via the Project ➤ Add New Item menu option of Visual Studio 2005. Update the HelperFunctions module as follows:

```
Module HelperFunctions
    ' Subroutines have no return value.
    Public Sub PrintMessage(ByVal msg As String)
        Console.WriteLine(msg)
    End Sub

    ' Functions have a return value.
    Public Function Add(ByVal x As Integer, ByVal y As Integer) As Integer
        ' Return sum using VB 6.0-style syntax.
        Add = 5
    End Function
End Module
```

As seen here, Visual Basic 2005 supports the VB 6.0–style function return syntax, where a function's return value is denoted by assigning the function name to the resulting output. However, since the release of the .NET platform, we are now supplied with a Return keyword for an identical purpose. Thus, the Add() method could be implemented like so:

```
' VB 2005 code!
' Much cleaner!
Public Function Add(ByVal x As Integer, ByVal y As Integer) As Integer
    Return 5
End Function
```

The final introductory note regarding functions is that it is possible to forgo specifying an explicit return value for a function if (and only if) Option Strict is not enabled. If you do not specify a return value for a function, System.Object is assumed:

```
' This will not compile if Option Strict is on!
Function Test()    ' As Object assumed.
    Return 5
End Function
```

As you will see throughout the remainder of this book, subroutines and functions can be implemented within the scope of modules, classes, and structures (and prototyped within interface types). While the definition of a method in VB 2005 is quite straightforward, there are a handful of keywords that you can use to control how arguments are passed to the method in question, and these are listed in Table 4-1.

Table 4-1. *Visual Basic 2005 Parameter Modifier*

Parameter Modifier Keyword	Meaning in Life
ByVal	The method is passed a copy of the original data. This is the default parameter passing behavior.
ByRef	The method is passed a reference to the original data in memory.
Optional	Marks an argument that does not need to be specified by the caller.
ParamArray	Defines an argument that may be passed a variable number of arguments of the same type.

Let's walk through the role of each keyword in turn.

The ByVal Parameter Modifier

Under Visual Basic 2005, all parameters are passed *by value* by default. When an argument is marked with the ByVal keyword, the method receives a copy of the original data declared elsewhere. Given that this is indeed a local copy, the method is free to change the parameter's value; however, the caller will *not* see the change. For example, if our Add() function were to reassign the values of the incoming Integer data types as follows:

```
Function Add(ByVal x As Integer, ByVal y As Integer) As Integer
    Dim answer As Integer = x + y
    ' Try to set the params to a new value.
    x = 22 : y = 30
    Return answer
End Function
```

the caller (Main() in this case) would be totally unaware of this attempted reassignment, given that a *copy* of the data was modified, not the caller's original data. This can be verified by printing out the input values after the call to Add():

```
Sub Main()
  Console.WriteLine("***** Fun with Methods *****")
  ' Pass two Integers by value.
  Dim x, y As Integer
  x = 10 : y = 20
  Console.WriteLine("{0} + {1} = {2}", x, y, Add(x, y))

  ' X is still 10 and y is still 20.
  Console.WriteLine("After call x = {0} and y = {1}", x, y)
End Sub
```

It is also worth pointing out that the ByVal keyword is technically optional, given that this is the default assumption:

```
' These args are implicitly ByVal.
Function Add(x As Integer, y As Integer) As Integer
End Function
```

However, if you do not specify ByVal or ByRef for a given parameter, Visual Studio 2005 will automatically add the ByVal modifier when you hit the Enter key.

■Note If you have a background in earlier versions of VB, do be very aware that this default setting is the exact opposite behavior as we had in the past! Before the release of .NET, VB passed parameters by reference (ByRef) as the default.

The ByRef Parameter Modifier

Some methods need to be created in such a way that the caller should be able to realize any reassignments that have taken place within the method scope. For example, you might have a method that needs to alter the state of a string (e.g., uppercase the characters), assign an incoming reference to a new object, or simply modify the value of a numerical argument. For this very reason, VB 2005 supplies the ByRef keyword. Consider the following update to the PrintMessage() method:

```
Sub PrintMessage(ByRef msg As String)
  Console.WriteLine("Your message is: {0}", msg)
  ' Caller will see this change!
  msg = "Thank you for calling this method"
End Sub
```

If we were to update Main() as follows:

```
Sub Main()
  Console.WriteLine("***** Fun with Methods *****")
...
  Dim msg As String = "Hello from Main!"
  PrintMessage(msg)
  Console.WriteLine("After call msg = {0}", msg)
End Sub
```

and you were to compile and run your project, you would find the output shown in Figure 4-1.

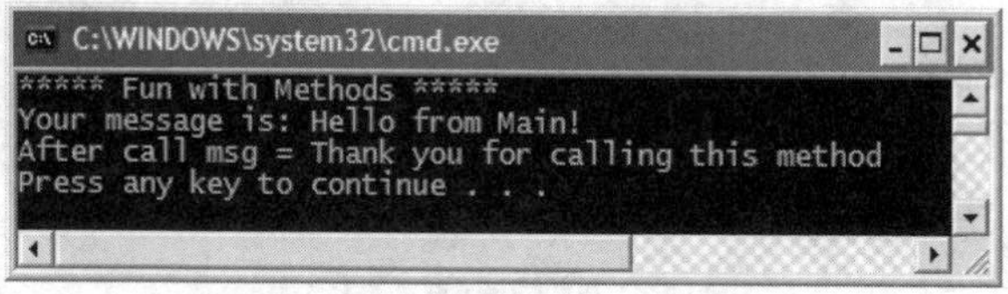

Figure 4-1. ByRef *arguments can be changed (and seen) by the caller.*

There is one additional parameter-passing-centric language feature of VB 2005, which is a carryover from earlier versions of the language. If you are calling a method prototyped to take a parameter ByRef, you can force the runtime to pass in a copy of the data (thereby treating it as if it were defined with the ByVal keyword). To do so, wrap the ByRef argument within an extra set of parentheses. For example, if you were to update the call to PrintMessage() like so:

```
Sub Main()
  Console.WriteLine("***** Fun with Methods *****")
...
  ' Pass a string by value
  Dim msg As String = "Hello from Main!"
  PrintMessage((msg))
  Console.WriteLine("After call msg = {0}", msg)
End Sub
```

you will now find that the string reassignment is not "remembered" as indicated in Figure 4-2.

Figure 4-2. *Wrapping a* ByRef *argument within parentheses forces* ByVal *semantics.*

■**Note** The ByRef and ByVal keywords will be revisited in Chapter 11. As you will see, the behaviors of these keywords change just a bit depending on whether the argument is a "value type" or "reference type."

Defining Optional Arguments

VB has long supported the use of optional arguments. Simply put, this language feature allows you to define a set of parameters that are not required to be supplied by the caller. If the caller chooses not to pass these optional elements, the argument will be assigned to a predefined default value. As you would hope, this feature is also part of VB 2005 with one important distinction—all optional parameters must now be set to an *explicit* default value. In contrast, under Visual Basic 6.0, optional arguments were assigned to their default values (0 for numerical and "" for strings) automatically.

Assume we have defined a new subroutine named PrintFormattedMessage() within the HelperFunctions module, which takes three optional arguments that are used to control how the incoming String is to be printed to the console:

```
Sub PrintFormattedMessage(ByVal msg As String, _
  Optional ByVal upperCase As Boolean = False, _
  Optional ByVal timesToRepeat As Integer = 0, _
  Optional ByVal textColor As ConsoleColor = ConsoleColor.Green)
    ' Store current console foreground color.
    Dim fGroundColor As ConsoleColor = Console.ForegroundColor
    ' Set Console foreground color.
    Console.ForegroundColor = textColor
    ' Print mesage in correct case x number of times.
    For i As Integer = 0 To timesToRepeat
      Console.WriteLine(msg)
    Next
    ' Reset current console forground color.
    Console.ForegroundColor = fGroundColor
End Sub
```

Given this definition, we are now able to call `PrintFormattedMessage()` in a variety of ways. First, if we wish to accept all defaults, we can simply supply the mandatory `String` argument as follows:

```
' Accept all defaults for the optional args.
PrintFormattedMessage("Call One")
```

If we would rather provide custom values for each optional argument, we can do so explicitly as follows:

```
' Provide each optional argument.
PrintFormattedMessage("Call Two", True, 5, ConsoleColor.Yellow)
```

Furthermore, when you are calling a method that has some number of optional arguments, you may be interested in only providing a subset of specific values, given that some of the default values fit the bill. To do so, your first approach is to skip over the optional arguments for which you wish to accept the defaults using a blank parameter:

```
' Print this message in current case, one time, in gray.
PrintFormattedMessage("Call Three", , , ConsoleColor.Gray)
```

While skipping over optional arguments is syntactically valid, it does not necessarily lend itself to readable (or easily maintainable) code. A more elegant manner in which to skip over select optional arguments is using *named arguments*:

```
' Same as previously shown, but cleaner!
PrintFormattedMessage("Call Four", textColor:=ConsoleColor.Gray)
```

As you can see, an argument is named by using the `:=` operator. The left side is the name of the parameter itself, while the right side is the value to pass this argument. Using this approach, the unnamed optional arguments will still be assigned to their predefined default.

As an interesting side note, given that VB 2005 supports named arguments, it is possible to call a method and pass in each argument in any order you so choose. This behavior is possible for any method, not simply for methods that define optional parameters. For example, the `Add()` method could be legally called like so:

```
' Pass x and y values out of order.
Add(y:=10, x:=90)
```

Of course, if you overuse this language feature, you not only incur additional keystrokes, but your code can also be much harder on the eyes. By and large, you should limit your use of named arguments to the invocation of methods that define optional arguments.

Working with ParamArrays

In addition to optional parameters, Visual Basic 2005 supports the use of *parameter arrays*. To understand the role of the ParamArray argument, you must (as the name implies) understand how to manipulate VB 2005 arrays. If this is not the case, you may wish to return to this section once you have finished this chapter. However, if you are already comfortable with the process of defining and initializing a VB array under the .NET platform, read on.

In a nutshell, a ParamArray allows you to pass into a method a variable number of parameters (of the same type) as a *single logical parameter*. As well, arguments marked with the ParamArray keyword can be processed if the caller sends in a strongly typed array or a comma-delimited list of items. Yes, this can be confusing. To clear things up, assume you wish to create a function named CalculateAverage(). Given the nature of this method, you would like to allow the caller to pass in any number of arguments, and return the calculated average.

If you were to prototype this method to take an array of Integers, this would force the caller to first define the array, then fill the array, and finally pass it into the method. However, if you define CalculateAverage() to take a ParamArray of Integer data types, the caller can simply pass a comma-delimited list of Integers. The .NET runtime will automatically package the set of Integers into an array of type Integer behind the scenes:

```
Function CalculateAverage(ByVal ParamArray itemsToAvg() As Integer) As Double
  Dim itemCount As Integer = UBound(itemsToAvg)
  Dim result As Integer
  For i As Integer = 0 To itemCount
    result += itemsToAvg(i)
  Next
  Return result / itemCount
End Function
```

As mentioned, when calling this method, you may send in an explicitly defined array of Integers, or alternatively, implicitly specify an array of Integers as a comma-delimited list. For example:

```
Sub Main()
  ...
  ' ParamArray data can be sent as a caller supplied array
  ' or a comma-delimited list of arguments.
  Console.WriteLine(CalculateAverage(10, 11, 12, 44))
  Dim data() As Integer = {22, 33, 44, 55}
  Console.WriteLine(CalculateAverage(data))
End Sub
```

As you might guess, this technique is nothing more than a convenience for the caller, given that the array is created by the CLR as necessary. By the time the array is within the scope of the method being called, you are able to treat it as a full-blown .NET array that contains all the function of the System.Array base class library type.

■**Note** To avoid any ambiguity, VB 2005 demands a method only support a single ParamArray argument, which must be the final argument in the parameter list.

Method Calling Conventions

The next aspect of building VB 2005 methods to be aware of is that *all* methods (subroutines and functions) are now called by wrapping arguments in parentheses (even if the method in question takes no arguments whatsoever). In stark contrast, VB 6.0 supported some rather ridiculous calling conventions that forced you to call subs using a different syntax than functions. In general, under VB 6.0, subs do not require parentheses, while functions do. However, the following variations do occur:

```
' VB 6.0 function calling insanity.
Dim i as Integer
i = myFunction(myArg)     ' Use () to capture return value.
MyFunction myArg          ' Forgo () if you don't care about return value.
Call myFunction(myArg)    ' Same as previous line.
myFunction(myArg)         ' Pass myArg by value.

' VB 6.0 Subroutine calling insanity.
mySub myArg          ' Subs don't take ()...
Call mySub (myArg)   ' ...unless you use the Call keyword...
mySub (myArg)        ' ...or you want to pass by value.
```

VB 2005 stops the madness once and for all by stating that all functions and all subs must be called using parentheses. Thus, if a sub or function does not require arguments, parentheses are still used:

```
' VB 2005 simplicity.
Dim i as Integer
i = AFuncWithNoArgs()                        ' Use ()
ASubWithNoArgs()                             ' Use ()
ASubWithArgs(89, 44, "Ahhh. Better")         ' Use ()
Dim IAmPassedByValue as Boolean
SomeMethod((IAmPassedByValue))               ' Use ()
```

Methods Containing Static Data

In VB 2005 (as well as earlier versions of the language), the Static keyword is used to define a point of data that is in memory as long as the application is running, but is visible only within the function in which it was declared. Assume you have added the following subroutine to your HelperFunctions module:

```
Sub PrintLocalCounter()
  ' Note the Static keyword.
  Static Dim localCounter As Integer
  localCounter += 1
  Console.Write("{0} ", localCounter)
End Sub
```

As you would expect, the first time this function is called, the static data is allocated and initialized to its default value (0 in the case of an Integer). However, because the local variable has been defined with the Static keyword, its previous value is retained across each method invocation. Therefore, if you invoke PrintLocalCounter() a handful of times within your Main() method as follows:

```
Sub Main()
...
  For i As Integer = 0 To 10
    PrintLocalCounter()
  Next
End Sub
```

you would see the printout to the console shown in Figure 4-3.

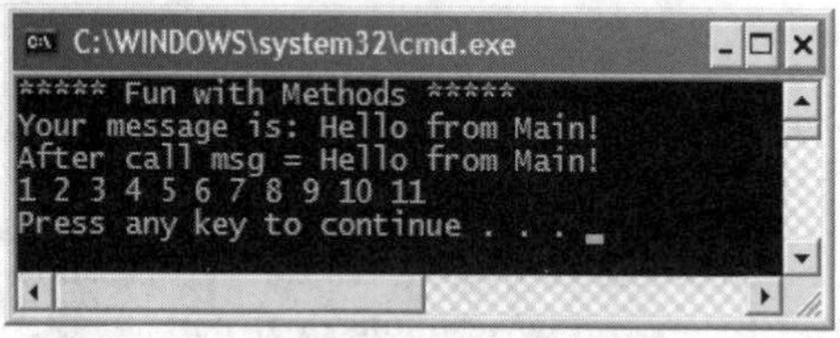

Figure 4-3. *Static data is retained between invocations.*

Of course, if a local variable is not defined with the Static keyword:

```
Sub PrintLocalCounter()
  Dim localCounter As Integer
  localCounter += 1
  Console.Write("{0} ", localCounter)
End Sub
```

you would see "1" printed out 11 times, as the Integer is re-created between calls.

■**Note** Unlike VB 6.0, VB 2005 no longer allows you to apply the Static keyword on the method level (in order to treat all local variables as Static). If you require the same behavior from a VB 2005 application, you need to explicitly define each data point using the Static keyword.

Understanding Member Overloading

Like other modern object-oriented languages, VB 2005 allows a method to be *overloaded*. Simply put, when you define a set of identically named members that differ by the number (or type) of parameters, the member in question is said to be overloaded.

To understand why overloading is so useful, consider life as a VB 6.0 developer. Assume you are using VB 6.0 to build a set of methods that return the sum of various incoming types (Integers, Doubles, and so on). Given that VB 6.0 does not support method overloading, we would be required to define a unique set of methods that essentially do the same thing (return the sum of the arguments):

```
' VB 6.0 code.
Public Function AddInts(ByVal x As Integer, ByVal y As Integer) As Integer
  AddInts = x + y
End Function
Public Function AddDoubles(ByVal x As Double, ByVal y As Double) As Double
  AddDoubles = x + y
End Function
Public Function AddLongs(ByVal x As Long, ByVal y As Long) As Long
  AddLongs = x + y
End Function
```

Not only can code such as this become tough to maintain, but the object user must now be painfully aware of the name of each method. Using overloading, we are able to allow the caller to call a single method named Add(). Again, the key is to ensure that each version of the method has a distinct set of arguments (members differing only by return type are *not* unique enough):

```
' VB 2005 code.
Public Function Add(ByVal x As Integer, ByVal y As Integer) As Integer
  Return x + y
End Function
```

```
Public Function Add(ByVal x As Double, ByVal y As Double) As Double
  Return x + y
End Function
Public Function Add(ByVal x As Long, ByVal y As Long) As Long
  Return x + y
End Function
```

The caller can now simply invoke Add() with the required arguments and the compiler is happy to comply, given the fact that the compiler is able to resolve the correct implementation to invoke given the provided arguments:

```
Sub Main()
...
  ' Calls Integer version of Add()
  Console.WriteLine(Add(10, 10))
  ' Calls Long verson of Add()
  Console.WriteLine(Add(900000000000, 900000000000))
  ' Calls Double version of Add()
  Console.WriteLine(Add(4.3, 4.4))
End Sub
```

The Overloads Keyword

Also know that VB 2005 provides the Overloads keyword, which can be used when you want to explicitly mark a member as overloaded. Using this keyword, however, is completely optional. The compiler assumes you are overloading if it finds identically named methods with varying arguments:

```
' VB 2005 code.
Public Overloads Function Add(ByVal x As Integer, ByVal y As Integer) As Integer
  Return x + y
End Function
Public Overloads Function Add(ByVal x As Double, ByVal y As Double) As Double
  Return x + y
End Function
Public Overloads Function Add(ByVal x As Long, ByVal y As Long) As Long
  Return x + y
End Function
```

Details of Method Overloading

When you are overloading a method, the VB 2005 parameter modifiers come into play to define valid forms of overloading. First of all, if the only point of differentiation between two methods is the ByVal/ByRef parameter modifier, it is *not unique* enough to be overloaded:

```
' Compiler error!  Methods can't differ only by
' ByRef / ByVal
Sub TestSub(ByVal a As Integer)
End Sub
Sub TestSub(ByRef a As Integer)
End Sub
```

Also, if a method is overloaded by nothing more than an argument marked with the Optional keyword, you will once again receive a compiler error. Consider the following:

```
Sub TestSub(ByVal a As Integer)
End Sub
Sub TestSub(ByVal a As Integer, Optional ByVal b As Integer = 0)
End Sub
```

The reason the compiler refuses to allow this overload is due to the fact that it cannot disambiguate the following code:

```
Sub Main()
...
  ' Are you calling the one arg version,
  ' or the two arg version and omitting the second parameter?
  TestSub(1)
End Sub
```

■**Source Code** The FunWithMethods application is located under the Chapter 4 subdirectory.

That wraps up our examination of building methods using the syntax of VB 2005. Next up, let's check out how to build and manipulate arrays, enumerations, and structures.

Array Manipulation in VB 2005

As I would guess you are already aware, an *array* is a set of data points, accessed using a numerical index. More specifically, an array is a set of contiguous data points of the same type (an array of Integers, an array of Strings, an array of SportsCars, and so on). Declaring an array with Visual Basic 2005 is quite straightforward. For example, here are three arrays of varying types:

```
Module Program
  Sub Main()
    Console.WriteLine("***** Fun with Arrays *****")
    ' An array of 11 Strings
    Dim myStrings(10) As String
    ' An array of 3 Integers
    Dim myInts(2) As Integer
    ' An array of 5 Objects
    Dim myObjs(4) As Object
  End Sub
End Module
```

Look closely at the code comments. When declaring a VB 2005 array, the number used in the array declaration represents the *upper bound* of the array, not the *maximum number* of elements. Thus, unlike C-based languages, when you write Dim myInts(2) As Integer you end up with *three* elements (0 through 2, inclusive).

Once you have defined an array, you are then able to fill the elements index by index as shown in the following Main() method:

```
Module Program
  Sub Main()
    Console.WriteLine("***** Fun with Arrays *****")
    ' Create and fill an array of 3 Integers
    Dim myInts(2) As Integer
    myInts(0) = 100
    myInts(1) = 200
    myInts(2) = 300
    ' Now print each value.
    For Each i As Integer In myInts
      Console.WriteLine(i)
    Next
  End Sub
End Module
```

Do be aware that if you declare an array, but do not explicitly fill each index, each item will be set the default value of the data type (e.g., an array of Booleans will be set to False, an array of Integers will be set to zero, and so forth). Given this, the following code will first print out three blank lines, followed by the names Cerebus, Jaka, and Astoria:

```
Module Program
  Sub Main()
    Console.WriteLine("***** Fun with Arrays *****")
...
    ' An array of (empty) Strings.
    Dim myStrs(2) As String
    For Each s As String In myStrs
      Console.WriteLine(s)
    Next
    ' Fill and print again.
    myStrs(0) = "Cerebus"
    myStrs(1) = "Jaka"
    myStrs(2) = "Astoria"
    For Each s As String In myStrs
      Console.WriteLine(s)
    Next
  End Sub
End Module
```

VB 2005 Array Initialization Syntax

In addition to filling an array using an item-by-item approach, you are also able to fill the items of an array using the VB 2005 member initialization syntax. To do so, specify each array item within the scope of curly brackets ({ }). This syntax can be helpful when you are creating an array of a known size, and wish to quickly specify the initial values. For example, the values of the myInts array could be established as follows:

```
Module Program
  Sub Main()
    Console.WriteLine("***** Fun with Arrays *****")
...
    ' An array of 3 Integers
    Dim myInts() As Integer = {100, 200, 300}
    For Each i As Integer In myInts
      Console.WriteLine(i)
    Next
  End Sub
End Module
```

Notice that when you make use of this "curly bracket array" syntax, you do not specify the size of the array, given that this will be inferred by the number of items within the scope of the curly brackets. Thus, the following statement results in a compiler error:

```
' OOPS! Don't specify upper bound when using
' curly bracket array initialization syntax!
Dim myInts(2) As Integer = {100, 200, 300}
```

Defining an Array of Objects

As mentioned, when you define an array, you do so by specifying the type of item that can be within the array variable. While this seems quite straightforward, there is one notable twist. As you will come to understand in Chapter 6, System.Object is the ultimate base class to each and every type (including fundamental data types) in the .NET type system. Given this fact, if you were to define an array of Objects, the subitems could be anything at all:

```
Module Program
  Sub Main()
    Console.WriteLine("***** Fun with Arrays *****")
...
    ' An array of Objects can be anything at all.
    Dim myObjects(3) As Object
    myObjects(0) = 10
    myObjects(1) = False
    myObjects(2) = New DateTime(1969, 3, 24)
    myObjects(3) = "Form & Void"

    For Each obj As Object In myObjects
      ' Print the type and value for each item in array.
      Console.WriteLine("Type: {0}, Value: {1}", obj.GetType(), obj)
    Next
  End Sub
End Module
```

Here, as we are iterating over the contents of myObjects, we print out the underlying type of each item using the GetType() method of System.Object as well as the value of the current item. Without going into too much detail regarding System.Object.GetType() at this point in the text, simply understand that this method can be used to obtain the fully qualified name of the item (Chapter 14 fully examines the topic of type information and reflection services). Figure 4-4 shows the output of the previous snippet.

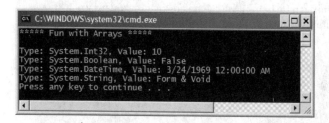

Figure 4-4. *Investigating an array of* Objects *using* Object.GetType()

Defining the Lower Bound of an Array

Visual Basic 6.0 allows developers to build an array with an arbitrary lower bound using the To keyword. To determine the upper and lower bounds of an array, we were provided with the LBound() and UBound() helper functions:

```
' VB 6.0 code!
Dim myNumbers(5 To 7) As Integer
myNumbers(5) = 10
myNumbers(6) = 10
myNumbers(7) = 10
Dim i As Integer
For i = LBound(myNumbers) To UBound(myNumbers)
  MsgBox i
Next i
```

Although the To keyword can still be used under VB 2005, the lower bound of an array is *always* zero in order to keep VB 2005 in step with the rules of the Common Type System (CTS). Given this point, the To keyword is more or less optional under the .NET platform:

```
' Under VB 2005, the To keyword does not bring much to the table.
Dim myNumbers(0 To 5) as Integer
Dim moreNumbers(5) as Integer
```

For new VB 2005 projects, the fact should pose no problems; however, if you are building an application that needs to communicate with a legacy VB 6.0 COM application that sends or receives arrays with arbitrary lower bounds, this can be an issue. For example, assume you are building a new .NET application that is making use of an ActiveX *.dll that contains a COM object that returns an array with a lower bound of 5. Given all .NET arrays have a lower bound of zero, how would you be able to process this array back within the .NET program?

Under the .NET platform, the only way to create (or represent) an array with a lower bound other than zero is to use the shared CreateInstance() method of System.Array. We will examine the role of System.Array in just a moment; however, ponder the following code, which does indeed build an array with a lower bound of 5 and an upper bound of 7:

```
Module Program
  Sub Main()
    Console.WriteLine("***** Fun with Arrays *****")
...
    ' An array representing the length of each dimension
    Dim myLengths() As Integer = {3}
    ' An array representing the lower bound of each dimension.
    Dim myBounds() As Integer = {5}

    ' Call Array.CreateInstance() specifying
    ' the type of array, length and bounds.
    Dim mySpecialArray As Array = _
      Array.CreateInstance(GetType(Integer), myLengths, myBounds)
    Console.WriteLine("Lower Bound: {0}", LBound(mySpecialArray))
    Console.WriteLine("Upper Bound: {0}", UBound(mySpecialArray))
  End Sub
End Module
```

While this code is more verbose than simply using the To keyword to set up a lower bound, it is not as complex as it might look. We begin by declaring two arrays of Integers that represent the length and lower bounds of each dimension of the array we are interested in building. The reason we have to represent the length and lower bound as an array of Integers (rather than two simple numbers) is due to the fact that Array.CreateInstance() can create single or multidimensional arrays. Here, we are creating an array of a single dimension, given that the myLengths and myBounds variables contain a single item. If you were to run this application, you would find the output shown in Figure 4-5.

Figure 4-5. *Creating an array with a lower bound of 5 using VB 2005*

The Redim/Preserve Syntax

VB 2005 allows you to dynamically reestablish the upper bound of a previous allocated array using the Redim/Preserve syntax. For example, assume you created an array of 10 Integers somewhere within your program. At a later time, you realize that this array needs to grow by 5 items (to hold a maximum of 16 Integers). To do so, you are able to author the following code:

```
' Make an array with 10 slots.
Dim myValues(9) As Integer
For i As Integer = 0 To 9
  myValues(i) = i
Next
For i As Integer = 0 To UBound(myValues)
  Console.Write("{0} ", myValues(i))
Next

' ReDim the array with extra slots.
ReDim Preserve myValues(15)
For i As Integer = 9 To UBound(myValues)
  myValues(i) = i
Next
For i As Integer = 0 To UBound(myValues)
  Console.Write("{0} ", myValues(i))
Next
```

Now, be very aware that the ReDim/Preserve syntax generates quite a bit of CIL code behind the scenes. You would be correct to assume that a new array will be created followed by a member-by-member transfer of the items from the old array into the new array (load your assembly into ildasm.exe to check out the code first hand).

Simply put, overuse of the ReDim/Preserve syntax can be inefficient. When you wish to use a container whose contents can dynamically grow (or shrink) on demand, you will always prefer using members from the System.Collections (Chapter 9) or System.Collections.Generic (Chapter 12) namespaces.

■**Note** This System.Array class provides the language-neutral Resize() method, which serves a similar function as VB 2005's ReDim/Preserve syntax.

Working with Multidimensional Arrays

In addition to the single dimensional arrays you have seen thus far, VB 2005 also supports the creation of multidimensional arrays. To declare and fill a multidimensional array, proceed as follows:

```
Sub Main()
...
  Dim myMatrix(6, 6) As Integer   ' makes a 7x7 array
  ' Populate array.
  Dim k As Integer, j As Integer
  For k = 0 To 6
    For j = 0 To 6
      myMatrix(k, j) = k * j
    Next j
  Next k
  ' Show array.
  For k = 0 To 6
    For j = 0 To 6
      Console.Write(myMatrix(k, j) & "  ")
```

```
      Next j
        Console.WriteLine()
   Next k
End Sub
```

So, at this point you should (hopefully) feel comfortable with the process of defining, filling, and examining the contents of a VB 2005 array type. To complete the picture, let's now examine the role of the System.Array class.

The System.Array Base Class

The most striking difference between VB 6.0 and VB 2005 arrays is the fact that every array you create gathers much of its functionality from the .NET System.Array class. Using these common members, we are able to operate on an array using a consistent object model. In fact, in most cases you are able to simply use the members of System.Array rather than the VB 6.0 style array functions (LBound(), UBound(), and so on). Table 4-2 gives a rundown of some of the more interesting members (be sure to check the .NET Framework 2.0 SDK for full details).

Table 4-2. *Select Members of* System.Array

Member of Array Class	Meaning in Life
Clear()	This shared method sets a range of elements in the array to empty values (0 for value items, shared for object references).
CopyTo()	Used to copy elements from the source array into the destination array.
GetEnumerator()	Returns the IEnumerator interface for a given array. I address interfaces in Chapter 9, but for the time being, keep in mind that this interface is required by the For Each construct.
Length	This property returns the number of items within the array.
Rank	This property returns the number of dimensions of the current array.
Reverse()	This shared method reverses the contents of a one-dimensional array.
Sort()	This shared method sorts a one-dimensional array of intrinsic types. If the elements in the array implement the IComparer interface, you can also sort your custom types (see Chapter 9).

Let's see some of these members in action. The following code makes use of the shared Reverse() and Clear() methods to pump out information about an array of string types to the console:

```
' Create some string arrays and exercise some System.Array members.
Sub Main()
...
  ' Initialize items at startup.
  Console.WriteLine("* Fun with System.Array *")
  Dim gothicBands() As String = _
    {"Tones on Tail", "Bauhaus", "Sisters of Mercy"}

  ' Print out names in declared order.
  Console.WriteLine(" -> " & "Here is the array:")
  For i As Integer = 0 To gothicBands.GetUpperBound(0)
    ' Print a name
    Console.Write(gothicBands(i) & " ")
  Next
  Console.WriteLine()
```

```
    ' Reverse them...
    Array.Reverse(gothicBands)
    Console.WriteLine(" -> " & "The reversed array")
    ' ... and print them.
    For i As Integer = 0 To gothicBands.GetUpperBound(0)
      ' Print a name
      Console.Write(gothicBands(i) & " ")
    Next
    Console.WriteLine()

    ' Clear out all but the final member.
    Console.WriteLine(" -> " & "Cleared out all but one...")
    Array.Clear(gothicBands, 1, 2)
    For i As Integer = 0 To gothicBands.GetUpperBound(0)
        ' Print a name
      Console.Write(gothicBands(i) & " ")
    Next
End Sub
```

The output can be seen in Figure 4-6.

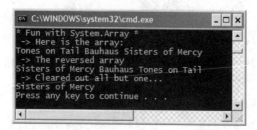

Figure 4-6. *Fun with* System.Array

Notice that many members of System.Array are defined as shared members and are therefore called at the class level (for example, the Array.Sort() or Array.Reverse() methods). Methods such as these are passed in the array you wish to process. Other methods of System.Array (such as the GetUpperBound() method or Length property) are bound at the object level, and thus you are able to invoke the member directly on the array.

Source Code The FunWithArrays application is located under the Chapter 4 subdirectory.

Understanding VB 2005 Enumerations

Recall from Chapter 1 that the .NET type system is composed of classes, structures, enumerations, interfaces, and delegates (also recall that a module is nothing more than a class type in disguise). To begin our exploration of these types, let's check out the role of the *enumeration*.

When building a system, it is often convenient to create a set of symbolic names that map to known numerical values. For example, if you are creating a payroll system, you may want to refer to the type of employees using constants such as VP, Manager, Grunt, and Contractor rather than raw numerical values such as {0, 1, 2, 3}. Like other managed languages, VB 2005 supports the notion of custom enumerations for this very reason. For example, here is an enumeration named EmpType:

```
' A custom enumeration.
Enum EmpType
    Manager     ' = 0
    Grunt       ' = 1
    Contractor  ' = 2
    VP          ' = 3
End Enum
```

The EmpType enumeration defines four named constants, corresponding to discrete numerical values. In VB 2005, the numbering scheme sets the first element to zero (0) by default, followed by an *n+1* progression. You are free to change the initial value as you see fit. For example, if it made sense to number the members of EmpType as 102 through 105, you could do so as follows:

```
' Begin with 102.
Enum EmpType
    Manager = 102
    Grunt       ' = 103
    Contractor  ' = 104
    VP          ' = 105
End Enum
```

Enumerations do not necessarily need to follow a sequential ordering. If (for some reason or another) it makes sense to establish your EmpType as seen here, the compiler continues to be happy:

```
' Elements of an enumeration need not be sequential!
Enum EmpType
    Manager = 10
    Grunt = 1
    Contractor = 100
    VP = 9
End Enum
```

Controlling the Underlying Storage for an Enum

By default, the storage type used to hold the values of an enumeration is a System.Int32 (the VB 2005 Integer); however, you are free to change this to your liking. VB 2005 enumerations can be defined in a similar manner for any of the core system types (Byte, Short, Integer, or Long). For example, if you want to set the underlying storage value of EmpType to be a Byte rather than an Integer, you can write the following:

```
' This time, EmpType maps to an underlying Byte.
Enum EmpType As Byte
    Manager = 10,
    Grunt = 1,
    Contractor = 100,
    VP = 9
End Enum
```

Changing the underlying type of an enumeration can be helpful if you are building a .NET application that will be deployed to a low-memory device (such as a .NET-enabled cell phone or PDA) and need to conserve memory wherever possible. Of course, if you do establish your enumeration to use a Byte as storage, each value must be within its range!

Declaring and Using Enums

Once you have established the range and storage type of your enumeration, you can use them in place of so-called magic numbers. Because enumerations are nothing more than a user-defined type, you are able to use them as function return values, method parameters, local variables, and so forth. Assume you have a module defining a public method, taking `EmpType` as the sole parameter:

```
Module Program
  ' Enums as parameters.
  Public Sub AskForBonus(ByVal e As EmpType)
    Select Case (e)
      Case EmpType.Contractor
        Console.WriteLine("You already get enough cash...")
      Case EmpType.Grunt
        Console.WriteLine("You have got to be kidding...")
      Case EmpType.Manager
        Console.WriteLine("How about stock options instead?")
      Case EmpType.VP
        Console.WriteLine("VERY GOOD, Sir!")
    End Select
  End Sub

  Sub Main()
    Console.WriteLine("**** Fun with Enums *****")
    ' Make a contractor type.
    Dim emp as EmpType
    emp = EmpType.Contractor
    AskForBonus(emp)
  End Sub
End Module
```

Notice that when you are assigning a value to an `Enum` variable, you must scope the `Enum` name (`EmpType`) to the value (`Grunt`). Because enumerations are a fixed set of name/value pairs, it is illegal to set an `Enum` variable to a value that is not defined directly by the enumerated type:

```
Sub Main()
  Console.WriteLine("**** Fun with Enums *****")
  Dim emp as EmpType
  ' Error!  SalesManager is not in the EmpType enum!
  emp = EmpType.SalesManager

  ' Error!  Forgot to scope Grunt to EmpType!
  emp= Grunt
End Sub
```

The System.Enum Class (and a Lesson in Resolving Keyword Name Clashes)

The interesting thing about .NET enumerations is that they gain functionality from the `System.Enum` class type. This class defines a number of methods that allow you to interrogate and transform a given enumeration. Before seeing some of this functionality first hand, you have one VB-ism to be aware of. As you know, VB is a case-insensitive language. Therefore, in the eyes of `vbc.exe`, `Enum`, `enum`, and `ENUM` all refer to the intrinsic `Enum` keyword.

While this can in fact be helpful (given that the Visual Studio 2005 IDE transforms keywords to the correct case), there is one problem. Specifically, if you attempt to access the shared members of `Enum` directly using the dot operator, you will be issued a compiler error. Assume you have updated your `Main()` method with the following call to `Enum.GetUnderlyingType()`. As the name implies, this method returns the data type used to store the values of the enumerated type (`System.Byte` in the case of `EmpType`):

```
' Print out the data type used to store the values?
Sub Main()
  Console.WriteLine("**** Fun with Enums *****")
  Dim emp As EmpType
  emp = EmpType.Contractor
  AskForBonus(emp)
  ' Compiler error!
  Console.WriteLine("EmpType uses a {0} for storage", _
    Enum.GetUnderlyingType(emp.GetType()))
End Sub
```

The problem is that the compiler assumes "Enum" refers to the VB 2005 keyword, *not* the System.Enum type! To resolve this name clash, you have a few choices. First, you could explicitly specify System.Enum everywhere in your code base:

```
Sub Main()
  Console.WriteLine("**** Fun with Enums *****")
  Dim emp As EmpType
  emp = EmpType.Contractor
  AskForBonus(emp)
  ' Use fully qualified name.
  Console.WriteLine("EmpType uses a {0} for storage", _
    System.Enum.GetUnderlyingType(emp.GetType()))
End Sub
```

While this fits the bill, it can be cumbersome to use fully qualified names. To help lessen your typing burden, you can make use of a variation of the VB 2005 Imports statement that allows you to define a simple token that maps to a fully qualified name:

```
' Build an alias to System.Enum
Imports DotNetEnum = System.Enum

Module Program
...
End Module
```

In this case, you defined an alias to System.Enum, called DotNetEnum. In your code, you can make use of this moniker whenever you want to make use of the members of the Enum type. At compile time, however, all occurences of DotNetEnum are replaced with System.Enum.

The final manner to resolve this nameclash is to wrap the Enum token within square brackets. This informs the compiler that you are refering to the Enum *type* not the Enum *keyword*:

```
Sub Main()
  Console.WriteLine("**** Fun with Enums *****")
  Dim emp As EmpType
  emp = EmpType.Contractor
  AskForBonus(emp)
  ' Wrap token in square brackets.
  Console.WriteLine("EmpType uses a {0} for storage", _
    [Enum].GetUnderlyingType(emp.GetType()))
End Sub
```

In any case, of greater interest than extracting the underlying type of an enumeration is the ability to extract the string names behind the numerical values. All VB 2005 enumerations support a method named ToString(), which as you would expect returns the string name of the current enumeration's value. For example:

```
Sub Main()
  Console.WriteLine("**** Fun with Enums *****")
```

```
...
   ' Prints out "emp is a Contractor".
   Console.WriteLine("emp is a {0}", emp.ToString())
End Sub
```

Using the shared Enum.Format() method, you gain a finer level of formatting options by specifying the desired format flag (the same formatting flags used when formatting data using the Console.WriteLine() method). In this context, "g" is the string value, the hexadecimal value is marked by "x" while the decimal value is obtained using "d". Format() takes two parameters, the first of which is the type information of the Enum you want to examine, while the second is the format flag.

System.Enum also defines another shared method named GetValues(). This method returns an instance of System.Array. Each item in the array corresponds to a member of the specified enumeration. Thus the following code will print out each name/value pair within the EmpType enumeration:

```
Sub Main()
   Console.WriteLine("**** Fun with Enums *****")
   ' Make a contractor type.
   Dim emp As EmpType
   emp = EmpType.Contractor
...
   ' Get all stats for EmpType.
   Dim obj As Array = DotNetEnum.GetValues(emp.GetType())
   Console.WriteLine("This enum has {0} members.", obj.Length)

   ' Now show the string name and associated value.
   Dim e As EmpType
   For Each e In obj
     Console.Write("String name: {0}", DotNetEnum.Format(emp.GetType(), e, "G"))
     Console.Write(" ({0})", DotNetEnum.Format(emp.GetType(), e, "D"))
     Console.WriteLine(" hex: {0}", DotNetEnum.Format(emp.GetType(), e, "X"))
   Next
End Sub
```

The output is shown in Figure 4-7.

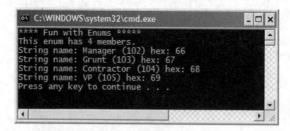

Figure 4-7. *Fun with* System.Enum

System.Enum also supports the IsDefined property. This allows you to determine whether a given string name is a member of the current enumeration. For example, assume you want to know whether the value "SalesPerson" is part of the EmpType enumeration:

```
' Does EmpType have a SalesPerson value?
If (DotNetEnum.IsDefined(emp.GetType(), "SalesPerson")) Then
   Console.WriteLine("Yep, we have sales people.")
```

```
Else
  Console.WriteLine("No, we have no profits....")
End If
```

As you will see over the course of this text, enumerations are used extensively throughout the .NET base class libraries. For example, ADO.NET makes use of numerous enums to represent the state of a connection (opened, closed, etc.), the state of a row in a DataTable (changed, new, detached, etc.), and so forth. Therefore, when you make use of a system-supplied enumeration, always remember that you are able to interact with the name/value pairs using the members of System.Enum.

■**Source Code** The FunWithEnums project is located under the Chapter 4 subdirectory.

Introducing the VB 2005 Structure Type

Now that you understand the role of enumeration types, let's conclude this chapter by introducing the .NET *structure*. A structure (like an enumeration) is a user-defined type; however, structures are not simply a collection of name/value pairs. Rather, structures are types that can contain any number of fields and members that operate on these fields. For example, structures can define constructors, can implement interfaces, and can contain any number of properties, methods, events, and fields (if some of these terms are unfamiliar at this point, don't fret. All of these topics are fully examined in later chapters).

■**Note** If you have a background in OOP, you can think of a structure as a "lightweight class type," given that structures provide a way to define a type that supports encapsulation, but cannot be used to build a family of related types (as structures are implicitly sealed).

To define a structure in VB 2005, you use the Structure keyword (and the required End Structure scope marker):

```
Structure Point
  Public x, y As Integer
  Public Sub Display()
    Console.WriteLine("{0}, {1}", x, y)
  End Sub
  Public Sub Increment()
    x += 1 : y += 1
  End Sub
  Public Sub Decrement()
    x -= 1 : y -= 1
  End Sub
  Public Function PointAsHexString() As String
    Return String.Format("{0:x}, {1:x}", x, y)
  End Function
End Structure
```

Structures are types that are well suited for modeling mathematical, geometric, and numerical types. Here, the Point structure is modeling an (*x, y*) coordinate represented by two Integer types, which can be altered via a handful of members.

Unlike arrays, strings, or enumerations, VB 2005 structures do not have an identically named class representation in the .NET library (that is, there is no System.Structure class), but are implicitly derived from System.ValueType.

Simply put, the role of System.ValueType is to ensure that the derived type (e.g., any structure) is allocated on the *stack* rather than the garbage collected heap. Given this, the lifetime of a structure is very predictable. When a structure variable falls out of the defining scope, it is removed from memory immediately:

```
Module Program
  Sub Main()
    Console.WriteLine("***** Fun with Structs *****")
    ' Create a Point
    Dim myPoint As Point
    myPoint.x = 100
    myPoint.y = 200
    myPoint.Display()

    ' Increase value of Point
    myPoint.Increment()
    myPoint.Display()

    Console.WriteLine("Value of Point in hex: {0}", _
      myPoint.PointAsHexString())
  End Sub     ' myPoint destroyed here!
End Module
```

We will revisit Structure types (and System.ValueType) and learn about numerous additional details in Chapter 11 when we drill into the distinction between value types and reference types. Until that point, just understand that a Structure allows you to define types that have a fixed and predictable lifetime.

■**Source Code**   The FunWithStructures project is located under the Chapter 4 subdirectory.

Summary

This chapter began with an examination of several VB 2005 keywords that allow you to build custom subroutines and functions. Recall that by default, parameters are passed by value (via the ByVal keyword); however, you may pass a parameter by reference if you mark it with ByRef. You also learned about the role of optional parameters and how to define and invoke methods taking parameter arrays.

Once we investigated the topic of method overloading, the remainder of this chapter examined several details regarding how arrays, enumerations, and structures are defined in Visual Basic 2005 and represented within the .NET base class libraries.

With this, our initial investigation of the Visual Basic 2005 programming language is complete! In the next chapter, we will begin to dig into the details of object-oriented development.

PART 3

■■■

Core Object-Oriented Programming Techniques

CHAPTER 5

■■■

Defining Encapsulated Class Types

In the previous two chapters, you investigated a number of core syntactical constructs that are commonplace to any .NET application you may be developing. Here, you will begin your examination of the object-oriented capabilities of VB 2005. Unlike Visual Basic 6.0, VB 2005 is a full-blown object-oriented programming language that has complete support for the famed "pillars of OOP" (encapsulation, inheritance, and polymorphism) and is therefore (for the most part) just as powerful as other OO languages such as Java, C++, or C#.

The first order of business is to examine the process of building well-defined class types with any number of *constructors*. Once you understand the basics of defining and allocating class types, the remainder of this chapter will examine the role of *encapsulation*. Along the way you will understand how to define class properties as well as the role of shared fields and members, read-only fields, and constant data. We wrap up by examining the new VB 2005 XML code documentation syntax.

Introducing the VB 2005 Class Type

As far as the .NET platform is concerned, the most fundamental programming construct is the *class type*. Formally, a class is a user-defined type that is composed of field data (often called *member variables*) and members that operate on this data (such as constructors, properties, subroutines, functions, events, and so forth). Collectively, the set of field data represents the "state" of a class instance (otherwise known as an *object*). The power of object-based languages such as Visual Basic 2005 is that by grouping data and related functionality in a class definition, you are able to model your software after entities in the real world.

To get the ball rolling, create a new VB 2005 console application named SimpleClassExample. Next, insert a new class file (named Car.vb) into your project using the Project ➤ Add New Item menu selection, choose the Class icon from the resulting dialog box as shown in Figure 5-1, and click the Add button.

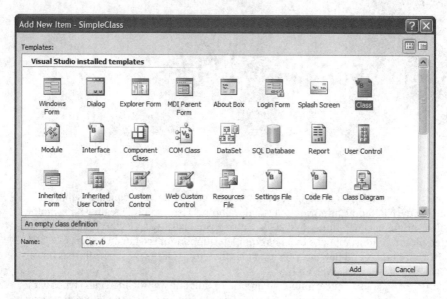

Figure 5-1. *Inserting a new* Class *type*

A class is defined in VB 2005 using the Class keyword. Like other constructs in the language, the scope of a class is terminated using the End keyword (End Class to be specific):

```
Public Class Car
End Class
```

Once you have defined a class type, you will need to consider the set of member variables that will be used to represent its state. For example, you may decide that cars maintain an Integer data type to represent the current speed and a String data type to represent the car's friendly pet name. Given these initial design notes, update your Car class as follows:

```
Public Class Car
  ' The 'state' of the Car.
  Public petName As String
  Public currSpeed As Integer
End Class
```

Notice that these member variables are declared using the Public access modifier. Public members of a class are directly accessible once an *object* of this type has been created. As you may already know, the term "object" is used to represent an instance of a given class type created using the New keyword.

Note Field data of a class should seldom (if ever) be defined as Public. To preserve the integrity of your state data, it is a far better design to define data as Private and allow controlled access to the data via type properties (as shown later in this chapter). However, to keep this first example as simple as possible, Public data fits the bill.

After you have defined the set of member variables that represent the state of the type, the next design step is to establish to members that model its behavior. For this example, the Car class will define one subroutine name SpeedUp() and another named PrintState():

```vb
Public Class Car
  ' The 'state' of the Car.
  Public petName As String
  Public currSpeed As Integer

  ' The functionality of the Car.
  Public Sub PrintState()
    Console.WriteLine("{0} is going {1} MPH.", _
      petName, currSpeed)
  End Sub
  Public Sub SpeedUp(ByVal delta As Integer)
    currSpeed += delta
  End Sub
End Class
```

As you can see, PrintState() is more or less a diagnostic function that will simply dump the current state of a given Car object to the command window. SpeedUp() will increase the speed of the Car by the amount specified by the incoming Integer parameter. Now, update your module's Main() method with the following code:

```vb
' If you rename your module, don't forget to reset the startup object
' using the My Project dialog box (see Chapter 3).
Module Program
  Sub Main()
    Console.WriteLine("***** Fun with Class Types *****")
    ' Allocate and configure a Car object.
    Dim myCar As New Car()
    myCar.petName = "Sven"
    myCar.currSpeed = 10

    ' Speed up the car a few times and print out the
    ' new state.
    For i As Integer = 0 To 10
      myCar.SpeedUp(5)
      myCar.PrintState()
    Next
  End Sub
End Module
```

Once you run your program, you will see that the Car object (myCar) maintains its current state throughout the life of the application, as shown in Figure 5-2.

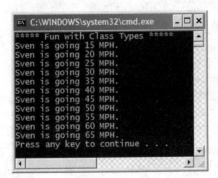

Figure 5-2. *Taking the* Car *for a test drive (pun intended)*

Allocating Objects with the New Keyword

As shown in the previous code example, objects must be allocated into memory using the New keyword. If you do not make use of the New keyword and attempt to make use of your class variable in a subsequent statement, you will receive a compiler warning. Even worse, if you execute code that makes use of an unallocated object, you will receive a runtime error (specifically, an exception of type NullReferenceException, which is the .NET equivalent of the dreaded VB 6.0 runtime error 91 "Object variable or With block variable not set"):

```
Sub Main()
  ' Runtime error! Forgot to use 'New'!
  Dim myCar As Car
  myCar.petName = "Fred"
End Sub
```

To correctly create a class type variable, you may define and allocate a Car object on a single line of code as follows:

```
Sub Main()
  Dim myCar As New Car()
  myCar.petName = "Fred"
End Sub
```

As an alternative, you can allocate an object using the assignment operator in conjunction with the New keyword. This syntax is provided to offer consistency within the language, given that this approach mimics the initialization of simple data types (such as an Integer). For example:

```
Sub Main()
  ' An alternative manner to allocate an object.
  Dim myInt as Integer = 10
  Dim myCar As Car = New Car()
End Sub
```

Note Unlike Visual Basic 6.0, there is no longer a performance penalty incurred when defining and allocating an object on a single line of code.

Finally, if you wish to define and allocate an object on separate lines of code, you may do so as follows:

```
Sub Main()
  Dim myCar as Car
  myCar = New Car()
  myCar.petName = "Fred"
End Sub
```

Note Under the .NET platform, the Set keyword has been deprecated. Thus, you no longer allocate objects using the VB 6.0 Set keyword (if you do so, Visual Studio 2005 will delete Set from the code statement when you hit the Enter key).

Here, the first code statement simply declares *a reference* to a yet-to-be-determined Car object. It is not until you assign a reference to an object via the New keyword that this reference points to a valid class instance. Without "new-ing" the reference, class variables are automatically assigned the value Nothing, as verified with the following If statement:

```
Sub Main()
  Dim ref As Car
  ' The following condition is true!
  If ref Is Nothing Then
    Console.WriteLine("ref is not initialized!")
  End If
End Sub
```

So at this point we have a trivial class type that defines a few points of data and some basic methods. To enhance the functionality of the current Car type, we need to understand the role class *constructors*.

Understanding Class Constructors

Given that objects have state (represented by the values of an object's member variables), the object user will typically want to assign relevant values to the object's field data before use. Currently, the Car type demands that the petName and currSpeed fields be assigned on a field-by-field basis. For the current example, this is not too problematic, given that we have only two data points. However, it is not uncommon for a class to have dozens of fields to contend with. Clearly, it would be undesirable to author 20 initialization statements to set 20 points of data. Even using the With construct we are at a disadvantage. By way of illustration:

```
Sub Main()
  Dim o As New SomeClass()
  With o
    .Field1 = 10
    .Field2 = True
    .Field3 = New AnotherClass()
    .Field4 = 9.99
    ...
    .Field20 = "Gad, this is nasty!"
End Sub
```

Before the release of the .NET platform, VB class designers handled the Initialize event to establish default values of an object's field data. Within the handler for the Initialize event, you were able to perform any necessary startup logic, to ensure the object came to life in a proper state. Thus, if you were to define a Car type in Visual Basic 6.0, and wish to assume that all car objects begin life named "Clunker" moving at 10 MPH, you might define the VB 6.0 Car.cls file shown in Figure 5-3.

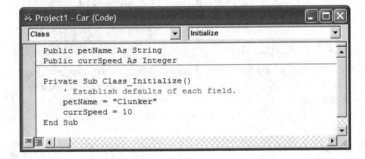

Figure 5-3. *A VB 6.0* Car *class*

The problem with this approach is that the `Initialize` event handler does not allow the object user to supply initialization parameters. Without this possibility, the object user is still required to establish the state of the object on a member-by-member basis:

```
' A VB 6.0 would require something like so.
Dim vb6Car As Car
Set vb6Car = New Car  ' Initialize event fired!
With vb6Car
  .currSpeed = 90
  .petName = "Chucky"
End With
```

To help the object user along, and reduce the number of "hits" required to establish the state of the object, many VB 6.0 developers created an ad hoc construction subroutine, often named `Create()`. For example, assume we have added the following method to the VB 6.0 `Car.cls` file:

```
Public Sub Create(ByVal pn As String, ByVal cs As Integer)
  petName = pn
  currSpeed = cs
End Sub
```

Although this technique does indeed reduce the number of hits to construct the object, it is now the responsibility *of the caller* to invoke the custom `Create()` method. If this step is forgotten, the object's state data is assigned to the values established within the `Initialize` event handler. In any case, here is an example of invoking our ad hoc VB 6.0 `Create()` method:

```
' A slightly better VB 6.0 solution.
Dim vb6Car As Car
Set vb6Car = New Car        ' Initialize fired! Default values established.
Vb6Car.Create "Zippy", 90   ' Supply custom values.
```

In an ideal world, the object user could specify startup values at the time of creation. In essence, you would *like* to be able to write the following VB 6.0 code:

```
' ILLEGAL VB 6.0 code!!!
Dim vb6Car As New Car("Zippy", 90)
```

While illegal in VB 6.0, using VB 2005 you are able to do this very thing by defining any number of class constructors. Simply put, a constructor is a subroutine of a class that is called *by the CLR at runtime* when you allocate an object into memory using the `New` keyword.

■Note The VB 6.0 class `Initialize` (and `Terminate`) events are no longer available under VB 2005. However, the default constructor (examined next) is the functional equivalent of `Initialize`. On a related note, Chapter 8 examines the garbage collection process and the logical replacement of the VB 6.0 `Terminate` event.

The Role of the Default Constructor

First of all, understand that every VB 2005 class is provided with a freebee *default constructor* that you may redefine if need be. By definition, default constructors never take arguments. Beyond allocating the new object into memory, the default constructor ensures that all state data is set to an appropriate default value (see Chapter 3 for information regarding the default values of VB 2005 data types).

If you are not satisfied with these default assignments, you may redefine the default constructor by defining a `Public` subroutine named `New()` on any VB 2005 class type. To illustrate, update your VB 2005 `Car` class as follows:

```
Public Class Car
  ' The 'state' of the Car.
  Public petName As String
  Public currSpeed As Integer

  ' A custom default constructor.
  Public Sub New()
    petName = "Chuck"
    currSpeed = 10
  End Sub
...
End Class
```

In this case, we are forcing all Car objects to begin life named Chuck, and are moving down the road at 10 MPH. With this, you are able to create a Car object set to these default values as follows:

```
Sub Main()
  ' Invoking the default constructor.
  Dim chuck As New Car()
  ' Prints "Chuck is going 10 MPH."
  chuck.PrintState()
End Sub
```

Strictly speaking, the VB 2005 compiler allows you to omit the empty parentheses when invoking the default constructor. This is purely a typing time saver and has no effect on performance or code size. Given this point, we could allocate a Car type using the default constructor as follows:

```
Sub Main()
  ' Note lack of () on constructor call.
  Dim chuck As New Car
End Sub
```

Defining Custom Constructors

Typically, classes define additional constructors beyond the default. In doing so, you provide the object user with a simple and consistent way to initialize the state of an object directly at the time of creation. Given this fact, VB 2005 developers have no need to author VB 6.0–style ad hoc creations methods (such as a Create() method) to allow the caller to set the object's state data. Ponder the following update to the Car class, which now supports a total of three class constructors:

```
Public Class Car
...
  ' A custom default constructor.
  Public Sub New()            ·
    petName = "Chuck"
    currSpeed = 10
  End Sub

  ' Here, currSpeed will receive the
  ' default value of an Integer (zero).
  Public Sub New(ByVal pn As String)
    petName = pn
  End Sub

  Public Sub New(ByVal pn As String, ByVal cs As Integer)
    petName = pn
    currSpeed = cs
  End Sub
End Class
```

Keep in mind that what makes one constructor different from another (in the eyes of the VB 2005 compiler) is the number of and type of constructor arguments. Recall from Chapter 4, when you define a method of the same name that differs by the number or type of arguments, you have *overloaded* the method. Thus, the Car type has *overloaded* the constructor to provide a number of ways to create the object at the time of declaration. In any case, you are now able to create Car objects using any of the public constructors. For example:

```
Sub Main()
  ' Make a Car called Chuck going 10 MPH.
  Dim chuck As New Car()
  chuck.PrintState()

  ' Make a Car called Mary going 0 MPH.
  Dim mary As New Car("Mary")
  mary.PrintState()

  ' Make a Car called Daisy going 75 MPH.
  Dim daisy As New Car("Daisy", 75)
  daisy.PrintState()
End Sub
```

The Default Constructor Revisited

As you have just learned, all classes are endowed with a free default constructor. Thus, if you insert a new class into your current project named Motorcycle, defined like so:

```
Public Class Motorcycle
  Public Sub PopAWheely()
    Console.WriteLine("Yeeeeeee Haaaaaeewww!")
  End Sub
End Class
```

you are able to create an instance of the Motorcycle type via the default constructor out of the box:

```
Sub Main()
  Dim mc As New Motorcycle()
  mc.PopAWheely()
End Sub
```

However, as soon as you define a custom constructor, the default constructor is *silently removed* from the class and is no longer available! Think of it this way: if you do not define a custom constructor, the VB 2005 compiler grants you a default in order to allow the object user to allocate an instance of your type with field data set to their default values. However, when you define a unique constructor, the compiler assumes you have taken matters into your own hands.

Therefore, if you wish to allow the object user to create an instance of your type with the default constructor, as well as your custom constructor, you must *explicitly* redefine the default. To this end, understand that in a vast majority of cases, the implementation of the default constructor of a class is intentionally empty, as all you require is the ability to create an object with default values:

```
Public Class Motorcycle
  Public driverIntensity As Integer

  Public Sub PopAWheely()
    For i As Integer = 0 To driverIntensity
      Console.WriteLine("Yeeeeeee Haaaaaeewww!")
    Next
  End Sub
```

```
' Put back the default constructor.
Public Sub New()
End Sub

' Our custom constructor.
Public Sub New(ByVal intensity As Integer)
   driverIntensity = intensity
End Sub
End Class
```

The Role of the Me Keyword

Like earlier additions of Visual Basic, VB 2005 supplies a Me keyword that provides access to the current class instance. One possible use of the Me keyword is to resolve scope ambiguity, which can arise when an incoming parameter is named identically to a data field of the type. Of course, ideally you would simply adopt a naming convention that does not result in such ambiguity; however, to illustrate this use of the Me keyword, update your Motorcycle class with a new String field (named name) to represent the driver's name. Next, add a subroutine named SetDriverName() implemented as follows:

```
Public Class Motorcycle
   Public driverIntensity As Integer
   Public name As String

   Public Sub SetDriverName(ByVal name As String)
      name = name
   End Sub
...
End Class
```

Although this code will compile just fine, if you update Main() to call SetDriverName() and then print out the value of the name field, you may be surprised to find that the value of the name field is an empty string!

```
' Make a Motorcycle named Tiny?
Dim c As New Motorcycle(5)
c.SetDriverName("Tiny")
c.PopAWheely()
Console.WriteLine("Rider name is {0}", c.name) ' Prints an empty name value!
```

The problem is that the implementation of SetDriverName() is assigning the incoming parameter *back to itself* given that the compiler assumes name is referring to the variable currently in the method scope rather than the name field at the class scope. To inform the compiler that you wish to set the current object's name data field to the incoming name parameter, simply use Me:

```
Public Sub SetDriverName(ByVal name As String)
   Me.name = name
End Sub
```

Do understand that if there is no ambiguity, you are not required to make use of the Me keyword when a class wishes to access its own data or members. For example, if we rename the String data member to driverName, the use of Me is optional as there is no longer a scope ambiguity:

```
Public Class Motorcycle
   Public driverIntensity As Integer
   Public driverName As String
```

```
Public Sub SetDriverName(ByVal name As String)
  ' These two line are functionally identical.
  driverName = name
  Me.driverName = name
End Sub
...
End Class
```

Even though there is little to be gained when using Me in unambiguous situations, you may still find this keyword useful when implementing members, as IDEs such as SharpDevelop and Visual Studio 2005 will enable IntelliSense when Me is specified. This can be very helpful when you have forgotten the name of a class item and want to quickly recall the definition. Consider Figure 5-4.

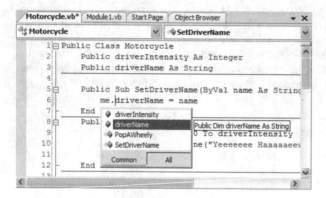

Figure 5-4. *The IntelliSense of* Me

■**Note** It is a compiler error to use the Me keyword within the implementation of a Shared member (explained shortly). As you will see, shared methods operate on the class (not object) level, and therefore at the class level, there is no current object (thus no Me)!

Chaining Constructor Calls Using Me

Another use of the Me keyword is to design a class using a technique termed *constructor chaining*. This design pattern is helpful when you have a class that defines multiple constructors. Given the fact that constructors often validate the incoming arguments to enforce various business rules, it can be quite common to find redundant validation logic within a class's constructor set. Consider the following updated Motorcycle:

```
Public Class Motorcycle
  Public driverIntensity As Integer
  Public driverName As String
...
  ' Redundant constructor logic.
  Public Sub New()
  End Sub
  Public Sub New(ByVal intensity As Integer)
    If intensity > 10 Then
      intensity = 10
```

```
    End If
    driverIntensity = intensity
  End Sub
  Public Sub New(ByVal intensity As Integer, ByVal name As String)
    If intensity > 10 Then
      intensity = 10
    End If
    driverIntensity = intensity
    driverName = name
  End Sub
End Class
```

Here (perhaps in an attempt to ensure the safety of the rider), each constructor is ensuring that the intensity level is never greater than 10. While this is all well and good, we do have redundant code statements in two constructors. This is less than ideal, as we are now required to update code in multiple locations if our rules change (for example, if the intensity should not be greater than 5).

One way to improve the current situation is to define a method in the Motorcycle class that will validate the incoming argument(s). If we were to do so, each constructor could make a call to this method before making the field assignment(s). While this approach does allow us to isolate the code we need to update when the business rules change, we are now dealing with the following redundancy:

```
Public Class Motorcycle
  Public driverIntensity As Integer
  Public driverName As String
...
  ' Constructors.
  Public Sub New()
  End Sub
  Public Sub New(ByVal intensity As Integer)
    ValidateIntensity(intensity)
    driverIntensity = intensity
  End Sub
  Public Sub New(ByVal intensity As Integer, ByVal name As String)
    ValidateIntensity(intensity)
    driverIntensity = intensity
    driverName = name
  End Sub
  Sub ValidateIntensity(ByRef intensity As Integer)
    If intensity > 10 Then
      intensity = 10
    End If
  End Sub
End Class
```

Under VB 2005, a cleaner approach is to designate the constructor that takes the *greatest number of arguments* as the "master constructor" and have its implementation perform the required validation logic. The remaining constructors can make use of the Me keyword to forward the incoming arguments to the master constructor and provide any additional parameters as necessary. In this way, we only need to worry about maintaining a single constructor for the entire class, while the remaining constructors are basically empty. Here is the final iteration of the Motorcycle class (with one additional constructor for the sake of illustration):

```
Public Class Motorcycle
  Public driverIntensity As Integer
  Public driverName As String
...
  ' Constructors.
```

```
  Public Sub New()
  End Sub
  Public Sub New(ByVal intensity As Integer)
    Me.New(intensity, "")
  End Sub
  Public Sub New(ByVal name As String)
    Me.New(5, name)
  End Sub

  ' This is the 'master' constructor that does all the real work.
  Public Sub New(ByVal intensity As Integer, ByVal name As String)
    If intensity > 10 Then
      intensity = 10
    End If
    driverIntensity = intensity
    driverName = name
  End Sub
End Class
```

Note When a constructor forwards parameters to the master constructor using Me.New(), it must do so on the very first line within the constructor body. If you fail to do so, you will receive a compiler error.

Understand that using the Me keyword to chain constructor calls is never mandatory. However, when you make use of this technique, you do tend to end up with a more maintainable and concise class definition. Again, using this technique you can simplify your programming tasks, as the real work is delegated to a single constructor (typically the constructor that has the most parameters), while the other constructors simply "pass the buck."

Observing Constructor Flow

On a final note, do know that once a constructor passes arguments to the designated master constructor (and that constructor has processed the data), the constructor invoked originally by the object user will finish executing any remaining code statements. To clarify, update each of the constructors of the Motorcycle class with a fitting call to Console.WriteLine():

```
Public Class Motorcycle
...
  ' Constructors.
  Public Sub New()
    Console.WriteLine("In default c-tor")
  End Sub

  Public Sub New(ByVal intensity As Integer)
    Me.New(intensity, "")
    Console.WriteLine("In c-tor taking an Integer")
  End Sub

  Public Sub New(ByVal name As String)
    Me.New(5, name)
    Console.WriteLine("In c-tor taking a String")
  End Sub
```

```
Public Sub New(ByVal intensity As Integer, ByVal name As String)
    Console.WriteLine("In master c-tor")
    If intensity > 10 Then
        intensity = 10
    End If
    driverIntensity = intensity
    driverName = name
End Sub
End Class
```

Now, ensure your Main() method exercises a Motorcycle object as follows:

```
Sub Main()
...
    ' Make a Motorcycle.
    Dim c As New Motorcycle(5)
    c.SetDriverName("Tiny")
    c.PopAWheely()
    Console.WriteLine("Rider name is {0}", c.name)
End Sub
```

With this, ponder the output in Figure 5-5.

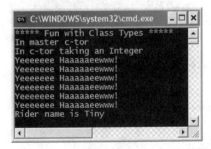

Figure 5-5. *Constructor chaining at work*

As you can see, the flow of constructor logic is as follows:

- We create our object by invoking the constructor requiring a single Integer.
- This constructor forwards the supplied data to the master constructor and provides any additional startup arguments not specified by the caller.
- The master constructor assigns the incoming data to the object's field data.
- Control is returned to the constructor originally called, and executes any remaining code statements.

Great! At this point you are able to define a class with field data and various members that can be created using any number of constructors. Next up, let's formalize the role of the Shared keyword.

■**Source Code** The SimpleClassExample project is included under the Chapter 5 subdirectory.

Understanding the Shared Keyword

A VB 2005 class (or structure) may define any number of *shared members* via the Shared keyword. When you do so, the member in question must be invoked directly from the class level, rather than from a type instance. To illustrate the distinction, consider our good friend System.Console. As you have seen, you do not invoke the WriteLine() method from the object level:

```
' Error!  WriteLine() is not an instance level method!
Dim c As New Console()
c.WriteLine("I can't be printed...")
```

but instead simply prefix the type name to the shared WriteLine() member:

```
' Correct!  WriteLine() is a Shared method.
Console.WriteLine("Thanks...")
```

Simply put, Shared members are items that are deemed (by the type designer) to be so commonplace that there is no need to create an instance of the type when invoking the member.

Defining Shared Methods (and Fields)

Assume you have a new console project named SharedMethods and have inserted a class named Teenager that defines a Shared method named Complain(). This method returns a random string, obtained in part by calling a helper function named GetRandomNumber():

```
Class Teenager
  Public Shared r As Random = New Random()

  Public Shared Function GetRandomNumber(ByVal upperLimit As Short) As Integer
    Return r.Next(upperLimit)
  End Function

  Public Shared Function Complain() As String
    Dim messages As String() = _
      {"Do I have to?", "He started it!", "I'm too tired...", _
       "I hate school!", "You are sooo wrong."}
    Return messages(GetRandomNumber(5))
  End Function
End Class
```

Notice that the System.Random member variable and the GetRandomNumber() helper function method have also been declared as Shared members of the Teenager class, given the rule that Shared members can operate only on other Shared members.

Note Allow me to repeat myself. Shared members can operate only on Shared data and call Shared methods of the defining class. If you attempt to make use of non-Shared data or call a non-Shared method within a Shared member, you'll receive a compiler error.

Like any Shared member, to call Complain(), prefix the name of the defining class:

```
Sub Main()
  Console.WriteLine("***** Shared Methods *****")
  For i As Integer = 0 To 5
    Console.WriteLine(Teenager.Complain())
  Next
End Sub
```

As stated, shared members are bound at the *class* not *object* level. However, a strange VB-ism exists that allows us to invoke the shared Complain() method as follows:

```
Sub Main()
  Console.WriteLine("***** Shared Methods *****")

  ' VB-ism!
  Dim bob As New Teenager()
  For i As Integer = 0 To 5
    Console.WriteLine(bob.Complain())
  Next
End Sub
```

Although the previous code will result in invoking the Complain() method, you will also receive a compiler warning:

```
warning BC42025: Access of shared member, constant member, enum member or nested
type through an instance; qualifying expression will not be evaluated.
```

Basically, this warning is informing us that Complain() cannot be invoked from our Teenager object named bob. How then is Complain() invoked? Under the covers, the VB 2005 compiler simply substitutes a correct call to Teenager.Complain() in the CIL code, which can be verified using ildasm.exe (see Chapter 1):

```
.method public static void  Main() cil managed
{
...
  IL_002c: call string SharedMethods.Teenager::Complain()
...
} // end of method Program::Main
```

As you might agree, the VB-ism is confusing at best. If you wish to inform the VB 2005 compiler to emit an error (rather than a warning) when invoking a shared member from an object variable, you can do so by opening the My Project icon, selecting the Compile tab, and setting the Instance variable accesses shared member condition to Error. By doing so, we would now receive a compile-time error when writing code such as

```
Sub Main()
  Dim bob as New Teenager()
  For i As Integer = 0 To 5
    ' Now an compile time error.
    Console.WriteLine(bob.Complain())
  Next
End Sub
```

Source Code The SharedMethods application is located under the Chapter 5 subdirectory.

Defining Shared Data

In addition to Shared members, a type may also define Shared field data (such as the Random member variable seen in the previous Teenager class). Understand that when a class defines non-Shared data (properly referred to as *instance data*), each object of this type maintains an independent copy of the field. For example, assume a class that models a savings account is defined in a new console application named SharedData:

```
' This class has a single piece of non-Shared data.
Class SavingsAccount
  Public currBalance As Double

  Public Sub New(ByVal balance As Double)
    currBalance = balance
  End Sub
End Class
```

When you create SavingsAccount objects, memory for the currBalance field is allocated for each class instance. Shared data, on the other hand, is allocated once and shared among all objects of the same type. To illustrate the usefulness of Shared data, assume you add piece of Shared data named currInterestRate to the SavingsAccount class:

```
Class SavingsAccount
  Public currBalance As Double

  ' A Shared point of data.
  Public Shared currInterestRate As Double = 0.04

  Public Sub New(ByVal balance As Double)
    currBalance = balance
  End Sub
End Class
```

If you were to create three instances of SavingsAccount as follows:

```
Sub Main()
  Console.WriteLine("***** Fun with Shared Data *****")
  Dim s1 As New SavingsAccount(50)
  Dim s2 As New SavingsAccount(100)
  Dim s3 As New SavingsAccount(10000.75)
End Sub
```

the in-memory data allocation would look something like Figure 5-6.

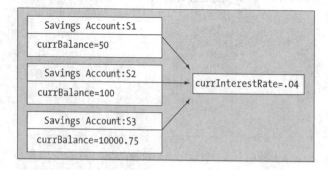

Figure 5-6. *Shared data is allocated once and shared among all instances of the class.*

Let's update the SavingsAccount class to define two Shared methods to get and set the interest rate value:

```
Class SavingsAccount
  Public currBalance As Double
  Public Shared currInterestRate As Double = 0.04
```

```
Public Sub New(ByVal balance As Double)
  currBalance = balance
End Sub

' Shared members to get/set interest rate.
Public Shared Sub SetInterestRate(ByVal newRate As Double)
  currInterestRate = newRate
End Sub
Public Shared Function GetInterestRate() As Double
  Return currInterestRate
End Function

' Instance members to get/set interest rate.
Public Sub SetInterestRateObj(ByVal newRate As Double)
  currInterestRate = newRate
End Sub
Public Function GetInterestRateObj() As Double
  Return currInterestRate
End Function
End Class
```

As stated, Shared methods can operate only on Shared data. However, a non-Shared method can make use of both Shared and non-Shared data. This should make sense, given that Shared data is available to all instances of the type. Now, observe the following usage and the output in Figure 5-7:

```
Sub Main()
  Console.WriteLine("***** Fun with Shared Data *****")
  Dim s1 As New SavingsAccount(50)
  Dim s2 As New SavingsAccount(100)

  ' Get and Set interest rate at object level.
  Console.WriteLine("Interest Rate is: {0}", s1.GetInterestRateObj())
  s2.SetInterestRateObj(0.08)

  ' Make new object, this does NOT 'reset' the interest rate.
  Dim s3 As New SavingsAccount(10000.75)
  Console.WriteLine("Interest Rate is: {0}", SavingsAccount.GetInterestRate())
  Console.ReadLine()
End Sub
```

Figure 5-7. Shared *data is allocated only once.*

As you can see, when you create new instances of the SavingsAccount class, the value of the Shared data is not reset, as the CLR will allocate the data into memory exactly one time. After that point, all objects of type SavingsAccount operate on the same value. Thus, if one object were to change the interest rate, all other objects report the same value:

```
Sub Main()
...
  SavingsAccount.SetInterestRate(0.09)
  ' All three lines print out "Interest Rate is: 0.09"
  Console.WriteLine("Interest Rate is: {0}", s1.GetInterestRateObj())
  Console.WriteLine("Interest Rate is: {0}", s2.GetInterestRateObj())
  Console.WriteLine("Interest Rate is: {0}", SavingsAccount.GetInterestRate())
  Console.ReadLine()
End Sub
```

Defining Shared Constructors

As you know, constructors are used to set the value of a type's data at the time of construction. Thus, if you were to assign the value to a piece of Shared data within an instance-level constructor, you would be saddened to find that the value is reset each time you create a new object! For example, assume you have updated the SavingsAccount class as follows:

```
Class SavingsAccount
  Public currBalance As Double
  Public Shared currInterestRate As Double

  Public Sub New(ByVal balance As Double)
    currBalance = balance
    currInterestRate = 0.04
  End Sub
...
End Class
```

If you execute the previous Main() method, notice how the currInterestRate variable is reset each time you create a new SavingsAccount object (see Figure 5-8).

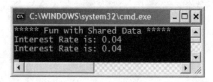

Figure 5-8. *Assigning* Shared *data in a constructor "resets" the value.*

While you are always free to establish the initial value of Shared data using the member initialization syntax, what if the value for your Shared data needed to be obtained from a database or external file? To perform such tasks requires a method scope (such as a constructor) to execute the code statements. For this very reason, VB 2005 allows you to define a Shared constructor:

```
Class SavingsAccount
  Public currBalance As Double
  Public Shared currInterestRate As Double

  ' A shared constructor.
  Shared Sub New()
    Console.WriteLine("In Shared ctor!")
    currInterestRate = 0.04
  End Sub
...
End Class
```

Simply put, a *shared constructor* is a special constructor that is an ideal place to initialize the values of shared data when the value is not known at compile time (e.g., you need to read in the value from an external file, etc.). Here are a few points of interest regarding Shared constructors:

- A given class (or structure) may define only a single Shared constructor.
- A Shared constructor does not take an access modifier and cannot take any parameters.
- A Shared constructor executes exactly one time, regardless of how many objects of the type are created.
- The runtime invokes the Shared constructor when it creates an instance of the class or before accessing the first Shared member invoked by the caller.
- The Shared constructor executes before any instance-level constructors.

Given this modification, when you create new SavingsAccount objects, the value of the Shared data is preserved, and the output is identical to Figure 5-7 (shown previously).

■**Source Code** The SharedData project is located under the Chapter 5 subdirectory.

Sweet! At this point in the chapter you (hopefully) feel comfortable defining simple class types containing constructors, fields, and various shared members. Now that you have the basics under your belt, we can formally investigate the three pillars of object-oriented programming.

Defining the Pillars of OOP

All object-based languages must contend with three core principals of object-oriented programming, often called the "pillars of object-oriented programming (OOP)":

- *Encapsulation*: How does this language hide an object's internal implementation details and preserve data integrity?
- *Inheritance*: How does this language promote code reuse?
- *Polymorphism*: How does this language let you treat related objects in a similar way?

As you are most likely already aware, VB 6.0 did not support each pillar of object technology. Specifically, VB 6.0 lacked inheritance (and therefore lacked true polymorphism). VB 2005, on the other hand, supports each aspect of OOP, and is on par with any other modern-day OO language (C#, Java, C++, Delphi, etc.). Before digging into the syntactic details of each pillar, it is important that you understand the basic role of each. Here is an overview of each pillar, which will be examined in full detail over the remainder of this chapter and the next.

The Role of Encapsulation

The first pillar of OOP is called *encapsulation*. This trait boils down to the language's ability to hide unnecessary implementation details from the object user. For example, assume you are using a class named DatabaseReader, which has two primary methods: Open() and Close():

```
' This object encapsulates the details of opening and closing a database.
Dim dbReader As New DatabaseReader()
dbReader.Open("C:\MyCars.mdf")
  ' Do something with data file...
dbReader.Close()
```

The fictitious DatabaseReader class encapsulates the inner details of locating, loading, manipulating, and closing the data file. Object users love encapsulation, as this pillar of OOP keeps programming task simpler. There is no need to worry about the numerous lines of code that are working behind the scenes to carry out the work of the DatabaseReader class. All you do is create an instance and send the appropriate messages (e.g., "Open the file named MyCars.mdf located on my C drive").

Closely related to the notion of encapsulating programming logic is the idea of data hiding. Ideally, an object's state data should be specified as Private (or possibly Protected). In this way, the outside world must ask politely in order to change or obtain the underlying value. This is a good thing, as publicly declared data points can easily become corrupted (hopefully by accident rather than intent!). You will formally examine this aspect of encapsulation in just a bit.

The Role of Inheritance

The next pillar of OOP, *inheritance*, boils down to the language's ability to allow you to build *new* class definitions based on *existing* class definitions. In essence, inheritance allows you to extend the behavior of a base (or "parent") class by inheriting core functionality into the derived subclass (also called a "child class"). Figure 5-9 shows a simple example.

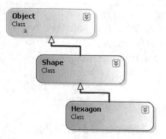

Figure 5-9. *The "is-a" relationship*

You can read the diagram in Figure 5-9 as "A hexagon is-a shape that is-an object." When you have classes related by this form of inheritance, you establish "is-a" relationships between types. The is-a relationship is often termed *classical inheritance*. Under Visual Basic 2005, System.Object is always the topmost base class in any .NET hierarchy, which defines some bare-bones functionality fully described in the next chapter. The Shape class extends Object. You can assume that Shape defines some number of members that are common to all descendents. The Hexagon class extends Shape, and inherits the core functionality defined by Shape and Object, as well as defines additional hexagon-related details of its own (whatever those may be).

There is another form of code reuse in the world of OOP: the containment/delegation model (also known as the "has-a" relationship or "aggregation"). This form of reuse (used exclusively by VB 6.0) is *not* used to establish parent/child relationships. Rather, the "has-a" relationship allows one class to contain an instance of another class and expose its functionality (if required) to the object user indirectly.

For example, assume you are again modeling an automobile. You might want to express the idea that a car "has-a" radio. It would be illogical to attempt to derive the Car class from a Radio, or vice versa (a Car "is-a" Radio? I think not!). Rather, you have two independent classes working together, where the Car class creates and exposes the Radio's functionality:

```
Public Class Radio
  Public Sub Power(ByVal turnOn As Boolean)
    Console.WriteLine("Radio on: {0}", turnOn)
  End Sub
End Class
```

```
Public Class Car
  ' Car 'has-a' Radio
  Private myRadio As Radio = New Radio()

  Public Sub TurnOnRadio(ByVal onOff As Boolean)
    ' Delegate call to inner object.
    myRadio.Power(onOff)
  End Sub
End Class
```

Notice that the object user has no clue that the Car class is making use of an inner object.

```
Sub Main()
  ' Call is forwarded to Radio internally.
  Dim viper as New Car()
  viper.TurnOnRadio(False)
End Sub
```

The Role of Polymorphism

The final pillar of OOP is *polymorphism*. This trait captures a language's ability to treat related objects in a similar manner. Specifically, this tenant of an object-oriented language allows a base class to define a set of members (formally termed the *polymorphic interface*) that are available to all descendents. A class's polymorphic interface is constructed using any number of *virtual* or *abstract* members (see Chapter 6 for full details).

In a nutshell, a *virtual member* is a member in a base class that defines a default implementation that may be changed (or more formally speaking, *overridden*) by a derived class. In contrast, an *abstract method* is a member in a base class that does *not* provide a default implementation, but does provide a signature. When a class derives from a base class defining an abstract method, it *must* be overridden by a derived type. In either case, when derived types override the members defined by a base class, they are essentially redefining how they respond to the same request.

To preview polymorphism, let's provide some details behind the shapes hierarchy shown in Figure 5-9. Assume that the Shape class has defined a virtual subroutine named Draw() that takes no parameters. Given the fact that every shape needs to render itself in a unique manner, subclasses (such as Hexagon and Circle) are free to override this method to their own liking (see Figure 5-10).

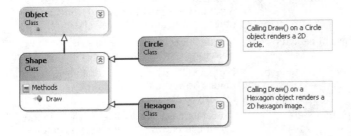

Figure 5-10. *Classical polymorphism*

Once a polymorphic interface has been designed, you can begin to make various assumptions in your code. For example, given that Hexagon and Circle derive from a common parent (Shape), an array of Shape types could contain anything deriving from this base class. Furthermore, given that Shape defines a polymorphic interface to all derived types (the Draw() method in this example), we can assume each member in the array has this functionality.

Consider the following Main() method, which instructs an array of Shape-derived types to render themselves using the Draw() method:

```
Module Program
  Sub Main()
    Dim myShapes(2) As Shape
    myShapes(0) = New Hexagon()
    myShapes(1) = New Circle()
    myShapes(2) = New Hexagon()

    For Each s As Shape In myShapes
      s.Draw()
    Next
    Console.ReadLine()
  End Sub
End Class
```

This wraps up our brisk overview of the pillars of OOP. Now that you have the theory in your mind, the remainder of this chapter explores further details of how encapsulation is handled under Visual Basic 2005. The next chapter will tackle the details of inheritance and polymorphism.

Visual Basic 2005 Access Modifiers

When working with encapsulation, you must always take into account which aspects of a type are visible to various parts of your application. Specifically, types (classes, interfaces, structures, enumerations, delegates) and their members (properties, subroutines, functions, constructors, fields, and so forth) are always defined using a specific keyword to control how "visible" the item is to other parts of your application. Although VB 2005 defines numerous keywords to control access, they differ on where they can be successfully applied (type or member). Table 5-1 documents the role of each access modifier and where they may be applied.

Table 5-1. *Visual Basic Access Modifiers*

Visual Basic 2005 Access Modifier	May Be Applied To	Meaning in Life
Public	Types or type members	Public items have no access restrictions. A public item can be accessed from an object as well as any derived class.
Private	Type members or nested types	Private items can only be accessed by the class (or structure) that defines the item.
Protected	Type members or nested types	Protected items are not accessible from an object; however, they are directly accessible by derived classes.
Friend	Types or type members	Friend items are accessible only within the current assembly. Therefore, if you define a set of Friend-level types within a .NET class library, other assemblies are not able to make use of them.
Protected Friend	Type members or nested types	When the Protected and Friend members are combined on an item, the item is accessible within the defining assembly, the defining class, and by derived classes.

In this chapter, we are only concerned with the `Public` and `Private` keywords. Later chapters will examine the role of the `Friend` and `Protected Friend` modifiers (useful when you build .NET code libraries) and the `Protected` modifier (useful when you are creating class hierarchies).

Access Modifiers and Nested Types

Notice that the `Private`, `Protected`, and `Protected Friend` access modifiers can be applied to a "nested type." Chapter 6 will examine nesting in detail. What you need to know at this point, however, is that a nested type is a type declared directly within the scope of `Class` or `Structure`. By way of example, here is a `Private Enum` (named `Color`) nested within a `Public` class (named `SportsCar`):

```
Public Class SportsCar
  ' OK!  Nested types can be marked Private.
  Private Enum CarColor
    Red
    Green
    Blue
  End Enum
End Class
```

Here, it is permissible to apply the `Private` access modifier on the nested type. However, nonnested types (such as the `SportsCar`) can only be defined with the `Public` or `Friend` modifiers. Therefore, the following `Class` is illegal:

```
' Error!  Non-nested types cannot be marked Private!
Private Class Radio
End Class
```

The Default Access Modifier

By default, a type's set of properties, subroutines, and functions are implicitly `Public`:

```
' A public class with a public default constructor.
Public Class Radio
  Sub New()
  End Sub
End Class
```

If you wish to be very clear in your intentions, you are free to explicitly mark a member with the `Public` keyword; however, the end result is identical in terms of performance and the size of the output assembly:

```
' Functionally identical to the previous class definition.
Public Class Radio
  Public Sub New()
  End Sub
End Class
```

Access Modifiers and Field Data

Fields of a `Class` or `Structure` *must* be defined with an access modifier. Unlike type members (constructors, properties, subroutines, or functions), there is not a "default" access level for field data. Consider the following illegal update to the `Radio` class:

```
Public Class Radio
  ' Error!  Must define access modifer
  ' for field data!
  favoriteStation as Double
```

```
  Sub New()
  End Sub
End Class
```

To rectify the situation, simply define the type with your access modifier of choice:

```
Public Class Radio
  Private favoriteStation as Double
  Sub New()
  End Sub
End Class
```

■Note It is possible to define a data field of a Class or Structure using the Dim keyword (although it is considered bad style). If you do so, the variable behaves as if it were declared with the Private access modifier.

The First Pillar: VB 2005's Encapsulation Services

The concept of encapsulation revolves around the notion that an object's internal data should not be directly accessible from an object instance. Rather, if the caller wants to alter the state of an object, the user does so indirectly using accessor (e.g., "getter") and mutator (e.g., "setter") methods. In VB 2005, encapsulation is enforced at the syntactic level using the Public, Private, Friend, and Protected keywords. To illustrate the need for encapsulation services, assume you have created the following class definition:

```
' A class with a single field.
Public Class Book
  Public numberOfPages As Integer
End Class
```

The problem with public field data is that the items have no ability to intrinsically "understand" whether the current value to which they are assigned is valid with regard to the current business rules of the system. As you know, the upper range of a VB 2005 Integer is quite large (2,147,483,647). Therefore, the compiler allows the following assignment:

```
' Humm. That is one heck of a mini-novel!
Sub Main()
  Dim miniNovel As New Book()
  miniNovel.numberOfPages = 30000000
End Sub
```

Although you have not overflowed the boundaries of an integer data type, it should be clear that a mini-novel with a page count of 30,000,000 pages is a bit unreasonable. As you can see, public fields do not provide a way to trap logical upper (or lower) limits. If your current system has a business rule that states a book must be between 1 and 1,000 pages, you are at a loss to enforce this programmatically. Because of this, public fields typically have no place in a production-level class definition.

Encapsulation provides a way to preserve the integrity of an object's state data. Rather than defining public fields (which can easily foster data corruption), you should get in the habit of defining *private data*, which is indirectly manipulated using one of two main techniques:

- Define a pair of accessor (get) and mutator (set) methods.

- Define a type property.

Additionally, VB 2005 supports the special keywords ReadOnly and WriteOnly, which also deliver a level of data protection. Whichever technique you choose, the point is that a well-encapsulated class should hide the details of how it operates from the prying eyes of the outside world. This is often termed *black box programming*. The beauty of this approach is that an object is free to change how a given method is implemented under the hood. It does this without breaking any existing code making use of it, provided that the signature of the method remains constant.

Encapsulation Using Traditional Accessors and Mutators

Over the remaining pages in this chapter, we will be building a fairly complete class that models a general employee. To get the ball rolling, create a new console application named EmployeeApp and insert a new Class (named Employee.vb) using the Project ➤ Add Class menu item. Update the Employee class with the following fields, subroutines, and constructors:

```
Public Class Employee
  ' Field data.
  Private empName As String
  Private empID As Integer
  Private currPay As Single

  ' Constructors
  Sub New()
  End Sub
  Sub New(ByVal name As String, ByVal id As Integer, ByVal pay As Single)
    empName = name
    empID = id
    currPay = pay
  End Sub

  ' Members.
  Sub GiveBonus(ByVal amount As Single)
    currPay += amount
  End Sub
  Sub DisplayStats()
    Console.WriteLine("Name: {0}", empName)
    Console.WriteLine("ID: {0}", empID)
    Console.WriteLine("Pay: {0}", currPay)
  End Sub
End Class
```

Notice that the fields of the Employee class are currently defined using the Private access keyword. Given this, the empName, empID, and currPay fields are not directly accessible from an object:

```
Sub Main()
  ' Error!  Cannot directly access Private members
  ' from an object!
  Dim emp As New Employee()
  emp.empName = "Marv"
End Sub
```

If you want the outside world to interact with your private string representing a worker's full name, tradition dictates defining an accessor (get method) and mutator (set method). For example, to encapsulate the empName field, you could add the following Public members to the existing Employee class type:

```
' Traditional accessor and mutator for a point of private data.
Public Class Employee
  ' Field data.
  Private empName As String
  ...
  ' Accessor (get method)
```

```vb
Public Function GetName() As String
  Return empName
End Function

' Mutator (set method)
Public Sub SetName(ByVal name As String)
  ' Remove any illegal characters (!,@,#,$,%),
  ' check maximum length or case before making assignment.
  empName = name
End Sub
End Class
```

This technique requires two uniquely named methods to operate on a single data point. To illustrate, update your Main() method as follows:

```vb
Sub Main()
  Console.WriteLine("***** Fun with Encapsulation *****")
  Dim emp As New Employee("Marvin", 456, 30000)
  emp.GiveBonus(1000)
  emp.DisplayStats()

  ' Use the get/set methods to interact with the object's name.
  emp.SetName("Marv")
  Console.WriteLine("Employee is named: {0}", emp.GetName())
  Console.ReadLine()
End Sub
```

Encapsulation Using Type Properties

Although you can encapsulate a piece of field data using traditional get and set methods, .NET languages prefer to enforce data protection using *properties* that are defined via the Property keyword. Visual Basic 6.0 programmers have long used properties to simulate direct access to field data; however, the syntax to do so has been modified under the .NET platform.

First of all, understand that properties always map to "real" accessor and mutator methods in terms of CIL code. Therefore, as a class designer, you are still able to perform any internal logic necessary before making the value assignment (e.g., uppercase the value, scrub the value for illegal characters, check the bounds of a numerical value, and so on). Here is the updated Employee class, now enforcing encapsulation of each field using property syntax rather than get and set methods:

```vb
Public Class Employee
  ' Field data.
  Private empName As String
  Private empID As Integer
  Private currPay As Single

  ' Properties
  Public Property Name() As String
    Get
      Return empName
    End Get
    Set(ByVal value As String)
      empName = value
    End Set
  End Property
```

```
  Public Property ID() As Integer
    Get
      Return empID
    End Get
    Set(ByVal value As Integer)
      empID = value
    End Set
  End Property

  Public Property Pay() As Single
    Get
      Return currPay
    End Get
    Set(ByVal value As Single)
      currPay = value
    End Set
  End Property
...
End Class
```

Unlike VB 6.0, a property is not represented by independent Get, Let, or Set members. Rather, a VB 2005 property is composed by defining a Get scope (accessor) and Set scope (mutator) directly within the property scope itself. Once we have these properties in place, it appears to the object user that they are getting and setting a public point of data; however, the correct Get and Set block is called behind the scenes:

```
Sub Main()
  Console.WriteLine("***** Fun with Encapsulation *****")
  Dim emp As New Employee("Marvin", 456, 30000)
  emp.GiveBonus(1000)
  emp.DisplayStats()

  ' Set and Get the Name property.
  emp.Name = "Marv"
  Console.WriteLine("Employee is named: {0}", emp.Name)
  Console.ReadLine()
End Sub
```

Properties (as opposed to accessors and mutators) also make your types easier to manipulate, in that properties are able to respond to the intrinsic operators of VB 2005. To illustrate, assume that the Employee class type has an internal private member variable representing the age of the employee. Here is our update:

```
Public Class Employee
...
  Private empAge As Integer
...
  Public Property Age() As Integer
    Get
      Return empAge
    End Get
    Set(ByVal value As Integer)
      empAge = value
    End Set
  End Property
```

```
  ' Constructors
  Sub New()
  End Sub
  Sub New(ByVal name As String, ByVal age As Integer, _
    ByVal id As Integer, ByVal pay As Single)
    empName = name
    empAge = age
    empID = id
    currPay = pay
  End Sub

  ' Members.
...
  Sub DisplayStats()
    Console.WriteLine("Name: {0}", empName)
    Console.WriteLine("Age: {0}", empAge)
    Console.WriteLine("ID: {0}", empID)
    Console.WriteLine("Pay: {0}", currPay)
  End Sub
End Class
```

Now assume you have created an Employee object named joe. On his birthday, you wish to increment the age by one. Using traditional accessor and mutator methods, you would need to write code such as the following:

```
Dim joe As New Employee()
joe.SetAge(joe.GetAge() + 1)
```

However, if you encapsulate empAge using property syntax, you are able to simply write

```
Dim joe As New Employee()
joe.Age = joe.Age + 1
```

Internal Representation of Properties

Many programmers (especially those who program with a C-based language such as C++) tend to design traditional accessor and mutator methods using "get_" and "set_" prefixes (e.g., get_Name() and set_Name()). This naming convention itself is not problematic as far as VB 2005 is concerned. However, it is important to understand that under the hood, a property is represented in CIL code using these same prefixes. For example, if you open up the EmployeeApp.exe assembly using ildasm.exe, you see that each property is mapped to hidden get_XXX()/set_XXX() methods called internally by the CLR (see Figure 5-11).

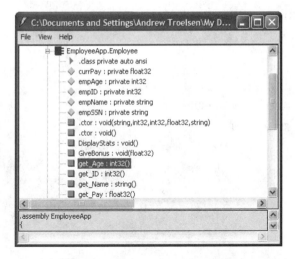

Figure 5-11. *A property is represented by get/set methods internally.*

Assume the Employee type now has a private member variable named empSSN to represent an individual's Social Security number, which is manipulated by a property named SocialSecurityNumber:

```vb
' Add support for a new field representing the employee's SSN.
Public Class Employee
...
  Private empSSN As String
...
  Public Property SocialSecurityNumber() As String
    Get
      Return empSSN
    End Get
    Set(ByVal value As String)
      empSSN = value
    End Set
  End Property
  ' Constructors
  Sub New()
  End Sub
  Sub New(ByVal name As String, ByVal age As Integer, _
    ByVal id As Integer, ByVal pay As Single, _
    ByVal ssn As String)
    empName = name
    empAge = age
    empID = id
    empSSN = ssn
    currPay = pay
  End Sub
  ' Members.
...
  Sub DisplayStats()
    Console.WriteLine("Name: {0}", empName)
    Console.WriteLine("Age: {0}", empAge)
```

```
    Console.WriteLine("SSN: {0}", empSSN)
    Console.WriteLine("ID: {0}", empID)
    Console.WriteLine("Pay: {0}", currPay)
  End Sub
End Class
```

If you were to also define two methods named get_SocialSecurityNumber() and set_SocialSecurityNumber(), you would be issued compile-time errors:

```
' Remember, a property really maps to a get_/set_ pair.
Public Class Employee
...
  Public Function get_SocialSecurityNumber() As String
    Return empSSN
  End Function
  Public Sub set_SocialSecurityNumber(ByVal val As String)
    empSSN = val
  End Sub
End Class
```

■**Note** The .NET base class libraries always favor type properties over traditional accessor and mutator methods. Therefore, if you wish to build custom types that integrate well with the .NET platform, avoid defining traditional get and set methods.

Controlling Visibility Levels of Property Get/Set Statements

Prior to VB 2005, the visibility of get and set logic was solely controlled by the access modifier of the property declaration:

```
' The get and set logic is both public,
' given the declaration of the property.
Public Property SocialSecurityNumber() As String
  Get
    Return empSSN
  End Get
  Set(ByVal value As String)
    empSSN = value
  End Set
End Property
```

In some cases, it would be helpful to specify unique accessibility levels for get and set logic. To do so, simply prefix an accessibility keyword to the appropriate Get or Set keyword (the unqualified scope takes the visibility of the property's declaration):

```
' Object users can only get the value, however
' the Employee class and derived types can set the value.
Public Property SocialSecurityNumber() As String
  Get
    Return empSSN
  End Get
  Protected Set(ByVal value As String)
    empSSN = value
  End Set
End Property
```

In this case, the set logic of SocialSecurityNumber can only be called by the current class and derived classes and therefore cannot be called from an object instance.

Read-Only and Write-Only Properties

When creating class types, you may wish to configure a *read-only property*. To do so, simply build a property using the ReadOnly keyword and omit the Set block. Likewise, if you wish to have a *write-only property*, build a property using the WriteOnly keyword and omit the Get block. For example, here is how the SocialSecurityNumber property could be retrofitted as read-only:

```
Public Class Employee
...
  ' Now as a  read-only property.
  Public ReadOnly Property SocialSecurityNumber() As String
    Get
      Return empSSN
    End Get
  End Property
End Class
```

Given this adjustment, the only manner in which an employee's US Social Security number can be set is through a constructor argument.

Shared Properties

VB 2005 also supports shared properties. Recall from earlier in this chapter that shared members are accessed at the class level, not from an instance (object) of that class. For example, assume that the Employee type defines a shared point of data to represent the name of the organization employing these workers. You may encapsulate a shared property as follows:

```
' Shared properties must operate on static data!
Public Class Employee
...
  Private Shared companyName As String
...
  Public Shared Property Company() As String
    Get
      Return companyName
    End Get
    Set(ByVal value As String)
      companyName = value
    End Set
  End Property
End Class
```

Shared properties are manipulated in the same manner as static methods, as seen here:

```
' Interact with the Shared property.
Sub Main()
  Employee.Company = "Intertech Training"
  Console.WriteLine("These folks work at {0}", Employee.Company)
End Sub
```

Finally, recall that classes can support shared constructors. Thus, if you wanted to ensure that the name of the static CompName field was always assigned to "Intertech Training", you would write the following:

```
' Shared constructors are used to initialize shared data.
Public Class Employee
  Private Shared companyName As String
    ....
```

```
    Shared Sub New()
       companyName = "Intertech Training"
    End Sub
End Class
```

Using this approach, there is no need to explicitly set the companyName value:

```
' Set to Intertech Training via Shared constructor.
Sub Main()
   Console.WriteLine("These folks work at {0}", Employee.Company)
End Sub
```

To wrap up the examination of encapsulation using VB 2005 properties, understand that these syntactic entities are used for the same purpose as a classical accessor/mutator pair. The benefit of properties is that the users of your objects are able to manipulate the internal data point using a single named item.

Understanding Constant Data

Now that you can create fields that can be modified using type properties, allow me to illustrate how to define data that can never change after the initial assignment. VB 2005 offers the Const keyword to define constant data. As you might guess, this can be helpful when you are defining a set of known values for use in your applications that are logically connected to a given class or structure.

Turning away from the Employee example for a moment, assume you are building a utility class named MyMathClass that needs to define a value for the value PI (which we will assume to be 3.14). Given that we would not want to allow other developers to change this value in code, PI could be modeled with the following constant:

```
Public Class MyMathClass
   Public Const PI As Double = 3.14
End Class

Module Program
   Sub Main()
      Console.WriteLine("The value of PI is: {0}", MyMathClass.PI)
   End Sub
End Module
```

Because PI has been defined as constant, it would be a compile-time error to attempt to modify this value within our code base:

```
Module Program
   Sub Main()
      Console.WriteLine("The value of PI is: {0}", MyMathClass.PI)

      ' Error! Can't change a constant!
      MyMathClass.PI = 3.1444
   End Sub
End Module
```

Notice that we are referencing the constant data defined by the MyConstants class using a class name prefix. This is due to the fact that constant fields of a class or structure are implicitly *shared*. As mentioned early in this chapter, VB 2005 does allow you to access shared members from an object (provided you have not altered your compiler error settings!). Thus, you could write the following code to access the value of PI:

```
Module Program
  Sub Main()
    Dim m As New MyMathClass()
    Console.WriteLine("The value of PI is: {0}", m.PI)
  End Sub
End Module
```

As well, it is permissible to define a local piece of constant data within a type member. By way of example:

```
Module Program
  Sub Main()
    Console.WriteLine("The value of PI is: {0}", MyMathClass.PI)

    ' A local constant data point.
    Const fixedStr As String = "Fixed String Data"
    Console.WriteLine(fixedStr)

    ' Error!
    fixedStr = "This will not work!"
  End Sub
End Module
```

Regardless of where you define a constant piece of data, the one point to always remember is that the initial value assigned to the constant must be specified at the time you define the constant. Thus, if you were to modify your MyMathClass in such a way that the value of PI is assigned in a class constructor as follows:

```
Public Class MyMathClass
  Public Const PI As Double
  Public Sub New()
  ' Nope!  Compiler error!
    PI = 3.14
  End Sub
End Class
```

you would receive a compile-time error. The reason for this restriction has to do with the fact the value of constant data must be known *at compile time*. Constructors, as you know, are invoked *at runtime*.

Understanding Read-Only Fields

Closely related to constant data is the notion of *read-only field data*. Like a constant, a read-only field cannot be changed after the initial assignment. However, unlike a constant, the value assigned to a read-only field can be determined at runtime, and therefore can legally be assigned within the scope of a constructor (but nowhere else).

This can be very helpful when you don't know the value of a field until runtime (perhaps because you need to read an external file to obtain the value), but wish to ensure that the value will not change after that point. For the sake of illustration, assume the following update to MyMathClass:

```
Public Class MyMathClass
  ' Now as a read only field.
  Public ReadOnly PI As Double
  Public Sub New()
    ' This is now OK.
    PI = 3.14
  End Sub
End Class
```

Again, any attempt to make assignments to a field marked ReadOnly outside the scope of a constructor results in a compiler error:

```
Module Program
  Sub Main()
    Dim m As New MyMathClass()
    ' Error.
    m.PI = 9
  End Sub
End Module
```

Shared Read-Only Fields

Unlike a constant field, read-only fields are not implicitly shared. Thus, if you wish to expose PI from the class level, you must explicitly make use of the Shared keyword. If you know the value of a shared read-only field at compile time, the initial assignment looks very similar to that of a constant:

```
Public Class MyMathClass
  Public Shared ReadOnly PI As Double = 3.14
End Class

Module Program
  Sub Main()
    Console.WriteLine("The value of PI is {0}", MyMathClass.PI)
  End Sub
End Module
```

However, if the value of a shared read-only field is not known until runtime, you must make use of a shared constructor as described earlier in this chapter:

```
Public Class MyMathClass
  Public Shared ReadOnly PI As Double
  Shared Sub New()
    PI = 3.14
  End Sub
End Class

Module Program
  Sub Main()
    Console.WriteLine("The value of PI is {0}", MyMathClass.PI)
  End Sub
End Module
```

Now that we have examined the role of constant data and read-only fields, we can return to the Employee example and put the wraps on this chapter.

Understanding Partial Types

VB 2005 introduces a new type modifier named Partial that allows you to define a type across multiple *.vb files. Earlier versions of the VB programming language required all code for a given type be defined within a single *.vb file. Given the fact that a production-level VB 2005 class may be hundreds of lines of code (or more), this can end up being a mighty lengthy file indeed.

In these cases, it would be ideal to partition a type's implementation across numerous *.vb files in order to separate code that is in some way more important for other details. For example, using the Partial class modifier, you could place all of the Employee constructors and properties into a new file named Employee.Internals.vb:

```
Partial Public Class Employee
  ' Constructors
  ...
  ' Properties
  ...
End Class
```

while the private field data and type methods are defined within the initial Employee.vb:

```
Partial Public Class Employee
  ' Field data.
  Private empName As String
  Private empID As Integer
  Private currPay As Single
  Private empAge As Integer
  Private empSSN As String
  Private Shared companyName As String

  ' Public methods.
  Sub GiveBonus(ByVal amount As Single)
    currPay += amount
  End Sub
  Sub DisplayStats()
    Console.WriteLine("Name: {0}", empName)
    Console.WriteLine("Age: {0}", empAge)
    Console.WriteLine("SSN: {0}", empSSN)
    Console.WriteLine("ID: {0}", empID)
    Console.WriteLine("Pay: {0}", currPay)
  End Sub
End Class
```

As you might guess, this can be helpful to new team members who need to quickly learn about the public interface of the type. Rather than reading though a single (lengthy) VB 2005 file to find the members of interest, they can focus on the public members. Of course, once these files are compiled by the VB 2005 compiler, the end result is a single unified type. To this end, the Partial modifier is purely a design-time construct.

■**Note** As you will see during our examination of Windows Forms and ASP.NET, Visual Studio 2005 makes use of the Partial keyword to partition code generated by the IDE's designer tools. Using this approach, you can keep focused on your current solution, and be blissfully unaware of the designer-generated code.

Documenting VB 2005 Source Code via XML

To wrap this chapter up, the final task is to examine VB 2005–specific comment tokens that yield XML-based code documentation. If you have worked with the Java programming language, you may be familiar with the javadoc utility. Using javadoc, you are able to turn Java source code into a corresponding HTML representation. The VB 2005 documentation model is slightly different, in that the "code comments to XML" conversion process is the job of the VB 2005 compiler (via the /doc option) rather than a stand-alone utility.

So, why use XML to document our type definitions rather than HTML? The main reason is that XML is a very "enabling technology." Given that XML separates the definition of data from the presentation of that data, we can apply any number of XML transformations to the underlying XML to display the code documentation in a variety of formats (MSDN format, HTML, etc.).

When you wish to document your VB 2005 types in XML, your first step is to make use of the new triple tick (`'''`) code comment notations. Once a documentation comment has been declared, you are free to use any well-formed XML elements, including the recommended set shown in Table 5-2.

Table 5-2. *Recommended Code Comment XML Elements*

Predefined XML Documentation Element	Meaning in Life
`<c>`	Indicates that the following text should be displayed in a specific "code font"
`<code>`	Indicates multiple lines should be marked as code
`<example>`	Mocks up a code example for the item you are describing
`<exception>`	Documents which exceptions a given class may throw
`<list>`	Inserts a list or table into the documentation file
`<param>`	Describes a given parameter
`<paramref>`	Associates a given XML tag with a specific parameter
`<permission>`	Documents the security constraints for a given member
`<remarks>`	Builds a description for a given member
`<returns>`	Documents the return value of the member
`<see>`	Cross-references related items in the document
`<seealso>`	Builds an "also see" section within a description
`<summary>`	Documents the "executive summary" for a given member
`<value>`	Documents a given property

If you are making use of the new VB 2005 XML code comment notation, do be aware the Visual Studio 2005 IDE will generate documentation skeletons on your behalf. For example, if you right-click the `Employee` class definition and select the Insert Comment menu option, as shown in Figure 5-12, the IDE will autocomplete the initial set of XML elements.

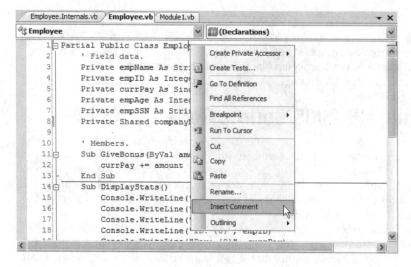

Figure 5-12. *Inserting an XML comment via Visual Studio 2005*

Simply fill in the blanks with your custom content:

```
''' <summary>
''' This is the employee class.
''' </summary>
''' <remarks></remarks>
Partial Public Class Employee
...
End Class
```

By way of another example, right-click your custom five-argument constructor and insert a code comment. This time the comment builder utility has been kind enough to add `<param>` elements:

```
''' <summary>
'''
''' </summary>
''' <param name="name"></param>
''' <param name="age"></param>
''' <param name="id"></param>
''' <param name="pay"></param>
''' <param name="ssn"></param>
''' <remarks></remarks>
Sub New(ByVal name As String, ByVal age As Integer, _
  ByVal id As Integer, ByVal pay As Single, _
  ByVal ssn As String)
...
End Sub
```

Once you have documented your code with XML comments, you will need to generate a corresponding `*.xml` file. If you are building your VB 2005 programs using the command-line compiler (`vbc.exe`), the `/doc` flag is used to generate a specified `*.xml` file based on your XML code comments:

```
vbc /doc:XmlCarDoc.xml *.vb
```

Visual Studio 2005 projects allow you to specify the name of an XML documentation file using the Generate XML documentation file check box option found on the Build tab of the Properties window (see Figure 5-13).

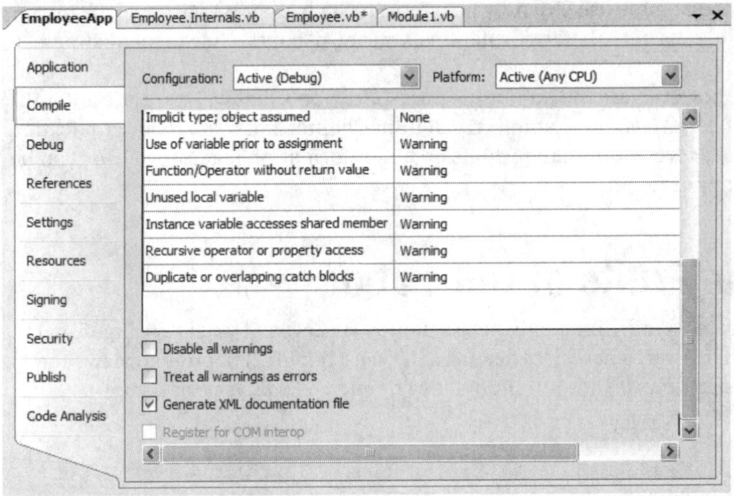

Figure 5-13. *Generating an XML code comment file via Visual Studio 2005*

Once you have enabled this behavior, the compiler will place the generated `*.xml` file within your project's `\bin\Debug` folder. You can verify this for yourself by clicking the Show All Files button on the Solution Explorer, generating the result in Figure 5-14.

Figure 5-14. *Locating the generated XML documentation file*

■**Note** There are many other elements and notations that may appear in VB 2005 XML code comments. If you are interested in more details, look up the topic "Documenting Your Code with XML (Visual Basic)" within the .NET Framework SDK 2.0 documentation.

Transforming XML Code Comments via NDoc

Now that you have generated an `*.xml` file that contains your source code comments, you may be wondering exactly what to do with it. Sadly, Visual Studio 2005 does not provide a built-in utility that transforms XML data into a more user-friendly help format (such as an HTML page). If you are comfortable with the ins and outs of XML transformations, you are, of course, free to manually create your own style sheets.

A simpler alternative, however, are the numerous third-party tools that will translate an XML code file into various helpful formats. For example, recall from Chapter 2 that the NDoc application generates documentation in several different formats. Again, information regarding NDoc can be found at `http://ndoc.sourceforge.net`.

Visualizing the Fruits of Our Labor

At this point, you have created a fairly interesting class named `Employee`. If you are using Visual Studio 2005, you may wish to insert a new class diagram file (see Chapter 2) in order to view (and maintain) your class at design time. Figure 5-15 shows the completed `Employee` class type.

Figure 5-15. *The completed* Employee *class*

As you will see in the next chapter, this Employee class will function as a base class for a family of derived class types (WageEmployee, SalesEmployee, and Manager).

Source Code The EmployeeApp project can be found under the Chapter 5 subdirectory.

Summary

The point of this chapter was to introduce you to the role of the VB 2005 class type. As you have seen, classes can take any number of *constructors* that enable the object user to establish the state of the object upon creation. This chapter also illustrated several class design techniques (and related keywords). Recall that the Me keyword can be used to obtain access to the current object, the Shared keyword allows you to define fields and members that are bound at the class (not object) level, and the Const keyword allows you to define a point of data that can never change after the initial assignment.

The bulk of this chapter dug into the details of the first pillar of OOP: encapsulation. Here you learned about the access modifiers of Visual Basic 2005 and the role of type properties, partial classes, and XML code documentation.

CHAPTER 6

■■■

Understanding Inheritance and Polymorphism

The previous chapter examined the first pillar of OOP: encapsulation. At that time you learned how to build a single well-defined class type with constructors and various members (fields, properties, constants, read-only fields, etc.). This chapter will focus on the remaining two pillars of OOP: inheritance and polymorphism.

First, you will learn how to build families of related classes using *inheritance*. As you will see, this form of code reuse allows you to define common functionality in a parent class that can be leveraged (and possibly altered) by child classes. Along the way, you will learn how to establish a *polymorphic interface* into the class hierarchies using virtual and abstract members. We wrap up by examining the role of the ultimate parent class in the .NET base class libraries: System.Object.

The Basic Mechanics of Inheritance

Recall from the previous chapter that *inheritance* is the aspect of OOP that facilitates code reuse. Specifically speaking, inheritance comes in two flavors: classical inheritance (the "is-a" relationship) and the containment/delegation model (the "has-a" relationship). Let's begin by examining the classical "is-a" model.

When you establish "is-a" relationships between classes, you are building a dependency between two or more class types. The basic idea behind classical inheritance is that new classes may leverage (and possibily extend) the functionality of existing classes. To illustrate, assume you have designed a simple class named Car that models some basic details of an automobile:

```
' A simple base class.
Public Class Car
  Public ReadOnly MaxSpeed As Integer
  Private currSpeed As Integer

  Public Sub New(ByVal max As Integer)
    MaxSpeed = max
  End Sub
  Public Sub New()
    MaxSpeed = 55
  End Sub
  Public Property Speed() As Integer
    Get
      Return currSpeed
    End Get
```

```
    Set(ByVal value As Integer)
      currSpeed += value
      If currSpeed > MaxSpeed Then
        currSpeed = MaxSpeed
      End If
    End Set
  End Property
End Class
```

Notice that the Car class is making use of encapsulation services to control access to the private currSpeed field using a public property named Speed. At this point you can exercise your Car type as follows:

```
Module Program
  Sub Main()
    ' Make a Car type.
    Dim myCar As New Car(80)
    myCar.Speed = 50
    Console.WriteLine("My car is going {0} MPH", _
      myCar.Speed)
  End Sub
End Module
```

The Inherits Keyword

Now assume you wish to build a new class named MiniVan. Like a basic Car, you wish to define the MiniVan class to support a maximum speed, current speed, and a property named Speed to allow the object user to modify the object's state. Clearly, the Car and MiniVan classes are related, in fact we can say that a MiniVan "*is-a*" Car. The "is-a" relationship (formally termed *classical inheritance*) allows you to build new class definitions that extend the functionality of an existing class.

The existing class that will serve as the basis for the new class is termed a *base* or *parent* class. The role of a base class is to define all the common data and members for the classes that extend it. The "extending" classes are formally termed *derived* or *child* classes. In VB 2005, we make use of the Inherits keyword to establish an "is-a" relationship between classes:

```
' MiniVan derives from Car
Public Class MiniVan
  Inherits Car
End Class
```

So, what have we gained by building our MiniVan by deriving from the Car base class? Simply put, the MiniVan class automatically gains the functionality of each and every member in the parent class declared as Public or Protected. Do know that inheritance preserves encapsulation! Therefore, the MiniVan class cannot directly access Private members of the parent. Given the relation between these two class types, we could now make use of the MiniVan type like so:

```
Module Program
  Sub Main()
...
    ' Make a MiniVan
    Dim myVan As New MiniVan()
    myVan.Speed = 10
    Console.WriteLine("My van is going {0} MPH", _
      myVan.Speed)
  End Sub
End Module
```

Notice that although we have not added any members to the `MiniVan` type, we have direct access to the public `Speed` property (thus we have reused code). Recall, however, that encapsulation is preserved, therefore the following code results in a compiler error:

```
Module Program
  Sub Main()
...
    ' Make a MiniVan
    Dim myVan As New MiniVan()
    myVan.Speed = 10
    Console.WriteLine("My van is going {0} MPH", _
      myVan.Speed)

    ' Error! Cannot access private data of the parent from an object!
    myVan.currSpeed = 10
  End Sub
End Module
```

As well, if the `MiniVan` defined its own set of members, it would not be able to access any private member of the `Car` base class:

```
Public Class MiniVan
  Inherits Car
  Public Sub TestMethod()
    ' OK!  Can use public members
    ' within derived type.
    Speed = 10
    ' Error!  Cannot access private
    ' members within derived type.
    currSpeed = 10
  End Sub
End Class
```

Regarding Multiple Base Classes

Speaking of base classes, it is important to keep in mind that the .NET platform demands that a given class have exactly *one* direct base class. It is not possible to create a class type that derives from two or more base classes (this technique is known as *multiple inheritance*, or simply *MI*):

```
' Illegal! The .NET platform does not allow
' multiple inheritance for classes!
Public Class WontWork
  Inherits BaseClassOne
  Inherits BaseClassTwo
End Class
```

As you will see in Chapter 9, VB 2005 does allow a given type to implement any number of discrete interfaces. In this way, a VB 2005 class can exhibit a number of behaviors while avoiding the complexities associated with MI. On a related note, it is permissible for a single interface to derive from multiple interfaces (again, see Chapter 9).

The NotInheritable Keyword

VB 2005 supplies another keyword, named `NotInheritable`, that *prevents* inheritance from occurring. When you mark a class as `NotInheritable`, the compiler will not allow you to derive from this type. For example, assume you have decided that it makes no sense to further extend the `MiniVan` class:

```
' This class cannot be extended!
Public NotInheritable Class MiniVan
  Inherits Car
End Class
```

If you (or a teammate) were to attempt to derive from this class, you would receive a compile-time error:

```
' Error! Cannot extend
' a class marked NotInheritable!
Public Class TryAnyway
  Inherits MiniVan
End Class
```

Formally speaking, the MiniVan class has been *sealed*. Most often, sealing a class makes the most sense when you are designing a utility class. For example, the System namespace defines numerous sealed classes (System.Console, System.Math, System.Environment, System.Sting, etc.). You can verify this for yourself by opening up the Visual Studio 2005 Object Browser (via the View menu) and selecting the System.Console type defined within mscorlib.dll. Notice in Figure 6-1 the use of the NotInheritable keyword.

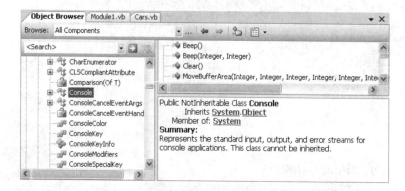

Figure 6-1. *The base class libraries define numerous sealed types.*

Thus, just like the MiniVan, if you attempted to build a new class that extends System.Console, you will receive a compile-time error:

```
' Another error! Cannot extend
' a class marked NotInheritable!
Public Class MyConsole
  Inherits Console
End Class
```

■**Note** In Chapter 4, you were introduced to the structure type. Structures are always implicitly sealed. Therefore, you can never derive one structure from another structure, a class from a structure or a structure from a class.

As you would guess, there are many more details to inheritance that you will come to know during the remainder of this chapter. For now, simply keep in mind that the `Inherits` keyword allows you to establish base/derived class relationships, while the `NotInheritable` keyword prevents inheritance from occurring.

Revising Visual Studio 2005 Class Diagrams

Back in Chapter 2, I briefly mentioned that Visual Studio 2005 now allows you to establish base/ derived class relationships visually at design time. To leverage this aspect of the IDE, your first step is to include a new class diagram file into your current project. To do so, access the Project ➤ Add New Item menu option and select the Class Diagram icon (in Figure 6-2, I renamed the file from `ClassDiagram1.cd` to `Cars.cd`).

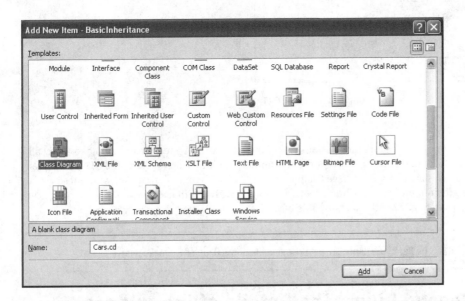

Figure 6-2. *Inserting a new class diagram*

When you do, the IDE responds by automatically including all types, including a set of types that are not directly visible from the Solution Explorer such as `MySettings`, `Resources`, etc. Realize that if you delete an item from the visual designer, this will not delete the associated source code. Given this, delete all visual icons except the `Car`, `MiniVan`, and `Program` types, as shown in Figure 6-3.

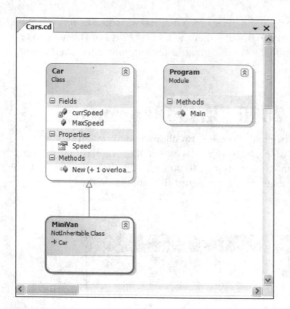

Figure 6-3. *The visual designer of Visual Studio 2005*

Beyond simply displaying the relationships of the types within your current application, recall that you can also create brand new types (and populate their members) using the Class Designer toolbox and Class Details window (see Chapter 2 for details). If you wish to make use of these visual tools during the remainder of the book, feel free. However! Always make sure you analyze the generated code so you have a solid understanding of what these tools have done on your behalf.

Source Code   The BasicInheritance project is located under the Chapter 6 subdirectory.

The Second Pillar: The Details of Inheritance

Now that you have seen the basics of inheritance, let's create a more complex example and get to know the numerous details of building class hierarchies. To do so, we will be reusing the Employee class we designed in Chapter 5. To begin, create a brand new console application named Employees. Next, activate the Project ➤ Add Existing Item menu option and navigate to the location of your Employee.vb and Employee.Internals.vb files. Select each of them (via a Ctrl+left click) and click the OK button. Visual Studio 2005 responds by copying each file into the current project. Once you have done so, compile your current application just to ensure you are up and running.

Our goal is to create a family of classes that model various types of employees in a company. Assume that you wish to leverage the functionality of the Employee class to create two new classes (SalesPerson and Manager). The class hierarchy we will be building initially looks something like what you see in Figure 6-4.

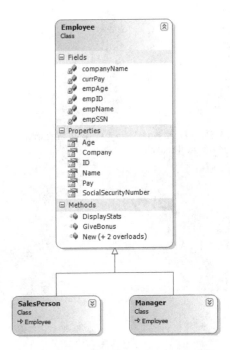

Figure 6-4. *The initial* Employees *hierarchy*

As illustrated in Figure 6-4, you can see that a SalesPerson "is-a" Employee (as is a Manager). Remember that under the classical inheritance model, base classes (such as Employee) are used to define general characteristics that are common to all descendents. Subclasses (such as SalesPerson and Manager) extend this general functionality while adding more specific behaviors.

For our example, we will assume that the Manager class extends Employee by recording the number of stock options, while the SalesPerson class maintains the number of sales made. Insert a new class file (Manager.vb) that defines the Manager type as follows:

```
' Managers need to know their number of stock options.
Public Class Manager
  Inherits Employee
  Private numberOfOptions As Integer
  Public Property StockOptions() As Integer
    Get
      Return numberOfOptions
    End Get
    Set(ByVal value As Integer)
      numberOfOptions = value
    End Set
  End Property
End Class
```

Next, add another new class file (SalesPerson.vb) that defines the SalesPerson type:

```
' Salespeople need to know their number of sales.
Public Class SalesPerson
  Inherits Employee
  Private numberOfSales As Integer
  Public Property SalesNumber() As Integer
```

```
    Get
        Return numberOfSales
    End Get
    Set(ByVal value As Integer)
        numberOfSales = value
    End Set
  End Property
End Class
```

Now that you have established an "is-a" relationship, `SalesPerson` and `Manager` have automatically inherited all public members of the `Employee` base class. To illustrate:

```
' Create a subclass and access base class functionality.
Module Program
  Sub Main()
    Console.WriteLine("***** The Employee Class Hierarchy *****")
    Console.WriteLine()

    ' Make a salesperson.
    Dim danny As New SalesPerson()
    With danny
      .Age = 29
      .ID = 100
      .SalesNumber = 50
      .Name = "Dan McCabe"
    End With
  End Sub
End Module
```

Controlling Base Class Creation with MyBase

Currently, `SalesPerson` and `Manager` can only be created using the freebee default constructor (see Chapter 5). With this in mind, assume you have added a new six-argument constructor to the `Manager` type, which is invoked as follows:

```
Sub Main()
...
  ' Assume we now have the following constructor.
  ' (name, age, ID, pay, SSN, number of stock options).
  Dim chucky As New Manager("Chucky", 45, 101, 30000, "222-22-2222", 90)
End Sub
```

If you look at the argument list, you can clearly see that most of these parameters should be stored in the member variables defined by the `Employee` base class. To do so, you might implement this custom constructor on the `Manager` class as follows:

```
Public Sub New(ByVal fullName As String, ByVal age As Integer, _
  ByVal empID As Integer, ByVal currPay As Single, _
  ByVal ssn As String, ByVal numbOfOpts As Integer)
  ' This field is defined by the Manager class.
  numberOfOptions = numbOfOpts

  ' Assign incoming parameters using the
  ' inherited properties of the parent class.
  ID = empID
  age = age
  Name = fullName
  Pay = currPay
```

```
' OOPS! This would be a compiler error,
' as the SSN property is read-only!
 SocialSecurityNumber = ssn
End Sub
```

The first issue with this approach is that we defined the SocialSecurityNumber property in the parent as read-only, therefore we are unable to assign the incoming String parameter to this field.

The second issue is that we have indirectly created a rather inefficient constructor, given the fact that under VB 2005, unless you say otherwise, the default constructor of a base class is called automatically before the logic of the custom Manager constructor is executed. After this point, the current implementation accesses numerous public properties of the Employee base class to establish its state. Thus, you have really made seven hits (five inherited properties and two constructor calls) during the creation of a Manager object!

To help optimize the creation of a derived class, you will do well to implement your subclass constructors to explicitly call an appropriate custom base class constructor, rather than the default. In this way, you are able to reduce the number of calls to inherited initialization members (which saves processing time). Let's retrofit the custom constructor to do this very thing using the MyBase keyword:

```
' This time, use the VB 2005 "MyBase" keyword to call a custom
' constructor on the base class.
Public Sub New(ByVal fullName As String, ByVal age As Integer, _
  ByVal empID As Integer, ByVal currPay As Single, _
  ByVal ssn As String, ByVal numbOfOpts As Integer)
  ' Pass these arguments to the parent's constructor.
  MyBase.New(fullName, age, empID, currPay, ssn)

  ' This belongs with us!
  numberOfOptions = numbOfOpts
End Sub
```

Here, the first statement within your custom constructor is making use of the MyBase keyword. In this situation, you are explicitly calling the five-argument constructor defined by Employee and saving yourself unnecessary calls during the creation of the child class. The custom SalesPerson constructor looks almost identical:

```
' As a general rule, all subclasses should explicitly call an appropriate
' base class constructor.
Public Sub New(ByVal fullName As String, ByVal age As Integer, _
  ByVal empID As Integer, ByVal currPay As Single, _
  ByVal ssn As String, ByVal numbOfSales As Integer)
  ' Pass these arguments to the parent's constructor.
  MyBase.New(fullName, age, empID, currPay, ssn)

  ' This belongs with us!
  numberOfSales = numbOfSales
End Sub
```

Also be aware that you may use the MyBase keyword anytime a subclass wishes to access a public or protected member defined by a parent class. Use of this keyword is not limited to constructor logic. You will see examples using MyBase in this manner during our examination of polymorphism later in this chapter.

Note When using MyBase to call a parent's constructor, the MyBase.New() statement must be the very first executable code statement within the constructor body. If this is not the case, you will receive a compiler error.

Keeping Family Secrets: The Protected Keyword

As you already know, public items are directly accessible from anywhere, while private items cannot be accessed from any object beyond the class that has defined it. Recall from Chapter 5 that VB 2005 takes the lead of many other modern object languages and provides an additional keyword to define member accessibility: `Protected`.

When a base class defines protected data or protected members, it establishes a set of items that can be accessed directly by any descendent. If you wish to allow the `SalesPerson` and `Manager` child classes to directly access the data sector defined by `Employee`, you can update the original `Employee` class definition as follows:

```
' Protected state data.
Partial Public Class Employee
  ' Derived classes can directly access this information.
  Protected empName As String
  Protected empID As Integer
  Protected currPay As Single
  Protected empAge As Integer
  Protected empSSN As String
  Protected Shared companyName As String
...
End Class
```

The benefit of defining protected members in a base class is that derived types no longer have to access the data using public methods or properties. The possible downfall, of course, is that when a derived type has direct access to its parent's internal data, it is very possible to accidentally bypass existing business rules found within public properties. When you define protected members, you are creating a level of trust between the parent and child class, as the compiler will not catch any violation of your type's business rules.

Finally, understand that as far as the object user is concerned, protected data is regarded as private (as the user is "outside" of the family). Therefore, the following is illegal:

```
Sub Main()
  ' Error! Can't access protected data from object instance.
  Dim emp As New Employee()
  emp.empSSN = "111-11-1111"
End Sub
```

■**Note** Although `Protected` field data can break encapsulation, it is quite safe (and useful) to define `Protected` subroutines and functions. When building class hierarchies, it is very common to define a set of methods that are only for use by derived types.

Adding a Sealed Class

Recall that a *sealed* class cannot be extended by other classes. As mentioned, this technique is most often used when you are designing a utility class. However, when building class hierarchies, you might find that a certain branch in the inheritance chain should be "capped off," as it makes no sense to further extend the linage. For example, assume you have added yet another class to your program (`PTSalesPerson`) that extends the existing `SalesPerson` type. Figure 6-5 shows the current update.

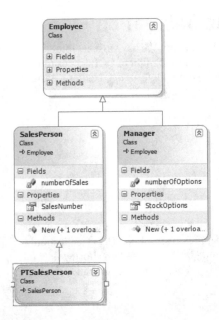

Figure 6-5. *The part-time salesperson class*

PTSalesPerson is a class representing (of course) a part-time salesperson. For the sake of argument, let's say that you wish to ensure that no other developer is able to subclass from PTSalesPerson. (After all, how much more part-time can you get than "part-time"?) To prevent others from extending a class, make use of the VB 2005 NotInheritable keyword:

```
Public NotInheritable Class PTSalesPerson
  Inherits SalesPerson

  Public Sub New(ByVal fullName As String, ByVal age As Integer, _
    ByVal empID As Integer, ByVal currPay As Single, _
    ByVal ssn As String, ByVal numbOfSales As Integer)
    ' Pass these arguments to the parent's constructor.
    MyBase.New(fullName, age, empID, currPay, ssn, numbOfSales)
  End Sub
  ' Assume other members here...
End Class
```

Given that sealed classes cannot be extended, you may wonder if it is possible to reuse the code within a class marked NotInheritable. If you wish to build a new class that leverages the functionality of a sealed class, your only option is to forego classical inheritance and make use of the containment/delegation model (aka the "has-a" relationship).

Programming for Containment/Delegation

As noted a bit earlier in this chapter, inheritance comes in two flavors. We have just explored the classical "is-a" relationship. To conclude the exploration of the second pillar of OOP, let's examine the "has-a" relationship (also known as the *containment/delegation model* or *aggregation*). Assume you have created a new class that models an employee benefits package:

```
' This type will function as a contained class.
Public Class BenefitPackage
  ' Assume we have other members that represent
  ' 401K plans, dental/health benefits, and so on.
  Public Function ComputePayDeduction() As Double
    Return 125.0
  End Function
End Class
```

Obviously, it would be rather odd to establish an "is-a" relationship between the BenefitPackage class and the employee types. (Manager "is-a" BenefitPackage? I don't think so.) However, it should be clear that some sort of relationship between the two could be established. In short, you would like to express the idea that each employee "has-a" BenefitPackage. To do so, you can update the Employee class definition as follows:

```
' Employees now have benefits.
Partial Public Class Employee
  ' Contain a BenefitPackage object.
  Protected empBenefits As BenefitPackage = New BenefitPackage()
...
End Class
```

At this point, you have successfully contained another object. However, to expose the functionality of the contained object to the outside world requires delegation. *Delegation* is simply the act of adding members to the containing class that make use of the contained object's functionality. For example, we could update the Employee class to expose the contained empBenefits object using a custom property as well as make use of its functionality internally using a new method named GetBenefitCost():

```
Partial Public Class Employee
  ' Contain a BenefitPackage object.
  Protected empBenefits As BenefitPackage = New BenefitPackage()
  ' Expose certain benefit behaviors of object.
  Public Function GetBenefitCost() As Double
    Return empBenefits.ComputePayDeduction()
  End Function
  ' Expose object through a custom property.
  Public Property Benefits() As BenefitPackage
    Get
      Return empBenefits
    End Get
    Set(ByVal value As BenefitPackage)
      empBenefits = value
    End Set
  End Property
...
End Class
```

In the following updated Main() method, notice how we can interact with the internal BenefitsPackage type defined by the Employee type:

```
Module Program
  Sub Main()
...
    Dim chucky As New Manager("Chucky", 45, 101, 30000, "222-22-2222", 90)
    Dim cost As Double = chucky.GetBenefitCost()
  End Sub
End Module
```

Nested Type Definitions

Before examining the final pillar of OOP (polymorphism), let's explore a programming technique termed *nesting types* (briefly mentioned in the previous chapter). In VB 2005, it is possible to define a type (enum, class, interface, struct, or delegate) directly within the scope of a class or structure. When you have done so, the nested (or "inner") type is considered a member of the nesting (or "outer") class, and in the eyes of the runtime can be manipulated like any other member (fields, properties, methods, events, etc.). The syntax used to nest a type is quite straightforward:

```
Public Class OuterClass
  ' A public nested type can be used by anybody.
  Public Class PublicInnerClass
  End Class

  ' A private nested type can only be used by members
  ' of the containing class.
  Private Class PrivateInnerClass
  End Class
End Class
```

Although the syntax is clean, understanding why you might do this is not readily apparent. To understand this technique, ponder the following traits of nesting a type:

- Nesting types is similar to aggregation ("has-a"), except that you have complete control over the access level of the inner type instead of a contained object.

- Because a nested type is a member of the containing class, it can access private members of the containing class.

- Oftentimes, a nested type is only useful as a helper for the outer class, and is not intended for use by the outside world.

When a type nests another class type, it can create member variables of the type, just as it would for any point of data. However, if you wish to make use of a nested type from outside of the containing type, you must qualify it by the scope of the nesting type. Consider the following code:

```
Sub Main()
  ' Create And use the Public inner Class. OK!
  Dim inner As OuterClass.PublicInnerClass
  inner = New OuterClass.PublicInnerClass

  ' Compiler Error! Cannot access the private class.
  Dim inner2 As OuterClass.PrivateInnerClass
  inner2 = New OuterClass.PrivateInnerClass
End Sub
```

To make use of this concept within our employees example, assume we have now nested the BenefitPackage directly within the Employee class type:

```
Partial Public Class Employee
  Public Class BenefitPackage
```

```
' Assume we have other members that represent
' 401K plans, dental/health benefits, and so on.
Public Function ComputePayDeduction() As Double
   Return 125.0
End Function
End Class
...
End Class
```

The nesting process can be as "deep" as you require. For example, assume we wish to create an enumeration named BenefitPackageLevel, which documents the various benefit levels an employee may choose. To programmatically enforce the tight connection between Employee, BenefitPackage, and BenefitPackageLevel, we could nest the enumeration as follows:

```
' Employee nests BenefitPackage.
Partial Public Class Employee
  ' BenefitPackage nests BenefitPackageLevel.
  Public Class BenefitPackage
     Public Enum BenefitPackageLevel
        Standard
        Gold
        Platinum
     End Enum
     Public Function ComputePayDeduction() As Double
        Return 125.0
     End Function
  End Class
...
End Class
```

Because of the nesting relationships, note how we are required to make use of this enumeration:

```
Sub Main()
...
  ' Define my benefit level.
  Dim myBenefitLevel As Employee.BenefitPackage.BenefitPackageLevel = _
     Employee.BenefitPackage.BenefitPackageLevel.Platinum
End Sub
```

Excellent! At this point you have been exposed to a number of keywords (and concepts) that allow you to build hierarchies of related types via inheritance. If the overall process is not quite crystal clear, don't sweat it. You will be building a number of additional hierarchies over the remainder of this text. Next up, let's examine the final pillar of OOP: polymorphism.

The Third Pillar: VB 2005's Polymorphic Support

Recall that the Employee base class defined a method named GiveBonus(), which was originally implemented as follows:

```
Partial Public Class Employee
  Public Sub GiveBonus(ByVal amount As Single)
     currPay += amount
  End Sub
...
End Class
```

Because this method has been defined with the Public keyword, you can now give bonuses to salespeople and managers (as well as part-time salespeople):

```
Module Program
  Sub Main()
    Console.WriteLine("***** The Employee Class Hierarchy *****")
    Console.WriteLine()
    ' Give each employee a bonus?
    Dim chucky As New Manager("Chucky", 50, 92, 100000, "333-23-2322", 9000)
    chucky.GiveBonus(300)
    chucky.DisplayStats()

    Dim fran As New SalesPerson("Fran", 43, 93, 3000, "932-32-3232", 31)
    fran.GiveBonus(200)
    fran.DisplayStats()
    Console.ReadLine()
  End Sub
End Module
```

The problem with the current design is that the inherited GiveBonus() method operates identically for all subclasses. Ideally, the bonus of a salesperson or part-time salesperson should take into account the number of sales. Perhaps managers should gain additional stock options in conjunction with a monetary bump in salary. Given this, you are suddenly faced with an interesting question: "How can related types respond differently to the same request?" Glad you asked!

The Overridable and Overrides Keywords

Polymorphism provides a way for a subclass to define its own version of a method defined by its base class, using the process termed *method overriding*. To retrofit your current design, you need to understand the meaning of the VB 2005 Overridable and Overrides keywords. If a base class wishes to define a method that *may be* (but does not have to be) overridden by a subclass, it must mark the method with the Overridable keyword:

```
Partial Public Class Employee
  ' This method may now be "overridden" by derived classes.
  Public Overridable Sub GiveBonus(ByVal amount As Single)
    currPay += amount
  End Sub
...
End Class
```

Note Methods that have been marked with the Overridable keyword are termed *virtual methods*.

When a subclass wishes to redefine a virtual method, it does so using the Overrides keyword. For example, the SalesPerson and Manager could override GiveBonus() as follows (assume that PTSalesPerson will not override GiveBonus() and therefore simply inherit the version defined by SalesPerson):

```
Public Class SalesPerson
  Inherits Employee
...
  ' A salesperson's bonus is influenced by the number of sales.
  Public Overrides Sub GiveBonus(ByVal amount As Single)
    Dim salesBonus As Integer = 0
    If numberOfSales >= 0 AndAlso numberOfSales <= 100 Then
        salesBonus = 10
```

```
      Else
        If numberOfSales >= 101 AndAlso numberOfSales <= 200 Then
          salesBonus = 15
        Else
          salesBonus = 20
        End If
      End If
      MyBase.GiveBonus(amount * salesBonus)
    End Sub
End Class

Public Class Manager
  Inherits Employee
...
  Public Overrides Sub GiveBonus(ByVal amount As Single)
    MyBase.GiveBonus(amount)
    Dim r As Random = New Random()
    numberOfOptions += r.Next(500)
  End Sub
End Class
```

Notice how each overridden method is free to leverage the default behavior using the Mybase keyword. In this way, you have no need to completely reimplement the logic behind GiveBonus(), but can reuse (and possibly extend) the default behavior of the parent class.

Also assume that Employee.DisplayStats() has been declared virtual, and has been overridden by each subclass to account for displaying the number of sales (for salespeople) and current stock options (for managers). Now that each subclass can interpret what these virtual methods means to itself, each object instance behaves as a more independent entity:

```
Module Program
  Sub Main()
    Console.WriteLine("***** The Employee Class Hierarchy *****")
    Console.WriteLine()
    ' A better bonus system!
    Dim chucky As New Manager("Chucky", 50, 92, 100000, "333-23-2322", 9000)
    chucky.GiveBonus(300)
    chucky.DisplayStats()
    Console.WriteLine()

    Dim fran As New SalesPerson("Fran", 43, 93, 3000, "932-32-3232", 31)
    fran.GiveBonus(200)
    fran.DisplayStats()
    Console.ReadLine()
  End Sub
End Module
```

Overriding with Visual Studio 2005

As you may have already noticed, when you are overriding a member, you must recall the type of each and every parameter—not to mention the method name and parameter passing conventions (ByRef, ParamArray, etc.). Visual Studio 2005 has a very helpful feature that you can make use of when overriding a virtual member. If you type the word "Overrides" within the scope of a class type, IntelliSense will automatically display a list of all the overridable members defined in your parent classes, as you see in Figure 6-6.

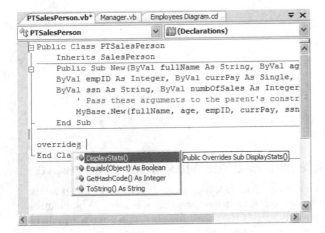

Figure 6-6. *Quickly viewing virtual methods a la Visual Studio 2005*

When you select a member and hit the Enter key, the IDE responds by automatically filling in the method stub on your behalf. Note that you also receive a code statement that calls your parent's version of the virtual member (you are free to delete this line if it is not required):

```
Public Overrides Sub DisplayStats()
  MyBase.DisplayStats()
End Sub
```

The NotOverridable Keyword

Recall that the NotInheritable keyword can be applied to a class type to prevent other types from extending its behavior via inheritance. As you may remember, we sealed PTSalesPerson as we assumed it made no sense for other developers to extend this line of inheritance any further.

On a related note, sometimes you may not wish to seal an entire class, but simply want to prevent derived types from overriding particular virtual methods. For example, assume we do not want part-time salespeople to obtain customized bonuses. To prevent the PTSalesPerson class from overriding the virtual GiveBonus(), we could effectively seal this method in the SalesPerson class with the NotOverridable keyword:

```
' SalesPerson has sealed the GiveBonus() method!
Public Class SalesPerson
  Inherits Employee
...
  Public NotOverridable Overrides Sub GiveBonus()
    ...
  End Sub
End Class
```

Here, SalesPerson has indeed overridden the virtual GiveBonus() method defined in the Employee class; however, it has explicitly marked it as NotOverridable. Thus, if we attempted to override this method in the PTSalesPerson class:

```
Public Class PTSalesPerson
    Inherits SalesPerson
...
  ' No bonus for you!
  Public Overrides Sub GiveBonus()
    ' Rats. Can't change this method any further.
  End Sub
End Class
```

we receive compile-time errors.

Understanding Abstract Classes and the MustInherit Keyword

Currently, the Employee base class has been designed to supply protected member variables for its descendents, as well as supply two virtual methods (GiveBonus() and DisplayStats()) that may be overridden by a given descendent. While this is all well and good, there is a rather odd byproduct of the current design: you can directly create instances of the Employee base class:

```
' What exactly does this mean?
Dim X As New Employee()
```

In this example, the only real purpose of the Employee base class is to define common members for all subclasses. In all likelihood, you did not intend anyone to create a direct instance of this class, reason being that the Employee type itself is too general of a concept. For example, if I were to walk up to you and say, "I'm an employee!" I would bet your very first question to me would be, "What *kind* of employee are you?" (a consultant, trainer, admin assistant, copy editor, White House aide, etc.).

Given that many base classes tend to be rather nebulous entities, a far better design for our example is to prevent the ability to directly create a new Employee object in code. In VB 2005, you can enforce this programmatically by using the MustInherit keyword. Formally speaking, classes marked with the MustInherit keyword are termed *abstract base classes*:

```
' Update the Employee class as abstract
' to prevent direct instantiation.
Partial Public MustInherit Class Employee
...
End Class
```

With this, if you now attempt to create an instance of the Employee class, you are issued a compile-time error:

```
' Error!  Cannot create an abstract class!
Dim X As New Employee()
```

Excellent! At this point you have constructed a fairly interesting employee hierarchy. We will add a bit more functionality to this application later in this chapter when examining VB 2005 casting rules. Until then, Figure 6-7 illustrates the core design of our current types.

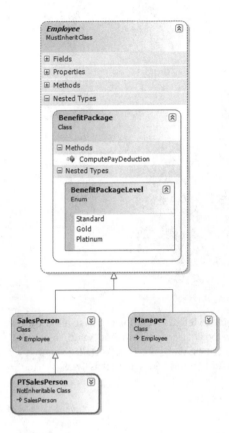

Figure 6-7. *The completed* Employee *hierarchy*

Source Code The Employees project is included under the Chapter 6 subdirectory.

Building a Polymorphic Interface with MustOverride

When a class has been defined as an abstract base class (via the MustInherit keyword), it may define any number of *abstract members*. Abstract members can be used whenever you wish to define a member that does *not* supply a default implementation. By doing so, you enforce a *polymorphic interface* on each descendent, leaving them to contend with the task of providing the details behind your abstract methods.

Simply put, an abstract base class's polymorphic interface simply refers to its set of virtual (Overridable) and abstract (MustOverride) methods. This is much more interesting than first meets the eye, as this trait of OOP allows us to build very extendable and flexible software applications. To illustrate, we will be implementing (and slightly modifying) the shapes hierarchy briefly examined in Chapter 5 during our overview of the pillars of OOP.

In Figure 6-8, notice that the Hexagon and Circle types each extend the Shape base class. Like any base class, Shape defines a number of members (a PetName property and Draw() method in this case) that are common to all descendents.

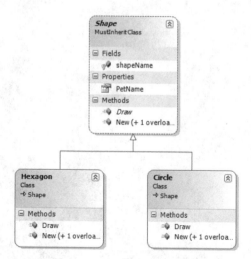

Figure 6-8. *The shapes hierarchy*

Much like the employee hierarchy, you should be able to tell that you don't want to allow the object user to create an instance of Shape directly, as it is too abstract of a concept. Again, to prevent the direct creation of the Shape type, you could define it as a MustInherit class. As well, given that we wish the derived types to respond uniquely to the Draw() method, let's mark it as Overridable and define a default implementation:

```
' The abstract base class of the hierarchy.
Public MustInherit Class Shape
  Protected shapeName As String

  Public Sub New()
    shapeName = "NoName"
  End Sub
  Public Sub New(ByVal s As String)
    shapeName = s
  End Sub

  Public Overridable Sub Draw()
    Console.WriteLine("Inside Shape.Draw()")
  End Sub

  Public Property PetName() As String
    Get
      Return shapeName
    End Get
    Set(ByVal value As String)
      shapeName = value
    End Set
  End Property
End Class
```

Notice that the virtual Draw() method provides a default implementation that simply prints out a message that informs us we are calling the Draw() method within the Shape base class. Now recall that when a method is marked with the Overridable keyword, the method provides a default implementation that all derived types automatically inherit. If a child class so chooses, it *may* override the method but does not *have* to. Given this, consider the following implementation of the Circle and Hexagon types:

```
'Circle DOES NOT override Draw().
Public Class Circle
  Inherits Shape
  Public Sub New()
  End Sub
  Public Sub New(ByVal name As String)
    MyBase.New(name)
  End Sub
End Class
```

```
' Hexagon DOES override Draw().
Public Class Hexagon
  Inherits Shape
  Public Sub New()
  End Sub
  Public Sub New(ByVal name As String)
    MyBase.New(name)
  End Sub
  Public Overrides Sub Draw()
    Console.WriteLine("Drawing {0} the Hexagon", shapeName)
  End Sub
End Class
```

The usefulness of abstract methods becomes crystal clear when you once again remember that subclasses are never required to override virtual methods (as in the case of Circle). Therefore, if you create an instance of the Hexagon and Circle types, you'd find that the Hexagon understands how to draw itself correctly. The Circle, however, is more than a bit confused (see Figure 6-9 for output):

```
Sub Main()
  Console.WriteLine("***** Fun with Polymorphism *****")
  Console.WriteLine()
  Dim hex As New Hexagon("Beth")
  hex.Draw()

  Dim cir As New Circle("Cindy")
  ' Calls base class implementation!
  cir.Draw()
  Console.ReadLine()
End Sub
```

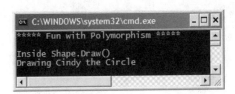

Figure 6-9. *Humm...something is not quite right.*

Clearly, this is not a very intelligent design for the current hierarchy. To force each child class to override the Draw() method, you can define Draw() as an abstract method of the Shape class, which by definition means you provide no default implementation whatsoever. To mark a method as abstract in VB 2005, you use the MustOverride keyword and define your member *without* an expected End construct:

```
' Force all child classes to define how to be rendered.
Public MustInherit Class Shape
...
   Public MustOverride Sub Draw()
...
End Class
```

Note MustOverride methods can only be defined in MustInherit classes. If you attempt to do otherwise, you will be issued a compiler error.

Methods marked with MustOverride are pure protocol. They simply define the name, return value (if any), and argument set. Here, the abstract Shape class informs the derived types "I have a subroutine named Draw() that takes no arguments. If you derive from me, you figure out the details."

Given this, we are now obligated to override the Draw() method in the Circle class. If you do not, Circle is also assumed to be a noncreatable abstract type that must be adorned with the MustInherit keyword (which is obviously not very useful in this example). Here is the code update:

```
' If we did not implement the MustOverride Draw() method, Circle would also be
' considered abstract, and would have to be marked MustInherit!
Public Class Circle
  Inherits Shape
  Public Sub New()
  End Sub
  Public Sub New(ByVal name As String)
    MyBase.New(name)
  End Sub
  Public Overrides Sub Draw()
    Console.WriteLine("Drawing {0} the Circle", shapeName)
  End Sub
End Class
```

The short answer is that we can now make the assumption that anything deriving from Shape does indeed have a unique version of the Draw() method. To illustrate the full story of polymorphism, consider the following code:

```
Module Program
  Sub Main()
    Console.WriteLine("***** Fun with Polymorphism *****")
    Console.WriteLine()

    ' Make an array of Shape compatible objects.
    Dim myShapes As Shape() = {New Hexagon, New Circle, _
      New Hexagon("Mick"), New Circle("Beth"), _
      New Hexagon("Linda")}

    ' Loop over each items and interact with the
    ' polymorphic interface.
    For Each s As Shape In myShapes
      s.Draw()
```

```
    Next
        Console.ReadLine()
    End Sub
End Module
```

Figure 6-10 shows the output.

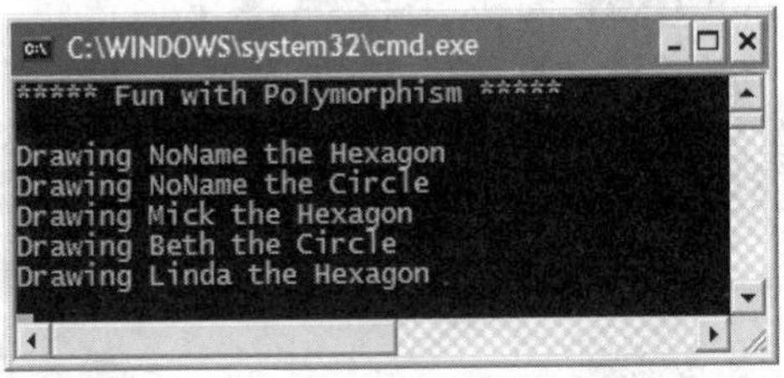

Figure 6-10. *Polymorphism in action*

This Main() method illustrates polymorphism at its finest. Although it is not possible to directly create an abstract base class (the Shape), you are able to freely store references to any subclass with an abstract base variable. Therefore, when you are creating an array of Shapes, the array can hold any object deriving from the Shape base class (if you attempt to place Shape-incompatible objects into the array, you receive a compiler error).

Given that all items in the myShapes array do indeed derive from Shape, we know they all support the same polymorphic interface (or said more plainly, they all have a Draw() method). As you iterate over the array of Shape references, it is at runtime that the underlying type is determined. At this point, the correct version of the Draw() method is invoked.

This technique also makes it very simple to safely extend the current hierarchy. For example, assume we derived five more classes from the abstract Shape base class (Triangle, Square, etc.). Due to the polymorphic interface, the code within our For loop would not have to change in the slightest as the compiler enforces that only Shape-compatible types are placed within the myShapes array.

Understanding Member Shadowing

VB 2005 provides a facility that is the logical opposite of method overriding termed *shadowing*. Formally speaking, if a derived class defines a member that is identical to a member defined in a base class, the derived class has *shadowed* the parent's version. In the real world, the possibility of this occurring is the greatest when you are subclassing from a class you (or your team) did not create yourselves (for example, if you purchase a third- party .NET software package).

For the sake of illustration, assume you receive a class named ThreeDCircle from a coworker (or classmate) that defines a subroutine named Draw() taking no arguments:

```
Public Class ThreeDCircle
    Public Sub Draw()
        Console.WriteLine("Drawing a 3D Circle")
    End Sub
End Class
```

You figure that a ThreeDCircle "is-a" Circle, so you derive from your existing Circle type:

```
Public Class ThreeDCircle
    Inherits Circle
    Public Sub Draw()
```

```
      Console.WriteLine("Drawing a 3D Circle")
    End Sub
End Class
```

Once you recompile, you find the warning you see in Figure 6-11 shown in Visual Studio 2005.

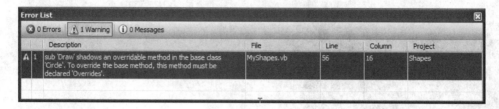

Figure 6-11. *Oops! We just shadowed a member in our parent class.*

To address this issue, you have two options. You could simply update the parent's version of Draw()
using the Overrides keyword (as suggested by the compiler). With this approach, the ThreeDCircle
type is able to extend the parent's default behavior as required.

As an alternative, you can include the Shadows keyword to the offending Draw() member of the
ThreeDCircle type. Doing so explicitly states that the derived type's implementation is intentionally
designed to hide the parent's version (again, in the real world, this can be helpful if external .NET
software somehow conflicts with your current software).

```
' This class extends Circle and hides the inherited Draw() method.
Public Class ThreeDCircle
  Inherits Circle

  ' Hide any Draw() implementation above me.
  Public Shadows Sub Draw()
    Console.WriteLine("Drawing a 3D Circle")
  End Sub
End Class
```

You can also apply the Shadows keyword to any member type inherited from a base class (field,
constant, shared member, property, etc.). As a further example, assume that ThreeDCircle wishes to
hide the inherited shapeName field:

```
' This class extends Circle and hides the inherited Draw() method.
Public Class ThreeDCircle
  Inherits Circle

  ' Hide the shapeName field above me.
  Protected Shadows shapeName As String

  ' Hide any Draw() implementation above me.
  Public Shadows Sub Draw()
    Console.WriteLine("Drawing a 3D Circle")
  End Sub
End Class
```

Finally, be aware that it is still possible to trigger the base class implementation of a shadowed
member using an explicit cast (described in the next section). For example:

```
Module Program
  Sub Main()
  ...
    ' Fun with shadowing.
    Dim o As ThreeDCircle = New ThreeDCircle()
    o.Draw()
    CType(o, Circle).Draw()
    Console.ReadLine()
  End Sub
End Module
```

■Source Code The Shapes project can be found under the Chapter 6 subdirectory.

Understanding Base Class/Derived Class Casting Rules

Now that you can build a family of related class types, you need to learn the laws of VB 2005 casting operations. To do so, let's return to the Employees hierarchy created earlier in this chapter. Under the .NET platform, the ultimate base class in the system is System.Object. Therefore, everything "is-a" Object and can be treated as such. Given this fact, it is legal to store an instance of any type within an object variable:

```
' A Manager "is-a" System.Object.
Dim frank As Object = _
  New Manager("Frank Zappa", 9, 3000, 40000, "111-11-1111", 5)
```

In the Employees system, Managers, SalesPerson, and PTSalesPerson types all extend Employee, so we can store any of these objects in a valid base class reference. Therefore, the following statements are also legal:

```
' A Manager "is-a" Employee too.
Dim moonUnit As Employee = New Manager("MoonUnit Zappa", 2, 3001, _
  20000, "101-11-1321", 1)
```

```
' A PTSalesPerson "is-a" SalesPerson.
Dim jill As SalesPerson = New PTSalesPerson("Jill", 834, 3002, _
  100000, "111-12-1119", 90)
```

The first law of casting between class types is that when two classes are related by an "is-a" relationship, it is always safe to store a derived type within a base class reference. Formally, this is called an *implicit cast*, as "it just works" given the laws of inheritance. This leads to some powerful programming constructs. For example, assume you have defined a new method within your current module:

```
Sub FireThisPerson(ByVal emp As Employee)
  ' Remove from database...
  ' Get key and pencil sharpener from fired employee...
End Sub
```

Because this method takes a single parameter of type Employee, you can effectively pass any descendent from the Employee class into this method directly, given the "is-a" relationship:

```
' Streamline the staff.
FireThisPerson(moonUnit)    ' "moonUnit" was declared as an Employee.
FireThisPerson(jill)        ' "jill" was declared as a SalesPerson.
```

The following code compiles given the implicit cast from the base class type (Employee) to the derived type. However, what if you also wanted to fire Frank Zappa (currently stored in a generic System.Object reference)? If you pass the frank object directly into TheMachine.FireThisPerson() as follows:

```
' This will only work if Option Strict is Off!
Dim frank As Object = _
  New Manager("Frank Zappa", 9, 3000, 40000, "111-11-1111", 5)
FireThisPerson(frank)
```

you will find the code will only work if Option Strict is disabled. However, if you were to enable this option for your project (which is always a good idea), you are issued a compiler error. The reason is you cannot automatically treat a System.Object as a derived Employee directly, given that Object "is-not-a" Employee. As you can see, however, the object reference is pointing to an Employee-compatible object. You can satisfy the compiler by performing an explicit cast.

This is the second law of casting: you must explicitly downcast using the VB 2005 CType() function. Recall that CType() takes two parameters. The first parameter is the object you currently have access to. The second parameter is the name of the type you want to have access to. The value returned from CType() is the result of the downward cast. Thus, the previous problem can be avoided as follows:

```
' OK even with Option Strict enabled.
FireThisPerson(CType(frank, Manager))
```

As you will see in Chapter 9, CType() is also the safe way of obtaining an interface reference from a type. Furthermore, CType() may operate safely on numerical types, but don't forget you have a number of related conversion functions at your disposal (CInt() and so on). Finally, be aware that if you attempt to cast an object into an incompatible type, you receive an invalid cast exception at runtime. Chapter 7 examines the details of structured exception handling.

Note In Chapter 11 you will examine two additional manners in which you can perform explicit casts using the DirectCast and TryCast keywords of VB 2005.

Determining the "Type of" Employee

Given that the FireThisPerson() method has been designed to take any possible type derived from Employee, one question on your mind may be how this method can determine which derived type was sent into the method. On a related note, given that the incoming parameter is of type Employee, how can you gain access to the specialized members of the SalesPerson and Manager types?

The VB 2005 language provides the TypeOf/Is statement to determine whether a given base class reference is actually referring to a derived type. Consider the following updated FireThisPerson() method:

```
Public Sub FireThisPerson(ByVal emp As Employee)
  If TypeOf emp Is SalesPerson Then
    Console.WriteLine("Lost a sales person named {0}", emp.Name)
    Console.WriteLine("{0} made {1} sale(s)...", emp.Name, _
      CType(emp, SalesPerson).SalesNumber)
  End If
  If TypeOf emp Is Manager Then
    Console.WriteLine("Lost a suit named {0}", emp.Name)
    Console.WriteLine("{0} had {1} stock options...", emp.Name, _
      CType(emp, Manager).StockOptions)
  End If
End Sub
```

Here you are performing a runtime check to determine what the incoming base class reference is actually pointing to in memory. Once you determine whether you received a SalesPerson or Manager type, you are able to perform an explicit cast via CType() to gain access to the specialized members of the class.

The Master Parent Class: System.Object

To wrap up this chapter, I'd like to examine the details of the master parent class in the .NET platform: Object. As you were reading the previous section, you may have noticed that the base classes in our hierarchies (Car, Shape, Employee) never explicitly marked their parent classes using the Inherits keyword:

```
' Who is the parent of Car?
Public Class Car
...
End Class
```

In the .NET universe, every type ultimately derives from a common base class named System.Object. The Object class defines a set of common members for every type in the framework. In fact, when you do build a class that does not explicitly define its parent, the compiler automatically derives your type from Object. If you want to be very clear in your intentions, you are free to define classes that derive from Object as follows:

```
' Here we are explicitly deriving from System.Object.
Class Car
   Inherits System.Object
End Class
```

Like any class, System.Object defines a set of members. In the following formal VB 2005 definition, note that some of these items are declared Overridable, which specifies that a given member may be overridden by a subclass, while others are marked with Shared (and are therefore called at the class level):

```
' The top-most class in the .NET world: System.Object
Public Class Object
   Public Overridable Function Equals(ByVal obj As Object) As Boolean
   Public Shared Function Equals(ByVal objA As Object, _
      ByVal objB As Object) As Boolean
   Public Overridable Function GetHashCode() As Integer
   Public Function GetType() As Type
   Protected Function MemberwiseClone() As Object
   Public Shared Function ReferenceEquals(ByVal objA As Object, _
      ByVal objB As Object) As Boolean
   Public Overridable Function ToString() As String
End Class
```

Table 6-1 offers a rundown of the functionality provided by each method.

Table 6-1. *Core Members of* System.Object

Instance Method of Object Class	Meaning in Life
Equals()	By default, this method returns True only if the items being compared refer to the exact same item in memory. Thus, Equals() is used to compare object references, not the state of the object. Typically, this method is overridden to return True only if the objects being compared have the same internal state values (that is, value-based semantics). Be aware that if you override Equals(), you should also override GetHashCode().
GetHashCode()	Returns an Integer that identifies a specific object instance.
GetType()	This method returns a Type object that fully describes the object you are currently referencing. In short, this is a Runtime Type Identification (RTTI) method available to all objects (discussed in greater detail in Chapter 14).
ToString()	Returns a string representation of this object, using the <namespace>.<type name> format (termed the *fully qualified name*). This method can be overridden by a subclass to return a tokenized string of name/value pairs that represent the object's internal state, rather than its fully qualified name.
Finalize()	For the time being, you can understand this method (when overridden) is called to free any allocated resources before the object is destroyed. I talk more about the CLR garbage collection services in Chapter 8.
MemberwiseClone()	This method exists to return a member by member copy of the current object. This method cannot be overridden or accessed by the outside world from an object instance. If you need to allow the outside world to obtain deep copies of a given type, implement the ICloneable interface, which you do in Chapter 9.

To illustrate some of the default behavior provided by the Object base class, create a new console application named ObjectOverrides. Add an empty class definition for a type named Person (shown in the following code snippet). Finally, update your Main() subroutine to interact with the inherited members of System.Object.

■**Note** By default, the members of Object are not shown through IntelliSense. To do so, activate the Tools ➤ Options menu item, and uncheck Hide Advanced Members located under the Text Editor ➤ Basic node of the tree view control.

```
' Remember! Person extends Object!
Public Class Person
End Class

Module Program
  Sub Main()
    Console.WriteLine("***** Fun with System.Object *****")
    Dim p1 As New Person()
```

```vbnet
        ' Use inherited members of System.Object.
        Console.WriteLine("ToString: {0}", p1.ToString())
        Console.WriteLine("Hash code: {0}", p1.GetHashCode())
        Console.WriteLine("Type: {0}", p1.GetType())

        ' Make some other references to hc.
        Dim p2 As Person = p1
        Dim o As Object = p2

        ' Are the references pointing to the same object in memory?
        If o.Equals(p1) AndAlso p2.Equals(o) Then
            Console.WriteLine("Same instance!")
        End If
    End Sub
End Module
```

Figure 6-12 shows the output.

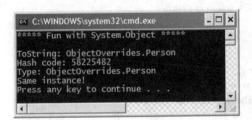

Figure 6-12. *Invoking the inherited members of* System.Object

First, notice how the default implementation of ToString() returns the fully qualified name of the current type (ObjectOverrides.Person). The default behavior of Equals() is to test whether two variables are pointing to the same object in memory. Here, you create a new Person variable named p1. At this point, a new Person object is placed on the managed heap. p2 is also of type Person. However, you are not creating a *new* instance, but rather assigning this variable to reference p1. Therefore, p1 and p2 are both pointing to the same object in memory, as is the variable o (of type Object, which was thrown in for good measure). Given that p1, p2, and o all point to the same memory location, the equality test succeeds.

Although the canned behavior of System.Object can fit the bill in a number of cases, it is quite common for your custom types to override some of these inherited methods. To illustrate, update the Person class to support some state data representing an individual's first name, last name, and age, each of which can be set by a custom constructor:

```vbnet
' Remember! Person extends Object.
Class Person
    Public Sub New(ByVal firstName As String, ByVal lastName As String, _
        ByVal age As Byte)
        fName = firstName
        lName = lastName
        personAge = age
    End Sub
    Sub New()
    End Sub
```

```
    ' Public only for simplicity. Properties and Private data
    ' would obviously be perferred.
    Public fName As String
    Public lName As String
    Public personAge As Byte
End Class
```

Overriding System.Object.ToString()

Many classes (and structures) that you create can benefit from overriding ToString() in order to return a string textual representation of the type's state. This can be quite helpful for purposes of debugging (among other reasons). How you choose to construct this string is a matter of personal choice; however, a recommended approach is to separate each name/value pair with semicolons and wrap the entire string within square brackets (many types in the .NET base class libraries follow this approach). Consider the following overridden ToString() for our Person class:

```
Public Overrides Function ToString() As String
  Dim myState As String
  myState = String.Format("[First Name: {0}; Last Name: {1}; Age: {2}]",
    fName, lName, personAge)
  Return myState
End Function
```

This implementation of ToString() is quite straightforward, given that the Person class only has three pieces of state data. However, always remember that a proper ToString() override should also account for any data defined up the chain of inheritance. When you override ToString() for a class extending a custom base class, the first order of business is to obtain the ToString() value from your parent using MyBase.

Overriding System.Object.Equals()

Let's also override the behavior of Object.Equals() to work with *value-based semantics*. Recall that by default, Equals() returns True only if the two objects being compared reference the same object instance in memory. For the Person class, it may be helpful to implement Equals() to return True if the two variables being compared contain the same state values (e.g., first name, last name, and age).

First of all, notice that the incoming argument of the Equals() method is a generic System.Object. Given this, our first order of business is to ensure the caller has indeed passed in a Person type, and as an extra safeguard, to make sure the incoming parameter is not an unallocated object.

Once we have established the caller has passed us an allocated Person, one approach to implement Equals() is to perform a field-by-field comparison against the data of the incoming object to the data of the current object:

```
Public Overrides Function Equals(ByVal obj As Object) As Boolean
    If TypeOf obj Is Person AndAlso obj IsNot Nothing Then
      Dim temp As Person
      temp = CType(obj, Person)
      If temp.fName = Me.fName AndAlso _
        temp.lName = Me.fName AndAlso _
        temp.personAge = Me.personAge Then
        Return True
      Else
        Return False
      End If
      Return False
    End If
End Function
```

Here, you are examining the values of the incoming object against the values of our internal values (note the use of the Me keyword). If the name and age of each are identical, you have two objects with the exact same state data and therefore return True. Any other possibility results in returning False.

While this approach does indeed work, you can certainly imagine how labor intensive it would be to implement a custom Equals() method for nontrivial types that may contain dozens of data fields. One common shortcut is to leverage your own implementation of ToString(). If a class has a prim-and-proper implementation of ToString() that accounts for all field data up the chain of inheritance, you can simply perform a comparison of the object's string data:

```
Public Overrides Function Equals(ByVal obj As Object) As Boolean
  ' No need to cast 'obj' to a Person anymore,
  ' as everyting has a ToString() method.
  Return obj.ToString = Me.ToString()
End Function
```

Overriding System.Object.GetHashCode()

When a class overrides the Equals() method, you should also override the default implementation of GetHashCode(). Simply put, a *hash code* is a numerical value that represents an object as a particular state. For example, if you create two string objects that hold the value Hello, you would obtain the same hash code. However, if one of the string objects were in all lowercase (hello), you would obtain different hash codes.

By default, System.Object.GetHashCode() uses your object's current location in memory to yield the hash value. However, if you are building a custom type that you intend to store in a Hashtable type (within the System.Collections namespace), you should always override this member, as the Hashtable will be internally invoking Equals() and GetHashCode() to retrieve the correct object.

Although we are not going to place our Person into a System.Collections.Hashtable, for completion, let's override GetHashCode(). There are many algorithms that can be used to create a hash code, some fancy, others not so fancy. Most of the time, you are able to generate a hash code value by leveraging the System.String's GetHashCode() implementation.

Given that the String class already has a solid hash code algorithm that is using the character data of the String to compute a hash value, if you can identify a piece of field data on your class that should be unique for all instances (such as the Social Security number), simply call GetHashCode() on that point of field data. If this is not the case, but you have overridden ToString(), call GetHashCode() on your own string representation:

```
' Return a hash code based on the person's ToString() value.
Public Overrides Function GetHashCode() As Integer
  Return Me.ToString().GetHashCode()
End Function
```

Testing Our Modified Person Class

Now that we have overridden the Overridable members of Object, update Main() to test your updates (see Figure 6-13 for output).

```
Module Program
  Sub Main()
    Console.WriteLine("***** Fun with System.Object *****")
    Console.WriteLine()
```

```vb
    ' NOTE:  We want these to be identical to test
    ' the Equals() and GetHashCode() methods.
    Dim p1 As Person = New Person("Homer", "Simpson", 50)
    Dim p2 As Person = New Person("Homer", "Simpson", 50)

    ' Get stringified version of objects.
    Console.WriteLine("p1.ToString() = {0}", p1.ToString())
    Console.WriteLine("p2.ToString() = {0}", p2.ToString())

    ' Test Overridden Equals()
    Console.WriteLine("p1 = p2?: {0}", p1.Equals(p2))

    ' Test hash codes.
    Console.WriteLine("Same hash codes?: {0}", _
      p1.GetHashCode() = p2.GetHashCode())
    Console.WriteLine()

    ' Change age of p2 and test again.
    p2.personAge = 45
    Console.WriteLine("p1.ToString() = {0}", p1.ToString())
    Console.WriteLine("p2.ToString() = {0}", p2.ToString())
    Console.WriteLine("p1 = p2?: {0}", p1.Equals(p2))
    Console.WriteLine("Same hash codes?: {0}", _
      p1.GetHashCode() = p2.GetHashCode())
    Console.ReadLine()
  End Sub
End Module
```

Figure 6-13. *Our customized* Person *type*

The Shared Members of System.Object

In addition to the instance-level members you have just examined, System.Object does define two (very helpful) shared members that also test for value-based or reference-based equality. Consider the following code:

```vb
'  Shared members of System.Object.
Dim p3 As Person = New Person("Sally", "Jones", 4)
Dim p4 As Person = New Person("Sally", "Jones", 4)
Console.WriteLine("P3 and P4 have same state: {0}", Object.Equals(p3, p4))
Console.WriteLine("P3 and P4 are pointing to same object: {0}", _
  Object.ReferenceEquals(p3, p4))
```

Here, you are able to simply send in two objects (of any type) and allow the System.Object class to determine the details automatically.

■**Source Code** The ObjectOverrides project is located under the Chapter 6 subdirectory.

Summary

This chapter explored the role and details of inheritance and polymorphism. Over these pages you were introduced to numerous new keywords to support each of these techniques. For example, recall that the Inherits keyword is used to establish the parent class of a given type. Parent types are able to define any number of virtual (Overridable) and/or abstract (MustOverride) members to establish a polymorphic interface. Derived types override such members using the Overrides keyword.

In addition to building numerous class hierarchies, this chapter also examined how to explicitly cast between base and derived types using the CType() operator, and wrapped up by diving into the details of the cosmic parent class in the .NET base class libraries: System.Object.

CHAPTER 7

■ ■ ■

Understanding Structured Exception Handling

The point of this chapter is to understand how to handle runtime anomalies in your VB 2005 code base through the use of *structured exception handling*. Not only will you learn about the VB 2005 keywords that allow you to handle such matters (Try, Catch, Throw, Finally), but you will also come to understand the distinction between application-level and system-level exceptions. This discussion will also serve as a lead-in to the topic of building custom exceptions, as well as how to leverage the exception-centric debugging tools of Visual Studio 2005.

Ode to Errors, Bugs, and Exceptions

Despite what our (sometimes inflated) egos may tell us, no programmer is perfect. Writing software is a complex undertaking, and given this complexity, it is quite common for even the best software to ship with various *problems*. Sometimes the problem is caused by "bad code" (such as overflowing the bounds of an array). Other times, a problem is caused by bogus user input that has not been accounted for in the application's code base (e.g., a phone number field assigned "Chucky"). Now, regardless of the cause of said problem, the end result is that your application does not work as expected. To help frame the upcoming discussion of structured exception handling, allow me to provide definitions for three commonly used anomaly-centric terms:

- *Bugs*: This is, simply put, an error on the part of the programmer. For example, assume you are programming with unmanaged C++. If you make calls on a NULL pointer or fail to delete allocated memory (resulting in a memory leak), you have a bug.

- *User errors*: Unlike bugs, user errors are typically caused by the individual running your application, rather than by those who created it. For example, an end user who enters a malformed string into a text box could very well generate an error *if* you fail to handle this faulty input in your code base.

- *Exceptions*: Exceptions are typically regarded as runtime anomalies that are difficult, if not impossible, to account for while programming your application. Possible exceptions include attempting to connect to a database that no longer exists, opening a corrupted file, or contacting a machine that is currently offline. In each of these cases, the programmer (and end user) has little control over these "exceptional" circumstances.

Given the previous definitions, it should be clear that .NET structured *exception* handling is a technique well suited to deal with runtime *exceptions*. However, as for the bugs and user errors that have escaped your view, the CLR will often generate a corresponding exception that identifies the problem at hand. The .NET base class libraries define numerous exceptions such as `FormatException`, `IndexOutOfRangeException`, `FileNotFoundException`, `ArgumentOutOfRangeException`, and so forth.

Before we get too far ahead of ourselves, let's formalize the role of structured exception handling and check out how it differs from traditional error handling techniques.

■**Note** To make the code examples used in this book as clean as possible, I will not catch every possible exception that may be thrown by a given method in the base class libraries. In your production-level projects, you should, of course, make liberal use of the techniques presented in this chapter.

The Role of .NET Exception Handling

Prior to .NET, error handling under the Windows operating system was a confused mishmash of techniques. Many programmers rolled their own error handling logic within the context of a given application. For example, a development team may define a set of numerical constants that represent known error conditions, and make use of them as function return values.

This approach is less than ideal, given the fact that raw numerical values are not self-describing and offer little detail regarding how to deal with the problem at hand. Ideally, you would like to wrap the name, message, and other helpful information regarding this error condition into a single, well-defined package (which is exactly what happens under structured exception handling).

In addition to a developer's ad hoc techniques, the Windows API defines hundreds of predefined error codes. Also, many COM developers have made use of a small set of standard COM interfaces (e.g., `ISupportErrorInfo`, `IErrorInfo`, `ICreateErrorInfo`) and COM objects (the VB 6.0 `Err` object) to return meaningful error information to a COM client.

The obvious problem with these previous techniques is the tremendous lack of symmetry. Each approach is more or less tailored to a given technology, a given language, and perhaps even a given project. In order to put an end to this madness, the .NET platform provides a standard technique to send and trap runtime errors: structured exception handling (SEH).

The beauty of this approach is that developers now have a unified approach to error handling, which is common to all languages targeting the .NET universe. Therefore, the way in which a VB 2005 programmer handles errors is syntactically similar to that of a C# programmer. As an added bonus, the syntax used to throw and catch exceptions across assemblies and machine boundaries is identical.

Another bonus of .NET exceptions is the fact that rather than receiving a raw numerical value that identifies the problem at hand, exceptions are objects that contain a human-readable description of the problem, as well as a detailed snapshot of the call stack that triggered the exception in the first place. Furthermore, you are able to provide the end user with help link information that points the user to a URL that provides detailed information regarding the error at hand as well as custom user-defined data.

The Atoms of .NET Exception Handling

Programming with structured exception handling involves the use of four interrelated entities:

- A class that represents the exception itself
- A member (property, subroutine, or function) that *throws* an instance of the exception class to the caller

- A block of code on the caller's side that invokes the exception-prone member

- A block of code on the caller's side that will process (or *catch*) the exception should it occur

The VB 2005 programming language offers four keywords (Try, Catch, Throw, and Finally) that allow you to throw and handle exceptions. The type that represents the problem at hand is a class derived from System.Exception (or a descendent thereof). Given this fact, let's check out the role of this exception-centric base class.

The System.Exception Base Class

All user- and system-defined exceptions ultimately derive from the System.Exception base class (which in turn derives from System.Object). In the member prototypes that follow, notice that some of these members are declared with the Overridable keyword and may thus be overridden by derived types:

```
' Member prototypes of select members.
Public Class Exception
  Implements ISerializable, _Exception

  ' Methods
  Public Sub New(ByVal message As String, ByVal innerException As Exception)
  Public Overridable Function GetBaseException() As Exception
  Public Function GetType() As Type
  Public Overrides Function ToString() As String
...
  ' Properties
  Public Overridable ReadOnly Property Data As IDictionary
  Public Overridable Property HelpLink As String
  Protected Property HResult As Integer
  Public ReadOnly Property InnerException As Exception
  Public Overridable ReadOnly Property Message As String
  Public Overridable Property Source As String
  Public Overridable ReadOnly Property StackTrace As String
  Public ReadOnly Property TargetSite As MethodBase
End Class
```

As you can see, many of the properties defined by System.Exception are read-only in nature. This is due to the simple fact that derived types will typically supply default values for each property (for example, the default message of the IndexOutOfRangeException type is "Index was outside the bounds of the array").

■**Note** As of .NET 2.0, the _Exception interface is implemented by System.Exception to expose its functionality to unmanaged code via the interoperability layer.

Table 7-1 describes the details of some (but not all) of the members of System.Exception.

Table 7-1. *Core Members of the* System.Exception *Type*

System.Exception Property	Meaning in Life
Data	This property (which is new to .NET 2.0) retrieves a collection of key/value pairs (represented by an object implementing IDictionary) that provides additional, user-defined information about the exception. By default, this collection is empty.
HelpLink	This property returns a URI to a help file describing the error in full detail.
InnerException	This read-only property can be used to obtain information about the previous exception(s) that caused the current exception to occur. The previous exception(s) are recorded by passing them into the constructor of the most current exception.
Message	This read-only property returns the textual description of a given error. The error message itself is set as a constructor parameter.
Source	This property returns the name of the assembly that threw the exception.
StackTrace	This read-only property contains a string that identifies the sequence of calls that triggered the exception. As you might guess, this property is very useful during debugging.
TargetSite	This read-only property returns a MethodBase type, which describes numerous details about the method that threw the exception (ToString() will identify the method by name).

The Simplest Possible Example

To illustrate the usefulness of structured exception handling, we need to create a type that may throw an exception under the correct circumstances. Assume we have created a new console application project (named SimpleException) that defines two class types (Car and Radio) associated using the "has-a" relationship. The Radio type defines a single method that turns the radio's power on or off:

```
Public Class Radio
  Public Sub TurnOn(ByVal state As Boolean)
    If state = True Then
      Console.WriteLine("Jamming...")
    Else
      Console.WriteLine("Quiet time...")
    End If
  End Sub
End Class
```

In addition to leveraging the Radio type, the Car type is defined in such a way that if the user accelerates a Car object beyond a predefined maximum speed (specified using a constant member variable), its engine explodes, rendering the Car unusable (captured by a Boolean member variable named carIsDead). Beyond these points, the Car type has a few member variables to represent the current speed and a user-supplied "pet name" as well as various constructors. Here is the complete definition (with code annotations):

```
Public Class Car
  ' Constant for maximum speed.
  Public Const maxSpeed As Integer = 100
```

```vbnet
' Internal state data.
Private currSpeed As Integer
Private petName As String

' Is the car still operational?
Private carIsDead As Boolean

' A car has a radio.
Private theMusicBox As Radio = New Radio()

' Constructors.
Public Sub New()
End Sub
Public Sub New(ByVal name As String, ByVal currSp As Integer)
  currSpeed = currSp
  petName = name
End Sub


Public Sub CrankTunes(ByVal state As Boolean)
  theMusicBox.TurnOn(state)
End Sub

' See if Car has overheated.
Public Sub Accelerate(ByVal delta As Integer)
  If carIsDead Then
    Console.WriteLine("{0} is out of order...", petName)
  Else
    currSpeed += delta
    If currSpeed > maxSpeed Then
      Console.WriteLine("{0} has overheated!", petName)
      currSpeed = 0
      carIsDead = True
    Else
      Console.WriteLine("=> CurrSpeed = {0}", currSpeed)
    End If
  End If
End Sub
End Class
```

Now, if we were to implement a Main() method that forces a Car object to exceed the predefined maximum speed (represented by the maxSpeed constant) as shown here:

```vbnet
Module Program
  Sub Main()
    Console.WriteLine("***** Creating a car and stepping on it *****")
    Dim myCar As Car = New Car("Zippy", 20)
    myCar.CrankTunes(True)

    For i As Integer = 0 To 10
      myCar.Accelerate(10)
    Next
    Console.ReadLine()
  End Sub
End Module
```

we would see the output displayed in Figure 7-1.

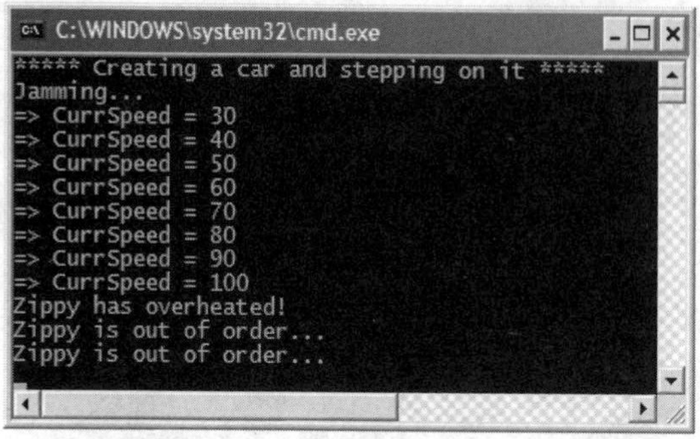

Figure 7-1. *The initial* Car *type in action*

Throwing a Generic Exception

Now that we have a functional Car type, I'll illustrate the simplest way to throw an exception. The current implementation of Accelerate() displays an error message if the caller attempts to speed up the Car beyond its upper limit. To retrofit this method to throw an exception if the user attempts to speed up the automobile after it has met its maker, you want to create and configure a new instance of the System.Exception class, setting the value of the read-only Message property via the class constructor. When you wish to send the error object back to the caller, make use of the VB 2005 Throw keyword. Here is the relevant code update to the Accelerate() method (the remainder of the Car class has been unchanged):

```
' See if Car has overheated.
Public Sub Accelerate(ByVal delta As Integer)
  If carIsDead Then
    Console.WriteLine("{0} is out of order...", petName)
  Else
    currSpeed += delta
    If currSpeed >= maxSpeed Then
      carIsDead = True
      currSpeed = 0
      ' Throw new exception!  This car is toast!
      Throw New Exception(String.Format("{0} has overheated!", petName))
    Else
      Console.WriteLine("=> CurrSpeed = {0}", currSpeed)
    End If
  End If
End Sub
```

Before examining how a caller would catch this exception, a few points of interest. First of all, when you are throwing an exception, it is always up to you to decide exactly what constitutes the error in question, and when it should be thrown. Here, you are making the assumption that if the program attempts to increase the speed of a car that has expired, a System.Exception type should be thrown to indicate the Accelerate() method cannot continue (which may or may not be a valid assumption).

Alternatively, you could implement Accelerate() to recover automatically without needing to throw an exception in the first place. By and large, exceptions should be thrown only when a more terminal condition has been met (for example, not finding a necessary file, failing to connect to a database, and whatnot). Deciding exactly what constitutes throwing an exception is a design issue you must always contend with. For our current purposes, assume that asking a doomed automobile to increase its speed justifies a cause to throw an exception.

Catching Exceptions

Because the Accelerate() method now throws an exception, the caller needs to be ready to handle the exception should it occur. When you are invoking a method that may throw an exception, you make use of a Try/Catch block. Once you have caught the exception type, you are able to invoke the members of the System.Exception type to extract the details of the problem.

What you do with this data is largely up to you. You may wish to log this information to a report file, write the data to the Windows event log, e-mail a system administrator, or display the problem to the end user. Here, you will simply dump the contents to the console window:

```
Module Program
  Sub Main()
    Console.WriteLine("***** Creating a car and stepping on it *****")
    Dim myCar As Car = New Car("Zippy", 20)
    myCar.CrankTunes(True)

    Try
      For i As Integer = 0 To 10
        myCar.Accelerate(10)
      Next
    Catch ex As Exception
      Console.WriteLine("*** Error! ***")
      Console.WriteLine("Method: {0}", ex.TargetSite)
      Console.WriteLine("Message: {0}", ex.Message)
      Console.WriteLine("Source: {0}", ex.Source)
    End Try

    ' The error has been handled, processing continues with the next statement.
    Console.WriteLine("***** Out of exception logic *****")
    Console.ReadLine()
  End Sub
End Module
```

In essence, a Try block is a group of statements that *may* throw an exception during execution. If an exception is detected, the flow of program execution is sent to the appropriate Catch block (as you will see in just a bit, it is possible to define multiple Catch blocks for a single Try). On the other hand, if the code within a Try block does not trigger an exception, the Catch block is skipped entirely, and all is right with the world. Figure 7-2 shows a test run of this program.

Figure 7-2. *Dealing with the error using structured exception handling*

As you can see, once an exception has been handled, the application is free to continue on from the point after the Catch block. In some circumstances, a given exception may be critical enough to warrant the termination of the application. However, in a good number of cases, the logic within the exception handler will ensure the application will be able to continue on its merry way (although it may be slightly less functional, such as the case of not being able to connect to a remote data source).

Configuring the State of an Exception

Currently, the System.Exception object configured within the Accelerate() method simply establishes a value exposed by the Message property (via a constructor parameter). As shown in Table 7-1, however, the Exception class also supplies a number of additional members (TargetSite, StackTrace, HelpLink, and Data) that can be useful in further qualifying the nature of the problem. To spruce up our current example, let's examine further details of these members on a case-by-case basis.

The TargetSite Property

The System.Exception.TargetSite property allows you to determine various details about the method that threw a given exception. As shown in the previous Main() method, printing the value of TargetSite will display the return value, name, and parameters of the method that threw the exception. However, TargetSite does not simply return a vanilla-flavored string, but a strongly typed System.Reflection. MethodBase object. This type can be used to gather numerous details regarding the offending method as well as the class that defines the offending method. To illustrate, assume the previous Catch logic has been updated as follows:

```
Module Program
  Sub Main()
...
    Try
      For i As Integer = 0 To 10
        myCar.Accelerate(10)
      Next
    Catch ex As Exception
      Console.WriteLine("*** Error! ***")
      Console.WriteLine("Member name: {0}", ex.TargetSite)
      Console.WriteLine("Class defining member: {0}", _
        ex.TargetSite.DeclaringType)
      Console.WriteLine("Member type: {0}", ex.TargetSite.MemberType)
      Console.WriteLine("Message: {0}", ex.Message)
      Console.WriteLine("Source: {0}", ex.Source)
    End Try
    ...
  End Sub
End Module
```

This time, you make use of the MethodBase.DeclaringType property to determine the fully qualified name of the class that threw the error (SimpleException.Car in this case) as well as the MemberType property of the MethodBase object to identify the type of member (such as a property versus a method) where this exception originated. Figure 7-3 shows the updated output.

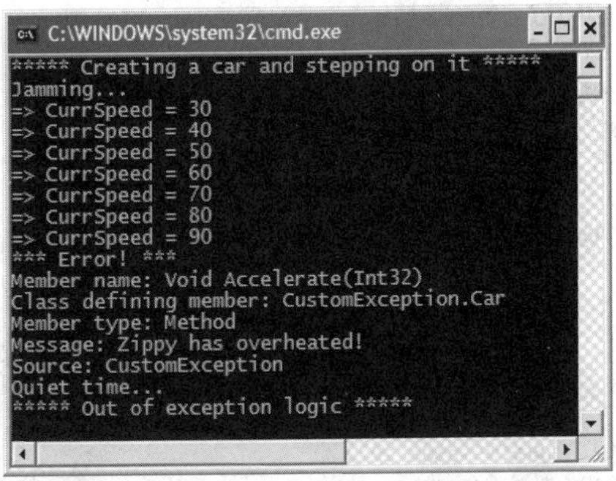

Figure 7-3. *Obtaining aspects of the target site*

The StackTrace Property

The System.Exception.StackTrace property allows you to identify the series of calls that resulted in the exception. Be aware that you never set the value of StackTrace as it is established automatically at the time the exception is created. To illustrate, assume you have once updated your Catch logic with the following additional statement:

```
Try
  For i As Integer = 0 To 10
    myCar.Accelerate(10)
  Next
Catch ex As Exception
...
  Console.WriteLine("Stack: {0}", ex.StackTrace)
End Try
```

If you were to run the program, you would find the following stack trace is printed to the console (your line numbers and application path may differ, of course):

```
Stack: at SimpleException.Car.Accelerate(Int32 delta)
in C:\Ch_07 Code\SimpleException\Car.vb:line 36
at SimpleException.Program.Main() in C:\SimpleException\Program.vb:line 9
```

The string returned from StackTrace documents the sequence of calls that resulted in the throwing of this exception. Notice how the bottommost line number of this string identifies the first call in the sequence, while the topmost line number identifies the exact location of the offending member. Clearly, this information can be quite helpful during the debugging of a given application, as you are able to "follow the flow" of the error's origin.

The HelpLink Property

While the TargetSite and StackTrace properties allow programmers to gain an understanding of a given exception, this information is of little use to the end user. As you have already seen, the System.Exception.Message property can be used to obtain human-readable information that may be displayed to the current user. In addition, the HelpLink property can be set to point the user to a specific URL or standard Windows help file that contains more detailed information.

By default, the value managed by the HelpLink property is an empty string. If you wish to fill this property with an interesting value, you will need to do so before throwing the System.Exception type. Here are the relevant updates to the Car.Accelerate() method:

```
' See if Car has overheated.
Public Sub Accelerate(ByVal delta As Integer)
  If carIsDead Then
    Console.WriteLine("{0} is out of order...", petName)
  Else
    currSpeed += delta
    If currSpeed >= maxSpeed Then
      carIsDead = True
      currSpeed = 0

      ' We need to call the HelpLink property, thus we need to
      ' create a local variable before throwing the Exception object.
      Dim ex As New Exception(String.Format("{0} has overheated!", petName))
      ex.HelpLink = "http://www.CarsRUs.com"
        Throw ex
    Else
        Console.WriteLine("=> CurrSpeed = {0}", currSpeed)
    End If
  End If
End Sub
```

The Catch logic could now be updated to print out this help link information as follows:

```
Catch ex As Exception
...
  Console.WriteLine("Help Link: {0}", ex.HelpLink)
End Try
```

The Data Property

The Data property of System.Exception is new to .NET 2.0, and allows you to fill an exception object with any additional relevant bits of information (such as a time stamp or what have you). The Data property returns an object implementing an interface named IDictionary, defined in the System.Collection namespace. Chapter 9 examines the role of interface-based programming as well as the System.Collections namespace. For the time being, just understand that dictionary collections allow you to create a set of values that are retrieved using a specific key value. Observe the next relevant update to the Car.Accelerate() method:

```
' See if Car has overheated.
Public Sub Accelerate(ByVal delta As Integer)
  If carIsDead Then
    Console.WriteLine("{0} is out of order...", petName)
  Else
    currSpeed += delta
    If currSpeed >= maxSpeed Then
      carIsDead = True
      currSpeed = 0

      ' We need to call the HelpLink property, thus we need to
      ' create a local variable before throwing the Exception object.
      Dim ex As New Exception(String.Format("{0} has overheated!", petName))
      ex.HelpLink = "http://www.CarsRUs.com"
      ' Stuff in custom data regarding the error.
      ex.Data.Add("TimeStamp", _
```

```
        String.Format("The car exploded at {0}", DateTime.Now))
      ex.Data.Add("Cause", "You have a lead foot.")
      Throw ex
    Else
      Console.WriteLine("=> CurrSpeed = {0}", currSpeed)
    End If
  End If
End Sub
```

To successfully enumerate over the key/value pairs, you first must make sure to specify an Imports directive for the System.Collection namespace, given we will make use of a DictionaryEntry type in the file containing the module implementing your Main() method:

```
Imports System.Collections
```

Next, we need to update the catch logic to test that the value returned from the Data property is not Nothing (the default setting). After this point, we make use of the Key and Value properties of the DictionaryEntry type to print the custom user data to the console:

```
Catch ex As Exception
...
  ' By default, the data field is empty, so check for Nothing.
  Console.WriteLine("-> Custom Data:")
  If (ex.Data IsNot Nothing) Then
    For Each de As DictionaryEntry In ex.Data
      Console.WriteLine("-> {0} : {1}", de.Key, de.Value)
    Next
  End If
End Try
```

With this, we would now find the update shown in Figure 7-4.

Figure 7-4. *Obtaining custom data*

Cool! At this point you hopefully have a better idea how to throw and catch exception objects to account for runtime errors. Next, let's examine the process of building strongly typed custom exception objects.

■**Source Code** The SimpleException project is included under the Chapter 7 subdirectory.

System-Level Exceptions (System.SystemException)

The .NET base class libraries define many classes derived from System.Exception. For example, the System namespace defines core error objects such as ArgumentOutOfRangeException, IndexOutOfRangeException, StackOverflowException, and so forth. Other namespaces define exceptions that reflect the behavior of that namespace (e.g., System.Drawing.Printing defines printing exceptions, System.IO defines IO-based exceptions, System.Data defines database-centric exceptions, and so forth).

Exceptions that are thrown by the CLR are (appropriately) called *system exceptions*. These exceptions are regarded as nonrecoverable, fatal errors. System exceptions derive directly from a base class named System.SystemException, which in turn derives from System.Exception (which derives from System.Object):

```
Public Class SystemException
  Inherits Exception
  ' Various constructors.
End Class
```

Given that the System.SystemException type does not add any additional functionality beyond a set of constructors, you might wonder why SystemException exists in the first place. Simply put, when an exception type derives from System.SystemException, you are able to determine that the .NET runtime is the entity that has thrown the exception, rather than the code base of the executing application. For example, the NullReferenceException class extends SystemException. You can verify this quite simply using the VB 2005 TypeOf/Is construct:

```
' True!
Dim nullRefEx As New NullReferenceException
Console.WriteLine("NullReferenceException is-a SystemException? : {0}", _
  TypeOf nullRefEx Is SystemException)
```

Application-Level Exceptions (System.ApplicationException)

Given that all .NET exceptions are class types, you are free to create your own application-specific exceptions. However, due to the fact that the System.SystemException base class represents exceptions thrown from the CLR, you may naturally assume that you should derive your custom exceptions from the System.Exception type. While you could do so, best practice dictates that you instead derive from the System.ApplicationException type:

```
Public Class ApplicationException
  Inherits Exception
  ' Various constructors.
End Class
```

Like SystemException, ApplicationException does not define any additional members beyond a set of constructors. Functionally, the only purpose of System.ApplicationException is to identify the source of the (nonfatal) error. When you handle an exception deriving from System.ApplicationException, you can assume the exception was raised by the code base of the executing application, rather than by the .NET base class libraries.

Building Custom Exceptions, Take One

While you can always throw instances of System.Exception to signal a runtime error (as shown in our first example), it is sometimes advantageous to build a *strongly typed exception* that represents the unique details of your current problem. For example, assume you wish to build a custom exception (named CarIsDeadException) to represent the error of speeding up a doomed automobile. The first step is to derive a new class from System.ApplicationException (by convention, all exception classes end with the "Exception" suffix; in fact, this is a .NET best practice).

```
' This custom exception describes the details of the car-is-dead condition.
Public Class CarIsDeadException
  Inherits ApplicationException
End Class
```

Like any class, you are free to include any number of custom members that can be called within the Catch block of the calling logic. You are also free to override any virtual members defined by your parent classes. For example, we could implement CarIsDeadException by overriding the virtual Message property:

```
Public Class CarIsDeadException
  Inherits ApplicationException

  Private messageDetails As String

  Public Sub New()
  End Sub
  Public Sub New(ByVal msg As String)
    messageDetails = msg
  End Sub

  ' Override the Exception.Message property.
  Public Overrides ReadOnly Property Message() As String
    Get
      Return String.Format("Car Error Message: {0}", messageDetails)
    End Get
  End Property
End Class
```

Here, the CarIsDeadException type maintains a private data member (messageDetails) that represents data regarding the current exception, which can be set using a custom constructor. Throwing this error from the Accelerate() is straightforward. Simply allocate, configure, and throw a CarIsDeadException type rather than a generic System.Exception:

```
' Throw the custom CarIsDeadException.
Public Sub Accelerate(ByVal delta As Integer)
...
 Dim ex As New CarIsDeadException(String.Format("{0} has overheated!", petName))
...
End Sub
```

To catch this incoming exception explicitly, your Catch scope can now be updated to catch a specific CarIsDeadException type (however, given that CarIsDeadException "is-a" System.Exception, it is still permissible to catch a generic System.Exception as well):

```
Sub Main()
...
 Catch ex As CarIsDeadException
   ' Process incoming exception.
 End Try
...
End Sub
```

So, now that you understand the basic process of building a custom exception, you may wonder when you are required to do so. Typically, you only need to create custom exceptions when the error is tightly bound to the class issuing the error (for example, a custom File class that throws a number of file-related errors, a Car class that throws a number of car-related errors, and so forth). In doing so, you provide the caller with the ability to handle numerous exceptions on an error-by-error basis.

Building Custom Exceptions, Take Two

The current CarIsDeadException type has overridden the System.Exception.Message property in order to configure a custom error message. However, we can simplify our programming tasks if we set the parent's Message property via an incoming constructor parameter. By doing so, we have no need to write anything other than the following:

```
Public Class CarIsDeadException
  Inherits ApplicationException
  Public Sub New()
  End Sub
  Public Sub New(ByVal msg As String)
    MyBase.New(msg)
  End Sub
End Class
```

Notice that this time you have *not* defined a string variable to represent the message, and have *not* overridden the Message property. Rather, you are simply passing the parameter to your base class constructor. With this design, a custom exception class is little more than a uniquely named class deriving from System.ApplicationException, devoid of any member variables (or base class overrides).

Don't be surprised if most (if not all) of your custom exception classes follow this simple pattern. Many times, the role of a custom exception is not necessarily to provide additional functionality beyond what is inherited from the base classes, but to provide a strongly named type that clearly identifies the nature of the error.

Building Custom Exceptions, Take Three

If you wish to build a truly prim-and-proper custom exception class, you would want to make sure your type adheres to the exception-centric .NET best practices. Specifically, this requires that your custom exception

- Derives from Exception/ApplicationException
- Is marked with the <System.Serializable> attribute
- Defines a default constructor
- Defines a constructor that sets the inherited Message property
- Defines a constructor to handle "inner exceptions"
- Defines a constructor to handle the serialization of your type

Now, based on your current background with .NET, you may have no idea regarding the role of attributes or object serialization, which is just fine. I'll address these topics later in the text (Chapters 14 and 19, respectively). However, to finalize our examination of building custom exceptions, here is the final iteration of CarIsDeadException:

```
<Serializable()> _
Public Class CarIsDeadException
  Inherits ApplicationException
  Public Sub New()
  End Sub
```

```
Public Sub New(ByVal message As String)
   MyBase.New(message)
End Sub
Public Sub New(ByVal message As String, ByVal inner As System.Exception)
   MyBase.New(message, inner)
End Sub
Protected Sub New(ByVal info As System.Runtime.Serialization.SerializationInfo, _
   ByVal context As System.Runtime.Serialization.StreamingContext)
   MyBase.New(info, context)
End Sub
End Class
```

So, at this point, you are able to build custom strongly typed exceptions that represent the application-specific errors your program may generate. Next up, we need to examine the process of handling multiple exceptions that may result from a single Try scope.

Processing Multiple Exceptions

In its simplest form, a Try block has a single Catch block. In reality, you often run into a situation where the statements within a Try block could trigger *numerous* possible exceptions. For example, assume the car's Accelerate() method also throws the predefined ArgumentOutOfRangeException if you pass an invalid parameter (which we will assume is any value less than zero):

```
Public Sub Accelerate(ByVal delta As Integer)
   If delta < 0 Then
      Throw New ArgumentOutOfRangeException()
   End If
...
End Sub
```

The Catch logic could now specifically respond to each type of exception:

```
Module Program
   Sub Main()
      Console.WriteLine("***** Creating a car and stepping on it *****")
      Dim myCar As Car = New Car("Zippy", 20)
      myCar.CrankTunes(True)
      Try
         For i As Integer = 0 To 10
            myCar.Accelerate(10)
         Next
      Catch ex As ArgumentOutOfRangeException
         ' Process bad arguments.
      Catch ex As CarIsDeadException
         ' Process CarIsDeadException.
      End Try
...
   End Sub
End Module
```

When you are authoring multiple Catch blocks, you must be aware that when an exception is thrown, it will be processed by the "first available" catch. To illustrate exactly what the "first available" catch means, assume you retrofitted the previous logic with an additional Catch scope that attempts to handle all exceptions beyond CarIsDeadException and ArgumentOutOfRangeException by catching a generic System.Exception as follows:

```
' This code will generate warnings!
Module Program
  Sub Main()
    Console.WriteLine("***** Creating a car and stepping on it *****")
    Dim myCar As Car = New Car("Zippy", 20)
    myCar.CrankTunes(True)

    Try
      For i As Integer = 0 To 10
        myCar.Accelerate(10)
      Next
    Catch ex As Exception
      ' Try to catch all other exceptions here?
    Catch ex As ArgumentOutOfRangeException
      ' Process bad arguments.
    Catch ex As CarIsDeadException
      ' Process CarIsDeadException.
    End Try
...
  End Sub
End Module
```

This exception handling logic generates several warnings. The problem is due to the fact that the first Catch block can handle anything derived from System.Exception (given the "is-a" relationship), including the CarIsDeadException and ArgumentOutOfRangeException types. Therefore, the final two Catch blocks are unreachable!

The rule of thumb to keep in mind is to make sure your Catch blocks are structured such that the very first Catch is the most specific exception (i.e., the most derived type in an exception type inheritance chain), leaving the final Catch for the most general (i.e., the base class of a given exception inheritance chain, in this case System.Exception).

Thus, if you wish to define a Catch statement that will handle any errors beyond CarIsDeadException and ArgumentOutOfRangeException, you would write the following:

```
' This code compiles without warning.
Module Program
  Sub Main()
    Console.WriteLine("***** Creating a car and stepping on it *****")
    Dim myCar As Car = New Car("Zippy", 20)
    myCar.CrankTunes(True)

    Try
      For i As Integer = 0 To 10
        myCar.Accelerate(10)
      Next
    Catch ex As ArgumentOutOfRangeException
      ' Process bad arguments.
    Catch ex As CarIsDeadException
      ' Process CarIsDeadException.
    Catch ex As Exception
      ' Try to catch all other exceptions here? Ok!
    End Try
...
  End Sub
End Module
```

Generic Catch Statements

VB 2005 also supports a "generic" Catch scope that does not explicitly receive the exception object thrown by a given member:

```
' A generic catch.
Module Program
  Sub Main()
    Console.WriteLine("***** Creating a car and stepping on it *****")
    Dim myCar As Car = New Car("Zippy", 20)
    myCar.CrankTunes(True)

    Try
      For i As Integer = 0 To 10
        myCar.Accelerate(10)
      Next
    Catch
      Console.WriteLine("Oops!  Something bad happened...")
    End Try
  End Sub
End Module
```

Obviously, this is not the most informative way to handle exceptions, given that you have no way to obtain meaningful data about the error that occurred (such as the method name, call stack, or custom message). Nevertheless, VB 2005 does allow for such a construct, which can be helpful when you wish to handle all errors in a very generic fashion.

Rethrowing Exceptions

Be aware that it is permissible for logic in a Try block to *rethrow* an exception up the call stack to the previous caller. To do so, simply make use of the Throw keyword within a Catch block. This passes the exception up the chain of calling logic, which can be helpful if your Catch block is only able to partially handle the error at hand:

```
' Passing the buck.
Module Program
  Sub Main()
    Console.WriteLine("***** Creating a car and stepping on it *****")
    Dim myCar As Car = New Car("Zippy", 20)
    myCar.CrankTunes(True)

    Try
      For i As Integer = 0 To 10
        myCar.Accelerate(10)
      Next
    Catch ex As ArgumentOutOfRangeException
      ' Process bad arguments.
    Catch ex As CarIsDeadException
      ' Do any partial processing of this error and pass the buck.
      ' Here, we are rethrowing the incoming CarIsDeadException object.
      ' However, you are also free to throw a different exception if need be.
      Throw ex
    Catch ex As Exception
      ' Try to catch all other exceptions here? Ok!
    End Try
...
  End Sub
End Module
```

Be aware that in this example code, the ultimate receiver of CarIsDeadException is the CLR, given that it is the Main() method rethrowing the exception. Given this point, your end user is presented with a system-supplied error dialog box. Typically, you would only rethrow a partially handled exception to a caller that has the ability to handle the incoming exception more gracefully.

Inner Exceptions

As you may suspect, it is entirely possible to trigger an exception at the time you are handling another exception. For example, assume that you are handing a CarIsDeadException within a particular Catch scope, and during the process you attempt to record the stack trace to a file on your C drive named carErrors.txt. Although we have not yet examined the topic of file IO, assume you have imported the System.IO namespace (via the Imports keyword) and authored the following code:

```
Catch ex As CarIsDeadException
  ' Attempt to open a file named carErrors.txt on the C drive.
  Dim fs As FileStream = File.Open("C:\carErrors.txt", FileMode.Open)
...
End Try
```

Now, if the specified file is not located on your C drive, the call to File.Open() results in a FileNotFoundException! Later in this text, you will learn all about the System.IO namespace where you will discover how to programmatically determine whether a file exists on the hard drive before attempting to open the file in the first place (thereby avoiding the exception altogether). However, to keep focused on the topic of exceptions, assume the exception has been raised.

When you encounter an exception while processing another exception, best practice states that you should record the new exception object as an "inner exception" within a new object of the same type as the initial exception (that was a mouthful). The reason we need to allocate a new object of the exception being handled is that the only way to document an inner exception is via a constructor parameter. Consider the following code:

```
Module Program
  Sub Main()
...
    Try
      For i As Integer = 0 To 10
        myCar.Accelerate(10)
      Next
    Catch ex As ArgumentOutOfRangeException
      ' process any bad arguments here.
    Catch ex As CarIsDeadException
      Try
        ' Attempt to open a file named carErrors.txt on the C drive.
        Dim fs As FileStream = File.Open("C:\carErrors.txt", FileMode.Open)
      Catch ex2 As Exception
        ' Throw a exception that records the new exception,
        ' as well as the message of the first exception.
        Throw New CarIsDeadException(ex.Message, ex2)
      End Try
...
    Catch ex As Exception
      ' Try to catch all other exceptions here? OK!
    End Try
...
  End Sub
End Module
```

Notice in this case, we have passed in the FileNotFoundException object as the second parameter to the CarIsDeadException constructor. Once we have configured this new object, we throw it up the call stack to the next caller, which in this case would be the Main() method.

Given that there is no "next caller" beyond the CLR after Main() to catch the exception, we would be again presented with an error dialog box. Much like the act of rethrowing an exception, recording inner exceptions is usually only useful when the caller has the ability to gracefully catch the exception in the first place. If this is the case, the caller's catch logic can make use of the InnerException property to extract the details of the inner exception object.

The Finally Block

A Try/Catch scope may also define an optional Finally block. The motivation behind a Finally block is to ensure that a set of code statements will *always* execute, exception (of any type) or not. To illustrate, assume you wish to always power down the car's radio before exiting Main(), regardless of any handled exception:

```
Module Program
  Sub Main()
    Console.WriteLine("***** Creating a car and stepping on it *****")
    Dim myCar As Car = New Car("Zippy", 20)
    myCar.CrankTunes(True)

    Try
      ' Speed up logic
    Catch ex As ArgumentOutOfRangeException
      ' Process arg out of range.
    Catch ex As CarIsDeadException
      ' Process car is dead.
    Catch ex As Exception
      ' Try to catch all other exceptions here.
    Finally
      ' This will always execute, error or not.
      myCar.CrankTunes(False)
    End Try
    ' The error has been handled, processing continues with the next statement.
    Console.WriteLine("***** Out of exception logic *****")
    Console.ReadLine()
  End Sub
End Module
```

If you did not include a Finally block, the radio would not be turned off if an exception is encountered (which may or may not be problematic). In a more real-world scenario, when you need to dispose of objects, close a file, detach from a database (or whatever), a Finally block ensures a location for proper cleanup.

Who Is Throwing What?

Given that a method in the .NET Framework could throw any number of exceptions (under various circumstances), a logical question would be "How do I know which exceptions may be thrown by a given base class library method?" The ultimate answer is simple: consult the .NET Framework 2.0 SDK documentation. Each method in the help system documents the exceptions a given member may throw.

For example, if you wish to see the exceptions the `Console.ReadLine()` method could throw, click the `ReadLine()` method and press the F1 key. This will open up the correct help page for the method in question. From here, simply consult the Exceptions table (see Figure 7-5).

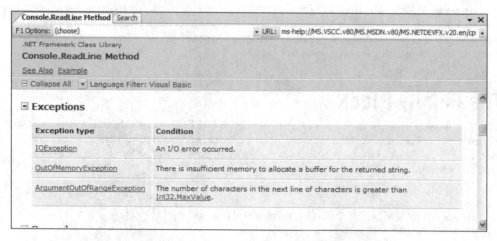

Figure 7-5. *Identifying the exceptions thrown from a given method*

Do understand that if a given member throws multiple exceptions, you are not literally required to catch each object within a separate `Catch` block. In many cases, you can handle all possible errors thrown from a set scope by catching a single `System.Exception`:

```
Sub Main()
  Try
    ' This one catch will handle all exceptions
    ' thrown from the Open() method.
    File.Open("IDontExist.txt", FileMode.Open)
  Catch ex As Exception
    Console.WriteLine(ex.Message)
  End Try
End Sub
```

However, if you do wish to handle specific exceptions uniquely, just make use of multiple `Catch` blocks as shown throughout this chapter. Using this approach, you can take unique courses of action based on the type of exception object, and therefore have a finer grain of control.

The Result of Unhandled Exception

At this point, you might be wondering what would happen if you do not handle an exception thrown your direction. Assume that the logic in `Main()` increases the speed of the `Car` object beyond the maximum speed, without the benefit of `Try/Catch` logic. The result of ignoring an exception would be highly obstructive to the end user of your application, as an "unhandled exception" dialog box is displayed. On a machine where .NET debugging tools are installed, you would see something similar to Figure 7-6 (a nondevelopment machine would display a similar intrusive dialog box).

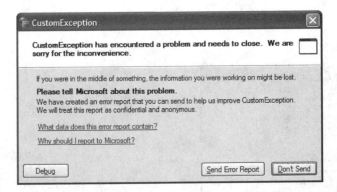

Figure 7-6. *The result of not dealing with exceptions*

Source Code The CustomException project is included under the Chapter 7 subdirectory.

Debugging Unhandled Exceptions Using Visual Studio 2005

As you would hope, Visual Studio 2005 provides a number of tools that help you debug exceptions. Again, assume you have increased the speed of a Car object beyond the maximum and are not making use of structured exception handling. If you were to start a debugging session (using the Debug ➤ Start menu selection), Visual Studio automatically breaks at the time the uncaught exception is thrown. Better yet, you are presented with a window (see Figure 7-7) displaying the value of the Message property.

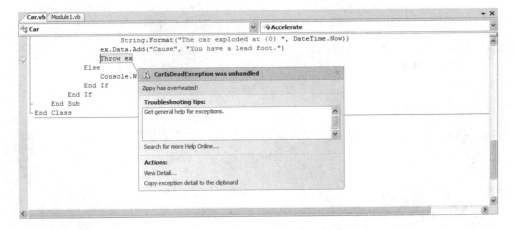

Figure 7-7. *Debugging unhandled custom exceptions with Visual Studio 2005*

If you click the View Detail link, you will find the details regarding the state of the object (see Figure 7-8).

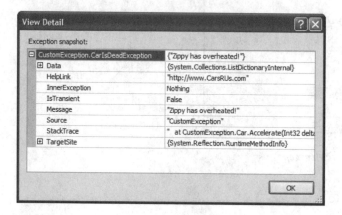

Figure 7-8. *Viewing the details of an exception with Visual Studio 2005*

■**Note** If you fail to handle an exception thrown by a method in the .NET base class libraries, the Visual Studio 2005 debugger breaks at the statement that called the offending method.

Blending VB 6.0 Error Processing and Structured Exception Handling

To wrap up this chapter, allow me to point out that the VB 6.0 error handling constructs are still supported under Visual Basic 2005. As you may know, the On Error GoTo construct allows you to define a label in the scope of a method, where control will be transferred in the event of an error. At this point, you can make use of the intrinsic Err object to scrape out select details of the problem at hand.

Since the release of the .NET platform, the VB Err object has been enhanced with a new method named GetException(), which returns a reference to the underlying System.Exception derived type. Consider the following code, which blends both approaches to handle the CarIsDeadException:

```
Module Program
  Sub Main()
    On Error GoTo OOPS

    Dim myCar As New Car("Sven", 80)
    For i As Integer = 0 To 10
      myCar.Accelerate(10)
    Next
OOPS:
    ' Use Err object.
    Console.WriteLine("=> Handling error with Err object.")
    Console.WriteLine(Err.Description)
    Console.WriteLine(Err.Source)
```

```
    ' Use Err object to get exception object.
    Console.WriteLine("=> Handling error with exception.")
    Console.WriteLine(Err.GetException().StackTrace)
    Console.WriteLine(Err.GetException().TargetSite)
  End Sub
End Module
```

Although the On Error construct is still supported, I prefer to make use of the structured exception handling techniques presented in this chapter. As you build new VB 2005 programs, it is best to regard the legacy VB 6.0 style of error handling as little more than a vehicle for backwards compatibility.

Source Code The Vb6StyleErrorHandling project is included under the Chapter 7 subdirectory.

Summary

In this chapter, you examined the role of structured exception handling. When a method needs to send an error object to the caller, it will allocate, configure, and throw a specific System.Exception derived type via the VB 2005 Throw keyword. The caller is able to handle any possible incoming exceptions using the VB 2005 Try/Catch keywords and an optional Finally scope.

When you are creating your own custom exceptions, you ultimately create a class type deriving from System.ApplicationException, which denotes an exception thrown from the currently executing application. In contrast, error objects deriving from System.SystemException represent critical (and fatal) errors thrown by the CLR.

This chapter also illustrated various tools within Visual Studio 2005 that can be used to debug exceptions as they occur. Last but not least, I pointed out that the legacy VB 6.0 style of error handling (On Error) is still supported under Visual Basic 2005 for purposes of backwards compatibility.

CHAPTER 8

■■■

Understanding Object Lifetime

At this point in the text, you learned a good deal about how to build custom class types using VB 2005. Here, you will come to understand how the CLR is managing allocated objects via *garbage collection*. VB 2005 programmers never directly deallocate a managed object from memory and, unlike classic COM, we are no longer required to interact with finicky interface reference counting logic (which occurred behind the scenes by VB 6.0). Rather, .NET objects are allocated onto a region of memory termed the *managed heap*, where they will be automatically destroyed by the garbage collector at "some time in the future."

Once you have examined the core details of the collection process, you will learn how to programmatically interact with the garbage collector using the System.GC class type. Next you examine how the virtual System.Object.Finalize() method and IDisposable interface can be used to build types that release internal *unmanaged resources* in a timely manner. By the time you have completed this chapter, you will have a solid understanding of how .NET objects are managed by the CLR.

Classes, Objects, and References

To frame the topics examined in this chapter, it is important to further clarify the distinction between classes, objects, and references. Recall that a class is nothing more than a blueprint that describes how an instance of this type will look and feel in memory. Classes, of course, are defined within a code file (which in VB 2005 takes a *.vb extension by convention). Consider a simple Car class defined within Car.vb:

```vb
' Car.vb
Public Class Car
  Private currSp As Integer
  Private petName As String

  Public Sub New()
  End Sub

  Public Sub New(ByVal name As String, ByVal speed As Integer)
    petName = name
    currSp = speed
  End Sub

  Public Overrides Function ToString() As String
    Return String.Format("{0} is going {1} MPH", petName, currSp)
  End Function
End Class
```

Once a class is defined, you can create any number of objects using the VB 2005 New keyword. Understand, however, that the New keyword returns a *reference* to the object on the heap, not the actual object itself. This reference variable is stored on the stack for further use in your application. When you wish to invoke members on the object, apply the VB 2005 dot operator on the stored reference:

```
Module Program
  Sub Main()
    ' Create a new Car object on
    ' the managed heap. We are
    ' returned a reference to this
    ' object ('refToMyCar').
    Dim refToMyCar As New Car("Zippy", 50)

    ' The VB 2005 dot operator (.) is used
    ' to invoke members on the object
    ' using our reference variable.
    Console.WriteLine(refToMyCar.ToString())
    Console.ReadLine()
  End Sub
End Module
```

Figure 8-1 illustrates the class, object, and reference relationship.

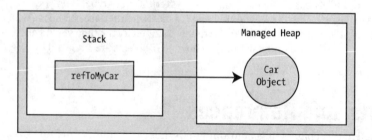

Figure 8-1. *References to objects on the managed heap*

The Basics of Object Lifetime

When you are building your VB 2005 applications, you are correct to assume that the managed heap will take care of itself without your direct intervention. In fact, the golden rule of .NET memory management is simple:

■**Rule** Allocate an object onto the managed heap using the New keyword and forget about it.

Once instantiated, the garbage collector will destroy the object when it is no longer needed. The next obvious question, of course, is, "How does the garbage collector determine when an object is no longer needed"? The short (i.e., incomplete) answer is that the garbage collector removes an object from the heap when it is *unreachable* by any part of your code base. Assume you have a method that allocates a local Car object:

```
Sub MakeACar()
  ' If myCar is the only reference to the Car object,
  ' it may be destroyed when the method returns.
  Dim myCar As New Car()
End Sub
```

Notice that the Car reference (myCar) has been created directly within the MakeACar() method and has not been passed outside of the defining scope. Thus, once this method call completes, the myCar reference is no longer reachable, and the associated Car object is now a *candidate* for garbage collection. Understand, however, that you cannot guarantee that this object will be reclaimed from memory immediately after MakeACar() has completed. All you can assume at this point is that when the CLR performs the next garbage collection, the myCar object could be safely destroyed.

As you will most certainly discover, programming in a garbage-collected environment will greatly simplify your application development. By allowing the garbage collector to be in charge of destroying objects, the burden of memory management has been taken from your shoulders and placed onto those of the CLR.

■**Note** If you happen to have a background in COM development, do know that .NET objects do not maintain an internal reference counter, and therefore managed objects do not expose methods such as AddRef() or Release().

The CIL of New

Before we examine the exact rules that determine when an object is removed from the managed heap, let's check out the role of the New keyword a bit more closely. First, understand that the managed heap is more than just a random chunk of memory accessed by the CLR. The .NET garbage collector is quite a tidy housekeeper of the heap, given that it will compact empty blocks of memory (when necessary) to optimize the process of locating allocated objects. To aid in this endeavor, the managed heap maintains a pointer (commonly referred to as the *next object pointer* or *new object pointer*) that identifies exactly where the next object will be located.

To better understand the dirty details of exactly how objects are allocated on the heap requires us to examine a bit of CIL code. When the VB 2005 compiler encounters the New keyword, it will emit a CIL newobj instruction into the method implementation. If you were to compile the current example code and investigate the resulting assembly using ildasm.exe, (see Chapter 1), you would find the following CIL statements within the MakeACar() method:

```
.method public static void MakeACar() cil managed
{
  // Code size 9 (0x9)
  .maxstack  1
  .locals init ([0] class SimpleGC.Car myCar)
  IL_0000:  nop
  IL_0001:  newobj instance void SimpleGC.Car::.ctor()
  IL_0006:  stloc.0
  IL_0007:  nop
  IL_0008:  ret
} // end of method Program::MakeACar
```

The newobj instruction informs the CLR to perform the following core tasks:

- Calculate the total amount of memory required for the object to be allocated (including the necessary memory required by the type's member variables and the type's base classes).

- Examine the managed heap to ensure that there is indeed enough room to host the object to be allocated. If this is the case, the type's constructor is called, and the caller is ultimately returned a reference to the new object in memory, whose address just happens to be identical to the last position of the next object pointer.

- Finally, before returning the reference to the caller, advance the next object pointer to point to the next available slot on the managed heap.

The basic process is illustrated in Figure 8-2.

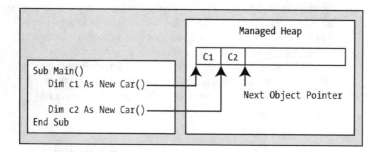

Figure 8-2. *The details of allocating objects onto the managed heap*

As you are busy allocating objects in your application, the space on the managed heap may eventually become full. When processing the newobj instruction, if the CLR determines that the managed heap does not have sufficient memory to allocate the requested type, it will perform a garbage collection in an attempt to free up memory. Thus, the next rule of garbage collection is also quite simple:

■**Rule** If the managed heap does not have sufficient memory to allocate a requested object, a garbage collection will occur.

When a collection does take place, the garbage collector temporarily suspends all active *threads* within the current process to ensure that the application does not access the heap during the collection process. We will examine the topic of threads in Chapter 16; however, for the time being, simply regard a thread as a path of execution within a running executable. Once the garbage collection cycle has completed, the suspended threads are permitted to carry on their work. Thankfully, the .NET garbage collector is highly optimized; you will seldom (if ever) notice this brief interruption in your application.

Setting Object References to Nothing

Those who have created COM objects using Visual Basic 6.0 were well aware that it was always preferable to set their references to Nothing when they were finished using them. Under the covers, the reference count of the COM object was decremented by one, and may be removed from memory if the object's reference count equaled zero.

Of course, .NET objects do *not* make use of the COM reference counting scheme. Given this fact, you might wonder what the end result is of assigning object references to Nothing under Visual Basic 2005. For example, assume the MakeACar() subroutine has now been updated as follows:

```
Sub MakeACar()
  Dim myCar As New Car()
  myCar = Nothing
End Sub
```

When you assign references to Nothing, the compiler will generate CIL code that ensures the reference (myCar in this example) no longer points to any object. If you were once again to make use of ildasm.exe to view the CIL code of the modified MakeACar(), you would find the ldnull opcode:

```
.method public static void  MakeACar() cil managed
{
  // Code size 11 (0xb)
  .maxstack  1
  .locals init ([0] class SimpleGC.Car myCar)
  IL_0000:  nop
  IL_0001:  newobj instance void SimpleGC.Car::.ctor()
  IL_0006:  stloc.0
  IL_0007:  ldnull
  IL_0008:  stloc.0
  IL_0009:  nop
  IL_000a:  ret
} // end of method Program::MakeACar
```

What you must understand, however, is that assigning a reference to Nothing does not in any way force the garbage collector to fire up at that exact moment and remove the object from the heap. The only thing you have accomplished is explicitly clipping the connection between the reference and the object it previously pointed to.

The Role of Application Roots

Now, back to the topic of how the garbage collector determines when an object is "no longer needed." To understand the details, you need to be aware of the notion of *application roots*. Simply put, a *root* is a storage location containing a reference to an object on the heap. Strictly speaking, a root can fall into any of the following categories:

- References to global objects (while not allowed in VB 2005, CIL code does permit allocation of global objects)
- References to currently used shared objects/shared fields
- References to local objects within a given method
- References to object parameters passed into a method
- References to objects waiting to be *finalized* (described later in this chapter)
- Any CPU register that references a local object

During a garbage collection process, the runtime will investigate objects on the managed heap to determine whether they are still reachable (aka *rooted*) by the application. To do so, the CLR will build an *object graph,* which represents each reachable object on the heap. Object graphs will be explained in greater detail during our discussion of object serialization (in Chapter 19). For now, just understand that object graphs are used to document all reachable objects. As well, be aware that the garbage collector will never graph the same object twice, thus avoiding the nasty circular reference count that could be found in classic COM programming.

Assume the managed heap contains a set of objects named A, B, C, D, E, F, and G. During a garbage collection, these objects (as well as any internal object references they may contain) are examined for active roots. Once the graph has been constructed, unreachable objects (which we will assume are objects C and F) are marked as garbage. Figure 8-3 diagrams a possible object graph for the scenario just described (you can read the directional arrows using the phrase *depends on* or *requires,* for example, "E depends on G and indirectly B," "A depends on nothing," and so on).

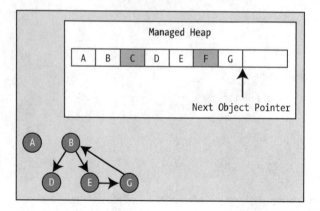

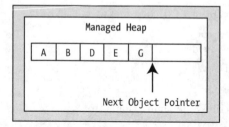

Figure 8-3. *Object graphs are constructed to determine which objects are reachable by application roots.*

Once an object has been marked for termination (C and F in this case—as they are not accounted for in the object graph), they are swept from memory. At this point, the remaining space on the heap is compacted, which in turn will cause the CLR to modify the set of active application roots to refer to the correct memory location (this is done automatically and transparently). Last but not least, the next object pointer is readjusted to point to the next available slot. Figure 8-4 illustrates the resulting readjustment.

Figure 8-4. *A clean and compacted heap*

Note Strictly speaking, the garbage collector makes use of *two* distinct heaps, one of which is specifically used to store very large objects. This heap is less frequently consulted during the collection cycle, given possible performance penalties involved with relocating large objects. Regardless of this fact, it is safe to consider the "managed heap" as a single region of memory.

Understanding Object Generations

When the CLR is attempting to locate unreachable objects, is does *not* literally examine each and every object placed on the managed heap. Obviously, doing so would involve considerable time, especially in larger (i.e., real-world) applications.

To help optimize the process, each object on the heap is assigned to a specific "generation." The idea behind generations is simple: the longer an object has existed on the heap, the more likely it is to stay there. For example, the object representing the main Form of a Windows Forms application will be in memory until the program terminates. Conversely, objects that have been recently placed on the heap are likely to be unreachable rather quickly (such as an object created within a local method scope). Given these assumptions, each object on the heap belongs to one of the following generations:

- *Generation 0*: Identifies a newly allocated object that has never been marked for collection
- *Generation 1*: Identifies an object that has survived a garbage collection (i.e., it was marked for collection, but was not removed due to the fact that the sufficient heap space was acquired)
- *Generation 2*: Identifies an object that has survived more than one sweep of the garbage collector

The garbage collector will investigate all generation 0 objects first. If marking and sweeping these objects results in the required amount of free memory, any surviving objects are promoted to generation 1. To illustrate how an object's generation affects the collection process, ponder Figure 8-5, which diagrams how a set of surviving generation 0 objects (A, B, and E) are promoted once the required memory has been reclaimed.

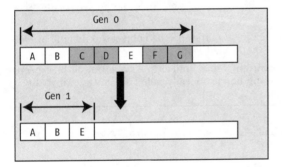

Figure 8-5. *Generation 0 objects that survive a garbage collection are promoted to generation 1.*

If all generation 0 objects have been evaluated, but additional memory is still required, generation 1 objects are then investigated for their "reachability" and collected accordingly. Surviving generation 1 objects are then promoted to generation 2. If the garbage collector *still* requires additional memory, generation 2 objects are then evaluated for their reachability. At this point, if a generation 2 object survives a garbage collection, it remains a generation 2 object given the predefined upper limit of object generations. (As of .NET 2.0, that is. Future versions of the platform may increase this upper generational limit.)

The bottom line is that by assigning a generational value to objects on the heap, newer objects (such as local variables) will be removed quickly, while older objects (such as a program's main Form) are not "bothered" as often.

The System.GC Type

The base class libraries provide a class type named System.GC that allows you to programmatically interact with the garbage collector using a set of shared members. Now, do be very aware that you will seldom (if ever) need to make use of this type directly in your code. Typically speaking, the only time you will make use of the members of System.GC is when you are creating types that make use of *unmanaged resources*. Table 8-1 provides a rundown of some of the more interesting members (consult the .NET Framework 2.0 SDK documentation for complete details).

Table 8-1. *Select Members of the* System.GC *Type*

System.GC Member	Meaning in Life
AddMemoryPressure() RemoveMemoryPressure()	Allow you to specify a numerical value that represents the calling object's "urgency level" regarding the garbage collection process. Be aware that these methods should alter pressure *in tandem* and thus never remove more pressure than the total amount you have added.
Collect()	Forces the GC to perform a garbage collection.
CollectionCount()	Returns a numerical value representing how many times a given generation has been swept.
GetGeneration()	Returns the generation to which an object currently belongs.
GetTotalMemory()	Returns the estimated amount of memory (in bytes) currently allocated on the managed heap. The Boolean parameter specifies whether the call should wait for garbage collection to occur before returning.
MaxGeneration	Returns the maximum of generations supported on the target system. Under Microsoft's .NET 2.0, there are three possible generations (0, 1, and 2).
SuppressFinalize()	Sets a flag indicating that the specified object should not have its Finalize() method called.
WaitForPendingFinalizers()	Suspends the current thread until all finalizable objects have been finalized. This method is typically called directly after invoking GC.Collect().

Ponder the following Main() method, which illustrates select members of System.GC:

```
Sub Main()
  ' Print out estimated number of bytes on heap.
  Console.WriteLine("Estimated bytes on heap: {0}", _
    GC.GetTotalMemory(False))

  ' MaxGeneration is zero based, so add 1 for display purposes.
  Console.WriteLine("This OS has {0} object generations.", _
    (GC.MaxGeneration + 1))

  Dim refToMyCar As New Car("Zippy", 100)
  Console.WriteLine(refToMyCar.ToString())

  ' Print out generation of refToMyCar object.
  Console.WriteLine("Generation of refToMyCar is: {0}", _
    GC.GetGeneration(refToMyCar))
  Console.ReadLine()
End Sub
```

Forcing a Garbage Collection

Again, the whole purpose of the .NET garbage collector is to manage memory on our behalf. However, under some very rare (and I do mean *very rare*) circumstances, it may be beneficial to programmatically force a garbage collection using GC.Collect(). Specifically:

- Your application is about to enter into a block of code that you do not wish to be interrupted by a possible garbage collection.

- Your application has just finished allocating an extremely large number of objects and you wish to clean up as much of the acquired memory as possible.

If you determine it may be beneficial to have the garbage collector check for unreachable objects, you could explicitly trigger a garbage collection, as follows:

```
Sub Main()
...
    ' Force a garbage collection and wait for
    ' each object to be finalized.
    GC.Collect()
    GC.WaitForPendingFinalizers()
...
End Sub
```

When you manually force a garbage collection, you should always make a call to GC.WaitForPendingFinalizers(). With this approach, you can rest assured that all *finalizable objects* (described in detail later in this chapter) have had a chance to perform any necessary cleanup before your program continues forward. Under the hood, GC.WaitForPendingFinalizers() will suspend the calling thread during the collection process. This is a good thing, as it ensures your code does not invoke methods on an object currently being destroyed!

The GC.Collect() method can also be supplied a numerical value that identifies the oldest generation on which a garbage collection will be performed. For example, if you wished to instruct the CLR to only investigate generation 0 objects, you would write the following:

```
Sub Main()
...
    ' Only investigate generation 0 objects.
    GC.Collect(0)
    GC.WaitForPendingFinalizers()
...
End Sub
```

Like any garbage collection, calling GC.Collect() will promote surviving generations. To illustrate, assume that our Main() method has been updated as follows:

```
Sub Main()
    Console.WriteLine("***** Fun with System.GC *****")

    ' Print out estimated number of bytes on heap.
    Console.WriteLine("Estimated bytes on heap: {0}", _
        GC.GetTotalMemory(False))

    ' MaxGeneration is zero based.
    Console.WriteLine("This OS has {0} object generations.", _
        (GC.MaxGeneration + 1))

    Dim refToMyCar As New Car("Zippy", 100)
    Console.WriteLine(refToMyCar.ToString())

    ' Print out generation of refToMyCar.
    Console.WriteLine("Generation of refToMyCar is: {0}", _
        GC.GetGeneration(refToMyCar))
```

```vb
' Make a ton of objects for testing purposes.
Dim tonsOfObjects(5000) As Object
For i As Integer = 0 To UBound(tonsOfObjects)
  tonsOfObjects(i) = New Object()
Next

' Collect only gen 0 objects.
GC.Collect(0)
GC.WaitForPendingFinalizers()

' Print out generation of refToMyCar.
Console.WriteLine("Generation of refToMyCar is: {0}", _
  GC.GetGeneration(refToMyCar))

' See if tonsOfObjects(4000) is still alive.
If (tonsOfObjects(4000) IsNot Nothing)
  Console.WriteLine("Generation of tonsOfObjects(4000) is: {0}", _
    GC.GetGeneration(tonsOfObjects(4000)))
Else
  Console.WriteLine("tonsOfObjects(4000) is no longer alive.")
End If

' Print out how many times a generation has been swept.
Console.WriteLine("Gen 0 has been swept {0} times", _
  GC.CollectionCount(0))
Console.WriteLine("Gen 1 has been swept {0} times", _
  GC.CollectionCount(1))
Console.WriteLine("Gen 2 has been swept {0} times", _
  GC.CollectionCount(2))
Console.ReadLine()
End Sub
```

Here, we have purposely created a very large array of System.Objects for testing purposes. As you can see from the output shown in Figure 8-6, even though this Main() method only made one explicit request for a garbage collection, the CLR performed a number of them in the background.

Figure 8-6. *Interacting with the CLR garbage collector via* System.GC

At this point in the chapter, I hope you feel more comfortable regarding the details of object lifetime. The remainder of this chapter examines the garbage collection process a bit further by addressing how you can build *finalizable objects* as well as *disposable objects*. Be very aware that the following techniques will only be useful if you are building managed classes that maintain internal unmanaged resources.

■**Source Code** The SimpleGC project is included under the Chapter 8 subdirectory.

Building Finalizable Objects

In Chapter 6, you learned that the supreme base class of .NET, System.Object, defines a virtual method named Finalize(). The default implementation of this method does nothing whatsoever, however do note this method has been marked as Overridable:

```
' System.Object
Class Object
...
  Protected Overridable Sub Finalize()
  End Sub
End Class
```

When you override Finalize() for your custom classes, you establish a specific location to perform any necessary cleanup logic for your type. Given that this member is defined as protected, it is not possible to directly call an object's Finalize() method. Rather, the *garbage collector* will call an object's Finalize() method (if supported) before removing the object from memory.

Of course, a call to Finalize() will (eventually) occur during a "natural" garbage collection or possibly when you programmatically force a collection via GC.Collect(). In addition, a type's finalizer method will automatically be called when the *application domain* hosting your application is unloaded from memory.

Based on your current background in .NET, you may know that application domains (or simply AppDomains) are used to host an executable assembly and any necessary external code libraries. If you are not familiar with this .NET concept, you will be by the time you've finished Chapter 15. The short answer is that when your AppDomain is unloaded from memory, the CLR automatically invokes finalizers for every finalizable object created during its lifetime.

Now, despite what your developer instincts may tell you, a *vast majority* of your VB 2005 classes will not require any explicit cleanup logic. The reason is simple: if your types are simply making use of other managed objects, everything will eventually be garbage collected. The only time you would need to design a class that can clean up after itself is when you are making use of *unmanaged resources* (such as raw OS file handles, raw unmanaged database connections, or other unmanaged resources).

As you may know, unmanaged resources are obtained by directly calling into the API of the operating system using PInvoke (platform invocation) services or due to some very elaborate COM interoperability scenarios. We will examine interoperability in Chapter 17; however, consider the next rule of garbage collection:

■**Rule** The only reason to override Finalize() is if your VB 2005 class is making use of unmanaged resources via PInvoke or complex COM interoperability tasks (typically via the System.Runtime.InteropServices.Marshal type).

■**Note** As you will see in Chapter 11, it is illegal to override Finalize() on structure types. This makes perfect sense given that structures are value types, which are never allocated on the heap to begin with, and therefore are not garbage collected!

Overriding System.Object.Finalize()

In the rare case that you do build a VB 2005 class that makes use of unmanaged resources, you will obviously wish to ensure that the underlying memory is released in a predictable manner. Assume you have created a class named `MyResourceWrapper` that makes use of an unmanaged resource (whatever that may be) and you wish to override `Finalize()`.

Perhaps because the act of overriding `Finalize()` is considered a rather rare task, the Visual Studio 2005 IDE does not display `Finalize()` as an `Overridable` method when you type the `Overrides` keyword, as you see in Figure 8-7.

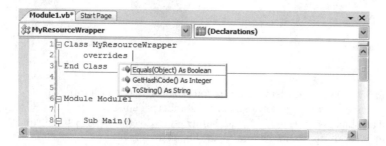

Figure 8-7. *Although not displayed, it is still legal to override* `Finalize()`*!*

Given this, you are required to manually type the definition of `Finalize()` within the code editor. Here is a custom finalizer for a class named `MyResourceWrapper` that will issue a system beep when invoked. Obviously this is only for instructional purposes. A real-world finalizer would do nothing more than free any unmanaged resources and would *not* interact with the members of other managed objects, as you cannot assume they are still alive at the point the garbage collector invokes your `Finalize()` method:

```
Class MyResourceWrapper
  ' Override System.Object.Finalize()
  Protected Overrides Sub Finalize()
    ' Clean up any unmanaged resources here!

    ' Beep when destroyed (testing purposes only!)
    Console.Beep()
  End Sub
End Class
```

While the previous implementation of `Finalize()` is syntactically correct, best practices state that a proper finalization routine should explicitly call the `Finalize()` method of its base class, to ensure that any unmanaged resources up the chain of inheritance are cleaned up as well. Furthermore, to make a `Finalize()` method as robust as possible, you should wrap your code statements within a `Try/Finally` construct. Given these notes, here is a prim-and-proper `Finalize()` method:

```
Class MyResourceWrapper
  ' Override System.Object.Finalize()
  Protected Overrides Sub Finalize()
    Try
      ' Clean up any unmanaged resources here!

      ' Beep when destroyed (testing purposes only!)
      Console.Beep()
```

```
    Finally
      MyBase.Finalize()
    End Try
  End Sub
End Class
```

If you were to now test the MyResourceWrapper type, you would find that a system beep occurs when the application terminates, given that the CLR will automatically invoke finalizers upon AppDomain shutdown:

```
Sub Main()
  Console.WriteLine("***** Fun with Finalizers *****")
  Console.WriteLine("Hit the return key to shut down this app")
  Console.WriteLine("and force the GC to invoke Finalize()")
  Console.WriteLine("for finalizable objects created in this AppDomain.")
  Console.ReadLine()
  Dim rw As New MyResourceWrapper()
End Sub
```

■**Source Code** The SimpleFinalize project is included under the Chapter 8 subdirectory.

Detailing the Finalization Process

Not to beat a dead horse, but always remember that the role of the Finalize() method is to ensure that a .NET object can clean up *unmanaged resources* when garbage collected. Thus, if you are building a type that does not make use of unmanaged entities (by far the most common case), finalization is of little use. In fact, if at all possible, you should design your types to avoid supporting a Finalize() method for the very simple reason that *finalization takes time.*

When you allocate an object onto the managed heap, the runtime automatically determines whether your object supports a custom Finalize() method. If so, the object is marked as *finalizable*, and a pointer to this object is stored on an internal queue named the *finalization queue.* The finalization queue is a table maintained by the garbage collector that points to each and every object that must be finalized before it is removed from the heap.

When the garbage collector determines it is time to free an object from memory, it examines each entry on the finalization queue, and copies the object off the heap to yet another managed structure termed the *finalization reachable* table (often abbreviated as freachable, and pronounced "eff-reachable"). At this point, a separate thread is spawned to invoke the Finalize() method for each object on the freachable table *at the next garbage collection.* Given this, it will take at the very least *two* garbage collections to truly finalize an object.

The bottom line is that while finalization of an object does ensure an object can clean up unmanaged resources, it is still nondeterministic in nature, and due to the extra behind-the-curtains processing, considerably slower.

Building Disposable Objects

Given that so many unmanaged resources are "precious items" that should be cleaned up ASAP, allow me to introduce you to another possible technique used to handle an object's cleanup. As an alternative to overriding Finalize(), your class could implement the IDisposable interface, which defines a single method named Dispose():

```
Public Interface IDisposable
  Sub Dispose()
End Interface
```

If you are new to interface-based programming, Chapter 9 will take you through the details. In a nutshell, an interface is a collection of abstract members a class or structure may support. When you do support the IDisposable interface, the assumption is that when the *object user* is finished using the object, it manually calls Dispose() before allowing the object reference to drop out of scope. In this way, your objects can perform any necessary cleanup of unmanaged resources without incurring the hit of being placed on the finalization queue and without waiting for the garbage collector to trigger the class's finalization logic.

■**Note** Structures and class types can both implement IDisposable (unlike overriding Finalize(), which is reserved for class types), as the object user (not the garbage collector) invokes the Dispose() method.

Here is an updated MyResourceWrapper class that now implements IDisposable, rather than overriding System.Object.Finalize():

```
' Implementing IDisposable.
Class MyResourceWrapper
  Implements IDisposable

  ' The object user should call this method
  ' when they finished with the object.
  Public Sub Dispose() Implements IDisposable.Dispose
    ' Clean up unmanaged resources here.
    ' Dispose other contained disposable objects.
    End Sub
End Class
```

■**Note** Visual Studio 2005 will autocomplete interface implementation as soon as you hit the Enter key. In fact, when implementing IDisposable, the IDE injects a good deal of code statements, which will become more understandable once you complete this chapter.

Notice that a Dispose() method is not only responsible for releasing the type's unmanaged resources, but should also call Dispose() on any other contained disposable methods. Unlike Finalize(), it is perfectly safe to communicate with other managed objects within a Dispose() method. The reason is simple: the garbage collector has no clue about the IDisposable interface and will never call Dispose(). Therefore, when the object user calls this method, the object is still living a productive life on the managed heap and has access to all other heap-allocated objects. The calling logic is straightforward:

```
Sub Main
  Dim rw As New MyResourceWrapper()
  rw.Dispose()
  Console.ReadLine()
End Sub
```

Of course, before you attempt to call Dispose() on an object, you will want to ensure the type supports the IDisposable interface. While you will typically know which objects implement IDisposable by consulting the .NET Framework 2.0 SDK documentation, a programmatic check can be accomplished using the TypeOf/Is syntax discussed in Chapter 6:

```
Sub Main()
  Dim rw As New MyResourceWrapper()
  If (TypeOf rw Is IDisposable) Then
```

```
      rw.Dispose()
    End If
    Console.ReadLine()
End Sub
```

This example exposes yet another rule of working with .NET memory management:

■**Rule** Always call Dispose() on any object you directly create if the object implements IDisposable. The assumption you should make is that if the class designer chose to support the Dispose() method, the type has some cleanup to perform.

The VB 2005 Using Keyword

When you are handling a managed object that implements IDisposable, it will be quite common to make use of structured exception handling (see Chapter 7) to ensure the type's Dispose() method is called in the event of a runtime exception:

```
Module Program
  Sub Main()
    Dim rw As New MyResourceWrapper()
    Try
      ' Call members of rw.
    Finally
      rw.Dispose()
    End Try
      Console.ReadLine()
  End Sub
End Module
```

While this is a fine example of defensive programming, the truth of the matter is that few developers are thrilled by the prospects of wrapping each and every disposable type within a Try/Catch/Finally block just to ensure the Dispose() method is called. To achieve the same result in a much less obtrusive manner, VB 2005 supports a special bit of syntax that looks like this:

```
Module Program
  Sub Main()
    Using rw As New MyResourceWrapper()
      ' Use the object, Dispose() automatically called!
    End Using

    Console.ReadLine()
  End Sub
End Module
```

Notice that the Using keyword (which is new as of .NET 2.0) allows you to establish a scope within a given method. Within this scope, you are free to call any methods of the type, and once the scope has ended, the type's Dispose() method is called *automatically*. As you might agree, this can certainly simplify your coding efforts. Also be aware that a single scope defined with the Using keyword can define multiple objects, each of which is denoted using a comma-delimited list. For example:

```
Module Program
  Sub Main()
    Using rw As New MyResourceWrapper(), _
        rw2 As New MyResourceWrapper(), _
        myCar As New Car()
      ' Use the objects, Dispose() automatically called!
```

```
      End Using
   Console.ReadLine()
   End Sub
End Module
```

■ Note If you attempt to "use" an object that does not implement IDisposable, you will receive a compiler error.

Even better, if you were to look at the CIL code behind this Main() method using ildasm.exe, you will find the Using construct informs the compiler to wrap your code within Try/Finally logic, with the expected call to Dispose() in the Finally scope. In this light, the new VB 2005 Using keyword is simply a shortcut for wrapping disposable objects within exception handling logic.

■ Source Code The SimpleDispose project is included under the Chapter 8 subdirectory.

Building Finalizable and Disposable Types

At this point, we have seen two different approaches to construct a class that cleans up internal unmanaged resources. On the one hand, we could override System.Object.Finalize(). Using this technique, we have the peace of mind that comes with knowing the object cleans itself up when garbage collected (whenever that may be) without the need for user interaction. On the other hand, we could implement IDisposable to provide a way for the object user to clean up the object as soon as it is finished. However, if the caller forgets to call Dispose(), the unmanaged resources may be held in memory indefinitely.

As you might suspect, it is possible to blend both techniques into a single class definition. By doing so, you gain the best of both models. If the object user *does* remember to call Dispose(), you can inform the garbage collector to bypass the finalization process by calling GC.SuppressFinalize(). If the object user *forgets* to call Dispose(), the object will eventually be finalized. The good news is that the object's internal unmanaged resources will be freed one way or another in the most optimal manner. Here is the next iteration of MyResourceWrapper, which is now finalizable and disposable:

```
' A sophisticated resource wrapper.
Class MyResourceWrapper
   Implements IDisposable

   ' The object user should call this method
   ' when they finished with the object.
   Public Sub Dispose() Implements IDisposable.Dispose
      ' Clean up unmanaged resources here.
      ' Dispose other contained disposable objects.

      ' No need to finalize if user called Dispose(),
      ' so suppress finalization.
      GC.SuppressFinalize(Me)
   End Sub

   ' The garbage collector will call this method if the
   ' object user forgets to call Dispose().
   Protected Overrides Sub Finalize()
      Try
         ' Clean up any internal unmanaged resources.
         ' Do **not** call Dispose() on any managed objects.
```

```
    Finally
        MyBase.Finalize()
    End Try
  End Sub
End Class
```

Notice that this `Dispose()` method has been updated to call `GC.SuppressFinalize()`, which informs the CLR that it is no longer necessary to call the destructor when this object is garbage collected, given that the unmanaged resources have already been freed via the `Dispose()` logic.

A Formalized Disposal Pattern

The current implementation of `MyResourceWrapper` does work fairly well; however, we are left with a few minor drawbacks. First, the `Finalize()` and `Dispose()` method each have to clean up the same unmanaged resources. This of course results in duplicate code, which can easily become a nightmare to maintain. Ideally, you would define a private helper function that is called by either method. Next, you would like to make sure that the `Finalize()` method does not attempt to dispose of any managed objects, while the `Dispose()` method should do so. Finally, you would also like to make sure that the object user can safely call `Dispose()` multiple times without error. Currently our `Dispose()` method has no such safeguards.

To address these design issues, Microsoft has defined a formal, prim-and-proper disposal pattern that strikes a balance between robustness, maintainability, and performance. Here is the final (and annotated) version of `MyResourceWrapper`, which makes use of this official pattern (and is very similar to the autogenerated code injected by the IDE when implementing the `IDisposable` interface using Visual Studio 2005):

```
Public Class MyResourceWrapper
  Implements IDisposable

  ' Used to determine if Dispose()
  ' has already been called.
  Private disposed As Boolean = False

  Public Sub Dispose() Implements IDisposable.Dispose
    ' Call our helper method.
    ' Specifying True signifies that
    ' the object user triggered the clean up.
    CleanUp(True)
    GC.SuppressFinalize(Me)
  End Sub

  Private Sub CleanUp(ByVal disposing As Boolean)
    ' Be sure we have not already been disposed!
    If Not Me.disposed Then
      If disposing Then
        ' Dispose managed resources.
      End If
      ' Clean up unmanaged resources here.
    End If
    disposed = True
  End Sub

  Protected Overrides Sub Finalize()
    ' Call our helper method.
    ' Specifying False signifies that
    ' the GC triggered the clean up.
```

```
      CleanUp(False)
   End Sub
End Class
```

Notice that MyResourceWrapper now defines a private helper method named CleanUp(). When specifying True as an argument, we are signifying that the object user has initiated the cleanup, therefore we should clean up all managed *and* unmanaged resources. However, when the garbage collector initiates the cleanup, we specify False when calling CleanUp() to ensure that internal disposable objects are *not* disposed (as we can't assume they are still in memory!). Last but not least, our Boolean member variable (disposed) is set to true before exiting CleanUp() to ensure that Dispose() can be called numerous times without error.

■**Source Code** The FinalizableDisposableClass project is included under the Chapter 8 subdirectory.

That wraps up our investigation of how the CLR is managing your objects via garbage collection. While there are additional advanced details regarding the collection process I have not examined here (such as weak references and object resurrection), you are certainly in a perfect position for further exploration on your own terms if you so choose.

Summary

The point of this chapter was to demystify the garbage collection process. As you have seen, the garbage collector will only run when it is unable to acquire the necessary memory from the managed heap (or when a given AppDomain unloads from memory). When a collection does occur, you can rest assured that Microsoft's collection algorithm has been optimized by the use of object generations, secondary threads for the purpose of object finalization, and a managed heap dedicated to host large objects.

This chapter also illustrated how to programmatically interact with the garbage collector using the System.GC class type. As mentioned, the only time when you will really need to do so is when you are building finalizable or disposable class types. Recall that finalizable types are classes that have overridden the virtual System.Object.Finalize() method to clean up unmanaged resources (at some time in the future). Disposable objects, on the other hand, are classes (or structures) that implement the IDisposable interface. Using this technique, you expose a public method to the object user that can be called to perform internal cleanup ASAP. Finally, you learned about an official "disposal" pattern that blends both approaches.

PART 4

■■■

Advanced Object-Oriented Programming Techniques

■ ■ ■

## CHAPTER 9

Working with Interfaces and Collections

This chapter builds on your current understanding of object-oriented development by examining the topic of interface-based programming. Here you learn how to use VB 2005 to define and implement interfaces, and come to understand the benefits of building types that support "multiple behaviors."

Once you understand how to build and implement custom interfaces, the remainder of this chapter is spent examining a number of interfaces defined within the .NET base class libraries. As you will see, your custom types are free to implement these predefined interfaces to support a number of advanced behaviors such as object cloning, object enumeration, and object sorting.

To showcase how interfaces are leveraged in the .NET base class libraries, this chapter will also examine numerous predefined interfaces implemented by various collection classes (ArrayList, Stack, etc.) defined by the System.Collections namespace. The information presented here will equip you to understand the topic of Chapter 12: generics and the System.Collections.Generic namespace.

Understanding Interface Types

To begin this chapter, allow me to provide a formal definition of the "interface type." An *interface* is nothing more than a named set of *abstract members*. Recall from Chapter 6 that abstract methods (defined using the VB 2005 MustOverride keyword) are pure protocol, in that they do not provide a default implementation. The specific members defined by an interface depend on the exact *behavior* it is modeling. Yes, it's true. An interface expresses a *behavior* that a given class or structure may choose to implement.

As you might guess, the .NET base class libraries ship with hundreds of predefined interface types that are implemented by various classes and structures. For example, as you will see in Chapter 24, ADO.NET ships with multiple data providers that allow you to communicate with a particular database management system. Thus, unlike COM-based ADO, under ADO.NET we have numerous connection objects we may choose between (SqlConnection, OracleConnection, OdbcConnection, etc.).

Regardless of the fact that each connection object has a unique name, are defined within different namespaces, and (in some cases) are bundled within different assemblies, they all implement a common interface named IDbConnection:

```
' The IDbConnection interface defines a common
' set of members supported by all connection objects.
Public Interface IDbConnection
  Implements IDisposable
```

```
' Methods
Function BeginTransaction() As IDbTransaction
Function BeginTransaction(ByVal il As IsolationLevel) As IDbTransaction
Sub ChangeDatabase(ByVal databaseName As String)
Sub Close()
Function CreateCommand() As IDbCommand
Sub Open()

' Properties
Property ConnectionString As String
ReadOnly Property ConnectionTimeout As Integer
ReadOnly Property Database As String
ReadOnly Property State As ConnectionState
End Interface
```

■**Note** By convention, .NET interface types are prefixed with a capital letter "I." When you are creating your own custom interfaces, it is considered a best practice to do the same.

Don't sweat the details of what these members actually do at this point. Simply understand that the IDbConnection interface defines a set of members that are common to all ADO.NET connection objects. Given this, you are guaranteed that each and every connection object supports members such as Open(), Close(), CreateCommand(), and so forth.

Another example: the System.Windows.Forms namespace defines a class named Control, which is a base class to a number of UI widgets (DataGrid, Label, StatusBar, TreeView, etc.). The Control class implements an interface named IDropTarget, which defines drag-and-drop functionality:

```
Public Interface IDropTarget
  ' Methods
  Sub OnDragDrop(ByVal e As DragEventArgs)
  Sub OnDragEnter(ByVal e As DragEventArgs)
  Sub OnDragLeave(ByVal e As EventArgs)
  Sub OnDragOver(ByVal e As DragEventArgs)
End Interface
```

Based on this interface, we can now correctly assume that any class that extends System.Windows.Forms.Control supports four subroutines named OnDragDrop(), OnDragEnter(), OnDragLeave(), and OnDragOver().

As we work through the remainder of this text, you will be exposed to dozens of interfaces that ship with the .NET base class libraries. As well, you will discover that you are free to implement these standard interfaces on your own custom classes and structures to define types that integrate tightly within the framework.

Contrasting Interface Types to Abstract Base Classes

Given your work in Chapter 6, the interface type may seem functionally equivalent to abstract base classes. Recall that when a class is marked as abstract (via the MustInherit keyword), it *may* define any number of abstract members to define a polymorphic interface to all derived types. However, when a class type does define a set of abstract members, it is also free to define any number of constructors, field data, nonabstract members (with implementation), and so on.

The polymorphic interface established by a parent class suffers from one major limitation in that only *derived types* are forced to support a set of members. However, in larger systems, it is very common to develop multiple class hierarchies that have no common parent beyond System.Object. Given that abstract members in an abstract base class *only* apply to derived types, we have no way to configure types in different hierarchies to support the same polymorphic interface.

As you would guess, interface types come to the rescue. When you define an interface, they can be implemented by any type, in any hierarchy, within any namespaces. Given this, interfaces are *highly* polymorphic. By way of a simple example, consider a standard .NET interface named ICloneable. This interface defines a single method named Clone():

```
Public Interface ICloneable
  Function Clone() As Object
End Interface
```

If you were to examine the .NET Framework 2.0 SDK documentation, you would find that a large number of seemingly unrelated types (System.Array, System.Data.SqlClient.SqlConnection, System.OperatingSystem, System.String, etc.) all implement this interface type. Although these types have no common parent (other than System.Object), we can treat them polymorphically via the ICloneable interface type.

Another limitation of traditional abstract base classes is that *each and every derived type* must contend with the set of abstract members and provide an implementation. In fact, the only way that a type can "ignore" abstract members is if the derived class is also defined as abstract (aka MustInherit). To see the problem, recall the shapes hierarchy we defined in Chapter 6. Assume we wish to define an abstract method in the Shape base class named GetNumberOfPoints(), which allows the derived type to return the number of points required to render the shape:

```
Public MustInherit Class Shape
...
  Public MustOverride Function GetNumberOfPoints() As Byte
End Class
```

Clearly, the only type that has any points in the first place is Hexagon. However, with this update, *every* derived type (Circle, Hexagon, and ThreeDCircle) must now provide a concrete implementation of this function even if it makes no sense to do so.

Again, the interface type provides a solution. If we were to define an interface that represents the behavior of "having points," we could simply plug it into the Hexagon type, leaving Circle and ThreeDCircle untouched.

Defining Custom Interfaces

Now that you better understand the overall role of interface types, let's see an example of defining custom interfaces. To begin, create a brand new console application named CustomInterface. Using the Project ➤ Add Existing Item menu option, insert the MyShapes.vb file you created back in Chapter 6 during the Shapes example. Finally, insert a new interface into your project named IPointy using the Project ➤ Add New Item menu option, as shown in Figure 9-1.

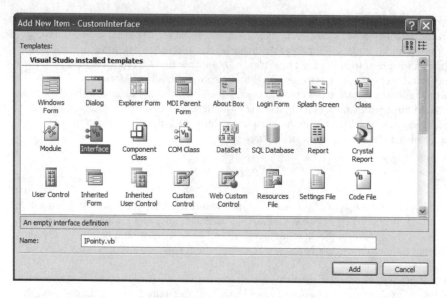

Figure 9-1. *Interfaces, like classes, can be defined in any* *.vb *file.*

An interface is defined using the VB 2005 Interface keyword. Unlike .NET class types, interfaces never specify a base class (not even System.Object) and contain members that are always implicitly Public and abstract (MustOverride). Our custom IPointy interface will model the behavior of "having points." Therefore, we could define a single function as follows:

```
' This interface defines the behavior of "having points."
Public Interface IPointy
  ' Implicitly public and abstract.
  Function GetNumberOfPoints() As Byte
End Interface
```

Notice that when you define a function or subroutine within an interface, you do *not* close the member with the expected End Sub/End Function syntax. Interfaces are pure protocol, and therefore never define an implementation (that is up to the supporting class or structure). Therefore, the following version of IPointy would result in compiler errors:

```
' Ack!  Compiler errors abound!
Public Interface IPointy
  ' Error!  Interfaces can't define field data!
  Public myInt as Integer
  ' Error!  Interfaces can't provide implementation!
  Function GetNumberOfPoints() As Byte
    Return 0
  End Function
End Interface
```

.NET interface types are also able to define any number of properties. For example, you could define the IPointy interface to use a read-only property rather than a function:

```
' The pointy behavior as a read-only property.
Public Interface IPointy
  ReadOnly Property Points() As Byte
End Point
```

Interface types are quite useless on their own, as they are nothing more than a named collection of abstract members. Given this, you cannot allocate interface types as you would a class or structure:

```
Module Program
  Sub Main()
    ' It is a compiler error to directly create
    ' interface types!
    Dim i As New IPointy
  End Sub
End Module
```

Interfaces do not bring much to the table until they are implemented by a class or structure. As you might already suspect, the IPointy behavior might be useful in the shapes hierarchy developed in Chapter 6. The idea is simple: some classes in the shapes hierarchy have points (such as the Hexagon), while others (such as the Circle and ThreeDCircle) do not.

Implementing an Interface

When a class (or structure) chooses to extend its functionality by supporting interface types, it does so using the Implements keyword. To illustrate, insert a brand new class into your project named Triangle that extends the abstract Shape base class and implements the IPointy interface. If you are using Visual Studio 2005 or Visual Basic 2005 Express, you will find that the integrated IntelliSense will automatically define skeleton code for each member defined by the interface (as well as any MustOverride methods in the parent class) as soon as you press the Enter key. Given this, our Triangle initially appears like so:

```
Public Class Triangle
  Inherits Shape
  Implements IPointy

  Public Overrides Sub Draw()
  End Sub

  Public ReadOnly Property Points() As Byte Implements IPointy.Points
    Get
    End Get
  End Property
End Class
```

Notice that the Implements keyword is used *twice*. First, the class definition is updated to list each interface supported by the type. Second, the Implements keyword is used to "attach" the interface member to a member on the class itself. At first glance, this can appear to be quite redundant; however, as you will see later in this chapter, this approach can be quite helpful when you need to resolve name clashes that can occur when a type implements multiple interfaces.

Recall that when a class or structure supports an interface, it is now under obligation to provide a fitting implementation for each member. Given that the IPointy interface defines a single read-only property, this is not too much of a burden. However, if you are implementing an interface that defines ten members, the type is now responsible for fleshing out the details of the ten abstract entities.

To complete the Triangle class, we will simply return the correct number of points (3), provide a fitting implementation of the abstract Draw() method defined by the Shape parent class, and define a set of constructors:

```
Public Class Triangle
  Inherits Shape
  Implements IPointy
```

```
    Public Sub New()
    End Sub
    Public Sub New(ByVal name As String)
      MyBase.New(name)
    End Sub

    Public Overrides Sub Draw()
      Console.WriteLine("Drawing {0} the Triangle", shapeName)
    End Sub

    Public ReadOnly Property Points() As Byte Implements IPointy.Points
      Get
        Return 3
      End Get
    End Property
End Class
```

Updating the Hexagon Class

Given that the Hexagon class also has some number of points, let's update the class definition to now support the IPointy interface as well. This time, our read-only Points property returns the expected value of 6.

```
' The Hexagon now supports the IPointy interface
Public Class Hexagon
  Inherits Shape
  Implements IPointy
...
  Public ReadOnly Property Points() As Byte Implements IPointy.Points
    Get
      Return 6
    End Get
  End Property
End Class
```

Each class now returns its number of points to the caller when asked to do so. To sum up the story so far, the Visual Studio 2005 class diagram shown in Figure 9-2 illustrates IPointy-compatible classes using the popular "lollipop" notation.

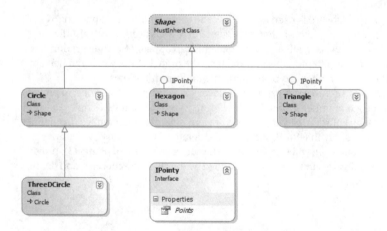

Figure 9-2. *The shapes hierarchy, now with interfaces*

Again notice that Circle and ThreeDCircle do not support the IPointy interface, and therefore do not have a Points property. In contrast, if we defined Points as an abstract member in the Shapes base class, we would be forced to do so (which, again, really makes no sense for these classes).

Types Supporting Multiple Interfaces

As far as the .NET platform is concerned, a class can only have one direct base class. However, a class or structure can implement any number of interfaces, each of which defines some number of members that models a particular behavior. When you wish to show support for numerous interfaces on a single type, you may either list each interface using a comma-delimited list or specify each interface with a discrete Implements statement.

We have no need to do so at this point; however, if we did wish to update the Hexagon to support System.ICloneable as well as IPointy, either of the following class definitions would do:

```
' Multiple interfaces via a comma-delimited list.
Public Class Hexagon
   Inherits Shape
   Implements IPointy, ICloneable
...
End Class
```

or

```
' Multiple interfaces via multiple Implements statements
Public Class Hexagon
   Inherits Shape
   Implements IPointy
   Implements ICloneable
...
End Class
```

As you can see, interface types are quite helpful given that VB 2005 (and .NET-aware languages in general) only support single inheritance; the interface-based protocol allows a given type to support numerous behaviors, while avoiding the issues that arise when deriving from extending multiple-base classes.

Interacting with Types Supporting Interfaces

Now that you have a set of types that support the IPointy interface, the next question is how you interact with the new functionality. The most straightforward way to interact with functionality supplied by a given interface is to invoke the members directly from the object level:

```
Module Program
   Sub Main()
      Console.WriteLine("***** Fun with Interfaces *****")
      Dim hex As New Hexagon()
      Console.WriteLine("Number of Points: {0}", hex.Points)
      Console.ReadLine()
   End Sub
End Module
```

This approach works fine in this particular case, given that you are well aware that the Hexagon type has implemented the interface in question. In fact, if you attempted to invoke the Points property on a type that did not implement IPointy, you will receive a compile-time error:

```
Module Program
  Sub Main()
...
    ' Compiler error!  Circle does not implement IPointy!
    Dim c As New Circle()
    Console.WriteLine("Number of Points: {0}", c.Points)
    Console.ReadLine()
  End Sub
End Module
```

Other times, however, you will not be able to determine at compile time which interfaces are supported by a given type. For example, assume you have an array containing 50 Shape-compatible types, only some of which support IPointy. Obviously, if you attempt to invoke the Points property on a type that has not implemented IPointy, you receive a runtime error. This brings up a very important question: how can we determine at runtime which interfaces are supported by a given type?

Obtaining Interface References Using CType()

The first way you can determine at runtime whether a type supports a specific interface is to perform an explicit cast via CType(). If the type does not support the requested interface, you receive an InvalidCastException. On the other hand, if the type does support the interface, you are returned a reference to the implemented interface. Using this variable, you are able to call any member defined by the interface itself. Because explicit casting is not evaluated until runtime, you will most certainly want to make use of structured exception handling to account for the possibility of an invalid cast:

```
Module Program
  Sub Main()
...
  ' Circle does not support IPointy!
  Dim c As New Circle()
  Dim itfPointy As IPointy

  ' Try to get IPointy from Circle.
  Try
    itfPointy = CType(c, IPointy)
    Console.WriteLine("Number of Points: {0}", itfPointy.Points)
  Catch ex As Exception
    Console.WriteLine("{0} does not implement IPointy!", c)
  End Try
    Console.ReadLine()
  End Sub
End Module
```

Although we could make use of Try/Catch logic to determine whether a given type supports an interface, it would be ideal to determine which interfaces are supported before invoking the interface members prior to casting in the first place. If we were able to do so, we would have no need to account for a possible InvalidCastException object being thrown at runtime when performing the explicit cast.

Obtaining Interface References Using TypeOf/Is

A more type-safe manner to determine whether a given type supports an interface is to make use of the TypeOf/Is construct, which was first introduced in Chapter 6. Recall that this construct can be used to test whether a given object derives from a particular base class. This same syntax can be used to determine whether a type implements a given interface. If the variable in question is not compatible with the specified interface, you are returned the value False. Consider the following runtime tests:

```
Module Program
  Sub Main()
    Console.WriteLine("***** Fun with Interfaces *****")
    Dim hex As New Hexagon()
    Dim c As New Circle()
...
    ' See which objects support IPointy.
    Console.WriteLine("Circle implements IPointy?: {0}", TypeOf c Is IPointy)
    Console.WriteLine("Hexagon implements IPointy?: {0}", TypeOf hex Is IPointy)
    Console.ReadLine()
  End Sub
End Module
```

Now assume we have defined an array of Shape-compatible types, only some of which implement IPointy. Notice how simple it is to dynamically determine which members of the array support IPointy. If the type is compatible with the interface in question, you can safely call the members without needing to make use of Try/Catch logic, given that you would never fall into the scope of the If block when the evaluation returns False:

```
Module Program
  Sub Main()
...
    ' Make an array of Shape-compatible types.
    Dim myShapes() As Shape = {New Hexagon("Fred"), New Circle("Angie"), _
      New ThreeDCircle(), New Triangle("Adam")}

    ' Now figure out which ones support IPointy.
    For Each s As Shape In myShapes
      If TypeOf s Is IPointy Then
        itfPointy = CType(s, IPointy)
        Console.WriteLine("{0} has {1} points.", _
          s.PetName, itfPointy.Points)
      Else
        Console.WriteLine("{0} does not implement IPointy!", s)
      End If
    Next
    Console.ReadLine()
  End Sub
End Module
```

The output can be seen in Figure 9-3.

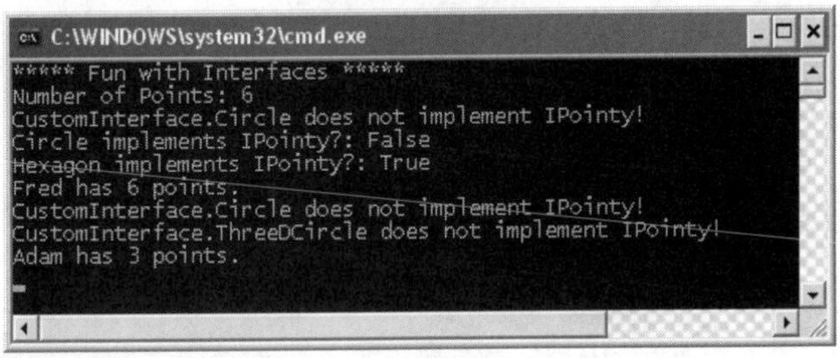

Figure 9-3. *Who supports* IPointy?

Interfaces As Member Parameters

Given that interfaces are valid .NET types, you may construct methods that take interfaces as parameters. To illustrate, assume you have defined another interface named IDraw3D that supports a single subroutine named Draw3D():

```
' Models the ability to render a type in stunning 3D.
Public Interface IDraw3D
   Sub Draw3D()
End Interface
```

Next, assume that two of your shapes (Circle and Hexagon) have been configured to support this new behavior:

```
' Circle supports IDraw3D.
Public Class Circle
   Inherits Shape
   Implements IDraw3D
...
   Public Sub Draw3D() Implements IDraw3D.Draw3D
      Console.WriteLine("Drawing circle in 3D!")
   End Sub
End Class
```

```
' Hexagon supports IPointy and IDraw3D.
Public Class Hexagon
   Inherits Shape
   Implements IPointy, IDraw3D
...
   Public Sub Draw3D() Implements IDraw3D.Draw3D
      Console.WriteLine("Drawing Hexagon in 3D!")
   End Sub
End Class
```

Figure 9-4 presents the updated Visual Studio 2005 class diagram.

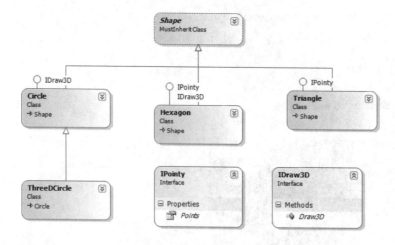

Figure 9-4. *The updated shapes hierarchy*

If you now define a new method within your module taking an IDraw3D interface as a parameter, you are able to effectively send in *any* object implementing IDraw3D. Furthermore, because interfaces are strongly typed entities, if you attempt to pass into this method a type that does not support IDraw3D, you will receive a compile-time error:

```
' This method can receive anything implementing IDraw3D.
Sub DrawIn3D(ByVal itf3d As IDraw3D)
  Console.WriteLine("-> Drawing IDraw3D compatible type")
  itf3d.Draw3D()
End Sub
```

If we were to now call this method while cycling through the array of Shapes, only the IDraw3D-compatible types are sent into our new subroutine (see Figure 9-5 for output).

```
Sub Main()
...
  For Each s As Shape In myShapes
    If TypeOf s Is IPointy Then
      itfPointy = CType(s, IPointy)
      Console.WriteLine("{0} has {1} points.", s.PetName, itfPointy.Points)
    Else
      Console.WriteLine("{0} does not implement IPointy!", s)
    End If
    If TypeOf s Is IDraw3D Then
      DrawIn3D(CType(s, IDraw3D))
    End If
  Next
  Console.ReadLine()
End Sub
```

Figure 9-5. *Rendering the* IDraw3D-*compatible types*

Interfaces As Return Values

Interfaces can also be used as function return values. For example, you could write a method that takes any System.Object, checks for IPointy compatibility, and returns a reference to the extracted interface (if it exists):

```
' This method tests for IPointy-compatibility and,
' if able, returns an interface reference.
Function ExtractPointyness(ByVal o As Object) As IPointy
```

```
If TypeOf o Is IPointy Then
  Return CType(o, IPointy)
Else
  Return Nothing
End If
End Function
```

We could interact with this method as follows:

```
Sub Main()
...
  ' Can we extract IPointy from an Array of Integers?
  Dim myInts() As Integer = {10, 20, 30}
  Dim i As IPointy = ExtractPointyness(myInts)

  ' Nope!
  If i Is Nothing Then
    Console.WriteLine("Sorry, this object was not IPointy compatible")
  End If
End Sub
```

Arrays of Interface Types

The true power of interfaces comes through loud and clear when you recall that the same interface can be implemented by numerous types, even if they are not defined within the same class hierarchy and do not share a common base class beyond System.Object. This can yield some very powerful programming constructs.

For example, assume that you have developed a brand new class hierarchy modeling kitchen utensils and another modeling gardening equipment. Although these hierarchies are completely unrelated from a classical inheritance point of view, you can treat them polymorphically using a common interface. Consider Figure 9-6.

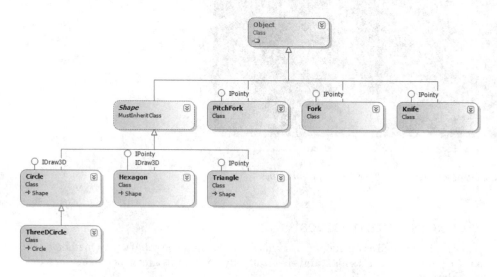

Figure 9-6. *Recall that interfaces can be "plugged into" any type in any part of a class hierarchy.*

If you did create the `PitchFork`, `Fork`, and `Knife` types, you could now define an array of `IPointy`-compatible objects. Given that these members all support the same interface, you are able to iterate through the array and treat each object as an `IPointy`-compatible object, regardless of the overall diversity of the class hierarchies:

```
Sub Main()
...
    ' This array can only contain types that
    ' implement the IPointy interface.
    Dim pointyThings() As IPointy = {New Hexagon(), New Knife(), _
        New Triangle(), New Fork(), New PitchFork()}

    For Each p As IPointy In pointyThings
        Console.WriteLine("Object has {0} points.", p.Points)
    Next
End Sub
```

Source Code The CustomInterface project is located under the Chapter 9 subdirectory.

Resolving Name Clashes with the Implements Keyword

As you have seen earlier in this chapter, a single class or structure can implement any number of interfaces. Given this, there is always a possibility that you may implement interfaces that contain identically named members, and therefore have a name clash to contend with. To illustrate various manners in which you can resolve this issue, create a brand new console application named (not surprisingly) InterfaceNameClash.

Now design three custom interfaces that represent various locations to which an implementing type could render their data:

```
' Draw image to a Form.
Public Interface IDrawToForm
    Sub Draw()
End Interface

' Draw to buffer in memory.
Public Interface IDrawToMemory
    Sub Draw()
End Interface

' Render to the printer
Public Interface IDrawToPrinter
    Sub Draw()
End Interface
```

Notice that each of these methods have been named `Draw()`. If you now wish to support each of these interfaces on a single class type named `Octagon`, the IDE will automatically generate three different `Public` members on the class, following the rather nondescript naming convention of suffixing a numerical value after the interface member name:

```
' To resolve name clashes,
' the IDE will autogenerate unique names where necessary.
Public Class Octagon
    Implements IDrawToForm, IDrawToMemory, IDrawToPrinter
```

```
    Public Sub Draw() Implements IDrawToForm.Draw
    End Sub

    Public Sub Draw1() Implements IDrawToMemory.Draw
    End Sub

    Public Sub Draw2() Implements IDrawToPrinter.Draw
    End Sub
End Class
```

Although the generated method names are a bit ambiguous, it should be clear that the coding logic used to render image data to a Form, a region of memory, or a piece of paper is quite different. Therefore, the most straightforward manner to clean up the Octagon type is to simply rename the autogenerated class members to a more fitting title:

```
Public Class Octagon
    Implements IDrawToForm, IDrawToMemory, IDrawToPrinter

    Public Sub Draw() Implements IDrawToForm.Draw
        ' Insert interesting code here...
    End Sub

    Public Sub RenderToMemory() Implements IDrawToMemory.Draw
        ' Insert interesting code here...
    End Sub

    Public Sub Print() Implements IDrawToPrinter.Draw
        ' Insert interesting code here...
    End Sub
End Class
```

Notice that the name of the method defined on the class does not necessarily need to match the name of the interface method, given the fact that it is the Implements keyword that binds an interface member to a supporting class member. Thus, if we were to create an instance of Octagon, we would find the members shown in Figure 9-7 exposed through IntelliSense.

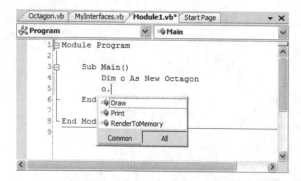

Figure 9-7. *Triggering interface members from the object level*

However, if the caller obtains an interface reference using an explicit cast, only the specific interface methods are exposed. Consider the following code:

```
Module Program
  Sub Main()
    Dim o As New Octagon

    ' Call IDrawToMemory.Draw()
    Dim iMem As IDrawToMemory
    iMem = CType(o, IDrawToMemory)
    iMem.Draw()

    ' Call IDrawToPrinter.Draw()
    Dim iPrint As IDrawToPrinter
    iPrint = CType(o, IDrawToPrinter)
    iPrint.Draw()

    ' Call IDrawToForm.Draw()
    Dim iForm As IDrawToForm
    iForm = CType(o, IDrawToForm)
    iForm.Draw()
    End Sub
End Module
```

Defining a Common Implementation with the Implements Keyword

Given the fact that the Implements keyword allows you to explicitly bind an interface member to a class (or structure) member, it is permissible to define a single member that implements the members of multiple interfaces (provided each interface member has an identical signature). By way of example:

```
Public Class Line
  Implements IDrawToForm, IDrawToMemory, IDrawToPrinter

  ' This single class method defines an implementation for
  ' each interface method.
  Public Sub Draw() Implements IDrawToForm.Draw, _
    IDrawToMemory.Draw, IDrawToPrinter.Draw
  End Sub
End Class
```

Of course, in this example, it really makes no sense to share the implementation of each version of Draw() given the semantics of the interface types. Nevertheless, under some circumstances it can be the case that a shared implementation of multiple interface members fits the bill. Using this approach, you are able to simplify the overall class design.

Hiding Interface Methods from the Object Level Using the Implements Keyword

The final aspect of the Implements keyword to be aware of is that it is perfectly fine to bind an interface member to a *private* class member:

```
' Notice each class method has been defined as Private
' and has been given very a nondescript name.
Public Class BlackAndWhiteBitmap
  Implements IDrawToForm, IDrawToMemory, IDrawToPrinter
```

```
    Private Sub X() Implements IDrawToForm.Draw
        ' Insert interesting code...
    End Sub

    Private Sub Y() Implements IDrawToMemory.Draw
        ' Insert interesting code...
    End Sub

    Private Sub Z() Implements IDrawToPrinter.Draw
        ' Insert interesting code...
    End Sub
End Class
```

When you map an interface member to a `Private` type member, it is now illegal to call the interface members from the object level. Thus, if we were to create an instance of `BlackAndWhiteBitmap`, we would only see the inherited members of our good friend `System.Object`, as shown in Figure 9-8.

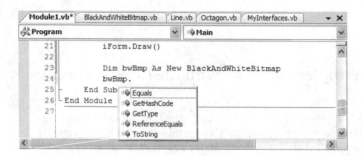

Figure 9-8. *Explicitly implemented interface members are not visible from the object level.*

When you hide interface members from the implementing type, the only possible way to call these members is by extracting out the interface using an explicit cast:

```
Dim bwBmp As New BlackAndWhiteBitmap
Dim i As IDrawToForm
i = CType(bwBmp, IDrawToForm)
i.Draw()
```

Notice that the actual methods that implement the interface members (`X()`, `Y()`, and `Z()`) are never exposed in any manner. Like any other `Private` member, the only part of your system that can directly call these members is the type that defines them (`BlackAndWhiteBitmap` in this case).

So, when would you choose to explicitly implement an interface member? Truth be told, this class design technique is never mandatory. However, by doing so you can hide some more "advanced" members from the object level. In this way, when the object user applies the dot operator, they will only see a subset of the type's overall functionality. However, those who require the more advanced behaviors can extract out the desired interface via an explicit cast.

■**Source Code** The InterfaceNameClash project is located under the Chapter 9 subdirectory.

Designing Interface Hierarchies

Before we turn our attention to working with various predefined interfaces that ship with the .NET base class libraries, it is worth pointing out that interfaces can be arranged into an interface hierarchy. Like a class hierarchy, when an interface extends an existing interface, it inherits the abstract members defined by the parent type(s). Of course, unlike class inheritance, derived interfaces never inherit true implementation. Rather, a derived interface simply extends its own definition with additional abstract members.

Interface hierarchies can be useful when you wish to extend the functionality of an existing interface without breaking existing code bases. To illustrate, let's redesign the previous set of interfaces (from the InterfaceNameClash example) such that IDrawable is the root of the family tree:

```
Public Interface IDrawable
    Sub Draw()
End Interface
```

Given that IDrawable defines a basic drawing behavior, we could now create a derived interface that extends this type with the ability to render its output to the printer:

```
Public Interface IPrintable
    Inherits IDrawable
    Sub Print()
End Interface
```

And just for good measure, we could define a final interface named IRenderToMemory, which extends IPrintable:

```
Public Interface IRenderToMemory
    Inherits IPrintable
    Sub Render()
End Interface
```

Given our design, if a type were to implement IRenderToMemory, we would now be required to implement each and every member defined up the chain of inheritance (specifically, the Render(), Print(), and Draw() subroutines). On the other hand, if a type were to only implement IPrintable, we would only need to contend with Print() and Draw(). For example:

```
Public Class SuperShape
    Implements IRenderToMemory
    Public Sub Draw() Implements IDrawable.Draw
        ' Code...
    End Sub

    Public Sub Print() Implements IPrintable.Print
        ' Code...
    End Sub

    Public Sub Render() Implements IRenderToMemory.Render
        ' Code...
    End Sub
End Class
```

Now, when we make use of the SuperShape, we are able to invoke each method at the object level (as they are all Public) as well as extract out a reference to each supported interface explicitly via casting:

```
Module Program
    Sub Main()
        Console.WriteLine("***** The SuperShape *****")
```

```
    ' Call from object level.
    Dim myShape As New SuperShape
    myShape.Draw()

    ' Get IPrintable explicitly.
    ' (and IDrawable implicitly!)
    Dim iPrint As IPrintable
    iPrint = CType(myShape, IPrintable)
    iPrint.Draw()
    iPrint.Print()
  End Sub
End Module
```

At this point, you hopefully feel more comfortable with the process of defining and implementing custom interfaces using the syntax of Visual Basic 2005. To be honest, interface-based programming can take awhile to get comfortable with, so if you are in fact still scratching your head just a bit, this is a perfectly normal reaction. To summarize the story thus far, remember that interfaces can be extremely useful when

- You have a single hierarchy where only a subset of the derived types support a common behavior.

- You need to model a common behavior that is found across multiple hierarchies.

Next up, let's check out the role of several predefined interfaces found within the .NET base class libraries.

Source Code The InterfaceHierarchy project is located under the Chapter 9 subdirectory.

Building Enumerable Types (IEnumerable and IEnumerator)

The System.Collections namespace defines two interfaces named IEnumerable and IEnumerator. When you build a type that supports these behaviors, you are able to iterate over any contained subitems using the For Each construct of Visual Basic 2005. Assume you have developed a class named Garage that contains a set of individual Car types (see Chapter 7) stored within a System.Array:

```
' Garage contains a set of Car objects.
Public Class Garage
  Private myCars() As Car = New Car(3) {}

  Public Sub New()
    myCars(0) = New Car("Fred", 40)
    myCars(1) = New Car("Zippy", 60)
    myCars(2) = New Car("Mabel", 0)
    myCars(3) = New Car("Max", 80)
  End Sub
End Class
```

Ideally, it would be convenient to iterate over the Garage object's subitems using the VB 2005 For Each construct. Assuming your Car class now supports two new properties (Name and Speed) that encapsulate the petName and currSpeed member variables, the following logic would be ideal:

```
' This seems reasonable...
Module Program
  Sub Main()
    Dim myCars As New Garage
    ' Hand over each car in the collection?
    For Each c As Car In myCars
      Console.WriteLine("{0} is going {1} MPH", _
        c.Name, c.Speed)
    Next
  End Sub
End Module
```

Sadly, the compiler informs you that the Garage class is not a "collection type." Specifically, collection types support a method named GetEnumerator(), which is formalized by the IEnumerable interface:

```
' This interface informs the caller
' that the object's subitems can be enumerated.
Public Interface IEnumerable
  Function GetEnumerator() As IEnumerator
End Interface
```

As you can see, the GetEnumerator() method returns a reference to yet another interface named System.Collections.IEnumerator. This interface provides the infrastructure to allow the caller to traverse the internal objects contained by the IEnumerable-compatible container:

```
Public Interface IEnumerator
  ' Advance to the next object in collection.
  Function MoveNext() As Boolean

  ' Reset to first object in collection.
  Sub Reset()

  ' Pluck out current object pointed to.
  ReadOnly Property Current As Object
End Interface
```

If you wish to update the Garage type to support these interfaces, you could take the long road and implement each method manually. While you are certainly free to provide customized versions of GetEnumerator(), MoveNext(), Current, and Reset(), there is a simpler way. As the System.Array type (as well as many other types) already implements IEnumerable and IEnumerator, you can simply forward the request to the System.Array as follows:

```
Public Class Garage
  Implements System.Collections.IEnumerable

  Private myCars() As Car = New Car(3) {}

  Public Sub New()
    myCars(0) = New Car("Fred", 40)
    myCars(1) = New Car("Zippy", 60)
    myCars(2) = New Car("Mabel", 0)
    myCars(3) = New Car("Max", 80)
  End Sub
```

```
    Public Function GetEnumerator() As System.Collections.IEnumerator _
      Implements System.Collections.IEnumerable.GetEnumerator
      Return myCars.GetEnumerator()
    End Function
End Class
```

Once you have updated your Garage type, you can now safely use the type within the VB 2005 For Each construct. Furthermore, given that the GetEnumerator() method has been defined publicly, the object user could also interact with the IEnumerator type:

```
Module Program
  Sub Main()
...
    ' Get IEnumerable directly.
    Dim iEnum As IEnumerator
    iEnum = myCars.GetEnumerator()
    iEnum.Reset()
    iEnum.MoveNext()

    Dim firstCar As Car = CType(iEnum.Current, Car)
    Console.WriteLine("First car in collection is: {0}", firstCar.Name)
  End Sub
End Module
```

Given that the only part of your system that is typically interested in manipulating the IEnumerator interface directly is indeed the For Each construct, you may wish to define GetEnumerator() as Private, to hide this member from the object level:

```
Private Function GetEnumerator() As System.Collections.IEnumerator _
  Implements System.Collections.IEnumerable.GetEnumerator
    Return myCars.GetEnumerator()
End Function
```

Source Code The CustomEnumerator project is located under the Chapter 9 subdirectory.

Building Cloneable Objects (ICloneable)

As you recall from Chapter 6, System.Object defines a member named MemberwiseClone(). This method is used to obtain a *shallow copy* of the current object. Object users do not call this method directly (as it is protected); however, a given object may call this method itself during the *cloning* process. Simply put, a shallow copy produces a copy of an object where each point of field data is copied verbatim. To illustrate, assume you have a class named Point:

```
' A class named Point.
Public Class Point
  ' Public for easy access.
  Public xPos, yPos As Integer

  Public Sub New()
  End Sub
  Public Sub New(ByVal x As Integer, ByVal y As Integer)
    xPos = x : yPos = y
  End Sub
```

```
  Public Overrides Function ToString() As String
    Return String.Format("X = {0} ; Y = {1}", xPos, yPos)
  End Function
End Class
```

As fully described in Chapter 11, when you assign one reference type to another, you are simply redirecting which object the reference is pointing to in memory. Thus, the following assignment operation results in two references to the same Point instance; modifications using either reference affect the same object on the heap. Therefore, each of the following calls to Console.WriteLine() prints the string "X = 0 ; Y = 50":

```
Sub Main()
  ' Two references to same object!
  Dim p1 As New Point(50, 50)
  Dim p2 As Point = p1
  p2.xPos = 0
  Console.WriteLine(p1)
  Console.WriteLine(p2)
End Sub
```

When you wish to equip your custom types to support the ability to return an identical copy of itself to the caller, you may implement the standard ICloneable interface. As shown at the beginning of this chapter, this type defines a single method named Clone():

```
Public Interface ICloneable
  Function Clone() As Object
End Interface
```

Obviously, the implementation of the Clone() method varies between objects. However, the basic functionality tends to be the same: copy the values of your member variables into a new instance, and return it to the user. To illustrate, ponder the following update to the Point class:

```
' The Point now supports "clone-ability."
Public Class Point
  Implements ICloneable
...
  Public Function Clone() As Object Implements System.ICloneable.Clone
    Return New Point(xPos, yPos)
  End Function
End Class
```

In this way, you can create exact stand-alone copies of the Point type, as illustrated by the following code:

```
Module Program
  Sub Main()
    ' Two references to same object!
    Dim p1 As New Point(50, 50)

    ' If Option Strict is enabled, you must
    ' perform an explicit cast, as Clone()
    ' returns a generic System.Object.
    Dim p2 As Point = CType(p1.Clone(), Point)
    p2.xPos = 0

    ' Prints X = 50 ; Y = 50
    Console.WriteLine(p1)
```

```
      ' Prints X = 0 ; Y = 50
      Console.WriteLine(p2)
   End Sub
End Module
```

While the current implementation of `Point` fits the bill, you can streamline things just a bit. Because the `Point` type does not contain reference type variables, you could simplify the implementation of the `Clone()` method as follows:

```
Public Function Clone() As Object
   ' Copy each field of the Point member by member.
   Return Me.MemberwiseClone()
End Function
```

Be aware, however, that if the `Point` did contain any reference type member variables, `MemberwiseClone()` will copy the references to those objects (aka a *shallow copy*). If you wish to support a true deep copy, you will need to create a new instance of any reference type variables during the cloning process. Let's see an example.

A More Elaborate Cloning Example

Now assume the `Point` class contains a reference type member variable of type `PointDescription`. This class maintains a point's friendly name as well as an identification number expressed as a `System.Guid` (if you don't come from a COM background, know that a Globally Unique Identifier [GUID] is a statistically unique 128-bit number). Here is the implementation:

```
Public Class PointDescription
   Public petName As String
   Public pointID As Guid
   Public Sub New()
      Me.petName = "No-name"
      pointID = Guid.NewGuid
   End Sub
End Class
```

The initial updates to the `Point` class itself included modifying `ToString()` to account for these new bits of state data, as well as defining and creating the `PointDescription` reference type. To allow the outside world to establish a string moniker for the `Point`, you also update the arguments passed into the overloaded constructor:

```
Public Class Point
   Implements ICloneable
   Public xPos, yPos As Integer
   Public desc As New PointDescription()

   Sub New()
   End Sub
   Sub New(ByVal x As Integer, ByVal y As Integer)
      xPos = x : yPos = y
   End Sub
   Sub New(ByVal x As Integer, ByVal y As Integer, ByVal name As String)
      xPos = x : yPos = y
      desc.petName = name
   End Sub
```

```
  Public Overrides Function ToString() As String
    Return String.Format("X = {0} ; Y = {1} ; Name = {2} : ID = {3}", _
      xPos, yPos, desc.petName, desc.pointID)
  End Function

  Public Function Clone() As Object Implements System.ICloneable.Clone
    ' Return New Point(xPos, yPos)
    Return Me.MemberwiseClone()
  End Function
End Class
```

Notice that you did not yet update your Clone() method. Therefore, when the object user asks for a clone using the current implementation, a shallow (member-by-member) copy is achieved. To illustrate, assume you have updated Main() as follows:

```
Module Program
  Sub Main()
    Dim p1 As New Point(50, 50, "Brad")
    Dim p2 As Point = CType(p1.Clone(), Point)

    Console.WriteLine("Before modification:")
    Console.WriteLine("p1: {0} ", p1)
    Console.WriteLine("p2: {0} ", p2)

    p2.desc.petName = "Mr. X"
    p2.xPos = 9
    Console.WriteLine("Changed p2.desc.petName and p2.x")

    Console.WriteLine("After modification:")
    Console.WriteLine("p1: {0} ", p1)
    Console.WriteLine("p2: {0} ", p2)
  End Sub
End Module
```

Now, observe the output in Figure 9-9.

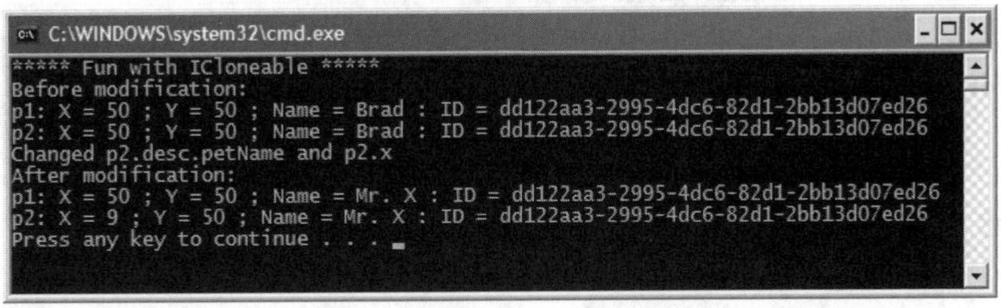

```
C:\WINDOWS\system32\cmd.exe
***** Fun with ICloneable *****
Before modification:
p1: X = 50 ; Y = 50 ; Name = Brad : ID = dd122aa3-2995-4dc6-82d1-2bb13d07ed26
p2: X = 50 ; Y = 50 ; Name = Brad : ID = dd122aa3-2995-4dc6-82d1-2bb13d07ed26
Changed p2.desc.petName and p2.x
After modification:
p1: X = 50 ; Y = 50 ; Name = Mr. X : ID = dd122aa3-2995-4dc6-82d1-2bb13d07ed26
p2: X = 9 ; Y = 50 ; Name = Mr. X : ID = dd122aa3-2995-4dc6-82d1-2bb13d07ed26
Press any key to continue . . .
```

Figure 9-9. *Oops! We just copied the* PointDescription *reference!*

In order for your Clone() method to make a complete deep copy of the internal reference types, you need to configure the object returned by MemberwiseClone() to account for the current point's name (the System.Guid type is in fact a structure, so the numerical data is indeed copied). Here is one possible implementation:

```vbnet
' Now we need to adjust for the PointDescription member.
Public Function Clone() As Object Implements System.ICloneable.Clone
  Dim newPoint As Point = CType(Me.MemberwiseClone(), Point)
  Dim currentDesc As PointDescription = New PointDescription()
  currentDesc.petName = Me.desc.petName
  currentDesc.pointID = Me.desc.pointID
  newPoint.desc = currentDesc
  Return newPoint
End Function
```

If you rerun the application once again, you see that the Point returned from Clone() does copy its internal reference type member variables (see Figure 9-10).

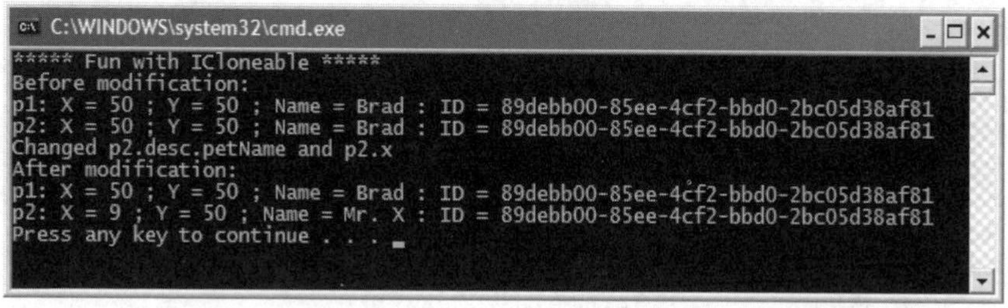

Figure 9-10. *Much better! We now copied the* PointDescription *object!*

To summarize the cloning process, if you have a class or structure that contains nothing but value types, implement your Clone() method using MemberwiseClone(). However, if you have a custom type that maintains other reference types, you need to establish a new object that takes into account the state of each member variable.

■**Source Code** The CloneablePoint project is located under the Chapter 9 subdirectory.

Building Comparable Objects (IComparable)

The System.IComparable interface specifies a behavior that allows an object to be sorted based on some specified key. Here is the formal definition:

```vbnet
' This interface allows an object to specify its
' relationship between other like objects.
Public Interface IComparable
  Function CompareTo(ByVal obj As Object) As Integer
End Interface
```

Let's assume you have updated the Car class to maintain a numerical identifier (represented by a simple integer named carID) that can be set via a constructor parameter and manipulated using a new property named ID. Here are the relevant updates to the Car type:

```vbnet
Public Class Car
...
  Private carID As Integer
  Public Property ID() As Integer
```

```
      Get
         Return carID
      End Get
      Set(ByVal value As Integer)
         carID = value
      End Set
   End Property

   Public Sub New(ByVal name As String, _
      ByVal currSp As Integer, ByVal id As Integer)
      currSpeed = currSp
      petName = name
      carID = id
   End Sub
...
End Class
```

Object users might create an array of Car types as follows:

```
Module Program
   Sub Main()
      ' Make an array of Car types.
      Dim myAutos(4) As Car
      myAutos(0) = New Car("Rusty", 80, 1)
      myAutos(1) = New Car("Mary", 40, 234)
      myAutos(2) = New Car("Viper", 40, 34)
      myAutos(3) = New Car("Mel", 40, 4)
      myAutos(4) = New Car("Chucky", 40, 5)
      For Each c As Car In myAutos
         Console.WriteLine("Car {0} is named {1}.", c.ID, c.Name)
      Next
   End Sub
End Module
```

As you may recall from Chapter 4, the System.Array class defines a shared method named Sort(). When you invoke this method on an array of intrinsic types (Integer, Short, String, etc.), you are able to sort the items in the array in numerical/alphabetic order as these intrinsic data types implement IComparable. However, what if you were to send an array of Car types into the Sort() method as follows?

```
' Sort my cars?
Array.Sort(myAutos)
```

If you run this test, you would find that an ArgumentException exception is thrown by the runtime, with the following message: "At least one object must implement IComparable." When you build custom types, you can implement IComparable to allow arrays of your types to be sorted. When you flesh out the details of CompareTo(), it will be up to you to decide what the baseline of the ordering operation will be. For the Car type, the internal carID seems to be the most logical candidate:

```
' The iteration of the Car can be ordered
' based on the carID.
Public Function CompareTo(ByVal obj As Object) As Integer _
   Implements System.IComparable.CompareTo
   Dim temp As Car = CType(obj, Car)
   If Me.carID > temp.carID Then
      Return 1
   End If
```

```
    If Me.carID < temp.carID Then
        Return -1
    Else
        Return 0
    End If
End Function
```

As you can see, the logic behind CompareTo() is to test the incoming type against the current instance based on a specific point of data. The return value of CompareTo() is used to discover if this type is less than, greater than, or equal to the object it is being compared with (see Table 9-1).

Table 9-1. CompareTo() *Return Values*

CompareTo() Return Value	Meaning in Life
Any number less than zero	This instance comes before the specified object in the sort order.
Zero	This instance is equal to the specified object.
Any number greater than zero	This instance comes after the specified object in the sort order.

Now that your Car type understands how to compare itself to like objects, you can write the following user code:

```
Module Program
  Sub Main()
    Console.WriteLine("***** Fun with IComparable *****")

    ' Make an array of Car types.
    Dim myAutos(4) As Car
    myAutos(0) = New Car("Rusty", 80, 1)
    myAutos(1) = New Car("Mary", 40, 234)
    myAutos(2) = New Car("Viper", 40, 34)
    myAutos(3) = New Car("Mel", 40, 4)
    myAutos(4) = New Car("Chucky", 40, 5)

    Console.WriteLine("-> Before Sorting:")
    For Each c As Car In myAutos
      Console.WriteLine("Car {0} is named {1}.", c.ID, c.Name)
    Next
    Console.WriteLine()

    ' Sort my cars?
    Array.Sort(myAutos)
    Console.WriteLine("-> After Sorting:")
    For Each c As Car In myAutos
      Console.WriteLine("Car {0} is named {1}.", c.ID, c.Name)
    Next
  End Sub
End Module
```

Figure 9-11 illustrates a test run.

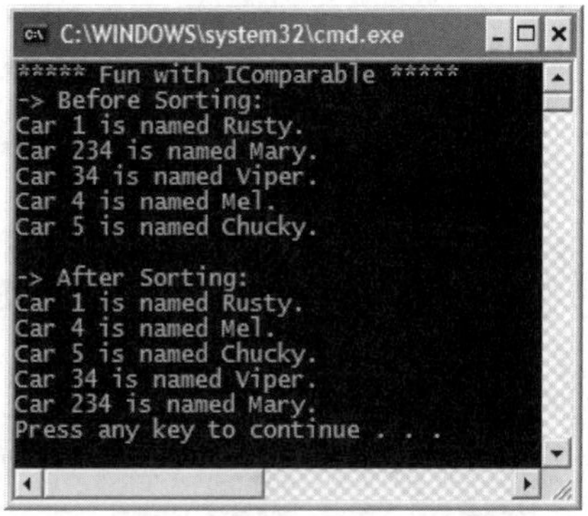

Figure 9-11. *Sorting* Cars *by ID via* IComparable

Specifying Multiple Sort Orders (IComparer)

In this version of the Car type, you made use of the car's ID to function as the baseline of the sort order. Another design might have used the pet name of the car as the basis of the sorting algorithm (to list cars alphabetically). Now, what if you wanted to build a Car that could be sorted by ID *as well as* by pet name? If this is the behavior you are interested in, you need to make friends with another standard interface named IComparer, defined within the System.Collections namespace as follows:

```
' A generic way to compare two objects.
Public Interface IComparer
  Function Compare(ByVal x As Object, ByVal y As Object) As Integer
End Interface
```

Unlike the IComparable interface, IComparer is typically *not* implemented on the type you are trying to sort (i.e., the Car). Rather, you implement this interface on any number of helper classes, one for each sort order (pet name, car ID, etc.). Currently, the Car type already knows how to compare itself against other cars based on the internal car ID. Therefore, to allow the object user to sort an array of Car types by pet name will require an additional helper class that implements IComparer. Here's the code:

```
' This helper class is used to sort an array of Cars by pet name.
Imports System.Collections

Public Class PetNameComparer
  Implements IComparer

  Public Sub New()
  End Sub
  Public Function Compare(ByVal x As Object, ByVal y As Object) _
    As Integer Implements System.Collections.IComparer.Compare
    Dim t1 As Car = CType(x, Car)
    Dim t2 As Car = CType(y, Car)
    Return String.Compare(t1.Name, t2.Name)
  End Function
End Class
```

The object user code is able to make use of this helper class. System.Array has a number of overloaded Sort() methods, one that just happens to take an object implementing IComparer (see Figure 9-12 for output):

```
Module Program
  Sub Main()
...
    ' Now sort by pet name.
    Array.Sort(myAutos, New PetNameComparer())
    Console.WriteLine("-> Ordering by pet name:")
    For Each c As Car In myAutos
      Console.WriteLine("{0} has the ID of {1}.", c.Name, c.ID)
    Next
  End Sub
End Module
```

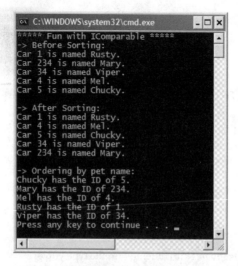

Figure 9-12. *Sorting* Cars *via* IComparable

Custom Properties, Custom Sort Types

When building custom types that can be sorted in a variety of manners, it is common to define the related IComparer helper class directly within the type. Assume the Car class has added a shared read-only property named SortByPetName() that returns an instance of an object implementing the IComparer interface (PetNameComparer, in this case):

```
' We now support a custom property to return
' the correct IComparer interface.
Public Class Car
  Implements IComparable
...
  ' Property to return the pet name comparer.
  Public Shared ReadOnly Property SortByPetName() As IComparer
    Get
      Return CType(New PetNameComparer(), IComparer)
    End Get
  End Property
End Class
```

The object user code can now sort by pet name using a strongly associated property, rather than just "having to know" to use the stand-alone PetNameComparer class type:

```
' Sorting by pet name made a bit cleaner.
Array.Sort(myAutos, Car.SortByPetName)
```

■Source Code The ComparableCar project is located under the Chapter 9 subdirectory.

So, at this point, you not only understand how to define and implement interface types, but have examined a few useful interfaces defined in the .NET base class libraries. To be sure, interfaces will be found within every major .NET namespace. As you would expect, some interfaces are more immediately useful than others, so be sure to consult the .NET Framework SDK 2.0 documentation for full details regarding the interfaces you encounter throughout the remainder of this text. To wrap up this chapter, let's check out the interfaces (and core classes) of the System.Collections namespace.

The Interfaces of the System.Collections Namespace

The most primitive of all containers in the .NET universe would have to be our good friend System. Array. As you have already seen in Chapter 4, this class provides a number of services (e.g., reversing, sorting, clearing, and enumerating). However, the simple Array class has a number of limitations, most notably it does not dynamically resize itself as you add or clear items. When you need to contain types in a more flexible container, you may wish to leverage the types defined within the System.Collections namespace (or as discussed in Chapter 12, the System.Collections.Generic namespace).

The System.Collections namespace defines a number of interfaces, some of which you have already implemented during the course of this chapter. As you might guess, a majority of the collection classes implement these interfaces to provide access to their contents. Table 9-2 gives a breakdown of the core collection-centric interfaces.

Table 9-2. *Interfaces of* System.Collections

System.Collections Interface	Meaning in Life
ICollection	Defines generic characteristics (e.g., count and thread safety) for a collection type.
IComparer	Allows two objects to be compared.
IDictionary	Allows an object to represent its contents using name/value pairs.
IDictionaryEnumerator	Enumerates the contents of a type supporting IDictionary.
IEnumerable	Returns the IEnumerator interface for a given object.
IEnumerator	Generally supports foreach-style iteration of subtypes.
IHashCodeProvider	Returns the hash code for the implementing type using a customized hash algorithm.
IKeyComparer	(This interface is new to .NET 2.0.) Combines the functionality of IComparer and IHashCodeProvider to allow objects to be compared in a "hash-code-compatible manner" (e.g., if the objects are indeed equal, they must also return the same hash code value).
IList	Provides behavior to add, remove, and index items in a list of objects. Also, this interface defines members to determine whether the implementing collection type is read-only and/or a fixed-size container.

Many of these interfaces are related by an interface hierarchy, while others are stand-alone entities. Figure 9-13 illustrates the relationship between each type (recall that it is permissible for a single interface to derive from multiple interfaces).

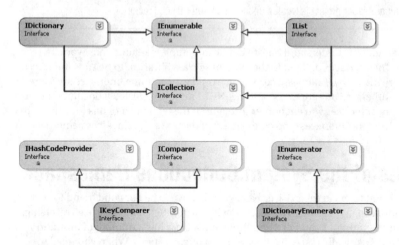

Figure 9-13. *The interfaces of* System.Collections

The Role of ICollection

The ICollection interface is the most primitive interface of the System.Collections namespace in that it defines a behavior supported by a collection type. In a nutshell, this interface provides a small set of properties that allow you to determine (a) the number of items in the container, (b) the thread safety of the container, as well as (c) the ability to copy the contents into a System.Array type. Formally, ICollection is defined as follows (note that ICollection extends IEnumerable):

```
Public Interface ICollection
    Inherits IEnumerable
    Sub CopyTo(ByVal array As Array, ByVal index As Integer)
    ReadOnly Property Count As Integer
    ReadOnly Property IsSynchronized As Boolean
    ReadOnly Property SyncRoot As Object
End Interface
```

The Role of IDictionary

As you may already be aware, a *dictionary* is simply a collection that maintains a set of name/value pairs. For example, you could build a custom type that implements IDictionary such that you can store Car types (the values) that may be retrieved by ID or pet name (e.g., names). Given this functionality, you can see that the IDictionary interface defines a Keys and Values property as well as Add(), Remove(), and Contains() methods. The individual items may be obtained by the type indexer. Here is the formal definition:

```
Public Interface IDictionary
  Inherits ICollection, IEnumerable
  Sub Add(ByVal key As Object, ByVal value As Object)
  Sub Clear()
  Function Contains(ByVal key As Object) As Boolean
  Function GetEnumerator() As IDictionaryEnumerator
  Sub Remove(ByVal key As Object)
  ReadOnly Property IsFixedSize As Boolean
  ReadOnly Property IsReadOnly As Boolean
  Property Item(ByVal key As Object) As Object
  ReadOnly Property Keys As ICollection
  ReadOnly Property Values As ICollection
End Interface
```

The Role of IDictionaryEnumerator

If you were paying attention, you may have noted that IDictionary.GetEnumerator() returns an instance of the IDictionaryEnumerator type. IDictionaryEnumerator is simply a strongly typed enumerator, given that it extends IEnumerator by adding the following functionality:

```
Public Interface IDictionaryEnumerator
  Inherits IEnumerator
  ReadOnly Property Entry As DictionaryEntry
  ReadOnly Property Key As Object
  ReadOnly Property Value As Object
End Interface
```

Notice how IDictionaryEnumerator allows you to enumerate over items in the dictionary via the generic Entry property, which returns a System.Collections.DictionaryEntry class type. In addition, you are also able to traverse the name/value pairs using the Key/Value properties.

The Role of IList

The final key interface of System.Collections is IList, which provides the ability to insert, remove, and index items into (or out of) a container:

```
Public Interface IList
  Inherits ICollection, IEnumerable
  Function Add(ByVal value As Object) As Integer
  Sub Clear()
  Function Contains(ByVal value As Object) As Boolean
  Function IndexOf(ByVal value As Object) As Integer
  Sub Insert(ByVal index As Integer, ByVal value As Object)
  Sub Remove(ByVal value As Object)
  Sub RemoveAt(ByVal index As Integer)
  ReadOnly Property IsFixedSize As Boolean
  ReadOnly Property IsReadOnly As Boolean
  Property Item(ByVal index As Integer) As Object
End Interface
```

The Class Types of System.Collections

As I hope you understand by this point in the chapter, interfaces by themselves are not very useful until they are implemented by a given class or structure. Table 9-3 provides a rundown of the core classes in the System.Collections namespace and the key interfaces they support.

Table 9-3. *Classes of* System.Collections

System.Collections Class	Meaning in Life	Key Implemented Interfaces
ArrayList	Represents a dynamically sized array of objects.	IList, ICollection, IEnumerable, and ICloneable
Hashtable	Represents a collection of objects identified by a numerical key. Custom types stored in a Hashtable should always override System.Object.GetHashCode().	IDictionary, ICollection, IEnumerable, and ICloneable
Queue	Represents a standard first-in, first-out (FIFO) queue.	ICollection, ICloneable, IEnumerable
SortedList	Like a dictionary; however, the elements can also be accessed by ordinal position (e.g., index).	IDictionary, ICollection, IEnumerable, and ICloneable
Stack	A last-in, first-out (LIFO) queue and provides push and pop (and peek) functionality.	ICollection, ICloneable, IEnumerable

In addition to these key types, System.Collections defines some minor players (at least in terms of their day-to-day usefulness) such as BitArray, CaseInsensitiveComparer, and CaseInsensitiveHashCodeProvider. Furthermore, this namespace also defines a small set of abstract base classes (CollectionBase, ReadOnlyCollectionBase, and DictionaryBase) that can be used to build strongly typed containers.

As you begin to experiment with the System.Collections types, you will find they all tend to share common functionality (that's the point of interface-based programming). Thus, rather than listing out the members of each and every collection class, the next task of this chapter is to illustrate how to interact with three common collection types: ArrayList, Queue, and Stack. Once you understand the functionality of these types, gaining an understanding of the remaining collection classes should naturally follow (especially since each of the types is fully documented within online help).

Working with the ArrayList Type

The ArrayList type is bound to be your most frequently used type in the System.Collections namespace in that it allows you to dynamically resize the contents at your whim. To illustrate the basics of this type, ponder the following code, which leverages the ArrayList to manipulate a set of Car objects:

```
Module Program
  Sub Main()
    ' Make ArrayList and add a range of Cars.
    Dim carArList As ArrayList = New ArrayList
    carArList.AddRange(New Car() {New Car("Fred", 90, 10), _
      New Car("Mary", 100, 50), New Car("MB", 190, 11)})
    Console.WriteLine("Items in carArList: {0}", carArList.Count)

    ' Iterate over contents.
    For Each c As Car In carArList
      Console.WriteLine("Car pet name: {0}", c.Name)
    Next

    ' Insert new car.
    Console.WriteLine("->Inserting new Car.")
    carArList.Insert(2, New Car("TheNewCar", 0, 12))
    Console.WriteLine("Items in carArList: {0}", carArList.Count)
```

```
  ' Get the subobjects as an array.
  Dim arrayOfCars As Object() = carArList.ToArray()
  Dim i As Integer = 0

  ' Now iterate over array
  While i < arrayOfCars.Length
    Console.WriteLine("Car pet name: {0}", CType(arrayOfCars(i), Car).Name)
    i = i + 1
  End While
  End Sub
End Module
```

Here you are making use of the AddRange() method to populate your ArrayList with a set of Car types (as you can tell, this is basically a shorthand notation for calling Add() *n* number of times). Once you print out the number of items in the collection (as well as enumerate over each item to obtain the pet name), you invoke Insert(). As you can see, Insert() allows you to plug a new item into the ArrayList at a specified index. Finally, notice the call to the ToArray() method, which returns a generic array of System.Object types based on the contents of the original ArrayList.

Working with the Queue Type

Queues are containers that ensure items are accessed using a first-in, first-out manner. Sadly, we humans are subject to queues all day long: lines at the bank, lines at the movie theater, and lines at the morning coffeehouse. When you are modeling a scenario in which items are handled on a first-come, first-served basis, System.Collections.Queue is your type of choice. In addition to the functionality provided by the supported interfaces, Queue defines the key members shown in Table 9-4.

Table 9-4. *Members of the* Queue *Type*

Member of System.Collection.Queue	Meaning in Life
Dequeue()	Removes and returns the object at the beginning of the Queue
Enqueue()	Adds an object to the end of the Queue
Peek()	Returns the object at the beginning of the Queue without removing it

To illustrate these methods, we will leverage our automobile theme once again and build a Queue object that simulates a line of cars waiting to enter a car wash. First, assume the following shared helper method to your Module type:

```
Public Sub WashCar(ByVal c As Car)
  Console.WriteLine("Cleaning {0}", c.Name)
End Sub
```

Now, consider the following code:

```
Sub Main()
...
  ' Make a Q with three items.
  Dim carWashQ As New Queue()
  carWashQ.Enqueue(New Car("FirstCar", 0, 1))
  carWashQ.Enqueue(New Car("SecondCar", 0, 2))
  carWashQ.Enqueue(New Car("ThirdCar", 0, 3))
```

```
' Peek at first car in Q.
Console.WriteLine("First in Q is {0}", _
    CType(carWashQ.Peek(), Car).Name)

' Remove each item from Q.
WashCar(CType(carWashQ.Dequeue(), Car))
WashCar(CType(carWashQ.Dequeue(), Car))
WashCar(CType(carWashQ.Dequeue(), Car))

' Try to de-Q again?
Try
    WashCar(CType(carWashQ.Dequeue(), Car))
Catch ex As Exception
    Console.WriteLine("Error!! {0}", ex.Message)
End Try
End Sub
```

Here, you insert three items into the Queue type via its Enqueue() method. The call to Peek() allows you to view (but not remove) the first item currently in the Queue, which in this case is the car named FirstCar. Finally, the call to Dequeue() removes the item from the line and sends it into the WashCar() helper function for processing. Do note that if you attempt to remove items from an empty queue, a runtime exception is thrown.

Working with the Stack Type

The System.Collections.Stack type represents a collection that maintains items using a last-in, first-out manner. As you would expect, Stack defines a member named Push() and Pop() (to place items onto or remove items from the stack). The following stack example makes use of the standard System.String:

```
Sub Main()
...
  Dim stringStack As New Stack()
  stringStack.Push("One")
  stringStack.Push("Two")
  stringStack.Push("Three")

  ' Now look at the top item, pop it, and look again.
  Console.WriteLine("Top item is: {0}", stringStack.Peek())
  Console.WriteLine("Popped off {0}", stringStack.Pop())
  Console.WriteLine("Top item is: {0}", stringStack.Peek())
  Console.WriteLine("Popped off {0}", stringStack.Pop())
  Console.WriteLine("Top item is: {0}", stringStack.Peek())
  Console.WriteLine("Popped off {0}", stringStack.Pop())

  Try
    Console.WriteLine("Top item is: {0} ", stringStack.Peek())
    Console.WriteLine("Popped off {0} ", stringStack.Pop())
  Catch ex As Exception
    Console.WriteLine("Error!! {0} ", ex.Message)
  End Try
End Sub
```

Here, you build a stack that contains three string types (named according to their order of insertion). As you peek onto the stack, you will always see the item at the very top, and therefore the first call to Peek() reveals the third string. After a series of Pop() and Peek() calls, the stack is eventually empty, at which time additional Peek()/Pop() calls raise a system exception.

■**Source Code** The CollectionTypes project can be found under the Chapter 9 subdirectory.

System.Collections.Specialized Namespace

In addition to the types defined within the System.Collections namespace, you should also be aware that the .NET base class libraries provide the System.Collections.Specialized namespace, which defines another set of types that are more (pardon the redundancy) specialized. For example, the StringDictionary and ListDictionary types each provide a stylized implementation of the IDictionary interface. Table 9-5 documents the key class types.

Table 9-5. *Types of the* System.Collections.Specialized *Namespace*

Member of System.Collections.Specialized	Meaning in Life
CollectionsUtil	Creates collections that ignore the case in strings.
HybridDictionary	Implements IDictionary by using a ListDictionary while the collection is small, and then switching to a Hashtable when the collection gets large.
ListDictionary	Implements IDictionary using a singly linked list. Recommended for collections that typically contain ten items or fewer.
NameValueCollection	Represents a sorted collection of associated String keys and String values that can be accessed either with the key or with the index.
StringCollection	Represents a collection of strings.
StringDictionary	Implements a hashtable with the key strongly typed to be a string rather than an object.
StringEnumerator	Supports a simple iteration over a StringCollection.

Summary

An interface can be defined as a named collection of *abstract members*. Because an interface does not provide any implementation details, it is common to regard an interface as a behavior that may be supported by a given type. When two or more classes implement the same interface, you are able to treat each type the same way (via interface-based polymorphism) even if the types are defined within unique class hierarchies.

VB 2005 provides the Interface keyword to allow you to define a new interface. As you have seen, a type can support as many interfaces as necessary using the Implements keyword. Furthermore, it is permissible to build interfaces that derive from multiple base interfaces.

In addition to building your custom interfaces, the .NET libraries define a number of framework-supplied interfaces. As you have seen, you are free to build custom types that implement these predefined interfaces to gain a number of desirable traits such as cloning, sorting, and enumerating. Finally, you spent some time investigating the stock collection classes defined within the System.Collections namespace and examining a number of common interfaces used by the collection-centric types.

CHAPTER 10

■■■

Callback Interfaces, Delegates, and Events

Up to this point in the text, every application you have developed added various bits of code to Main(), which, in some way or another, sent requests *to* a given object by invoking its members. However, you have not yet examined how an object can *talk back* to the entity that created it. In most programs, it is quite common for objects to engage in a two-way conversation through the use of callback interfaces, events, and other programming constructs. Although we most often think of events in the context of a GUI environment (for example, handling the Click event of a button or detecting mouse movement), the truth of the matter is events can be used to allow any two objects in memory to communicate (visible or not).

This chapter opens by examining how interface types may be used to enable callback functionality. Although the .NET event architecture is not directly tied to interface-based programming techniques, callback interfaces can be quite useful given that they are language and architecture neutral.

Next, you learn about the .NET delegate type, which is a type-safe object that "points to" other method(s) that can be invoked at a later time. As you will see, .NET delegates are quite sophisticated, in that they have built-in support for *multicasting* and asynchronous (e.g., nonblocking) invocations.

Once you learn how to create and manipulate delegate types, you then investigate a set of VB 2005 keywords (Event, Handles, RaiseEvent, etc.) that simplify the process of working with delegate types in the raw. Finally, this chapter examines a new language feature provided by Visual Basic 2005, specifically the ability to build "custom events" in order to intercept the process of registering with, detaching from, and sending an event notification.

■**Note** You will be happy to know that the event-centric techniques shown in this chapter are found all throughout the .NET platform. In fact, when you are handling Windows Forms or ASP.NET events, you will be using the exact same syntax.

Using Interfaces As a Callback Mechanism

As you have seen in the previous chapter, interfaces can be used to define a behavior that may be supported by various types in your system. Beyond using interfaces to establish polymorphism across hierarchies, interfaces may also be used as a *callback mechanism*. This technique enables objects to engage in a two-way conversation using an agreed upon set of members.

To illustrate the use of callback interfaces (also termed *event interfaces*), let's retrofit the now familiar Car type (first defined in Chapter 6) in such a way that it is able to inform the caller when the engine is about to explode (when the current speed is 10 miles below the maximum speed) and has exploded (when the current speed is at or above the maximum speed). The ability to send and receive these events will be facilitated with a custom interface named IEngineStatus:

```
' The callback interface.
Public Interface IEngineStatus
  Sub AboutToBlow(msg As String)
  Sub Exploded(msg As String)
End Interface
```

In order to keep an application's code base as flexible and reusable as possible, callback interfaces are not typically implemented directly by the object interested in receiving the events, but rather by a helper object called a *sink object*. Assume we have created a class named CarEventSink that implements IEngineStatus by printing the incoming messages to the console. As well, our sink will also maintain a string used as a textual identifier. As you will see, it is possible to register multiple sink objects for a given event source; therefore, it will prove helpful to identify a sink by name. This being said, consider the following implementation:

```
' Car event sink.
Public Class CarEventSink
  Implements IEngineStatus
  Private name As String

  Public Sub New(ByVal sinkName As String)
    name = sinkName
  End Sub

  Public Sub AboutToBlow(ByVal msg As String) _
    Implements IEngineStatus.AboutToBlow
    Console.WriteLine("{0} reporting: {1}", name, msg)
  End Sub
  Public Sub Exploded(ByVal msg As String) _
    Implements IEngineStatus.Exploded
    Console.WriteLine("{0} reporting: {1}", name, msg)
  End Sub
End Class
```

Now that you have a sink object that implements the event interface, your next task is to pass a reference to this sink into the Car type. The Car holds onto this object and makes calls back on the sink when appropriate. In order to allow the Car to receive the caller-supplied sink reference, we will need to add a public helper member to the Car type that we will call Connect(). Likewise, to allow the caller to detach from the event source, we will define another helper method on the Car type named Disconnect(). Finally, to enable the caller to register multiple sink objects (for the purposes of *multicasting*), the Car now maintains an ArrayList to represent each outstanding connection. Here are the relevant updates to the Car type:

```
' This iteration of the Car type maintains a list of
' objects implementing the IEngineStatus interface.
Public Class Car
  ' The set of connected clients.
  Private clientSinks As New ArrayList()

  ' The client calls these methods to connect
  ' to, or detach from, the event notification.
  Public Sub Connect(ByVal sink As IEngineStatus)
    clientSinks.Add(sink)
  End Sub
  Public Sub Disconnect(ByVal sink As IEngineStatus)
    clientSinks.Remove(sink)
  End Sub
...
End Class
```

To actually send the events, let's update the `Car.Accelerate()` method to iterate over the list of sinks maintained by the `ArrayList` and send the correct notification when appropriate. Here is the updated member in question:

```vb
' The Accelerate method now fires event notifications to the caller,
' rather than throwing a custom exception.
Public Sub Accelerate(ByVal delta As Integer)
  ' If the car is doomed, sent out event to
  ' each connected client.
  If carIsDead Then
    For Each i As IEngineStatus In clientSinks
      i.Exploded("Sorry!  This car is toast!")
    Next
  Else
    currSpeed += delta
    ' Send out 'about to blow' event?
    If (maxSpeed - currSpeed) = 10 Then
      For Each i As IEngineStatus In clientSinks
        i.AboutToBlow("Careful! About to blow!")
      Next
    End If
    ' Is the car doomed?
    If currSpeed >= maxSpeed Then
      carIsDead = True
    Else
      ' We are OK, just print out speed.
      Console.WriteLine("=> CurrSpeed = {0}", currSpeed)
    End If
  End If
End Sub
```

To complete the example, here is a `Main()` method making use of a callback interface to listen to the Car events:

```vb
' Make a car and listen to the events.
Module Program
  Sub Main()
    Console.WriteLine("***** Interfaces as event enablers *****")
    Dim myCar As New Car("SlugBug", 10)

    ' Make sink object.
    Dim sink As New CarEventSink("MySink")

    ' Register the sink with the Car.
    myCar.Connect(sink)

    ' Speed up (this will trigger the event notifications).
    For i As Integer = 0 To 5
      myCar.Accelerate(20)
    Next

    ' Detach from event source.
    myCar.Disconnect(sink)
    Console.ReadLine()
  End Sub
End Module
```

Figure 10-1 shows the end result of this interface-based event protocol.

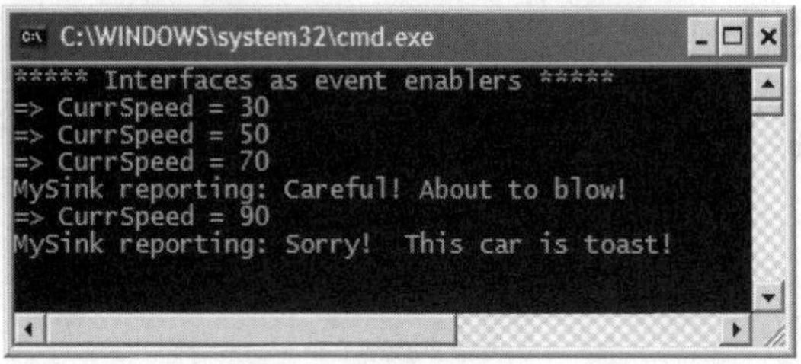

```
C:\WINDOWS\system32\cmd.exe                    _ □ ×
***** Interfaces as event enablers *****
=> CurrSpeed = 30
=> CurrSpeed = 50
=> CurrSpeed = 70
MySink reporting: Careful! About to blow!
=> CurrSpeed = 90
MySink reporting: Sorry!  This car is toast!
```

Figure 10-1. *Interfaces as event protocols*

Notice that we call `Disconnect()` before exiting `Main()`, although this is not actually necessary for the example to function as intended. However, the `Disconnect()` method can be very helpful in that it allows the caller to selectively detach from an event source at will. Assume that the application now wishes to register two sink objects, dynamically remove a particular sink during the flow of execution, and continue processing the program at large:

```
Module Program
  Sub Main()
    Console.WriteLine("***** Interfaces as event enablers *****")
    Dim myCar As New Car("SlugBug", 10)

    ' Make sink object.
    Console.WriteLine("***** Creating Sinks! *****")
    Dim sink As New CarEventSink("First Sink")
    Dim otherSink As New CarEventSink("Second Sink")

    ' Pass both sinks to car.
    myCar.Connect(sink)
    myCar.Connect(otherSink)

    ' Speed up (this will trigger the events).
    For i As Integer = 0 To 5
      myCar.Accelerate(20)
    Next

    ' Detach from first sink.
    myCar.Disconnect(sink)

    ' Speed up again (only otherSink will be called).
    For i As Integer = 0 To 5
      myCar.Accelerate(20)
    Next

    ' Detach from other sink.
    myCar.Disconnect(otherSink)
    Console.ReadLine()
  End Sub
End Module
```

Figure 10-2 shows the update.

```
C:\WINDOWS\system32\cmd.exe                              _ □ ×
***** Interfaces as event enablers *****
***** Creating Sinks! *****
=> CurrSpeed = 30
=> CurrSpeed = 50
=> CurrSpeed = 70
First Sink reporting: Careful! About to blow!
Second Sink reporting: Careful! About to blow!
=> CurrSpeed = 90
First Sink reporting: Sorry!  This car is toast!
Second Sink reporting: Sorry!  This car is toast!
Second Sink reporting: Sorry!  This car is toast!
Second Sink reporting: Sorry!  This car is toast!
Second Sink reporting: Sorry!  This car is toast!
Second Sink reporting: Sorry!  This car is toast!
Second Sink reporting: Sorry!  This car is toast!
Second Sink reporting: Sorry!  This car is toast!
```

Figure 10-2. *Working with multiple sinks*

So! Hopefully you agree that event interfaces can be helpful in that they can be used under any language (VB 6.0, VB 2005, C++, etc.) or platform (COM, .NET, or J2EE) that supports interface-based programming. However, as you may be suspecting, the .NET platform defines an "official" event protocol that is not dependent on the construction of interfaces. To understand .NET's intrinsic event architecture, we begin by examining the role of the *delegate type*.

■**Source Code** The EventInterface project is located under the Chapter 10 subdirectory.

Understanding the .NET Delegate Type

Before formally defining .NET delegates, let's gain a bit of historical perspective regarding the Windows platform. Since its inception many years ago, the Win32 API made use of C-style function pointers to support *callback functionality*. Using these function pointers, programmers were able to configure one function in the program to invoke another function in the application. As you would imagine, this approach allowed applications to handle events from various UI elements, intercept messages in a distributed system, and numerous other techniques. Although BASIC-style languages have historically avoided the complexity of working with function pointers (thankfully), the callback construct is burned deep into the fabric of the Windows API.

One of the problems found with C-style callback functions is that they represent little more than a raw address in memory, which offers little by way of type safety or object orientation. Ideally, callback functions could be configured to include additional type-safe information such as the number of (and types of) parameters and the return value (if any) of the method being "pointed to." Alas, this is not the case in traditional callback functions, and, as you may suspect, can therefore be a frequent source of bugs, hard crashes, and other runtime disasters.

Nevertheless, callbacks are useful entities in that they can be used to build event architectures. In the .NET Framework, callbacks are still possible, and their functionality is accomplished in a much safer and more object-oriented manner using *delegates*. In essence, a delegate is a type-safe object that points to another method (or possibly multiple methods) in the application, which can be invoked at a later time. Specifically speaking, a delegate type maintains three important pieces of information:

- The *address* of the method on which it will make calls
- The *arguments* (if any) required by this method
- The *return value* (if any) returned from this method

Once a delegate has been defined and provided the necessary information, you may dynamically invoke the method(s) it points to at runtime. As you will see, every delegate in the .NET Framework (including your custom delegates) is automatically endowed with the ability to call their methods *synchronously* (using the calling thread) or *asynchronously* (on a secondary thread in a nonblocking manner). This fact greatly simplifies programming tasks, given that we can call a method on a secondary thread of execution without manually creating and managing a Thread object. This chapter will focus on the synchronous aspect of the delegate type. We will examine the asynchronous behavior of delegate types during our investigation of the System.Threading namespace in Chapter 16.

Defining a Delegate in VB 2005

When you want to create a delegate in VB 2005, you make use of the Delegate keyword. The name of your delegate can be whatever you desire. However, you must define the delegate to match the signature of the method it will point to. For example, assume you wish to build a delegate named BinaryOp that can point to any method that returns an Integer and takes two Integers as input parameters:

```
' This delegate can point to any method,
' taking two Integers and returning an
' Integer.
Public Delegate Function BinaryOp(ByVal x as Integer, _
   ByVal y as Integer) As Integer
```

When the VB 2005 compiler processes a delegate type, it automatically generates a sealed class deriving from System.MulticastDelegate. This class (in conjunction with its base class, System.Delegate) provides the necessary infrastructure for the delegate to hold onto the list of methods to be invoked at a later time. For example, if you examine the BinaryOp delegate using ildasm.exe, you would find the autogenerated class type depicted in Figure 10-3.

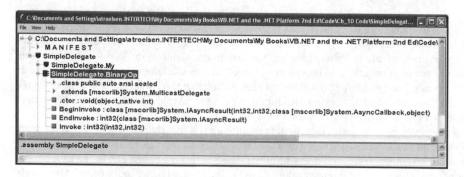

Figure 10-3. *The* BinaryOp *delegate under the hood*

As you can see, the generated BinaryOp class defines three public methods. Invoke() is perhaps the core method, as it is used to invoke each method maintained by the delegate type in a *synchronous* manner, meaning the caller must wait for the call to complete before continuing on its way. Strangely enough, the synchronous Invoke() method is typically not directly called in code. As you will see in just a bit, Invoke() is called behind the scenes when you make use of the appropriate VB 2005 syntax.

BeginInvoke() and EndInvoke() provide the ability to call the method pointed to by the delegate *asynchronously* on a second thread of execution. If you have a background in multithreading, you are aware that one of the most common reasons developers create secondary threads of execution is to invoke methods that require a good deal of time to complete. Although the .NET base class libraries provide an entire namespace devoted to multithreaded programming (System.Threading), delegates provide this functionality out of the box.

Investigating the Autogenerated Class Type

So, how exactly does the compiler know how to define the Invoke(), BeginInvoke(), and EndInvoke() methods? To understand the process, here is the crux of the generated BinaryOp class type, shown in dazzling pseudo-code:

```
' This is only pseudo-code!
NotInheritable Class BinaryOp
  Inherits System.MulticastDelegate
  ' Compiler generated constructor.
  Public Sub New(ByVal target As Object, ByVal functionAddress As System.UInt32)
  End Sub
  ' Used for synchronous calls.
  Public Sub Invoke(ByVal x As Integer, ByVal y As Integer)
  End Sub
  ' Used for asynchronous calls on a second thread.
  Public Function BeginInvoke(ByVal x As Integer, ByVal y As Integer, _
    ByVal cb As AsyncCallback, ByVal state As Object) As IAsyncResult
  End Function
  Public Function EndInvoke(ByVal result As IAsyncResult) As Integer
  End Function
End Class
```

First, notice that the parameters and return value defined for the Invoke() method exactly match the definition of the BinaryOp delegate. The initial parameters to BeginInvoke() members (two Integers in our case) are also based on the BinaryOp delegate; however, BeginInvoke() will always provide two final parameters (of type AsyncCallback and Object) that are used to facilitate asynchronous method invocations. Finally, the return value of EndInvoke() is identical to the original delegate declaration and will always take as a sole parameter an object implementing the IAsyncResult interface.

Let's see another example. Assume you have defined a delegate that can point to any method returning a String and receiving three Boolean input parameters:

```
Public Delegate Function MyDelegate(ByVal a As Boolean, ByVal b As Boolean, _
  ByVal c As Boolean) As String
```

This time, the autogenerated class breaks down as follows:

```
NotInheritable Class MyDelegate
Inherits System.MulticastDelegate
  Public Sub New(ByVal target As Object, ByVal functionAddress As System.UInt32)
  End Sub
  Public Function Invoke(ByVal a As Boolean, ByVal b As Boolean, _
    ByVal c As Boolean) As String
  End Function
  Public Function BeginInvoke(ByVal a As Boolean, ByVal b As Boolean, _
    ByVal c As Boolean, ByVal cb As AsyncCallback, _
    ByVal state As Object) As IAsyncResult
  End Function
```

```
   Public Function EndInvoke(ByVal result As IAsyncResult) As String
   End Function
End Class
```

Delegates can also "point to" methods that contain any number of ByRef parameters. For example, assume the following delegate type definition:

```
Public Delegate Function MyOtherDelegate(ByRef a As Boolean, _
  ByRef b As Boolean, ByVal c As Integer) As String
```

The signatures of the Invoke() and BeginInvoke() methods look as you would expect; however, check out the EndInvoke() method, which now includes the set of all ByRef arguments defined by the delegate type:

```
NotInheritable Class MyOtherDelegate
  Inherits System.MulticastDelegate
  Public Sub New(ByVal target As Object, ByVal functionAddress As System.UInt32)
  End Sub
  Public Function Invoke(ByRef a As Boolean, ByRef b As Boolean, _
    ByVal c As Integer) As String
  End Function
  Public Function BeginInvoke(ByRef a As Boolean, ByRef b As Boolean, _
    ByVal c As Integer, ByVal cb As AsyncCallback, _
    ByVal state As Object) As IAsyncResult
  End Function
  Public Function EndInvoke(ByRef a As Boolean, ByRef b As Boolean, _
    ByVal result As IAsyncResult) As String
  End Function
End Class
```

To summarize the story thus far, a VB 2005 delegate definition results in a compiler-generated sealed class containing three methods (as well as an internally called constructor) whose parameter and return types are based on the delegate's declaration. Again, the good news is that the VB 2005 compiler is the entity in charge of defining the actual delegate definition on our behalf.

The System.MulticastDelegate and System.Delegate Base Classes

So, when you build a type using the VB 2005 Delegate keyword, you indirectly declare a class type that derives from System.MulticastDelegate. This class provides descendents with access to a list that contains the addresses of the methods maintained by the delegate type, as well as several additional methods to interact with the invocation list. MulticastDelegate obtains additional functionality from its parent class, System.Delegate.

Now, do understand that you will never directly derive from these base classes (in fact it is a compiler error to do so). However, all delegate types inherit the members documented in Table 10-1 (consult the .NET Framework 2.0 documentation for full details).

Table 10-1. *Select Members of* System.MultcastDelegate/System.Delegate

Inherited Member	Meaning in Life
Method	This property returns a System.Reflection.MethodInfo type that represents details of a shared method that is maintained by the delegate.
Target	If the method to be called is defined at the object level (rather than a shared method), Target returns the name of the method maintained by the delegate. If the value returned from Target equals Nothing, the method to be called is a shared member.
Combine()	This shared method adds a method to the list maintained by the delegate.
GetInvocationList()	This method returns an array of System.Delegate types, each representing a particular method maintained by the delegate's invocation list.
Remove() RemoveAll()	These shared methods removes a method (or all methods) from the invocation list.

The Simplest Possible Delegate Example

Delegates tend to cause a great deal of confusion when encountered for the first time (even for those who do have experience with C-style callback functions). Thus, to get the ball rolling, let's take a look at a very simple console application (named SimpleDelegate) that makes use of our BinaryOp delegate type. Here is the complete code (defined within a single *.vb file), with analysis to follow:

```
' Our delegate type can point to any method
' taking two integers and returning an integer.
Public Delegate Function BinaryOp(ByVal x As Integer, _
   ByVal y As Integer) As Integer

' This class defines the methods that will be 'pointed to' by the delegate.
Public Class SimpleMath
   Public Shared Function Add(ByVal x As Integer, ByVal y As Integer) As Integer
      Return x + y
   End Function
   Public Shared Function Subtract(ByVal x As Integer, _
      ByVal y As Integer) As Integer
      Return x - y
   End Function
End Class

Module Program
   Sub Main()
      Console.WriteLine("***** Simple Delegate Example *****")

      ' Make a delegate object and add method to invocation
      ' list using the AddressOf keyword.
      Dim b As BinaryOp = New BinaryOp(AddressOf SimpleMath.Add)

      ' Invoke the method 'pointed to'
      Console.WriteLine("10 + 10 is {0}", b(10, 10))
      Console.ReadLine()
   End Sub
End Module
```

Again notice the format of the BinaryOp delegate, which can point to any method taking two Integers and returning an Integer. Given this, we have created a class named SimpleMath, which defines two shared methods that (surprise, surprise) match the pattern defined by the BinaryOp delegate. When you want to insert the target method to a given delegate, simply pass in the name of the method to the delegate's constructor using the VB 2005 AddressOf keyword.

At this point, you are able to invoke the member pointed to using a syntax that looks like a direct method invocation:

```
' Invoke() is really called here!
Console.WriteLine("10 + 10 is {0}", b(10, 10))
```

Under the hood, the runtime actually calls the compiler-generated Invoke() method. You can verify this fact for yourself if you open your assembly in ildasm.exe and investigate the CIL code within the Main() method. Here is a partial code snippet:

```
.method private hidebysig static void Main(string[] args) cil managed
{
...
   callvirt instance int32 SimpleDelegate.BinaryOp::Invoke(int32, int32)
...
}
```

If you wish to call the Invoke() method directly, you are free to do so:

```
' Call Invoke() directly.
Console.WriteLine("10 + 10 is {0}", b.Invoke(10, 10))
```

Recall that .NET delegates are intrinsically *type safe*. Therefore, if you attempt to pass a delegate the address of a method that does not "match the pattern," you receive a compile-time error. To illustrate, assume the SimpleMath class now defines an additional method named SquareNumber() as follows:

```
Public Class SimpleMath
...
   Public Shared Function SquareNumber(ByVal a As Integer) As Integer
      Return a * a
   End Function
End Class
```

Given that the BinaryOp delegate can *only* point to methods that take two Integers and return an Integer, the following code is illegal and will not compile:

```
' Error! Method does not match delegate pattern!
Dim b As New BinaryOp(AddressOf SimpleMath.SquareNumber)
```

Interacting with a Delegate Object

Let's spice up the current example by defining a helper function within our module named DisplayDelegateInfo(). This method will print out names of the methods maintained by the incoming delegate type as well as the name of the class defining the method. To do so, we will iterate over the System.Delegate array returned by GetInvocationList(), invoking each object's Target and Method properties:

```
Sub DisplayDelegateInfo(ByVal delObj As System.Delegate)
  For Each d As System.Delegate In delObj.GetInvocationList()
    Console.WriteLine("Method Name: {0}", d.Method)
    Console.WriteLine("Type Name: {0}", d.Target)
  Next
End Sub
```

Assuming you have updated your `Main()` method to actually call this new helper method by passing in your `BinaryOp` object:

```
Sub Main()
...
  Dim b As BinaryOp = New BinaryOp(AddressOf SimpleMath.Add)
  ' Invoke the method 'pointed to' as before.
  Console.WriteLine("10 + 10 is {0}", b(10, 10))
  DisplayDelegateInfo(b)
...
End Sub
```

you would find the output shown in Figure 10-4.

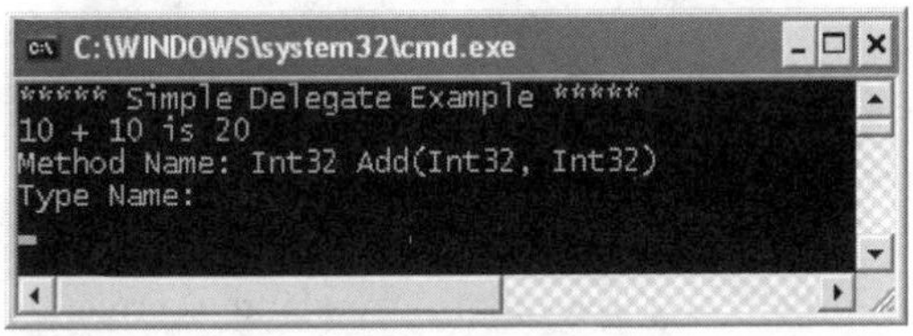

Figure 10-4. *Investigation our* `BinaryOp` *delegate*

Notice that the name of the type (`SimpleMath`) is currently not displayed by the `Target` property. The reason has to do with the fact that our `BinaryOp` delegate is pointing to *shared* methods and therefore there is no object to reference! However, if we update the `Add()` and `Subtract` methods to be instance-level members (simply by deleting the `Shared` keywords), we could create an instance of the `SimpleMath` type and specify the methods to invoke as follows:

```
Sub Main()
  Console.WriteLine("***** Simple Delegate Example *****")

  ' Make a new SimpleMath object.
  Dim myMath As New SimpleMath()

  ' Use this object to specify the address of the Add method.
  Dim b As BinaryOp = New BinaryOp(AddressOf myMath.Add)

  ' Invoke the method 'pointed to' as before.
  Console.WriteLine("10 + 10 is {0}", b(10, 10))
  DisplayDelegateInfo(b)
  Console.ReadLine()
End Sub
```

In this case, we would find the output shown in Figure 10-5.

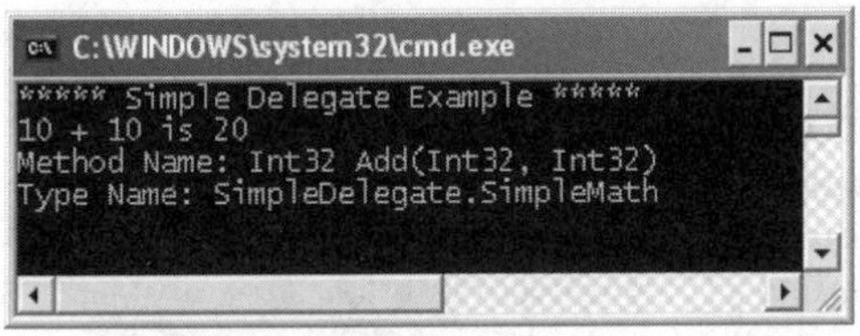

Figure 10-5. *"Pointing to" instance-level methods*

■Source Code The SimpleDelegate project is located under the Chapter 10 subdirectory.

Retrofitting the Car Type with Delegates

Clearly, the previous SimpleDelegate example was intended to be purely illustrative in nature, given that there would be no compelling reason to build a delegate simply to add two numbers. Hopefully, however, this example demystifies the basic process of working with delegate types.

To provide a more realistic use of delegate types, let's retrofit our Car type to send the Exploded and AboutToBlow notifications using .NET delegates rather than a custom event interface. Beyond no longer implementing IEngineStatus, here are the steps we will take:

- Define the AboutToBlow and Exploded delegates.

- Declare member variables of each delegate type in the Car class.

- Create helper functions on the Car that allow the caller to specify the methods to add to the delegate member variable's invocation lists.

- Update the Accelerate() method to invoke the delegate's invocation list under the correct circumstances.

First, consider the following updates to the Car class, which address the first three points:

```
Public Class Car
  ' Our delegate types are nested in the Car type.
  Public Delegate Sub AboutToBlow(ByVal msg As String)
  Public Delegate Sub Exploded(ByVal msg As String)

  ' Because delegates are simply classes, we can create
  ' member variables of delegate types.
  Private almostDeadList As AboutToBlow
  Private explodedList As Exploded

  ' To allow the caller to pass us a delegate object.
  Public Sub OnAboutToBlow(ByVal clientMethod As AboutToBlow)
    almostDeadList = clientMethod
  End Sub
  Public Sub OnExploded(ByVal clientMethod As Exploded)
    explodedList = clientMethod
  End Sub
...
End Class
```

Notice in this example that we define the delegate types directly within the scope of the Car type. From a design point of view, it is quite natural to define a delegate within the scope of the type it naturally works with given that it illustrates a tight association between the two types. Furthermore, given that the compiler transforms a delegate into a full class definition, what we have actually done is indirectly created two nested classes.

Next, note that we declare two member variables (one for each delegate type) and two helper functions (OnAboutToBlow() and OnExploded()) that allow the client to add a method to the delegate's invocation list. In concept, these methods are similar to the Connect() and Disconnect() methods we created during the EventInterface example. Of course, in this case, the incoming parameter is a client-allocated delegate object rather than a sink implementing a specific event interface.

At this point, we need to update the Accelerate() method to invoke each delegate, rather than iterate over an ArrayList of client-supplied sinks:

```
Public Sub Accelerate(ByVal delta As Integer)
  If carIsDead Then
    ' If the car is doomed, send out the Exploded notification.
    If Not (explodedList Is Nothing) Then
      explodedList("Sorry, this car is dead...")
    End If
  Else
    currSpeed += delta
    ' Are we almost doomed?  If so, send out AboutToBlow notification.
    If 10 = maxSpeed - currSpeed AndAlso Not (almostDeadList Is Nothing) Then
      almostDeadList("Careful buddy!  Gonna blow!")
    End If
    If currSpeed >= maxSpeed Then
      carIsDead = True
    Else
      Console.WriteLine("->CurrSpeed = {0}", currSpeed)
    End If
  End If
End Sub
```

Notice that before we invoke the methods maintained by the almostDeadList and explodedList member variables, we are checking them against the value Nothing. The reason is that it will be the job of the caller to allocate these objects when calling the OnAboutToBlow() and OnExploded() helper methods. If the caller does not call these methods (given that it may not wish to hear about these events), and we attempt to invoke the delegate's invocation list, we will trigger a NullReferenceException and bomb at runtime (which would obviously be a bad thing!).

Now that we have the delegate infrastructure in place, observe the updates to the Program module:

```
Module Program
  Sub Main()
    Console.WriteLine("***** Delegates as event enablers *****")
    Dim c1 As Car = New Car("SlugBug", 10)

    ' Pass the address of the methods that will be maintained
    ' by the delegate member variables of the Car type.
    c1.OnAboutToBlow(AddressOf CarAboutToBlow)
    c1.OnExploded(AddressOf CarExploded)

    Console.WriteLine("***** Speeding up *****")
    For i As Integer = 0 To 5
      c1.Accelerate(20)
    Next
    Console.ReadLine()
  End Sub

  ' These are called by the Car object.
  Public Sub CarAboutToBlow(ByVal msg As String)
    Console.WriteLine(msg)
  End Sub
  Public Sub CarExploded(ByVal msg As String)
    Console.WriteLine(msg)
  End Sub
End Module
```

Notice that in this code example, we are not directly allocating an instance of the Car.AboutToBlow or Car.Exploded delegate objects. However, when we make use of the VB 2005 AddressOf keyword, the compiler will automatically generate a new instance of the related delegate type. This can be verified using ildasm.exe (which I will leave as an exercise to the interested reader).

While the fact that the AddressOf keyword automatically generates the delegate objects in the background is quite helpful, there will be times when you will prefer to allocate the delegate object manually for later use in your application. We will see a practical reason to do so in the next section; however, to illustrate the process, consider the following iteration of Main():

```
Module Program
  Sub Main()
    Console.WriteLine("***** Delegates as event enablers *****")
    Dim c1 As Car = New Car("SlugBug", 10)

    ' Manually create the delegate objects.
    Dim aboutToBlowDel As New Car.AboutToBlow(AddressOf CarAboutToBlow)
    Dim explodedDel As New Car.Exploded(AddressOf CarExploded)

    ' Now pass in delegate objects.
    c1.OnAboutToBlow(aboutToBlowDel)
    c1.OnExploded(explodedDel)
...
  End Sub

  Public Sub CarAboutToBlow(ByVal msg As String)
    Console.WriteLine(msg)
  End Sub
  Public Sub CarExploded(ByVal msg As String)
    Console.WriteLine(msg)
  End Sub
End Module
```

The only major point to be made here is because of the fact that the AboutToBlow and Exploded delegates are nested within the Car class, we must allocate them using their full name (e.g., Car.AboutToBlow). Like any delegate constructor, we pass in the name of the method to add to the invocation list.

Enabling Multicasting

Recall that .NET delegates have the intrinsic ability to *multicast*. In other words, a delegate object can maintain a *list* of methods to call (provided they match the pattern defined by the delegate), rather than a single method. When you wish to add multiple methods to a delegate object, you will need to call System.Delegate.Combine(). To enable multicasting on the Car type, we could update the OnAboutToBlow() and OnExploded() methods as follows:

```
Class Car
...
  ' Now with multicasting!
  Public Sub OnAboutToBlow(ByVal clientMethod As AboutToBlow)
    almostDeadList = System.Delegate.Combine(almostDeadList, clientMethod)
  End Sub
  Public Sub OnExploded(ByVal clientMethod As Exploded)
    explodedList = System.Delegate.Combine(explodedList, clientMethod)
  End Sub
...
End Class
```

Be aware that the previous code will only compile if Option Strict is not enabled in your project. Since this is always good practice, here would be a more type-safe (and compiler acceptable) implementation of these methods using explicit casting:

```
' Now with type-safe multicasting!
Public Sub OnAboutToBlow(ByVal clientMethod As AboutToBlow)
```

```
    almostDeadList = CType(System.Delegate.Combine(almostDeadList, _
      clientMethod), AboutToBlow)
End Sub
Public Sub OnExploded(ByVal clientMethod As Exploded)
  explodedList = CType(System.Delegate.Combine(explodedList, _
    clientMethod), Exploded)
End Sub
```

In either case, the first argument to pass into Combine() is the delegate object that is maintaining the current invocation list, while the second argument is the new delegate object you wish to add to the list. At this point, the caller can now register multiple targets as follows:

```
Module Program
  Sub Main()
    Console.WriteLine("***** Delegates as event enablers *****")
    Dim c1 As Car = New Car("SlugBug", 10)

    ' Register multiple event handlers!
    c1.OnAboutToBlow(AddressOf CarAboutToBlow)
    c1.OnAboutToBlow(AddressOf CarIsAlmostDoomed)
    c1.OnExploded(AddressOf CarExploded)
...
  End Sub

  ' This time, two methods are called
  ' when the AboutToBlow notification fires.
  Public Sub CarAboutToBlow(ByVal msg As String)
    Console.WriteLine(msg)
  End Sub
  Public Sub CarIsAlmostDoomed(ByVal msg As String)
    Console.WriteLine("Critical Message from Car: {0}", msg)
  End Sub
  Public Sub CarExploded(ByVal msg As String)
    Console.WriteLine(msg)
  End Sub
End Module
```

Removing a Target from a Delegate's Invocation List

The Delegate class also defines a shared Remove() method that allows a caller to dynamically remove a member from the invocation list. If you wish to allow the caller the option to detach from the AboutToBlow and Exploded notifications, you could add the following additional helper methods to the Car type:

```
Class Car
...
  ' To remove a target from the list.
  Public Sub RemoveAboutToBlow(ByVal clientMethod As AboutToBlow)
    almostDeadList = CType(System.Delegate.Remove(almostDeadList, _
      clientMethod), AboutToBlow)
  End Sub
  Public Sub RemoveExploded(ByVal clientMethod As Exploded)
    explodedList = CType(System.Delegate.Remove(explodedList, _
      clientMethod), Exploded)
  End Sub
...
End Class
```

Thus, we could stop receiving the Exploded notification by updating Main() as follows:

```
Sub Main()
  Console.WriteLine("***** Delegates as event enablers *****")
  Dim c1 As Car = New Car("SlugBug", 10)

  ' Register multiple event handlers!
  c1.OnAboutToBlow(AddressOf CarAboutToBlow)
  c1.OnAboutToBlow(AddressOf CarIsAlmostDoomed)
  c1.OnExploded(AddressOf CarExploded)

  Console.WriteLine("***** Speeding up *****")
  For i As Integer = 0 To 5
    c1.Accelerate(20)
  Next

  ' Remove CarExploded from invocation list.
  c1.RemoveExploded(AddressOf CarExploded)

  ' This will not fire the Exploded event.
  For i As Integer = 0 To 5
    c1.Accelerate(20)
  Next
  Console.ReadLine()
End Sub
```

The final output of our CarDelegate application can be seen in Figure 10-6.

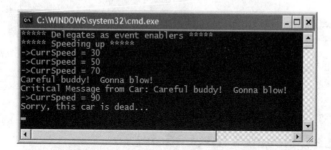

Figure 10-6. *The* Car *type, now with delegates*

■**Source Code** The CarDelegate project is located under the Chapter 10 subdirectory.

Understanding (and Using) Events

Delegates are fairly interesting constructs in that they enable two objects in memory to engage in a two-way conversation in a type-safe and object-oriented manner. As you may agree, however, working with delegates in the raw does entail a good amount of boilerplate code (defining the delegate, declaring any necessary member variables, and creating custom registration/unregistration methods).

Because the ability for one object to call back to another object is such a helpful construct, VB 2005 provides a small set of keywords to lessen the burden of using delegates in the raw. For example, when the compiler processes the Event keyword, you are automatically provided with registration and unregistration methods that allow the caller to hook into an event notification. Better yet, using the Event keyword removes the need to define delegate objects in the first place. In this light, the Event keyword is little more than syntactic sugar, which can be used to save you some typing time.

To illustrate these new keywords, let's reconfigure the Car class to make use of VB 2005 events, rather than raw delegates. First, you need to define the events themselves using the VB .NET Event keyword. Notice that events are defined with regards to the set of parameters passed into the registered handler:

```
Public Class Car
...
  ' This car can send these events.
  Public Event Exploded(ByVal msg As String)
  Public Event AboutToBlow(ByVal msg As String)
...
End Class
```

Firing an Event Using the RaiseEvent Keyword

Firing an event is as simple as specifying the event by name (with any specified parameters) using the RaiseEvent keyword. To illustrate, update the previous implementation of Accelerate() to send each event accordingly:

```
Public Sub Accelerate(ByVal delta As Integer)
  If carIsDead Then
    ' If the car is doomed, raise Exploded event.
    RaiseEvent Exploded("Sorry, this car is dead...")
  Else
    currSpeed += delta
    ' Are we almost doomed?  If so, send out AboutToBlow event.
    If 10 = maxSpeed - currSpeed Then
      RaiseEvent AboutToBlow("Careful buddy!  Gonna blow!")
    End If
    If currSpeed >= maxSpeed Then
      carIsDead = True
    Else
      Console.WriteLine("->CurrSpeed = {0}", currSpeed)
    End If
  End If
End Sub
```

With this, you have configured the car to send two custom events (under the correct conditions). You will see the usage of this new automobile in just a moment, but first, let's dig a bit deeper into the VB 2005 Event keyword.

Events Under the Hood

A VB 2005 event actually encapsulates a good deal of information. Each time you declare an event with the Event keyword, the compiler generates the following information within the defining class:

- A new hidden, nested delegate is created automatically and added to your class. The name of this delegate is always *EventName*+EventHandler. For example, if you have an event named Exploded, the autogenerated delegate is named ExplodedEventHandler.

- Two hidden public functions, one having an "add_" prefix, the other having a "remove_" prefix, are automatically added to your class. These are used internally to call Delegate.Combine() and Delegate.Remove(), in order to add and remove methods to/from the list maintained by the delegate.

- A new hidden member variable is added to your class that represents a new instance of the autogenerated delegate type (see the first bullet item).

As you can see, the Event keyword is indeed a timesaver as it instructs the compiler to author the same sort of code you created manually when using the delegate type directly!

If you were to compile the CarEvent example and load the assembly into ildasm.exe, you could check out the CIL instructions behind the compiler-generated add_AboutToBlow(). Notice it calls Delegate.Combine() on your behalf. Also notice that the parameter passed to add_AboutToBlow() is an instance of the autogenerated AboutToBlowEventHandler delegate:

```
.method public specialname instance void
  add_AboutToBlow(class CarEvent.Car/AboutToBlowEventHandler obj)
  cil managed synchronized
{
...
  IL_0008:  call class [mscorlib]System.Delegate
    [mscorlib]System.Delegate::Combine(class [mscorlib]System.Delegate,
    class [mscorlib]System.Delegate)
...
} // end of method Car::add_AboutToBlow
```

Furthermore, remove_AboutToBlow() makes the call to Delegate.Remove() automatically, passing in the incoming AboutToBlowEventHandler delegate:

```
.method public specialname instance void
  remove_AboutToBlow(class CarEvent.Car/AboutToBlowEventHandler obj)
  cil managed synchronized
{
...
  IL_0008:  call class [mscorlib]System.Delegate
    [mscorlib]System.Delegate::Remove(class [mscorlib]System.Delegate,
    class [mscorlib]System.Delegate)
...
} // end of method Car::remove_AboutToBlow
```

The CIL instructions for the event declaration itself makes use of the .addon and .removeon CIL tokens to connect the correct add_XXX() and remove_XXX() methods:

```
.event CarEvents.Car/EngineHandler AboutToBlow
{
  .addon
  void CarEvents.Car::add_AboutToBlow(class CarEvents.Car/EngineHandler)
  .removeon
  void CarEvents.Car::remove_AboutToBlow(class CarEvents.Car/EngineHandler)
} // end of event Car::AboutToBlow
```

Perhaps most important, if you check out the CIL behind this iteration of the Accelerate() method, you find that the delegate is invoked on your behalf. Here is a partial snapshot of the CIL that invokes the invocation list maintained by the ExplodedEventHandler delegate:

```
.method public instance
  void Accelerate(int32 delta) cil managed
{
...
  IL_001d:  callvirt
    instance void CarEvents.Car/ExplodedEventHandler::Invoke(string)
...
}
```

As you can see, the VB 2005 Event keyword is quite helpful, given that it builds and manipulates raw delegates on your behalf. As you saw earlier in this chapter, however, you are able to directly manipulate delegates if you so choose.

Hooking into Incoming Events Using WithEvents and Handles

Now that you understand how to build a class that can send events, the next big question is how you can configure an object to receive these events. Assume you have now created an instance of the Car class and want to listen to the events it is capable of sending.

The first step is to declare a member variable for which you wish to process incoming events using the WithEvents keyword. Next, you will associate an event to a particular event handler using the Handles keyword. For example:

```
Module Program
  ' Declare member variables 'WithEvents' to
  ' capture the events.
  Dim WithEvents c As New Car("NightRider", 50)

  Sub Main()
    Console.WriteLine("***** Fun with Events *****")
    Dim i As Integer
    For i = 0 To 5
      c.Accelerate(10)
    Next
  End Sub

  ' Event Handlers.
  Public Sub MyExplodedHandler(ByVal s As String) _
    Handles c.Exploded
    Console.WriteLine(s)
  End Sub
  Public Sub MyAboutToDieHandler(ByVal s As String) _
    Handles c.AboutToBlow
    Console.WriteLine(s)
  End Sub
End Module
```

In many ways, things look more or less like traditional VB 6.0 event logic. The only new spin is the fact that the Handles keyword is now used to connect the handler to an object's event.

■**Note** As you may know, VB 6.0 demanded that event handlers always be named using very strict naming conventions (*NameOfTheObject_NameOfTheEvent*) that could easily break as you renamed the objects in your code base. With the VB 2005 Handles keyword, however, the name of your event handlers can be anything you choose.

Multicasting Using the Handles Keyword

Another extremely useful aspect of the Handles statement is the fact that you are able to configure multiple methods to process the same event. For example, if you update your module as follows:

```
Module Program
...
  Public Sub MyExplodedHandler(ByVal s As String) _
    Handles c.Exploded
    Console.WriteLine(s)
  End Sub

  ' Both of these handlers will be called when AboutToBlow is fired.
  Public Sub MyAboutToDieHandler(ByVal s As String) _
    Handles c.AboutToBlow
    Console.WriteLine(s)
  End Sub
  Public Sub MyAboutToDieHandler2(ByVal s As String) _
    Handles c.AboutToBlow
    Console.WriteLine(s)
  End Sub
End Module
```

you would see the incoming String object sent by the AboutToBlow event print out twice, as we have handled this event using two different event handlers.

Defining a Single Handler for Multiple Events

The Handles keyword also allows you to define a single handler to (pardon the redundancy) handle multiple events, provided that the events are passing in the same set of arguments. This should make sense, as the VB 2005 Event keyword is simply a shorthand notation for working with type-safe delegates. In our example, given that the Exploded and AboutToBlow events are both passing a single string by value, we could intercept each event using the following handler:

```
Module Program
  Dim WithEvents c As New Car("NightRider", 50)

  Sub Main()
    Console.WriteLine("***** Fun with Events *****")
    Dim i As Integer
    For i = 0 To 5
      c.Accelerate(10)
    Next
  End Sub

  ' A single handler for each event.
  Public Sub MyExplodedHandler(ByVal s As String) _
    Handles c.Exploded, c.AboutToBlow
    Console.WriteLine(s)
  End Sub
End Module
```

Source Code The CarEvents project is located under the Chapter 10 subdirectory.

Dynamically Hooking into Incoming Events with AddHandler/RemoveHandler

Currently, we have been hooking into an event by explicitly declaring the variable using the WithEvents keyword. When you do so, you make a few assumptions in your code:

- The variable is *not* a local variable, but a member variable of the defining type (Module, Class, or Structure).

- You wish to be informed of the event throughout the lifetime of your application.

Given these points, it is not possible to declare a local variable using the WithEvents keyword:

```
Sub Main()
  ' Error!  Local variables cannot be
  ' declared 'with events'.
  Dim WithEvents myCar As New Car()
End Sub
```

However, under the .NET platform, you do have an alternative method that may be used to hook into an event. It is possible to declare a local object (as well as a member variable of a type) without using the WithEvents keyword, and dynamically rig together an event handler at runtime.

To do so, you ultimately need to call the correct autogenerated add_XXX() method to ensure that your method is added to the list of function pointers maintained by the Car's internal delegate (remember, the Event keyword expands to produce—among other things—a delegate type). Of course, you do not call add_XXX() directly, but rather use the VB 2005 AddHandler statement.

As well, if you wish to dynamically *remove* an event handler from the underlying delegate's invocation list, you can indirectly call the compiler-generated remove_XXX() method using the RemoveHandler statement.

In a nutshell, AddHandler/RemoveHandler allows us to gain "delegate-like" functionality without directly interacting defining the delegate types. Consider the following reworked Main() method:

```
Module Program
  Sub Main()
    Console.WriteLine("***** Fun with AddHandler/RemoveHandler *****")

    ' Note lack of WithEvents keyword.
    Dim c As New Car("NightRider", 50)

    ' Dynamically hook into event using AddHandler.
    AddHandler c.Exploded, AddressOf CarEventHandler
    AddHandler c.AboutToBlow, AddressOf CarEventHandler

    For i As Integer = 0 To 5
      c.Accelerate(10)
    Next
    Console.ReadLine()
  End Sub

  ' Event Handler for both events
  ' (note lack of Handles keyword).
  Public Sub CarEventHandler(ByVal s As String)
    Console.WriteLine(s)
  End Sub
End Module
```

As you can see, the `AddHandler` statement requires the name of the event you want to listen to, and the address of the method that will be invoked when the event is sent. Here, you also routed each event to a single handler (which is of course not required). As well, if you wish to enable multicasting, simple use the `AddHandler` statement multiple times and specify unique targets:

```
' Multicasting!
AddHandler c.Exploded, AddressOf MyExplodedHandler
AddHandler c. Exploded, AddressOf MySecondExplodedHandler
```

`RemoveHandler` works in the same manner. If you wish to stop receiving events from a particular object, you may do so using the following syntax:

```
' Dynamically unhook a handler using RemoveHandler.
RemoveHandler c. Exploded, AddressOf MySecondExplodedHandler
```

At this point you may wonder when (or if) you would ever need to make use of the `AddHandler` and `RemoveHandler` statements, given that VB 2005 supports the `WithEvents` syntax. Again, understand that this approach is very powerful, given that you have the ability to detach from an event source at will.

When you make use of the `WithEvent` keyword, you will continuously receive events from the source object until the object dies (which typically means until the client application is terminated). Using the `RemoveHandler` statements, you can simply tell the object "Stop sending me this event," even though the object may be alive and well in memory.

Source Code The DynamicCarEvents project is located under the Chapter 10 subdirectory.

Defining a "Prim-and-Proper" Event

Truth be told, there is one final enhancement we could make to our `CarEvents` examples that mirrors Microsoft's recommended event pattern. As you begin to explore the events sent by a given type in the base class libraries, you will find that the target method's first parameter is a `System.Object`, while the second parameter is a type deriving from `System.EventArgs`.

The `System.Object` argument represents a reference to the object that sent the event (such as the Car), while the second parameter represents information regarding the event at hand. The `System.EventArgs` base class represents an event that is not sending any custom information:

```
Public Class EventArgs
   Public Shared ReadOnly Empty As EventArgs
   Shared Sub New()
   End Sub
   Public Sub New()
   End Sub
End Class
```

Our current examples have specified the parameters they send directly within the definition of the event itself:

```
Public Class Car
...
   ' Notice we are specifying the event arguments directly.
   Public Event Exploded(ByVal msg As String)
   Public Event AboutToBlow(ByVal msg As String)
...
End Class
```

As you have learned, the compiler will take these arguments to define a proper delegate behind the scenes. While this approach is very straightforward, if you do wish to follow the recommended design pattern, the Exploded and AboutToBlow events should be retrofitted to send a System.Object and System.EventArgs descendent.

Although you can pass an instance of EventArgs directly, you lose the ability to pass in custom information to the registered event handler. Thus, when you wish to pass along custom data, you should build a suitable class deriving from EventArgs. For our example, assume we have a class named CarEventArgs, which maintains a string representing the message sent to the receiver:

```
Public Class CarEventArgs
  Inherits EventArgs
  Public ReadOnly msgData As String
  Public Sub New(ByVal msg As String)
    msgData = msg
  End Sub
End Class
```

With this, we would now update the events sent from the Car type like so:

```
Public Class Car
...
  ' These events follow Microsoft design guidelines.
  Public Event Exploded(ByVal sender As Object, ByVal e As CarEventArgs)
  Public Event AboutToBlow(ByVal sender As Object, ByVal e As CarEventArgs)
...
End Class
```

When firing our events from within the Accelerate() method, we would now need to supply a reference to the current Car (via the Me keyword) and an instance of our CarEventArgs type:

```
Public Sub Accelerate(ByVal delta As Integer)
  If carIsDead Then
    ' If the car is doomed, send out the Exploded notification.
    RaiseEvent Exploded(Me, New CarEventArgs("This car is doomed..."))
  Else
    currSpeed += delta
    ' Are we almost doomed?  If so, send out AboutToBlow notification.
    If 10 = maxSpeed - currSpeed Then
      RaiseEvent AboutToBlow(Me, New CarEventArgs("Slow down!"))
    End If
    If currSpeed >= maxSpeed Then
      carIsDead = True
    Else
      Console.WriteLine("->CurrSpeed = {0}", currSpeed)
    End If
  End If
End Sub
```

On the caller's side, all we would need to do is update our event handlers to receive the incoming parameters and obtain the message via our read-only field. For example:

```
' Assume this event was handled using AddHandler.
Public Sub AboutToBlowHandler(ByVal sender As Object, ByVal e As CarEventArgs)
  Console.WriteLine("{0} says: {1}", sender, e.msgData)
End Sub
```

If the receiver wishes to interact with the object that sent the event, we can explicitly cast the System.Object. Thus, if we wish to power down the radio when the Car object is about to meet its maker, we could author an event handler looking something like the following:

```
' Assume this event was handled using AddHandler.
Public Sub ExplodedHandler(ByVal sender As Object, ByVal e As CarEventArgs)
  If TypeOf sender Is Car Then
    Dim c As Car = CType(sender, Car)
    c.CrankTunes(False)
  End If
  Console.WriteLine("Critical message from {0}: {1}", sender, e.msgData)
End Sub
```

■**Source Code** The PrimAndProperEvent project is located under the Chapter 10 subdirectory.

Defining Events in Terms of Delegates

As I am sure you have figured out by now (given that I have mentioned it numerous times), the VB 2005 Event keyword automatically creates a delegate behind the scenes. However, if you have already defined a delegate type, you are able to associate it to an event using the As keyword. By doing so, you inform the VB 2005 compiler to make use of your delegate-specific type, rather than generating a delegate class on the fly. For example:

```
Public Class Car
...
  ' Define the delegate used for these events
  Public Delegate Sub CarDelegate(ByVal sender As Object, ByVal e As CarEventArgs)

  ' Now associate the delegate to the event.
  Public Event Exploded As CarDelegate
  Public Event AboutToBlow As CarDelegate
...
End Class
```

The truth of the matter is that you would seldom (if ever) need to follow this approach to define an event using VB 2005. However, now that you understand this alternative syntax for event declaration, we can address the final topic of this chapter and come to understand a new event-centric keyword introduced with Visual Basic 2005: Custom.

Customizing the Event Registration Process

Although a vast majority of your applications will simply make use of the Event, Handles, and RaiseEvent keywords, .NET 2.0 now supplies Visual Basic 2005 with a new event-centric keyword named Custom. As the name implies, this allows you to author custom code that will execute when a caller interacts with an event or when the event is raised in your code.

The first question probably on your mind is what exactly is meant by "customizing the event process"? Simply put, using the Custom keyword, you are able to author code that will execute when the caller registers with an event via AddHandler or detaches from an event via RemoveHandler, or when your code base sends the event via RaiseEvent. Custom events also have a very important restriction:

- The event must be defined in terms of a specific delegate.

In many cases, the delegate you associate to the event will be a standard type that ships with the base class libraries named `System.EventHandler` (although as you will see, you can make use of any delegate, including custom delegates you have created yourself). The `System.EventHandler` delegate can point to any method that takes a `System.Object` as the first parameter and a `System.EventArgs` as the second. Given this requirement, here is a skeleton of what a custom event looks like in the eyes of VB 2005:

```
Public Custom Event MyEvent As RelatedDelegate
  ' Triggered when caller uses AddHandler.
  AddHandler(ByVal value As RelatedDelegate)
  End AddHandler

  ' Triggered when caller uses RemoveHandler.
  RemoveHandler(ByVal value As RelatedDelegate)
  End RemoveHandler

  ' Triggered when RaiseEvent is called.
  RaiseEvent(Parameters required by RelatedDelegate)
  End RaiseEvent
End Event
```

As you can see, a custom event is defined in terms of the associated delegate via the As keyword. Next, notice that within the scope of the custom event we have three subscopes that allow us to author code to execute when the AddHandler, RemoveHandler, or RaiseEvent statements are used.

Defining a Custom Event

To illustrate, assume a simple `Car` type that defines a custom event named `EngineStart`, defined in terms of the standard `System.EventHandler` delegate. The `Car` defines a member variable of type `ArrayList` that will be used to hold onto each of the incoming delegate objects passed by the caller (very much like our interface-based approach shown at the beginning of this chapter).

Furthermore, when the `Car` fires the `EngineStart` event (from a method named `Start()`) our customization of RaiseEvent will iterate over each connection to invoke the client-side event handler. Ponder the following class definition:

```
Public Class Car
  ' This ArrayList will hold onto the delegates
  ' sent from the caller.
  Private arConnections As New ArrayList

  ' This event has been customized!
  Public Custom Event EngineStart As System.EventHandler
    AddHandler(ByVal value As EventHandler)
      Console.WriteLine("Added connection")
      arConnections.Add(value)
    End AddHandler

    RemoveHandler(ByVal value As System.EventHandler)
      Console.WriteLine("Removed connection")
      arConnections.Remove(value)
    End RemoveHandler

    RaiseEvent(ByVal sender As Object, ByVal e As System.EventArgs)
      For Each h As EventHandler In arConnections
        Console.WriteLine("Raising event")
        h(sender, e)
```

```
      Next
    End RaiseEvent
  End Event

  Public Sub Start()
    RaiseEvent EngineStart(Me, New EventArgs())
  End Sub
End Class
```

Beyond adding (and removing) System.EventHandler delegates to the ArrayList member variable, the other point of interest to note is that the implementation of Start() must now raise the EngineStart event by passing a System.Object (representing the sender of the event) and a new System.EventArgs, given the use of the System.EventHandler delegate (that was a mouthful!). Also recall that we are indirectly calling Invoke() on each System.EventHandler delegate to invoke the target in a synchronous manner:

```
' We could also call Invoke() directly
' like so: h.Invoke(sender, e)
h(sender, e)
```

On the caller's side, we could now proceed as expected using AddHandler and RemoveHandler:

```
Module Program
  Sub Main()
    Console.WriteLine("***** Fun with Custom Events *****")
    Dim c As New Car()

    ' Dynamically hook into event.
    AddHandler c.EngineStart, AddressOf EngineStartHandler
    c.Start()

    ' Just to trigger our custom logic.
    RemoveHandler c.EngineStart, AddressOf EngineStartHandler

    ' Just to test we are no longer sending event.
    c.Start()
    Console.ReadLine()
  End Sub

  ' Our handler must match this signature given that
  ' EngineStart has been prototyped using the System.EventHandler delegate.
  Public Sub EngineStartHandler(ByVal sender As Object, ByVal e As EventArgs)
    Console.WriteLine("Car has started")
  End Sub
End Module
```

The output can be seen in Figure 10-7. While not entirely fascinating, we are able to verify that our custom code statements are executing whenever AddHandler, RemoveHandler, or RaiseEvent is used in our code base.

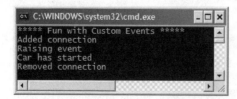

Figure 10-7. *Interacting with a custom event*

■**Note** If the caller invokes an event on a member variable declared using the WithEvents modifier, the custom AddHandler and RemoveHandler scope is (obviously) not executed.

■**Source Code** The CustomEvent project is located under the Chapter 10 subdirectory.

Custom Events Using Custom Delegates

Currently, our custom event has been defined in terms of a standard delegate named System. EventHandler. As you would guess, however, we can make use of any delegate that meets our requirements, including our own custom delegate. Here would be a retrofitted Car type that is now making use of a custom delegate named CarDelegate (which takes our CarEventArgs as a second parameter):

```
Public Class Car
  ' The custom delegate.
  Public Delegate Sub CarDelegate(ByVal sender As Object, _
    ByVal args As CarEventArgs)
  Private arConnections As New ArrayList

  ' Now using CarDelegate.
  Public Custom Event EngineStart As CarDelegate
    AddHandler(ByVal value As CarDelegate)
      Console.WriteLine("Added connection")
      arConnections.Add(value)
    End AddHandler

    RemoveHandler(ByVal value As CarDelegate)
      Console.WriteLine("Removed connection")
      arConnections.Remove(value)
    End RemoveHandler

    RaiseEvent(ByVal sender As Object, ByVal e As CarEventArgs)
      For Each h As CarDelegate In arConnections
        Console.WriteLine("Raising event")
        h.Invoke(sender, e)
      Next
    End RaiseEvent
  End Event

  Public Sub Start()
    RaiseEvent EngineStart(Me, New CarEventArgs("Enjoy the ride"))
  End Sub
End Class
```

The caller's code would now be modified to make sure that the event handlers take a CarEventArgs as the second parameter, rather than the System.EventArgs type required by the System.EventHandler delegate:

```
Module Program
...
  Public Sub EngineStartHandler(ByVal sender As Object, ByVal e As CarEventArgs)
    Console.WriteLine("Message from {0}: {1}", sender, e.msgData)
  End Sub
End Module
```

The output can be seen in Figure 10-8.

Figure 10-8. *Interacting with a custom event, take two*

Now that you have seen the process of building a custom event, you might be wondering when you might need to do so. While the simple answer is "whenever you want to customize the event process," a very common use of this technique is when you wish to fire out events in a nonblocking manner using secondary threads of execution. However, at this point in the text, I have yet to dive into the details of the System.Threading namespace or the asynchronous nature of the delegate type (see Chapter 16 for details). In any case, just understand that the Custom keyword allows you to author custom code statements that will execute during the handing and sending of events.

■**Source Code** The CustomEventWithCustomDelegate project is located under the Chapter 10 subdirectory.

Summary

Over the course of this chapter you have seen numerous approaches that can be used to "connect" two objects in order to enable a two-way conversation (interface types, delegates, and the VB 2005 event architecture). Recall that the Delegate keyword is used to indirectly construct a class derived from System.MulticastDelegate. As you have seen, a delegate is simply an object that maintains a list of methods to call when told to do so (most often using the Invoke() method).

Next, we examined the Event, RaiseEvent, and WithEvents keywords. Although they have been retrofitted under the hood to work with .NET delegates, they look and feel much the same as the legacy event-centric keywords of VB 6.0. As you have seen, VB .NET now supports the Handles statement, which is used to syntactically associate an event to a given method (as well as enable multicasting).

You also examined the process of hooking into (and detaching from) an event dynamically using the AddHandler and RemoveHandler statements. This is a very welcome addition to the Visual Basic language, given that you now have a type-safe way to dynamically intercept events on the fly. Finally, you learned about the new Custom keyword, which allows you to control how events are handled and sent by a given type.

■ ■ ■

Advanced VB 2005 Programming Constructs

This chapter will complete your investigation of the core syntax and semantics of the Visual Basic 2005 language by examining a number of slightly more advanced programming techniques. We begin by examining the various "preprocessor" directives that are supported by the VB 2005 compiler (#If, #ElseIf, etc.) and the construction of code regions (à la #Region/#End Region).

Next up, you will come to understand the gory details of value types and reference types (and various combinations thereof). As you will see, the CLR handles structure and class variables very differently in regards to their memory allocation. At this time, you will revisit the ByVal and ByRef keywords to see how they handle value types and reference types under the hood. At this time, you will also come to understand the role of *boxing* and *unboxing* operations.

The remainder of this chapter will concentrate on several new programming constructs supported by VB 2005 with the release of .NET 2.0. Here you will come to understand the role of operator overloading and the creation of explicit (and implicit) conversion routines. To wrap up, you'll check out the role of two new casting-centric keywords (DirectCast and TryCast). At the conclusion of this chapter, you will have a very solid grounding on the core features of the language, and be in a perfect position to understand the topic of generics in Chapter 12.

The VB 2005 Preprocessor Directives

VB 2005, like many other C-based programming languages, supports the use of various tokens that allow you to interact with the compilation process. Before examining various VB 2005 preprocessor directives, let's get our terminology correct. The term "VB 2005 preprocessor directive" is not entirely accurate. In reality, this term is used only for consistency with the C and C++ programming languages. In VB 2005, there is no separate preprocessing step. Rather, preprocessor directives are processed as part of the lexical analysis phase of the compiler.

In any case, the syntax of the VB 2005 preprocessor directives is very similar to that of the other members of the C family, in that the directives are always prefixed with the pound sign (#). Table 11-1 defines some of the more commonly used directives (consult the .NET Framework 2.0 SDK documentation for complete details).

Table 11-1. *Common VB 2005 Preprocessor Directives*

Directives	Meaning in Life
#Region, #End Region	Although not technically "preprocessor directives" in the classic definition of the term (as they are ignored by the compiler), these tokens are used to mark sections of collapsible source code within the editor.
#Const	Used to define conditional compilation symbols.
#If, #ElseIf, #Else, #End If	Used to conditionally skip sections of source code (based on specified compilation symbols).

Specifying Code Regions

Perhaps some of the most useful of all directives are #Region and #End Region. Using these tags, you are able to specify a block of code that may be hidden from view and identified by a friendly textual marker. Use of regions can help keep lengthy *.vb files more manageable. For example, you could create one region for a type's constructors, another for type properties, and so forth:

```
Class Car
    Private petName As String
    Private currSp As Integer

    #Region "Constructors"
    Public Sub New()
    ...
    End Sub
    Public Sub New(ByVal currSp As Integer, ByVal petName As String)
    ...
    End Sub
    #End Region

    #Region "Properties"
    Public Property Speed() As Integer
    ...
    End Property
    Public Property Name() As String
    ...
    End Property
    #End Region
End Class
```

When you place your mouse cursor over a collapsed region, you are provided with a snapshot of the code lurking behind, as you see in Figure 11-1.

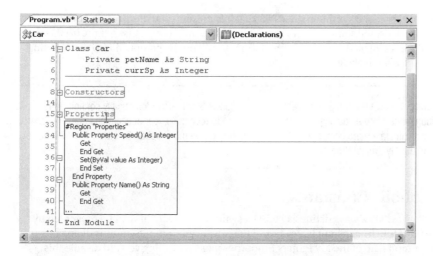

Figure 11-1. *Code regions allow you to define a set of collapsible code statements.*

Do be aware that not all .NET IDEs support the use of regions. If you are making use of Visual Studio 2005, Visual Basic 2005 Express, or SharpDevelop, you will be happy to find regions are supported. Other .NET IDEs (including simple text editors such as TextPad or NotePad) ignore the #Region and #End Region directives completely.

■**Note** Visual Basic 2005 does not allow you to define regions within the scope of a property or method. Rather, regions are used to group related members or types.

Conditional Code Compilation

The next batch of preprocessor directives (#If, #ElseIf, #Else, #End If) allow you to conditionally compile a block of code, based on predefined symbols. The classic use of these directives is to identify a block of code that is compiled only under a debug (rather than a release) build:

```
Module Program
  Sub Main()
    ' This code will only execute if the project is
    ' compiled as a Debug build.
#If DEBUG Then
    Console.WriteLine("***** In Debug Mode! *****")
    Console.WriteLine("App directory: {0}", _
      Environment.CurrentDirectory)
    Console.WriteLine("Box: {0}", _
      Environment.MachineName)
    Console.WriteLine("OS: {0}", _
      Environment.OSVersion)
    Console.WriteLine(".NET Version: {0}", _
      Environment.Version)
#End If
  End Sub
End Module
```

Here, you are checking for a symbol named DEBUG. If it is present, you dump out a number of interesting statistics using some shared members of the System.Environment class. If the DEBUG symbol is not defined, the code placed between #If and #End If will not be compiled into the resulting assembly, and it will be effectively ignored.

■**Note** When you create a new VB 2005 project with Visual Studio 2005, you are automatically configured to compile under a Debug mode. Before you ship the software, be sure to recompile your application under Release mode as this typically results in a more compact and better performing assembly. Debug/Release mode can be set using the Debug tab of the My Project Properties page.

Defining Symbolic Constants

By default, Visual Studio 2005 always defines a DEBUG symbol; however, this can be prevented by deselecting the Define DEBUG constant check box of the Advanced Compile Options dialog box located under the Compile tab of the My Project Properties page. Assuming you did disable this autogenerated DEBUG symbol, you could now define this symbol on a file-by-file basis using the #Const preprocessor directive.

When you use this directive, you must make a value assignment to your symbol. If this value is zero, you have just disabled this constant for the given file. This can be helpful when you wish to define an application-wide constant, but selectively ignore its presence on a file-by-file basis. When the value is set to any value other than zero, the constant is enabled. For example:

```
' The DEBUG constant was disabled in the My Project
' property page, but defined and enabled in this file.
#Const DEBUG = 1

Module Program
  Sub Main()
    ' This code will only execute if the project is
    ' compiled as a Debug build.
#If DEBUG Then
...
#End If
  End Sub
End Module
```

While you typically would have no need to disable the autogenerated DEBUG constant, the #Const directive allows you to define any number of custom preprocessor symbols for your projects. For example, assume you have authored a VB 2005 class that should be compiled a bit differently under the Mono distribution of .NET (see Chapter 1). Using #Const, you can define a symbol named MONO_BUILD on a file-by-file basis:

```
#Const MONO_BUILD = 1

Class SomeClass
  Public Sub SomeMethod()
#If MONO_BUILD Then
    Console.WriteLine("Compiling under Mono!")
#Else
    Console.WriteLine("Compiling under Microsoft .NET")
#End If
  End Sub
End Class
```

Here, the #Const directive has been used to define (or disable) a preprocessor constant on a file-by-file basis. To create a project-wide symbol, make use of the Custom Constants text box located in the Advanced Compile Options dialog box located under the Compile tab of the My Project Properties page (see Figure 11-2).

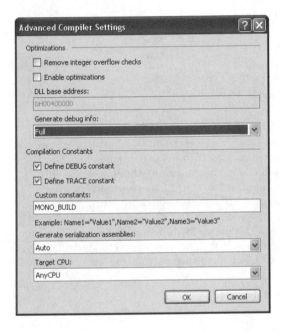

Figure 11-2. *Defining project-wide symbolic precompilation constants*

Cool! Now that you understand the role of the VB 2005 preprocessor directives, we can turn our attention to a meatier topic that you should be well aware of: the value type/reference type distinction.

■**Source Code** The Preprocessor project is located under the Chapter 11 subdirectory.

Understanding Value Types and Reference Types

Like any programming language, VB 2005 defines a number of keywords that represent basic data types such as whole numbers, character data, floating-point numbers, and Boolean values. Each of these intrinsic types are fixed entities in the CTS, meaning that when you create an integer variable (which is captured using the Integer keyword in VB 2005), all .NET-aware languages understand the fixed nature of this type, and all agree on the range it is capable of handling.

Specifically speaking, a .NET data type may be *value-based* or *reference-based*. Value-based types, which include all numerical data types (Integer, Double, etc.), as well as enumerations and structures, are allocated *on the stack*. Given this factoid, value types can be quickly removed from memory once they fall out of the defining scope:

```
' Integers are value types!
Public Sub SomeMethod()
  Dim i As Integer = 0
```

```
  Console.WriteLine("Value of i is: {0}", i)
End Sub   ' i is popped off the stack here!
```

When you assign one value type to another, a member-by-member copy is achieved by default. In terms of numerical or Boolean data types, the only "member" to copy is the value of the variable itself:

```
' Assigning two intrinsic value types results in
' two independent variables on the stack.
Public Sub SomeOtherMethod()
  Dim i As Integer = 99
  Dim k As Integer = i

  ' After the following assignment, 'i' is still 99.
  k = 8732
End Sub
```

While the previous example is no major newsflash, understand that .NET structures and enumerations are also value types. Structures, as you may recall from Chapter 4, provide a way to achieve the bare-bones benefits of object orientation (i.e., encapsulation) while having the efficiency of stack-allocated data. Like a class, structures can take constructors (provided they have arguments) and define any number of members (properties, fields, subroutines, etc.).

All structures are implicitly derived from a class named System.ValueType. Functionally, the only purpose of System.ValueType is to override the virtual methods defined by System.Object to honor value-based, versus reference-based, semantics. In fact, the instance methods defined by System.ValueType are identical to those of System.Object, as you can see from the following method prototypes:

```
' Structures and enumerations extend System.ValueType.
Public MustInherit Class ValueType
  Inherits Object
  Public Overrides Function Equals(ByVal obj As Object) As Boolean
  Public Overrides Function GetHashCode() As Integer
  Public Overrides Function ToString() As String
End Class
```

Assume you have created a VB 2005 structure named MyPoint, using the VB 2005 Structure keyword:

```
' Structures are value types!
Structure MyPoint
  Public x, y As Integer
End Structure
```

To allocate a structure type, you may make use of the New keyword, which may seem counterintuitive given that we typically think New always implies heap allocation. This is part of the smoke and mirrors maintained by the CLR. As programmers, we can assume everything can be treated as an object. However, when the runtime encounters a type derived from System.ValueType, stack allocation is achieved:

```
' Still on the stack!
Dim p As New MyPoint()
```

As an alternative, structures can be allocated without using the New keyword:

```
Dim p1 As MyPoint
p1.x = 100
p1.y = 100
```

In either case, the MyPoint variable is allocated on the stack, and will be removed from memory as soon as the defining scope exits.

Value Types, References Types, and the Assignment Operator

Now, consider the following Main() method and observe the output shown in Figure 11-3:

```
Sub Main()
  Console.WriteLine("***** Value Types / Reference Types *****")
  Console.WriteLine("-> Creating p1")
  Dim p1 As New MyPoint()
  p1.x = 100
  p1.y = 100
  Console.WriteLine("-> Assigning p2 to p1")
  Dim p2 As MyPoint = p1

  ' Here is p1.
  Console.WriteLine("p1.x = {0}", p1.x)
  Console.WriteLine("p1.y = {0}", p1.y)

  ' Here is p2.
  Console.WriteLine("p2.x = {0}", p2.x)
  Console.WriteLine("p2.y = {0}", p2.y)

  ' Change p2.x. This will NOT change p1.x.
  Console.WriteLine("-> Changing p2.x to 900")
  p2.x = 900

  ' Print again.
  Console.WriteLine("-> Here are the X values again...")
  Console.WriteLine("p1.x = {0}", p1.x)
  Console.WriteLine("p2.x = {0}", p2.x)
  Console.ReadLine()
End Sub
```

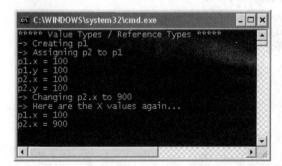

Figure 11-3. *Assigning one value type to another results in a bitwise copy of the field data.*

Here you have created a variable of type MyPoint (named p1) that is then assigned to another MyPoint (p2). Because MyPoint is a value type, you have two copies of the MyPoint type on the stack, each of which can be independently manipulated. Therefore, when you change the value of p2.x, the value of p1.x is unaffected (just like the behavior seen in the previous Integer example).

In stark contrast, reference types (classes) are allocated on the managed heap. These objects stay in memory until the .NET garbage collector destroys them. By default, assignment of reference types results in a new reference to the *same* object on the heap. To illustrate, let's change the definition of the MyPoint type from a VB 2005 structure to a VB 2005 class:

```vb
' Classes are always reference types.
Class MyPoint
    Public x, y As Integer
End Class ' Now a class!
```

If you were to run the test program once again, you would notice a change in behavior (see Figure 11-4).

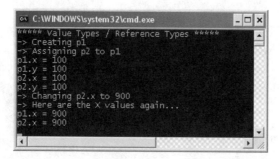

Figure 11-4. *Assigning one reference type to another results in redirecting the reference.*

In this case, you have two references pointing to the same object on the managed heap. Therefore, when you change the value of x using the p2 reference, p1.x reports the same value.

Value Types Containing Reference Types

Now that you have a better feeling for the differences between value types and reference types, let's examine a more complex example. Assume you have the following reference (class) type that maintains an informational string that can be set using a custom constructor:

```vb
Class ShapeInfo
    Public infoString As String
    Public Sub New(ByVal info As String)
        infoString = info
    End Sub
End Class
```

Now assume that you want to contain a variable of this class type within a value type named MyRectangle. To allow the outside world to set the value of the inner ShapeInfo, you also provide a custom constructor (as explained in just a bit, the default constructor of a structure is reserved and cannot be redefined):

```vb
Structure MyRectangle
    ' The MyRectangle structure contains a reference type member.
    Public rectInfo As ShapeInfo

    Public top, left, bottom, right As Integer
```

```
  Public Sub New(ByVal info As String)
    rectInfo = New ShapeInfo(info)
    top = 10 : left = 10
    bottom = 10 : right = 100
  End Sub
End Structure
```

At this point, you have contained a reference type within a value type. The million-dollar question now becomes, what happens if you assign one MyRectangle variable to another? Given what you already know about value types, you would be correct in assuming that the Integer field data (which are indeed structures) should be independent entities for each MyRectangle variable. But what about the internal reference type? Will the object's state be fully copied, or will the *reference* to that object be copied? Consider the following updated Main() method and check out Figure 11-5 for the answer.

```
Sub Main()
  ' Previous code commented out...

  ' Create the first MyRectangle.
  Console.WriteLine("-> Creating r1")
  Dim r1 As New MyRectangle("This is my first rect")

  ' Now assign a new MyRectangle to r1.
  Console.WriteLine("-> Assigning r2 to r1")
  Dim r2 As MyRectangle
  r2 = r1

  ' Change values of r2.
  Console.WriteLine("-> Changing all values of r2")
  r2.rectInfo.infoString = "This is new info!"
  r2.bottom = 4444

  ' Print values
  Console.WriteLine("-> Values after change:")
  Console.WriteLine("-> r1.rectInfo.infoString: {0}", r1.rectInfo.infoString)
  Console.WriteLine("-> r2.rectInfo.infoString: {0}", r2.rectInfo.infoString)
  Console.WriteLine("-> r1.bottom: {0}", r1.bottom)
  Console.WriteLine("-> r2.bottom: {0}", r2.bottom)
End Sub
```

When you run this program, you will find that when you change the value of the informational string using the r2 reference, the r1 reference displays the same value.

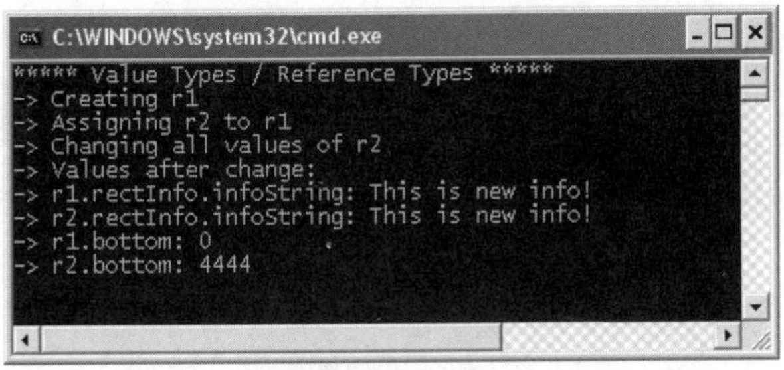

Figure 11-5. r1 *and* r2 *are both pointing to the same* ShapeInfo *object!*

By default, when a value type contains other reference types, assignment results in a copy *of the references*. In this way, you have two independent structures, each of which contains a reference pointing to the same object in memory (i.e., a "shallow copy"). When you want to perform a "deep copy," where the state of internal references is fully copied into a new object, you need to implement the ICloneable interface (as you did in Chapter 9).

Source Code The ValAndRef project is located under the Chapter 11 subdirectory.

Passing Reference Types by Value

Reference types can obviously be passed as parameters to functions and subroutines. However, passing an object by reference is quite different from passing it by value. To understand the distinction, assume you have a simple Person class, defined as follows:

```
Class Person
  Public fullName As String
  Public age As Integer

  Public Sub New(ByVal n As String, ByVal a As Integer)
    fullName = n
    age = a
  End Sub
  Public Sub New()
  End Sub

  Public Sub PrintInfo()
    Console.WriteLine("{0} is {1} years old", fullName, age)
  End Sub
End Class
```

Now, what if you create a method that allows the caller to send in the Person type by value:

```
Sub SendAPersonByValue(ByVal p As Person)
  ' Change the age of 'p'?
  p.age = 99

  ' Will the caller see this reassignment?
  p = New Person("Nikki", 999)
End Sub
```

Notice how the SendAPersonByValue() method attempts to reassign the incoming Person reference to a new Person object as well as change some state data. Now let's test this method using the following Main() method:

```
Sub Main()
  ' Passing ref types by value.
  Console.WriteLine("***** Passing Person object by value *****")
  Dim fred As Person = New Person("Fred", 12)
  Console.WriteLine("Before by value call, Person is:")
  fred.PrintInfo()
  SendAPersonByValue(fred)
  Console.WriteLine("After by value call, Person is:")
  fred.PrintInfo()
End Sub
```

Figure 11-6 shows the output of this code.

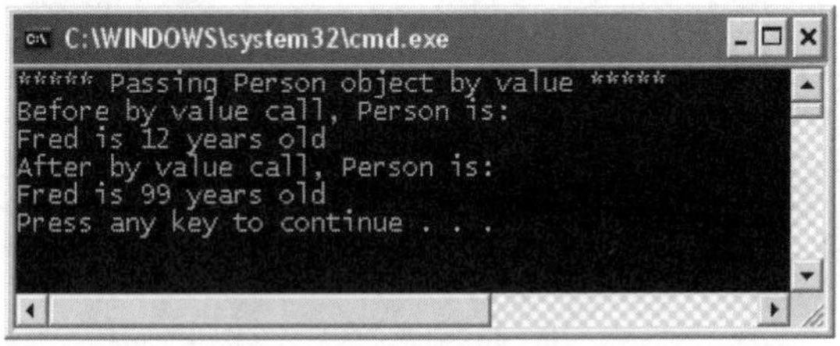

Figure 11-6. *Passing reference types by value "locks" which object the reference points to.*

As you can see, the value of age has been modified. This behavior seems to fly in the face of what it means to pass a parameter "by value." Given that you were able to change the state of the incoming Person, what was copied? The answer: a copy of the *reference* to the caller's object. Therefore, as the SendAPersonByValue() method is pointing to the same object as the caller, it is possible to alter the object's state data. What is *not* possible is to reassign what the reference is pointing to.

Passing Reference Types by Reference

Now assume you have a SendAPersonByReference() method, which passes a reference type by reference (note the ByRef parameter modifier):

```
Sub SendAPersonByReference(ByRef p As Person)
  ' Change some data of 'p'.
  p.age = 555

  ' 'p' is now pointing to a new object on the heap!
  p = New Person("Nikki", 999)
End Sub
```

As you might expect, this allows complete flexibility of how the callee is able to manipulate the incoming parameter. Not only can the callee change the state of the object, but if it so chooses, it may also reassign the reference to a new Person object. Now ponder the following usage:

```
Sub Main()
  ' Previous code commented out...

  ' Passing ref types by ref.
  Console.WriteLine("***** Passing Person object by reference *****")
  Dim mel As New Person("Mel", 23)
  Console.WriteLine("Before by ref call, Person is:")
  mel.PrintInfo()
  SendAPersonByReference(mel)
  Console.WriteLine("After by ref call, Person is:")
  mel.PrintInfo()
End Sub
```

As you can see from Figure 11-7, the object named mel returns after the call as an object named Nikki.

Figure 11-7. *Passing reference types by reference allows you to reset what the reference points to on the heap.*

The golden rule to keep in mind when passing reference types by reference is as follows:

- If a reference type is passed by reference, the callee may change the values of the object's state data as well as the object it is referencing.

■**Source Code**   The RefTypeValTypeParams project is located under the Chapter 11 subdirectory.

Value and Reference Types: Final Details

To wrap up this topic, ponder the information in Table 11-2, which summarizes the core distinctions between value types and reference types.

Table 11-2. *Value Types and Reference Types Side by Side*

Intriguing Question	Value Type	Reference Type
Where is this type allocated?	Allocated on the stack.	Allocated on the managed heap.
How is a variable represented?	Value type variables are local copies.	Reference type variables are pointing to the memory occupied by the allocated instance.
What is the base type?	Must derive from System.ValueType.	Can derive from any other type (except System. ValueType), as long as that type is not "sealed" (see Chapter 6).
Can this type function as a base to other types?	No. Value types are always sealed and cannot be extended.	Yes. If the type is not sealed, it may function as a base to other types.
What is the default parameter passing behavior?	Variables are passed by value (i.e., a copy of the variable is passed into the called function).	Variables are passed by reference (e.g., the address of the variable is passed into the called function).
Can this type override System.Object.Finalize()?	No. Value types are never placed onto the heap and therefore do not need to be finalized.	Yes (see Chapter 8).
Can I define constructors for this type?	Yes, but the default constructor is reserved (i.e., your custom constructors must all have arguments).	But of course!
When do variables of this type die?	When they fall out of the defining scope.	When the managed heap is garbage collected.

Despite their differences, value types and reference types both have the ability to implement interfaces and may support any number of fields, methods, overloaded operators, constants, properties, and events.

Understanding Boxing and Unboxing Operations

Given that .NET defines two major categories of types (value based and reference based), you may occasionally need to represent a variable of one category as a variable of the other category. The .NET platform provides a very simple mechanism, known as *boxing*, to convert a value type to a reference type. Assume that you have created a variable of type Short:

```
' Make a short value type.
Dim s As Short = 25
```

If, during the course of your application, you wish to represent this value type as a reference type, you would box the value as follows:

```
' Box the value into an object reference.
Dim objShort As Object = s
```

Boxing can be formally defined as the process of assigning a value type to a System.Object variable. When you do so, the CLR allocates a new object on the heap and copies the value type's value (in this case, 25) into that instance. What is returned to you is a reference to the newly allocated object. Using this technique, .NET developers have no need to make use of a set of wrapper classes used to temporarily treat stack data as heap-allocated objects.

The opposite operation is also permitted through *unboxing*. Unboxing is the process of converting the value held in the object back into a corresponding value type on the stack. The unboxing operation begins by verifying that the receiving data type is equivalent to the boxed type, and if so, it copies the value back into a local stack-based variable. For example, the following unboxing operation works successfully, given that the underlying type of the objShort is indeed a Short:

```
' Unbox the reference back into a corresponding short.
Dim anotherShort As Short = CType(objShort, Short)
```

Note If you do not have Option Strict enabled, you are not required to explicitly cast via CType() to perform an unboxing operation. However, given that enabling Option Strict is always a good idea, use of CType() is necessary.

Some Practical (Un)Boxing Examples

So, you may be thinking, when would you really need to manually box (or unbox) a data type? The previous examples were purely illustrative in nature, as there was no good reason to box (and then unbox) the Short variable. The truth of the matter is that you will seldom—if ever—need to manually box data types. Much of the time, the VB 2005 compiler automatically boxes variables when appropriate. For example, if you pass a value type into a method requiring an Object parameter, boxing occurs behind the curtains.

```
Module Program
  Sub Main()
    ' Make a value type.
    Dim s As Short = 25

    ' Because 's' is passed into a
    ' method prototyped to take an Object,
    ' it is 'boxed' automatically.
```

```
    UseThisObject(s)
    Console.ReadLine()
  End Sub

  Sub UseThisObject(ByVal o As Object)
    Console.WriteLine("Value of o is: {0}", o)
  End Sub
End Module
```

Automatic boxing also occurs when working with the types of the .NET base class libraries. For example, recall that the System.Collections namespace (examined in Chapter 9) defines a class type named ArrayList. Like most collection types, ArrayList provides members that allow you to insert, obtain, and remove items. Consider the following member prototypes:

```
Public Class ArrayList
  Implements IList, ICollection, IEnumerable, ICloneable
...
  Public Overrideable Function Add(ByVal value As Object) As Integer
  Public Overrideable Sub Insert(ByVal index As Integer, ByVal value As Object)
  Public Overrideable Sub Remove(ByVal value As Object)
End Class
```

As you can see, these members operate on generic System.Object types. Given that everything ultimately derives from this common base class, the following code is perfectly legal:

```
Sub Main()
...
  Dim myData As New ArrayList()
  myData.Add(88)
  myData.Add(3.33)
  myData.Add(False)
  Console.ReadLine()
End Sub
```

However, given your understanding of value types and reference types, you might wonder exactly what was placed into the ArrayList type. (References? Copies of references? Copies of structures?) Just like with the previous UseThisObject() method, it should be clear that each of these value types were indeed boxed before being placed into the ArrayList type. To retrieve an item from the ArrayList type, you are required to unbox accordingly:

```
Sub Main()
...
  Dim myData As New ArrayList()
  myData.Add(88)
  myData.Add(3.33)
  myData.Add(False)

  ' Unbox first item from ArrayList.
  Dim firstItem As Integer = CType(myData(0), Integer)
  Console.WriteLine("First item is {0}", firstItem)
  Console.ReadLine()
End Sub
```

To be sure, boxing and unboxing types takes some processing time and, if used without restraint, could hurt the performance of your application. However, with this technique, you are able to symmetrically operate on value-based and reference-based types.

■**Note** Under .NET 2.0, boxing and unboxing penalties can be eliminated using generics, which you'll examine in Chapter 12.

Unboxing Custom Value Types

When you pass custom structures or enumerations into a method prototyped to take a System.Object, a boxing operation also occurs. However, once the incoming parameter has been received by the called method, you will not be able to access any members of the structure (or enum) until you unbox the type. Recall the MyPoint structure defined previously in this chapter:

```
' Structures are value types!
Structure MyPoint
   Public x, y As Integer
End Structure
```

Assume you now send a MyPoint variable into a new method named UseBoxedMyPoint():

```
Sub Main()
...
  Dim p As MyPoint
  p.x = 10
  p.y = 20
  UseBoxedMyPoint(p)
  Console.ReadLine()
End Sub
```

If you attempt to access the field data of MyPoint, you receive a compiler error (assuming Option Strict is enabled), as the method assumes you are operating on a strongly typed System.Object:

```
Sub UseBoxedMyPoint(ByVal o As Object)
  ' Error!  System.Object does not have
  ' member variables named 'x' or 'y'.
  Console.WriteLine("{0}, {1}", o.x, o.y)
End Sub
```

To access the field data of MyPoint, you must first unbox the parameter:

```
Sub UseBoxedMyPoint(ByVal o As Object)
  If TypeOf o Is MyPoint Then
    Dim p As MyPoint = CType(o, MyPoint)
    Console.WriteLine("{0}, {1}", p.x, p.y)
  End If
End Sub
```

■**Source Code** The Boxing project is included under the Chapter 11 subdirectory.

Understanding Operator Overloading

Visual Basic 2005, like any programming language, has a canned set of tokens that are used to perform basic operations on intrinsic types. For example, you know that the + operator can be applied to two Integers in order to yield a larger Integer (assuming the numbers are both positive!):

```
' The + operator with Integers.
Dim a As Integer = 100
Dim b As Ingeter = 240
Dim c As Integer = a + b   ' c is now 340
```

Again, this is no major newsflash, but have you ever stopped and noticed how the same +
operator can be applied to most intrinsic VB 2005 data types? For example, consider this code:

```
' The + operator with Strings.
Dim s1 As String = "Hello"
Dim s2 As String = " world!"
Dim s3 As String = s1 + s2    ' s3 is now "Hello world!"
```

In essence, the + operator functions in unique ways based on the supplied data types (Strings
or Integers in this case). When the + operator is applied to numerical types, the result is the summation of the operands. However, when the + operator is applied to string types, the result is string
concatenation.

As of .NET 2.0, the VB 2005 language now provides the capability for you to build custom
classes and structures that also respond uniquely to the same set of basic tokens (such as the +
operator). As you will see over the next several pages, if you use this language feature correctly, your
custom classes and structures can be used in a more intuitive manner. However, you should also
understand that if used *incorrectly*, types that support overloaded operators can make your code
much more confusing to other developers.

Before you see a working example of overloading operators, be aware that although VB 2005
defines many operators, only a subset can be redefined for your custom types. Table 11-3 lists the
possibilities.

Table 11-3. *Valid Overloadable Operators*

VB 2005 Operator	Overloadability
Not, IsTrue, IsFalse	This set of unary operators can be overloaded.
+, -, *, /, \, &, |, ^, <<, >>, Mod, And, Or, Xor, Like	These binary operators can be overloaded.
=, <>, <, >, <=, >=	The comparison operators can be overloaded. VB 2005 will demand that "like" operators (i.e., < and >, <= and >=, = and <>) are overloaded together.
CType	The CType operator can be overloaded to implement a custom conversion method.

Overloading Binary Operators

To illustrate the process of overloading binary operators, assume again our simple MyPoint structure,
now with an overridden ToString() implementation and a custom constructor:

```
Public Structure MyPoint
  Private x As Integer, y As Integer
  Public Sub New(ByVal xPos As Integer, ByVal yPos As Integer)
    x = xPos
    y = yPos
  End Sub
  Public Overrides Function ToString() As String
    Return String.Format("[{0}, {1}]", Me.x, Me.y)
  End Function
End Structure
```

Now, logically speaking, it makes sense to add MyPoints together to yield a new, larger MyPoint
that is based on the "x" and "y" values of objects. On a related note, it may be helpful to subtract one
MyPoint from another (to obtain a smaller MyPoint). For example, you would like to be able to author
the following code, which sadly will not yet compile:

```
' Adding and subtracting two MyPoints?
Sub Main()
  Console.WriteLine("***** Fun with Overloaded Operators *****")
  Console.WriteLine()

  ' Make two MyPoints.
  Dim ptOne As MyPoint = New MyPoint(100, 100)
  Dim ptTwo As MyPoint = New MyPoint(40, 40)
  Console.WriteLine("ptOne = {0}", ptOne)
  Console.WriteLine("ptTwo = {0}", ptTwo)

  ' Add the points to make a bigger point?
  Console.WriteLine("ptOne + ptTwo: {0}", ptOne + ptTwo)

  ' Subtract the points to make a smaller point?
  Console.WriteLine("ptOne - ptTwo: {0}", ptOne - ptTwo)
  Console.ReadLine()
End Sub
```

To allow a custom type to respond uniquely to intrinsic operators, VB 2005 provides the Operator keyword, which you can only use in conjunction with shared methods. When you are overloading a binary operator (such as + and -), you will pass in two arguments that are the same type as the defining class (a MyPoint in this example), as illustrated in the following code update:

```
' A more intelligent MyPoint type.
Public Structure MyPoint
...
  ' overloaded operator +.
  Public Shared Operator +(ByVal p1 As MyPoint, ByVal p2 As MyPoint) As MyPoint
    Return New MyPoint(p1.x + p2.x, p1.y + p2.y)
  End Operator

  ' overloaded operator -.
  Public Shared Operator -(ByVal p1 As MyPoint, ByVal p2 As MyPoint) As MyPoint
    Return New MyPoint(p1.x - p2.x, p1.y - p2.y)
  End Operator
End Struture
```

The logic behind operator + is simply to return a brand new MyPoint based on the summation of the fields of the incoming MyPoint parameters. Thus, when you write pt1 + pt2, under the hood you can envision the following hidden call to the shared operator + method:

```
' p3 = MyPoint.Operator+ (p1, p2)
Dim p3 As MyPoint = p1 + p2
```

Likewise, p1 - p2 maps to the following:

```
' p3 = MyPoint.operator- (p1, p2)
Dim p3 As MyPoint = p1 - p2
```

Overloading Equality Operators

As you may recall from Chapter 6, System.Object.Equals() can be overridden to perform value-based (rather than referenced-based) comparisons between types. If you choose to override Equals() (and the often-related System.Object.GetHashCode() method), it is trivial to overload the equality operators (= and <>). To illustrate, here is the updated MyPoint type:

```
' This incarnation of MyPoint also overloads the = and <> operators.
Public Structure MyPoint
...
  ' Overridden methods of System.Object.
  Public Overrides Function Equals(ByVal o As Object) As Boolean
    If TypeOf o Is MyPoint Then
      If Me.ToString() = o.ToString() Then
        Return True
      End If
    End If
    Return False
  End Function
  Public Overrides Function GetHashCode() As Integer
    Return Me.ToString().GetHashCode()
  End Function

  ' Now let's overload the = and <> operators.
  Public Shared Operator =(ByVal p1 As MyPoint, ByVal p2 As MyPoint) As Boolean
    Return p1.Equals(p2)
  End Operator
  Public Shared Operator <>(ByVal p1 As MyPoint, ByVal p2 As MyPoint) As Boolean
    Return Not p1.Equals(p2)
  End Operator
End Structure
```

Notice how the implementation of operator = and operator <> simply makes a call to the overridden Equals() method to get the bulk of the work done. Given this, you can now exercise your MyPoint class as follows:

```
' Make use of the overloaded equality operators.
Sub Main()
...
  Console.WriteLine("ptOne = ptTwo : {0}", ptOne = ptTwo)
  Console.WriteLine("ptOne <> ptTwo : {0}", ptOne <> ptTwo)
End Sub
```

As you can see, it is quite intuitive to compare two objects using the well-known = and <> operators rather than making a call to Object.Equals(). If you do overload the equality operators for a given class, keep in mind that VB 2005 demands that if you override the = operator, you *must* also override the <> operator (if you forget, the compiler will let you know).

Overloading Comparison Operators

In Chapter 9, you learned how to implement the IComparable interface in order to compare the relative relationship between two like objects. Additionally, you may also overload the comparison operators (<, >, <=, and >=) for the same class. Like the equality operators, VB 2005 demands that if you overload <, you must also overload >. The same holds true for the <= and >= operators. If the MyPoint type overloaded these comparison operators, the object user could now compare MyPoints as follows:

```
' Using the overloaded < and > operators.
Sub Main()
...
  Console.WriteLine("ptOne < ptTwo : {0}", ptOne < ptTwo)
  Console.WriteLine("ptOne > ptTwo : {0}", ptOne > ptTwo)
End Sub
```

Assuming you have implemented the IComparable interface, overloading the comparison operators is trivial. Here is the updated class definition:

```
' MyPoint is also comparable using the comparison operators.
Public Structure MyPoint
  Implements IComparable
...
  Public Function CompareTo(ByVal obj As Object) As Integer _
    Implements IComparable.CompareTo
    If TypeOf obj Is MyPoint Then
      Dim p As MyPoint = CType(obj, MyPoint)
      If Me.x > p.x AndAlso Me.y > p.y Then
        Return 1
      End If
      If Me.x < p.x AndAlso Me.y < p.y Then
        Return -1
      Else
        Return 0
      End If
    Else
      Throw New ArgumentException()
    End If
  End Function

  ' The overloaded comparison ops.
  Public Shared Operator <(ByVal p1 As MyPoint, ByVal p2 As MyPoint) As Boolean
    Return (p1.CompareTo(p2) < 0)
  End Operator
  Public Shared Operator >(ByVal p1 As MyPoint, ByVal p2 As MyPoint) As Boolean
    Return (p1.CompareTo(p2) > 0)
  End Operator
  Public Shared Operator <=(ByVal p1 As MyPoint, ByVal p2 As MyPoint) As Boolean
    Return (p1.CompareTo(p2) <= 0)
  End Operator
  Public Shared Operator >=(ByVal p1 As MyPoint, ByVal p2 As MyPoint) As Boolean
    Return (p1.CompareTo(p2) >= 0)
  End Operator
End Structure
```

Final Thoughts Regarding Operator Overloading

As you have seen, VB 2005 now provides the capability to build types that can respond uniquely to various intrinsic, well-known operators. Now, before you go and retrofit all your classes to support such behavior, you must be sure that the operator(s) you are about to overload make some sort of logical sense in the world at large.

For example, let's say you overloaded the multiplication operator for the Engine class. What exactly would it mean to multiply two Engine objects? Not much. Overloading operators is generally only useful when you're building utility types. Strings, points, rectangles, fractions, and hexagons make good candidates for operator overloading. People, managers, cars, database connections, and dialog boxes do not. As a rule of thumb, if an overloaded operator makes it *harder* for the user to understand a type's functionality, don't do it. Use this feature wisely.

■**Source Code** The OverloadedOps project is located under the Chapter 11 subdirectory.

Understanding Custom Type Conversions

Let's now examine a topic closely related to operator overloading: custom type conversions. To set the stage for the discussion to follow, let's quickly review the notion of explicit and implicit conversions between numerical data and related class types.

Recall: Numerical Conversions

In terms of the intrinsic numerical types (Byte, Integer, Double, etc.), an *explicit conversion* (or *narrowing conversion*) is required when you attempt to store a larger value in a smaller container, as this may result in a loss of data. Basically, this is your way to tell the compiler, "Leave me alone, I know what I am trying to do." Conversely, an *implicit conversion* (or *widening conversion*) happens automatically when you attempt to place a smaller type in a destination type that will not result in a loss of data:

```
Sub Main()
  Dim a As Integer = 123
  Dim b As Long = a                     ' Implicit conversion from Integer to Long
  Dim c As Integer = CType(b, Integer)  ' Explicit conversion from Long to Integer
End Sub
```

Recall: Conversions Among Related Class Types

As shown in Chapter 6, class types may be related by classical inheritance (the "is-a" relationship). In this case, the VB 2005 conversion process allows you to cast up and down the class hierarchy. For example, a derived class can always be implicitly cast into a given base type. However, if you wish to store a base class type in a derived variable, you must perform an explicit cast:

```
' Two related class types.
Class Base
End Class

Class Derived
  Inherits Base
End Class

Module Program
  Sub Main()
    ' Implicit cast between derived to base.
    Dim myBaseType As Base
    myBaseType = New Derived()

    ' Must explicitly cast to store base reference
    ' in derived type.
    Dim myDerivedType As Derived = CType(myBaseType, Derived)
  End Sub
End Module
```

This explicit cast works due to the fact that the Base and Derived classes are related by classical inheritance. However, what if you have two class types in *different hierarchies* that require conversions? Given that they are not related by classical inheritance, explicit casting offers no help.

On a related note, consider value types. Assume you have two .NET structures named Square and Rectangle. Given that structures cannot leverage classic inheritance, you have no natural way to cast between these seemingly related types (assuming it made sense to do so).

While you could build helper methods in the structures (such as `Rectangle.ToSquare()`), VB 2005 allows you to build custom conversion routines that allow your types to respond to the `CType()` operator. Therefore, if you configured the `Square` structure correctly, you would be able to use the following syntax to explicitly convert between these structure types:

```
' Convert a Rectangle structure to a Square structure.
Dim rect As Rectangle
rect.Width = 3
rect.Height = 10
Dim sq As Square = CType(rect, Square)
```

Creating Custom Conversion Routines

VB 2005 provides two keywords, `Widening` and `Narrowing`, that can be used when redefining how your class or structure responds to the `CType()` operator. The difference between these conversion routines can be summarized as follows:

- Narrowing conversions do not always succeed at runtime, and may result in loss of data. If `Option Strict` is enabled, `CType` must be used for all narrowing conversions.

- Widening conversion always succeeds at runtime and never incurs data loss.

To illustrate, assume you have the following structure definitions:

```
Public Structure Rectangle
  ' Public for ease of use;
  ' however, feel free to encapsulate with properties.
  Public Width As Integer, Height As Integer

  Public Sub Draw()
    Console.WriteLine("Drawing a rect.")
  End Sub
  Public Overloads Overrides Function ToString() As String
    Return String.Format("[Width = {0}; Height = {1}]", Width, Height)
  End Function
End Structure

Public Structure Square
  Public Length As Integer

  Public Sub Draw()
    Console.WriteLine("Drawing a square.")
  End Sub
  Public Overloads Overrides Function ToString() As String
    Return String.Format("[Length = {0}]", Length)
  End Function

  ' Rectangles can be explicitly converted
  ' into Squares.
  Public Shared Narrowing Operator CType(ByVal r As Rectangle) As Square
    Dim s As Square
    s.Length = r.Width
    Return s
  End Operator
End Structure
```

Notice that this iteration of the Square type defines a custom narrowing conversion operation. Like the process of overloading an operator, conversion routines make use of the VB 2005 Operator keyword (in conjunction with the Narrowing or Widening keyword) and must be defined as a shared member. The incoming parameter is the entity you are converting *from*, while the return value is the entity you are converting *to*:

```
Public Shared Narrowing Operator CType(ByVal r As Rectangle) As Square
...
End Operator
```

In any case, the assumption is that a square (being a geometric pattern in which all sides are of equal length) can be obtained from the width of a rectangle. Thus, you are free to convert a Rectangle into a Square as follows:

```
Module Program
  Sub Main()
    Console.WriteLine("***** Fun with Custom Conversions *****")
    Console.WriteLine()

    ' Create a 5 * 10 Rectangle.
    Dim rect As Rectangle
    rect.Width = 10
    rect.Height = 5
    Console.WriteLine("rect = {0}", rect)

    ' Convert Rectangle to a 10 * 10 Square.
    Dim sq As Square = CType(rect, Square)
    Console.WriteLine("sq = {0}", sq)
    Console.ReadLine()
  End Sub
End Module
```

While it may not be all that helpful to convert a Rectangle into a Square within the same scope, assume you have a function that has been prototyped to take Square types.

```
' This method requires a Square type.
Sub DrawSquare(ByVal sq As Square)
  sq.Draw()
End Sub
```

Using your explicit conversion operation, you can safely pass in Rectangle types for processing:

```
Sub Main()
  Console.WriteLine("***** Fun with Custom Conversions *****")
  Console.WriteLine()

  ' Create a 5 * 10 Rectangle.
  Dim rect As Rectangle
  rect.Width = 10
  rect.Height = 5
  Console.WriteLine("rect = {0}", rect)

  ' This is all right, as the Square has
  ' a custom narrowing CType() implementation.
  DrawSquare(CType(rect, Square))
End Sub
```

Additional Explicit Conversions for the Square Type

Now that you can explicitly convert Rectangles into Squares, let's examine a few additional explicit conversions. Given that a square is symmetrical on each side, it might be helpful to provide an explicit conversion routine that allows the caller to cast from an Integer type into a Square (which, of course, will have a side length equal to the incoming Integer). Likewise, what if you were to update Square such that the caller can cast *from* a Square into an Integer? Here is the calling logic:

```
Sub Main()
...
    ' Converting an Integer to a Square.
    Dim sq2 As Square = CType(90, Square)
    Console.WriteLine("sq2 = {0}", sq2)

    ' Converting a Square to an Integer.
    Dim side As Integer = CType(sq2, Integer)
    Console.WriteLine("Side length of sq2 = {0}", side)
End Sub
```

and here is the update to the Square type:

```
Structure Square
...
  Public Shared Narrowing Operator CType(ByVal sideLength As Integer) As Square
    Dim newSq As Square
    newSq.Length = sideLength
    Return newSq
  End Operator

  Public Shared Narrowing Operator CType(ByVal s As Square) As Integer
    Return s.Length
  End Operator
End Structure
```

Wild, huh? To be honest, converting from a Square into an Integer may not be the most intuitive (or useful) operation. However, this does point out a very important fact regarding custom conversion routines: the compiler does not care what you convert to or from, as long as you have written syntactically correct code. Thus, as with overloading operators, just because you can create an explicit cast operation for a given type does not mean you should. Typically, this technique will be most helpful when you're creating .NET structure types, given that they are unable to participate in classical inheritance (where casting comes for free).

Defining Implicit Conversion Routines

Thus far, you have created various custom *explicit* (e.g., *narrowing*) conversion operations. However, what about the following *implicit* (e.g., *widening*) conversion?

```
Sub Main()
...
    ' Attempt to make an implicit cast?
    Dim s3 As Square
    s3.Length = 83
    Dim rect2 As Rectangle = s3
...
End Sub
```

As you might expect, this code will not compile, given that you have not provided an implicit conversion routine for the Rectangle type. Now here is the catch: it is illegal to define explicit and implicit conversion functions on the same type, if they do not differ by their return type or parameter set. This might seem like a limitation; however, the second catch is that when a type defines an *implicit* conversion routine, it is legal for the caller to make use of the *explicit* cast syntax!

Confused? To clear things up, let's add an implicit conversion routine to the Rectangle structure using the VB 2005 Widening keyword (note that the following code assumes the width of the resulting Rectangle is computed by multiplying the side of the Square by 2):

```
Public Structure Rectangle
...
  Public Shared Widening Operator CType(ByVal s As Square) As Rectangle
    Dim r As Rectangle
    r.Height = s.Length

    ' Assume the length of the new Rectangle with
    ' (Length x 2)
    r.Width = s.Length * 2
    Return r
  End Operator
End Structure
```

With this update, you are now able to convert between types as follows:

```
Sub Main()
...
  ' Implicit cast OK!
  Dim s3 As Square
  s3.Length= 83
  Dim rect2 As Rectangle = s3
  Console.WriteLine("rect2 = {0}", rect2)
  DrawSquare(s3)

  ' Explicit cast syntax still OK!
  Dim s4 As Square
  s4.Length = 3
  Dim rect3 As Rectangle = CType(s4, Rectangle)
  Console.WriteLine("rect3 = {0}", rect3)
...
End Sub
```

Again, be aware that it is permissible to define explicit and implicit conversion routines for the same type as long as their signatures differ. Thus, you could update the Square as follows:

```
Public Structure Square
...
  ' Can call as:
  ' Dim sq2 As Square = CType(90, Square)
  ' or as:
  ' Dim sq2 As Square = 90
  Public Shared Widening Operator CType(ByVal sideLength As Integer) As Square
    Dim newSq As Square
    newSq.Length = sideLength
    Return newSq
  End Operator

  ' Must call as:
  ' Dim side As Integer = CType(mySquare, Square)
  Public Shared Narrowing Operator CType(ByVal s As Square) As Integer
```

```
    return s.Length
  End Operator
End Structure
```

Source Code The CustomConversions project is located under the Chapter 11 subdirectory.

The VB 2005 DirectCast Keyword

To wrap things up for this chapter, allow me to comment on two new keywords introduced with Visual Basic 2005 that can be used as alternatives to CType(). As you know by this point in the text, CType() can be used to explicitly convert an expression to a specified data type, object, structure, class, or interface.

Also recall that when you use CType(), the CLR will throw a runtime exception if the arguments are incompatible. To illustrate, assume you have two class types and a single interface related as follows:

```
Interface ITurboBoost
  Sub TurboCharge(ByVal onOff As Boolean)
End Interface

Class Car
End Class

Class SportsCar
  Inherits Car
  Implements ITurboBoost
  Public Sub TurboCharge(ByVal onOff As Boolean) _
    Implements ITurboBoost.TurboCharge
  End Sub
End Class
```

Now observe the following CType() statements, all of which compile, and some of which cause a runtime exception (an InvalidCastException to be exact):

```
Sub Main()
  Console.WriteLine("***** Fun with CType / DirectCast / TryCast ******")
  Console.WriteLine()

  ' This CType() throws an exception,
  ' as Car does not implement ITurboBoost.
  Dim myCar As New Car
  Dim iTB As ITurboBoost
  iTB = CType(myCar, ITurboBoost)

  ' This CType() is a-OK, as SportsCar does
  ' implement ITurboBoost.
  Dim myViper As New SportsCar
  iTB = CType(myViper, ITurboBoost)

  ' CType() can also be used to narrow or widen
  ' between primitive types.
  Dim i As Integer = 200
  Dim b As Byte = CType(i, Byte)
End Sub
```

While using CType() to convert between types is always permissible, VB 2005 now provides an alternative keyword named DirectCast(). Syntactically, DirectCast() looks identical to CType(). Under the hood, however, DirectCast() offers better performance when converting to or from reference types. The reason is that DirectCast(), unlike CType(), does not make use of the Visual Basic runtime helper routines for conversion. However, remember that DirectCast can only be used if the arguments are related by the "is-a" relationship or interface implementation (and could therefore never be used to convert between structures [and thus numerical types]). Consider the following update to the previous Main() method:

```
Sub Main()
  Console.WriteLine("***** Fun with CType / DirectCast / TryCast ******")
  Console.WriteLine()

  Dim myCar As New Car
  Dim iTB As ITurboBoost
  iTB = DirectCast(myCar, ITurboBoost)

  Dim myViper As New SportsCar
  iTB = DirectCast(myViper, ITurboBoost)

  ' Compiler error! Integer and Byte
  ' are not related to inheritance/interface
  ' implementation!
  Dim i As Integer = 200
  Dim b As Byte = DirectCast(i, Byte)
End Sub
```

Note that the first two DirectCast() calls function identically to CType(). The final call to DirectCast() is a compile-time error, however. While it is true that DirectCast() can result in greater performance for large-scale applications, this is not to say the CType() is obsolete. In fact, in most applications, these two calls can be used interchangeably with little or no noticeable effect. However, when you wish to squeeze out every drop of performance from a VB 2005 application, DirectCast() is one part of the puzzle.

The VB 2005 TryCast Keyword

On a final note, VB 2005 now offers one final manner to perform runtime type conversions using TryCast(). Again, syntactically, TryCast() looks identical to CType(). The difference is that TryCast() returns Nothing if the arguments are not related by inheritance or interface implementation, rather than throwing a runtime exception. Thus, rather than wrapping a call to CType() or DirectCast() within Try/Catch logic, you can simply test the returned reference within a conditional statement.

This being said, here is the final iteration of our Main() method, which makes use of structured exception handling/conditional tests for Nothing as required by each of the conversion operators.

```
Sub Main()
  Console.WriteLine("***** Fun with CType / DirectCast / TryCast ******")
  Console.WriteLine()
```

```
Dim myCar As New Car
Dim iTB As ITurboBoost

' CType() throws
' exceptions if the types are not compatible.
Try
  iTB = CType(myCar, ITurboBoost)
Catch ex As InvalidCastException
  Console.WriteLine(ex.Message)
  Console.WriteLine()
End Try

' Like CType(), DirectCast() throws
' exceptions if the types are not compatible.
Dim myViper As New SportsCar
Try
  iTB = DirectCast(myViper, ITurboBoost)
Catch ex As Exception
  Console.WriteLine(ex.Message)
  Console.WriteLine()
End Try

' TryCast() returns Nothing if the types are not
' compatible.
Dim c As Car = TryCast(myViper, Car)
If c Is Nothing Then
  Console.WriteLine("Sorry, types are not compatable...")
Else
  Console.WriteLine(c.ToString())
End If
End Sub
```

Source Code The Casting project is located under the Chapter 11 subdirectory.

Summary

This chapter has illustrated a number of more advanced aspects of the Visual Basic 2005 programming language. We began by looking at the various preprocessor directives supported by VB 2005, and saw how to conditionally compile blocks of code based on predefined constants. The first "meaty" topic of this chapter was a detailed examination of the value type/reference type distinction and the related topic of boxing and unboxing. Next up, you learned about several new features introduced with the release of .NET 2.0, specifically support for overloading operators and defining custom type conversions for your classes and structures. We wrapped up by examining two new conversion keywords (DirectCast() and TryCast()) that can be used in place of traditional calls to CType().

CHAPTER 12

■■■

Understanding Generics and Nullable Data Types

With the release of .NET 2.0, the VB 2005 programming language has been enhanced to support a new feature of the Common Type System (CTS) termed *generics*. Simply put, generics provide a way for programmers to define "placeholders" (formally termed *type parameters*) for members (subroutines, functions, fields, properties, etc.) and type definitions (classes, structures, etc.), which are specified at the time of invoking the generic member or creating the generic type.

While it's true that you could build an entire .NET 2.0 application without ever using a generic item in your code, you gain several benefits by doing so. Given this, the chapter opens by qualifying the need for generic types. Once you understand the problems generics attempt to solve, you will then learn how to make use of existing generic types defined within the System.Collections.Generic namespace.

Next, you will get to know the role of the System.Nullable(Of T) generic type and come to understand a new language feature termed *nullable data types*. As you will see, this generic type allows you to define numerical data that can be set to the value Nothing (which can be particularly helpful when working with relational databases).

After you've seen generic support within the base class libraries, the remainder of this chapter examines how you can build your own generic members, classes, structures, interfaces, and delegates (and when you might wish to do so).

Revisiting the Boxing, Unboxing, and System.Object Relationship

To understand the benefits provided by generics, it's helpful to understand the issues programmers had without them. As you recall from Chapter 11, the .NET platform supports automatic conversion between stack-allocated and heap-allocated memory through *boxing* and *unboxing*. At first glance, this may seem like a rather uneventful language feature that is more academic than practical. In reality, the (un)boxing process is very helpful in that it allows us to assume everything can be treated as a System.Object, while the CLR takes care of the memory-related details on our behalf.

To review the boxing process, assume you have created a System.Collections.ArrayList to hold numeric (and therefore stack-allocated) data. Recall that the members that insert or remove items into (or out of) the ArrayList are all prototyped to receive and return System.Object types. However, rather than forcing programmers to manually wrap a numeric value into a related object wrapper, the runtime will automatically do so via a boxing operation:

```
Sub Main()
  ' Value types are automatically boxed when
  ' passed to a member requesting an object.
  Dim myInts As New ArrayList()
  myInts.Add(10)
  Console.ReadLine()
End Sub
```

If you wish to retrieve this value from the ArrayList object using the type's default property, you must unbox the heap-allocated object into a stack-allocated integer using an explicit casting operation (recall that explicit casting using CType() is required when Option Strict is enabled):

```
Sub Main()
  ' Value types are automatically boxed when
  ' passed to a member requesting an Object.
  Dim myInts As New ArrayList()
  myInts.Add(10)

  ' Value is now unboxed...then reboxed!
  Console.WriteLine("Value of your int: {0}", _
    CType(myInts(0), Integer))
  Console.ReadLine()
End Sub
```

When the VB 2005 compiler transforms a boxing operation into terms of CIL code, you find the box opcode is used internally. Likewise, the unboxing operation is transformed into a CIL unbox operation. Here is the relevant CIL code for the previous Main() method (which can be viewed using ildasm.exe):

```
.method private hidebysig static void Main() cil managed
{
...
  box    [mscorlib]System.Int32
  callvirt   instance int32
  [mscorlib]System.Collections.ArrayList::Add(object)
  pop
  ldstr   "Value of your int: {0}"
  ldloc.0
  ldc.i4.0
  callvirt   instance object [mscorlib]
  System.Collections.ArrayList::get_Item(int32)
  unbox   [mscorlib]System.Int32
  ldind.i4
  box    [mscorlib]System.Int32
  call  void [mscorlib]System.Console::WriteLine(string, object)
...
}
```

Note that the stack-allocated System.Int32 is boxed prior to the call to ArrayList.Add() in order to pass in the required System.Object. Also note that System.Object is unboxed back into a System.Int32 once retrieved from the ArrayList using the type indexer (which maps to the hidden get_Item() method), only to be *boxed again* when it's passed to the Console.WriteLine() method.

The Problem with (Un)Boxing Operations

Although boxing and unboxing are very convenient from a programmer's point of view, this approach to stack/heap memory transfer comes with the baggage of performance issues. To understand the performance issues, consider the steps that must occur to box and unbox a simple integer:

1. A new object must be allocated on the managed heap.

2. The value of the stack-based data must be transferred into that memory location.

3. When unboxed, the value stored on the heap-based object must be transferred back to the stack using an explicit cast (via CType).

4. The now unused object on the heap will (eventually) be garbage collected.

Although the current `Main()` method won't cause a major bottleneck in terms of performance, you could certainly feel the impact if an `ArrayList` contained thousands of integers that are manipulated by your program on a somewhat regular basis. This would result in numerous objects on the heap that must be managed by the garbage collector, which can be yet another possible performance penalty.

In an ideal world, the VB 2005 compiler would be able to store sets of value types in a container that did not require boxing in the first place. If this were the case, we not only gain a higher degree of type safety (as this would remove the need for explicit casting), but also build more performance-driven code. As you would guess, .NET 2.0 generics are the solution to each of these issues.

Type Safety and Strongly Typed Collections

Another issue we have in a generic-less world has to do with the construction of strongly typed collections. Again, recall that a majority of the class types within the `System.Collections` namespace have been constructed to contain `System.Object` types, which resolves to anything at all. In some cases, this is the exact behavior you require given the extreme flexibility:

```
Sub Main()
  ' The ArrayList can hold any item whatsoever.
  Dim myStuff As New ArrayList()
  myStuff.Add(10)
  myStuff.Add(New ArrayList())
  myStuff.Add(True)
  myStuff.Add("Some text data")
  Console.ReadLine()
End Sub
```

While this loose typing can be helpful in some circumstances, it's often advantageous to build a *strongly-typed* collection. Prior to .NET version 2.0, this was most often achieved by leveraging the container types of `System.Collections`. To illustrate, assume you wish to create a custom collection that can only contain objects of type `Person`:

```
Public Class Person
  ' Made public for simplicity.
  Public currAge As Integer
  Public fName As String
  Public lName As String

  Public Sub New()
  End Sub
  Public Sub New(ByVal firstName As String, ByVal lastName As String, _
    ByVal age As Integer)
    currAge = age
```

```
      fName = firstName
      lName = lastName
    End Sub
    Public Overrides Function ToString() As String
      Return String.Format("{0}, {1} is {2} years old.", _
        lName, fName, currAge)
    End Function
End Class
```

To build a person collection, you could define a System.Collections.ArrayList member variable within a class named PeopleCollection and configure all members to operate on strongly typed Person objects, rather than on System.Objects:

```
Public Class PeopleCollection
  Implements IEnumerable
  Private arPeople As ArrayList = New ArrayList()

  Public Function GetPerson(ByVal pos As Integer) As Person
    Return CType(arPeople(pos), Person)
  End Function
  Public Sub AddPerson(ByVal p As Person)
    arPeople.Add(p)
  End Sub
  Public Sub ClearPeople()
    arPeople.Clear()
  End Sub
  Public ReadOnly Property Count() As Integer
    Get
      Return arPeople.Count
    End Get
  End Property
  Public Function GetEnumerator() As IEnumerator _
    Implements IEnumerable.GetEnumerator
    Return arPeople.GetEnumerator()
  End Function
End Class
```

With these types defined, you are now assured of type safety, given that the VB 2005 compiler will be able to determine any attempt to insert an incompatible type:

```
Sub Main()
  Console.WriteLine("***** Strongly Typed Collections *****")
  Console.WriteLine()

  Dim myPeople As PeopleCollection = New PeopleCollection()
  myPeople.AddPerson(New Person("Homer", "Simpson", 40))
  myPeople.AddPerson(New Person("Marge", "Simpson", 38))
  myPeople.AddPerson(New Person("Lisa", "Simpson", 9))
  myPeople.AddPerson(New Person("Bart", "Simpson", 7))
  myPeople.AddPerson(New Person("Maggie", "Simpson", 2))

  ' This would be a compile-time error!
  myPeople.AddPerson(New Car())

  For Each p As Person In myPeople
    Console.WriteLine(p)
  Next
  Console.ReadLine()
End Sub
```

While custom collections do ensure type safety, this approach leaves you in a position where you must create a (almost identical) custom collection for each type you wish to contain. Thus, if you need a custom collection that will be able to operate only on classes deriving from the Car base class, you need to build a very similar type:

```
Public Class CarCollection
  Implements IEnumerable
  Private arCars As ArrayList = New ArrayList()

  Public Function GetCar(ByVal pos As Integer) As Car
    Return CType(arCars(pos), Car)
  End Function
  Public Sub AddCar(ByVal c As Car)
    arCars.Add(c)
  End Sub
  Public Sub ClearCars()
    arCars.Clear()
  End Sub
  Public ReadOnly Property Count() As Integer
    Get
      Return arCars.Count
    End Get
  End Property
  Public Function GetEnumerator() As IEnumerator _
    Implements IEnumerable.GetEnumerator
    Return arCars.GetEnumerator()
  End Function
End Class
```

As you may know from firsthand experience, the process of creating multiple strongly typed collections to account for various types is not only labor intensive, but also a nightmare to maintain. Generic collections allow us to delay the specification of the contained type until the time of creation. Don't fret about the syntactic details just yet, however. Consider the following code, which makes use of a generic class named System.Collections.Generic.List(Of T) to create two type-safe container objects:

```
Module Program
  Sub Main()
    ' Use the generic List type to hold only people.
    Dim morePeople As New List(Of Person)
    morePeople.Add(New Person())

    ' Use the generic List type to hold only cars.
    Dim moreCars As New List(Of Car)
    moreCars.Add(New Car())

    ' Compile-time error!
    moreCars.Add(New Person())
  End Sub
End Module
```

Boxing Issues and Strongly Typed Collections

Strongly typed collections are found throughout the .NET base class libraries and are very useful programming constructs. However, these custom containers do little to solve the issue of boxing penalties. Even if you were to create a custom collection named IntegerCollection that was constructed to operate only on Integer data types, you must allocate some type of reference type to hold the numerical data (System.Array, System.Collections.ArrayList, etc.). Again, given that the nongeneric types operate on System.Objects, we incur boxing and unboxing penalties:

```
Public Class IntegerCollection
  Implements IEnumerable
  Private arInts As ArrayList = New ArrayList()

  Public Function GetInt(ByVal pos As Integer) As Integer
    ' Unboxing!
    Return CType(arInts(pos), Integer)
  End Function
  Public Sub AddInt(ByVal i As Integer)
    ' Boxing!
    arInts.Add(i)
  End Sub
  Public Sub ClearInts()
    arInts.Clear()
  End Sub
  Public ReadOnly Property Count() As Integer
    Get
      Return arInts.Count
    End Get
  End Property
  Public Function GetEnumerator() As IEnumerator _
    Implements IEnumerable.GetEnumerator
    Return arInts.GetEnumerator()
  End Function
End Class
```

Regardless of which type you may choose to hold the integers (System.Array, System.Collections.ArrayList, etc.), you cannot escape the boxing dilemma using .NET 1.x. As you might guess, generics come to the rescue again. The following code leverages the System.Collections.Generic.List(Of T) type to create a container of integers that does *not* incur any boxing or unboxing penalties when inserting or obtaining the value type:

```
Module Program
  Sub Main()
    ' No boxing!
    Dim myInts As New List(Of Integer)
    myInts.Add(10)

    ' No unboxing!
    Console.WriteLine("Int value is: {0}", myInts(0))
  End Sub
End Module
```

To summarize the story thus far, generics address the following issues:

- Performance issues incurred with boxing and unboxing
- Type safety issues found with loosely typed collections
- Code maintenance issues incurred with the construction of strongly typed collections

So now that you have a better feel for the problems generics attempt to solve, you're ready to dig into the details. To begin, allow me to formally introduce the System.Collections.Generic namespace.

Source Code   The StronglyTypedCollections project is located under the Chapter 12 subdirectory.

The System.Collections.Generic Namespace

Generic types are found sprinkled throughout the .NET 2.0 base class libraries; however, the System. Collections.Generic namespace is chock full of them (as its name implies). Like its nongeneric counterpart (System.Collections), the System.Collections.Generic namespace contains numerous class and interface types that allow you to contain subitems in a variety of containers. Not surprisingly, the generic interfaces mimic the corresponding nongeneric types in the System.Collections namespace:

- ICollection(Of T)
- IComparer(Of T)
- IDictionary(Of K, V)
- IEnumerable(Of T)
- IEnumerator(Of T)
- IList(Of T)

■**Note** By convention, generic types specify their placeholders using uppercase letters. Although any letter (or word) will do, typically T is used to represent types, K is used for keys, and V is used for values.

The System.Collections.Generic namespace also defines a number of classes that implement many of these key interfaces. Table 12-1 describes the core class types of this namespace, the interfaces they implement, and any corresponding type in the System.Collections namespace.

Table 12-1. *Classes of* System.Collections.Generic

Generic Type	Nongeneric Counterpart Class in System.Collections	Meaning in Life
Collection(Of T)	CollectionBase	The basis for a generic collection
Comparer(Of T)	Comparer	Compares two generic objects for equality
Dictionary(Of K, V)	Hashtable	A generic collection of name/value pairs
List(Of T)	ArrayList	A dynamically resizable list of items
Queue(Of T)	Queue	A generic implementation of a first-in, first-out (FIFO) list
SortedDictionary(Of K, V)	SortedList	A generic implementation of a sorted set of name/value pairs
Stack(Of T)	Stack	A generic implementation of a last-in, first-out (LIFO) list
LinkedList(Of T)	N/A	A generic implementation of a doubly linked list
ReadOnlyCollection(Of T)	ReadOnlyCollectionBase	A generic implementation of a set of read-only items

The System.Collections.Generic namespace also defines a number of "helper" classes and structures that work in conjunction with a specific container. For example, the LinkedListNode(Of T) type represents a node within a generic LinkedList(Of T), the KeyNotFoundException exception is raised when attempting to grab an item from a container using a nonexistent key, and so forth.

As you can see from Table 12-1, many of the generic collection classes have a nongeneric counterpart in the System.Collections namespace (some of which are identically named). Given that Chapter 9 illustrated how to work with these nongeneric types, I will not provide a detailed examination of each generic counterpart, as they work more or less the same as the nongeneric types. Rather, I'll make use of List(Of T) to illustrate the process of working with generics. If you require details regarding other members of the System.Collections.Generic namespace, consult the .NET Framework 2.0 SDK documentation.

Examining the List(Of T) Type

Like nongeneric classes, generic types are created via the New keyword and any necessary constructor arguments. In addition, you are required to specify the type(s) to be substituted for the type parameter(s) defined by the generic type. For example, System.Collections.Generic.List(Of T) requires you to specify a single type parameter that describes the type of item the List(Of T) will operate upon. Therefore, if you wish to create three List(Of T) objects to contain integers and Person and Car objects, you would make use of the VB 2005 Of keyword as follows:

```
Module Program
  Sub Main()
    ' A list of Integers.
    Dim myInts As New List(Of Integer)

    ' A list of Person objects.
    Dim myPeople As New List(Of Person)

    ' A list of Cars.
    Dim myCars As New List(Of Car)
  End Sub
End Module
```

At this point, you might wonder what exactly becomes of the specified placeholder value. If you were to make use of the Visual Studio 2005 Object Browser, you will find that the placeholder T is used throughout the definition of the List(Of T) type, as you see in Figure 12-1.

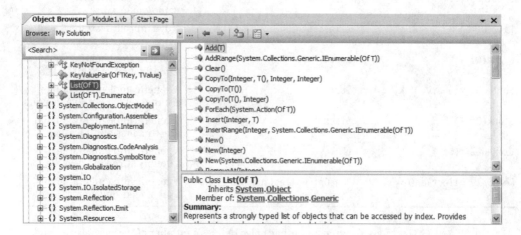

Figure 12-1. *A type parameter can be used as a placeholder throughout a type definition.*

Thus, when you create a List(Of T) specifying Car types, Car is substituted for T throughout the List type. Likewise, if you were to build a List(Of T) of type Integers, T is of type Integer. Of course, when you create a generic List(Of T), the compiler does not literally create a brand new implementation of the List(Of T) type. Rather, it will address only the members of the generic type you actually invoke. For example, if you were to author the following Main() method, which invokes the Add() and Count members of the List(Of T) type:

```
Module Program
  Sub Main()
    ' A list of Cars.
    Dim myCars As New List(Of Car)
    myCars.Add(New Car())
    Console.WriteLine("myCars contains {0} items", _
      myCars.Count)
    Console.ReadLine()
  End Sub
End Module
```

you would find the VB 2005 compiler generates the following (slightly edited and annotated) CIL code (which can be verified using ildasm.exe):

```
.method public static void  Main() cil managed
{
...
  // Create the List(Of T) type where 'T' is of type Car.
  .locals init ([0]  class
  [mscorlib]System.Collections.Generic.List`1
  <class SimpleGenerics.Car> myCars)
  IL_0001:  newobj instance void class
  [mscorlib]System.Collections.Generic.List`1
  <class SimpleGenerics.Car>::.ctor()
...
  // Create a Car and add it into the List of
  // Cars via the Add() method.
  IL_0008:  newobj     instance void SimpleGenerics.Car::.ctor()
  IL_000d:  callvirt   instance void class
  [mscorlib]System.Collections.Generic.List`1
  <class SimpleGenerics.Car>::Add(!0)
...
  // Call the ReadOnly Count property.
  IL_0019: callvirt instance int32 class
  [mscorlib]System.Collections.Generic.List`1
  <class SimpleGenerics.Car>::get_Count()
...
}
```

Notice that in terms of CIL code, a type parameter is specified using angled brackets. Thus, the Visual Basic 2005 List(Of T) syntax translates into List`1<T> in terms of CIL. Also notice the type parameters of the List(Of T) constructor, Add() method, and Count property have all been set to be of type Car.

Now assume you have created a List(Of T) generic type where you specify T to be of type Integer:

```
Module Program
  Sub Main()
...
    ' A list of Ingeters.
    Dim myInts As New List(Of Integer)
```

```
    ' No boxing!
    myInts.Add(50)

    ' No unboxing!
    Dim val As Integer = myInts.Count
    Console.WriteLine("myInts contains {0} items", myInts.Count)
    Console.ReadLine()
  End Sub
End Module
```

This time, the compiler generates CIL code wherein each occurrence of T is now of type int32 (the internal representation of the VB 2005 Integer type):

```
.method public static void  Main() cil managed
{
...
  // Make a List of Integers.
  .locals init ([0] class  [mscorlib]
  System.Collections.Generic.List`1<int32> MyInts)
  IL_0001:  newobj  instance void class
  [mscorlib]System.Collections.Generic.List`1<int32>::.ctor()

  // Add the value '50' to the List.
  IL_0008:  ldc.i4.s    50
  IL_000a:  callvirt    instance void class
  [mscorlib]System.Collections.Generic.List`1<int32>::Add(!0)
...
  // Call the ReadOnly Count property.
  IL_0016:  callvirt  instance int32 class
  [mscorlib]System.Collections.Generic.List`1<int32>::get_Count()
...
}
```

The most telling aspect of this CIL code snippet is the fact that we have not incurred any boxing or unboxing penalties when inserting or obtaining the numerical data from the List type! This is in stark contrast to inserting numerical data (or any structure) within the nongeneric System.Collections.ArrayList.

Source Code The SimpleGenerics project is located under the Chapter 12 subdirectory.

So, at this point you've looked at the process of working with the generic List(Of T) type. Again, do understand that the remaining types of System.Collections.Generic would be manipulated in a similar manner. Next up, let's turn our attention to the use of another generic type within the System namespace named Nullable(Of T).

Understanding Nullable Data Types and the System.Nullable(Of T) Generic Type

Another very interesting generic class is System.Nullable(Of T), which allows you to define *nullable data types*. As you know, CLR data types have a fixed range of possible values. For example, the System.Boolean data type can be assigned a value from the set {True, False}. As of .NET 2.0, it's now possible to create nullable data types. Simply put, a nullable type can represent all the values of its underlying type, plus an empty (aka, *undefined*) value. Thus, if we declare a nullable System.Boolean, it could be assigned a value from the set {True, False, Nothing}.

To define a nullable variable type, simply create a new Nullable(Of T) type and specify the type parameter. Be aware, however, that the specified type must be a value type! If you attempt to create a nullable reference type (including Strings), you are issued a compile-time error. For example:

```
Sub Main()
  ' Define some local nullable types.
  Dim nullableInt As New Nullable(Of Integer)
  Dim nullableDouble As New Nullable(Of Double)
  Dim nullableBool As New Nullable(Of Boolean)

  ' Error!  Strings are reference types!
  Dim s As New Nullable(Of String)
End Sub
```

Like any type, System.Nullable(Of T) provides a set of members that all nullable types can make use of. For example, you are able to programmatically discover whether the nullable variable indeed has been assigned an undefined Nothing value using the HasValue property. The assigned value of a nullable type may be obtained via the Value property.

Working with Nullable Types

Nullable data types can be particularly useful when you are interacting with databases, given that columns in a data table may be intentionally empty (e.g., undefined). To illustrate, assume the following class, which simulates the process of accessing a database containing a table of two columns that may be undefined. Note that the GetIntFromDatabase() method has assigned the value Nothing to the nullable Integer member variable, while GetBoolFromDatabase() is assigning the value True to the Boolean member:

```
Class DatabaseReader
  ' Nullable data fields.
  Public numbericValue As Nullable(Of Integer) = Nothing
  Public boolValue As Nullable(Of Boolean) = True

  ' Note the nullable return type.
  Public Function GetIntFromDatabase() As Nullable(Of Integer)
    Return numbericValue
  End Function

  ' Note the nullable return type.
  Public Function GetBoolFromDatabase() As Nullable(Of Boolean)
    Return boolValue
  End Function
End Class
```

Now, assume the following Main() method, which invokes each member of the DatabaseReader class, and discovers the assigned values using the HasValue and Value members:

```
Module Program
  Sub Main()
    Console.WriteLine("***** Fun with Nullable Data *****")
    Console.WriteLine()

    Dim dr As New DatabaseReader()

    ' Get integer from 'database'.
    Dim i As Nullable(Of Integer) = dr.GetIntFromDatabase()
```

```
    If (i.HasValue) Then
      Console.WriteLine("Value of 'i' is: {0}", i.Value)
    Else
      Console.WriteLine("Value of 'i' is undefined.")
    End If

    ' Get boolean from 'database'.
    Dim b As Nullable(Of Boolean) = dr.GetBoolFromDatabase()
    If (b.HasValue) Then
      Console.WriteLine("Value of 'b' is: {0}", b.Value)
    Else
      Console.WriteLine("Value of 'b' is undefined.")
    End If
    Console.ReadLine()
  End Sub
End Module
```

Cool! At this point, you hopefully understand how to interact with generic types that lurk within the .NET base class libraries. During the remainder of this chapter, you'll examine how to create your own generic methods, types, and collections. First up, let's check out how to build a custom generic method.

■**Source Code** The NullableData project is located under the Chapter 12 subdirectory.

Creating Generic Methods

As you learned back in Chapter 4, methods can be *overloaded*. Recall that this language feature allows you to define multiple versions of the same method, provided each variation differs by the number (or type) of parameters. For example, assume you wish to build a method that can swap two Integer data types. To do so, simply pass in each argument by reference and flip the values around with the help of a local Integer variable:

```
Module NonGenericMethods
  Public Function Swap(ByRef a As Integer, _
    ByRef b As Integer) As Integer
    Dim temp As Integer
    temp = a
    a = b
    b = temp
  End Function
End Module
```

With this, we could now call our Swap() method like so:

```
Module Program
  Sub Main()
    ' Call the nongeneric Swap() methods.
    Dim a, b As Integer
    a = 10
    b = 40
    Console.WriteLine("Before swap: a={0}, b={1}", a, b)
    Swap(a, b)
    Console.WriteLine("After swap: a={0}, b={1}", a, b)
    Console.ReadLine()
  End Sub
End Module
```

Although this Swap() method works as expected, assume you now wish to build a method that can swap two Doubles. This would require you to build a second version of Swap() that now operates on floating-point data:

```
Public Function Swap(ByRef a As Double, _
  ByRef b As Double) As Double
  Dim temp As Double
  temp = a
  a = b
  b = temp
End Function
```

As you would expect, if you require other swap routines to operate on Strings, Booleans, SportsCars, and whatnot, you would need to build new versions of the Swap() function. Clearly, this would be a pain to maintain over the long run, not to mention the fact that each version of Swap() is doing more-or-less the same thing.

Before the use of generics, one way to avoid this redundancy was to create a single Swap() method that operates on Object data types. Because everything in .NET can be represented as a System.Object, this approach would allow us to have a single version of Swap(); however, we are once again incurring boxing and unboxing penalties when operating on value types.

To simplify our coding (and avoid undesirable boxing/unboxing operations), we could author a generic Swap() method. Consider the following generic Swap() method, which can swap any two data types of type T (remember, the name you give to a type parameter is entirely up to you):

```
' This generic method can swap any two items of type 'T'
Public Function Swap(Of T)(ByRef a As T, ByRef b As T) As T
  Console.WriteLine("T is a {0}.", GetType(T))
  Dim temp As T
  temp = a
  a = b
  b = temp
End Function
```

Notice how a generic method is defined by specifying the type parameter after the method name but before the parameter list. Here, you're stating that the Swap() method can operate on any two parameters of type T. Just to spice things up a bit, you're printing out the type name of the supplied placeholder to the console using the VB 2005 GetType() operator.

Now ponder the following Main() method, which swaps integer and string types:

```
Sub Main()
  Console.WriteLine("***** Fun with Generic Methods *****")
  Console.WriteLine()

  ' Swap two Integers.
  Dim a, b As Integer
  a = 10 : b = 40
  Console.WriteLine("Before swap: a={0}, b={1}", a, b)
  Swap(Of Integer)(a, b)
  Console.WriteLine("After swap: a={0}, b={1}", a, b)
  Console.WriteLine()

  ' Swap two Strings.
  Dim s1, s2 As String
  s1 = "Generics" : s2 = "Rock"
  Console.WriteLine("Before swap: s1={0}, s2={1}", s1, s2)
  Swap(Of String)(s1, s2)
  Console.WriteLine("After swap: s1={0}, s2={1}", s1, s2)
  Console.ReadLine()
End Sub
```

The output of this program can be seen in Figure 12-2.

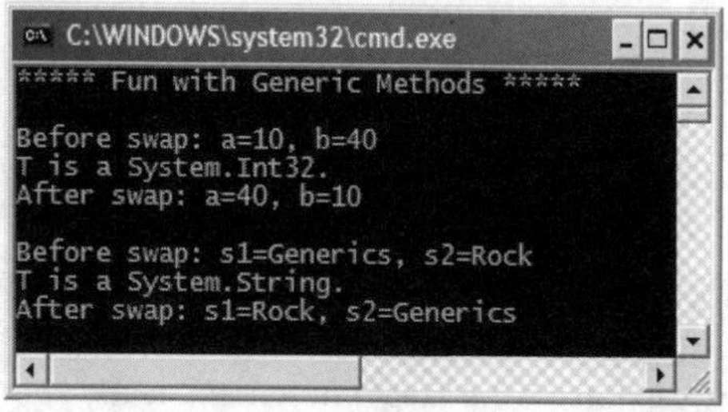

Figure 12-2. *Our generic swap method in action*

Omission of Type Parameters

When you invoke generic methods such as Swap(Of T), you can optionally omit the type parameter if (and only if) the generic method requires arguments, as the compiler can infer the type parameter based on the member parameters. For example, you could swap two System.Boolean types as follows:

```
' Compiler will infer System.Boolean.
Dim b1, b2 As Boolean
b1 = True : b2 = False
Console.WriteLine("Before swap: b1={0}, b2={1}", b1, b2)
Swap(b1, b2)
Console.WriteLine("Before swap: b1={0}, b2={1}", b1, b2)
```

However, if you have another generic method named DisplayBaseClass(Of T) that does not take any incoming parameters, as follows:

```
Sub DisplayBaseClass(Of T)()
  Console.WriteLine("Base class of {0} is: {1}.", _
    GetType(T), GetType(T).BaseType)
End Sub
```

you are required to supply the type parameter upon invocation:

```
Sub Main()
...
  ' Must specify 'T' when a generic
  ' method takes no parameters.
  DisplayBaseClass(Of Boolean)()
  DisplayBaseClass(Of String)()
  DisplayBaseClass(Of Integer)()
End Sub
```

■**Source Code** The GenericSwapMethod project is located under the Chapter 12 subdirectory.

Creating Generic Structures (or Classes)

Now that you understand how to define and invoke generic methods, let's turn our attention to the construction of a generic structure (the process of building a generic class is identical). Assume you have built a flexible Point structure that supports a single type parameter representing the underlying storage for the (x, y) coordinates. The caller would then be able to create Point(Of T) types as follows:

```
' Point using Integer.
Dim intPt As New Point(Of Integer)(100, 100)

' Point using Double.
Dim dblPt As New Point(Of Double)(5.6, 3.23)
```

Here is the complete definition of Point(Of T), with analysis to follow:

```
Public Structure Point(Of T)
  Private xPos, yPos As T

  Public Sub New(ByVal x As T, ByVal y As T)
    xPos = x : yPos = y
  End Sub
  Public Property X() As T
    Get
      Return xPos
    End Get
    Set(ByVal value As T)
      xPos = value
    End Set
  End Property
  Public Property Y() As T
    Get
      Return xPos
    End Get
    Set(ByVal value As T)
      yPos = value
    End Set
  End Property
  Public Overrides Function ToString() As String
    Return String.Format("({0}, {1}", xPos, yPos)
  End Function
End Structure
```

Notice that our Point structure has been defined to operate internally with type T, just like the previous generic Swap() method. Given that the caller must specify T at the time of creating a Point type, we are free to use T throughout the definition, as we have here for field data, property definitions, and member arguments.

Assuming this new example has implemented the Swap(Of T) method from the previous example, we can now create, manipulate, and swap instances of the Point(Of T) type like so:

```
Sub Main()
  Console.WriteLine("***** Fun with Custom Generic Types *****")
  Console.WriteLine()

  ' Make a Point using Integers.
  Dim intPt As New Point(Of Integer)(100, 100)
  Console.WriteLine("intPt.ToString()={0}", intPt.ToString())
  Console.WriteLine()
```

```
' Point using Double.
Dim dblPt As New Point(Of Double)(5.6, 3.23)
Console.WriteLine("dblPt.ToString()={0}", dblPt.ToString())
Console.WriteLine()

' Swap 2 Points.
Dim p1 As New Point(Of Integer)(10, 43)
Dim p2 As New Point(Of Integer)(6, 987)
Console.WriteLine("Before swap: {0} , {1}", p1, p2)

' Here we are swapping two points of type Integer.
Swap(Of Point(Of Integer))(p1, p2)
Console.WriteLine("Before swap: {0} , {1}", p1, p2)
Console.ReadLine()
End Sub
```

Notice when we swap our two Point types, we are explicitly specifying the type parameters for the Point's T as well as the Swap() method's T. While this approach makes our code very explicit, type inference allows us to simply call Swap() as follows:

```
' The compiler is able to infer we are using Points
' of type Integer.
Swap(p1, p2)
```

In either case, Figure 12-3 shows the output.

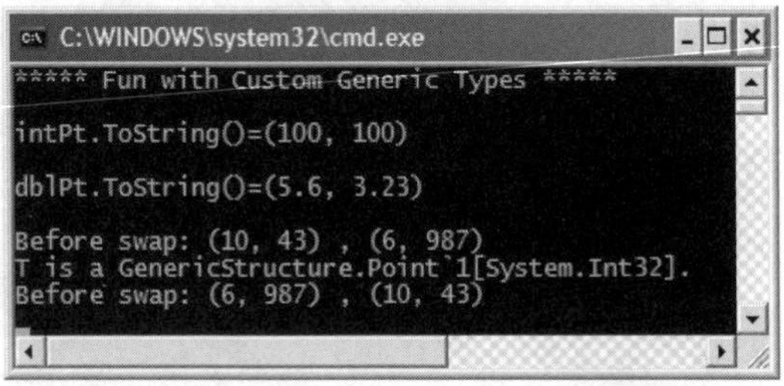

Figure 12-3. *Working with our generic structure*

■**Source Code** The GenericStructure project is located under the Chapter 12 subdirectory.

Creating a Custom Generic Collection

As you have seen, the System.Collections.Generic namespace provides numerous types that allow you to create type-safe and efficient containers. Given the set of available choices, the chances are quite good that you will not need to build custom collection types when programming with .NET 2.0. Nevertheless, to illustrate how you could build a stylized generic container, the next task is to build a generic collection class named CarCollection(Of T).

Like the nongeneric CarCollection created earlier in this chapter, this iteration will leverage an existing collection type to hold the subitems (a List(Of T) in this case). As well, you will support For Each iteration by implementing the generic IEnumerable(Of T) interface. Do note that IEnumerable(Of T) extends the nongeneric IEnumerable interface; therefore, the compiler expects you to implement *two* versions of the GetEnumerator() method. Here is the definition of our type:

```
Public Class CarCollection(Of T)
  Implements IEnumerable(Of T)

  Private myCars As New List(Of T)

  ' Generic default property.
  Default Public Property Item(ByVal index As Integer) As T
    Get
       Return myCars(index)
    End Get
    Set(ByVal value As T)
      myCars.Add(value)
    End Set
  End Property
  Public Sub ClearCars()
    myCars.Clear()
  End Sub
  Public Function CarCount() As Integer
    Return myCars.Count()
  End Function
  Public Function GetEnumeratorGeneric() As IEnumerator(Of T) _
    Implements IEnumerable(Of T).GetEnumerator
    Return myCars.GetEnumerator()
  End Function
  Public Function GetEnumerator() As IEnumerator _
    Implements IEnumerable.GetEnumerator
    Return myCars.GetEnumerator()
  End Function
End Class
```

You could make use of this updated CarCollection(Of T) as follows:

```
Module Program
  Sub Main()
    Console.WriteLine("***** Custom Generic Collection *****")
    Console.WriteLine()

    ' Make a collection of Cars.
    Dim myCars As New CarCollection(Of Car)
    myCars(0) = New Car("Rusty", 20)
    myCars(1) = New Car("Zippy", 90)

    For Each c As Car In myCars
      Console.WriteLine("PetName: {0}, Speed: {1}", _
      c.PetName, c.Speed)
    Next
    Console.ReadLine()
  End Sub
End Module
```

Here you are creating a CarCollection(Of T) type that contains only Car types. Again, you could achieve a similar end result if you make use of the List(Of T) type directly. The only real benefit at this point is the fact that you are free to define uniquely named methods to the CarCollection that delegate the request to the internal List(Of T). For example, notice that we have defined two members that clearly express we are operating on the Car type (ClearCars() and CarCount()).

While this benefit may be quite negligible, another possible benefit of building a custom generic container is that you gain the ability to author custom code statements that should execute during the scope of your methods. For example, the Add() method of List(Of T) simply inserts the new item into the internally maintained list. However, if you needed to ensure that when a type was added to the List(of T) you wrote data out to an event log, fired out a custom event, or what have you, a custom container is the most straightforward way to do so.

Constraining Type Parameters

Currently, the CarCollection(Of T) class does not buy you much beyond uniquely named public methods. Furthermore, given that T (or any type parameter) by default can be used to specify anything at all, an object user could create an instance of CarCollection(Of T) and specify a completely unrelated type parameter:

```
' This is syntactically correct, but confusing at best...
Dim myInts As New CarCollection(Of Integer)
myInts(0) = 4
myInts(1) = 44
```

To illustrate another form of generics abuse, assume that you have now created two new classes (SportsCar and MiniVan) that derive from the Car type:

```
Public Class SportsCar
  Inherits Car
  Public Sub New(ByVal p As String, ByVal s As Integer)
    MyBase.New(p, s)
  End Sub
  ' Assume additional SportsCar methods.
End Class

Public Class MiniVan
  Inherits Car
  Public Sub New(ByVal p As String, ByVal s As Integer)
    MyBase.New(p, s)
  End Sub
  ' Assume additional MiniVan methods.
End Class
```

Given the laws of inheritance, it's permissible to add a MiniVan or SportsCar type directly into a CarCollection(Of T) created with a type parameter of Car:

```
' CarCollection(Of Car) can hold any type deriving from Car.
Dim otherCars As New CarCollection(Of Car)
otherCars(0) = New MiniVan("Mel", 10)
otherCars(1) = New SportsCar("Suzy", 30)
```

Although this is syntactically correct, what if you wished to update CarCollection(Of T) with a new public method named PrintPetName()? This seems simple enough—just access the correct item in the List(Of T) and invoke the PetName property:

```
' Error! System.Object does not have a
' property named PetName.
Public Sub PrintPetName(ByVal pos As Integer)
  Console.WriteLine(myCars(pos).PetName)
End Sub
```

However, this will not compile, given that the true identity of T is not yet known, and you cannot say for certain whether the item in the List(Of T) type has a PetName property. When a type parameter is not constrained in any way (as is the case here), the generic type is said to be *unbound*. By design, unbound type parameters are assumed to have only the members of System.Object (which clearly does not provide a PetName property).

You may try to trick the compiler by casting the item returned from the List(Of T)'s indexer method into a strongly typed Car, and invoking PetName from the returned object:

```
' Error! System.Object does not have a
' property named PetName.
Public Sub PrintPetName(ByVal pos As Integer)
    Console.WriteLine(CType(myCars(pos), Car).PetName)
End Sub
```

This again does not compile, given that the compiler does not yet know the value of the type parameter (Of T) and cannot guarantee the cast would be legal.

To address such issues, .NET generics may be defined with optional constraints using the As keyword. As of .NET 2.0, generics may be constrained in the ways listed in Table 12-2.

Table 12-2. *Possible Constraints for Generic Type Parameters*

Generic Constraint	Meaning in Life
Of T As Structure	The type parameter (Of T) must have System.ValueType in its chain of inheritance.
Of T As Class	The type parameter (Of T) must *not* have System.ValueType in its chain of inheritance (e.g., (Of T) must be a reference type).
Of T As New	The type parameter (Of T) must have a default constructor. This is very helpful if your generic type must create an instance of the type parameter, as you cannot assume the format of custom constructors. Note that this constraint must be listed last on a multiconstrained type.
Of T As NameOfBaseClass	The type parameter (Of T) must be derived from the class specified by NameOfBaseClass.
Of T As NameOfInterface	The type parameter (Of T) must implement the interface specified by NameOfInterface.

When you wish to apply constraints on a type parameter, simply make use of the As keyword. Furthermore, a single type parameter may be assigned multiple constraints by grouping them within curly brackets. By way of a few concrete examples, consider the following constraints of a generic class named MyGenericClass:

```
' Contained items must have a default ctor.
Public Class MyGenericClass(Of T As New)
End Class
```

```
' Contained items must implement ICloneable
' and support a default ctor.
Public Class MyGenericClass(Of T As {ICloneable, New})
End Class
```

```
' MyGenericClass derives from SomeBaseClass
' and implements ISomeInterface,
' while the contained items must be structures.
Public Class MyGenericClass(Of T As Structure)
    Inherits SomeBaseClass
    Implements ISomeInterface
End Class
```

On a related note, if you are building a generic type that specifies multiple type parameters, you can specify a unique set of constraints for each:

```
' (Of K) must have a default ctor, while (Of T) must
' implement the generic IComparable interface.
Public Class MyGenericClass(Of K As New, T As IComparable(Of T))
End Class
```

If you wish to update `CarCollection(Of T)` to ensure that only `Car`-derived types can be placed within it, you could write the following:

```
Public Class CarCollection(Of T As Car)
  Implements IEnumerable(Of T)

  Private myCars As New List(Of T)

  ' This is now a-OK, as the compiler knows 'T' must derive from Car.
  Public Sub PrintPetName(ByVal pos As Integer)
    Console.WriteLine(myCars(pos).PetName)
  End Sub
...
End Class
```

Notice that once you constrain `CarCollection(Of T)` such that it can contain only `Car`-derived types, the implementation of `PrintPetName()` is straightforward, given that the compiler now assumes `(Of T)` is a `Car`-derived type. Furthermore, if the specified type parameter is not `Car`-compatible, you are issued a compiler error:

```
' Now a compile-time error!
Dim myInts As New CarCollection(Of Integer)
myInts(0) = 4
myInts(1) = 44
```

Do be aware that type parameters of generic methods can also be constrained. For example, if you wish to ensure that only value types are passed into the `Swap()` method created previously in this chapter, update the code accordingly:

```
' Type 'T' must be a structure.
Public Function Swap(Of T As Structure) _
  (ByRef a As T, ByRef b As T) As T
  ...
End Function
```

Understand of course, that if you were to constrain the `Swap()` method in this manner, you would no longer be able to swap `String` types (as they are reference types).

The Lack of Operator Constraints

When you are creating generic methods, it may come as a surprise to you that it's a compiler error to apply any VB 2005 operators (+, -, *, etc.) on the type parameters. As an example, I am sure you could imagine the usefulness of a class that can add or subtract generic types:

```
' Compiler error!  Cannot apply
' operators to type parameters!
Public Class BasicMath(Of T)
  Public Function Add(ByVal a As T, _
    ByVal b As T) As T
    Return a + b  ' Error!
  End Function
```

```
  Public Function Subtract(ByVal a As T, _
    ByVal b As T) As T
    Return a - b   ' Error!
  End Function
End Class
```

Sadly, the preceding BasicMath(Of T) class will not compile, as the compiler cannot guarantee that T has overloaded the + and - operators (see Chapter 11 for details of operator overloading). While this may seem like a major restriction, you need to remember that generics *are* generic.

Of course, the Integer type can work just fine with the binary operators of VB 2005. However, for the sake of argument, if (Of T) were a custom class or structure type, the compiler cannot assume it has overloaded the +, -, *, and / operators. Ideally, VB 2005 would allow a generic type to be constrained by supported operators, for example:

```
' Illustrative code only!
' This is not legal code under VB 2005.
Public Class BasicMath(Of T As Operator +, -)
    Public Function Add(ByVal a As T, _
      ByVal b As T) As T
        Return a + b
    End Function
    Public Function Subtract(ByVal a As T, _
      ByVal b As T) As T
        Return a - b
    End Function
End Class
```

Alas, operator constraints are not supported on .NET 2.0 generics.

■**Source Code** The CustomGenericCollection project is located under the Chapter 12 subdirectory.

Creating Generic Interfaces

As you saw earlier in the chapter during the examination of the System.Collections.Generic namespace, generic interfaces are also permissible (e.g., IEnumerable(Of T)). You are, of course, free to define your own generic interfaces (with or without constraints). Assume you wish to define an interface that can perform binary operations on a generic type parameter:

```
Public Interface IBasicMath(Of T)
  Function Add(ByVal a As T, ByVal b As T) As T
  Function Subtract(ByVal a As T, ByVal b As T) As T
  Function Multiply(ByVal a As T, ByVal b As T) As T
  Function Divide(ByVal a As T, ByVal b As T) As T
End Interface
```

Of course, interfaces are more or less useless until they are implemented by a class or structure. When you implement a generic interface, the supporting type specifies the placeholder type:

```
Public Class BasicMath
  Implements IBasicMath(Of Integer)

  Public Function Add(ByVal a As Integer, ByVal b As Integer) _
    As Integer Implements IBasicMath(Of Integer).Add
    Return a + b
  End Function
```

```
   Public Function Divide(ByVal a As Integer, ByVal b As Integer) _
      As Integer Implements IBasicMath(Of Integer).Divide
      Return CInt(a / b)
   End Function

   Public Function Multiply(ByVal a As Integer, ByVal b As Integer) _
      As Integer Implements IBasicMath(Of Integer).Multiply
      Return a * b
   End Function

   Public Function Subtract(ByVal a As Integer, ByVal b As Integer) _
      As Integer Implements IBasicMath(Of Integer).Subtract
      Return a - b
   End Function
End Class
```

At this point, you make use of BasicMath as you would expect:

```
Module Program
   Sub Main()
      Console.WriteLine("***** Generic Interfaces *****")
      Dim m As New BasicMath()
      Console.WriteLine("1 + 1 = {0}", m.Add(1, 1))
      Console.ReadLine()
   End Sub
End Module
```

If you would rather create a BasicMath class that operates on floating-point numbers, you could specify the type parameter like so:

```
Public Class BasicMath
   Implements IBasicMath(Of Double)

   Public Function Add(ByVal a As Double, ByVal b As Double) _
      As Double Implements IBasicMath(Of Double).Add
      Return a + b
   End Function
...
End Class
```

■**Source Code** The GenericInterface project is located under the Chapter 12 subdirectory.

Creating Generic Delegates

Last but not least, .NET 2.0 does allow you to define generic delegate types. For example, assume you wish to define a delegate that can call any subroutine taking a single argument. If the argument in question may differ, you could model this using a type parameter. To illustrate, ponder the following code:

```vb
' This generic delegate can point to any method
' taking a single argument (specified at the time
' of creation).
Public Delegate Sub MyGenericDelegate(Of T)(ByVal arg As T)

Module Program
  Sub Main()
    Console.WriteLine("***** Fun with generic delegates *****")
    Console.WriteLine()

    ' Make instance of delegate pointing to method taking an
    ' integer.
    Dim d As New MyGenericDelegate(Of Integer) _
      (AddressOf IntegerTarget)
    d(100)

    ' Now pointing to a method taking a string.
    Dim d2 As New MyGenericDelegate(Of String)(AddressOf StringTarget)
    d2("Cool!")
    Console.ReadLine()
  End Sub

  Public Sub IntegerTarget(ByVal arg As Integer)
    Console.WriteLine("You passed me a {0} with the value of {1}", _
      arg.GetType().Name, arg)
  End Sub
  Public Sub StringTarget(ByVal arg As String)
    Console.WriteLine("You passed me a {0} with the value of {1}", _
      arg.GetType().Name, arg)
  End Sub
End Module
```

Notice that `MyGenericDelegate(Of T)` defines a single type parameter that represents the argument to pass to the delegate target. When creating an instance of this type, you are required to specify the value of the type parameter as well as the name of the method the delegate will invoke. Thus, if you specified a string type, you send a string value to the target method:

```vb
' Create an instance of MyGenericDelegate(Of T)
' with string as the type parameter.
Dim d2 As New MyGenericDelegate(Of String)(AddressOf StringTarget)
d2("Cool!")
```

Given the format of the `strTarget` object, the `StringTarget()` method must now take a single string as a parameter:

```vb
Public Sub StringTarget(ByVal arg As String)
  Console.WriteLine("You passed me a {0} with the value of {1}", _
    arg.GetType().Name, arg)
End Sub
```

■**Source Code** The GenericDelegate project is located under the Chapter 12 directory.

Summary

Generics can arguably be viewed as the major enhancement provided by VB 2005. As you have seen, a generic item allows you to specify "placeholders" (i.e., type parameters) that are specified at the time of creation (or invocation, in the case of generic methods). Essentially, generics provide a solution to the boxing and type-safety issues that plagued .NET 1.1 development.

While you will most often simply make use of the generic types provided in the .NET base class libraries, you are also able to create your own generic types. When you do so, you have the option of specifying any number of constraints to increase the level of type safety and ensure that you are performing operations on types of a "known quantity."

■■■

## PART 5

Programming with .NET Assemblies

▪▪▪

## CHAPTER 13

Introducing .NET Assemblies

Each of the applications developed in this book's first 12 chapters were along the lines of traditional "stand-alone" applications, given that all of your custom programming logic was contained within a single executable file (*.exe). However, one major aspect of the .NET platform is the notion of *binary reuse*, where applications make use of the types contained within various external assemblies (aka code libraries). The point of this chapter is to examine the core details of creating, deploying, and configuring .NET assemblies.

Once you examine the .NET assembly format and understand how to define your own custom namespaces, you'll then learn the distinction between single-file and multifile assemblies, as well as "private" and "shared" assemblies. Next, you'll examine exactly how the .NET runtime resolves the location of an assembly and come to understand the role of the Global Assembly Cache (GAC), application configuration files (*.config files), publisher policy assemblies, and the role of the System.Configuration namespace.

The Role of .NET Assemblies

.NET applications are constructed by piecing together any number of *assemblies*. Simply put, an assembly is a versioned, self-describing binary file hosted by the CLR. Now, despite the fact that .NET assemblies have exactly the same file extensions (*.exe or *.dll) as previous Win32 binaries (including legacy COM servers), they have very little in common under the hood. Thus, to set the stage for the information to come, let's ponder some of the benefits provided by the assembly format.

Assemblies Promote Code Reuse

As you have been building your console applications over the previous chapters, it may have seemed that *all* of the applications' functionality was contained within the executable assembly you were constructing. In reality, your applications were leveraging numerous types contained within the always accessible .NET code library, mscorlib.dll (recall that the VB 2005 compiler references mscorlib.dll automatically), as well as System.Windows.Forms.dll, which was required for the occasional call to MessageBox.Show().

As you may know, a *code library* (also termed a *class library*) is a *.dll that contains types intended to be used by external applications. When you are creating executable assemblies, you will no doubt be leveraging numerous system-supplied and custom code libraries as you create the application at hand. Do be aware, however, that a code library need not take a *.dll file extension. It is perfectly possible for an executable assembly to make use of types defined within an external executable file. In this light, a referenced *.exe can also be considered a "code library."

■**Note** Before the release of Visual Studio 2005, the only way to reference an executable code library was using the /reference flag of the VB 2005 compiler. However, the Add Reference dialog box of Visual Studio 2005 now allows you to reference *.exe assemblies.

Regardless of how a code library is packaged, the .NET platform allows you to reuse types in a language-independent manner. For example, you could create a code library in VB 2005 and reuse that library in any other .NET programming language. It is possible to not only *allocate* types across languages, but derive from them as well. A base class defined in VB 2005 could be extended by a class authored in C#. Interfaces defined in Pascal .NET can be implemented by structures defined in VB 2005, and so forth. The point is that when you begin to break apart a single monolithic executable into numerous .NET assemblies, you achieve a *language-neutral* form of code reuse.

Assemblies Establish a Type Boundary

In Chapter 1, you were introduced to the topic of .NET namespaces, which were defined as a collection of semantically related types (for example, the System.IO namespace contains file I/O types, the System.Windows.Forms namespace defines GUI types, and so forth). Recall that a type's *fully qualified name* is composed by prefixing the type's namespace (e.g., System) to its name (e.g., Console). Strictly speaking, however, the assembly in which a type resides further establishes a type's identity. For example, if you have two uniquely named assemblies (say, MyCars.dll and YourCars.dll) that both define a namespace (CarLibrary) containing a class named SportsCar, they are considered unique types in the .NET universe.

Assemblies Are Versionable Units

.NET assemblies are assigned a four-part numerical version number of the form *<major>.<minor>. <build>.<revision>* (if you do not provide a version number explicitly, your assembly is automatically assigned a version of 0.0.0.0). This number, in conjunction with an optional *public key value*, allows multiple versions of the same assembly to coexist in harmony on a single machine. Formally speaking, assemblies that provide public key information are termed *strongly named*. As you will see in this chapter, using a strong name, the CLR is able to ensure that the correct version of an assembly is loaded on behalf of the calling client.

Assemblies Are Self-Describing

Assemblies are regarded as *self-describing* in part because they record every external assembly they must have access to in order to function correctly. Thus, if your assembly requires System.Windows. Forms.dll and System.Drawing.dll, they will be documented in the assembly's *manifest*. Recall from Chapter 1 that a manifest is a blob of metadata that describes the assembly itself (name, version, external assemblies, etc.).

In addition to manifest data, an assembly contains metadata that describes the composition (member names, implemented interfaces, base classes, constructors, and so forth) of every contained type. Given that an assembly is documented in such vivid detail, the CLR does *not* consult the Win32 system registry to resolve its location (quite the radical departure from Microsoft's legacy COM programming model). As you will discover during this chapter, the CLR makes use of an entirely new scheme to resolve the location of external code libraries.

Assemblies Are Configurable

Assemblies can be deployed as "private" or "shared." Private assemblies reside in the same directory (or possibly a subdirectory) as the client application making use of them. Shared assemblies, on the other hand, are libraries intended to be consumed by numerous applications on a single machine and are deployed to a specific directory termed the *Global Assembly Cache,* or *GAC.*

Regardless of how you deploy your assemblies, you are free to author XML-based configuration files. Using these configuration files, the CLR can be instructed to "probe" for assemblies under a specific location, load a specific version of a referenced assembly for a particular client, or consult an arbitrary directory on your local machine, your network location, or a web-based URL. You'll learn a good deal more about XML configuration files throughout this chapter.

Understanding the Format of a .NET Assembly

Now that you've learned about several benefits provided by the .NET assembly, let's shift gears and get a better idea of how an assembly is composed under the hood. Structurally speaking, a .NET assembly (*.dll or *.exe) consists of the following elements:

- A Win32 file header
- A CLR file header
- CIL code
- Type metadata
- An assembly manifest
- Optional embedded resources

While the first two elements (the Win32 and CLR headers) are blocks of data that you can typically ignore, they do deserve some brief consideration. This being said, an overview of each element follows.

The Win32 File Header

The Win32 file header establishes the fact that the assembly can be loaded and manipulated by the Windows family of operating systems. This header data also identifies the kind of application (console-based, GUI-based, or *.dll code library) to be hosted by the Windows operating system. If you open a .NET assembly using the dumpbin.exe command-line utility (using a .NET Framework 2.0 SDK command prompt) and specify the /headers flag, you can view an assembly's Win32 header information. Figure 13-1 shows (partial) Win32 header information for the CarLibrary.dll assembly you will build a bit later in this chapter.

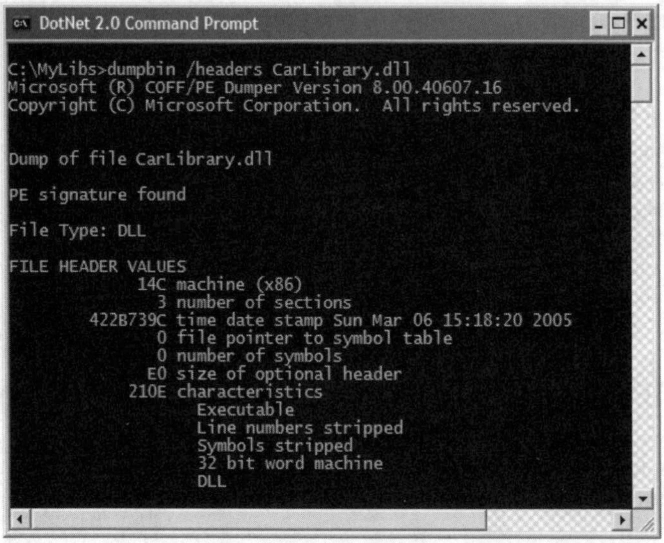

Figure 13-1. *An assembly's Win32 file header information*

The CLR File Header

The CLR header is a block of data that all .NET files must support (and do support, courtesy of the VB 2005 compiler) in order to be hosted by the CLR. In a nutshell, this header defines numerous flags that enable the runtime to understand the layout of the managed file. For example, flags exist that identify the location of the metadata and resources within the file, the version of the runtime the assembly was built against, the value of the (optional) public key, and so forth. If you supply the /clrheader flag to dumpbin.exe, you are presented with the internal CLR header information for a given .NET assembly, as shown in Figure 13-2.

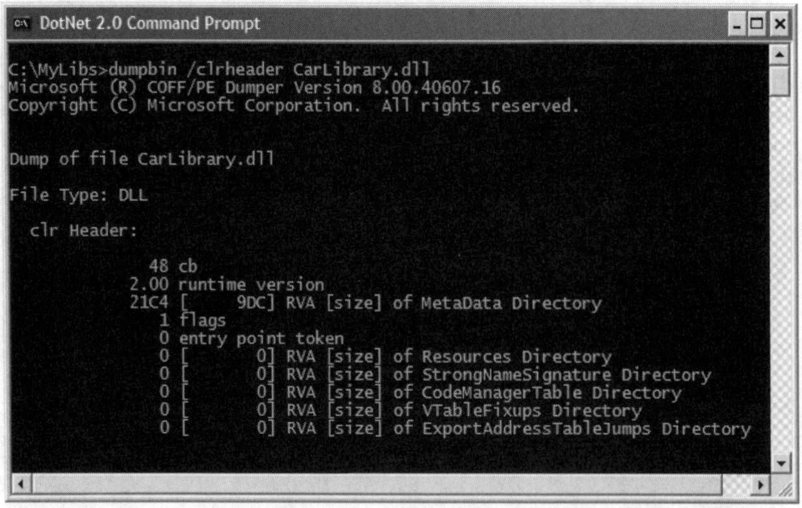

Figure 13-2. *An assembly's CLR file header information*

CLR header data is represented by an unmanaged C-style structure (IMAGE_COR20_HEADER) defined in the C-based header file, corhdr.h (located by default under C:\Program Files\Microsoft Visual Studio 8\SDK\v2.0\include if you install the C++ development environment). For those who are interested, here is the layout of the structure in question:

```
// CLR 2.0 header structure.
typedef struct IMAGE_COR20_HEADER
{
  // Header versioning
  ULONG    cb;
  USHORT   MajorRuntimeVersion;
  USHORT   MinorRuntimeVersion;

  // Symbol table and startup information
  IMAGE_DATA_DIRECTORY    MetaData;
  ULONG      Flags;
  ULONG      EntryPointToken;

  // Binding information
  IMAGE_DATA_DIRECTORY    Resources;
  IMAGE_DATA_DIRECTORY    StrongNameSignature;

  // Regular fixup and binding information
  IMAGE_DATA_DIRECTORY    CodeManagerTable;
  IMAGE_DATA_DIRECTORY    VTableFixups;
  IMAGE_DATA_DIRECTORY    ExportAddressTableJumps;

  // Precompiled image info (internal use only - set to zero)
  IMAGE_DATA_DIRECTORY    ManagedNativeHeader;
} IMAGE_COR20_HEADER;
```

Again, as a .NET developer you will not need to concern yourself with the gory details of Win32 or CLR header information (unless perhaps you are building a compiler for a new .NET programming language!). Just understand that every .NET assembly contains this data, which is used behind the scenes by the .NET runtime and Win32 operating system.

CIL Code, Type Metadata, and the Assembly Manifest

At its core, an assembly contains CIL code, which as you recall is a platform- and CPU-agnostic intermediate language. At runtime, the internal CIL is compiled on the fly (using a just-in-time [JIT] compiler) to platform- and CPU-specific instructions. Given this architecture, .NET assemblies can indeed execute on a variety of architectures, devices, and operating systems. Thankfully, it is always the job of the VB 2005 compiler to generate CIL code based on your VB 2005 code base.

An assembly also contains metadata that completely describes the format of the contained types as well as the format of external types referenced by this assembly. The .NET runtime uses this metadata to resolve the location of types (and their members) within the binary, lay out types in memory, and facilitate remote method invocations. You'll check out the details of the .NET metadata format in Chapter 14 during our examination of reflection services.

An assembly must also contain an associated *manifest* (also referred to as *assembly metadata*). The manifest documents each module within the assembly, establishes the version of the assembly, and also documents any *external* assemblies referenced by the current assembly (unlike legacy COM type libraries, which did not provide a way to document external dependencies). As you will see over the course of this chapter, the CLR makes extensive use of an assembly's manifest during the process of locating external assembly references.

■**Note** Needless to say by this point in the book, when you wish to view an assembly's CIL code, type metadata, or manifest, `ildasm.exe` is the tool of choice. I will assume you will make extensive use of `ildasm.exe` as you work through the code examples in this chapter (see Chapter 1 for coverage of the `ildasm.exe` utility).

Optional Assembly Resources

Finally, a .NET assembly may contain any number of embedded resources such as application icons, image files, sound clips, or string tables. In fact, the .NET platform supports *satellite assemblies* that contain nothing but localized resources. This can be useful if you wish to partition your resources based on a specific culture (English, German, etc.) for the purposes of building international software. The topic of building satellite assemblies is outside the scope of this text; however, you *will* learn how to embed application resources into an assembly during our examination of GDI+ in Chapter 22.

Single-File and Multifile Assemblies

Technically speaking, an assembly can be composed of multiple *modules*. A module is really nothing more than a generic term for a valid .NET binary file. In most situations, an assembly is in fact composed of a single module. In this case, there is a one-to-one correspondence between the (logical) assembly and the underlying (physical) binary (hence the term *single-file assembly*).

Single-file assemblies contain all of the necessary elements (header information, CIL code, type metadata, manifest, and required resources) in a single *.exe or *.dll package. Figure 13-3 illustrates the composition of a single-file assembly.

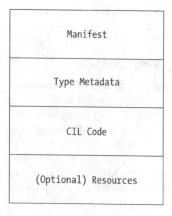

Figure 13-3. *A single-file assembly*

A multifile assembly, on the other hand, is a set of .NET *.dlls that are deployed and versioned as a single logic unit. Formally speaking, one of these *.dlls is termed the *primary module* and contains the assembly-level manifest (as well as any necessary CIL code, metadata, header information, and optional resources). The manifest of the primary module records each of the related *.dll files it is dependent upon.

As a naming convention, the secondary modules in a multifile assembly take a *.netmodule file extension; however, this is not a requirement of the CLR. Secondary *.netmodules also contain CIL code and type metadata, as well as a *module-level manifest*, which simply records the externally required assemblies of that specific module.

The major benefit of constructing multifile assemblies is that they provide a very efficient way to download content. For example, assume you have a machine that is referencing a remote multifile assembly composed of three modules, where the primary module is installed on the client. If the client requires a type within a secondary remote *.netmodule, the CLR will download the binary to the local machine on demand to a specific location termed the *download cache*. If each *.netmodule is 1MB, I'm sure you can see the benefit.

Another benefit of multifile assemblies is that they enable modules to be authored using multiple .NET programming languages (which is very helpful in larger corporations, where individual departments tend to favor a specific .NET language). Once each of the individual modules has been compiled, the modules can be logically "connected" into a logical assembly using tools such as the assembly linker (al.exe).

In any case, do understand that the modules that compose a multifile assembly are *not* literally linked together into a single (larger) file. Rather, multifile assemblies are only logically related by information contained in the primary module's manifest. Figure 13-4 illustrates a multifile assembly composed of three modules, each authored using a unique .NET programming language.

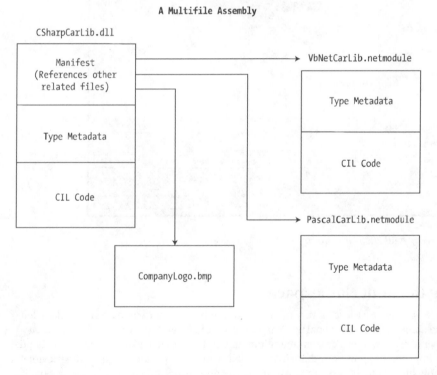

Figure 13-4. *The primary module records secondary modules in the assembly manifest.*

At this point you (hopefully) have a better understanding about the internal composition of a .NET binary file. With this necessary preamble out of the way, we are ready to dig into the details of building and configuring a variety of code libraries, beginning with the topic of defining custom namespaces.

Constructing Custom .NET Namespaces

During the previous 12 chapters, as you created your stand-alone *.exe assemblies, Visual Basic 2005 was secretly grouping each one of your types within a *default namespace* (also known as the *root* namespace). By default, when you create a new VB 2005 Visual Studio 2005 project, your custom types are wrapped within a namespace that takes the identical name of the project itself. As you would expect, it is possible to change the name of this root namespace as well as define any number of additional namespaces via the VB 2005 Namespace keyword.

When you begin to build .NET *.dll assemblies, it is very important that you take time to organize your types into namespaces that make sense for the code library at hand, given that other developers will reference these libraries and need to know the set of Import statements required to make use of your types. To illustrate the ins-and-outs of namespace definitions, create a new Class Library project named MyCodeLibrary using Visual Studio 2005, as shown in Figure 13-5.

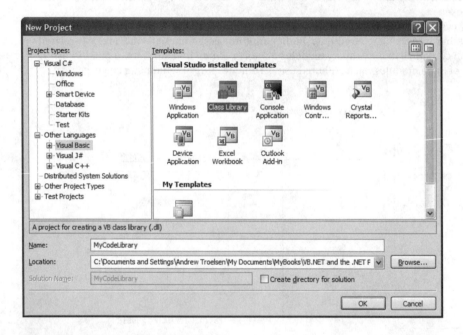

Figure 13-5. *Creating a VB 2005 class library*

Observing the Root Namespace

Notice that when you create a Class Library project, you receive little more than an empty class definition for a type named Class1. Your goal when building a *.dll assembly is to populate the binary with any number of classes, interfaces, enumerations, structures, and delegates for the task at hand. Given this, it is important to point out that all of the skills you have developed during the previous 12 chapters apply directly to a Class Library project. The only noticeable difference between a *.dll and *.exe assembly is how the image is loaded from disk.

In any case, double-click the My Project icon within the Solution Explorer. Notice that the Application tab contains a text area that defines the root namespace, which as mentioned is by default named identically to the project you have just created, as you see in Figure 13-6.

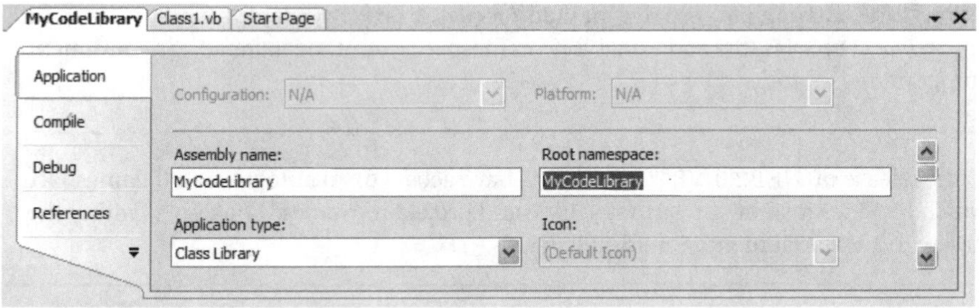

Figure 13-6. *The root namespace*

You are always free to rename your root namespace as you see fit. Recall that a namespace does not need to be defined within an identically named assembly. Consider again our good friend mscorlib.dll. This core .NET assembly does *not* define a namespace named mscorlib. Rather the mscorlib.dll assembly defines a good number of unique namespaces (System.IO, System, System.Threading, System. Collections, etc.). This brings up another very important point: the fact that a single assembly can contain any number of uniquely named namespaces. In fact, it is also possible to have a single namespace defined within multiple assemblies. For example, the System.IO namespace is partially defined in mscorlib.dll as well as System.dll.

Defining Namespaces Beyond the Root

To illustrate the role of the VB 2005 Namespace keyword, update your initial *.vb file with the following code:

```
' This type is in the root namespace,
' which is (by default) the same name
' as the initial project.
Public Class SomeClass
End Class

' This namespace is nested within the
' root.  Therefore the fully qualified
' name of this class is MyCodeLibrary.MyTypes.SomeClass
Namespace MyTypes
  Public Class SomeClass
  End Class

  ' It is possible to nest namespaces within other
  ' namespaces to gain a greater level of structure.
  ' Thus, the fully qualified name of this enum is:
  ' MyCodeLibrary.MyTypes.MyEnums.TestEnum
  Namespace MyEnums
    Public Enum TestEnum
      TestValue
    End Enum
  End Namespace
End Namespace
```

Notice that the Namespace keyword allows us to create customized namespaces that are nested within the root. To see the impact of this firsthand, open the Visual Studio 2005 Object Browser (via the View menu) and expand the tree view representing your project. As you can see, your single assembly defines three custom namespaces named MyCodeLibrary, MyCodeLibrary.MyTypes, and MyCodeLibrary.MyTypes.MyEnums (the additional "My" namespaces are autogenerated as a convenience for VB 2005 programmers).

Note With the release of .NET 2.0, VB 2005 projects have access to an autogenerated namespace named My, which provides instant access to machine and project resources. Look up My within the .NET 2.0 Framework SDK documentation for full details.

Importing Custom Namespaces

Given the way we have organized our types, if you were to build another assembly that referenced MyCodeLibrary.dll, you would need to add the following Imports statements to gain access to each type:

```
Imports MyCodeLibrary
Imports MyCodeLibrary.MyTypes
Imports MyCodeLibrary.MyTypes.MyEnums
```

Also be aware that when you are building an assembly that contains multiple namespaces (such as MyCodeLibrary.dll), you may need to make use of the Imports keyword on a file-by-file basis where necessary. To illustrate, insert a new Class file into your current project (via the Project ➤ Add Class menu). Now, attempt to update the new Class with the following method:

```
Public Class Class2
  Public Sub MySub()
    Dim e As TestEnum
  End Sub
End Class
```

If you were to compile your assembly, you might be surprised to find a compiler error that states the TestEnum is not defined, regardless of the fact that this type is defined within a *.vb file in the same project! The reason, of course, is due to the fact that the Class2 class type is defined within the root namespace, while TestEnum is within MyCodeLibrary.MyTypes.MyEnums. Therefore, this new *.vb file must import the defining namespace before we can compile the file successfully:

```
Imports MyCodeLibrary.MyTypes.MyEnums

Public Class Class2
  Public Sub MySub()
    Dim e As TestEnum
  End Sub
End Class
```

Note The References tab of the My Project namespace allows you to select any number of namespaces that should be automatically imported into each *.vb file within your current project. If a namespace is selected in this manner, you are not required to explicitly import the namespace using the Imports keyword.

Building Type Aliases Using the Imports Keyword

Before we build our first official code library, there is one final aspect of the Imports keyword I'd like to point out. In our current example, you may have noticed that we have two classes named SomeClass, one defined within MyCodeLibrary and the other within MyCodeLibrary.MyTypes. Surprisingly, if you wish to make use of the SomeClass defined within MyCodeLibrary, you are not required to add any additional Imports statements. Given that Class2 is defined within the MyCodeLibrary namespace, the compiler assumes you are requesting the SomeClass within the shared namespace scope:

```
Imports MyCodeLibrary.MyTypes.MyEnums

Public Class Class2
  Public Sub MySub()
    Dim e As TestEnum
    ' This is really MyCodeLibrary.SomeClass
    Dim s As New SomeClass
  End Sub
End Class
```

However, for the sake of argument, what if you wished to make use of the SomeClass defined within MyCodeLibrary.MyTypes? You might think that you would simply add an Imports statement for MyCodeLibrary.MyTypes, as follows:

```
Imports MyCodeLibrary.MyTypes.MyEnums
Imports MyCodeLibrary.MyTypes

Public Class Class2
  Public Sub MySub()
    Dim e As TestEnum
    ' This is STILL MyCodeLibrary.SomeClass
    Dim s As New SomeClass
  End Sub
End Class
```

However, s is still of type MyCodeLibrary.SomeClass (this can be verified using ildasm.exe)! To inform the compiler you explicitly wish to have the SomeClass defined within MyCodeLibrary.MyTypes, you can either use fully qualified names:

```
Imports MyCodeLibrary.MyTypes.MyEnums

Public Class Class2
  Public Sub MySub()
    Dim e As TestEnum
    Dim s As New MyCodeLibrary.MyTypes.SomeClass
  End Sub
End Class
```

or make use of a specialized form of the Imports statement shown here:

```
Imports MyCodeLibrary.MyTypes.MyEnums

' A type alias!
Imports TypeIWant = MyCodeLibrary.MyTypes.SomeClass

Public Class Class2
  Public Sub MySub()
    Dim e As TestEnum
    ' 's' is now of type MyCodeLibrary.MyTypes.SomeClass
    Dim s As New TypeIWant
    MsgBox(s.GetType().FullName)
  End Sub
End Class
```

This format of the Imports keyword is used to build a type *alias*. Simply put, this allows you to define a symbolic token (in this case TypeIWant) that is replaced at compile time with the assigned fully qualified name (MyCodeLibrary.MyTypes.SomeClass) of a type.

■**Source Code**   The MyCodeLibrary project is located under the Chapter 13 subdirectory.

Building and Consuming a Single-File Assembly

Now that you better understand the nature of defining and using custom .NET namespaces, our next task is to create a single-file *.dll assembly (named CarLibrary) that contains a small set of public types. To build a code library using Visual Studio 2005, simply select the Class Library project workspace (again, see Figure 13-5 earlier).

The design of your automobile library begins with an abstract base class named Car that defines a number of protected data members exposed through custom properties. This class has a single abstract method named TurboBoost(), which makes use of a custom enumeration (EngineState) representing the current condition of the car's engine. As all of these types will be in the root namespace, we have no need to make use of the VB 2005 Namespace keyword:

```vb
' Represents the state of the engine.
Public Enum EngineState
  engineAlive
  engineDead
End Enum

' The abstract base class in the hierarchy.
Public MustInherit Class Car
  Protected name As String
  Protected speed As Short
  Protected max_speed As Short
  Protected egnState As EngineState = EngineState.engineAlive

  Public MustOverride Sub TurboBoost()

  Public Sub New()
  End Sub

  Public Sub New(ByVal name As String, ByVal max As Short, ByVal curr As Short)
    name = name
    max_speed = max
    speed = curr
  End Sub

  Public Property PetName() As String
    Get
      Return name
    End Get
    Set(ByVal value As String)
      name = value
    End Set
  End Property

  Public Property CurrSpeed() As Short
    Get
      Return speed
    End Get
    Set(ByVal value As Short)
      speed = value
    End Set
  End Property
```

```vbnet
   Public ReadOnly Property MaxSpeed() As Short
     Get
       Return max_speed
     End Get
   End Property

   Public ReadOnly Property EngineState() As EngineState
     Get
       Return egnState
     End Get
   End Property
End Class
```

Now assume that you have two direct descendents of the Car type named MiniVan and SportsCar. Each overrides the abstract TurboBoost() method in an appropriate manner.

```vbnet
Imports System.Windows.Forms

Public Class SportsCar
  Inherits Car

  Public Sub New()
  End Sub

  Public Sub New(ByVal name As String, ByVal max As Short, ByVal curr As Short)
    MyBase.New(name, max, curr)
  End Sub

  Public Overrides Sub TurboBoost()
    MessageBox.Show("Ramming speed!", "Faster is better...")
  End Sub
End Class

Public Class MiniVan
  Inherits Car

  Public Sub New()
  End Sub

  Public Sub New(ByVal name As String, ByVal max As Short, ByVal curr As Short)
    MyBase.New(name, max, curr)
  End Sub

  ' Minivans have poor turbo capabilities!
  Public Overrides Sub TurboBoost()
    egnState = EngineState.engineDead
    MessageBox.Show("Time to call AAA", "Your car is dead")
  End Sub
End Class
```

Notice how each subclass implements TurboBoost() using the MessageBox class, which is defined in the System.Windows.Forms.dll assembly. For your assembly to make use of the types defined within this external assembly, the CarLibrary project must set a reference to this binary via the Add Reference dialog box (see Figure 13-7), which you can access through the Visual Studio 2005 Project ➤ Add Reference menu selection.

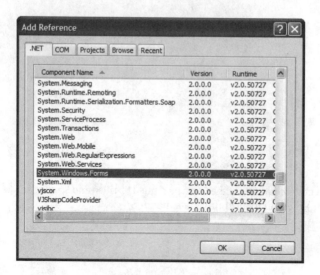

Figure 13-7. *Referencing external .NET assemblies begins here.*

It is *really* important to understand that the assemblies displayed in the .NET tab of the Add Reference dialog box do not represent each and every assembly on your machine. The Add Reference dialog box will *not* display your custom assemblies, and it does *not* display all assemblies located in the GAC. Rather, this dialog box simply presents a list of common assemblies that Visual Studio 2005 is preprogrammed to display. When you are building applications that require the use of an assembly not listed within the Add Reference dialog box, you need to click the Browse tab to manually navigate to the *.dll or *.exe in question.

■Note Although it is technically possible to have your custom assemblies appear in the Add Reference dialog box's list by deploying a copy to C:\Program Files\Microsoft Visual Studio 8\Common7\IDE\ PublicAssemblies, there is little benefit in doing so. The Recent tab keeps a running list of previously referenced assemblies.

Exploring the Manifest

Before making use of CarLibrary.dll from a client application, let's check out how the code library is composed under the hood. Assuming you have compiled this project, load CarLibrary.dll into ildasm.exe (see Figure 13-8).

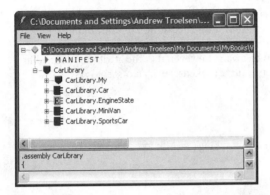

Figure 13-8. `CarLibrary.dll` *loaded into* `ildasm.exe`

Now, open the manifest of `CarLibrary.dll` by double-clicking the MANIFEST icon. The first code block encountered in a manifest is used to specify all external assemblies that are required by the current assembly to function correctly. As you recall, `CarLibrary.dll` made use of types within `mscorlib.dll` and `System.Windows.Forms.dll`, both of which are listed in the manifest using the `.assembly` extern token. As well, given that all VB 2005 applications created with Visual Studio 2005 automatically reference the VB 6.0 backwards-compatibility assembly, you will also find references to `System.dll` and `Microsoft.VisualBasic` assemblies:

```
.assembly extern mscorlib
{
  .publickeytoken = (B7 7A 5C 56 19 34 E0 89 )
  .ver 2:0:0:0
}
.assembly extern Microsoft.VisualBasic
{
  .publickeytoken = (B0 3F 5F 7F 11 D5 0A 3A )
  .ver 8:0:0:0
}
.assembly extern System
{
  .publickeytoken = (B7 7A 5C 56 19 34 E0 89 )
  .ver 2:0:0:0
}
.assembly extern System.Windows.Forms
{
  .publickeytoken = (B7 7A 5C 56 19 34 E0 89 )
  .ver 2:0:0:0
}
```

Here, each `.assembly` extern block is qualified by the `.publickeytoken` and `.ver` directives. The `.publickeytoken` instruction is present only if the assembly has been configured with a *strong name* (more details later in this chapter). The `.ver` token marks (of course) the numerical version identifier.

After cataloging each of the external references, you will find a number of `.custom` tokens that identify assembly-level attributes. If you examine the `AssemblyInfo.vb` file created by Visual Studio 2005, you will find these attributes represent basic characteristics about the assembly such as company

name, trademark, and so forth (all of which are currently empty). By default, AssemblyInfo.vb is
hidden from view. To see this file, you must click the Show All Files button on the Solution
Explorer and expand the plus node under the My Project icon. Chapter 14 examines attributes in
detail, so don't sweat the details at this point. Do be aware, however, that the attributes defined in
AssemblyInfo.vb update the manifest with various .custom tokens, such as <AssemblyTitle>:

```
.assembly CarLibrary
{
...
  .custom instance void [mscorlib]
  System.Reflection.AssemblyTitleAttribute::.ctor(string) = ( 01 00 00 00 00 )
  .hash algorithm 0x00008004
  .ver 1:0:454:30104
}
.module CarLibrary.dll
```

Finally, you can also see that the .assembly token is used to mark the friendly name of your
assembly (CarLibrary), while the .module token specifies the name of the module itself (CarLibrary.
dll). The .ver token defines the version number assigned to this assembly, as specified by the
<AssemblyVersion> attribute within AssemblyInfo.vb.

Exploring the CIL

Recall that an assembly does not contain platform-specific instructions; rather, it contains
platform-agnostic CIL. When the .NET runtime loads an assembly into memory, the underlying CIL
is compiled (using the JIT compiler) into instructions that can be understood by the target platform.
If you double-click the TurboBoost() method of the SportsCar class, ildasm.exe will open a new
window showing the CIL instructions:

```
.method public hidebysig virtual instance void
  TurboBoost() cil managed
{
  // Code size        17 (0x11)
  .maxstack  2
  IL_0000:  ldstr      "Ramming speed!"
  IL_0005:  ldstr      "Faster is better..."
  IL_000a:  call       valuetype [System.Windows.Forms]
    System.Windows.Forms.DialogResult [System.Windows.Forms]
    System.Windows.Forms.MessageBox::Show(string, string)
  IL_000f:  pop
  IL_0010:  ret
}  // end of method SportsCar::TurboBoost
```

Notice that the .method tag is used to identify a method defined by the SportsCar type. Member
variables defined by a type are marked with the .field tag. Recall that the Car class defined a set of
protected data, such as currSpeed:

```
.field family int16 currSpeed
```

Properties are marked with the .property tag. Here is the CIL describing the public CurrSpeed
property (note that the read/write nature of a property is marked by .get and .set tags):

```
.property instance int16 CurrSpeed()
{
  .get instance int16 CarLibrary.Car::get_CurrSpeed()
  .set instance void CarLibrary.Car::set_CurrSpeed(int16)
}  // end of property Car::CurrSpeed
```

Exploring the Type Metadata

Finally, if you now press Ctrl+M, `ildasm.exe` displays the metadata for each type within the `Vb2005CarClient` assembly, as you see in Figure 13-9.

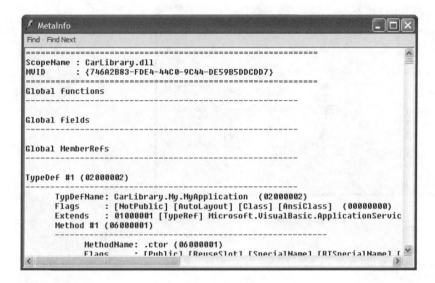

Figure 13-9. *Type metadata for the types within* `CarLibrary.dll`

Now that you have looked inside the `CarLibrary.dll` assembly, you can build some client applications.

■**Source Code**   The CarLibrary project is located under the Chapter 13 subdirectory.

Building a VB 2005 Client Application

Because each of the `CarLibrary` types has been declared using the `Public` keyword, other assemblies are able to make use of them. Recall that you may also define types using the VB 2005 `Friend` keyword. Friend types can be used only by the assembly in which they are defined. External clients can neither see nor create friend types.

■**Note**   .NET 2.0 now provides a way to specify "friend assemblies" that allow `Friend` types to be consumed by specific assemblies. Look up the `InternalsVisibleToAttribute` class in the .NET Framework 2.0 SDK documentation for details.

To consume these types, create a new VB 2005 console application project (Vb2005CarClient). Once you have done so, set a reference to `CarLibrary.dll` using the Browse tab of the Add Reference dialog box (if you compiled `CarLibrary.dll` using Visual Studio 2005, your assembly is located under the \Bin\Debug subdirectory of the CarLibrary project folder). Once you click the OK button, Visual Studio 2005 responds by placing a copy of CarLibrary.dll into the \bin\Debug folder of the Vb2005CarClient project folder, as shown in Figure 13-10.

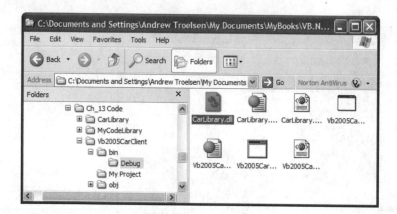

Figure 13-10. *Visual Studio 2005 copies private assemblies to the client's directory.*

At this point you can build your client application to make use of the external types. Update your initial VB 2005 file like so:

```
' Import the CarLibrary namespace
' defined in the CarLibrary.dll assembly.
Imports CarLibrary

Module Program
  Sub Main()
    Console.WriteLine("***** Visual Basic 2005 Client *****")
    Dim myMiniVan As New MiniVan()
    myMiniVan.TurboBoost()

    Dim mySportsCar As New SportsCar()
    mySportsCar.TurboBoost()
  End Sub
End Module
```

This code looks just like the other applications developed thus far. The only point of interest is that the VB 2005 client application is now making use of types defined within a separate custom assembly. Go ahead and run your program. As you would expect, the execution of this program results in the display of various message boxes.

■**Source Code**   The Vb2005CarClient project is located under the Chapter 13 subdirectory.

Building a C# Client Application

To illustrate the language-agnostic attitude of the .NET platform, let's create another console application (CSharpCarClient), this time using the C# programming (see Figure 13-11). Once you have created the project, set a reference to CarLibrary.dll using the Add Reference dialog box.

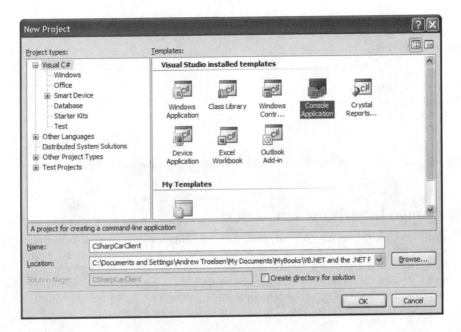

Figure 13-11. *Creating a C# console application*

Like VB 2005, C# requires you to list each namespace used within the current file. However, C# offers the using keyword rather than the VB 2005 Imports keyword. Given this, add the following using statement within the Class1.cs code file (remember, C# is a *case-sensitive* programming language!):

```
using System;
using System.Collections.Generic;
using System.Text;
using CarLibrary;

namespace CSharpCarClient
{
  class Program
  {
    static void Main(string[] args)
    {
    }
  }
}
```

Notice that the Main() method is defined within a C# class type (rather than the VB 2005 specific Module type). In any case, to exercise the MiniVan and SportsCar types using the syntax of C#, update your Main() method like so:

```
class Program
{
  static void Main(string[] args)
  {
    Console.WriteLine("***** Fun with C# *****");
```

```
    // Make a sports car.
    SportsCar viper = new SportsCar("Viper", 240, 40);
    viper.TurboBoost();

    // Make a minivan.
    MiniVan mv = new MiniVan();
    mv.TurboBoost();
    Console.ReadLine();
  }
}
```

When you compile and run your application, you will once again find a series of message boxes displayed.

Cross-Language Inheritance in Action

A very enticing aspect of .NET development is the notion of *cross-language inheritance*. To illustrate, let's create a new C# class that derives from SportsCar (which was authored using VB 2005). First, add a new class file to your current C# application (by selecting Project ➤ Add Class) named PerformanceCar.cs. Update the initial class definition by deriving from the SportsCar type using the C# inheritance token (a single colon, which is functionally equivalent to the Inherits keyword). Furthermore, override the abstract TurboBoost() method using the override keyword:

```
using System;
using System.Collections.Generic;
using System.Text;
using CarLibrary;

namespace CSharpCarClient
{
  public class PerformanceCar : SportsCar
  {
    // This C# type is deriving from the VB 2005 SportsCar.
    public override void TurboBoost()
    {
      Console.WriteLine("Zero to 60 in a cool 4.8 seconds...");
    }
  }
}
```

To test this new class type, update the Main() method as follows:

```
static void Main(string[] args)
{
  Console.WriteLine("***** Fun with C# *****");

  // Make a sports car.
  SportsCar viper = new SportsCar("Viper", 240, 40);
  viper.TurboBoost();

  // Make a minivan.
  MiniVan mv = new MiniVan();
  mv.TurboBoost();

  PerformanceCar dreamCar = new PerformanceCar();
  // Inherited property.
  dreamCar.PetName = "Hank";
```

```
  dreamCar.TurboBoost();
  Console.ReadLine();
}
```

Notice that the dreamCar object is able to invoke any public member (such as the PetName property) found up the chain of inheritance, regardless of the fact that the base class has been defined in a completely different language and is defined in a completely different code library.

Source Code The CSharpCarClient project is located under the Chapter 13 subdirectory.

Building and Consuming a Multifile Assembly

Now that you have constructed and consumed a single-file assembly, let's examine the process of building a multifile assembly. Recall that a multifile assembly is simply a collection of related modules (which has nothing to do with the Visual Basic 2005 Module keyword!) that are deployed and versioned as a single unit. At the time of this writing, Visual Studio 2005 does not support a VB 2005 multifile assembly project template. Therefore, you will need to make use of the command-line compiler (vbc.exe) if you wish to build such as beast (see Chapter 2 for details of the command-line compiler).

To illustrate the process, you will build a multifile assembly named AirVehicles. The primary module (airvehicles.dll) will contain a single class type named Helicopter. The related manifest (also contained in airvehicles.dll) catalogs an additional *.netmodule file named ufo.netmodule, which contains another class type named (of course) Ufo. Although both class types are physically contained in separate binaries, you will group them into a single namespace named AirVehicles. Finally, both classes are created using VB 2005 (although you could certainly mix and match languages if you desire).

To begin, open a simple text editor (such as Notepad or TextPad) and create the following Ufo class definition saved to a file named ufo.vb:

```
' This type will be placed
' within a *.netmodule binary,
' and it thus part of a multifile
' Assembly.
Namespace AirVehicles
  Public Class Ufo
    Public Sub AbductHuman()
      Console.WriteLine("Resistance is futile")
    End Sub
  End Class
End Namespace
```

To compile this class into a .NET module, navigate to the folder containing ufo.vb and issue the following command to the VB 2005 compiler (the module option of the /target flag instructs vbc.exe to produce a *.netmodule as opposed to a *.dll or an *.exe file):

```
vbc.exe /t:module ufo.vb
```

If you now look in the folder that contains the ufo.vb file, you should see a new file named ufo.netmodule (take a peek). Next, create a new file named helicopter.vb that contains the following class definition:

```
' This type will be in the
' primary module of the multifile
' assembly, therefore this assembly
' will contain the assembly manifest.
```

```
Namespace AirVehicles
  Public Class Helicopter
    Public Sub TakeOff()
      Console.WriteLine("Helicopter taking off!")
    End Sub
  End Class
End Namespace
```

Given that airvehicles.dll is the intended name of the primary module of this multifile assembly, you will need to compile helicopter.vb using the /t:library and /out: options. To enlist the ufo.netmodule binary into the assembly manifest, you must also specify the /addmodule flag. The following command does the trick:

```
vbc /t:library /addmodule:ufo.netmodule /out:airvehicles.dll helicopter.vb
```

At this point, your directory should contain the primary airvehicles.dll module as well as the secondary ufo.netmodule binary.

Exploring the ufo.netmodule File

Now, using ildasm.exe, open ufo.netmodule. As you can see, *.netmodules contain a *module-level manifest*; however, its sole purpose is to list each external assembly referenced by the code base. Given that the Ufo class did little more than make a call to Console.WriteLine(), you find the following:

```
.assembly extern mscorlib
{
  .publickeytoken = (B7 7A 5C 56 19 34 E0 89 )
  .ver 2:0:0:0
}
.assembly extern Microsoft.VisualBasic
{
  .publickeytoken = (B0 3F 5F 7F 11 D5 0A 3A )
  .ver 8:0:0:0
}
.module ufo.netmodule
```

Exploring the airvehicles.dll File

Next, using ildasm.exe, open the primary airvehicles.dll module and investigate the assembly-level manifest. Notice that the .file token documents the associated modules in the multifile assembly (ufo.netmodule in this case). The .class extern tokens are used to document the names of the external types referenced for use from the secondary module (ufo):

```
.assembly extern mscorlib
{
  .publickeytoken = (B7 7A 5C 56 19 34 E0 89 )
  .ver 2:0:0:0
}

.assembly airvehicles
{
...
  .hash algorithm 0x00008004
  .ver 0:0:0:0
}
```

```
.file ufo.netmodule
...
.class extern public AirVehicles.Ufo
{
  .file ufo.netmodule
  .class 0x02000002
}
.module airvehicles.dll
```

Again, realize that the only entity that links together `airvehicles.dll` and `ufo.netmodule` is the assembly manifest. These two binary files have not been merged into a single, larger *.dll.

Consuming a Multifile Assembly

The consumers of a multifile assembly couldn't care less that the assembly they are referencing is composed of numerous modules. To keep things simple, let's create a new Visual Basic .NET client application at the command line. Create a new file named `Client.vb` with the following `Module` definition. When you are done, save it in the same location as your multifile assembly.

```
Imports AirVehicles

Module Program
  Sub Main()
    Dim h As New AirVehicles.Helicopter()
    h.TakeOff()

    ' This will load the *.netmodule on demand.
    Dim u As New UFO()
    u.AbductHuman()
  End Sub
End Module
```

To compile this executable assembly at the command line, you will make use of the Visual Basic .NET command-line compiler, `vbc.exe`, with the following command set:

```
vbc /r:airvehicles.dll Client.vb
```

Notice that when you are referencing a multifile assembly, the compiler needs to be supplied only with the name of the primary module (the *.netmodules are loaded on demand when used by the client's code base). In and of themselves, *.netmodules do not have an individual version number and cannot be directly loaded by the CLR. Individual *.netmodules can be loaded only by the primary module (e.g., the file that contains the assembly manifest).

Note Visual Studio 2005 also allows you to reference a multifile assembly. Simply use the Add References dialog box and select the primary module. Any related *.netmodules are copied during the process.

At this point, you should feel comfortable with the process of building both single-file and multifile assemblies. To be completely honest, chances are that 99.99 percent of your assemblies will be single-file entities. Nevertheless, multifile assemblies can prove helpful when you wish to break a large physical binary into more modular units (and they are quite useful for remote download scenarios). Next up, let's formalize the concept of a private assembly.

Source Code The MultifileAssembly project is included under the Chapter 13 subdirectory.

Understanding Private Assemblies

Technically speaking, the assemblies you've created thus far in this chapter have been deployed as *private assemblies*. Private assemblies are required to be located within the same directory as the client application (termed the *application directory*) or a subdirectory thereof. Recall that when you set a reference to CarLibrary.dll while building the VbNetCarClient.exe and CSharpCarClient.exe applications, Visual Studio 2005 responded by placing a copy of CarLibrary.dll within the client's application directory.

When a client program uses the types defined within this external assembly, the CLR simply loads the local copy of CarLibrary.dll. Because the .NET runtime does not consult the system registry when searching for referenced assemblies, you can relocate the VbNetCarClient.exe (or CSharpCarClient.exe) and CarLibrary.dll assemblies to a location on your machine and run the application (this is often termed *Xcopy deployment*).

Uninstalling (or replicating) an application that makes exclusive use of private assemblies is a no-brainer: simply delete (or copy) the application folder. Unlike with COM applications, you do not need to worry about dozens of orphaned registry settings. More important, you do not need to worry that the removal of private assemblies will break any other applications on the machine.

The Identity of a Private Assembly

The full identity of a private assembly consists of the friendly name and numerical version, both of which are recorded in the assembly manifest. The *friendly name* simply is the name of the module that contains the assembly's manifest minus the file extension. For example, if you examine the manifest of the CarLibrary.dll assembly, you find the following:

```
.assembly CarLibrary
{
...
    .ver 1:0:0:0
}
```

Given the isolated nature of a private assembly, it should make sense that the CLR does not bother to make use of the version number when resolving its location. The assumption is that private assemblies do not need to have any elaborate version checking, as the client application is the only entity that "knows" of its existence. Given this, it is (very) possible for a single machine to have multiple copies of the same private assembly in various application directories.

Understanding the Probing Process

The .NET runtime resolves the location of a private assembly using a technique termed *probing*, which is much less invasive than it sounds. Probing is the process of mapping an external assembly request to the location of the requested binary file. Strictly speaking, a request to load an assembly may be either *implicit* or *explicit*. An implicit load request occurs when the CLR consults the manifest in order to resolve the location of an assembly defined using the .assembly extern tokens:

```
.assembly extern CarLibrary
{...}
```

An explicit load request occurs programmatically using the Load() or LoadFrom() method of the System.Reflection.Assembly class type, typically for the purposes of late binding and dynamic invocation of type members. You'll examine these topics further in Chapter 14, but for now you can see an example of an explicit load request in the following code:

```
' An explicit load request.
Dim asm As Assembly = Assembly.Load("CarLibrary")
```

In either case, the CLR extracts the friendly name of the assembly and begins probing the client's application directory for a file named `CarLibrary.dll`. If this file cannot be located, an attempt is made to locate an executable assembly based on the same friendly name (`CarLibrary.exe`). If neither of these files can be located in the application directory, the runtime gives up and throws a `FileNotFound` exception at runtime.

Note Technically speaking, if a copy of the requested assembly cannot be found within the client's application directory, the CLR will also attempt to locate a client subdirectory with the exact same name as the assembly's friendly name (e.g., C:\MyClient\CarLibrary). If the requested assembly resides within this subdirectory, the CLR will load the assembly into memory.

Configuring Private Assemblies

While it is possible to deploy a .NET application by simply copying all required assemblies to a single folder on the user's hard drive, you will most likely wish to define a number of subdirectories to group related content. For example, assume you have an application directory named C:\MyApp that contains `Vb2005CarClient.exe`. Under this folder might be a subfolder named MyLibraries that contains `CarLibrary.dll`.

Regardless of the intended relationship between these two directories, the CLR will *not* probe the MyLibraries subdirectory unless you supply a configuration file. Configuration files contain various XML elements that allow you to influence the probing process. Configuration files must have the same name as the launching application and take a `*.config` file extension, and they must be deployed in the client's application directory. Thus, if you wish to create a configuration file for `Vb2005CarClient.exe`, it must be named `Vb2005CarClient.exe.config`.

To illustrate the process, create a new directory on your C drive named MyApp using Windows Explorer. Next, copy `Vb2005CarClient.exe` and `CarLibrary.dll` to this new folder, and run the program by double-clicking the executable. Your program should run successfully at this point (remember, assemblies are not registered!). Next, create a new subdirectory under C:\MyApp named MyLibraries, as shown in Figure 13-12, and move `CarLibrary.dll` to this location.

Figure 13-12. `CarLibrary.dll` *now resides under the MyLibraries subdirectory.*

Try to run your client program again. Because the CLR could not locate "CarLibrary" directly within the application directory, you are presented with a rather nasty unhandled `FileNotFound` exception.

To rectify the situation, create a new configuration file named Vb2005CarClient.exe.config and save it in the *same* folder containing the Vb2005CarClient.exe application, which in this example would be C:\MyApp. Open this file and enter the following content exactly as shown (be aware that XML is case sensitive!):

```
<configuration>
  <runtime>
    <assemblyBinding xmlns="urn:schemas-microsoft-com:asm.v1">
      <probing privatePath="MyLibraries"/>
    </assemblyBinding>
  </runtime>
</configuration>
```

.NET *.config files always open with a root element named <configuration>. The nested <runtime> element may specify an <assemblyBinding> element, which nests a further element named <probing>. The privatePath attribute is the key point in this example, as it is used to specify the subdirectories relative to the application directory where the CLR should probe.

Do note that the <probing> element does not specify *which* assembly is located under a given subdirectory. In other words, you cannot say, "CarLibrary is located under the MyLibraries subdirectory, but MathUtils is located under the Bin subdirectory." The <probing> element simply instructs the CLR to investigate all specified subdirectories for the requested assembly until the first match is encountered.

■**Note** Be very aware that the privatePath attribute *cannot be used* to specify an absolute (C:\SomeFolder\ SomeSubFolder) or relative (..\SomeFolder\AnotherFolder) path! If you wish to specify a directory outside the client's application directory, you will need to make use of a completely different XML element named <codeBase>, described later in the chapter.

Multiple subdirectories can be assigned to the privatePath attribute using a semicolon-delimited list. You have no need to do so at this time, but here is an example that informs the CLR to consult the MyLibraries and MyLibraries\Tests client subdirectories:

```
<probing privatePath="MyLibraries;MyLibraries\Tests"/>
```

Once you've finished creating Vb2005CarClient.exe.config, run the client by double-clicking the executable in Windows Explorer. You should find that Vb2005CarClient.exe executes without a hitch (if this is not the case, double-check it for typos in your XML document).

Next, for testing purposes, change the name of your configuration file (in one way or another) and attempt to run the program once again. The client application should now fail. Remember that *.config files must be prefixed with the same name as the related client application. By way of a final test, open your configuration file for editing and capitalize any of the XML elements. Once the file is saved, your client should fail to run once again (as XML is case sensitive).

Configuration Files and Visual Studio 2005

While you are always able to create XML configuration files by hand using your text editor of choice, Visual Studio 2005 allows you create a configuration file during the development of the client program. To illustrate, load the Vb2005CarClient (or CSharpCarClient) solution into Visual Studio 2005 and insert a new Application Configuration File item (see Figure 13-13) using the Project ➤ Add New Item menu selection. Before you click the OK button, take note that the file is named app.config (don't rename it!). If you look in the Solution Explorer window, you will now find app.config has been inserted into your current project.

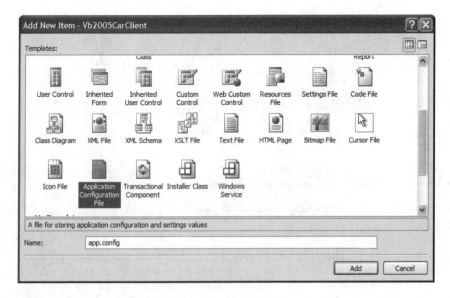

Figure 13-13. *The Visual Studio 2005* app.config *file*

At this point, you are free to enter the necessary XML elements for the client you happen to be creating. Now, here is the cool thing. Each time you compile your project, Visual Studio 2005 will automatically copy the data in app.config to the \bin\Debug directory using the proper naming convention (such as Vb2005CarClient.exe.config). However, this behavior will happen only if your configuration file is indeed named app.config.

Using this approach, all you need to do is maintain app.config, and Visual Studio 2005 will ensure your application directory contains the latest and greatest content (even if you happen to rename your project).

■**Note** For better or for worse, when you insert a new app.config file into a VB 2005 project, the IDE will add a good deal of data within an element named <system.diagnostics>, which has nothing to do with assembly binding. For the remainder of this chapter, I will assume that you will delete this unnecessary XML data and author the XML elements as shown in the remaining code examples.

Introducing the .NET Framework 2.0 Configuration Utility

Although authoring a *.config file by hand is not too traumatic, the .NET Framework 2.0 SDK does ship with a tool that allows you to build XML configuration files using a friendly GUI editor. You can find the .NET Framework 2.0 Configuration utility under the Administrative folder of your Control Panel. Once you launch this tool, you will find a number of configuration options, as shown in Figure 13-14.

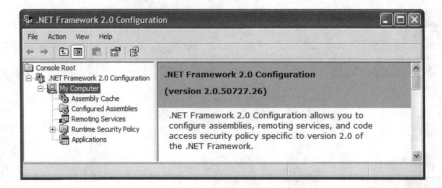

Figure 13-14. *The .NET Framework 2.0 Configuration utility*

To build a client *.config file using this utility, your first step is to add the application to configure by right-clicking the Applications node and selecting Add. In the resulting dialog box, you *may* find the application you wish to configure, provided that you have executed it using Windows Explorer. If this is not the case, click the Other button and navigate to the location of the client program you wish to configure. For this example, select the CSharpCarClient.exe application created earlier in this chapter (look under the Bin folder). Once you have done so, you will now find a new subnode, as shown in Figure 13-15.

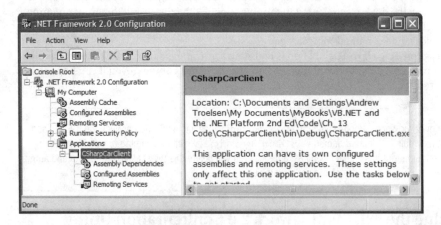

Figure 13-15. *Preparing to configure* CSharpCarClient.exe

If you right-click the CSharpCarClient node and activate the Properties page, you will notice a text field located at the bottom of the dialog box where you can enter the values to be assigned to the privatePath attribute. Just for testing purposes, enter a subdirectory named MyLibraries (see Figure 13-16).

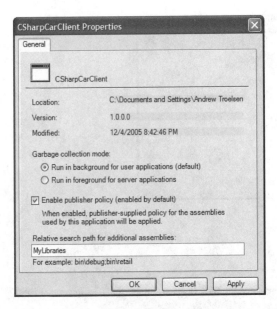

Figure 13-16. *Configuring a private probing path graphically*

Once you click the OK button, you can examine the CSharpCarClient\Bin\Debug directory and find that a new *.config file has been updated with the correct <probing> element.

■**Note** As you may guess, you can copy the XML content generated by the .NET Framework 2.0 Configuration utility into a Visual Studio 2005 app.config file for further editing. Using this approach, you can certainly decrease your typing burden by allowing the tool to generate the initial content.

Understanding Shared Assemblies

Now that you understand how to deploy and configure a private assembly, you can begin to examine the role of a *shared assembly*. Like a private assembly, a shared assembly is a collection of types and (optional) resources. The most obvious difference between shared and private assemblies is the fact that a single copy of a shared assembly can be used by several applications on a single machine.

Consider all the applications created in this text that required you to set a reference to System. Windows.Forms.dll. If you were to look in the application directory of each of these clients, you would *not* find a private copy of this .NET assembly. The reason is that System.Windows.Forms.dll has been deployed as a shared assembly. Clearly, if you need to create a machine-wide class library, this is the way to go.

As suggested in the previous paragraph, a shared assembly is not deployed within the same directory as the application making use of it. Rather, shared assemblies are installed into the Global Assembly Cache. The GAC is located under a subdirectory of your Windows directory named Assembly (e.g., C:\WINDOWS\Assembly), as shown in Figure 13-17.

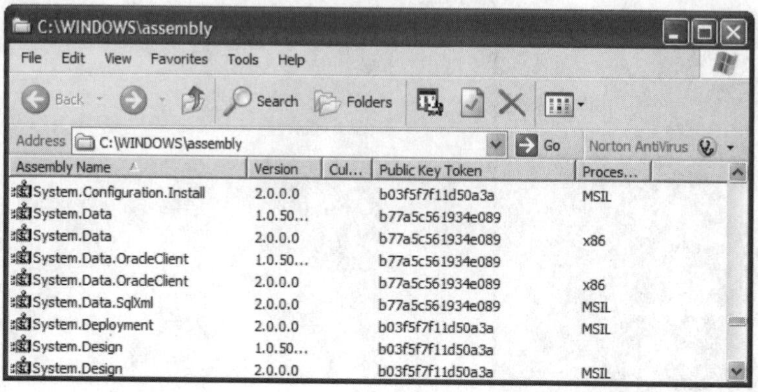

Figure 13-17. *The GAC*

■**Note** You cannot install executable assemblies (*.exe) into the GAC. Only assemblies that take the *.dll file extension can be deployed as a shared assembly.

Understanding Strong Names

Before you can deploy an assembly to the GAC, you must assign it a *strong name*, which is used to uniquely identify the publisher of a given .NET binary. Understand that a "publisher" could be an individual programmer, a department within a given company, or an entire company at large.

In some ways, a strong name is the modern day .NET equivalent of the COM globally unique identifier (GUID) identification scheme. If you have a COM background, you may recall that AppIDs are GUIDs that identify a particular COM application. Unlike COM GUID values (which are nothing more than 128-bit numbers), strong names are based (in part) on two cryptographically related keys (termed the *public key* and the *private key*), which are much more unique and resistant to tampering than a simple GUID.

Formally, a strong name is composed of a set of related data, much of which is specified using assembly-level attributes:

- The friendly name of the assembly (which you recall is the name of the assembly minus the file extension)

- The version number of the assembly (assigned using the <AssemblyVersion> attribute)

- The public key value (assigned using the <AssemblyKeyFile> attribute)

- An optional culture identity value for localization purposes (assigned using the <AssemblyCulture> attribute)

- An embedded *digital signature* created using a hash of the assembly's contents and the private key value

To provide a strong name for an assembly, your first step is to generate public/private key data using the .NET Framework 2.0 SDK's sn.exe utility (which you'll do momentarily). The sn.exe utility responds by generating a file (typically ending with the *.snk [Strong Name Key] file extension) that contains data for two distinct but mathematically related keys, the "public" key and the "private" key. Once the VB 2005 compiler is made aware of the location for your *.snk file, it will record the full public key value in the assembly manifest using the .publickey at the time of compilation.

The VB 2005 compiler will also generate a hash code based on the contents of the entire assembly (CIL code, metadata, and so forth). As you recall from Chapter 6, a *hash code* is a numerical value that is unique for a fixed input. Thus, if you modify any aspect of a .NET assembly (even a single character in a string literal), the compiler yields a unique hash code. This hash code is combined with the private key data within the *.snk file to yield a digital signature embedded within the assembly's CLR header data. The process of strongly naming an assembly is illustrated in Figure 13-18.

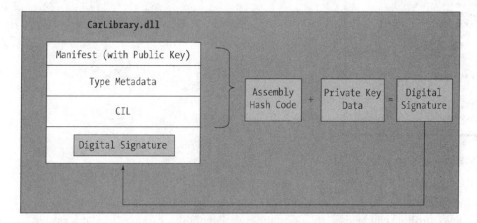

Figure 13-18. *At compile time, a digital signature is generated and embedded into the assembly based in part on public and private key data.*

Understand that the actual *private* key data is not listed anywhere within the manifest, but is used only to digitally sign the contents of the assembly (in conjunction with the generated hash code). Again, the whole idea of making use of public/private key data is to ensure that no two companies, departments, or individuals have the same identity in the .NET universe. In any case, once the process of assigning a strong name is complete, the assembly may be installed into the GAC.

___

■**Note** Strong names also provide a level of protection against potential evildoers tampering with your assembly's contents. Given this point, it is considered a .NET best practice to strongly name every assembly regardless of whether it is deployed to the GAC.

___

Strongly Naming CarLibrary.dll Using sn.exe

Let's walk through the process of assigning a strong name to the CarLibrary assembly created earlier in this chapter (go ahead and open up that project using your IDE of choice). The first order of business is to generate the required key data using the sn.exe utility. Although this tool has numerous command-line options, all you need to concern yourself with for the moment is the -k flag, which instructs the tool to generate a new file containing the public/private key information. Create a new folder on your C drive named MyTestKeyPair and change to that directory using the .NET Command Prompt. Now, issue the following command to generate a file named MyTestKeyPair.snk:

```
sn -k MyTestKeyPair.snk
```

Now that you have your key data, you need to inform the VB 2005 compiler exactly where MyTestKeyPair.snk is located. When you create any new VB 2005 project workspace using Visual

Studio 2005, you will receive a project file (located under the My Project node of Solution Explorer) named AssemblyInfo.vb. By default, you cannot see this file; however, if you click the Show All Files button on the Solution Explorer, you will see this is the case, as shown in Figure 13-19.

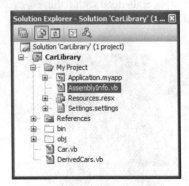

Figure 13-19. *The hidden* AssemblyInfo.vb *file*

This file contains a number of attributes that describe the assembly itself. The AssemblyKeyFile assembly-level attribute can be used to inform the compiler of the location of a valid *.snk file. Simply specify the path as a string parameter, for example:

```
<Assembly: AssemblyKeyFile("C:\MyTestKeyPair\MyTestKeyPair.snk")>
```

In the AssemblyInfo.vb file, you will find another attribute named <AssemblyVersion>. Initially the value is set to 1.0.0.0. Recall that a .NET version number is composed of these four parts: (*<major>.<minor>.<build>.<revision>*).

```
<Assembly: AssemblyVersion("1.0.0.0")>
```

At this point, the VB 2005 compiler has all the information needed to generate strong name data (as you are not specifying a unique culture value via the <AssemblyCulture> attribute, you "inherit" the culture of your current machine). Compile your CarLibrary code library and open the manifest using ildasm.exe. You will now see a new .publickey tag is used to document the full public key information, while the .ver token records the version specified via the <AssemblyVersion> attribute, as shown in Figure 13-20.

```
MANIFEST
Find  Find Next
  .publickey = (00 24 00 00 04 80 00 00 94 00 00 00 06 02 00 00   // .$.....
                00 24 00 00 52 53 41 31 00 04 00 00 01 00 01 00   // .$..RSA
                3F 56 80 E9 7C D0 9A 1E 2B 3C C7 20 4A B8 E3 2B   // ?V..|..
                E6 CC 75 A8 71 F0 87 91 06 C3 3E 8E A5 42 FC      // ..u.q..
                C7 1D 8B 4E 0D 01 12 53 C5 7D 54 E5 47 26 1A 87   // ...N...
                35 D8 85 7D 5B 0C 45 A7 43 63 59 A3 BA 11 7D EF   // 5..}[.E
                14 ED 18 11 18 85 F8 27 C3 99 07 FE 66 D2 FC 3A   // .......
                0D C7 66 35 01 26 3C CC B3 C7 30 3E 81 24 9B AB   // ..F5.&<
                EE 95 8D 9C 5C CD 9C E6 D3 94 6C 30 58 10 1C 2A   // ....\..
                28 3D C8 5E DD 3F 99 B8 D8 3E 65 AD B6 96 34 E4 ) // (=.^.?.
  .hash algorithm 0x00008004
  .ver 1:0:0:0
```

Figure 13-20. *A strongly named assembly records the public key in the manifest.*

Assigning Strong Names Using Visual Studio 2005

Before you deploy CarLibrary.dll to the GAC, let me point out that Visual Studio 2005 allows you to specify the location of your *.snk file using the project's Properties page (in fact, this is now considered the preferred approach). To do so, select the Signing node, supply the path to the *.snk file, and select the "Sign the assembly" check box (see Figure 13-21).

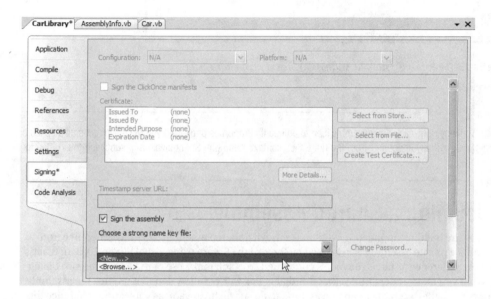

Figure 13-21. *Specifying an *.snk file via the Properties page*

Installing/Removing Shared Assemblies to/from the GAC

The final step is to install the (now strongly named) CarLibrary.dll into the GAC. The simplest way to install a shared assembly into the GAC is to drag and drop the assembly to C:\WINDOWS\Assembly using Windows Explorer, which is ideal for a quick test (know that copy/paste operations will *not* work when deploying to the GAC).

In addition, the .NET Framework 2.0 SDK provides a command-line utility named gacutil.exe that allows you to examine and modify the contents of the GAC. Table 13-1 documents some relevant options of gacutil.exe (specify the /? flag to see each option).

Table 13-1. *Various Options of gacutil.exe*

Option	Meaning in Life
/i	Installs a strongly named assembly into the GAC
/u	Uninstalls an assembly from the GAC
/l	Displays the assemblies (or a specific assembly) in the GAC

Using either technique, deploy CarLibrary.dll to the GAC. Once you've finished, you should see your library present and accounted for, as shown in Figure 13-22.

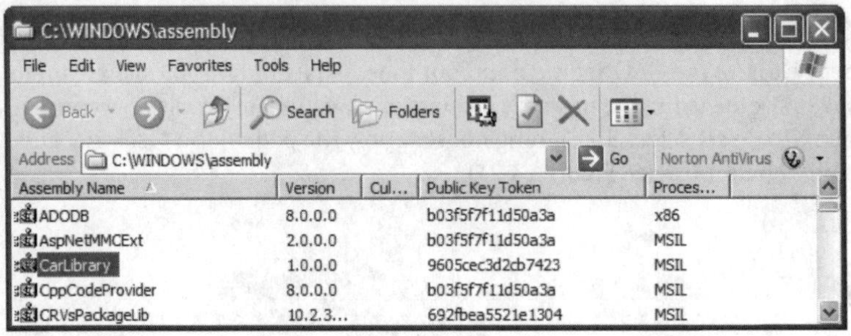

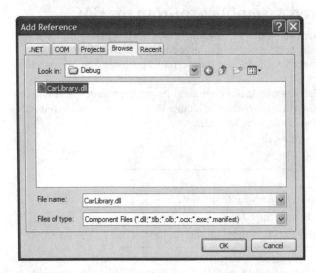

Figure 13-22. *The strongly named, shared* CarLibrary *(version 1.0.0.0)*

■**Note** You may right-click any assembly icon to pull up its Properties page, and you may also uninstall a specific version of an assembly altogether from the right-click context menu (the GUI equivalent of supplying the /u flag to gacutil.exe).

Consuming a Shared Assembly

When you are building applications that make use of a shared assembly, the only difference from consuming a private assembly is in how you reference the library using Visual Studio 2005. In reality, there is no difference as far as the tool is concerned (you still make use of the Add Reference dialog box). What you must understand is that this dialog box will *not* allow you to reference the assembly by browsing to the Assembly folder. Any efforts to do so will be in vain, as you cannot reference the assembly you have highlighted. Rather, you will need to browse to the \bin\Debug directory of the *original* project via the Browse tab, which is shown in Figure 13-23.

Figure 13-23. *Correct! You must reference shared assemblies by navigating to the project's \bin\Debug directory using Visual Studio 2005.*

This (somewhat annoying) fact aside, create a new VB 2005 console application named SharedCarLibClient and exercise your types as you wish:

```
Imports CarLibrary

Module Program
  Sub Main()
    Dim mycar As New SportsCar()
    mycar.TurboBoost()
    Console.ReadLine()
  End Sub
End Module
```

Once you have compiled your client application, navigate to the directory that contains SharedCarLibClient.exe using Windows Explorer and notice that Visual Studio 2005 has *not* copied CarLibrary.dll to the client's application directory. When you reference an assembly whose manifest contains a .publickey value, Visual Studio 2005 assumes the strongly named assembly will most likely be deployed in the GAC, and therefore does not bother to copy the binary.

Exploring the Manifest of SharedCarLibClient

Recall that when you generate a strong name for an assembly, the entire public key is recorded in the assembly manifest. On a related note, when a client references a strongly named assembly, its manifest records a condensed hash-value of the full public key, denoted by the .publickeytoken tag. If you were to open the manifest of SharedCarLibClient.exe using ildasm.exe, you would find the following:

```
.assembly extern CarLibrary
{
  .publickeytoken = (21 9E F3 80 C9 34 8A 38)
  .ver 1:0:0:0
}
```

If you compare the value of the public key token recorded in the client manifest with the public key token value shown in the GAC, you will find a dead-on match. Recall that a public key represents one aspect of the strongly named assembly's identity. Given this, the CLR will only load version 1.0.0.0 of an assembly named CarLibrary that has a public key that can be hashed down to the value 219EF380C9348A38. If the CLR does not find an assembly meeting this description in the GAC (and cannot find a private assembly named CarLibrary in the client's directory), a FileNotFound exception is thrown.

■**Source Code** The SharedCarLibClient application can be found under the Chapter 13 subdirectory.

Configuring Shared Assemblies

Like a private assembly, shared assemblies can be configured using a client *.config file. Of course, because shared assemblies are found in a well-known location (the GAC), you will not specify a <privatePath> element as you did for private assemblies (although if the client is using both shared and private assemblies, the <privatePath> element may still exist in the *.config file).

You can use application configuration files in conjunction with shared assemblies whenever you wish to instruct the CLR to bind to a *different* version of a specific assembly, effectively bypassing the value recorded in the client's manifest. This can be useful for a number of reasons. For example, imagine that you have shipped version 1.0.0.0 of an assembly and discover a major bug sometime after the fact. One corrective action would be to rebuild the client application to reference the correct version of the bug-free assembly (say, 1.1.0.0) and redistribute the updated client and new library to each and every target machine.

Another option is to ship the new code library and a *.config file that automatically instructs the runtime to bind to the new (bug-free) version. As long as the new version has been installed into the GAC, the original client runs without recompilation, redistribution, or fear of having to update your resume.

Here's another example: you have shipped the first version of a bug-free assembly (1.0.0.0), and after a month or two, you add new functionality to the assembly in question to yield version 2.0.0.0. Obviously, existing client applications that were compiled against version 1.0.0.0 have no clue about these new types, given that their code base makes no reference to them.

New client applications, however, wish to make reference to the new functionality found in version 2.0.0.0. Under .NET, you are free to ship version 2.0.0.0 to the target machines, and have version 2.0.0.0 run alongside the older version 1.0.0.0. If necessary, existing clients can be dynamically redirected to load version 2.0.0.0 (to gain access to the implementation refinements), using an application configuration file without needing to recompile and redeploy the client application.

Freezing the Current Shared Assembly

To illustrate how to dynamically bind to a specific version of a shared assembly, open Windows Explorer and copy the current version of CarLibrary (1.0.0.0) into a distinct subdirectory (I called mine "Version 1.0.0.0") off the project root to symbolize the freezing of this version (see Figure 13-24).

Figure 13-24. *Freezing the current version of* CarLibrary.dll

Building Shared Assembly Version 2.0.0.0

Now, update your CarLibrary project to define a new Enum named MusicMedia that defines four possible musical devices:

```
' Holds source of music.
Public Enum MusicMedia
  musicCd
  musicTape
  musicRadio
  musicMp3
End Enum
```

As well, add a new public method to the Car type that allows the caller to turn on one of the given media players (be sure to import the System.Windows.Forms namespace):

```
Public MustInherit Class Car
...
  Public Sub TurnOnRadio(ByVal musicOn As Boolean, ByVal mm As MusicMedia)
    If musicOn Then
      MessageBox.Show(String.Format("Jamming {0}", mm))
    Else
      MessageBox.Show("Quiet time...")
    End If
  End Sub
...
End Class
```

Update the constructors of the Car class to display a MessageBox that verifies you are indeed using CarLibrary 2.0.0.0:

```
Public MustInherit Class Car
...
  Public Sub New()
    MessageBox.Show("Car 2.0.0.0")
  End Sub
  Public Sub New(ByVal name As String, ByVal max As Short, ByVal curr As Short)
    MessageBox.Show("Car 2.0.0.0")
    name = name
    max_speed = max
    speed = curr
  End Sub
...
End Class
```

Finally, before you recompile, be sure to update this version of this assembly to 2.0.0.0 by updating the value passed to the <AssemblyVersion> and <AssemblyFileVersion> attributes within the AssemblyInfo.vb file:

```
' CarLibrary version 2.0.0.0 (now with music!)
<Assembly: AssemblyFileVersion("2.0.0.0")>
<Assembly: AssemblyVersion("2.0.0.0")>
```

If you look in your project's \Bin\Debug folder, you'll see that you have a new version of this assembly (2.0.0.0), while version 1.0.0.0 is safe in storage under the Version 1 subdirectory. Install this new assembly into the GAC as described earlier in this chapter. Notice that you now have two versions of the same assembly, as shown in Figure 13-25.

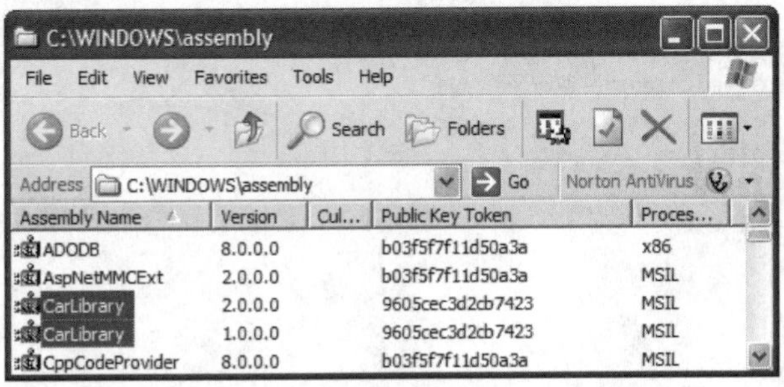

Figure 13-25. *Side-by-side execution*

If you were to run the current `SharedCarLibClient.exe` program by double-clicking the icon using Windows Explorer, you should *not* see the "Car 2.0.0.0" message box appear, as the manifest is specifically requesting version 1.0.0.0. How then can you instruct the CLR to bind to version 2.0.0.0? Glad you asked.

Dynamically Redirecting to Specific Versions of a Shared Assembly

When you wish to inform the CLR to load a version of a shared assembly other than the version listed in its manifest, you may build a `*.config` file that contains a `<dependentAssembly>` element. When doing so, you will need to create an `<assemblyIdentity>` subelement that specifies the friendly name of the assembly listed in the client manifest (`CarLibrary`, for this example) and an optional culture attribute (which can be assigned an empty string or omitted altogether if you wish to specify the default culture for the machine). Moreover, the `<dependentAssembly>` element will define a `<bindingRedirect>` subelement to define the version *currently* in the manifest (via the `oldVersion` attribute) and the version in the GAC to load instead (via the `newVersion` attribute).

Create a new configuration file in the application directory of SharedCarLibClient named `SharedCarLibClient.exe.config` that contains the following XML data. Of course, the value of your public key token will be different from what you see in the following code, and it can be obtained either by examining the client manifest using `ildasm.exe` or via the GAC.

```
<configuration>
  <runtime>
    <assemblyBinding xmlns="urn:schemas-microsoft-com:asm.v1">
      <dependentAssembly>
        <assemblyIdentity name="CarLibrary"
         publicKeyToken="219ef380c9348a38"/>
          <bindingRedirect oldVersion= "1.0.0.0"
          newVersion= "2.0.0.0"/>
      </dependentAssembly>
    </assemblyBinding>
  </runtime>
</configuration>
```

Now run the `SharedCarLibClient.exe` program. You should see the message that displays version 2.0.0.0 has loaded. If you set the `newVersion` attribute to 1.0.0.0 (or if you simply deleted the `*.config` file), you now see the message that version 1.0.0.0 has loaded, as the CLR found version 1.0.0.0 listed in the client's manifest.

Multiple `<dependentAssembly>` elements can appear within a client's configuration file. Although you have no need to do so, assume that the manifest of `SharedCarLibClient.exe` also references version 2.5.0.0 of an assembly named `MathLibrary`. If you wished to redirect to version 3.0.0.0 of `MathLibrary` (in addition to version 2.0.0.0 of `CarLibrary`), the `SharedCarLibClient.exe.config` file would look like the following:

```
<configuration>
  <runtime>
    <assemblyBinding xmlns="urn:schemas-microsoft-com:asm.v1">
      <dependentAssembly>
        <assemblyIdentity name="CarLibrary"
          publicKeyToken="219ef380c9348a38"/>
        <bindingRedirect oldVersion= "1.0.0.0"
          newVersion= "2.0.0.0"/>
      </dependentAssembly>
      <dependentAssembly>
        <assemblyIdentity name="MathLibrary"
          publicKeyToken="219ef380c9348a38"/>
        <bindingRedirect oldVersion= "2.5.0.0"
```

```
            newVersion= "3.0.0.0"/>
        </dependentAssembly>
      </assemblyBinding>
    </runtime>
</configuration>
```

Revisiting the .NET Framework 2.0 Configuration Utility

As you would hope, you can generate shared assembly–centric *.config files using the graphical .NET Framework 2.0 Configuration utility. Like the process of building a *.config file for private assemblies, the first step is to reference the *.exe to configure. To illustrate, delete the SharedCarLibClient.exe.config you just authored. Now, add a reference to SharedCarLibClient.exe by right-clicking the Applications node. Once you do, expand the plus sign (+) icon and select the Configured Assemblies subnode. From here, click the Configure an Assembly link on the right side of the utility.

At this point, you are presented with a dialog box that allows you to establish a <dependentAssembly> element using a number of friendly UI elements. First, select the "Choose an assembly from the list of assemblies this application uses" radio button (which simply means, "Show me the manifest!") and click the Choose Assembly button.

A dialog box now displays that shows you not only the assemblies specifically listed in the client manifest, but also the assemblies referenced by these assemblies. For this example's purposes, select CarLibrary. When you click the Finish button, you will be shown a Properties page for this one small aspect of the client's manifest. Here, you can generate the <dependentAssembly> using the Binding Policy tab.

Once you select the Binding Policy tab, you can set the oldVersion attribute (1.0.0.0) via the Requested Version text field and the newVersion attribute (2.0.0.0) using the New Version text field. Once you have committed the settings, you will find the following configuration file is generated for you:

```xml
<?xml version="1.0"?>
<configuration>
    <runtime>
      <assemblyBinding xmlns="urn:schemas-microsoft-com:asm.v1">
        <dependentAssembly>
          <assemblyIdentity name="CarLibrary"
            publicKeyToken="219ef380c9348a38"/>
          <publisherPolicy apply="yes"/>
          <bindingRedirect oldVersion="1.0.0.0" newVersion="2.0.0.0"/>
        </dependentAssembly>
      </assemblyBinding>
    </runtime>
</configuration>
```

Understanding Publisher Policy Assemblies

The next configuration issue you'll examine is the role of *publisher policy assemblies*. As you've just seen, *.config files can be constructed to bind to a specific version of a shared assembly, thereby bypassing the version recorded in the client manifest. While this is all well and good, imagine you're an administrator who now needs to reconfigure all client applications on a given machine to rebind to version 2.0.0.0 of the CarLibrary.dll assembly. Given the strict naming convention of a configuration file, you would need to duplicate the same XML content in numerous locations (assuming you are, in fact, aware of the locations of the executables using CarLibrary!). Clearly this would be a maintenance nightmare.

Publisher policy allows the publisher of a given assembly (you, your department, your company, or what have you) to ship a binary version of a `*.config` file that is installed into the GAC along with the newest version of the associated assembly. The benefit of this approach is that client application directories do *not* need to contain specific `*.config` files. Rather, the CLR will read the current manifest and attempt to find the requested version in the GAC. However, if the CLR finds a publisher policy assembly, it will read the embedded XML data and perform the requested redirection *at the level of the GAC*.

Publisher policy assemblies are created at the command line using a .NET utility named `al.exe` (the assembly linker). While this tool provides a large number of options, building a publisher policy assembly requires you only to pass in the following input parameters:

- The location of the `*.config` or `*.xml` file containing the redirecting instructions
- The name of the resulting publisher policy assembly
- The location of the `*.snk` file used to sign the publisher policy assembly
- The version numbers to assign the publisher policy assembly being constructed

If you wish to build a publisher policy assembly that controls `CarLibrary.dll`, the command set is as follows (which should be entered on a single line):

```
al /link: CarLibraryPolicy.xml /out:policy.1.0.CarLibrary.dll
/keyf:C:\ MyKey\ myKey.snk /v:1.0.0.0
```

Here, the XML content is contained within a file named `CarLibraryPolicy.xml`. The name of the output file (which must be in the format *policy.<major>.<minor>.assemblyToConfigure*) is specified using the obvious /out flag. In addition, note that the name of the file containing the public/private key pair will also need to be supplied via the /keyf option. (Remember, publisher policy files are deployed to the GAC, and therefore must have a strong name!)

Once the `al.exe` tool has executed, the result is a new assembly that can be placed into the GAC to force all clients to bind to version 2.0.0.0 of `CarLibrary.dll`, without the use of a specific client application configuration file.

Disabling Publisher Policy

Now, assume you (as a system administrator) have deployed a publisher policy assembly (and the latest version of the related assembly) to a client machine's GAC. As luck would have it, nine of the ten affected applications rebind to version 2.0.0.0 without error. However, the remaining client application (for whatever reason) blows up when accessing `CarLibrary.dll` 2.0.0.0 (as we all know, it is next to impossible to build backward-compatible software that works 100 percent of the time).

In such a case, it is possible to build a configuration file for a specific troubled client that instructs the CLR to *ignore* the presence of any publisher policy files installed in the GAC. The remaining client applications that are happy to consume the newest .NET assembly will simply be redirected via the installed publisher policy assembly. To disable publisher policy on a client-by-client basis, author a (properly named) `*.config` file that makes use of the `<publisherPolicy>` element and set the `apply` attribute to no. When you do so, the CLR will load the version of the assembly originally listed in the client's manifest.

```
<configuration>
  <runtime>
    <assemblyBinding xmlns="urn:schemas-microsoft-com:asm.v1">
      <publisherPolicy apply="no" />
    </assemblyBinding>
  </runtime>
</configuration>
```

Understanding the <codeBase> Element

Application configuration files can also specify *code bases*. The <codeBase> element can be used to instruct the CLR to probe for dependent assemblies located at arbitrary locations (such as network share points, or simply a local directory outside a client's application directory).

■Note If the value assigned to a <codeBase> element is located on a remote machine, the assembly will be downloaded on demand to a specific directory in the GAC termed the *download cache*. You can view the content of your machine's download cache by supplying the /ldl option to gacutil.exe.

Given what you have learned about deploying assemblies to the GAC, it should make sense that assemblies loaded from a <codeBase> element will need to be assigned a strong name (after all, how else could the CLR install remote assemblies to the GAC?).

■Note Technically speaking, the <codeBase> element can be used to probe for assemblies that do not have a strong name. However, the assembly's location must be relative to the client's application directory (and thus is little more than an alternative to the <privatePath> element).

Create a console application named CodeBaseClient, set a reference to CarLibrary.dll version 2.0.0.0, and update the initial file as follows:

```
Imports CarLibrary

Module Program
  Sub Main()
    Console.WriteLine("***** Fun with CodeBases *****")
    Dim c As SportsCar = New SportsCar()
    Console.WriteLine("Sports car has been allocated.")
    Console.ReadLine()
  End Sub
End Module
```

Given that CarLibrary.dll has been deployed to the GAC, you are able to run the program as is. However, to illustrate the use of the <codeBase> element, create a new folder under your C drive (perhaps C:\MyAsms) and place a copy of CarLibrary.dll version 2.0.0.0 into this directory.

Now, add an app.config file to the CodeBaseClient project (as explained earlier in this chapter) and author the following XML content (remember that your .publickeytoken value will differ; consult your GAC as required):

```
<configuration>
  <runtime>
    <assemblyBinding xmlns="urn:schemas-microsoft-com:asm.v1">
      <dependentAssembly>
        <assemblyIdentity name="SharedAssembly" publicKeyToken="219ef380c9348a38" />
        <codeBase version="2.0.0.0" href="file:///C:\MyAsms\CarLibrary.dll" />
      </dependentAssembly>
    </assemblyBinding>
  </runtime>
</configuration>
```

As you can see, the <codeBase> element is nested within the <assemblyIdentity> element, which makes use of the name and publicKeyToken attributes to specify the friendly name as associated publicKeyToken values. The <codeBase> element itself specifies the version and location (via the href property) of the assembly to load. If you were to delete version 2.0.0.0 of CarLibrary.dll from the GAC, this client would still run successfully, as the CLR is able to locate the external assembly under C:\MyAsms.

However, if you were to delete the MyAsms directory from your machine, the client would now fail. Clearly the <codeBase> elements (if present) take precedence over the investigation of the GAC.

■**Note** If you place assemblies at random locations on your development machine, you are in effect re-creating the system registry (and the related DLL hell), given that if you move or rename the folder containing your binaries, the current bind will fail. Given this point, use <codeBase> with caution.

The <codeBase> element can also be helpful when referencing assemblies located on a remote networked machine. Assume you have permission to access a folder located at http:// www.IntertechTraining.com. To download the remote *.dll to the GAC's download cache on your location machine, you could update the <codeBase> element as follows:

```
<codeBase version="2.0.0.0"
  href="http://www.IntertechTraining.com/Assemblies/CarLibrary.dll" />
```

■**Source Code** The CodeBaseClient application can be found under the Chapter 13 subdirectory.

The System.Configuration Namespace

Currently, all of the *.config files shown in this chapter have made use of well-known XML elements that are read by the CLR to resolve the location of external assemblies. In addition to these recognized elements, it is perfectly permissible for a client configuration file to contain application-specific data that has nothing to do with binding heuristics. Given this, it should come as no surprise that the .NET Framework provides a namespace that allows you to programmatically read the data within a client configuration file.

The System.Configuration namespace provides a small set of types you may use to read custom data from a client's *.config file. These custom settings must be contained within the scope of an <appSettings> element. The <appSettings> element contains any number of <add> elements that define a key/value pair to be obtained programmatically.

For example, assume you have a *.config file for a console application named AppConfigReaderApp that defines a database connection string and a point of data named timesToSayHello:

```
<configuration>
  <appSettings>
    <add key="appConStr"
        value="server=localhost;uid='sa';pwd='';database=Cars" />
      <add key="timesToSayHello" value="8" />
  </appSettings>
</configuration>
```

Reading these values for use by the client application is as simple as calling the instance-level GetValue() method of the System.Configuration.AppSettingsReader type. As shown in the following code, the first parameter to GetValue() is the name of the key in the *.config file, whereas the second parameter is the underlying type of the key (obtained via the VB 2005 GetType operator):

```
Imports System.Configuration

Module Program
  Sub Main()
```

```
    Dim ar As AppSettingsReader = New AppSettingsReader
    Console.WriteLine(ar.GetValue("appConStr", GetType(String)))
    Dim numbOfTimes As Integer = CType(ar.GetValue("timesToSayHello", _
      GetType(Integer)), Integer)

    For i As Integer = 0 To numbOfTimes
      Console.WriteLine("Yo!")
    Next
    Console.ReadLine()
  End Sub
End Module
```

The AppSettingsReader class type does *not* provide a way to write application-specific data to a *.config file. While this may seem like a limitation at first encounter, it actually makes good sense. The whole idea of a *.config file is that it contains read-only data that is consulted by the CLR (or possibly the AppSettingsReader type) after an application has already been deployed to a target machine.

■**Note** During our examination of ADO.NET (Chapter 24), you will learn about the new <connectionStrings> configuration element and new types within the System.Configuration namespace. These .NET 2.0–specific items provide a standard manner to handle connection string data.

■**Source Code** The AppConfigReaderApp application can be found under the Chapter 13 subdirectory.

The Machine Configuration File

The configuration files you've examined in this chapter have a common theme: they apply only to a specific application (that is why they have the same name as the launching application). In addition, each .NET-aware machine has a file named machine.config that contains a vast number of configuration details (many of which have nothing to do with resolving external assemblies) that control how the .NET platform operates.

The .NET platform maintains a separate *.config file for each version of the framework installed on the local machine. The machine.config file for .NET 2.0 can be found under the C:\WINDOWS\Microsoft.NET\Framework\v2.0.50727\CONFIG directory (your version may differ). If you were to open this file, you would find numerous XML elements that control ASP.NET settings, various security details, debugging support, and so forth.

Although this file can be directly edited using Notepad, be warned that if you alter this file incorrectly, you may cripple the ability of the runtime to function correctly. This scenario can be far more painful than a malformed application *.config file, given that XML errors in an application configuration file affect only a single application, but erroneous XML in the machine.config file can break a specific version of the .NET platform.

The Assembly Binding "Big Picture"

Now that you have drilled down into the details regarding how the CLR resolves the location of requested external assemblies, remember that the simple case is, indeed, simple. Many (if not most) of your .NET applications will consist of nothing more than a group of private assemblies deployed to a single directory. In this case, simply copy the folder to a location of your choosing and run the client executable.

As you have seen, however, the CLR will check for client configuration files and publisher policy assemblies during the resolution process. To summarize the path taken by the CLR to resolve an external assembly reference, ponder Figure 13-26.

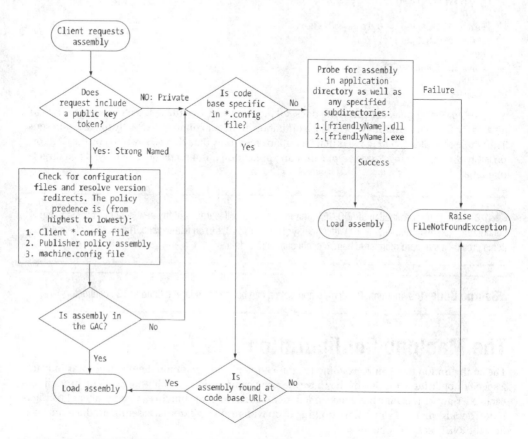

Figure 13-26. *Behold the CLR's path of assembly resolution*

Summary

This chapter drilled down into the details of how the CLR resolves the location of externally referenced assemblies. You began by examining the content within an assembly: headers, metadata, manifests, and CIL. Then you constructed single-file and multifile assemblies and a handful of client applications (written in a language-agonistic manner).

As you have seen, assemblies may be private or shared. Private assemblies are copied to the client's subdirectory, whereas shared assemblies are deployed to the Global Assembly Cache (GAC), provided they have been assigned a strong name. Finally, as you have seen, private and shared assemblies can be configured using a client-side XML configuration file or, alternatively, via a publisher policy assembly.

CHAPTER 14

■■■

Type Reflection, Late Binding, and Attribute-based Programming

As shown in the previous chapter, assemblies are the basic unit of deployment in the .NET universe. Using the integrated object browsers of Visual Studio 2005, you are able to examine the types within a project's referenced set of assemblies. Furthermore, external tools such as ildasm.exe allow you to peek into the underlying CIL code, type metadata, and assembly manifest for a given .NET binary. In addition to this design-time investigation of .NET assemblies, you are also able to *programmatically* obtain this same information using the System.Reflection namespace. To this end, the first task of this chapter is to define the role of reflection and the necessity of .NET metadata.

The remainder of the chapter examines a number of closely related topics, all of which hinge upon reflection services. For example, you'll learn how a .NET client may employ dynamic loading and late binding to activate types it has no compile-time knowledge of. You'll also learn how to insert custom metadata into your .NET assemblies through the use of system-supplied and custom attributes. To put all of these (seemingly esoteric) topics into perspective, the chapter closes by demonstrating how to build several "snap-in objects" that you can plug into an extendable Windows Forms application.

The Necessity of Type Metadata

The ability to fully describe types (classes, interfaces, structures, enumerations, and delegates) using metadata is a key element of the .NET platform. Numerous .NET technologies, such as object serialization, .NET remoting, and XML web services, require the ability to discover the format of types at runtime. Furthermore, COM interoperability, compiler support, and an IDE's IntelliSense capabilities all rely on a concrete description of *type*.

Regardless of (or perhaps due to) its importance, metadata is not a new idea supplied by the .NET Framework. Java, CORBA, and COM all have similar concepts. For example, COM type libraries (which are little more than compiled IDL code) are used to describe the types contained within a COM server. Like COM, .NET code libraries also support type metadata. Of course, .NET metadata has no syntactic similarities to COM IDL. Recall that the ildasm.exe utility allows you to view an assembly's type metadata using the Ctrl+M keyboard option (see Chapter 1). Thus, if you were to open any of the *.dll or *.exe assemblies created over the course of this book (such as CarLibrary.dll) using ildasm.exe and then press Ctrl+M, you would find the relevant type metadata (see Figure 14-1).

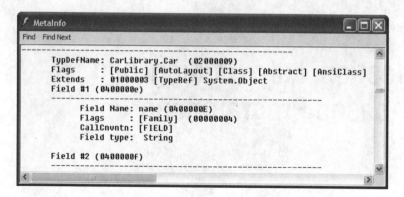

Figure 14-1. *Viewing an assembly's metadata*

As you can see, `ildasm.exe`'s display of .NET type metadata is very verbose (the actual binary format is much more compact). In fact, if I were to list the entire metadata description representing the `CarLibrary.dll` assembly, it would span several pages. Given that this act would be a woeful waste of paper, let's just glimpse into some key metadata tokens within the `CarLibrary.dll` assembly.

Viewing (Partial) Metadata for the EngineState Enumeration

Each type defined within the current assembly is documented using a `TypeDef` `#n` token (where `TypeDef` is short for *type definition*). If the type being described uses a type defined within a separate .NET assembly, the referenced type is documented using a `TypeDef` `#n` token (where `TypeRef` is short for *type reference*). A `TypeRef` token is a pointer (if you will) to the referenced type's full metadata definition. In a nutshell, .NET metadata is a set of tables that clearly mark all type definitions (`TypeDefs`) and referenced entities (`TypeRefs`), all of which can be viewed using `ildasm.exe`'s metadata window.

As far as `CarLibrary.dll` goes, one `TypeDef` we encounter is the metadata description of the `CarLibrary.EngineState` enumeration (your number may differ; `TypeDef` numbering is based on the order in which the VB 2005 compiler processes the source code files):

TypeDef #6 (02000007)

```
---------------------------------------------------------
TypDefName: CarLibrary.EngineState  (02000007)
Flags     : [Public] [AutoLayout] [Class] [Sealed] [AnsiClass]  (00000101)
Extends   : 01000007 [TypeRef] System.Enum
...
Field #2 (04000007)
---------------------------------------------------------
  Field Name: engineAlive (04000007)
  Flags     : [Public] [Shared] [Literal] [HasDefault]  (00008056)
  DefltValue: (I4) 0
  CallCnvntn: [FIELD]
  Field type:  ValueClass CarLibrary.EngineState
...
```

Here, the `TypDefName` token is used to establish the name of the given type. The `Extends` metadata token is used to document the base class of a given .NET type (in this case, the referenced type, `System.Enum`). Each field of an enumeration is marked using the `Field` `#n` token. For brevity, I have simply listed the metadata for `EngineState.engineAlive`.

Viewing (Partial) Metadata for the Car Type

Here is a partial dump of the Car type that illustrates the following:

- How fields are defined in terms of .NET metadata
- How methods are documented via .NET metadata
- How a single type property is mapped to two discrete member functions

```
TypeDef #3
-------------------------------------------------------
  TypDefName: CarLibrary.Car  (02000004)
  Flags     : [Public] [AutoLayout] [Class] [Abstract] [AnsiClass]  (00100081)
  Extends   : 01000002 [TypeRef] System.Object
  Field #1
  -------------------------------------------------------
    Field Name: petName (04000008)
    Flags     : [Family]  (00000004)
    CallCnvntn: [FIELD]
    Field type:  String
...
  Method #1
  -------------------------------------------------------
    MethodName: .ctor (06000001)
    Flags     : [Public] [HideBySig] [ReuseSlot] [SpecialName]
    [RTSpecialName] [.ctor]  (00001886)
    RVA        : 0x00002050
    ImplFlags : [IL] [Managed]  (00000000)
    CallCnvntn: [DEFAULT]
    hasThis
    ReturnType: Void
    No arguments.
...
  Property #1
  -------------------------------------------------------
    Prop.Name : PetName (17000001)
    Flags     : [none] (00000000)
    CallCnvntn: [PROPERTY]
    hasThis
    ReturnType: String
    No arguments.
    DefltValue:
      Setter    : (06000004) set_PetName
      Getter    : (06000003) get_PetName
      0 Others
...
```

First, note that the Car class metadata marks the type's base class and includes various flags that describe how this type was constructed (e.g., [public], [abstract], and whatnot). Methods (such as our Car's constructor, denoted by .ctor) are described in regard to their parameters, return value, and name. Finally, note how properties are mapped to their internal get/set methods using the .NET metadata Setter/Getter tokens. As you would expect, the derived Car types (SportsCar and MiniVan) are described in a similar manner.

Examining a TypeRef

Recall that an assembly's metadata will describe not only the set of internal types (Car, EngineState, etc.), but also any external types the internal types reference. For example, given that CarLibrary.dll has defined two enumerations, you find a TypeRef block for the System.Enum type, which is defined in mscorlib.dll:

```
TypeRef #1 (01000001)
-------------------------------------------------------
Token:             0x01000001
ResolutionScope:   0x23000001
TypeRefName:       System.Enum
  MemberRef #1
  ---------------------------------------------------------
  Member: (0a00000f) ToString:
  CallCnvntn: [DEFAULT]
  hasThis
  ReturnType: String
  No arguments.
```

Documenting the Defining Assembly

The ildasm.exe metadata window also allows you to view the .NET metadata that describes the assembly itself using the Assembly token. As you can see from the following (partial) listing, information documented within the Assembly table is (surprise, surprise!) the same information that can be viewable via the MANIFEST icon. Here is a partial dump of the manifest of CarLibrary.dll (version 2.0.0.0):

```
Assembly
-----------------------------------------------------
  Token: 0x20000001
  Name : CarLibrary
  Public Key : 00 24 00 00 04 80 00 00   // Etc...

  Hash Algorithm : 0x00008004
  Major Version: 0x00000002
  Minor Version: 0x00000000
  Build Number: 0x00000000
  Revision Number: 0x00000000
  Locale: <null>
  Flags : [SideBySideCompatible]   (00000000)
```

Documenting Referenced Assemblies

In addition to the Assembly token and the set of TypeDef and TypeRef blocks, .NET metadata also makes use of AssemblyRef #n tokens to document each external assembly. Given that the CarLibrary.dll makes use of the MessageBox type, you find an AssemblyRef for System.Windows.Forms, for example:

```
AssemblyRef #2
-----------------------------------------------------
  Token: 0x23000002
  Public Key or Token: b7 7a 5c 56 19 34 e0 89
  Name: System.Windows.Forms
  Version: 2.0.3600.0
  Major Version: 0x00000002
  Minor Version: 0x00000000
  Build Number: 0x00000e10
```

```
Revision Number: 0x00000000
Locale: <null>
HashValue Blob:
Flags: [none] (00000000)
```

Documenting String Literals

The final point of interest regarding .NET metadata is the fact that each and every string literal in
your code base is documented under the User Strings token, for example:

```
User Strings
-------------------------------------------------------
70000001 : (11) L"Car 2.0.0.0"
70000019 : (11) L"Jamming {0} "
70000031 : (13) L"Quiet time..."
7000004d : (14) L"Ramming speed!"
7000006b : (19) L"Faster is better..."
70000093 : (16) L"Time to call AAA"
700000b5 : (16) L"Your car is dead"
700000d7 : ( 9) L"Be quiet "
700000eb : ( 2) L"!!"
```

Now, don't be too concerned with the exact syntax of each and every piece of .NET metadata.
The bigger point to absorb is that .NET metadata is very descriptive and lists each internally defined
(and externally referenced) type found within a given code base.

The next question on your mind may be (in the best-case scenario) "How can I leverage this
information in my applications?" or (in the worst-case scenario) "Why should I care about metadata
in the first place?" To address both points of view, allow me to introduce .NET reflection services. Be
aware that the usefulness of the topics presented over the pages that follow may be a bit of a head-
scratcher until this chapter's endgame. So hang tight.

■**Note** You will also find a number of .custom tokens displayed by the MetaInfo window, which documents the
attributes applied within the code base. You'll learn about the role of .NET attributes later in this chapter.

Understanding Reflection

In the .NET universe, *reflection* is the process of runtime type discovery. Using reflection services,
you are able to programmatically obtain the same metadata information displayed by ildasm.exe
using a friendly object model. For example, through reflection, you can obtain a list of all types contained within a given assembly (or *.netmodule, as discussed in Chapter 13), including the methods,
fields, properties, and events defined by a given type. You can also dynamically discover the set of
interfaces supported by a given class (or structure), the parameters of a method, and other related
details (base classes, namespace information, manifest data, and so forth).

Like any namespace, System.Reflection contains a number of related types. Table 14-1 lists
some of the core items you should be familiar with.

Table 14-1. *A Sampling of Members of the* System.Reflection *Namespace*

Type	Meaning in Life
Assembly	This class (in addition to numerous related types) contains a number of methods that allow you to load, investigate, and manipulate an assembly programmatically.
AssemblyName	This class allows you to discover numerous details behind an assembly's identity (version information, culture information, and so forth).
EventInfo	This class holds information for a given event.
FieldInfo	This class holds information for a given field.
MemberInfo	This is the abstract base class that defines common behaviors for the EventInfo, FieldInfo, MethodInfo, and PropertyInfo types.
MethodInfo	This class contains information for a given method.
Module	This class allows you to access a given module within a multifile assembly.
ParameterInfo	This class holds information for a given parameter.
PropertyInfo	This class holds information for a given property.

To understand how to leverage the System.Reflection namespace to programmatically read .NET metadata, you need to first come to terms with the System.Type class.

The System.Type Class

The System.Type class defines a number of members that can be used to examine a type's metadata, a great number of which return types from the System.Reflection namespace. For example, Type.GetMethods() returns an array of MethodInfo types, Type.GetFields() returns an array of FieldInfo types, and so on. The complete set of members exposed by System.Type is quite expansive; however, Table 14-2 offers a partial snapshot of the members supported by System.Type (see the .NET Framework 2.0 SDK documentation for full details).

Table 14-2. *Select Members of* System.Type

Type Member	Meaning in Life
IsAbstract IsArray IsClass IsCOMObject IsEnum IsGenericTypeDefinition IsGenericParameter IsInterfaceIsPrimitive IsNestedPrivate IsNestedPublic IsSealed IsValueType	These properties (among others) allow you to discover a number of basic traits about the Type you are referring to (e.g., if it is an abstract method, an array, a nested class, and so forth).
GetConstructors() GetEvents() GetFields() GetInterfaces() GetMembers() GetMethods() GetNestedTypes() GetProperties()	These methods (among others) allow you to obtain an array representing the items (interface, method, property, etc.) you are interested in. Each method returns a related array (e.g., GetFields() returns a FieldInfo array, GetMethods() returns a MethodInfo array, etc.). Be aware that each of these methods has a singular form (e.g., GetMethod(), GetProperty(), etc.) that allows you to retrieve a specific item by name, rather than an array of all related items.

Type Member	Meaning in Life
FindMembers()	This method returns an array of MemberInfo types based on search criteria.
GetType()	This shared method returns a Type instance given a string name.
InvokeMember()	This method allows late binding to a given item.

Obtaining a Type Reference Using System.Object.GetType()

You can obtain an instance of the Type class in a variety of ways. However, the one thing you cannot do is directly create a Type object using the New keyword, as Type is an abstract class. Regarding your first choice, recall that System.Object defines a method named GetType(), which returns an instance of the Type class that represents the metadata for the current object:

```
' Obtain type information using a SportsCar instance.
Dim sc As SportsCar = New SportsCar()
Dim t As Type = sc.GetType()
```

Obviously, this approach will only work if you have compile-time knowledge of the type you wish to investigate (SportsCar in this case). Given this restriction, it should make sense that tools such as ildasm.exe do not obtain type information by directly calling a custom type's GetType() method, given that ildasm.exe was not compiled against your custom assemblies!

Obtaining a Type Reference Using System.Type.GetType()

To obtain type information in a more flexible manner, you may call the shared GetType() member of the System.Type class and specify the fully qualified string name of the type you are interested in examining. Using this approach, you do *not* need to have compile-time knowledge of the type you are extracting metadata from, given that Type.GetType() takes an instance of the omnipresent System.String.

The Type.GetType() method has been overloaded to allow you to specify two Boolean parameters, one of which controls whether an exception should be thrown if the type cannot be found, and the other of which establishes the case sensitivity of the string. To illustrate, ponder the following code statements:

```
' Obtain type information using the shared Type.GetType() method.
' (don't throw an exception if SportsCar cannot be found and ignore case).
Dim t As Type = Type.GetType("CarLibrary.SportsCar", False, True)
```

In the previous example, notice that the string you are passing into GetType() makes no mention of the assembly containing the type. In this case, the assumption is that the type is defined within the currently executing assembly. However, when you wish to obtain metadata for a type within an external private assembly, the string parameter is formatted using the type's fully qualified name, followed by the friendly name of the assembly containing the type (each of which is separated by a comma):

```
' Obtain type information for a type within an external assembly.
Dim t As Type
t = Type.GetType("CarLibrary.SportsCar, CarLibrary")
```

As well, do know that the string passed into Type.GetType() may specify a plus token (+) to denote a nested type. Assume you wish to obtain type information for an enumeration (SpyOptions) nested within a class named JamesBondCar, defined in an external private assembly named CarLibrary.dll. To do so, you would write the following:

```
' Obtain type information for a nested enumeration
' within the current assembly.
Dim t As Type = _
  Type.GetType("CarLibrary.JamesBondCar+SpyOptions, CarLibrary")
```

Obtaining a Type Reference Using GetType()

The final way to obtain type information is using the VB 2005 GetType operator:

```
' Get the Type using GetType.
Dim t As Type = GetType(SportsCar)
```

Like Type.GetType(), the GetType operator is helpful in that you do not need to first create an object instance to extract type information. However, your code base must still have compile-time knowledge of the type you are interested in examining.

Building a Custom Metadata Viewer

To illustrate the basic process of reflection (and the usefulness of System.Type), let's create a console application named MyTypeViewer. This program will display details of the methods, properties, fields, and supported interfaces (in addition to some other points of interest) for any type within mscorlib.dll (recall all .NET applications have automatic access to this core framework class library) or a type within MyTypeViewer.exe itself.

Reflecting on Methods

The Program module will be updated to define a number of subroutines, each of which takes a single System.Type parameter. First you have ListMethods(), which (as you might guess) prints the name of each method defined by the incoming type. Notice how Type.GetMethods() returns an array of System.Reflection.MethodInfo types:

```
' Display method names of type.
Public Sub ListMethods(ByVal t As Type)
  Console.WriteLine("***** Methods *****")
  Dim mi As MethodInfo() = t.GetMethods()
  For Each m As MethodInfo In mi
   Console.WriteLine("->{0}", m.Name)
  Next
  Console.WriteLine("")
End Sub
```

Here, you are simply printing the name of the method using the MethodInfo.Name property. Of course, MethodInfo has many additional members that allow you to determine whether the method is shared, virtual, or abstract. As well, the MethodInfo type allows you to obtain the method's return value and parameter set. You'll spruce up the implementation of ListMethods() in just a bit.

Reflecting on Fields and Properties

The implementation of ListFields() is similar. The only notable difference is the call to Type.GetFields() and the resulting FieldInfo array. Again, to keep things simple, you are printing out only the name of each field.

```
' Display field names of type.
Public Sub ListFields(ByVal t As Type)
  Console.WriteLine("***** Fields *****")
  Dim fi As FieldInfo() = t.GetFields()
  For Each field As FieldInfo In fi
    Console.WriteLine("->{0}", field.Name)
  Next
  Console.WriteLine("")
End Sub
```

The logic to display a type's properties is similar:

```
' Display property names of type.
Public Sub ListProps(ByVal t As Type)
  Console.WriteLine("***** Properties *****")
  Dim pi As PropertyInfo() = t.GetProperties()
  For Each prop As PropertyInfo In pi
    Console.WriteLine("->{0}", prop.Name)
  Next
  Console.WriteLine("")
End Sub
```

Reflecting on Implemented Interfaces

Next, you will author a method named ListInterfaces() that will print out the names of any interfaces supported on the incoming type. The only point of interest here is that the call to GetInterfaces() returns an array of System.Types! This should make sense given that interfaces are, indeed, types:

```
' Display implemented interfaces.
Public Sub ListInterfaces(ByVal t As Type)
  Console.WriteLine("***** Interfaces *****")
  Dim ifaces As Type() = t.GetInterfaces()
  For Each i As Type In ifaces
    Console.WriteLine("->{0}", i.Name)
  Next
  Console.WriteLine("")
End Sub
```

Displaying Various Odds and Ends

Last but not least, you have one final helper method that will simply display various statistics (indicating whether the type is generic, what the base class is, whether the type is sealed, and so forth) regarding the incoming type:

```
' Just for good measure.
Public Sub ListVariousStats(ByVal t As Type)
  Console.WriteLine("***** Various Statistics *****")
  Console.WriteLine("Base class is: {0}", t.BaseType)
  Console.WriteLine("Is type abstract? {0}", t.IsAbstract)
  Console.WriteLine("Is type sealed? {0}", t.IsSealed)
  Console.WriteLine("Is type generic? {0}", t.IsGenericTypeDefinition)
  Console.WriteLine("Is type a class type? {0}", t.IsClass)
  Console.WriteLine("")
End Sub
```

Implementing Main()

The Main() method of the Program class prompts the user for the fully qualified name of a type. Once you obtain this string data, you pass it into the Type.GetType() method and send the extracted System.Type into each of your helper methods. This process repeats until the user enters **Q** to terminate the application:

```vb
' Need to make use of the reflection namespace.
Imports System.Reflection

Module Program
  Sub Main()
    Console.WriteLine("***** Welcome to MyTypeViewer *****")
    Dim typeName As String = ""
    Dim userIsDone As Boolean = False

    Do
      Console.WriteLine()
      Console.WriteLine("Enter a type name to evaluate")
      Console.Write("or enter Q to quit: ")

      ' Get name of type.
      typeName = Console.ReadLine()

      ' Does user want to quit?
      If typeName.ToUpper = "Q" Then
        userIsDone = True
        Exit Do
      End If

      ' Try to display type
      Try
        Dim t As Type = Type.GetType(typeName)
        Console.WriteLine("")
        ListVariousStats(t)
        ListFields(t)
        ListProps(t)
        ListMethods(t)
        ListInterfaces(t)
      Catch
        Console.WriteLine("Sorry, can't find {0}.", typeName)
      End Try
    Loop While Not userIsDone
  End Sub
  ' Assume all the helper methods are defined below.
...
End Module
```

At this point, MyTypeViewer.exe is ready to take out for a test drive. For example, run your
application and enter the following fully qualified names (be aware that the manner in which you
invoked Type.GetType() requires *case-sensitive* string names):

- System.Int32
- System.Collections.ArrayList
- System.Threading.Thread
- System.Void
- System.IO.BinaryWriter
- System.Math
- System.Console
- MyTypeViewer.Program

Figure 14-2 shows the partial output when specifying System.Math.

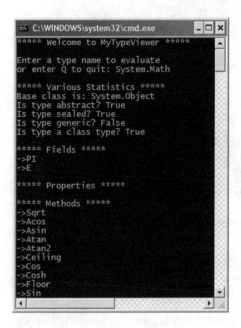

Figure 14-2. *Reflecting on* System.Math

Reflecting on Method Parameters and Return Values

So far, so good! Let's make one minor enhancement to the current application. Specifically, you will update the ListMethods() helper function to list not only the name of a given method, but also the return value and incoming parameters. The MethodInfo type provides the ReturnType property and GetParameters() method for these very tasks. In the following code, notice that you are building a string type that contains the type and name of each parameter using a nested For Each loop:

```
Public Sub ListMethods(ByVal t As Type)
  Console.WriteLine("***** Methods *****")
  Dim mi As MethodInfo() = t.GetMethods()
  For Each m As MethodInfo In mi
    Dim retVal As String = m.ReturnType.FullName()
    Dim paramInfo As String = "("
    For Each pi As ParameterInfo In m.GetParameters()
      paramInfo += String.Format("{0} {1}", pi.ParameterType, pi.Name)
    Next
      paramInfo += ")"
    Console.WriteLine("->{0} {1} {2}", retVal, m.Name, paramInfo)
  Next
  Console.WriteLine("")
End Sub
```

If you now run this updated application, you will find that the methods of a given type are much more detailed. Figure 14-3 shows the method metadata of the System.Globalization. GregorianCalendar type.

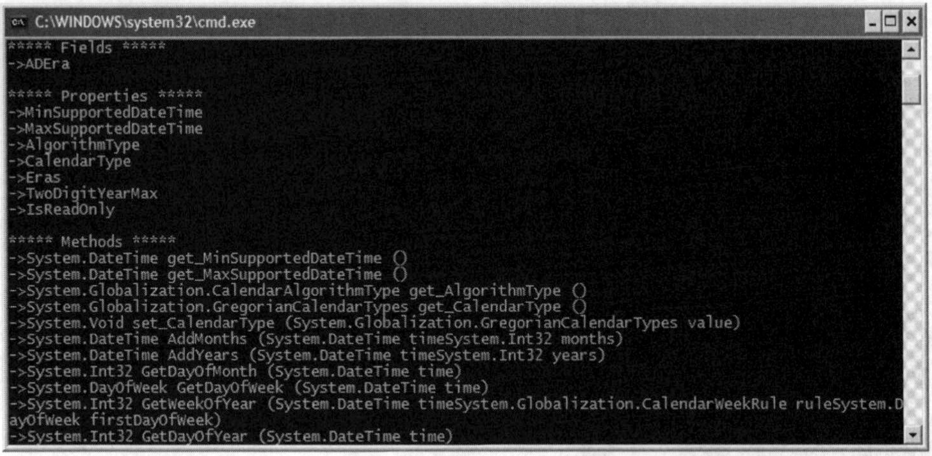

Figure 14-3. *Method details of* System.Globalization.GregorianCalendar

Interesting stuff, huh? Clearly the System.Reflection namespace and System.Type class allow you to reflect over many other aspects of a type beyond what MyTypeViewer is currently displaying. For example, you can obtain a type's events, get the list of any generic parameters for a given member, optional arguments, and glean dozens of other details.

Nevertheless, at this point you have created an (somewhat capable) object browser. The major limitation, of course, is that you have no way to reflect beyond the current assembly (MyTypeViewer.exe) or the always accessible mscorlib.dll. This begs the question, "How can I build applications that can load (and reflect over) assemblies not known at compile time?"

■**Source Code** The MyTypeViewer project can be found under the Chapter 14 subdirectory.

Dynamically Loading Assemblies

In the previous chapter, you learned all about how the CLR consults the assembly manifest when probing for an externally referenced assembly. While this is all well and good, there will be many times when you need to load assemblies on the fly programmatically, even if there is no record of said assembly in the manifest. Formally speaking, the act of loading external assemblies on demand is known as a *dynamic load*.

System.Reflection defines a class named Assembly. Using this type, you are able to dynamically load an assembly as well as discover properties about the assembly itself. Using the Assembly type, you are able to dynamically load private or shared assemblies, as well as load an assembly located at an arbitrary location. In essence, the Assembly class provides methods (Load() and LoadFrom() in particular) that allow you to programmatically supply the same sort of information found in a client-side *.config file.

To illustrate dynamic loading, create a brand-new console application named ExternalAssemblyReflector. Your task is to construct a Main() method that prompts for the friendly name of an assembly to load dynamically. You will pass the Assembly reference into a helper method named DisplayTypes(), which will simply print the names of each class, interface, structure, enumeration, and delegate it contains. The code is refreshingly simple:

```vb
Imports System.Reflection

Module Program
  Sub Main()
    Console.WriteLine("***** External Assembly Viewer *****")
    Dim asmName As String = ""
    Dim userIsDone As Boolean = False
    Dim asm As Assembly = Nothing
    Do
      Console.WriteLine()
      Console.WriteLine("Enter an assembly to evaluate")
      Console.Write("or enter Q to quit: ")

      ' Get name of assembly.
      asmName = Console.ReadLine()

      ' Does user want to quit?
      If asmName.ToUpper = "Q" Then
        userIsDone = True
        Exit Do
      End If

      Try ' Try to load assembly.
        asm = Assembly.Load(asmName)
        DisplayTypesInAsm(asm)
      Catch
        Console.WriteLine("Sorry, can't find assembly named {0}.", asmName)
      End Try
    Loop While Not userIsDone
  End Sub

  Sub DisplayTypesInAsm(ByVal asm As Assembly)
    Console.WriteLine()
    Console.WriteLine("***** Types in Assembly *****")
    Console.WriteLine("->{0}", asm.FullName)
    Dim types As Type() = asm.GetTypes()
    For Each t As Type In types
      Console.WriteLine("Type: {0}", t)
    Next
    Console.WriteLine("")
  End Sub
End Module
```

Notice that the shared `Assembly.Load()` method has been passed only the friendly name of the assembly you are interested in loading into memory. Thus, if you wish to reflect over `CarLibrary.dll`, you will need to copy the `CarLibrary.dll` binary to the `\bin\Debug` directory of the ExternalAssemblyReflector application to run this program. Once you do, you will find output similar to Figure 14-4.

Figure 14-4. *Reflecting on the external* CarLibrary *assembly*

■Note If you wish to make ExternalAssemblyReflector more flexible, load the external assembly using
Assembly.LoadFrom() rather than Assembly.Load(). By doing so, you can enter an absolute path to the
assembly you wish to view (e.g., C:\MyApp\MyAsm.dll).

■Source Code The ExternalAssemblyReflector project is included in the Chapter 14 subdirectory.

Reflecting on Shared Assemblies

As you may suspect, Assembly.Load() has been overloaded a number of times. One variation of the
Assembly.Load() method allows you to specify a culture value (for localized assemblies) as well as
a version number and public key token value (for shared assemblies).

Collectively speaking, the set of items identifying an assembly is termed the *display name*. The
format of a display name is a comma-delimited string of name/value pairs that begins with the friendly
name of the assembly, followed by optional qualifiers (that may appear in any order). Here is the
template to follow (optional items appear in parentheses):

```
Name (,Culture = culture token) (,Version = major.minor.build.revision)
(,PublicKeyToken = public key token)
```

When you're crafting a display name, the convention PublicKeyToken=null indicates that
binding and matching against a non–strongly-named assembly is required. Additionally, Culture=""
(or Culture+"neutral") indicates matching against the default culture of the target machine, for example:

```
' Load version 1.0.0.0 of CarLibrary using the default culture.
Dim a As Assembly = Assembly.Load( _
"CarLibrary, Version=1.0.0.0, PublicKeyToken=null, Culture=""")
```

Also be aware that the System.Reflection namespace supplies the AssemblyName type, which allows you to represent the preceding string information in a handy object variable. Typically, this class is used in conjunction with System.Version, which is an OO wrapper around an assembly's version number. Once you have established the display name, it can then be passed into the overloaded Assembly.Load() method:

```
' Make use of AssemblyName to define the display name.
Dim asmName As AssemblyName
asmName = New AssemblyName()
asmName.Name = "CarLibrary"
Dim v As Version = New Version("1.0.0.0")
asmName.Version = v
Dim a As Assembly = Assembly.Load(asmName)
```

To load a shared assembly from the GAC, the Assembly.Load() parameter must specify a publickeytoken value. For example, assume you wish to load version 2.0.0.0 of the System.Windows.Forms.dll assembly provided by the .NET base class libraries. Given that the number of types in this assembly is very large, the following application simply prints out the names of the first 20 types:

```
Imports System.Reflection

Module Program
  Sub DisplayInfo(ByVal a As Assembly)
    Console.WriteLine("***** Info about Assembly *****")
    Console.WriteLine("Loaded from GAC? {0}", a.GlobalAssemblyCache)
    Console.WriteLine("Asm Name: {0}", a.GetName.Name)
    Console.WriteLine("Asm Version: {0}", a.GetName.Version)
    Console.WriteLine("Asm Culture: {0}", a.GetName.CultureInfo.DisplayName)
    Dim types As Type() = a.GetTypes()

    ' Just print out the first 20 types.
    For i As Integer = 0 To 19
      Try
        Console.WriteLine("Type: {0}", types(i))
      Catch ex As Exception
        Console.WriteLine(ex.Message)
      End Try
    Next
  End Sub

  Sub Main()
    Console.WriteLine("***** The Shared Asm Reflector App *****")
    Console.WriteLine()
    Dim displayName As String = _
    "System.Windows.Forms, Version=2.0.0.0, " & _
      "PublicKeyToken=b77a5c561934e089, Culture=neutral"
    Dim asm As Assembly = Assembly.Load(displayName)
    DisplayInfo(asm)
    Console.ReadLine()
  End Sub
End Module
```

Source Code The SharedAssemblyReflector project is included in the Chapter 14 subdirectory.

Sweet! At this point you should understand how to use some of the core items defined within the System.Reflection namespace to discover metadata at runtime. Of course, I realize despite the "cool factor," you likely won't need to build custom object browsers at your place of employment. Do recall, however, that reflection services are the foundation for a number of very common programming activities, including *late binding*.

Understanding Late Binding

Simply put, *late binding* is a technique in which you are able to create an instance of a given type and invoke its members at runtime without having compile-time knowledge of its existence. When you are building an application that binds late to a type in an external assembly, you have no reason to set a reference to the assembly; therefore, the caller's manifest has no direct listing of the assembly.

At first glance, you may not understand the value of late binding. It is true that if you can "bind early" to a type (e.g., set an assembly reference and allocate the type using the VB 2005 New keyword), you should opt to do so. For one reason, early binding allows you to determine errors at compile time, rather than at runtime. Nevertheless, late binding does have a critical role in any extendable application you may be building.

Late Binding with the System.Activator Class

The System.Activator class is the key to the .NET late binding process. Beyond the methods inherited from System.Object, Activator defines only a small set of members, many of which have to do with .NET remoting (see Chapter 20). For our current example, we are only interested in the Activator.CreateInstance() method, which is used to create an instance of a type à la late binding.

This method has been overloaded numerous times to provide a good deal of flexibility. The simplest variation of the CreateInstance() member takes a valid Type object that describes the entity you wish to allocate on the fly. Create a new application named LateBinding, and update the Main() method as follows (be sure to place a copy of CarLibrary.dll in the project's \bin\Debug directory):

```
Imports System.Reflection
Imports System.IO

Module Program
  Sub Main()
    Console.WriteLine("***** Fun with Late Binding *****")
    ' Try to load a local copy of CarLibrary.
    Dim a As Assembly = Nothing
    Try
      a = Assembly.Load("CarLibrary")
    Catch e As FileNotFoundException
      Console.WriteLine(e.Message)
      Return
    End Try

    ' If we found it, get type information about
    ' the minivan and create an instance.
    Dim miniVan As Type = a.GetType("CarLibrary.MiniVan")
    Dim obj As Object = Activator.CreateInstance(miniVan)
    Console.ReadLine()
  End Sub
End Module
```

Notice that the Activator.CreateInstance() method returns a System.Object reference rather than a strongly typed MiniVan. Therefore, if you apply the dot operator on the obj variable, you will fail to see any members of the MiniVan type. At first glance, you may assume you can remedy this problem with an explicit cast; however, this program has no clue what a MiniVan is in the first place, therefore it would be a compiler error to attempt to use CType() to do so (as you must specify the name of the type to convert to).

Remember that the whole point of late binding is to create instances of objects for which there is no compile-time knowledge. Given this, how can you invoke the underlying methods of the MiniVan object stored in the System.Object variable? The answer, of course, is by using reflection.

Invoking Methods with No Parameters

Assume you wish to invoke the TurboBoost() method of the MiniVan. As you recall, this method will set the state of the engine to "dead" and display an informational message box. The first step is to obtain a MethodInfo type for the TurboBoost() method using Type.GetMethod(). From the resulting MethodInfo, you are then able to call MiniVan.TurboBoost using Invoke(). MethodInfo.Invoke() requires you to send in all parameters that are to be given to the method represented by MethodInfo. These parameters are represented by an array of System.Object types (as the parameters for a given method could be any number of various entities).

Given that TurboBoost() does not require any parameters, you can simply pass Nothing. Update your Main() method like so:

```
Sub Main()
    ' Try to load a local copy of CarLibrary.
    ...
    ' If we found it, get type information about
    ' the minivan and create an instance.
    Dim miniVan As Type = a.GetType("CarLibrary.MiniVan")
    Dim obj As Object = Activator.CreateInstance(miniVan)

    ' Get info for TurboBoost.
    Dim mi As MethodInfo = miniVan.GetMethod("TurboBoost")

    ' Invoke method (Nothing for no parameters).
    mi.Invoke(obj, Nothing)
End Sub
```

At this point you are happy to see the message box in Figure 14-5.

Figure 14-5. *Late-bound method invocation*

Invoking Methods with Parameters

To illustrate how to dynamically invoke a method that does take some number of parameters, assume the MiniVan type defines a method named TellChildToBeQuiet() (feel free to update CarLibrary.dll if you so choose):

```
' Quiet down the troops...
Public Sub TellChildToBeQuiet(ByVal kidName As String, _
```

```
    ByVal shameIntensity As Integer)
    For i As Integer = 0 to shameIntensity
        MessageBox.Show("Be quiet {0}!!", kidName)
    Next
End Sub
```

TellChildToBeQuiet() takes two parameters: a String representing the child's name and an Integer representing your current level of frustration. When using late binding, parameters are packaged as an array of System.Objects. To invoke the new method (assuming of course you have updated your MiniVan type), add the following code to your Main() method:

```
' Bind late to a method taking params.
Dim args(1) As Object
args(0) = "Fred"
args(1) = 4
mi = miniVan.GetMethod("TellChildToBeQuiet")
mi.Invoke(obj, args)
```

Hopefully at this point you can see the relationships among reflection, dynamic loading, and late binding. Again, you still may wonder exactly when you might make use of these techniques in your own applications. The conclusion of this chapter should shed light on this question; however, the next topic under investigation is the role of .NET attributes.

■**Note** If Option Strict is disabled (which is the case by default), you can simplify your late binding logic. See the source code for the LateBinding project for details.

■**Source Code** The LateBinding project is included in the Chapter 14 subdirectory.

Understanding Attributed Programming

As illustrated at the beginning of this chapter, one role of a .NET compiler is to generate metadata descriptions for all defined and referenced types. In addition to this standard metadata contained within any assembly, the .NET platform provides a way for programmers to embed additional metadata into an assembly using *attributes*. In a nutshell, attributes are nothing more than code annotations that can be applied to a given type (class, interface, structure, etc.), member (property, method, etc.), assembly, or module.

The idea of annotating code using attributes is not new. COM IDL provided numerous predefined attributes that allowed developers to describe the types contained within a given COM server. However, COM attributes were little more than a set of keywords. If a COM developer needed to create a custom attribute, they could do so, but it was referenced in code by a 128-bit number (GUID), which was cumbersome at best.

Unlike COM IDL attributes (which again were simply keywords), .NET attributes are class types that extend the abstract System.Attribute base class. As you explore the .NET namespaces, you will find many predefined attributes that you are able to make use of in your applications. Furthermore, you are free to build custom attributes to further qualify the behavior of your types by creating a new type deriving from Attribute.

Understand that when you apply attributes in your code, the embedded metadata is essentially useless until another piece of software explicitly reflects over the information. If this is not the case, the blurb of metadata embedded within the assembly is ignored and completely harmless.

Attribute Consumers

As you would guess, the .NET Framework 2.0 SDK ships with numerous utilities that are indeed on the lookout for various attributes. The VB 2005 compiler (vbc.exe) itself has been preprogrammed to discover the presence of various attributes during the compilation cycle. For example, if the VB 2005 compiler encounters the <CLSCompilant> attribute, it will automatically check the attributed item to ensure it is exposing only CLS-compliant constructs. By way of another example, if the VB 2005 compiler discovers an item attributed with the <Obsolete> attribute, it will display a compiler warning in the Visual Studio 2005 Error List window.

In addition to development tools, numerous methods in the .NET base class libraries are preprogrammed to reflect over specific attributes. For example, if you wish to persist the state of an object to a file, all you are required to do is annotate your class with the <Serializable> attribute. If the Serialize() method of the BinaryFormatter class encounters this attribute, the object's state data is automatically persisted to a stream as a compact binary format.

The .NET CLR is also on the prowl for the presence of certain attributes. Perhaps the most famous .NET attribute is <WebMethod>. If you wish to expose a method via HTTP requests and automatically encode the method return value as XML, simply apply <WebMethod> to the method and the CLR handles the details. Beyond web service development, attributes are critical to the operation of the .NET security system, .NET remoting layer, and COM/.NET interoperability (and so on).

Finally, you are free to build applications that are programmed to reflect over your own custom attributes as well as any attribute in the .NET base class libraries. By doing so, you are essentially able to create a set of "keywords" that are understood by a specific set of assemblies.

Applying Predefined Attributes in VB 2005

As previously mentioned, the .NET base class library provides a number of attributes in various namespaces. Table 14-3 gives a snapshot of some—but by *absolutely* no means all—predefined attributes.

Table 14-3. *A Tiny Sampling of Predefined Attributes*

Attribute	Meaning in Life
<CLSCompliant>	Enforces the annotated item to conform to the rules of the Common Language Specification (CLS). Recall that CLS-compliant types are guaranteed to be used seamlessly across all .NET programming languages.
<DllImport>	Allows .NET code to make calls to any unmanaged C- or C++-based code library, including the API of the underlying operating system. Do note that <DllImport> is not used when communicating with COM-based software.
<Obsolete>	Marks a deprecated type or member. If other programmers attempt to use such an item, they will receive a compiler warning describing the error of their ways.
<Serializable>	Marks a class or structure as being "serializable."
<NonSerialized>	Specifies that a given field in a class or structure should not be persisted during the serialization process.
<WebMethod>	Marks a method as being invokable via HTTP requests and instructs the CLR to serialize the method return value as XML (see Chapter 28 for complete details).

To illustrate the process of applying attributes in VB 2005, assume you wish to build a class named Motorcycle that can be persisted in a binary format. To do so, simply apply the <Serializable> attribute to the class definition. If you have a field that should not be persisted, you may apply the <NonSerialized> attribute:

```
' This class can be saved to a stream.
<Serializable()> _
Public Class Motorcycle
  ' However, this field will not be persisted.
  <NonSerialized()> _
  Private weightOfCurrentPassengers As Single

  ' These fields are still serializable.
  Private hasRadioSystem As Boolean
  Private hasHeadSet As Boolean
  Private hasSissyBar As Boolean
End Class
```

Note An attribute only applies to the "very next" item. For example, the only nonserialized field of the Motorcycle class is weightOfCurrentPassengers. The remaining fields are serializable given that the entire class has been annotated with <Serializable>.

At this point, don't concern yourself with the actual process of object serialization (Chapter 19 examines the details). Just notice that when you wish to apply an attribute, the name of the attribute is sandwiched between angled brackets.

Once this class has been compiled, you can view the extra metadata using ildasm.exe. Notice that these attributes are recorded using the serializable and notserialized tokens (see Figure 14-6).

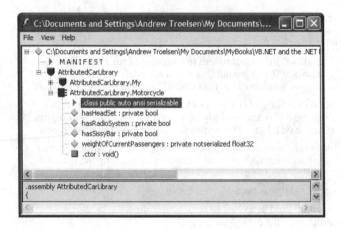

Figure 14-6. *Attributes shown in* ildasm.exe

As you might guess, a single item can be attributed with multiple attributes. Assume you have a legacy VB 2005 class type (HorseAndBuggy) that was marked as serializable, but is now considered obsolete for current development. To apply multiple attributes to a single item, simply use a comma-delimited list:

```
<Serializable(), _
Obsolete("This class is obsolete, use another vehicle!")> _
Public Class HorseAndBuggy
End Class
```

As an alternative, you can also apply multiple attributes on a single item by stacking each attribute as follows (the end result is identical):

```
<Serializable()> _
<Obsolete("This class is obsolete, use another vehicle!")> _
Public Class HorseAndBuggy
End Class
```

Specifying Constructor Parameters for Attributes

Notice that the <Obsolete> attribute is able to accept what appears to be a constructor parameter. In terms of VB 2005, the formal definition of the <Obsolete> attribute looks something like so:

```
Public NotInheritable Class ObsoleteAttribute
  Inherits System.Attribute
  Public ReadOnly Property IsError() As Boolean
  End Property
  Public ReadOnly Property Message() As String
  End Property
  Public Sub New(ByVal message As String, ByVal error As Boolean)
  End Sub
  Public Sub New(ByVal message As String)
  End Sub
  Public Sub New()
  End Sub
End Class
```

As you can see, this class indeed defines a number of constructors, including one that receives a System.String. However, do understand that when you supply constructor parameters to an attribute, the attribute is *not* allocated into memory until the parameters are reflected upon by another type or an external tool. The string data defined at the attribute level is simply stored within the assembly as a blurb of metadata.

The <Obsolete> Attribute in Action

Now that HorseAndBuggy has been marked as obsolete, if you were to allocate an instance of this type, you would find that the supplied string data is extracted and displayed within the Error List window of Visual Studio 2005, as you see Figure 14-7.

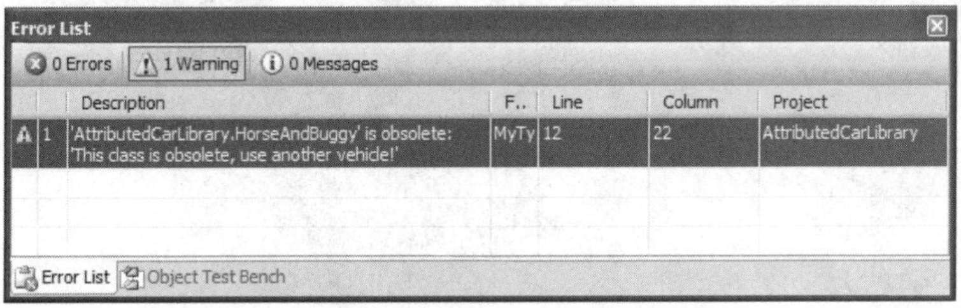

Figure 14-7. *Attributes in action*

In this case, the "other piece of software" that is reflecting on the `<Obsolete>` attribute is the VB 2005 compiler.

VB 2005 Attribute Shorthand Notation

If you were reading closely, you may have noticed that the actual class name of the `<Obsolete>` attribute is *ObsoleteAttribute*, not *Obsolete*. As a naming convention, all .NET attributes (including custom attributes you may create yourself) are suffixed with the `Attribute` token. However, to simplify the process of applying attributes, the VB 2005 language does not require you to type in the `Attribute` suffix. Given this, the following iteration of the `HorseAndBuggy` type is identical to the previous (it just involves a few more keystrokes):

```
<SerializableAttribute()> _
<ObsoleteAttribute("This class is obsolete, use another vehicle!")> _
Public Class HorseAndBuggy
End Class
```

Be aware that this is a courtesy provided by VB 2005. Not all .NET-enabled languages support this feature. In any case, at this point you should hopefully understand the following key points regarding .NET attributes:

- Attributes are classes that derive from `System.Attribute`.

- Attributes result in embedded metadata.

- Attributes are basically useless until another agent reflects upon them.

- Attributes are applied in VB 2005 using angled brackets.

Next up, let's examine how you can build your own custom attributes and a piece of custom software that reflects over the embedded metadata.

Building Custom Attributes

The first step in building a custom attribute is to create a new class deriving from `System.Attribute`. Keeping in step with the automobile theme used throughout this book, assume you have created a brand new VB 2005 class library named `AttributedCarLibrary`. This assembly will define a handful of vehicles (some of which you have already seen in this text), each of which is described using a custom attribute named `VehicleDescriptionAttribute`:

```
' A custom attribute.
Public NotInheritable Class VehicleDescriptionAttribute
  Inherits System.Attribute
  Private msgData As String

  Public Sub New(ByVal description As String)
    msgData = description
  End Sub
  Public Sub New()
  End Sub
  Public Property Description() As String
    Get
      Return msgData
    End Get
    Set(ByVal value As String)
      msgData = value
    End Set
  End Property
End Class
```

As you can see, VehicleDescriptionAttribute maintains a private internal string (msgData) that can be set using a custom constructor and manipulated using a type property (Description). Beyond the fact that this class derived from System.Attribute, there is nothing unique to this class definition.

■**Note** For security reasons, it is considered a .NET best practice to design all custom attributes as NonInheritable.

Applying Custom Attributes

Given that VehicleDescriptionAttribute is derived from System.Attribute, you are now able to annotate your vehicles as you see fit:

```
' Assign description using a 'named property'.
<Serializable()> _
<VehicleDescription(Description:="My rocking Harley")> _
Public Class Motorcycle
...
End Class

<SerializableAttribute()> _
<Obsolete("This class is obsolete, use another vehicle!"), _
VehicleDescription("The old grey Mare she ain't what she used to be...")> _
Public Class HorseAndBuggy
End Class

<VehicleDescription("A very long, slow but feature rich auto")> _
Public Class Winnebago
End Class
```

Notice that the description of Motorcycle is assigned a description using a new bit of attribute-centric syntax termed a *named property*. In the constructor of the first <VehicleDescription> attribute, you set the underlying System.String using a name/value pair. If this attribute is reflected upon by an external agent, the value is fed into the Description property (named property syntax is legal only if the attribute supplies a writable .NET property). In contrast, the HorseAndBuggy and Winnebago types are not making use of named property syntax and are simply passing the string data via the custom constructor.

Once you compile the AttributedCarLibrary assembly, you can make use of ildasm.exe to view the injected metadata descriptions for your type. For example, Figure 14-8 shows an embedded description of the Winnebago type.

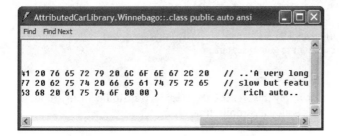

Figure 14-8. *Embedded vehicle description data*

Restricting Attribute Usage

By default, custom attributes can be applied to just about any aspect of your code (methods, classes, properties, and so on). Thus, if it made sense to do so, you could use VehicleDescription to qualify methods, properties, or fields (among other things):

```
<VehicleDescription("A very long, slow, but feature-rich auto")> _
Public Class Winnebago
  <VehicleDescription("My rocking CD player")> _
  Public Sub PlayMusic(bool On)
  End Sub
End Class
```

In some cases, this is exactly the behavior you require. Other times, however, you may want to build a custom attribute that can be applied only to select code elements. If you wish to constrain the scope of a custom attribute, you will need to apply the <AttributeUsage> attribute on the definition of your custom attribute. The <AttributeUsage> attribute allows you to supply any combination of values (via an OR operation) from the AttributeTargets enumeration:

```
' This enumeration defines the possible targets of an attribute.
Public Enum AttributeTargets
  All
  Assembly
  Class
  Constructor
  Delegate
  Enum
  Event
  Field
  Interface
  Method
  Module
  Parameter
  Property
  ReturnValue
  Struct
End Enum
```

Furthermore, <AttributeUsage> also allows you to optionally set a named property (AllowMultiple) that specifies whether the attribute can be applied more than once on the same item. As well, <AttributeUsage> allows you to establish whether the attribute should be inherited by derived classes using the Inherited named property.

To establish that the <VehicleDescription> attribute can be applied only once on a class or structure (and the value is not inherited by derived types), you can update the VehicleDescriptionAttribute definition as follows:

```
<AttributeUsage(AttributeTargets.Class Or _
 AttributeTargets.Struct, AllowMultiple:=False, Inherited:=False)> _
Public NotInheritable Class VehicleDescriptionAttribute
...
End Class
```

With this, if a developer attempted to apply the <VehicleDescription> attribute on anything other than a class or structure, he or she is issued a compile-time error.

■**Tip** Always get in the habit of explicitly marking the usage flags for any custom attribute you may create, as not all .NET programming languages honor the use of unqualified attributes!

Assembly-level (and Module-level) Attributes

It is also possible to apply attributes on all types within a given module or all modules within a given assembly using the `<Module:>` and `<Assembly:>` tags, respectively. For example, assume you wish to ensure that every public member of every public type defined within your assembly is CLS-compliant. To do so, simply add the following line in any one of your VB 2005 source code files (do note that assembly-level attributes must be outside the scope of a namespace definition):

```
' Enforce CLS compliance for all public types in this assembly.
<Assembly:System.CLSCompliantAttribute(True)>
```

If you now add a bit of code that falls outside the CLS specification (such as an exposed field of unsigned data) like so:

```
' UInt64 types don't jibe with the CLS.
<VehicleDescription("A very long, slow but feature rich auto")> _
Public Class Winnebago
   Public notCompliant As UInt64
End Class
```

you are issued a compiler error.

The Visual Studio 2005 AssemblyInfo.vb File

Visual Studio 2005 projects always contain a file named `AssemblyInfo.vb`; however, by default this file is not made visible until you click the Show All Files button of the Solution Explorer. Once you do, you can expand the My Project icon to reveal this file, as shown in Figure 14-9.

Figure 14-9. *The* AssemblyInfo.vb *file*

This file is a handy place to put attributes that are to be applied at the assembly level. Table 14-4 lists some assembly-level attributes to be aware of.

Table 14-4. *Select Assembly-level Attributes*

Attribute	Meaning in Life
AssemblyCompany	Holds basic company information
AssemblyCopyright	Holds any copyright information for the product or assembly
AssemblyCulture	Provides information on what cultures or languages the assembly supports
AssemblyDescription	Holds a friendly description of the product or modules that make up the assembly
AssemblyKeyFile	Specifies the name of the file containing the key pair used to sign the assembly (i.e., establish a shared name)
AssemblyOperatingSystem	Provides information on which operating system the assembly was built to support
AssemblyProcessor	Provides information on which processors the assembly was built to support
AssemblyProduct	Provides product information
AssemblyTrademark	Provides trademark information
AssemblyVersion	Specifies the assembly's version information, in the format *<major.minor.build.revision>*

■**Note** While you are free to update `AssemblyInfo.vb` directly, be aware that each of these attributes can be set using various areas of the My Project GUI editor (in fact, this is the preferred manner to establish assembly-level attributes). To do so, open the My Project editor, select the Application tab and click the Assembly Information button.

■**Source Code** The AttributedCarLibrary project is included in the Chapter 14 subdirectory.

Reflecting on Attributes Using Early Binding

As mentioned in this chapter, an attribute is quite useless until some piece of software reflects over its data. Once a given attribute has been discovered, that piece of software can take whatever course of action necessary. Now, like any application, this "other piece of software" could discover the presence of a custom attribute using either early binding or late binding. If you wish to make use of early binding, you'll require the client application to have a compile-time definition of the attribute in question (VehicleDescriptionAttribute in this case). Given that the AttributedCarLibrary assembly has defined this custom attribute as a public class, early binding is the best option.

To illustrate the process of reflecting on custom attributes, create a new VB 2005 console application named VehicleDescriptionReader. Next, set a reference to the AttributedCarLibrary assembly. Finally, update your initial *.cs file with the following code:

```
Imports AttributedCarLibrary

' Reflecting on custom attributes using early binding.
Module Program
  Sub Main()
    ' Get a Type representing the Winnebago.
    Dim t As Type = GetType(Winnebago)

    ' Get all attributes on the Winnebago.
    Dim customAtts As Object() = t.GetCustomAttributes(False)
```

```
    ' Print the description.
    Console.WriteLine("***** Value of VehicleDescriptionAttribute *****")
    For Each v As VehicleDescriptionAttribute In customAtts
      Console.WriteLine()
      Console.WriteLine("->{0}.", v.Description)
    Next
    Console.ReadLine()
  End Sub
End Module
```

As the name implies, Type.GetCustomAttributes() returns an object array that represents all the attributes applied to the member represented by the Type (the Boolean parameter controls whether the search should extend up the inheritance chain). Once you have obtained the list of attributes, iterate over each VehicleDescriptionAttribute class and print out the value obtained by the Description property.

Source Code The VehicleDescriptionAttributeReader application is included under the Chapter 14 subdirectory.

Reflecting on Attributes Using Late Binding

The previous example made use of early binding to print out the vehicle description data for the Winnebago type. This was possible due to the fact that the VehicleDescriptionAttribute class type was defined as a public member in the AttributedCarLibrary assembly. It is also possible to make use of dynamic loading and late binding to reflect over attributes.

Create a new project called VehicleDescriptionReaderLB (where LB stands for "late binding") and copy AttributedCarLibrary.dll to the project's \bin\Debug directory. Now, update your Main() method as follows:

```
Imports System.Reflection

Module Project
  Sub Main()
    Console.WriteLine("***** Descriptions of Your Vehicles *****")
    Console.WriteLine()

    ' Load the local copy of AttributedCarLibrary.
    Dim asm As Assembly = Assembly.Load("AttributedCarLibrary")

    ' Get type info of VehicleDescriptionAttribute.
    Dim vehicleDesc As Type = _
      asm.GetType("AttributedCarLibrary.VehicleDescriptionAttribute")

    ' Get type info of the Description property.
    Dim propDesc As PropertyInfo = vehicleDesc.GetProperty("Description")

    ' Get all types in the assembly.
    Dim types As Type() = asm.GetTypes()

    ' Iterate over each attribute.
    For Each t As Type In types
      Dim objs As Object() = t.GetCustomAttributes(vehicleDesc, False)
      For Each o As Object In objs
        Console.WriteLine("-> {0} : {1}", t.Name, propDesc.GetValue(o, Nothing))
      Next
    Next
```

```
      Console.ReadLine()
   End Sub
End Module
```

If you were able to follow along with the examples in this chapter, this `Main()` method should be (more or less) self-explanatory. The only point of interest is the use of the `PropertyInfo.GetValue()` method, which is used to trigger the property's get method. Figure 14-10 shows the output.

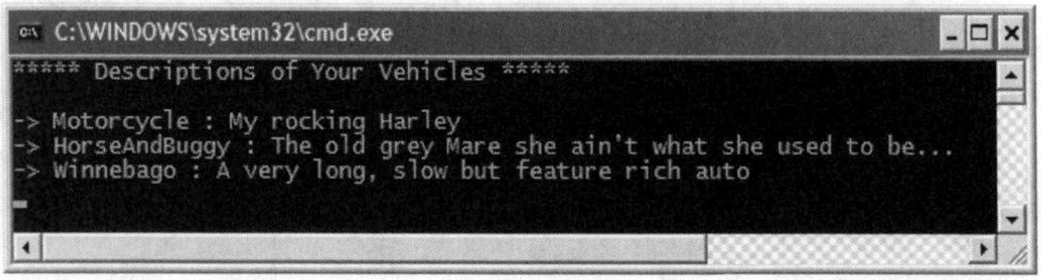

Figure 14-10. *Reflecting on attributes using late binding*

■ **Source Code** The VehicleDescriptionReaderLB application is included under the Chapter 14 subdirectory.

Putting Reflection, Late Binding, and Custom Attributes in Perspective

Even though you have seen numerous examples of these techniques in action, you may still be wondering when to make use of reflection, dynamic loading, late binding, and custom attributes in your programs. To be sure, these topics can seem a bit on the academic side of programming (which may or may not be a bad thing, depending on your point of view). To help map these topics to a real-world situation, you need a solid example. Assume for the moment that you are on a programming team that is building an application with the following requirement:

- The product must be extendable by the use of additional third-party tools.

So, what exactly is meant by *extendable*? Consider Visual Studio 2005. When this application was developed, various "hooks" were inserted to allow other software vendors to snap custom modules into the IDE. Obviously, the Visual Studio 2005 team had no way to set references to external .NET assemblies it had not programmed (thus, no early binding), so how exactly would an application provide the required hooks?

- First, an extendable application must provide some input vehicle to allow the user to specify the module to plug in (such as a dialog box or command-line flag). This requires *dynamic loading*.

- Second, an extendable application must be able to determine whether the module supports the correct functionality (such as a set of required interfaces) in order to be plugged into the environment. This requires *reflection*.

- Finally, an extendable application must obtain a reference to the required infrastructure (e.g., the interface types) and invoke the members to trigger the underlying functionality. This often requires *late binding*.

Simply put, if the extendable application has been preprogrammed to query for specific interfaces, it is able to determine at runtime whether the type can be activated. Once this verification test has been passed, the type in question may support additional interfaces that provide a polymorphic fabric to their functionality. This is the exact approach taken by the Visual Studio 2005 team, and despite what you may be thinking, it is not at all difficult.

Building an Extendable Application

In the sections that follow, I will take you through a complete example that illustrates the process of building an extendable Windows Forms application that can be augmented by the functionality of external assemblies. What I will not do at this point is comment on the process of programming Windows Forms applications (Chapters 21, 22, and 23 will tend to that chore). So, if you are not familiar with the process of building Windows Forms applications, feel free to simply open up the downloadable sample code and follow along (or build a console-based alternative). To serve as a road map, our extendable application entails the following assemblies:

- CommonSnappableTypes.dll: This assembly contains type definitions that will be implemented by each snap-in object as well as referenced by the extendable Windows Forms application.

- VbNetSnapIn.dll: A snap-in written in Visual Basic 2005 that leverages the types of CommonSnappableTypes.dll.

- CSharpSnapIn.dll: A snap-in written in C# that leverages the types of CommonSnappableTypes.dll.

- MyPluggableApp.exe: This Windows Forms application will be the entity that may be extended by the functionality of each snap-in. Again, this application will make use of dynamic loading, reflection, and late binding to dynamically gain the functionality of assemblies it has no prior knowledge of.

Building CommonSnappableTypes.dll

The first order of business is to create an assembly that contains the types that a given snap-in must leverage to be plugged into your expandable Windows Forms application. The CommonSnappableTypes class library project defines two types:

```
Public Interface IAppFunctionality
  Sub DoIt()
End Interface

<AttributeUsage(AttributeTargets.Class)> _
Public NotInheritable Class CompanyInfoAttribute
  Inherits System.Attribute
  Private companyName As String
  Private companyUrl As String

  Public Sub New()
  End Sub
  Public Property Name() As String
    Get
      Return companyName
    End Get
    Set(ByVal value As String)
      companyName = value
    End Set
  End Property
  Public Property Url() As String
```

```
    Get
        Return companyUrl
    End Get
    Set(ByVal value As String)
        companyUrl = value
    End Set
  End Property
End Class
```

The IAppFunctionality interface provides a polymorphic interface for all snap-ins that can be consumed by the extendable Windows Forms application. Of course, as this example is purely illustrative in nature, you supply a single method named DoIt(). To map this to a real-world example, imagine an interface (or a set of interfaces) that allows the snapper to generate scripting code, render an image onto the application's toolbox, or integrate into the main menu of the hosting application.

The CompanyInfoAttribute type is a custom attribute that will be applied on any class type that wishes to be snapped into the container. As you can tell by the definition of this class, <CompanyInfo> allows the developer of the snap-in to provide some basic details about the component's point of origin.

Building the VB 2005 Snap-In

Next up, you need to create a type that implements the IAppFunctionality interface. Again, to focus on the overall design of an extendable application, a trivial type is in order. Assume a new VB 2005 code library named VbNetSnapIn that defines a class type named VbNetSnapIn. Given that this class must make use of the types defined in CommonSnappableTypes, be sure to set a reference to this binary (as well as System.Windows.Forms.dll to display a noteworthy message). This being said, here is the code:

```
Imports System.Windows.Forms
Imports CommonSnappableTypes

<CompanyInfo(Name:="Chucky's Software", Url:="www.ChuckySoft.com")> _
Public Class VbNetSnapIn
  Implements IAppFunctionality
  Public Sub DoIt() Implements CommonSnappableTypes.IAppFunctionality.DoIt
    MessageBox.Show("You have just used the VB 2005 snap in!")
  End Sub
End Class
```

Building the C# Snap-In

Now, to simulate the role of a third-party vendor who prefers C# over VB 2005, create a new C# code library (CSharpSnapIn) that references the same external assemblies as the previous VbNetSnapIn project. The code is (again) intentionally simple:

```
using System;
using CommonSnappableTypes;
using System.Windows.Forms;

namespace CSharpSnapIn
{
  [CompanyInfo(Name = "Intertech Training",
  Url = "www.intertechtraining.com")]
  public class TheCSharpModule : IAppFunctionality
  {
    void IAppFunctionality.DoIt()
    {
```

```
      MessageBox.Show("You have just used the C# snap in!");
    }
  }
}
```

Without getting hung up on the syntax of the C# language, do notice that applying attributes in the syntax of C# requires square brackets ([ ]) rather than angled brackets (< >).

Building an Extendable Windows Forms Application

The final step of this example is to create a new Windows Forms application (MyExtendableApp) that allows the user to select a snap-in using a standard Windows Open dialog box. Next, set a reference to the CommonSnappableTypes.dll assembly, but *not* the CSharpSnapIn.dll or VbNetSnapIn.dll code libraries. Remember that the whole goal of this application is to make use of late binding and reflection to determine the "snapability" of independent binaries created by third-party vendors.

Again, I won't bother to examine all the details of Windows Forms development at this point in the text. However, assuming you have placed a MenuStrip component onto the Form template, define a topmost menu item named Tools that provides a single submenu named Snap In Module. This Windows Form will also contain a ListBox type (which I renamed as lstLoadedSnapIns) that will be used to display the names of each snap-in loaded by the user. Figure 14-11 shows the final GUI.

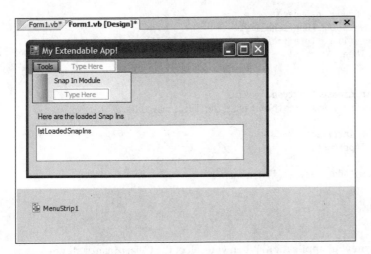

Figure 14-11. *Final GUI for MyExtendableApp*

The code that handles the Click event of the Tools ➤ Snap In Module menu item (which may be created simply by double-clicking the menu item from the design-time editor) displays a File Open dialog box and extracts the path to the selected file. This path is then sent into a helper function named LoadExternalModule() for processing. This method will return False when it is unable to find a class implementing IAppFunctionality:

```
Private Sub SnapInModuleToolStripMenuItem_Click(ByVal sender As System.Object, _
  ByVal e As System.EventArgs) Handles SnapInModuleToolStripMenuItem.Click
    ' Allow user to select an assembly to load.
    Dim dlg As OpenFileDialog = New OpenFileDialog()

    If dlg.ShowDialog = Windows.Forms.DialogResult.OK Then
      If LoadExternalModule(dlg.FileName) = False Then
        MessageBox.Show("Nothing implements IAppFunctionality!")
```

```
        End If
    End If
End Sub
```

The `LoadExternalModule()` method performs the following tasks:

- Dynamically loads the assembly into memory
- Determines whether the assembly contains a type implementing `IAppFunctionality`

If a type implementing `IAppFunctionality` is found, the `DoIt()` method is called, and the fully qualified name of the type is added to the `ListBox` (note that the `For` loop will iterate over all types in the assembly to account for the possibility that a single assembly has multiple snap-in objects):

```
Private Function LoadExternalModule(ByVal path As String) As Boolean
  Dim foundSnapIn As Boolean = False
  Dim itfAppFx As IAppFunctionality

  ' Dynamically load the selected assembly.
  Dim theSnapInAsm As Assembly = Assembly.LoadFrom(path)

  ' Get all types in assembly.
  Dim theTypes As Type() = theSnapInAsm.GetTypes()

  For i As Integer = 0 To UBound(theTypes)
    ' See if a type implements IAppFunctionality.
    Dim t As Type = theTypes(i).GetInterface("IAppFunctionality")
    If Not (t Is Nothing) Then
      foundSnapIn = True

      ' Use late binding to create the type.
      Dim o As Object = theSnapInAsm.CreateInstance(theTypes(i).FullName)

      ' Call DoIt() off the interface.
      itfAppFx = CType(o, IAppFunctionality)
      itfAppFx.DoIt()
      lstLoadedSnapIns.Items.Add(theTypes(i).FullName)
    End If
  Next
  Return foundSnapIn
End Function
```

At this point, you can run your application. When you select the `CSharpSnapIn.dll` or `VbNetSnapIn.dll` assemblies, you should see the correct message displayed. Figure 14-12 shows one possible run of this Windows Forms application.

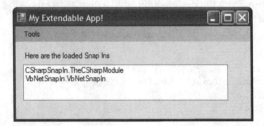

Figure 14-12. *Snapping in external assemblies*

The final task is to display the metadata provided by the <CompanyInfo>. To do so, simply update LoadExternalModule() to call a new helper function named DisplayCompanyData() before exiting the If scope. Notice this method takes a single System.Type parameter.

```
Private Function LoadExternalModule(ByVal path As String) As Boolean
...
  If Not (t Is Nothing) Then
...
    ' Show company info.
    DisplayCompanyData(theTypes(i))
  End If
...
End Function
```

Using the incoming type, simply reflect over the <CompanyInfo> attribute:

```
Private Sub DisplayCompanyData(ByVal t As Type)
  ' Get <CompanyInfo> type.
  Dim customAtts As Object() = t.GetCustomAttributes(False)
  For Each c As CompanyInfoAttribute In customAtts
    ' Show data.
    MessageBox.Show(c.Url, String.Format _
      ("More info about {0} can be found at", c.Name))
  Next
End Sub
```

Excellent! That wraps up the example application. I hope at this point you can see that the topics presented in this chapter can be quite helpful in the real world and are not limited to the tool builders of the world.

Source Code The CommonSnappableTypes, CSharpSnapIn, VbNetSnapIn, and MyExtendableApp applications are all included under the Chapter 14 subdirectory.

Summary

Reflection is a very powerful aspect of a robust OO environment. In the world of .NET, the keys to reflection services revolve around the System.Type class and the System.Reflection namespace. As you have seen, reflection is the process of placing a type under the magnifying glass at runtime to understand the who, what, where, when, why, and how of a given item.

Late binding is the process of creating a type and invoking its members without prior knowledge of the specific names of said members. As shown during this chapter's extendable application example, this is a very powerful technique used by tool builders as well as tool consumers. This chapter also examined the role of attribute-based programming. When you adorn your types with attributes, the result is the augmentation of the underlying assembly metadata.

■ ■ ■

## CHAPTER 15

Processes, AppDomains, Contexts, and CLR Hosts

In the previous two chapters, you examined the steps taken by the CLR to resolve the location of an externally referenced assembly as well as the role of .NET metadata. In this chapter, you'll drill deeper into the details of how an assembly is hosted by the CLR and come to understand the relationship between processes, application domains, and object contexts.

In a nutshell, *application domains* (or, simply, *AppDomains*) are logical subdivisions within a given process that host a set of related .NET assemblies. As you will see, an AppDomain is further subdivided into contextual boundaries, which are used to group together like-minded .NET objects. Using the notion of context, the CLR is able to ensure that objects with special runtime requirements are handled appropriately.

Once you have come to understand how an assembly is hosted by the CLR, it's time to address the next obvious question: what is hosting the CLR? As you recall from Chapter 1, the CLR itself is represented (in part) by mscoree.dll. When you launch an executable assembly, mscoree.dll is loaded automatically; however, as you will see, there are actually a number of transparent steps happening in the background.

Reviewing Traditional Win32 Processes

The concept of a "process" has existed within Windows-based operating systems well before the release of the .NET platform. Simply put, a *process* is the term used to describe the set of resources (such as external code libraries and the primary thread) and the necessary memory allocations used by a running application. For each *.exe loaded into memory, the OS creates a separate and isolated process for use during its lifetime. Using this approach to application isolation, the result is a much more robust and stable runtime environment, given that the failure of one process does not affect the functioning of another.

Now, every Win32 process is assigned a unique process identifier (PID) and may be independently loaded and unloaded by the OS as necessary (as well as programmatically using Win32 API calls). As you may be aware, the Processes tab of the Windows Task Manager utility (activated via the Ctrl+Shift+Esc keystroke combination) allows you to view various statistics regarding the processes running on a given machine, including its PID and image name, as you see Figure 15-1.

Figure 15-1. *Windows Task Manager*

■**Note** If you do not see a PID column listed in Task Manager, simply select View ➤ Select Columns and check the PID box.

An Overview of Threads

Every Win32 process has exactly one main "thread" that functions as the entry point for the application. The next chapter examines how to create additional threads and thread-safe code using the System.Threading namespace; however, to facilitate the topics presented here, we need a few working definitions. First of all, a *thread* is a path of execution within a process. Formally speaking, the first thread created by a process's entry point (the Main() method) is termed the *primary thread*.

Processes that contain a single primary thread of execution are intrinsically *thread-safe*, given the fact that there is only one thread that can access the data in the application at a given time. However, a single-threaded application (especially one that is GUI-based) may appear a bit unresponsive to the user if this single thread is performing a complex operation (such as printing out a lengthy text file, performing an exotic calculation, or attempting to connect to a remote server located thousands of miles away).

Given this potential drawback of single-threaded applications, the Win32 API makes it possible for the primary thread to spawn additional secondary threads using a handful of Win32 API functions such as CreateThread(). Each thread (primary or secondary) becomes a unique path of execution in the process and has concurrent access to all shared points of data.

As you may have guessed, developers typically create additional threads to help improve the program's overall responsiveness. Multithreaded processes provide the illusion that numerous activities are happening at more or less the same time. For example, an application may spawn a worker thread to perform a labor-intensive unit of work (such as printing a large text file). As this secondary thread is churning away, the main thread is still responsive to user input, which gives the entire process the potential of delivering greater performance. However, this may not actually be the case: using too many threads in a single process can actually *degrade* performance, as the CPU must switch between the active threads in the process (which takes time).

In reality, it is always worth keeping in mind that multithreading is most commonly an illusion provided by the OS. Machines that host a single CPU do not have the ability to literally handle multiple threads at the same exact time. Rather, a single CPU will execute one thread for a unit of time (called a *time slice*) based on the thread's priority level. When a thread's time slice is up, the existing thread is suspended to allow another thread to perform its business. For a thread to remember what was happening before it was kicked out of the way, each thread is given the ability to write to Thread Local Storage (TLS) and is provided with a separate call stack, as illustrated in Figure 15-2.

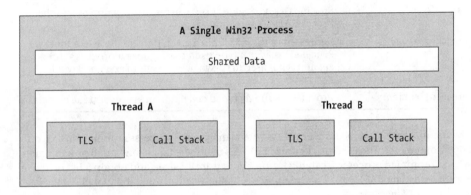

Figure 15-2. *The Win32 process/thread relationship*

If the subject of threads is new to you, don't sweat the details (again, see Chapter 16). At this point, just remember that a thread is a unique path of execution within a Win32 process. Every process has a primary thread (created via the executable's Main() method) and may contain additional threads that have been programmatically created.

■**Note** Newer Intel CPUs have a feature called *Hyper-Threading Technology* that allows a single CPU to handle multiple threads simultaneously under certain circumstances. See http://www.intel.com/info/hyperthreading for more details.

Interacting with Processes Under the .NET Platform

Although processes and threads are nothing new, the manner in which we interact with these primitives under the .NET platform has changed quite a bit (for the better). To pave the way to understanding the world of building multithreaded assemblies, let's begin by checking out how to interact with processes using the .NET base class libraries.

The System.Diagnostics namespace defines a number of types that allow you to programmatically interact with processes and various diagnostic-related types such as the system event log and performance counters. In this chapter, we are only concerned with the process-centric types defined in Table 15-1.

Table 15-1. *Select Members of the* System.Diagnostics *Namespace*

Process-Centric Types of the System.Diagnostics Namespace	Meaning in Life
Process	The Process class provides access to local and remote processes and also allows you to programmatically start and stop processes.
ProcessModule	This type represents a module (*.dll or *.exe) that is loaded into a particular process. Understand that the ProcessModule type can represent *any* module—COM-based, .NET-based, or traditional C-based binaries.
ProcessModuleCollection	Provides a strongly typed collection of ProcessModule objects.
ProcessStartInfo	Specifies a set of values used when starting a process via the Process.Start() method.
ProcessThread	Represents a thread within a given process. Be aware that ProcessThread is a type used to diagnose a process's thread set and is not used to spawn new threads of execution within a process.
ProcessThreadCollection	Provides a strongly typed collection of ProcessThread objects.

The System.Diagnostics.Process type allows you to analyze the processes running on a given machine (local or remote). The Process class also provides members that allow you to programmatically start and terminate processes, establish a process's priority level, and obtain a list of active threads and/or loaded modules within a given process. Table 15-2 lists some (but not all) of the key members of System.Diagnostics.Process.

Table 15-2. *Select Members of the* Process *Type*

Members	Meaning in Life
ExitCode	This property gets the value that the associated process specified when it terminated. Do note that you will be required to handle the Exited event (for asynchronous notification) or call the WaitForExit() method (for synchronous notification) to obtain this value.
ExitTime	This property gets the timestamp associated with the process that has terminated (represented with a DateTime type).
Handle	This property returns the handle associated to the process by the OS.
HandleCount	This property returns the number of handles opened by the process.
Id	This property gets the process ID (PID) for the associated process.
MachineName	This property gets the name of the computer the associated process is running on.
MainModule	This property gets the ProcessModule type that represents the main module for a given process.
MainWindowTitle	MainWindowTitle gets the caption of the main window of the process (if the process does not have a main window, you receive an empty string).
MainWindowHandle	MainWindowHandle gets the underlying handle (represented via a System.IntPtr type) of the associated window. If the process does not have a main window, the IntPtr type is assigned the value System.IntPtr.Zero.
Modules	This property provides access to the strongly typed ProcessModuleCollection type, which represents the set of modules (*.dll or *.exe) loaded within the current process.

Members	Meaning in Life
PriorityBoostEnabled	This property determines whether the OS should temporarily boost the process if the main window has the focus.
PriorityClass	This property allows you to read or change the overall priority for the associated process.
ProcessName	This property gets the name of the process (which, as you would assume, is the name of the application itself).
Responding	This property gets a value indicating whether the user interface of the process is responding (or not).
StartTime	This property gets the time that the associated process was started (via a DateTime type).
Threads	This property gets the set of threads that are running in the associated process (represented via an array of ProcessThread types).
CloseMainWindow()	This method closes a process that has a user interface by sending a close message to its main window.
GetCurrentProcess()	This shared method returns a new Process type that represents the currently active process.
GetProcesses()	This shared method returns an array of new Process components running on a given machine.
Kill()	This method immediately stops the associated process.
Start()	This method starts a process.

Enumerating Running Processes

To illustrate the process of manipulating Process types (pardon the redundancy), assume you have a VB 2005 console application named ProcessManipulator, which defines the following method in the main Module:

```
Public Sub ListAllRunningProcesses()
  ' Get all the processes on the local machine.
  Dim runningProcs As Process() = Process.GetProcesses(".")

  ' Print out PID and name of each process.
  For Each p As Process In runningProcs
    Dim info As String = String.Format("-> PID: {0}" & _
      Microsoft.VisualBasic.Chr(9) & "Name: {1}", p.Id, p.ProcessName)
    Console.WriteLine(info)
  Next
  Console.WriteLine("**********************************")
  Console.WriteLine()
End Sub
```

Notice how the shared Process.GetProcesses() method returns an array of Process types that represent the running processes on the target machine (the dot notation shown here represents the local computer). Once you have obtained the array of Process types, you are able to trigger any of the members seen in Table 15-2. Here, you are simply displaying the PID and the name of each process. Assuming the Main() method has been updated to call ListAllRunningProcesses(), you will see something like the output shown in Figure 15-3.

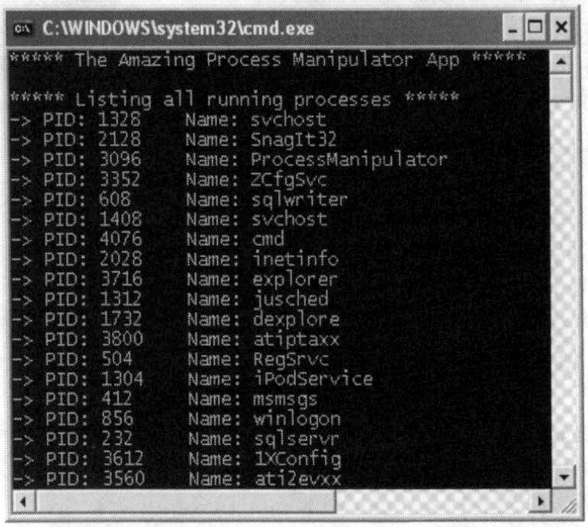

Figure 15-3. *Enumerating running processes*

Investigating a Specific Process

In addition to obtaining a full and complete list of all running processes on a given machine, the shared `Process.GetProcessById()` method allows you to obtain a single `Process` type via the associated PID. If you request access to a nonexistent process ID, an `ArgumentException` exception is thrown. For example, if you were interested in obtaining a `Process` object representing a process with the PID of 987, you could write the following:

```
' If there is no process with the PID of 987, a
' runtime exception will be thrown.
Sub Main()
  Dim theProc As Process
  Try
    theProc = Process.GetProcessById(987)
  Catch   ' Generic catch for used simplicity.
    Console.WriteLine("-> Sorry...bad PID!")
  End Try
End Sub
```

Investigating a Process's Thread Set

The `Process` class type also provides a manner to programmatically investigate the set of all threads currently used by a specific process. The set of threads is represented by the strongly typed `ProcessThreadCollection` collection, which contains some number of individual `ProcessThread` types. To illustrate, consider the implementation of the following additional subroutine:

```
Public Sub EnumThreadsForPid(ByVal pID As Integer)
  Dim theProc As Process
  Try
    theProc = Process.GetProcessById(pID)
  Catch
    Console.WriteLine("-> Sorry...bad PID!")
    Console.WriteLine("**********************************")
    Console.WriteLine()
    Return
  End Try
  Console.WriteLine("Here are the threads used by: {0}", theProc.ProcessName)
```

```
' List out stats for each thread in the specified process.
Dim theThreads As ProcessThreadCollection = theProc.Threads
For Each pt As ProcessThread In theThreads
  Dim info As String = String.Format("-> Thread ID: {0}" _
    & Microsoft.VisualBasic.Chr(9) & "Start Time {1}" & _
    Microsoft.VisualBasic.Chr(9) & "Priority {2}", _
    pt.Id, pt.StartTime.ToShortTimeString, pt.PriorityLevel)
  Console.WriteLine(info)
Next
Console.WriteLine("**********************************")
Console.WriteLine()
End Sub
```

As you can see, the Threads property of the System.Diagnostics.Process type provides access to the ProcessThreadCollection class. Here, you are printing out the assigned thread ID, start time, and priority level of each thread in the process specified by the client. Thus, if you update your program's Main() method to prompt the user for a PID to investigate, as follows:

```
Sub Main()
  Console.WriteLine("***** The Amazing Process Manipulator App *****")
  Console.WriteLine()
  Console.WriteLine("***** Listing all running processes *****")
  ListAllRunningProcesses()

  ' Prompt user for a PID and print out the set of active threads.
  Console.WriteLine("***** Enter PID of process to investigate *****")
  Console.Write("PID: ")
  Dim pID As String = Console.ReadLine()
  Try
    Dim theProcID As Integer = Integer.Parse(pID)
    EnumThreadsForPid(theProcID)
  Catch ex As Exception
    Console.WriteLine(ex.Message)
  End Try
  Console.ReadLine()
End Sub
```

you would find output along the lines of that shown in Figure 15-4.

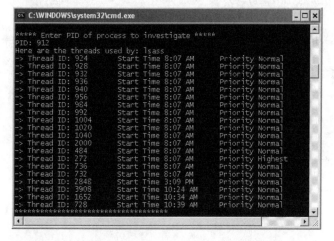

Figure 15-4. *Enumerating the threads within a running process*

The ProcessThread type has additional members of interest beyond Id, StartTime, and PriorityLevel. Table 15-3 documents some members of interest.

Table 15-3. *Select Members of the* ProcessThread *Type*

Member	Meaning in Life
BasePriority	Gets the base priority of the thread
CurrentPriority	Gets the current priority of the thread
Id	Gets the unique identifier of the thread
IdealProcessor	Sets the preferred processor for this thread to run on
PriorityLevel	Gets or sets the priority level of the thread
ProcessorAffinity	Sets the processors on which the associated thread can run
StartAddress	Gets the memory address of the function that the operating system called that started this thread
StartTime	Gets the time that the operating system started the thread
ThreadState	Gets the current state of this thread
TotalProcessorTime	Gets the total amount of time that this thread has spent using the processor
WaitReason	Gets the reason that the thread is waiting

Before you read any further, be very aware that the ProcessThread type is *not* the entity used to create, suspend, or kill threads under the .NET platform. Rather, ProcessThread is a vehicle used to obtain diagnostic information for the active Win32 threads within a running process.

Investigating a Process's Module Set

Next up, let's check out how to iterate over the number of loaded *modules* that are hosted within a given process. Recall that a *module* is a generic name used to describe a given *.dll (or the *.exe itself) that is hosted by a specific process. When you access the ProcessModuleCollection via the Process.Module property, you are able to enumerate over *all modules* hosted within a process: .NET-based, COM-based, or traditional C-based libraries. Ponder the following additional helper function that will enumerate the modules in a specific process based on the PID:

```
Public Sub EnumModsForPid(ByVal pID As Integer)
  Dim theProc As Process
  Try
    theProc = Process.GetProcessById(pID)
  Catch
    Console.WriteLine("-> Sorry...bad PID!")
    Console.WriteLine("***********************************")
    Console.WriteLine()
    Return
  End Try
  Console.WriteLine("Here are the loaded modules for: {0}", theProc.ProcessName)
  Try
    Dim theMods As ProcessModuleCollection = theProc.Modules
    For Each pm As ProcessModule In theMods
      Dim info As String = String.Format("-> Mod Name: {0}", pm.ModuleName)
      Console.WriteLine(info)
    Next
    Console.WriteLine("***********************************")
    Console.WriteLine()
```

```
  Catch
    Console.WriteLine("No mods!")
  End Try
End Sub
```

To see some possible output, let's check out the loaded modules for the process hosting the current console application (ProcessManipulator). To do so, run the application, identify the PID assigned to ProcessManipulator.exe, and pass this value to the EnumModsForPid() method (be sure to update your Main() method accordingly). Once you do, you may be surprised to see the list of *.dlls used for a simple console application. Figure 15-5 shows a test run.

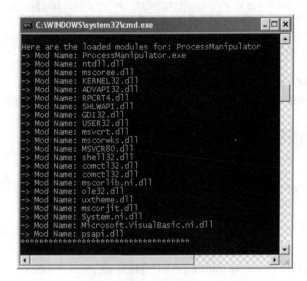

Figure 15-5. *Enumerating the loaded modules within a running process*

Starting and Stopping Processes Programmatically

The final aspects of the System.Diagnostics.Process type examined here are the Start() and Kill() methods. As you can gather by their names, these members provide a way to programmatically launch and terminate a process, respectively. For example, consider the following StartAndKillProcess() method:

```
Public Sub StartAndKillProcess()
  ' Launch Internet Explorer.
  Console.Write("--> Hit a key to launch IE")
  Console.ReadLine()
  Dim ieProc As Process = Process.Start("IExplore.exe", _
  "www.intertechtraining.com")
  Console.Write("--> Hit a key to kill {0}...", ieProc.ProcessName)
  Console.ReadLine()

  ' Kill the iexplorer.exe process.
  Try
    ieProc.Kill()
  Catch  ' In case the user already killed it...
  End Try
End Sub
```

The shared `Process.Start()` method has been overloaded a few times, however. At minimum, you will need to specify the friendly name of the process you wish to launch (such as `IExplore.exe`). This example makes use of a variation of the `Start()` method that allows you to specify any additional arguments to pass into the program's entry point (i.e., the `Main()` method), which in this case is the URL to navigate to upon startup.

Regardless of which version of the `Process.Start()` method you invoke, do note that you are returned a reference to the newly activated process. When you wish to terminate the process, simply call the instance-level `Kill()` method.

Note The `Start()` method also allows you to pass in a `System.Diagnostics.ProcessStartInfo` type to specify additional bits of information regarding how a given process should come to life. See the .NET Framework 2.0 SDK documentation for full details.

Source Code The ProcessManipulator application is included under the Chapter 15 subdirectory.

Understanding .NET Application Domains

Now that you understand the role of Win32 processes and how to interact with them from managed code, we need to investigate the concept of a .NET application domain. Under the .NET platform, assemblies are not hosted directly within a process (as is the case in traditional Win32 applications). Rather, a .NET executable is hosted by a logical partition within a process termed an application domain, or AppDomain. As you will see, a single process may contain multiple application domains, each of which is capable of hosting a .NET application. This additional subdivision of a traditional Win32 process offers several benefits, some of which are as follows:

- AppDomains are a key aspect of the OS-neutral nature of the .NET platform, given that this logical division abstracts away the differences in how an underlying OS represents a loaded executable.

- AppDomains are far less expensive in terms of processing power and memory than a full-blown process. Thus, the CLR is able to load and unload application domains much quicker than a formal process.

- AppDomains provide a deeper level of isolation for hosting a loaded application. If one AppDomain within a process fails, the remaining AppDomains remain functional.

As suggested in the previous hit list, a single process can host any number of AppDomains, each of which is fully and completely isolated from other AppDomains within this process (or any other process). Given this factoid, be very aware that an application running in one AppDomain is unable to obtain data of any kind within another AppDomain unless it makes use of the .NET remoting protocol (which you'll examine in Chapter 20).

While a single process *may* host multiple AppDomains, this is not always the case. At the very least, an OS process will host what is termed the *default application domain*. This specific application domain is automatically created by the CLR at the time the process launches.

After this point, the CLR creates additional application domains on an as-needed basis. If the need should arise (which it most likely *will not* for the majority of your .NET endeavors), you are also able to programmatically create application domains at runtime within a given process using various methods of the `System.AppDomain` class. This class is also useful for low-level control of application domains. Key members of this class are shown in Table 15-4.

Table 15-4. *Select Members of* AppDomain

Member	Meaning in Life
CreateDomain()	This shared method creates a new AppDomain in the current process. Understand that the CLR will create new application domains as necessary, and thus the chance of you absolutely needing to call this member is slim to none.
GetCurrentThreadId()	This shared method returns the ID of the active thread in the current application domain.
Unload()	This is another shared method that allows you to unload a specified AppDomain within a given process.
BaseDirectory	This property returns the base directory used to probe for dependent assemblies.
CreateInstance()	This method creates an instance of a specified type defined in a specified assembly file.
ExecuteAssembly()	This method executes an assembly within an application domain, given its file name.
GetAssemblies()	This method gets the set of .NET assemblies that have been loaded into this application domain (COM-based and other unmanaged binaries are ignored).
Load()	This method is used to dynamically load an assembly into the current application domain.

In addition, the AppDomain type also defines a small set of events that correspond to various aspects of an application domain's life cycle, as shown in Table 15-5.

Table 15-5. *Events of the* AppDomain *Type*

Event	Meaning in Life
AssemblyLoad	Occurs when an assembly is loaded
AssemblyResolve	Occurs when the resolution of an assembly fails
DomainUnload	Occurs when an AppDomain is about to be unloaded
ProcessExit	Occurs on the default application domain when the default application domain's parent process exits
ResourceResolve	Occurs when the resolution of a resource fails
TypeResolve	Occurs when the resolution of a type fails
UnhandledException	Occurs when an exception is not caught by an event handler

Enumerating a Process's AppDomains

To illustrate how to interact with .NET application domains programmatically, assume you have a new VB 2005 console application named AppDomainManipulator that defines a method named PrintAllAssembliesInAppDomain(). This method makes use of AppDomain.GetAssemblies() to obtain a list of all .NET binaries hosted within the application domain in question.

This list is represented by an array of System.Reflection.Assembly types, and thus you are required to use the System.Reflection namespace (see Chapter 14). Once you acquire the assembly array, you iterate over the array and print out the friendly name and version of each module:

```
Public Sub PrintAllAssembliesInAppDomain(ByVal ad As AppDomain)
  Dim loadedAssemblies() As Assembly = ad.GetAssemblies()
```

```
Console.WriteLine("***** Here are the assemblies loaded in {0} *****", _
  ad.FriendlyName)

' Remember!  We need to import System.Reflection to use
' the Assembly type.
For Each a As Assembly In loadedAssemblies
  Console.WriteLine("-> Name: {0}", a.GetName.Name)
  Console.WriteLine("-> Version: {0}", a.GetName.Version)
Next
End Sub
```

Now let's update the Main() method to obtain a reference to the current application domain before invoking PrintAllAssembliesInAppDomain(), using the AppDomain.CurrentDomain property. To make things a bit more interesting, notice that the Main() method launches a Windows Forms message box to force the CLR to load the System.Windows.Forms.dll, System.Drawing.dll, and System.dll assemblies (so be sure to set a reference to these assemblies and update your Imports statements appropriately):

```
Sub Main()
  Console.WriteLine("***** The Amazing AppDomain app *****")

  ' Get info for current AppDomain.
  Dim defaultAD As AppDomain = AppDomain.CurrentDomain()
  MessageBox.Show("Hello")
  PrintAllAssembliesInAppDomain(defaultAD)
  Console.ReadLine()
End Sub
```

Figure 15-6 shows the output (your version numbers may differ).

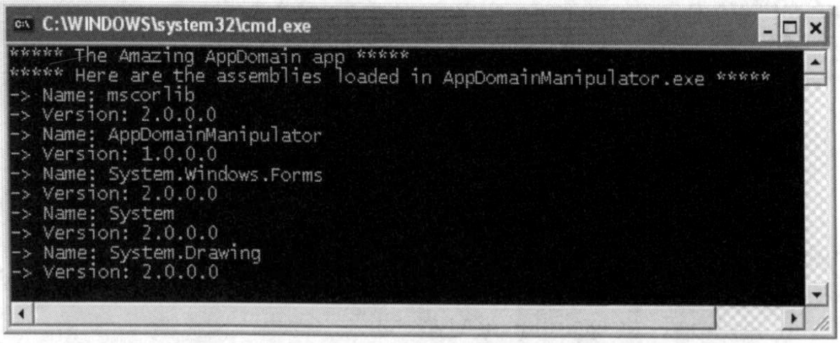

Figure 15-6. *Enumerating assemblies within the current application domain*

Programmatically Creating New AppDomains

Recall that a single process is capable of hosting multiple AppDomains. While it is true that you will seldom (if ever) need to manually create AppDomains in code, you are able to do so via the shared CreateDomain() method. As you would guess, AppDomain.CreateDomain() has been overloaded a number of times. At minimum, you will specify the friendly name of the new application domain, as shown here:

```
Sub Main()
...
  ' Programmatically make a new appdomain.
  Dim anotherAD As AppDomain = AppDomain.CreateDomain("SecondAppDomain")
```

```
  PrintAllAssembliesInAppDomain(anotherAD)
  Console.ReadLine()
End Sub
```

Now, if you run the application again, notice that the System.Windows.Forms.dll, System. Drawing.dll, and System.dll assemblies are only loaded within the default application domain, as shown in Figure 15-7. This may seem counterintuitive if you have a background in traditional unmanaged Win32 (as you might suspect, both application domains have access to the same assembly set). Recall, however, that an assembly loads into an *application domain*, not directly into the process itself.

Figure 15-7. *A single process with two application domains*

Next, notice how the SecondAppDomain application domain automatically contains its own copy of mscorlib.dll, as this key assembly is automatically loaded by the CLR for each and every application domain. This begs the question, "How can I programmatically load an assembly into an application domain?" Answer: with the AppDomain.Load() method (or, alternatively, AppDomain. ExecuteAssembly()). Assuming you have copied CarLibrary.dll to the application directory of AppDomainManipulator.exe, you may load CarLibrary.dll into the SecondAppDomain AppDomain like so:

```
Sub Main()
...
  ' Programmatically make a new appdomain.
  Dim anotherAD As AppDomain = AppDomain.CreateDomain("SecondAppDomain")

  ' Load CarLibrary.dll into this new appdomain.
  anotherAD.Load("CarLibrary")
  PrintAllAssembliesInAppDomain(anotherAD)
  Console.ReadLine()
End Sub
```

To solidify the relationship between processes, application domains, and assemblies, Figure 15-8 diagrams the internal composition of the AppDomainManipulator.exe process just constructed.

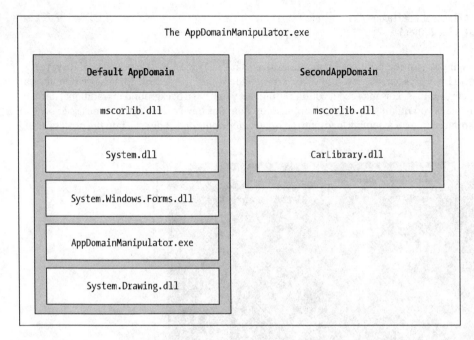

Figure 15-8. *The* AppDomainManipulator.exe *process under the hood*

Programmatically Unloading AppDomains

It is important to point out that the CLR does not permit unloading individual .NET assemblies. However, using the AppDomain.Unload() method, you are able to selectively unload a given application domain from its hosting process. When you do so, the application domain will unload each assembly in turn.

Recall that the AppDomain type defines a small set of events, one of which is DomainUnload. This event is fired when a (non-default) AppDomain is unloaded from the containing process. Another event of interest is the ProcessExit event, which is fired when the default application domain is unloaded from the process (which obviously entails the termination of the process itself). Thus, if you wish to programmatically unload anotherAD from the AppDomainManipulator.exe process and be notified when the associated application domain is torn down, you are able to write the following event logic:

```
Sub Main()
...
    ' Hook into DomainUnload event.
    AddHandler anotherAD.DomainUnload, AddressOf anotherAD_DomainUnload

    ' Now unload anotherAD.
    AppDomain.Unload(anotherAD)
    Console.ReadLine()
End Sub
```

Notice that the `DomainUnload` event works in conjunction with the `System.EventHandler` delegate, and therefore the format of `anotherAD_DomainUnload()` takes the following arguments:

```
Public Sub anotherAD_DomainUnload(ByVal sender As Object, ByVal e As EventArgs)
  Console.WriteLine("***** Unloaded anotherAD! *****")
End Sub
```

If you wish to be notified when the default AppDomain is unloaded, modify your `Main()` method to handle the `ProcessEvent` event of the default application domain:

```
Sub Main()
...
  ' Hook into DomainUnload event.
  AddHandler anotherAD.DomainUnload, AddressOf anotherAD_DomainUnload
  AppDomain.Unload(anotherAD)

  ' Hook into ProcessExit.
  AddHandler defaultAD.ProcessExit, AddressOf defaultAD_ProcessExit
  Console.ReadLine()
End Sub
```

and define an appropriate event handler:

```
Private Sub defaultAD_ProcessExit(ByVal sender As Object, ByVal e As EventArgs)
  Console.WriteLine("***** Unloaded defaultAD! *****")
End Sub
```

■**Source Code** The AppDomainManipulator project is included under the Chapter 15 subdirectory.

Understanding Object Context Boundaries

As you have just seen, AppDomains are logical partitions within a process used to host .NET assemblies. On a related note, a given application domain may be further subdivided into numerous *context boundaries*. In a nutshell, a .NET context provides a way for a single AppDomain to establish a "specific home" for a given object.

Using context, the CLR is able to ensure that objects that have special runtime requirements are handled in an appropriate and consistent manner by intercepting method invocations into and out of a given context. This layer of interception allows the CLR to adjust the current method invocation to conform to the contextual settings of a given object. For example, if you define a VB 2005 class type that requires automatic thread safety (using the `<Synchronization>` attribute), the CLR will create a "synchronized context" during allocation.

Just as a process defines a default AppDomain, every application domain has a default context. This default context (sometimes referred to as *context 0*, given that it is always the first context created within an application domain) is used to group together .NET objects that have no specific or unique contextual needs. As you may expect, a vast majority of .NET objects are loaded into context 0. If the CLR determines a newly created object has special needs, a new context boundary is created within the hosting application domain. Figure 15-9 illustrates the process/AppDomain/context relationship.

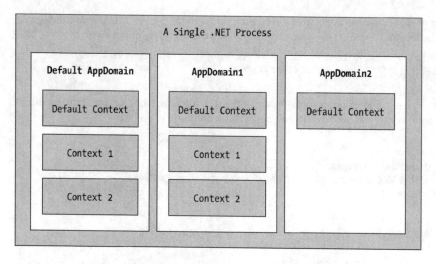

Figure 15-9. *Processes, application domains, and context boundaries*

Context-Agile and Context-Bound Types

.NET types that do not demand any special contextual treatment are termed *context-agile* objects. These objects can be accessed from anywhere within the hosting AppDomain without interfering with the object's runtime requirements. Building context-agile objects is a no-brainer, given that you simply do nothing (specifically, you do not adorn the type with any contextual attributes and do not derive from the System.ContextBoundObject base class):

```
' A context-agile object is loaded into context 0.
Class SportsCar
End Class
```

On the other hand, objects that do demand contextual allocation are termed *context-bound* objects, and they must derive from the System.ContextBoundObject base class. This base class solidifies the fact that the object in question can function appropriately only within the context in which it was created. Given the role of .NET context, it should stand to reason that if a context-bound object were to somehow end up in an incompatible context, bad things would be guaranteed to occur at the most inopportune times.

In addition to deriving from System.ContextBoundObject, a context-sensitive type will also be adorned by a special category of .NET attributes termed (not surprisingly) context attributes. All context attributes derive from the System.Runtime.Remoting.Contexts.ContextAttribute base class.

Given that the ContextAttribute class is not sealed, it is possible for you to build your own custom contextual attribute (simply derive from ContextAttribute and override the necessary virtual methods). Once you have done so, you are able to build a custom piece of software that can respond to the contextual settings.

Note This book doesn't dive into the details of building custom object contexts; however, if you are interested in learning more, check out *Applied .NET Attributes* (Apress, 2003).

Defining a Context-Bound Object

Assume that you wish to define a class (SportsCarTS) that is automatically thread-safe in nature, even though you have not hard-coded thread synchronization logic within the member implementations. To do so, derive from ContextBoundObject and apply the <Synchronization> attribute as follows:

```
Imports System.Runtime.Remoting.Contexts

' This context-bound type will only be loaded into a
' synchronized (hence thread-safe) context.
<Synchronization> _
Class SportsCarTS
  Inherits ContextBoundObject
End Class
```

Types that are attributed with the <Synchronization> attribute are loaded into a thread-safe context. Given the special contextual needs of the SportsCarTS class type, imagine the problems that would occur if an allocated object were moved from a synchronized context into a nonsynchronized context. The object is suddenly no longer thread-safe and thus becomes a candidate for massive data corruption, as numerous threads are attempting to interact with the (now thread-volatile) reference object. To ensure the CLR does not move SportsCarTS objects outside of a synchronized context, simply derive from ContextBoundObject.

Inspecting an Object's Context

Although very few of the applications you will write will need to programmatically interact with context, here is an illustrative example. Create a new console application named ContextManipulator. This application defines one context-agile class (SportsCar) and a single context-bound type (SportsCarTS):

```
Imports System.Runtime.Remoting.Contexts  ' For Context type.
Imports System.Threading  ' For Thread type.

' SportsCar has no special contextual
' needs and will be loaded into the
' default context of the app domain.
Public Class SportsCar
  Public Sub New()
    ' Get context information and print out context ID.
    Dim ctx As Context = Thread.CurrentContext()
    Console.WriteLine("{0} object in context {1}", Me.ToString, ctx.ContextID)
    For Each itfCtxProp As IContextProperty In ctx.ContextProperties
      Console.WriteLine("-> Ctx Prop: {0}", itfCtxProp.Name)
    Next
  End Sub
End Class

' SportsCarTS demands to be loaded in
' a synchronization context.
<Synchronization()> _
Public Class SportsCarTS
  Inherits ContextBoundObject

  Public Sub New()
    ' Get context information and print out context ID.
    Dim ctx As Context = Thread.CurrentContext()
```

```
      Console.WriteLine("{0} object in context {1}", Me.ToString, ctx.ContextID)
      For Each itfCtxProp As IContextProperty In ctx.ContextProperties
        Console.WriteLine("-> Ctx Prop: {0}", itfCtxProp.Name)
      Next
    End Sub
  End Class
```

Notice that each constructor obtains a `Context` type from the current thread of execution, via `Thread.CurrentContext()`. Using the `Context` object, you are able to print out statistics about the contextual boundary, such as its assigned ID, as well as a set of descriptors obtained via `Context.ContextProperties`. This property returns an object implementing the `IContextProperty` interface, which exposes each descriptor through the `Name` property. Now, update `Main()` to allocate an instance of each class type:

```
Sub Main()
  Console.WriteLine("***** The Amazing Context Application *****")
  Console.WriteLine()

  ' Objects will display contextual info upon creation.
  Dim sport As SportsCar = New SportsCar()
  Console.WriteLine()

  Dim sport2 As SportsCar = New SportsCar()
  Console.WriteLine()

  Dim synchroSport As SportsCarTS = New SportsCarTS()
  Console.ReadLine()
End Sub
```

As the objects come to life, the class constructors will dump out various bits of context-centric information, as shown in Figure 15-10.

Figure 15-10. *Investigating an object's context*

Given that the `SportsCar` class has not been qualified with a context attribute, the CLR has allocated `sport` and `sport2` into context 0 (i.e., the default context). However, the `SportsCarTS` object is loaded into a unique contextual boundary (which has been assigned a context ID of 1), given the fact that this context-bound type was adorned with the `<Synchronization>` attribute.

Source Code The ContextManipulator project is included under the Chapter 15 subdirectory.

Summarizing Processes, AppDomains, and Context

At this point, you hopefully have a much better idea about how a .NET assembly is hosted by the CLR. To summarize the key points:

- A .NET process hosts one to many application domains. Each AppDomain is able to host any number of related .NET assemblies and may be independently loaded and unloaded by the CLR (or programmatically via the System.AppDomain type).

- A given AppDomain consists of one to many contexts. Using a context, the CLR is able to place a "special needs" object into a logical container, to ensure that its runtime requirements are honored.

If the previous pages have seemed to be a bit too low level for your liking, fear not. For the most part, the .NET runtime automatically deals with the details of processes, application domains, and contexts on your behalf. The good news, however, is that this information provides a solid foundation for understanding multithreaded programming under the .NET platform. Before we turn our attention to the System.Threading namespace, though, we'll examine how the CLR itself is hosted by the Win32 OS.

Runtime Hosts of the CLR

To the end user, running a .NET executable is achieved simply by double-clicking the *.exe in Windows Explorer (or activating an associated shortcut). As you recall from Chapter 1, however, the .NET Framework is not (currently) incorporated directly into the Windows OS, but sits on top of the OS itself. When you install Visual Studio 2005 (or the .NET Framework 2.0 SDK) on your development machine, the .NET runtime environment (including the necessary base class libraries) is installed as well. Also recall that Microsoft provides a freely distributable .NET runtime setup program (dotnetfx.exe) to configure end user machines to host .NET assemblies.

Given that the Windows OS does not natively understand the format of a .NET assembly, it should be clear that various steps occur in the background when an executable assembly is activated. Under the Windows XP OS, the basic steps are as follows (do recall from Chapter 13 that all .NET assemblies contain Win32 header information):

1. The Windows OS loads the executable binary file into memory.

2. The Windows OS reads the embedded WinNT header to determine whether the binary file is a .NET assembly (via the IMAGE_DIRECTORY_ENTRY_COM_DESCRIPTOR flag).

3. If the image is a .NET assembly, mscoree.dll is loaded.

4. mscoree.dll then loads *one of two* implementations of the CLR (mscorwks.dll or mscorsvr.dll).

5. At this point, the CLR takes over the show, performing all .NET-centric details (finding external assemblies, performing security checks, processing CIL code, performing garbage collections, etc.).

As suggested by the previous list, mscoree.dll is *not* the CLR itself. Although it is safe to regard mscoree.dll as the actual CLR, in reality this binary file is a shim to one of two possible CLR implementations. If the host machine makes use of a single CPU, mscorwks.dll is loaded. If the machine supports multiple CPUs, mscorsvr.dll is loaded into memory (which is a version of the CLR optimized to execute on multiple-processor machines).

Side-by-Side Execution of the CLR

To dig just a bit deeper, realize that the .NET platform supports side-by-side execution, meaning that multiple versions of the .NET platform can be installed on a single machine (1.0, 1.1, and 2.0 at the time of this writing). mscoree.dll itself resides in the machine's System32 subdirectory of the registered Windows installation directory. On my machine, mscoree.dll lives under C:\WINDOWS\system32 (see Figure 15-11).

Figure 15-11. mscoree.dll *lives under the System32 directory.*

Once mscoree.dll has been loaded, the Win32 system registry (yes, *that* system registry) is consulted to determine the latest installed version and installation path of the .NET Framework via HKEY_LOCAL_MACHINE\Software\Microsoft\.NETFramework, as shown in Figure 15-12.

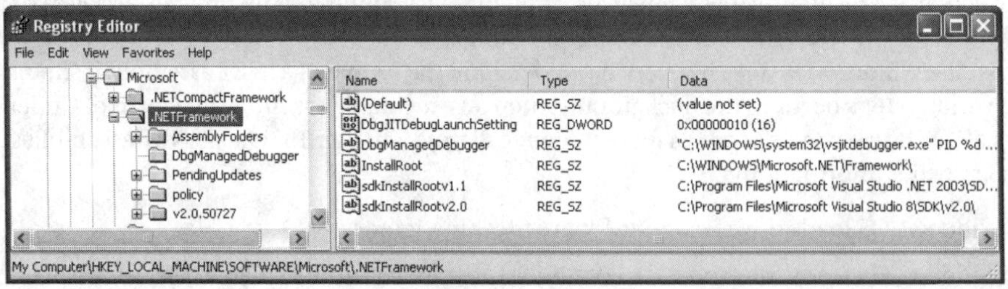

Figure 15-12. *Resolving the version and installation path of the .NET platform*

Once the version and installation path of the .NET platform have been determined, the correct version of mscorwks.dll/mscorsvr.dll is loaded into memory. Again, on my machine, the root installation path of the .NET platform is C:\WINDOWS\Microsoft.NET\Framework. Under this directory are specific subdirectories for .NET version 1.0, 1.1, and (at the time of this writing) the current build of 2.0 (see Figure 15-13; your version numbers may differ).

Figure 15-13. mscorwks.dll *version 2.0*

Loading a Specific Version of the CLR

When mscoree.dll determines which version of mscorwks.dll/mscorsrv.dll to load (by consulting the system registry), it will also read a subfolder under HKEY_LOCAL_MACHINE\Software\Microsoft\ .NET\Framework named "policy." This subfolder records the CLR upgrades that may be safely performed. For example, if you execute an assembly that was built using .NET version 1.0.3705, mscoree.dll learns from the policy file that it can safely load version 1.1.4322.

This promotion occurs silently in the background and only when the upgrade is known to produce compatible execution. In the rare case that you wish to instruct mscoree.dll to load a *specific* version of the CLR, you may do so using a client-side *.config file:

```xml
<?xml version="1.0" encoding="utf-8" ?>
<configuration>
  <startup>
    <requiredRuntime version ="1.0.3705"/>
  </startup>
</configuration>
```

Here, the <requiredRuntime> element expresses that only version 1.0.3705 should be used to host the assembly in question. Therefore, if the target machine does not have a complete installation of .NET version 1.0.3705, the end user is presented with a runtime error.

Additional CLR Hosts

The process just defined qualifies the basic steps taken by the Windows OS to host the CLR when an executable assembly is activated. However, Microsoft provides many applications that bypass this out-of-the-box behavior in favor of loading the CLR *programmatically*. For example, Microsoft Internet Explorer can natively host custom Windows Forms controls (the managed equivalent of the now legacy ActiveX controls). The latest version of Microsoft SQL Server (code-named Yukon and officially called SQL Server 2005) also has the ability to directly host the CLR internally.

As a final note, Microsoft has defined a set of interfaces that allow developers to build their own custom CLR host. This may be done using straight C/C++ code or via a COM type library (mscoree.tlb). While the process of building a custom CLR host is surprisingly simple (especially using the COM type library), this topic is outside the scope of this text. If you require further information, you can find numerous articles online (just do a search for "CLR hosts").

Summary

The point of this chapter was to examine exactly how a .NET executable image is hosted by the .NET platform. As you have seen, the long-standing notion of a Win32 process has been altered under the hood to accommodate the needs of the CLR. A single process (which can be programmatically manipulated via the System.Diagnostics.Process type) is now composed of multiple application domains, which represent isolated and independent boundaries within a process. As you have seen, a single process can host multiple application domains, each of which is capable of hosting and executing any number of related assemblies.

Furthermore, a single application domain can contain any number of contextual boundaries. Using this additional level of type isolation, the CLR can ensure that special-need objects are handled correctly. The chapter concluded by examining the details regarding how the CLR is hosted by the Win32 OS.

CHAPTER 16

■ ■ ■

Building Multithreaded Applications

In the previous chapter, you examined the relationship between processes, application domains, and contexts. This chapter builds on your newfound knowledge by examining how the .NET platform allows you to build multithreaded applications and how to keep shared resources thread-safe.

You'll begin by revisiting the .NET delegate type and come to understand its intrinsic support for asynchronous method invocations. As you'll see, this technique allows you to invoke a method on a secondary thread of execution automatically. Next, you'll investigate the types within the System. Threading namespace. Here you'll examine numerous types (Thread, ThreadStart, etc.) that allow you to easily create additional threads of execution.

As you will see, the complexity of multithreaded development isn't in the creation of threads, but in ensuring that your code base is well equipped to handle concurrent access to shared resources. Given this, the chapter closes by examining various synchronization primitives that the .NET Framework provides.

The Process/AppDomain/Context/Thread Relationship

In the previous chapter, a *thread* was defined as a path of execution within an executable application. While many .NET applications can live happy and productive single-threaded lives, an assembly's primary thread (spawned by the CLR when Main() executes) may create secondary threads of execution to perform additional units of work. By implementing additional threads, you can build more responsive (but not necessarily faster executing) applications.

The System.Threading namespace contains various types that allow you to create multithreaded applications. The Thread class is perhaps the core type, as it represents a given thread. If you wish to programmatically obtain a reference to the thread currently executing a given member, simply call the shared Thread.CurrentThread property:

```
Private Sub ExtractExecutingThread()
  ' Get the thread currently
  ' executing this method.
  Dim currThread As Thread = Thread.CurrentThread
End Sub
```

Under the .NET platform, there is *not* a direct one-to-one correspondence between application domains and threads. In fact, a given AppDomain can have numerous threads executing within it at any given time. Furthermore, a particular thread is not confined to a single application domain during its lifetime. Threads are free to cross application domain boundaries as the Win32 thread scheduler and CLR see fit.

Although active threads can be moved between AppDomain boundaries, a given thread can execute within only a single application domain at any point in time (in other words, it is impossible for a single thread to be doing work in more than one AppDomain). When you wish to programmatically gain access to the AppDomain that is hosting the current thread, call the shared Thread.GetDomain() method:

```
Private Sub ExtractAppDomainHostingThread()
  ' Obtain the AppDomain hosting the current thread.
  Dim ad As AppDomain = Thread.GetDomain()
End Sub
```

A single thread may also be moved into a particular context at any given time, and it may be relocated within a new context at the whim of the CLR. When you wish to obtain the current context a thread happens to be executing in, make use of the shared Thread.CurrentContext property:

```
Private Sub ExtractCurrentThreadContext()
  ' Obtain the Context under which the
  ' current thread is operating
  Dim ctx As Context = Thread.CurrentContext
End Sub
```

Again, the CLR is the entity that is in charge of moving threads into (and out of) application domains and contexts. As a .NET developer, you can usually remain blissfully unaware where a given thread ends up (or exactly when it is placed into its new boundary). Nevertheless, you should be aware of the various ways of obtaining the underlying primitives.

The Problem of Concurrency and the Role of Thread Synchronization

One of the many "joys" (read: *painful aspects*) of multithreaded programming is that you have little control over how the underlying operating system or the CLR makes use of its threads. For example, if you craft a block of code that creates a new thread of execution, you cannot guarantee that the thread executes immediately. Rather, such code only instructs the OS to execute the thread as soon as possible (which is typically when the thread scheduler gets around to it).

Furthermore, given that threads can be moved between application and contextual boundaries as required by the CLR, you must be mindful of which aspects of your application are *thread-volatile* (e.g., subject to multithreaded access) and which operations are *atomic* (thread-volatile operations are the dangerous ones!). To illustrate, assume a thread is executing a method of a specific object. Now assume that this thread is instructed by the thread scheduler to suspend its activity, in order to allow another thread to access the same method of the same object.

If the original thread was not completely finished with the current operation, the second incoming thread may be viewing an object in a partially modified state. At this point, the second thread is basically reading bogus data, which is sure to give way to extremely odd (and very hard to find) bugs, which are even harder to replicate and debug.

Atomic operations, on the other hand, are always safe in a multithreaded environment. Sadly, there are very few operations in the .NET base class libraries that are guaranteed to be atomic. Even the act of assigning a value to a member variable is not atomic! Unless the .NET Framework 2.0 SDK documentation specifically says an operation is atomic, you must assume it is thread-volatile and take precautions.

At this point, it should be clear that multithreaded application domains are in themselves quite volatile, as numerous threads can operate on the shared functionality at (more or less) the same time. To protect an application's resources from possible corruption, .NET developers must make use of any number of threading primitives (such as locks, monitors, and the <Synchronization> attribute) to control access to the data among the executing threads.

Although the .NET platform cannot make the difficulties of building robust multithreaded applications completely disappear, the process has been simplified considerably. Using types defined within the System.Threading namespace, you are able to spawn additional threads with minimal fuss and bother. Likewise, when it is time to lock down shared points of data, you will find additional types that provide the same functionality as the Win32 API threading primitives (using a much cleaner object model).

However, the System.Threading namespace is not the only way to build multithread .NET programs. During our examination of the .NET delegate (see Chapter 10), it was mentioned that all delegates have the ability to invoke members asynchronously. This is a *major* benefit of the .NET platform, given that one of the most common reasons a developer creates threads is for the purpose of invoking methods in a nonblocking (aka asynchronous) manner. Although you could make use of the System.Threading namespace to achieve a similar result, delegates make the whole process much easier.

A Brief Review of the .NET Delegate

Recall that the .NET delegate type is a type-safe, object-oriented function pointer. When you declare a .NET delegate, the VB 2005 compiler responds by building a sealed class that derives from System.MulticastDelegate (which in turn derives from System.Delegate). These base classes provide every delegate with the ability to maintain a list of method addresses, all of which may be invoked at a later time. Consider the BinaryOp delegate first defined in Chapter 10:

```
' A custom delegate type.
Public Delegate Function BinaryOp(ByVal x As Integer, _
  ByVal y As Integer) As Integer
```

Based on its definition, BinaryOp can point to any method taking two Integers as arguments and returning an Integer. Once compiled, the defining assembly now contains a full-blown class definition that is dynamically generated based on the delegate declaration. In the case of BinaryOp, this class looks more or less like the following:

```
NotInheritable Class BinaryOp
  Inherits System.MulticastDelegate

  Public Sub New(ByVal target As Object, ByVal functionAddress As System.UInt32)
  End Sub

  Public Sub Invoke(ByVal x As Integer, ByVal y As Integer)
  End Sub

  Public Function BeginInvoke(ByVal x As Integer, ByVal y As Integer, _
    ByVal cb As AsyncCallback, ByVal state As Object) As IAsyncResult
  End Function

  Public Function EndInvoke(ByVal result As IAsyncResult) As Integer
  End Function
End Class
```

Recall that the generated Invoke() method is used to invoke the methods maintained by a delegate object in a synchronous manner. Therefore, the calling thread (such as the primary thread of the application) is forced to wait until the delegate invocation completes. Also recall that in VB 2005, the Invoke() method is called behind the scenes when you apply "normal" method invocation syntax. Consider the following program, which invokes the shared Add() method in a synchronous (aka blocking) manner:

```vb
' Need this for the Thread.Sleep() call.
Imports System.Threading

' Our custom delegate.
Public Delegate Function BinaryOp(ByVal x As Integer, _
  ByVal y As Integer) As Integer

Module Program
  Sub Main()
    Console.WriteLine("***** Synch Delegate Review *****")
    Console.WriteLine()

    ' Print out the ID of the executing thread.
    Console.WriteLine("Main() invoked on thread {0}.", _
      Thread.CurrentThread.GetHashCode)

    ' Invoke Add() in a synchronous manner.
    Dim b As BinaryOp = AddressOf Add
    Dim answer As Integer = b(10, 10)

    ' These lines will not execute until
    ' the Add() method has completed.
    Console.WriteLine("Doing more work in Main()!")
    Console.WriteLine("10 + 10 is {0}.", answer)
    Console.ReadLine()
  End Sub

  Function Add(ByVal x As Integer, ByVal y As Integer) As Integer
    ' Print out the ID of the executing thread.
    Console.WriteLine("Add() invoked on thread {0}.", _
      Thread.CurrentThread.GetHashCode)

    '  Pause to simulate a lengthy operation.
    Thread.Sleep(5000)
    Return x + y
  End Function
End Module
```

Notice first of all that this program is making use of the System.Threading namespace. Within the Add() method, you are invoking the shared Thread.Sleep() method to suspend the calling thread for (more or less) 5 seconds to simulate a lengthy task. Given that you are invoking the Add() method in a *synchronous* manner, the Main() method will not print out the result of the operation until the Add() method has completed (again, approximately 5 seconds after the call).

Next, note that the Main() method is obtaining access to the currently executing thread (via Thread.CurrentThread) and printing out its hash code. Given that a hash code represents an object in a specific state, this value can be used as a quick-and-dirty thread ID. This same logic is repeated in the shared Add() method. As you might suspect, given that all the work in this application is performed exclusively by the primary thread, you find the same hash code value displayed to the console, as shown in Figure 16-1.

Figure 16-1. *Synchronous method invocations are "blocking" calls.*

When you run this program, you should notice that a 5-second delay takes place before you see the `Console.WriteLine()` logic execute. Although many (if not most) methods may be called synchronously without ill effect, .NET delegates can be instructed to call their methods asynchronously if necessary.

■**Source Code** The SyncDelegate project is located under the Chapter 16 subdirectory.

The Asynchronous Nature of Delegates

If you are new to the topic of multithreading, you may wonder what exactly an *asynchronous* method invocation is all about. As you are no doubt fully aware, some programming operations take time. Although the previous `Add()` was purely illustrative in nature, imagine that you built a single-threaded application that is invoking a method on a remote object, performing a long-running database query, or writing 500 lines of text to an external file. While performing these operations, the application may appear to hang for quite some time. Until the task at hand has been processed, all other aspects of this program (such as menu activation, toolbar clicking, or console output) are unresponsive.

The question therefore is, how can you tell a delegate to invoke a method on a separate thread of execution to simulate numerous tasks performing "at the same time"? The good news is that every .NET delegate type is automatically equipped with this capability. The even better news is that you are *not* required to directly dive into the details of the `System.Threading` namespace to do so (although these entities can quite naturally work hand in hand).

The BeginInvoke() and EndInvoke() Methods

When the VB 2005 compiler processes the `Delegate` keyword, the dynamically generated class defines two methods named `BeginInvoke()` and `EndInvoke()`. Given our definition of the `BinaryOp` delegate, these methods are prototyped as follows:

```
NotInheritable Class BinaryOp
  Inherits System.MulticastDelegate
...
  ' Used to invoke a method asynchronously.
  Public Function BeginInvoke(ByVal x As Integer, ByVal y As Integer, _
    ByVal cb As AsyncCallback, ByVal state As Object) As IAsyncResult
  End Function

  ' Used to fetch the return value
  ' of the invoked method.
  Public Function EndInvoke(ByVal result As IAsyncResult) As Integer
  End Function
End Class
```

The first stack of parameters passed into `BeginInvoke()` will be based on the format of the VB 2005 delegate (two `Integers` in the case of `BinaryOp`). The final two arguments will always be `System.AsyncCallback` and `System.Object`. We'll examine the role of these parameters shortly; for the time being, though, we'll supply `Nothing` for each.

The System.IAsyncResult Interface

Also note that the `BeginInvoke()` method always returns an object implementing the `IAsyncResult` interface, while `EndInvoke()` requires an `IAsyncResult`-compatible type as its sole parameter. The `IAsyncResult`-compatible object returned from `BeginInvoke()` is basically a coupling mechanism that allows the calling thread to obtain the result of the asynchronous method invocation at a later time via `EndInvoke()`. The `IAsyncResult` interface (defined in the `System` namespace) is defined as follows:

```
Public Interface IAsyncResult
  ReadOnly Property AsyncState() As Object
  ReadOnly Property AsyncWaitHandle() As WaitHandle
  ReadOnly Property CompletedSynchronously() As Boolean
  ReadOnly Property IsCompleted() As Boolean
End Interface
```

In the simplest case, you are able to avoid directly invoking these members. All you have to do is cache the `IAsyncResult`-compatible object returned by `BeginInvoke()` and pass it to `EndInvoke()` when you are ready to obtain the result of the function invocation. As you will see, you are able to invoke the members of an `IAsyncResult`-compatible object when you wish to become "more involved" with the process of fetching the method's return value.

■Note If you asynchronously invoke a method that does not provide a return value, you can simply "fire and forget." In such cases, you will never need to cache the `IAsyncResult`-compatible object or call `EndInvoke()` in the first place (as there is no return value to retrieve).

Invoking a Method Asynchronously

To instruct the `BinaryOp` delegate to invoke `Add()` asynchronously, you can update the previous `Main()` method as follows:

```
Sub Main()
  Console.WriteLine("***** Async Delegate Invocation *****")
  Console.WriteLine()

  ' Print out the ID of the executing thread.
  Console.WriteLine("Main() invoked on thread {0}.", _
    Thread.CurrentThread.GetHashCode)

  ' Invoke Add() on a secondary thread.
  Dim b As BinaryOp = New BinaryOp(Add)
  Dim itfAR As IAsyncResult = b.BeginInvoke(10, 10, Nothing, Nothing)

  ' Do other work on primary thread...
  Console.WriteLine("Doing more work in Main()!")
```

```
' Obtain the result of the Add()
' method when ready.
Dim answer As Integer = b.EndInvoke(itfAR)
Console.WriteLine("10 + 10 is {0}.", answer)
Console.ReadLine()
End Sub
```

If you run this application, you will find that two unique hash codes are displayed, given that there are in fact two threads working within the current AppDomain (see Figure 16-2).

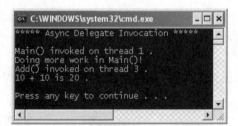

Figure 16-2. *Methods invoked asynchronously are done so on a unique thread.*

In addition to the unique hash code values, you will also notice upon running the application that the "Doing more work in Main()!" message displays immediately, while the secondary thread is occupied attending to its business.

Synchronizing the Calling Thread

If you take a moment to ponder the current implementation of Main(), you might have realized that the time span between calling BeginInvoke() and EndInvoke() is clearly less than 5 seconds. Therefore, once "Doing more work in Main()!" prints to the console, the calling thread is now blocked and waiting for the secondary thread to complete before being able to obtain the result of the Add() method. Therefore, you are effectively making yet another *synchronous call* (in a very roundabout fashion!):

```
Sub Main()
...
  Dim b As BinaryOp = New BinaryOp(Add)
  Dim itfAR As IAsyncResult = b.BeginInvoke(10, 10, Nothing, Nothing)

  ' This call takes far less than 5 seconds!
  Console.WriteLine("Doing more work in Main()!")

  ' The calling thread is now blocked until
  ' EndInvoke() completes.
  Dim answer As Integer = b.EndInvoke(itfAR)
...
End Sub
```

Obviously, asynchronous delegates would lose their appeal if the calling thread had the potential of being blocked under various circumstances. To allow the calling thread to discover whether the asynchronously invoked method has completed its work, the IAsyncResult interface provides the IsCompleted property.

Using this member, the calling thread is able to determine whether the asynchronous call has indeed completed before calling EndInvoke(). If the method has not completed, IsCompleted returns False, and the calling thread is free to carry on its work. If IsCompleted returns True, the calling thread is able to obtain the result in the "least blocking manner" possible. Ponder the following update to the Main() method:

```
Sub Main()
...
  Dim b As BinaryOp = New BinaryOp(Add)
  Dim itfAR As IAsyncResult = b.BeginInvoke(10, 10, Nothing, Nothing)

  ' This message will keep printing until
  ' the Add() method is finished.
  While Not itfAR.IsCompleted
    Console.WriteLine("Doing more work in Main()!")
    ' Just so we don't see hundreds of printouts!
    Thread.Sleep(1000)
  End While

  ' Now we know the Add() method is complete.
  Dim answer As Integer = b.EndInvoke(itfAR)
...
End Sub
```

Here, you enter a loop that will continue processing the Console.WriteLine() statement until the secondary thread has completed. Once this has occurred, you can obtain the result of the Add() method knowing full well the method has indeed completed.

In addition to the IsCompleted property, the IAsyncResult interface provides the AsyncWaitHandle property for more flexible waiting logic. This property returns an instance of the WaitHandle type, which exposes a method named WaitOne(). The benefit of WaitHandle.WaitOne() is that you can specify the maximum wait time. If the specified amount of time is exceeded, WaitOne() returns False. Ponder the following updated while loop:

```
While Not itfAR.AsyncWaitHandle.WaitOne(2000, true)
  Console.WriteLine("Doing more work in Main()!")
  ' Just so we don't see dozens of printouts!
  Thread.Sleep(1000)
End While
```

While these properties of IAsyncResult do provide a way to synchronize the calling thread, they are not the most efficient approach. In many ways, the IsCompleted property is much like a really annoying manager (or classmate) who is constantly asking, "Are you done yet?" Thankfully, delegates provide a number of additional (and more effective) techniques to obtain the result of a method that has been called asynchronously.

■**Source Code**   The AsyncDelegate project is located under the Chapter 16 subdirectory.

The Role of the AsyncCallback Delegate

Rather than polling a delegate to determine whether an asynchronous method has completed, it would be ideal to have the delegate inform the calling thread when the task is finished. When you wish to enable this behavior, you will need to supply an instance of the System.AsyncCallback delegate as a parameter to BeginInvoke(), which up until this point has been Nothing. However, when you do supply an AsyncCallback object, the delegate will call the specified method automatically when the asynchronous call has completed.

Like any delegate, `AsyncCallback` can only invoke methods that match a specific pattern, which in this case is a method taking `IAsyncResult` as the sole parameter and returning nothing:

```
Sub MyAsyncCallbackMethod(ByVal itfAR As IAsyncResult)
```

Assume you have another application making use of the `BinaryOp` delegate. This time, however, you will not poll the delegate to determine whether the `Add()` method has completed. Rather, you will define a shared method named `AddComplete()` to receive the notification that the asynchronous invocation is finished:

```
Imports System.Threading

' Our delegate.
Public Delegate Function BinaryOp(ByVal x As Integer, _
  ByVal y As Integer) As Integer

Module Program
  Sub Main()
    Console.WriteLine("***** AsyncCallbackDelegate Example *****")
    Console.WriteLine()

    Console.WriteLine("Main() invoked on thread {0}.", _
      Thread.CurrentThread.GetHashCode())
    Dim b As BinaryOp = New BinaryOp(AddressOf Add)
    Dim itfAR As IAsyncResult = _
      b.BeginInvoke(10, 10, New AsyncCallback(AddressOf AddComplete), _
                Nothing)

    ' Other work performed here...

    Console.ReadLine()
  End Sub

  Sub AddComplete(ByVal itfAR As IAsyncResult)
    Console.WriteLine("AddComplete() invoked on thread {0}.", _
      Thread.CurrentThread.GetHashCode())
    Console.WriteLine("Your addition is complete")
  End Sub

  Function Add(ByVal x As Integer, ByVal y As Integer) As Integer
    Console.WriteLine("Add() invoked on thread {0}.", _
      Thread.CurrentThread.GetHashCode())
    Thread.Sleep(5000)
    Return x + y
  End Function
End Module
```

Again, the shared `AddComplete()` method will be invoked by the `AsyncCallback` delegate when the `Add()` method has completed. If you run this program, you can confirm that the secondary thread is the thread invoking the `AddComplete()` callback, as shown in Figure 16-3.

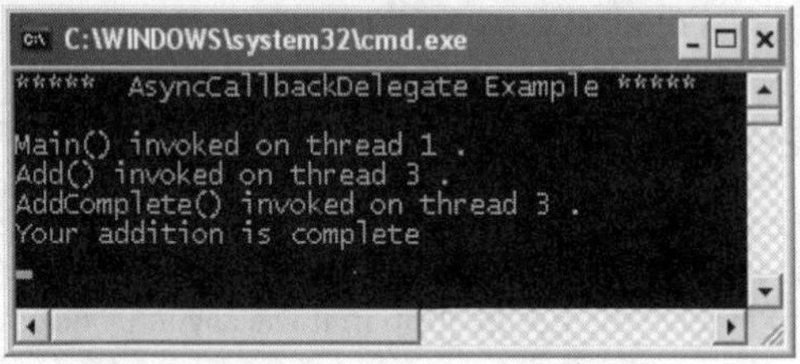

Figure 16-3. *The* AsyncCallback *delegate in action*

The Role of the AsyncResult Class

You may have noticed in the current example that the Main() method is not caching the IAsyncResult type returned from BeginInvoke() and is no longer calling EndInvoke(). The reason is that the target of the AsyncCallback delegate (AddComplete() in this example) does not have access to the original BinaryOp delegate created in the scope of Main(). While you could simply declare the BinaryOp variable as a shared member of the module to allow both methods to access the same object, a more elegant solution is to use the incoming IAsyncResult parameter.

The incoming IAsyncResult parameter passed into the target of the AsyncCallback delegate is actually an instance of the AsyncResult class (note the lack of an I prefix, which identifies interface types) defined in the System.Runtime.Remoting.Messaging namespace. The shared AsyncDelegate property returns a reference to the original asynchronous delegate that was created elsewhere. Therefore, if you wish to obtain a reference to the BinaryOp delegate object allocated within Main(), simply cast the System.Object returned by the AsyncDelegate property into type BinaryOp. At this point, you can trigger EndInvoke() as expected:

```
' Don't forget to Import the
' System.Runtime.Remoting.Messaging namespace!
Sub AddComplete(ByVal itfAR As IAsyncResult)
  Console.WriteLine("AddComplete() invoked on thread {0}.", _
    Thread.CurrentThread.GetHashCode)
  Console.WriteLine("Your addition is complete")

  ' Now get the result.
  Dim ar As AsyncResult = CType(itfAR, AsyncResult)
  Dim b As BinaryOp = CType(ar.AsyncDelegate, BinaryOp)
  Console.WriteLine("10 + 10 is {0}.", b.EndInvoke(itfAR))
End Sub
```

Passing and Receiving Custom State Data

The final aspect of asynchronous delegates we need to address is the final argument to the BeginInvoke() method (which has been Nothing up to this point). This parameter allows you to pass additional state information to the callback method from the primary thread. Because this argument is prototyped as a System.Object, you can pass in any type of data whatsoever, as long as the callback method knows what to expect. Assume for the sake of demonstration that the primary thread wishes to pass in a custom text message to the AddComplete() method:

```
Sub Main()
...
  Dim b As BinaryOp = New BinaryOp(AddressOf Add)
  Dim itfAR As IAsyncResult = _
    b.BeginInvoke(10, 10, New AsyncCallback(AddressOf AddComplete), _
    "Main() thanks you for adding these numbers.")

  ' Other work performed here...

  Console.ReadLine()
End Sub
```

To obtain this data within the scope of AddComplete(), make use of the AsyncState property of the incoming IAsyncResult parameter:

```
Sub AddComplete(ByVal itfAR As IAsyncResult)
...
  ' Retrieve the informational object and cast it to string
  Dim msg As String = CType(itfAR.AsyncState, String)
  Console.WriteLine(msg)
End Sub
```

Figure 16-4 shows the output of the current application.

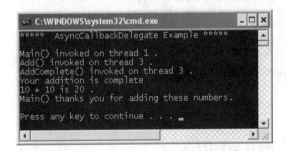

Figure 16-4. *Passing and receiving custom state data*

Cool! Now that you understand how a .NET delegate can be used to automatically spin off a secondary thread of execution to handle an asynchronous method invocation, let's turn our attention to interacting with threads directly using the System.Threading namespace.

■**Source Code** The AsyncCallbackDelegate project is located under the Chapter 16 subdirectory.

The System.Threading Namespace

Under the .NET platform, the System.Threading namespace provides a number of types that enable the construction of multithreaded applications. In addition to providing types that allow you to interact with a particular CLR thread, this namespace defines types that allow access to the CLR-maintained thread pool, a simple (non–GUI-based) Timer class, and numerous types used to provide synchronized access to shared resources. Table 16-1 lists some of the core members of this namespace. (Be sure to consult the .NET Framework 2.0 SDK documentation for full details.)

Table 16-1. *Select Types of the* System.Threading *Namespace*

Type	Meaning in Life
Interlocked	This type provides atomic operations for types that are shared by multiple threads.
Monitor	This type provides the synchronization of threading objects using locks and wait/signals. The VB 2005 SyncLock keyword makes use of a Monitor type under the hood.
Mutex	This synchronization primitive can be used for synchronization between application domain boundaries.
ParameterizedThreadStart	This delegate (which is new to .NET 2.0) allows a thread to call methods that take any number of arguments.
Semaphore	This type allows you to limit the number of threads that can access a resource, or a particular type of resource, concurrently.
Thread	This type represents a thread that executes within the CLR. Using this type, you are able to spawn additional threads in the originating AppDomain.
ThreadPool	This type allows you to interact with the CLR-maintained thread pool within a given process.
ThreadPriority	This enum represents a thread's priority level (Highest, Normal, etc.).
ThreadStart	This delegate is used to specify the method to call for a given thread. Unlike the ParameterizedThreadStart delegate, targets of ThreadStart must match a fixed prototype.
ThreadState	This enum specifies the valid states a thread may take (Running, Aborted, etc.).
Timer	This type provides a mechanism for executing a method at specified intervals.
TimerCallback	This delegate type is used in conjunction with Timer types.

The System.Threading.Thread Class

The most primitive of all types in the System.Threading namespace is Thread. This class represents an object-oriented wrapper around a given path of execution within a particular AppDomain. This type also defines a number of methods (both shared and instance level) that allow you to create new threads within the current AppDomain, as well as to suspend, stop, and destroy a particular thread. Consider the list of core shared members in Table 16-2.

Table 16-2. *Key Shared Members of the* Thread *Type*

Shared Member	Meaning in Life
CurrentContext	This read-only property returns the context in which the thread is currently running.
CurrentThread	This read-only property returns a reference to the currently running thread.
GetDomain() GetDomainID()	These methods return a reference to the current AppDomain or the ID of this domain in which the current thread is running.
Sleep()	This method suspends the current thread for a specified time.

The Thread class also supports several instance-level members, some of which are shown in Table 16-3.

Table 16-3. *Select Instance-Level Members of the* Thread *Type*

Instance-Level Member	Meaning in Life
IsAlive	Returns a Boolean that indicates whether this thread has been started.
IsBackground	Gets or sets a value indicating whether or not this thread is a "background thread" (more details in just a moment).
Name	Allows you to establish a friendly text name of the thread.
Priority	Gets or sets the priority of a thread, which may be assigned a value from the ThreadPriority enumeration.
ThreadState	Gets the state of this thread, which may be assigned a value from the ThreadState enumeration.
Abort()	Instructs the CLR to terminate the thread as soon as possible.
Interrupt()	Interrupts (e.g., wakes) the current thread from a suitable wait period.
Join()	Blocks the calling thread until the specified thread (the one on which Join() is called) exits.
Resume()	Resumes a thread that has been previously suspended.
Start()	Instructs the CLR to execute the thread ASAP.
Suspend()	Suspends the thread. If the thread is already suspended, a call to Suspend() has no effect.

Obtaining Statistics About the Current Thread

Recall that the entry point of an executable assembly (i.e., the Main() method) runs on the primary thread of execution. To illustrate the basic use of the Thread type, assume you have a new console application named ThreadStats. As you know, the shared Thread.CurrentThread property retrieves a Thread object that represents the currently executing thread. Once you have obtained the current thread, you are able to print out various statistics:

```
' Be sure to import the System.Threading namespace.
Sub Main()
  Console.WriteLine("***** Primary Thread stats *****")
  Console.WriteLine()

  ' Obtain and name the current thread.
  Dim primaryThread As Thread = Thread.CurrentThread
  primaryThread.Name = "ThePrimaryThread"

  ' Show details of hosting AppDomain/Context.
  Console.WriteLine("Name of current AppDomain: {0}", _
    Thread.GetDomain().FriendlyName)
  Console.WriteLine("ID of current Context: {0}", _
    Thread.CurrentContext.ContextID)

  ' Print out some stats about this thread.
  Console.WriteLine("Thread Name: {0}", _
    primaryThread.Name)
  Console.WriteLine("Has thread started?: {0}", _
    primaryThread.IsAlive)
  Console.WriteLine("Priority Level: {0}", _
    primaryThread.Priority)
  Console.WriteLine("Thread State: {0}", _
    primaryThread.ThreadState)
  Console.ReadLine()
End Sub
```

Figure 16-5 shows the output for the current application.

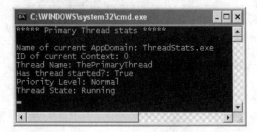

Figure 16-5. *Gathering thread statistics*

The Name Property

While this code is more or less self-explanatory, do notice that the Thread class supports a property called Name. If you do not set this value, Name will return an empty string. However, once you assign a friendly string moniker to a given Thread object, you can greatly simplify your debugging endeavors. If you are making use of Visual Studio 2005, you may access the Threads window during a debugging session (select Debug ➤ Windows ➤ Threads). As you can see from Figure 16-6, you can quickly identify the thread you wish to diagnose.

ID	Name	Location	Priority	Suspend
2384				0
1292	<No Name>		Highest	0
2768	<No Name>		Normal	0
2464	<No Name>		Normal	0
1488				0
2312	<No Name>		Normal	0
3900	<No Name>		Normal	0
3020	<No Name>		Normal	0
2272	.NET SystemEvents		Normal	0
1756	ThePrimaryThread	ThreadStats.Program.Main	Normal	0

Figure 16-6. *Debugging a thread with Visual Studio 2005*

The Priority Property

Next, notice that the Thread type defines a property named Priority. By default, all threads have a priority level of Normal. However, you can change this at any point in the thread's lifetime using the ThreadPriority property and the related System.Threading.ThreadPriority enumeration:

```
Public Enum ThreadPriority
   AboveNormal
   BelowNormal
   Highest
   Idle
   Lowest
   Normal      ' Default value.
   TimeCritical
End Enum
```

If you were to assign a thread's priority level to a value other than the default (ThreadPriority.Normal), understand that you would have little control over when the thread scheduler switches between threads. In reality, a thread's priority level offers a hint to the CLR regarding the importance of the thread's activity. Thus, a thread with the value ThreadPriority.Highest is not necessarily guaranteed to given the highest precedence. Again, if the thread scheduler is pre-occupied with a given task (e.g., synchronizing an object, switching threads, or moving threads), the priority level will most likely be altered accordingly.

However, all things being equal, the CLR will read these values and instruct the thread scheduler how to best allocate time slices. All things still being equal, threads with an identical thread priority should each receive the same amount of time to perform their work.

In most cases, you will seldom (if ever) need to directly alter a thread's priority level. In theory, it is possible to jack up the priority level on a set of threads, thereby preventing lower-priority threads from executing at their required levels (so use caution).

■**Source Code** The ThreadStats project is included under the Chapter 16 subdirectory.

Programmatically Creating Secondary Threads

When you wish to programmatically create additional threads to carry on some unit of work, you will follow a very predictable process:

1. Create a method to be the entry point for the new thread.

2. Create a new ParameterizedThreadStart (or legacy ThreadStart) delegate, passing the address of the method defined in step 1 to the constructor.

3. Create a Thread object, passing the ParameterizedThreadStart/ThreadStart delegate as a constructor argument.

4. Establish any initial thread characteristics (name, priority, etc.).

5. Call the Thread.Start() method. This starts the thread at the method referenced by the delegate created in step 2 as soon as possible.

As stated in step 2, you may make use of two distinct delegate types to "point to" the method that the secondary thread will execute. The ThreadStart delegate has been part of the System.Threading namespace since .NET 1.0, and it can point to any subroutine that takes no arguments. This delegate can be helpful when the method is designed to simply run in the background without further interaction.

The obvious limitation of ThreadStart is that you are unable to pass in parameters for processing. As of .NET 2.0, you are provided with the ParameterizedThreadStart delegate type, which allows a single parameter of type System.Object. Given that anything can be represented as a System.Object, you can pass in any number of parameters via a custom class or structure. Do note, however, that like ThreadStart the ParameterizedThreadStart delegate can only point to subroutines, not functions.

Working with the ThreadStart Delegate

To illustrate the process of building a multithreaded application (as well as to demonstrate the usefulness of doing so), assume you have a console application (SimpleMultiThreadApp) that allows the end user to choose whether the application will perform its duties using the single primary thread or split its workload using two separate threads of execution.

Assuming you have imported the System.Threading namespace via the VB 2005 Imports keyword, your first step is to define a type method to perform the work of the (possible) secondary thread. To keep focused on the mechanics of building multithreaded programs, this method will simply print out a sequence of numbers to the console window, pausing for approximately 2 seconds with each pass. Here is the full definition of the Printer class:

```vb
Public Class Printer
  Public Sub PrintNumbers()
    ' Display Thread info.
    Console.WriteLine("-> {0} is executing PrintNumbers()", _
      Thread.CurrentThread.Name)

    ' Print out numbers.
    Console.Write("Your numbers: ")
    For i As Integer = 0 To 10
      Console.Write(i & ", ")
      Thread.Sleep(2000)
    Next
    Console.WriteLine()
  End Sub
End Class
```

Now, within Main(), you will first prompt the user to determine whether one or two threads will be used to perform the application's work. If the user requests a single thread, you will simply invoke the PrintNumbers() method within the primary thread. However, if the user specifies two threads, you will create a ThreadStart delegate that points to PrintNumbers(), pass this delegate object into the constructor of a new Thread object, and call Start() to inform the CLR this thread is ready for processing.

To begin, set a reference to the System.Windows.Forms.dll assembly and display a message within Main() using MessageBox.Show() (you'll see the point of doing so once you run the program). Here is the complete implementation of Main():

```vb
Module Program
  Sub Main()
    Console.WriteLine("***** The Amazing Thread App *****")
    Console.Write("Do you want [1] or [2] threads?")
    Dim threadCount As String = Console.ReadLine()

    ' Name the current thread.
    Dim primaryThread As Thread = Thread.CurrentThread
    primaryThread.Name = "Primary"

    '  Display Thread info.
    Console.WriteLine("-> {0} is executing Main()", Thread.CurrentThread.Name)

    ' Make worker class.
    Dim p As Printer = New Printer()

    ' How many threads does the user want?
    Select Case threadCount
      Case "2"
        ' User wants an extra thread.
        Dim backgroundThread As Thread = _
          New Thread(New ThreadStart(AddressOf p.PrintNumbers))
        backgroundThread.Name = "Secondary"
        backgroundThread.Start()
```

```
      Case "1"
        p.PrintNumbers()
      Case Else
        Console.WriteLine("I don't know what you want...you get 1 thread.")
        p.PrintNumbers()
      End Select

    MessageBox.Show("I'm busy!", "Work on main thread...")
    Console.ReadLine()
  End Sub
End Module
```

Now, if you run this program with a single thread, you will find that the message box will not display until the entire sequence of numbers has printed to the console. As you are explicitly pausing for approximately 2 seconds after each number is printed, this will result in a less-than-stellar end user experience. However, if you select two threads, the message box displays instantly, given that a unique Thread object is responsible for printing out the numbers to the console (see Figure 16-7).

Figure 16-7. *Multithreaded applications result in more responsive applications.*

Before we move on, it is important to note that when you build multithreaded applications (which includes the use of asynchronous delegates) on single CPU machines, you do not end up with an application that *runs* any faster, as that is a function of a machine's CPU. When running this application using either one or two threads, the numbers are still displaying at the same pace.

In reality, multithreaded applications result in *more responsive* applications. To the end user, it may appear that the program is "faster," but this is not the case. Threads have no power to make For loops execute quicker, to make paper print faster, or to force numbers to be added together at rocket speed. Multithreaded applications simply allow multiple threads to share the workload.

■**Source Code** The SimpleMultiThreadApp project is included under the Chapter 16 subdirectory.

Creating Threads: A Shorthand Notation

In the previous example, you were shown the four steps the CLR expects you to take when you wish to spin off a new thread of execution. As you would suppose, however, some optional shorthand notations are available. Specifically, if you do not have a need to hold onto the instance of the ThreadStart delegate in your code, you can simply pass in the address of the method the Thread object is pointing to directly. Therefore, the following code:

```
' Directly create the ThreadStart delegate.
Dim backgroundThread As Thread = _
  New Thread(New ThreadStart(AddressOf p.PrintNumbers))
backgroundThread.Name = "Secondary"
backgroundThread.Start()
```

could be simplified like so:

```
' Indirectly create the ThreadStart delegate.
Dim backgroundThread As Thread = New Thread(AddressOf p.PrintNumbers)
backgroundThread.Name = "Secondary"
backgroundThread.Start()
```

As you might guess, the previous code snippet will force the Thread to create a new instance of the ThreadStart delegate behind the scenes.

Working with the ParameterizedThreadStart Delegate

Recall that the ThreadStart delegate can point only to subroutines that take no arguments. While this may fit the bill in many cases, if you wish to pass data to the method executing on the secondary thread, you will need to make use of the ParameterizedThreadStart delegate type (rather than ThreadStart). To illustrate, let's re-create the logic of the AsyncCallbackDelegate project created earlier in this chapter, this time making use of the ParameterizedThreadStart delegate type.

To begin, create a new console application named AddWithThreads and import the System.Threading namespace. Now, given that ParameterizedThreadStart can point to any method taking a System.Object parameter, you will create a custom type containing the numbers to be added:

```
Class AddParams
  Public a As Integer
  Public b As Integer
  Public Sub New(ByVal numb1 As Integer, ByVal numb2 As Integer)
    a = numb1
    b = numb2
  End Sub
End Class
```

Next, create a shared method in the Module type that will take an AddParams type and print out the summation of each value. The code within Main() is straightforward. Simply use ParameterizedThreadStart rather than ThreadStart. Here is the complete Module definition:

```
Module Program
  Public Sub Add(ByVal data As Object)
    If TypeOf data Is AddParams Then
      Console.WriteLine("ID of thread in Add(): {0}", _
        Thread.CurrentThread.GetHashCode())
      Dim ap As AddParams = CType(data, AddParams)
      Console.WriteLine("{0} + {1} is {2}", ap.a, ap.b, ap.a + ap.b)
    End If
  End Sub
```

```
  Sub Main(ByVal args As String())
    Console.WriteLine("***** Adding with Thread objects *****")
    Console.WriteLine("ID of thread in Main(): {0}", _
      Thread.CurrentThread.GetHashCode())
    Dim ap As AddParams = New AddParams(10, 10)
    Dim t As Thread = New Thread(New ParameterizedThreadStart(AddressOf Add))
    t.Start(ap)
    Console.ReadLine()
  End Sub
End Module
```

As in the previous example, you have the option of directly creating an instance of the ParameterizedThreadStart delegate, or allowing the Thread type to do so on your behalf. Therefore, we could allocate our new Thread object as follows:

```
' This time, because Add() is a method taking a System.Object,
' a new ParameterizedThreadStart delegate is created
' behind the scenes.
Dim t As Thread = New Thread(AddressOf Add)
```

■**Source Code** The AddWithThreads project is included under the Chapter 16 subdirectory.

Foreground Threads and Background Threads

Now that you have seen how to programmatically create new threads of execution using the System.Threading namespace, let's formalize the distinction between foreground threads and background threads:

- *Foreground threads* have the ability to prevent the current application from terminating. The CLR will not shut down an application (which is to say, unload the hosting AppDomain) until all foreground threads have ended.

- *Background threads* (sometimes called *daemon threads*) are viewed by the CLR as expendable paths of execution that can be ignored at any point in time (even if they are currently laboring over some unit of work). Thus, if all foreground threads have terminated, any and all background threads are automatically killed when the application domain unloads.

It is important to note that foreground and background threads are *not* synonymous with primary and worker threads. By default, every thread you create via the Thread.Start() method is automatically a *foreground* thread. Again, this means that the AppDomain will not unload until all threads of execution have completed their units of work. In most cases, this is exactly the behavior you require.

For the sake of argument, however, assume that you wish to invoke Printer.PrintNumbers() on a secondary thread that should behave as a background thread. Again, this means that the method pointed to by the Thread type (via the ThreadStart or ParameterizedThreadStart delegate) should be able to halt safely as soon as all foreground threads are done with their work. Configuring such a thread is as simple as setting the IsBackground property to True:

```
Sub Main()
  Console.WriteLine("***** Background Threads *****")
  Console.WriteLine()
```

```
    Dim p As Printer = New Printer()
    Dim bgroundThread As Thread = New Thread(AddressOf p.PrintNumbers)
    bgroundThread.IsBackground = True
    bgroundThread.Start()
End Sub
```

Notice that this `Main()` method is *not* making a call to `Console.ReadLine()` to force the console to remain visible until you press the Enter key. Thus, when you run the application, it will shut down immediately because the `Thread` object has been configured as a background thread. Given that the `Main()` method triggers the creation of the primary *foreground* thread, as soon as the logic in `Main()` completes, the AppDomain unloads before the secondary thread is able to complete its work.

However, if you comment out the line that sets the `IsBackground` property, you will find that each number prints to the console, as all foreground threads must finish their work before the AppDomain is unloaded from the hosting process.

For the most part, configuring a thread to run as a background type can be helpful when the worker thread in question is performing a noncritical task that is no longer needed when the main task of the program is finished.

Source Code The BackgroundThread project is included under the Chapter 16 subdirectory.

The Issue of Concurrency

All the multithreaded sample applications you have written over the course of this chapter have been thread-safe, given that only a single `Thread` object was executing the method in question. While some of your applications may be this simplistic in nature, a good deal of your multithreaded applications may contain numerous secondary threads. Given that all threads in an AppDomain have concurrent access to the shared data of the application, imagine what might happen if multiple threads were accessing the same point of data. As the thread scheduler will force threads to suspend their work seemingly at random, what if Thread A is kicked out of the way before it has fully completed its work? Thread B is now reading unstable data.

To illustrate the problem of concurrency, let's build another VB 2005 console application named MultiThreadedPrinting. This application will once again make use of the `Printer` class created previously, but this time the `PrintNumbers()` method will force the current thread to pause for a randomly generated amount of time:

```
Public Class Printer
  Public Sub PrintNumbers()
    Console.WriteLine("-> {0} is executing PrintNumbers()", _
      Thread.CurrentThread.Name)
    Console.Write("Your numbers: ")
    For i As Integer = 0 To 10
      Dim r As Random = New Random()
      Thread.Sleep(100 * r.Next(5))
      Console.Write(i & ", ")
    Next
    Console.WriteLine()
  End Sub
End Class
```

The `Main()` method is responsible for creating an array of eleven (uniquely named) `Thread` objects, each of which is making calls on the same instance of the `Printer` object:

```
Module Program
  Sub Main()
    Console.WriteLine("***** Synchronizing Threads *****")
    Console.WriteLine()

    Dim p As Printer = New Printer()

    ' Make 11 threads that are all pointing to the same
    ' method on the same object.
    Dim threads(10) As Thread
    For i As Integer = 0 To 10
      threads(i) = New Thread(AddressOf p.PrintNumbers)
      threads(i).Name = String.Format("Worker thread #{0}", i)
    Next

    ' Now start each one.
    For Each t As Thread In threads
      t.Start()
    Next
    Console.ReadLine()
  End Sub
End Module
```

Before looking at some test runs, let's recap the problem. The primary thread within this AppDomain begins life by spawning 11 secondary worker threads. Each worker thread is told to make calls on the `PrintNumbers()` method on the same `Printer` instance. Given that you have taken no precautions to lock down this object's shared resources (the console), there is a good chance that the current thread will be kicked out of the way before the `PrintNumbers()` method is able to print out the complete results. Because you don't know exactly when (or if) this might happen, you are bound to get unpredictable results. For example, you might find the output shown in Figure 16-8.

Figure 16-8. *Concurrency in action, take one*

Now run the application a few more times. Figure 16-9 shows another possibility (your results will obviously differ).

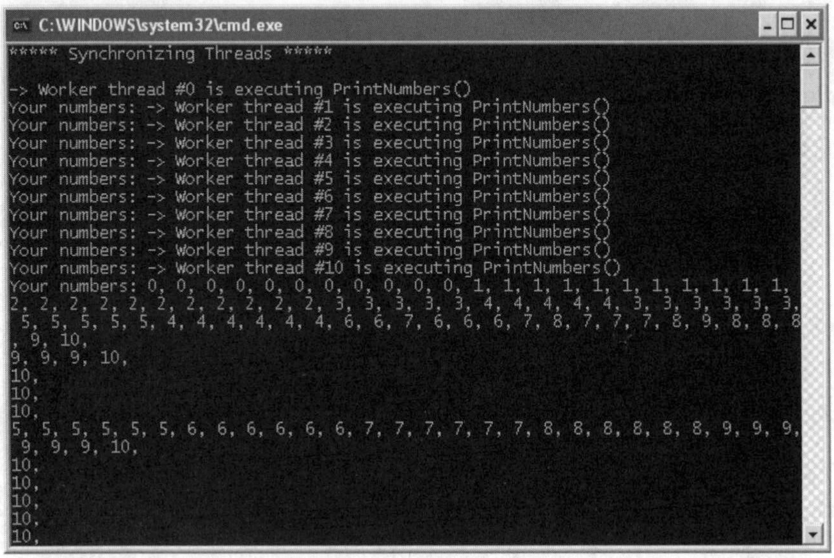

Figure 16-9. *Concurrency in action, take two*

There are clearly some problems here. As each thread is telling the Printer to print out the numerical data, the thread scheduler is happily swapping threads in the background. The result is inconsistent output. What we need is a way to programmatically enforce synchronized access to the shared resources. As you would guess, the System.Threading namespace provides a number of synchronization-centric types. The VB 2005 programming language also provides a particular keyword for the very task of synchronizing shared data in multithreaded applications.

■**Note** If you are unable to generate unpredictable outputs, increase the number of threads from 10 to 100 (for example) or introduce a call to Thread.Sleep() within your program. Eventually, you will encounter a concurrency issue.

Synchronization Using the VB 2005 SyncLock Keyword

The first technique you can use to synchronize access to shared resources is the VB 2005 SyncLock keyword. This keyword allows you to define a scope of statements that must be synchronized between threads. By doing so, incoming threads cannot interrupt the current thread, preventing it from finishing its work. The SyncLock keyword requires you to specify a *token* (an object reference) that must be acquired by a thread to enter within the lock scope. When you are attempting to lock down an instance-level method, you can simply pass in a reference to the current type:

```
' Use the current object as the thread token.
SyncLock Me
    ' All code within this scope is thread-safe.
End SyncLock
```

If you examine the PrintNumbers() method, you can see that the shared resource the threads are competing to gain access to is the console window. Therefore, if you scope all interactions with the Console type within a lock scope as follows:

```vb
Public Class Printer
  Public Sub PrintNumbers()
    SyncLock Me
      Console.WriteLine("-> {0} is executing PrintNumbers()", _
        Thread.CurrentThread.Name)
      Console.Write("Your numbers: ")
      For i As Integer = 0 To 10
        Dim r As Random = New Random()
        Thread.Sleep(100 * r.Next(5))
        Console.Write(i & ", ")
      Next
      Console.WriteLine()
    End SyncLock
  End Sub
End Class
```

you have effectively designed a method that will allow the current thread to complete its task. Once a thread enters into a SyncLock scope, the lock token (in this case, a reference to the current object) is inaccessible by other threads until the lock is released once the SyncLock scope has exited. Thus, if Thread A has obtained the lock token, other threads are unable to enter the scope until Thread A relinquishes the lock token. If you now run the application, you can see that each thread has ample opportunity to finish its business, as shown in Figure 16-10.

Figure 16-10. *Concurrency in action, take three*

■**Source Code** The MultiThreadedPrinting application is included under the Chapter 16 subdirectory.

Synchronization Using the System.Threading.Monitor Type

The VB 2005 SyncLock statement is really just a shorthand notation for working with the System.Threading.Monitor class type. Once processed by the VB 2005 compiler, a SyncLock scope actually resolves to the following (which you can verify using ildasm.exe):

```
Public Sub PrintNumbers()
  Monitor.Enter(Me)
  Try
    Console.WriteLine("-> {0} is executing PrintNumbers()", _
      Thread.CurrentThread.Name)
    Console.Write("Your numbers: ")
    For i As Integer = 0 To 10
      Dim r As Random = New Random()
      Thread.Sleep(100 * r.Next(5))
      Console.Write(i & ", ")
    Next
    Console.WriteLine()
  Finally
    Monitor.Exit(Me)
  End Try
End Sub
```

First, notice that the Monitor.Enter() method is the ultimate recipient of the thread token you specified as the argument to the SyncLock keyword. Next, all code within a lock scope is wrapped within a try block. The corresponding Finally clause ensures that the thread token is released (via the Monitor.Exit() method), regardless of any possible runtime exception. If you were to modify the MultiThreadSharedData program to make direct use of the Monitor type (as just shown), you will find the output is identical.

Now, given that the SyncLock keyword seems to require less code than making explicit use of the System.Threading.Monitor type, you may wonder about the benefits of using the Monitor type directly. The short answer is control. If you make use of the Monitor type, you are able to instruct the active thread to wait for some duration of time (via the Wait() method), inform waiting threads when the current thread is completed (via the Pulse() and PulseAll() methods), and so on.

As you would expect, in a great number of cases, the VB 2005 SyncLock keyword will fit the bill. However, if you are interested in checking out additional members of the Monitor class, consult the .NET Framework 2.0 SDK documentation.

Synchronization Using the System.Threading.Interlocked Type

Although it always is hard to believe until you look at the underlying CIL code, assignments and simple arithmetic operations are *not atomic*! For this reason, the System.Threading namespace provides a type that allows you to operate on a single point of data atomically with less overhead than with the Monitor type. The Interlocked class type defines the shared members shown in Table 16-4.

Table 16-4. *Members of the* System.Threading.Interlocked *Type*

Member	Meaning in Life
CompareExchange()	Safely tests two values for equality and, if equal, changes one of the values with a third
Decrement()	Safely decrements a value by 1
Exchange()	Safely swaps two values
Increment()	Safely increments a value by 1

Although it might not seem like it from the onset, the process of atomically altering a single value is quite common in a multithreaded environment. Assume you have a method named AddOne() that increments an integer member variable named intVal. Rather than writing synchronization code such as the following:

```
Public Sub AddOne()
  SyncLock Me
    initVal = intVal + 1
  End SyncLock
End Sub
```

you can simplify your code via the shared Interlocked.Increment() method. Simply pass in the variable to increment by reference. Do note that the Increment() method not only adjusts the value of the incoming parameter, but also returns the new value:

```
Public Sub AddOne()
  Dim newVal As Integer = Interlocked.Increment(ntVal)
End Sub
```

In addition to Increment() and Decrement(), the Interlocked type allows you to atomically assign numerical and object data. For example, if you wish to assign a member variable to the value 83, you can avoid the need to use an explicit SyncLock statement (or explicit Monitor logic) and make use of the Interlocked.Exchange() method:

```
Public Sub SafeAssignment()
  Interlocked.Exchange(myInt, 83)
End Sub
```

Finally, if you wish to test two values for equality to change the point of comparison in a thread-safe manner, you are able to leverage the Interlocked.CompareExchange() method as follows:

```
Public Sub CompareAndExchange()
  ' If the value of myInt is currently 83, change i to 99.
  Interlocked.CompareExchange(myInt, 99, 83)
End Sub
```

Synchronization Using the <Synchronization> Attribute

The final synchronization primitive examined here is the <Synchronization> attribute, which is a member of the System.Runtime.Remoting.Contexts namespace. In essence, this class-level attribute effectively locks down *all* instance member code of the object for thread safety. When the CLR allocates objects attributed with <Synchronization>, it will place the object within a synchronized context. As you may recall from Chapter 15, objects that should not be removed from a contextual boundary should derive from ContextBoundObject. Therefore, if you wish to make the Printer class type thread-safe (without explicitly writing thread-safe code within the class members), you could update the definition like so:

```
Imports System.Runtime.Remoting.Contexts
...

' All methods of Printer are now thread-safe!
<Synchronization> _
Public Class Printer
  Inherits ContextBoundObject
  Public Sub PrintNumbers()
    ...
  End Sub
End Class
```

In some ways, this approach can be seen as the lazy way to write thread-safe code, given that you are not required to dive into the details about which aspects of the type are truly manipulating thread-sensitive data. The major downfall of this approach, however, is that even if a given method is not making use of thread-sensitive data, the CLR will *still* lock invocations to the method. Obviously, this could degrade the overall functionality of the type, so use this technique with care.

At this point, you have seen a number of ways you are able to provide synchronized access to shared data. To be sure, additional types are available under the System.Threading namespace, which I will encourage you to explore at your leisure. To wrap up our examination of thread programming, allow me to introduce three additional types: TimerCallback, Timer, and ThreadPool.

Programming with Timer Callbacks

Many applications have the need to call a specific method during regular intervals of time. For example, you may have an application that needs to display the current time on a status bar via a given helper function. As another example, you may wish to have your application call a helper function every so often to perform noncritical background tasks such as checking for new e-mail messages. For situations such as these, you can use the System.Threading.Timer type in conjunction with a related delegate named TimerCallback.

To illustrate, assume you have a console application that will print the current time every second until the user presses a key to terminate the application. The first obvious step is to write the method that will be called by the Timer type:

```
Sub PrintTime(ByVal state As Object)
  Console.WriteLine("Time is: {0}", _
    DateTime.Now.ToLongTimeString())
End Sub
```

Notice how this method has a single parameter of type System.Object and is a subroutine, rather than a function. This is not optional, given that the TimerCallback delegate can only call methods that match this signature. The value passed into the target of your TimerCallback delegate can be any bit of information whatsoever (in the case of the e-mail example, this parameter might represent the name of the Microsoft Exchange server to interact with during the process). Also note that given that this parameter is indeed a System.Object, you are able to pass in multiple arguments using a System.Array or custom class/structure.

The next step is to configure an instance of the TimerCallback delegate and pass it into the Timer object. In addition to configuring a TimerCallback delegate, the Timer constructor allows you to specify the optional parameter information to pass into the delegate target (defined as a System.Object), the interval to poll the method, and the amount of time to wait (in milliseconds) before making the first call, for example:

```
Sub Main()
  Console.WriteLine("***** Working with Timer type *****")
  Console.WriteLine()

  ' Create the delegate for the Timer type.
  Dim timeCB As TimerCallback = AddressOf PrintTime

  ' Pass in the delegate instance, data to send the
  ' method 'pointed to', time to wait before starting
  ' and interval of time between calls.
  Dim t As Timer = New Timer(timeCB, Nothing, 0, 1000)

  Console.WriteLine("Hit key to terminate...")
  Console.ReadLine()
End Sub
```

As you would guess, if you don't need to use the `TimerCallback` delegate object directly, you can simply create your `Timer` object as follows:

```
Dim t As Timer = New Timer(AddressOf PrintTime, Nothing, 0, 1000)
```

In any case, the `PrintTime()` method will be called roughly every second and will pass in no additional information to said method. If you did wish to send in some information for use by the delegate target, simply substitute the null value of the second constructor parameter with the appropriate information:

```
Dim t As Timer = New Timer(AddressOf PrintTime, "Hi", 0, 1000)
```

We could now make use of this data within the `PrintTime()` method. Consider the following updates:

```
Sub PrintTime(ByVal state As Object)
  Console.WriteLine("Time is: {0}, Param is: {1}", _
    DateTime.Now.ToLongTimeString, state.ToString())
End Sub
```

Figure 16-11 shows the output.

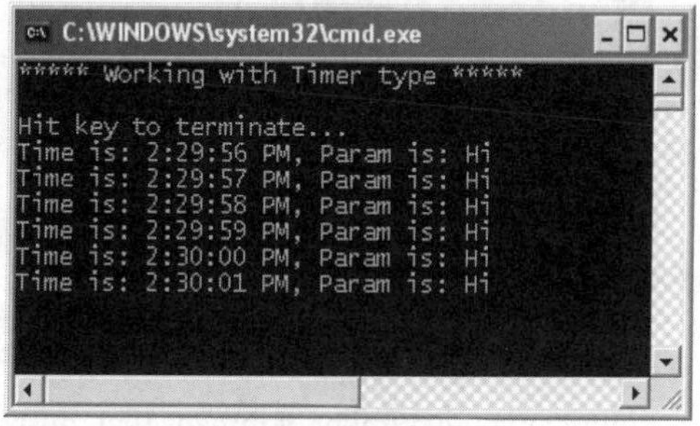

Figure 16-11. *Timers at work*

■**Source Code** The TimerApp application is included under the Chapter 16 subdirectory.

Understanding the CLR ThreadPool

The final thread-centric topic we will examine in this chapter is the CLR thread pool. When you invoke a method asynchronously using delegate types (via the `BeginInvoke()` method), the CLR does not literally create a brand-new thread. For purposes of efficiency, a delegate's `BeginInvoke()` method leverages a pool of worker threads that is maintained by the runtime. To allow you to interact with this pool of waiting threads, the `System.Threading` namespace provides the `ThreadPool` class type.

If you wish to queue a method call for processing by a worker thread in the pool, you can make use of the `ThreadPool.QueueUserWorkItem()` method. This method has been overloaded to allow you to specify an optional `System.Object` for custom state data in addition to an instance of the `WaitCallback` delegate.

The WaitCallback delegate can point to any subroutine that takes a System.Object as its sole parameter (which represents the optional state data). Do note that if you do not provide a System.Object when calling QueueUserWorkItem(), the CLR automatically passes the value Nothing. To illustrate queuing methods for use by the CLR thread pool, consider the following program, which makes use of the Printer type once again. In this case, however, you are not manually creating an array of Thread types; rather, you are assigning members of the pool to the PrintNumbers() method:

```
Module Program
  Sub Main()
    Console.WriteLine("Main thread started. ThreadID = {0}", _
      Thread.CurrentThread.GetHashCode)
    Dim p As Printer = New Printer
    Dim workItem As WaitCallback = AddressOf PrintTheNumbers

    ' Queue the method 10 times
    For i As Integer = 0 To 9
      ThreadPool.QueueUserWorkItem(workItem, p)
    Next
    Console.WriteLine("All tasks queued")
    Console.ReadLine()
  End Sub

  Sub PrintTheNumbers(ByVal state As Object)
    Dim task As Printer = CType(state, Printer)
    task.PrintNumbers()
  End Sub
End Module
```

At this point, you may be wondering whether it would be advantageous to make use of the CLR-maintained thread pool rather than explicitly creating Thread objects. Consider these major benefits of leveraging the thread pool:

- The thread pool manages threads efficiently by minimizing the number of threads that must be created, started, and stopped.

- By using the thread pool, you can focus on your business problem rather than the application's threading infrastructure.

However, using manual thread management is preferred in some cases, for example:

- If you require foreground threads or must set the thread priority. Pooled threads are *always* background threads with default priority (ThreadPriority.Normal).

- If you require a thread with a fixed identity in order to abort it, suspend it, or discover it by name.

Source Code The ThreadPoolApp application is included under the Chapter 16 subdirectory.

That wraps up our examination of multithreaded programming under .NET. To be sure, the System.Threading namespace defines numerous types beyond what I had the space to cover in this chapter. Nevertheless, at this point you should have a solid foundation to build on.

Summary

This chapter began by examining how .NET delegate types can be configured to execute a method in an asynchronous manner. As you have seen, the BeginInvoke() and EndInvoke() methods allow you to indirectly manipulate a background thread with minimum fuss and bother. During this discussion, you were also introduced to the IAsyncResult interface and AsyncResult class type. As you learned, these types provide various ways to synchronize the calling thread and obtain possible method return values.

The remainder of this chapter examined the role of the System.Threading namespace. As you learned, when an application creates additional threads of execution, the result is that the program in question is able to carry out numerous tasks at (what appears to be) the same time. You also examined several manners in which you can protect thread-sensitive blocks of code to ensure that shared resources do not become unusable units of bogus data. Last but not least, you learned that the CLR maintains an internal pool of threads for the purposes of performance and convenience.

CHAPTER 17

■ ■ ■

COM and .NET Interoperability

By now, you've gained a solid foundation in the VB 2005 language and the core services provided by the .NET platform. I suspect that when you contrast the object model provided by .NET to that of classic COM and VB 6.0, you'll no doubt be convinced that these are two entirely unique systems. Regardless of the fact that COM is now considered to be a legacy framework, few of us are in a position to completely abandon the ways of COM and Visual Basic 6.0 (after all, we'll always have legacy systems to maintain). The truth is that people have spent hundreds of thousands of hours building systems that make substantial use of these legacy technologies.

Thankfully, the .NET platform provides various types, tools, and namespaces that make the process of COM and .NET interoperability quite straightforward. The chapter begins by examining the process of .NET to COM interoperability and the related Runtime Callable Wrapper (RCW). The latter part of this chapter examines the opposite situation: a COM type communicating with a .NET type using a COM Callable Wrapper (CCW).

■**Note** A full examination of the .NET interoperability layer would require a book unto itself. If you require more details than presented in this introductory chapter, check out my book *COM and .NET Interoperability* (Apress, 2002).

The Scope of .NET Interoperability

Recall that when you build assemblies using a .NET-aware compiler, you are creating *managed code* that can be hosted by the Common Language Runtime (CLR). Managed code offers a number of benefits such as automatic memory management, a unified type system (the CTS), self-describing assemblies, and so forth. As you have also seen, .NET assemblies have a particular internal composition. In addition to CIL instructions and type metadata, assemblies contain a manifest that fully documents any required external assemblies as well as other file-related details (strong naming, version, etc.).

On the other side of the spectrum are legacy COM servers (which are, of course, *unmanaged code*). These binaries bear no relationship to .NET assemblies beyond a shared file extension (*.dll or *.exe). First of all, COM servers contain platform-specific machine code, not platform-agnostic CIL instructions, and work with a unique set of data types (often termed *oleautomation* or *variant-compliant* data types), none of which are directly understood by the CLR. In addition to the necessary COM-centric infrastructure required by all COM binaries (such as registry entries and support for core COM interfaces like IUnknown) is the fact that COM types demand to be *reference counted* in order to correctly control the lifetime of a COM object. This is in stark contrast, of course, to a .NET object, which is allocated on a managed heap and handled by the CLR garbage collector.

Given that .NET types and COM types have so little in common, you may wonder how these two architectures can make use of each others' services. Unless you are lucky enough to work for a company dedicated to "100% Pure .NET" development, you will most likely need to build .NET solutions that use legacy COM types. As well, you may find that a legacy COM server might like to communicate with the types contained within a shiny new .NET assembly.

The bottom line is that for some time to come, COM and .NET must learn how to get along. This chapter examines the process of managed and unmanaged types living together in harmony using the .NET interoperability layer. In general, the .NET Framework supports two core flavors of interoperability:

- .NET types using COM types
- COM types using .NET types

As you see throughout this chapter, the .NET Framework 2.0 SDK and Visual Studio 2005 supply a number of tools that help bridge the gap between these unique architectures. As well, the .NET base class library defines a namespace (`System.Runtime.InteropServices`) dedicated solely to the issue of interoperability. However, before diving in too far under the hood, let's look at a very simple example of .NET to COM interoperability.

■**Note** The .NET platform also makes it very simple for a .NET assembly to call into the underlying API of the operating system (as well as any C-based unmanaged *.dll) using a technology termed *platform invocation* (or simply *PInvoke*). From a VB 2005 point of view, working with PInvoke looks very similar to working with VB 6.0, as we can simply use the `Declare` statement. As an alternative, the .NET platform provides the language-neutral `<DllImport>` attribute, which performs the same function as the VB 2005–specific `Declare` statement. Although PInvoke is not examined in this chapter, check out the `Declare` keyword (and `<DllImport>` attribute) using the .NET Framework 2.0 SDK documentation for further details.

A Simple Example of .NET to COM Interop

To begin our exploration of interoperability services, let's see just how simple things appear on the surface. The goal of this section is to build a VB 6.0 ActiveX *.dll server, which is then consumed by a VB 2005 application. Fire up VB 6.0, and create a new ActiveX *.dll project named SimpleComServer and rename your initial class file to ComCalc.cs and name the class itself ComCalc. As you may know, the name of your project and the names assigned to the contained classes will be used to define the programmatic identifier (ProgID) of the COM types (SimpleComServer.ComCalc, in this case). Finally, define the following methods within ComCalc.cls:

```
' The VB 6.0 COM object
Option Explicit

Public Function Add(ByVal x As Integer, ByVal y As Integer) As Integer
  Add = x + y
End Function
Public Function Subtract(ByVal x As Integer, ByVal y As Integer) As Integer
  Subtract = x - y
End Function
```

At this point, compile your *.dll (via the File ➤ Make menu option) and, just to keep things peaceful in the world of COM, establish binary compatibility (via the Component tab of the project's Property page) before you exit the VB 6.0 IDE. This will ensure that if you recompile the application, VB 6.0 will preserve the assigned globally unique identifiers (GUIDs).

■**Source Code** The SimpleComServer is located under the Chapter 17 subdirectory.

Building the VB 2005 Client

Now open up Visual Studio 2005 and create a new VB 2005 console application named VBNetSimpleComClient. When you are building a .NET application that needs to communicate with a legacy COM application, the first step is to reference the COM server within your project (much like you reference a .NET assembly).

To do so, simply access the Project ➤ Add Reference menu selection and select the COM tab from the Add Reference dialog box. The name of your COM server will be listed alphabetically, as the VB 6.0 compiler updated the system registry with the necessary listings when you compiled your COM server. Go ahead and select the SimpleComServer.dll as shown in Figure 17-1 and close the dialog box.

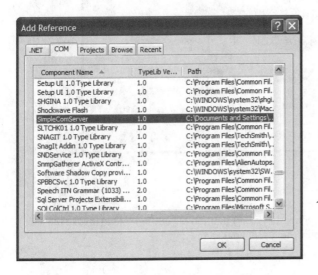

Figure 17-1. *Referencing a COM server using Visual Studio 2005*

Now, if you click the Show All Files button on the Solution Explorer, you see what looks to be a new .NET assembly reference added to your project, as illustrated in Figure 17-2. Formally speaking, assemblies that are generated when referencing a COM server are termed *interop assemblies*. Without getting too far ahead of ourselves at this point, simply understand that interop assemblies contain .NET descriptions of COM types.

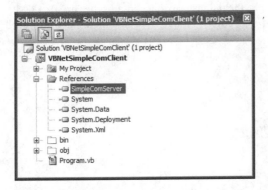

Figure 17-2. *The referenced interop assembly*

Although we have not added any code to our initial module, if you compile your application and examine the project's bin\Debug directory, you will find that a local copy of the generated interop assembly has been placed in the application directory (see Figure 17-3). Notice that Visual Studio 2005 automatically prefixes `Interop.` to interop assemblies generated when using the Add Reference dialog box—however, this is only a convention; the CLR does not demand that interop assemblies follow this particular naming convention.

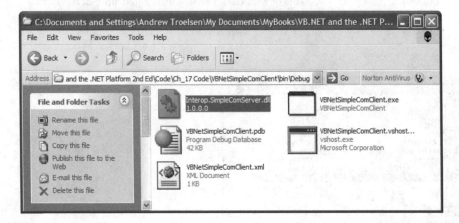

Figure 17-3. *The autogenerated interop assembly*

To complete this initial example, update the `Main()` method of your module to invoke the `Add()` method from a `ComCalc` object and display the result. For example:

```
Imports SimpleComServer

Module Program
  Sub Main()
    Console.WriteLine("***** The .NET COM Client App *****")
    Dim comObj As New ComCalc()
    Console.WriteLine("COM server says 10 + 832 is {0}", _
      comObj.Add(10, 832))
    Console.ReadLine()
  End Sub
End Module
```

As you can see from the previous code example, the namespace that contains the `ComCalc` COM object is named identically to the original VB 6.0 project (notice the `Imports` statement). The output shown in Figure 17-4 is as you would expect.

Figure 17-4. *Behold! .NET to COM interoperability*

As you can see, consuming a COM type from a .NET application can be a very transparent operation indeed. As you might imagine, however, a number of details are occurring behind the scenes to make this communication possible, the gory details of which you will explore throughout this chapter, beginning with taking a deeper look into the interop assembly itself.

Investigating a .NET Interop Assembly

As you have just seen, when you reference a COM server using the Visual Studio 2005 Add Reference dialog box, the IDE responds by generating a brand-new .NET assembly taking an `Interop.` prefix (such as `Interop.SimpleComServer.dll`). Just like an assembly that you would create yourself, interop assemblies contain type metadata, an assembly manifest, and under some circumstances *may* contain CIL code. As well, just like a "normal" assembly, interop assemblies can be deployed privately (e.g., within the directory of the client assembly) or assigned a strong name to be deployed to the GAC.

Interop assemblies are little more than containers to hold .NET metadata descriptions of the original COM types. In many cases, interop assemblies do not contain CIL instructions to implement their methods, as the real work is taking place in the COM server itself. The only time an interop assembly contains executable CIL instructions is if the COM server contains COM objects that have the ability to fire events to the client. In this case, the CIL code within the interop assembly is used by the CLR to manage the event handing logic.

At first glance, it may seem that interop assemblies are not entirely useful, given that they do not contain any implementation logic. However, the metadata descriptions within an interop assembly are extremely important, as it will be consumed by the CLR at runtime to build a runtime proxy (termed the *Runtime Callable Wrapper*, or simply *RCW*) that forms a bridge between the .NET application and the COM object it is communicating with.

You'll examine the details of the RCW in the next several sections; however, for the time being, open up the `Interop.SimpleComServer.dll` assembly using `ildasm.exe`, as you see in Figure 17-5.

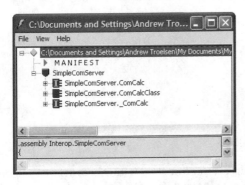

Figure 17-5. *The guts of the* `Interop.SimpleComServer.dll` *interop assembly*

As you can see, although the original VB6 project only defined a single COM class (`ComCalc`), the interop assembly contains *three* types. To make things even more confusing, if you were to examine the interop assembly using Visual Studio 2005, you only see a single type named `ComCalc`. Rest assured that `ComCalcClass` and `_ComCalc` are within the interop assembly. To view them, you simply need to elect to view hidden types with the VS 2005 Object Browser (see Figure 17-6).

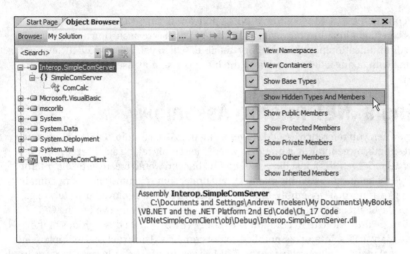

Figure 17-6. *Viewing hidden types within our interop assembly*

Simply put, each COM class is represented by three distinct .NET types. First, you have a .NET type that is identically named to the original COM type (ComCalc, in this case). Next, you have a second .NET type that takes a Class suffix (ComCalcClass). These types are very helpful when you have a COM type that implements several custom interfaces, in that the Class-suffixed types expose *all* members from *each* interface supported by the COM type. Thus, from a .NET programmer's point of view, there is no need to manually obtain a reference to a specific COM interface before invoking its functionality. Although ComCalc did not implement multiple custom interfaces, we are able to invoke the Add() and Subtract() methods from a ComCalcClass object (rather than a ComCalc object) as follows:

```
Module Program
  Sub Main()
  Console.WriteLine("***** The .NET COM Client App *****")

  ' Now using the Class-suffixed type.
  Dim comObj As New ComCalcClass()
    Console.WriteLine("COM server says 10 + 832 is {0}", _
      comObj.Add(10, 832))
    Console.ReadLine()
  End Sub
End Module
```

Finally, interop assemblies define .NET equivalents of any original COM interfaces defined within the COM server. In this case, we find a .NET interface named _ComCalc. Unless you are well versed in the mechanics of VB 6.0 COM, this is certain to appear strange, given that we never directly created an interface in our SimpleComServer project (let alone the oddly named _ComCalc interface). The role of these underscore-prefixed interfaces will become clear as you move throughout this chapter; for now, simply know that if you really wanted to, you could make use of interface-based programming techniques to invoke Add() or Subtract():

```
Module Program
  Sub Main()
    Console.WriteLine("***** The .NET COM Client App *****")

    ' Now manually obtain the hidden interface.
    Dim i As SimpleComServer._ComCalc
```

```
      Dim c As New ComCalc
      i = CType(c, _ComCalc)
      Console.WriteLine("COM server says 10 + 832 is {0}", _
        i.Add(10, 832))
      Console.ReadLine()
    End Sub
End Module
```

Now, do understand that invoking a method using the Class-suffixed or underscore-prefixed interface is seldom necessary (which is exactly why the Visual Studio 2005 Object Browser hides these types by default). However, as you build more complex .NET applications that need to work with COM types in more sophisticated manners, having knowledge of these types is critical.

■Source Code The VBNetSimpleComClient project is located under the Chapter 17 subdirectory.

Understanding the Runtime Callable Wrapper

As mentioned, at runtime the CLR will make use of the metadata contained within a .NET interop assembly to build a proxy type that will manage the process of .NET to COM communication. The proxy to which I am referring is the Runtime Callable Wrapper, which is little more than a bridge to the real COM class (officially termed a *coclass*). Every coclass accessed by a .NET client requires a corresponding RCW. Thus, if you have a single .NET application that uses three COM coclasses, you end up with three distinct RCWs that map .NET calls into COM requests. Figure 17-7 illustrates the big picture.

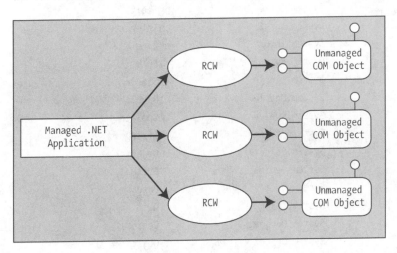

Figure 17-7. *RCWs sit between the .NET caller and the COM object.*

■Note There is always a single RCW per COM object, regardless of how many interfaces the .NET client has obtained from the COM type (you'll examine a multi-interfaced VB 6.0 COM object a bit later in this chapter). Using this technique, the RCW can maintain the correct COM identity (and reference count) of the COM object.

Again, the good news is that the RCW is created automatically when required by the CLR. The other bit of good news is that legacy COM servers do not require any modifications to be consumed by a .NET-aware language. The intervening RCW takes care of the internal work. To see how this is achieved, let's formalize some core responsibilities of the RCW.

The RCW: Exposing COM Types As .NET Types

The RCW is in charge of transforming COM data types into .NET equivalents (and vice versa). As a simple example, assume you have a VB 6.0 COM subroutine defined as follows:

```
' VB 6.0 COM method definition.
Public Sub DisplayThisString(ByVal s as String)
```

The interop assembly defines the method parameter as a .NET System.String:

```
' VB 2005 mapping of COM method.
Public Sub DisplayThisString(ByVal s as System.String)
```

When this method is invoked by the .NET code base, the RCW automatically takes the incoming System.String and transforms it into a VB 6.0 String data type (which, as you may know, is in fact a COM BSTR). As you would guess, all VB 6.0 COM data types have a corresponding .NET equivalent. To help you gain your bearings, Table 17-1 documents the mapping taking place between COM IDL (interface definition language) data types, the related .NET System data types, and the corresponding VB 2005 keyword.

Table 17-1. *Mapping Intrinsic COM Types to .NET Types*

COM IDL Data Type	System Types	Visual Basic 2005 Data Type
wchar_t, short	System.Int16	Short
long, int	System.Int32	Integer
Hyper	System.Int64	Long
unsigned char, byte	System.Byte	Byte
single	System.Single	Single
double	System.Double	Double
VARIANT_BOOL	System.Boolean	Boolean
BSTR	System.String	String
VARIANT	System.Object	Object
DECIMAL	System.Decimal	Decimal
DATE	System.DateTime	DateTime
GUID	System.Guid	Guid
CURRENCY	System.Decimal	Decimal
IUnknown	System.Object	Object
IDispatch	System.Object	Object

■**Note** You will come to understand the importance of having some knowledge of IDL data types as you progress through this chapter.

The RCW: Managing a Coclass's Reference Count

Another important duty of the RCW is to manage the reference count of the COM object. As you may know from your experience with COM, the COM reference-counting scheme is a joint venture between coclass and client and revolves around the proper use of AddRef() and Release() calls. COM classes self-destruct when they detect that they have no outstanding references (thankfully, VB 6.0 would call these low-level COM methods behind the scenes).

However, .NET types do not use the COM reference-counting scheme, and therefore a .NET client should not be forced to call Release() on the COM types it uses. To keep each participant happy, the RCW caches all interface references internally and triggers the final release when the type is no longer used by the .NET client. The bottom line is that similar to VB 6.0, .NET clients never explicitly call AddRef(), Release(), or QueryInterface().

■**Note** If you wish to directly interact with a COM object's reference count from a .NET application, the System.Runtime.InteropServices namespace provides a type named Marshal. This class defines a number of shared methods, many of which can be used to manually interact with a COM object's lifetime. Although you will typically not need to make use of Marshal in most of your applications, consult the .NET Framework 2.0 SDK documentation for further details.

The RCW: Hiding Low-level COM Interfaces

The final core service provided by the RCW is to consume a number of low-level COM interfaces. Because the RCW tries to do everything it can to fool the .NET client into thinking it is communicating with a native .NET type, the RCW must hide various low-level COM interfaces from view.

For example, when you build a COM class that supports IConnectionPointContainer (and maintains a subobject or two supporting IConnectionPoint), the coclass in question is able to fire events back to the COM client. VB 6.0 hides this entire process from view using the Event and RaiseEvent keywords. In the same vein, the RCW also hides such COM "goo" from the .NET client. Table 17-2 outlines the role of these hidden COM interfaces consumed by the RCW.

Table 17-2. *Hidden COM Interfaces*

Hidden COM Interface	Meaning in Life
IConnectionPointContainer IConnectionPoint	Enable a coclass to send events back to an interested client. VB 6.0 automatically provides a default implementation of each of these interfaces.
IDispatch IProvideClassInfo	Facilitate "late binding" to a coclass. Again, when you are building VB 6.0 COM types, these interfaces are automatically supported by a given COM type.
IErrorInfo ISupportErrorInfo ICreateErrorInfo	These interfaces enable COM clients and COM objects to send and respond to COM errors.
IUnknown	The granddaddy of COM. Manages the reference count of the COM object and allows clients to obtain interfaces from the coclass.

The Role of COM IDL

At this point you hopefully have a solid understanding of the role of the interop assembly and the RCW. Before you go much further into the COM to .NET conversion process, it is necessary to review some of the finer details of COM IDL. Understand, of course, that this chapter is *not* intended to function as a complete COM IDL tutorial; however, to better understand the interop layer, you only need to be aware of a few IDL constructs.

As you saw in Chapter 14, a .NET assembly contains *metadata*. Formally speaking, metadata is used to describe each and every aspect of a .NET assembly, including the internal types (their members, base class, and so on), assembly version, and optional assembly-level information (strong name, culture, and so on).

In many ways, .NET metadata is the big brother of an earlier metadata format used to describe classic COM servers. Classic ActiveX COM servers (*.dlls or *.exes) document their internal types using a *type library*, which may be realized as a stand-alone *.tlb file or bundled into the COM server as an internal resource (which is the default behavior of VB 6.0). COM type libraries are themselves created using a metadata language called the Interface Definition Language and a special compiler named midl.exe (the Microsoft IDL compiler).

VB 6.0 does a fantastic job of hiding type libraries and IDL from view. In fact, many skilled VB COM programmers can live a happy and productive life ignoring the syntax of IDL altogether. Nevertheless, whenever you compile ActiveX project workspace types, VB automatically generates and embeds the type library within the physical *.dll or *.exe COM server. Furthermore, VB 6.0 ensures that the type library is automatically registered under a very particular part of the system registry: HKEY_CLASSES_ROOT\TypeLib (see Figure 17-8).

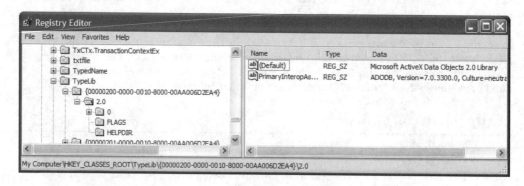

Figure 17-8. *HKCR\TypeLib lists all registered type libraries on a given machine.*

Type libraries are referenced all the time by numerous IDEs. For example, whenever you access the Project ➤ References menu selection of VB 6.0, the IDE consults HKCR\TypeLib to determine each and every registered type library, as shown in Figure 17-9.

■Note In reality, COM type library browser tools will only consult HKCR\TypeLib the first time the tool is activated, and cache the results for later use. This explains why the first time you load such tools, there is a noticeable delay.

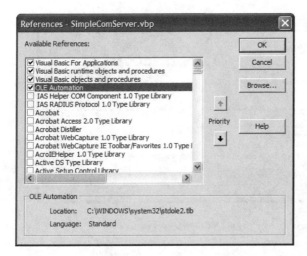

Figure 17-9. *Referencing COM type information from VB 6.0*

Likewise, when you open the VB 6.0 Object Browser, the VB 6.0 IDE reads the type information and displays the contents of the COM server using a friendly GUI, as shown in Figure 17-10.

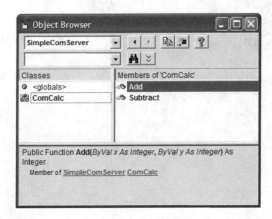

Figure 17-10. *Viewing type libraries using the VB 6.0 Object Browser*

Observing the Generated IDL for Your VB COM Server

Although the VB 6.0 Object Browser displays all COM types contained within a type library, the OLE View utility (oleview.exe) allows you to view the underlying IDL syntax used to build the corresponding type library. Again, few VB 6.0 developers need to know the gory details of the IDL language; however, to better understand the interoperability layer, open OLE View (via Start ➤ All Programs ➤ Microsoft Visual Studio 6.0 ➤ Microsoft Visual Studio 6.0 Tools) and locate the SimpleComServer server under the Type Libraries node of the tree view control, as shown in Figure 17-11.

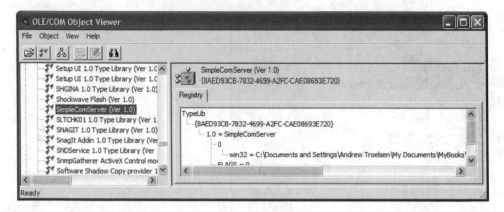

Figure 17-11. *Hunting down SimpleComServer using the OLE/COM object viewer*

If you were to double-click the type library icon, you would open a new window that shows you all of the IDL tokens that constitute the type library generated by the VB 6.0 compiler. Here is the relevant—and slightly reformatted—IDL (your [uuid] values will differ):

```
[uuid(8AED93CB-7832-4699-A2FC-CAE08693E720), version(1.0)]
library SimpleComServer
{
  importlib("stdole2.tlb");
  interface _ComCalc;

  [odl, uuid(5844CD28-2075-4E77-B619-9B65AA0761A3), version(1.0),
   hidden, dual, nonextensible, oleautomation]
  interface _ComCalc : IDispatch {
    [id(0x60030000)]
    HRESULT Add([in] short x, [in] short y,
                [out, retval] short* );
    [id(0x60030001)]
    HRESULT Subtract([in] short x, [in] short y,
                     [out, retval] short* );
  };

  [uuid(012B1485-6834-47FF-8E53-3090FE85050C), version(1.0)]
  coclass ComCalc {
      [default] interface _ComCalc;
  };
};
```

IDL Attributes

To begin parsing out this IDL, notice that IDL syntax contains blocks of code placed in square brackets ([. . .]). Within these brackets is a comma-delimited set of IDL keywords, which are used to disambiguate the "very next thing" (the item to the right of the block or the item directly below the block). These blocks are IDL *attributes* that serve the same purpose as .NET attributes (i.e., they describe something). One key IDL attribute is [uuid], which is used to assign the globally unique identifier (GUID) of a given COM type. As you may already know, just about everything in COM is assigned a GUID (interfaces, COM classes, type libraries, and so on), which is used to uniquely identify a given item.

The IDL Library Statement

Starting at the top, you have the COM "library statement," which is marked using the IDL *library* keyword. Contained within the library statement are each and every interface and COM class, and any enumeration (through the VB 6.0 Enum keyword) and user-defined type (through the VB 6.0 Type keyword). In the case of SimpleComServer, the type library lists exactly one COM class, ComCalc, which is marked using the *coclass* (i.e., COM class) keyword.

The Role of the [default] Interface

According to the laws of COM, the only possible way in which a COM client can communicate with a COM class is to use an interface reference (not an object reference). If you have created C++-based COM clients, you are well aware of the process of querying for a given interface, releasing the interface when it is no longer used, and so forth. However, when you make use of VB 6.0 to build COM clients, you receive a *default interface* on the COM class automatically.

When you build VB 6.0 COM servers, any public member on a *.cls file (such as your Add() function) is placed onto the "default interface" of the COM class. Now, if you examine the class definition of ComCalc, you can see that the name of the default interface is _ComCalc:

```
[uuid(012B1485-6834-47FF-8E53-3090FE85050C), version(1.0)]
coclass ComCalc {
  [default] interface _ComCalc;
};
```

In case you are wondering, the name of the default interface VB 6.0 constructs in the background is always *_NameOfTheClass* (the underscore is a naming convention used to specify a hidden interface, the very interface the VS 2005 Object Browser did not show by default). Thus, if you have a class named Car, the default interface is _Car, a class named DataConnector has a default interface named _DataConnector, and so forth.

Under VB 6.0, the default interface is completely hidden from view. However, when you write the following VB 6.0 code:

```
' VB 6.0 COM client code.
Dim c As ComCalc
Set c = New ComCalc ' [default] _ComCalc interface returned automatically!
```

the VB runtime automatically queries the object for the default interface (as specified by the type library) and returns it to the client. Because VB always returns the default interface on a COM class, you can pretend that you have a true object reference. However, this is only a bit of syntactic sugar provided by VB 6.0. In COM, there is no such thing as a direct object reference. You always have an interface reference (even if it happens to be the default).

The Role of IDispatch

If you examine the IDL description of the default _ComCalc interface, you see that this interface derives from a standard COM interface named IDispatch. While a full discussion concerning the role of IDispatch is well outside of the scope of this chapter, simply understand that this is the interface that makes it possible to interact with COM objects on the Web from within a classic Active Server Page, as well as anywhere else where late binding is required.

When you use VB proper (as opposed to VBScript), 99 percent of the time you want to avoid the use of IDispatch (it is slower, and errors are discovered at runtime rather than at compile time). However, just to illustrate, say you call the VB 6.0 CreateObject() method as follows:

```
' VB 6.0 late binding.
Dim o As Object
Set o = CreateObject("SimpleComServer.ComCalc")
```

You have actually instructed the VB runtime to query the COM type for the IDispatch interface. Note that calling CreateObject() alone does not trigger a query for IDispatch. In addition, you must store the return value in a VB 6.0 Object data type.

IDL Parameter Attributes

The final bit of IDL that you need to be aware of is how VB 6.0 parameters are expressed under the hood. As you know, under VB 6.0 all parameters are passed by reference, unless the ByVal keyword is used explicitly, which is represented using the IDL [in] attribute. Furthermore, a function's return value is marked using the [out, retval] attributes. Thus, the following VB 6.0 function:

```
' VB 6.0 function
Public Function Add(ByVal x as Integer, ByVal y as Integer) as Integer
  Add = x + y
End Function
```

would be expressed in IDL like so:

```
HRESULT Add([in] short* x, [in] short* y, [out, retval] short* );
```

On the other hand, if you do not mark a parameter using the VB 6.0 ByVal keyword, ByRef is assumed:

```
' These parameters are passed ByRef under VB 6.0!
Public Function Subtract(x As Integer, y As Integer) As Integer
  Subtract = x - y
End Function
```

ByRef parameters are marked in IDL via the [in, out] attributes:

```
HRESULT Subtract([in, out] short x,  [in, out] short y,  [out, retval] short* );
```

Using a Type Library to Build an Interop Assembly

To be sure, the VB 6.0 compiler generates many other IDL attributes under the hood, and you see additional bits and pieces where appropriate. However, at this point, I am sure you are wondering exactly why I spent the last several pages describing the COM IDL. The reason is simple: when you add a reference to a COM server using Visual Studio 2005, the IDE reads the type library to build the corresponding interop assembly. While VS 2005 does a very good job of generating an interop assembly, the Add Reference dialog box follows a default set of rules regarding how the interop assembly will be constructed and does not allow you to fine-tune this construction.

If you require a greater level of flexibility, you have the option of generating interop assemblies at the command prompt, using a .NET tool named tlbimp.exe (the type library importer utility). Among other things, tlbimp.exe allows you to control the name of the .NET namespace that will contain the types and the name of the output file. Furthermore, if you wish to assign a strong name to your interop assembly in order to deploy it to the GAC, tlbimp.exe provides the /keyfile flag to specify the *.snk file (see Chapter 13 for details regarding strong names). To view all of your options, simply type **tlbimp** at a Visual Studio 2005 command prompt and hit the Enter key, as shown in Figure 17-12.

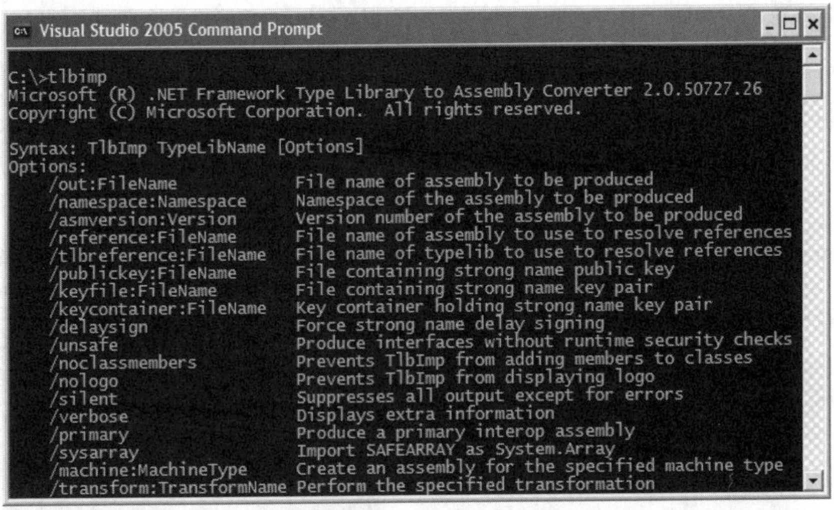

Figure 17-12. *Options of* tlbimp.exe

While this tool has numerous options, the following command could be used to generate a strongly named interop assembly named CalcInteropAsm.dll:

```
tlbimp SimpleComServer.dll /keyfile:myKeyPair.snk /out:CalcInteropAsm.dll
```

Again, if you are happy with the interop assembly created by Visual Studio 2005, you are not required to directly make use of tlbimp.exe.

Late Binding to the CoCalc Coclass

Once you have generated an interop assembly, your .NET applications are now able to make use of their types using early binding or late binding techniques. Given that you have already seen how to create a COM type using early binding at the opening of this chapter (via the VB 2005 New keyword), let's turn our attention to activating a COM object using late binding.

As you recall from Chapter 14, the System.Reflection namespace provides a way for you to programmatically inspect the types contained in a given assembly at runtime. In COM, the same sort of functionality is supported through the use of a set of standard interfaces (e.g., ITypeLib, ITypeInfo, and so on). When a client binds to a member at runtime (rather than at compile time), the client is said to exercise "late" binding.

By and large, you should always prefer the early binding technique using the VB 2005 New keyword. There are times, however, when you must use late binding to a coclass. For example, some legacy COM servers may have been constructed in such a way that they provide no type information whatsoever. If this is the case, it should be clear that you cannot run the tlbimp.exe utility in the first place. For these rare occurrences, you can access classic COM types using .NET reflection services.

The process of late binding begins with a client obtaining the IDispatch interface from a given coclass. This standard COM interface defines a total of four methods, only two of which you need to concern yourself with at the moment. First, you have GetIDsOfNames(). This method allows a late bound client to obtain the numerical value (called the dispatch ID, or DISPID) used to identify the method it is attempting to invoke.

In COM IDL, a member's DISPID is assigned using the [id] attribute. If you examine the IDL code generated by Visual Basic (using the OLE View tool), you will see that the DISPID of the Add() method has been assigned a DISPID such as the following:

```
[id(0x60030000)] HRESULT Add( [in] short x, [in] short y, [out, retval] short* );
```

This is the value that GetIDsOfNames() returns to the late bound client. Once the client obtains this value, it makes a call to the next method of interest, Invoke(). This method of IDispatch takes a number of arguments, one of which is the DISPID obtained using GetIDsOfNames(). In addition, the Invoke() method takes an array of COM VARIANT types that represent the parameters passed to the function. In the case of the Add() method, this array contains two shorts (of some value). The final argument of Invoke() is another VARIANT that holds the return value of the method invocation (again, a short).

Although a .NET client using late binding does not directly use the IDispatch interface, the same general functionality comes through using the System.Reflection namespace. To illustrate, the following is another VB 2005 client that uses late binding to trigger the Add() logic. Notice that this application does *not* make reference to the assembly in any way and therefore does not require the use of the tlbimp.exe utility.

```
Imports System.Reflection

Module Program
  Sub Main()
    Console.WriteLine("***** The Late Bound .NET Client *****")

    ' First get IDispatch reference from coclass.
    Dim calcObj As Type = _
      Type.GetTypeFromProgID("SimpleCOMServer.ComCalc")
    Dim calcDisp As Object = Activator.CreateInstance(calcObj)

    ' Make the array of args.
    Dim addArgs() As Object = {100, 24}

    ' Invoke the Add() method and obtain summation.
    Dim sum As Object
    sum = calcObj.InvokeMember("Add", BindingFlags.InvokeMethod, _
      Nothing, calcDisp, addArgs)

    ' Display result.
    Console.WriteLine("Late bound adding: 100 + 24 is: {0}", sum)
  End Sub
End Module
```

Finally, be aware that VB 2005 does allow you to simplify your late binding code by making use of the legacy CreateObject() method. However, the following VB 2005 late binding code would *only* work if Option Strict is disabled:

```
' This will only compile if Option Strict is disabled.
Dim c As Object = CreateObject("SimpleCOMServer.ComCalc")
Console.WriteLine("10 + 10 = {0}", c.Add(10, 10))
```

■**Source Code** The VBNetComClientLateBinding application is included under the Chapter 17 subdirectory.

Building a More Interesting VB 6.0 COM Server

So much for Math 101. It's time to build a more exotic VB 6.0 ActiveX server that makes use of more elaborate COM programming techniques. Create a brand-new ActiveX *.dll workspace named Vb6ComCarServer. Rename your initial class to CoCar, which is implemented like so:

```
Option Explicit

' A COM enum.
Enum CarType
  Viper
  Colt
  BMW
End Enum

' A COM Event.
Public Event BlewUp()

' Member variables.
Private currSp As Integer
Private maxSp As Integer
Private Make As CarType

' Remember! All Public members
' are exposed by the default interface!
Public Property Get CurrentSpeed() As Integer
  CurrentSpeed = currSp
End Property

Public Property Get CarMake() As CarType
  CarMake = Make
End Property

Public Sub SpeedUp()
  currSp = currSp + 10
  If currSp >= maxSp Then
    RaiseEvent BlewUp  ' Fire event If you max out the engine.
  End If
End Sub

Private Sub Class_Initialize()
  MsgBox "Init COM car"
End Sub

Public Sub Create(ByVal max As Integer, _
  ByVal cur As Integer, ByVal t As CarType)
  maxSp = max
  currSp = cur
  Make = t
End Sub
```

As you can see, this is a simple COM class that mimics the functionality of the VB 2005 Car class used throughout this text. The only point of interest is the Create() subroutine, which allows the caller to pass in the state data representing the Car object. (Remember, VB 6.0 has no support for class constructors!)

Supporting an Additional COM Interface

Now that you have fleshed out the details of building a COM class with a single (default) interface, insert a new *.cls file that defines the following IDriverInfo interface:

```
Option Explicit

' Driver has a name
Public Property Let driverName(ByVal s As String)
End Property
Public Property Get driverName() As String
End Property
```

If you have created COM objects supporting multiple interfaces, you are aware that VB 6.0 provides the *Implements* keyword. Once you specify the interfaces implemented by a given COM class, you are able to make use of the VB 6.0 code window to build the method stubs. Assume you have added a private String variable (driverName) to the CoCar class type and implemented the IDriverInfo interface as follows:

```
' Implemented interfaces
' [General][Declarations]
Implements IDriverInfo
...
' ***** IDriverInfo impl ***** '
Private Property Let IDriverInfo_driverName(ByVal RHS As String)
  driverName = RHS
End Property
Private Property Get IDriverInfo_driverName() As String
  IDriverInfo_driverName = driverName
End Property
```

To wrap up this interface implementation, set the Instancing property of IDriverInfo to PublicNotCreatable (given that the outside world should not be able to "New" an interface reference).

Exposing an Inner Object

Under VB 6.0 (as well as COM itself), we do not have the luxury of classical implementation inheritance. Rather, you are limited to the use of the containment/delegation model (the "has-a" relationship). For testing purposes, add a final *.cls file to your current VB 6.0 project named Engine, and set its instancing property to PublicNotCreatable (as you want to prevent the user from directly creating an Engine object).

The default public interface of Engine is short and sweet. Define a single function that returns an array of strings to the outside world representing pet names for each cylinder of the engine (okay, no right-minded person gives friendly names to his or her cylinders, but hey . . .):

```
Option Explicit

Public Function GetCylinders() As String()
  Dim c(3) As String
  c(0) = "Grimey"
  c(1) = "Thumper"
  c(2) = "Oily"
  c(3) = "Crusher"
  GetCylinders = c
End Function
```

Finally, add a method to the default interface of CoCar named GetEngine(), which returns an instance of the contained Engine (I assume you will create a Private member variable named eng of type Engine for this purpose):

```
' Return the Engine to the world.
Public Function GetEngine() As Engine
  Set GetEngine = eng
End Function
```

At this point you have an ActiveX server that contains a COM class supporting two interfaces. As well, you are able to return an internal COM type using the [default] interface of the CoCar and interact with some common programming constructs (enums and COM arrays). Go ahead and compile your sever (setting binary compatibility, once finished), and then close down your current VB 6.0 workspace.

■**Source Code**   The Vb6ComCarServer project is included under the Chapter 17 subdirectory.

Examining the Interop Assembly

Rather than making use of the tlbimp.exe utility to generate our interop assembly, simply create a new console project (named VbNetCarClient) using Visual Studio 2005 and set a reference to the Vb6ComCarServer.dll using the COM tab of the Add Reference dialog box. Now, examine the interop assembly using the VS 2005 Object Browser utility, as shown in Figure 17-13.

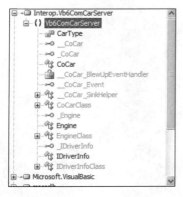

Figure 17-13. *The* Interop.VbComCarServer.dll *assembly*

Assuming you have configured the Object Browser to show hidden types, you will find that you once again have a number of Class-suffixed and underscore-prefixed interface types, as well as a number of new items we have not yet examined, whose names suggest they may be used to handle COM to .NET event notifications (_CoCar_Event, _CoCar_SinkHelper, and _CoCarBlewUpEventHandler in particular). Recall from earlier in this chapter, I mentioned that when a COM object exposes COM events, the interop assembly will contain additional CIL code that is used by the CLR to map COM events to .NET events (you'll see them in action in just a bit).

Building our VB 2005 Client Application

Given that the CLR will automatically create the necessary RCW at runtime, our VB 2005 application can program directly against the CoCar, CarType, Engine, and IDriveInfo types as if they were all implemented using managed code. Here is the complete module, with analysis to follow:

```
Imports Vb6ComCarServer

Module Program
  ' Create the COM class using
  ' early binding.
  Public WithEvents myCar As New CoCar()

  Sub Main()
    Console.WriteLine("***** CoCar Client App *****")

    ' Call the Create() method.
    myCar.Create(50, 10, CarType.BMW)

    ' Set name of driver.
    Dim itf As IDriverInfo
    itf = CType(myCar, IDriverInfo)
    itf.driverName = "Fred"
    Console.WriteLine("Drive is named: {0}", itf.driverName)

    ' Print type of car.
    Console.WriteLine("Your car is a {0}.", myCar.CarMake())
    Console.WriteLine()

    ' Get the Engine and print name of a Cylinders.
    Dim eng As Engine = myCar.GetEngine()
    Console.WriteLine("Your Cylinders are named:")
    Dim names() As String = CType(eng.GetCylinders(), String())
    For Each s As String In names
      Console.WriteLine(s)
    Next
    Console.WriteLine()

    ' Speed up car to trigger event.
    For i As Integer = 0 To 3
      myCar.SpeedUp()
    Next
  End Sub

  Private Sub myCar_BlewUp() Handles myCar.BlewUp
    Console.WriteLine("***** Ek!  Car is doomed...! *****")
  End Sub
End Module
```

Interacting with the CoCar Type

Recall that when we created the VB 6.0 CoCar, we defined and implemented a custom COM interface named IDriverInfo, in addition to the automatically generated default interface (_CoCar) created by the VB 6.0 compiler. When our Main() method creates an instance of CoCar, we only have direct access to the members of the _CoCar interface, which as you recall will be composed by each public member of the COM class:

```
' Here, you are really working with the [default] interface.
myCar.Create(50, 10, CarType.BMW)
```

Given this fact, in order to invoke the driverInfo property of the IDriverInfo interface, we must explicitly cast the CoCar object to an IDriverInfo interface as follows:

```
' Set name of driver.
Dim itf As IDriverInfo
itf = CType(myCar, IDriverInfo)
itf.driverName = "Fred"
Console.WriteLine("Drive is named: {0}", itf.driverName)
```

Recall, however, that when a type library is converted into an interop assembly, it will contain `Class`-suffixed types that expose every member of every interface. Therefore, if you so choose, you could simplify your programming if you create and make use of a `CoCarClass` object, rather than a `CoCar` object. For example, consider the following subroutine, which makes use of members of the default interface of `CoCar` as well as members of `IDriverInfo`:

```
Sub UseCar()
  Dim c As New CoCarClass()

  ' This property is a member of IDriverInfo.
  c.driverName = "Mary"

  ' This method is a member of _CoCar.
  c.SpeedUp()
End Sub
```

■**Note** Remember, because the `Class`-suffixed types are hidden by default, they will not appear in the Visual Studio 2005 IntelliSense.

If you are wondering exactly how this single type is exposing members of each implemented interface, check out the list of implemented interfaces and the base class of `CoCarClass` using the Visual Studio 2005 Object Browser (see Figure 17-14).

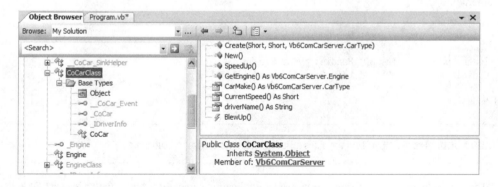

Figure 17-14. *The composition of* `CoCarClass`

As you can see, this type implements the hidden `_CoCar` and `_IDriverInfo` interfaces and exposes them as "normal" public members.

Intercepting COM Events

In Chapter 10, you learned about the .NET event model. Recall that this architecture is based on delegating the flow of logic from one part of the application to another. The entity in charge of forwarding a request is a type deriving from System.MulticastDelegate, which we create indirectly in VB 2005 using the Delegate keyword.

When the tlbimp.exe utility encounters event definitions in the COM server's type library, it responds by creating a number of managed types that wrap the low-level COM connection point architecture. Using these types, you can pretend to add a member to a System.MulticastDelegate's internal list of methods. Under the hood, of course, the proxy is mapping the incoming COM event to their managed equivalents. Table 17-3 briefly describes these types.

Table 17-3. *COM Event Helper Types*

Generated Type (Based on the _CarEvents [source] Interface)	Meaning in Life
__CoCar_Event	This is a managed interface that defines the add and remove members used to add (or remove) a method to (or from) the System.MulticastDelegate's linked list.
__CoCar_BlewUpEventHandler	This is the managed delegate (which derives from System.MulticastDelegate).
__CoCar_SinkHelper	This generated class implements the outbound interface in a .NET-aware sink object.

As you would hope, the VB 2005 language does not require you to make direct use of these types. Rather, you are able to handle the incoming COM events in the same way you handle events based on the .NET delegation architecture. Simply declare the COM type WithEvents, and use the Handles keyword to map the event to a given method (or make use of the AddHandler/RemoveHandler statements).

```
Module Program
  Public WithEvents myCar As New CoCar
...
  Private Sub myCar_BlewUp() Handles myCar.BlewUp
    Console.WriteLine("***** Ek!  Car is doomed...! *****")
  End Sub
End Module
```

■**Source Code** The VbNetCarClient project is included under the Chapter 17 subdirectory.

That wraps up our investigation of how a .NET application can communicate with a legacy COM application. Now be aware that the techniques you have just learned would work for *any* COM server at all. This is important to remember, given that many COM servers might never be rewritten as native .NET applications. For example, the object models of Microsoft Outlook and Microsoft Office products are currently exposed as COM types. Thus, if you needed to build a .NET program that interacted with these products, the interoperability layer is (currently) mandatory.

Understanding COM to .NET Interoperability

The next topic of this chapter is to examine the process of a COM application communicating with a .NET type. This "direction" of interop allows legacy COM code bases (such as your existing VB 6.0 projects) to make use of functionality contained within newer .NET assemblies. As you might imagine, this situation is less likely to occur than .NET to COM interop; however, it is still worth exploring.

For a COM application to make use of a .NET type, we somehow need to fool the COM program into believing that the managed .NET type is in fact *unmanaged*. In essence, you need to allow the COM application to interact with the .NET type using the functionality required by the COM architecture. For example, the COM type should be able to obtain new interfaces through QueryInterface() calls, simulate unmanaged memory management using AddRef() and Release(), make use of the COM connection point protocol, and so on. Again, although VB 6.0 does not expose this level of COM infrastructure to the surface, it must exist nonetheless.

Beyond fooling the COM client, COM to .NET interoperability also involves fooling the COM runtime. As you know, a COM server is activated using the COM runtime rather than the CLR. For this to happen, the COM runtime must look up numerous bits of information in the system registry (ProgIDs, CLSIDs, IIDs, and so forth). The problem, of course, is that .NET assemblies are not registered in the registry in the first place!

In a nutshell, to make your .NET assemblies available to COM clients, you must take the following steps:

1. Register your .NET assembly in the system registry to allow the COM runtime to locate it.

2. Generate a COM type library (*.tlb) file (based on the .NET metadata) to allow the COM client to interact with the public types.

3. Deploy the assembly in the same directory as the COM client or (more typically) install it into the GAC.

As you will see, these steps can be performed using Visual Studio 2005 or at the command line using various tools that ship with the .NET Framework 2.0 SDK.

The Attributes of System.Runtime.InteropServices

In addition to performing these steps, you will typically also need to decorate your VB 2005 types with various .NET attributes, all of which are defined in the System.Runtime.InteropServices namespace. These attributes ultimately control how the COM type library is created and therefore control how the COM application is able to interact with your managed types. Table 17-4 documents some (but not all) of the attributes you can use to control the generated COM type library.

Table 17-4. *Select Attributes of* System.Runtime.InteropServices

.NET Interop Attribute	Meaning in Life
<ClassInterface>	Used to create a default COM interface for a .NET class type.
<ComClass>	This attribute is similar to <ClassInterface>, except it also provides the ability to establish the GUIDs used for the class ID (CLSID) and interface IDs of the COM types within the type library.
<DispId>	Used to hard-code the DISPID values assigned to a member for purposes of late binding.
<Guid>	Used to hard-code a GUID value in the COM type library.
<In>	Exposes a member parameter as an input parameter in COM IDL.
<InterfaceType>	Used to control how a .NET interface should be exposed to COM (IDispatch-only, dual, or IUnknown-only).
<Out>	Exposes a member parameter as an output parameter in COM IDL.

Now do be aware that for simple COM to .NET interop scenarios, you are not required to adorn your .NET code with dozens of attributes in order to control how the underlying COM type library is defined. However, when you need to be very specific regarding how your .NET types will be exposed to COM, the more you understand COM IDL attributes the better, given that the attributes defined in System.Runtime.InteropServices are little more than managed definitions of these IDL keywords.

The Role of the CCW

Before we walk through the steps of exposing a .NET type to COM, let's take a look at exactly how COM programs interact with .NET types using a COM Callable Wrapper, or CCW. As you have seen, when a .NET program communicates with a COM type, the CLR creates a Runtime Callable Wrapper. In a similar vein, when a COM client accesses a .NET type, the CLR makes use of an intervening proxy termed the COM Callable Wrapper to negotiate the COM to .NET conversion (see Figure 17-15).

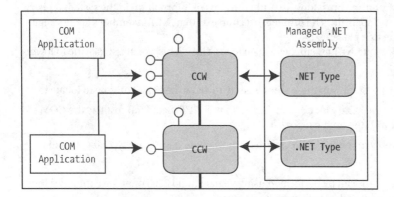

Figure 17-15. *COM types talk to .NET types using a CCW.*

Like any COM object, the CCW is a reference-counted entity. This should make sense, given that the COM client is assuming that the CCW is a real COM type and thus must abide by the rules of AddRef() and Release(). When the COM client has issued the final release, the CCW releases its reference to the real .NET type, at which point it is ready to be garbage collected.

The CCW implements a number of COM interfaces automatically to further the illusion that the proxy represents a genuine coclass. In addition to the set of custom interfaces defined by the .NET type (including an entity termed the *class interface* that you examine in just a moment), the CCW provides support for the standard COM behaviors described in Table 17-5.

Table 17-5. *The CCW Supports Many Core COM Interfaces*

CCW-implemented Interface	Meaning in Life
IConnectionPointContainer IConnectionPoint	If the .NET type supports any events, they are represented as COM connection points.
IEnumVariant	If the .NET type supports the IEnumerable interface, it appears to the COM client as a standard COM enumerator.
ISupportErrorInfo IErrorInfo	These interfaces allow coclasses to send COM error objects.

CCW-implemented Interface	Meaning in Life
ITypeInfo IProvideClassInfo	These interfaces allow the COM client to pretend to manipulate an assembly's COM type information. In reality, the COM client is interacting with .NET metadata.
IUnknown IDispatch IDispatchEx	These core COM interfaces provide support for early and late binding to the .NET type. IDispatchEx can be supported by the CCW if the .NET type implements the IExpando interface.

The Role of the .NET Class Interface

In classic COM, the only way a COM client can communicate with a COM object is to use an interface reference. In contrast, .NET types do not need to support any interfaces whatsoever, which is clearly a problem for a COM caller. Given that classic COM clients cannot work with object references, another responsibility of the CCW is to expose a *class interface* to represent each member defined by the type's public sector. As you can see, the CCW is taking the same approach as Visual Basic 6.0!

Defining a Class Interface

To define a class interface for your .NET types, you will need to apply the <ClassInterface> attribute on each public class you wish to expose to COM. Again, doing so will ensure that each public member of the class is exposed to a default autogenerated interface that follows the same exact naming convention as VB 6.0 (_NameOfTheClass). Technically speaking, applying this attribute is optional; however, you will almost always wish to do so. If you do not, the only way the COM caller can communicate with the type is using late binding (which is far less type safe and typically results in slower performance).

The <ClassInterface> attribute supports a named property (ClassInterfaceType) that controls exactly how this default interface should appear in the COM type library. Table 17-6 defines the possible settings.

Table 17-6. *Values of the* ClassInterfaceType *Enumeration*

ClassInterfaceType Member Name	Meaning in Life
AutoDispatch	Indicates the autogenerated default interface will only support late binding, and is equivalent to not applying the <ClassInterface> attribute at all.
AutoDual	Indicates that the autogenerated default interface is a "dual interface" and can therefore be interacted with using early binding or late binding. This would be the same behavior taken by VB 6.0 when it defines a default COM interface.
None	Indicates that no interface will be generated for the class. This can be helpful when you have defined your own strongly typed .NET interfaces that will be exposed to COM, and do not wish to have the "freebee" interface.

In the next example, you specify ClassInterfaceType.AutoDual as the class interface designation. In this way, late binding clients such as VBScript can access the Add() and Subtract() methods using IDispatch, while early bound clients (such as VB 6.0 or C++) can use the class interface (named _VbDotNetCalc).

Building Your .NET Types

To illustrate a COM type communicating with managed code, assume you have created a simple VB 2005 Class Library project named ComUsableDotNetServer, which defines a class named DotNetCalc. This class will define two simple methods named Add() and Subtract(). The implementation logic is trivial; however, notice the use of the <ClassInterface> attribute:

```
' We need this to obtain the necessary
' interop attributes.
Imports System.Runtime.InteropServices

<ClassInterface(ClassInterfaceType.AutoDual)> _
Public Class DotNetCalc
    Public Function Add(ByVal x As Integer, ByVal y As Integer) As Integer
        Return x + y
    End Function
    Public Function Subtract(ByVal x As Integer, ByVal y As Integer) As Integer
        Return x - y
    End Function
End Class
```

As mentioned earlier in this chapter, in the world of COM, just about everything is identified using a 128-bit number termed a GUID. These values are recorded into the system registry in order to define an identity of the COM type. Here, we have not specifically defined GUID values for our DotNetCalc class, and therefore the type library exporter tool (tlbexp.exe) will generate GUIDs on the fly. The problem with this approach, of course, is that each time you generate the type library (which we will do shortly), you receive unique GUID values, which can break existing COM clients.

To define specific GUID values, you may make use of the guidgen.exe utility, which is accessible from the Tools ➤ Create Guid menu item of Visual Studio 2005. Although this tool provides four GUID formats, the <Guid> attribute demands the GUID value be defined using the Registry Format option, as shown in Figure 17-16.

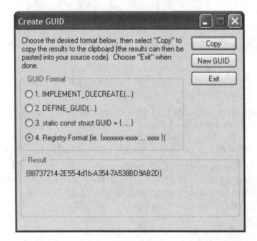

Figure 17-16. *Obtaining a GUID value*

Once you copy this value to your clipboard (via the Copy GUID button), you can then paste it in as an argument to the <Guid> attribute. Be aware that you must remove the curly brackets from the GUID value! This being said, here is our updated DotNetCalc class type:

```
<ClassInterface(ClassInterfaceType.AutoDual)> _
<Guid("88737214-2E55-4d1b-A354-7A538BD9AB2D")> _
Public Class DotNetCalc
  Public Function Add(ByVal x As Integer, ByVal y As Integer) As Integer
    Return x + y
  End Function
  Public Function Subtract(ByVal x As Integer, ByVal y As Integer) As Integer
    Return x - y
  End Function
End Class
```

On a related note, click the Show All Files button on the Solution Explorer and open up the assemblyInfo.vb file located under the My Project icon. By default, all Visual Studio 2005 project workspaces are provided with an assembly-level <Guid> attribute used to identify the GUID of the type library generated based on the .NET server (if exposed to COM).

```
' The following GUID is for the ID of the typelib if this project is exposed to COM
<Assembly: Guid("EB268C4F-EB36-464C-8A25-93212C00DC89")>
```

Inserting a COM Class Using Visual Studio 2005

While you are always able to manually add attributes to a .NET type for purposes of COM interop, Visual Studio 2005 provides a project item named Com Class, which can be inserted using the Project ➤ Add New Item dialog box. To illustrate, insert a new COM type named DotNetPerson, as you see in Figure 17-17.

Figure 17-17. *Inserting a Com Class using Visual Studio 2005*

Although the name of this project item is termed *Com Class*, it should be clear that what you are really inserting into your project is a .NET class type that is adorned with several attributes that expose this type to COM. Here is the initial code definition of the DotNetPerson:

```
<ComClass(DotNetPerson.ClassId, _
  DotNetPerson.InterfaceId, DotNetPerson.EventsId)> _
Public Class DotNetPerson

#Region "COM GUIDs"
  ' These GUIDs provide the COM identity for this class
  ' and its COM interfaces. If you change them, existing
  ' clients will no longer be able to access the class.
  Public Const ClassId As String = "ec2a6ec2-a681-41a1-a644-30c16c7409a9"
  Public Const InterfaceId As String = "ea905f17-5f7f-4958-b8c6-a95f419063a8"
  Public Const EventsId As String = "57c3d0e3-9e15-4b6a-a96e-b4c6736c7b6d"
#End Region

  ' A creatable COM class must have a Public Sub New()
  ' with no parameters; otherwise, the class will not be
  ' registered in the COM registry and cannot be created
  ' via CreateObject.
  Public Sub New()
    MyBase.New()
  End Sub
End Class
```

As you can see, DotNetPerson has been attributed with the <ComClass> attribute, rather than the <ClassInterface> attribute used previously. One benefit of <ComClass> is that it allows us to estab-lish the necessary GUIDs as direct arguments, as opposed to making use of additional attributes (such as <Guid>) individually. As well, notice that we have already been provided with a set of GUID values, and thus have no need to manually run the guidgen.exe utility.

■**Note** As explained in the generated code comments, all .NET types exposed to COM must have a default con-structor. Recall that when you define a custom constructor, the default is *removed* from the class definition. Here, the Com Class template ensures this does not happen by explicitly defining the default constructor in the initial code.

For testing purposes, add a single method to your DotNetPerson type that returns a hard-coded string.

```
Public Function GetMessage() As String
  Return "I am alive..."
End Function
```

Defining a Strong Name

As a best practice, all .NET assemblies that are exposed to COM should be assigned a strong name and installed into the global assembly cache (the GAC). Technically speaking, this is not required; however, if you do not deploy the assembly to the GAC, you will need to copy this assembly into the same folder as the COM application making use of it.

Given that Chapter 13 already walked you though the details of defining a strongly named assembly, simply generate a new *.snk file for signing purposes using the Signing tab of the My Project editor (see Figure 17-18).

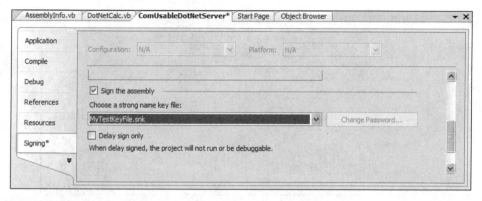

Figure 17-18. *Generating a strong name using Visual Studio 2005*

At this point, you can compile your assembly and install ComUsableDotNetServer.dll into the GAC using gacutil.exe (again, see Chapter 13 for details).

```
gacutil -i ComUsableDotNetServer.dll
```

Generating the Type Library and Registering the .NET Types

At this point, we are ready to generate the necessary COM type library and register our .NET assembly into the system registry for use by COM. Do to so, you can take two possible approaches. Your first approach is to use a command-line tool named regasm.exe, which ships with the .NET Framework 2.0 SDK. This tool will add several listings to the system registry, and when you specify the /tlb flag, it will also generate the required type library, as shown here:

```
regasm DotNetCalc.dll /tlb:VbDotNetCalc.tlb
```

■**Note** The .NET Framework 2.0 SDK also provides a tool named tlbexp.exe. Like regasm.exe, this tool will generate type libraries from a .NET assembly; however, it does not add the necessary registry entries. Given this, it is more common to simply use regasm.exe to perform each required step.

While regasm.exe provides the greatest level of flexibility regarding how the COM type library is to be generated, Visual Studio 2005 provides a handy alternative. Using the My Project editor, simply check the Register for COM Interop option on the Compile tab, as shown in Figure 17-19, and recompile your assembly.

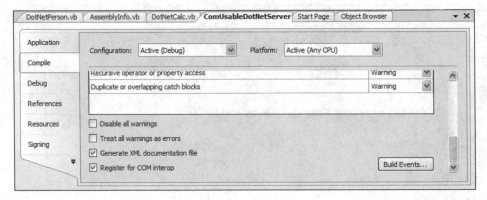

Figure 17-19. *Registering an assembly for COM interop using Visual Studio 2005*

Once you have run regasm.exe or enabled the Register for COM Interop option, you will find that your bin\Debug folder now contains a COM type library file (taking a *.tlb file extension).

■**Source Code** The ComUsableDotNetServer application is included under the Chapter 17 subdirectory.

Examining the Exported Type Information

Now that you have generated the corresponding COM type library, you can view its contents using the OLE View utility by loading the *.tlb file. If you load ComUsableDotNetServer.tlb (via the File ➤ View Type Library menu option), you will find the COM type descriptions for each of your .NET class types. For example, the DotNetCalc class has been defined to support the default _DotNetClass interface (due to the <ClassInterface> attribute, as well as an interface named (surprise, surprise) _Object. As you would guess, this is a unmanaged definition of the functionality defined by System.Object:

```
[uuid(88737214-2E55-4D1B-A354-7A538BD9AB2D),
 version(1.0), custom({0F21F359-AB84-41E8-9A78-36D110E6D2F9},
 "ComUsableDotNetServer.DotNetCalc")]
coclass DotNetCalc {
  [default] interface _DotNetCalc;
  interface _Object;
};
```

As specified by the <ClassInterface> attribute, the default interface has been configured as a dual interface, and can therefore be accessed using early or late binding:

```
[odl, uuid(AC807681-8C59-39A2-AD49-3072994C1EB1), hidden,
 dual, nonextensible, oleautomation,
 custom({0F21F359-AB84-41E8-9A78-36D110E6D2F9},
 "ComUsableDotNetServer.DotNetCalc")]
interface _DotNetCalc : IDispatch {
  [id(00000000), propget,
   custom({54FC8F55-38DE-4703-9C4E-250351302B1C}, "1")]
  HRESULT ToString([out, retval] BSTR* pRetVal);
  [id(0x60020001)]
  HRESULT Equals( [in] VARIANT obj,
                  [out, retval] VARIANT_BOOL* pRetVal);
```

```
[id(0x60020002)]
HRESULT GetHashCode([out, retval] long* pRetVal);
[id(0x60020003)]
HRESULT GetType([out, retval] _Type** pRetVal);
[id(0x60020004)]
HRESULT Add([in] long x, [in] long y,
    [out, retval] long* pRetVal);
[id(0x60020005)]
HRESULT Subtract( [in] long x, [in] long y,
                  [out, retval] long* pRetVal);
};
```

Notice that the _DotNetCalc interface not only describes the Add() and Subtract() methods, but also exposes the members inherited by System.Object! As a rule, when you expose a .NET class type to COM, all public methods defined up the chain of inheritance are also exposed through the autogenerated class interface.

Building a Visual Basic 6.0 Test Client

Now that the .NET assembly has been properly configured to interact with the COM runtime, you can build some COM clients. You can create a simple VB 6.0 Standard *.exe project type (named VB6_DotNetClient) and set a reference to the new generated type library (see Figure 17-20).

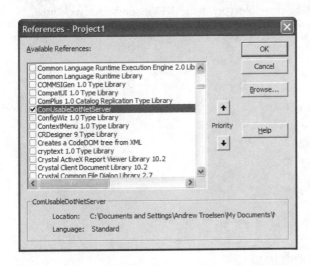

Figure 17-20. *Referencing your .NET server from VB 6.0*

As for the GUI front end, keep things really simple. A single Button object will be used to manipulate the DotNetCalc .NET type. Here is the code (notice that you are also invoking ToString(), defined by the _Object interface):

```
Private Sub btnUseDotNetObject_Click()
  ' Create the .NET object.
  Dim c As New DotNetCalc
  MsgBox c.Add(10, 10), , "Adding with .NET"
```

```
' Invoke some members of System.Object.
  MsgBox c.ToString, , "ToString value"
End Sub
```

Source Code The VB6_DotNetClient application is included under the Chapter 17 subdirectory.

So, at this point you have seen the process of building .NET applications that talk to COM types and COM applications that talk to .NET types. Again, while there are many additional topics regarding the role of interop services, you should be in a solid position for further exploration.

Summary

.NET is a wonderful thing. Nevertheless, managed and unmanaged code must learn to work together for some time to come. Given this fact, the .NET platform provides various techniques that allow you to blend the best of both worlds.

A major section of this chapter focused on the details of .NET types using legacy COM components. As you have seen, the process begins by generating an assembly proxy for your COM types. The RCW forwards calls to the underlying COM binary and takes care of the details of mapping COM types to their .NET equivalents.

The chapter concluded by examining how COM types can call on the services of newer .NET types. As you have seen, this requires that the creatable types in the .NET assembly are registered for use by COM, and that the .NET types are described via a COM type library.

PART 6

■ ■ ■

Exploring the .NET Base Class Libraries

CHAPTER 18

■ ■ ■

The System.IO Namespace

When you are creating full-blown desktop applications, the ability to save information between user sessions is imperative. This chapter examines a number of I/O-related topics as seen through the eyes of the .NET Framework. The first order of business is to explore the core types defined in the System.IO namespace and come to understand how to programmatically modify a machine's directory and file structure. Once you can do so, the next task is to explore various ways to read from and write to character-based, binary-based, string-based, and memory-based data stores.

Exploring the System.IO Namespace

In the framework of .NET, the System.IO namespace is the region of the base class libraries devoted to file-based (and memory-based) input and output (I/O) services. Like any namespace, System.IO defines a set of classes, interfaces, enumerations, structures, and delegates, most of which are contained in mscorlib.dll. In addition to the types contained within mscorlib.dll, the System.dll assembly defines additional types of the System.IO namespace (given that all Visual Studio 2005 projects automatically set a reference to both assemblies, you should be ready to go).

Many of the types within the System.IO namespace focus on the programmatic manipulation of physical directories and files. However, additional types provide support to read data from and write data to string buffers as well as raw memory locations. To give you a road map of the functionality in System.IO, Table 18-1 outlines the core (nonabstract) classes.

Table 18-1. *Key Members of the* System.IO *Namespace*

Nonabstract I/O Class Type	Meaning in Life
BinaryReader BinaryWriter	These types allow you to store and retrieve primitive data types (integers, Booleans, strings, and whatnot) as a binary value.
BufferedStream	This type provides temporary storage for a stream of bytes that may be committed to storage at a later time.
Directory DirectoryInfo	These types are used to manipulate a machine's directory structure. The Directory type exposes functionality primarily as *shared methods*. The DirectoryInfo type exposes similar functionality from a valid *object variable*.
DriveInfo	This type (new to .NET 2.0) provides detailed information regarding the drives on a given machine.
File FileInfo	These types are used to manipulate a machine's set of files. The type exposes functionality primarily as *shared methods*. The FileInfo type exposes similar functionality from a valid *object variable*.

Continued

Table 18-1. *Continued*

Nonabstract I/O Class Type	Meaning in Life
FileStream	This type allows for random file access (e.g., seeking capabilities) with data represented as a stream of bytes.
FileSystemWatcher	This type allows you to monitor the modification of a given external file.
MemoryStream	This type provides random access to streamed data stored in memory rather than a physical file.
Path	This type performs operations on System.String types that contain file or directory path information in a platform-neutral manner.
StreamWriter StreamReader	These types are used to store (and retrieve) textual information to (or from) a file. These types do not support random file access.
StringWriter StringReader	Like the StreamReader/StreamWriter types, these classes also work with textual information. However, the underlying storage is a string buffer rather than a physical file.

In addition to these creatable class types, System.IO defines a number of enumerations, as well as a set of abstract classes (Stream, TextReader, TextWriter, and so forth), that define a shared polymorphic interface to all descendents. You will read about many of these types in this chapter.

The Directory(Info) and File(Info) Types

System.IO provides four types that allow you to manipulate individual files, as well as interact with a machine's directory structure. The first two types, Directory and File, expose creation, deletion, copying, and moving operations using various shared members. The closely related FileInfo and DirectoryInfo types expose similar functionality as instance-level methods (and therefore these types must be instantiated with the VB 2005 New keyword). In Figure 18-1, notice that the Directory and File types directly extend System.Object, while DirectoryInfo and FileInfo derive from the abstract FileSystemInfo type.

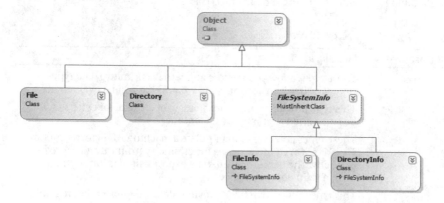

Figure 18-1. *The* File- *and* Directory-*centric types*

Generally speaking, FileInfo and DirectoryInfo are better choices for recursive operations (such as enumerating all subdirectories under a given root), as the Directory and File class members tend to return string values rather than strongly typed objects. However, as you will see, in many cases File and FileInfo (as well as Directory and DirectoryInfo) offer similar functionality.

The Abstract FileSystemInfo Base Class

The DirectoryInfo and FileInfo types receive many behaviors from the abstract FileSystemInfo base class. For the most part, the members of the FileSystemInfo class are used to discover general characteristics (such as time of creation, various attributes, and so forth) about a given file or directory. Table 18-2 lists some core properties of interest.

Table 18-2. FileSystemInfo *Properties*

Property	Meaning in Life
Attributes	Gets or sets the attributes associated with the current file that are represented by the FileAttributes enumeration.
CreationTime	Gets or sets the time of creation for the current file or directory.
Exists	Can be used to determine whether a given file or directory exists.
Extension	Retrieves a file's extension.
FullName	Gets the full path of the directory or file.
LastAccessTime	Gets or sets the time the current file or directory was last accessed.
LastWriteTime	Gets or sets the time when the current file or directory was last written to.
Name	For files, gets the name of the file. For directories, gets the name of the last directory in the hierarchy if a hierarchy exists. Otherwise, the Name property gets the name of the directory.

The FileSystemInfo type also defines the Delete() method. This is implemented by derived types to delete a given file or directory from the hard drive. As well, Refresh() can be called prior to obtaining attribute information to ensure that the statistics regarding the current file (or directory) are not outdated.

Working with the DirectoryInfo Type

The first creatable I/O-centric type you will examine is the DirectoryInfo class. This class contains a set of members used for creating, moving, deleting, and enumerating over directories and subdirectories. In addition to the functionality provided by its base class (FileSystemInfo), DirectoryInfo offers the key members in Table 18-3.

Table 18-3. *Key Members of the* DirectoryInfo *Type*

Members	Meaning in Life
Create() CreateSubdirectory()	Create a directory (or set of subdirectories), given a path name
Delete()	Deletes a directory and all its contents
GetDirectories()	Returns an array of strings that represent all subdirectories in the current directory
GetFiles()	Retrieves an array of FileInfo types that represent a set of files in the given directory
MoveTo()	Moves a directory and its contents to a new path
Parent	Retrieves the parent directory of the specified path
Root	Gets the root portion of a path

You begin working with the DirectoryInfo type by specifying a particular directory path as a constructor parameter. If you want to obtain access to the current application directory (i.e., the directory of the executing application), use the "." notation. Here are some examples:

```
' Bind to the current application directory.
Dim dir1 As DirectoryInfo = New DirectoryInfo(".")
```

```
' Bind to C:\Windows.
Dim dir2 As DirectoryInfo = New DirectoryInfo("C:\Windows")
```

In the second example, you are making the assumption that the path passed into the constructor (C:\Windows) already exists on the physical machine. However, if you attempt to interact with a nonexistent directory, a System.IO.DirectoryNotFoundException is thrown. Thus, if you specify a directory that is not yet created, you will need to call the Create() method before proceeding:

```
' Bind to a nonexistent directory, then create it.
Dim dir3 As DirectoryInfo = New DirectoryInfo("C:\Windows\Testing")
dir3.Create()
```

Once you have created a DirectoryInfo object, you can investigate the underlying directory contents using any of the properties inherited from FileSystemInfo. To illustrate, the following class creates a new DirectoryInfo object mapped to C:\Windows (adjust your path if need be) and displays a number of interesting statistics (see Figure 18-2 for the corresponding output):

```
Imports System.IO

Module Program
  Sub Main()
    Console.WriteLine("***** Fun with Directory(Info) *****")
    Console.WriteLine()

    ' Get basic info about C:\Windows
    Dim dir As DirectoryInfo = New DirectoryInfo("C:\Windows")
    Console.WriteLine("***** Directory Info *****")
    Console.WriteLine("FullName: {0}", dir.FullName)
    Console.WriteLine("Name: {0}", dir.Name)
    Console.WriteLine("Parent: {0}", dir.Parent)
    Console.WriteLine("Creation: {0}", dir.CreationTime)
    Console.WriteLine("Attributes: {0}", dir.Attributes)
    Console.WriteLine("Root: {0}", dir.Root)
    Console.WriteLine("*************************")
    Console.ReadLine()
  End Sub
End Module
```

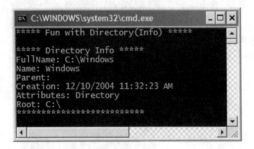

Figure 18-2. *Information about your Windows directory*

The FileAttributes Enumeration

The `Attributes` property exposed by `FileSystemInfo` provides various traits for the current directory or file, all of which are represented by the `FileAttributes` enumeration (enum). While the names of this enum are fairly self-describing (e.g., `Temporary`, `Encrypted`, etc.), some of the less obvious names are documented here (consult the .NET Framework 2.0 SDK documentation for full details):

```
Enum FileAttributes
  ReadOnly
  Hidden
  ' The file is part of the operating system or is used
  ' exclusively by the operating system.
  System
  Directory
  Archive
  ' This name is reserved for future use.
  Device
  ' The file is 'normal' as it has no other attributes set.
  Normal
  Temporary
  ' Sparse files are typically large files whose data are mostly zeros.
  SparseFile
  ' A block of user-defined data associated with a file or a directory
  ReparsePoint
  Compressed
  Offline
  ' The file will not be indexed by the operating system's
  ' content indexing service.
  NotContentIndexed
  Encrypted
End Enum
```

Enumerating Files with the DirectoryInfo Type

In addition to obtaining basic details of an existing directory, you can extend the current example to use some methods of the `DirectoryInfo` type. First, let's leverage the `GetFiles()` method to obtain information about all `*.bmp` files located under the C:\Windows directory. This method returns an array of `FileInfo` types, each of which exposes details of a particular file (full details of the `FileInfo` type are explored later in this chapter):

```
Module Program
  Sub Main()
    Console.WriteLine("***** Fun with Directory(Info) *****")
    Console.WriteLine()

    ' Get basic info about C:\Windows
    Dim dir As DirectoryInfo = New DirectoryInfo("C:\Windows")
...
    ' Get info about all *.bmp files in the C:\Windows directory.
    Dim bitmapFiles As FileInfo() = dir.GetFiles("*.bmp")
    Console.WriteLine("Found {0} *.bmp files", bitmapFiles.Length)
    For Each f As FileInfo In bitmapFiles
      Console.WriteLine()
      Console.WriteLine("File name: {0}", f.Name)
      Console.WriteLine("File size: {0}", f.Length)
      Console.WriteLine("Creation: {0}", f.CreationTime)
      Console.WriteLine("Attributes: {0}", f.Attributes)
```

```
      Console.WriteLine()
      Console.WriteLine("**************************")
    Next
    Console.ReadLine()
  End Sub
End Module
```

Once you run the application, you see a listing something like the one shown in Figure 18-3. (Your bitmaps may vary!)

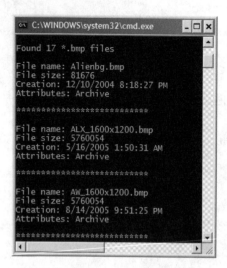

Figure 18-3. *Bitmap file information*

Creating Subdirectories with the DirectoryInfo Type

You can programmatically extend a directory structure using the DirectoryInfo.CreateSubdirectory() method. This method can create a single subdirectory, as well as multiple nested subdirectories, in a single function call. To illustrate, here is a block of code that extends the directory structure of C:\Windows with some custom subdirectories:

```
Module Program
  Sub Main()
    Console.WriteLine("***** Fun with Directory(Info) *****")
    Dim dir as DirectoryInfo = New DirectoryInfo("C:\Windows")
    ...
    ' Create C:\Windows\MyFoo.
    dir.CreateSubdirectory("MyFoo")

    ' Create C:\Windows\MyBar\MyQaaz.
    dir.CreateSubdirectory("MyBar\MyQaaz")
  End Sub
End Module
```

If you examine your Windows directory using Windows Explorer, you will see that the new subdirectories are present and accounted for (see Figure 18-4).

Figure 18-4. *Creating subdirectories*

Although you are not required to capture the return value of the CreateSubdirectory() method, be aware that a DirectoryInfo type representing the newly created item is passed back on successful execution:

```
' CreateSubdirectory() returns a DirectoryInfo item representing the new item.
Dim d As DirectoryInfo = dir.CreateSubdirectory("MyFoo")
Console.WriteLine("Created: {0}", d.FullName);

d = dir. CreateSubdirectory("MyBar\MyQaaz")
Console.WriteLine("Created: {0}", d.FullName)
```

Working with the Directory Type

Now that you have seen the DirectoryInfo type in action, you can learn about the Directory type. For the most part, the members of Directory mimic the functionality provided by the instance-level members defined by DirectoryInfo. Recall, however, that the members of Directory typically return String types rather than strongly typed FileInfo/DirectoryInfo types.

To illustrate some functionality of the Directory type, the final iteration of this example displays the names of all drives mapped to the current computer (via the Directory.GetLogicalDrives() method) and uses the shared Directory.Delete() method to remove the \MyFoo and \MyBar\MyQaaz subdirectories previously created:

```
Module Program
  Sub Main()
...
  ' Use Directory type.
  Dim drives As String() = Directory.GetLogicalDrives()
  Console.WriteLine("Here are your drives:")
  For Each s As String In drives
    Console.WriteLine("-> {0}", s)
  Next

  ' Delete the directories we created.
  Console.WriteLine("Press Enter to delete directories")
  Console.ReadLine()
  Try
    Directory.Delete("C:\Windows\MyFoo")
```

```
        Directory.Delete("C:\Windows\MyBar", True)
      Catch e As IOException
        Console.WriteLine(e.Message)
      End Try
        Console.ReadLine()
      End Sub
End Module
```

■**Source Code** The MyDirectoryApp project is located under the Chapter 18 subdirectory.

Working with the DriveInfo Class Type

As of .NET 2.0, the System.IO namespace provides a class named DriveInfo. Like Directory.
GetLogicalDrives(), the shared DriveInfo.GetDrives() method allows you to discover the names
of a machine's drives. Unlike Directory.GetLogicalDrives(), however, DriveInfo provides numerous other details (such as the drive type, available free space, volume label, and whatnot). Consider
the following sample code:

```
Imports System.IO

Module Program
  Sub Main()
    Console.WriteLine("***** Fun with DriveInfo *****")
    Dim myDrives As DriveInfo() = DriveInfo.GetDrives()

    ' Print stats about each drive.
    For Each d As DriveInfo In myDrives
      Console.WriteLine("******************************")
      Console.WriteLine("-> Name: {0}", d.Name)
      Console.WriteLine("-> Type: {0}", d.DriveType)

      ' Is the drive mounted?
      If d.IsReady Then
        Console.WriteLine("-> Free space: {0}", d.TotalFreeSpace)
        Console.WriteLine("-> Format: {0}", d.DriveFormat)
        Console.WriteLine("-> Label: {0}", d.VolumeLabel)
      End If
    Next
    Console.ReadLine()
  End Sub
End Module
```

Figure 18-5 shows the output based on my current machine.

At this point, you have investigated some core behaviors of the Directory, DirectoryInfo, and
DriveInfo classes. Next, you'll learn how to create, open, close, and destroy the files that populate
a given directory.

■**Source Code** The DriveTypeApp project is located under the Chapter 18 subdirectory.

Figure 18-5. *Gather drive details via* DriveInfo.

Working with the FileInfo Class

As shown in the MyDirectoryApp example, the FileInfo class allows you to obtain details regarding existing files on your hard drive (time created, size, file attributes, and so forth) and aids in the creation, copying, moving, and destruction of files. In addition to the set of functionality inherited by FileSystemInfo are some core members unique to the FileInfo class, which are described in Table 18-4.

Table 18-4. FileInfo *Core Members*

Member	Meaning in Life
AppendText()	Creates a StreamWriter type (described later) that appends text to a file
CopyTo()	Copies an existing file to a new file
Create()	Creates a new file and returns a FileStream type (described later) to interact with the newly created file
CreateText()	Creates a StreamWriter type that writes a new text file
Delete()	Deletes the file to which a FileInfo instance is bound
Directory	Gets an instance of the parent directory
DirectoryName	Gets the full path to the parent directory
Length	Gets the size of the current file or directory
MoveTo()	Moves a specified file to a new location, providing the option to specify a new file name
Name	Gets the name of the file
Open()	Opens a file with various read/write and sharing privileges
OpenRead()	Creates a read-only FileStream
OpenText()	Creates a StreamReader type (described later) that reads from an existing text file
OpenWrite()	Creates a write-only FileStream type

It is important to understand that a majority of the members of the `FileInfo` class return a specific I/O-centric object (`FileStream`, `StreamWriter`, and so forth) that allows you to begin reading and writing data to (or reading from) the associated file in a variety of formats. You will check out these types in just a moment, but until then, let's examine various ways to obtain a file handle using the `FileInfo` class type.

The FileInfo.Create() Method

The first way you can create a file handle is to make use of the `FileInfo.Create()` method:

```
Imports System.IO

Module Program
  Sub Main()
    ' Make a new file on the C drive.
    Dim f As FileInfo = New FileInfo("C:\Test.dat")
    Dim fs As FileStream = f.Create()

    ' Use the FileStream object...

    ' Close down file stream.
    fs.Close()
  End Sub
End Module
```

Notice that the `FileInfo.Create()` method returns a `FileStream` type, which exposes synchronous and asynchronous write/read operations to/from the underlying file.

The FileInfo.Open() Method

You can use the `FileInfo.Open()` method to open existing files as well as create new files with far more precision than `FileInfo.Create()`. Once the call to `Open()` completes, you are returned a `FileStream` object. Ponder the following logic:

```
Imports System.IO

Module Program
  Sub Main()
    ' Make a new file via FileInfo.Open().
    Dim f2 As FileInfo = New FileInfo("C:\Test2.dat")
    Dim fs2 As FileStream = f2.Open(FileMode.OpenOrCreate, _
      FileAccess.ReadWrite, FileShare.None)

    ' Use the FileStream object...

    ' Close down file stream.
    fs2.Close()
  End Sub
End Module
```

This version of the overloaded `Open()` method requires three parameters. The first parameter specifies the general flavor of the I/O request (e.g., make a new file, open an existing file, append to a file, etc.), which is specified using the `FileMode` enumeration:

```
Enum FileMode
  ' Specifies that the operating system should create a new file.
  ' If the file already exists, a System.IO.IOException is thrown.
```

```
CreateNew
' Specifies that the operating system should create a new file.
' If the file already exists, it will be overwritten.
Create
Open
' Specifies that the operating system should open a file if it exists;
' otherwise, a new file should be created.
OpenOrCreate
Truncate
Append
End Enum
```

The second parameter, a value from the `FileAccess` enumeration, is used to determine the read/write behavior of the underlying stream:

```
Enum FileAccess
  Read
  Write
  ReadWrite
End Enum
```

Finally, you have the third parameter, `FileShare`, which specifies how the file is to be shared among other file handlers. Here are the core names:

```
Enum FileShare
  None
  Read
  Write
  ReadWrite
End Enum
```

The FileInfo.OpenRead() and FileInfo.OpenWrite() Methods

While the `FileInfo.Open()` method allows you to obtain a file handle in a very flexible manner, the `FileInfo` class also provides members named `OpenRead()` and `OpenWrite()`. As you might imagine, these methods return a properly configured read-only or write-only `FileStream` type, without the need to supply various enumeration values. Like `FileInfo.Create()` and `FileInfo.Open()`, `OpenRead()` and `OpenWrite()` return a `FileStream` object:

```
Sub Main()
...
  ' Get a FileStream object with read-only permissions.
  Dim f3 As FileInfo = New FileInfo("C:\Test3.dat")
  Dim readOnlyStream As FileStream = f3.OpenRead()

  ' Use FileStream...

  readOnlyStream.Close()

  ' Get a FileStream object with write-only permissions.
  Dim f4 As FileInfo = New FileInfo("C:\Test4.dat")
  Dim writeOnlyStream As FileStream = f4.OpenWrite()

  ' Use FileStream...

  writeOnlyStream.Close()
End Sub
```

The FileInfo.OpenText() Method

Another open-centric member of the FileInfo type is OpenText(). Unlike Create(), Open(), OpenRead(), and OpenWrite(), the OpenText() method returns an instance of the StreamReader type, rather than a FileStream type:

```
Sub Main()
...
  ' Get a StreamReader object.
  Dim f5 As FileInfo = New FileInfo("C:\boot.ini")
  Dim sreader As StreamReader = f5.OpenText()

  ' Use the StreamReader object...

  sreader.Close()
End Sub
```

As you will see shortly, the StreamReader type provides a way to read character data from the underlying file.

The FileInfo.CreateText() and FileInfo.AppendText() Methods

The final two methods of interest at this point are CreateText() and AppendText(), both of which return a StreamWriter reference, as shown here:

```
Sub Main()
...
  Dim f6 As FileInfo = New FileInfo("C:\Test5.txt")
  Dim swriter As StreamWriter = f6.CreateText()

  ' Use the StreamWriter object...

  swriter.Close()

  Dim f7 As FileInfo = New FileInfo("C:\FinalTest.txt")
  Dim swriterAppend As StreamWriter = f7.AppendText()

  ' Use the StreamWriter object...

  swriterAppend.Close()
End Sub
```

As you would guess, the StreamWriter type provides a way to write character data to the underlying file.

Working with the File Type

The File type provides functionality almost identical to that of the FileInfo type, using a number of shared members. Like FileInfo, File supplies the AppendText(), Create(), CreateText(), Open(), OpenRead(), OpenWrite(), and OpenText() methods. In fact, in many cases, the File and FileStream types may be used interchangeably. To illustrate, each of the previous FileStream examples can be simplified by using the File type instead:

```
Sub Main()
  ' Obtain FileStream object via File.Create().
  Dim fs As FileStream = File.Create("C:\Test.dat")
  fs.Close()
```

```
' Obtain FileStream object via File.Open().
Dim fs2 As FileStream = File.Open("C:\Test2.dat", _
  FileMode.OpenOrCreate, _
  FileAccess.ReadWrite, FileShare.None)
fs2.Close()

' Get a FileStream object with read-only permissions.
Dim readOnlyStream As FileStream = File.OpenRead("Test3.dat")
readOnlyStream.Close()

' Get a FileStream object with write-only permissions.
Dim writeOnlyStream As FileStream = File.OpenWrite("Test4.dat")
writeOnlyStream.Close()

' Get a StreamReader object.
Dim sreader As StreamReader = File.OpenText("C:\boot.ini")
sreader.Close()

' Get some StreamWriters.
Dim swriter As StreamWriter = File.CreateText("C:\Test3.txt")
swriter.Close()
Dim swriterAppend As StreamWriter = File.AppendText("C:\FinalTest.txt")
swriterAppend.Close()
End Sub
```

New .NET 2.0 File Members

Unlike FileInfo, the File type supports a few unique members (as of .NET 2.0) shown in Table 18-5, which can greatly simplify the processes of reading and writing textual data.

Table 18-5. *Methods of the* File *Type*

Method	Meaning in Life
ReadAllBytes()	Opens the specified file, returns the binary data as an array of bytes, and then closes the file
ReadAllLines()	Opens a specified file, returns the character data as an array of strings, and then closes the file
ReadAllText()	Opens a specified file, returns the character data as a System.String, and then closes the file
WriteAllBytes()	Opens the specified file, writes out the byte array, and then closes the file
WriteAllLines()	Opens a specified file, writes out an array of strings, and then closes the file
WriteAllText()	Opens a specified file, writes the character data, and then closes the file

Using these new methods of the File type, you are able to read and write batches of data in just a few lines of code. Even better, each of these new members automatically closes down the underlying file handle, as in this example:

```
Imports System.IO

Module Program
  Sub Main()
    ' Write these strings to a new file on the C drive.
    Dim myTasks As String() = {"Fix bathroom sink", _
      "Call Dave", "Call Mom and Dad", _
```

```
          "Play Xbox 360"}
      File.WriteAllLines("C:\tasks.txt", myTasks)

      ' Now read in each one and print to the console.
      For Each task As String In File.ReadAllLines("C:\tasks.txt")
        Console.WriteLine("TODO: {0}.", task)
      Next
    End Sub
End Module
```

Clearly, when you wish to quickly obtain a file handle, the `File` type will save you some keystrokes. However, one benefit of first creating a `FileInfo` object is that you are able to investigate the file using the members of the abstract `FileSystemInfo` base class:

```
Imports System.IO

Module Program
  Sub Main()
    ' Display info about boot.ini and then open
    ' for read-only access.
    Dim bootFile As FileInfo = New FileInfo("C:\boot.ini")
    Console.WriteLine(bootFile.CreationTime)
    Console.WriteLine(bootFile.LastAccessTime)
    Dim readOnlyStream As FileStream = bootFile.OpenRead()
    readOnlyStream.Close()
  End Sub
End Module
```

The Abstract Stream Class

At this point, you have seen numerous ways to obtain `FileStream`, `StreamReader`, and `StreamWriter` objects, but you have yet to read data from, or write data to, a file using these types. To understand how to do so, you'll need to become familiar with the concept of a *stream*.

In the world of I/O manipulation, a stream represents a chunk of data. Streams provide a common way to interact with *a sequence of bytes*, regardless of what kind of device (file, network connection, printer, etc.) is storing or displaying the bytes in question.

The abstract `System.IO.Stream` class defines a number of members that provide support for synchronous and asynchronous interactions with the storage medium (e.g., an underlying file or memory location). Figure 18-6 shows a few descendents of the `Stream` type.

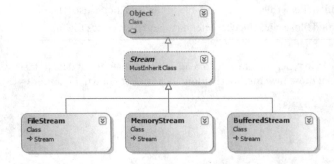

Figure 18-6. *Stream-derived types*

> **Note** Be aware that the concept of a stream is not limited to files or memory locations. To be sure, the .NET libraries provide stream access to networks and other stream-centric abstractions.

Again, Stream descendents represent data as a raw stream of bytes; therefore, working with raw streams can be quite cryptic. Some Stream-derived types support *seeking*, which refers to the process of obtaining and adjusting the current position in the stream. To begin understanding the functionality provided by the Stream class, take note of the core members described in Table 18-6.

Table 18-6. *Abstract* Stream *Members*

Members	Meaning in Life
CanRead CanSeek CanWrite	Determine whether the current stream supports reading, seeking, and/or writing.
Close()	Closes the current stream and releases any resources (such as sockets and file handles) associated with the current stream.
Flush()	Updates the underlying data source or repository with the current state of the buffer and then clears the buffer. If a stream does not implement a buffer, this method does nothing.
Length	Returns the length of the stream, in bytes.
Position	Determines the position in the current stream.
Read() ReadByte()	Read a sequence of bytes (or a single byte) from the current stream and advance the current position in the stream by the number of bytes read.
Seek()	Sets the position in the current stream.
SetLength()	Sets the length of the current stream.
Write() WriteByte()	Write a sequence of bytes (or a single byte) to the current stream and advance the current position in this stream by the number of bytes written.

Working with FileStreams

The FileStream class provides an implementation for the abstract Stream members in a manner appropriate for file-based streaming. It is a fairly primitive stream; it can read or write only a single byte or an array of bytes. In reality, you will not often need to directly interact with the members of the FileStream type. Rather, you will most likely make use of various *stream wrappers*, which make it easier to work with textual data or .NET types. Nevertheless, for illustrative purposes, let's experiment with the synchronous read/write capabilities of the FileStream type.

Assume you have a new console application named FileStreamApp. Your goal is to write a simple text message to a new file named myMessage.dat. However, given that FileStream can operate only on raw bytes, you will be required to encode the System.String type into a corresponding byte array. Luckily, the System.Text namespace defines a type named Encoding, which provides members that encode and decode strings to (or from) an array of bytes (check out the .NET Framework 2.0 SDK documentation for full details of the Encoding type).

Once encoded, the byte array is persisted to the file using the FileStream.Write() method. To read the bytes back into memory, you must reset the internal position of the stream (via the Position property) and call the ReadByte() method. Finally, you display the raw byte array and the decoded string to the console. Here is the complete Main() method:

```
Imports System.IO
Imports System.Text
```

```
Module Program
  Sub Main()
    Console.WriteLine("***** Fun with FileStreams *****")
    Console.WriteLine()

    ' Obtain a FileStream object.
    Dim fStream As FileStream = File.Open("C:\myMessage.dat", FileMode.Create)

    ' Encode a string as an array of bytes.
    Dim msg As String = "Hello!"
    Dim msgAsByteArray As Byte() = Encoding.Default.GetBytes(msg)

    ' Write array of bytes to file.
    fStream.Write(msgAsByteArray, 0, msgAsByteArray.Length)

    ' Reset internal position of stream.
    fStream.Position = 0

    ' Read the types from file and display to console.
    Console.Write("Your message as an array of bytes: ")
    Dim bytesFromFile(msgAsByteArray.Length) As Byte
    Dim i As Integer = 0
    While i < msgAsByteArray.Length
      bytesFromFile(i) = CType(fStream.ReadByte, Byte)
      Console.Write(bytesFromFile(i))
      i = i + 1
    End While

    ' Display decoded messages.
    Console.WriteLine()
    Console.Write("Decoded Message: ")
    Console.WriteLine(Encoding.Default.GetString(bytesFromFile))
    fStream.Close()
  End Sub
End Module
```

While this example does indeed populate the file with data, it punctuates the major downfall of working directly with the FileStream type: it demands to operate on raw bytes. Other Stream-derived types operate in a similar manner. For example, if you wish to write a sequence of bytes to a region of memory, you can allocate a MemoryStream. Likewise, if you wish to push an array of bytes through a network connection, you can make use of the NetworkStream type.

Thankfully, the System.IO namespace provides a number of "reader" and "writer" types that encapsulate the details of working with Stream-derived types.

■**Source Code** The FileStreamApp project is included under the Chapter 18 subdirectory.

Working with StreamWriters and StreamReaders

The StreamWriter and StreamReader classes are useful whenever you need to read or write character-based data (e.g., strings). Both of these types work by default with Unicode characters; however, you can change the underlying character encoding by supplying a properly configured System.Text. Encoding object reference. To keep things simple, let's assume that the default Unicode encoding fits the bill (as will be the case for almost all of your .NET applications).

StreamReader derives from an abstract type named TextReader, as does the related StringReader type (discussed later in this chapter). The TextReader base class provides a very limited set of functionality to each of these descendents, specifically the ability to read and peek into a character stream.

The StreamWriter type (as well as StringWriter, also examined later in this chapter) derives from an abstract base class named TextWriter. This class defines members that allow derived types to write textual data to a given character stream. The relationship between each of these new I/O-centric types is shown in Figure 18-7.

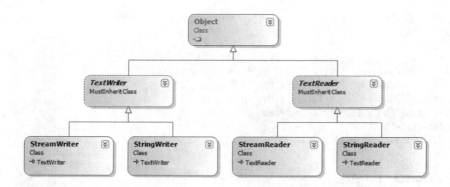

Figure 18-7. *Readers and writers*

To aid in your understanding of the core writing capabilities of the StreamWriter and StringWriter classes, Table 18-7 describes the core members of the abstract TextWriter base class.

Table 18-7. *Core Members of* TextWriter

Member	Meaning in Life
Close()	Closes the writer and frees any associated resources. In the process, the buffer is automatically flushed.
Flush()	Clears all buffers for the current writer and causes any buffered data to be written to the underlying device, but does not close the writer.
NewLine	Indicates the newline constant for the derived writer class. The default line terminator is a carriage return followed by a line feed (the equivalent to the VB VbLf constant).
Write()	Writes a line to the text stream without a newline constant.
WriteLine()	Writes a line to the text stream with a newline constant.

■**Note** The last two members of the TextWriter class probably look familiar to you. If you recall, the System.Console type has Write() and WriteLine() members that push textual data to the standard output device. In fact, the Console.In property wraps a TextWriter, and the Console.Out property wraps a TextReader.

The derived StreamWriter class provides an appropriate implementation for the Write(), Close(), and Flush() methods, and it defines the additional AutoFlush property. This property, when set to true, forces StreamWriter to flush all data every time you perform a write operation. Be aware that you can gain better performance by setting AutoFlush to false, provided you always call Close() when you are done writing with a StreamWriter.

Writing to a Text File

Now for an example of working with the StreamWriter type. The following class creates a new file named reminders.txt using the File.CreateText() method. Using the obtained StreamWriter object, you add some textual data to the new file, as shown here:

```
Imports System.IO

Module Program
  Sub Main()
    Console.WriteLine("***** Fun with StreamWriter / StreamReader *****")
    Console.WriteLine()

    ' Get a StreamWriter and write string data.
    Dim writer As StreamWriter = File.CreateText("reminders.txt")
    writer.WriteLine("Don't forget Mother's Day this year...")
    writer.WriteLine("Don't forget Father's Day this year...")
    writer.WriteLine("Don't forget these numbers:")
    For i As Integer = 0 To 10
      writer.Write(String.Format("{0},", i))
    Next

    ' Insert a new line and close.
    writer.Write(writer.NewLine)
    writer.Close()
      Console.WriteLine("Created file and wrote some thoughts...")
  End Sub
End Module
```

Notice that the parameter to File.CreateTest() is the full path of the file you wish to create. Here, however, I simply specified the file name itself, and therefore the file will be created in the application directory of the assembly (which will be under your bin\Debug folder). In any case, once you run this program, you can examine the contents of this new file, which should resemble what you see in Figure 18-8.

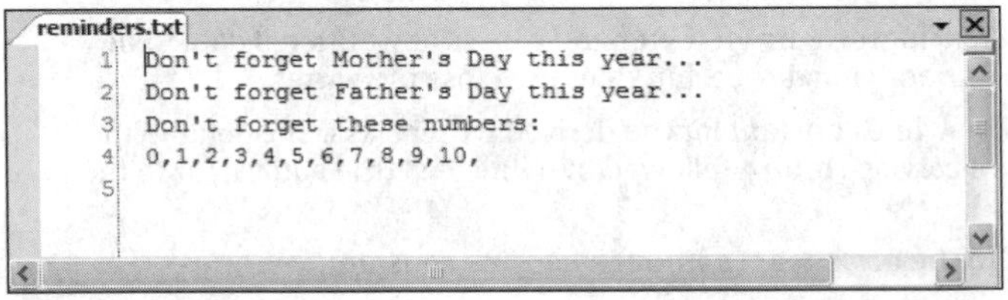

Figure 18-8. *The contents of your* *.txt *file*

Reading from a Text File

Now you need to understand how to programmatically read data from a file using the corresponding StreamReader type. As you recall, this class derives from TextReader, which offers the functionality described in Table 18-8.

Table 18-8. `TextReader` *Core Members*

Member	Meaning in Life
`Peek()`	Returns the next available character without actually changing the position of the reader. A value of –1 indicates you are at the end of the stream.
`Read()`	Reads data from an input stream.
`ReadBlock()`	Reads a maximum of count characters from the current stream and writes the data to a buffer, beginning at index.
`ReadLine()`	Reads a line of characters from the current stream and returns the data as a string (a null string indicates EOF).
`ReadToEnd()`	Reads all characters from the current position to the end of the stream and returns them as a single string.

If you now extend the current `MyStreamWriterReader` class to use a `StreamReader`, you can read in the textual data from the `reminders.txt` file as shown here:

```
Sub Main()
  Console.WriteLine("***** Fun with StreamWriter / StreamReader *****")
...
  Console.WriteLine("Here are your thoughts:")
  Dim sr As StreamReader = File.OpenText("reminders.txt")
  Console.WriteLine(sr.ReadToEnd())
  Console.ReadLine()
End Sub
```

Once you run the program, you will see the character data within `Thoughts.txt` displayed to the console.

Directly Creating StreamWriter/StreamReader Types

One of the slightly confusing aspects of working with the types within `System.IO` is that you can often achieve an identical result using numerous approaches. For example, you have already seen that you can obtain a `StreamWriter` via the `File` or `FileInfo` type using the `CreateText()` method. In reality, there is yet another way in which you can work with `StreamWriters` and `StreamReaders`: create them directly. For example, the current application could be retrofitted as follows:

```
Sub Main()
  Console.WriteLine("***** Fun with StreamWriter / StreamReader *****")
  ' Get a StreamWriter and write string data.
  Dim writer As StreamWriter = New StreamWriter("reminders.txt")
...
  ' Now read data from file.
  Dim sr As StreamReader = New StreamReader("reminders.txt")
...
End Sub
```

Although it can be a bit confusing to see so many seemingly identical approaches to file I/O, keep in mind that the end result is greater flexibility. In any case, now that you have seen how to move character data to and from a given file using the `StreamWriter` and `StreamReader` types, you will next examine the role of the `StringWriter` and `StringReader` classes.

___

■**Source Code** The StreamWriterReaderApp project is included under the Chapter 18 subdirectory.

Working with StringWriters and StringReaders

Using the StringWriter and StringReader types, you can treat textual information as a stream of in-memory characters. This can prove helpful when you wish to append character-based information to an existing buffer. To illustrate, the following example writes a block of string data to a StringWriter object rather than a file on the local hard drive:

```
Module Program
  Sub Main()
    Console.WriteLine("***** Fun with StringWriter / StringReader *****")
    Console.WriteLine()

    ' Create a StringWriter and emit character data
    ' to memory.
    Dim strWriter As StringWriter = New StringWriter()
    strWriter.Write("Don't forget Mother's Day this year...")
    strWriter.Close()

    ' Get a copy of the contents (stored in a string) and pump
    ' to console.
    Console.WriteLine("Contents of StringWriter: {0}", strWriter)
    Console.ReadLine()
  End Sub
End Module
```

Because StringWriter and StreamWriter both derive from the same base class (TextWriter), the writing logic is more or less identical. However, given that nature of StringWriter, be aware that this class allows you to extract a System.Text.StringBuilder object via the GetStringBuilder() method:

```
Module Program
  Sub Main()
    Console.WriteLine("***** Fun with StringWriter / StringReader *****")
    Console.WriteLine()

    ' Create a StringWriter and emit character data
    ' to memory.
    Dim strWriter As StringWriter = New StringWriter()
...
    ' Get the internal StringBuilder.
    Dim sb As StringBuilder = strWriter.GetStringBuilder()
    sb.Insert(0, "Hey!! ")
    Console.WriteLine("-> {0}", sb.ToString())

    ' Remove the inserted string.
    sb.Remove(0, "Hey!! ".Length)
    Console.WriteLine("-> {0}", sb.ToString())
    Console.ReadLine()
  End Sub
End Module
```

When you wish to read from a stream of character data, make use of the corresponding StringReader type, which (as you would expect) functions identically to the related StreamReader class. In fact, the StringReader class does nothing more than override the inherited members to read from a block of character data, rather than a file, as shown here:

```
Module Program
  Sub Main()
    Console.WriteLine("***** Fun with StringWriter / StringReader *****")
    Console.WriteLine()
```

```vb
' Create a StringWriter and emit character data
' to memory.
Dim strWriter As StringWriter = New StringWriter()
...
' Now dump using a StringReader.
Console.WriteLine("-> Here are your thoughts:")
Dim strReader As StringReader = New StringReader(strWriter.ToString())
Dim input As String = strReader.ReadToEnd()
Console.WriteLine(input)
strReader.Close()
Console.ReadLine()
End Sub
End Module
```

■**Source Code** The StringReaderWriterApp is included under the Chapter 18 subdirectory.

Working with BinaryWriters and BinaryReaders

The final writer/reader sets you will examine here are BinaryReader and BinaryWriter, both of which derive directly from System.Object. These types allow you to read and write discrete *data types* to an underlying stream in a compact binary format. The BinaryWriter class defines a highly overloaded Write() method to place a data type in the underlying stream. In addition to Write(), BinaryWriter provides additional members that allow you to get or set the Stream-derived type and offers support for random access to the data (see Table 18-9).

Table 18-9. BinaryWriter *Core Members*

Member	Meaning in Life
BaseStream	This read-only property provides access to the underlying stream used with the BinaryWriter object.
Close()	This method closes the binary stream.
Flush()	This method flushes the binary stream.
Seek()	This method sets the position in the current stream.
Write()	This method writes a value to the current stream.

The BinaryReader class complements the functionality offered by BinaryWriter with the members described in Table 18-10.

Table 18-10. BinaryReader *Core Members*

Member	Meaning in Life
BaseStream	This read-only property provides access to the underlying stream used with the BinaryReader object.
Close()	This method closes the binary reader.
PeekChar()	This method returns the next available character without actually advancing the position in the stream.
Read()	This method reads a given set of bytes or characters and stores them in the incoming array.
ReadXXXX()	The BinaryReader class defines numerous ReadXXXX() methods that grab the next type from the stream (ReadBoolean(), ReadByte(), ReadInt32(), and so forth).

The following example writes a number of data types to a new *.dat file in a binary format:

```vb
Module Program
  Sub Main()
    Console.WriteLine("***** Fun with BinaryWriter / BinaryReader *****")
    Console.WriteLine()

    ' Open a binary writer for a file.
    Dim f As FileInfo = New FileInfo("BinFile.dat")
    Dim bw As BinaryWriter = New BinaryWriter(f.OpenWrite)

    ' Print out the type of BaseStream.
    ' (System.IO.FileStream in this case).
    Console.WriteLine("Base stream is: {0}", bw.BaseStream)

    ' Create some data to save in the file
    Dim aDouble As Double = 1234.67
    Dim anInt As Integer = 34567
    Dim aCharArray As Char() = {"A"c, "B"c, "C"c}

    'Write the data
    bw.Write(aDouble)
    bw.Write(anInt)
    bw.Write(aCharArray)
    bw.Close()
    Console.WriteLine()
  End Sub
End Module
```

Notice how the FileStream object returned from FileInfo.OpenWrite() is passed to the constructor of the BinaryWriter type. Using this technique, it is very simple to "layer in" a stream before writing out the data. Do understand that the constructor of BinaryWriter takes any Stream-derived type (e.g., FileStream, MemoryStream, or BufferedStream). Thus, if you would rather write binary data to memory, simply supply a valid MemoryStream object.

To read the data out of the BinFile.dat file, the BinaryReader type provides a number of options. Here, you will make use of PeekChar() to determine whether the stream still has data to provide and, if so, use ReadByte() to obtain the value. Note that you are formatting the bytes in hexadecimal and inserting seven spaces between each:

```vb
Sub Main()
  ' Open a binary writer for a file.
  Dim f As FileInfo = New FileInfo("BinFile.dat")
  ...

  ' Read the data as raw bytes
  Dim br As BinaryReader = New BinaryReader(f.OpenRead)
  Dim temp As Integer = 0

  ' Print out in a formatted manner.
  While Not (br.PeekChar = -1)
    Console.Write("{0,7:x} ", br.ReadByte)
    temp = temp + 1
    If temp = 4 Then
      Console.WriteLine()
      temp = 0
    End If
  End While
  Console.WriteLine()
End Sub
```

The output of this program appears in Figure 18-9.

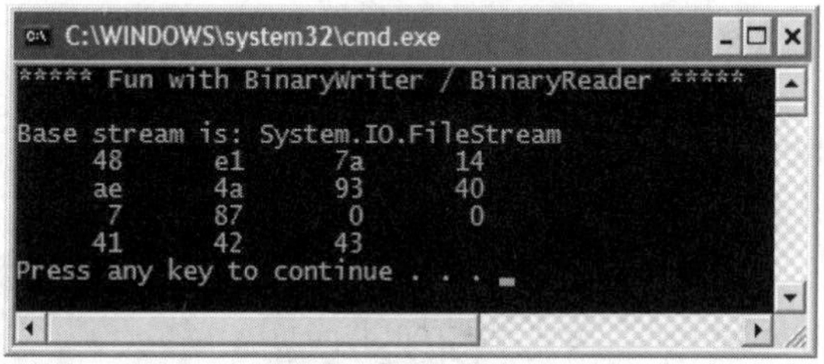

Figure 18-9. *Reading bytes from a binary file*

■**Source Code** The BinaryWriterReader application is included under the Chapter 18 subdirectory.

Revising the VB 2005 Using Keyword

As you may recall from Chapter 8, VB 2005 provides a Using keyword, which ensures that objects that implement IDisposable will automatically have their Dispose() method called when the member drops out of scope. It is worth pointing out that this same construct can be used with Stream-derived types (such as FileStream) to ensure that the underlying file handle is automatically released when the "used" type falls out of scope. Therefore, the following code:

```
Using fs As New FileStream("MyFile.txt", FileMode.OpenOrCreate)
   fs.WriteByte(20)
End Using ' Dispose() automatically called here.
```

is a more compact alternative to this functionally equivalent code:

```
Dim fs As New FileStream("MyFile.txt", FileMode.OpenOrCreate)
Try
   fs.WriteByte(20)
Finally
   fs.Dispose()
End Try
```

Although the code in this chapter explicitly called Close() on a Stream-derived type (which frees the underlying file handle, just like the Dispose() method), making use of the Using keyword can streamline your code, given that the compiler injects the Try/Finally logic into your assembly on your behalf.

Programmatically "Watching" Files and Directories

Now that you have a better handle on the use of various readers and writers, next you'll look at the role of the FileSystemWatcher class. This type can be quite helpful when you wish to programmatically monitor (or "watch") files on your system. Specifically, the FileSystemWatcher type can be instructed to monitor files for any of the actions specified by the NotifyFilters enumeration (while many of these members are self-explanatory, check the online help for further details):

```
Enum NotifyFilters
   Attributes
   CreationTime
   DirectoryName
   FileName
   LastAccess
   LastWrite,
   Security
   Size
End Enum
```

The first step you will need to take to work with the FileSystemWatcher type is to set the Path property to specify the name (and location) of the directory that contains the files to be monitored, as well as the Filter property that defines the file extensions of the files to be monitored.

At this point, you may choose to handle the Changed, Created, and Deleted events, all of which work in conjunction with the FileSystemEventHandler delegate. This delegate can call any method matching the following pattern:

```
' The FileSystemEventHandler delegate must point
' to methods matching the following signature.
Sub MyNotificationHandler(ByVal source As Object, ByVal e As FileSystemEventArgs)
```

As well, the Renamed event may also be handled via the RenamedEventHandler delegate type, which can call methods matching the following signature:

```
' The RenamedEventHandler delegate must point
' to methods matching the following signature.
Sub MyNotificationHandler(ByVal source As Object, ByVal e As RenamedEventArgs)
```

To illustrate the process of watching a file, assume you have created a new directory on your C drive named MyFolder that contains various *.txt files (named whatever you wish). The following console application will monitor the *.txt files within MyFolder and print out messages in the event that the files are created, deleted, modified, or renamed:

```
Sub Main()
  Console.WriteLine("***** The Amazing File Watcher App *****")

  ' Create and configure the watcher.
  Dim watcher As FileSystemWatcher = New FileSystemWatcher()
  Try
    watcher.Path = "C:\MyFolder"
  Catch ex As ArgumentException
    Console.WriteLine(ex.Message)
    Return
  End Try
  watcher.NotifyFilter = NotifyFilters.LastAccess Or _
                         NotifyFilters.LastWrite Or _
                         NotifyFilters.FileName Or _
                         NotifyFilters.DirectoryName
  watcher.Filter = "*.txt"

  ' Establish event handlers.
  AddHandler watcher.Changed, AddressOf OnFileModified
  AddHandler watcher.Created, AddressOf OnFileModified
  AddHandler watcher.Deleted, AddressOf OnFileModified
  AddHandler watcher.Renamed, AddressOf OnRenamed
  watcher.EnableRaisingEvents = True
```

```
' Keep alive until user hits enter key.
Console.ReadLine()
End Sub
```

The two event handlers simply print out the current file modification:

```
' Event handlers.
Sub OnFileModified(ByVal source As Object, ByVal e As FileSystemEventArgs)
  ' Specify what is done when a file is changed, created, or deleted.
  Console.WriteLine("File: {0} {1}!", e.FullPath, e.ChangeType)
End Sub

Sub OnRenamed(ByVal source As Object, ByVal e As RenamedEventArgs)
  ' Specify what is done when a file is renamed.
  Console.WriteLine("File: {0} renamed to {1}.", e.OldFullPath, e.FullPath)
End Sub
```

To test this program, run the application and open Windows Explorer. Try renaming your files, creating a *.txt file, deleting a *.txt file, or whatnot. You will see the console application print out various bits of information regarding the state of the text files within MyFolder, as shown in Figure 18-10.

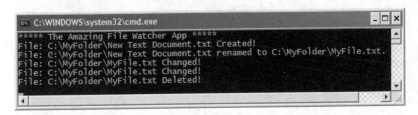

Figure 18-10. *Watching some text files*

■**Source Code** The MyDirectoryWatcher application is included under the Chapter 18 subdirectory.

Performing Asynchronous File I/O

To conclude our examination of the System.IO namespace, let's see how to interact with FileStream types asynchronously. You have already seen the asynchronous support provided by the .NET Framework during the examination of multithreading (see Chapter 16). Because I/O can be a lengthy task, all types deriving from System.IO.Stream inherit a set of methods (BeginRead(), BeginWrite(), EndRead(), and EndWrite(), specifically) that enable asynchronous processing of the data. As you would expect, these methods work in conjunction with the IAsyncResult type (again, see Chapter 16). Here are the prototypes of the members in question:

```
Public Class FileStream
  Inherits Stream
...
  Public Overrides Function BeginRead(ByVal array As Byte(), _
    ByVal offset As Integer, ByVal numBytes As Integer,
    ByVal userCallback As AsyncCallback,
    ByVal stateObject As Object) As IAsyncResult
```

```
  Public Overrides Function BeginWrite(ByVal array As Byte(), _
    ByVal offset As Integer, ByVal numBytes As Integer, _
    ByVal userCallback As AsyncCallback, _
    ByVal stateObject As Object) As IAsyncResult

  Public Overrides Function EndRead(ByVal asyncResult As IAsyncResult) _
    As Integer

  Public Overrides Sub EndWrite(ByVal asyncResult As IAsyncResult)
...
End Class
```

The process of working with the asynchronous behavior of Stream-derived types is identical to working with asynchronous delegates and asynchronous remote method invocations. While it's unlikely that asynchronous behaviors will greatly improve file access, other streams (e.g., socket-based streams) are much more likely to benefit from asynchronous handling. In any case, the following example illustrates one manner in which you can asynchronously interact with a FileStream type:

```
Imports System.IO
Imports System.Text
Imports System.Threading

Module Program
  Sub Main()
    Console.WriteLine("**** Asynch File IO *****")
    Console.WriteLine()

    Console.WriteLine("Main thread started. ThreadID = {0}", _
      Thread.CurrentThread.GetHashCode)

    ' Must use this ctor to get a FileStream with asynchronous
    ' read or write access.
    Dim fs As FileStream = New FileStream("logfile.txt", FileMode.Append, _
      FileAccess.Write, FileShare.None, 4096, True)
    Dim msg As String = "this is a test"
    Dim buffer As Byte() = Encoding.ASCII.GetBytes(msg)

    ' Start the asynchronous write. WriteDone invoked when finished.
    ' Note that the FileStream object is passed as state info to the
    ' callback method.
    fs.BeginWrite(buffer, 0, buffer.Length, AddressOf WriteDone, fs)
  End Sub

  Private Sub WriteDone(ByVal ar As IAsyncResult)
    Console.WriteLine("AsyncCallback method on ThreadID = {0}", _
      Thread.CurrentThread.GetHashCode)
    Dim s As Stream = CType(ar.AsyncState, Stream)
    s.EndWrite(ar)
    s.Close()
  End Sub
End Module
```

The only point of interest in this example (assuming you recall the process of working with delegates!) is that in order to enable the asynchronous behavior of the FileStream type, you must make use of a specific constructor (shown here). The final System.Boolean parameter (when set to True) informs the FileStream object to perform its work on a secondary thread of execution.

■**Source Code** The AsyncFileStream application is included under the Chapter 18 subdirectory.

Summary

This chapter began by examining the use of the `Directory(Info)` and `File(Info)` types. As you learned, these classes allow you to manipulate a physical file or directory on your hard drive. Next, you examined a number of types derived from the abstract `Stream` class, specifically `FileStream`. Given that `Stream`-derived types operate on a raw stream of bytes, the `System.IO` namespace provides numerous reader/writer types (`StreamWriter`, `StringWriter`, `BinaryWriter`, etc.) that simplify the process. Along the way, you also checked out a new I/O-centric type provided by .NET 2.0 (`DriveInfo`), and you learned how to monitor files using the `FileSystemWatcher` type and how to interact with streams in an asynchronous manner.

■ ■ ■

## CHAPTER 19

Understanding Object Serialization

In Chapter 18, you learned about the functionality provided by the System.IO namespace. As shown, this namespace provides numerous reader/writer types that can be used to persist data to a given location (in a given format). This chapter examines the related topic of *object serialization*. Using object serialization, you are able to persist and retrieve the state of an object to (or from) any System.IO.Stream-derived type.

As you might imagine, the ability to serialize types is critical when attempting to copy an object to a remote machine (the subject of the next chapter). Understand, however, that serialization is quite useful in its own right and will likely play a role in many of your .NET applications (distributed or not). Over the course of this chapter, you will be exposed to numerous aspects of the .NET serialization scheme, including a set of new attributes introduced with .NET 2.0 that allow you to customize the process.

Understanding Object Serialization

The term *serialization* describes the process of persisting (and possibly transferring) the state of an object to a stream. The persisted data sequence contains all necessary information needed to reconstruct (or *deserialize*) the state of the object for use later. Using this technology, it is trivial to save vast amounts of data (in various formats) with minimal fuss and bother. In fact, in many cases, saving application data using serialization services is much less cumbersome than making direct use of the readers/writers found within the System.IO namespace.

For example, assume you have created a GUI-based desktop application and wish to provide a way for end users to save their preferences. To do so, you might define a class named UserPrefs that encapsulates 20 or so pieces of field data. If you were to make use of a System.IO.BinaryWriter type, you would need to *manually* save each field of the UserPrefs object. Likewise, when you wish to load the data from the file back into memory, you would need to make use of a System.IO.BinaryReader and (once again) *manually* read in each value to reconfigure a new UserPrefs object.

While this is certainly doable, you would save yourself a good amount of time simply by marking the UserPrefs class with the <Serializable> attribute. In this case, the entire state of the object can be persisted out using a few lines of code:

```
Sub Main()
    ' Assume UserPrefs is marked with the <Serializable> attribute.
    Dim userData As UserPrefs = New UserPrefs()
    userData.WindowColor = "Yellow"
    userData.FontSize = "50"
    userData.IsPowerUser = False
```

```
' Create a new binary formatter to perform the persistence.
Dim binFormat As BinaryFormatter = New BinaryFormatter()
Dim fStream As Stream = New FileStream("user.dat", _
  FileMode.Create, FileAccess.Write, FileShare.None)
binFormat.Serialize(fStream, userData)
fStream.Close()
Console.ReadLine()
End Sub
```

While it is quite simple to persist objects using .NET object serialization, the processes used behind the scenes are quite sophisticated. For example, when an object is persisted to a stream, all associated data (base classes, contained objects, etc.) are automatically serialized as well. Therefore, if you are attempting to persist a derived class, all data up the chain of inheritance comes along for the ride. As you will see, a set of interrelated objects is represented using an *object graph*.

.NET serialization services also allow you to persist an object graph in a variety of formats. The previous code example made use of the BinaryFormatter type; therefore, the state of the UserPrefs object was persisted as a compact binary format. You are also able to persist an object graph into a Simple Object Access Protocol (SOAP) or XML format using other types. These formats can be quite helpful when you wish to ensure that your persisted objects travel well across operating systems, languages, and architectures.

Finally, do know that an object graph can be persisted into *any* System.IO.Stream-derived type. In the previous example, you persisted a UserPrefs object into a local file via the FileStream type. However, if you would rather persist an object to memory, you could make use of a MemoryStream type instead. All that matters is the fact that the sequence of data correctly represents the state of objects within the graph.

The Role of Object Graphs

As mentioned, when an object is serialized, the CLR will account for all related objects. The set of related objects is collectively referred to as an object graph. Object graphs provide a simple way to document how a set of objects refer to each other and do not necessarily map to classic OO relationships (such as the "is-a" or "has-a" relationship), although they do model this paradigm quite well.

Each object in an object graph is assigned a unique numerical value. Keep in mind that the numbers assigned to the members in an object graph are arbitrary and have no real meaning to the outside world. Once all objects have been assigned a numerical value, the object graph can record each object's set of dependencies.

As a simple example, assume you have created a set of classes that model some automobiles (of course). You have a base class named Car, which "has-a" Radio. Another class named JamesBondCar extends the Car base type. Figure 19-1 shows a possible object graph that models these relationships.

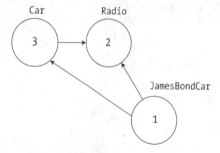

Figure 19-1. *A simple object graph*

When reading object graphs, you can use the phrase "depends on" or "refers to" when connecting the arrows. Thus, in Figure 19-1 you can see that the Car class refers to the Radio class (given the "has-a" relationship). JamesBondCar refers to Car (given the "is-a" relationship) as well as Radio (as it inherits this member variable).

Of course, the CLR does not paint pictures in memory to represent a graph of related objects. Rather, the relationship documented in the previous diagram is represented by a flattened mathematical formula that looks something like this:

```
[Car 3, ref 2], [Radio 2], [JamesBondCar 1, ref 3, ref 2]
```

If you parse this formula, you can again see that object 3 (the Car) has a dependency on object 2 (the Radio). Object 2, the Radio, is a lone wolf and requires nobody. Finally, object 1 (the JamesBondCar) has a dependency on object 3 as well as object 2. In any case, when you serialize or deserialize an instance of JamesBondCar, the object graph ensures that the Radio and Car types also participate in the process.

The beautiful thing about the serialization process is that the graph representing the relationships among your objects is established automatically behind the scenes. As you will see later in this chapter, however, if you do wish to become more involved in the construction of a given object graph, it is possible to do so.

Configuring Objects for Serialization

To make an object available to .NET serialization services, all you need to do is decorate each type in the object graph with the <Serializable> attribute. That's it (really). If you determine that a given class has some member data that should not (or perhaps cannot) participate in the serialization scheme, you can mark such fields with the <NonSerialized> attribute. This can be helpful if you have member variables in a serializable class that do not need to be "remembered" (e.g., fixed values, random values, transient data, etc.) and you wish to reduce the size of the persisted graph.

To get the ball rolling, here is the Radio class, which has been marked <Serializable>, excluding a single member variable (radioID) that has been marked <NonSerialized> and will therefore not be persisted into the specified data stream:

```
<Serializable> _
Public Class Radio
    Public hasTweeters As Boolean
    Public hasSubWoofers As Boolean
    Public stationPresets As Double()
    <NonSerialized()> _
    Public radioID As String = "XF-552RR6"
End Class
```

The JamesBondCar class and Car base class are also marked <Serializable> and define the following pieces of field data:

```
<Serializable()> _
Public Class Car
    Public theRadio As Radio = New Radio
    Public isHatchBack As Boolean
End Class

<Serializable()> _
Public Class JamesBondCar
    Inherits Car
    Public canFly As Boolean
    Public canSubmerge As Boolean
End Class
```

Be aware that the `<Serializable>` attribute cannot be inherited. Therefore, if you derive a class from a type marked `<Serializable>`, the child class must be marked `<Serializable>` as well, or it cannot be persisted. In fact, all objects in an object graph must be marked with the `<Serializable>` attribute. If you attempt to serialize a nonserializable object using the `BinaryFormatter` or `SoapFormatter`, you will receive a `SerializationException` at runtime.

Public Fields, Private Fields, and Public Properties

Notice that in each of these classes, I have defined the field data as public, just to simplify the example. Of course, private data exposed using public properties would be preferable from an OO point of view. Also, for the sake of simplicity, I have not defined any custom constructors on these types, and therefore all unassigned field data will receive the expected default values.

OO design principles aside, you may wonder how the various formatters expect a type's field data to be defined in order to be serialized into a stream. The answer is, it depends. If you are persisting an object using the `BinaryFormatter`, it makes absolutely no difference. This type is programmed to serialize *all* serializable fields of a type, regardless of whether they are public fields, private fields, or private fields exposed through public properties. The situation is quite different if you make use of the `XmlSerializer` or `SoapFormatter` type, however. These types will *only* serialize public pieces of field data or private data exposed through public properties.

Do recall, however, that if you have points of data that you do not want to be persisted into the object graph, you can selectively mark public or private fields as `<NonSerialized>`, as done with the string field of the `Radio` type.

Choosing a Serialization Formatter

Once you have configured your types to participate in the .NET serialization scheme, your next step is to choose which format should be used when persisting your object graph. As of .NET 2.0, you have three choices out of the box:

- `BinaryFormatter`
- `SoapFormatter`
- `XmlSerializer`

The `BinaryFormatter` type serializes your object graph to a stream using a compact binary format. This type is defined within the `System.Runtime.Serialization.Formatters.Binary` namespace that is part of `mscorlib.dll`. Therefore, to serialize your objects using a binary format, all you need to do is specify the following VB 2005 `Imports` directive:

```
' Gain access to the BinaryFormatter in mscorlib.dll.
Imports System.Runtime.Serialization.Formatters.Binary
```

The `SoapFormatter` type represents your graph as a SOAP message. This type is defined within the `System.Runtime.Serialization.Formatters.Soap` namespace that is defined within a *separate assembly*. Thus, to format your object graph into a SOAP message, you must set a reference to `System.Runtime.Serialization.Formatters.Soap.dll` and specify the following VB 2005 `Imports` directive:

```
' Must reference System.Runtime.Serialization.Formatters.Soap.dll!
Imports System.Runtime.Serialization.Formatters.Soap
```

Finally, if you wish to persist an object graph as an XML document, you will need to specify that you are using the `System.Xml.Serialization` namespace, which is also defined in a separate assembly: `System.Xml.dll`. As luck would have it, all Visual Studio 2005 project templates automatically reference `System.Xml.dll`, therefore you will simply need to import the following namespace:

```
' Defined within System.Xml.dll.
Imports System.Xml.Serialization
```

The IFormatter and IRemotingFormatting Interfaces

Regardless of which formatter you choose to make use of, be aware that each of them derives directly from System.Object, and therefore they do not share a common set of members from a serialization-centric base class. However, the BinaryFormatter and SoapFormatter types do support common members through the implementation of the IFormatter and IRemotingFormatter interfaces (of which XmlSerializer implements neither).

System.Runtime.Serialization.IFormatter defines the core Serialize() and Deserialize() methods, which do the grunt work to move your object graphs into and out of a specific stream. Beyond these members, IFormatter defines a few properties that are used behind the scenes by the implementing type:

```
Public Interface IFormatter
  Function Deserialize(ByVal serializationStream As Stream) As Object
  Sub Serialize(ByVal serializationStream As Stream, ByVal graph As Object)
  Property Binder As SerializationBinder
  Property Context As StreamingContext
  Property SurrogateSelector As ISurrogateSelector
End Interface
```

The System.Runtime.Remoting.Messaging.IRemotingFormatter interface (which is leveraged internally by the .NET remoting layer) overloads the Serialize() and Deserialize() members into a manner more appropriate for distributed persistence. Note that IRemotingFormatter derives from the more general IFormatter interface:

```
Public Interface IRemotingFormatter
  Inherits IFormatter
  Function Deserialize(ByVal serializationStream As Stream, _
    ByVal handler As HeaderHandler) As Object
  Sub Serialize(ByVal serializationStream As Stream, _
    ByVal graph As Object, ByVal headers As Header())
End Interface
```

Although you may not need to directly interact with these interfaces for most of your serialization endeavors, recall that interface-based polymorphism allows you to hold an instance of BinaryFormatter or SoapFormatter using an IFormatter reference. Therefore, if you wish to build a method that can serialize an object graph using either of these classes, you could write the following:

```
Sub SerializeObjectGraph(ByVal itfFormat As IFormatter, _
 ByVal destStream As Stream, ByVal graph As Object)
  ' Serialize the object graph here!
  itfFormat.Serialize(destStream, graph)
End Sub
```

Type Fidelity Among the Formatters

The most obvious difference among the three formatters is how the object graph is persisted to the stream (binary, SOAP, or pure XML). You should be aware of a few more subtle points of distinction, specifically how the formatters contend with *type fidelity*. When you make use of the BinaryFormatter type, it will not only persist the serializable field data of the objects in the graph, but also each type's fully qualified name and the full name of the defining assembly. These extra points of data make the BinaryFormatter an ideal choice when you wish to transport objects by value (e.g., as a full copy) across machine boundaries using the .NET remoting layer (see Chapter 20). As noted, to achieve this level of type fidelity, the BinaryFormatter will account for all field data of a type (public or private).

The SoapFormatter and XmlSerializer, on the other hand, do *not* attempt to preserve full type fidelity and therefore do not record the type's fully qualified name or assembly of origin, and only persist public field data/public properties. While this may seem like a limitation at first glance, the reason has to do with the open-ended nature of XML data representation. If you wish to persist object graphs that can be used by any operating system (Windows XP, Mac OS X, and Unix distributions), application framework (.NET, J2EE, COM, etc.), or programming language, you do not want to maintain full type fidelity, as you cannot assume all possible recipients can understand .NET-specific data types. Given this, SoapFormatter and XmlSerializer are ideal choices when you wish to ensure as broad a reach as possible for the persisted object graph.

Serializing Objects Using the BinaryFormatter

To illustrate how easy it is to persist an instance of the JamesBondCar to a physical file, let's make use of the BinaryFormatter type. Again, the two key methods of the BinaryFormatter type to be aware of are Serialize() and Deserialize():

- Serialize(): Persists an object graph to a specified stream as a sequence of bytes
- Deserialize(): Converts a persisted sequence of bytes to an object graph

Assume you have created an instance of JamesBondCar, modified some state data, and want to persist your spy-mobile into a *.dat file. The first task is to create the *.dat file itself. This can be achieved by creating an instance of the System.IO.FileStream type (see Chapter 18). At this point, simply create an instance of the BinaryFormatter and pass in the FileStream and object graph to persist:

```
Imports System.Runtime.Serialization.Formatters.Binary
Imports System.IO

Module Program
  Sub Main()
    Console.WriteLine("***** Fun with Object Serialization *****")
    ' Make a new object to persist.
    Dim jbc As JamesBondCar = New JamesBondCar()
    jbc.canFly = True
    jbc.canSubmerge = False
    jbc.theRadio.stationPresets = New Double() {89.3, 105.1, 97.1}
    jbc.theRadio.hasTweeters = True

    ' Save the object in a binary format to
    ' a local file.
    Dim binFormat As BinaryFormatter = New BinaryFormatter()
    Dim fStream As Stream = New FileStream("CarData.dat", FileMode.Create, _
      FileAccess.Write, FileShare.None)
    binFormat.Serialize(fStream, jbc)
    fStream.Close()
    Console.ReadLine()
  End Sub
End Module
```

As you can see, the BinaryFormatter.Serialize() method is the member responsible for composing the object graph and moving the byte sequence to some Stream-derived type. In this case, the stream happens to be a physical file. However, you could also serialize your object types to any Stream-derived type such as a memory location, given that MemoryStream is a descendent of the Stream type. At this point, you can open the CarData.dat file to view the binary data that represents this instance of the JamesBondCar, as shown in Figure 19-2.

```
CarData.dat                                                          ▼ ×
00000000  00 01 00 00 00 FF FF FF  FF 01 00 00 00 00 00 00   ...............
00000010  00 0C 02 00 00 00 4A 53  69 6D 70 6C 65 53 65 72   ......JSimpleSer
00000020  69 61 6C 69 7A 61 74 69  6F 6E 2C 20 56 65 72 73   ialization, Vers
00000030  69 6F 6E 3D 31 2E 30 2E  30 2E 30 2C 20 43 75 6C   ion=1.0.0.0, Cul
00000040  74 75 72 65 3D 6E 65 75  74 72 61 6C 2C 20 50 75   ture=neutral, Pu
00000050  62 6C 69 63 4B 65 79 54  6F 6B 65 6E 3D 6E 75 6C   blicKeyToken=nul
00000060  6C 05 01 00 00 00 20 53  69 6D 70 6C 65 53 65 72   l..... SimpleSer
00000070  69 61 6C 69 7A 61 74 69  6F 6E 2E 4A 61 6D 65 73   ialization.James
00000080  42 6F 6E 64 43 61 72 04  00 00 00 06 63 61 6E 46   BondCar.....canF
00000090  6C 79 0B 63 61 6E 53 75  62 6D 65 72 67 65 08 74   ly.canSubmerge.t
000000a0  68 65 52 61 64 69 6F 0B  69 73 48 61 74 63 68 42   heRadio.isHatchB
000000b0  61 63 6B 00 00 04 00 01  01 19 53 69 6D 70 6C 65   ack.......Simple
000000c0  53 65 72 69 61 6C 69 7A  61 74 69 6F 6E 2E 52 61   Serialization.Ra
000000d0  64 69 6F 02 00 00 00 01  02 00 00 00 01 00 09 03   dio.............
000000e0  00 00 00 00 05 03 00 00  00 19 53 69 6D 70 6C 65   ..........Simple
000000f0  53 65 72 69 61 6C 69 7A  61 74 69 6F 6E 2E 52 61   Serialization.Ra
00000100  64 69 6F 03 00 00 00 0B  68 61 73 54 77 65 65 74   dio.....hasTweet
00000110  65 72 73 0D 68 61 73 53  75 62 57 6F 6F 66 65 72   ers.hasSubWoofer
00000120  73 0E 73 74 61 74 69 6F  6E 50 72 65 73 65 74 73   s.stationPresets
00000130  00 00 07 01 01 06 02 00  00 00 01 00 09 04 00 00   ................
00000140  00 0F 04 00 00 00 03 00  00 00 06 33 33 33 33 33   ...........33333
00000150  53 56 40 66 66 66 66 66  46 5A 40 66 66 66 66 66   SV@fffffFZ@fffff
00000160  46 58 40 0B                                        FX@.
```

Figure 19-2. JamesBondCar *serialized using a* BinaryFormatter

Deserializing Objects Using the BinaryFormatter

Now suppose you want to read the persisted JamesBondCar from the binary file back into an object variable. Once you have programmatically opened CarData.dat (via the File.OpenRead() method), simply call the Deserialize() method of the BinaryFormatter. Be aware that Deserialize() returns a generic System.Object type, so you need to impose an explicit cast, as shown here:

```
Sub Main()
...
  ' Now read the JamesBondCar from the binary file.
  fStream = File.OpenRead("CarData.dat")
  Dim carFromDisk As JamesBondCar = _
    CType(binFormat.Deserialize(fStream), JamesBondCar)
  Console.WriteLine("Can this car fly? : {0}", carFromDisk.canFly)
  fStream.Close()
  Console.ReadLine()
End Sub
```

Notice that when you call Deserialize(), you pass the Stream-derived type that represents the location of the persisted object graph (again, a file stream in this case). Now if that is not painfully simple, I'm not sure what is. In a nutshell, mark each class you wish to persist to a stream with the <Serializable> attribute. After this point, use the BinaryFormatter type to move your object graph to and from a binary stream.

Serializing Objects Using the SoapFormatter

Your next choice of formatter is the SoapFormatter type. The SoapFormatter will persist an object graph into a SOAP message, which makes this formatter a solid choice when you wish to distribute objects remotely using HTTP. If you are unfamiliar with the SOAP specification, don't sweat the details right now. In a nutshell, SOAP defines a standard process in which methods may be invoked in a platform- and OS-neutral manner (we'll examine SOAP in a bit more detail in the final chapter of this book during a discussion of XML web services).

Assuming you have referenced the System.Runtime.Serialization.Formatters.Soap.dll assembly, you could persist and retrieve a JamesBondCar as a SOAP message simply by replacing each occurrence of BinaryFormatter with SoapFormatter. Consider the following code, which serializes an object to a local file named CarData.soap:

```
Imports System.Runtime.Serialization.Formatters.Soap
...
Sub Main()
...
    ' Save object to a file named CarData.soap in SOAP format.
    Dim soapForamt As SoapFormatter = New SoapFormatter
    fStream = New FileStream("CarData.soap", _
      FileMode.Create, FileAccess.Write, FileShare.None)
    soapForamt.Serialize(fStream, jbc)
    fStream.Close()
    Console.ReadLine()
End Sub
```

As before, simply use Serialize() and Deserialize() to move the object graph in and out of the stream. If you open the resulting *.soap file, you can locate the XML elements that mark the stateful values of the current JamesBondCar as well as the relationship between the objects in the graph via the #ref tokens. Consider the following end result (XML namespaces snipped for brevity):

```
<SOAP-ENV:Envelope xmlns:xsi="...">
  <SOAP-ENV:Body>
    <a1:JamesBondCar id="ref-1" xmlns:a1="...">
      <canFly>true</canFly>
      <canSubmerge>false</canSubmerge>
      <theRadio href="#ref-3"/>
      <isHatchBack>false</isHatchBack>
    </a1:JamesBondCar>
    <a1:Radio id="ref-3" xmlns:a1="...">
      <hasTweeters>true</hasTweeters>
      <hasSubWoofers>false</hasSubWoofers>
      <stationPresets href="#ref-4"/>
    </a1:Radio>
    <SOAP-ENC:Array id="ref-4" SOAP-ENC:arrayType="xsd:double[3]">
      <item>89.3</item>
      <item>105.1</item>
      <item>97.1</item>
    </SOAP-ENC:Array>
  </SOAP-ENV:Body>
</SOAP-ENV:Envelope>
```

Serializing Objects Using the XmlSerializer

In addition to the SOAP and binary formatters, the System.Xml.dll assembly provides a third formatter, System.Xml.Serialization.XmlSerializer, which can be used to persist the state of a given object as pure XML, as opposed to a SOAP message. Working with this type is a bit different from working with the SoapFormatter or BinaryFormatter type. Consider the following code:

```
Imports System.Xml.Serialization
...
Sub Main()
...
    ' Save object to a file named CarData.xml in XML format.
```

```
Dim xmlForamt As XmlSerializer = _
  New XmlSerializer(GetType(JamesBondCar), _
  New Type() {GetType(Radio), GetType(Car)})
fStream = New FileStream("CarData.xml", FileMode.Create, _
  FileAccess.Write, FileShare.None)
xmlForamt.Serialize(fStream, jbc)
fStream.Close()
...
End Sub
```

The key difference is that the XmlSerializer type requires you to specify type information (which can be obtained using GetType()) that represents the items in the object graph. Notice that the first constructor argument of the XmlSerializer defines the root element of the XML file, while the second argument is an array of System.Type types that hold metadata regarding the subelements. If you were to look within the newly generated CarData.xml file, you would find the following (abbreviated) XML data:

```
<?xml version="1.0" encoding="utf-8"?>
<JamesBondCar xmlns:xsi="...">
  <theRadio>
    <hasTweeters>true</hasTweeters>
    <hasSubWoofers>false</hasSubWoofers>
    <stationPresets>
      <double>89.3</double>
      <double>105.1</double>
      <double>97.1</double>
    </stationPresets>
  </theRadio>
  <isHatchBack>false</isHatchBack>
  <canFly>true</canFly>
  <canSubmerge>false</canSubmerge>
</JamesBondCar>
```

■**Note** The XmlSerializer demands that all serialized types in the object graph support a default constructor (so be sure to add it back if you define custom constructors). If this is not the case, you will receive an InvalidOperationException at runtime.

Controlling the Generated XML Data

If you have a background in XML technologies, you are well aware that it is often critical to ensure the elements within an XML document conform to a set of rules that establish the "validity" of the data. Understand that a "valid" XML document does not have to do with the syntactic well-being of the XML elements (e.g., all opening elements must have a closing element). Rather, valid documents conform to agreed-upon formatting rules (e.g., field *x* must be expressed as an attribute and not a subelement), which are typically defined by an XML schema or document-type definition (DTD) file.

By default, all field data of a <Serializable> type is formatted as elements rather than XML attributes. If you wish to control how the XmlSerializer generates the resulting XML document, you may decorate your <Serializable> types with any number of additional attributes from the System. Xml.Serialization namespace. Table 19-1 documents some (but not all) of the attributes that influence how XML data is encoded to a stream.

Table 19-1. *Serialization-centric Attributes of the* System.Xml.Serialization *Namespace*

Attribute	Meaning in Life
<XmlAttribute>	The member will be serialized as an XML attribute.
<XmlElement>	The field or property will be serialized as an XML element.
<XmlEnum>	The element name of an enumeration member.
<XmlRoot>	This attribute controls how the root element will be constructed (namespace and element name).
<XmlText>	The property or field should be serialized as XML text.
<XmlType>	The name and namespace of the XML type.

By way of a simple example, first consider how the field data of JamesBondCar is currently persisted as XML:

```
<?xml version="1.0" encoding="utf-8"?>
<JamesBondCar xmlns:xsi="http://www.w3.org/2001/XMLSchema-instance"
  xmlns:xsd="http://www.w3.org/2001/XMLSchema">
...
  <canFly>true</canFly>
  <canSubmerge>false</canSubmerge>
</JamesBondCar>
```

If you wished to specify a custom XML namespace that qualifies the JamesBondCar as well as encodes the canFly and canSubmerge values as XML attributes, you can do so by modifying the VB 2005 definition of JamesBondCar as follows (be sure to import the System.Xml.Serialization namespace to gain access to these new attributes):

```
<Serializable(), XmlRoot(Namespace:="http://www.intertechtraining.com")> _
Public Class JamesBondCar
  Inherits Car
  <XmlAttribute()> _
  Public canFly As Boolean
  <XmlAttribute()> _
  Public canSubmerge As Boolean
End Class
```

This would yield the following XML document (note the opening <JamesBondCar> element):

```
<?xml version="1.0" encoding="utf-8"?>
<JamesBondCar xmlns:xsi="http://www.w3.org/2001/XMLSchema-instance"
  xmlns:xsd="http://www.w3.org/2001/XMLSchema"
  canFly="true" canSubmerge="false"
  xmlns="http://www.intertechtraining.com">
...
</JamesBondCar>
```

Of course, there are numerous other attributes that can be used to control how the XmlSerializer generates the resulting XML document. If you wish to see all of your options, look up the System.Xml.Serialization namespace using the .NET Framework 2.0 SDK documentation.

Persisting Collections of Objects

Now that you have seen how to persist a single object to a stream, let's examine how to save a set of objects. As you may have noticed, the Serialize() method of the IFormatter interface does not provide a way to specify an arbitrary number of objects (only a single System.Object). On a related note, the return value of Deserialize() is, again, a single System.Object:

```
Public Interface IFormatter
  Function Deserialize(ByVal serializationStream As Stream) As Object
  Sub Serialize(ByVal serializationStream As Stream, ByVal graph As Object)
...
End Interface
```

Recall that the System.Object in fact represents a complete object graph. Given this, if you pass in an object that has been marked as <Serializable> and contains other <Serializable> objects, the entire set of objects is persisted right away. As luck would have it, most of the types found within the System.Collections and System.Collections.Generic namespaces have already been marked as <Serializable>. Therefore, if you wish to persist a set of objects, simply add the set to the container (such as an ArrayList or generic List(Of T)) and serialize the object to your stream of choice.

Assume you have updated the JamesBondCar class with a two-argument constructor to set a few pieces of state data (note that you add back the default constructor as required by the XmlSerializer):

```
<Serializable(), XmlRoot(Namespace:="http://www.intertechtraining.com")> _
Public Class JamesBondCar
  Inherits Car

  Public Sub New(ByVal SkyWorthy As Boolean, ByVal SeaWorthy As Boolean)
    canFly = SkyWorthy
    canSubmerge = SeaWorthy
  End Sub

  ' The XmlSerializer demands a default constructor!
  Public Sub New()
  End Sub

  <XmlAttribute()> _
  Public canFly As Boolean
  <XmlAttribute()> _
  Public canSubmerge As Boolean
End Class
```

With this, you are now able to persist any number of JamesBondCars like so:

```
Sub Main()
...
  ' Now persist a List<> of JamesBondCars.
  Dim myCars As List(Of JamesBondCar) = New List(Of JamesBondCar)
  myCars.Add(New JamesBondCar(True, True))
  myCars.Add(New JamesBondCar(True, False))
  myCars.Add(New JamesBondCar(False, True))
  myCars.Add(New JamesBondCar(False, False))

  fStream = New FileStream("CarCollection.xml", _
    FileMode.Create, FileAccess.Write, FileShare.None)
  xmlForamt = New XmlSerializer(GetType(List(Of JamesBondCar)), _
    New Type() {GetType(JamesBondCar), GetType(Car), GetType(Radio)})
  xmlForamt.Serialize(fStream, myCars)
  fStream.Close()
  Console.ReadLine()
End Sub
```

Again, because you made use of the XmlSerializer, you are required to specify type information for each of the subobjects within the root object (which in this case is the ArrayList). Had you made use of the BinaryFormatter or SoapFormatter type, the logic would be even more straightforward, for example:

```
Sub Main()
...
  ' Save List object (myCars) as binary.
  Dim myCars As List(Of JamesBondCar) = New List(Of JamesBondCar)
...
  Dim binFormat As BinaryFormatter = New BinaryFormatter()
  Dim fStream As Stream = New FileStream("CarData.dat", FileMode.Create, _
    FileAccess.Write, FileShare.None)
  binFormat.Serialize(fStream, myCars)
  fStream.Close()
  Console.ReadLine()
End Sub
```

Excellent! At this point, you should see how you can use object serialization services to simplify the process of persisting and resurrecting your application's data. Next up, allow me to illustrate how you can customize the default serialization process.

■**Source Code** The SimpleSerialize application is located under the Chapter 19 subdirectory.

Customizing the Serialization Process

In a vast majority of cases, the default serialization scheme just examined will fit the bill. Simply apply the <Serializable> attribute accordingly and pass the object graph to your formatter of choice. In some cases, however, you may wish to become more involved with how an object graph is handled during the serialization process in order to customize the formatting of the data (among other tasks). For example, maybe you have a business rule that says all field data must be persisted in a given text format, or perhaps you wish to add additional bits of data to the stream that do not directly map to fields in the object being persisted (time stamps, unique identifiers, or whatnot) or interact with an external log file.

When you wish to become more involved with the process of object serialization, the System.Runtime.Serialization namespace provides several types that allow you to do so. Table 19-2 describes some of the core types to be aware of.

Table 19-2. System.Runtime.Serialization *Namespace Core Types*

Type	Meaning in Life
ISerializable	Before the release of .NET 2.0, implementing this interface was the preferred way to perform custom serialization. As of .NET 2.0, however, the preferred way to customize the serialization process is to apply a new set of serialization-centric attributes (described in just a bit).
<OnDeserialized>	This .NET 2.0 attribute allows you to specify a method that will be called immediately after the object has been deserialized.
<OnDeserializing>	This .NET 2.0 attribute allows you to specify a method that will be called during the deserialization process.
<OnSerialized>	This .NET 2.0 attribute allows you to specify a method that will be called immediately after the object has been serialized.

Type	Meaning in Life
`<OnSerializing>`	This .NET 2.0 attribute allows you to specify a method that will be called during the serialization process.
`<OptionalField>`	This .NET 2.0 attribute allows you to define a field on a type that can be missing from the specified stream.
`SerializationInfo`	In essence, this class is a "property bag" that maintains name/value pairs representing the state of an object during the serialization process.

A Deeper Look at Object Serialization

Before we examine various ways in which you can customize the serialization process, it will be helpful to take a deeper look at what takes place behind the scenes. When the `BinaryFormatter` serializes an object graph, it is in charge of transmitting the following information into the specified stream:

- The fully qualified name of the objects in the graph (e.g., `MyApp.JamesBondCar`)
- The name of the assembly defining the object graph (e.g., `MyApp.exe`)
- An instance of the `SerializationInfo` class that contains all stateful data maintained by the members in the object graph

During the deserialization process, the `BinaryFormatter` uses this same information to build an identical copy of the object, using the information extracted from the underlying stream. The actual state of the object graph itself is represented by an instance of the `SerializationInfo` type, which is created and populated automatically by the formatter when required.

■**Note** Recall that the `SoapFormatter` and `XmlSerializer` do not persist a type's fully qualified name or the name of the defining assembly. These types are concerned only with persisting exposed field data.

The big picture can be visualized as shown in Figure 19-3.

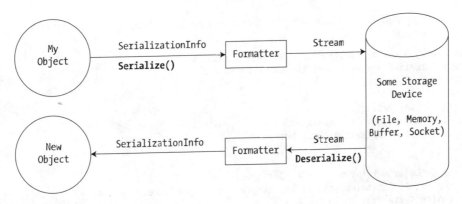

Figure 19-3. *The serialization process*

Beyond moving the required data into and out of a stream, formatters also analyze the members in the object graph for the following pieces of infrastructure:

- A check is made to determine whether the object is marked with the <Serializable> attribute. If the object is not, a SerializationException is thrown.

- If the object is marked <Serializable>, a check is made to determine whether the object implements the ISerializable interface. If this is the case, ISerializable.GetObjectData() is called on the object.

- If the object does not implement ISerializable, the default serialization process is used, serializing all fields not marked as <NonSerialized>.

In addition to determining whether the type supports ISerializable, formatters (as of .NET 2.0) are also responsible for discovering whether the types in question support members that have been adorned with the <OnSerializing>, <OnSerialized>, <OnDeserializing>, or <OnDeserialized> attribute. We'll examine the role of these attributes in just a bit, but first let's look at the role of ISerializable.

Customizing Serialization Using ISerializable

Objects that are marked <Serializable> have the option of implementing the ISerializable interface. By doing so, you are able to "get involved" with the serialization process and perform any pre-data formatting. This interface is quite simple, given that it defines only a single method, GetObjectData(), which is called by the formatter when the object is being serialized into a stream:

```
' The formatter will call this method with serializing
' an object.
Public Interface ISerializable
  Sub GetObjectData(ByVal info As SerializationInfo, _
  ByVal context As StreamingContext)
End Interface
```

The implementation of this method populates the incoming SerializationInfo parameter with a series of name/value pairs that (typically) map to the field data of the object being persisted. SerializationInfo defines numerous variations on the overloaded AddValue() method, in addition to a small set of properties that allow the type to get and set the type's name, defining assembly, and member count.

Types that implement the ISerializable interface must also define a special constructor taking the following signature:

```
' You must supply a custom constructor with this signature
' to allow the runtime engine to set the state of your object.
<Serializable()> _
Class SomeClass
  Implements ISerializable
  Private Sub New(ByVal si As SerializationInfo, ByVal ctx As StreamingContext)
    ' Add custom deserialization logic here.
  End Sub

  Public Sub GetObjectData(ByVal info As SerializationInfo, _
    ByVal context As StreamingContext) Implements ISerializable.GetObjectData
    ' Add custom serialization logic here.
  End Sub
End Class
```

This special constructor is only intended to be called by a given formatter when the object is being deserialized, and therefore best practice is to define the visibility of this constructor as *private*. This is permissible given that the formatter will have access to this member regardless of its visibility.

As you can see, the first parameter of this constructor must be an instance of the SerializationInfo type (which again holds the state of the object's members).

The second parameter of this special constructor is a StreamingContext type, which contains information regarding the source or destination of the bits. The most informative member of this type is the State property, which represents a value from the StreamingContextStates enumeration. The values of this enumeration represent the basic composition of the current stream. To be honest, unless you are implementing some low-level custom remoting services, you will seldom need to deal with this enumeration directly. Nevertheless, here are the possible names of the StreamingContextStates enum (consult the .NET Framework 2.0 SDK documentation for full details):

```
Enum StreamingContextStates
  CrossProcess
  CrossMachine
  File
  Persistence
  Remoting
  Other
  Clone
  CrossAppDomain
  All
End Enum
```

To illustrate customizing the serialization process using ISerializable, assume you have a class type that defines two points of string data. Furthermore, assume that you must ensure the string values are serialized to the stream in all uppercase and deserialized from the stream in all lowercase. To account for such rules, you could implement ISerializable as follows (be sure to import the System.Runtime.Serialization namespace):

```
<Serializable()> _
Class MyStringData
  Implements ISerializable

  Public dataItemOne As String
  Public dataItemTwo As String

  Public Sub New()
  End Sub

  ' Called by formatter when object graph is being deseralized.
  Private Sub New(ByVal si As SerializationInfo, ByVal ctx As StreamingContext)
    dataItemOne = si.GetString("First_Item").ToLower()
    dataItemTwo = si.GetString("dataItemTwo").ToLower()
  End Sub

  ' Called by formatter when object is being serialized.
  Public Sub GetObjectData(ByVal info As SerializationInfo, _
    ByVal context As StreamingContext) Implements ISerializable.GetObjectData
    info.AddValue("First_Item", dataItemOne.ToUpper())
    info.AddValue("dataItemTwo", dataItemTwo.ToUpper())
  End Sub
End Class
```

Notice that when you are filling the SerializationInfo type from within the GetObjectData() method, you are not required to name the data points identically to the type's internal member variables. This can obviously be helpful if you need to further decouple the type's data from the persisted format. Do be aware, however, that you will need to obtain the values from within the private constructor using the same names assigned within GetObjectData().

To test your customization, assume you have persisted an instance of `MyStringData` using a `SoapFormatter`. When you view the resulting `*.soap` file, you will note that the string fields have indeed been persisted in uppercase:

```
<SOAP-ENV:Envelope xmlns:xsi="...">
  <SOAP-ENV:Body>
    <a1:MyStringData id="ref-1" xmlns:a1="...">
      <First_Item id="ref-3">THIS IS SOME DATA.</First_Item>
      <dataItemTwo id="ref-4">HERE IS SOME MORE DATA</dataItemTwo>
    </a1:MyStringData>
  </SOAP-ENV:Body>
</SOAP-ENV:Envelope>
```

When deserializing these same values, they would be converted back into lowercase given the custom code within the "special hidden" constructor. While this example was intended to be only illustrative in nature, is does point out the fact that customizing how your object's data is (de)serialized involves support of the `ISerializable` interface and support for a specific hidden constructor invoked behind the scenes by the formatter.

Customizing Serialization Using Attributes

Although the previously examined approach to customizing the object serialization process is still possible under .NET 2.0, the preferred manner to do so is to define methods that are attributed with any of the new serialization-centric attributes: `<OnSerializing>`, `<OnSerialized>`, `<OnDeserializing>`, or `<OnDeserialized>`. The roles of each of these new attributes are documented in Table 19-3.

Table 19-3. *Custom Serialization Attributes of .NET 2.0*

Serialization Attribute	Meaning in Life
`<OnDeserializing>`	The method marked with this attribute will be called before the deserialization process begins. Here you can initialize default values for optional fields (these being fields marked with the `<OptionalField>` attribute).
`<OnDeserialized>`	The method marked with this attribute will be called once the deserialization process is complete. Here you are able to establish optional field values based on the contents of other fields.
`<OnSerializing>`	The method marked with this attribute will be called before the serialization process begins. Here you can prep for the serialization process (e.g., create optional data structures, write to event logs, etc.).
`<OnSerialized>`	The method marked with this attribute will be called after the serialization process is complete. Typically this method would be used to log serialization events.

Using these attributes to control object serialization is typically less cumbersome than implementing `ISerializable` (and the obligatory private "special constructor"), given that you do not need to manually interact with an incoming `SerializationInfo` parameter. Instead, you are able to directly modify your state data while the formatter is operating on the type. Also be aware that you are not required to capture each step of the serialization/deserialization process. Thus, if you only are interested in attributing methods with the `<OnDeserialized>` and `<OnSerialized>` attributes (to account for when the object is fully serialized or deserialized), you are free to do so.

The subroutines that are decorated with any of the attributes described in Table 19-3 must be defined to receive a `StreamingContext` parameter as their only parameter (otherwise, you will receive a runtime exception). To illustrate, here is a new `<Serializable>` type that has the same requirements as `MyStringData`, this time accounted for using the `<OnSerializing>` and `<OnDeserialized>` attributes:

```vb
<Serializable()> _
Class MoreStringData
  Public dataItemOne As String
  Public dataItemTwo As String

  ' This method is called by the formatter when the
  ' object is being serialized.
  <OnSerializing()> _
  Private Sub OnSerializing(ByVal context As StreamingContext)
    dataItemOne = dataItemOne.ToUpper()
    dataItemTwo = dataItemTwo.ToUpper()
  End Sub

  ' This method is called by the formatter when the
  ' object is being deserialized.
  <OnDeserialized()> _
  Private Sub OnDeserialized(ByVal context As StreamingContext)
    dataItemOne = dataItemOne.ToLower()
    dataItemTwo = dataItemTwo.ToLower()
  End Sub
End Class
```

If you were to serialize this new type, you would again find that the data has been persisted as uppercase and deserialized as lowercase.

■**Source Code** The CustomSerialization project is included under the Chapter 19 subdirectory.

■**Note** The .NET platform provides another new serialization-centric attribute named <OptionalField>. This attribute can be applied to new fields of a previously serializable type to help safely version an object (and prevent the CLR from throwing runtime exceptions when incompatibilities are found). Look up the topic "Version Tolerant Serialization" within the .NET 2.0 Framework SDK documentation for further information.

Summary

This chapter introduced the topic of object serialization services. As you have seen, the .NET platform makes use of an object graph to correctly account for the full set of related objects that are to be persisted to a stream. As long as each member in the object graph has been marked with the <Serializable> attribute, the data is persisted using your format of choice (binary, SOAP, or XML).

You also learned that it is possible to customize the out-of-the-box serialization process using two possible approaches. First, you learned how to implement the ISerializable interface (and support a special private constructor) to become more involved with how formatters persist the supplied data. Next, you came to know a set of new attributes introduced with .NET 2.0, which simplifies the process of custom serialization. Just apply the <OnSerializing>, <OnSerialized>, <OnDeserializing>, or <OnDeserialized> attribute on members taking a StreamingContext parameter, and the formatters will invoke them accordingly.

CHAPTER 20

■ ■ ■

The .NET Remoting Layer

Developers who are new to the .NET platform often assume that .NET is all about building Internet-centric applications (given that the term ".NET" often conjures the notion of "interNET" software). As you have already seen, however, this is simply not the case. In fact, the construction of web-based programs is simply one small (but quite well-touted) aspect of the .NET platform. In this same vein of misinformation, many new .NET developers tend to assume that XML web services are the only way to interact with remote objects. Again, this is not true. Using the .NET remoting layer, you are able to build peer-to-peer distributed applications that have nothing whatsoever to do with HTTP or XML (if you so choose).

The first goal of this chapter is to examine the low-level grunge used by the CLR to move information between application boundaries. Along the way, you will come to understand the numerous terms used when discussing .NET remoting, such as proxies, channels, marshaling by reference (as opposed to by value), server-activated (versus client-activated) objects, and so forth. After these background elements are covered, the remainder of the chapter offers numerous code examples that illustrate the process of building distributed systems using the .NET platform.

Defining .NET Remoting

As you recall from your reading in Chapter 15, an *application domain* (*AppDomain*) is a logical boundary for a .NET assembly, which is itself housed within a Win32 process. Understanding this concept is critical when discussing distributed computing under .NET, given that *remoting* is nothing more than the act of two objects communicating across application domains. The two application domains in question could be physically configured in any of the following manners:

- Two application domains in the same process (and thus on the same machine)
- Two application domains in separate processes on the same machine
- Two application domains in separate processes on different machines

Given these three possibilities, you can see that remoting does not necessarily need to involve two networked computers. In fact, each of the examples presented in this chapter can be successfully run on a single, stand-alone machine. Regardless of the distance between two objects, it is common to refer to each agent using the terms "client" and "server." Simply put, the *client* is the entity that attempts to interact with remote objects. The *server* is the software agent that houses the remote objects.

The .NET Remoting Namespaces

Before we dive too deep into the details of the .NET remoting layer, we need to check out the functionality provided by the remoting-centric namespaces. The .NET base class libraries provide numerous namespaces that allow you to build distributed applications. The bulk of the types found within these namespaces are contained within mscorlib.dll, but the System.Runtime.Remoting.dll assembly does complement and extend the core namespaces. Table 20-1 briefly describes the role of the remoting-centric namespaces as of .NET 2.0.

Table 20-1. *.NET Remoting-centric Namespaces*

Namespace	Meaning in Life
System.Runtime.Remoting	This is the core namespace you must use when building any sort of distributed .NET application.
System.Runtime.Remoting.Activation	This relatively small namespace defines a handful of types that allow you to fine-tune the process of activating a remote object.
System.Runtime.Remoting.Channels	This namespace contains types that represent channels and channel sinks.
System.Runtime.Remoting.Channels.Http	This namespace contains types that use the HTTP protocol to transport messages and objects to and from remote locations.
System.Runtime.Remoting.Channels.Ipc	This namespace (which is new to .NET 2.0) contains types that leverage the Win32 inter-process communication (IPC) architecture. As you may know, IPC proves fast communications between AppDomains on the *same* physical machine.
System.Runtime.Remoting.Channels.Tcp	This namespace contains types that use the TCP protocol to transport messages and objects to and from remote locations.
System.Runtime.Remoting.Contexts	This namespace allows you to configure the details of an object's context.
System.Runtime.Remoting.Lifetime	This namespace contains types that manage the lifetime of remote objects.
System.Runtime.Remoting.Messaging	This namespace contains types used to create and transmit message objects.
System.Runtime.Remoting.Metadata	This namespace contains types that can be used to customize the generation and processing of SOAP formatting.
System.Runtime.Remoting.Metadata.W3cXsd2001	Closely related to the previous namespace, this namespace contains types that represent the XML Schema Definition (XSD) defined by the World Wide Web Consortium (W3C) in 2001.
System.Runtime.Remoting.MetadataServices	This namespace contains the types used by the soapsuds.exe command-line tool to convert .NET metadata to and from an XML schema for the remoting infrastructure.
System.Runtime.Remoting.Proxies	This namespace contains types that provide functionality for proxy objects.
System.Runtime.Remoting.Services	This namespace defines a number of common base classes (and interfaces) that are typically only leveraged by other intrinsic remoting agents.

Understanding the .NET Remoting Framework

When clients and servers exchange information across application boundaries, the CLR makes use of several low-level primitives to ensure the entities in question are able to communicate with each other as transparently as possible. This means that as a .NET programmer, you are *not* required to provide reams and reams of grungy networking code to invoke a method on a remote object. Likewise, the server process is *not* required to manually pluck a network packet out of the queue and reformat the message into terms the remote object can understand.

As you would hope, the CLR takes care of such details automatically using a default set of remoting primitives (although you are certainly able to get involved with the process if you so choose).

In a nutshell, the .NET remoting layer revolves around a careful orchestration that takes place between four key players:

- Proxies
- Messages
- Channels
- Formatters

Let's check out each entity in turn and see how their combined functionality facilitates remote method invocations.

Understanding Proxies and Messages

Clients and server objects do not communicate via a direct connection, but rather through the use of an intermediary termed a *proxy*. The role of a .NET proxy is to fool the client into believing it is communicating with the requested remote object in the *same application domain*. To facilitate this illusion, a proxy has the identical members (i.e., methods, properties, fields, and whatnot) as the remote type it represents. As far as the client is concerned, a given proxy *is* the remote object. Under the hood, however, the proxy is forwarding calls to the remote object.

Formally speaking, the proxy invoked directly by the client is termed the *transparent proxy*. This CLR-autogenerated entity is in charge of ensuring that the client has provided the correct number of (and type of) parameters to invoke the remote method. Given this, you can regard the transparent proxy as a fixed interception layer that *cannot* be modified or extended programmatically.

Assuming the transparent proxy is able to verify the validity of the incoming arguments, this information is packaged up into another CLR-generated type termed the *message object*. By definition, all message objects implement the System.Runtime.Remoting.Messaging.IMessage interface:

```
Public Interface IMessage
  ReadOnly Property Properties() As IDictionary
End Interface
```

As you can see, the IMessage interface defines a single read-only property (named Properties) that provides access to a collection used to hold the client-supplied arguments. Once this message object has been populated by the CLR, it is then passed into a closely related type termed the *real proxy*.

The real proxy is the entity that actually passes the message object into the channel (described momentarily). Unlike the transparent proxy, the real proxy *can* be extended by the programmer and is represented by a base class type named (of course) RealProxy. Again, it is worth pointing out that the CLR will always generate a default implementation of the client-side real proxy, which will serve your needs most (if not all) of the time. If you are interested in the formal definition of the RealProxy type, consult the .NET 2.0 Framework SDK documentation.

Understanding Channels

Once the proxies have validated and formatted the client-supplied arguments into a message object, this IMessage-compatible type is passed from the real proxy into a channel object. *Channels* are the entities in charge of transporting a message to the remote object and, if necessary, ensuring that any function return value is passed from the remote object back to the client. The .NET 2.0 base class libraries provide three channel implementations out of the box:

- TCP channel
- HTTP channel
- IPC channel

The *TCP channel* is represented by the TcpChannel class type and is used to pass messages using the TCP/IP network protocol. TcpChannel is helpful in that the formatted packets are quite lightweight, given that the messages are converted into a tight binary format using a related BinaryFormatter (yes, the same BinaryFormatter you saw in Chapter 19). Use of the TcpChannel type tends to result in faster remote access. The downside is that TCP channels are not firewall friendly and may require the services of a system administrator to allow messages to pass across machine boundaries.

In contrast, the *HTTP channel* is represented by the HttpChannel class type, which converts message objects into a SOAP format using a related SOAP formatter. As you have seen, SOAP is XML based and thus tends to result in beefier payloads than the payloads used by the TcpChannel type. Given this, using the HttpChannel can result in slightly slower remote access. On the plus side, HTTP is far more firewall friendly, given that most firewalls allow textual packets to be passed over port 80.

Finally, as of .NET 2.0, we have access to the *IPC channel*, represented by the IpcChannel type, which defines a communication channel for remoting using the IPC system of the Windows operating system. Because IpcChannel bypasses traditional network communication to cross AppDomains, the IpcChannel is much faster than the HTTP and TCP channels; however, it can be used only for communication between application domains *on the same physical computer*. Given this, you could never use IpcChannel to build a distributed application that spans multiple physical computers. IpcChannel can be an ideal option, however, when you wish to have two local programs share information in the fastest possible manner.

Regardless of which channel type you choose to use, understand that the HttpChannel, TcpChannel, and IpcChannel types all implement the IChannel, IChannelSender, and IChannelReceiver interfaces. The IChannel interface (as you will see in just a bit) defines a small set of members that provide common functionality to all channel types. The role of IChannelSender is to define a common set of members for channels that are able to send information *to* a specific receiver. On the other hand, IChannelReceiver defines a set of members that allow a channel to receive information *from* a given sender.

To allow the client and server applications to register their channel of choice, you will make use of the ChannelServices.RegisterChannel() method, which takes a type implementing IChannel. Just to preview things to come, the following code snippet illustrates how a server-side application domain can register an HTTP channel on port 32469 (you'll see the client's role shortly):

```
' Create and register a server-side HttpChannel on port 32469.
Dim c As HttpChannel = New HttpChannel(32469)
ChannelServices.RegisterChannel(c)
```

Revisiting the Role of .NET Formatters

The final piece of the .NET remoting puzzle is the role of *formatter* objects. The TcpChannel and HttpChannel types both leverage an internal formatter, whose job it is to translate the message object into protocol-specific terms. As mentioned, the TcpChannel type makes use of the BinaryFormatter type, while the HttpChannel type uses the functionality provided by the SoapFormatter type. Given your work in the previous chapter, you should already have some insights as to how a given channel will format the incoming messages.

Once the formatted message has been generated, it is passed into the channel, where it will eventually reach its destination application domain, at which time the message is formatted from protocol-specific terms back to .NET-specific terms, at which point an entity termed the *dispatcher* invokes the correct method on the remote object.

All Together Now!

If your head is spinning from reading the previous sections, fear not! The transparent proxy, real proxy, message object, and dispatcher can typically be completely ignored, provided you are happy with the default remoting plumbing. To help solidify the sequence of events, ponder Figure 20-1, which illustrates the basic process of two objects communicating across distinct application domains.

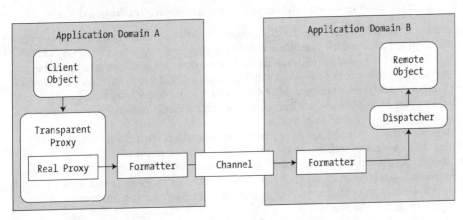

Figure 20-1. *A high-level view of the default .NET remoting architecture*

A Brief Word Regarding Extending the Default Plumbing

A key aspect of the .NET remoting API is the fact that most of the default layers can be extended or completely replaced at the whim of the developer. Thus, if you truly want (or possibly need) to build a custom message dispatcher, custom formatter, or custom real proxy, you are free to do so. You are also able to inject *additional* levels of indirection by plugging in custom types that stand between a given layer (e.g., a custom sink used to perform preprocessing or postprocessing of a given message). Now, to be sure, you may never need to retrofit the core .NET remoting layer in such ways. However, the fact remains that the .NET platform does provide the namespaces to allow you to do so.

■**Note** This chapter does not address the topic of extending the default .NET remoting layer. If you wish to learn how to do so, check out *Advanced .NET Remoting, Second Edition* by Ingo Rammer and Mario Szpuszta (Apress, 2005).

Terms of the .NET Remoting Trade

Like any new paradigm, .NET remoting brings a number of TLAs (three-letter acronyms) into the mix. Thus, before you see your first code example, we do need to define a few terms used when describing the composition of a .NET remoting application. As you would guess, this terminology is used to describe a number of details regarding common questions that arise during the construction of a distributed application: How do we pass a type across application domain boundaries? When exactly is a remote type activated? How do we manage the lifetime of a remote object (and so forth)? Once you have an understanding of the related terminology, the act of building a distributed .NET application will be far less perplexing.

Object Marshaling Choices: MBR or MBV?

Under the .NET platform, you have two options regarding how a remote object is marshaled to the client. Simply put, *marshaling* describes how a remote object is passed between application domains. When you are designing a remotable object, you may choose to employ *marshal-by-reference* (*MBR*) or *marshal-by-value* (*MBV*) semantics. The distinction is as follows:

- *MBR objects*: The caller communicates with the remote object via a proxy.
- *MBV objects*: The caller receives a full copy of the object in its own application domain.

If you configure an MBR object type, the CLR ensures that the transparent and real proxies are created in the client's application domain, while the MBR object itself remains in the server's application domain. As the client invokes methods on the remote type, the .NET remoting plumbing (examined previously) takes over the show and will package, pass, and return information between application domain boundaries. To be sure, MBR objects have a number of traits above and beyond their physical location. As you will see, MBR objects have various configuration options regarding their activation options and lifetime management.

MBV objects, on the other hand, are *local copies* of remote objects (which leverage the .NET serialization protocol examined in Chapter 19). MBV objects have far fewer configuration settings, given that their lifetime is directly controlled by the client code base. Like any .NET object, once a client has released all references to an MBV type, it is a candidate for garbage collection. Given that MBV types are local copies of remote objects, as a client invokes members on the type, no network activity occurs during the process.

Now, understand that it will be quite common for a single server to provide access to numerous MBR and MBV types. As you may also suspect, MBR types tend to support methods that return various MBV types, which gives way to the familiar factory pattern (e.g., an object that creates and returns other related objects). The next question is, How do you configure your custom class types as MBR or MBV entities?

Configuring an MBV Object

The process of configuring an object as an MBV type is identical to the process of configuring an object for serialization. Simply annotate the type with the `<Serializable>` attribute:

```
<Serializable> _
Public Class SportsCar
...
End Class
```

Configuring an MBR Object

MBR objects are not marked as such using a .NET attribute, but rather by deriving (directly or indirectly) from the `System.MarshalByRefObject` base class:

```
Public Class SportsCarFactory
  Inherits MarshalByRefObject
...
End Class
```

As you will see over the course of this chapter, `MarshalByRefObject` proves a handful of members that can be used to control the lifetime of the remote object. Table 20-2 describes the role of the core members of this type.

Table 20-2. *Key Members of* `System.MarshalByRefObject`

Member	Meaning in Life
`CreateObjRef()`	Creates an object that contains all the relevant information required to generate a proxy used to communicate with a remote object
`GetLifetimeServices()`	Retrieves the current lifetime service object that controls the lifetime policy for this instance
`InitializeLifetimeServices()`	Obtains a lifetime service object to control the lifetime policy for this instance

■**Note** Just because you have configured a type as an MBV or MBR entity does not mean it is only usable within a remoting application, just that it may be used in a remoting application. For example, the `System.Windows.Forms.Form` type is a descendent of `MarshalByRefObject`; thus, if accessed remotely, it is realized as an MBR type. If not, it is just another local object in the client's application domain.

Now that you understand the distinct traits of MBR and MBV types, let's check out some issues that are specific to MBR types (MBV types need not apply).

■**Note** As a corollary to the previous note, understand that if a .NET type is not serializable and does not include `MarshalByRefObject` in its inheritance chain, the type in question can only be activated and used in the originating application domain (meaning, the type is context bound; see Chapter 15 for more details).

Activation Choices for MBR Types: WKO or CAO?

Another remoting-centric choice you face as a .NET programmer has to do with exactly *when* an MBR object is activated and *when* it should be a candidate for garbage collection on the server. This might seem like a strange choice to make, as you might naturally assume that MBR objects are created when the client requests them and die when the client is done with them. While it is true that the client is the entity in charge of instructing the remoting layer it wishes to communicate with a remote type, the server application domain may (or may not) create the type at the exact moment the client's code base requests it.

The reason for this seemingly strange behavior has to do with the optimization. Specifically, every MBR type may be configured to be activated using one of two techniques:

- As a well-known object (WKO)
- As a client-activated object (CAO)

■**Note** A potential point of confusion is that fact that the acronym WKO is also called a server-activated object (SAO) in the .NET literature. In fact, you may see the SAO acronym in various .NET-centric articles and books. In keeping with the current terminology, I will use WKO throughout this chapter.

WKO objects are MBR types whose lifetimes are directly controlled by the server's application domain. The client-side application activates the remote type using a friendly, well-known string name (hence the acronym WKO). The server's application domain allocates WKO types when the client makes the first method call on the object (via the transparent proxy), *not* when the client's code base makes use of the New keyword or via the shared Activator.GetObject() method, for example:

```
' Get a proxy to remote object. This line does NOT create the WKO type!
' (you'll see the parameters to GetObject() later in this chapter)
Dim remoteObj As Object = Activator.GetObject(...)

' Invoke a method on remote WKO type. This WILL create the WKO object
' and invoke the SomeFunction() method.
Dim simple As SomeRemoteObject = CType(remoteObj, SomeRemoteObject)
Console.WriteLine("Remote object says: {0}", simple.SomeFunction())
```

The rationale for this behavior? This approach saves a network round-trip solely for the purpose of creating the object. As another interesting corollary, WKO types can *be created only via the type's default constructor*. This should make sense, given that the remote type's constructor is triggered only when the client makes the initial member invocation. Thus, the runtime has no other option than to invoke the type's default constructor.

Note Always remember: all WKO types must define a default constructor! Thus, if you define custom constructors for your WKO types, be sure to redefine the default.

If you wish to allow the client to create a remote MBR object using a custom constructor, the server must configure the object as a CAO. CAO objects are entities whose lifetime is controlled by the client's application domain. When accessing a CAO type, a round-trip to the server occurs at the time the client makes use of the New keyword (using any of the type's constructors) or via the Activator type.

Stateful Configuration of WKO Types: Singleton or Single Call?

The final .NET design choice to consider with regard to MBR types has to do with how the server should handle multiple requests to a WKO type. CAO types need not apply, given that there is always a one-to-one correspondence between a client and a remote CAO type (because they are stateful).

Your first option is to configure a WKO type to function as a *singleton type*. The CLR will create a single instance of the remote type that will take requests from any number of clients, and it is a natural choice if you need to maintain stateful information among multiple remote callers. Given the fact that multiple clients could invoke the same method at the same time, the CLR places each client invocation on a new thread. It is *your* responsibility, however, to ensure that your objects are thread-safe using the same techniques described in Chapter 16.

In contrast, a *single call* object is a WKO type that exists only during the context of a single method invocation. Thus, if there are 20 clients making use of a WKO type configured with single-call semantics, the server will create 20 distinct objects (one for each client), all of which are candidates for garbage collection directly after the method invocation. As you can guess, single-call objects are far more scalable than singleton types, given that they are invariably stateless entities.

The server is the entity in charge of determining the stateful configuration of a given WKO type. Programmatically, these options are expressed via the System.Runtime.Remoting.WellKnownObjectMode enumeration:

```
Enum WellKnownObjectMode
   SingleCall
   Singleton
End Enum
```

Summarizing the Traits of MBR Object Types

As you have seen, configuring an MBV object is a no-brainer: apply the `<Serializable>` attribute to allow copies of the type to be returned to the client's application domain. At this point, all interaction with the MBV type takes place in the client's locale. When the client is finished using the MBV type, it is a candidate for garbage collection, and all is well with the world.

With MBR types, however, you have a number of possible configuration choices. As you have seen, a given MBR type can be configured with regard to its time of activation, statefulness, and lifetime management. To summarize the array of possibilities, Table 20-3 documents how WKO and CAO types stack up against the traits you have just examined.

Table 20-3. *Configuration Options for MBR Types*

MBR Object Trait	WKO Behavior	CAO Behavior
Instantiation options	WKO types can only be activated using the default constructor of the type, which is triggered when the client makes the first method invocation.	CAO types can be activated using any constructor of the type. The remote object is created at the point the caller makes use of constructor semantics (or via the `Activator` type).
State management	WKO types can be configured as singleton or single-call entities. Singleton types can service multiple clients and are therefore stateful. Single-call types are alive only during a specific client-side invocation and are therefore stateless.	The lifetime of a CAO type is dictated by the caller; therefore, CAO types are stateful entities.
Lifetime management	Singleton WKO types make use of a lease-based management scheme (described later in this chapter). Single-call WKO types are candidates for garbage collection after the current method invocation.	CAO types make use of a lease-based management scheme (described later in this chapter).

Basic Deployment of a .NET Remoting Project

Enough acronyms! At this point you are almost ready to build your first .NET remoting application (finally). Before you do, however, I need to discuss one final detail: deployment. When you are building a .NET remoting application, you are almost certain to end up with three (yes, three, not two) distinct .NET assemblies that will constitute the entirety of your remote application. I am sure you can already account for the first two assemblies:

- *The client*: This assembly is the entity that is interested in obtaining access to a remote object (such as a Windows Forms or console application).

- *The server*: This assembly is the entity that receives channel requests from the remote client and hosts the remote objects.

So then, where does the third assembly fit in? In many cases, the server application is typically a host to a third assembly that defines and implements the remote objects. For convenience, I'll call this assembly the *general assembly*. This decoupling of the assembly containing the remote objects and server host is quite important, in that both the client and the server assemblies typically set a reference to the general assembly to obtain the metadata definitions of the remotable types.

In the simplest case, the general assembly is placed into the application directory of the client and server. The only possible drawback to this approach is the fact that the client has a reference to an assembly that contains CIL code that is never used (which may be a problem if you wish to ensure that the end user cannot view proprietary code). Specifically, the only reason the client requires a reference to the general assembly is to obtain the metadata descriptions of the remotable types. You can overcome this glitch in several ways, for example:

- Construct your remote objects to make use of interface-based programming techniques. Given this, the client is able to set a reference to a .NET binary that contains nothing but interface definitions.

- Make use of the soapsuds.exe command-line application. Using this tool, you are able to generate an assembly that contains nothing but metadata descriptions of the remote types.

- Manually build an assembly that contains nothing but metadata descriptions of the remote types.

To keep things simple over the course of this chapter, you will build and deploy general assemblies that contain the required metadata as well as the CIL implementation.

■**Note** If you wish to examine how to implement general assemblies using each of these alternatives, check out *Distributed .NET Programming in VB .NET* by Tom Barnaby (Apress, 2002).

Building Your First Distributed Application

There is nothing more satisfying than building a distributed application using a new platform. To illustrate how quickly you're able to get up and running with the .NET remoting layer, let's build a simple example. As mentioned, the entirety of this example consists of three .NET assemblies:

- A general assembly named SimpleRemotingAsm.dll
- A client assembly named SimpleRemoteObjectClient.exe
- A server assembly named SimpleRemoteObjectServer.exe

Building the General Assembly

First, let's create the general assembly, SimpleRemotingAsm.dll, which will be referenced by both the server and client applications. SimpleRemotingAsm.dll defines a single MBR type named RemoteMessageObject, which supports two public members. The DisplayMessage() method prints a client-supplied message on the server's console window, while ReturnMessage() returns a message to the client. Here is the complete code of this new VB 2005 class library:

```
' This is a type that will be
' marshaled by reference (MBR) if accessed remotely.
Public Class RemoteMessageObject
  Inherits MarshalByRefObject

  Public Sub New()
    Console.WriteLine("Constructing RemoteMessageObject!")
  End Sub

  ' This method takes an input string
  ' from the caller.
  Public Sub DisplayMessage(ByVal msg As String)
```

```
    Console.WriteLine("Message is: {0}", msg)
  End Sub

  ' This method returns a value to the caller.
  Public Function ReturnMessage() As String
    Return "Hello from the remote object!"
  End Function
End Class
```

The major point of interest is the fact that the type derives from the System.MarshalByRefObject base class, which ensures that the derived class will be accessible via a client-side proxy. Also note the custom default constructor that will print out a message when an instance of the type comes to life. That's it. Go ahead and build your new SimpleRemotingAsm.dll assembly.

Building the Server Assembly

Recall that server assemblies are essentially hosts for general assemblies that contain the remotable objects. Create a console program named SimpleRemoteObjectServer. The role of this assembly is to open a channel for the incoming requests and register RemoteMessageObject as a WKO. To begin, reference the System.Runtime.Remoting.dll and SimpleRemotingAsm.dll assemblies, and update Main() as follows:

```
' Be sure to reference SimpleRemotingAsm.dll
' and System.Runtime.Remoting.dll
Imports SimpleRemotingAsm
Imports System.Runtime.Remoting
Imports System.Runtime.Remoting.Channels
Imports System.Runtime.Remoting.Channels.Http

Module Program
  Sub Main()
    Console.WriteLine("***** SimpleRemoteObjectServer started! *****")
    Console.WriteLine("Hit enter to end.")

    ' Register a new HttpChannel
    Dim c As HttpChannel = New HttpChannel(32469)

    ' The second Boolean parameter controls if the
    ' channel is to be secured.
    ChannelServices.RegisterChannel(c, False)

    ' Register a WKO type, using singleton activation.
    RemotingConfiguration.RegisterWellKnownServiceType( _
      GetType(SimpleRemotingAsm.RemoteMessageObject), _
      "RemoteMsgObj.soap", _
      WellKnownObjectMode.Singleton)
    Console.ReadLine()
  End Sub
End Module
```

Main() begins by creating a new HttpChannel type using an arbitrary port ID. This port is opened on registering the channel via the shared ChannelServices.RegisterChannel() method. Once the channel as been registered, the remote server assembly is now equipped to process incoming messages via port number 32469.

Note The number you assign to a port is typically up to you (or your system administrator). Do be aware, however, that port IDs below 1024 are reserved for system use.

Next, to register the `SimpleRemotingAsm.RemoteMessageObject` type as a WKO requires the use of the `RemotingConfiguration.RegisterWellKnownServiceType()` method. The first argument to this method is the type information of the type to be registered. The second parameter to `RegisterWellKnownServiceType()` is a simple string (of your choosing) that will be used to identify the object across application domain boundaries. Here, you are informing the CLR that this object is to be realized by the client using the name `RemoteMsgObj.soap`.

The final parameter is a member of the `WellKnownObjectMode` enumeration, which you have specified as `WellKnownObjectMode.Singleton`. Recall that singleton WKO types ensure that a single instance of the `RemoteMessageObject` will service all incoming requests. Build your server assembly and let's move on to the client-side code.

Building the Client Assembly

Now that you have a listener that is hosting your remotable object, the final step is to build an assembly that will request access to its services. Again, let's use a simple console application (named `SimpleRemoteObjectClient`). Set a reference to `System.Runtime.Remoting.dll` and `SimpleRemotingAsm.dll`. Implement `Main()` as follows:

```vb
Imports System.Runtime.Remoting
Imports System.Runtime.Remoting.Channels
Imports System.Runtime.Remoting.Channels.Http
Imports SimpleRemotingAsm

Module Program
  Sub Main()
    Console.WriteLine("***** SimpleRemoteObjectClient started! *****")
    Console.WriteLine("Hit enter to end.")

    ' Create a new HttpChannel.
    Dim c As HttpChannel = New HttpChannel()
    ChannelServices.RegisterChannel(c, False)

    ' Get a proxy to remote WKO type.
    Dim remoteObj As Object = Activator.GetObject( _
      GetType(SimpleRemotingAsm.RemoteMessageObject), _
      "http://localhost:32469/RemoteMsgObj.soap")

    ' Now use the remote object.
    Dim simple As RemoteMessageObject = CType(remoteObj, RemoteMessageObject)
    simple.DisplayMessage("Hello from the client!")
    Console.WriteLine("Server says: {0}", simple.ReturnMessage())
    Console.ReadLine()
  End Sub
End Module
```

A few notes about this client application. First, notice that the client is also required to register an HTTP channel, but the client does not specify a port ID, as the end point is specified by the client-supplied activation URL. Given that the client is interacting with a registered WKO type, you are limited to triggering the type's default constructor. To do so, make use of the `Activator.GetObject()` method, specifying two parameters. The first is the type information that describes the remote object you are interested in interacting with. Read that last sentence again. Given that the `Activator.GetObject()` method requires the object's metadata description, it should make more sense as to why the client is *also* required to reference the general assembly! Again, at the end of the chapter you'll examine various ways to clean up this aspect of your client-side assembly.

The second parameter to `Activator.GetObject()` is termed the *activation URL*. Activation URLs that describe a WKO type can be generalized into the following format:

```
ProtocolScheme://ComputerName:Port/ObjectUri
```

Finally, note that the `Activator.GetObject()` method returns a generic `System.Object` type, and thus you must make use of an explicit cast to gain access to the members of the `RemoteMessageObject`.

Testing the Remoting Application

To test your application, begin by launching the server application, which will open an HTTP channel and register `RemoteMessageObject` for remote for access. Next, launch an instance of the client application. If all is well, your server window should appear as shown in Figure 20-2, while the client application displays what you see in Figure 20-3.

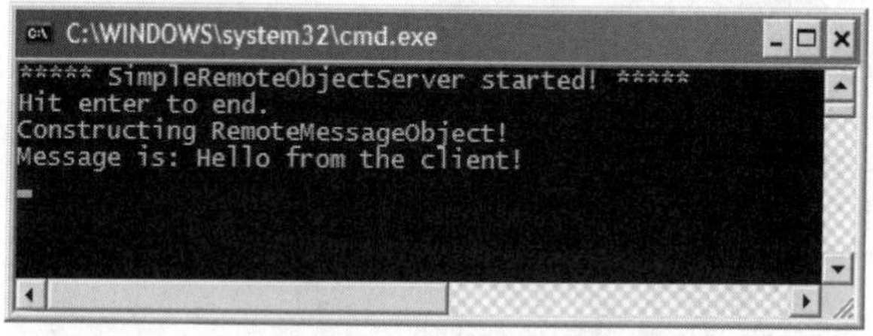

Figure 20-2. *The server's output*

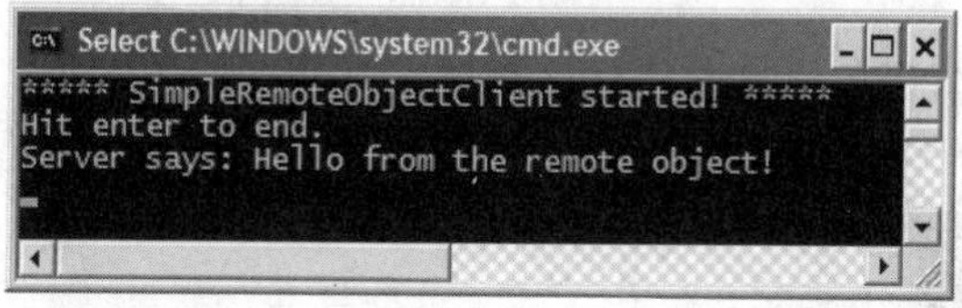

Figure 20-3. *The client's output*

Understanding the ChannelServices Type

As you have seen, when a server application wishes to advertise the existence of a remote object, it makes use of the `System.Runtime.Remoting.Channels.ChannelServices` type. `ChannelServices` provides a small set of shared methods that aid in the process of remoting channel registration, resolution, and URL discovery. Table 20-4 documents some of the core members.

Table 20-4. *Select Members of the* ChannelServices *Type*

Member	Meaning in Life
RegisteredChannels	This property gets or sets a list of currently registered channels, each of which is represented by the IChannel interface.
DispatchMessage()	This method dispatches incoming remote calls.
GetChannel()	This method returns a registered channel with the specified name.
GetUrlsForObject()	This method returns an array of all the URLs that can be used to reach the specified object.
RegisterChannel()	This method registers a channel with the channel services.
UnregisterChannel()	This method unregisters a particular channel from the registered channels list.

In addition to the aptly named RegisterChannel() and UnregisterChannel() methods, ChannelServices defines the RegisteredChannels property. This member returns an array of IChannel interfaces, each representing a handle to each channel registered in a given application domain. The definition of the IChannel interface is quite straightforward:

```
Public Interface IChannel
  ReadOnly Property ChannelName() As String
  ReadOnly Property ChannelPriority() As Integer
  Function Function Parse(ByVal url As String, _
    ByRef objectURI As String) As String
End Interface
```

As you can see, each channel is given a friendly string name as well as a priority level. To illustrate, if you were to update the Main() method of the SimpleRemoteObjectClient application with the following logic (just before you invoke ReturnMessage()):

```
' List all registered channels.
Dim channelObjs() As IChannel = ChannelServices.RegisteredChannels()
For Each i As IChannel In channelObjs
  Console.WriteLine("Channel name: {0}", i.ChannelName)
  Console.WriteLine("Channel Priority: {0}", i.ChannelPriority)
Next
```

you would find the client-side console now looks like Figure 20-4.

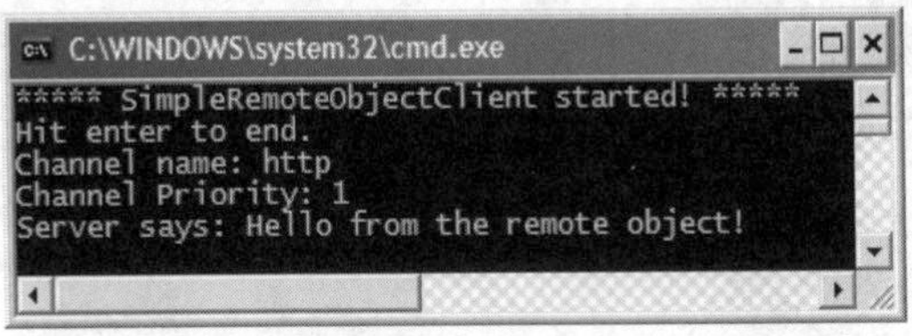

Figure 20-4. *Enumerating client-side channels*

Understanding the RemotingConfiguration Type

Another key remoting-centric type is RemotingConfiguration, which as its name suggests is used to configure various aspects of a remoting application. Currently, you have seen this type in use on the server side (via the call to the RegisterWellKnownServiceType() method). Table 20-5 lists additional shared members of interest, some of which you'll see in action over the remainder of this chapter.

Table 20-5. *Members of the* RemotingConfiguration *Type*

Member	Meaning in Life
ApplicationId	Gets the ID of the currently executing application
ApplicationName	Gets or sets the name of a remoting application
ProcessId	Gets the ID of the currently executing process
Configure()	Reads the configuration file and configures the remoting infrastructure
GetRegisteredActivatedClientTypes()	Retrieves an array of object types registered on the client as types that will be activated remotely
GetRegisteredActivatedServiceTypes()	Retrieves an array of object types registered on the service end that can be activated on request from a client
GetRegisteredWellKnownClientTypes()	Retrieves an array of object types registered on the client end as well-known types
GetRegisteredWellKnownServiceTypes()	Retrieves an array of object types registered on the service end as well-known types
IsWellKnownClientType()	Checks whether the specified object type is registered as a well-known client type
RegisterActivatedClientType()	Registers an object on the client end as a type that can be activated on the server
RegisterWellKnownClientType()	Registers an object on the client end as a well-known type (single call or singleton)
RegisterWellKnownServiceType()	Registers an object on the service end as a well-known type (single call or singleton)

Recall that the .NET remoting layer distinguishes between two types of MBR objects: WKO (server activated) and CAO (client activated). Furthermore, WKO types can be configured to make use of singleton or single-call activations. Using the functionality of the RemotingConfiguration type, you are able to dynamically obtain such information at runtime. For example, if you update the Main() method of your SimpleRemoteObjectServer application with the following:

```
Sub Main()
  Console.WriteLine("***** SimpleRemoteObjectServer started! *****")
  Console.WriteLine("Hit enter to end.")
...
  ' Set a friendly name for this server app.
  RemotingConfiguration.ApplicationName = "First server app!"
  Console.WriteLine("App Name: {0}", _
    RemotingConfiguration.ApplicationName)

  ' Get an array of WellKnownServiceTypeEntry types
  ' that represent all the registered WKOs.
  Dim WKOs() As WellKnownServiceTypeEntry = _
    RemotingConfiguration.GetRegisteredWellKnownServiceTypes()

  ' Now print their statistics.
  For Each wko As WellKnownServiceTypeEntry In WKOs
    Console.WriteLine("Asm name containing WKO: {0}", wko.AssemblyName)
    Console.WriteLine("URL to WKO: {0}", wko.ObjectUri)
    Console.WriteLine("Type of WKO: {0}", wko.ObjectType)
    Console.WriteLine("Mode of WKO: {0}", wko.Mode)
  Next
  Console.ReadLine()
End Sub
```

you would find a list of all WKO types registered by this server application domain. As you iterate over the array of WellKnownServiceTypeEntry types, you are able to print out various points of interest regarding each WKO. Given that your server's application registered only a single type (SimpleRemotingAsm.RemoteMessageObject), you'll receive the output shown in Figure 20-5.

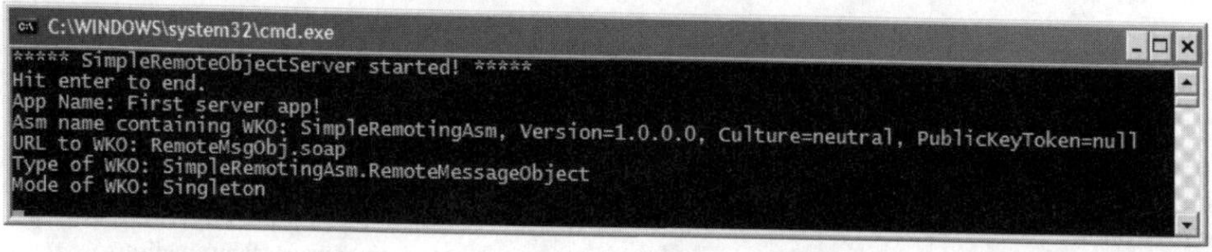

Figure 20-5. *Server-side statistics*

The other major method of the RemotingConfiguration type is Configure(). As you'll see in just a bit, this shared member allows the client- and server-side application domains to make use of remoting configuration files.

Revisiting the Activation Mode of WKO Types

Recall that WKO types can be configured to function under singleton or single-call activation. Currently, your server application has registered your WKO to employ singleton activation semantics:

```
' Singletons can service multiple clients.
RemotingConfiguration.RegisterWellKnownServiceType( _
  GetType(SimpleRemotingAsm.RemoteMessageObject), _
  "RemoteMsgObj.soap", _
  WellKnownObjectMode.Singleton)
```

Again, singleton WKOs are capable of receiving requests from multiple clients. Thus, singleton objects maintain a one-to-many relationship between themselves and the remote clients. To test this behavior for yourself, run the server application (if it is not currently running) and launch three separate client applications. If you look at the output for the server, you will find a single call to the RemoteMessageObject's default constructor. Now to test the behavior of single-call objects, modify the server to register the WKO to support single-call activation:

```
' Single-call types maintain a 1-to-1 relationship
' between client and WKO.
RemotingConfiguration.RegisterWellKnownServiceType( _
  GetType(SimpleRemotingAsm.RemoteMessageObject), _
  "RemoteMsgObj.soap", _
  WellKnownObjectMode.SingleCall)
```

Once you have recompiled and run the server application, again launch three clients. This time you can see that a new RemoteMessageObject is created for each client request. As you might be able to gather, if you wish to share stateful data between multiple remote clients, singleton activation provides one possible alternative, as all clients are communicating with a single instance of the remote object.

■**Source Code** The SimpleRemotingAsm, SimpleRemoteObjectServer, and SimpleRemoteObjectClient projects are located under the Chapter 20 directory.

Deploying the Server to a Remote Machine

At this point, you have just crossed an application and process boundary on a single machine. If you're connected to an additional machine, let's extend this example to allow the client to interact with the RemoteMessageObject type across a machine boundary. To do so, follow these steps:

1. On your server machine, create and share a folder to hold your server-side assemblies.

2. Copy the SimpleRemoteObjectServer.exe and SimpleRemotingAsm.dll assemblies to this server-side share point.

3. Open your SimpleRemoteObjectClient project workspace and retrofit the activation URL to specify the name of the remote machine, for example:

```
' Get a proxy to remote object.
Dim remoteObj As Object = Activator.GetObject( _
    GetType(SimpleRemotingAsm.RemoteMessageObject), _
    "http://YourRemoteBoxName:32469/RemoteMsgObj.soap")
```

4. Execute the SimpleRemoteObjectServer.exe application on the server machine.

5. Execute the SimpleRemoteObjectClient.exe application on the client machine.

6. Sit back and grin.

■**Note** Activation URLs may specify a machine's IP address in place of its friendly name.

Leveraging the TCP Channel

Currently, your remote object is accessible via the HTTP network protocol. As mentioned, this protocol is quite firewall friendly, but the resulting SOAP packets are a bit on the bloated side (given the nature of XML data representation). To lighten the payload, you can update the client and server assemblies to make use of the TCP channel, and therefore make use of the BinaryFormatter type behind the scenes. Here are the relevant updates to the server assembly:

■**Note** When you are defining an object to be URI accessible via a TCP endpoint, it is common (but not required) to make use of the *.rem (i.e., remote) extension.

```
' Server-side code adjustments!
Imports System.Runtime.Remoting.Channels.Tcp
...

Sub Main()
...
    ' Create a new TcpChannel
    Dim c As TcpChannel = New TcpChannel(32469)
    ChannelServices.RegisterChannel(c, False)

    ' Register a 'well-known' object in single-call mode.
    RemotingConfiguration.RegisterWellKnownServiceType( _
        GetType(SimpleRemotingAsm.RemoteMessageObject), _
        "RemoteMsgObj.rem", _
```

```
            WellKnownObjectMode.SingleCall)
    Console.ReadLine()
End Sub
```

Notice that you are now registering a System.Runtime.Remoting.Channels.Tcp.TcpChannel type to the .NET remoting layer. Also note that the object URI has been altered to support a more generic name (RemoteMsgObj.rem) rather than the SOAP-centric *.soap extension. The client-side updates are equally as simple:

```
' Client adjustments!
Imports System.Runtime.Remoting.Channels.Tcp
...
Sub Main()
...
    ' Create a new TcpChannel
    Dim c As TcpChannel = New TcpChannel()
    ChannelServices.RegisterChannel(c, False)

    ' Get a proxy to remote object.
    Dim remoteObj As Object = Activator.GetObject( _
        GetType(SimpleRemotingAsm.RemoteMessageObject), _
        "tcp://localhost:32469/RemoteMsgObj.rem")

    ' Use object.
    Dim simple As RemoteMessageObject = _
        CType(remoteObj, RemoteMessageObject)
    simple.DisplayMessage("Hello from the client!")
    Console.WriteLine("Server says: {0}", simple.ReturnMessage())
    Console.ReadLine()
End Sub
```

The only point to be aware of here is that the client's activation URL now must specify the tcp:// channel qualifier rather than http://. Beyond that, the bulk of the code base is identical to the previous HttpChannel logic.

Source Code The TCPSimpleRemoteObjectServer and TCPSimpleRemoteObjectClient projects are located under the Chapter 20 directory (both projects reference the SimpleRemotingAsm.dll created previously).

A Brief Word Regarding the IpcChannel

Before moving on to an examination of remoting configuration files, recall that .NET 2.0 also provides the IpcChannel type, which provides the fastest possible manner in which two applications *on the same machine* can exchange information. Given that this chapter is geared toward covering distributed programs that involve two or more computers, interested readers should look up IpcChannel in the .NET Framework 2.0 SDK documentation (as you might guess, the code is just about identical to working with HttpChannel and TcpChannel).

Remoting Configuration Files

At this point you have successfully built a distributed application using the .NET remoting layer. One issue you may have noticed in these first examples is the fact that the client and the server applications have a good deal of hard-coded logic within their respective binaries. For example, the server specifies a fixed port ID, fixed activation mode, and fixed channel type. The client, on the other hand, hard-codes the name of the remote object it is attempting to interact with.

As you might agree, it is wishful thinking to assume that initial design notes remain unchanged once an application is deployed. Ideally, details such as port ID and object activation mode (and whatnot) could be altered on the fly without needing to recompile and redistribute the client or server code bases. Under the .NET remoting scheme, all the aforementioned issues can be circumvented using the remoting configuration file.

As you will recall from Chapter 13, *.config can be used to provide hints to the CLR regarding the loading of externally referenced assemblies. The same *.config files can be used to inform the CLR of a number of remoting-related details, on both the client side and the server side.

When you build a remoting *.config file, the <system.runtime.remoting> element is used to hold various remoting-centric details. Do be aware that if you're building an application that already has a *.config file that specifies assembly resolution details, you're free to add remoting elements within the same file. Thus, a single *.config file that contains remoting and binding information would look something like this:

```
<configuration>
  <system.runtime.remoting>
    <! -- configure client/server remoting settings here -- >
  </system.runtime.remoting>
  <runtime>
    <! -- assembly binding settings here -- >
  </runtime>
</configuration>
```

If your configuration file has no need to specify assembly binding logic, you can omit the <runtime> element and make use of the following skeleton *.config file:

```
<configuration>
  <system.runtime.remoting>
    <! -- configure client/server remoting settings here -- >
  </system.runtime.remoting>
</configuration>
```

Building Server-side *.config Files

Server-side configuration files allow you to declare the objects that are to be reached via remote invocations as well as channel and port information. Basically, using the <service>, <wellknown>, and <channels> elements, you are able to replace the following server-side logic:

```
' Hard-coded HTTP server logic.
Dim c As HttpChannel = New HttpChannel(32469)
ChannelServices.RegisterChannel(c, False)
RemotingConfiguration.RegisterWellKnownServiceType( _
  GetType(SimpleRemotingAsm.RemoteMessageObject), _
  "RemoteMsgObj.soap", _
WellKnownObjectMode.Singleton)
```

with the following *.config file:

```
<configuration>
  <system.runtime.remoting>
    <application>
      <service>
        <wellknown
          mode="Singleton"
          type="SimpleRemotingAsm.RemoteMessageObject, SimpleRemotingAsm"
          objectUri="RemoteMsgObj.soap"/>
      </service>
      <channels>
          <channel ref="http" port="32469"/>
      </channels>
    </application>
  </system.runtime.remoting>
</configuration>
```

Notice that much of the relevant server-side remoting information is wrapped within the scope of the <service> (not *server*) element. The child <wellknown> element makes use of three attributes (mode, type, and objectUri) to specify the well-known object to register with the .NET remoting layer. The child <channels> element contains any number of <channel> elements that allow you to define the type of channel (in this case, HTTP) to open on the server. TCP channels would simply make use of the tcp string token in place of http.

As the *.config file contains all the necessary information, the server-side Main() method cleans up considerably. All you are required to do is make a single call to RemotingConfiguration.Configure() and specify the name of your configuration file.

```
Imports System.Runtime.Remoting

Module Program
  Sub Main()
    Console.WriteLine("***** Server with *.config file *****")
    Console.WriteLine()
    ' Register a 'well-known' object using a *.config file.
    ' Second parameter specifies if the connection is secure.
    RemotingConfiguration.Configure( _
      "SimpleRemoteObjectServerWithConfig.exe.config", False)
    Console.WriteLine("Server started!  Hit enter to end")
    Console.ReadLine()
  End Sub
End Module
```

Building Client-side *.config Files

Clients are also able to leverage remoting *.config files. Unlike a server-side configuration file, client-side configuration files make use of the <client> element to identify the name of the well-known object the caller wishes to interact with. In addition to providing the ability to dynamically change the remoting information without the need to recompile the code base, client-side *.config files allow you to create the proxy type directly using the VB 2005 New keyword, rather than the Activator.GetObject() method. Thus, if you have the following client-side *.config file:

```
<configuration>
  <system.runtime.remoting>
    <application>
      <client displayName = "SimpleRemoteObjectClientWithConfig">
```

```
      <wellknown
        type="SimpleRemotingAsm.RemoteMessageObject, SimpleRemotingAsm"
        url="http://localhost:32469/RemoteMsgObj.soap"/>
    </client>
    <channels>
      <channel ref="http"/>
    </channels>
  </application>
 </system.runtime.remoting>
</configuration>
```

you are able to update the client's `Main()` method as follows:

```
Imports System.Runtime.Remoting
Imports SimpleRemotingAsm

Module Program
  Sub Main()
    Console.WriteLine("***** Client with *.config *****")
    Console.WriteLine()

    RemotingConfiguration.Configure( _
      "SimpleRemoteObjectClientWithConfig.exe.config", False)

    ' Using *.config file, the client is able to directly 'New' the type.
    Dim simple As RemoteMessageObject = New RemoteMessageObject()
    simple.DisplayMessage("Hello from the client!")
    Console.WriteLine("Server says: {0}", simple.ReturnMessage())
    Console.WriteLine("Client started!  Hit enter to end")
    Console.ReadLine()
  End Sub
End Module
```

When you run the application, the output is identical to the previous assemblies that hard-coded the remoting logic. If the client wishes to make use of the TCP channel, the url property of the `<wellknown>` element and `<channel>` ref property must make use of the tcp token in place of http.

■ **Source Code** The SimpleRemoteObjectServerWithConfig and SimpleRemoteObjectClientWithConfig projects are located under the Chapter 20 subdirectory (both of which reference `SimpleRemotingAsm.dll`).

Working with MBV Objects

Our first remoting applications allowed client-side access to a single WKO type. Recall that WKO types are (by definition) MBR types, and therefore client access takes place via an intervening proxy. In contrast, MBV types are local copies of a server-side object, which (not surprisingly) are typically returned from a public member of an MBR type. Although you already know how to configure an MBV type (mark a class with the `<Serializable>` attribute), you have not yet seen an example of MBV types in action (beyond passing String data between the two parties, as String types are indeed marked with the `<Serializable>` attribute). To illustrate the interplay of MBR and MBV types, let's see another example involving three assemblies:

- The general assembly named `CarGeneralAsm.dll`
- The client assembly named `CarProviderClient.exe`
- The server assembly named `CarProviderServer.exe`

As you might assume, the code behind the client and server applications is more or less identical to the previous example, especially since these applications will again make use of *.config files. Nevertheless, let's step through the process of building each assembly one at a time.

Building the General Assembly

To begin, create a new VB 2005 Code Library project named CarGeneralAsm. During our examination of object serialization in Chapter 19, you created a type named JamesBondCar (in addition to the dependent Radio and Car classes). The CarGeneralAsm.dll code library will reuse these types, so begin by using the Project ➤ Add Existing Item menu command and include these *.vb files in this new Class Library project. Given that each of these types has already been marked with the <Serializable> attribute, they are ready to be marshaled by value to a remote client. By way of a quick reminder, here are the definitions of the types in question (note that I have removed the XML-centric attributes from the definitions):

```
<Serializable()> _
Public Class Radio
  Public hasTweeters As Boolean
  Public hasSubWoofers As Boolean
  Public stationPresets As Double()
  <NonSerialized()> _
  Public radioID As String = "XF-552RR6"
End Class

<Serializable()> _
Public Class Car
  Public theRadio As Radio = New Radio
  Public isHatchBack As Boolean
End Class

<Serializable()> _
Public Class JamesBondCar
  Inherits Car
  Public Sub New(ByVal SkyWorthy As Boolean, ByVal SeaWorthy As Boolean)
    canFly = SkyWorthy
    canSubmerge = SeaWorthy
  End Sub
  Public Sub New()
  End Sub
  Public canFly As Boolean
  Public canSubmerge As Boolean
End Class
```

All you need now is an MBR type that provides access to the JamesBondCar type. To make things a bit more interesting, however, your MBR object (CarProvider) will maintain a generic List(Of T) of JamesBondCar types. CarProvider will also define two members that allow the caller to obtain a specific JamesBondCar as well as receive the entire List(Of T) of types. Here is the complete code for the new class type:

```
' This type is an MBR object that provides
' access to related MBV types.
Public Class CarProvider
  Inherits MarshalByRefObject

  Private theJBCars As List(Of JamesBondCar) = _
    New List(Of JamesBondCar)()
```

```
' Add some cars to the list.
Public Sub New()
  Console.WriteLine("Car provider created")
  theJBCars.Add(New JamesBondCar(True, True))
  theJBCars.Add(New JamesBondCar(True, False))
  theJBCars.Add(New JamesBondCar(False, True))
  theJBCars.Add(New JamesBondCar(False, False))
End Sub

' Get all the JamesBondCars.
Public Function GetAllAutos() As List(Of JamesBondCar)
  Return theJBCars
End Function

' Get one JamesBondCar.
Public Function GetJBCByIndex(ByVal i As Integer) As JamesBondCar
  Return CType(theJBCars(i), JamesBondCar)
End Function
End Class
```

Notice that the GetAllAutos() method returns the internal List(Of T) type. The obvious question is how this member of the System.Collections.Generic namespace is marshaled back to the caller. If you look up this type using the .NET Framework 2.0 SDK documentation, you will find that List(Of T) has been decorated with the <Serializable> attribute:

```
<SerializableAttribute> _
Public Class List(Of T)
  Implements IList(Of T), ICollection(Of T), _
  IEnumerable(Of T), IList, ICollection, _
  IEnumerable
...
End Class
```

Therefore, the entire contents of the List(Of T) type will be marshaled by value to the caller (provided the contained types are also serializable)! This brings up a very good point regarding .NET remoting and members of the base class libraries. In addition to the custom MBV and MBR types you may create yourself, understand that any type in the base class libraries that is decorated with the <Serializable> attribute is able to function as an MBV type in the .NET remoting architecture. Likewise, any type that derives (directly or indirectly) from MarshalByRefObject will function as an MBR type.

Note Be aware that the SoapFormatter does not support serialization of generic types. If you build methods that receive or return generic types (such as the List(Of T) type), you must make use of the BinaryFormatter and the TcpChannel object.

Building the Server Assembly

Next, create a new console application named CarProviderServer and add a reference to CarGeneralAsm.dll. The server host assembly (CarProviderServer.exe) has the following logic within the Main() method:

```
Imports CarGeneralAsm
Imports System.Runtime.Remoting

Module Project
  Sub Main()
```

```
      RemotingConfiguration.Configure("CarProviderServer.exe.config", False)
      Console.WriteLine("Car server started!  Hit enter to end")
      Console.ReadLine()
    End Sub
End Module
```

The related *.config file is just about identical to the server-side *.config file you created in the previous example. The only point of interest is to define an object URI value that makes sense for the CarProvider type:

```
<configuration>
  <system.runtime.remoting>
    <application>
      <service>
        <wellknown mode="Singleton"
          type="CarGeneralAsm.CarProvider, CarGeneralAsm"
          objectUri="carprovider.rem" />
      </service>
      <channels>
        <channel ref="tcp" port="32469" />
      </channels>
    </application>
  </system.runtime.remoting>
</configuration>
```

Building the Client Assembly

Last but not least, we have the client application (a console application named CarProviderClient) that will make use of the MBR CarProvider type in order to obtain discrete JamesBondCars types as well as the List(Of T) type. Once you obtain a type from the CarProvider, you'll send it into the UseCar() helper function from processing:

```
Imports CarGeneralAsm
Imports System.Runtime.Remoting

Module Program
  Sub Main()
    Console.WriteLine("Client started!  Hit enter to end")
    RemotingConfiguration.Configure("CarProviderClient.exe.config", False)

    ' Make the car provider.
    Dim cp As CarProvider = New CarProvider()

    ' Get first JBC.
    Dim jbCar As JamesBondCar = cp.GetJBCByIndex(0)

    ' Get all JBCs.
    Dim JBCs As List(Of JamesBondCar) = cp.GetAllAutos()

    ' Use first car.
    UseCar(jbCar)

    ' Use all cars in List.
    For Each j As JamesBondCar In JBCs
      UseCar(j)
    Next
    Console.ReadLine()
  End Sub
```

```
  Private Sub UseCar(ByVal c As JamesBondCar)
    Console.WriteLine("-> Flight worthy? {0}", c.canFly)
    Console.WriteLine("-> Seaworthy? {0}", c.canSubmerge)
    Console.WriteLine("-> Has hatch back? {0}", c.isHatchBack)
    Console.WriteLine("-> Radio has sub woofers? {0}", c.theRadio.hasSubWoofers)
    Console.WriteLine()
  End Sub
End Module
```

The client-side *.config file is also what you would expect. Simply update the activation URL:

```
<configuration>
  <system.runtime.remoting>
    <application>
      <client displayName = "CarClient">
        <wellknown
          type="CarGeneralAsm.CarProvider, CarGeneralAsm"
          url="tcp://localhost:32469/carprovider.rem"/>
      </client>
      <channels>
        <channel ref="http"/>
      </channels>
    </application>
  </system.runtime.remoting>
</configuration>
```

Now, run your server and client applications (in that order, of course) and observe the output. Your client-side console window will whirl through the JamesBondCars and print out the statistics of each type. Recall that as you interact with the List(Of T) and JamesBondCar types, you are operating on their members within the client's application domain, as they have both been marked with the <Serializable> attribute.

■Source Code The CarGeneralAsm, CarProviderServer, and CarProviderClient projects are located under the Chapter 20 subdirectory.

Understanding Client-activated Objects

All of these current remoting examples have made use of WKOs. Recall that WKOs have the following characteristics:

- WKOs can be configured either as singleton or single call.
- WKOs can only be activated using the type's default constructor.
- WKOs are instantiated on the server on the first client-side member invocation.

CAO types, on the other hand, can be instantiated using any constructor on the type and are created at the point the client makes use of the VB 2005 New keyword or Activator type. Furthermore, the lifetime of CAO types is monitored by the .NET leasing mechanism. Do be aware that when you configure a CAO type, the .NET remoting layer will generate a specific CAO remote object to service each client. Again, the big distinction is the fact that CAOs are always alive (and therefore stateful) beyond a single method invocation.

To illustrate the construction, hosting, and consumption of CAO types, let's retrofit the previous CarGeneralAsm.dll general assembly. Assume that your MBR CarProvider class has defined an additional constructor that allows the client to pass in an array of JamesBondCar types that will be used to populate the generic List(Of T):

```
Public Class CarProvider
  Inherits MarshalByRefObject

  Private theJBCars As List(Of JamesBondCar) = _
    New List(Of JamesBondCar)()

  Public Sub New(ByVal theCars() As JamesBondCar)
    Console.WriteLine("Car provider created with custom ctor")
    theJBCars.AddRange(theCars)
  End Sub
...
End Class
```

To allow the caller to activate the CarProvider using your new constructor syntax, you need to build a server application (a console project named CAOCarProviderServer) that registers CarProvider as a CAO type rather than a WKO type. This may be done programmatically (à la the RemotingConfiguration.RegisterActivatedServiceType() method) or using a server-side *.config file. If you wish to hard-code the name of the CAO object within the host server's code base, all you need to do is pass in the type information of the type(s) (after creating and registering a channel) as follows:

```
' Hard-code the fact that CarProvider is a CAO type.
RemotingConfiguration.RegisterActivatedServiceType( _
  GetType(CAOCarGeneralAsm.CarProvider))
```

If you would rather leverage the *.config file, replace the <wellknown> element with the <activated> element as follows:

```
<configuration>
  <system.runtime.remoting>
    <application>
      <service>
        <activated type = "CAOCarGeneralAsm.CarProvider,
          CAOCarGeneralAsm"/>
      </service>
      <channels>
        <channel ref="tcp" port="32469" />
      </channels>
    </application>
  </system.runtime.remoting>
</configuration>
```

Finally, you need to update the client application (or create a new console application named CAOCarProviderClient), not only by way of the *.config file (or programmatically in the code base) to request access to the remote CAO, but also to indeed trigger the custom constructor of the CarProvider type. Here are the relevant updates to the client-side Main() method:

```
Sub Main()
  Console.WriteLine("Client started!  Hit enter to end")
  RemotingConfiguration.Configure("CAOCarProviderClient.exe.config", False)

  ' Create array of types to pass to provider.
  Dim cars() As JamesBondCar = {New JamesBondCar(False, False), _
    New JamesBondCar(True, False), _
    New JamesBondCar(True, False)}

  ' Now trigger the custom ctor.
  Dim cp As CarProvider = New CarProvider(cars)
```

```
' Get first JBC.
Dim jbCar As JamesBondCar = cp.GetJBCByIndex(0)

' Use all cars in List.
UseCar(jbCar)

Console.ReadLine()
End Sub
```

The updated client-side *.config file also makes use of the <activated> element, as opposed to <wellknown>. In addition, the <client> element now requires the url property to define the location of the registered CAO. Recall that when the server registered the CarProvider as a WKO, the client specified such information within the <wellknown> element.

```
<configuration>
  <system.runtime.remoting>
    <application>
      <client displayName = "CarClient" url = "tcp://localhost:32469">
        <activated type = "CAOCarGeneralAsm.CarProvider, CAOCarGeneralAsm" />
      </client>
      <channels>
        <channel ref="tcp"/>
      </channels>
    </application>
  </system.runtime.remoting>
</configuration>
```

If you would rather hard-code the client's request to the CAO type, you can make use of the RegistrationServices.RegisterActivatedClientType() method as follows:

```
Sub Main()
  ' Use hard-coded values.
  RemotingConfiguration.RegisterActivatedClientType( _
    GetType(CAOCarGeneralAsm.CarProvider), _
    "tcp://localhost:32469")
...
End Sub
```

If you now execute the updated server and client assemblies, you will be pleased to find that you are able to pass your custom array of JamesBondCar types to the remote CarProvider via the overloaded constructor.

■**Source Code** The CAOCarGeneralAsm, CAOCarProviderServer, and CAOCarProviderClient projects are located under the Chapter 20 subdirectory.

The Lease-based Lifetime of CAO/WKO-Singleton Objects

As you have seen, WKO types configured with single-call activation are alive only for the duration of the current method call. Given this fact, WKO single-call types are stateless entities. As soon as the current invocation has completed, the WKO single-call type is a candidate for garbage collection.

On the other hand, CAO types and WKO types that have been configured to use singleton activation are both, by their nature, stateful entities. Given these two object configuration settings, the question that must be asked is, How does the server process know when to destroy these MBR objects? Clearly, it would be a huge problem if the server machine garbage-collected MBR objects that were currently in use by a remote client. If the server machine waits too long to release its set of MBR types, this may place undue stress on the system, especially if the MBR object(s) in question maintain valuable system resources (database connections, unmanaged types, and whatnot).

The lifetime of a CAO/WKO-singleton MBR type is governed by a "lease time" that is tightly integrated with the .NET garbage collector. If the lease time of a CAO/WKO-singleton MBR type expires, the object is ready to be garbage-collected on the next collection cycle. Like any .NET type, if the remote object has overridden `System.Object.Finalize()`, the .NET runtime will indeed trigger the finalization logic.

The Default Leasing Behavior

CAO and WKO-singleton MBR types have what is known as a *default lease*, which lasts for five minutes. If the runtime detects five minutes of inactivity have passed for a CAO/WKO-singleton MBR type, the assumption is that the client is no longer making use of the object and therefore the remote object may be garbage-collected. However, when the default lease expires, this does not imply that the object is *immediately* marked for garbage collection. In reality, there are many ways to influence the behavior of the default lease.

First and foremost, anytime the remote client invokes a member of the remote CAO/WKO-singleton MBR type, the lease is renewed back to its five-minute limit. In addition to the automatic client-invocation–centric renew policy, the .NET runtime provides three additional alternatives:

- `*.config` files can be authored that override the default lease settings for remote objects.
- Server-side lease sponsors can be used to act on behalf of a remote object whose lease time has expired.
- Client-side lease sponsors can be used to act on behalf of a remote object whose lease time has expired.

For the time being, let's examine the default lease settings of a remote type. Recall that the `MarshalByRefObject` base class defines a member named `GetLifetimeService()`. This method returns a reference to an internally implemented object that supports the `System.Runtime.Remoting.Lifetime.ILease` interface. As you would guess, the `ILease` interface can be used to interact with the leasing behavior of a given CAO/WKO-singleton type. Here is the formal definition:

```
Public Interface ILease
    ReadOnly Property CurrentLeaseTime() As TimeSpan
    ReadOnly Property CurrentState() As LeaseState
    Property InitialLeaseTime() As TimeSpan
    Property RenewOnCallTime() As TimeSpan
    Property SponsorshipTimeout() As TimeSpan
    Sub Register(ByVal obj As ISponsor)
    Sub Register(ByVal obj As ISponsor, ByVal renewalTime As TimeSpan)
    Function Renew(ByVal renewalTime As TimeSpan) As TimeSpan
    Sub Unregister(ByVal obj As ISponsor)
End Interface
```

The `ILease` interface not only allows you to obtain information regarding the current lease (via `CurrentLeaseTime`, `CurrentState`, and `InitialLeaseTime`), but also provides the ability to build lease "sponsors" (more details on this later). Table 20-6 documents the role of each `ILease` member.

Table 20-6. *Members of the* ILease *Interface*

Member	Meaning in Life
CurrentLeaseTime	Gets the amount of time remaining before the object deactivates, if it does not receive further method invocations.
CurrentState	Gets the current state of the lease, represented by the LeaseState enumeration.
InitialLeaseTime	Gets or sets the initial amount of time for a given lease. The initial lease time of an object is the amount of time following the initial activation before the lease expires if no other method calls occur.
RenewOnCallTime	Gets or sets the amount of time by which a call to the remote object increases the CurrentLeaseTime.
SponsorshipTimeout	Gets or sets the amount of time to wait for a sponsor to return with a lease renewal time.
Register()	Overloaded. Registers a sponsor for the lease.
Renew()	Renews a lease for the specified time.
Unregister()	Removes a sponsor from the sponsor list.

To illustrate the characteristics of the default lease of a CAO/WKO-singleton remote object, assume that your current CAOCarGeneralAsm project has defined a new internal class named LeaseInfo. LeaseInfo supports a shared member named LeaseStats(), which dumps select statistics regarding the current lease for the CarProvider type to the server-side console window (be sure to import the System.Runtime.Remoting.Lifetime namespace to inform the compiler where the ILease type is defined):

```
Imports System.Runtime.Remoting.Lifetime

Friend Class LeaseInfo
  Public Shared Sub LeaseStats(ByVal itfLease As ILease)
    Console.WriteLine("***** Lease Stats *****")
    Console.WriteLine("Lease state: {0}", itfLease.CurrentState)
    Console.WriteLine("Initial lease time: {0}:{1}", _
      itfLease.InitialLeaseTime.Minutes, itfLease.InitialLeaseTime.Seconds)
    Console.WriteLine("Current lease time: {0}:{1}", _
      itfLease.CurrentLeaseTime.Minutes, itfLease.CurrentLeaseTime.Seconds)
    Console.WriteLine("Renew on call time: {0}:{1}", _
      itfLease.RenewOnCallTime.Minutes, itfLease.RenewOnCallTime.Seconds)
    Console.WriteLine()
  End Sub
End Class
```

Now that you have this helper type in place, assume LeaseInfo.LeaseStats() is called within the GetJBCByIndex() and GetAllAutos() methods of the CarProvider type. To obtain the current ILease-compatible object, you must explicitly cast the System.Object returned by the inherited GetLifetimeServices() method:

```
Public Function GetAllAutos() As List(Of JamesBondCar)
  LeaseInfo.LeaseStats(CType(GetLifetimeService(), ILease))
  Return theJBCars
End Function

Public Function GetJBCByIndex(ByVal i As Integer) As JamesBondCar
  LeaseInfo.LeaseStats(CType(GetLifetimeService(), ILease))
  Return CType(theJBCars(i), JamesBondCar)
End Function
```

Once you recompile the server and client assemblies (again, simply to ensure Visual Studio 2005 copies the latest and greatest version of the CarGeneralAsm.dll to the client and server application directories), run the application once again. Your server's console window should now look something like Figure 20-6.

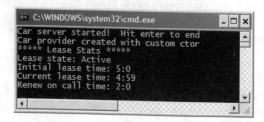

Figure 20-6. *The default lease information for CarProvider*

Altering the Default Lease Characteristics

Obviously, the default lease characteristics of a CAO/WKO-singleton type may not be appropriate for each and every CAO/WKO-singleton remote object. If you wish to alter these default settings, you have two approaches:

- You can adjust the default lease settings using a server-side *.config file.
- You can programmatically alter the settings of a MBR type's default lease by overriding members of the MarshalByRefObject base class.

While each of these options will indeed alter the default lease settings, there is a key difference. When you make use of a server-side *.config file, the lease settings affect *all* objects hosted by the server process. In contrast, when you override select members of the MarshalByRefObject type, you are able to change lease settings on an object-by-object basis.

To illustrate changing the default lease settings via a remoting *.config file, assume you have updated the server-side XML data with the following additional <lifetime> element:

```
<configuration>
  <system.runtime.remoting>
    <application>
      <lifetime leaseTime = "15M" renewOnCallTime = "5M"/>
      <service>
        <activated type = "CAOCarGeneralAsmLease.CarProvider,
          CAOCarGeneralAsmLease"/>
      </service>
      <channels>
        <channel ref="tcp" port="32469" />
      </channels>
    </application>
  </system.runtime.remoting>
</configuration>
```

Notice how the leaseTime and renewOnCallTime properties have been marked with the M suffix, which as you might guess stands for the number of minutes to set for each lease-centric unit of time. If you wish, your <lifetime> element may also suffix the numerical values with MS (milliseconds), S (seconds), H (hours), or even D (days). If you were to run the server and then run the client program, you would now find the lease output shown in Figure 20-7.

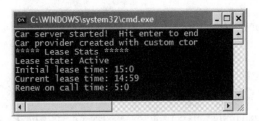

Figure 20-7. *The lease information as specified by* *.config

Now recall that when you update the server's *.config file, you have effectively changed the leasing characteristics for each CAO/WKO-singleton object hosted by the server. As an alternative, you may choose to programmatically override the InitializeLifetime() method in a specific remote type:

```vb
Public Class CarProvider
  Inherits MarshalByRefObject

  Public Overrides Function InitializeLifetimeService() As Object
    ' Obtain the current lease info.
    Dim itfLeaseInfo As ILease = _
      CType(MyBase.InitializeLifetimeService(), ILease)
    ' Adjust settings.
    itfLeaseInfo.InitialLeaseTime = TimeSpan.FromMinutes(50)
    itfLeaseInfo.RenewOnCallTime = TimeSpan.FromMinutes(10)
    Return itfLeaseInfo
  End Function
  ...
End Class
```

Here, the CarProvider has altered its InitialLeaseTime value to 50 minutes and its RenewOnCallTime value to 10. Again, the benefit of overriding InitializeLifetimeServices() is the fact that you can configure each remote type individually.

Note If you wish to disable lease-based lifetime management for a given CAO/WKO-singleton object type, you may override InitializeLifetimeServices() and simply return Nothing. If you do so, you have basically configured an MBR type that will *never* die as long as the hosting server application is alive and kicking.

So at this point you should have a better idea how the lifetime of remote objects is handled by the CLR. To be honest, there are additional techniques that can be used to manage the life of remote types beyond what I have examined here (lease sponsors, etc.). If you require a deeper treatment of the topic, I would again recommend checking out *Advanced .NET Remoting, Second Edition* by Ingo Rammer and Mario Szpuszta (Apress, 2005). In any case, before we wrap things up, there are two final topics that are worth addressing: object hosting options and asynchronous remote invocations.

■**Source Code** The CAOCarGeneralAsmLease, CAOCarProviderServerLease, and CAOCarProviderClientLease projects are located under the Chapter 20 subdirectory.

Alternative Hosts for Remote Objects

Over the course of this chapter, you have constructed numerous console-based server hosts, which provide access to some set of remote objects. If you have a background in the classic Distributed Component Object Model (DCOM), this step may have seemed a bit odd. In the world of DCOM, it was not unusual to build a single server-side COM server that contained the remote objects and was also in charge of receiving incoming requests from some remote client. This single *.exe DCOM application would quietly load in the background without presenting a looming command window.

When you are building a .NET server assembly, the chances are quite good that the remote machine does not need to display any sort of UI. Rather, all you really wish to do is build a server-side entity that opens the correct channel(s) and registers the remote object(s) for client-side access. Moreover, when you build a simple console host, you are (or someone else is) required to manually run the server-side *.exe assembly, due to the fact that .NET remoting will not automatically run a server-side *.exe when called by a remote client.

Given these two issues, the question then becomes, How can you build an invisible listener that loads automatically? .NET programmers have two major choices at their disposal when they wish to build a transparent host for various remote objects:

- Build a .NET Windows service application to host the remote objects.
- Allow IIS to host the remote objects.

Hosting Remote Objects Using a Windows Service

Perhaps the ideal host for remote objects is a Windows service, given that it

- Can be configured to load automatically on system startup
- Runs as an invisible background process
- Can be run under specific user accounts

As luck would have it, building a custom Windows service using the .NET platform is extremely simple. To illustrate, let's create a Windows Service project named CarWinService (see Figure 20-8) that will be in charge of hosting the remote types contained within the CarGeneralAsm.dll.

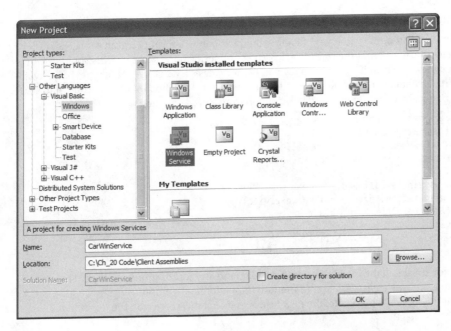

Figure 20-8. *Creating a new Windows Service project workspace*

Visual Studio 2005 responds by generating a class (named Service1 by default) that defines two overridden methods named OnStart() and OnEnd(). As you would guess, this is where you are able to author code that will execute when your service starts and stops:

```
Public Class Service1
    Protected Overrides Sub OnStart(ByVal args() As String)
        ' Add code here to start your service. This method should set things
        ' in motion so your service can do its work.
    End Sub
    Protected Overrides Sub OnStop()
        ' Add code here to perform any tear-down necessary to stop your service.
    End Sub
End Class
```

Given that Service1 is a rather nondescript name for your custom service, the first order of business is to change the values of the (Name) and ServiceName properties to CarService using the IDE's Properties window. The distinction between these two settings is that the (Name) value is used to define the name used to refer to your type in the code base, while the ServiceName property marks the name to display to Windows service–centric configuration tools.

Before moving on, be sure you set a reference to the CarGeneralAsm.dll and System.Remoting.dll assemblies, and import the following namespaces in the initial *.vb file:

```
Imports System.Runtime.Remoting
Imports System.Runtime.Remoting.Channels.Http
Imports System.Runtime.Remoting.Channels
Imports CarGeneralAsm
```

Implementing CarService.OnStart()

You can likely already assume what sort of logic should happen when your custom service is started on a given machine. Recall that the role of CarService is to perform the same tasks as your custom console-based service. Thus, if you wish to register CarService as a WKO-singleton type that is available via HTTP, you could add the following code to the OnStart() method (of course, you could also choose to dynamically read the remoting information from a *.config file):

```
Protected Overrides Sub OnStart(ByVal args() As String)
  ' Create a new HttpChannel.
  Dim c As HttpChannel = New HttpChannel(32469)
  ChannelServices.RegisterChannel(c, False)

  ' Register as single-call WKO.
  RemotingConfiguration.RegisterWellKnownServiceType( _
    GetType(CarGeneralAsm.CarProvider), _
    "CarProvider.soap", _
    WellKnownObjectMode.SingleCall)
End Sub
```

Technically speaking, the CarService does not demand any sort of shutdown logic. Therefore, for this example, we can leave the OnStop() method implementation empty.

Now that the service is complete, the next task is to install this service on the target machine.

Adding a Service Installer

Before you can install your service on a given machine, you need to add an additional type into your current CarWinService project. Specifically, any Windows service (written using .NET or the Win32 API) requires a number of registry entries to be made to allow the OS to interact with the service itself. Rather than making these entries manually, you can simply add an Installer type to a Windows service project, which will configure your ServiceBase-derived type correctly when installed on the target machine.

To add an installer for the CarService, open the design-time service editor (by double-clicking the CarService.vb file from Solution Explorer), right-click anywhere within the designer, and select Add Installer (see Figure 20-9).

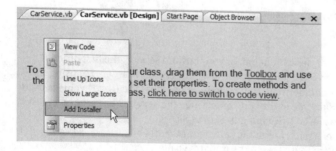

Figure 20-9. *Including an installer for the custom Windows service*

This selection will add a new component that derives from the `System.Configuration.Install.Installer` base class. On your designer will be two components. The `ServiceInstaller1` type represents a specific service installer for a specific service in your project. If you select this icon and view the Properties window, you will find that the `ServiceName` property has been set to the `CarService` class type.

The second component (`ServiceProcessInstaller1`) allows you to establish the identity under which the installed service will execute. By default, the `Account` property is set to `User`. Using the Properties window of Visual Studio 2005, change this value to `LocalService` (see Figure 20-10).

Figure 20-10. *Establishing the identity of the* `CarService`

That's it! Now compile your project.

Installing the CarWinService

Installing `CarService.exe` on a given machine (local or remote) requires two steps:

1. Move the compiled service assembly (and any necessary external assemblies; `CarGeneralAsm.dll` in this example) to the remote machine.

2. Run the `installutil.exe` command-line tool, specifying your service as an argument.

Assuming step 1 is complete, open a Visual Studio 2005 command window, navigate to the location of the `CarWinService.exe` assembly, and issue the following command (note that this same tool can be used to uninstall a service as well using the `-u` options):

```
installutil carwinservice.exe
```

Once this Windows service has been properly installed, you are now able to start and configure it using the Services applet, which is located under the Administrative Tools folder of your system's Control Panel. Once you have located your `CarService` (see Figure 20-11), click the Start link to load and run the binary.

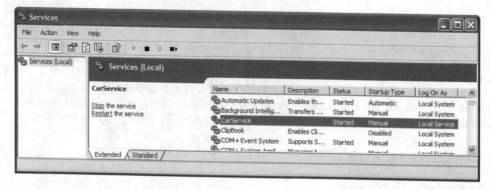

Figure 20-11. *The Windows Services applet*

At this point, you can build any number of clients that can communicate with the remote objects hosted by the Windows service.

Source Code The CarWinService project is located under the Chapter 20 subdirectory.

Hosting Remote Objects Using IIS

Hosting a remote assembly under IIS is even simpler than building a Windows service, as IIS is preprogrammed to allow incoming HTTP requests via port 80. Now, given the fact that IIS is a *web* server, it should stand to reason that IIS is only able to host remote objects using the HttpChannel type (unlike a Windows service, which can also leverage the TcpChannel type). Assuming this is not perceived as a limitation, follow these steps to leverage the remoting support of IIS:

1. On your hard drive, create a new folder to hold your CarGeneralAsm.dll. Within this folder, create a subdirectory named \Bin. Now, copy the CarGeneralAsm.dll to this subdirectory (e.g., C:\IISCarService\Bin).

2. Open the Internet Information Services applet on the host machine (located under the Administrative Tools folder in your system's Control Panel).

3. Right-click the Default Web Site node and select New ➤ Virtual Directory.

4. Create a virtual directory that maps to the root folder you just created (C:\IISCarService). The remaining default settings presented by the New Virtual Directory Wizard are fine.

5. Finally, create a new configuration file named web.config to control how this virtual directory should register the remote type (see the following code). Make sure this file is saved under the root folder (in this example, C:\IISCarService).

```
<configuration>
  <system.runtime.remoting>
    <application>
      <service>
        <wellknown mode="Singleton"
          type="CarGeneralAsm.CarProvider, CarGeneralAsm"
          objectUri="carprovider.soap" />
      </service>
      <channels>
      <channel ref="http"/>
      </channels>
```

```
        </application>
      </system.runtime.remoting>
    </configuration>
```

Now that your CarGeneralAsm.dll has been configured to be reachable via HTTP requests under IIS, you can update your client-side *.config file as follows (using the name of your IIS host, of course):

```
<configuration>
  <system.runtime.remoting>
    <application>
      <client displayName = "CarClient">
        <wellknown
          type="CarGeneralAsm.CarProvider, CarGeneralAsm"
          url="http://NameTheRemoteIISHost/IISCarHost/carprovider.soap"/>
      </client>
      <channels>
        <channel ref="http"/>
      </channels>
    </application>
  </system.runtime.remoting>
</configuration>
```

At this point, you are able to build a client application that loads the *.config file to make use of the remote objects now hosted under IIS.

Asynchronous Remoting

To wrap things up, let's examine how to invoke members of a remote type asynchronously. In Chapter 16, you were first introduced to the topic of asynchronous method invocations using delegate types. As you would expect, if a client assembly wishes to call a remote object asynchronously, the first step is to define a custom delegate to represent the remote method in question. At this point, the caller can make use of any of the techniques seen in Chapter 16 to invoke and receive the method return value.

By way of a simple illustration, create a new console application (AsyncWKOCarProviderClient) and set a reference to the first iteration of the CarGeneralAsm.dll assembly. Now, update the Program module as follows:

```
Imports CarGeneralAsm
Imports System.Runtime.Remoting

' The delegate for the GetAllAutos() method.
Public Delegate Function GetAllAutosDelegate() As List(Of JamesBondCar)

Module Program
  Sub Main()
    Console.WriteLine("Client started!  Hit enter to end")
    RemotingConfiguration.Configure( _
      "AsyncWKOCarProviderClient.exe.config", False)

    ' Make the car provider.
    Dim cp As CarProvider = New CarProvider()

    ' Make the delegate.
    Dim getCarsDel As GetAllAutosDelegate = _
      New GetAllAutosDelegate(AddressOf cp.GetAllAutos)
```

```
    ' Call GetAllAutos() asynchronously.
    Dim ar As IAsyncResult = getCarsDel.BeginInvoke(Nothing, Nothing)

    ' Simulate client-side activity.
    While Not ar.IsCompleted
      Console.WriteLine("Client working...")
    End While

    ' All done!  Get return value from delegate.
    Dim allJBCs As List(Of JamesBondCar) = getCarsDel.EndInvoke(ar)

    ' Use all cars in List.
    For Each j As JamesBondCar In allJBCs
      UseCar(j)
    Next
    Console.ReadLine()
  End Sub

  Public Sub UseCar(ByVal j As JamesBondCar)
    Console.WriteLine("Can car fly? {0}", j.canFly)
    Console.WriteLine("Can car swim? {0}", j.canSubmerge)
  End Sub
End Module
```

Notice how the client application first declares a delegate that matches the signature of the GetAllAutos() method of the remote CarProvider type. When the delegate is created, you pass in the name of the method to call (GetAllAutos), as always. Next, you trigger the BeginInvoke() method, cache the resulting IAsyncResult interface, and simulate some work on the client side (recall that the IAsyncResult.IsCompleted property allows you to monitor whether the associated method has completed processing).

Finally, once the client's work has completed, you obtain the List(Of T) returned from the CarProvider.GetAllAutos() method by invoking the EndInvoke() member, and pass each JamesBondCar into a shared helper function named UseCar(). Again, the beauty of the .NET delegate type is the fact that the logic used to invoke remote methods asynchronously is identical to the process of local method invocations.

■**Source Code**   The AsyncWKOCarProviderClient project is located under the Chapter 20 subdirectory.

Summary

In this chapter, you examined how to configure distinct .NET assemblies to share types between application boundaries. As you have seen, a remote object may be configured as an MBV or MBR type. This choice ultimately controls how a remote type is realized in the client's application domain (a copy or transparent proxy).

If you have configured a type to function as an MBR entity, you are suddenly faced with a number of related choices (WKO versus CAO, single call versus singleton, and so forth), each of which was addressed during this chapter. As well, you examined the process of tracking the lifetime of a remote object via the use of leases and lease sponsorship. Finally, you revisited the role of the .NET delegate type to understand how to asynchronously invoke a remote method (which, as luck would have it, is identical to the process of asynchronously invoking a local type).

CHAPTER 21

■■■

Building a Better Window with System.Windows.Forms

If you have read through the previous 20 chapters, you should have a solid handle on the VB 2005 programming language as well as the foundation of the .NET architecture. While you could take your newfound knowledge and begin building the next generation of console applications (boring!), you are more likely to be interested in building an attractive graphical user interface (GUI) to allow users to interact with your system.

This chapter is the first of three aimed at introducing you to the process of building traditional form-based desktop applications. Here, you'll learn how to build a highly stylized main window using the Form and Application classes. This chapter also illustrates how to capture and respond to user input (i.e., handle mouse and keyboard events) within the context of a GUI desktop environment. Finally, you will learn to construct menu systems, toolbars, status bars, and multiple document interface (MDI) applications, both by hand and using the designers incorporated into Visual Studio 2005.

Overview of the System.Windows.Forms Namespace

Like any namespace, System.Windows.Forms is composed of various classes, structures, delegates, interfaces, and enumerations. Although the difference in appearance between a console UI (CUI) and graphical UI (GUI) seems at first glance like night and day, in reality the process of building a Windows Forms application involves nothing more than learning how to manipulate a new set of types using the VB 2005 syntax you already know. From a high level, the many types within the System.Windows.Forms namespace can be grouped into the following broad categories:

- *Core infrastructure*: These are types that represent the core operations of a .NET Forms program (Form, Application, etc.) and various types to facilitate interoperability with legacy ActiveX controls.

- *Controls*: These are types used to create rich UIs (Button, MenuStrip, ProgressBar, DataGridView, etc.), all of which derive from the Control base class. Controls are configurable at design time and are visible (by default) at runtime.

- *Components*: These are types that do not derive from the Control base class but still provide visual features to a .NET Forms program (ToolTip, ErrorProvider, etc.). Many components (such as the Timer) are not visible at runtime, but can be configured visually at design time.

- *Common dialog boxes*: Windows Forms provides a number of canned dialog boxes for common operations (OpenFileDialog, PrintDialog, etc.). As you would hope, you can certainly build your own custom dialog boxes if the standard dialog boxes do not suit your needs.

Given that the total number of types within System.Windows.Forms is well over 100 strong, it would be redundant (not to mention a terrible waste of paper) to list every member of the Windows Forms family. To set the stage for the next several chapters, however, Table 21-1 lists some of the core .NET 2.0 System.Windows.Forms types (consult the .NET Framework 2.0 SDK documentation for full details).

Table 21-1. *Core Types of the* System.Windows.Forms *Namespace*

Classes	Meaning in Life
Application	This class encapsulates the runtime operation of a Windows Forms application.
Button, CheckBox, ComboBox, DateTimePicker, ListBox, LinkLabel, MaskedTextBox, MonthCalendar, PictureBox, TreeView	These classes (in addition to many others) correspond to various GUI widgets. You'll examine many of these items in detail in Chapter 23.
FlowLayoutPanel, TableLayoutPanel	.NET 2.0 now supplies various *layout managers* that automatically arrange a Form's controls during resizing.
Form	This type represents a main window, dialog box, or MDI child window of a Windows Forms application.
ColorDialog, OpenFileDialog, SaveFileDialog, FontDialog, PrintPreviewDialog, FolderBrowserDialog	These are various standard dialog boxes for common GUI operations.
Menu, MainMenu, MenuItem, ContextMenu, MenuStrip, ContextMenuStrip	These types are used to build topmost and context-sensitive menu systems. These controls (new to .NET 2.0) allow you to build menus that may contain traditional drop-down menu items as well as other controls (text boxes, combo boxes, and so forth).
StatusBar, Splitter, ToolBar, ScrollBar, StatusStrip, ToolStrip	These types are used to adorn a Form with common child controls.

■**Note** In addition to System.Windows.Forms, the System.Windows.Forms.dll assembly defines additional GUI-centric namespaces. For the most part, these additional types are used internally by the Forms engine and/or the designer tools of Visual Studio 2005. Given this fact, we will keep focused on the core System.Windows.Forms namespace.

Working with the Windows Forms Types

When you build a Windows Forms application, you may choose to write all the relevant code by hand (using Notepad or TextPad, perhaps) and feed the resulting *.vb files into the VB 2005 compiler using the /target:winexe flag. Taking time to build some Windows Forms applications by hand not only is a great learning experience, but also helps you understand the code generated by the various graphics designers found within various .NET IDEs.

To make sure you truly understand the basic process of building a Windows Forms application, the initial examples in this chapter will avoid the use of graphics designers. Once you feel comfortable with the process of building a Windows Forms application "wizard-free," you will then leverage the various designer tools provided by Visual Studio 2005.

Building a Main Window by Hand

To begin learning about Windows Forms programming, you'll build a minimal main window from scratch. Create a new folder on your hard drive (e.g., C:\MyFirstWindow) and create a new file within this directory named MainWindow.vb using your text editor of choice.

In the world of Windows Forms, the Form class is used to represent any window in your application. This includes a topmost main window in a single-document interface (SDI) application, modeless and modal dialog boxes, and the parent and child windows of a multiple-document interface (MDI) application. When you are interested in creating and displaying the main window in your program, you have two mandatory steps:

1. Derive a new class from System.Windows.Forms.Form.

2. Configure your application's Main() method to invoke Application.Run(), passing an instance of your Form-derived type as an argument.

Given this, update your MainWindow.vb file with the following class definition (note that because our Main() subroutine is within a Class type (not a Module), we are required to define Main() using the Shared keyword):

```
Imports System.Windows.Forms

Namespace MyWindowsApp
  Public Class MainWindow
  Inherits Form
    ' Run this application and identify the main window.
    Shared Sub Main()
      Application.Run(New MainWindow())
    End Sub
  End Class
End Namespace
```

In addition to the always present mscorlib.dll, a Windows Forms application needs to reference the System.dll and System.Windows.Forms.dll assemblies. As you may recall from Chapter 2, the default VB 2005 response file (vbc.rsp) instructs vbc.exe to automatically include these assemblies during the compilation process, so you are good to go. Also recall that the /target:winexe option of vbc.exe instructs the compiler to generate a Windows executable.

■**Note** Technically speaking, you can build a Windows application at the command line using the /target:exe option; however, if you do, you will find that a command window will be looming in the background (and it will stay there until you shut down the main window). When you specify /target:winexe, your executable runs as a native Windows Forms application (without the looming command window).

To compile your VB 2005 code file, open a Visual Studio 2005 command prompt, change to the directory containing your *.vb file, and issue the following command:

```
vbc /target:winexe *.vb
```

Figure 21-1 shows a test run.

Figure 21-1. *A simple main window à la Windows Forms*

Granted, the Form is not altogether that interesting at this point. But simply by deriving from Form, you have a minimizable, maximizable, resizable, and closable main window (with a default system-supplied icon to boot!). Unlike other Microsoft GUI frameworks you may have used in the past (Microsoft Foundation Classes, in particular), there is no need to bolt in hundreds of lines of coding infrastructure. Unlike a C-based Win32 API Windows application, there is no need to manually implement WinProc() or WinMain() procedures. Under the .NET platform, those dirty details have been encapsulated within the Form and Application types.

Honoring the Separation of Concerns

Currently, the MainWindow class defines the Main() method directly within its scope. If you prefer, you may create a dedicated module (I named mine Program) that is responsible for the task of launching the main window, leaving the Form-derived class responsible for representing the window itself:

```
Imports System.Windows.Forms

Namespace MyWindowsApp
  Public Class MainWindow
    Inherits Form
  End Class

  Public Module Program
    ' Run this application and identify the main window.
    Sub Main()
      Application.Run(New MainWindow())
    End Sub
  End Module
End Namespace
```

By doing so, you are abiding by an OO design principle termed *the separation of concerns.* Simply put, this rule of OO design states that a class should be in charge of doing the least amount of work possible. Given that you have refactored the initial class into two unique classes, you have decoupled the Form from the class that creates it. The end result is a more portable window, as it can be dropped into any project without carrying the extra baggage of a project-specific Main() method.

Source Code The MyFirstWindow project can be found under the Chapter 21 subdirectory.

The Role of the Application Class

The Application class defines numerous shared members that allow you to control various low-level behaviors of a Windows Forms application. For example, the Application class defines a set of events that allow you to respond to events such as application shutdown and idle-time processing. In addition to the Run() method, here are some other methods to be aware of:

- DoEvents(): Provides the ability for an application to process messages currently in the message queue during a lengthy operation.

- Exit(): Terminates the Windows application and unloads the hosting AppDomain.

- EnableVisualStyles(): Configures your application to support Windows XP visual styles. Do note that if you enable XP styles, this method must be called before loading your main window via Application.Run().

The Application class also defines a number of properties, many of which are read-only in nature. As you examine Table 21-2, note that most of these properties represent an application-level trait such as company name, version number, and so forth. In fact, given what you already know about assembly-level attributes (see Chapter 14), many of these properties should look vaguely familiar.

Table 21-2. *Core Properties of the* Application *Type*

Property	Meaning in Life
CompanyName	Retrieves the value of the assembly-level <AssemblyCompany> attribute
ExecutablePath	Gets the path for the executable file
ProductName	Retrieves the value of the assembly-level <AssemblyProduct> attribute
ProductVersion	Retrieves the value of the assembly-level <AssemblyVersion> attribute
StartupPath	Retrieves the path for the executable file that started the application

Finally, the Application class defines various shared events, some of which are as follows:

- ApplicationExit: Occurs when the application is just about to shut down.

- Idle: Occurs when the application's message loop has finished processing the current batch of messages and is about to enter an idle state (as there are no messages to process at the current time).

- ThreadExit: Occurs when a thread in the application is about to terminate. If the exiting thread is the main thread of the application, ThreadExit is fired before the ApplicationExit event.

Fun with the Application Class

To illustrate some of the functionality of the Application class, let's enhance your current MainWindow to perform the following:

- Reflect over select assembly-level attributes.

- Handle the shared ApplicationExit event.

The first task is to make use of select properties in the Application class to reflect over some assembly-level attributes. To begin, add the following attributes to your MainWindow.vb file (note you are now importing the System.Reflection namespace):

```
Imports System.Windows.Forms
Imports System.Reflection

' Assembly-level attributes.
<assembly:AssemblyCompany("Intertech Training")>
<assembly:AssemblyProduct("A Better Window")>
<assembly:AssemblyVersion("1.1.0.0")>

Namespace MyWindowsApp
...
End Namespace
```

Rather than manually reflecting over the <AssemblyCompany> and <AssemblyProduct> attributes using the techniques illustrated in Chapter 14, the Application class will do so automatically using various shared properties. To illustrate, implement the default constructor of MainForm as follows:

```
Public Class MainWindow
  Inherits Form

  ' Reflect over attributes using Application type.
  Public Sub New
    MessageBox.Show(Application.ProductName, _
      string.Format("This app brought to you by {0}", _
      Application.CompanyName))
  End Sub
End Class
```

When you recompile and run this application, you'll see a message box that displays various bits of information (see Figure 21-2).

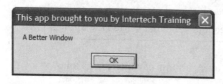

Figure 21-2. *Reading attributes via the* Application *type*

Now, let's equip this Form to respond to the ApplicationExit event. When you wish to respond to events from within a Windows Forms application, you will be happy to find that the same event syntax detailed in Chapter 10 is used to handle GUI-based events. Therefore, if you wish to intercept the shared ApplicationExit event, simply register an event handler using the AddHandler statement:

```
Public Class MainWindow
  Inherits Form

  ' Reflect over attributes using Application type.
  Public Sub New
...
    ' Handle Application.Exit event.
    AddHandler Application.ApplicationExit, AddressOf MainWindow_OnExit
  End Sub
```

```
Public Sub MainWindow_OnExit(ByVal sender As Object, ByVal args As EventArgs)
   MessageBox.Show(string.Format("Form version {0} has terminated.", _
      Application.ProductVersion))
   End Sub
End Class
```

The System.EventHandler Delegate

Notice that the ApplicationExit event works in conjunction with the System.EventHandler delegate. This delegate must point to subroutines that conform to the following signature:

```
Sub MyEventHandler(ByVal sender As Object, ByVal args As EventArgs)
```

System.EventHandler is the most primitive delegate used to handle events within Windows Forms, but many variations do exist for other events. As far as EventHandler is concerned, the first parameter of the assigned method is of type System.Object, which represents the object sending the event. The second EventArgs parameter contains any relevant information regarding the current event.

■**Note** EventArgs is the base class to numerous derived types that contain information for a family of related events. For example, mouse events work with the MouseEventArgs parameter, which contains details such as the (x, y) position of the cursor. Many keyboard events work with the KeyEventArgs type, which contains details regarding the current keypress, and so forth.

In any case, if you now recompile and run the application, you will find your message box appears upon the termination of the application.

■**Source Code** The AppClassExample project can be found under the Chapter 21 subdirectory.

The Anatomy of a Form

Now that you understand the role of the Application type, the next task is to examine the functionality of the Form class itself. Not surprisingly, the Form class inherits a great deal of functionality from its parent classes. Figure 21-3 shows the inheritance chain (including the set of implemented interfaces) of a Form-derived type using the Visual Studio 2005 Object Browser.

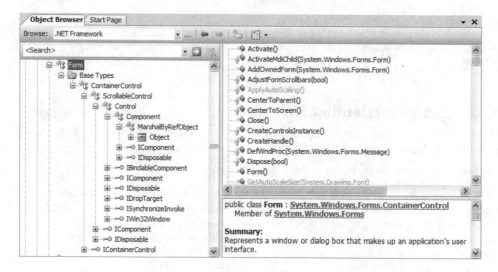

Figure 21-3. *The derivation of the* Form *type*

Although the complete derivation of a Form type involves numerous base classes and interfaces, do understand that you are *not* required to learn the role of each and every member from each and every parent class or implemented interface to be a proficient Windows Forms developer. In fact, the majority of the members (properties and events in particular) you will use on a daily basis are easily set using the Visual Studio 2005 IDE Properties window. Before we move on to examine some specific members inherited from these parent classes, take a look at Table 21-3, which outlines the basic role of each base class.

Table 21-3. *Base Classes in the* Form *Inheritance Chain*

Parent Class	Meaning in Life
System.Object	Like any class in .NET, a Form "is-a" object.
System.MarshalByRefObject	Recall during our examination of .NET remoting (see Chapter 20) that types deriving from this class are accessed remotely via a *reference* (not a copy) of the remote type.
System.ComponentModel.Component	This class provides a default implementation of the IComponent interface. In the .NET universe, a component is a type that supports design-time editing, but is not necessarily visible at runtime.
System.Windows.Forms.Control	This class defines common UI members for all Windows Forms UI controls, including the Form type itself.
System.Windows.Forms.ScrollableControl	This class defines support for auto-scrolling behaviors.
System.Windows.Forms.ContainerControl	This class provides focus-management functionality for controls that can function as a container for other controls.
System.Windows.Forms.Form	This class represents any custom Form, MDI child, or dialog box.

As you might guess, detailing each and every member of each class in the Form's inheritance chain would require a large book in itself. However, it is important to understand the behavior supplied by the Control and Form types. I'll assume that you will spend time examining the full details behind each class at your leisure using the .NET Framework 2.0 SDK documentation.

The Functionality of the Control Class

The System.Windows.Forms.Control class establishes the common behaviors required by any GUI type. The core members of Control allow you to configure the size and position of a control, capture keyboard and mouse input, get or set the focus/visibility of a member, and so forth. Table 21-4 defines some (but not all) properties of interest, grouped by related functionality.

Table 21-4. *Core Properties of the* Control *Type*

Properties	Meaning in Life
BackColor, ForeColor, BackgroundImage, Font, Cursor	These properties define the core UI of the control (colors, font for text, mouse cursor to display when the mouse is over the widget, etc.).
Anchor, Dock, AutoSize	These properties control how the control should be positioned within the container.
Top, Left, Bottom, Right, Bounds, ClientRectangle, Height, Width	These properties specify the current dimensions of the control.
Enabled, Focused, Visible	These properties each return a Boolean that specifies the state of the current control.
ModifierKeys	This shared property checks the current state of the modifier keys (Shift, Ctrl, and Alt) and returns the state in a Keys type.
MouseButtons	This shared property checks the current state of the mouse buttons (left, right, and middle mouse buttons) and returns this state in a MouseButtons type.
TabIndex, TabStop	These properties are used to configure the tab order of the control.
Opacity	This property determines the opacity of the control, in fractions (0.0 is completely transparent; 1.0 is completely opaque).
Text	This property indicates the string data associated with this control.
Controls	This property allows you to access a strongly typed collection (ControlsCollection) that contains any child controls within the current control.

As you would guess, the Control class also defines a number of events that allow you to intercept mouse, keyboard, painting, and drag-and-drop activities (among other things). Table 21-5 lists some (but not all) events of interest, grouped by related functionality.

Table 21-5. *Events of the* Control *Type*

Events	Meaning in Life
Click, DoubleClick, MouseEnter, MouseLeave, MouseDown, MouseUp, MouseMove, MouseHover, MouseWheel	Various events that allow you to interact with the mouse
KeyPress, KeyUp, KeyDown	Various events that allow you to interact with the keyboard
DragDrop, DragEnter, DragLeave, DragOver	Various events used to monitor drag-and-drop activity
Paint	An event that allows you to interact with GDI+ (see Chapter 22)

Finally, the Control base class also defines a number of methods that allow you to interact with any Control-derived type. As you examine the methods of the Control type, you will notice that a good number of them have an On prefix followed by the name of a specific event (OnMouseMove, OnKeyUp, OnPaint, etc.). Each of these On-prefixed virtual methods is the default event handler for its respective event. If you override any of these virtual members, you gain the ability to perform any necessary pre- or postprocessing of the event before (or after) invoking your parent's default implementation:

```
Imports System.Windows.Forms

Public Class MainForm
  Protected Overrides Sub OnMouseDown(ByVal e As MouseEventArgs)
    ' Add code for MouseDown event.

    ' Call parent implementation when finished.
    MyBase.OnMouseDown(e)
  End Sub
End Class
```

While this can be helpful in some circumstances (especially if you are building a custom control that derives from a standard control), you will often handle events using the VB 2005 Handles keyword (in fact, this is the default behavior of the Visual Studio 2005 designers). When you do so, the framework will call your custom event handler once the parent's implementation has completed:

```
Imports System.Windows.Forms

Public Class MainForm
  Private Sub MainForm_MouseDown(ByVal sender As Object, _
    ByVal e As MouseEventArgs) Handles Me.MouseDown
    ' Add code for MouseDown event.
  End Sub
End Class
```

Beyond these OnXXX() methods, here are a few other methods provided by the Control class to be aware of:

- Hide(): Hides the control and sets the Visible property to False
- Show(): Shows the control and sets the Visible property to True
- Invalidate(): Forces the control to redraw itself by sending a Paint event

To be sure, the Control class does define additional properties, methods, and events beyond the subset you've just examined. You should, however, now have a solid understanding regarding the overall functionality of this base class. Let's see it in action.

Fun with the Control Class

To illustrate the usefulness of some members from the Control class, let's build a new Form that is capable of handling the following events:

- Respond to the MouseMove and MouseDown events.
- Capture and process keyboard input via the KeyUp event.

To begin, create a new class derived from Form. In the default constructor, you'll make use of various inherited properties to establish the initial look and feel. Note you're now importing the

System.Drawing namespace to gain access to the Color structure (you'll examine this namespace in detail in the next chapter):

```
Imports System.Windows.Forms
Imports System.Drawing

Namespace MyWindowsApp
  Public Class MainWindow
    Inherits Form

    Public Sub New()
      ' Use inherited properties to set basic UI.
      Text = "My Fantastic Form"
      Height = 300
      Width = 500
      BackColor = Color.LemonChiffon
      Cursor = Cursors.Hand
    End Sub
  End Class

  Public Module Program
    ' Run this application and identify the main window.
    Sub Main()
      Application.Run(New MainWindow())
    End Sub
  End Module
End Namespace
```

Compile your application at this point, just to make sure you have not injected any typing errors:

```
vbc /target:winexe *.vb
```

Responding to the MouseMove Event

Next, you need to handle the MouseMove event. The goal is to display the current (x, y) location within the Form's caption area. All mouse-centric events (MouseMove, MouseUp, etc.) work in conjunction with the MouseEventHandler delegate, which can call any method matching the following signature:

```
Sub MyMouseHandler(ByVal sender As Object, ByVal e As MouseEventArgs)
```

The incoming MouseEventArgs structure extends the general EventArgs base class by adding a number of members particular to the processing of mouse activity (see Table 21-6).

Table 21-6. *Properties of the* MouseEventArgs *Type*

Property	Meaning in Life
Button	Gets which mouse button was pressed, as defined by the MouseButtons enumeration
Clicks	Gets the number of times the mouse button was pressed and released
Delta	Gets a signed count of the number of detents the mouse wheel has rotated
X	Gets the x-coordinate of a mouse click
Y	Gets the y-coordinate of a mouse click

Here, then, is the updated MainForm class that handles the MouseMove event as intended:

```
Public Class MainWindow
  Inherits Form
...
  Public Sub MainForm_MouseMove(ByVal sender As Object, _
    ByVal e As MouseEventArgs) Handles Me.MouseMove
    Text = string.Format("Current Pos: ({0} , {1})", e.X, e.Y)
  End Sub
End Class
```

If you now run your program and move the mouse over your Form, you will find the current (x, y) value display on the caption area as shown in Figure 21-4.

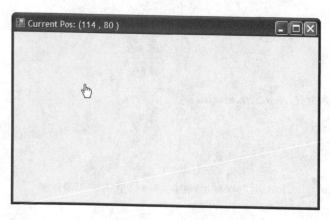

Figure 21-4. *Monitoring mouse movement*

Determining Which Mouse Button Was Clicked

One thing to be aware of is that the MouseUp (or MouseDown) event is sent whenever any mouse button is clicked. If you wish to determine exactly which button was clicked (such as left, right, or middle), you need to examine the Button property of the MouseEventArgs class. The value of the Button property is constrained by the related MouseButtons enumeration defined in the System.Windows.Forms namespace. The following MouseUp event handler displays which mouse button was clicked inside a message box:

```
Public Sub MainForm_MouseUp(ByVal sender As Object, _
  ByVal e As MouseEventArgs) Handles Me.MouseUp
    If e.Button = System.Windows.Forms.MouseButtons.Left Then
      MessageBox.Show("Left click!")
    End If
    If e.Button = System.Windows.Forms.MouseButtons.Right Then
      MessageBox.Show("Right click!")
    End If
    If e.Button = System.Windows.Forms.MouseButtons.Middle Then
      MessageBox.Show("Middle click!")
    End If
End Sub
```

Responding to Keyboard Events

Processing keyboard input is almost identical to responding to mouse activity. The KeyUp and KeyDown events work in conjunction with the KeyEventHandler delegate, which can point to any method taking an object as the first parameter and KeyEventArgs as the second:

```
Sub MyKeyboardHandler(ByVal sender As Object, ByVal e As KeyEventArgs)
```

KeyEventArgs has the members of interest shown in Table 21-7.

Table 21-7. *Properties of the* KeyEventArgs *Type*

Property	Meaning in Life
Alt	Gets a value indicating whether the Alt key was pressed
Control	Gets a value indicating whether the Ctrl key was pressed
Handled	Gets or sets a value indicating whether the event was fully handled in your handler
KeyCode	Gets the keyboard code for a KeyDown or KeyUp event
Modifiers	Indicates which modifier keys (Ctrl, Shift, and/or Alt) were pressed
Shift	Gets a value indicating whether the Shift key was pressed

Update your MainForm to handle the KeyUp event. Once you do, display the name of the key that was pressed inside a message box using the KeyCode property.

```
Public Sub MainForm_KeyUp(ByVal sender As Object, _
  ByVal e As KeyEventArgs) Handles Me.KeyUp
    MessageBox.Show(e.KeyCode.ToString(), "Key Pressed!")
End Sub
```

Now compile and run your program. You should be able to determine not only which mouse button was clicked, but also which keyboard key was pressed.

That wraps up our look at the core functionality of the Control base class. Next up, let's check out the role of Form.

■**Source Code** The ControlBehaviors project is included under the Chapter 21 subdirectory.

The Functionality of the Form Class

The Form class is typically (but not necessarily) the direct base class for your custom Form types. In addition to the large set of members inherited from the Control, ScrollableControl, and ContainerControl classes, the Form type adds additional functionality in particular to main windows, MDI child windows, and dialog boxes. Let's start with the core properties in Table 21-8.

Table 21-8. *Properties of the* Form *Type*

Properties	Meaning in Life
AcceptButton	Gets or sets the button on the Form that is clicked when the user presses the Enter key.
ActiveMDIChild IsMDIChildIsMDIContainer	Used within the context of an MDI application.
CancelButton	Gets or sets the button control that will be clicked when the user presses the Esc key.
ControlBox	Gets or sets a value indicating whether the Form has a control box.
FormBorderStyle	Gets or sets the border style of the Form. Used in conjunction with the FormBorderStyle enumeration.
Menu	Gets or sets the menu to dock on the Form.
MaximizeBox MinimizeBox	Used to determine whether this Form will enable the maximize and minimize boxes.
ShowInTaskbar	Determines whether this Form will be seen on the Windows taskbar.
StartPosition	Gets or sets the starting position of the Form at runtime, as specified by the FormStartPosition enumeration.
WindowState	Configures how the Form is to be displayed on startup. Used in conjunction with the FormWindowState enumeration.

In addition to the expected On-prefixed default event handlers, the Form type defines several core methods, as listed in Table 21-9.

Table 21-9. *Key Methods of the* Form *Type*

Method	Meaning in Life
Activate()	Activates a given Form and gives it focus.
Close()	Closes a Form.
CenterToScreen()	Places the Form in the dead-center of the screen.
LayoutMDI()	Arranges each child Form (as specified by the LayoutMDI enumeration) within the parent Form.
ShowDialog()	Displays a Form as a modal dialog box. More on dialog box programming in Chapter 23.

Finally, the Form class defines a number of events, many of which fire during the Form's lifetime. Table 21-10 hits the highlights.

Table 21-10. *Select Events of the* Form *Type*

Events	Meaning in Life
Activated	Occurs whenever the Form is *activated*, meaning the Form has been given the current focus on the desktop
Closed, Closing	Used to determine when the Form is about to close or has closed
Deactivate	Occurs whenever the Form is *deactivated*, meaning the Form has lost current focus on the desktop
Load	Occurs after the Form has been allocated into memory, but is not yet visible on the screen
MDIChildActive	Sent when a child window is activated

The Life Cycle of a Form Type

If you have programmed user interfaces using GUI toolkits such as Java Swing, Mac OS X Cocoa, or the raw Win32 API, you are aware that window types have a number of events that fire during their lifetime. The same holds true for Windows Forms. As you have seen, the life of a Form begins when the type constructor is called prior to being passed into the `Application.Run()` method.

Once the object has been allocated on the managed heap, the framework fires the `Load` event. Within a `Load` event handler, you are free to configure the look and feel of the Form, prepare any contained child controls (such as `ListBoxes`, `TreeViews`, and whatnot), or simply allocate resources used during the Form's operation (database connections, proxies to remote objects, and whatnot).

Once the `Load` event has fired, the next event to fire is `Activated`. This event fires when the Form receives focus as the active window on the desktop. The logical counterpart to the `Activated` event is (of course) `Deactivate`, which fires when the Form loses focus as the active window. As you can guess, the `Activated` and `Deactivate` events can fire numerous times over the life of a given Form type as the user navigates between active applications.

When the user has chosen to close the Form in question, two close-centric events fire: `Closing` and `Closed`. The `Closing` event is fired first and is an ideal place to prompt the end user with the much hated (but useful) "Are you *sure* you wish to close this application?" message. This confirmational step is quite helpful to ensure the user has a chance to save any application-centric data before terminating the program.

The `Closing` event works in conjunction with the `CancelEventHandler` delegate defined in the `System.ComponentModel` namespace. If you set the `CancelEventArgs.Cancel` property to `True`, you prevent the Form from being destroyed and instruct it to return to normal operation. If you set `CancelEventArgs.Cancel` to `False`, the `Close` event fires and the Windows Forms application terminates, which unloads the AppDomain and terminates the process.

To solidify the sequence of events that take place during a Form's lifetime, assume you have a new `MainWindow.vb` file that handles the `Load`, `Activated`, `Deactivate`, `Closing`, and `Close` events (be sure to add a `using` directive for the `System.ComponentModel` namespace to obtain the definition of `CancelEventArgs`).

In the `Load`, `Closed`, `Activated`, and `Deactivate` event handlers, you are going to update the value of a new Form-level `System.String` member variable (named `lifeTimeInfo`) with a simple message that displays the name of the event that has just been intercepted. As well, notice that within the `Closed` event handler, you will display the value of this string within a message box:

```
Public Class MainWindow
   Inherits Form
   Private lifeTimeInfo As String

   ' Handle the Load, Activated, Deactivate, and Closed events.
   Public Sub MainForm_Load(ByVal sender As Object, _
      ByVal e as EventArgs) Handles Me.Load
      lifeTimeInfo = lifeTimeInfo & "Load event" & VbLf
   End Sub
   Public Sub MainForm_Activated(ByVal sender As Object, _
      ByVal e as EventArgs) Handles Me.Activated
      lifeTimeInfo = lifeTimeInfo & "Activated event" & VbLf
   End Sub
   Public Sub MainForm_Deactivate(ByVal sender As Object, _
      ByVal e as EventArgs) Handles Me.Deactivate
      lifeTimeInfo = lifeTimeInfo & "Deactivate event" & VbLf
   End Sub
```

```
   Public Sub MainForm_Closed(ByVal sender As Object, _
     ByVal e as EventArgs) Handles Me.Closed
     lifeTimeInfo = lifeTimeInfo & "Closed event" & VbLf
     MessageBox.Show(lifeTimeInfo)
   End Sub
End Class
```

Within the Closing event handler, you will prompt the user to ensure he or she wishes to terminate the application using the incoming CancelEventArgs:

```
Private Sub MainForm_Closing(ByVal sender As Object, _
   ByVal e As CancelEventArgs) Handles Me.Closing
   Dim dr As System.Windows.Forms.DialogResult = _
     MessageBox.Show("Do you REALLY want to close this app?", _
       "Closing event!", MessageBoxButtons.YesNo)
   If dr = System.Windows.Forms.DialogResult.No Then
     e.Cancel = True
   Else
     e.Cancel = False
   End If
End Sub
```

Notice that the MessageBox.Show() method returns a DialogResult type, which has been set to a value representing the button clicked by the end user (Yes or No). Now, compile your code at the command line:

```
vbc /target:winexe *.vb
```

Run your application and shift the Form into and out of focus a few times (to trigger the Activated and Deactivate events). Once you shut down the Form, you will see a message box that looks something like Figure 21-5.

Figure 21-5. *The life and times of a* Form-*derived type*

Now, most of the really interesting aspects of the Form type have to do with its ability to create and host menu systems, toolbars, and status bars. While the code to do so is not complex, you will be happy to know that Visual Studio 2005 defines a number of graphical designers that take care of most of the mundane code on your behalf. Given this, let's say goodbye to the command-line compiler for the time being and turn our attention to the process of building Windows Forms applications using Visual Studio 2005.

■**Source Code** The FormLifeTime project can be found under the Chapter 21 subdirectory.

Building Windows Applications with Visual Studio 2005

Visual Studio 2005 has a specific project type dedicated to the creation of Windows Forms applications. When you select the Windows Application project type, you not only receive an initial Form-derived type, but you also can make use of the VB 2005–specific *startup object*. As you may know, VB 2005 allows you to declaratively specify which Form to show upon application startup, thereby removing the need to manually define a Main() method. However, if you do need to add additional startup logic, you are able to define a dedicated Main() method that will be called when your program launches.

Better yet, the IDE provides a number of graphical designers that make the process of building a UI child's play. Just to learn the lay of the land, create a new Windows Application project workspace, as shown in Figure 21-6. You are not going to build a working example just yet, so name this project whatever you desire (for example, MyTesterWindowsApp).

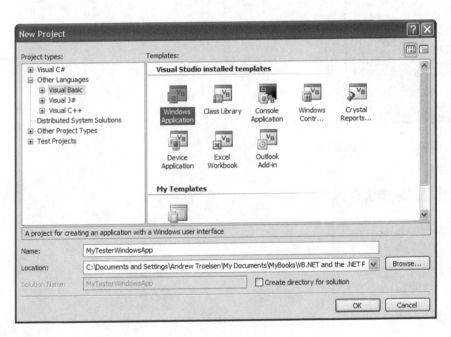

Figure 21-6. *The Visual Studio 2005 Windows Application project*

Once the project has loaded, you will no doubt notice the Forms designer, which allows you to build a UI by dragging controls/components from the Toolbox (see Figure 21-7) and configuring their properties and events using the Properties window (see Figure 21-8).

Figure 21-7. *The Visual Studio 2005 Toolbox*

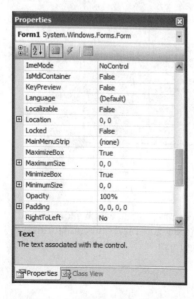

Figure 21-8. *The Visual Studio 2005 Properties window*

As you can see, the Toolbox groups UI controls by various categories. While most are self-explanatory (e.g., Printing contains printing controls, Menus & Toolbars contains recommended menu/toolbar controls, etc.), a few categories deserve special mention:

- *Common Controls*: Members in this category are considered the "recommended set" of common UI controls.

- *All Windows Forms*: Here you will find the full set of Windows Forms controls, including various .NET 1.*x* controls that are considered deprecated.

The second bullet point is worth reiterating. If you have worked with Windows Forms using .NET 1.*x*, be aware that many of your old friends (such as the DataGrid control) have been placed under the All Windows Forms category. Furthermore, many common UI controls you may have used under .NET 1.*x* (such as MainMenu, ToolBar, and StatusBar) are *not* shown in the Toolbox by default.

Enabling the Deprecated Controls

The first bit of good news is that these (deprecated) UI elements are still completely usable under .NET 2.0. The second bit of good news is that if you still wish to program with them, you can add them back to the Toolbox by right-clicking anywhere in the Toolbox and selecting Choose Items. From the resulting dialog box, check off the items of interest, as shown in Figure 21-9.

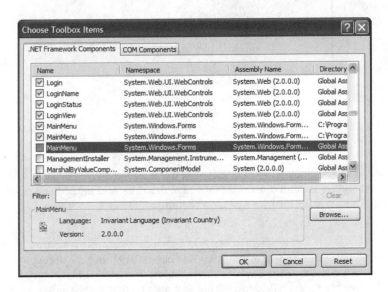

Figure 21-9. *Adding additional controls to the Toolbox*

■**Note** At first glance, it might appear that there are redundant listings for a given control (such as the MainMenu). In reality, each listing is unique, as a control may be versioned (1.0 versus 2.0) and/or may be a member of the .NET Compact Framework. Be sure to examine the directory path to select the correct item.

At this point, I am sure you are wondering why many of these old standbys have been hidden from view. The reason is that .NET 2.0 provides a set of new menu-, toolbar-, and status bar–centric controls that are now favored. For example, rather than using the legacy MainMenu control to build a menu, you can use the MenuStrip control, which provides a number of new bells and whistles in addition to the functionality found within MainMenu.

■Note In this chapter, I will favor the use of this new recommended set of UI elements. If you wish to work with the legacy MainMenu, StatusBar, or ToolBar types, consult the .NET Framework 2.0 SDK documentation.

Dissecting a Visual Studio 2005 Windows Forms Project

Each Form in a Visual Studio 2005 Windows Application project is composed of two related VB 2005 files, which can be verified using Solution Explorer (note that I renamed this initial class from Form1 to MainWindow). Be aware that the *.Designer.vb file is hidden until you click the Show All Files button on the Solution Explorer, as shown in Figure 21-10.

Figure 21-10. *Under Visual Studio 2005, each Form is composed of two* *.vb *files.*

Right-click the MainForm.vb icon and select View Code. Here you will see a class type that will contain all of the Form's event handlers, custom constructors, member overrides, and any additional member you author yourself. Upon startup, the Form type is quite empty:

```
Public Class MainForm
End Class
```

The first point of interest is it does not appear that the MainForm class is extending the necessary Form base class. Rest assured this is the case; however, this detail has been established in the related *.Designer.vb file. If you open up the *.Designer.vb file, you will find that your MainForm class is further defined via the Partial keyword examined in Chapter 5. Recall this keyword allows a single type to be defined across multiple files. Visual Studio 2005 uses this technique to hide the designer-generated code, allowing you to keep focused on the core logic of your Form-derived type. Here is the initial definition of this Partial class:

```
<Global.Microsoft.VisualBasic.CompilerServices.DesignerGenerated()> _
Partial Class MainForm
  Inherits System.Windows.Forms.Form
```

```
'Form overrides dispose to clean up the component list.
<System.Diagnostics.DebuggerNonUserCode()> _
Protected Overrides Sub Dispose(ByVal disposing As Boolean)
  If disposing AndAlso components IsNot Nothing Then
    components.Dispose()
  End If
  MyBase.Dispose(disposing)
End Sub

'Required by the Windows Forms designer
Private components As System.ComponentModel.IContainer

'NOTE: The following procedure is required by the Windows Forms designer
'It can be modified using the Windows Forms designer.
'Do not modify it using the code editor.
<System.Diagnostics.DebuggerStepThrough()> _
Private Sub InitializeComponent()
  components = New System.ComponentModel.Container()
  Me.AutoScaleMode = System.Windows.Forms.AutoScaleMode.Font
  Me.Text = "Form1"
End Sub
End Class
```

Notice the InitializeComponent() method. This method is maintained on your behalf by Visual Studio 2005, and it contains all of the code representing your design-time modifications. To illustrate, switch back to the Forms designer and locate the Text property in the Properties window. Change this value to something like My Test Window. Now open your MainForm.Designer.vb file and notice that InitializeComponent() has been updated accordingly:

```
Private Sub InitializeComponent()
...
  Me.Text = "My Test Window"
  Me.ResumeLayout(False)
End Sub
```

In addition to maintaining InitializeComponent(), the *.Designer.vb file will define the member variables that represent each control placed on the designer. Again, to illustrate, drag a Button control onto the Forms designer. Now, using the Properties window, rename your member variable from button1 to btnTestButton via the Name property.

Note It is always a good idea to rename the controls you place on the designer before handling events. If you fail to do so, you will most likely end up with a number of nondescript event handlers, such as button27_Click, given that the default names simply suffix a numerical value to the variable name.

Once you do, you will find that the *.Designer.vb file now contains a new member variable definition of type Button, which was defined using the WithEvents keyword:

```
Friend WithEvents btnTestButton As System.Windows.Forms.Button
```

Implementing Events at Design Time

Notice that the Properties window has a button depicting a lightning bolt. Although you are always free to handle Form-level or widget-level events by authoring the necessary logic by hand (as done in the previous examples), this event button allows you to visually handle an event for a given item. Simply select the control you wish to interact with from the drop-down list box (mounted at the top of the Properties window), locate the event you are interested in handling, and type in the name to be used as an event handler (or simply double-click the event to generate a default name of the form ControlName_EventName).

> **Note** The "lighting bolt button" approach to handling events is new to Visual Basic 2005. If you would rather make use of the drop-down list boxes supported by a *.vb code file to handle events, you are free to do so. Simply pick the item you wish to interact with in the left drop-down list box and the event you wish to handle from the right drop-down list box.

Assuming you have handled the Click event for the Button control, you will find that the MainForm.vb file contains the following event handler:

```
Public Class MainForm
  Private Sub btnTestButton_Click(ByVal sender As System.Object, _
    ByVal e As System.EventArgs) Handles btnTestButton.Click
    ' Add your code here!
  End Sub
End Class
```

> **Note** Every control has a default event, which refers to the event that will be handled if you double-click the item on the control using the Forms designer. For example, a Form's default event is Load, and if you double-click anywhere on a Form type, the IDE will automatically write code to handle this event.

The StartUp Object/Main() Sub Distinction

In the initial examples in this chapter, we were manually defining a Main() method that called Application.Run() in order to specify the main window of the program. However, when you create a new Windows Application project using Visual Studio 2005, you will not find similar code. The reason is that VB 2005 honors the notion of a startup object that is automatically created upon application launch. By default, the startup object will always be the initial Form-derived type in your application, which can be viewed using the Application tab of the My Project dialog box, shown in Figure 21-11.

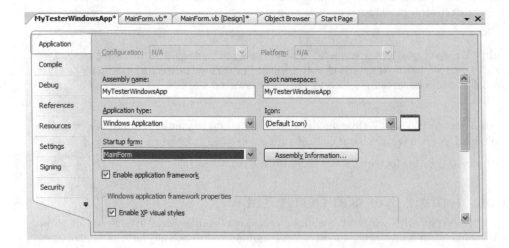

Figure 21-11. *Viewing the startup object*

While this approach can simplify your project development, many times it is preferred to specify a custom `Main()` method in order to perform custom startup logic before the main Form is shown (such as showing a splash screen while your program loads into memory). To do so, you must manually define a `Class` or `Module` that defines a proper `Main()` method. For example:

```
Module Program
  Sub Main()
    Application.EnableVisualStyles()
    Application.Run(New MainForm())
  End Sub
End Module
```

To instruct the IDE to invoke your custom `Main()` method (rather than create an instance of the startup object automatically), uncheck the Enable application framework check box from the Application tab of the My Project dialog box, and select `Sub Main()` from the Startup Object drop-down list, as shown in Figure 21-12.

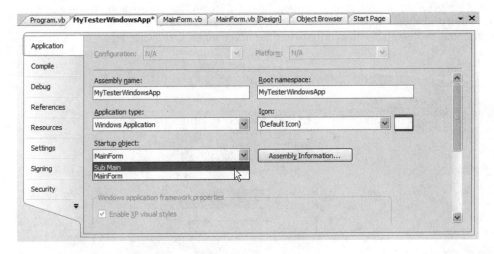

Figure 21-12. *Specifying a custom* `Main()` *method*

Autoreferenced Assemblies

To wrap up our initial look at the Visual Studio 2005 Windows Application project template, be aware that you automatically receive references to a number of necessary assemblies, including `System.Windows.Forms.dll` and `System.Drawing.dll`. Again, the details of `System.Drawing.dll` will be examined in the next chapter.

Working with MenuStrips and ContextMenuStrips

As of .NET 2.0, the recommended control for building a menu system is `MenuStrip`. This control allows you to create "normal" menu items such as File ➤ Exit, and you may also configure it to contain any number of relevant controls within the menu area. Here are some common UI elements that may be contained within a `MenuStrip`:

- `ToolStripMenuItem`: A traditional menu item

- `ToolStripComboBox`: An embedded `ComboBox`

- `ToolStripSeparator`: A simple line that separates content

- `ToolStripTextBox`: An embedded `TextBox`

Programmatically speaking, the `MenuStrip` control contains a strongly typed collection named `ToolStripItemCollection`. Like other collection types, this object supports members such as `Add()`, `AddRange()`, `Remove()`, and the `Count` property. While this collection is typically populated indirectly using various design-time tools, you are able to manually manipulate this collection if you so choose.

To illustrate the process of working with the `MenuStrip` control, create a new Windows Forms application named MenuStripApp. Using the Forms designer, place a `MenuStrip` control named `mainFormMenuStrip` onto your Form. When you do so, your `*.Designer.vb` file is updated with a new `MenuStrip` member variable:

```
Friend WithEvents mainFormMenuStrip As System.Windows.Forms.MenuStrip
```

`MenuStrips` can be highly customized using the Visual Studio 2005 Forms designer. For example, if you look at the extreme upper left of the control, you will notice a small arrow icon. After you select this icon, you are presented with a context-sensitive *inline editor*, as shown in Figure 21-13.

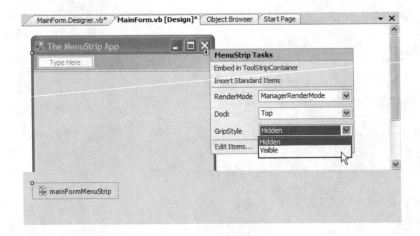

Figure 21-13. *The inline* MenuStrip *editor*

Many Windows Forms controls support such context-sensitive inline editors. As far as `MenuStrip` is concerned, the editor allows you to quickly do the following:

- Insert a "standard" menu system (File, Save, Tools, Help, etc.) using the Insert Standard Items link.

- Change the docking and gripping behaviors of the `MenuStrip`.

- Edit each item in the `MenuStrip` (this is simply a shortcut to selecting a specific item in the Properties window).

For this example, you'll ignore the options of the inline editor and stay focused on the design of the menu system. To begin, select the `MenuStrip` control on the designer and define a standard File ➤ Exit menu by typing in the names within the Type Here prompts, as shown in Figure 21-14.

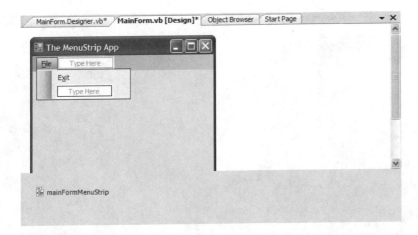

Figure 21-14. *Designing a menu system*

■**Note** As you may know, when the ampersand character (&) is placed before a letter in a menu item, it denotes
the item's shortcut key. In this example, you are creating &File ➤ E&xit; therefore, the user may activate the Exit
menu by pressing Alt+F, and then X.

Each menu item you type into the designer is represented by the `ToolStripMenuItem` class type.
If you open your `*.Designer.vb` file, you will find two new member variables for each item:

```
Partial Class MainForm
  Inherits Form
...
  Friend WithEvents mainFormMenuStrip As System.Windows.Forms.MenuStrip
  Friend WithEvents FileToolStripMenuItem As System.Windows.Forms.ToolStripMenuItem
  Friend WithEvents ExitToolStripMenuItem As System.Windows.Forms.ToolStripMenuItem
End Class
```

To finish the initial code of this example, return to the designer and handle the `Click` event for
the Exit menu item using the events button of the Properties window. Within the generated event
handler, make a call to `Application.Exit()`:

```
Public Class MainForm
    Private Sub ExitToolStripMenuItem_Click(ByVal sender As System.Object, _
    ByVal e As System.EventArgs) Handles ExitToolStripMenuItem.Click
        Application.Exit()
    End Sub
End Class
```

At this point, you should be able to compile and run your program. Verify that you can terminate
the application via File ➤ Exit as well as pressing Alt+F and then X on the keyboard.

Adding a TextBox to the MenuStrip

Now, let's create a new topmost menu item named Change Background Color. The subitem in this
case will not be a menu item, but a `ToolStripTextBox` (see Figure 21-15). Once you have added the
new control, rename this control to `toolStripTextBoxColor` using the Properties window.

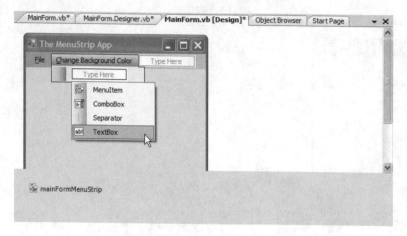

Figure 21-15. *Adding* TextBoxes *to a* MenuStrip

The goal here is to allow the user to enter the name of a color (red, green, pink, etc.) that will be used to set the BackColor property of the Form. First, handle the LostFocus event for the new ToolStripTextBox member variable (as you would guess, this event fires when the TextBox within the ToolStrip is no longer the active UI element).

Within the event handler, you will extract the string data entered within the ToolStripTextBox (via the Text property) and make use of the System.Drawing.Color.FromName() method. This shared method will return a Color type based on a known string value. To account for the possibility that the user enters an unknown color (or types bogus data), you will make use of some simple Try/Catch logic:

```vb
Public Class MainForm
  Private Sub ExitToolStripMenuItem_Click(ByVal sender As System.Object, _
  ByVal e As System.EventArgs) Handles ExitToolStripMenuItem.Click
    Application.Exit()
  End Sub

  Private Sub toolStripTextBoxColor_LostFocus(ByVal sender As System.Object, _
  ByVal e As System.EventArgs) Handles toolStripTextBoxColor.LostFocus
    Try
      BackColor = Color.FromName(toolStripTextBoxColor.Text)
    Catch ' Just do nothing if the user provides bad data
    End Try
  End Sub
End Class
```

Go ahead and take your updated application out for another test drive and try entering in the names of various colors (red, green, blue, for example). Once you do, you should see your Form's background color change as soon as you press the Tab key. If you are interested in checking out some valid color names, look up the System.Drawing.Color type using the Visual Studio 2005 Object Browser or the .NET Framework 2.0 SDK documentation.

Creating a Context Menu

Let's now examine the process of building a context-sensitive pop-up (i.e., right-click) menu. Under .NET 1.1, the ContextMenu type was the class of choice for building context menus, but under .NET 2.0 the preferred type is ContextMenuStrip. Like the MenuStrip type, ContextMenuStrip maintains a `ToolStripItemCollection` to represent the possible subitems (such as `ToolStripMenuItem`, `ToolStripComboBox`, `ToolStripSeperator`, `ToolStripTextBox`, etc.).

Drag a new `ContextMenuStrip` control from the Toolbox onto the Forms designer and rename the control to `fontSizeContextStrip` using the Properties window. Notice that you are able to populate the subitems graphically in much the same way you would edit the Form's main `MenuStrip` (a welcome change from the method used in Visual Studio .NET 2003). For this example, add three `ToolStripMenuItems` named `Huge`, `Normal`, and `Tiny`, as shown in Figure 21-16.

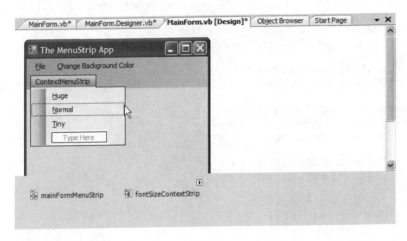

Figure 21-16. *Designing a* `ContextMenuStrip`

This context menu will be used to allow the user to select the size to render a message within the Form's client area. To facilitate this endeavor, create an `Enum` type named `TextFontSize` and declare a new member variable of this type within your `Form` type (set to `TextFontSize.FontSizeNormal`):

```
Public Class MainForm
  Private currFontSize As TextFontSize = TextFontSize.FontSizeNormal
...
End Class
```

```
' Helper enum for font size.
Enum TextFontSize
  FontSizeHuge = 30
  FontSizeNormal = 20
  FontSizeTiny = 8
End Enum
```

The next step is to handle the Form's `Paint` event using the Properties window. As described in greater detail in the next chapter, the `Paint` event allows you to render graphical data (including stylized text) onto a Form's client area. Here, you are going to draw a textual message using a font of user-specified size. Don't sweat the details at this point, but do update your `Paint` event handler as follows:

```
Private Sub MainForm_Paint(ByVal sender As System.Object, _
  ByVal e As System.Windows.Forms.PaintEventArgs) Handles MyBase.Paint
  Dim g As Graphics = e.Graphics
  g.DrawString("Right click on me...", _
    New Font("Times New Roman", currFontSize), _
    New SolidBrush(Color.Black), 50, 50)
End Sub
```

Last but not least, you need to handle the Click events for each of the ToolStripMenuItem types maintained by the ContextMenuStrip. While you could have a separate Click event handler for each, you will simply specify a single event handler that will be called when any of the three ToolStripMenuItems have been clicked, therefore you will have a single event handler with multiple Handles statements. Using the Properties window, specify the name of the Click event handler as ContextMenuItemSelection_Clicked for each of the three ToolStripMenuItems and implement this method like so:

```
' This one event handler handles the Click event from each context menu item.
Private Sub ContextMenuItemSelection_Clicked(ByVal sender As System.Object, _
  ByVal e As System.EventArgs) Handles HugeToolStripMenuItem.Click, _
  TinyToolStripMenuItem.Click, NormalToolStripMenuItem.Click

    ' Obtain the currently clicked ToolStripMenuItem.
    Dim miClicked As ToolStripMenuItem = CType(sender, ToolStripMenuItem)

    ' Figure out which item was clicked using its Name.
    If miClicked.Name = "HugeToolStripMenuItem" Then
      currFontSize = TextFontSize.FontSizeHuge
    End If
    If miClicked.Name = "NormalToolStripMenuItem" Then
      currFontSize = TextFontSize.FontSizeNormal
    End If
    If miClicked.Name = "TinyToolStripMenuItem" Then
      currFontSize = TextFontSize.FontSizeTiny
    End If

    ' Tell the Form to repaint itself.
    Invalidate()
End Sub
```

Notice that using the "sender" argument, you are able to determine the name of the ToolStripMenuItem member variable in order to set the current text size. Once you have done so, the call to Invalidate() fires the Paint event, which will cause your Paint event handler to execute.

The final step is to inform the Form which ContextMenuStrip it should display when the right mouse button is clicked in its client area. To do so, simply use the Properties window to set the ContextMenuStrip property equal to the name of your context menu item. Once you have done so, you will find the following line within InitializeComponent():

```
    Me.ContextMenuStrip = Me.fontSizeContextStrip
```

■**Note** Be aware that any control can be assigned a context menu via the ContextMenuStrip property. For example, you could create a Button object on a dialog box that responds to a particular context menu. In this way, the menu would be displayed only if the mouse button were right-clicked within the bounding rectangle of the button.

If you now run the application, you should be able to change the size of the rendered text message via a right-click of your mouse.

Checking Menu Items

ToolStripMenuItem defines a number of members that allow you to check, enable, and hide a given item. Table 21-11 gives a rundown of some (but not all) of the interesting properties.

Table 21-11. *Members of the* ToolStripMenuItem *Type*

Member	Meaning in Life
Checked	Gets or sets a value indicating whether a check mark appears beside the text of the ToolStripMenuItem
CheckOnClick	Gets or sets a value indicating whether the ToolStripMenuItem should automatically appear checked/unchecked when clicked
Enabled	Gets or sets a value indicating whether the ToolStripMenuItem is enabled

Let's extend the previous pop-up menu to display a check mark next to the currently selected menu item. Setting a check mark on a given menu item is not at all difficult (just set the Checked property to True). However, tracking which menu item should be checked does require some additional logic. One possible approach is to define a distinct ToolStripMenuItem member variable that represents the currently checked item:

```
Public Class MainForm
...
  ' Marks the item checked.
  Private WithEvents currentCheckedItem As ToolStripMenuItem
End Form
```

Recall that the default text size is TextFontSize.FontSizeNormal. Given this, the initial item to be checked is the normalToolStripMenuItem ToolStripMenuItem member variable. Add a default constructor to your Form-derived type, implemented like so:

```
Public Sub New()
  ' Call InitializeComponent() when defining your own constructor!
  InitializeComponent()

  ' Inherited method to center the Form.
  CenterToScreen()

  ' Now check the 'Normal' menu item.
  currentCheckedItem = normalToolStripMenuItem
  currentCheckedItem.Checked = True
End Sub
```

■**Note** When you redefine the default constructor for a Form-derived type, you must manually make a call to InitializeComponent() within its scope, as this will no longer automatically be done on your behalf. Thankfully, Visual Studio 2005 will automatically insert a call to InitializeComponent() when you press the Enter key after typing **Sub New()**.

Now that you have a way to programmatically identify the currently checked item, the last step is to update the ContextMenuItemSelection_Clicked() event handler to uncheck the previous item and check the new current ToolStripMenuItem object in response to the user selection:

```
' This one event handler handles the Click event from each context menu item.
Private Sub ContextMenuItemSelection_Clicked(ByVal sender As System.Object, _
  ByVal e As System.EventArgs) Handles HugeToolStripMenuItem.Click, _
  TinyToolStripMenuItem.Click, NormalToolStripMenuItem.Click

  ' Obtain the currently clicked ToolStripMenuItem.
  Dim miClicked As ToolStripMenuItem = CType(sender, ToolStripMenuItem)
```

```
' Uncheck the currently checked item.
currentCheckedItem.Checked = False

' Figure out which item was clicked using its Name.
If miClicked.Name = "HugeToolStripMenuItem" Then
  currFontSize = TextFontSize.FontSizeHuge
End If
If miClicked.Name = "NormalToolStripMenuItem" Then
  currFontSize = TextFontSize.FontSizeNormal
End If
If miClicked.Name = "TinyToolStripMenuItem" Then
  currFontSize = TextFontSize.FontSizeTiny
End If

' Tell the Form to repaint itself.
Invalidate()

' Establish which item to check.
If miClicked.Name = "HugeToolStripMenuItem" Then
  currFontSize = TextFontSize.FontSizeHuge
  currentCheckedItem = HugeToolStripMenuItem
End If
If miClicked.Name = "NormalToolStripMenuItem" Then
  currFontSize = TextFontSize.FontSizeNormal
  currentCheckedItem = NormalToolStripMenuItem
End If
If miClicked.Name = "TinyToolStripMenuItem" Then
  currFontSize = TextFontSize.FontSizeTiny
  currentCheckedItem = TinyToolStripMenuItem
End If

  ' Check new item.
  currentCheckedItem.Checked = True
End Sub
```

Figure 21-17 shows the completed MenuStripApp project in action.

Figure 21-17. *Checking/unchecking* ToolStripMenuItems

■**Source Code** The MenuStripApp application is located under the Chapter 21 subdirectory.

Working with StatusStrips

In addition to a menu system, many Forms also maintain a *status bar* that is typically mounted at the bottom of the Form. A status bar may be divided into any number of "panes" that hold some textual (or graphical) information such as menu help strings, the current time, or other application-specific information.

Although status bars have been supported since the release of the .NET platform (via the System.Windows.Forms.StatusBar type), as of .NET 2.0 the simple StatusBar has been ousted by the new StatusStrip type. Like a status bar, a StatusStrip can consist of any number of panes to hold textual/graphical data using a ToolStripStatusLabel type. However, status strips have the ability to contain additional tool strip items such as the following:

- ToolStripProgressBar: An embedded progress bar.
- ToolStripDropDownButton: An embedded button that displays a drop-down list of choices when clicked.
- ToolStripSplitButton: This is similar to the ToolStripDropDownButton, but the items of the drop-down list are displayed only if the user clicks directly on the drop-down area of the control. The ToolStripSplitButton also has normal buttonlike behavior and can thus support the Click event.

In this example, you will build a new MainWindow that supports a simple menu (File ➤ Exit and Help ➤ About) as well as a StatusStrip. The leftmost pane of the status strip will be used to display help string data regarding the currently selected menu subitem (e.g., if the user selects the Exit menu, the pane will display "Exits the app").

The far-right pane will display one of two dynamically created strings that will show either the current time or the current date. Finally, the middle pane will be a ToolStripDropDownButton type that allows the user to toggle the date/time display (with a happy face icon to boot!). Figure 21-18 shows the application in its completed form.

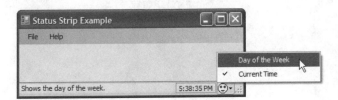

Figure 21-18. *The StatusStrip application*

Designing the Menu System

To begin, create a new Windows Forms application project named StatusStripApp. Place a MenuStrip control onto the Forms designer and build the two menu items (File ➤ Exit and Help ➤ About). Once you have done so, handle the Click and MouseHover events for each subitem (Exit and About) using the Properties window.

The implementation of the File ➤ Exit Click event handler will simply terminate the application, while the Help ➤ About Click event handler shows a friendly MessageBox.

```
Public Class MainForm
  Private Sub exitToolStripMenuItem_Click(ByVal sender As System.Object, _
     ByVal e As System.EventArgs) Handles exitToolStripMenuItem.Click
       Application.Exit()
  End Sub

  Private Sub aboutToolStripMenuItem_Click(ByVal sender As System.Object, _
     ByVal e As System.EventArgs) Handles aboutToolStripMenuItem.Click
       MessageBox.Show("My StatusStripApp!")
  End Sub

  Private Sub exitToolStripMenuItem_MouseHover(ByVal sender As System.Object, _
  ByVal e As System.EventArgs) Handles exitToolStripMenuItem.MouseHover
  End Sub

  Private Sub aboutToolStripMenuItem_MouseHover(ByVal sender As System.Object, _
  ByVal e As System.EventArgs) Handles aboutToolStripMenuItem.MouseHover
  End Sub
End Class
```

You will update the MouseHover event handlers to display the correct prompt in the leftmost pane of the StatusStrip in just a bit, so leave them empty for the time being.

Designing the StatusStrip

Next, place a StatusStrip control onto the designer and rename this control to mainStatusStrip. Understand that by default a StatusStrip contains no panes whatsoever. To add the three panes, you may take various approaches:

- Author the code by hand without designer support (perhaps using a helper method named CreateStatusStrip() that is called in the Form's constructor).

- Add the items via a dialog box activated through the Edit Items link using the StatusStrip context-sensitive inline editor (see Figure 21-19).

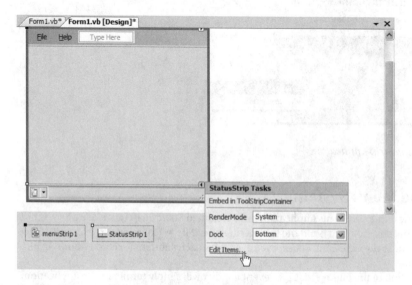

Figure 21-19. *The StatusStrip context editor*

- Add the items one by one via the new item drop-down editor mounted on the StatusStrip (see Figure 21-20).

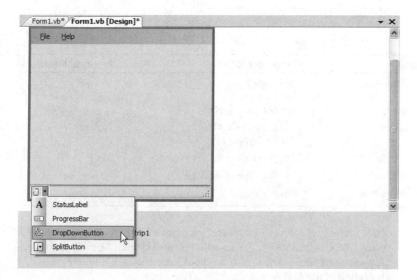

Figure 21-20. *Adding items via the* StatusStrip *new item drop-down editor*

For this example, you will leverage the new item drop-down editor. Add two new ToolStripStatusLabel types named toolStripStatusLabelMenuState and toolStripStatusLabelClock, and a ToolStripDropDownButton named toolStripDropDownButtonDateTime. As you would expect, this will add new member variables in the *.Designer.vb file and update InitializeComponent() accordingly. Now, select the ToolStripDropDownButton on the designer and add two new menu items named currentTimeToolStripMenuItem and dayoftheWeekToolStripMenuItem (see Figure 21-21).

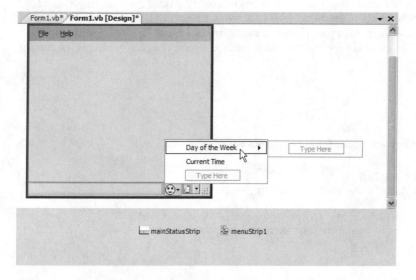

Figure 21-21. *Adding menu items to the* ToolStripDropDownButton

To configure your panes to reflect the look and feel shown in Figure 21-21, you will need to set several properties, which you do using the Visual Studio 2005 Properties window. Table 21-12 documents the necessary properties to set and events to handle for each item on your StatusStrip (of course, feel free to stylize the panes with additional settings as you see fit).

Table 21-12. StatusStrip *Pane Configuration*

Pane Member Variable	Properties to Set	Events to Handle
toolStripStatusLabelMenuState	Spring = True Text = (empty) TextAlign = TopLeft	None
toolStripStatusLabelClock	BorderSides = All Text = (empty)	None
toolStripDropDownButtonDateTime	Image = (see text that follows)	None
dayoftheWeekToolStripMenuItem	Text = "Day of the Week"	MouseHoverClick
currentTimeToolStripMenuItem	Text = "Current Time"	MouseHoverClick

The Image property of the toolStripDropDownButtonDateTime member can be set to any image file on your machine (of course, extremely large image files will be quite skewed). For this example, you may wish to use the happyDude.bmp file included with this book's downloadable source code (please visit the Downloads section of the Apress website, http://www.apress.com).

So at this point, the GUI design is complete! Before you implement the remaining event handlers, you need to get to know the role of the Timer component.

Working with the Timer Type

Recall that the second pane should display the current time or current date based on user preference. The first step to take to achieve this design goal is to add a Timer member variable to the Form. A Timer is a component that calls some method (specified using the Tick event) at a given interval (specified by the Interval property).

Drag a Timer component onto your Forms designer and rename it to timerDateTimeUpdate. Using the Properties window, set the Interval property to 1,000 (the value in milliseconds) and set the Enabled property to True. Finally, handle the Tick event. Before implementing the Tick event handler, define a new enum type in your project named DateTimeFormat. This enum will be used to determine whether the second ToolStripStatusLabel should display the current time or the current day of the week:

```
Enum DateTimeFormat
  ShowClock
  ShowDay
End Enum
```

With this enum in place, update your MainWindow with the following code:

```
Public Class MainForm
  ' Which format to display?
  Private dtFormat As DateTimeFormat = DateTimeFormat.ShowClock

  Private Sub timerDateTimeUpdate_Tick(ByVal sender As System.Object, _
  ByVal e As System.EventArgs) Handles timerDateTimeUpdate.Tick
    Dim panelInfo As String = ""
```

```
  ' Create current format.
  If dtFormat = DateTimeFormat.ShowClock Then
    panelInfo = DateTime.Now.ToLongTimeString
  Else
    panelInfo = DateTime.Now.ToLongDateString
  End If

  ' Set text on pane.
  toolStripStatusLabelClock.Text = panelInfo
End Sub
...
End Class
```

Notice that the Timer event handler makes use of the DateTime type. Here, you simply find the current system time or date using the Now property and use it to set the Text property of the toolStripStatusLabelClock member variable.

Toggling the Display

At this point, the Tick event handler should be displaying the current time within the toolStripStatusLabelClock pane, given that the default value of your DateTimeFormat member variable has been set to DateTimeFormat.ShowClock. To allow the user to toggle between the date and time display, update your MainWindow as follows (note you are also toggling which of the two menu items in the ToolStripDropDownButton should be checked):

```
Public Class MainForm
  ' Which format to display?
  Private dtFormat As DateTimeFormat = DateTimeFormat.ShowClock

  ' Marks the item checked.
  Private currentCheckedItem As ToolStripMenuItem

  Public Sub New()
    ' This call is required by the Windows Forms designer.
    InitializeComponent()

    ' These properties can also be set
    ' with the Properties window.
    Text = "Status Strip Example"
    CenterToScreen()
    currentCheckedItem = currentTimeToolStripMenuItem
    currentCheckedItem.Checked = True
  End Sub
...
  Private Sub currentTimeToolStripMenuItem_Click(ByVal sender As System.Object, _
  ByVal e As System.EventArgs) Handles currentTimeToolStripMenuItem.Click
    ' Toggle check mark and set pane format to time.
    currentCheckedItem.Checked = False
    dtFormat = DateTimeFormat.ShowClock
    currentCheckedItem = currentTimeToolStripMenuItem
    currentCheckedItem.Checked = True
  End Sub

  Private Sub dayoftheWeekToolStripMenuItem_Click(ByVal sender As System.Object, _
  ByVal e As System.EventArgs) Handles dayoftheWeekToolStripMenuItem.Click
```

```
        ' Toggle check mark and set pane format to date.
        currentCheckedItem.Checked = False
        dtFormat = DateTimeFormat.ShowDay
        currentCheckedItem = dayoftheWeekToolStripMenuItem
        currentCheckedItem.Checked = True
    End Sub
End Class
```

Displaying the Menu Selection Prompts

Finally, you need to configure the first pane to hold menu help strings. As you know, most applications send a small bit of text information to the first pane of a status bar whenever the end user selects a menu item (e.g., "This terminates the application"). Given that you have already handled the MouseHover events for each submenu on the MenuStrip and TooStripDropDownButton, all you need to do is assign a proper value to the Text property for the toolStripStatusLabelMenuState member variable, for example:

```
Private Sub exitToolStripMenuItem_MouseHover(ByVal sender As System.Object, _
   ByVal e As System.EventArgs) Handles exitToolStripMenuItem.MouseHover
   toolStripStatusLabelMenuState.Text = "Exits the app."
End Sub

Private Sub aboutToolStripMenuItem_MouseHover(ByVal sender As System.Object, _
   ByVal e As System.EventArgs) Handles aboutToolStripMenuItem.MouseHover
   toolStripStatusLabelMenuState.Text = "Shows about box."
End Sub

Private Sub dayoftheWeekToolStripMenuItem_MouseHover(ByVal sender As System.Object, _
   ByVal e As System.EventArgs) Handles dayoftheWeekToolStripMenuItem.MouseHover
   toolStripStatusLabelMenuState.Text = "Shows the day of the week."
End Sub

Private Sub currentTimeToolStripMenuItem_MouseHover(ByVal sender As System.Object, _
   ByVal e As System.EventArgs) Handles currentTimeToolStripMenuItem.MouseHover
   toolStripStatusLabelMenuState.Text = "Shows the current time."
End Sub
```

Take your updated project out for a test drive. You should now be able to find these informational help strings in the first pane of your StatusStrip as you select each menu item.

Establishing a "Ready" State

The final thing to do for this example is ensure that when the user deselects a menu item, the first text pane is set to a default message (e.g., "Ready"). With the current design, the previously selected menu prompt remains on the leftmost text pane, which is confusing at best. To rectify this issue, handle the MouseLeave event for the Exit, About, Day of the Week, and Current Time menu items. To simplify coding, we will make use of a single handler for each widget (note the multiple Handles statements):

```
Private Sub Handle_MouseLeave(ByVal sender As System.Object, _
   ByVal e As System.EventArgs) Handles currentTimeToolStripMenuItem.MouseLeave, _
   exitToolStripMenuItem.MouseLeave, _
   dayoftheWeekToolStripMenuItem.MouseLeave, _
   aboutToolStripMenuItem.MouseLeave
   toolStripStatusLabelMenuState.Text = "Ready."
End Sub
```

With this, you should find that the first pane resets to this default message as soon as the mouse cursor leaves any of your four menu items.

■**Source Code** The StatusStripApp project is included under the Chapter 21 subdirectory.

Working with ToolStrips

The next Form-level GUI item to examine in this chapter is the .NET 2.0 `ToolStrip` type, which overshadows the functionality found within the deprecated .NET 1.*x* `ToolBar` class. As you know, toolbars typically provide an alternate means to activate a given menu item. Thus, if the user clicks a Save button, this has the same effect as selecting File ➤ Save. Much like `MenuStrip` and `StatusStrip`, the `ToolStrip` type can contain numerous toolbar items, some of which you have already encountered in previous examples:

- `ToolStripButton`
- `ToolStripLabel`
- `ToolStripSplitButton`
- `ToolStripDropDownButton`
- `ToolStripSeparator`
- `ToolStripComboBox`
- `ToolStripTextBox`
- `ToolStripProgressBar`

Like other Windows Forms controls, the `ToolStrip` supports an inline editor that allows you to quickly add standard button types (File, Exit, Help, Copy, Paste, etc.) to a `ToolStrip`, change the docking position, and embed the `ToolStrip` in a `ToolStripContainer` (more details in just a bit). Figure 21-22 illustrates the designer support for `ToolStrips`.

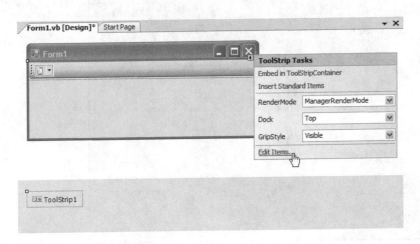

Figure 21-22. *Designing* `ToolStrips`

To illustrate working with `ToolStrips`, the following Windows Forms application creates a `ToolStrip` containing two `ToolStripButton` types (named `toolStripButtonGrowFont` and `toolStripButtonShrinkFont`), a `ToolBarSeparator`, and a `ToolBarTextBox` (named `toolStripTextBoxMessage`). The end user is able to enter a message to be rendered on the Form via the `ToolBarTextBox`, and the two `ToolBarButton` types will be used to increase or decrease the font size. Figure 21-23 shows the end result of the project you will construct.

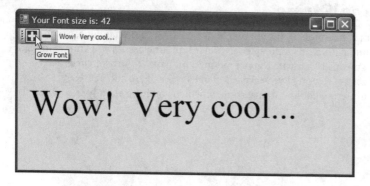

Figure 21-23. `ToolStripApp` *in action*

By now I'd guess you have a handle on working with the Visual Studio 2005 Forms designer, so I won't belabor the point of building the `ToolStrip`. Do note, however, that each `ToolStripButton` has a custom (albeit poorly drawn by yours truly) icon that was created using the Visual Studio 2005 image editor. If you wish to create image files for your project, simply select the Project ➤ Add New Item menu option, and from the resulting dialog box add a new icon file (see Figure 21-24).

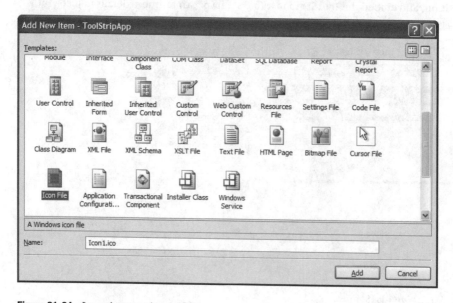

Figure 21-24. *Inserting new image files*

Once you have done so, you are able to edit your images using the Colors tab on the Toolbox and the Image Editor toolbox. In any case, once you have designed your icons, you are able to associate them with the ToolStripButton types via the Image property in the Properties window. Once you are happy with the ToolStrip's look and feel, handle the Click event for each ToolStripButton.

The necessary code is extremely straightforward. In the following updated MainWindow, notice that the current font size is constrained between 12 and 70:

```vb
Public Class MainWindow
  ' The current, max, and min font sizes.
  Private currFontSize As Integer = 12
  Const MinFontSize As Integer = 12
  Const MaxFontSize As Integer = 70

  Public Sub New()
    InitializeComponent()
    CenterToScreen()
    Text = String.Format("Your Font size is: {0}", currFontSize)
  End Sub

  Private Sub toolStripButtonShrinkFont_Click(ByVal sender As System.Object, _
  ByVal e As System.EventArgs) Handles toolStripButtonShrinkFont.Click
    ' Reduce font size by 5 and refresh display.
    currFontSize -= 5
    If (currFontSize <= MinFontSize) Then
      currFontSize = MinFontSize
    End If
    Text = String.Format("Your Font size is: {0}", currFontSize)
    Invalidate()
  End Sub

  Private Sub toolStripButtonGrowFont_Click(ByVal sender As System.Object, _
  ByVal e As System.EventArgs) Handles toolStripButtonGrowFont.Click
    ' Increase font size by 5 and refresh display.
    currFontSize += 5
    If (currFontSize >= MaxFontSize) Then
      currFontSize = MaxFontSize
    End If
    Text = String.Format("Your Font size is: {0}", currFontSize)
    Invalidate()
  End Sub

  Private Sub MainWindow_Paint(ByVal sender As Object, _
  ByVal e As System.Windows.Forms.PaintEventArgs) Handles Me.Paint
    ' Paint the user-defined message.
    Dim g As Graphics = e.Graphics
    g.DrawString(toolStripTextBoxMessage.Text, _
      New Font("Times New Roman", currFontSize), _
        Brushes.Black, 10, 60)
  End Sub
End Class
```

Working with ToolStripContainers

A ToolStrip, if required, can be configured to be "dockable" against any or all sides of the Form that contain it. To illustrate how you can accomplish this, right-click your current ToolStrip using the designer and select the Embed in ToolStripContainer menu option. Once you have done so, you will find that the ToolStrip has been contained within a ToolStripContainer. For this example, select the Dock Fill in Form option (see Figure 21-25).

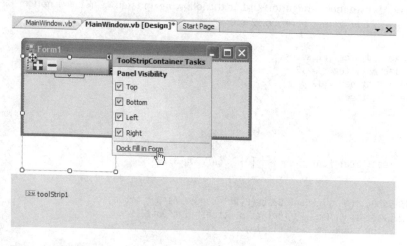

Figure 21-25. *Docking the* ToolStripContainer *within the entire Form*

If you run your current update, you will find that the ToolStrip can be moved and docked to each side of the container. However, your custom message has now vanished. The reason for this is that ToolStripContainers are actually *child controls* of the Form. Therefore, the graphical render is still taking place, but the output is being hidden by the container that now sits on top of the Form's client area.

To fix this problem, you will need to handle the Paint event on the ToolStripContainer rather than on the Form. First, handle the Paint event for the ToolStripContainer and move the rendering code from the existing Form's Paint event handler into the container's Paint event handler (and delete the Form's Paint handler when finished). Finally, you will need to replace each occurrence of the call to the Form's Invalidate() method to the container's Invalidate() method. Here are the relevant code updates:

```
Public Class MainWindow
...
  Private Sub ContentPanel_Paint(ByVal sender As System.Object, _
  ByVal e As System.Windows.Forms.PaintEventArgs) _
  Handles toolStripContainer1.ContentPanel.Paint
    ' Paint the user-defined message.
    Dim g As Graphics = e.Graphics
    g.DrawString(toolStripTextBoxMessage.Text, _
      New Font("Times New Roman", currFontSize), _
      Brushes.Black, 10, 60)
  End Sub

  Private Sub toolStripButtonShrinkFont_Click(ByVal sender As System.Object, _
  ByVal e As System.EventArgs) Handles toolStripButtonShrinkFont.Click
...
    toolStripContainer1.Invalidate(True)
  End Sub
```

```
Private Sub toolStripButtonGrowFont_Click(ByVal sender As System.Object, _
ByVal e As System.EventArgs) Handles toolStripButtonGrowFont.Click
...
    toolStripContainer1.Invalidate(True)
  End Sub
End Class
```

Of course, the `ToolStripContainer` can be configured in various ways to tweak how it operates. I leave it to you to check out the .NET Framework 2.0 SDK documentation for complete details. Figure 21-26 shows the completed project.

Figure 21-26. *ToolStripApp, now with a dockable* `ToolStrip`

■**Source Code** The ToolStripApp project is included under the Chapter 21 subdirectory.

Building an MDI Application

To wrap up our initial look at Windows Forms, I'll close this chapter by discussing how to configure a Form to function as a parent to any number of child windows (i.e., an MDI container). MDI applications allow users to have multiple child windows open at the same time within the same topmost window. In the world of MDIs, each window represents a given "document" of the application. For example, Visual Studio 2005 is an MDI application in that you are able to have multiple documents open from within an instance of the application.

When you are building MDI applications using Windows Forms, your first task is to (of course) create a brand-new Windows application. The initial Form of the application typically hosts a menu system that allows you to create new documents (such as File ➤ New) as well as arrange existing open windows (cascade, vertical tile, and horizontal tile).

Creating the child windows is interesting, as you typically define a prototypical Form that functions as a basis for each child window. Given that Forms are class types, any private data defined in the child Form will be unique to a particular instance. For example, if you were to create an MDI word processing application, you might create a child Form that maintains a `StringBuilder` to represent the text. If a user created five new child windows, each Form would maintain its own `StringBuilder` instance, which could be individually manipulated.

Additionally, MDI applications allow you to *merge menus*. As mentioned previously, parent windows typically have a menu system that allows the user to spawn and organize additional child windows. However, what if the child window also maintains a menuing system? If the user maximizes a particular child window, you need to merge the child's menu system within the parent Form to allow the user to activate items from each menu system. The Windows Forms namespace defines a number of properties, methods, and events that allow you to programmatically merge menu systems. In addition, there is a "default merge" system, which works in a good number of cases.

Building the Parent Form

To illustrate the basics of building an MDI application, begin by creating a brand-new Windows application named SimpleMdiApp. Almost all of the MDI infrastructure can be assigned to your initial Form using various design-time tools. To begin, locate the IsMdiContainer property in the Properties window and set it to true. If you look at the design-time Form, you'll see that the client area has been modified to visually represent a container of child windows.

Next, place a new MenuStrip control on your main Form. This menu specifies three topmost items named File, Window, and Arrange Windows. The File menu contains two subitems named New and Exit. The Window menu does not contain any subitems, because you will programmatically add new items as the user creates additional child windows. Finally, the Arrange Window menu defines three subitems named Cascade, Vertical, and Horizontal.

Once you have created the menu UI, handle the Click event for the Exit, New, Cascade, Vertical, and Horizontal menu items (remember, the Window menu does not have any subitems just yet). You'll implement the File ➤ New handler in the next section, but for now here is the code behind the remaining menu selections:

```
' Handle File | Exit event and arrange all child windows.
Private Sub exitToolStripMenuItem_Click(ByVal sender As System.Object, _
  ByVal e As System.EventArgs) Handles exitToolStripMenuItem.Click
  Application.Exit()
End Sub

Private Sub cascadeToolStripMenuItem_Click(ByVal sender As System.Object, _
  ByVal e As System.EventArgs) Handles cascadeToolStripMenuItem.Click
  LayoutMdi(MdiLayout.Cascade)
End Sub

Private Sub verticalToolStripMenuItem_Click(ByVal sender As System.Object, _
  ByVal e As System.EventArgs) Handles verticalToolStripMenuItem.Click
  LayoutMdi(MdiLayout.TileVertical)
End Sub

Private Sub horizontalToolStripMenuItem_Click(ByVal sender As System.Object, _
  ByVal e As System.EventArgs) Handles horizontalToolStripMenuItem.Click
  LayoutMdi(MdiLayout.TileHorizontal)
End Sub
```

The main point of interest here is the use of the LayoutMdi() method and the corresponding MdiLayout enumeration. The code behind each menu select handler should be quite clear. When the user selects a given arrangement, you tell the parent Form to automatically reposition any and all child windows.

Before you move on to the construction of the child Form, you need to set one additional property of the MenuStrip. The MdiWindowListItem property is used to establish which topmost menu item should be used to automatically list the name of each child window as a possible menu selection. Set this property to the windowToolStripMenuItem member variable. By default, this list is the value of the child's Text property followed by a numerical suffix (i.e., Form1, Form2, Form3, etc.).

Building the Child Form

Now that you have the shell of an MDI container, you need to create an additional Form that functions as the prototype for a given child window. Begin by inserting a new Form type into your current project (using Project ➤ Add Windows Form) named ChildPrototypeForm and handle the Click event for this Form. In the generated event handler, randomly set the background color of the client area. In addition, print out the "stringified" value of the new Color object into the child's caption bar. The following logic should do the trick:

```
Public Class ChildPrototypeForm
  Private Sub ChildPrototypeForm_Click(ByVal sender As System.Object, _
  ByVal e As System.EventArgs) Handles MyBase.Click
    ' Get three random numbers
    Dim r, g, b As Integer
    Dim ran As Random = New Random()
    r = ran.Next(0, 255)
    g = ran.Next(0, 255)
    b = ran.Next(0, 255)

    ' Now create a color for the background.
    Dim currColor As Color = Color.FromArgb(r, g, b)
    Me.BackColor = currColor
    Me.Text = currColor.ToString()
  End Sub
End Class
```

Spawning Child Windows

Your final order of business is to flesh out the details behind the parent Form's File ➤ New event handler. Now that you have defined a child Form, the logic is simple: create and show a new instance of the ChildPrototypeForm type. As well, you need to set the value of the child Form's MdiParent property to point to the containing Form (in this case, your main window). Here is the update:

```
Private Sub newToolStripMenuItem_Click(ByVal sender As System.Object, _
  ByVal e As System.EventArgs) Handles newToolStripMenuItem.Click
  ' Make a new child window.
  Dim newChild As ChildPrototypeForm = New ChildPrototypeForm()

  ' Set the Parent Form of the Child window.
  newChild.MdiParent = Me

  ' Display the new form.
  newChild.Show()
End Sub
```

■**Note** A child Form may access the MdiParent property directly whenever it needs to manipulate (or communicate with) its parent window.

To take this application out for a test drive, begin by creating a set of new child windows and click each one to establish a unique background color. If you examine the subitems under the Windows menu, you should see each child Form present and accounted for. As well, if you access the Arrange Window menu items, you can instruct the parent Form to vertically tile, horizontally tile, or cascade the child Forms. Figure 21-27 shows the completed application.

Figure 21-27. *An MDI application*

■**Source Code** The SimpleMdiApp project can be found under the Chapter 21 subdirectory.

Summary

This chapter introduced the fine art of building a UI with the types contained in the System.Windows.Forms namespace. You began by building a number of applications by hand, and you learned along the way that at a minimum, a GUI application needs a class that derives from Form and a Main() method that invokes Application.Run().

During the course of this chapter, you learned how to build topmost menus (and pop-up menus) and how to respond to a number of menu events. You also came to understand how to further enhance your Form types using toolbars and status bars. As you have seen, .NET 2.0 prefers to build such UI elements using MenuStrips, ToolStrips, and StatusStrips rather than the older .NET 1.x MainMenu, ToolBar, and StatusBar types (although these deprecated types are still supported). Finally, this chapter wrapped up by illustrating how to construct MDI applications using Windows Forms.

CHAPTER 22

■ ■ ■

Rendering Graphical Data with GDI+

The previous chapter introduced you to the process of building a GUI-based desktop application using System.Windows.Forms. The point of this chapter is to examine the details of rendering graphics (including stylized text and image data) onto a Form's surface area. We'll begin by taking a high-level look at the numerous drawing-related namespaces, and we'll examine the role of the Paint event and the almighty Graphics object.

The remainder of this chapter covers how to manipulate colors, fonts, geometric shapes, and graphical images. This chapter also explores a number of rendering-centric programming techniques, such as nonrectangular hit testing, drag-and-drop logic, and the .NET resource format. While *technically* not part of GDI+ proper, resources often involve the manipulation of graphical data (which, in my opinion, is "GDI+ enough" to be presented here).

■**Note** If you are a web programmer by trade, you may think that GDI+ is of no use to you. However, GDI+ is not limited to traditional desktop applications and is extremely relevant for web applications.

A Survey of the GDI+ Namespaces

The .NET platform provides a number of namespaces devoted to two-dimensional graphical rendering. In addition to the basic functionality you would expect to find in a graphics toolkit (colors, fonts, pens, brushes, etc.), you also find types that enable geometric transformations, antialiasing, palette blending, and document printing support. Collectively speaking, these namespaces make up the .NET facility we call *GDI+*, which is a managed alternative to the Win32 Graphical Device Interface (GDI) API. Table 22-1 gives a high-level view of the core GDI+ namespaces.

Table 22-1. *Core GDI+ Namespaces*

Namespace	Meaning in Life
System.Drawing	This is the core GDI+ namespace that defines numerous types for basic rendering (fonts, pens, basic brushes, etc.) as well as the almighty Graphics type.
System.Drawing.Drawing2D	This namespace provides types used for more advanced two-dimensional/vector graphics functionality (e.g., gradient brushes, pen caps, geometric transforms, etc.).
System.Drawing.Imaging	This namespace defines types that allow you to manipulate graphical images (e.g., change the palette, extract image metadata, manipulate metafiles, etc.).
System.Drawing.Printing	This namespace defines types that allow you to render images to the printed page, interact with the printer itself, and format the overall appearance of a given print job.
System.Drawing.Text	This namespace allows you to manipulate collections of fonts.

■**Note** All of the GDI+ namespaces are defined within the System.Drawing.dll assembly. While many Visual Studio 2005 project types automatically set a reference to this code library, you can manually reference System.Drawing.dll using the Add References dialog box if necessary.

An Overview of the System.Drawing Namespace

The vast majority of the types you'll use when programming GDI+ applications are found within the System.Drawing namespace. As you would expect, there are classes that represent images, brushes, pens, and fonts. Furthermore, System.Drawing defines a number of related utility types such as Color, Point, and Rectangle. Table 22-2 lists some (but not all) of the core types.

Table 22-2. *Core Types of the* System.Drawing *Namespace*

Type	Meaning in Life
Bitmap	This type encapsulates image data (*.bmp or otherwise).
Brush Brushes SolidBrush SystemBrushes TextureBrush	Brush objects are used to fill the interiors of graphical shapes such as rectangles, ellipses, and polygons.
BufferedGraphics	This new .NET 2.0 type provides a graphics buffer for double buffering, which is used to reduce or eliminate flicker caused by redrawing a display surface.
Color SystemColors	The Color and SystemColors types define a number of shared read-only properties used to obtain specific colors for the construction of various pens/brushes.
Font FontFamily	The Font type encapsulates the characteristics of a given font (i.e., type name, bold, italic, point size, etc.). FontFamily provides an abstraction for a group of fonts having a similar design but with certain variations in style.
Graphics	This core class represents a valid drawing surface, as well as a number of methods to render text, images, and geometric patterns.
Icon SystemIcons	These classes represent custom icons, as well as the set of standard system-supplied icons.

Type	Meaning in Life
Image ImageAnimator	Image is an abstract base class that provides functionality for the Bitmap, Icon, and Cursor types. ImageAnimator provides a way to iterate over a number of Image-derived types at some specified interval.
Pen Pens SystemPens	Pens are objects used to draw lines and curves. The Pens type defines a number of shared properties that return a new Pen of a given color.
Point PointF	These structures represent an (x, y) coordinate mapping to an underlying integer or float, respectively.
Rectangle RectangleF	These structures represent a rectangular dimension (again mapping to an underlying integer or float).
Size SizeF	These structures represent a given height/width (again mapping to an underlying integer or float).
StringFormat	This type is used to encapsulate various features of textual layout (i.e., alignment, line spacing, etc.).
Region	This type describes the interior of a geometric image composed of rectangles and paths.

The System.Drawing Utility Types

Many of the drawing methods defined by the System.Drawing.Graphics object require you to specify the position or area in which you wish to render a given item. For example, the DrawString() method requires you to specify the location to render the text string on the Control-derived type. Given that DrawString() has been overloaded a number of times, this positional parameter may be specified using an (x, y) coordinate or the dimensions of a "box" to draw within. Other GDI+ type methods may require you to specify the width and height of a given item, or the internal bounds of a geometric region.

To specify such information, the System.Drawing namespace defines the Point, Rectangle, Region, and Size types. Obviously, a Point represents an (x, y) coordinate. Rectangle types capture a pair of points representing the upper-left and bottom-right bounds of a rectangular region. Size types are similar to Rectangles, but this structure represents a particular dimension using a given length and width. Finally, Regions provide a way to represent and qualify nonrectangular surfaces.

The member variables used by the Point, Rectangle, and Size types are internally represented as an integer data type. If you need a finer level of granularity, you are free to make use of the corresponding PointF, RectangleF, and SizeF types, which (as you might guess) map to an underlying float. Regardless of the underlying data representation, each type has an identical set of members, including a number of overloaded operators.

The Point and PointF Types

The first utility types you should be aware of are Point and PointF, which define a number of helpful members, including

- +, -, =, <>: The Point type overloads various VB 2005 operators.
- X, Y: These members provide access to the underlying (x, y) values of the Point.
- IsEmpty: This member returns true if x and y are both set to 0.

To illustrate working with the GDI+ utility types, here is a console application (named DrawingUtilTypes) that makes use of the System.Drawing.Point type (be sure to set a reference to System.Drawing.dll, as this is not done automatically when building console projects).

```
Imports System.Drawing

Module Program
  Sub Main()
    Console.WriteLine("***** Working with Drawing-centric util types *****")
    Console.WriteLine()
    Console.WriteLine("***** Exercise Point type *****")

    ' Create and offset a point.
    Dim pt As Point = New Point(100, 72)
    Console.WriteLine(pt)
    pt.Offset(20, 20)
    Console.WriteLine(pt)

    ' Overloaded Point operators.
    Dim pt2 As Point = pt
    If pt = pt2 Then
      Console.WriteLine("Points are the same")
    Else
      Console.WriteLine("Different points")
    End If

    ' Change pt2's X value.
    pt2.X = 4000

    ' Now show each point's value
    Console.WriteLine("First point: {0}", pt)
    Console.WriteLine("Second point: {0}", pt2)
    Console.ReadLine()
  End Sub
End Module
```

The Rectangle and RectangleF Types

Rectangles, like Points, are useful in many applications (GUI based or otherwise). One of the more useful methods of the Rectangle type is Contains(). This method allows you to determine whether a given Point or Rectangle is within the current bounds of another object. Later in this chapter, you'll see how to make use of this method to perform hit testing of GDI+ images. Until then, here is a simple example:

```
Sub Main()
...
  Console.WriteLine("***** Point in Rect? *****")
  Dim r1 As Rectangle = New Rectangle(0, 0, 100, 100)
  Dim pt3 As Point = New Point(101, 101)
  If r1.Contains(pt3) Then
    Console.WriteLine("Point is within the rect!")
  Else
    Console.WriteLine("Point is not within the rect!")
  End If

  ' Now place point in rectangle's area.
  pt3.X = 50
  pt3.Y = 30
  If r1.Contains(pt3) Then
    Console.WriteLine("Point is within the rect!")
```

```
   Else
      Console.WriteLine("Point is not within the rect!")
   End If
   Console.ReadLine()
End Sub
```

The Region Class

The Region type represents the interior of a geometric shape. Given this last statement, it should make sense that the constructors of the Region class require you to send an instance of some existing geometric pattern. For example, assume you have created a 100×100-pixel rectangle. If you wish to gain access to the rectangle's interior region, you could write the following:

```
' Get the interior of this rectangle.
Dim r As Rectangle = New Rectangle(0, 0, 100, 100)
Dim rgn As Region = New Region(r)
```

Once you have the interior dimensions of a given shape, you may manipulate it using various members such as the following:

- Complement(): Updates this Region to the portion of the specified graphics object that does not intersect with this Region

- Exclude(): Updates this Region to the portion of its interior that does not intersect with the specified graphics object

- GetBounds(): Returns a Rectangle that represents a rectangular region that bounds this Region

- Intersect(): Updates this Region to the intersection of itself with the specified graphics object

- Transform(): Transforms a Region by the specified Matrix object

- Union(): Updates this Region to the union of itself and the specified graphics object

- Translate(): Offsets the coordinates of this Region by a specified amount

I'm sure you get the general idea behind these coordinate primitives; please consult the .NET Framework 2.0 SDK documentation if you require further details.

■**Note** The Size and SizeF types require little comment. These types each define Height and Width properties and a handful of overloaded operators.

■**Source Code** The DrawingUtilTypes project is included under the Chapter 22 subdirectory.

Understanding the Graphics Class

The System.Drawing.Graphics class is the gateway to GDI+ rendering functionality. This class not only represents the surface you wish to draw upon (such as a Form's surface, a control's surface, or region of memory), but also defines dozens of members that allow you to render text, images (icons, bitmaps, etc.), and numerous geometric patterns. Table 22-3 gives a partial list of members.

Table 22-3. *Members of the* Graphics *Class*

Methods	Meaning in Life
FromHdc() FromHwnd() FromImage()	These shared methods provide a way to obtain a valid Graphics object from a given image (e.g., icon, bitmap, etc.) or GUI widget.
Clear()	Fills a Graphics object with a specified color, erasing the current drawing surface in the process.
DrawArc() DrawBezier() DrawBeziers() DrawCurve() DrawEllipse() DrawIcon() DrawLine() DrawLines() DrawPie() DrawPath() DrawRectangle() DrawRectangles() DrawString()	These methods are used to render a given image or geometric pattern. As you will see, DrawXXX() methods require the use of GDI+ Pen objects.
FillEllipse() FillPath() FillPie() FillPolygon() FillRectangle()	These methods are used to fill the interior of a given geometric shape. As you will see, FillXXX() methods require the use of GDI+ Brush objects.

As well as providing a number of rendering methods, the Graphics class defines additional members that allow you to configure the "state" of the Graphics object. By assigning values to the properties shown in Table 22-4, you are able to alter the current rendering operation.

Table 22-4. *Stateful Properties of the* Graphics *Class*

Properties	Meaning in Life
Clip ClipBounds VisibleClipBounds IsClipEmpty IsVisibleClipEmpty	These properties allow you to set the clipping options used with the current Graphics object.
Transform	This property allows you to transform "world coordinates" (more details on this later).
PageUnit PageScale DpiX DpiY	These properties allow you to configure the point of origin for your rendering operations, as well as the unit of measurement.
SmoothingMode PixelOffsetMode TextRenderingHint	These properties allow you to configure the smoothness of geometric objects and text.
CompositingMode	This property determines whether drawing overwrites the background or is blended with the background.
InterpolationMode	This property specifies how data is interpolated between end points.

■Note As of .NET 2.0, the System.Drawing namespace provides a BufferedGraphics type that allows you to render graphics using a double-buffering system to minimize or eliminate the flickering that can occur during a rendering operation. Consult the .NET Framework 2.0 SDK documentation for full details.

Now, despite what you may be thinking, the Graphics class is not directly creatable via the New keyword, as there are no publicly defined constructors. How, then, do you obtain a valid Graphics object? Glad you asked.

Understanding Paint Sessions

The most common way to obtain a Graphics object is to interact with the Paint event. Recall from the previous chapter that the Control class defines a virtual method named OnPaint(). When you want a Form to render graphical data to its surface, you may override this method and extract a Graphics object from the incoming PaintEventArgs parameter. To illustrate, create a new Windows Forms application named BasicPaintForm, and update the Form-derived class as follows:

```
Public Class MainForm
  Sub New()
    ' This call is required by the Windows Forms designer.
    InitializeComponent()

    ' Add any initialization after the InitializeComponent() call.
    CenterToScreen()
  End Sub

  Protected Overrides Sub OnPaint(ByVal e As System.Windows.Forms.PaintEventArgs)
    ' If overriding OnPaint(), be sure to call base class implementation.
    MyBase.OnPaint(e)

    ' Obtain a Graphics object from the incoming
    ' PaintEventArgs.
    Dim g As Graphics = e.Graphics

    ' Render a textual message in a given font and color.
    g.DrawString("Hello GDI+", New Font("Times New Roman", 20), _
            Brushes.Green, 0, 0)
  End Sub
End Class
```

While overriding OnPaint() is permissible, it is more common to handle the Paint event using the associated PaintEventHandler delegate (in fact, this is the default behavior taken by Visual Studio 2005 when handling events with the Properties window). This delegate can point to any method taking a System.Object as the first parameter and a PaintEventArgs as the second. Assuming you have handled the Paint event, you are once again able to extract a Graphics object from the incoming PaintEventArgs. Here is the update:

```
Public Class MainForm
  Sub New()
    ' This call is required by the Windows Forms designer.
    InitializeComponent()
```

```
        ' Add any initialization after the InitializeComponent() call.
        CenterToScreen()
    End Sub

    Private Sub MainForm_Paint(ByVal sender As System.Object, _
    ByVal e As System.Windows.Forms.PaintEventArgs) Handles MyBase.Paint
        ' Obtain a Graphics object from the incoming
        ' PaintEventArgs.
        Dim g As Graphics = e.Graphics

        ' Render a textual message in a given font and color.
        g.DrawString("Hello GDI+", New Font("Times New Roman", 20), _
                Brushes.Green, 0, 0)
    End Sub
End Class
```

Regardless of how you respond to the Paint event, be aware that whenever a window becomes "dirty," the Paint event will fire. As you may be aware, a window is considered "dirty" whenever it is resized, uncovered by another window (partially or completely), or minimized and then restored. In all these cases, the .NET platform ensures that when your Form needs to be redrawn, the Paint event handler (or overridden OnPaint() method) is called automatically.

Invalidating the Form's Client Area

During the flow of a GDI+ application, you may need to explicitly fire the Paint event, rather than waiting for the window to become "naturally dirty." For example, you may be building a program that allows the user to select from a number of bitmap images using a custom dialog box. Once the dialog box is dismissed, you need to draw the newly selected image onto the Form's client area. Obviously, if you waited for the window to become "naturally dirty," the user would not see the change take place until the window was resized or uncovered by another window. To force a window to repaint itself programmatically, simply call the inherited Invalidate() method:

```
Public Class MainForm
...
    Private Sub MainForm_Paint(ByVal sender As System.Object, _
    ByVal e As System.Windows.Forms.PaintEventArgs) Handles MyBase.Paint
        Dim g As Graphics = e.Graphics
        ' Render a bitmap here...
    End Sub

    Private Sub RenderMyBitmap()
        ' Assume we have code here to load
        ' a bitmap from disk...
        Invalidate() ' Fires Paint event!
    End Sub
End Class
```

The Invalidate() method has been overloaded a number of times to allow you to specify a specific rectangular region to repaint, rather than repainting the entire client area (which is the default). If you wish to only update the extreme upper-left rectangle of the client area, you could write the following:

```
' Repaint a given rectangular area of the Form.
Private Sub UpdateUpperArea()
    Dim myRect As Rectangle = New Rectangle(0, 0, 75, 150)
    Invalidate(myRect)
End Sub
```

Obtaining a Graphics Object Outside of a Paint Event Handler

In some cases, you may need to access a Graphics object *outside* the scope of a Paint event handler. For example, assume you wish to draw a small circle at the (*x*, *y*) position where the mouse has been clicked. To obtain a valid Graphics object from within the scope of a MouseDown event handler, one approach is to call the shared Graphics.FromHwnd() method. Based on your background in Win32 development, you may know that an HWND is a data structure that represents a given Win32 window. Under the .NET platform, the inherited Handle property extracts the underlying HWND, which can be used as a parameter to Graphics.FromHwnd():

```
Private Sub MainForm_MouseDown(ByVal sender As System.Object, _
   ByVal e As System.Windows.Forms.MouseEventArgs) Handles MyBase.MouseDown
   ' Grab a Graphics object via Hwnd.
   Dim g As Graphics = Graphics.FromHwnd(Me.Handle)

   ' Now draw a 10*10 circle at mouse click.
   g.FillEllipse(Brushes.Firebrick, e.X, e.Y, 10, 10)

   ' Dispose of all Graphics objects you create directly.
   g.Dispose()
End Sub
```

While this logic renders a circle outside an OnPaint() event handler, it is very important to understand that when the form is invalidated (and thus redrawn), each of the circles is erased! This should make sense, given that this rendering happens only within the context of a MouseDown event. A far better approach is to have the MouseDown event handler create a new Point type, which is then added to an internal collection (such as a generic List(Of T)), followed by a call to Invalidate(). At this point, the Paint event handler can simply iterate over the collection and draw each Point:

```
Public Class MainForm
   ' Used to hold all the Points.
   Private myPts As New List(Of Point)
...
   Private Sub MainForm_Paint(ByVal sender As System.Object, _
      ByVal e As System.Windows.Forms.PaintEventArgs) Handles MyBase.Paint
      Dim g As Graphics = e.Graphics
      g.DrawString("Hello GDI+", New Font("Times New Roman", 20), _
               Brushes.Green, 0, 0)

      ' Now render all the Points.
      For Each p As Point In myPts
         g.FillEllipse(Brushes.DarkOrange, p.X, p.Y, 10, 10)
      Next
   End Sub

   Private Sub MainForm_MouseDown(ByVal sender As System.Object, _
   ByVal e As System.Windows.Forms.MouseEventArgs) Handles MyBase.MouseDown
      ' Add new point to list.
      myPts.Add(New Point(e.X, e.Y))
      Invalidate()
   End Sub
End Class
```

Using this approach, the rendered circles are always present and accounted for, as the graphical rendering has been handled within the Paint event. Figure 22-1 shows a test run of this initial GDI+ application.

Figure 22-1. *A simple painting application*

■**Source Code** The BasicPaintForm project is included under the Chapter 22 subdirectory.

Regarding the Disposal of a Graphics Object

If you were reading closely over the last several pages, you may have noticed that *some* of the sample code directly called the Dispose() method of the Graphics object, while other sample code did not. Given that a Graphics type is manipulating various underlying unmanaged resources, it should make sense that it would be advantageous to release said resources via Dispose() as soon as possible (rather than via the garbage collector in the finalization process). The same can be said for any type that supports the IDisposable interface. When working with GDI+ Graphics objects, remember the following rules of thumb:

- If you directly create a Graphics object, dispose of it when you are finished.

- If you reference an existing Graphics object, do *not* dispose of it.

To clarify, consider the following Paint event handler:

```
Private Sub MainForm_Paint(ByVal sender As System.Object, _
  ByVal e As System.Windows.Forms.PaintEventArgs) Handles MyBase.Paint
  ' Load a local *.jpg file.
  Dim myImageFile As Image = Image.FromFile("landscape.jpg")

  ' Create new Graphics object based on the image.
  Dim imgGraphics As Graphics = Graphics.FromImage(myImageFile)

  ' Render new data onto the image.
  imgGraphics.FillEllipse(Brushes.DarkOrange, 50, 50, 150, 150)

  ' Draw image to Form.
  Dim g As Graphics = e.Graphics
  g.DrawImage(myImageFile, New Point(0, 0))

  ' Release Graphics object we created.
  imgGraphics.Dispose()
End Sub
```

Now at this point in the chapter, don't become concerned if some of this GDI+ logic looks a bit foreign. However, notice that you are obtaining a Graphics object from a *.jpg file loaded from the local application directory (via the shared Graphics.FromImage() method). Because you have explicitly created this Graphics object, best practice states that you should Dispose() of the object when you have finished making use of it, to free up the internal resources for use by other parts of the system.

However, notice that you did not explicitly call Dispose() on the Graphics object you obtained from the incoming PaintEventArgs. This is due to the fact that you did not directly create the object and cannot ensure other parts of the program are making use of it. Clearly, it would be a problem if you released a Graphics object used elsewhere!

On a related note, recall from our examination of the .NET garbage collector in Chapter 8 that if you do forget to call Dispose() on a method implementing IDisposable, the internal resources will eventually be freed when the object is garbage collected at a later time. In this light, the manual disposal of the imgGraphics object is not technically necessary. Although explicitly disposing of GDI+ objects you directly created is smart programming, in order to keep the code examples in this chapter crisp, I will not manually dispose of each GDI+ type and allow the garbage collector to reclaim the underlying memory.

The GDI+ Coordinate Systems

Our next task is to examine the underlying coordinate system. GDI+ defines three distinct coordinate systems, which are used by the runtime to determine the location and size of the content to be rendered. First we have what are known as *world coordinates*. World coordinates represent an abstraction of the size of a given GDI+ type, irrespective of the unit of measurement. For example, if you draw a rectangle using the dimensions (0, 0, 100, 100), you have specified a rectangle 100×100 "things" in size. As you may guess, the default "thing" is a pixel; however, it can be configured to be another unit of measure (inch, centimeter, etc.).

Next, we have *page coordinates*. Page coordinates represent an offset applied to the original world coordinates. This is helpful in that you are not the one in charge of manually applying offsets in your code (should you need them). For example, if you have a Form that needs to maintain a 100×100-pixel border, you can specify a (100*100) page coordinate to allow all rending to begin at point (100*100). In your code base, however, you are able to specify simple world coordinates (thereby avoiding the need to manually calculate the offset).

Finally, we have *device coordinates*. Device coordinates represent the result of applying page coordinates to the original world coordinates. This coordinate system is used to determine exactly where the GDI+ type will be rendered. When you are programming with GDI+, you will typically think in terms of world coordinates, which are the baselines used to determine the size and location of a GDI+ type. To render in world coordinates requires no special coding actions—simply pass in the dimensions for the current rendering operation:

```
Private Sub MainForm_Paint(ByVal sender As System.Object, _
  ByVal e As System.Windows.Forms.PaintEventArgs) _
  Handles MyBase.Paint
  Dim g As Graphics = e.Graphics

  ' Render a rectangle in world coordinates.
  g.DrawRectangle(Pens.Black, 10, 10, 100, 100)
End Sub
```

Under the hood, your world coordinates are automatically mapped in terms of page coordinates, which are then mapped into device coordinates. In many cases, you will never directly make use of page or device coordinates unless you wish to apply some sort of graphical transformation. Given that the previous code did not specify any transformational logic, the world, page, and device coordinates are identical.

If you do wish to apply various transformations before rendering your GDI+ logic, you will make use of various members of the Graphics type (such as the TranslateTransform() method) to specify various "page coordinates" to your existing world coordinate system before the rendering operation. The result is the set of device coordinates that will be used to render the GDI+ type to the target device:

```
Private Sub MainForm_Paint(ByVal sender As System.Object, _
  ByVal e As System.Windows.Forms.PaintEventArgs) _
  Handles MyBase.Paint
  Dim g As Graphics = e.Graphics
  ' Specify page coordinate offsets (10 * 10).
  g.TranslateTransform(10, 10)
  g.DrawRectangle(10, 10, 100, 100)
End Sub
```

In this case, the rectangle is actually rendered with a top-left point of (20, 20), given that the world coordinates have been offset by the call to TranslateTransform().

The Default Unit of Measure

Under GDI+, the default unit of measure is pixel based. The origin begins in the upper-left corner with the x-axis increasing to the right and the y-axis increasing downward (see Figure 22-2).

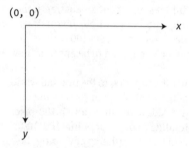

Figure 22-2. *The default coordinate system of GDI+*

Thus, if you render a Rectangle using a 5-pixel thick red pen as follows:

```
Private Sub MainForm_Paint(ByVal sender As System.Object, _
  ByVal e As System.Windows.Forms.PaintEventArgs) _
  Handles MyBase.Paint
  Dim g As Graphics = e.Graphics
  ' Set up world coordinates using the default unit of measure.
  g.DrawRectangle(New Pen(Color.Red, 5), 0, 0, 100, 100)
End Sub
```

you would see a square rendered starting on the top-left client edge of the Form, as shown in Figure 22-3.

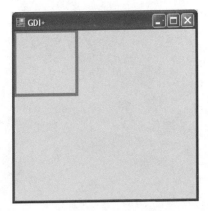

Figure 22-3. *Rendering via pixel units*

Specifying an Alternative Unit of Measure

If you do not wish to render images using a pixel-based unit of measure, you are able to change this default setting by setting the PageUnit property of the Graphics object to alter the units used by the page coordinate system. The PageUnit property can be assigned any member of the GraphicsUnit enumeration:

```
Enum GraphicsUnit
  ' Specifies world coordinates.
  World
  ' Pixels for video displays and 1/100 inch for printers.
  Display
  ' Specifies a pixel.
  Pixel
  ' Specifies a printer's point (1/72 inch).
  Point
  ' Specifies an inch.
  Inch
  ' Specifies a document unit (1/300 inch).
  Document
  ' Specifies a millimeter.
  Millimeter
End Sub
```

To illustrate how to change the underlying GraphicsUnit, update the previous rendering code as follows:

```
Private Sub MainForm_Paint(ByVal sender As System.Object, _
  ByVal e As System.Windows.Forms.PaintEventArgs) _
  Handles MyBase.Paint
  ' Draw a rectangle in inches...not pixels.
  Dim g As Graphics = e.Graphics
  g.PageUnit = GraphicsUnit.Inch
  ' Set up world coordinates using the default unit of measure.
  g.DrawRectangle(New Pen(Color.Red, 5), 0, 0, 100, 100)
End Sub
```

You would find a *radically* different rectangle, as shown in Figure 22-4.

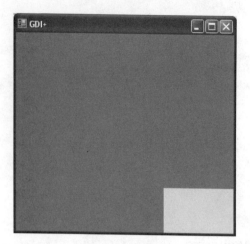

Figure 22-4. *Rendering using inch units*

The reason that 95 percent (or so) of the Form's client area is now filled with red is because you have configured a Pen with a 5-*inch* nib! The rectangle itself is 100×100 *inches* in size. In fact, the small gray box you see located in the lower-right corner is the upper-left interior of the rectangle.

Specifying an Alternative Point of Origin

Recall that when you make use of the default coordinate and measurement system, point (0, 0) is at the extreme upper left of the surface area. While this is often what you desire, what if you wish to alter the location where rendering begins? For example, let's assume that your application always needs to reserve a 100-pixel boundary around the Form's client area (for whatever reason). You need to ensure that all GDI+ operations take place somewhere within this internal region.

One approach you could take is to offset all your rendering code manually. This, of course, would be bothersome, as you would need to constantly apply some offset value to each and every rendering operation. It would be far better (and simpler) if you could set a property that says in effect, "Although *I* might say render a rectangle with a point of origin at (0, 0), make sure *you* begin at point (100, 100)." This would simplify your life a great deal, as you could continue to specify your plotting points without modification.

In GDI+, you can adjust the point of origin by setting the transformation value using the TranslateTransform() method of the Graphics class, which allows you to specify a page coordinate system that will be applied to your original world coordinate specifications, for example:

```
Private Sub MainForm_Paint(ByVal sender As System.Object, _
  ByVal e As System.Windows.Forms.PaintEventArgs) _
  Handles MyBase.Paint
  Dim g As Graphics = e.Graphics
  ' Set page coordinate to (100, 100).
  g.TranslateTransform(100, 100)

  ' World origin is still (0, 0, 100, 100),
  ' however, device origin is now (100, 100, 200, 200).
  g.DrawRectangle(New Pen(Color.Red, 5), 0, 0, 100, 100)
End Sub
```

Here, you have set the world coordinate values (0, 0, 100, 100). However, the page coordinate values have specified an offset of (100, 100). Given this, the device coordinates map to (100, 100, 200, 200). Thus, although the call to DrawRectangle() looks as if you are rendering a rectangle on the upper left of the Form, the rendering shown in Figure 22-5 has taken place.

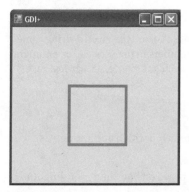

Figure 22-5. *The result of applying page offsets*

To help you experiment with some of the ways to alter the GDI+ coordinate system, this book's downloadable source code (visit the Downloads section of the Apress website at www.apress.com) provides a sample application named CoorSystem. Using two menu items, you are able to alter the point of origin as well as the unit of measurement (see Figure 22-6).

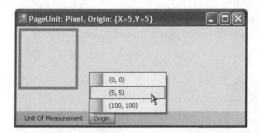

Figure 22-6. *Altering coordinate and measurement modes*

Now that you have a better understanding of the underlying transformations used to determine where to render a given GDI+ type onto a target device, the next order of business is to examine details of color manipulation.

■**Source Code** The CoorSystem project is included under the Chapter 22 subdirectory.

Defining a Color Value

Many of the rendering methods defined by the Graphics class require you to specify the color that should be used during the drawing process. The System.Drawing.Color structure represents an alpha-red-green-blue (ARGB) color constant. Most of the Color type's functionality comes by way of a number of shared read-only properties, which return a specific Color type:

```
' One of many predefined colors...
Dim c As Color = Color.PapayaWhip
```

If the default color values do not fit the bill, you are also able to create a new Color type and specify the A, R, G, and B values using the FromArgb() method:

```
' Specify ARGB manually.
Dim myColor As Color = Color.FromArgb(0, 255, 128, 64)
```

As well, using the FromName() method, you are able to generate a Color type given a string value. The characters in the string parameter must match one of the members in the KnownColor enumeration (which includes values for various Windows color elements such as KnownColor.WindowFrame and KnownColor.WindowText):

```
' Get Color from a known name.
Dim myColor As Color = Color.FromName("Red")
```

Regardless of the method you use, the Color type can be interacted with using a variety of members:

- GetBrightness(): Returns the brightness of the Color type based on hue-saturation-brightness (HSB) measurements

- GetSaturation(): Returns the saturation of the Color type based on HSB measurements

- GetHue(): Returns the hue of the Color type based on HSB measurements

- IsSystemColor: Determines whether the Color type is a registered system color

- A, R, G, B: Returns the value assigned to the alpha, red, green, and blue aspects of a Color type

The ColorDialog Class

If you wish to provide a way for the end user of your application to configure a Color type, the System.Windows.Forms namespace provides a predefined dialog box class named ColorDialog, as shown in Figure 22-7.

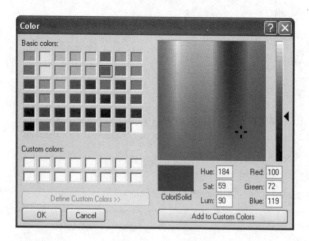

Figure 22-7. *The Windows Forms color dialog box*

Working with this dialog box is quite simple. Using a valid instance of the ColorDialog type, call ShowDialog() to display the dialog box modally. Once the user has closed the dialog box, you can extract the corresponding Color object using the ColorDialog.Color property.

Assume you wish to allow the user to configure the background color of the Form's client area using the ColorDialog. To keep things simple, you will display the ColorDialog when the user clicks anywhere on the client area:

```
Public Class MainForm
  Private colorDlg As ColorDialog
  Private currColor As Color = Color.DimGray

  Sub New()
    ' This call is required by the Windows Forms designer.
    InitializeComponent()

    ' Add any initialization after the InitializeComponent() call.
    CenterToScreen()
    colorDlg = New ColorDialog()
    Text = "Click on me to change the color"
  End Sub

  Private Sub MainForm_MouseDown(ByVal sender As System.Object, _
  ByVal e As System.Windows.Forms.MouseEventArgs) _
  Handles MyBase.MouseDown
    If colorDlg.ShowDialog() <> Windows.Forms.DialogResult.Cancel Then
      currColor = colorDlg.Color
      Me.BackColor = currColor
      ' Show current color.
      Dim strARGB As String = colorDlg.Color.ToString()
      MessageBox.Show(strARGB, "Color is:")
    End If
  End Sub
End Class
```

Source Code The ColorDlg application is included under the Chapter 22 subdirectory.

Manipulating Fonts

Next, let's examine how to programmatically manipulate fonts. The System.Drawing.Font type represents a given font installed on the user's machine. Font types can be defined using any number of overloaded constructors. Here are a few examples:

```
' Create a Font of a given type name and size.
Dim f As Font = New Font("Times New Roman", 12)

' Create a Font with a given name, size, and style set.
Dim f2 As Font = New Font("WingDings", 50, FontStyle.Bold Or FontStyle.Underline)
```

Here, f2 has been created by OR-ing together a set of values from the FontStyle enumeration:

```
Enum FontStyle
  Regular
  Bold
  Italic
  Underline
  Strikeout
End Enum
```

Once you have configured the look and feel of your Font object, the next task is to pass it as a parameter to the Graphics.DrawString() method. Although DrawString() has also been overloaded a number of times, each variation typically requires the same basic information: the text to draw, the font to draw it in, a brush used for rendering, and a location in which to place it.

```
Private Sub MainForm_Paint(ByVal sender As System.Object, _
  ByVal e As System.Windows.Forms.PaintEventArgs) _
  Handles MyBase.Paint
  Dim g As Graphics = e.Graphics

  ' Specify (String, Font, Brush, Point) as args.
  g.DrawString("My string", New Font("WingDings", 25), _
    Brushes.Black, New Point(0, 0))

  ' Specify (String, Font, Brush, Integer, Integer)
  g.DrawString("Another string", New Font("Times New Roman", 16), _
    Brushes.Red, 40, 40)
End Sub
```

Working with Font Families

The System.Drawing namespace also defines the FontFamily type, which abstracts a group of typefaces having a similar basic design but with certain style variations. A family of fonts, such as Verdana, can include several fonts that differ in style and size. For example, Verdana 12-point bold and Verdana 24-point italic are different fonts within the Verdana font family.

The constructor of the FontFamily type takes a string representing the name of the font family you are attempting to capture. Once you create the "generic family," you are then able to create a more specific Font object:

```
Private Sub MainForm_Paint(ByVal sender As System.Object, _
  ByVal e As System.Windows.Forms.PaintEventArgs) _
  Handles MyBase.Paint
  Dim g As Graphics = e.Graphics

  ' Make a family of fonts.
  Dim myFamily As FontFamily = New FontFamily("Verdana")

  ' Pass family into ctor of Font.
  Dim myFont As Font = New Font(myFamily, 12)
  g.DrawString("Hello!", myFont, Brushes.Blue, 10, 10)
End Sub
```

Of greater interest is the ability to gather statistics regarding a given family of fonts. For example, say you are building a text-processing application and wish to determine the average width of a character in a particular FontFamily. What if you wish to know the ascending and descending values for a given character? To answer such questions, the FontFamily type defines the key members shown in Table 22-5.

Table 22-5. *Members of the* FontFamily *Type*

Member	Meaning in Life
GetCellAscent()	Returns the ascender metric for the members in this family
GetCellDescent()	Returns the descender metric for members in this family
GetLineSpacing()	Returns the distance between two consecutive lines of text for this FontFamily with the specified FontStyle
GetName()	Returns the name of this FontFamily in the specified language
IsStyleAvailable()	Indicates whether the specified FontStyle is available

To illustrate, here is a `Paint` event handler that prints a number of characteristics of the Verdana font family:

```
Public Class MainForm
  Private Sub MainForm_Paint(ByVal sender As System.Object, _
  ByVal e As System.Windows.Forms.PaintEventArgs) _
  Handles MyBase.Paint
    Dim g As Graphics = e.Graphics
    Dim myFamily As FontFamily = New FontFamily("Verdana")
    Dim myFont As Font = New Font(myFamily, 12)
    Dim y As Integer = 0
    Dim fontHeight As Integer = myFont.Height

    ' Show units of measurement for FontFamily members.
    Me.Text = "Measurements are in GraphicsUnit." & myFont.Unit.ToString()
    g.DrawString("The Verdana family.", myFont, Brushes.Blue, 10, y)
    y += 20
    ' Print our family ties...
    g.DrawString("Ascent for bold Verdana: " _
      & myFamily.GetCellAscent(FontStyle.Bold), _
      myFont, Brushes.Black, 10, y + fontHeight)
    y += 20
    g.DrawString("Descent for bold Verdana: " _
      & myFamily.GetCellDescent(FontStyle.Bold), _
      myFont, Brushes.Black, 10, y + fontHeight)
    y += 20
    g.DrawString("Line spacing for bold Verdana: " _
      & myFamily.GetLineSpacing(FontStyle.Bold), _
      myFont, Brushes.Black, 10, y + fontHeight)
    y += 20
    g.DrawString("Height for bold Verdana: " & _
      myFamily.GetEmHeight(FontStyle.Bold), _
      myFont, Brushes.Black, 10, y + fontHeight)
    y += 20
  End Sub
End Class
```

Figure 22-8 shows the result.

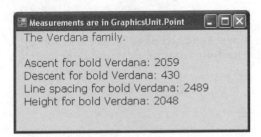

Figure 22-8. *Gathering statistics of the Verdana font family*

Note that these members of the `FontFamily` type return values using `GraphicsUnit.Point` (not `Pixel`) as the unit of measure, which corresponds to 1/72 inch. You are free to transform these values to other units of measure as you see fit.

Source Code The FontFamilyApp application is included under the Chapter 22 subdirectory.

Working with Font Faces and Font Sizes

Next, you'll build a more complex application that allows the user to manipulate a Font object main-tained by a Form. The application will allow the user to select the current font face from a predefined set using the Configure ➤ Font Face menu selection. You'll also allow the user to indirectly control the size of the Font object using a Windows Forms Timer object. If the user activates the Timer using the Configure ➤ Swell? menu item, the size of the Font object increases at a regular interval (to a maximum upper limit). In this way, the text appears to swell and thus provides an animation of "breathing" text. Finally, you'll use a final menu item under the Configure menu named List All Fonts, which will be used to list all fonts installed on the end user's machine. Figure 22-9 shows the menu UI logic (notice that this Form maintains a Timer member variable that has been named swellTimer).

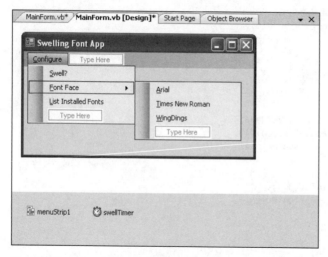

Figure 22-9. *Menu layout (and* Timer) *of the FontApp project*

To begin implementing the application, update the Form with a Timer member variable (named swellTimer), a string (strFontFace) to represent the current font face, and an Integer (swellValue) to represent the amount to adjust the font size. Within the Form's constructor, configure the Timer to emit a Tick event every 100 milliseconds:

```vb
Public Class MainForm
  Private swellValue As Integer
  Private strFontFace As String = "WingDings"

  Sub New()
    ' This call is required by the Windows Forms designer.
    InitializeComponent()

    ' Add any initialization after the InitializeComponent() call.
    BackColor = Color.Honeydew
    CenterToScreen()
    ' Configure the Timer.
    swellTimer.Enabled = True
```

```
      swellTimer.Interval = 100
    End Sub
End Class
```

Now, handle the Tick event, and within the generated handler, increase the value of the swellValue data member by 5. Recall that the swellValue integer will be added to the current font size to provide a simple animation (assume swellValue has a maximum upper limit of 50). To help reduce the flicker that can occur when redrawing the entire client area, notice how the call to Invalidate() is only refreshing the upper rectangular area of the Form:

```
Private Sub swellTimer_Tick(ByVal sender As System.Object, _
  ByVal e As System.EventArgs) Handles swellTimer.Tick
  ' Increase current swellValue by 5.
  swellValue += 5
  ' If this value is greater than or equal to 50, reset to zero.
  If swellValue >= 50 Then
    swellValue = 0
  End If
  ' Just invalidate the 'minimal dirty rectangle' to help reduce flicker.
  Invalidate(New Rectangle(0, 0, ClientRectangle.Width, 100))
End Sub
```

Now that the upper 100 pixels of your client area are refreshed with each tick of the Timer, you had better have something to render! In the Form's Paint handler, create a Font object based on the user-defined font face (as selected from the appropriate menu item) and current swellValue (as dictated by the Timer). Once you have your Font object fully configured, render a message into the center of the dirty rectangle:

```
Private Sub MainForm_Paint(ByVal sender As System.Object, _
  ByVal e As System.Windows.Forms.PaintEventArgs) _
  Handles MyBase.Paint
  Dim g As Graphics = e.Graphics
  Dim theFont As Font = New Font(strFontFace, 12 + swellValue)
  Dim message As String = "Hello GDI+"

  ' Display message in the center of the window!
  Dim windowCenter As Single = CSng(Me.DisplayRectangle.Width / 2)
  Dim stringSize As SizeF = e.Graphics.MeasureString(message, theFont)
  Dim startPos As Single = windowCenter - (stringSize.Width / 2)
  g.DrawString(message, theFont, Brushes.Blue, startPos, 10)
End Sub
```

As you would guess, if a user selects a specific font face, the Clicked handler for each menu selection is in charge of updating the fontFace string variable and invalidating the client area, for example:

```
Private Sub arialToolStripMenuItem_Click(ByVal sender As System.Object, _
  ByVal e As System.EventArgs) Handles arialToolStripMenuItem.Click
  strFontFace = "Arial"
  Invalidate()
End Sub
```

The Click menu handler for the Swell menu item will be used to allow the user to stop or start the swelling of the text (i.e., enable or disable the animation). To do so, toggle the Enabled property of the Timer as follows:

```
Private Sub swellToolStripMenuItem_Click(ByVal sender As System.Object, _
  ByVal e As System.EventArgs) Handles swellToolStripMenuItem.Click
  swellTimer.Enabled = Not swellTimer.Enabled
End Sub
```

Enumerating Installed Fonts

Next, let's expand this program to display the set of installed fonts on the target machine using types within System.Drawing.Text. This namespace contains a handful of types that can be used to discover and manipulate the set of fonts installed on the target machine. For our purposes, we are only concerned with the InstalledFontCollection class.

When the user selects the Configure ➤ List Installed Fonts menu item, the corresponding Clicked handler creates an instance of the InstalledFontCollection class. This class maintains an array named FontFamily, which represents the set of all fonts on the target machine and may be obtained using the InstalledFontCollection.Families property. Using the FontFamily.Name property, you are able to extract the font face (e.g., Times New Roman, Arial, etc.) for each font.

Add a private String data member to your Form named installedFonts to hold each font face. The logic in the List Installed Fonts menu handler creates an instance of the InstalledFontCollection type, reads the name of each string, and adds the new font face to the private installedFonts data member:

```
' Need this!
Imports System.Drawing.Text

Class MainForm
' Holds the list of fonts.
  Private installedFonts As String

  ' Menu handler to get the list of installed fonts.
  Private Sub listInstalledFontsToolStripMenuItem_Click( _
    ByVal sender As System.Object, _
    ByVal e As System.EventArgs) Handles listInstalledFontsToolStripMenuItem.Click
    Dim fonts As InstalledFontCollection = New InstalledFontCollection()
    For i As Integer = 0 To fonts.Families.Length - 1
      installedFonts &= fonts.Families(i).Name & " "
    Next

    ' This time, we need to invalidate the entire client area,
    ' as we will paint the installedFonts string on the lower half
    ' of the client rectangle.
    Invalidate()
  End Sub
...
End Class
```

The final task is to render the installedFonts string to the client area, directly below the screen real estate that is used for your swelling text:

```
Private Sub MainForm_Paint(ByVal sender As System.Object, _
  ByVal e As System.Windows.Forms.PaintEventArgs) Handles MyBase.Paint
  Dim g As Graphics = e.Graphics
  Dim theFont As Font = New Font(strFontFace, 12 + swellValue)
  Dim message As String = "Hello GDI+"

  ' Display message in the center of the window!
  Dim windowCenter As Single = CSng(Me.DisplayRectangle.Width / 2)
  Dim stringSize As SizeF = e.Graphics.MeasureString(message, theFont)
  Dim startPos As Single = windowCenter - (stringSize.Width / 2)
  g.DrawString(message, theFont, Brushes.Blue, startPos, 10)
```

```
' Show installed fonts in the rectangle below the swell area.
Dim myRect As Rectangle = _
  New Rectangle(0, 100, ClientRectangle.Width, ClientRectangle.Height)

' Paint this area of the Form black.
g.FillRectangle(New SolidBrush(Color.Black), myRect)
g.DrawString(installedFonts, New Font("Arial", 12), Brushes.White, myRect)
End Sub
```

Recall that the size of the "dirty rectangle" has been mapped to the upper 100 pixels of the client rectangle. Because your `Tick` handler invalidates only a portion of the Form, the remaining area is not redrawn when the `Tick` event has been sent (to help optimize the rendering of the client area).

As a final touch to ensure proper redrawing, let's handle the Form's `Resize` event to ensure that if the user resizes the Form, the lower part of client rectangle is redrawn correctly:

```
Private Sub MainForm_Resize(ByVal sender As System.Object, _
  ByVal e As System.EventArgs) Handles MyBase.Resize
  Dim myRect As Rectangle = New Rectangle(0, 100, _
  ClientRectangle.Width, ClientRectangle.Height)
  Invalidate(myRect)
End Sub
```

Figure 22-10 shows the result (with the text rendered in Wingdings!).

Figure 22-10. *The FontApp application in action*

■Source Code The SwellingFontApp project is included under the Chapter 22 subdirectory.

The FontDialog Class

As you might assume, there is an existing font dialog box (FontDialog), as shown in Figure 22-11.

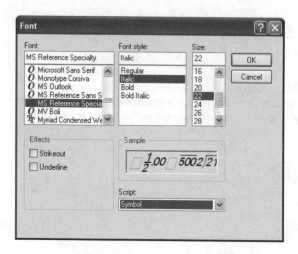

Figure 22-11. *The Windows Forms Font dialog box*

Like the ColorDialog type examined earlier in this chapter, when you wish to work with the FontDialog, simply call the ShowDialog() method. Using the Font property, you may extract the characteristics of the current selection for use in the application. To illustrate, here is a Form that mimics the logic of the previous ColorDlg project. When the user clicks anywhere on the Form, the Font dialog box displays and renders a message with the current selection:

```
Public Class MainForm
  Private fontDlg As New FontDialog()
  Private currFont As New Font("Times New Roman", 12)

  Private Sub MainForm_MouseDown(ByVal sender As System.Object, _
    ByVal e As System.Windows.Forms.MouseEventArgs) Handles MyBase.MouseDown
    If fontDlg.ShowDialog() <> Windows.Forms.DialogResult.Cancel Then
      currFont = fontDlg.Font
      Me.Text = String.Format("Selected Font: {0} ", currFont)
      Invalidate()
    End If
  End Sub

  Private Sub MainForm_Paint(ByVal sender As System.Object, _
  ByVal e As System.Windows.Forms.PaintEventArgs) Handles MyBase.Paint
    Dim g As Graphics = e.Graphics
    g.DrawString("Testing...", currFont, Brushes.Black, 0, 0)
  End Sub
End Class
```

■**Source Code** The FontDlgForm application is included under the Chapter 22 subdirectory.

Survey of the System.Drawing.Drawing2D Namespace

Now that you have manipulated Font types, the next task is to examine how to manipulate Pen and Brush objects to render geometric patterns. While you could do so making use of nothing more than Brushes and Pens helper types to obtain preconfigured types in a solid color, you should be aware that many of the more "exotic" pens and brushes are found within the System.Drawing.Drawing2D namespace.

This additional GDI+ namespace provides a number of classes that allow you to modify the end cap (triangle, diamond, etc.) used for a given pen, build textured brushes, and work with vector graphic manipulations. Some core types to be aware of (grouped by related functionality) are shown in Table 22-6.

Table 22-6. *Classes of* System.Drawing.Drawing2D

Classes	Meaning in Life
AdjustableArrowCap CustomLineCap	Pen caps are used to paint the beginning and end points of a given line. These types represent an adjustable arrow-shaped and user-defined cap.
Blend ColorBlend	These classes are used to define a blend pattern (and colors) used in conjunction with a LinearGradientBrush.
GraphicsPath GraphicsPathIterator PathData	A GraphicsPath object represents a series of lines and curves. This class allows you to insert just about any type of geometrical pattern (arcs, rectangles, lines, strings, polygons, etc.) into the path. PathData holds the graphical data that makes up a path.
HatchBrush LinearGradientBrush PathGradientBrush	These are exotic brush types.

Also be aware that the System.Drawing.Drawing2D namespace defines another set of enumerations (DashStyle, FillMode, HatchStyle, LineCap, and so forth) that are used in conjunction with these core types.

Working with Pens

GDI+ Pen types are used to draw lines between two end points. However, a Pen in and of itself is of little value. When you need to render a geometric shape onto a Control-derived type, you send a valid Pen type to any number of render methods defined by the Graphics class. In general, the DrawXXX() methods are used to render some set of lines to a graphics surface and are typically used with Pen objects.

The Pen type defines a small set of constructors that allow you to determine the initial color and width of the pen nib. Most of a Pen's functionality comes by way of its supported properties. Table 22-7 gives a partial list.

Table 22-7. *Pen Properties*

Properties	Meaning in Life
Brush	Determines the Brush used by this Pen.
Color	Determines the Color type used by this Pen.
CustomStartCap CustomEndCap	Gets or sets a custom cap style to use at the beginning or end of lines drawn with this Pen. *Cap style* is simply the term used to describe how the initial and final stroke of the Pen should look and feel. These properties allow you to build custom caps for your Pen types.
DashCap	Gets or sets the cap style used at the beginning or end of dashed lines drawn with this Pen.
DashPattern	Gets or sets an array of custom dashes and spaces. The dashes are made up of line segments.
DashStyle	Gets or sets the style used for dashed lines drawn with this Pen.
StartCap EndCap	Gets or sets the predefined cap style used at the beginning or end of lines drawn with this Pen. Set the cap of your Pen using the LineCap enumeration defined in the System.Drawing.Drawing2D namespace.
Width	Gets or sets the width of this Pen.
DashOffset	Gets or sets the distance from the start of a line to the beginning of a dash pattern.

Remember that in addition to the Pen type, GDI+ provides a Pens collection. Using a number of shared properties, you are able to retrieve a Pen (or a given color) on the fly, rather than creating a custom Pen by hand. Be aware, however, that the Pen types returned will always have a width of 1. If you require a more exotic pen, you will need to build a Pen type by hand. This being said, let's render some geometric images using simple Pen types. Assume you have a main Form object that is capable of responding to paint requests. The implementation is as follows:

```
Imports System.Drawing.Drawing2D

Public Class MainForm
  Private Sub MainForm_Paint(ByVal sender As System.Object, _
    ByVal e As System.Windows.Forms.PaintEventArgs) Handles MyBase.Paint
    Dim g As Graphics = e.Graphics
    ' Make a big blue pen.
    Dim bluePen As Pen = New Pen(Color.Blue, 20)

    ' Get a stock pen from the Pens type.
    Dim pen2 As Pen = Pens.Firebrick

    ' Render some shapes with the pens.
    g.DrawEllipse(bluePen, 10, 10, 100, 100)
    g.DrawLine(pen2, 10, 130, 110, 130)
    g.DrawPie(Pens.Black, 150, 10, 120, 150, 90, 80)

    ' Draw a purple dashed polygon as well...
    Dim pen3 As Pen = New Pen(Color.Purple, 5)
    pen3.DashStyle = DashStyle.DashDotDot
    g.DrawPolygon(pen3, New Point() {New Point(30, 140), _
      New Point(265, 200), New Point(100, 225), _
      New Point(190, 190), New Point(50, 330), _
      New Point(20, 180)})

    ' And a rectangle containing some text...
    Dim r As Rectangle = New Rectangle(150, 10, 130, 60)
```

```
    g.DrawRectangle(Pens.Blue, r)
    g.DrawString("Hello out there...How are ya?", _
    New Font("Arial", 12), Brushes.Black, r)
  End Sub

  Private Sub MainForm_Resize(ByVal sender As System.Object, _
    ByVal e As System.EventArgs) Handles MyBase.Resize
    Invalidate()
  End Sub
End Class
```

Notice that the Pen used to render your polygon makes use of the DashStyle enumeration (defined in System.Drawing.Drawing2D):

```
Enum DashStyle
  Solid
  Dash
  Dot
  DashDot
  DashDotDot
  Custom
End Enum
```

In addition to the preconfigured DashStyles, you are able to define custom patterns using the DashPattern property of the Pen type:

```
Private Sub MainForm_Paint(ByVal sender As System.Object, _
  ByVal e As System.Windows.Forms.PaintEventArgs) Handles MyBase.Paint
  Dim g As Graphics = e.Graphics
...
  ' Draw custom dash pattern all around the border of the form.
  Dim customDashPen As Pen = New Pen(Color.BlueViolet, 10)
  Dim myDashes As Single() = {5.0F, 2.0F, 1.0F, 3.0F}
  customDashPen.DashPattern = myDashes
  g.DrawRectangle(customDashPen, ClientRectangle)
End Sub
```

Figure 22-12 shows the final output of this Paint event handler.

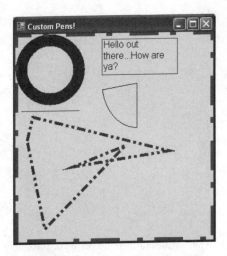

Figure 22-12. *Working with* Pen *types*

Source Code The CustomPenApp project is included under the Chapter 22 subdirectory.

Working with Pen Caps

If you examine the output of the previous pen example, you should notice that the beginning and end of each line was rendered using a standard pen protocol (an end cap composed of 90 degree angles). Using the LineCap enumeration, however, you are able to build Pens that exhibit a bit more flair:

```
Enum LineCap
   Flat
   Square
   Round
   Triangle
   NoAnchor
   SquareAnchor
   RoundAnchor
   DiamondAnchor
   ArrowAnchor
   AnchorMask
   Custom
End Enum
```

To illustrate, the following Pens application draws a series of lines using each of the LineCap styles. The end result can be seen in Figure 22-13.

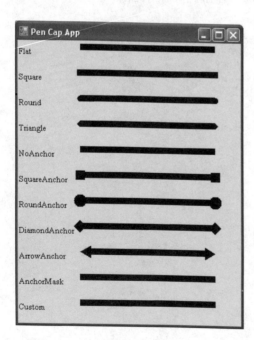

Figure 22-13. *Working with pen caps*

The code simply loops through each member of the LineCap enumeration and prints out the name of the item (e.g., ArrowAnchor). It then configures and draws a line with the current cap:

```vb
Imports System.Drawing.Drawing2D

Public Class MainForm
  Private Sub MainForm_Paint(ByVal sender As System.Object, _
    ByVal e As System.Windows.Forms.PaintEventArgs) Handles MyBase.Paint
    Dim g As Graphics = e.Graphics
    Dim thePen As Pen = New Pen(Color.Black, 10)
    Dim yOffSet As Integer = 10

    ' Get all members of the LineCap enum.
    Dim obj As Array = [Enum].GetValues(GetType(LineCap))

    For x As Integer = 0 To obj.Length - 1
      ' Draw a line with a LineCap member.
      ' Get next cap and configure pen.
      Dim temp As LineCap = CType(obj.GetValue(x), LineCap)
      thePen.StartCap = temp
      thePen.EndCap = temp
      ' Print name of LineCap enum.
      g.DrawString(temp.ToString(), New Font("Times New Roman", 10), _
        New SolidBrush(Color.Black), 0, yOffSet)
      ' Draw a line with the correct cap.
      g.DrawLine(thePen, 100, yOffSet, Width - 50, yOffSet)
      yOffSet += 40
    Next
  End Sub

  Private Sub MainForm_Resize(ByVal sender As System.Object, _
    ByVal e As System.EventArgs) Handles MyBase.Resize
    Invalidate()
  End Sub
End Class
```

Source Code The PenCapApp project is included under the Chapter 22 subdirectory.

Working with Brushes

System.Drawing.Brush-derived types are used to fill a region with a given color, pattern, or image. The Brush class itself is an abstract type and cannot be directly created. However, Brush serves as a base class to the other related brush types (e.g., SolidBrush, HatchBrush, LinearGradientBrush, and so forth). In addition to specific Brush-derived types, the System.Drawing namespace also defines two helper classes that return a configured brush using a number of shared properties: Brushes and SystemBrushes. In any case, once you obtain a brush, you are able to call any number of the FillXXX() methods of the Graphics type.

Interestingly enough, you are also able to build a custom Pen type based on a given brush. In this way, you are able to build some brush of interest (e.g., a brush that paints a bitmap image) and render geometric patterns with configured Pen. To illustrate, here is a small sample program that makes use of various Brush types:

```vb
Public Class MainForm
  Private Sub MainForm_Paint(ByVal sender As System.Object, _
    ByVal e As System.Windows.Forms.PaintEventArgs) Handles MyBase.Paint
    Dim g As Graphics = e.Graphics
```

```
      ' Make a blue SolidBrush.
      Dim blueBrush As SolidBrush = New SolidBrush(Color.Blue)

      ' Get a stock brush from the Brushes type.
      Dim pen2 As SolidBrush = CType(Brushes.Firebrick, SolidBrush)

      ' Render some shapes with the brushes.
      g.FillEllipse(blueBrush, 10, 10, 100, 100)
      g.FillPie(Brushes.Black, 150, 10, 120, 150, 90, 80)

      ' Draw a purple polygon as well...
      Dim brush3 As SolidBrush = New SolidBrush(Color.Purple)
      g.FillPolygon(brush3, New Point() {New Point(30, 140), _
        New Point(265, 200), New Point(100, 225), _
        New Point(190, 190), New Point(50, 330), _
        New Point(20, 180)})

      ' And a rectangle with some text...
      Dim r As Rectangle = New Rectangle(150, 10, 130, 60)
      g.FillRectangle(Brushes.Blue, r)
      g.DrawString("Hello out there...How are ya?", _
        New Font("Arial", 12), Brushes.White, r)
   End Sub
End Class
```

If you can't tell, this application is little more than the CustomPenApp program, this time making use of the FillXXX() methods and SolidBrush types, rather than pens and the related DrawXXX() methods. Figure 22-14 shows the output.

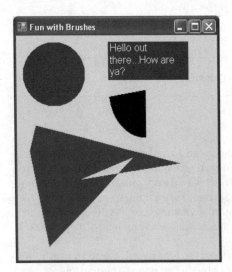

Figure 22-14. *Working with* Brush *types*

Source Code   The SolidBrushApp project is included under the Chapter 22 subdirectory.

Working with HatchBrushes

The System.Drawing.Drawing2D namespace defines a Brush-derived type named HatchBrush. This type allows you to fill a region using a (very large) number of predefined patterns, represented by the HatchStyle enumeration. Here is a partial list of names:

```
Enum HatchStyle
  Horizontal
  Vertical
  ForwardDiagonal,
  BackwardDiagonal
  Cross
  DiagonalCross
  LightUpwardDiagonal
...
End Enum
```

When constructing a HatchBrush, you need to specify the foreground and background colors to use during the fill operation. To illustrate, let's rework the logic seen previously in the PenCapApp example:

```
Imports System.Drawing.Drawing2D

Public Class MainForm
  Private Sub MainForm_Paint(ByVal sender As System.Object, _
  ByVal e As System.Windows.Forms.PaintEventArgs) Handles MyBase.Paint
    Dim g As Graphics = e.Graphics
    Dim yOffSet As Integer = 10

    ' Get all members of the HatchStyle enum.
    Dim obj As Array = [Enum].GetValues(GetType(HatchStyle))

    For x As Integer = 0 To 4
      ' Draw an oval with first 5 HatchStyle values.
      ' Configure Brush.
      Dim temp As HatchStyle = CType(obj.GetValue(x), HatchStyle)
      Dim theBrush As HatchBrush = New HatchBrush(temp, Color.White, Color.Black)

      ' Print name of HatchStyle enum.
      g.DrawString(temp.ToString(), New Font("Times New Roman", 10), _
      Brushes.Black, 0, yOffSet)

      ' Fill a rectangle with the correct brush.
      g.FillEllipse(theBrush, 150, yOffSet, 200, 25)
      yOffSet += 40
    Next
  End Sub
End Class
```

The output renders a filled oval for the first five hatch values (see Figure 22-15).

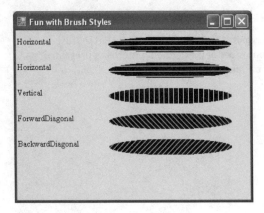

Figure 22-15. *Select hatch styles*

■**Source Code** The BrushStyles application is included under the Chapter 22 subdirectory.

Working with TextureBrushes

The TextureBrush type allows you to attach a bitmap image to a brush, which can then be used in conjunction with a fill operation. In just a few pages, you will learn about the details of the GDI+ Image class. For the time being, understand that a TextureBrush is assigned an Image reference for use during its lifetime. The image itself is typically found stored in some local file (*.bmp, *.gif, *.jpg) or embedded into a .NET assembly.

Let's build a sample application that makes use of the TextureBrush type. One brush is used to paint the entire client area with the image found in a file named clouds.bmp, while the other brush is used to paint text with the image found within soap bubbles.bmp. The output is shown in Figure 22-16.

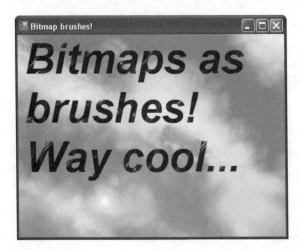

Figure 22-16. *Bitmaps as brushes*

To begin, your Form-derived class maintains two Brush member variables, which are assigned to a new TextureBrush in the constructor. Notice that the constructor of the TextureBrush type requires a type derived from Image. With these two TextureBrush types to use for rendering, the Paint event handler is quite straightforward:

Note The *.bmp files used in this example must be in the same folder as the application (or specified using hard-coded paths). We'll address this limitation later in this chapter.

```
Public Class MainForm
  Private texturedTextBrush As Brush
  Private texturedBGroundBrush As Brush

  Sub New()
    ' This call is required by the Windows Forms designer.
    InitializeComponent()

    ' Add any initialization after the InitializeComponent() call.
    CenterToScreen()

    ' Load images brushes.
    Try
      Dim bGroundBrushImage As Image = New Bitmap("Clouds.bmp")
      texturedBGroundBrush = New TextureBrush(bGroundBrushImage)
      Dim textBrushImage As Image = New Bitmap("Soap Bubbles.bmp")
      texturedTextBrush = New TextureBrush(textBrushImage)
    Catch
      MessageBox.Show("Can't find bitmap files!")
    End Try
  End Sub

  Private Sub MainForm_Paint(ByVal sender As System.Object, _
    ByVal e As System.Windows.Forms.PaintEventArgs) Handles MyBase.Paint
    Dim g As Graphics = e.Graphics
    Dim r As Rectangle = ClientRectangle

    ' Paint the clouds on the client area.
    g.FillRectangle(texturedBGroundBrush, r)

    ' Some big bold text with a textured brush.
    g.DrawString("Bitmaps as brushes!  Way cool...", _
      New Font("Arial", 50, FontStyle.Bold Or FontStyle.Italic), _
      texturedTextBrush, r)
  End Sub
End Class
```

Source Code The TexturedBrushes application is included under the Chapter 22 subdirectory.

Working with LinearGradientBrushes

Last but not least is the LinearGradientBrush type, which you can use whenever you want to blend two colors together in a gradient pattern. Working with this type is just as simple as working with the other brush types. The only point of interest is that when you build a LinearGradientBrush, you need to specify a pair of Color types and the direction of the blend via the LinearGradientMode enumeration:

```
Enum LinearGradientMode
   Horizontal
   Vertical
   ForwardDiagonal
   BackwardDiagonal
End Enum
```

To test each value, let's render a series of rectangles using a LinearGradientBrush:

```
Imports System.Drawing.Drawing2D

Public Class MainForm
   Private Sub MainForm_Paint(ByVal sender As System.Object, _
   ByVal e As System.Windows.Forms.PaintEventArgs) Handles MyBase.Paint
      Dim g As Graphics = e.Graphics
      Dim r As Rectangle = New Rectangle(10, 10, 100, 100)

      ' A gradient brush.
      Dim theBrush As LinearGradientBrush = Nothing
      Dim yOffSet As Integer = 10

      ' Get all members of the LinearGradientMode enum.
      Dim obj As Array = [Enum].GetValues(GetType(LinearGradientMode))

      For x As Integer = 0 To obj.Length - 1
         ' Draw an oval with a LinearGradientMode member.
         ' Configure Brush.
         Dim temp As LinearGradientMode = CType(obj.GetValue(x), LinearGradientMode)
         theBrush = New LinearGradientBrush(r, Color.GreenYellow, Color.Blue, temp)

         ' Print name of LinearGradientMode enum.
         g.DrawString(temp.ToString(), _
            New Font("Times New Roman", 10), _
            New SolidBrush(Color.Black), 0, yOffSet)

         ' Fill a rectangle with the correct brush.
         g.FillRectangle(theBrush, 150, yOffSet, 200, 50)
         yOffSet += 80
      Next
   End Sub
End Class
```

Figure 22-17 shows the end result.

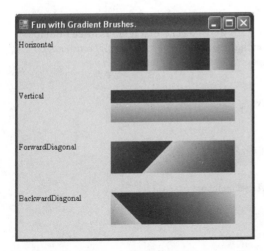

Figure 22-17. *Gradient brushes at work*

■**Source Code** The GradientBrushes application is included under the Chapter 22 subdirectory.

Rendering Images

At this point, you have examined how to manipulate three of the four major GDI+ types: fonts, pens, and brushes. The final type you'll examine in this chapter is the Image class and related subtypes. The abstract System.Drawing.Image type defines a number of methods and properties that hold various bits of information regarding the underlying image data it represents. For example, the Image class supplies the Width, Height, and Size properties to retrieve the dimensions of the image. Other properties allow you to gain access to the underlying palette. The Image class defines the core members shown in Table 22-8.

Table 22-8. *Members of the* Image *Type*

Members	Meaning in Life
FromFile()	This shared method creates an Image from the specified file.
FromStream()	This shared method creates an Image from the specified data stream.
Height Width Size HorizontalResolution VerticalResolution	These properties return information regarding the dimensions of this Image.
Palette	This property returns a ColorPalette data type that represents the underlying palette used for this Image.
GetBounds()	This method returns a Rectangle that represents the current size of this Image.
Save()	This method saves the data held in an Image-derived type to file.

Given that the abstract Image class cannot be directly created, you typically make a direct instance of the Bitmap type. Assume you have some Form-derived class that renders three bitmaps into the client area. Once you fill the Bitmap types with the correct image file, simply render each one within your Paint event handler using the Graphics.DrawImage() method:

```
Public Class MainForm
  ' To hold the *.bmp data.
  Private myImages As Bitmap() = New Bitmap(2) {}

  Sub New()
    ' This call is required by the Windows Forms designer.
    InitializeComponent()

    ' Add any initialization after the InitializeComponent() call.
    myImages(0) = New Bitmap("imageA.bmp")
    myImages(1) = New Bitmap("imageB.bmp")
    myImages(2) = New Bitmap("imageC.bmp")
    CenterToScreen()
  End Sub

  Private Sub MainForm_Paint(ByVal sender As System.Object, _
      ByVal e As System.Windows.Forms.PaintEventArgs) Handles MyBase.Paint
    Dim g As Graphics = e.Graphics
    ' Render all three images.
    Dim yOffset As Integer = 10
    For Each b As Bitmap In myImages
      g.DrawImage(b, 10, yOffset, 90, 90)
      yOffset += 100
    Next
  End Sub
End Class
```

Figure 22-18 shows the output.

■**Note** The *.bmp files used in this example must be in the same folder as the application (or specified using hard-coded paths). We'll resolve this limitation later in this chapter.

Finally, be aware that regardless of its name, the Bitmap class can contain image data stored in any number of file formats (*.tif, *.gif, *.bmp, etc.).

■**Source Code** The BasicImages application is included under the Chapter 22 subdirectory.

Figure 22-18. *Rendering images*

Dragging and Hit Testing the PictureBox Control

While you are free to render Bitmap images directly onto any Control-derived class, you will find that you gain far greater control and functionality if you instead choose to make use of a PictureBox type to contain your image. For example, because the PictureBox type "is-a" Control, you inherit a great deal of functionality, such as the ability to handle various events, assign a tool tip or context menu, and so forth. While you could achieve similar behaviors using a raw Bitmap, you would be required to author a fair amount of boilerplate code.

To showcase the usefulness of the PictureBox type, let's create a simple "game" that illustrates the ability to capture mouse activity over a graphical image. If the user clicks the mouse somewhere within the bounds of the image, he is in "dragging" mode and can move the image around the Form. To make things more interesting, let's monitor where the user releases the image. If it is within the bounds of a GDI+-rendered rectangle, you'll take some additional course of action (seen shortly). As you may know, the process of testing for mouse click events within a specific region is termed *hit testing*.

The PictureBox type gains most of its functionality from the Control base class. You've already explored a number of Control's members in the previous chapter, so let's quickly turn our attention to the process of assigning an image to the PictureBox member variable using the Image property (again, the happyDude.bmp file must be in the application directory):

```
Public Class MainForm
  Private happyBox As PictureBox = New PictureBox()
  Private oldX As Integer, oldY As Integer
```

```
Private isDragging As Boolean
Private dropRect As Rectangle = New Rectangle(100, 100, 140, 170)

Sub New()
    ' This call is required by the Windows Forms designer.
    InitializeComponent()

    ' Add any initialization after the InitializeComponent() call.
    ' Configure the PictureBox and add to
    ' the Form's Controls collection.
    happyBox.SizeMode = PictureBoxSizeMode.StretchImage
    happyBox.Location = New System.Drawing.Point(64, 32)
    happyBox.Size = New System.Drawing.Size(50, 50)
    happyBox.Cursor = Cursors.Hand
    happyBox.Image = New Bitmap("happyDude.bmp")

    ' Add handlers for the following events.
    AddHandler happyBox.MouseDown, AddressOf happyBox_MouseDown
    AddHandler happyBox.MouseUp, AddressOf happyBox_MouseUp
    AddHandler happyBox.MouseMove, AddressOf happyBox_MouseMove
    Controls.Add(happyBox)
End Sub
End Class
```

Beyond the Image property, the only other property of interest is SizeMode, which makes use of the PictureBoxSizeMode enumeration. This type is used to control how the associated image should be rendered within the bounding rectangle of the PictureBox. Here, you assigned PictureBoxSizeMode. StretchImage, indicating that you wish to skew the image over the entire area of the PictureBox type (which is set to 50×50 pixels).

The next task is to handle the MouseMove, MouseUp, and MouseDown events for the PictureBox member variable using the expected VB 2005 event syntax:

```
' Add handlers for the following events.
AddHandler happyBox.MouseDown, AddressOf happyBox_MouseDown
AddHandler happyBox.MouseUp, AddressOf happyBox_MouseUp
AddHandler happyBox.MouseMove, AddressOf happyBox_MouseMove
```

The MouseDown event handler is in charge of storing the incoming (x, y) location of the cursor within two Integer member variables (oldX and oldY) for later use, as well as setting a System.Boolean member variable (isDragging) to True, to indicate that a drag operation is in process. Add these member variables to your Form and implement the MouseDown event handler as follows:

```
Private Sub happyBox_MouseDown(ByVal sender As System.Object, _
  ByVal e As System.Windows.Forms.MouseEventArgs)
  isDragging = True
  ' Save the (x, y) of the mouse down click,
  ' because we need it as an offset when dragging the image.
  oldX = e.X
  oldY = e.Y
End Sub
```

The MouseMove event handler simply relocates the position of the PictureBox (using the Top and Left properties) by offsetting the current cursor location with the integer data captured during the MouseDown event:

```
Private Sub happyBox_MouseMove(ByVal sender As System.Object, _
  ByVal e As System.Windows.Forms.MouseEventArgs)
  If isDragging Then
    ' Need to figure new Y value based on where the mouse
```

```
    ' down click happened.
    happyBox.Top = happyBox.Top + (e.Y - oldY)

    ' Same deal for X (use oldX as a base line).
    happyBox.Left = happyBox.Left + (e.X - oldX)
  End If
End Sub
```

The MouseUp event handler sets the isDragging Boolean to False, to signal the end of the drag operation. As well, if the MouseUp event occurs when the PictureBox is contained within our GDI+-rendered Rectangle image, you can assume the user has won the (albeit rather simplistic) game. Given the Rectangle member variable (named dropRect) we added to the Form class, the MouseUp event handler can now be implemented like so:

```
Private Sub happyBox_MouseUp(ByVal sender As System.Object, _
  ByVal e As System.Windows.Forms.MouseEventArgs)
  isDragging = False
  ' Is the mouse within the area of the drop rect?
  If dropRect.Contains(happyBox.Bounds) Then
    MessageBox.Show("You win!", "What an amazing test of skill...")
  End If
End Sub
```

Finally, you need to render the rectangular area (maintained by the dropRect member variable) on the Form within a Paint event handler:

```
Private Sub MainForm_Paint(ByVal sender As System.Object, _
  ByVal e As System.Windows.Forms.PaintEventArgs) Handles MyBase.Paint
  ' Draw the drop box.
  Dim g As Graphics = e.Graphics
  g.FillRectangle(Brushes.BlueViolet, dropRect)
  ' Display instructions.
  g.DrawString("Drag the happy guy in here...", _
  New Font("Times New Roman", 25), Brushes.WhiteSmoke, dropRect)
End Sub
```

When you run the application, you are presented with what appears in Figure 22-19.

Figure 22-19. *The amazing happy-dude game*

If you have what it takes to win the game, you are rewarded with the kudos shown in Figure 22-20.

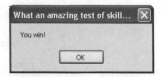

Figure 22-20. *You have nerves of steel!*

■**Source Code**   The DraggingImages application is included under the Chapter 22 subdirectory.

Hit Testing Rendered Images

Validating a hit test against a Control-derived type (such as the PictureBox) is very simple, as it can respond directly to mouse events. However, what if you wish to perform a hit test on a geometric shape rendered directly on the surface of a Form?

To illustrate the process, let's revisit the previous BasicImages application and add some new functionality. The goal is to determine when the user clicks one of the three images. Once you discover which image was clicked, you'll adjust the Text property of the Form and highlight the image with a 5-pixel outline.

The first step is to define a new set of member variables in the Form type that represents the Rectangles you will be testing against in the MouseDown event. When this event occurs, you need to programmatically figure out whether the incoming (*x*, *y*) coordinate is somewhere within the bounds of the Rectangles used to represent the dimension of each Image. If the user does click a given image, you set a private Boolean member variable (isImageClicked) to true and indicate which image was selected via another member variable of a custom enumeration named ClickedImage, defined as follows:

```
Enum ClickedImage
   ImageA
   ImageB
   ImageC
End Enum
```

With this, here is the initial update to the Form-derived class:

```
Public Class MainForm
...
   Private imageRects As Rectangle() = New Rectangle(2) {}
   Private isImageClicked As Boolean = False
   Private imageClicked As ClickedImage = ClickedImage.ImageA

   Sub New()
...
      ' Set up the rectangles.
      imageRects(0) = New Rectangle(10, 10, 90, 90)
      imageRects(1) = New Rectangle(10, 110, 90, 90)
      imageRects(2) = New Rectangle(10, 210, 90, 90)
      CenterToScreen()
   End Sub
...
```

```
Private Sub MainForm_MouseDown(ByVal sender As System.Object, _
  ByVal e As System.Windows.Forms.MouseEventArgs) Handles MyBase.MouseDown
  ' Get (x, y) of mouse click.
  Dim mousePt As Point = New Point(e.X, e.Y)

  ' See if the mouse is anywhere in the 3 Rectangles.
  If imageRects(0).Contains(mousePt) Then
    isImageClicked = True
    imageClicked = ClickedImage.ImageA
    Me.Text = "You clicked image A"
  ElseIf imageRects(1).Contains(mousePt) Then
    isImageClicked = True
    imageClicked = ClickedImage.ImageB
    Me.Text = "You clicked image B"
  ElseIf imageRects(2).Contains(mousePt) Then
    isImageClicked = True
    imageClicked = ClickedImage.ImageC
    Me.Text = "You clicked image C"
  Else
    ' Not in any shape, set defaults.
    isImageClicked = False
    Me.Text = "Hit Testing Images"
  End If
  ' Redraw the client area.
  Invalidate()
End Sub
End Class
```

Notice that the final conditional check sets the isImageClicked member variable to False, indicating that the user did not click one of the three images. This is important, as you want to erase the outline of the previously selected image. Once all items have been checked, invalidate the client area. Here is the updated Paint handler:

```
Private Sub MainForm_Paint(ByVal sender As System.Object, _
  ByVal e As System.Windows.Forms.PaintEventArgs) Handles MyBase.Paint
  Dim g As Graphics = e.Graphics
...
  ' Draw outline (if clicked)
  If isImageClicked = True Then
    Dim outline As Pen = New Pen(Color.Red, 5)
    Select Case imageClicked
      Case ClickedImage.ImageA
        g.DrawRectangle(outline, imageRects(0))
        Exit Select
      Case ClickedImage.ImageB
        g.DrawRectangle(outline, imageRects(1))
        Exit Select
      Case ClickedImage.ImageC
        g.DrawRectangle(outline, imageRects(2))
        Exit Select
      Case Else
        Exit Select
    End Select
  End If
End Sub
```

At this point, you should be able to run your application and validate that an outline appears around each image that has been clicked (and that no outline is present when you click outside the bounds of said images).

Hit Testing Nonrectangular Images

Now, what if you wish to perform a hit test in a nonrectangular region, rather than a simple square? Assume you updated your application to render an oddball geometric shape that will also sport an outline when clicked (see Figure 22-21).

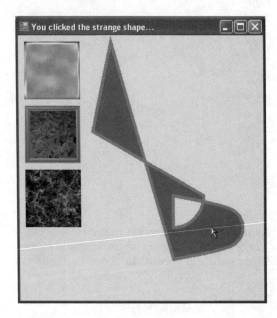

Figure 22-21. *Hit-testing polygons*

This geometric image was rendered on the Form using the FillPath() method of the Graphics type. This method takes an instance of a GraphicsPath object, which encapsulates a series of connected lines, curves, and strings. Adding new items to a GraphicsPath instance is achieved using a number of related Add methods, as described in Table 22-9.

Table 22-9. Add-*Centric Methods of the* GraphicsPath *Class*

Methods	Meaning in Life
AddArc()	Appends an elliptical arc to the current figure
AddBezier() AddBeziers()	Adds a cubic Bezier curve (or set of Bezier curves) to the current figure
AddClosedCurve()	Adds a closed curve to the current figure
AddCurve()	Adds a curve to the current figure
AddEllipse()	Adds an ellipse to the current figure
AddLine() AddLines()	Appends a line segment (or a set of lines) to the current figure

Methods	Meaning in Life
AddPath()	Appends the specified GraphicsPath to the current figure
AddPie()	Adds the outline of a pie shape to the current figure
AddPolygon()	Adds a polygon to the current figure
AddRectangle() AddRectangles()	Adds one rectangle (or more) to the current figure
AddString()	Adds a text string to the current figure

Assuming you have imported the System.Drawing.Drawing2D namespace, add a new GraphicsPath member variable to your Form-derived class. In the Form's constructor, build the set of items that represent your path as follows:

```
Imports System.Drawing.Drawing2D

Public Class MainForm
...
  Private myPath As GraphicsPath = New GraphicsPath()

  Sub New()
...
    ' Create an interesting path.
    myPath.StartFigure()
    myPath.AddLine(New Point(150, 10), New Point(120, 150))
    myPath.AddArc(200, 200, 100, 100, 0, 90)
    Dim point1 As Point = New Point(250, 250)
    Dim point2 As Point = New Point(350, 275)
    Dim point3 As Point = New Point(350, 325)
    Dim point4 As Point = New Point(250, 350)
    Dim points As Point() = {point1, point2, point3, point4}
    myPath.AddCurve(points)
    myPath.CloseFigure()
  End Sub
...
End Class
```

Notice the calls to StartFigure() and CloseFigure(). When you call StartFigure(), you are able to insert a new item into the current path you are building. A call to CloseFigure() closes the current figure and begins a new figure (if you require one). Also know that if the figure contains a sequence of connected lines and curves (as in the case of the myPath instance), the loop is closed by connecting a line from the end point to the starting point. First, add an additional name to the ImageClicked enumeration named StrangePath:

```
Enum ClickedImage
  ImageA
  ImageB
  ImageC
  StrangePath
End Enum
```

Next, update your existing MouseDown event handler to test for the presence of the cursor's (x, y) position within the bounds of the GraphicsPath. Like a Region type, this can be discovered using the IsVisible() member:

```
Private Sub MainForm_MouseDown(ByVal sender As System.Object, _
  ByVal e As System.Windows.Forms.MouseEventArgs) Handles MyBase.MouseDown
  ' Get (x, y) of mouse click.
  Dim mousePt As Point = New Point(e.X, e.Y)

  If imageRects(0).Contains(mousePt) Then
    isImageClicked = True
    imageClicked = ClickedImage.ImageA
    Me.Text = "You clicked image A"
  ElseIf imageRects(1).Contains(mousePt) Then
    isImageClicked = True
    imageClicked = ClickedImage.ImageB
    Me.Text = "You clicked image B"
  ElseIf imageRects(2).Contains(mousePt) Then
    isImageClicked = True
    imageClicked = ClickedImage.ImageC
    Me.Text = "You clicked image C"
  ElseIf myPath.IsVisible(mousePt) Then
    isImageClicked = True
    imageClicked = ClickedImage.StrangePath
    Me.Text = "You clicked the strange shape..."
  Else
    ' Not in any shape, set defaults.
    isImageClicked = False
    Me.Text = "Hit Testing Images"
  End If
  ' Redraw the client area.
  Invalidate()
End Sub
```

Finally, update the Paint handler as follows:

```
Private Sub MainForm_Paint(ByVal sender As System.Object, _
  ByVal e As System.Windows.Forms.PaintEventArgs) Handles MyBase.Paint
  Dim g As Graphics = e.Graphics
...
  ' Draw the graphics path.
  g.FillPath(Brushes.Sienna, myPath)

  ' Draw outline (if clicked)
  If isImageClicked = True Then
    Dim outline As Pen = New Pen(Color.Red, 5)
    Select Case imageClicked
    ...
      Case ClickedImage.StrangePath
        g.DrawPath(outline, myPath)
        Exit Select
      Case Else
        Exit Select
    End Select
  End If
End Sub
```

Source Code   The HitTestingImages project is included under the Chapter 22 subdirectory.

Understanding the .NET Resource Format

Up to this point in the chapter, each application that made use of external resources (such as bitmap files) demanded that the image files be within the client's application directory. Given this, you loaded your *.bmp files using an absolute name:

```
' Fill the images with bitmaps.
bMapImageA = New Bitmap("imageA.bmp")
bMapImageB = New Bitmap("imageB.bmp")
bMapImageC = New Bitmap("imageC.bmp")
```

This logic, of course, demands that the application directory does indeed contain three files named imageA.bmp, imageB.bmp, and imageC.bmp; otherwise, you will receive a runtime exception.

As you may recall from Chapter 13, an assembly is a collection of types and *optional resources*. Given this, your final task of the chapter is to learn how to bundle external resources (such as image files and strings) into the assembly itself. In this way, your .NET binary is truly self-contained. At the lowest level, bundling external resources into a .NET assembly involves the following steps:

1. Create a *.resx file that establishes name/value pairs for each resource in your application via XML data representation.

2. Use the resgen.exe command-line utility to convert your XML-based *.resx file into a binary equivalent (a *.resources file).

3. Using the /resource flag of the VB 2005 compiler, embed the binary *.resources file into your assembly.

As you might suspect, these steps are automated when using Visual Studio 2005. You'll examine how this IDE can assist you in just a moment. For the time being, let's check out how to generate and embed .NET resources at the command line.

The System.Resources Namespace

The key to understanding the .NET resource format is to know the types defined within the System.Resources namespace. This set of types provides the programmatic means to read and write *.resx (XML-based) and *.resources (binary) files, as well as obtain resources embedded in a given assembly. Table 22-10 provides a rundown of the core types.

Table 22-10. *Members of the* System.Resources *Namespace*

Members	Meaning in Life
ResourceReader ResourceWriter	These types allow you to read from and write to binary *.resources files.
ResXResourceReader ResXResourceWriter	These types allow you to read from and write to XML-based *.resx files.
ResourceManager	This type allows you to programmatically obtain embedded resources from a given assembly.

Programmatically Creating a *.resx File

As mentioned, a *.resx file is a block of XML data that assigns name/value pairs for each resource in your application. The ResXResourceWriter class provides a set of members that allow you to create the *.resx file, add binary and string-based resources, and commit them to storage. To illustrate, let's create a simple application (ResXWriter) that will generate a *.resx file containing an entry for the happyDude.bmp file (first seen in the DraggingImages example) and a single string resource. The GUI consists of a single Button type as shown in Figure 22-22.

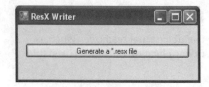

Figure 22-22. *The ResX application*

The `Click` event handler for the `Button` adds the `happyDude.bmp` and string resource to the `*.resx` file, which is saved on the local C drive:

```
Imports System.Resources

Public Class MainForm
  Private Sub btnGenResX_Click(ByVal sender As System.Object, _
  ByVal e As System.EventArgs) Handles btnGenResX.Click
    ' Make an resx writer & specify the file to write to.
    Dim w As ResXResourceWriter = New ResXResourceWriter("C:\ResXForm.resx")
    ' Add happy dude & string.
    Dim bMap As Bitmap = New Bitmap("happyDude.bmp")
    w.AddResource("happyDude", bMap)
    w.AddResource("welcomeString", "Hello new resource format!")
    ' Commit it.
    w.Generate()
    w.Close()
  End Sub
End Class
```

The member of interest is `ResXResourceWriter.AddResource()`. This method has been overloaded a few times to allow you to insert binary data (as you did with the `happyDude.bmp` image), as well as textual data (as you have done for your test string). Notice that each version takes two parameters: the name of a given resource in the `*.resx` file and the data itself. The `Generate()` method commits the information to file. At this point, you have an XML description of the image and string resources. To verify, open the new `ResXForm.resx` file using a text editor (see Figure 22-23).

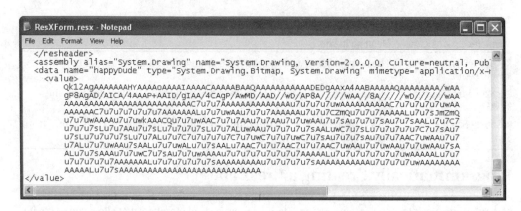

Figure 22-23. `*.resx` *expressed as XML*

Building the *.resources File

Now that you have a *.resx file, you can make use of the resgen.exe utility to produce the binary equivalent. To do so, open a Visual Studio 2005 command prompt, navigate to your C drive, and issue the following command:

```
resgen resxform.resx resxform.resources
```

You can now open the new *.resources file using Visual Studio 2005 and view the binary format, as shown in Figure 22-24.

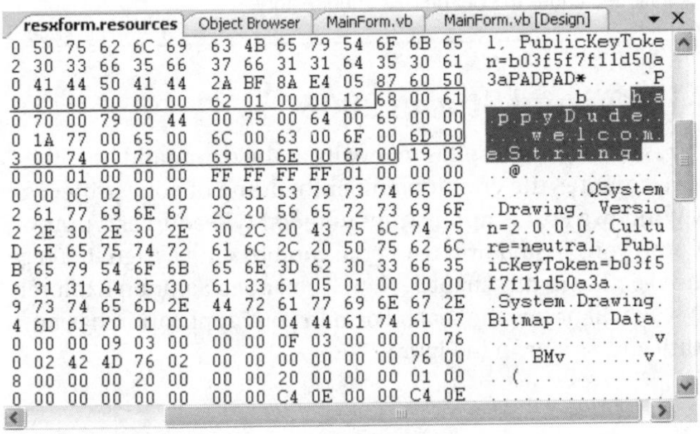

Figure 22-24. *The binary* *.resources *file*

Binding the *.resources File into a .NET Assembly

At this point, you are able to embed the *.resources file into a .NET assembly using the /resources command-line argument of the VB 2005 compiler. As you would hope, Visual Studio 2005 will auto-mate this process; however, for the sake of illustration, assume you have copied all the necessary *.vb files to the folder containing your *.resources file. The following command set could then be used to embed the binary data directly into the assembly:

```
vbc /resource:resxform.resources *.vb
```

Working with ResourceWriters

The previous example made use of the ResXResourceWriter types to generate an XML file that con-tains name/value pairs for each application resource. The resulting *.resx file was then run through the resgen.exe utility. Finally, you saw how you could manually embed the *.resources file into the assembly using the /resource flag of the VB 2005 compiler. The truth of the matter is that you do not need to build a *.resx file (although having an XML representation of your resources can come in handy and is easily readable). If you do not require a *.resx file, you can make use of the ResourceWriter type to directly create a binary *.resources file:

```
Private Sub GenerateResourceFile()
    ' Make a new *.resources file.
    Dim rw As ResourceWriter
    rw = New ResourceWriter("C:\myResources.resources")
```

```
' Add 1 image and 1 string.
rw.AddResource("happyDude", New Bitmap("happyDude.bmp"))
rw.AddResource("welcomeString", "Hello new resource format!")
rw.Generate()
rw.Close()
End Sub
```

At this point, the *.resources file can be bundled into an assembly using the /resources option:

```
vbc /resource:myresources.resources *.vb
```

■**Source Code**   The ResXWriter project is included under the Chapter 22 subdirectory.

Generating Resources using Visual Studio 2005

Although it is possible to work with *.resx/*.resources files manually at the command line, the good news is that Visual Studio 2005 automates the creation and embedding of your project's resources. To illustrate, create a new Windows Forms application named MyResourcesWinApp. Next, place a PictureBox component onto your main Form using the Toolbox, and assign its Image property to the happyDude.bmp image used earlier in this chapter. Now, if you open Solution Explorer (and select the Show All Files button), you will notice that each Form in your application has an associated *.resx file in place automatically, as shown in Figure 22-25.

Figure 22-25. *The autogenerated* *.resx *files of Visual Studio 2005*

This *.resx file will be maintained automatically while you naturally add resources (such as an image in a PictureBox widget) using the visual designers. Now, despite what you may be thinking, you should *not* manually update this file to specify your custom resources, as Visual Studio 2005 regenerates this file with each compilation. To be sure, you will do well if you allow the IDE to manage a Form's *.resx file on your behalf.

When you want to maintain a custom set of resources that are not directly mapped to a given Form, simply insert a new *.resx file (named MyResources.resx in this example) using the Project ➤ Add New Item menu item (see Figure 22-26).

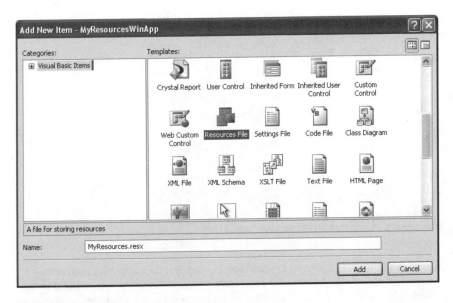

Figure 22-26. *Inserting a new* `*.resx` *file*

If you open your new `*.resx` file, a friendly GUI editor appears that allows you to insert string data, image files, sound clips, and other resources. The leftmost drop-down menu item allows you to select the type of resource you wish to add. First, add a new string resource named `WelcomeString` that is set to a message of your liking, as shown in Figure 22-27.

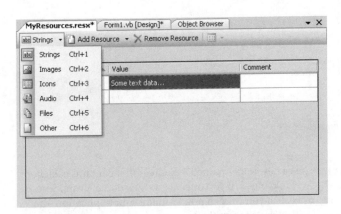

Figure 22-27. *Inserting new string resources with the* `*.resx` *editor*

Next, add the `happyDude.bmp` image file by selecting Images from the leftmost drop-down, choosing the Add Existing File option, as shown in Figure 22-28, and navigating to the `happyDude.bmp` file.

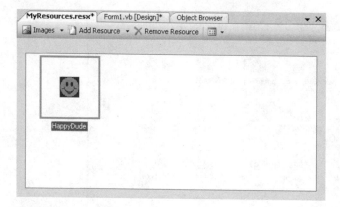

Figure 22-28. *Inserting new* *.bmp *resources with the* *.resx *editor*

At this point, you will find that the *.bmp file has been copied into your application directory. If you select the happyDude icon from the *.resx editor, you can now specify that this image should be embedded directly into the assembly (rather than linked as an external stand-alone file) by adjusting the Persistence property, as you see in Figure 22-29.

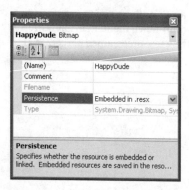

Figure 22-29. *Embedding specified resources*

Furthermore, Solution Explorer now has a new folder named Resources that contains each item to be embedded into the assembly. As you would guess, if you open a given resource, Visual Studio 2005 launches an associated editor. In any case, if you were to now compile your application, the string and image data will be embedded within your assembly.

Programmatically Reading Resources

Now that you understand the process of embedding resources into your assembly (using vbc.exe or Visual Studio 2005), you'll need to learn how to programmatically read them for use in your program using the ResourceManager type. To illustrate, add a new Button and an additional PictureBox widget on your Form type, as shown in Figure 22-30.

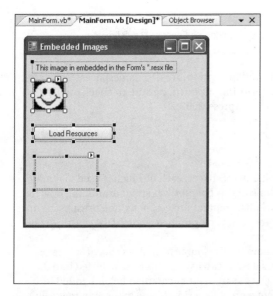

Figure 22-30. *The updated UI*

Next, handle the Button's Click event. Update the event handler with the following code:

```
Imports System.Resources
Imports System.Reflection

Public Class MainForm
  Private Sub btnLoadResources_Click(ByVal sender As System.Object, _
  ByVal e As System.EventArgs) Handles btnLoadResources.Click
    ' Make a resource manager.
    Dim rm As ResourceManager = _
      New ResourceManager("MyResourcesWinApp.MyResources", _
      Assembly.GetExecutingAssembly())

    ' Get the embedded string (case sensitive!)
    MessageBox.Show(rm.GetString("WelcomeString"))

    ' Get the embedded bitmap (case sensitive!)
    myPictureBox.Image = CType(rm.GetObject("HappyDude"), Bitmap)

    ' Clean up.
    rm.ReleaseAllResources()
  End Sub
End Class
```

Notice that the first constructor argument to the ResourceManager is the fully qualified name of your *.resx file (minus the file extension). The second parameter is a reference to the assembly that contains the embedded resource (which is the current assembly in this case). Once you have created the ResourceManager, you can call GetString() or GetObject() to extract the embedded data. If you were to run the application and click the button, you would find that the string data is displayed in the MessageBox and the image data has been extracted from the assembly and placed into the PictureBox.

■**Source Code** The MyResourcesWinApp project is included under the Chapter 22 subdirectory.

Well, that wraps up our examination of GDI+ and the System.Drawing namespaces. If you are interested in exploring GDI+ further (including printing support), be sure to check out *GDI+ Programming in C# and VB .NET* by Nick Symmonds (Apress, 2002).

Summary

GDI+ is the name given to a number of related .NET namespaces, each of which is used to render graphic images to a Control-derived type. The bulk of this chapter was spent examining how to work with core GDI+ object types such as colors, fonts, graphics images, pens, and brushes in conjunction with the almighty Graphics type. Along the way, you examined some GDI+-centric details such as hit testing and how to drag and drop images.

This chapter wrapped up by examining the new .NET resource format. As shown, a *.resx denotes resources using a set of name/value pairs describes as XML. This file can be fed into the resgen.exe utility, resulting in a binary format (*.resources) that can then be embedded into a related assembly. Finally, the ResourceManager type provides a simple way to programmatically retrieve embedded resources at runtime.

CHAPTER 23

■■■

Programming with Windows Forms Controls

This chapter is concerned with providing a road map of the controls defined in the
System.Windows.Forms namespace. Chapter 21 already gave you a chance to work with some
controls mounted onto a main Form such as MenuStrip, ToolStrip, and StatusStrip. In this chapter,
however, you will examine various types that tend to exist within the boundaries of a Form's client
area (e.g., Button, MaskedTextBox, WebBrowser, MonthCalendar, TreeView, and the like). Once you
look at the core UI widgets, you will then cover the process of building custom Windows Forms
controls that integrate into the Visual Studio 2005 IDE.

The chapter then investigates the process of building custom dialog boxes and the role of *form
inheritance*, which allows you to build hierarchies of related Form types. The chapter wraps up with
a discussion of how to establish the *docking* and *anchoring* behaviors for your family of GUI types,
and the role of the FlowControlPanel and TableControlPanel types supplied by .NET 2.0.

The World of Windows Forms Controls

The System.Windows.Forms namespace contains a number of types that represent common GUI
widgets typically used to allow you to respond to user input in a Windows Forms application. Many
of the controls you will work with on a day-to-day basis (such as Button, TextBox, and Label) are quite
intuitive to work with. Other, more exotic controls and components (such as TreeView, ErrorProvider,
and TabControl) require a bit more explanation.

As you learned in Chapter 21, the System.Windows.Forms.Control type is the base class for all
derived widgets. Recall that Control provides the ability to process mouse and keyboard events,
establish the physical dimensions and position of the widget using various properties (Height, Width,
Left, Right, Location, etc.), manipulate background and foreground colors, establish the active
font/cursor, and so forth. As well, the Control base type defines members that control a widget's
anchoring and docking behaviors (explained at the conclusion of this chapter).

As you read through this chapter, remember that the widgets you examine here gain a good deal
of their functionality from the Control base class. Thus, we'll focus (more or less) on the unique
members of a given widget. Do understand that this chapter does not attempt to fully describe each
and every member of each and every control (that is a task for the .NET Framework 2.0 SDK documentation). Rest assured, though, that once you complete this chapter, you will have no problem
understanding the widgets I have not directly described.

■**Note** Windows Forms provide a number of controls that allow you to display relational data (DataGridView,
BindingSource, etc.). Some of these data-centric controls are examined in Chapter 24 during our discussion of ADO.NET.

Adding Controls to Forms by Hand

Regardless of which type of control you choose to place on a Form, you will follow an identical set of steps to do so. First of all, you must define member variables that represent the controls themselves. Next, inside the Form's constructor (or within a helper method called by the constructor), you'll configure the look and feel of each control using the exposed properties, methods, and events. Finally (and most important), once you've set the control to its initial state, you must add it into the Form's internal controls collection using the inherited Controls property. If you forget this final step, your widgets will *not* be visible at runtime.

To illustrate the process of adding controls to a Form, let's begin by building a Form type "wizard-free" using your text editor of choice and the VB 2005 command-line compiler. Create a new VB 2005 file named ControlsByHand.vb and code a new MainWindow class as follows:

```
Imports System.Windows.Forms
Imports System.Drawing

Class MainWindow
Inherits Form
  ' Form widget member variables.
  Private firstNameBox As TextBox = New TextBox()
  Private WithEvents btnShowControls As Button = New Button()

  Public Sub New()
    ' Configure Form.
    Me.Text = "Simple Controls"
    Me.Width = 300
    Me.Height = 200
    CenterToScreen()

    ' Add a new textbox to the Form.
    firstNameBox.Text = "Hello"
    firstNameBox.Size = New Size(150, 50)
    firstNameBox.Location = New Point(10, 10)
    Me.Controls.Add(firstNameBox)

    ' Add a new button to the Form.
    btnShowControls.Text = "Click Me"
    btnShowControls.Size = New Size(90, 30)
    btnShowControls.Location = New Point(10, 70)
    btnShowControls.BackColor = Color.DodgerBlue
    Me.Controls.Add(btnShowControls)
  End Sub

  ' Handle Button's Click event.
  Private Sub btnShowControls_Clicked(ByVal sender As Object, _
  ByVal e As EventArgs) Handles btnShowControls.Click
    ' Call ToString() on each control in the
    ' Form's Controls collection
    Dim ctrlInfo As String = ""
    For Each c As Control In Me.Controls
      ctrlInfo += String.Format("Control: {0}" & Chr(10), c.ToString())
    Next
    MessageBox.Show(ctrlInfo, "Controls on Form")
  End Sub
End Class
```

Now, add a second class to the `ControlsByHand.vb` file that implements the program's `Main()` method:

```
Class Program
  Public Shared Sub Main()
    Application.Run(New MainWindow())
  End Sub
End Class
```

At this point, compile your VB 2005 file at the command line using the following command:

```
vbc/target:winexe *.vb
```

When you run your program and click the Form's button, you will find a message box that lists each item on the Form, as you see in Figure 23-1.

Figure 23-1. *Interacting with the Form's controls collection*

The Control.ControlCollection Type

While the process of adding a new widget to a Form is quite simple, I'd like to discuss the `Controls` property in a bit more detail. This property returns a reference to a nested class named `ControlCollection` defined within the `Control` class. The nested `ControlCollection` type maintains an entry for each widget placed on the Form. You can obtain a reference to this collection anytime you wish to "walk the list" of child widgets:

```
' Get access to the nested ControlCollection for this Form.
Dim coll As Control.ControlCollection = Me.Controls
```

Once you have a reference to this collection, you can manipulate its contents using the members shown in Table 23-1.

Table 23-1. `ControlCollection` *Members*

Member	Meaning in Life
`Add()` `AddRange()`	Used to insert a new `Control`-derived type (or array of types) in the collection
`Clear()`	Removes all entries in the collection
`Count`	Returns the number of items in the collection
`GetEnumerator()`	Returns the `IEnumerator` interface for this collection
`Remove()` `RemoveAt()`	Used to remove a control from the collection

Given that a Form maintains a collection of its controls, it is very simple under Windows Forms to dynamically create, remove, or otherwise manipulate visual elements. For example, assume you wish to disable all Button types on a given Form (or some such similar operation, such as change the background color of all TextBoxes). To do so, you can leverage the VB 2005 TypeOf/Is construct to determine who's who and change the state of the widgets accordingly:

```
Private Sub DisableAllButtons()
  For Each c As Control In Me.Controls
    If TypeOf c Is Button Then
      CType(c, Button).Enabled = False
    End If
    Next
End Sub
```

Source Code The ControlsByHand project is included under the Chapter 23 subdirectory.

Adding Controls to Forms Using Visual Studio 2005

Now that you understand the process of adding controls to a Form by hand, let's see how Visual Studio 2005 can automate the process. Create a new Windows Application project for testing purposes named whatever you choose. Similar to the process of designing with menu, toolbar, or status bar controls, when you drop a control from the Toolbox onto the Forms designer, the IDE responds by automatically adding the correct member variable to the *.Designer.vb file. As well, when you design the look and feel of the widget using the IDE's Properties window, the related code changes are added to the InitializeComponent() member function (also located within the *.Designer.vb file).

Note Recall that the Properties window also allows you to handle events for a given control when you click the lightning bolt icon. Simply select the widget from the drop-down list and type in the name of the method to be called for the events you are interested in responding to (or just double-click the event to generate a default event handler name, which always takes the form *NameOfControl_NameOfEvent()*).

Assume you have added a TextBox and Button type to the Forms designer. Notice that when you reposition a control on the designer, the Visual Studio 2005 IDE provides visual hints regarding the spacing and alignment of the current widget (see Figure 23-2).

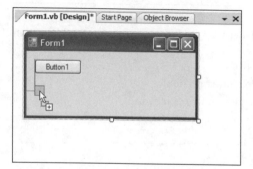

Figure 23-2. *Alignment and spacing hints*

Once you have placed the `Button` and `TextBox` on the designer, examine the code generated in the `InitializeComponent()` method. Here you will find that the types have been allocated and inserted into the Form's `ControlCollection` automatically (in addition to any settings you may have made using the Properties window):

```
Private Sub InitializeComponent()
  Me.Button1 = New System.Windows.Forms.Button
  Me.TextBox1 = New System.Windows.Forms.TextBox
...
  Me.Controls.Add(Me.TextBox1)
  Me.Controls.Add(Me.Button1)
End Sub
```

As you can see, a tool such as Visual Studio 2005 simply saves you some typing time (and helps you avoid hand cramps). Although `InitializeComponent()` is maintained on your behalf, do understand that you are free to configure a given control directly in code anywhere you see necessary (constructors, event handlers, helper functions, etc.). The role of `InitializeComponent()` is simply to establish the initial state of your UI elements. If you want to keep your life simple, I suggest allowing Visual Studio 2005 to maintain `InitializeComponent()` on your behalf, given that the designers may ignore or overwrite edits you make within this method.

Working with the Basic Controls

The `System.Windows.Forms` namespace defines numerous "basic controls" that are commonplace to any windowing framework (buttons, labels, text boxes, check boxes, etc.). Although I would guess you are familiar with the basic operations of such types, let's examine some of the more interesting aspects of the following basic UI elements:

- `Label`, `TextBox`, and `MaskedTextBox`
- `Button`
- `CheckBox`, `RadioButton`, and `GroupBox`
- `CheckedListBox`, `ListBox`, and `ComboBox`

Once you have become comfortable with these basic `Control`-derived types, we will turn our attention to more exotic widgets such as `MonthCalendar`, `TabControl`, `TrackBar`, `WebBrowser`, and so forth.

Fun with Labels

The `Label` control is capable of holding read-only information (text or image based) that explains the role of the other controls to help the user along. Assume you have created a new Visual Studio 2005 Windows Forms project named LabelsAndTextBoxes. Define a method called `CreateLabelControl` in your `Form`-derived type that creates and configures a `Label` type, and then adds it to the Form's controls collection:

```
Private Sub CreateLabelControl()
  ' Create and configure a Label.
  Dim lblInstructions As Label = New Label()
  lblInstructions.Name = "lblInstructions"
  lblInstructions.Text = "Please enter values in all the text boxes"
  lblInstructions.Font = New Font("Times New Roman", 10, FontStyle.Bold)
  lblInstructions.AutoSize = True
```

```
lblInstructions.Location = New System.Drawing.Point(16, 13)
lblInstructions.Size = New System.Drawing.Size(240, 16)
' Add to Form's controls collection.
Me.Controls.Add(lblInstructions)
End Sub
```

If you were to call this helper function within your Form's constructor, you would find your prompt displayed in the upper portion of the main window:

```
Sub New()
  ' This call is required by the Windows Form Designer.
  InitializeComponent()

  ' Add any initialization after the InitializeComponent() call.
  CreateLabelControl()

  ' Inherited method to center form on the screen.
  CenterToScreen()
End Sub
```

Unlike most other widgets, Label controls cannot receive focus via a Tab keypress. However, under .NET 2.0, it is now possible to create *mnemonic keys* for any Label by setting the UseMnemonic property to True (which happens to be the default setting). Once you have done so, a Label's Text property can define a shortcut key (via the ampersand symbol, &), which is used to tab to the control that follows it in the tab order.

Note You'll learn more about configuring tab order later in this chapter, but for the time being, understand that a control's tab order is established via the TabIndex property. By default, a control's TabIndex is set based on the order in which it was added to the Forms designer. Thus, if you add a Label followed by a TextBox, the Label is set to TabIndex 0 while the TextBox is set to TabIndex 1.

To illustrate, let's now leverage the Forms designer to build a UI containing a set of three Labels and three TextBoxes (be sure to leave room on the upper part of the Form to display the Label dynamically created in the CreateLabelControl() method). In Figure 23-3, note that each label has an underlined letter that was identified using the & character in the value assigned to the Text property (as you might know, &-specified characters allow the user to activate an item using the Alt+<*assigned key*> keystroke).

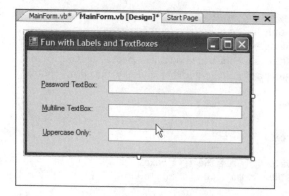

Figure 23-3. *Assigning mnemonics to* Label *controls*

If you now run your project, you will be able to tab between each TextBox using the Alt+P, Alt+M, or Alt+U keystrokes.

Fun with TextBoxes

Unlike the Label control, the TextBox control is typically not read-only (although it could be if you set the ReadOnly property to True), and it is commonly used to allow the user to enter textual data for processing. The TextBox type can be configured to hold a single line or multiple lines of text, it can be configured with a *password character* (such as an asterisk, *), and it may support scroll bars in the case of multiline text boxes. In addition to the behavior inherited by its base classes, TextBox defines a few particular properties of interest (see Table 23-2).

Table 23-2. TextBox *Properties*

Property	Meaning in Life
AcceptsReturn	Gets or sets a value indicating whether pressing Enter in a multiline TextBox control creates a new line of text in the control or activates the "default button" for the Form
CharacterCasing	Gets or sets whether the TextBox control modifies the case of characters as they are typed
PasswordChar	Gets or sets the character used to mask characters in a single-line TextBox control used to enter passwords
ScrollBars	Gets or sets which scroll bars should appear in a multiline TextBox control
TextAlign	Gets or sets how text is aligned in a TextBox control, using the HorizontalAlignment enumeration

To illustrate some aspects of the TextBox, let's configure the three TextBox controls on the current Form. The first TextBox (named txtPassword) should be configured as a password text box, meaning the characters typed into the TextBox should not be directly visible, but are instead masked with a predefined password character via the PasswordChar property.

Note Be aware that the PasswordChar property does not encrypt the password data! It simply prevents the password data from being viewed within the TextBox.

The second TextBox (named txtMultiline) will be a multiline text area that has been configured to accept Enter key processing and displays a vertical scroll bar when the text entered exceeds the space of the TextBox area. Finally, the third TextBox (named txtUppercase) will be configured to translate the entered character data into uppercase.

Configure each TextBox accordingly via the Properties window and use the following (partial) InitializeComponent() implementation as a guide:

```
Private Sub InitializeComponent()
...
' txtPassword
'
Me.txtPassword.PasswordChar = '*'
...
' txtMultiline
'
Me.txtMultiline.Multiline = True
```

```
  Me.txtMultiline.ScrollBars = System.Windows.Forms.ScrollBars.Vertical
...
' txtUpperCase
'
  Me.txtUpperCase.CharacterCasing = _
    System.Windows.Forms.CharacterCasing.Upper
...
End Sub
```

Notice that the ScrollBars property is assigned a value from the ScrollBars enumeration, which defines the following values:

```
Enum ScrollBars
  Both
  Horizontal
  None
  Vertical
End Enum
```

The CharacterCasing property works in conjunction with the CharacterCasing enum, which is defined like so:

```
Enum CharacterCasing
  Normal
  Upper
  Lower
End Enum
```

Now assume you have placed a Button on the Form (named btnDisplayData) and added an event handler for the Button's Click event. The implementation of this method simply displays the value in each TextBox within a message box:

```
Private Sub btnDisplayData_Click(ByVal sender As System.Object, _
  ByVal e As System.EventArgs) Handles btnDisplayData.Click
  ' Get data from all the text boxes.
  Dim textBoxData As String = ""
  textBoxData &= String.Format("MultiLine: {0}" & Chr(10), txtMultiline.Text)
  textBoxData &= String.Format("Password: {0}" & Chr(10), _
    txtPassword.Text)
  textBoxData &= String.Format("Uppercase: {0}" & Chr(10), txtUpperCase.Text)
  ' Display all the data.
  MessageBox.Show(textBoxData, "Here is the data in your TextBoxes")
End Sub
```

Figure 23-4 shows one possible input session (note that you need to hold down the Alt key to see the label mnemonics).

Figure 23-5 shows the result of clicking the Button type.

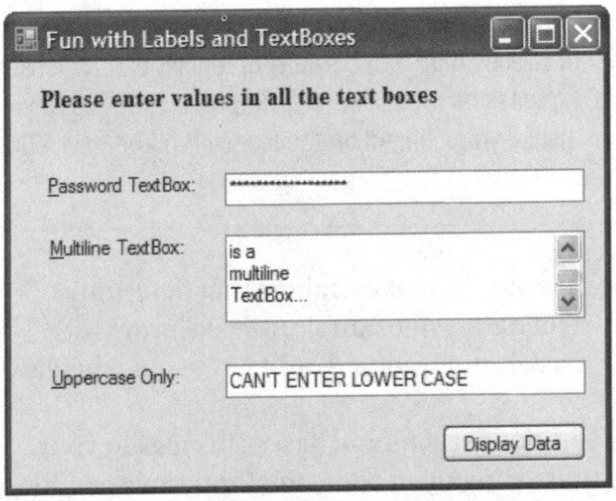

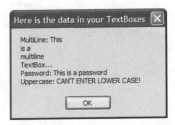

Figure 23-4. *The many faces of the* TextBox *type*

Figure 23-5. *Extracting values from* TextBox *types*

Fun with MaskedTextBoxes

As of .NET 2.0, we now have a *masked* text box that allows us to specify a valid sequence of characters that will be accepted by the input area (Social Security number, phone number with area code, zip code, or whatnot). The mask to test against (termed a *mask expression*) is established using specific tokens embedded into a string literal. Once you have created a mask expression, this value is assigned to the Mask property. Table 23-3 documents some (but not all) valid masking tokens.

Table 23-3. *Mask Tokens of* MaskedTextBox

Mask Token	Meaning in Life
0	Represents a mandatory digit with the value 0–9
9	Represents an optional digit or a space
L	Required letter (in uppercase or lowercase), A–Z
?	Optional letter (in uppercase or lowercase), A–Z
,	Represents a thousands separator placeholder
:	Represents a time placeholder
/	Represents a date placeholder
$	Represents a currency symbol

■**Note** The characters understood by the MaskedTextBox *do not* directly map to the syntax of regular expressions. Although .NET provides namespaces to work with proper regular expressions (System.Text.RegularExpressions and System.Web.RegularExpressions), the MaskedTextBox uses syntax based on the legacy MaskedEdit VB6 COM control.

In addition to the Mask property, the MaskedTextBox has additional members that determine how this control should respond if the user enters incorrect data. For example, BeepOnError will cause the control to (obviously) issue a beep when the mask is not honored, and it prevents the illegal character from being processed.

To illustrate the use of the MaskedTextBox, add an additional Label and MaskedTextBox to your current Form. Although you are free to build a mask pattern directly in code, the Properties window provides an ellipsis button for the Mask property that will launch a dialog box with a number of predefined masks, as shown in Figure 23-6.

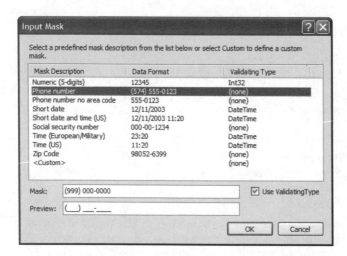

Figure 23-6. *Predefined mask values of the* Mask *property*

Find a masking pattern (such as Phone number), enable the BeepOnError property, and take your program out for another test run. You should find that you are unable to enter any alphabetic characters (in the case of the Phone number mask).

As you would expect, the MaskedTextBox will send out various events during its lifetime, one of which is MaskInputRejected, which is fired when the end user enters erroneous input. Handle this event using the Properties window and notice that the second incoming argument of the generated event handler is of type MaskInputRejectedEventArgs. This type has a property named RejectionHint that contains a brief description of the input error. For testing purposes, simply display the error on the Form's caption.

```
Private Sub txtMaskedTextBox_MaskInputRejected(ByVal sender As System.Object, _
  ByVal e As System.Windows.Forms.MaskInputRejectedEventArgs) _
  Handles txtMaskedTextBox.MaskInputRejected
  Me.Text = String.Format("Error: {0}", e.RejectionHint)
End Sub
```

■**Source Code** The LabelsAndTextBoxes project is included under the Chapter 23 subdirectory.

Fun with Buttons

The role of the System.Windows.Forms.Button type is to provide a vehicle for user confirmation, typically in response to a mouse click or keypress. The Button class immediately derives from an abstract type named ButtonBase, which provides a number of key behaviors for all derived types (such as CheckBox, RadioButton, and Button). Table 23-4 describes some (but by no means all) of the core properties of ButtonBase.

Table 23-4. ButtonBase *Properties*

Property	Meaning in Life
FlatStyle	Gets or sets the flat style appearance of the Button control, using members of the FlatStyle enumeration.
Image	Configures which (optional) image is displayed somewhere within the bounds of a ButtonBase-derived type. Recall that the Control class also defines a BackgroundImage property, which is used to render an image over the entire surface area of a widget.
ImageAlign	Sets the alignment of the image on the Button control, using the ContentAlignment enumeration.
TextAlign	Gets or sets the alignment of the text on the Button control, using the ContentAlignment enumeration.

The TextAlign property of ButtonBase makes it extremely simple to position text at just about any location. To set the position of your Button's caption, use the ContentAlignment enumeration (defined in the System.Drawing namespace). As you will see, this same enumeration can be used to place an optional image on the Button type:

```
Enum ContentAlignment
    BottomCenter
    BottomLeft
    BottomRight
    MiddleCenter
    MiddleLeft
    MiddleRight
    TopCenter
    TopLeft
    TopRight
End Enum
```

FlatStyle is another property of interest. It is used to control the general look and feel of the Button control, and it can be assigned any value from the FlatStyle enumeration (defined in the System.Windows.Forms namespace):

```
Enum FlatStyle
    Flat
    Popup
    Standard
    System
End Enum
```

To illustrate working with the Button type, create a new Windows Forms application named Buttons. On the Forms designer, add three Button types (named btnFlat, btnPopup, and btnStandard) and set each Button's FlatStyle property value accordingly (e.g., FlatStyle.Flat, FlatStyle.Popup, or FlatStyle.Standard). As well, set the Text value of each Button to a fitting value and handle the Click event for the btnStandard Button. As you will see in just a moment, when the user clicks this button, you will reposition the button's text using the TextAlign property.

Now, add a final fourth Button (named btnImage) that supports a background image (set via the BackgroundImage property) and a small bull's-eye icon (set via the Image property), which will also be dynamically relocated when the btnStandard Button is clicked. Feel free to use any image files to assign to the BackgroundImage and Image properties, but do note that the downloadable source code contains the images used here.

Given that the designer has authored all the necessary UI prep code within InitializeComponent(), the remaining code makes use of the ContentAlignment enumeration to reposition the location of the text on btnStandard and the icon on btnImage. In the following code, notice that you are calling the shared Enum.GetValues() method to obtain the list of names from the ContentAlignment enumeration:

```
Public Class MainForm
  ' Hold the current text alignment
  Private currAlignment As ContentAlignment = ContentAlignment.MiddleCenter
  Private currEnumPos As Integer = 0

  Private Sub btnStandard_Click(ByVal sender As System.Object, _
  ByVal e As System.EventArgs) Handles btnStandard.Click
    ' Get all possible values
    ' of the ContentAlignment enum.
    Dim values As Array = [Enum].GetValues(currAlignment.GetType())

    ' Bump the current position in the enum.
    ' & check for wrap around.
    currEnumPos += 1
    If currEnumPos >= values.Length Then
      currEnumPos = 0
    End If

    ' Bump the current enum value.
    currAlignment = CType([Enum].Parse(currAlignment.GetType(), _
      values.GetValue(currEnumPos).ToString()), ContentAlignment)
    btnStandard.TextAlign = currAlignment

    ' Paint enum value name on button.
    btnStandard.Text = currAlignment.ToString()

    ' Now assign the location of the icon on
    ' btnImage...
    btnImage.ImageAlign = currAlignment
  End Sub
End Class
```

Now run your program. As you click the middle button, you will see its text is set to the current name and position of the currAlignment member variable. As well, the icon within the btnImage is repositioned based on the same value. Figure 23-7 shows the output.

Figure 23-7. *The many faces of the* Button *type*

■**Source Code** The Buttons project is included under the Chapter 23 directory.

Fun with CheckBoxes, RadioButtons, and GroupBoxes

The System.Windows.Forms namespace defines a number of other types that extend ButtonBase, specifically CheckBox (which can support up to three possible states) and RadioButton (which can be either selected or not selected). Like the Button, these types also receive most of their functionality from the Control base class. However, each class defines some additional functionality. First, consider the core properties of the CheckBox widget described in Table 23-5.

Table 23-5. CheckBox *Properties*

Property	Meaning in Life
Appearance	Configures the appearance of a CheckBox control, using the Appearance enumeration.
AutoCheck	Gets or sets a value indicating if the Checked or CheckState value and the CheckBox's appearance are automatically changed when it is clicked.
CheckAlign	Gets or sets the horizontal and vertical alignment of a CheckBox on a CheckBox control, using the ContentAlignment enumeration (much like the Button type).
Checked	Returns a Boolean value representing the state of the CheckBox (checked or unchecked). If the ThreeState property is set to true, the Checked property returns true for either checked or indeterminately checked values.
CheckState	Gets or sets a value indicating whether the CheckBox is checked, using a CheckState enumeration rather than a Boolean value.
ThreeState	Configures whether the CheckBox supports three states of selection (as specified by the CheckState enumeration) rather than two.

The RadioButton type requires little comment, given that it is (more or less) just a slightly redesigned CheckBox. In fact, the members of a RadioButton are almost identical to those of the CheckBox type. The only notable difference is the CheckedChanged event, which (not surprisingly) is fired when the Checked value changes. Also, the RadioButton type does not support the ThreeState property, as a RadioButton must be on or off.

Typically, multiple RadioButton objects are logically and physically grouped together to function as a whole. For example, if you have a set of four RadioButton types representing the color choice of a given automobile, you may wish to ensure that only one of the four types can be checked at a time. Rather than writing code programmatically to do so, simply use the GroupBox control to ensure all RadioButtons are mutually exclusive.

To illustrate working with the CheckBox, RadioButton, and GroupBox types, let's create a new Windows Forms application named CarConfig, which you will extend over the next few sections. The main Form allows users to enter (and confirm) information about a new vehicle they intend to purchase. The order summary is displayed in a Label type once the Confirm Order button has been clicked. Figure 23-8 shows the initial UI.

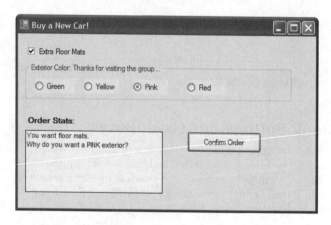

Figure 23-8. *The initial UI of the CarConfig Form*

Assuming you have leveraged the Forms designer to build your UI, you will now have numerous member variables representing each GUI widget. As well, the InitializeComponent() method will be updated accordingly. The first point of interest is the construction of the CheckBox type. As with any Control-derived type, once the look and feel has been established, it must be inserted into the Form's internal collection of controls:

```
Private Sub InitializeComponent()
...
    ' checkFloorMats
    '
    Me.checkFloorMats.Name = "checkFloorMats"
    Me.checkFloorMats.TabIndex = 0
    Me.checkFloorMats.Text = "Extra Floor Mats"
...
    Me.Controls.Add(Me.checkFloorMats)
End Sub
```

Next, you have the configuration of the GroupBox and its contained RadioButton types. When you wish to place a control under the ownership of a GroupBox, you want to add each item to the GroupBox's Controls collection (in the same way you add widgets to the Form's Controls collection).

```vb
Private Sub InitializeComponent()
...
' radioRed
'
Me.radioRed.Name = "radioRed"
Me.radioRed.Size = new System.Drawing.Size(64, 23)
Me.radioRed.Text = "Red"
'
' groupBoxColor
'
...
Me.groupBoxColor.Controls.Add(Me.radioRed)
Me.groupBoxColor.Text = "Exterior Color"
...
End Sub
```

To make things a bit more interesting, use the Properties window to handle the Enter and Leave
events sent by the GroupBox object. Understand, of course, that you do not need to capture the Enter
or Leave event for a GroupBox. However, to illustrate, the event handlers update the caption text of
the GroupBox as shown here:

```vb
Public Class MainForm
  Private Sub groupBoxColor_Enter(ByVal sender As System.Object, _
  ByVal e As System.EventArgs) Handles groupBoxColor.Enter
    groupBoxColor.Text = "Exterior Color: You are in the group..."
  End Sub

  Private Sub groupBoxColor_Leave(ByVal sender As System.Object, _
  ByVal e As System.EventArgs) Handles groupBoxColor.Leave
    groupBoxColor.Text = "Exterior Color: Thanks for visiting the group..."
  End Sub
End Class
```

The final GUI widgets on this Form (the Label and Button types) will also be configured and
inserted in the Form's Controls collection via InitializeComponent(). The Label is used to display
the order confirmation, which is formatted in the Click event handler of the order Button, as
shown here:

```vb
Private Sub btnOrder_Click(ByVal sender As Object, _
  ByVal e As System.EventArgs) Handles btnOrder.Click
  ' Build a string to display information.
  Dim orderInfo As String = ""
  If checkFloorMats.Checked Then
    orderInfo += "You want floor mats." & Chr(10) & ""
  End If
  If radioRed.Checked Then
    orderInfo += "You want a red exterior." & Chr(10) & ""
  End If
  If radioYellow.Checked Then
    orderInfo += "You want a yellow exterior." & Chr(10) & ""
  End If
  If radioGreen.Checked Then
    orderInfo += "You want a green exterior." & Chr(10) & ""
  End If
  If radioPink.Checked Then
    orderInfo += "Why do you want a PINK exterior?" & Chr(10) & ""
  End If
```

```
' Send this string to the Label.
  infoLabel.Text = orderInfo
End Sub
```

Notice that both the CheckBox and RadioButton support the Checked property, which allows you to investigate the state of the widget. Finally, recall that if you have configured a tri-state CheckBox, you will need to check the state of the widget using the CheckState property.

Fun with CheckedListBoxes

Now that you have explored the basic Button-centric widgets, let's move on to the set of list selection–centric types, specifically CheckedListBox, ListBox, and ComboBox. The CheckedListBox widget allows you to group related CheckBox options in a scrollable list control. Assume you have added such a control to your CarConfig Form that allows users to configure a number of options regarding an automobile's sound system (see Figure 23-9).

Figure 23-9. *The* CheckedListBox *type*

To insert new items in a CheckedListBox, call Add() for each item, or use the AddRange() method and send in an array of objects (strings, to be exact) that represent the full set of checkable items. Be aware that you can fill any of the list types at design time using the Items property located on the Properties window (just click the ellipsis button and type the string values). Here is the relevant code within InitializeComponent() that configures the CheckedListBox:

```
Private Sub InitializeComponent()
...
  ' checkedBoxRadioOptions
  '
  Me.checkedBoxRadioOptions.Items.AddRange(New Object() _
  {"Front Speakers", "8-Track Tape Player", _
  "CD Player", "Cassette Player", "Rear Speakers", "Ultra Base Thumper"})
...
```

```
Me.Controls.Add (Me.checkedBoxRadioOptions)
End Sub
```

Now update the logic behind the Click event for the Confirm Order button. Ask the CheckedListBox which of its items are currently selected and add them to the orderInfo string. Here are the relevant code updates:

```
Private Sub btnOrder_Click(ByVal sender As Object, _
  ByVal e As EventArgs) Handles btnOrder.Click
  ' Build a string to display information.
  Dim orderInfo As String = ""
  ...
  orderInfo += "-------------------------------" & Chr(10) & ""
  For i As Integer = 0 To checkedBoxRadioOptions.Items.Count - 1
    ' For each item in the CheckedListBox:
    ' Is the current item checked?
    If checkedBoxRadioOptions.GetItemChecked(i) Then
      ' Get text of checked item and append to orderinfo string.
      orderInfo &= "Radio Item: "
      orderInfo &= checkedBoxRadioOptions.Items(i).ToString()
      orderInfo &= "" & Chr(10) & ""
    End If
    ...
  Next
End Sub
```

The final note regarding the CheckedListBox type is that it supports the use of multiple columns through the inherited MultiColumn property. Thus, if you make the following update:

```
checkedBoxRadioOptions.MultiColumn = True
```

you see the multicolumn CheckedListBox shown in Figure 23-10.

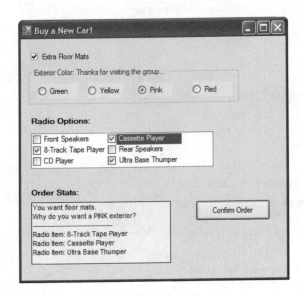

Figure 23-10. *Multicolumn* CheckedListBox *type*

Fun with ListBoxes

As mentioned earlier, the CheckedListBox type inherits most of its functionality from the ListBox type. To illustrate using the ListBox type, let's add another feature to the current CarConfig application: the ability to select the make (BMW, Yugo, etc.) of the automobile. Figure 23-11 shows the desired UI.

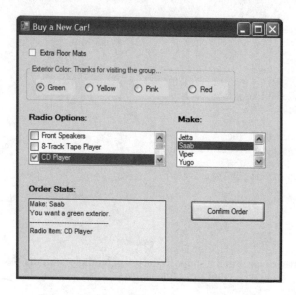

Figure 23-11. *The* ListBox *type*

As always, begin by creating a member variable to manipulate your type (in this case, a ListBox type). Next, configure the look and feel using the following snapshot from InitializeComponent():

```
Private Sub InitializeComponent()
...
  ' carMakeList
  '
  Me.carMakeList.Items.AddRange(New Object() {"BMW", "Caravan", "Ford", _
  "Grand Am", "Jeep", "Jetta", _
  "Saab", "Viper", "Yugo"})
...
  Me.Controls.Add (Me.carMakeList)
End Sub
```

The update to the btnOrder_Click() event handler is also simple:

```
Private Sub btnOrder_Click(ByVal sender As Object, _
  ByVal e As EventArgs) Handles btnOrder.Click
  ' Build a string to display information.
  Dim orderInfo As String = ""
...
  ' Get the currently selected item (not index of the item).
  If carMakeList.SelectedItem IsNot Nothing Then
    orderInfo += "Make: " + carMakeList.SelectedItem + "" & Chr(10) & ""
...
  End If
End Sub
```

Fun with ComboBoxes

Like a ListBox, a ComboBox allows users to make a selection from a well-defined set of possibilities. However, the ComboBox type is unique in that users can also insert additional items. Recall that ComboBox derives from ListBox (which then derives from Control). To illustrate its use, add yet another GUI widget to the CarConfig Form that allows a user to enter the name of a preferred salesperson. If the salesperson in question is not on the list, the user can enter a custom name. One possible UI update is shown in Figure 23-12 (feel free to add your own salesperson monikers).

Figure 23-12. *The* ComboBox *type*

This modification begins with configuring the ComboBox itself. As you can see here, the logic looks identical to that for the ListBox:

```
Private Sub InitializeComponent()
...
    ' comboSalesPerson
    '
    Me.comboSalesPerson.Items.AddRange(New Object() _
    {"Baby Ry-Ry", "Dan 'the Machine'", _
    "Cowboy Dan", "Tom 'the Style' "})
...
    Me.Controls.Add (Me.comboSalesPerson)
End Sub
```

The update to the btnOrder_Click() event handler is again simple, as shown here:

```
Private Sub btnOrder_Click(ByVal sender As Object, _
ByVal e As EventArgs) Handles btnOrder.Click
    ' Build a string to display information.
    Dim orderInfo As String = ""
...
    ' Use the Text property to figure out the user's salesperson.
    If comboSalesPerson.Text <> "" Then
        orderInfo += "Sales Person: " + comboSalesPerson.Text & "" & Chr(10) & ""
```

```
    Else
       orderInfo += "You did not select a sales person!" & "" & Chr(10) & ""
...
  End If
End Sub
```

Configuring the Tab Order

Now that you have created a somewhat interesting Form, let's formalize the issue of tab order. As you may know, when a Form contains multiple GUI widgets, users expect to be able to shift focus using the Tab key. Configuring the tab order for your set of controls requires that you understand two key properties: TabStop and TabIndex.

The TabStop property can be set to true or false, based on whether or not you wish this GUI item to be reachable using the Tab key. Assuming the TabStop property has been set to true for a given widget, the TabOrder property is then set to establish its order of activation in the tabbing sequence (which is zero based). Consider this example:

```
' Configure tabbing properties.
radioRed.TabIndex = 2
radioRed.TabStop = True
```

The Tab Order Wizard

The Visual Studio 2005 IDE supplies a Tab Order Wizard, which you access by choosing View ➤ Tab Order (be aware that you will not find this menu option unless the Forms designer is active). Once activated, your design-time Form displays the current TabIndex value for each widget. To change these values, click each item in the order you choose (see Figure 23-13).

To exit the Tab Order Wizard, simply press the Esc key.

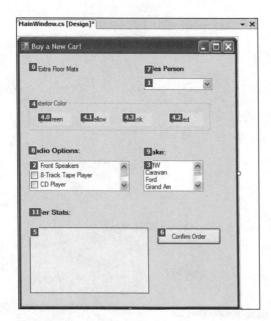

Figure 23-13. *The Tab Order Wizard*

Setting the Form's Default Input Button

Many user-input forms (especially dialog boxes) have a particular Button that will automatically respond to the user pressing the Enter key. For the current Form, if you wish to ensure that when the user presses the Enter key, the Click event handler for btnOrder is invoked, simply set the Form's AcceptButton property as follows:

```
' When the Enter key is pressed, it is as if
' the user clicked the btnOrder button.
Me.AcceptButton = btnOrder
```

■**Note** Some Forms require the ability to simulate clicking the Form's Cancel button when the user presses the Esc key. This can be done by assigning the CancelButton property to the Button object representing the Cancel button.

Working with More Exotic Controls

At this point, you have seen how to work most of the basic Windows Forms controls (Labels, TextBoxes, and the like). The next task is to examine some GUI widgets, which are a bit more high-powered in their functionality. Thankfully, just because a control may seem "more exotic" does not mean it is hard to work with, only that it requires a bit more elaboration from the outset. Over the next several pages, we will examine the following GUI elements:

- MonthCalendar
- ToolTip
- TabControl
- TrackBar
- Panel
- The UpDown controls
- ErrorProvider
- TreeView
- WebBrower

To begin, let's wrap up the CarConfig project by examining the MonthCalendar and ToolTip controls.

Fun with MonthCalendars

The System.Windows.Forms namespace provides an extremely useful widget, the MonthCalendar control, that allows the user to select a date (or range of dates) using a friendly UI. To showcase this new control, update the existing CarConfig application to allow the user to enter in the new vehicle's delivery date. Figure 23-14 shows the updated (and slightly rearranged) Form.

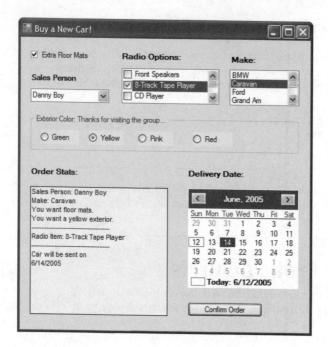

Figure 23-14. *The* MonthCalendar *type*

Although the MonthCalendar control offers a fair bit of functionality, it is very simple to programmatically capture the range of dates selected by the user. The default behavior of this type is to always select (and mark) today's date automatically. To obtain the currently selected date programmatically, you can update the Click event handler for the order Button, as shown here:

```
Private Sub btnOrder_Click(ByVal sender As System.Object, _
ByVal e As System.EventArgs) Handles btnOrder.Click
  ' Build a string to display information.
  Dim orderInfo As String = ""
...
  ' Get ship date.
  Dim d As DateTime = monthCalendar.SelectionStart
  Dim dateStr As String = _
    String.Format("{0}/{1}/{2} ", d.Month, d.Day, d.Year)
  orderInfo &= "Car will be sent: " & dateStr
...
End Sub
```

Notice that you can ask the MonthCalendar control for the currently selected date by using the SelectionStart property. This property returns a DateTime reference, which you store in a local variable. Using a handful of properties of the DateTime type, you can extract the information you need in a custom format.

At this point, I assume the user will specify exactly one day on which to deliver the new automobile. However, what if you want to allow the user to select a range of possible shipping dates? In that case, all the user needs to do is drag the cursor across the range of possible shipping dates. You already have seen that you can obtain the start of the selection using the SelectionStart property. The end of the selection can be determined using the SelectionEnd property. Here is the code update:

```
Private Sub btnOrder_Click(ByVal sender As System.Object, _
ByVal e As System.EventArgs) Handles btnOrder.Click
  ' Build a string to display information.
  Dim orderInfo As String = ""
...
  ' Get ship date range....
  Dim startD As DateTime = monthCalendar.SelectionStart
  Dim endD As DateTime = monthCalendar.SelectionEnd
  Dim dateStartStr As string = _
    String.Format("{0}/{1}/{2} ", startD.Month, startD.Day, startD.Year)
  Dim dateEndStr As string = _
    String.Format("{0}/{1}/{2} ", endD.Month, endD.Day, endD.Year)

  ' The DateTime type supports overloaded operators!
  If dateStartStr <> dateEndStr Then
    orderInfo &= "Car will be sent between " & _
    dateStartStr & " and" & Chr(10) & "" & dateEndStr
  Else
    orderInfo &= "Car will be sent on " & dateStartStr
    ' They picked a single date.
...
  End If
End Sub
```

■**Note** The Windows Forms toolkit also provides the `DateTimePicker` control, which exposes a `MonthCalendar` from a `DropDown` control.

Fun with ToolTips

As far as the CarConfig Form is concerned, we have one final point of interest. Most modern UIs support *tool tips*. In the `System.Windows.Forms` namespace, the `ToolTip` type represents this functionality. These widgets are simply small floating windows that display a helpful message when the cursor hovers over a given item.

To illustrate, add a tool tip to the CarConfig's `Calendar` type. Begin by dragging a new `ToolTip` control from the Toolbox onto your Forms designer, and rename it to `calendarTip`. Using the Properties window, you are able to establish the overall look and feel of the `ToolTip` widget, for example:

```
Private Sub InitializeComponent()
...
  ' calendarTip
  '
  Me.calendarTip.IsBalloon = True
  Me.calendarTip.ShowAlways = True
  Me.calendarTip.ToolTipIcon = System.Windows.Forms.ToolTipIcon.Info
...
End Sub
```

To associate a `ToolTip` with a given control, select the control that should activate the `ToolTip` and set the "ToolTip on *controlName*" property (see Figure 23-15).

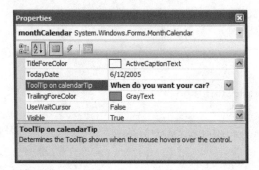

Figure 23-15. *Associating a* ToolTip *to a given widget*

At this point, the CarConfig project is complete. Figure 23-16 shows the ToolTip in action.

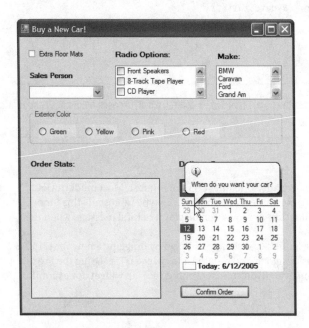

Figure 23-16. *The* ToolTip *in action*

■**Source Code** The CarConfig project is included under the Chapter 23 directory.

Fun with TabControls

To illustrate the remaining "exotic" controls, you will build a new Form that maintains a TabControl. As you may know, TabControls allow you to selectively hide or show pages of related GUI content via clicking a given tab. To begin, create a new Windows Forms application named ExoticControls and rename your initial Form to MainWindow.

Next, add a TabControl onto the Forms designer and, using the Properties window, open the page editor via the TabPages collection (just click the ellipsis button on the Properties window). A dialog configuration tool displays. Add a total of six pages, setting each page's Text and Name properties based on the completed TabControl shown in Figure 23-17.

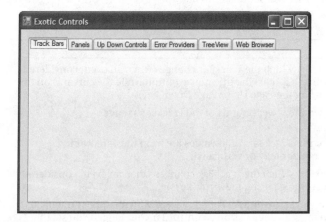

Figure 23-17. *A multipage* TabControl

As you are designing your TabControl, be aware that each page is represented by a TabPage object, which is inserted into the TabControl's internal collection of pages. Once the TabControl has been configured, this object (like any other GUI widget within a Form) is inserted into the Form's Controls collection. Consider the following partial InitializeComponent() method:

```
Private Sub InitializeComponent()
...
    'tabControlExoticControls
    '
    Me.tabControlExoticControls.Controls.Add(Me.pageTrackBars)
    Me.tabControlExoticControls.Controls.Add(Me.pagePanels)
    Me.tabControlExoticControls.Controls.Add(Me.pageUpDown)
    Me.tabControlExoticControls.Controls.Add(Me.pageErrorProvider)
    Me.tabControlExoticControls.Controls.Add(Me.pageTreeView)
    Me.tabControlExoticControls.Controls.Add(Me.pageWebBrowser)
    Me.tabControlExoticControls.Location = New System.Drawing.Point(11, 16)
    Me.tabControlExoticControls.Name = "tabControlExoticControls"
    Me.tabControlExoticControls.SelectedIndex = 0
    Me.tabControlExoticControls.Size = New System.Drawing.Size(644, 367)
    Me.tabControlExoticControls.TabIndex = 1
...
    Me.Controls.Add(Me.tabControlExoticControls)
End Sub
```

Now that you have a basic Form supporting multiple tabs, you can build each page to illustrate the remaining exotic controls. First up, let's check out the role of the TrackBar.

■**Note** The TabControl widget supports Selected, Selecting, Deselected, and Deselecting events. These can prove helpful when you need to dynamically generate the elements within a given page.

Fun with TrackBars

The TrackBar control allows users to select from a range of values, using a scroll bar–like input mechanism. When working with this type, you need to set the minimum and maximum range, the minimum and maximum change increments, and the starting location of the slider's thumb. Each of these aspects can be set using the properties described in Table 23-6.

Table 23-6. TrackBar *Properties*

Properties	Meaning in Life
LargeChange	The number of ticks by which the TrackBar changes when an event considered a large change occurs (e.g., clicking the mouse button while the cursor is on the sliding range and using the Page Up or Page Down key).
Maximum Minimum	Configure the upper and lower bounds of the TrackBar's range.
Orientation	The orientation for this TrackBar. Valid values are from the Orientation enumeration (i.e., horizontally or vertically).
SmallChange	The number of ticks by which the TrackBar changes when an event considered a small change occurs (e.g., using the arrow keys).
TickFrequency	Indicates how many ticks are drawn. For a TrackBar with an upper limit of 200, it is impractical to draw all 200 ticks on a control 2 inches long. If you set the TickFrequency property to 5, the TrackBar draws 20 total ticks (each tick represents 5 units).
TickStyle	Indicates how the TrackBar control draws itself. This affects both where the ticks are drawn in relation to the movable thumb and how the thumb itself is drawn (using the TickStyle enumeration).
Value	Gets or sets the current location of the TrackBar. Use this property to obtain the numeric value contained by the TrackBar for use in your application.

To illustrate, you'll update the first tab of your TabControl with three TrackBars, each of which has an upper range of 255 and a lower range of 0. As the user slides each thumb, the application intercepts the Scroll event and dynamically builds a new System.Drawing.Color type based on the value of each slider. This Color type will be used to display the color within a PictureBox widget (named colorBox) and the RGB values within a Label type (named lblCurrColor). Figure 23-18 shows the (completed) first page in action.

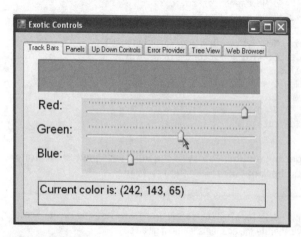

Figure 23-18. *The* TrackBar *page*

First, place three TrackBars onto the first tab using the Forms designer and rename your member variables with an appropriate value (redTrackBar, greenTrackBar, and blueTrackBar). Next, handle the Scroll event for each of your TrackBar controls. Here is the relevant code within InitializeComponent() for blueTrackBar (the remaining bars look almost identical):

```
Private Sub InitializeComponent()
...
'
'blueTrackBar
'
Me.blueTrackBar.Location = New System.Drawing.Point(132, 151)
Me.blueTrackBar.Maximum = 255
Me.blueTrackBar.Name = "blueTrackBar"
Me.blueTrackBar.Size = New System.Drawing.Size(310, 45)
Me.blueTrackBar.TabIndex = 18
Me.blueTrackBar.TickFrequency = 5
Me.blueTrackBar.TickStyle = System.Windows.Forms.TickStyle.TopLeft
...
End Sub
```

Note that the default minimum value of the TrackBar is 0 and thus does not need to be explicitly set. Now, to handle the Scroll event handlers for each TrackBar, you make a call to a yet-to-be-written helper function named UpdateColor():

```
Private Sub blueTrackBar_Scroll(ByVal sender As System.Object, _
  ByVal e As System.EventArgs) Handles blueTrackBar.Scroll
  UpdateColor()
End Sub
```

UpdateColor() is responsible for two major tasks. First, you read the current value of each TrackBar and use this data to build a new Color variable using Color.FromArgb(). Once you have the newly configured color, update the PictureBox member variable (again, named colorBox) with the current background color. Finally, UpdateColor() formats the thumb values in a string placed on the Label (lblCurrColor), as shown here:

```
Private Sub UpdateColor()
  ' Get the new color based on track bars.
  Dim c As Color = Color.FromArgb(redTrackBar.Value, _
    greenTrackBar.Value, blueTrackBar.Value)
  ' Change the color in the PictureBox.
  colorBox.BackColor = c
  ' Set color label.
  lblCurrColor.Text = _
  String.Format("Current color is: (R:{0}, G:{1}, B:{2})", _
  redTrackBar.Value, greenTrackBar.Value, blueTrackBar.Value)
End Sub
```

The final detail is to set the initial values of each slider when the Form comes to life and render the current color, within a custom default constructor:

```
Sub New()
  ' This call is required by the Windows Form Designer.
  InitializeComponent()

  CenterToScreen()
  ' Set initial position of each slider.
  redTrackBar.Value = 100
  greenTrackBar.Value = 255
  blueTrackBar.Value = 0
```

```
    UpdateColor()
End Sub
```

Fun with Panels

As you saw earlier in this chapter, the GroupBox control can be used to logically bind a number of controls (such as RadioButtons) to function as a collective. Closely related to the GroupBox is the Panel control. Panels are also used to group related controls in a logical unit. One difference is that the Panel type derives from the ScrollableControl class, thus it can support scroll bars, which is not possible with a GroupBox.

Panels can also be used to conserve screen real estate. For example, if you have a group of controls that takes up the entire bottom half of a Form, you can contain the group in a Panel that is half the size and set the AutoScroll property to true. In this way, the user can use the scroll bar(s) to view the full set of items. Furthermore, if a Panel's BorderStyle property is set to None, you can use this type to simply group a set of elements that can be easily shown or hidden from view in a manner transparent to the end user.

To illustrate, let's update the second page of the TabControl with two Button types (btnShowPanel and btnHidePanel) and a single Panel that contains a pair of text boxes (txtNormalText and txtUpperText) and an instructional Label. (Mind you, the widgets on the Panel are not terribly important for this example.) Figure 23-19 shows the final GUI.

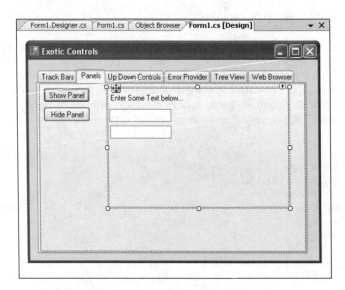

Figure 23-19. *The* TrackBar *page*

Using the Properties window, handle the TextChanged event for the first TextBox, and within the generated event handler, place an uppercase version of the text entered within txtNormalText into txtUpperText:

```
Private Sub txtNormalText_TextChanged(ByVal sender As System.Object, _
  ByVal e As System.EventArgs) Handles txtNormalText.TextChanged
  txtUpperText.Text = txtNormalText.Text.ToUpper()
End Sub
```

Now, handle the Click event for each button. As you might suspect, you will simply hide or show the Panel (and all of its contained UI elements):

```
Private Sub btnShowPanel_Click(ByVal sender As System.Object, _
  ByVal e As System.EventArgs) Handles btnShowPanel.Click
  panelTextBoxes.Visible = True
End Sub

Private Sub btnHidePanel_Click(ByVal sender As System.Object, _
  ByVal e As System.EventArgs) Handles btnHidePanel.Click
  panelTextBoxes.Visible = False
End Sub
```

If you now run your program and click either button, you will find that the Panel's contents are shown and hidden accordingly. While this example is hardly fascinating, I am sure you can see the possibilities. For example, you may have a menu option (or security setting) that allows the user to see a "simple" or "complex" view. Rather than having to manually set the Visible property to false for multiple widgets, you can group them all within a Panel and set its Visible property accordingly.

Fun with the UpDown Controls

Windows Forms provide two widgets that function as *spin controls* (also known as *up/down controls*). Like the ComboBox and ListBox types, these new items also allow the user to choose an item from a range of possible selections. The difference is that when you're using a DomainUpDown or NumericUpDown control, the information is selected using a pair of small up and down arrows. For example, check out Figure 23-20.

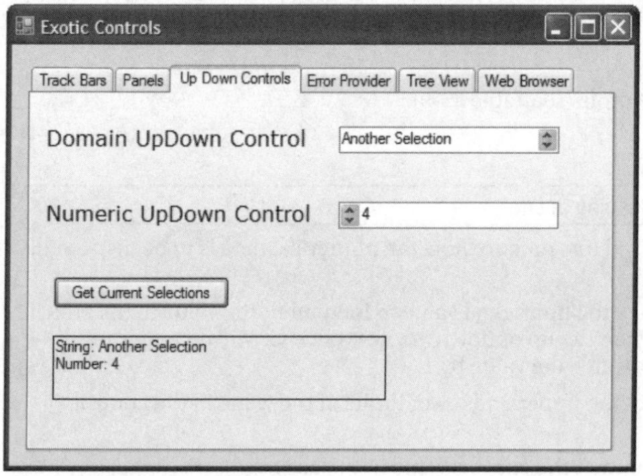

Figure 23-20. *Working with* UpDown *types*

Given your work with similar types, you should find working with the UpDown widgets painless. The DomainUpDown widget allows the user to select from a set of string data. NumericUpDown allows selections from a range of numeric data points. Each widget derives from a common direct base class, UpDownBase. Table 23-7 describes some important properties of this class.

Table 23-7. `UpDownBase` *Properties*

Property	Meaning in Life
InterceptArrowKeys	Gets or sets a value indicating whether the user can use the up arrow and down arrow keys to select values
ReadOnly	Gets or sets a value indicating whether the text can only be changed by the use of the up and down arrows and not by typing in the control to locate a given string
Text	Gets or sets the current text displayed in the spin control
TextAlign	Gets or sets the alignment of the text in the spin control
UpDownAlign	Gets or sets the alignment of the up and down arrows on the spin control, using the `LeftRightAlignment` enumeration

The `DomainUpDown` control adds a small set of properties (see Table 23-8) that allow you to configure and manipulate the textual data in the widget.

Table 23-8. `DomainUpDown` *Properties*

Property	Meaning in Life
Items	Allows you to gain access to the set of items stored in the widget
SelectedIndex	Returns the zero-based index of the currently selected item (a value of –1 indicates no selection)
SelectedItem	Returns the selected item itself (not its index)
Sorted	Configures whether or not the strings should be alphabetized
Wrap	Controls whether the collection of items continues to the first or last item if the user continues past the end of the list

The `NumericUpDown` type is just as simple (see Table 23-9).

Table 23-9. `NumericUpDown` *Properties*

Property	Meaning in Life
DecimalPlaces ThousandsSeparatorHexadecimal	Used to configure how the numerical data is to be displayed.
Increment	Sets the numerical value to increment the value in the control when the up or down arrow is clicked. The default is to advance the value by 1.
Minimum Maximum	Set the upper and lower limits of the value in the control.
Value	Returns the current value in the control.

The `Click` event handler for this page's `Button` type simply asks each type for its current value and places it in the appropriate `Label` (`lblCurrSel`) as a formatted string, as shown here:

```
Private Sub btnGetSelections_Click(ByVal sender As System.Object, _
    ByVal e As System.EventArgs) Handles btnGetSelections.Click
    ' Get info from updowns...
    lblCurrSel.Text = _
        String.Format("String: {0}" & Chr(13) & "Number: {1}", _
        domainUpDown.Text, numericUpDown.Value)
End Sub
```

Fun with ErrorProviders

Most Windows Forms applications will need to validate user input in one way or another. This is especially true with dialog boxes, as you should inform users if they make a processing error before continuing forward. The ErrorProvider type can be used to provide a visual cue of user input error. For example, assume you have a Form containing a TextBox and Button widget. If the user enters more than five characters in the TextBox and the TextBox loses focus, the error information shown in Figure 23-21 could be displayed.

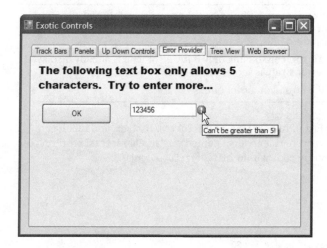

Figure 23-21. *The* ErrorProvider *in action*

Here, you have detected that the user entered more than five characters and responded by placing a small error icon (!) next to the TextBox object. When the user places his cursor over this icon, the descriptive error text appears as a pop-up. Also, this ErrorProvider is configured to cause the icon to blink a number of times to strengthen the visual cue (which, of course, you can't see without running the application).

If you wish to support this type of input validation, the first step is to understand the properties of the Control class shown in Table 23-10.

Table 23-10. Control *Properties*

Property	Meaning in Life
CausesValidation	Indicates whether selecting this control causes validation on the controls requiring validation
Validated	Occurs when the control is finished performing its validation logic
Validating	Occurs when the control is validating user input (e.g., when the control loses focus)

Every GUI widget can set the CausesValidation property to true or false (the default is true). If you set this bit of state data to true, the control forces the other controls on the Form to validate themselves when it receives focus. Once a validating control has received focus, the Validating and Validated events are fired for each control. In the scope of the Validating event handler, you configure a corresponding ErrorProvider. Optionally, the Validated event can be handled to determine when the control has finished its validation cycle.

The ErrorProvider type has a small set of members. The most important item for your purposes is the BlinkStyle property, which can be set to any of the values of the ErrorBlinkStyle enumeration described in Table 23-11.

Table 23-11. ErrorBlinkStyle *Properties*

Property	Meaning in Life
AlwaysBlink	Causes the error icon to blink when the error is first displayed or when a new error description string is set for the control and the error icon is already displayed
BlinkIfDifferentError	Causes the error icon to blink only if the error icon is already displayed, but a new error string is set for the control
NeverBlink	Indicates the error icon never blinks

To illustrate, update the UI of the Error Provider page with a Button, TextBox, and Label as shown in Figure 23-21. Next, drag an ErrorProvider widget named tooManyCharactersErrorProvider onto the designer. Here is the configuration code within InitializeComponent():

```
Private Sub InitializeComponent()
...
    'tooManyCharactersErrorProvider
    '
    Me.tooManyCharactersErrorProvider.BlinkRate = 500
    Me.tooManyCharactersErrorProvider.BlinkStyle = _
        System.Windows.Forms.ErrorBlinkStyle.AlwaysBlink
    Me.tooManyCharactersErrorProvider.ContainerControl = Me
...
End Sub
```

Once you have configured how the ErrorProvider looks and feels, you bind the error to the TextBox within the scope of its Validating event handler, as shown here:

```
Private Sub txtInput_Validating(ByVal sender As System.Object, _
  ByVal e As System.ComponentModel.CancelEventArgs) Handles txtInput.Validating
    ' Check if the text length is greater than 5.
    If txtInput.Text.Length > 5 Then
        tooManyCharactersErrorProvider.SetError(txtInput, "Can't be greater than 5!")
    Else
        tooManyCharactersErrorProvider.SetError(txtInput, "")
        ' Things are OK, don't show anything.
    End If
End Sub
```

Fun with TreeViews

TreeView controls are very helpful types in that they allow you to visually display hierarchical data (such as a directory structure or any other type of parent/child relationship). As you would expect, the Window Forms TreeView control can be highly customized. If you wish, you can add custom images, node colors, node subcontrols, and other visual enhancements. (I'll assume interested readers will consult the .NET Framework 2.0 SDK documentation for full details of this widget.)

To illustrate the basic use of the TreeView, the next page of your TabControl will programmatically construct a TreeView defining a series of topmost nodes that represent a set of Car types. Each Car node has two subnodes that represent the selected car's current speed and favorite radio station. In Figure 23-22, notice that the selected item will be highlighted. Also note that if the selected node has a parent (and/or sibling), its name is presented in a Label widget.

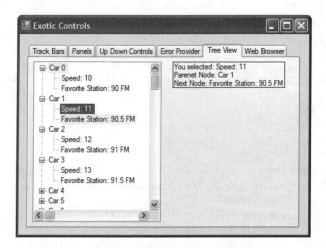

Figure 23-22. *The* TreeView *in action*

Assuming your Tree View UI is composed of a TreeView control (named treeViewCars) and a Label (named lblNodeInfo), insert a new VB 2005 file into your ExoticControls project that models a trivial Car that "has-a" Radio:

```
Class Car
  Public Sub New(ByVal pn As String, ByVal cs As Integer)
    petName = pn
    currSp = cs
  End Sub
  ' Public to keep the example simple.
  Public petName As String
  Public currSp As Integer
  Public r As Radio
End Class

Class Radio
  Public favoriteStation As Double
  Public Sub New(ByVal station As Double)
    favoriteStation = station
  End Sub
End Class
```

The Form-derived type will maintain a generic List(Of T) (named listCars) of 100 Car types, which will be populated in the default constructor of the MainForm type. As well, the constructor will call a new subroutine named BuildCarTreeView() which takes no arguments. Here is the initial update:

```
Public Class MainForm
  ' Create a new generic List to hold the Car objects.
  Private listCars As List(Of Car) = New List(Of Car)()

  Sub New()
...
    ' Fill List(Of T) and build TreeView.
    Dim offset As Double = 0.5
    For x As Integer = 0 To 99
      listCars.Add(New Car(String.Format("Car {0}", x), 10 + x))
      offset += 0.5
      listCars(x).r = New Radio(89 + offset)
    Next
    BuildCarTreeView()
  End Sub

...
End Class
```

Note that the petName of each car is based on the current value of x (Car 0, Car 1, Car 2, etc.). As well, the current speed is set by offsetting x by 10 (10 mph to 109 mph), while the favorite radio station is established by offsetting the value 89.0 by 0.5 (90, 90.5, 91, 91.5, etc.).

Now that you have a list of Cars, you need to map these values to nodes of the TreeView control. The most important aspect to understand when working with the TreeView widget is that each topmost node and subnode is represented by a System.Windows.Forms.TreeNode object. As you would expect, TreeNode has numerous members of interest that allow you to control the UI of a given node (IsExpanded, IsVisible, BackColor, ForeColor, NodeFont). As well, the TreeNode provides members to navigate to the next (or previous) TreeNode. Given this, consider the initial implementation of BuildCarTreeView():

```
Sub BuildCarTreeView()
  ' Don't paint the TreeView until all the nodes have been created.
  treeViewCars.BeginUpdate()

  ' Clear the TreeView of any current nodes.
  treeViewCars.Nodes.Clear()

  ' Add a TreeNode for each Car object in the List(Of T).
  For Each c As Car In listCars
    ' Add the current Car as a topmost node.
    treeViewCars.Nodes.Add(New TreeNode(c.petName))
    ' Now, get the Car you just added to build
    ' two subnodes based on the speed and
    ' internal Radio object.
    treeViewCars.Nodes(listCars.IndexOf(c)).Nodes.Add(New _
      TreeNode(String.Format("Speed: {0}", c.currSp.ToString())))
    treeViewCars.Nodes(listCars.IndexOf(c)).Nodes.Add(New _
      TreeNode(String.Format("Favorite Station: {0} FM", _
      c.r.favoriteStation)))
  Next
  ' Now paint the TreeView.
  treeViewCars.EndUpdate()
End Sub
```

As you can see, the construction of the TreeView nodes are sandwiched between a call to BeginUpdate() and EndUpdate(). This can be helpful when you are populating a massive TreeView with a great many nodes, given that the widget will wait to display the items until you have finished filling the Nodes collection. In this way, the end user does not see the gradual rendering of the TreeView's elements.

The topmost nodes are added to the TreeView simply by iterating over the generic List(Of T) type and inserting a new TreeNode object into the TreeView's Nodes collection. Once a topmost node has been added, you pluck it from the Nodes collection (via the type indexer) to add its subnodes (which are also represented by TreeNode objects). As you might guess, if you wish to add subnodes to a current subnode, simply populate its internal collection of nodes via the Nodes property.

The next task for this page of the TabControl is to highlight the currently selected node (via the BackColor property) and display the selected item (as well as any parent or subnodes) within the Label widget. All of this can be accomplished by handling the TreeView control's AfterSelect event via the Properties window. This event fires after the user has selected a node via a mouse click or keyboard navigation. Here is the complete implementation of the AfterSelect event handler:

```
Private Sub treeViewCars_AfterSelect(ByVal sender As System.Object, _
  ByVal e As System.Windows.Forms.TreeViewEventArgs) _
  Handles treeViewCars.AfterSelect
  Dim nodeInfo As String = ""
  ' Build info about selected node.
  nodeInfo = String.Format("You selected: {0}" & Chr(10) & "", e.Node.Text)
  If e.Node.Parent IsNot Nothing Then
    nodeInfo &= String.Format("Parent Node: {0}" & Chr(10) & "", _
    e.Node.Parent.Text)
  End If
  If e.Node.NextNode IsNot Nothing Then
    nodeInfo &= String.Format("Next Node: {0}", e.Node.NextNode.Text)
  End If
  ' Show info and highlight node.
  lblNodeInfo.Text = nodeInfo
  e.Node.BackColor = Color.AliceBlue
End Sub
```

The incoming TreeViewEventArgs object contains a property named Node, which returns a TreeNode object representing the current selection. From here, you are able to extract the node's name (via the Text property) as well as the parent and next node (via the Parent/NextNode properties). Note you are explicitly checking the TreeNode objects returned from Parent/NextNode for Nothing, in case the user has selected the topmost node or the very last subnode (if you did not do this, you might trigger a NullReferenceException).

Adding Node Images

To wrap up our examination of the TreeView type, let's spruce up the current example by defining three new *.bmp images that will be assigned to each node type. To do so, add a new ImageList component (named imageListTreeView) to the designer of the MainForm type. Next, add three new bitmap images to your project via the Project ➤ Add New Item menu selection (or make use of the supplied *.bmp files within this book's downloadable code) that represent (or at least closely approximate) a car, radio, and "speed" image. Do note that each of these *.bmp files is 16×16 pixels (set via the Properties window) so that they have a decent appearance within the TreeView.

Once you have created these image files, select the ImageList on your designer and populate the Images property with each of these three images, ordered as shown in Figure 23-23, to ensure you can assign the correct ImageIndex (0, 1, or 2) to each node.

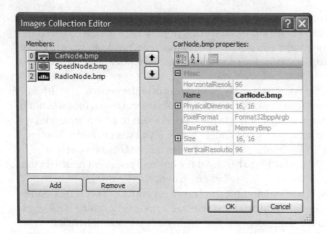

Figure 23-23. *Populating the* ImageList

As you recall from Chapter 22, when you incorporate resources (such as bitmaps) into your
Visual Studio 2005 solutions, the underlying *.resx file is automatically updated. Therefore, these
images will be embedded into your assembly with no extra work on your part. Now, using the Properties window, set the TreeView control's ImageList property to your ImageList member variable
(see Figure 23-24).

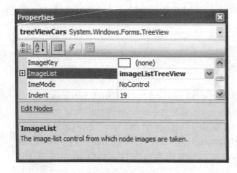

Figure 23-24. *Associating the* ImageList *to the* TreeView

Last but not least, update your BuildCarTreeView() method to specify the correct ImageIndex
(via constructor arguments) when creating each TreeNode:

```
Sub BuildCarTreeView()
...
  ' Add a root TreeNode for each Car object in the List(Of T).
  For Each c As Car In listCars
    ' Add the current Car as a topmost node.
    treeViewCars.Nodes.Add(New TreeNode(c.petName, 0, 0))
    ' Now, get the Car you just added to build
    ' two subnodes based on the speed and
    ' internal Radio object.
```

```
    treeViewCars.Nodes(listCars.IndexOf(c)).Nodes.Add(New _
      TreeNode(String.Format("Speed: {0}", c.currSp.ToString()), 1, 1))
    treeViewCars.Nodes(listCars.IndexOf(c)).Nodes.Add(New _
      TreeNode(String.Format("Favorite Station: {0} FM", _
    c.r.favoriteStation), 2, 2))
  Next
...
End Sub
```

Notice that you are specifying each ImageIndex twice. The reason for this is that a given TreeNode can have two unique images assigned to it: one to display when unselected and another to display when selected. To keep things simple, you are specifying the same image for both possibilities. In any case, Figure 23-25 shows the updated TreeView type.

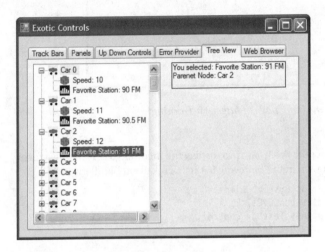

Figure 23-25. *The* TreeView *with images*

Fun with WebBrowsers

The final page of this example will make use of the System.Windows.Forms.WebBrowser widget, which is new to .NET 2.0. This widget is a highly configurable mini web browser that may be embedded into any Form-derived type. As you would expect, this control defines a Url property that can be set to any valid URI, formally represented by the System.Uri type. On the Web Browser page, add a WebBrowser (configured to your liking), a TextBox (to enter the URL), and a Button (to perform the HTTP request). Figure 23-26 shows the runtime behavior of assigning the Url property to http:// www.intertechtraining.com (yes, a shameless promotion for the company I am employed with).

Figure 23-26. *The* WebBrowser *showing the homepage of Intertech Training*

The only necessary code to instruct the WebBrowser to display the incoming HTTP request form data is to assign the Url property, as shown in the following Button Click event handler:

```
Private Sub btnGO_Click(ByVal sender As System.Object, _
  ByVal e As System.EventArgs) Handles btnGO.Click
  ' Set URL based on value within page's TextBox control.
  myWebBrowser.Url = New System.Uri(txtUrl.Text)
End Sub
```

That wraps up our examination of the widgets of the System.Windows.Forms namespace. Although I have not commented on each possible UI element, you should have no problem investigating the others further on your own time. Next up, let's look at the process of building *custom* Windows Forms controls.

■**Source Code** The ExoticControls project is included under the Chapter 23 directory.

Building Custom Windows Forms Controls

The .NET platform provides a very simple way for developers to build custom UI elements. Unlike (the now legacy) ActiveX controls, Windows Forms controls do not require vast amounts of COM infrastructure or complex memory management. Rather, .NET developers simply build a new class deriving from UserControl and populate the type with any number of properties, methods, and events. To demonstrate this process, during the next several pages you'll construct a custom control named CarControl using Visual Studio 2005.

Note As with any .NET application, you are always free to build a custom Windows Forms control using nothing more than the command-line compiler and a simple text editor. As you will see, custom controls reside in a *.dll assembly; therefore, you may specify the /target:dll option of vbc.exe.

To begin, fire up Visual Studio 2005 and select a new Windows Control Library workspace named CarControlLibrary (see Figure 23-27).

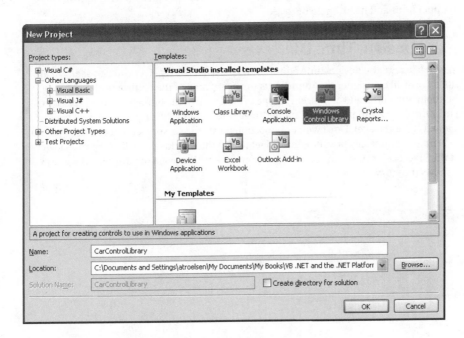

Figure 23-27. *Creating a new Windows Control Library workspace*

When you are finished, rename the initial VB 2005 class to CarControl. Like a Windows Application project workspace, your custom control is composed of two partial classes. The *.Designer.vb file contains all of the designer-generated code, and derives your type from System.Windows.Forms. UserControl:

```
Partial Class CarControl
  Inherits System.Windows.Forms.UserControl
  ...
End Class
```

Before we get too far along, let's establish the big picture of where you are going with this example. The CarControl type is responsible for animating through a series of bitmaps that will change based on the internal state of the automobile. If the car's current speed is safely under the car's maximum speed limit, the CarControl loops through three bitmap images that render an automobile driving safely along. If the current speed is 10 mph below the maximum speed, the CarControl loops through four images, with the fourth image showing the car slowly breaking down. Finally, if the car has surpassed its maximum speed, the CarControl loops over five images, where the fifth image represents a doomed automobile.

Creating the Images

Given the preceding design notes, the first order of business is to create a set of five *.bmp files for use by the animation loop. If you wish to create custom images, begin by activating the Project ▶ Add New Item menu selection and insert five new bitmap files. If you would rather not showcase your artistic abilities, feel free to use the images that accompany this sample application (keep in mind that I in *no way* consider myself a graphic artist!). The first of these three images (Lemon1.bmp, Lemon2.bmp, and Lemon3.bmp) illustrates a car navigating down the road in a safe and orderly fashion. The final two bitmap images (AboutToBlow.bmp and EngineBlown.bmp) represent a car approaching its maximum upper limit and its ultimate demise.

Building the Design-Time UI

The next step is to leverage the design-time editor for the CarControl type. As you can see, you are presented with a Form-like designer that represents the client area of the control under construction. Using the Toolbox window, add an ImageList type to hold each of the bitmaps (named carImages), a Timer type to control the animation cycle (named imageTimer), and a PictureBox to hold the current image (named currentImage). Don't worry about configuring the size or location of the PictureBox type, as you will programmatically position this widget within the bounds of the CarControl. However, be sure to set the SizeMode property of the PictureBox to StretchImage via the Properties window. Figure 23-28 shows the story thus far.

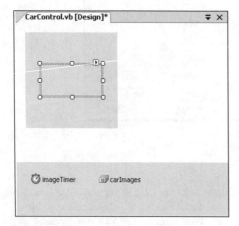

Figure 23-28. *Creating the design-time GUI*

Now, using the Properties window, configure the ImageList's Images collection by adding each bitmap to the list. Be aware that you will want to add these items sequentially (Lemon1.bmp, Lemon2.bmp, Lemon3.bmp, AboutToBlow.bmp, and EngineBlown.bmp) to ensure a linear animation cycle. Also be aware that the default width and height of *.bmp files inserted by Visual Studio 2005 is 47×47 pixels. Thus, the ImageSize of the ImageList should also be set to 47×47 (or else you will have with some skewed rendering). Finally, configure the state of your Timer type such that the Interval property is set to 200 and is initially disabled.

Implementing the Core CarControl

With this UI prep work out of the way, you can now turn to implementation of the type members. To begin, create a new public enumeration named AnimFrames, which has a member representing each item maintained by the ImageList. You will make use of this enumeration to determine the current frame to render into the PictureBox:

```
' Helper enum for images.
Public Enum AnimFrames
  Lemon1
  Lemon2
  Lemon3
  AboutToBlow
  EngineBlown
End Enum
```

The CarControl type maintains a good number of private data points to represent the animation logic. Here is the rundown of each member:

```
Public Class CarControl
  ' State data.
  Private currFrame As AnimFrames = AnimFrames.Lemon1
  Private currMaxFrame As AnimFrames = AnimFrames.Lemon3
  Private IsAnim As Boolean
  Private currSp As Integer = 50
  Private maxSp As Integer = 100
  Private carPetName As String = "Lemon"
  Private bottomRect As Rectangle = New Rectangle()
End Class
```

As you can see, you have data points that represent the current and maximum speed, the pet name of the automobile, and two members of type AnimFrames. The currFrame variable is used to specify which member of the ImageList is to be rendered. The currMaxFrame variable is used to mark the current upper limit in the ImageList (recall that the CarControl loops through three to five images based on the current speed). The IsAnim data point is used to determine whether the car is currently in animation mode. Finally, you have a Rectangle member (bottomRect), which is used to represent the bottom region of the CarControl type. Later, you render the pet name of the automobile into this piece of control real estate.

To divide the CarControl into two rectangular regions, create a private helper function named StretchBox(). The role of this member is to calculate the correct size of the bottomRect member and to ensure that the PictureBox widget is stretched out over the upper two-thirds (or so) of the CarControl type.

```
Private Sub StretchBox()
  ' Configure picture box.
  currentImage.Top = 0
  currentImage.Left = 0
  currentImage.Height = Me.Height - 50
  currentImage.Width = Me.Width
  currentImage.Image = carImages.Images(CType(AnimFrames.Lemon1, Integer))
  ' Figure out size of bottom rect.
  bottomRect.X = 0
  bottomRect.Y = Me.Height - 50
  bottomRect.Height = Me.Height - currentImage.Height
  bottomRect.Width = Me.Width
End Sub
```

Once you have carved out the dimensions of each rectangle, call StretchBox() from the default constructor:

```
Sub New()
  ' This call is required by the Windows Form Designer.
  InitializeComponent()
  StretchBox()
End Sub
```

Defining the Custom Events

The CarControl type supports two events that are fired back to the host Form based on the current speed of the automobile. The first event, AboutToBlow, is sent out when the CarControl's speed approaches the upper limit. BlewUp is sent to the container when the current speed is greater than the allowed maximum. Each of these events send out a single System.String as its parameter. You'll fire these events in just a moment, but for the time being, add the following members to the public sector of the CarControl:

```
' Car events.
Public Event AboutToBlow(ByVal msg As String)
Public Event BlewUp(ByVal msg As String)
```

Defining the Custom Properties

Like any class type, custom controls may define a set of properties to allow the outside world to interact with the state of the widget. For your current purposes, you are interested only in defining three properties. First, you have Animate. This property enables or disables the Timer type:

```
' Used to configure the internal Timer type.
Public Property Animate() As Boolean
  Get
    Return IsAnim
  End Get
  Set
    IsAnim = value
    imageTimer.Enabled = IsAnim
  End Set
End Property
```

The PetName property is what you would expect and requires little comment. Do notice, however, that when the user sets the pet name, you make a call to Invalidate() to render the name of the CarControl into the bottom rectangular area of the widget (you'll do this step in just a moment):

```
' Configure pet name.
Public Property PetName() As String
  Get
    Return carPetName
  End Get
  Set
    carPetName = value
    Invalidate()
  End Set
End Property
```

Next, you have the Speed property. In addition to simply modifying the currSp data member, Speed is the entity that fires the AboutToBlow and BlewUp events based on the current speed of the CarControl. Here is the complete logic:

```
' Adjust currSp and currMaxFrame, and fire our events.
Public Property Speed() As Integer
  Get
    Return currSp
  End Get
  Set(ByVal value As Integer)
    ' Within safe speed?
    If currSp <= maxSp Then
      currSp = value
      currMaxFrame = AnimFrames.Lemon3
    End If
    ' About to explode?
    If (maxSp - currSp) <= 10 Then
      RaiseEvent AboutToBlow("Slow down dude!")
      currMaxFrame = AnimFrames.AboutToBlow
    End If
    ' Maxed out?
    If currSp >= maxSp Then
      currSp = maxSp
      RaiseEvent BlewUp("Ug...you're toast...")
      currMaxFrame = AnimFrames.EngineBlown
    End If
    End Set
End Property
```

As you can see, if the current speed is 10 mph below the maximum upper speed, you fire the AboutToBlow event and adjust the upper frame limit to AnimFrames.AboutToBlow. If the user has pushed the limits of your automobile, you fire the BlewUp event and set the upper frame limit to AnimFrames.EngineBlown. If the speed is below the maximum speed, the upper frame limit remains as AnimFrames.Lemon3.

Controlling the Animation

The next detail to attend to is ensuring that the Timer type advances the current frame to render within the PictureBox. Again, recall that the number of frames to loop through depends on the current speed of the automobile. You only want to bother adjusting the image in the PictureBox if the Animate property has been set to true. Begin by handling the Tick event for the Timer type, and flesh out the details as follows:

```
Private Sub imageTimer_Tick(ByVal sender As System.Object, _
  ByVal e As System.EventArgs) Handles imageTimer.Tick
  If IsAnim Then
    currentImage.Image = carImages.Images(CType(currFrame, Integer))
  End If
  ' Bump frame.
  Dim nextFrame As Integer = (CType(currFrame, Integer)) + 1
  currFrame = CType(nextFrame, AnimFrames)
  If currFrame > currMaxFrame Then
    currFrame = AnimFrames.Lemon1
  End If
End Sub
```

Rendering the Pet Name

Before you can take your control out for a spin, you have one final detail to attend to: rendering the car's moniker. To do this, handle the Paint event for your CarControl, and within the handler, render the CarControl's pet name into the bottom rectangular region of the client area:

```
Private Sub CarControl_Paint(ByVal sender As System.Object, _
  ByVal e As System.Windows.Forms.PaintEventArgs) _
  Handles MyBase.Paint
  ' Render the pet name on the bottom of the control.
  Dim g As Graphics = e.Graphics
  g.FillRectangle(Brushes.GreenYellow, bottomRect)
  g.DrawString(PetName, _
    New Font("Times New Roman", 15), _
    Brushes.Black, bottomRect)
End Sub
```

At this point, your initial crack at the CarControl is complete. Go ahead and build your project.

Testing the CarControl Type

When you run or debug a Windows Control Library project within Visual Studio 2005, the UserControl Test Container (a managed replacement for the now legacy ActiveX Control Test Container) automatically loads your control into its designer test bed. As you can see from Figure 23-29, this tool allows you to set each custom property (as well as all inherited properties) for testing purposes.

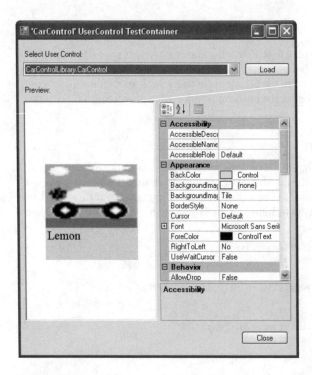

Figure 23-29. *Testing the CarControl with the UserControl Test Container*

If you set the Animate property to true, you should see the CarControl cycle through the first three *.bmp files. What you are unable to do with this testing utility, however, is handle events. To test this aspect of your UI widget, you need to build a custom Form.

Building a Custom CarControl Form Host

As with all .NET types, you are now able to make use of your custom control from any language targeting the CLR. Begin by closing down the current workspace and creating a new VB 2005 Windows Application project named CarControlTestForm. To reference your custom controls from within the Visual Studio 2005 IDE, right-click anywhere within the Toolbox window and select the Choose Item menu selection. Using the Browse button on the .NET Framework Components tab, navigate to your CarControlLibrary.dll library. Once you click OK, you will find a new icon on the Toolbox named, of course, CarControl.

Next, place a new CarControl widget onto the Forms designer. Notice that the Animate, PetName, and Speed properties are all exposed through the Properties window. Again, like the UserControl Test Container, the control is "alive" at design time. Thus, if you set the Animate property to true, you will find your car is animating on the Forms designer.

Once you have configured the initial state of your CarControl, add additional GUI widgets that allow the user to increase and decrease the speed of the automobile, and view the string data sent by the incoming events as well as the car's current speed (Label controls will do nicely for these purposes). One possible GUI design is shown in Figure 23-30.

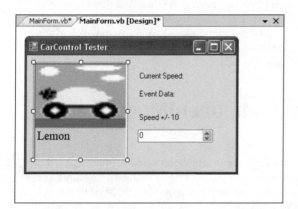

Figure 23-30. *The client-side GUI*

Provided you have created a GUI identical to mine, the code within the Form-derived type is quite straightforward (here I am assuming you have handled each of the CarControl events using the Properties window):

```
Public Class MainForm
  Sub New()
    ' This call is required by the Windows Form Designer.
    InitializeComponent()
    lblCurrentSpeed.Text = String.Format("Current Speed: {0}", _
      Me.myCarControl.Speed.ToString())
    numericUpDownCarSpeed.Value = myCarControl.Speed
```

```
' Configure the car control.
  myCarControl.Animate = True
  myCarControl.PetName = "Zippy"
End Sub
Private Sub myCarControl_AboutToBlow(ByVal msg As System.String) _
  Handles myCarControl.AboutToBlow
  lblEventData.Text = String.Format("Event Data: {0}", msg)
End Sub

Private Sub myCarControl_BlewUp(ByVal msg As System.String) _
  Handles myCarControl.BlewUp
  lblEventData.Text = String.Format("Event Data: {0}", msg)
End Sub

Private Sub numericUpDownCarSpeed_ValueChanged(ByVal sender As System.Object, _
  ByVal e As System.EventArgs) Handles numericUpDownCarSpeed.ValueChanged
  ' Assume the min of this NumericUpDown is 0 and max is 300.
  Me.myCarControl.Speed = CType(numericUpDownCarSpeed.Value, Integer)
  lblCurrentSpeed.Text = String.Format("Current Speed: {0}", _
  Me.myCarControl.Speed.ToString())
  End Sub
End Class
```

At this point, you are able to run your client application and interact with the CarControl. As you can see, building and using custom controls is a fairly straightforward task, given what you already know about OOP, the .NET type system, GDI+ (aka System.Drawing.dll), and Windows Forms.

While you now have enough information to continue exploring the process of .NET Windows controls development, there is one additional programmatic aspect you have to contend with: design-time functionality. Before I describe exactly what this boils down to, you'll need to understand the role of the System.ComponentModel namespace.

The Role of the System.ComponentModel Namespace

The System.ComponentModel namespace defines a number of attributes (among other types) that allow you to describe how your custom controls should behave at design time. For example, you can opt to supply a textual description of each property, define a default event, or group related properties or events into a custom category for display purposes within the Visual Studio 2005 Properties window. When you are interested in making the sorts of modifications previously mentioned, you will want to make use of the core attributes shown in Table 23-12.

Table 23-12. *Select Members of* System.ComponentModel

Attribute	Applied To	Meaning in Life
Browsable	Properties and events	Specifies whether a property or an event should be displayed in the property browser. By default, all custom properties and events can be browsed.
Category	Properties and events	Specifies the name of the category in which to group a property or event.
Description	Properties and events	Defines a small block of text to be displayed at the bottom of the property browser when the user selects a property or event.

Attribute	Applied To	Meaning in Life
DefaultProperty	Properties	Specifies the default property for the component. This property is selected in the property browser when a user selects the control.
DefaultValue	Properties	Defines a default value for a property that will be applied when the control is "reset" within the IDE.
DefaultEvent	Events	Specifies the default event for the component. When a programmer double-clicks the control, stub code is automatically written for the default event.

Enhancing the Design-Time Appearance of CarControl

To illustrate the use of some of these new attributes, close down the CarControlTestForm project and reopen your CarControlLibrary project. Let's create a custom category called "Car Configuration" to which each property and event of the CarControl belongs. Also, let's supply a friendly description for each member and default value for each property. To do so, simply update each of the properties and events of the CarControl type to support the <Category>, <DefaultValue>, and <Description> attributes as required:

```
Public Class CarControl
...
    ' Car events.
    <Category("Car Configuration"), _
     Description("Sent when the car is approaching terminal speed.")> _
    Public Event AboutToBlow(ByVal msg As String)
...
    ' Configure pet name.
    <Category("Car Configuration"), _
     Description("Name your car!"), _
     DefaultValue("Lemon")> _
    Public Property PetName() As String
...
    End Property
...
End Class
```

Now, let me make a comment on what it means to assign a *default value* to a property, because I can almost guarantee you it is not what you would (naturally) assume. Simply put, the <DefaultValue> attribute does *not* ensure that the underlying value of the data point wrapped by a given property will be automatically initialized to the default value. Thus, although you specified a default value of "No Name" for the PetName property, the carPetName member variable will not be set to "Lemon" unless you do so via the type's constructor or via member initialization syntax (as you have already done):

```
Private carPetName As String = "Lemon"
```

Rather, the <DefaultValue> attribute comes into play when the programmer "resets" the value of a given property using the Properties window. To reset a property using Visual Studio 2005, select the property of interest, right-click it, and select Reset. In Figure 23-31, notice that the <Description> value appears in the bottom pane of the Properties window.

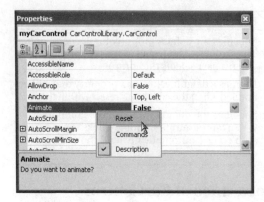

Figure 23-31. *Resetting a property to the default value*

The `<Category>` attribute will be realized only if the programmer selects the categorized view of the Properties window (as opposed to the default alphabetical view) as shown in Figure 23-32.

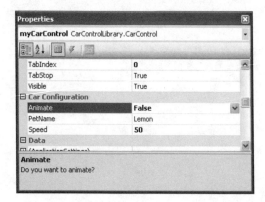

Figure 23-32. *The custom category*

Defining a Default Property and Default Event

In addition to describing and grouping like members into a common category, you may want to configure your controls to support default behaviors. A given control may support a default property. When you define the default property for a class using the `<DefaultProperty>` attribute as follows:

```
' Mark the default property for this control.
<DefaultProperty("Animate")> _
Public Class CarControl
...
End Class
```

you ensure that when the user selects this control at design time, the `Animate` property is automatically highlighted in the Properties window. Likewise, if you configure your control to have a default event as follows:

```
' Mark the default event and property for this control.
<DefaultEvent("AboutToBlow"), _
DefaultProperty("Animate")> _
Public Class CarControl
...
End Class
```

you ensure that when the user double-clicks the widget at design time, stub code is automatically written for the default event (which explains why when you double-click a Button, the Click event is automatically handled; when you double-click a Form, the Load event is automatically handled; and so on).

Specifying a Custom Toolbox Bitmap

A final design-time bell-and-whistle any polished custom control should sport is a custom toolbox bitmap image. Currently, when the user selects the CarControl, the IDE will show this type within the Toolbox using the default "gear" icon. If you wish to specify a custom image, your first step is to insert a new *.bmp file into your project (CarControl.bmp) that is configured to be 16×16 pixels in size (established via the Width and Height properties). Here, I simply reused the Car image used in the TreeView example.

Once you have created the image as you see fit, use the <ToolboxBitmap> attribute (which is applied at the type level) to assign this image to your control. The first argument to the attribute's constructor is the type information for the control itself, while the second argument is the friendly name of the *.bmp file.

```
<DefaultEvent("AboutToBlow"), _
DefaultProperty("Animate"), _
ToolboxBitmap(GetType(CarControl), "CarControl")> _
Public Class CarControl
...
End Class
```

The final step is to make sure you set the Build Action value of the control's icon image to Embedded Resource (via the Properties window) to ensure the image data is embedded within your assembly, as shown in Figure 23-33.

Figure 23-33. *Embedding the image resource*

> **■Note** The reason you are manually embedding the *.bmp file (in contrast to when you make use of the
> ImageList type) is that you are not assigning the CarControl.bmp file to a UI element at design time, therefore
> the underlying *.resx file will not automatically update.

Once you recompile your Windows Controls library, you can now load your previous
CarControlTestForm project. Right-click the current CarControl icon within the Toolbox and select
Delete. Next, re-add the CarControl widget to the Toolbox (by right-clicking and selecting Choose
Items). This time, you should see your custom toolbox bitmap (see Figure 23-34).

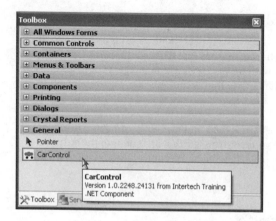

Figure 23-34. *The custom toolbox bitmap*

So, that wraps up our examination of the process of building custom Windows Forms controls.
I hope this example sparked your interest in custom control development. Here, I stuck with the
book's automobile theme. Imagine, though, the usefulness of a custom control that will render a pie
chart based on the current inventory of a given table in a given database, or a control that extends
the functionality of standard UI widgets.

> **■Source Code** The CarControlLibrary and CarControlTestForm projects are included under the Chapter 23
> directory.

Building Custom Dialog Boxes

Now that you have a solid understanding of the core Windows Forms controls and the process of
building custom controls, let's examine the construction of custom dialog boxes. The good news is
that everything you have already learned about Windows Forms applies directly to dialog box programming. By and large, creating (and showing) a dialog box is no more difficult than inserting
a new Form into your current project.

There is no "Dialog" base class in the System.Windows.Forms namespace. Rather, a dialog box is
simply a stylized Form. For example, many dialog boxes are intended to be nonsizable, therefore
you will typically want to set the FormBorderStyle property to FormBorderStyle.FixedDialog. As
well, dialog boxes typically set the MinimizeBox and MaximizeBox properties to false. In this way, the

dialog box is configured to be a fixed constant. Finally, if you set the ShowInTaskbar property to false, you will prevent the Form from being visible in the Windows XP task bar.

To illustrate the process of working with dialog boxes, create a new Windows application named SimpleModalDialog. The main Form type supports a MenuStrip that contains a File ➤ Exit menu item as well as Tools ➤ Configure. Build this UI now, and handle the Click event for the Exit and Enter Message menu items. As well, define a string member variable in your main Form type (named userMessage), and render this data within a Paint event handler of your main Form. Here is the current code within the MainForm.vb file:

```vb
Public Class MainForm
  Private userMessage As String = "Default Message"

  ' We will implement this method in just a bit...
  Private Sub configureToolStripMenuItem_Click(ByVal sender As System.Object, _
  ByVal e As System.EventArgs) Handles configureToolStripMenuItem.Click
  End Sub

  Private Sub exitToolStripMenuItem_Click(ByVal sender As System.Object, _
  ByVal e As System.EventArgs) Handles exitToolStripMenuItem.Click
    Application.Exit()
  End Sub

  Private Sub MainForm_Paint(ByVal sender As System.Object, _
  ByVal e As System.Windows.Forms.PaintEventArgs) Handles MyBase.Paint
  Dim g As Graphics = e.Graphics
  g.DrawString(userMessage, New Font("Times New Roman", 24), _
    Brushes.DarkBlue, 50, 50)
  End Sub
End Class
```

Now add a new Form to your current project using the Project ➤ Add Windows Form menu item named UserMessageDialog.vb. Set the ShowInTaskbar, MinimizeBox, and MaximizeBox properties to False. Next, build a UI that consists of two Button types (for the OK and Cancel buttons), a single TextBox (to allow the user to enter her message), and an instructive Label. Figure 23-35 shows one possible UI.

Figure 23-35. *A custom dialog box*

Finally, expose the Text value of the Form's TextBox using a custom property named Message:

```
Public Class UserMessageDialog
  Public Property Message() As String
    Get
      Return txtUserInput.Text
    End Get
    Set(ByVal value As String)
      txtUserInput.Text = value
    End Set
  End Property
End Class
```

The DialogResult Property

As a final UI task, select the OK button on the Forms designer and find the DialogResult property. Assign DialogResult.OK to your OK button and DialogResult.Cancel to your Cancel button. Formally, you can assign the DialogResult property to any value from the DialogResult enumeration:

```
Public Enum DialogResult
  Abort
  Cancel
  Ignore
  No
  None
  OK
  Retry
  Yes
End Enum
```

So, what exactly does it mean to assign a Button's DialogResult value? This property can be assigned to any Button type (as well as the Form itself) and allows the parent Form to determine which button the end user selected. To illustrate, update the Tools ➤ Configure menu handler on the MainForm type as follows:

```
Private Sub configureToolStripMenuItem_Click(ByVal sender As System.Object, _
  ByVal e As System.EventArgs) Handles configureToolStripMenuItem.Click
  ' Create an instance of UserMessageDialog.
  Dim dlg As UserMessageDialog = New UserMessageDialog()

  ' Place the current message in the TextBox.
  dlg.Message = userMessage

  ' If user clicked OK button, render his message.
  If Windows.Forms.DialogResult.OK = dlg.ShowDialog() Then
    userMessage = dlg.Message
    Invalidate()
  End If

  ' Have dialog clean up internal widgets now, rather
  ' than when the GC destroys the object.
  dlg.Dispose()
End Sub
```

Here, you are showing the UserMessageDialog via a call to ShowDialog(). This method will launch the Form as a *modal* dialog box which, as you may know, means the user is unable to activate the main form until she dismisses the dialog box. Once the user does dismiss the dialog box (by clicking the OK or Cancel button), the Form is no longer visible, but it is still in memory. Therefore, you are able to ask the UserMessageDialog instance (dlg) for its new Message value in the event the user has clicked the OK button. If so, you render the new message. If not, you do nothing.

■**Note** If you wish to show a modeless dialog box (which allows the user to navigate between the parent and dialog Forms), call Show() rather than ShowDialog().

Understanding Form Inheritance

One very appealing aspect of building dialog boxes under Windows Forms is *form inheritance*. As you are no doubt aware, inheritance is the pillar of OOP that allows one class to extend the functionality of another class. Typically, when you speak of inheritance, you envision one non-GUI type (e.g., SportsCar) deriving from another non-GUI type (e.g., Car). However, in the world of Windows Forms, it is possible for one Form to derive from another Form and in the process inherit the base class's widgets and implementation.

   Form-level inheritance is a very powerful technique, as it allows you to build a base Form that provides core-level functionality for a family of related dialog boxes. If you were to bundle these base-level Forms into a .NET assembly, other members of your team could extend these types using the .NET language of their choice.

   For the sake of illustration, assume you wish to subclass the UserMessageDialog to build a new dialog box that also allows the user to specify whether the message should be rendered in italics. To do so, active the Project ➤ Add Windows Form menu item, but this time add a new Inherited Form named ItalicUserMessageDialog.vb, as shown in Figure 23-36.

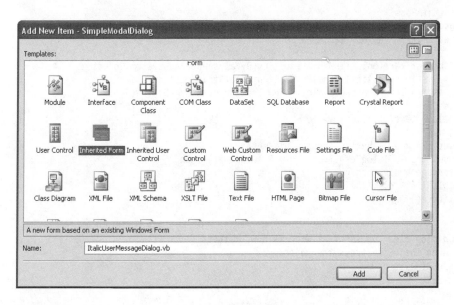

Figure 23-36. *A derived Form*

Once you select Add, you will be shown the *Inheritance Picker* utility, which allows you to choose from a Form in your current project or select a Form in an external assembly via the Browse button. For this example, select your existing UserMessageDialog type.

Note If you cannot find your Form listed in the Inheritance Picker, you have not yet built your project! This dialog box is using reflection to find all Form derived types in your assembly, therefore if your build is out of date, the metadata has not been refreshed.

If you look in your `*.designer.vb` file, you will find that your new Form type extends your current dialog type rather than directly from Form. At this point, you are free to extend this derived Form any way you choose. For test purposes, simply add a new CheckBox control (named checkBoxItalic) that is exposed through a property named Italic:

```
Public Class ItalicUserMessageDialog
  Public Property Italic() As Boolean
    Get
      Return checkBoxItalic.Checked
    End Get
    Set(ByVal value As Boolean)
      checkBoxItalic.Checked = value
    End Set
  End Property
End Class
```

Now that you have subclassed the basic UserMessageDialog type, update your MainForm to leverage the new Italic property. Simply add a new Boolean member variable that will be used to build an italic Font object, and update your Tools ➤ Configure Click menu handler to make use of ItalicUserMessageDialog. Here is the complete update:

```
Public Class MainForm
  Private userMessage As String = "Default Message"
  Private textIsItalic As Boolean = False

  Private Sub configureToolStripMenuItem_Click(ByVal sender As System.Object, _
  ByVal e As System.EventArgs) Handles configureToolStripMenuItem.Click
    Dim dlg As ItalicUserMessageDialog = New ItalicUserMessageDialog()
    dlg.Message = userMessage
    dlg.Italic = textIsItalic

    ' If user clicked OK button, render his message.
    If Windows.Forms.DialogResult.OK = dlg.ShowDialog() Then
      userMessage = dlg.Message
      textIsItalic = dlg.Italic
      Invalidate()
    End If

    ' Have dialog clean up internal widgets now, rather
    ' than when the GC destroys the object.
    dlg.Dispose()
  End Sub
...
  Private Sub MainForm_Paint(ByVal sender As System.Object, _
  ByVal e As System.Windows.Forms.PaintEventArgs) Handles MyBase.Paint
    Dim g As Graphics = e.Graphics
    Dim f As Font = Nothing
    If textIsItalic Then
      f = New Font("Times New Roman", 24, FontStyle.Italic)
    Else
      f = New Font("Times New Roman", 24)
```

```
      End If
      g.DrawString(userMessage, f, Brushes.DarkBlue, 50, 50)
   End Sub
End Class
```

■**Source Code** The SimpleModalDialog application is included under the Chapter 23 directory.

Dynamically Positioning Windows Forms Controls

To wrap up this chapter, let's examine a few techniques you can use to control the layout of widgets on a Form. By and large, when you build a Form type, the assumption is that the controls are rendered using *absolute position*, meaning that if you placed a Button on your Forms designer 10 pixels down and 10 pixels over from the upper left portion of the Form, you expect the Button to stay put during its lifetime.

On a related note, when you are creating a Form that contains UI controls, you need to decide whether the Form should be resizable. Typically speaking, main windows are resizable, whereas dialog boxes are not. Recall that the resizability of a Form is controlled by the FormBorderStyle property, which can be set to any value of the FormBorderStyle enum.

```
Public Enum FormBorderStyle
   None
   FixedSingle
   Fixed3D
   FixedDialog
   Sizable
   FixedToolWindow
   SizableToolWindow
End Enum
```

Assume that you have allowed your Form to be resizable. This brings up some interesting questions regarding the contained controls. For example, if the user makes the Form smaller than the rectangle needed to display each control, should the controls adjust their size (and possibly location) to morph correctly with the Form?

The Anchor Property

In Windows Forms, the Anchor property is used to define a relative fixed position in which the control should always be rendered. Every Control-derived type has an Anchor property, which can be set to any of the values from the AnchorStyles enumeration described in Table 23-13.

Table 23-13. AnchorStyles *Values*

Value	Meaning in Life
Bottom	The control's bottom edge is anchored to the bottom edge of its container.
Left	The control's left edge is anchored to the left edge of its container.
None	The control is not anchored to any edges of its container.
Right	The control's right edge is anchored to the right edge of its container.
Top	The control's top edge is anchored to the top edge of its container.

To anchor a widget at the upper-left corner, you are free to OR styles together (e.g., AnchorStyles.Top ➤ AnchorStyles.Left). Again, the idea behind the Anchor property is to configure which edges of the control are anchored to the edges of its container. For example, if you configure a Button with the following Anchor value:

```
' Anchor this widget relative to the right position.
myButton.Anchor = AnchorStyles.Right
```

you are ensured that as the Form is resized, this Button maintains its position relative to the right side of the Form.

The Dock Property

Another aspect of Windows Forms programming is establishing the *docking behavior* of your controls. If you so choose, you can set a widget's Dock property to configure which side (or sides) of a Form the widget should be attached to. The value you assign to a control's Dock property is honored, regardless of the Form's current dimensions. Table 23-14 describes possible options.

Table 23-14. DockStyle *Values*

Value	Meaning in Life
Bottom	The control's bottom edge is docked to the bottom of its containing control.
Fill	All the control's edges are docked to all the edges of its containing control and sized appropriately.
Left	The control's left edge is docked to the left edge of its containing control.
None	The control is not docked.
Right	The control's right edge is docked to the right edge of its containing control.
Top	The control's top edge is docked to the top of its containing control.

So, for example, if you want to ensure that a given widget is always docked on the left side of a Form, you would write the following:

```
' This item is always located on the left of the Form, regardless
' of the Form's current size.
myButton.Dock = DockStyle.Left
```

To help you understand the implications of setting the Anchor and Dock properties, the downloadable code for this book contains a project named AnchoringControls. Once you build and run this application, you can make use of the Form's menu system to set various AnchorStyles and DockStyle values and observe the change in behavior of the Button type (see Figure 23-37).

Be sure to resize the Form when changing the Anchor property to observe how the Button responds.

■Source Code   The AnchoringControls application is included under the Chapter 23 directory.

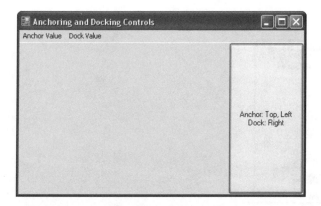

Figure 23-37. *The AnchoringControls application*

Table and Flow Layout

.NET 2.0 offers an additional way to control the layout of a Form's widgets using one of two layout managers. The TableLayoutPanel and FlowLayoutPanel types can be docked into a Form's client area to arrange the internal controls. For example, assume you place a new FlowLayoutPanel widget onto the Forms designer and configure it to dock fully within the parent Form, as you see in Figure 23-38.

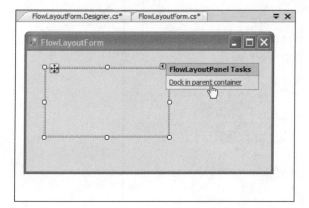

Figure 23-38. *Docking a FlowLayoutPanel into a Form*

Now, add ten new Button types within the FlowLayoutPanel using the Forms designer. If you now run your application, you will notice that the ten Buttons automatically rearrange themselves in a manner very close to standard HTML.

On the other hand, if you create a Form that contains a TableLayoutPanel, you are able to build a UI that is partitioned into various "cells," as shown in Figure 23-39.

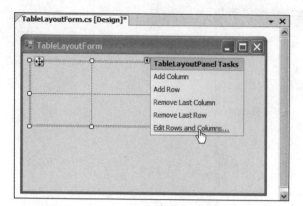

Figure 23-39. *The* TableLayoutPanel *type*

If you select the Edit Rows and Columns inline menu option using the Forms designer (as shown in Figure 23-39), you are able to control the overall format of the TableLayoutPanel on a cell-by-cell basis (see Figure 23-40).

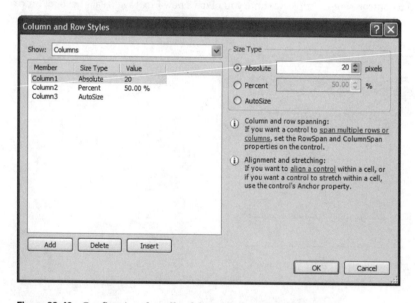

Figure 23-40. *Configuring the cells of the* TableLayoutPanel *type*

Truth be told, the only way to see the effects of the TableLayoutPanel type is to do so in a hands-on manner. I'll let interested readers handle that task.

Summary

This chapter rounded off your understanding of the Windows Forms namespace by examining the programming of numerous GUI widgets, from the simple (e.g., Label) to the more exotic (e.g., TreeView). After examining numerous control types, you moved on to cover the construction of custom controls, including the topic of design-time integration.

In the latter half of this chapter, you learned how to build custom dialog boxes and how to derive a new Form from an existing Form type using form inheritance. This chapter concluded by briefly exploring the various anchoring and docking behaviors you can use to enforce a specific layout of your GUI types, as well as the new .NET 2.0 layout managers.

CHAPTER 24

■■■

Database Access with ADO.NET

Unless you are a video game developer by trade, you are probably interested in the topic of database access. As you would expect, the .NET platform defines a number of namespaces that allow you to interact with local and remote data stores. Collectively speaking, these namespaces are known as *ADO.NET*.

In this chapter, once I frame the overall role of ADO.NET, I'll move on to discuss the topic of ADO.NET data providers. The .NET platform supports numerous data providers, each of which is optimized to communicate with a specific database management system (Microsoft SQL Server, Oracle, MySQL, etc.). After you understand how to manipulate a specific data provider, you will then examine the new data provider factory pattern offered by .NET 2.0. Using types within the System. Data.Common namespace (and a related app.config file), you are able to build a single code base that can dynamically pick and choose the underlying data provider without the need to recompile or redeploy the application's code base.

The remaining part of this chapter examines how to programmatically interact with relational databases using your data provider of choice. As you will see, ADO.NET provides two distinct ways to interface with a data source, often termed the *connected layer* and the *disconnected layer*. You will come to know the role of connection objects, command objects, data readers, data adapters, and numerous types within the System.Data namespace (specifically, DataSet, DataTable, DataRow, DataColumn, DataView, and DataRelation). I'll wrap up by showing you several tools of Visual Studio 2005 that allow you to rapidly build Windows Forms applications that interact with external data stores.

A High-level Definition of ADO.NET

If you have a background in Microsoft's previous COM-based data access model (Active Data Objects, or ADO), understand that ADO.NET has very little to do with ADO beyond the letters "A," "D," and "O." While it is true that there is some relationship between the two systems (e.g., each has the concept of connection and command objects), some familiar ADO types (e.g., the Recordset) no longer exist. Furthermore, there are a number of new ADO.NET types that have no direct equivalent under classic ADO (e.g., the data adapter).

Unlike classic ADO, which was primarily designed for tightly coupled client/server systems, ADO.NET was built with the disconnected world in mind, using DataSets. This type represents a local copy of any number of related tables. Using the DataSet, the client tier is able to manipulate and update its contents while disconnected from the data source, and it can submit the modified data back for processing using a related data adapter.

Another major difference between classic ADO and ADO.NET is that ADO.NET has deep support for XML data representation. In fact, the data obtained from a data store is serialized (by default) as XML. Given that XML is often transported between layers using standard HTTP, ADO.NET is not limited by firewall constraints.

■**Note** As of .NET 2.0, `DataSets` (and `DataTables`) can now be serialized in a binary format via the `RemotingFormat` property. This can be helpful when building distributed systems using the .NET remoting layer (see Chapter 20), as binary data is much more compact than XML data.

Perhaps the most fundamental difference between classic ADO and ADO.NET is that ADO.NET is a managed library of code, therefore it plays by the same rules as any managed library. The types that make up ADO.NET use the CLR memory management protocol, adhere to the same type system (classes, interfaces, enums, structures, and delegates), and can be accessed by any .NET language.

The Two Faces of ADO.NET

The ADO.NET libraries can be used in two conceptually unique manners: connected or disconnected. When you are making use of the *connected layer*, your code base will explicitly connect to and disconnect from the underlying data store. When you are using ADO.NET in this manner, you typically interact with the data store using connection objects, command objects, and data reader objects. As you will see later in this chapter, data readers provide a way to pull records from a data store using a forward-only, read-only approach (much like a fire-hose cursor).

The disconnected layer, on the other hand, allows you to obtain a set of `DataTable` objects (contained within a `DataSet`) that functions as a client-side copy of the external data. When you obtain a `DataSet` using a related data adapter object, the connection is automatically opened and closed on your behalf. As you would guess, this approach helps quickly free up connections for other callers. Once the client receives a `DataSet`, it is able to traverse and manipulate the contents without incurring the cost of network traffic. As well, if the client wishes to submit the changes back to the data store, the data adapter (in conjunction with a set of SQL statements) is used once again to update the data source, at which point the connection is closed immediately.

Understanding ADO.NET Data Providers

Unlike classic ADO, ADO.NET does not provide a single set of types that communicate with multiple database management systems (DBMSs). Rather, ADO.NET supports multiple *data providers*, each of which is optimized to interact with a specific DBMS. The first benefit of this approach is that a specific data provider can be programmed to access any unique features of the DBMS. Another benefit is that a specific data provider is able to directly connect to the underlying engine of the DBMS without an intermediate mapping layer standing between the tiers.

Simply put, a *data provider* is a set of types defined in a given namespace that understand how to communicate with a specific data source. Regardless of which data provider you make use of, each defines a set of class types that provide core functionality. Table 24-1 documents some (but not all) of the core common objects, their base class (all defined in the `System.Data.Common` namespace), and their implemented data-centric interfaces (each defined in the `System.Data` namespace).

Table 24-1. *Core Objects of an ADO.NET Data Provider*

Object	Base Class	Implemented Interfaces	Meaning in Life
Connection	DbConnection	IDbConnection	Provides the ability to connect to and disconnect from the data store. Connection objects also provide access to a related transaction object.
Command	DbCommand	IDbCommand	Represents a SQL query or name of a stored procedure. Command objects also provide access to the provider's data reader object.
DataReader	DbDataReader	IDataReader, IDataRecord	Provides forward-only, read-only access to data.
DataAdapter	DbDataAdapter	IDataAdapter, IDbDataAdapter	Transfers DataSets between the caller and the data store. Data adapters contain a set of four internal command objects used to select, insert, update, and delete information from the data store.
Parameter	DbParameter	IDataParameter, IDbDataParameter	Represents a named parameter within a parameterized query.
Transaction	DbTransaction	IDbTransaction	Performs a database transaction.

Although the names of these types will differ among data providers (e.g., SqlConnection versus OracleConnection versus OdbcConnection versus MySqlConnection), each object derives from the same base class that implements identical interfaces. Given this, you are correct to assume that once you learn how to work with one data provider, the remaining providers are quite straightforward.

■**Note** As a naming convention, the objects in a specific data provider are prefixed with the name of the related DBMS (for example, SqlDataReader, OracleCommand, MySqlParameter, etc.).

Figure 24-1 illustrates the big picture behind ADO.NET data providers. Note that in the diagram, the "Client Assembly" can literally be any type of .NET application: console program, Windows Forms application, ASP.NET web page, XML web service, .NET code library, and so on.

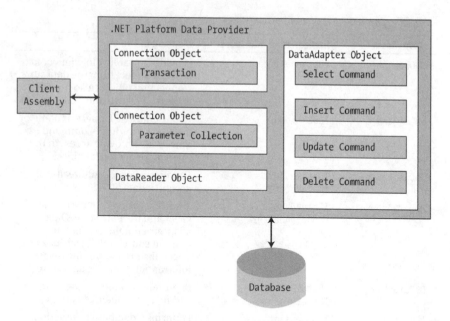

Figure 24-1. *ADO.NET data providers provide access to a given DBMS.*

Now, to be sure, a data provider will supply you with other types beyond the objects shown in Figure 24-1. However, these core objects define a common baseline across all data providers.

Microsoft-supplied Data Providers

As of version 2.0, Microsoft's .NET distribution ships with numerous data providers, including a provider for Oracle, SQL Server, and ODBC-style connectivity. Table 24-2 documents the namespace and containing assembly for each Microsoft ADO.NET data provider.

Table 24-2. *Microsoft ADO.NET Data Providers*

Data Provider	Namespace	Assembly
OLE DB	System.Data.OleDb	System.Data.dll
Microsoft SQL Server	System.Data.SqlClient	System.Data.dll
Microsoft SQL Server Mobile	System.Data.SqlServerCe	System.Data.SqlServerCe.dll
ODBC	System.Data.Odbc	System.Data.dll
Oracle	System.Data.OracleClient	System.Data.OracleClient.dll

■**Note** There is no specific data provider that maps directly to the Jet engine (and therefore Microsoft Access). If you wish to interact with an Access data file, you can do so using the OLE DB or ODBC data provider.

The OLE DB data provider, which is composed of the types defined in the System.Data.OleDb namespace, allows you to access data located in any data store that supports the classic COM-based OLE DB protocol. Using this provider, you may communicate with any OLE DB–compliant database simply by tweaking the Provider segment of your connection string. Be aware, however, that the OLE DB provider interacts with various COM objects behind the scenes, which can affect the performance of your application. By and large, the OLE DB data provider is only useful if you are interacting with a DBMS that does not define a specific .NET data provider.

The Microsoft SQL Server data provider offers direct access to Microsoft SQL Server data stores, and *only* SQL Server data stores (version 7.0 and greater). The `System.Data.SqlClient` namespace contains the types used by the SQL Server provider and offers the same basic functionality as the OLE DB provider. The key difference is that the SQL Server provider bypasses the OLE DB layer and thus gives numerous performance benefits. As well, the Microsoft SQL Server data provider allows you to gain access to the unique features of this particular DBMS.

Note If you are interested in making use of the `System.Data.SqlServerCe`, `System.Data.Odbc`, or `System.Data.Oracle` namespaces, check out the details as you see fit using the .NET Framework 2.0 SDK documentation.

Select Third-party Data Providers

In addition to the data providers that ship from Microsoft, numerous third-party data providers exist for various open source and commercial databases. Table 24-3 documents where to obtain managed providers for several popular databases that do not directly ship with Microsoft .NET 2.0 (please note that the provided URLs are subject to change).

Table 24-3. *Third-party ADO.NET Data Providers*

Data Provider	Website
Firebird Interbase	http://www.mono-project.com/Firebird_Interbase
IBM DB2 Universal Database	http://www-306.ibm.com/software/data/db2
MySQL	http://dev.mysql.com/downloads/connector/net/1.0.html
PostgreSQL	http://www.mono-project.com/PostgreSQL
Sybase	http://www.mono-project.com/Sybase

Note There are many websites that catalog known ADO.NET data providers. Check out http://www.sqlsummit.com/DataProv.htm to view a very inclusive listing.

Additional ADO.NET Namespaces

In addition to the .NET namespaces that define the types of a specific data provider, the base class libraries provide a number of additional ADO.NET-centric namespaces, as shown in Table 24-4.

Table 24-4. *Additional ADO.NET-centric Namespaces*

Namespace	Meaning in Life
`Microsoft.SqlServer.Server`	This new .NET 2.0 namespace provides types that allow you to author stored procedures via managed languages for SQL Server 2005.
`System.Data`	This namespace defines the core ADO.NET types used by all data providers.
`System.Data.Common`	This namespace contains types shared between data providers, including the .NET 2.0 data provider factory types.

Continued

Table 24-4. *Continued*

Namespace	Meaning in Life
System.Data.Design	This new .NET 2.0 namespace contains various types used to construct a design-time appearance for custom data components.
System.Data.Sql	This new .NET 2.0 namespace contains types that allow you to discover Microsoft SQL Server instances installed on the current local network.
System.Data.SqlTypes	This namespace contains native data types used by Microsoft SQL Server. Although you are always free to use the corresponding CLR data types, the SqlTypes are optimized to work with SQL Server.

Do understand that this chapter will not examine each and every type within each and every ADO.NET namespace (that task would require a large book in and of itself). However, it is quite important for you to understand the types within the System.Data namespace.

The System.Data Types

Of all the ADO.NET namespaces, System.Data is the lowest common denominator. You simply cannot build ADO.NET applications without specifying this namespace in your data access applications. This namespace contains types that are shared among all ADO.NET data providers, regardless of the underlying data store. In addition to a number of database-centric exceptions (NoNullAllowedException, RowNotInTableException, MissingPrimaryKeyException, and the like), System.Data contains types that represent various database primitives (tables, rows, columns, constraints, etc.), as well as the common interfaces implemented by data provider objects. Table 24-5 lists some of the core types to be aware of.

Table 24-5. *Core Members of the* System.Data *Namespace*

Type	Meaning in Life
Constraint	Represents a constraint for a given DataColumn object.
DataColumn	Represents a single column within a DataTable object.
DataRelation	Represents a parent/child relationship between two DataTable objects.
DataRow	Represents a single row within a DataTable object.
DataSet	Represents an in-memory cache of data consisting of any number of interrelated DataTable objects.
DataTable	Represents a tabular block of in-memory data.
DataTableReader	Allows you to treat a DataTable as a fire-hose cursor (forward only, read-only data access). New in .NET 2.0.
DataView	Represents a customized view of a DataTable for sorting, filtering, searching, editing, and navigation.
IDataAdapter	Defines the core behavior of a data adapter object.
IDataParameter	Defines the core behavior of a parameter object.
IDataReader	Defines the core behavior of a data reader object.
IDbCommand	Defines the core behavior of a command object.
IDbDataAdapter	Extends IDataAdapter to provide additional functionality of a data adapter object.
IDbTransaction	Defines the core behavior of a transaction object.

Later in this chapter, you will get to know the role of the DataSet and its related cohorts (DataTable, DataRelation, DataRow, etc.). However, your next task is to examine the core interfaces of System.Data at a high level, to better understand the common functionality offered by any data provider. You will learn specific details throughout this chapter, so for the time being let's simply focus on the overall behavior of each interface type.

The Role of the IDbConnection Interface

First up is the IDbConnection type, which is implemented by a data provider's *connection object*. This interface defines a set of members used to configure a connection to a specific data store, and it also allows you to obtain the data provider's transactional object. Here is the formal definition of IDbConnection:

```
Public Interface IDbConnection
  Inherits IDisposable
  Property ConnectionString() As String
  ReadOnly Property ConnectionTimeout() As Integer
  ReadOnly Property Database() As String
  ReadOnly Property State() As ConnectionState
  Function BeginTransaction() As IDbTransaction
  Function BeginTransaction(ByVal il As IsolationLevel) As IDbTransaction
  Sub ChangeDatabase(ByVal databaseName As String)
  Sub Close()
  Function CreateCommand() As IDbCommand
  Sub Open()
End Interface
```

The Role of the IDbTransaction Interface

As you can see, the overloaded BeginTransaction() method defined by IDbConnection provides access to the provider's *transaction object*. Using the members defined by IDbTransaction, you are able to programmatically interact with a transactional session and the underlying data store:

```
Public Interface IDbTransaction
  Inherits IDisposable
  ReadOnly Property Connection() As IDbConnection
  ReadOnly Property IsolationLevel() As IsolationLevel
  Sub Commit()
  Sub Rollback()
End Interface
```

The Role of the IDbCommand Interface

Next, we have the IDbCommand interface, which will be implemented by a data provider's *command object*. Like other data access object models, command objects allow programmatic manipulation of SQL statements, stored procedures, and parameterized queries. In addition, command objects provide access to the data provider's data reader type via the overloaded ExecuteReader() method:

```
Public Interface IDbCommand
  Inherits IDisposable
  Property CommandText() As String
  Property CommandTimeout() As Integer
  Property CommandType() As CommandType
  Property Connection() As IDbConnection
  ReadOnly Property Parameters() As IDataParameterCollection
  Property Transaction() As IDbTransaction
```

```
  Property UpdatedRowSource() As UpdateRowSource
  Sub Cancel()
  Function CreateParameter() As IDbDataParameter
  Function ExecuteNonQuery() As Integer
  Function ExecuteReader() As IDataReader
  Function ExecuteReader(ByVal behavior As CommandBehavior) As IDataReader
  Function ExecuteScalar() As Object
  Sub Prepare()
End Interface
```

The Role of the IDbDataParameter and IDataParameter Interfaces

Notice that the Parameters property of IDbCommand returns a strongly typed collection that implements IDataParameterCollection. This interface provides access to a set of IDbDataParameter-compliant class types (e.g., parameter objects):

```
Public Interface IDbDataParameter
  Inherits IDataParameter
  Property Precision() As Byte
  Property Scale() As Byte
  Property Size() As Integer
End Interface
```

IDbDataParameter extends the IDataParameter interface to obtain the following additional behaviors:

```
Public Interface IDataParameter
  Property DbType() As DbType
  Property Direction() As ParameterDirection
  ReadOnly Property IsNullable() As Boolean
  Property ParameterName() As String
  Property SourceColumn() As String
  Property SourceVersion() As DataRowVersion
  Property Value() As Object
End Interface
```

As you will see, the functionality of the IDbDataParameter and IDataParameter interfaces allows you to represent parameters within a SQL command (including stored procedures) via specific ADO.NET parameter objects rather than hard-coded string literals.

The Role of the IDbDataAdapter and IDataAdapter Interfaces

Data adapters are used to push and pull DataSets to and from a given data store. Given this, the IDbDataAdapter interface defines a set of properties that are used to maintain the SQL statements for the related select, insert, update, and delete operations:

```
Public Interface IDbDataAdapter
  Inherits IDataAdapter
  Property DeleteCommand() As IDbCommand
  Property InsertCommand() As IDbCommand
  Property SelectCommand() As IDbCommand
  Property UpdateCommand() As IDbCommand
End Interface
```

In addition to these four properties, an ADO.NET data adapter also picks up the behavior defined in the base interface, IDataAdapter. This interface defines the key function of a data adapter type:

the ability to transfer DataSets between the caller and underlying data store using the Fill() and Update() methods.

As well, the IDataAdapter interface allows you to map database column names to more user-friendly display names via the TableMappings property:

```
Public Interface IDataAdapter
    Property MissingMappingAction() As MissingMappingAction
    Property MissingSchemaAction() As MissingSchemaAction
    ReadOnly Property TableMappings() As ITableMappingCollection
    Function Fill(ByVal dataSet As System.Data.DataSet) As Integer
    Function FillSchema(ByVal dataSet As DataSet, _
        ByVal schemaType As SchemaType) As DataTable()
    Function GetFillParameters() As IDataParameter()
    Function Update(ByVal dataSet As DataSet) As Integer
End Interface
```

The Role of the IDataReader and IDataRecord Interfaces

The next key interface to be aware of is IDataReader, which represents the common behaviors supported by a given data reader object. When you obtain an IDataReader-compatible type from an ADO.NET data provider, you are able to iterate over the result set in a forward-only, read-only manner.

```
Public Interface IDataReader
    Inherits IDisposable
    Inherits IDataRecord
    ReadOnly Property Depth() As Integer
    ReadOnly Property IsClosed() As Boolean
    ReadOnly Property RecordsAffected() As Integer
    Sub Close()
    Function GetSchemaTable() As DataTable
    Function NextResult() As Boolean
    Function Read() As Boolean
End Interface
```

Finally, as you can see, IDataReader extends IDataRecord, which defines a good number of members that allow you to extract a strongly typed value from the stream, rather than casting the generic System.Object retrieved from the data reader's overloaded indexer method. Here is a partial listing of the various GetXXX() methods defined by IDataRecord (see the .NET Framework 2.0 SDK documentation for a complete listing):

```
Public Interface IDataRecord
    ReadOnly Property FieldCount() As Integer
    Function GetBoolean(ByVal i As Integer) As Boolean
    Function GetByte(ByVal i As Integer) As Byte
    Function GetChar(ByVal i As Integer) As Char
    Function GetDateTime(ByVal i As Integer) As DateTime
    Function GetDecimal(ByVal i As Integer) As Decimal
    Function GetFloat(ByVal i As Integer) As Single
    Function GetInt16(ByVal i As Integer) As Short
    Function GetInt32(ByVal i As Integer) As Integer
    Function GetInt64(ByVal i As Integer) As Long
    Function IsDBNull(ByVal i As Integer) As Boolean
...
End Interface
```

Note The IDataReader.IsDBNull() method can be used to programmatically discover whether a specified field is set to Nothing before obtaining a value from the data reader (to avoid triggering a runtime exception).

Abstracting Data Providers Using Interfaces

At this point, you should have a better idea of the common functionality found among all .NET data providers, based on the core interfaces you just examined. Recall that even though the exact names of the implementing types will differ among data providers, you are able to program against these types in a similar manner—that's the beauty of interface-based polymorphism. Therefore, if you define a method that takes an IDbConnection parameter, you can pass in any ADO.NET connection object:

```
Public Sub OpenConnection(ByVal cn As IDbConnection)
  ' Open the incoming connection for the caller.
  cn.Open()
End Sub
```

The same holds true for a member return value. For example, consider the following example VB 2005 program, which allows the caller to obtain a specific connection object using the value of a custom enumeration and a custom function named GetConnection():

```
Enum DataProvider
  SqlServer
  OleDb
  Odbc
  Oracle
End Enum

Module Program
  Sub Main()
    ' Get a specific connection via GetConnection() helper function.
    Dim myCn As IDbConnection = GetConnection(DataProvider.SqlServer)

    ' Assume we wish to connect to the SQL Server Pubs database.
    myCn.ConnectionString = _
      "Data Source=localhost;uid=sa;pwd=;Initial Catalog=Pubs"

    ' Now open connection via our other helper function.
    OpenConnection(myCn)

    ' Use connection and close when finished.
    ...
    myCn.Close()
  End Sub

  Function GetConnection(ByVal dp As DataProvider) As IDbConnection
    Dim conn As IDbConnection = Nothing
    Select dp
      Case DataProvider.SqlServer
        conn = New SqlConnection()
        Exit Select
      Case DataProvider.OleDb
        conn = New OleDbConnection()
        Exit Select
      Case DataProvider.Odbc
```

```
            conn = New OdbcConnection()
            Exit Select
        Case DataProvider.Oracle
            conn = New OracleConnection()
            Exit Select
        End Select
    Return conn
  End Function
End Module
```

The benefit of working with the general interfaces of System.Data is that you have a much better chance of building a flexible code base that can evolve over time. For example, perhaps today you are building an application targeting Microsoft SQL Server, but what if your company switches to Oracle months down the road? If you hard-code the types of System.Data.SqlClient, you will obviously need to edit, recompile, and redeploy the assembly.

Increasing Flexibility Using Application Configuration Files

To further increase the flexibility of your ADO.NET applications, you could incorporate a client-side *.config file that makes use of custom key/value pairs within the <appSettings> element. Recall from Chapter 13 that custom data can be programmatically obtained using types within the System.Configuration namespace. For example, assume you have specified the connection string and data provider values within a configuration file as follows:

```
<configuration>
  <appSettings>
    <add key="provider" value="SqlServer" />
    <add key="cnStr" value=
      "Data Source=localhost;uid=sa;pwd=;Initial Catalog=Pubs"/>
  </appSettings>
</configuration>
```

With this, you could update Main() to programmatically read these values. By doing so, you essentially build a *data provider factory*. Here are the relevant updates:

```
Sub Main()
    ' Read the provider key from *.config file.
    Dim dpStr As String = ConfigurationManager.AppSettings("provider")
    Dim dp As DataProvider = _
      CType([Enum].Parse(GetType(DataProvider), dpStr), DataProvider)
    Console.WriteLine("You specified the {0} provider.", dp)

    ' Read the cnStr.
    Dim cnStr As String = ConfigurationManager.AppSettings("cnStr")
    Console.WriteLine("Cn string: {0}", cnStr)

    ' Get a specific connection.
    Dim myCn As IDbConnection = GetConnection(dp)
    myCn.ConnectionString = cnStr
...
End Sub
```

> **Note** The ConfigurationManager type is new to .NET 2.0. Be sure to set a reference to the System.Configuration.dll assembly and import the System.Configuration namespace.

If the previous example were reworked into a .NET code library (rather than a console application), you would be able to build any number of clients that could obtain specific connections using various layers of abstraction. However, to make a worthwhile data provider factory library, you would also have to account for command objects, data readers, data adapters, and other data-centric types. While building such a code library would not necessarily be difficult, it would require a good amount of code. Thankfully, as of .NET 2.0, the kind folks in Redmond have built this very thing into the base class libraries.

> **Source Code** The MyConnectionFactory project is included under the Chapter 24 subdirectory.

The .NET 2.0 Provider Factory Model

Under .NET 2.0, we are now offered a data provider factory pattern that allows us to build a single code base using generalized data access types. Furthermore, using application configuration files (and the spiffy new <connectionStrings> section), we are able to obtain providers and connection strings declaratively without the need to recompile or redeploy the client software.

To understand the data provider factory implementation, recall from Table 24-1 that the objects within a data provider each derive from the same base classes defined within the System.Data.Common namespace:

- DbCommand: Abstract base class for all command objects
- DbConnection: Abstract base class for all connection objects
- DbDataAdapter: Abstract base class for all data adapter objects
- DbDataReader: Abstract base class for all data reader objects
- DbParameter: Abstract base class for all parameter objects
- DbTransaction: Abstract base class for all transaction objects

In addition, as of .NET 2.0, each of the Microsoft-supplied data providers now provides a specific class deriving from System.Data.Common.DbProviderFactory. This base class defines a number of methods that retrieve provider-specific data objects. Here is a snapshot of the relevant members of DbProviderFactory:

```
Public MustOverride Class DbProviderFactory
  ...
  Public Overridable Function CreateCommand() As DbCommand
  End Function
  Public Overridable Function CreateCommandBuilder() As DbCommandBuilder
  End Function
  Public Overridable Function CreateConnection() As DbConnection
  End Function
  Public Overridable Function CreateConnectionStringBuilder() _
  As DbConnectionStringBuilder
  End Function
  Public Overridable Function CreateDataAdapter() As DbDataAdapter
  End Function
```

```
    Public Overridable Function CreateDataSourceEnumerator() _
      As DbDataSourceEnumerator
    End Function
    Public Overridable Function CreateParameter() As DbParameter
    End Function
End Class
```

To obtain the DbProviderFactory-derived type for your data provider, the System.Data.Common namespace provides a class type named DbProviderFactories (note the plural in this type's name). Using the shared GetFactory() method, you are able to obtain the specific (which is to say, singular) DbProviderFactory of the specified data provider, for example:

```
Sub Main()
  ' Get the factory for the SQL data provider.
  Dim sqlFactory As DbProviderFactory = _
    DbProviderFactories.GetFactory("System.Data.SqlClient")
...
  ' Get the factory for the Oracle data provider.
  Dim oracleFactory As DbProviderFactory = _
    DbProviderFactories.GetFactory("System.Data.OracleClient")
...
End Sub
```

As you might be thinking, rather than obtaining a factory using a hard-coded string literal, you could read in this information from a client-side *.config file (much like the previous MyConnectionFactory example). You will do so in just a bit. However, in any case, once you have obtained the factory for your data provider, you are able to obtain the associated provider-specific data objects (connections, commands, etc.).

Registered Data Provider Factories

Before you look at a full example of working with ADO.NET data provider factories, it is important to point out that the DbProviderFactories type (as of .NET 2.0) is able to fetch factories for only a subset of all possible data providers. The list of valid provider factories is recorded within the <DbProviderFactories> element within the machine.config file for your .NET 2.0 installation (note that the value of the invariant attribute is identical to the value passed into the DbProviderFactories. GetFactory() method):

```
<system.data>
  <DbProviderFactories>
    <add name="Odbc Data Provider" invariant="System.Data.Odbc"
      description=".Net Framework Data Provider for Odbc"
      type="System.Data.Odbc.OdbcFactory,
      System.Data, Version=2.0.0.0, Culture=neutral,
      PublicKeyToken=b77a5c561934e089" />
    <add name="OleDb Data Provider" invariant="System.Data.OleDb"
      description=".Net Framework Data Provider for OleDb"
      type="System.Data.OleDb.OleDbFactory,
      System.Data, Version=2.0.0.0, Culture=neutral,
      PublicKeyToken=b77a5c561934e089" />
    <add name="OracleClient Data Provider" invariant="System.Data.OracleClient"
      description=".Net Framework Data Provider for Oracle"
      type="System.Data.OracleClient.OracleClientFactory, System.Data.OracleClient,
      Version=2.0.0.0, Culture=neutral, PublicKeyToken=b77a5c561934e089" />
    <add name="SqlClient Data Provider" invariant="System.Data.SqlClient"
      description=".Net Framework Data Provider for SqlServer"
      type="System.Data.SqlClient.SqlClientFactory, System.Data,
      Version=2.0.0.0, Culture=neutral, PublicKeyToken=b77a5c561934e089" />
```

```
    </DbProviderFactories>
</system.data>
```

Note If you wish to leverage a similar data provider factory pattern for DMBSs not accounted for in the
`machine.config` file, note that the Mono distribution of .NET (see Chapter 1) provides a similar data factory that
accounts for numerous open source and commercial data providers.

A Complete Data Provider Factory Example

For a complete example, let's build a console application (named DataProviderFactory) that prints
out the first and last names of individuals in the Authors table of a database named Pubs residing
within Microsoft SQL Server (as you may know, Pubs is a sample database modeling a fictitious
book publishing company).

First, add a reference to the `System.Configuration.dll` assembly, insert an `app.config` file to the
current project, and define an `<appSettings>` element. Remember that the format of the "official"
provider value is the full namespace name for the data provider, rather than the string name of the
ad hoc `DataProvider` enumeration used in the MyConnectionFactory example:

```
<configuration>
  <appSettings>
    <!-- Which provider? -->
    <add key="provider" value="System.Data.SqlClient" />
    <!-- Which connection string? -->
    <add key="cnStr" value=
    "Data Source=localhost;uid=sa;pwd=;Initial Catalog=Pubs"/>
  </appSettings>
</configuration>
```

Now that you have a proper *.config file, you can read in the provider and `cnStr` values
using the `ConfigurationManager.AppSettings()` method. The provider value will be passed to
`DbProviderFactories.GetFactory()` to obtain the data provider–specific factory type. The `cnStr`
value will be used to set the `ConnectionString` property of the `DbConnection`-derived type. To illustrate, update your initial `Module` as follows:

```
Imports System.Configuration
Imports System.Data.Common

Module Project
  Sub Main()
    Console.WriteLine("***** Fun with Data Provider Factories *****")
    Console.WriteLine()
    ' Get Connection string/provider from *.config.
    Dim dp As String = ConfigurationManager.AppSettings("provider")
    Dim cnStr As String = ConfigurationManager.AppSettings("cnStr")

    ' Make the factory provider.
    Dim df As DbProviderFactory = DbProviderFactories.GetFactory(dp)

    ' Now make connection object.
    Dim cn As DbConnection = df.CreateConnection()
    Console.WriteLine("Your connection object is a: {0}", _
      cn.GetType().FullName)
    cn.ConnectionString = cnStr
    cn.Open()
```

```
    ' Make command object.
    Dim cmd As DbCommand = df.CreateCommand()
    Console.WriteLine("Your command object is a: {0}", cmd.GetType().FullName)
    cmd.Connection = cn
    cmd.CommandText = "Select * From Authors"

    ' Print out data with data reader.
    Dim dr As DbDataReader = cmd.ExecuteReader(CommandBehavior.CloseConnection)
    Console.WriteLine("Your data reader object is a: {0}", _
      dr.GetType().FullName)
    Console.WriteLine()
    Console.WriteLine("***** Authors in Pubs *****")
    While dr.Read()
      Console.WriteLine("-> {0} , {1}", dr("au_lname"), dr("au_fname"))
    End While
    dr.Close()
  End Sub
End Module
```

Notice that for diagnostic purposes, you are printing out the fully qualified name of the under-lying connection, command, and data reader using reflection services. If you run this application, you will find that the Microsoft SQL Server provider has been used to read data from the Authors table of the Pubs database, as shown in Figure 24-2.

Figure 24-2. *Obtaining the SQL Server data provider via the .NET 2.0 data provider factory*

Now, if you change the *.config file to specify System.Data.OleDb as the data provider (and update your connection string) as follows:

```
<configuration>
  <appSettings>
    <!-- Which provider? -->
    <add key="provider" value="System.Data.OleDb" />
    <!-- Which connection string? -->
    <add key="cnStr" value=
    "Provider=SQLOLEDB.1;Data Source=localhost;uid=sa;pwd=;Initial Catalog=Pubs"/>
  </appSettings>
</configuration>
```

you will find the System.Data.OleDb types are used behind the scenes (see Figure 24-3).

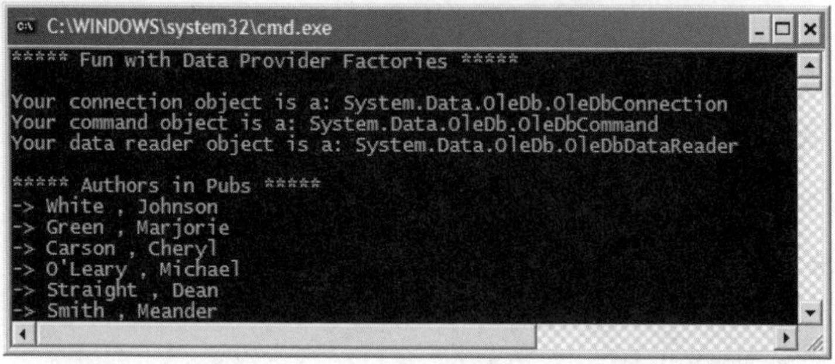

Figure 24-3. *Obtaining the OLE DB data provider via the .NET 2.0 data provider factory*

Of course, based on your experience with ADO.NET, you may be a bit unsure exactly what the connection, command, and data reader objects are actually doing. Don't sweat the details for the time being (quite a few pages remain in this chapter, after all!). At this point, just understand that under .NET 2.0, it is possible to build a single code base that can consume various data providers in a declarative manner.

Although this is a very powerful model, you must make sure that the code base does indeed make use only of types and methods that are common to all providers. Therefore, when authoring your code base, you will be limited to the members exposed by DbConnection, DbCommand, and the other types of the System.Data.Common namespace. Given this, you may find that this "generalized" approach will prevent you from directly accessing some of the bells and whistles of a particular DBMS (so be sure to test your code!).

The <connectionStrings> Element

As of .NET 2.0, application configuration files may define a new element named <connectionStrings>. Within this element, you are able to define any number of name/value pairs that can be programmatically read into memory using the ConfigurationManager.ConnectionStrings indexer. The chief advantage of this approach (rather than using the <appSettings> element and the ConfigurationManager.AppSettings indexer) is that you can define multiple connection strings for a single application in a consistent manner.

To illustrate, update your current app.config file as follows (note that each connection string is documented using the name and connectionString attributes rather than the key and value attributes as found in <appSettings>):

```
<configuration>
  <appSettings>
  <!-- Which provider? -->
    <add key="provider" value="System.Data.SqlClient" />
  </appSettings>
  <connectionStrings>
    <add name ="SqlProviderPubs"  connectionString =
    "Data Source=localhost;uid=sa;pwd=;Initial Catalog=Pubs"/>
    <add name ="OleDbProviderPubs"  connectionString =
    " Provider=SQLOLEDB.1;Data Source=localhost;uid=sa;pwd=;Initial Catalog=Pubs"/>
  </connectionStrings>
</configuration>
```

With this, you can now update your `Main()` method as follows:

```
Sub Main()
  Console.WriteLine("***** Fun with Data Provider Factories *****")
  Console.WriteLine()
  ' Get Connection string/provider from *.config.
  Dim dp As String = ConfigurationManager.AppSettings("provider")
  Dim cnStr As String = _
    ConfigurationManager.ConnectionStrings("SqlProviderPubs").ConnectionString
...
End Sub
```

At this point, you should be clear on how to interact with the .NET 2.0 data provider factory (and the new `<connectionStrings>` element).

■**Note** Now that you understand the role of ADO.NET data provider factories, the remaining examples in this chapter will make explicit use of the types within `System.Data.SqlClient` and hard-coded connection strings, just to keep focused on the task at hand.

■**Source Code** The DataProviderFactory project is included under the Chapter 24 subdirectory.

Installing the Cars Database

Now that you understand the basic properties of a .NET data provider, you can begin to dive into the specifics of coding with ADO.NET. As mentioned earlier, the examples in this chapter will make use of Microsoft SQL Server. In keeping with the automotive theme used throughout this text, I have included a sample Cars database that contains three interrelated tables named Inventory, Orders, and Customers.

■**Note** If you do not have a copy of Microsoft SQL Server, you can download a (free) copy of Microsoft SQL Server 2005 Express Edition (http://lab.msdn.microsoft.com/express). While this tool does not have all the bells and whistles of the full version of Microsoft SQL Server, it will allow you to host the provided Cars database. Do be aware, however, that this chapter was written with Microsoft SQL Server in mind, so be sure to consult the provided SQL Server 2005 Express Edition documentation.

To install the Cars database on your machine, begin by opening the Query Analyzer utility that ships with SQL Server. Next, connect to your machine and open the provided `Cars.sql` file. Before you run the script, make sure that the path listed in the SQL file points to your installation of Microsoft SQL Server. Edit the following lines (in bold) as necessary:

```
CREATE DATABASE [Cars]  ON (NAME = N'Cars_Data', FILENAME = N
'C:\Program Files\Microsoft SQL Server\MSSQL\Data\Cars_Data.MDF',
SIZE = 2, FILEGROWTH = 10%)

LOG ON (NAME = N'Cars_Log', FILENAME = N
'C:\Program Files\Microsoft SQL Server\MSSQL\Data\Cars_Log.LDF',
SIZE = 1, FILEGROWTH = 10%)
GO
```

Now run the script. Once you do, open up SQL Server Enterprise Manager. You should see three interrelated tables (with some sample data to boot) and a single stored procedure. Figure 24-4 shows the tables that populate the Cars database.

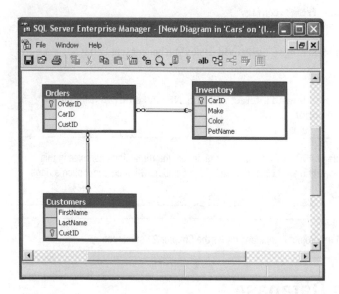

Figure 24-4. *The sample Cars database*

Connecting to the Cars Database from Visual Studio 2005

Now that you have the Cars database installed, you may wish to create a data connection to the database from within Visual Studio 2005. This will allow you to view and edit the various database objects from within the IDE. To do so, open the Server Explorer window using the View menu. Next, right-click the Data Connections node and select Add Connection from the context menu. From the resulting dialog box, select Microsoft SQL Server as the data source. As well, select your machine name (or simply *localhost*) from the Server name drop-down list and specify the correct logon information. Finally, choose the Cars database from the Select or enter a database name drop-down list, as shown in Figure 24-5.

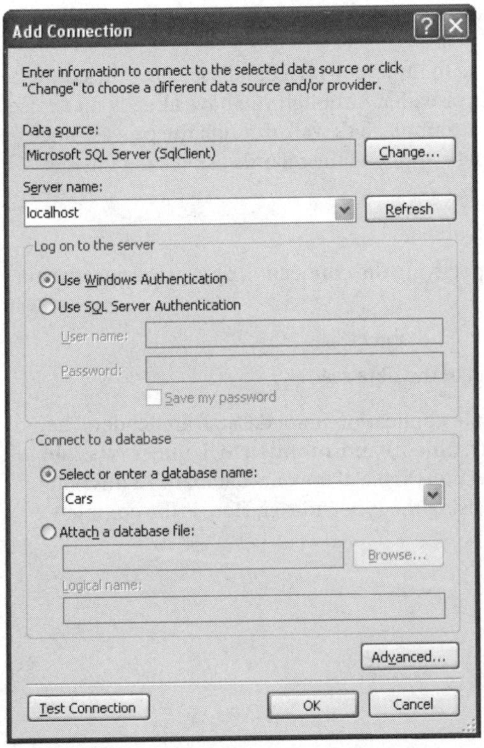

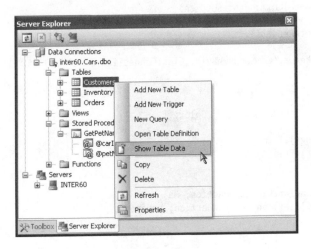

Figure 24-5. *Connecting to the Cars database from Visual Studio 2005*

Once you've finished, you should now see a node for Cars under Data Connections. Notice that you can pull up the records for a given data table simply by right-clicking and selecting Show Table Data, as you see in Figure 24-6.

Figure 24-6. *Viewing table data*

Understanding the Connected Layer of ADO.NET

Recall that the *connected layer* of ADO.NET allows you to interact with a database using the connection, command, and data reader objects of your data provider. Although you have already made use of these objects in the previous DataProviderFactory example, let's walk through the process once again in detail. When you wish to connect to a database and read the records using a data reader object, you need to perform the following steps:

1. Create, configure, and open your connection object.
2. Allocate and configure a command object, specifying the connection object as a constructor argument or via the `Connection` property.
3. Call `ExecuteReader()` on the configured command object.
4. Process each record using the `Read()` method of the data reader.

To get the ball rolling, create a brand-new console application named CarsDataReader. The goal is to open a connection (via the `SqlConnection` object) and submit a SQL query (via the `SqlCommand` object) to obtain all records within the Inventory table of the Cars database. At this point, you will use a `SqlDataReader` to print out the results using the type indexer. Here is the complete code within `Main()`, with analysis to follow:

```vb
Imports System.Data.SqlClient

Module Program
  Sub Main()
    Console.WriteLine("***** Fun with Data Readers *****")
    Console.WriteLine()

    ' Create an open a connection.
    Dim cn As SqlConnection = New SqlConnection()
    cn.ConnectionString = _
      "uid=sa;pwd=;Initial Catalog=Cars; Data Source=(local)"
    cn.Open()

    ' Create a SQL command object.
    Dim strSQL As String = "Select * From Inventory"
    Dim myCommand As SqlCommand = New SqlCommand(strSQL, cn)

    ' Obtain a data reader a la ExecuteReader().
    Dim myDataReader As SqlDataReader
    myDataReader = myCommand.ExecuteReader(CommandBehavior.CloseConnection)

    ' Loop over the results.
    While myDataReader.Read()
      Console.WriteLine("-> Make: {0} , PetName: {1} , Color: {2}.", _
      myDataReader("Make").ToString().Trim(), _
      myDataReader("PetName").ToString().Trim(), _
      myDataReader("Color").ToString().Trim())
    End While

    ' Because we specified CommandBehavior.CloseConnection, we
    ' don't need to explicitly call Close() on the connection; however,
    ' it is safe to do so.
    myDataReader.Close()
    Console.WriteLine()
    Console.ReadLine()
  End Sub
End Module
```

Working with Connection Objects

The first step to take when working with a data provider is to establish a session with the data source using the connection object (which, as you recall, derives from DbConnection). .NET connection types are provided with a formatted *connection string*, which contains a number of name/value pairs separated by semicolons. This information is used to identify the name of the machine you wish to connect to, required security settings, the name of the database on that machine, and other data provider–specific information.

As you can infer from the preceding code, the Initial Catalog name refers to the database you are attempting to establish a session with (Pubs, Northwind, Cars, etc.). The Data Source name identifies the name of the machine that maintains the database (for simplicity, I have assumed no specific password is required for local system administrators).

Note Look up the ConnectionString property of your data provider's connection object in the .NET Framework 2.0 SDK documentation to learn about each name/value pair for your specific DBMS. Also, keep in mind that some providers support multiple versions of a single connection string segment (for example, localhost and (local) both can be used to establish the server machine accessed by the SqlConnection type).

Once your construction string has been established, a call to Open() establishes your connection with the DBMS. In addition to the ConnectionString, Open(), and Close() members, a connection object provides a number of members that let you configure attritional settings regarding your connection, such as timeout settings and transactional information. Table 24-6 lists some (but not all) members of the DbConnection base class.

Table 24-6. *Members of the* DbConnection *Type*

Member	Meaning in Life
BeginTransaction()	This method is used to begin a database transaction.
ChangeDatabase()	This method changes the database on an open connection.
ConnectionTimeout	This read-only property returns the amount of time to wait while establishing a connection before terminating and generating an error (the default value is 15 seconds). If you wish to change the default, specify a Connect Timeout segment in the connection string (e.g., Connect Timeout=30).
Database	This property gets the name of the database maintained by the connection object.
DataSource	This property gets the location of the database maintained by the connection object.
GetSchema()	This method returns a DataSet that contains schema information from the data source.
State	This property sets the current state of the connection, represented by the ConnectionState enumeration.

Many of the properties of the DbConnection type are read-only in nature and are only useful when you wish to obtain the characteristics of a connection at runtime. When you wish to override default settings, you typically alter the construction string itself. For example, the connection string sets the connection timeout setting from 15 seconds to 30 seconds (via the Connect Timeout segment of the connection string):

```
Sub Main()
  Console.WriteLine("***** Fun with Data Readers *****")
  Console.WriteLine()

  ' Create an open a connection.
  Dim cn As SqlConnection = New SqlConnection()
  cn.ConnectionString = _
  "uid=sa;pwd=;Initial Catalog=Cars; Data Source=(local);Connect Timeout=30"
  cn.Open()
...
End Sub
```

In the preceding code, notice you have now passed your connection object as a parameter to a new helper method in the Program module named ShowConnectionStatus(), implemented as follows:

```
' Be sure to import the System.Data.Common namespace!
Sub ShowConnectionStatus(ByVal cn As DbConnection)
  ' Show various stats about current connection object.
  Console.WriteLine("***** Info about your connection *****")
  Console.WriteLine("Database location: {0}", cn.DataSource)
  Console.WriteLine("Database name: {0}", cn.Database)
  Console.WriteLine("Timeout: {0}", cn.ConnectionTimeout)
  Console.WriteLine("Connection state: {0}", cn.State.ToString())
  Console.WriteLine()
End Sub
```

While most of these properties are self-explanatory, the State property is worth special mention. Although this property may be assigned any value of the ConnectionState enumeration:

```
Enum ConnectionState
  Broken
  Closed
  Connecting
  Executing
  Fetching
  Open
End Enum
```

the only valid ConnectionState values are ConnectionState.Open and ConnectionState.Closed (the remaining members of this enum are reserved for future use). Also, understand that it is always safe to close a connection whose connection state is currently ConnectionState.Closed.

Working with .NET 2.0 ConnectionStringBuilders

Working with connection strings programmatically can be a bit clunky, given that they are often represented as string literals, which are difficult to maintain and error prone at best. Under .NET 2.0, the Microsoft-supplied ADO.NET data providers now support *connection string builder objects*, which allow you to establish the name/value pairs using strongly typed properties. Consider the following update to the current Main() method:

```
Sub Main()
  Console.WriteLine("***** Fun with Data Readers *****")
  Console.WriteLine()
```

```
' Create a connection string via the builder object.
Dim cnStrBuilder As SqlConnectionStringBuilder = _
    New SqlConnectionStringBuilder()
cnStrBuilder.UserID = "sa"
cnStrBuilder.Password = ""
cnStrBuilder.InitialCatalog = "Cars"
cnStrBuilder.DataSource = "(local)"
cnStrBuilder.ConnectTimeout = 30

Dim cn As SqlConnection = New SqlConnection()
cn.ConnectionString = cnStrBuilder.ConnectionString
cn.Open()
ShowConnectionStatus(cn)
...
End Sub
```

In this iteration, you create an instance of SqlConnectionStringBuilder, set the properties accordingly, and obtain the internal string via the ConnectionString property. Also note that you make use of the default constructor of the type. If you so choose, you can also create an instance of your data provider's connection string builder object by passing in an existing connection string as a starting point (which can be helpful when you are reading these values dynamically from an app.config file). Once you have hydrated the object with the initial string data, you can change specific name/value pairs using the related properties, for example:

```
Sub Main()
    Console.WriteLine("***** Fun with Data Readers *****")
    Console.WriteLine()

    ' Assume you really obtained cnStr from a *.config file.
    Dim cnStr As String = "uid=sa;pwd=;Initial Catalog=Cars;" & _
        "Data Source=(local);Connect Timeout=30"

    Dim cnStrBuilder As SqlConnectionStringBuilder = _
        New SqlConnectionStringBuilder(cnStr)

    ' Change timeout value.
    cnStrBuilder.ConnectTimeout = 5
...
End Sub
```

Working with Command Objects

Now that you better understand the role of the connection object, the next order of business is to check out how to submit SQL queries to the database in question. The SqlCommand type (which derives from DbCommand) is an OO representation of a SQL query, table name, or stored procedure. The type of command is specified using the CommandType property, which may take any value from the CommandType enum:

```
Enum CommandType
    StoredProcedure
    TableDirect
    Text   ' Default value.
End Enum
```

When creating a command object, you may establish the SQL query as a constructor parameter or via the CommandText property. Also when you are creating a command object, you need to specify the connection to be used. Again, you may do so as a constructor parameter or via the Connection property:

```
Sub Main()
  Dim cn As SqlConnection = New SqlConnection()
...
  ' Create command object via ctor args.
  Dim strSQL As String = "Select * From Inventory"
  Dim myCommand As SqlCommand = New SqlCommand(strSQL, cn)

  ' Create another command object via properties.
  Dim testCommand As SqlCommand = New SqlCommand()
  testCommand.Connection = cn
  testCommand.CommandText = strSQL
...
End Sub
```

Realize that at this point, you have not literally submitted the SQL query to the Cars database, but rather prepped the state of the command type for future use. Table 24-7 highlights some additional members of the DbCommand type.

Table 24-7. *Members of the* DbCommand *Type*

Member	Meaning in Life
CommandTimeout	Gets or sets the time to wait while executing the command before terminating the attempt and generating an error. The default is 30 seconds.
Connection	Gets or sets the DbConnection used by this instance of the DbCommand.
Parameters	Gets the collection of DbParameter types used for a parameterized query.
Cancel()	Cancels the execution of a command.
ExecuteReader()	Returns the data provider's DbDataReader object, which provides forward-only, read-only access to the underlying data.
ExecuteNonQuery()	Issues the command text to the data store.
ExecuteScalar()	A lightweight version of the ExecuteNonQuery() method, designed specifically for singleton queries (such as obtaining a record count).
ExecuteXmlReader()	Microsoft SQL Server (2000 and higher) is capable of returning result sets as XML. As you might suspect, this method returns a System.Xml.XmlReader that allows you to process the incoming stream of XML.
Prepare()	Creates a prepared (or compiled) version of the command on the data source. As you may know, a prepared query executes slightly faster and is useful when you wish to execute the same query multiple times.

Note As illustrated later in this chapter, as of .NET 2.0, the SqlCommand object has been updated with additional members that facilitate asynchronous database interactions.

Working with Data Readers

Once you have established the active connection and SQL command, the next step is to submit the query to the data source. As you might guess, you have a number of ways to do so. The DbDataReader type (which implements IDataReader) is the simplest and fastest way to obtain information from a data store. Recall that data readers represent a read-only, forward-only stream of data returned one record at a time. Given this, it should stand to reason that data readers are useful only when submitting SQL selection statements to the underlying data store.

Data readers are useful when you need to iterate over large amounts of data very quickly and have no need to maintain an in-memory representation. For example, if you request 20,000 records from a table to store in a text file, it would be rather memory-intensive to hold this information in a DataSet. A better approach is to create a data reader that spins over each record as rapidly as possible. Be aware, however, that data reader objects (unlike data adapter objects, which you'll examine later) maintain an open connection to their data source until you explicitly close the session.

Data reader objects are obtained from the command object via a call to ExecuteReader(). When invoking this method, you may optionally instruct the reader to automatically close down the related connection object by specifying CommandBehavior.CloseConnection.

The following use of the data reader leverages the Read() method to determine when you have reached the end of your records (via a false return value). For each incoming record, you are making use of the type indexer to print out the make, pet name, and color of each automobile. Also note that you call Close() as soon as you are finished processing the records, to free up the connection object:

```
Sub Main()
...
  ' Obtain a data reader a la ExecuteReader().
  Dim myDataReader As SqlDataReader
  myDataReader = myCommand.ExecuteReader(CommandBehavior.CloseConnection)

  ' Loop over the results.
  While myDataReader.Read()
    Console.WriteLine("-> Make: {0} , PetName: {1} , Color: {2}.", _
      myDataReader("Make").ToString().Trim(), _
      myDataReader("PetName").ToString().Trim(), _
      myDataReader("Color").ToString().Trim())
  End While

  myDataReader.Close()
  ShowConnectionStatus(cn)
End Sub
```

■**Note** The trimming of the string data shown here is only used to remove trailing blank spaces in the database entries; it is not directly related to ADO.NET!

The indexer of a data reader object has been overloaded to take either a string (representing the name of the column) or an integer (representing the column's ordinal position). Thus, you could clean up the current reader logic (and avoid hard-coded string names) with the following update (note the use of the FieldCount property):

```
While myDataReader.Read()
  Console.WriteLine("***** Record *****")
  For i As Integer = 0 To myDataReader.FieldCount - 1
    Console.WriteLine("{0} = {1}", _
      myDataReader.GetName(i), _
      myDataReader.GetValue(i).ToString().Trim())
  Next
  Console.WriteLine()
End While
```

If you compile and run your project, you should be presented with a list of all automobiles in the Inventory table of the Cars database like the one in Figure 24-7.

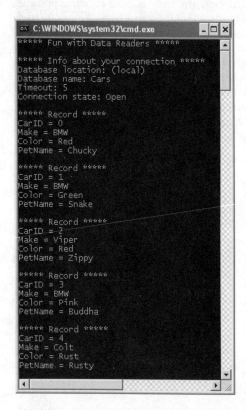

Figure 24-7. *Fun with data reader objects*

Obtaining Multiple Result Sets Using a Data Reader

Data reader objects are able to obtain multiple result sets from a single command object. For example, if you are interested in obtaining all rows from the Inventory table as well as all rows from the Customers table, you are able to specify both SQL Select statements using a semicolon delimiter:

```
Dim theSQL As String = "Select * From Inventory;Select * from Customers"
```

Once you obtain the data reader, you are able to iterate over each result set via the NextResult() method. Do be aware that you are always returned the first result set automatically. Thus, if you wish to read over the rows of each table, you will be able to build the following iteration construct:

```
Do
  While myDataReader.Read()
    Console.WriteLine("***** Record *****")
    For i As Integer = 0 To myDataReader.FieldCount - 1
      Console.WriteLine("{0} = {1}", _
        myDataReader.GetName(i), _
        myDataReader.GetValue(i).ToString().Trim())
    Next
    Console.WriteLine()
  End While
Loop While myDataReader.NextResult()
```

So, at this point, you should be more aware of the functionality data reader objects bring to the table. While these objects provide additional bits of functionality than I have shown here (such as the ability to execute scalars and single-row queries), I'll leave it to interested readers to consult the .NET Framework 2.0 SDK documentation for complete details.

Source Code The CarsDataReader project is included under the Chapter 24 subdirectory.

Modifying Tables Using Command Objects

As you have just seen, the `ExecuteReader()` method extracts a data reader object that allows you to examine the results of a SQL `Select` statement using a forward-only, read-only flow of information. However, when you wish to submit SQL commands that result in the modification of a given table, you will call the `ExecuteNonQuery()` method of your command object. This single method will perform inserts, updates, and deletes based on the format of your command text.

To illustrate how to modify an existing database using nothing more than a call to `ExecuteNonQuery()`, you will now build a new console application (CarsInventoryUpdater) that allows the caller to modify the Inventory table of the Cars database. Like in other examples in this text, the `Main()` method is responsible for prompting the user for a specific course of action and executing that request via a `Select Case` statement. This program will allow the user to enter the following commands:

- *I*: Inserts a new record into the Inventory table
- *U*: Updates an existing record in the Inventory table
- *D*: Deletes an existing record from the Inventory table
- *L*: Displays the current inventory using a data reader
- *S*: Shows these options to the user
- *C*: Clears the console and shows these options to the user
- *Q*: Quits the program

Each possible option is handled by a unique method within the `Program` module (each of which is seen momentarily). Here is the implementation of `Main()`, which I assume requires no further comment:

```
Sub Main()
  ' Display options to user.
  ShowInstructions()

  Dim userDone As Boolean = False
  Dim userCommand As String = ""
```

```vb
Dim cn As SqlConnection = New SqlConnection()
cn.ConnectionString = _
  "uid=sa;pwd=;Initial Catalog=Cars;Data Source=(local)"
cn.Open()

' Keep looping until user enters 'q'.
Do
  Console.Write("Please enter your command: ")
  userCommand = Console.ReadLine()
  Console.WriteLine()
  Select Case userCommand.ToUpper()
    Case "I"
      InsertNewCar(cn)
      Exit Select
    Case "U"
      UpdateCarPetName(cn)
      Exit Select
    Case "D"
      DeleteCar(cn)
      Exit Select
    Case "L"
      ListInventory(cn)
      Exit Select
    Case "S"
      ShowInstructions()
      Exit Select
    Case "P"
      LookUpPetName(cn)
      Exit Select
    Case "Q"
      userDone = True
      Exit Select
    Case "C"
      Console.Clear()
      ShowInstructions()
      Exit Select
    Case Else
      Console.WriteLine("Bad data!  Try again")
      Exit Select
  End Select
Loop While Not userDone
cn.Close()
End Sub
```

The ShowInstructions() method does what you would expect:

```vb
Sub ShowInstructions()
  Console.WriteLine("***** Car Inventory Updater *****")
  Console.WriteLine()
  Console.WriteLine("I: Inserts a new car.")
  Console.WriteLine("U: Updated an existing car.")
  Console.WriteLine("D: Deletes an existing car.")
  Console.WriteLine("L: List current inventory.")
  Console.WriteLine("S: Show these instructions.")
  Console.WriteLine("C: Clear console and show instructions.")
  Console.WriteLine("P: Look up pet name for existing car.")
  Console.WriteLine("Q: Quits program.")
End Sub
```

As mentioned, ListInventory() prints out the current rows of the Inventory table using a data reader object (the code is identical to the previous CarsDataReader example):

```
Sub ListInventory(ByVal cn As SqlConnection)
  Dim strSQL As String = "Select * From Inventory"
  Dim myCommand As SqlCommand = New SqlCommand(strSQL, cn)
  Dim myDataReader As SqlDataReader
  myDataReader = myCommand.ExecuteReader()
  While myDataReader.Read()
    For i As Integer = 0 To myDataReader.FieldCount - 1
      Console.Write("{0} = {1} ", _
        myDataReader.GetName(i).Trim(), _
        myDataReader.GetValue(i).ToString().Trim())
    Next
    Console.WriteLine()
  End While
  myDataReader.Close()
End Sub
```

Now that the basic console user interface (CUI) is in place, let's move on to the good stuff.

Inserting New Records

Inserting a new record into the Inventory table is as simple as formatting the SQL insert statement (based on user input) and calling ExecuteNonQuery():

```
Sub InsertNewCar(ByVal cn As SqlConnection)
  ' Gather info about new car.
  Console.Write("Enter CarID: ")
  Dim newCarID As Integer = 0
  Try
    newCarID = Integer.Parse(Console.ReadLine())
  Catch
    Console.WriteLine("Bad input!  Canceling request")
    Return
  End Try
  Console.Write("Enter Make: ")
  Dim newCarMake As String = Console.ReadLine()
  Console.Write("Enter Color: ")
  Dim newCarColor As String = Console.ReadLine()
  Console.Write("Enter PetName: ")
  Dim newCarPetName As String = Console.ReadLine()

  ' Format and execute SQL statement.
  Dim sql As String = String.Format("Insert Into Inventory" & _
    "(CarID, Make, Color, PetName) Values" & _
    "('{0}', '{1}', '{2}', '{3}')", _
    newCarID, newCarMake, newCarColor, newCarPetName)
  Dim cmd As SqlCommand = New SqlCommand(sql, cn)
  Try
    cmd.ExecuteNonQuery()
  Catch
    Console.WriteLine("Bad input!  Canceling request")
    Return
  End Try
End Sub
```

■**Note** As you may know, building a SQL statement using string concatenation can be risky from a security point of view (think SQL injection attacks). While I use this approach during this chapter for purposes of brevity, the preferred way to build command text is using a parameterized query, which I describe shortly.

Deleting Existing Records

Deleting an existing record is just as simple as inserting a new record. Simply build the SQL query and call ExecuteNonQuery():

```
Sub DeleteCar(ByVal cn As SqlConnection)
  ' Get ID of car to delete, then do so.
  Dim carToDelete As Integer = 0
  Console.Write("Enter CarID of car to delete: ")
  Try
    carToDelete = Integer.Parse(Console.ReadLine())
  Catch ex As FormatException
    Console.WriteLine(ex.Message)
    Return
  End Try

  Dim sql As String = _
    String.Format("Delete from Inventory where CarID = '{0}'", carToDelete)
  Dim cmd As SqlCommand = New SqlCommand(sql, cn)
  Try
    cmd.ExecuteNonQuery()
  Catch
    Console.WriteLine("Sorry!  That car is on order! Terminating request...")
  End Try
End Sub
```

Updating Existing Records

If you followed the code behind DeleteCar() and InsertNewCar(), then UpdateCarPetName() is a no-brainer:

```
Sub UpdateCarPetName(ByVal cn As SqlConnection)
  Dim carToUpdate As Integer = 0
  Dim newPetName As String = ""
  Console.Write("Enter CarID of car to modify: ")
  Try
    carToUpdate = Integer.Parse(Console.ReadLine())
  Catch ex As FormatException
    Console.WriteLine(ex.Message)
    Return
  End Try
  Console.Write("Enter new pet name: ")
  newPetName = Console.ReadLine()
  Dim sql As String = _
    String.Format("Update Inventory Set PetName = '{0}' Where CarID = '{1}'", _
    newPetName, carToUpdate)
  Dim cmd As SqlCommand = New SqlCommand(sql, cn)
  cmd.ExecuteNonQuery()
End Sub
```

With this, our application is feature complete! Figure 24-8 shows a test run (notice the deletion of the car with the ID of 99).

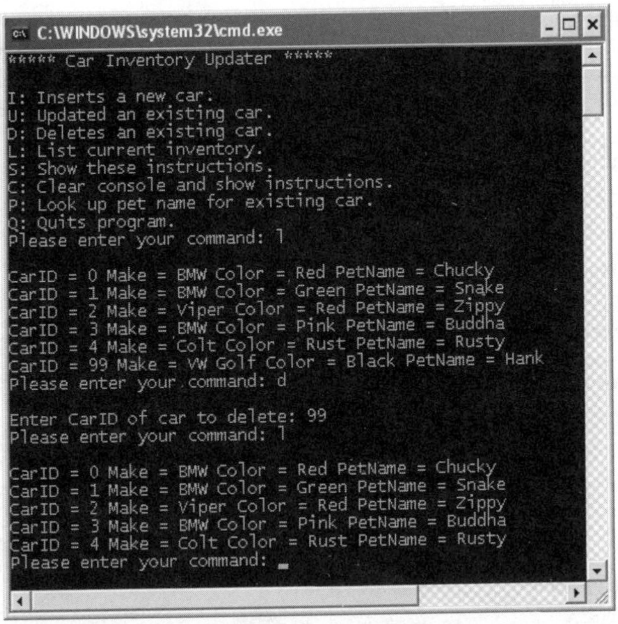

Figure 24-8. *Inserting, updating, and deleting records via command objects*

Working with Parameterized Command Objects

The previous insert, update, and delete logic works as expected; however, note that each of your SQL queries is represented using hard-coded string literals. As you may know, a *parameterized query* can be used to treat SQL parameters as objects, rather than simple blobs of text. Typically, parameterized queries execute much faster than a literal SQL string, in that they are parsed exactly once (rather than each time the SQL string is assigned to the CommandText property). As well, parameterized queries also help protect against SQL injection attacks (a well-known data access security issue).

ADO.NET command objects maintain a collection of discrete parameter types. By default this collection is empty, but you are free to insert any number of parameter objects that map to a "placeholder parameter" in the SQL query. When you wish to associate a parameter within a SQL query to a member in the command object's parameters collection, prefix the SQL text parameter with an at (@) symbol (at least when using Microsoft SQL Server; not all DBMSs support this notation so be sure to consult the documentation for your .NET data provider).

Specifying Parameters Using the DbParameter Type

Before you build a parameterized query, let's get to know the DbParameter type (which is the base class to a provider's specific parameter object). This class maintains a number of properties that allow you to configure the name, size, and data type of the parameter, as well as other characteristics such as the parameter's direction of travel. Table 24-8 describes some key properties of the DbParameter type.

Table 24-8. *Key Members of the* DbParameter *Type*

Property	Meaning in Life
DbType	Gets or sets the native data type from the data source, represented as a CLR data type
Direction	Gets or sets whether the parameter is input-only, output-only, bidirectional, or a return value parameter
IsNullable	Gets or sets whether the parameter accepts null values
ParameterName	Gets or sets the name of the DbParameter
Size	Gets or sets the maximum parameter size of the data
Value	Gets or sets the value of the parameter

To illustrate, let's rework the previous InsertNewCar() method to make use of parameter objects. Here is the code update:

```
Sub InsertNewCar(ByVal cn As SqlConnection)
  ' Gather info about new car.
  Console.Write("Enter CarID: ")
  Dim newCarID As Integer = 0
  Try
    newCarID = Integer.Parse(Console.ReadLine())
  Catch
    Console.WriteLine("Bad input!  Canceling request")
    Return
  End Try
  Console.Write("Enter Make: ")
  Dim newCarMake As String = Console.ReadLine()
  Console.Write("Enter Color: ")
  Dim newCarColor As String = Console.ReadLine()
  Console.Write("Enter PetName: ")
  Dim newCarPetName As String = Console.ReadLine()

  ' Format and execute SQL statement.
  Dim sql As String = String.Format("Insert Into Inventory" & _
    "(CarID, Make, Color, PetName) Values" & _
    "(@CarID, @Make, @Color, @PetName)")
  Dim cmd As SqlCommand = New SqlCommand(sql, cn)

  ' Fill params collection.
  Dim param As SqlParameter = New SqlParameter()
  param.ParameterName = "@CarID"
  param.Value = newCarID
  param.SqlDbType = SqlDbType.Int
  cmd.Parameters.Add(param)

  param = New SqlParameter()
  param.ParameterName = "@Make"
  param.Value = newCarMake
  param.SqlDbType = SqlDbType.Char
  param.Size = 20
  cmd.Parameters.Add(param)
```

```
    param = New SqlParameter()
    param.ParameterName = "@Color"
    param.Value = newCarColor
    param.SqlDbType = SqlDbType.Char
    param.Size = 20
    cmd.Parameters.Add(param)

    param = New SqlParameter()
    param.ParameterName = "@PetName"
    param.Value = newCarPetName
    param.SqlDbType = SqlDbType.Char
    param.Size = 20
    cmd.Parameters.Add(param)

    Try
        cmd.ExecuteNonQuery()
    Catch
        Console.WriteLine("Bad input!  Canceling request")
        Return
    End Try
End Sub
```

While building a parameterized query requires a larger amount of code, the end result is a more convenient way to tweak SQL statements programmatically as well as better overall performance. While you are free to make use of this technique whenever a SQL query is involved, parameterized queries are most helpful when you wish to trigger a stored procedure.

■**Note** Here, I made use of various properties to establish a parameter object. Do know, however, that parameter objects support a number of overloaded constructors that allow you to set the values of various properties (which will result in a more compact code base). Furthermore, be aware that the Visual Studio 2005 IDE will autogenerate most (if not all) of this ADO.NET code when you make use of various visual designers (as we will do at the conclusion of this chapter).

Executing a Stored Procedure Using DbCommand

A *stored procedure* is a named block of SQL code stored in the database. Stored procedures can be constructed to return a set of rows or scalar data types and may take any number of optional parameters. The end result is a unit of work that behaves like a typical function, with the obvious difference of being located on a data store rather than a binary business object.

■**Note** Although I don't cover this topic in this chapter, it is worth pointing out that the newest version of Microsoft SQL Server (2005) is a CLR host! Therefore, stored procedures (and other database atoms) can be authored using managed languages (such as VB 2005) rather than traditional SQL. Consult http://www.microsoft.com/sql/2005 for further details.

To illustrate the process, let's add a new option to the CarInventoryUpdate program that allows the caller to look up a car's pet name via the GetPetName stored procedure. This database object was established when you installed the Cars database and looks like this:

```
CREATE PROCEDURE GetPetName
@carID int,
@petName char(20) output
AS
SELECT @petName = PetName from Inventory where CarID = @carID
```

First, update the current switch statement in Main() to handle a new case for "P" that calls a new helper function named LookUpPetName() that takes a SqlConnection parameter and returns void. Update your ShowInstructions() method to account for this new option.

When you wish to execute a stored procedure, you begin as always by creating a new connection object, configuring your connection string, and opening the session. However, when you create your command object, the CommandText property is set to the name of the stored procedure (rather than a SQL query). As well, you must be sure to set the CommandType property to CommandType.StoredProcedure (the default is CommandType.Text).

Given that this stored procedure has one input and one output parameter, your goal is to build a command object that contains two SqlParameter objects within its parameter collection:

```
Sub LookUpPetName(ByVal cn As SqlConnection)
  ' Get the CarID.
  Console.Write("Enter CarID: ")
  Dim carID As Integer = Integer.Parse(Console.ReadLine())

  ' Establish name of stored proc.
  Dim cmd As SqlCommand = New SqlCommand("GetPetName", cn)
  cmd.CommandType = CommandType.StoredProcedure

  ' Input param.
  Dim param As SqlParameter = New SqlParameter()
  param.ParameterName = "@carID"
  param.SqlDbType = SqlDbType.Int
  param.Value = carID
  param.Direction = ParameterDirection.Input
  cmd.Parameters.Add(param)

  ' Output param.
  param = New SqlParameter()
  param.ParameterName = "@petName"
  param.SqlDbType = SqlDbType.Char
  param.Size = 20
  param.Direction = ParameterDirection.Output
  cmd.Parameters.Add(param)

  ' Execute the stored proc.
  cmd.ExecuteNonQuery()
  ' Print output param.
  Console.WriteLine("Pet name for car {0} is {1}", carID, _
    cmd.Parameters("@petName").Value)
End Sub
```

Notice that the Direction property of the parameter object allows you to specify input and output parameters. Once the stored procedure completes via a call to ExecuteNonQuery(), you are able to obtain the value of the output parameter by investigating the command object's parameter collection. Figure 24-9 shows one possible test run.

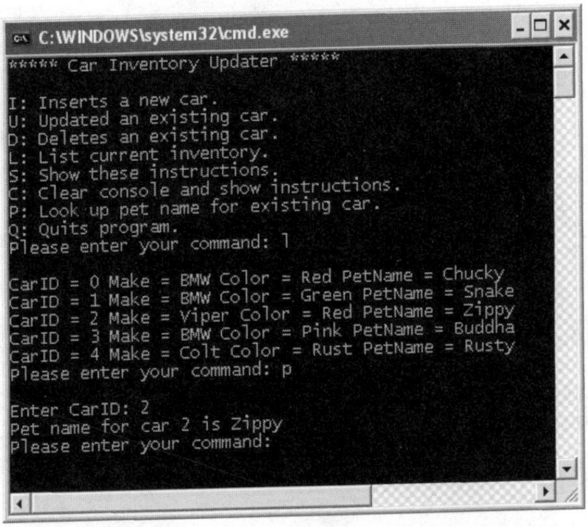

Figure 24-9. *Triggering a stored procedure*

Source Code The CarsInventoryUpdater application is included under the Chapter 24 subdirectory.

Asynchronous Data Access Under .NET 2.0

As of .NET 2.0, the SQL data provider (represented by the System.Data.SqlClient namespace) has been enhanced to support asynchronous database interactions via the following new members of SqlCommand:

- BeginExecuteReader()/EndExecuteReader()
- BeginExecuteNonQuery()/EndExecuteNonQuery()
- BeginExecuteXmlReader()/EndExecuteXmlReader()

Given your work in Chapter 16, the naming convention of these method pairs may ring a bell. Recall that the .NET asynchronous delegate pattern makes use of a "begin" method to execute a task on a secondary thread, whereas the "end" method can be used to obtain the result of the asynchronous invocation using the members of IAsyncResult and the optional AsyncCallback delegate. Because the process of working with asynchronous commands is modeled after the standard delegate patterns, a simple example should suffice (so be sure to consult Chapter 16 for full details of asynchronous delegates).

Assume you wish to select the records from the Inventory table on a secondary thread of execution using a data reader object. Here is the complete Main() method, with analysis to follow:

```
' Note we need to import the threading
' namespace!
Imports System.Data
Imports System.Data.SqlClient
Imports System.Threading
```

```vb
Module Program
  Sub Main()
    Console.WriteLine("***** Fun with ASNYC Data Readers *****")
    Console.WriteLine()

    ' Create an open a connection that is async-aware.
    Dim cn As SqlConnection = New SqlConnection()
    cn.ConnectionString = "uid=sa;pwd=;Initial Catalog=Cars;" & _
      "Asynchronous Processing=true;Data Source=(local)"
    cn.Open()

    ' Create a SQL command object.
    Dim strSQL As String = "WaitFor Delay '00:00:02';Select * From Inventory"
    Dim myCommand As SqlCommand = New SqlCommand(strSQL, cn)

    ' Execute the reader on a second thread.
    Dim itfAsynch As IAsyncResult
    itfAsynch = myCommand.BeginExecuteReader(CommandBehavior.CloseConnection)

    ' Do something while other thread works.
    While Not itfAsynch.IsCompleted
      Console.WriteLine("Working on main thread...")
      Thread.Sleep(1000)
    End While
    Console.WriteLine()

    ' Loop over the results.
    Dim myDataReader As SqlDataReader = myCommand.EndExecuteReader(itfAsynch)
    While myDataReader.Read()
      Console.WriteLine("-> Make: {0}, PetName: {1}, Color: {2}.", _
        myDataReader("Make").ToString().Trim(), _
        myDataReader("PetName").ToString().Trim(), _
        myDataReader("Color").ToString().Trim())
    End While
    myDataReader.Close()
  End Sub
End Module
```

The first point of interest is the fact that you need to enable asynchronous activity using the new Asynchronous Processing segment of the connection string. Also note that you have padded into the command text of your SqlCommand object a new WaitFor Delay segment simply to simulate a long-running database interaction.

Beyond these points, notice that the call to BeginExecuteDataReader() returns the expected IasyncResult-compatible type, which is used to synchronize the calling thread (via the IsCompleted property) as well as obtain the SqlDataReader once the query has finished executing.

■**Source Code** The AsyncCmdObject application is included under the Chapter 24 subdirectory.

Understanding the Disconnected Layer of ADO.NET

As you have seen, working with the connected layer allows you to interact with a database using connection, command, and data reader objects. With this small handful of types, you are able to select, insert, update, and delete records to your heart's content (as well as trigger stored procedures).

In reality, however, you have seen only half of the ADO.NET story. Recall that the ADO.NET object model can be used in a *disconnected* manner.

When you work with the disconnected layer of ADO.NET, you will still make use of connection and command objects. In addition, you will leverage a specific object named a *data adapter* (which extends the abstract DbDataAdapter) to fetch and update data. Unlike the connected layer, data obtained via a data adapter is not processed using data reader objects. Rather, data adapter objects make use of DataSet objects to move data between the caller and data source. The DataSet type is a container for any number of DataTable objects, each of which contains a collection of DataRow and DataColumn objects.

The data adapter object of your data provider handles the database connection automatically. In an attempt to increase scalability, data adapters keep the connection open for the shortest possible amount of time. Once the caller receives the DataSet object, he is completely disconnected from the DBMS and left with a local copy of the remote data. The caller is free to insert, delete, or update rows from a given DataTable, but the physical database is not updated until the caller explicitly passes the DataSet to the data adapter for updating. In a nutshell, DataSets allow the clients to pretend they are indeed always connected, when in fact they are operating on an in-memory database, as Figure 24-10 illustrates.

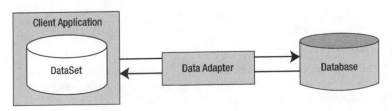

Figure 24-10. *Data adapter objects move* DataSet*s to and from the client tier.*

Given that the centerpiece of the disconnected layer is the DataSet type, your next task is to learn how to manipulate a DataSet manually. Once you understand how to do so, you will have no problem manipulating the contents of a DataSet retrieved from a data adapter object.

Understanding the Role of the DataSet

Simply put, a DataSet is an in-memory representation of data. More specifically, a DataSet is a class type that maintains three internal strongly typed collections, as Figure 24-11 demonstrates.

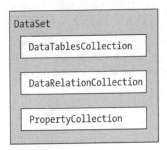

Figure 24-11. *The anatomy of a* DataSet

The Tables property of the DataSet allows you to access the DataTableCollection that contains the individual DataTables. Another important collection used by the DataSet is the DataRelationCollection. Given that a DataSet is a disconnected version of a database schema, it can programmatically represent the parent/child relationships between its tables. For example, a relation can be created between two tables to model a foreign key constraint using the DataRelation type. This object can then be added to the DataRelationCollection through the Relations property. At this point, you can navigate between the connected tables as you search for data. You will see how this is done a bit later in the chapter.

The ExtendedProperties property provides access to the PropertyCollection object, which allows you to associate any extra information to the DataSet as name/value pairs. This information can literally be anything at all, even if it has no bearing on the data itself. For example, you can associate your company's name to a DataSet, which can then function as in-memory metadata. Other examples of extended properties might include timestamps, an encrypted password that must be supplied to access the contents of the DataSet, a number representing a data refresh rate, and so forth.

Note Like the DataSet, the DataTable class also supports extended properties via the ExtendedProperties property.

Members of the DataSet

Before exploring too many other programmatic details, take a look at some core members of the DataSet. Beyond the Tables, Relations, and ExtendedProperties properties, Table 24-9 describes some additional properties of interest.

Table 24-9. *Properties of the Mighty* DataSet

Property	Meaning in Life
CaseSensitive	Indicates whether string comparisons in DataTable objects are case sensitive (or not).
DataSetName	Represents the friendly name of this DataSet. Typically this value is established as a constructor parameter.
EnforceConstraints	Gets or sets a value indicating whether constraint rules are followed when attempting any update operation.
HasErrors	Gets a value indicating whether there are errors in any of the rows in any of the DataTables of the DataSet.
RemotingFormat	This new .NET 2.0 property allows you to define how the DataSet should serialize its content (binary or XML) for the .NET remoting layer.

The methods of the DataSet mimic some of the functionality provided by the aforementioned properties. In addition to interacting with XML streams, the DataSet provides methods that allow you to copy/clone the contents of your DataSet, as well as establish the beginning and ending points of a batch of updates. Table 24-10 describes some core methods.

Table 24-10. *Methods of the Mighty* DataSet

Methods	Meaning in Life
AcceptChanges()	Commits all the changes made to this DataSet since it was loaded or the last time AcceptChanges() was called.
Clear()	Completely clears the DataSet data by removing every row in each DataTable.
Clone()	Clones the structure of the DataSet, including all DataTables, as well as all relations and any constraints.
Copy()	Copies both the structure and data for this DataSet.
GetChanges()	Returns a copy of the DataSet containing all changes made to it since it was last loaded or since AcceptChanges() was called.
GetChildRelations()	Returns the collection of child relations that belong to a specified table.
GetParentRelations()	Gets the collection of parent relations that belong to a specified table.
HasChanges()	Overloaded. Gets a value indicating whether the DataSet has changes, including new, deleted, or modified rows.
Merge()	Overloaded. Merges this DataSet with a specified DataSet.
ReadXml() ReadXmlSchema()	Allow you to read XML data from a valid stream (file based, memory based, or network based) into the DataSet.
RejectChanges()	Rolls back all the changes made to this DataSet since it was created or the last time DataSet.AcceptChanges was called.
WriteXml() WriteXmlSchema()	Allow you to write out the contents of a DataSet into a valid stream.

Now that you have a better understanding of the role of the DataSet (and some idea of what you can do with one), create a new console application named SimpleDataSet. Within the Main() method, define a new DataSet object that contains two extended properties representing your company name and timestamp (don't forget to import System.Data):

```
Sub Main()
  Console.WriteLine("***** Fun with DataSets *****")
  Console.WriteLine()

  ' Create the DataSet object.
  Dim carsInventoryDS As DataSet = New DataSet("Car Inventory")
  carsInventoryDS.ExtendedProperties("TimeStamp") = DateTime.Now
  carsInventoryDS.ExtendedProperties("Company") = "Intertech Training"
End Sub
```

A DataSet without DataTables is a bit like a workweek without a weekend. Therefore, the next task is to examine the internal composition of the DataTable, beginning with the DataColumn type.

Working with DataColumns

The DataColumn type represents a single column within a DataTable. Collectively speaking, the set of all DataColumn types bound to a given DataTable represents the foundation of a table's schema information. For example, if you were to model the Inventory table of the Cars database, you would create four DataColumns, one for each column (CarID, Make, Color, and PetName). Once you have created your DataColumn objects, they are typically added into the columns collection of the DataTable type (via the Columns property).

If you have a background in relational database theory, you know that a given column in a data table can be assigned a set of constraints (e.g., configured as a primary key, assigned a default value, configured to contain read-only information, etc.). Also, every column in a table must map to an underlying data type. For example, the Inventory table's schema requires that the CarID column map to an integer, while Make, Color, and PetName map to an array of characters. The DataColumn class has numerous properties that allow you to configure these very things. Table 24-11 provides a rundown of some core properties.

Table 24-11. *Properties of the* DataColumn

Properties	Meaning in Life
AllowDBNull	This property is used to indicate whether a row can specify null values in this column. The default value is true.
AutoIncrement AutoIncrementSeed AutoIncrementStep	These properties are used to configure the autoincrement behavior for a given column. This can be helpful when you wish to ensure unique values in a given DataColumn (such as a primary key). By default, a DataColumn does not support autoincrement behavior.
Caption	This property gets or sets the caption to be displayed for this column (e.g., what the end user sees in a DataGridView).
ColumnMapping	This property determines how a DataColumn is represented when a DataSet is saved as an XML document using the DataSet.WriteXml() method.
ColumnName	This property gets or sets the name of the column in the Columns collection (meaning how it is represented internally by the DataTable). If you do not set the ColumnName explicitly, the default values are Column with (n+1) numerical suffixes (i.e., Column1, Column2, Column3, etc.).
DataType	This property defines the data type (Boolean, string, float, etc.) stored in the column.
DefaultValue	This property gets or sets the default value assigned to this column when inserting new rows. This is used if not otherwise specified.
Expression	This property gets or sets the expression used to filter rows, calculate a column's value, or create an aggregate column.
Ordinal	This property gets the numerical position of the column in the Columns collection maintained by the DataTable.
ReadOnly	This property determines whether this column can be modified once a row has been added to the table. The default is false.
Table	This property gets the DataTable that contains this DataColumn.
Unique	This property gets or sets a value indicating whether the values in each row of the column must be unique or whether repeating values are permissible. If a column is assigned a primary key constraint, the Unique property should be set to true.

Building a DataColumn

To continue with the SimpleDataSet project (and illustrate the use of the DataColumn), assume you wish to model the columns of the Inventory table. Given that the CarID column will be the table's primary key, you will configure the DataColumn object as read-only, unique, and non-null (using the ReadOnly, Unique, and AllowDBNull properties). Update the Main() method to build four DataColumn objects:

```
Sub Main()
...
  ' Create data columns that map to the
  ' 'real' columns in the Inventory table
  ' of the Cars database.
  Dim carIDColumn As DataColumn = _
    New DataColumn("CarID", GetType(Integer))
  carIDColumn.ReadOnly = True
  carIDColumn.Caption = "Car ID"
  carIDColumn.AllowDBNull = False
  carIDColumn.Unique = True

  Dim carMakeColumn As DataColumn = _
    New DataColumn("Make", GetType(String))

  Dim carColorColumn As DataColumn = _
    New DataColumn("Color", GetType(String))

  Dim carPetNameColumn As DataColumn = _
    New DataColumn("PetName", GetType(String))
  carPetNameColumn.Caption = "Pet Name"
End Sub
```

Enabling Autoincrementing Fields

One aspect of the DataColumn you may choose to configure is its ability to *autoincrement*. Simply put, autoincrementing columns are used to ensure that when a new row is added to a given table, the value of this column is assigned automatically, based on the current step of the incrementation. This can be helpful when you wish to ensure that a column has no repeating values (such as a primary key).

This behavior is controlled using the AutoIncrement, AutoIncrementSeed, and AutoIncrementStep properties. The seed value is used to mark the starting value of the column, whereas the step value identifies the number to add to the seed when incrementing. Consider the following update to the construction of the carIDColumn DataColumn:

```
Sub Main()
...
  Dim carIDColumn As DataColumn = New DataColumn("CarID", GetType(Integer))
  carIDColumn.ReadOnly = True
  carIDColumn.Caption = "Car ID"
  carIDColumn.AllowDBNull = False
  carIDColumn.Unique = True
  carIDColumn.AutoIncrement = True
  carIDColumn.AutoIncrementSeed = 0
  carIDColumn.AutoIncrementStep = 1
End Sub
```

Here, the carIDColumn object has been configured to ensure that as rows are added to the respective table, the value for this column is incremented by 1. Because the seed has been set at 0, this column would be numbered 0, 1, 2, 3, and so forth.

Adding a DataColumn to a DataTable

The DataColumn type does not typically exist as a stand-alone entity, but is instead inserted into a related DataTable. To illustrate, create a new DataTable type (fully detailed in just a moment) and insert each DataColumn object in the columns collection using the Columns property:

```
Sub Main()
...
  ' Now add DataColumns to a DataTable.
  Dim inventoryTable As DataTable = New DataTable("Inventory")
  inventoryTable.Columns.AddRange(New DataColumn() _
    {carIDColumn, carMakeColumn, carColorColumn, carPetNameColumn})
End Sub
```

Working with DataRows

As you have seen, a collection of DataColumn objects represents the schema of a DataTable. In contrast, a collection of DataRow types represents the actual data in the table. Thus, if you have 20 listings in the Inventory table of the Cars database, you can represent these records using 20 DataRow types. Using the members of the DataRow class, you are able to insert, remove, evaluate, and manipulate the values in the table. Table 24-12 documents some (but not all) of the members of the DataRow type.

Table 24-12. *Key Members of the* DataRow *Type*

Members	Meaning in Life
HasErrors GetColumnsInError() GetColumnError() ClearErrors() RowError	The HasErrors property returns a Boolean value indicating whether there are errors. If so, the GetColumnsInError() method can be used to obtain the offending members, and GetColumnError() can be used to obtain the error description, while the ClearErrors() method removes each error listing for the row. The RowError property allows you to configure a textual description of the error for a given row.
ItemArray	This property gets or sets all of the values for this row using an array of objects.
RowState	This property is used to pinpoint the current "state" of the DataRow using values of the RowState enumeration.
Table	This property is used to obtain a reference to the DataTable containing this DataRow.
AcceptChanges() RejectChanges()	These methods commit or reject all changes made to this row since the last time AcceptChanges() was called.
BeginEdit() EndEdit() CancelEdit()	These methods begin, end, or cancel an edit operation on a DataRow object.
Delete()	This method marks this row to be removed when the AcceptChanges() method is called.
IsNull()	This method gets a value indicating whether the specified column contains a null value.

Working with a DataRow is a bit different from working with a DataColumn, because you cannot create a direct instance of this type; rather, you obtain a reference from a given DataTable. For example, assume you wish to insert two rows in the Inventory table. The DataTable.NewRow() method allows you to obtain the next slot in the table, at which point you can fill each column with new data via the type indexer, as shown here:

```
Sub Main()
...
  ' Now add some rows to the Inventory Table.
  Dim carRow As DataRow = inventoryTable.NewRow()
  carRow("Make") = "BMW"
  carRow("Color") = "Black"
  carRow("PetName") = "Hamlet"
  inventoryTable.Rows.Add(carRow)

  carRow = inventoryTable.NewRow()
  carRow("Make") = "Saab"
  carRow("Color") = "Red"
  carRow("PetName") = "Sea Breeze"
  inventoryTable.Rows.Add(carRow)
End Sub
```

Notice how the DataRow class defines an indexer that can be used to gain access to a given DataColumn by numerical position as well as column name. At this point, you have a single DataTable containing two rows.

Understanding the DataRow.RowState Property

The RowState property is useful when you need to programmatically identify the set of all rows in a table that have changed, have been newly inserted, and so forth. This property may be assigned any value from the DataRowState enumeration, as shown in Table 24-13.

Table 24-13. *Values of the* DataRowState *Enumeration*

Value	Meaning in Life
Added	The row has been added to a DataRowCollection, and AcceptChanges() has not been called.
Deleted	The row has been deleted via the Delete() method of the DataRow.
Detached	The row has been created but is not part of any DataRowCollection. A DataRow is in this state immediately after it has been created and before it is added to a collection, or if it has been removed from a collection.
Modified	The row has been modified, and AcceptChanges() has not been called.
Unchanged	The row has not changed since AcceptChanges() was last called.

While you are programmatically manipulating the rows of a given DataTable, the RowState property is set automatically:

```
Sub Main()
...
  Dim carRow As DataRow = inventoryTable.NewRow()
  ' Prints out: Row State is: Detached.
  Console.WriteLine("Row State is: {0} .", carRow.RowState)
  carRow("Make") = "BMW"
  carRow("Color") = "Black"
  carRow("PetName") = "Hamlet"
  inventoryTable.Rows.Add(carRow)
  ' Prints out: Row State is: Added.
  Console.WriteLine("Row State is: {0} .", inventoryTable.Rows(0).RowState);
...
End Sub
```

As you can see, the ADO.NET DataRow is smart enough to remember its current state of affairs. Given this, the owning DataTable is able to identify which rows have been modified. This is a key feature of the DataSet, as when it comes time to send updated information to the data store, only the modified data is submitted.

Working with DataTables

The DataTable defines a good number of members, many of which are identical in name and functionality to those of the DataSet. Table 24-14 describes some core properties of the DataTable type beyond Rows and Columns.

Table 24-14. *Key Members of the* DataTable *Type*

Property	Meaning in Life
CaseSensitive	Indicates whether string comparisons within the table are case sensitive (or not). The default value is false.
ChildRelations	Returns the collection of child relations for this DataTable (if any).
Constraints	Gets the collection of constraints maintained by the table.
DataSet	Gets the DataSet that contains this table (if any).
DefaultView	Gets a customized view of the table that may include a filtered view or a cursor position.
MinimumCapacity	Gets or sets the initial number of rows in this table (the default is 25).
ParentRelations	Gets the collection of parent relations for this DataTable.
PrimaryKey	Gets or sets an array of columns that function as primary keys for the data table.
RemotingFormat	Allows you to define how the DataSet should serialize its content (binary or XML) for the .NET remoting layer. This property is new in .NET 2.0.
TableName	Gets or sets the name of the table. This same property may also be specified as a constructor parameter.

For the current example, let's set the PrimaryKey property of the DataTable to the carIDColumn DataColumn object:

```
Sub Main()
...
  ' Mark the primary key of this table.
  inventoryTable.PrimaryKey = New DataColumn() _
    {inventoryTable.Columns(0)}
End Sub
```

Once you do this, the DataTable example is complete. The final step is to insert your DataTable into the carsInventoryDS DataSet object. Then you'll pass your DataSet to a (yet to be written) helper method named PrintDataSet():

```
Sub Main()
...
  ' Finally, add our table to the DataSet.
  carsInventoryDS.Tables.Add(inventoryTable)

  ' Now print the DataSet.
  PrintDataSet(carsInventoryDS)
End Sub
```

The PrintDataSet() method simply iterates over each DataTable in the DataSet, printing out the column names and row values using the type indexers:

```
Sub PrintDataSet(ByVal ds As DataSet)
  Console.WriteLine("Tables in '{0}' DataSet." _
    & Chr(10) & "", ds.DataSetName)
  For Each dt As DataTable In ds.Tables
    Console.WriteLine("{0} Table." & Chr(10) & "", dt.TableName)
      For curCol As Integer = 0 To dt.Columns.Count - 1
      ' Print out the column names.
      Console.Write(dt.Columns(curCol).ColumnName.Trim() _
        & "" & Chr(9) & "")
  Next
  Console.WriteLine("" & Chr(10) & "----------------------------------")
  For curRow As Integer = 0 To dt.Rows.Count - 1
    ' Print the DataTable.
    For curCol As Integer = 0 To dt.Columns.Count - 1
      Console.Write(dt.Rows(curRow)(curCol).ToString().Trim() & "" & Chr(9) & "")
    Next
    Console.WriteLine()
    Next
  Next
End Sub
```

Figure 24-12 shows the program's output.

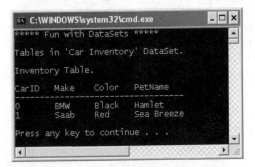

Figure 24-12. *Contents of the example's* DataSet *object*

Working with .NET 2.0 DataTableReaders

DataTables provide a number of methods beyond what we've examined thus far. For example, like DataSets, DataTables support AcceptChanges(), GetChanges(), Copy(), and ReadXml()/WriteXml() methods. As of .NET 2.0, DataTables also now support a method named CreateDataReader(). This method allows you to obtain the data within a DataTable using a data reader–like navigation scheme (forward-only, read-only). To illustrate, create a new helper function named PrintTable(), implemented as follows:

```
Private Sub PrintTable(ByVal dt As DataTable)
  Console.WriteLine("" & Chr(10) & "***** Rows in DataTable *****")
  ' Now, get the new .NET 2.0 DataTableReader type.
  Dim dtReader As DataTableReader = dt.CreateDataReader()
```

```
' The DataTableReader works just like the DataReader.
While dtReader.Read()
  For i As Integer = 0 To dtReader.FieldCount - 1
    Console.Write("{0} = {1}", dtReader.GetName(i).Trim(), _
      dtReader.GetValue(i).ToString().Trim())
  Next
  Console.WriteLine()
End While
dtReader.Close()
End Sub
```

Notice that the DataTableReader works identically to the data reader object of your data provider. Using a DataTableReader can be an ideal choice when you wish to quickly pump out the data within a DataTable without needing to traverse the internal row and column collections. To call this method, simply pass in the correct table:

```
Sub Main()
...
  ' Print out the DataTable via 'table reader'.
  PrintTable(carsInventoryDS.Tables("Inventory"))
End Sub
```

Persisting DataSets (and DataTables) As XML

To wrap up the current example, recall that DataSets and DataTables both support WriteXml() and ReadXml() methods. WriteXml() allows you to persist the object's content to a local file (as well as into any System.IO.Stream-derived type) as an XML document. ReadXml() allows you to hydrate the state of a DataSet (or DataTable) from a given XML document. In addition, DataSets and DataTables both support WriteXmlSchema() and ReadXmlSchema() to save or load an *.xsd file. To test this out for yourself, update your Main() method with the final set of code statements:

```
Sub Main()
...
  ' Save this DataSet as XML.
  carsInventoryDS.WriteXml("carsDataSet.xml")
  carsInventoryDS.WriteXmlSchema("carsDataSet.xsd")

  ' Clear out the DataSet and reload from XML.
  carsInventoryDS.Clear()

  ' Print the DataSet (will be empty)
  PrintDataSet(carsInventoryDS)
  carsInventoryDS.ReadXml("carsDataSet.xml")
  PrintDataSet(carsInventoryDS)
  Console.WriteLine()
End Sub
```

If you open the carsDataSet.xml file, you will find that each column in the table has been encoded as an XML element:

```
<?xml version="1.0" standalone="yes"?>
<Car_x0020_Inventory>
  <Inventory>
    <CarID>0</CarID>
    <Make>BMW</Make>
    <Color>Black</Color>
    <PetName>Hamlet</PetName>
  </Inventory>
```

```
<Inventory>
  <CarID>1</CarID>
  <Make>Saab</Make>
  <Color>Red</Color>
  <PetName>Sea Breeze</PetName>
</Inventory>
</Car_x0020_Inventory>
```

Finally, recall that the DataColumn type supports a property named ColumnMapping, which can be used to control how a column should be represented in XML. The default setting is MappingType.Element. However, if you establish the CarID column as an XML attribute as follows by updating your existing carIDColumn DataColumn object:

```
Sub Main()
  ...
  Dim carIDColumn As DataColumn = New DataColumn("CarID", GetType(Integer))
  ...
  carIDColumn.ColumnMapping = MappingType.Attribute
End Sub
```

you will find the following XML:

```
<?xml version="1.0" standalone="yes"?>
<Car_x0020_Inventory>
  <Inventory CarID="0">
    <Make>BMW</Make>
    <Color>Black</Color>
    <PetName>Hamlet</PetName>
  </Inventory>
  <Inventory CarID="1">
    <Make>Saab</Make>
    <Color>Red</Color>
    <PetName>Sea Breeze</PetName>
  </Inventory>
</Car_x0020_Inventory>
```

■**Source Code** The SimpleDataSet application is included under the Chapter 24 subdirectory.

Binding DataTables to User Interfaces

Now that you have been exposed to the process of interacting with DataSets in the raw, let's see a Windows Forms example. Your goal is to build a Form that displays the contents of a DataTable within a DataGridView widget. Figure 24-13 shows the final UI design (which is implemented in the next several sections).

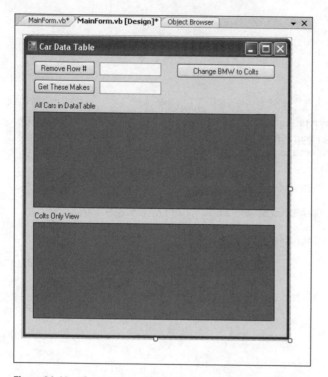

Figure 24-13. *The Windows Forms CarDataTableViewer GUI*

■**Note** As of .NET 2.0, the DataGridView widget is the preferred UI control used to bind relational data. Do be aware, however, that the legacy .NET 1.*x* DataGrid control is still available.

To begin, create a new Windows Forms application named CarDataTableViewer. Add a DataGridView widget (named carInventoryGridView) and descriptive Label to your designer. Next, insert a new VB 2005 class into your project (named Car), which is defined as follows:

```
Public Class Car
  ' Made public for ease of use.
  Public carPetName As String, carMake As String, carColor As String
  Public Sub New(ByVal petName As String, _
    ByVal make As String, ByVal color As String)
    carPetName = petName
    carColor = color
    carMake = make
  End Sub
End Class
```

Now, implement the Form's default constructor to populate a generic List(Of Car) member variable:

```
Public Class MainForm
  ' A generic list of cars.
  Private arTheCars As New List(Of Car)
```

```
Public Sub New()
  ' This call is required by the Windows Forms designer.
  InitializeComponent()

  ' Inherited member to center the form.
  CenterToScreen()

  ' Fill the list with some cars.
  arTheCars.Add(New Car("Chucky", "BMW", "Green"))
  arTheCars.Add(New Car("Tiny", "Yugo", "White"))
  arTheCars.Add(New Car("", "Jeep", "Tan"))
  arTheCars.Add(New Car("Pain Inducer", "Caravan", "Pink"))
  arTheCars.Add(New Car("Fred", "BMW", "Pea Soup Green"))
  arTheCars.Add(New Car("Buddha", "BMW", "Black"))
  arTheCars.Add(New Car("Mel", "Firebird", "Red"))
  arTheCars.Add(New Car("Sarah", "Colt", "Black"))
End Sub
End Class
```

Like the previous SimpleDataSet example, the CarDataTableViewer application will construct a DataTable that contains four DataColumns to represent the columns of the Inventory table within the Cars database. As well, this DataTable will contain a set of DataRows to represent a list of automobiles. This time, however, you will fill the rows using your generic List(Of T) member variable.

First, add a new member variable named inventoryTable of type DataTable to your Form. Next, add a new helper function to your Form class named CreateDataTable(), and call this method within the Form's default constructor. The code required to add the DataColumns to the DataTable object is identical to that in the previous example, so I'll omit it here (consult this book's code download for complete details). Do note, though, that you are iterating over each member of the List(Of T) to build your row set:

```
Private Sub CreateDataTable()
  ' Create DataColumns and add to DataTable.
...
  ' Now add DataColumns to a DataTable.
  inventoryTable.Columns.AddRange(New DataColumn() _
    {carIDColumn, carMakeColumn, carColorColumn, carPetNameColumn})

  ' Mark the primary key of this table.
  inventoryTable.PrimaryKey = New DataColumn() {inventoryTable.Columns(0)}

  ' Iterate over the array list to make rows.
  For Each c As Car In arTheCars
    Dim newRow As DataRow = inventoryTable.NewRow()
    newRow("Make") = c.carMake
    newRow("Color") = c.carColor
    newRow("PetName") = c.carPetName
    inventoryTable.Rows.Add(newRow)
  Next
  ' Bind the DataTable to the carInventoryGridView.
  carInventoryGridView.DataSource = inventoryTable
End Sub
```

Notice that the final line of code within the CreateDataTable() method assigns the inventoryTable to the DataSource property. This single property is all you need to set to bind a DataTable to a DataGridView object. As you might guess, this GUI widget is reading the rows and column collections internally to establish the UI. At this point, you should be able to run your application and see the DataTable within the topmost DataGridView control.

Programmatically Deleting Rows

Now, what if you wish to remove a row from a DataTable? One approach is to call the Delete()
method of the DataRow object that represents the row to terminate. Simply specify the index (or
DataRow object) representing the row to remove. The following logic behind the Remove Row #
Button's Click event handler removes the specified row from your in-memory DataTable:

```
' Remove this row from the DataRowCollection.
Private Sub btnRemoveRow_Click(ByVal sender As System.Object, _
  ByVal e As System.EventArgs) Handles btnRemoveRow.Click
  Try
    inventoryTable.Rows((Integer.Parse(txtRowToRemove.Text))).Delete()
    inventoryTable.AcceptChanges()
  Catch ex As Exception
    MessageBox.Show(ex.Message)
  End Try
End Sub
```

The Delete() method might have been better named MarkedAsDeletable(), as the row is not
literally removed until the DataTable.AcceptChanges() method is called. In effect, the Delete() method
simply sets a flag that says, "I am ready to die when my table tells me to." Also understand that if a row
has been marked for deletion, a DataTable may reject the delete operation via RejectChanges(), as
shown here:

```
' Mark a row as deleted, but reject the changes.
Private Sub btnRemoveRow_Click(ByVal sender As System.Object, _
  ByVal e As System.EventArgs) Handles btnRemoveRow.Click
  ...
  inventoryTable.Rows((Integer.Parse(txtRowToRemove.Text))).Delete()
  ' Do more work
  ...
  inventoryTable.RejectChanges() ' Restore previous RowState value.
End Sub
```

Applying Filters and Sort Orders

You may wish to see a small subset of a DataTable's data, as specified by some sort of filtering criteria.
For example, what if you wish to see only a certain make of automobile from the in-memory Inventory table? The Select() method of the DataTable class provides this very functionality. Update your
GUI once again, this time allowing users to specify a string that represents the make of the automobile
they are interested in viewing. The result will be placed into a Windows Forms message box.

The Select() method has been overloaded a number of times to provide different selection
semantics. At its most basic level, the parameter sent to Select() is a string that contains some conditional operation. To begin, observe the following logic for the Click event handler of the Get These
Makes Button:

```
Private Sub btnGetMakes_Click(ByVal sender As System.Object, _
  ByVal e As System.EventArgs) Handles btnGetMakes.Click
  ' Build a filter based on user input.
  Dim filterStr As String = String.Format("Make= '{0}'", txtMakeToGet.Text)

  ' Find all rows matching the filter.
  Dim makes As DataRow() = inventoryTable.Select(filterStr, "PetName DESC")

  ' Show what we got!
  If makes.Length = 0 Then
    MessageBox.Show("Sorry, no cars...", "Selection error!")
```

```
Else
  Dim strMake As String = Nothing
  For i As Integer = 0 To makes.Length - 1
    Dim temp As DataRow = makes(i)
      strMake &= temp("PetName").ToString() & "" & Chr(10) & ""
  Next
    MessageBox.Show(strMake, txtMakeToGet.Text & " type(s):")
  End If
End Sub
```

Here, you first build a simple filter based on the value in the associated TextBox. If you specify BMW, your filter is Make = 'BMW'. When you send this filter to the Select() method, you get back an array of DataRow types that represent each row that matches the filter (see Figure 24-14).

Figure 24-14. *Displaying filtered data*

As you can see, filtering logic is standard SQL syntax. To prove the point, assume you wish to obtain the results of the previous Select() invocation alphabetically based on pet name. In terms of SQL, this translates into a sort based on the PetName column. Luckily, the Select() method has been overloaded to send in a sort criterion, as shown here:

```
' Sort by PetName.
makes = inventoryTable.Select(filterStr, "PetName")
```

If you want the results in descending order, call Select(), as shown here:

```
' Return results in descending order.
makes = inventoryTable.Select(filterStr, "PetName DESC")
```

In general, the sort string contains the column name followed by "ASC" (ascending, which is the default) or "DESC" (descending). If need be, multiple columns can be separated by commas. Finally, understand that a filter string can be composed of any number of relational operators. For example, what if you want to find all cars with an ID greater than 5? Here is a helper function that does this very thing:

```
Private Sub ShowCarsWithIdLessThanFive()
  ' Now show the pet names of all cars with ID greater than 5.
  Dim properIDs As DataRow()
  Dim newFilterStr As String = "ID > '5'"
  properIDs = inventoryTable.Select(newFilterStr)
  Dim strIDs As String = Nothing
  For i As Integer = 0 To properIDs.Length - 1
    Dim temp As DataRow = properIDs(i)
      strIDs &= temp("PetName").ToString() & " is ID " _
      & temp("ID").ToString() & "" & Chr(10) & ""
  Next
  MessageBox.Show(strIDs, "Pet names of cars where ID > 5")
End Sub
```

Updating Rows

The final aspect of the DataTable you should be aware of is the process of updating an existing row with new values. One approach is to first obtain the row(s) that match a given filter criterion using the Select() method. Once you have the DataRow(s) in question, modify them accordingly. For example, assume you have a new Button that (when clicked) searches the DataTable for all rows where Make is equal to BMW. Once you identify these items, you change the Make from BMW to Colt:

```
Private Sub btnChangeBeemersToColts_Click(ByVal sender As System.Object, _
  ByVal e As System.EventArgs) Handles btnChangeBeemersToColts.Click
  ' Make sure user has not lost their mind.
  If Windows.Forms.DialogResult.Yes = _
    MessageBox.Show("Are you sure?? BMWs are much nicer than Colts!", _
    "Please Confirm!", MessageBoxButtons.YesNo) Then

    ' Build a filter.
    Dim filterStr As String = "Make='BMW'"

    ' Find all rows matching the filter.
    For Each r As DataRow In inventoryTable.Select(filterStr)
      ' Change all Beemers to Colts!
      r("Make") = "Colt"
    Next
  End If
End Sub
```

The DataRow class also provides the BeginEdit(), EndEdit(), and CancelEdit() methods, which allow you to edit the content of a row while temporarily suspending any associated validation rules. In the previous logic, each row was validated with each assignment. (Also, if you capture any events from the DataRow, they fire with each modification.) When you call BeginEdit() on a given DataRow, the row is placed in edit mode. At this point you can make your changes as necessary and call either EndEdit() to commit these changes or CancelEdit() to roll back the changes to the original version, for example:

```
Private Sub UpdateSomeRow()
  ' Assume you have obtained a row to edit.
  ' Now place this row in edit mode.
  rowToUpdate.BeginEdit()
  ' Send the row to a helper function, which returns a Boolean.
  If ChangeValuesForThisRow(rowToUpdate) Then
    rowToUpdate.EndEdit()
  Else
    rowToUpdate.CancelEdit()
    ' OK!
  End If
    ' Forget it.
End Sub
```

Although you are free to manually call these methods on a given DataRow, these members are automatically called when you edit a DataGridView widget that has been bound to a DataTable. For example, when you select a row to edit from a DataGridView, that row is automatically placed in edit mode. When you shift focus to a new row, EndEdit() is called automatically.

Working with the DataView Type

In database nomenclature, a *view object* is a stylized representation of a table (or set of tables). For example, using Microsoft SQL Server, you could create a view for your current Inventory table that returns a new table containing automobiles only of a given color. In ADO.NET, the DataView type allows you to programmatically extract a subset of data from the DataTable into a stand-alone object.

One great advantage of holding multiple views of the same table is that you can bind these views to various GUI widgets (such as the DataGridView). For example, one DataGridView might be bound to a DataView showing all autos in the Inventory, while another might be configured to display only green automobiles.

To illustrate, update the current UI with an additional DataGridView type named dataGridColtsView and a descriptive Label. Next, define a member variable named coltsOnlyView of type DataView:

```
Public Class MainForm
  ' I only show red colts.
  Private coltsOnlyView As DataView
...
End Class
```

Now, create a new helper function named CreateDataView(), and call this method within the Form's default constructor directly after the DataTable has been fully constructed, as shown here:

```
Public Sub New()
...
  CreateDataTable()

  ' Make View.
  CreateDataView()
End Sub
```

Here is the implementation of this new helper function. Notice that the constructor of each DataView has been passed the DataTable that will be used to build the custom set of data rows.

```
Private Sub CreateDataView()
  ' Set the table that is used to construct this view.
  coltsOnlyView = New DataView(inventoryTable)
  ' Now configure the views using a filter.
  coltsOnlyView.RowFilter = "Make = 'Colt'"
  ' Bind to grid.
  dataGridColtsView.DataSource = coltsOnlyView
End Sub
```

As you can see, the DataView class supports a property named RowFilter, which contains the string representing the filtering criteria used to extract matching rows. Once you have your view established, set the grid's DataSource property accordingly. Figure 24-15 shows the completed application in action.

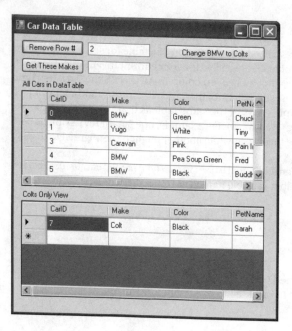

Figure 24-15. *Viewing filtered data with* DataViews

■**Source Code** The CarDataTableViewer project is included under the Chapter 24 subdirectory.

Working with Data Adapters

Now that you understand the ins and outs of manipulating ADO.NET DataSets by hand, let's turn our attention to the topic of data adapters. Recall that data adapter objects are used to fill a DataSet with DataTable objects and send modified DataTables back to the database for processing. Table 24-15 documents the core members of the DbDataAdapter base class.

Table 24-15. *Core Members of the* DbDataAdapter *Class*

Members	Meaning in Life
SelectCommand InsertCommand UpdateCommand DeleteCommand	Establish SQL commands that will be issued to the data store when the Fill() and Update() methods are called.
Fill()	Fills a given table in the DataSet with some number of records based on the command object–specified SelectCommand.
Update()	Updates a DataTable using command objects within the InsertCommand, UpdateCommand, or DeleteCommand property. The exact command that is executed is based on the RowState value for a given DataRow in a given DataTable (of a given DataSet).

In the examples that follow, remember that data adapter objects manage the underlying connection to the database on your behalf; therefore, you will not need to explicitly open or close your session with the DBMS. However, you will still need to supply the data adapter with a valid connection object or a connection string (which will be used to build a connection object internally) as a constructor argument.

Filling a DataSet Using a Data Adapter

Create a new console application named FillDataSetWithSqlDataAdapter and import the System. Data.Common and System.Data.SqlClient namespaces. Update your Main() method as follows:

```
Sub Main()
  Console.WriteLine("***** Fun with Data Adapters *****")
  Console.WriteLine()

  ' Ideally we'd read this from a *.config file.
  Dim cnStr As String = "uid=sa;pwd=;Initial Catalog=Cars;Data Source=(local)"

  ' Fill the DataSet with a new DataTable.
  Dim myDS As DataSet = New DataSet("Cars")
  Dim dAdapt As SqlDataAdapter = _
    New SqlDataAdapter("Select * From Inventory", cnStr)
  Try
    dAdapt.Fill(myDS, "Inventory")
  Catch ex As Exception
    Console.WriteLine(ex.Message)
  End Try
  ' Display contents.
  PrintDataSet(myDS)
End Sub
```

Notice that the data adapter has been constructed by specifying a SQL Select statement. This value will be used to build a command object internally, which can be later obtained via the SelectCommand property. Next, notice that the Fill() method takes an instance of the DataSet type and optionally a string name that will be used to set the TableName property of the new DataTable (if you do not specify a table name, the data adapter will simply name the table "Table").

■**Note** The Fill() method returns an Integer that represents the number of rows affected by the SQL query.

As you would expect, when you pass the DataSet to the PrintDataSet() method (implemented earlier in this chapter), you are presented with a list of all rows in the Inventory table of the Cars database, as shown in Figure 24-16.

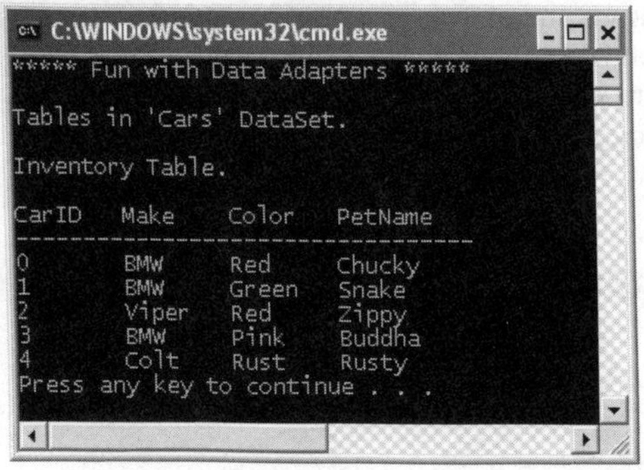

Figure 24-16. *Filling a* DataSet *with a data adapter object*

Mapping Database Names to Friendly Names

As you most certainly know, database administrators (DBAs) tend to create table and column names that can be less than friendly to end users. The good news is that data adapter objects maintain an internal strongly named collection (DataTableMappingCollection) of System.Data.Common.DataTableMapping types, accessed via the TableMappings property.

If you so choose, you may manipulate this collection to inform a DataTable about which "display names" it should use when asked to print its contents. For example, assume that you wish to map the DBMS table name Inventory to "Current Inventory" for display purposes. Furthermore, say you wish to display the CarID column name as "Car ID" (note the extra space) and the PetName column name as "Name of Car." To do so, add the following code before calling the Fill() method of your data adapter object (and be sure to "use" the System.Data.Common namespace):

```
Sub Main()
...
  ' Create table mappings.
  Dim custMap As DataTableMapping = _
    dAdapt.TableMappings.Add("Inventory", "Current Inventory")
  custMap.ColumnMappings.Add("CarID", "Car ID")
  custMap.ColumnMappings.Add("PetName", "Name of Car")
...
End Sub
```

If you were to run this program once again, you would find that the PrintDataSet() method now displays the "friendly names" of the DataTable and DataRow objects, rather than the names established by the database schema.

■**Source Code** The FillDataSetWithSqlDataAdapter project is included under the Chapter 24 subdirectory.

Updating a Database Using Data Adapter Objects

Not only do data adapters fill the tables of a DataSet on your behalf, but they are also in charge of maintaining a set of core SQL command objects used to push updates back to the data store. When you call the Update() method of a given data adapter, it will examine the RowState property for each row in the DataTable and use the correct SQL commands assigned to the DeleteCommand, InsertCommand, and UpdateCommand properties to push the changes within a given DataTable back to the data source.

To illustrate the process of using a data adapter to push back modifications in a DataTable, the next example will reengineer the CarsInventoryUpdater example developed earlier in the chapter to now make use of DataSet and data adapter objects. Given that you have already created a bulk of the application, let's focus on the changes to the DeleteCar(), UpdateCarPetName(), and InsertNewCar() methods (check out the downloadable code for full details).

The first basic adjustment to make to the application is to define two new member variables of the Program Module to represent your DataSet and connection object. As well, the Main() method will be modified to fill the DataSet with the initial data upon startup:

```
Module Program
  ' The applicaion-wide DataSet.
  Public dsCarInventory As DataSet = New DataSet("CarsDatabase")

  ' The application-wide connection object.
  Public cnObj As SqlConnection = _
    New SqlConnection("uid=sa;pwd=;Initial Catalog=Cars;Data Source=(local)")

  Sub Main()
    Console.WriteLine("***** Car Inventory Updater (with DataSets) *****")
    Dim userDone As Boolean = False
    Dim userCommand As String = ""

    ' Create the adapter.
    Dim dAdapter As SqlDataAdapter = _
      New SqlDataAdapter("Select * From Inventory", cnObj)

    ' Fill the DataSet.
    dAdapter.Fill(dsCarInventory, "Inventory")
    ShowInstructions()

    ' Keep looping until user enters 'q'.
  ...
End Sub
```

Also note in the code that follows that the ListInventory(), DeleteCar(), UpdateCarPetName(), and InsertNewCar() methods have all been updated to take a SqlDataAdapter as the sole parameter (so be sure to update the calls to these functions within your Do/While loop!).

Setting the InsertCommand Property

When you are using a data adapter to update a DataSet, the first order of business is to assign the UpdateCommand, DeleteCommand, and InsertCommand properties with valid command objects (until you do so, these properties return null!). By "valid" command objects, I am referring to the fact that the set of command objects you plug into a data adapter will change based on the table you are attempting to update. In this example, the table in question is Inventory. Here is the modified InsertNewCar() method:

```
Private Sub InsertNewCar(ByVal dAdpater As SqlDataAdapter)
  ' Gather info about new car.
  ...
  ' Format SQL Insert and plug into DataAdapter.
    Dim sql As String = String.Format("Insert Into Inventory" & _
      "(CarID, Make, Color, PetName) Values" & _
      "('{0}', '{1}', '{2}', '{3}')", _
      newCarID, newCarMake, newCarColor, newCarPetName)
    dAdpater.InsertCommand = New SqlCommand(sql)
    dAdpater.InsertCommand.Connection = cnObj
```

```
' Update Inventory Table with new row.
Dim newCar As DataRow = dsCarInventory.Tables("Inventory").NewRow()
newCar("CarID") = newCarID
newCar("Make") = newCarMake
newCar("Color") = newCarColor
newCar("PetName") = newCarPetName
dsCarInventory.Tables("Inventory").Rows.Add(newCar)
Try
    dAdpater.Update(dsCarInventory.Tables("Inventory"))
Catch
    Console.WriteLine("Sorry!  Error!  Canceling request")
End Try
End Sub
```

Once you have created your command object, you plug it into the adapter via the InsertCommand property. Next, you add a new row to the Inventory DataTable maintained by the dsCarInventory object. Once you have added this DataRow back into the DataTable, the adapter will execute the SQL found within the InsertCommand property, given that the RowState of this new row is DataRowState.Added.

Setting the UpdateCommand Property

The modification of the UpdateCarPetName() method is more or less identical. Simply build a new command object and plug it into the UpdateCommand property.

```
Private Sub UpdateCarPetName(ByVal dAdpater As SqlDataAdapter)
  Dim carToUpdate As Integer = 0
  Dim newPetName As String = ""
  Console.Write("Enter CarID of car to modify: ")
  Try
    carToUpdate = Integer.Parse(Console.ReadLine())
  Catch ex As FormatException
    Console.WriteLine(ex.Message)
    Return
  End Try
  Console.Write("Enter new pet name: ")
  newPetName = Console.ReadLine()

  Dim sql As String = _
    String.Format("Update Inventory Set PetName = '{0}' Where CarID = '{1}'", _
    newPetName, carToUpdate)
  Dim cmd As SqlCommand = New SqlCommand(sql, cnObj)
  dAdpater.UpdateCommand = cmd
  Dim carRowToUpdate As DataRow() = _
    dsCarInventory.Tables("Inventory").Select(String.Format("CarID = '{0}'", _
    carToUpdate))
  carRowToUpdate(0)("PetName") = newPetName
  Try
      dAdpater.Update(dsCarInventory.Tables("Inventory"))
    Catch
      Console.WriteLine("Sorry!  Error!  Canceling request")
  End Try
End Sub
```

In this case, when you select a specific row (via the Select() method), the RowState value of said row is automatically set to DataRowState.Modified. The only other point of interest here is that the Select() method returns an array of DataRow objects; therefore, you must specify the exact row you wish to modify.

Setting the DeleteCommand Property

Last but not least, you have the following update to the DeleteCar() method:

```
Private Sub DeleteCar(ByVal dAdpater As SqlDataAdapter)
  ' Get ID of car to delete, then do so.
...
  Dim sql As String = _
    String.Format("Delete from Inventory where CarID = '{0}'", carToDelete)
  Dim cmd As SqlCommand = New SqlCommand(sql, cnObj)
  dAdpater.DeleteCommand = cmd
  Dim carRowToDelete As DataRow() = _
    dsCarInventory.Tables("Inventory").Select(String.Format("CarID = '{0}'", _
    carToDelete))
  carRowToDelete(0).Delete()
  Try
    dAdpater.Update(dsCarInventory.Tables("Inventory"))
  Catch
    Console.WriteLine("Sorry!  Error!  Canceling request")
  End Try
End Sub
```

In this case, you find the row you wish to delete (again using the Select() method) and then set the RowState property to DataRowState.Deleted by calling Delete().

Source Code The CarsInvertoryUpdaterDS project is included under the Chapter 24 subdirectory.

Autogenerating SQL Commands Using CommandBuilder Types

You might agree that working with data adapters can entail a fair amount of code, given the need to build each of the four command objects and the associated connection string (or DbConnection-derived object). To help simplify matters, each of the ADO.NET data providers that ships with .NET 2.0 provides a *command builder* type. Using this type, you are able to automatically obtain command objects that contain the correct Insert, Delete, and Update command types based on the initial Select statement.

The SqlCommandBuilder automatically generates the values contained within the SqlDataAdapter's InsertCommand, UpdateCommand, and DeleteCommand properties based on the initial SelectCommand. Clearly, the benefit is that you have no need to build all the SqlCommand and SqlParameter types by hand.

An obvious question at this point is how a command builder is able to build these SQL command objects on the fly. The short answer is metadata. At runtime, when you call the Update() method of a data adapter, the related command builder will read the database's schema data to autogenerate the underlying insert, delete, and update command objects.

Consider the following example, which deletes a row in a DataSet using the autogenerated SQL statements.

```
Sub Main()
  Dim theCarsInventory As DataSet = New DataSet("CarsDS")
  ' Make connection.
  Dim cn As SqlConnection = _
    New SqlConnection("server=(local);User ID=sa;Pwd=;database=Cars")
```

```
' Autogenerate INSERT, UPDATE, and DELETE commands
' based on exiting SELECT command.
Dim da As SqlDataAdapter = New SqlDataAdapter("SELECT * FROM Inventory", cn)
Dim invBuilder As SqlCommandBuilder = New SqlCommandBuilder(da)

' Fill data set.
da.Fill(theCarsInventory, "Inventory")
PrintDataSet(theCarsInventory)

' Delete row based on user input and update database.
Try
  Console.Write("Row # to delete: ")
  Dim rowToDelete As Integer = Integer.Parse(Console.ReadLine())
  theCarsInventory.Tables("Inventory").Rows(rowToDelete).Delete()
  da.Update(theCarsInventory, "Inventory")
Catch e As Exception
  Console.WriteLine(e.Message)
End Try

' Refill and reprint Inventory table.
theCarsInventory = New DataSet()
da.Fill(theCarsInventory, "Inventory")
PrintDataSet(theCarsInventory)
End Sub
```

In the previous code, notice that you made no use of the command builder object (`SqlCommandBuilder` in this case) beyond passing in the data adapter object as a constructor parameter. As odd as this may seem, this is all you are required to do (at a minimum). Under the hood, this type will configure the data adapter with the remaining command objects.

Now, while you may love the idea of getting something for nothing, do understand that command builders come with some critical restrictions. Specifically, a command builder is only able to autogenerate SQL commands for use by a data adapter if all of the following conditions are true:

- The `Select` command interacts with only a single table (e.g., no joins).
- The single table has been attributed with a primary key.
- The column(s) representing the primary key is accounted for in your SQL Select statement.

If these restrictions are unacceptable, rest assured that much of the ADO.NET "grunge" code will be autogenerated by the Visual Studio 2005 Windows Forms and ASP.NET designer surfaces and integrated wizards. You'll see the Windows Forms ADO.NET wizards in action at the conclusion of this chapter (and their ASP.NET counterparts in Part 7).

Source Code   The MySqlCommandBuilder project is found under the Chapter 24 subdirectory.

Multitabled DataSets and DataRelation Objects

Currently, all of this chapter's examples involved DataSets that contained a single DataTable object. However, the power of the disconnected layer really comes to light when a DataSet object contains numerous interrelated DataTables. In this case, you are able to insert any number of DataRelation objects into the DataSet's DataRelation collection to account for the interdependencies of the tables. Using these objects, the client tier is able to navigate between the table data without incurring network round-trips.

To illustrate the use of data relation objects, create a new Windows Forms project called Multi-tabledDataSet. The GUI is simple enough. In Figure 24-17 you can see three `DataGridView` widgets that hold the data retrieved from the Inventory, Orders, and Customers tables of the Cars database. In addition, the single `Button` pushes any and all changes back to the data store.

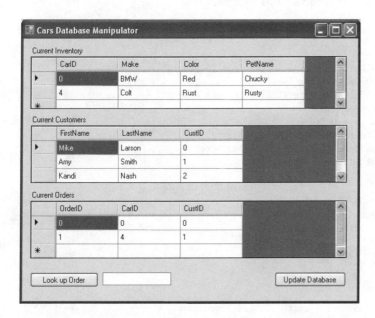

Figure 24-17. *Viewing related* `DataTables`

To keep things simple, the `MainForm` will make use of command builders to autogenerate the SQL commands for each of the three `SqlDataAdapters` (one for each table). Here is the initial update to the `Form`-derived type:

```
Public Class MainForm
  ' Formwide DataSet.
  Private carsDS As DataSet = New DataSet("CarsDataSet")

  ' Make use of command builders to simplify data adapter configuration.
  Private sqlCBInventory As SqlCommandBuilder
  Private sqlCBCustomers As SqlCommandBuilder
  Private sqlCBOrders As SqlCommandBuilder

  ' Our data adapters (for each table).
  Private invTableAdapter As SqlDataAdapter
  Private custTableAdapter As SqlDataAdapter
  Private ordersTableAdapter As SqlDataAdapter

  ' Formwide connection object.
  Private cn As SqlConnection = _
    New SqlConnection("server=(local);uid=sa;pwd=;database=Cars")
...
End Class
```

The Form's constructor does the grunge work of creating your data-centric member variables and filling the DataSet. Also note that there is a call to a private helper function, BuildTableRelationship(), as shown here:

```
Sub New()
  ' This call is required by the Windows Forms designer.
  InitializeComponent()
  CenterToScreen()

  ' Create adapters.
  invTableAdapter = New SqlDataAdapter("Select * from Inventory", cn)
  custTableAdapter = New SqlDataAdapter("Select * from Customers", cn)
  ordersTableAdapter = New SqlDataAdapter("Select * from Orders", cn)

  ' Autogenerate commands.
  sqlCBInventory = New SqlCommandBuilder(invTableAdapter)
  sqlCBOrders = New SqlCommandBuilder(ordersTableAdapter)
  sqlCBCustomers = New SqlCommandBuilder(custTableAdapter)

  ' Add tables to DS.
  invTableAdapter.Fill(carsDS, "Inventory")
  custTableAdapter.Fill(carsDS, "Customers")
  ordersTableAdapter.Fill(carsDS, "Orders")

  ' Build relations between tables.
  BuildTableRelationship()

  ' Bind to grids
  dataGridViewInventory.DataSource = carsDS.Tables("Inventory")
  dataGridViewCustomers.DataSource = carsDS.Tables("Customers")
  dataGridViewOrders.DataSource = carsDS.Tables("Orders")
End Sub
```

The BuildTableRelationship() helper function does just what you would expect. Recall that the Cars database expresses a number of parent/child relationships, accounted for with the following code:

```
Private Sub BuildTableRelationship()
  ' Create CustomerOrder data relation object.
  Dim dr As DataRelation = New DataRelation("CustomerOrder", _
    carsDS.Tables("Customers").Columns("CustID"), _
    carsDS.Tables("Orders").Columns("CustID")) _
    carsDS.Relations.Add(dr)

  ' Create InventoryOrder data relation object.
  dr = New DataRelation("InventoryOrder", _
    carsDS.Tables("Inventory").Columns("CarID"), _
    carsDS.Tables("Orders").Columns("CarID")) _
    carsDS.Relations.Add(dr)
End Sub
```

Now that the DataSet has been filled and disconnected from the data source, you can manipulate each table locally. To do so, simply insert, update, or delete values from any of the three DataGridViews. When you are ready to submit the data back for processing, click the Form's Update button. The code behind the Click event should be clear at this point:

```
Private Sub btnUpdate_Click(ByVal sender As System.Object, _
  ByVal e As System.EventArgs) Handles btnUpdate.Click
```

```
Try
    invTableAdapter.Update(carsDS, "Inventory")
    custTableAdapter.Update(carsDS, "Customers")
    ordersTableAdapter.Update(carsDS, "Orders")
Catch ex As Exception
    MessageBox.Show(ex.Message)
End Try
End Sub
```

Once you update, you will find that each table in the Cars database has been correctly altered.

Navigating Between Related Tables

To illustrate how a DataRelation allows you to move between related tables programmatically, extend your GUI to include a new Button type and a related TextBox. The end user is able to enter the ID of a customer and obtain all the information about that customer's order, which is placed in a simple message box. The Button's Click event handler is implemented as follows:

```
Private Sub btnGetInfo_Click(ByVal sender As System.Object, _
 ByVal e As System.EventArgs) Handles btnGetInfo.Click
    Dim strInfo As String = ""
    Dim drCust As DataRow = Nothing
    Dim drsOrder As DataRow() = Nothing
    ' Get the specified CustID from the TextBox.
    Dim theCust As Integer = Integer.Parse(Me.txtCustID.Text)
    ' Now based on CustID, get the correct row in Customers table.
    drCust = carsDS.Tables("Customers").Rows(theCust)
    strInfo &= "Cust #" & drCust("CustID").ToString() & "" & Chr(10) & ""

    ' Navigate from customer table to order table.
    drsOrder = drCust.GetChildRows(carsDS.Relations("CustomerOrder"))
    ' Get order number.
    For Each r As DataRow In drsOrder
        strInfo &= "Order Number: " & r("OrderID").ToString() & "" & Chr(10) & ""
    Next

    ' Now navigate from order table to inventory table.
    Dim drsInv As DataRow() = _
        drsOrder(0).GetParentRows(carsDS.Relations("InventoryOrder"))
    ' Get Car info.
    For Each r As DataRow In drsInv
        strInfo &= "Make: " & r("Make").ToString() & "" & Chr(10) & ""
        strInfo &= "Color: " & r("Color").ToString() & "" & Chr(10) & ""
        strInfo &= "Pet Name: " & r("PetName").ToString() & "" & Chr(10) & ""
    Next
    MessageBox.Show(strInfo, "Info based on cust ID")
End Sub
```

As you can see, the key to moving between data tables is to use a handful of methods defined by the DataRow type. Let's break this code down step by step. First, you obtain the correct customer ID from the text box and use it to grab the correct row in the Customers table (using the Rows property, of course). Next, you navigate from the Customers table to the Orders table, using the CustomerOrder data relation. Notice that the DataRow.GetChildRows() method allows you to grab rows from your child table. Once you do, you can read information out of the table.

Your final step is to navigate from the Orders table to its parent table (Inventory) using the GetParentRows() method. At this point, you can read information from the Inventory table using the Make, PetName, and Color columns. Figure 24-18 shows one possible output.

Figure 24-18. *Navigating data relations*

Hopefully, this last example has you convinced of the usefulness of the DataSet type. Given that a DataSet is completely disconnected from the underlying data source, you can work with an in-memory copy of data and navigate around each table to make any necessary updates, deletes, or inserts. Once you've finished, you can then submit your changes to the data store for processing.

■**Source Code** The MultitabledDataSetApp project is included under the Chapter 24 subdirectory.

We're Off to See the (Data) Wizard

At this point in the chapter, you have seen numerous ways to interact with the types of ADO.NET in a "wizard-free" manner. While it is (most definitely) true that understanding the ins and outs of working with your data provider is quite important, it is also true that this can lead to hand cramps from typing the large amount of boilerplate code. To wrap things up, therefore, I'd like to point out a few data-centric wizards you may wish to make use of when building Windows Forms applications.

Be aware that space does not allow me to comment on *all* of the UI-centric data wizards provided by Visual Studio 2005, but to illustrate the basics, let's examine some additional configuration options of the DataGridView widget. Assume you have created a new Windows Forms application (named EasyDataAccessForm) that has a single Form containing a DataGridView control named inventoryDataGridView. Using the designer, activate the inline editor for this widget, and from the Choose Data Source drop-down listbox, click the Add Project Data Source link (see Figure 24-19).

This will launch the Data Source Configuration Wizard. On the first step, simply select the Database icon and click Next. On the second step, click New Connection and establish a connection to the Cars database (using the same set of steps described earlier in this chapter within the "Connecting to the Cars Database from Visual Studio 2005" section). The third step allows you to inform the wizard to store the connection string within an external app.config file (which is generally a good idea) within a properly configured <connectionStrings> element. As the final step, you are able to select which database objects you wish to account for within the generated DataSet, which for your purposes here will simply be the Inventory table, as shown in Figure 24-20.

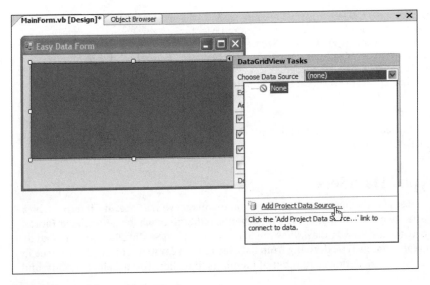

Figure 24-19. *Adding a data source*

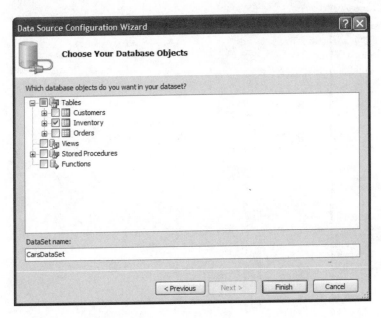

Figure 24-20. *Selecting the Inventory table*

Once you complete the wizard, you will notice that the DataGridView automatically displays the column names within the designer. In fact, if you run your application as is, you will find the contents of the Inventory table displayed within the grid's UI!

As you might be suspecting, this wizard updated your Form with numerous lines of code; however, if you examine the code behind the Forms designer, you find little else than the following implementation of the Form's Load event:

```
Public Class MainForm
  Private Sub MainForm_Load(ByVal sender As System.Object, _
    ByVal e As System.EventArgs) Handles MyBase.Load
    'TODO: This line of code loads data into the 'CarsDataSet.Inventory' table.
    'You can move, or remove it, as needed.
    Me.InventoryTableAdapter.Fill(Me.CarsDataSet.Inventory)
    End Sub
End Class
```

To understand what this code is in fact doing, you need to first understand the role of strongly typed DataSet objects.

Strongly Typed DataSets

Strongly typed DataSets (as the name implies) allow you to interact with a DataSet's internal tables using database-specific properties, methods, and events, rather than via the generalized Tables property. If you activate the View ➤ Class View menu option of Visual Studio 2005, you will find that the wizard has created a new type deriving from DataSet named CarsDataSet. As you can see in Figure 24-21, this class type defines a number of members that allow you to select, modify, and update its contents.

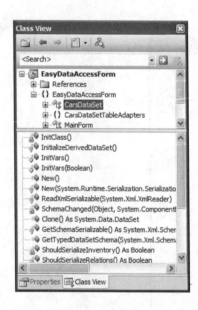

Figure 24-21. *The strongly typed* DataSet

Once the wizard completes its task, it places a member variable of type CarDataSet within your Form's *.Designer.vb file (which is the same member variable manipulated in the Load event of your Form):

```
Partial Class MainForm
  Inherits System.Windows.Forms.Form
...
  Friend WithEvents CarsDataSet As EasyDataAccessForm.CarsDataSet
End Class
```

The Autogenerated Data Component

In addition to the strongly typed DataSet, the wizard generated a data component (named InventoryTableAdapter in this example) that encapsulates the underlying data connection, data adapter, and command objects used to interact with the Inventory table, as you see in Figure 24-22.

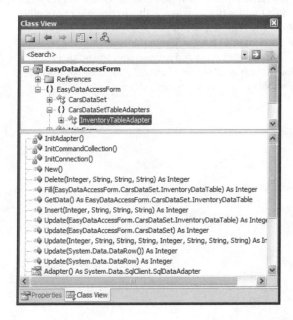

Figure 24-22. *The autogenerated table adapter data component*

As well, this component defines custom Fill() and Update() methods that are tailor-made to operate on your CarsDataSet, in addition to a set of members used to insert, update, or delete row data from the internal Inventory table. I'll leave it up to interested readers to dive into the implementation details of each member. The good news is that after all your work in this chapter, the code behind each member should look quite familiar.

■**Source Code** The EasyDataAccessForm project is included under the Chapter 24 subdirectory.

■**Note** If you are interested in taking a deeper look at the ADO.NET object model, including the numerous Visual Studio 2005 designers, check out *Pro ADO.NET 2.0* by Sahil Malik (Apress, 2005).

Summary

ADO.NET is a new data access technology developed with the disconnected *n*-tier application firmly in mind. The System.Data namespace contains most of the core types you need to programmatically interact with rows, columns, tables, and views. As you have seen, the .NET platform ships with numerous data providers that allow you to leverage the connected and disconnected layers of ADO.NET.

Using connection objects, command objects, and data reader objects of the connected layer, you are able to select, update, insert, and delete records. As you have seen, command objects support an internal parameter collection, which can be used to add some type safety to your SQL queries and is quite helpful when triggering stored procedures.

The centerpiece of the disconnected layer is the `DataSet`. This type is an in-memory representation of any number of tables and any number of optional interrelationships, constraints, and expressions. The beauty of establishing relations on your local tables is that you are able to programmatically navigate between them while disconnected from the remote data store.

You also examined the role of the data adapter in this chapter. Using this type (and the related `SelectCommand`, `InsertCommand`, `UpdateCommand`, and `DeleteCommand` properties), the adapter can resolve changes in the `DataSet` with the original data store. Also, you learned about the connected layer of ADO.NET and came to understand the role of data reader types.

PART 7

■■■

Web Applications and XML Web Services

CHAPTER 25

■■■

Building ASP.NET 2.0 Web Pages

Until now, all of the example applications in this text have focused on console-based and Windows Forms front ends. In the next three chapters, you'll explore how the .NET platform facilitates the construction of browser-based presentation layers using a technology named ASP.NET. To begin, you'll quickly review a number of key web-centric concepts (HTTP, HTML, client-side, and server-side script) and examine the role of the Microsoft's commercial web server (IIS) as well as the ASP.NET 2.0 development server, WebDev.WebServer.exe.

With this web primer out of the way, the remainder of this chapter concentrates on the structure of ASP.NET web pages (including the single-page and enhanced code-behind model) as well as the composition of a Page type. This chapter will also define the role of the web.config file, which will be used throughout the remainder of this text. Do be aware that the information presented here will serve as a foundation for the next two chapters, when we examine web controls, themes, master pages, and numerous state management techniques.

The Role of HTTP

Web applications are very different animals from traditional desktop applications (to say the least). The first obvious difference is that a production-level web application will always involve at least two networked machines (of course, during development it is entirely possible to have a single machine play the role of both client and server). Given this fact, the machines in question must agree upon a particular wire protocol to determine how to send and receive data. The wire protocol that connects the computers in question is the *Hypertext Transfer Protocol (HTTP)*.

When a client machine launches a web browser (such as Netscape Navigator, Mozilla Firefox, or Microsoft Internet Explorer), an HTTP request is made to access a particular resource (such as an *.aspx or *.htm file) on the remote server machine. HTTP is a text-based protocol that is built upon a standard request/response paradigm. For example, if you navigate to http://www.IntertechTraining.com, the browser software leverages a web technology termed *Domain Name Service* (*DNS*) that converts the registered URL into a four-part, 32-bit numerical value, termed an *IP address*. At this point, the browser opens a socket connection (typically via port 80) and sends the HTTP request for the default page at the http://www.IntertechTraining.com website, at which point the browser displays the site's default page.

Once the user posts back to the web server, it is then able to process the incoming HTTP request and may scrape out any client-supplied input values (such as values within a text box) in order to format a proper HTTP response. Web programmers may leverage any number of technologies (CGI, ASP, ASP.NET, Java servlets, etc.) to dynamically generate the content to be emitted into the HTTP response. At this point, the client-side browser renders the HTML sent from the web server. Figure 25-1 illustrates the basic HTTP request/response cycle.

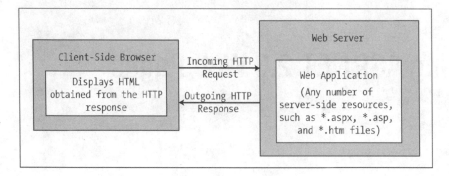

Figure 25-1. *The HTTP request-and-response cycle*

Another aspect of web development that is markedly different from traditional desktop programming is the fact that HTTP is an essentially *stateless* wire protocol. As soon as the web server emits a response to the client, everything about the previous interaction is forgotten. Therefore, as a web developer, it is up to you take specific steps to "remember" information (such as items in a shopping cart) about the users who are currently logged on to your site. As you will see in Chapter 27, ASP.NET provides numerous ways to handle state, many of which are commonplace to any web platform (session variables, cookies, and application variables) as well as some new techniques such as view state, the cache object, and the ASP.NET 2.0 profile management API.

Understanding Web Applications and Web Servers

A *web application* can be understood as a collection of files (*.htm, *.asp, *.aspx, image files, etc.) and related components (such as a .NET code library or legacy COM server) stored within a particular set of directories on a given web server. As shown in Chapter 27, ASP.NET web applications have a specific life cycle and provide numerous events (such as initial startup or final shutdown) that you can hook into to perform specialized processing.

A *web server* is a software product in charge of hosting your web applications, and it typically provides a number of related services such as integrated security, File Transfer Protocol (FTP) support, mail exchange services, and so forth. Internet Information Server (IIS) is Microsoft's enterprise-level web server product, and as you would guess, it has intrinsic support for classic ASP as well as ASP.NET web applications.

When you build ASP.NET web applications, you will often need to interact with IIS. Be aware, however, that IIS is *not* automatically selected when you install the Windows Server 2003 or Windows XP Professional Edition. Sadly, you can't install IIS on the Home editions of the Windows operating system, but hang tight! ASP.NET does provide an alternative server for testing and development, which I'll comment on shortly.

Depending on the configuration of your development machine, you may be required to manually install IIS before proceeding through this chapter. To do so, simply access the Add/Remove Program applet from the Control Panel folder and select Add/Remove Windows Components.

■**Note** Ideally, your development machine will have IIS installed *before* you install the .NET Framework. If you install IIS *after* you install the .NET Framework, none of your ASP.NET web applications will execute correctly (you will simply get back a blank page). Luckily, you can reconfigure IIS to host .NET applications by running the `aspnet_regiis.exe` command-line tool and specifying the `/i` option.

Assuming you have IIS properly installed on your workstation, you can interact with IIS from the Administrative Tools folder (located in the Control Panel folder) by double-clicking the Internet Information Services applet. For the purposes of this chapter, you are concerned only with the Default Web Site node (see Figure 25-2).

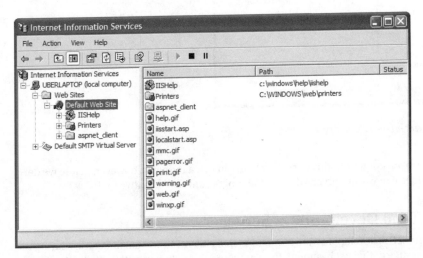

Figure 25-2. *The IIS applet*

Working with IIS Virtual Directories

A single IIS installation is able to host numerous web applications, each of which resides in a *virtual directory*. Each virtual directory is mapped to a physical directory on the local hard drive. Therefore, if you create a new virtual directory named CarsRUs, the outside world can navigate to this site using a URL such as http://www.CarsRUs.com (assuming your site's IP address has been registered with the world at large). Under the hood, the virtual directory maps to a physical root directory such as C:\inetpub\wwwroot\AspNetCarsSite, which contains the content of the web application.

When you create ASP.NET web applications using Visual Studio 2005, you have the option of generating a new virtual directory for the current website. However, you are also able to manually create a virtual directory by hand. For the sake of illustration, assume you wish to create a simple web application named Cars. The first step is to create a new folder on your machine to hold the collection of files that constitute this new site (which I will assume during this example is C:\CodeTests\CarsWebSite).

Next, you need to create a new virtual directory to host the Cars site. Simply right-click the Default Web Site node of IIS and select New ➤ Virtual Directory from the context menu. This menu selection launches an integrated wizard. Skip past the welcome screen and give your website a name (Cars). Next, you are asked to specify the physical folder on your hard drive that contains the various files and images that represent this site (in this case, C:\CodeTests\CarsWebSite).

The final step of the wizard prompts you for some basic traits about your new virtual directory (such as read/write access to the files it contains, the ability to view these files from a web browser, the ability to launch executables [e.g., CGI applications], etc.). For this example, the default selections are just fine (be aware that you can always modify your selections after running this tool using various right-click-activated Property dialog boxes integrated within IIS). When you are finished, you will see that your new virtual directory has been registered with IIS (see Figure 25-3).

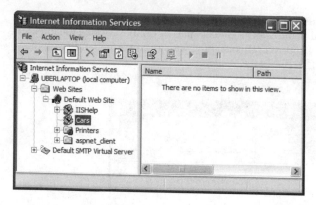

Figure 25-3. *The Cars virtual directory*

We'll add some web content to this virtual directory in just a moment; however, before we do, allow me to introduce a new web server, which is the programmer's alternative to IIS.

The ASP.NET 2.0 Development Server

Prior to .NET 2.0, ASP.NET developers were required to make use of IIS virtual directories during the development and testing of their web content. In many cases, this tight dependency to IIS made team development more complex than necessary (not to mention that many IT professionals frowned upon installing IIS on every developer's machine). Thankfully, as of ASP.NET 2.0, we are provided with a lightweight web server named WebDev.WebServer.exe. This utility allows developers to host an ASP.NET 2.0 web application outside the bounds of IIS. Using this tool, you can build and test your web pages from any directory on your machine (which is quite helpful for team development scenarios and for building ASP.NET 2.0 web programs on Windows XP Home Edition, which does not support IIS installations).

■**Note** WebDev.WebServer.exe cannot be used to test or host classic (COM-based) ASP web applications. This web server can only host ASP.NET web applications and/or .NET-based XML web services.

When building a website with Visual Studio 2005, you have the option of using WebDev.WebServer.exe to host your pages (as you will see a bit later in this chapter). However, you are also able to manually interact with this tool from a .NET command prompt. If you enter the following command:

```
WebDev.WebServer.exe -?
```

you will be presented with a message box that describes the valid command-line options. In a nutshell, you will need to specify an unused port (via the /port: option), the root directory of the web application (via the /path: option), and an optional virtual path using the /vpath: option (if you do not supply a /vpath: option, the default is simply /). Consider the following usage:

```
WebDev.WebServer.exe /port:12345 /path:"C:\CodeTests\CarsWebSite"
```

Once you have entered this command, you can launch your web browser of choice to request pages. Thus, if the CarsWebSite folder had a file named Default.aspx, you could enter the following URL:

```
http://localhost:12345/CarsWebSite/Default.aspx
```

Many of the examples in this chapter and the next will make use of `WebDev.WebServer.exe` via Visual Studio 2005, rather than manually constructing a virtual directory under IIS. While this approach can simplify the development of your web application, do be very aware that this web server is *not* intended to host production-level web applications. It is purely intended for development and testing purposes. Once a web application is ready for prime time, your site will need to be copied to an IIS virtual directory.

■**Note** As yet another alternative web server, be aware that the Mono project (see Chapter 1) provides a free ASP.NET plug-in for the Apache web server. This makes it possible to build and host ASP.NET web applications on operating systems other than MS Windows. If you are interested, check out `http://www.mono-project.com/ASP.NET` for details.

The Role of HTML

Now that you have configured a directory to host your web application, and have chosen a web server to serve as the host, you need to create the content itself. Recall that *web application* is simply the term given to the set of files that constitute the functionality of the site. To be sure, a vast number of these files will contain syntactic tokens defined by the *Hypertext Markup Language* (*HTML*). HTML is a standard markup language used to describe how literal text, images, external links, and various HTML-based UI widgets are to be rendered within the client-side browser.

This particular aspect of web development is one of the major reasons why many programmers dislike building web-based programs. While it is true that modern IDEs (including Visual Studio 2005) and web development platforms (such as ASP.NET) generate much of the HTML automatically, you will do well to have a working knowledge of HTML as you work with ASP.NET.

While this section will most certainly not cover all aspects of HTML (by any means), let's check out some basics and build a simple web application using HTML, classic (COM-based) ASP, and IIS. This will serve as a roadmap for those of you who are coming to ASP.NET from a traditional desktop application development background.

■**Note** If you are already comfortable with the overall process of web development, feel free to skip ahead to the section "Problems with Classic ASP."

HTML Document Structure

An HTML file consists of a set of tags that describe the look and feel of a given web page. As you would expect, the basic structure of an HTML document tends to remain the same. For example, `*.htm` files (or, alternatively, `*.html` files) open and close with `<html>` and `</html>` tags, typically define a `<body>` section, and so forth. Keep in mind that HTML is *not* case sensitive. Therefore, in the eyes of the hosting browser, `<HTML>`, `<html>`, and `<Html>` are identical.

To illustrate some HTML basics, open Visual Studio 2005, insert an empty HTML file using the File ➤ New ➤ File menu selection, and save this file under your C:\CodeTests\CarsWebSite directory as `default.htm`. As you can see, the initial markup is rather uneventful:

```
<!DOCTYPE html PUBLIC "-//W3C//DTD XHTML 1.0 Transitional//EN"
"http://www.w3.org/TR/xhtml1/DTD/xhtml1-transitional.dtd">
<html xmlns="http://www.w3.org/1999/xhtml" >
<head>
  <title>Untitled Page</title>
</head>
<body>
```

```
</body>
</html>
```

First of all, notice that this HTML file opens with a DOCTYPE processing instruction (at least when you use Visual Studio 2005). This informs the IDE that the contained HTML tags should be validated against the XHTML standard. As you may know, traditional HTML was very "loose" in its syntax. For example, it was permissible to define an opening element (such as <br>, for a line break) that did not have a corresponding closing break (</br> in this case). The XHTML standard is a W3C specification that adds some much needed rigor to the HTML markup language.

■**Note** By default, Visual Studio 2005 validates all HTML documents against the XHTML 1.0 Transitional validation scheme. Simply put, HTML *validation schemes* are used to ensure the markup is in sync with specific standards. If you wish to specify an alternative validation scheme, activate the Tools ➤ Options dialog box, then select the Validation node under HTML. If you would rather not see validation errors, simply uncheck the Show Errors check box (which I will assume you have done during the remainder of this chapter).

The <html> and </html> tags are used to mark the beginning and end of your document. Notice that the opening <html> tag is further qualified with an xmlns (XML namespace) attribute that qualifies the various tags that may appear within this document (again, by default these tags are based on the XHTML standard). Web browsers use these particular tags to understand where to begin applying the rendering formats specified in the body of the document. The <body> scope is where the vast majority of the actual content is defined. To spruce things up just a bit, update the title of your page as follows:

```
<head>
  <title>This is the Cars web site</title>
</head>
```

Not surprisingly, the <title> tags are used to specify the text string that should be placed in the title bar of the calling web browser.

HTML Form Development

The real meat of an *.htm file occurs within the scope of the <form> elements. An *HTML form* is simply a named group of related UI elements used to gather user input, which is then transmitted to the web application via HTTP. Do not confuse an HTML form with the entire display area shown by a given browser. In reality, an HTML form is more of a *logical grouping* of widgets placed in the <form> and </form> tag set:

```
<html xmlns="http://www.w3.org/1999/xhtml" >
<head>
  <title>This Is the Cars Web site</title>
</head>
<body>
  <form id="defaultPage">
    <!-- Insert web UI content here ->
  </form>
</body>
</html>
```

This form has been assigned the ID and name of "defaultPage". Typically, the opening <form> tag supplies an action attribute that specifies the URL to which to submit the form data, as well as the method of transmitting that data itself (POST or GET). You will examine this aspect of the <form>

tag in just a bit. For the time being, let's look at the sorts of items that can be placed in an HTML form (in addition to simple literal text). Visual Studio 2005 provides an HTML tab on the Toolbox that allows you to select each HTML-based UI widget, as shown in Figure 25-4.

Figure 25-4. *The HTML tab of the Toolbox*

Building an HTML-based User Interface

Before you add the HTML widgets to the HTML <form>, it is worth pointing out that Visual Studio 2005 allows you to edit the overall look and feel of the *.htm file itself using the integrated HTML designer and the Properties window. If you select DOCUMENT from the Properties window, as shown in Figure 25-5, you are able to configure various aspects of the HTML page, such as the background color.

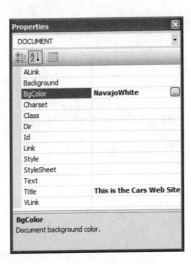

Figure 25-5. *Editing an HTML document via the VS 2005 Properties window*

Update the <body> of the default.htm file to display some literal text that prompts the user to enter a user name and password, and choose a background color of your liking (be aware that you can enter and format textual content by typing directly on the HTML designer):

```
<html xmlns="http://www.w3.org/1999/xhtml" >
<head>
  <title>This is the Cars Web Site</title>
</head>
<body bgcolor="NavajoWhite">
  <!-- Prompt for user input-->
  <h1 align="center"> The Cars Login Page</h1>
  <p align="center"> <br/>
    Please enter your <i>user name</i> and <i>password</i>.
  </p>
  <form id="defaultPage">
  </form>
</body>
</html>
```

Now let's build the HTML form itself. In general, each HTML widget is described using a name attribute (used to identify the item programmatically) and a type attribute (used to specify which UI element you are interested in placing in the <form> declaration). Depending on which UI widget you manipulate, you will find additional attributes specific to that particular item that can be modified using the Properties window.

The UI you will build here will contain two text fields (one of which is a Password widget) and two button types (one to submit the form data and the other to reset the form data to the default values):

```
<!-- Build a form to get user info -->
<form id="defaultPage">
  <p align="center">
    User Name:
    <input id="txtUserName" type="text" name="txtUserName"></p>
  <p align="center">
    Password:
    <input name="txtPassword" type="password" id="txtPassword"></p>
  <p align="center">
    <input name="btnSubmit" type="submit" value="Submit" id="btnSubmit">
    <input name="btnReset" type="reset" value="Reset" id="btnReset">
  </p>
</form>
```

Notice that you have assigned relevant names and IDs to each widget (txtUserName, txtPassword, btnSubmit, and btnReset). Of greater importance, note that each input item has an extra attribute named type that marks these buttons as UI items that automatically clear all fields to their initial values (type = "reset"), mask the input as a password (type="password"), or send the form data to the recipient (type = "submit"). Figure 25-6 displays the page thus far.

Figure 25-6. *The initial crack at the* default.htm *page*

The Role of Client-side Scripting

In addition to HTML UI elements, a given *.htm file may contain blocks of script code that will be emitted into the response stream and processed by the requesting browser. There are two major reasons why client-side scripting is used:

- To validate user input before posting back to the web server
- To interact with the Document Object Model (DOM) of the target browser

Regarding the first point, understand that the inherent evil of a web application is the need to make frequent round-trips (termed *postbacks*) to the server machine to update the HTML rendered into the browser. While postbacks are unavoidable, you should always be mindful of ways to minimize travel across the wire. One technique that saves round-trips is to use client-side scripting to validate user input before submitting the form data to the web server. If an error is found (such as not supplying data within a required field), you can prompt the user of the error without incurring the cost of posting back to the web server (after all, nothing is more annoying to users than posting back on a slow connection, only to receive instructions to address input errors!).

In addition to validating user input, client-side scripts can also be used to interact with the underlying object model (the DOM) of the web browser itself. Most commercial browsers expose a set of objects that can be leveraged to control how the browser should behave. One major annoyance is the fact that different browsers tend to expose similar, but not identical, object models. Thus, if you emit a block of client-side script code that interacts with the DOM, it may not work identically on all browsers.

■**Note** ASP.NET provides the HttpRequest.Browser property, which allows you to determine at runtime the capacities of the browser that sent the current request.

There are many scripting languages that can be used to author client-side script code. Two of the more popular are VBScript and JavaScript. VBScript is a subset of the Visual Basic 6.0 programming language. Be aware that Microsoft Internet Explorer (IE) is the only web browser that has built-in support for client-side VBScript support (other browsers may or may not provide optional plug-ins). Thus, if you wish your HTML pages to work correctly in any commercial web browser, do *not* use VBScript for your client-side scripting logic.

The other popular scripting language is JavaScript. Be very aware that JavaScript is in no way, shape, or form a subset of the Java language. While JavaScript and Java have a somewhat similar syntax, JavaScript is not a full-fledged OOP language, and thus is far less powerful than Java. The good news is that all modern-day web browsers support JavaScript, which makes it a natural candidate for client-side scripting logic.

Note To further confuse the issue, recall that JScript .NET is a managed language that can be used to build valid .NET assemblies using a scripting-like syntax.

A Client-side Scripting Example

To illustrate the role of client-side scripting, let's first examine how to intercept events sent from client-side HTML GUI widgets. Assume you have added an additional HTML button (btnHelp) to your default.htm page that allows the user to view help information. To capture the Click event for this button, activate the HTML view and select your button from the left drop-down list. Using the right drop-down list, select the onclick event. This will add an onclick attribute to the definition of the new Button type:

```
<input id="btnHelp" type="button" value="Help" language="javascript"
onclick="return btnHelp_onclick()" />
```

Visual Studio 2005 will also create an empty JavaScript function that will be called when the user clicks the button. Within this stub, simply make use of the alert() method to display a client-side message box:

```
<script language="javascript" type="text/javascript">
<!--
function btnHelp_onclick() {
  alert("Dude, it is not that hard. Click the Submit button!");
}
// -->
</script>
```

Note that the scripting block has been wrapped within HTML comments (<!-- -->). The reason is simple. If your page ends up on a browser that does not support JavaScript, the code will be treated as a comment block and ignored. Of course, your page may be less functional, but the upside is that your page will not blow up when rendered by the browser.

Validating the default.htm Form Data

Now, let's update the default.htm page to support some client-side validation logic. The goal is to ensure that when the user clicks the Submit button, you call a JavaScript function that checks each text box for empty values. If this is the case, you pop up an alert that instructs the user to enter the required data. First, handle an onclick event for the Submit button:

```
<input name="btnSubmit" type="submit" value="Submit" id="btnSubmit"
language="javascript" onclick="return btnSubmit_onclick()">
```

Implement this handler like so:

```
function btnSubmit_onclick(){
  // If they forget either item, pop up a message box.
  if((defaultPage.txtUserName.value == "") ||
    (defaultPage.txtPassword.value == ""))
  {
```

```
    alert("You must supply a user name and password!");
    return false;
  }
  return true;
}
```

At this point, you can open your browser of choice and navigate to the default.htm page hosted by your Cars virtual directory and test out your client-side script logic:

```
http://localhost/Cars/default.htm
```

Submitting the Form Data (GET and POST)

Now that you have a simple HTML page, you need to examine how to transmit the form data back to the web server for processing. When you build an HTML form, you typically supply an action attribute on the opening <form> tag to specify the recipient of the incoming form data. Possible receivers include mail servers, other HTML files, an Active Server Page file, and so forth. For this example, you'll use a classic ASP file named ClassicAspPage.asp. Update your default.htm file by specifying the following attribute in the opening <form> tag:

```
<form name="defaultPage" id="defaultPage"
  action="http://localhost/Cars/ClassicAspPage.asp" method = "GET">
...
</form>
```

These extra attributes ensure that when the Submit button for this form is clicked, the form data will be sent to the ClassicAspPage.asp at the specified URL. When you specify method = "GET" as the mode of transmission, the form data is appended to the query string as a set of name/value pairs separated by ampersands:

```
http://localhost/Cars/ClassicAspPage.asp?txtUserName=
Andrew&txtPassword=Foo$&btnSubmit=Submit
```

The other method of transmitting form data to the web server is to specify method = "POST":

```
<form name="defaultPage" id="defaultPage"
  action="http://localhost/Cars/ClassicAspPage.asp" method = "POST">
...
</form>
```

In this case, the form data is not appended to the query string, but instead is written to a separate line within the HTTP header. Using POST, the form data is not directly visible to the outside world. More important, POST data does not have a character-length limitation (many browsers have a limit for GET queries). For the time being, make use of HTTP GET to send the form data to the receiving *.asp page.

Building a Classic ASP Page

A classic ASP page is a hodgepodge of HTML and server-side script code. If you have never worked with classic ASP, understand that the goal of ASP is to dynamically build HTML on the fly using *server-side* script and a small set of COM objects. For example, you may have a server-side VBScript (or JavaScript) block that reads a table from a data source using classic ADO and returns the rows as a generic HTML table.

For this example, the ASP page uses the intrinsic ASP Request COM object to read the values of the incoming form data (appended to the query string) and echo them back to the caller (not terribly exciting, but it illustrates the point of the request/response cycle). The server-side script logic will make use of VBScript (as denoted by the language directive).

To do so, create a new HTML file using Visual Studio 2005 and save this file under the name ClassicAspPage.asp into the folder to which your virtual directory has been mapped (e.g., C:\ CodeTests\CarsWebSite). Implement this page as follows:

```
<%@ language="VBScript" %>
<html>
<head>
  <title>The Cars Page</title>
</head>
  <body>
    <h1 align="center">Here is what you sent me:</h1>
    <P align="center"> <b>User Name: </b>
    <%= Request.QueryString("txtUserName") %> <br>
    <b>Password: </b>
    <%= Request.QueryString("txtPassword") %> <br>
    </P>
  </body>
</html>
```

Here, you use the classic ASP Request COM object to call the QueryString() method to examine the values contained in each HTML widget submitted via method = "GET". The <%= ...%> notation is a shorthand way of saying, "Insert the following directly into the outbound HTTP response." To gain a finer level of flexibility, you could interact with the ASP Response COM object within a full server-side script block (denoted by the <%, %> notation). You have no need to do so here; however, the following is a simple example:

```
<%
  Dim pwd
  pwd = Request.QueryString("txtPassword")
  Response.Write(pwd)
%>
```

Obviously, the Request and Response objects of classic ASP provide a number of additional members beyond those shown here. Furthermore, classic ASP also defines a small number of additional COM objects (Session, Server, Application, and so on) that you can use while constructing your web application.

■Note Under ASP.NET, these COM objects are officially dead. However, you will see that the System.Web.UI.Page base class defines identically named properties that expose objects with similar functionality.

To test the ASP logic, simply load the default.htm page from a browser and submit the form data. Once the script is processed on the web server, you are returned a brand new (dynamically generated) HTML display, as you see in Figure 25-7.

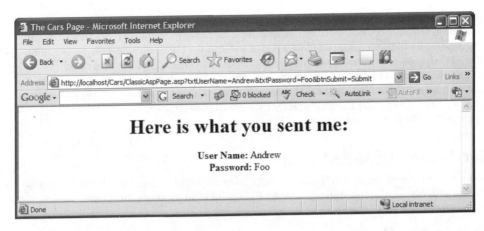

Figure 25-7. *The dynamically generated HTML*

Responding to POST Submissions

Currently, your `default.htm` file specifies HTTP GET as the method of sending the form data to the target `*.asp` file. Using this approach, the values contained in the various GUI widgets are appended to the end of the query string. It is important to note that the ASP `Request.QueryString()` method is *only* able to extract data submitted via the GET method.

If you would rather submit form data to the web resource using HTTP POST, you can use the `Request.Form` collection to read the values on the server, for example:

```
<body>
  <h1 align="center">Here is what you sent me:</h1>
  <P align="center">
    <b>User Name: </b>
    <%= Request.Form("txtUserName") %> <br>
    <b>Password: </b>
    <%= Request.Form("txtPassword") %> <br>
  </P>
</body>
```

That wraps up our web-centric primer. Hopefully, if you're new to web development you now have a better understanding of the basic building blocks of a web-based application. However, before we check out how the ASP.NET web platform improves upon the current state of affairs, let's take a brief moment to critique classic ASP and understand its core limitations.

■**Source Code** The ClassicAspCars example is included under the Chapter 25 subdirectory.

Problems with Classic ASP

While many successful websites have been created using classic ASP, this architecture is not without its downsides. Perhaps the biggest downfall of classic ASP is the same thing that makes it a powerful platform: server-side scripting languages. Scripting languages such as VBScript and JavaScript are interpreted, typeless entities that do not lend themselves to robust OO programming techniques.

Another problem with classic ASP is the fact that an `*.asp` page does not yield very modularized code. Given that ASP is a blend of HTML and script in a *single* page, most ASP web applications are a confused mix of two very different programming techniques. While it is true that classic ASP allows you to partition reusable code into distinct include files, the underlying object model does not support true separation of concerns. In an ideal world, a web framework would allow the presentation logic (i.e., HTML tags) to exist independently from the business logic (i.e., functional code).

A final issue to consider here is the fact that classic ASP demands a good deal of boilerplate, redundant script code that tends to repeat between projects. Almost all web applications need to validate user input, repopulate the state of HTML widgets before emitting the HTTP response, generate an HTML table of data, and so forth.

Major Benefits of ASP.NET 1.*x*

The first major release of ASP.NET (version 1.*x*) did a fantastic job of addressing each of the limitations found with classic ASP. In a nutshell, the .NET platform brought about the following techniques to the web paradigm:

- ASP.NET 1.*x* provides a model termed *code-behind*, which allows you to separate presentation logic from business logic.

- ASP.NET 1.*x* pages are coded using .NET programming languages, rather than interpreted scripting languages. The code files are compiled into valid .NET assemblies (which translates into much faster execution).

- Web controls allow programmers to build the GUI of a web application in a manner similar to building a Windows Forms application.

- ASP.NET web controls automatically maintain their state during postbacks using a hidden form field named __VIEWSTATE.

- ASP.NET web applications are completely object-oriented and make use of the Common Type System (CTS).

- ASP.NET web applications can be easily configured using standard IIS settings *or* using a web application configuration file (web.config).

While ASP.NET 1.*x* was a major step in the right direction, ASP.NET 2.0 provides even more bells and whistles. The good news is that (just about) everything you may already know about ASP.NET 1.*x* still applies to ASP.NET 2.0. In fact, it is perfectly fine to have a single IIS installation host .NET 1.*x* and .NET 2.0–based web content.

Major Enhancements of ASP.NET 2.0

ASP.NET 2.0 provides a number of new namespaces, types, utilities, and technologies to the .NET web development landscape. Consider this partial list:

- As you have seen, ASP.NET 2.0 no longer requires websites to be hosted under IIS during the testing and development of your site. You are now able to host your site from any directory on the hard drive using the WebDev.WebServer.exe utility.

- ASP.NET 2.0 ships with a large number of new web controls (navigation controls, security controls, new data controls, new UI controls, etc.) that complement the existing ASP.NET 1.*x* control set.

- ASP.NET 2.0 supports the use of *master pages*, which allow you to attach a common UI frame to a set of related pages.

- ASP.NET 2.0 supports *themes*, which offer a declarative manner to change the look and feel of the entire web application.

- ASP.NET 2.0 supports *web parts*, which can be used to allow end users to customize the look and feel of a web page.

- ASP.NET 2.0 supports a web-based configuration and management utility that maintains your web.config files.

Given that this book is not focused exclusively on web development, be sure to consult the .NET Framework 2.0 documentation for details of topics not covered here. The truth of the matter is that if I were to truly do justice to every aspect of ASP.NET 2.0, this book would easily double in size. Rest assured that by the time you complete this text, you will have a solid ASP.NET foundation to build upon.

The ASP.NET 2.0 Namespaces

As of .NET 2.0, there are no fewer than *34* web-centric namespaces in the base class libraries. From a high level, these namespaces can be grouped into four major categories:

- Core functionality (e.g., types that allow you to interact with the HTTP request and response, Web Form infrastructure, theme and profiling support, web parts, security, etc.)

- Web Form and HTML controls

- Mobile web development

- XML web services

This text will not examine the topic of mobile .NET development (web-based or otherwise); however, the role of XML web services will be examined in Chapter 28. Table 25-1 describes several of the core ASP.NET 2.0 namespaces.

Table 25-1. *The Core ASP.NET Web-centric Namespaces*

Namespaces	Meaning in Life
System.Web	Defines types that enable browser/web server communication (such as request and response capabilities, cookie manipulation, and file transfer)
System.Web.Caching	Defines types that facilitate caching support for a web application
System.Web.Hosting	Defines types that allow you to build custom hosts for the ASP.NET runtime
System.Web.Management	Defines types for managing and monitoring the health of an ASP.NET web application
System.Web.Profile	Defines types that are used to implement ASP.NET user profiles
System.Web.Security	Defines types that allow you to programmatically secure your site
System.Web.SessionState	Defines types that allow you to maintain stateful information on a per-user basis (e.g., session state variables)
System.Web.UI System.Web.UI.WebControls System.Web.UI.HtmlControls	Define a number of types that allow you to build a GUI front end for your web application

The ASP.NET Web Page Code Model

ASP.NET web pages can be constructed using one of two approaches. You are free to create a single *.aspx file that contains a blend of server-side code and HTML (much like classic ASP). Using the single-file page model, server-side code is placed within a <script> scope, but the code itself is *not* script code proper (e.g., VBScript/JavaScript). Rather, the code statements within a <script> block are written in your .NET language of choice (VB 2005, C#, etc.).

If you are building a page that contains very little code (but a good deal of HTML), a single-file page model may be easier to work with, as you can see the code and the markup in one unified *.aspx file. In addition, crunching your code and HTML into a single *.aspx file provides a few other advantages:

- Pages written using the single-file model are slightly easier to deploy or to send to another developer.

- Because there is no dependency between files, a single-file page is easier to rename.

- Managing files in a source code control system is slightly easier, as all the action is taking place in a single file.

The default approach taken by Visual Studio 2005 (when creating a new website solution) is to make use of a technique known as code-behind, which allows you to separate your programming code from your HTML presentation logic using two distinct files. This model works quite well when your pages contain significant amounts of code or when multiple developers are working on the same website. The code-behind model offers several benefits as well:

- Because code-behind pages offer a clean separation of HTML markup and code, it is possible to have designers working on the markup while programmers author the VB 2005 code.

- Code is not exposed to page designers or others who are working only with the page markup (as you might guess, HTML folks are not always interested in viewing reams of VB 2005 code).

- Code files can be used across multiple *.aspx files.

Regardless of which approach you take, do know that there is *no* difference in terms of performance. Also be aware that the single-file *.aspx model is no longer frowned upon as it was under .NET 1.*x*. In fact, many ASP.NET 2.0 web applications will benefit by building sites that make use of both approaches.

Working with the Single-file Page Model

First up, let's examine the single-file page model. Our goal is to build an *.aspx file (named Default.aspx) that displays the Inventory table of the Cars database (created in Chapter 24). While you could build this page using nothing but Notepad, Visual Studio 2005 can simplify matters via IntelliSense, code completion, and a visual page designer. To begin, open Visual Studio 2005 and create a new Web Form using the File ➤ New ➤ File menu option (see Figure 25-8).

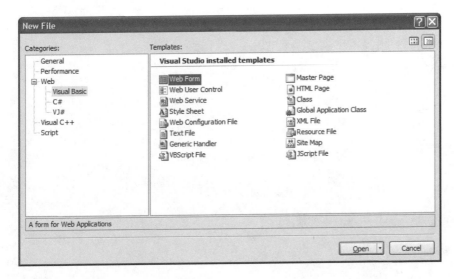

Figure 25-8. *Creating a new* *.aspx *file*

Once the page loads into the IDE, notice that the bottom area of the page designer allows you to view the *.aspx file in two distinct manners. If you select the Design button, you are shown a visual designer surface that allows you to build the UI of your page much like you would build a Windows Form (drag widgets to the surface, configure them via the Properties window, etc.). If you select the Source button, you can view the HTML and <script> blocks that compose the *.aspx file itself.

■**Note** Unlike earlier versions of Visual Studio, the Source view of Visual Studio 2005 has full-blown IntelliSense support for *.aspx files, and allows you to drag and drop UI elements directly from the Toolbox into the HTML document!

Using the Visual Studio 2005 Toolbox, select the Standard tab and drag and drop a Button, Label, and GridView control onto the page designer (the GridView widget can be found under the Data tab of the Toolbox). Feel free to make use of the Properties window (or the HTML IntelliSense) to set various UI properties and give each web widget a proper name via the ID property. Figure 25-9 shows one possible design (I kept my look and feel intentionally bland to minimize the amount of generated control markup, but feel free to use the Properties window to spruce things up to your liking).

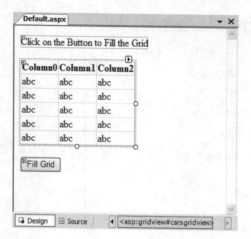

Figure 25-9. *The* Default.aspx *UI*

Now, click the Source button at the bottom of your code window and locate the <form> section of your page. Notice how each web control has been defined using an <asp:> tag. Before the closing tag, you will find a series of name/value pairs that correspond to the settings you made in the Properties window:

```
<form id="form1" runat="server">
<div>
  <asp:Label ID="lblInfo" runat="server"
    Text="Click on the Button to Fill the Grid">
  </asp:Label>
  <asp:GridView ID="carsGridView" runat="server">
  </asp:GridView>
  <asp:Button ID="btnFillData" runat="server" Text="Fill Grid" />
</div>
</form>
```

You will dig into the full details of ASP.NET web controls later in Chapter 26. Until then, understand that web controls are objects processed on the web server that emit back their HTML representation into the outgoing HTTP response automatically (that's right—you don't author the HTML!) Beyond this major benefit, ASP.NET web controls support a Windows Forms–like programming model, given that the names of the properties, methods, and events mimic their Windows Forms equivalents.

To illustrate, handle the Click event for the Button type using either the Visual Studio Properties window (via the lightning-bolt icon) or using the drop-down boxes mounted at the top of the Source view window. Once you do, you will find your Button's definition has been updated with an OnClick attribute that is assigned to the name of your Click event handler:

```
<asp:Button ID="btnFillData" runat="server"
Text="Fill Grid" OnClick="btnFillData_Click" />
```

As well, your `<script>` block has been updated with a server-side `Click` event handler (notice that the incoming parameters are a dead-on match for the target of the `System.EventHandler` delegate):

```
<script runat="server">
  Protected Sub btnFillData_Click(ByVal sender As Object, ByVal e As EventArgs)
  End Sub
</script>
```

Implement your server-side event handler to make use of an ADO.NET data reader to fill the `GridView`. Also add an `Import` directive (more details on this in just a moment) that specifies you are using the `System.Data.SqlClient` namespace. Here is the remaining relevant page logic of the `Default.aspx` file:

```
<%@ Page Language="VB" %>
<%@ Import Namespace = "System.Data.SqlClient" %>
...
<script runat="server">
Protected Sub btnFillData_Click(ByVal sender As Object, ByVal e As EventArgs)
  Dim sqlConn As New SqlConnection("Data Source=.;Initial Catalog=Cars;UID=sa;PWD=")
  sqlConn.Open()
  Dim cmd As New SqlCommand("Select * From Inventory", sqlConn)
  carsGridView.DataSource = cmd.ExecuteReader()
  carsGridView.DataBind()
  sqlConn.Close()
End Sub
</script>

<html xmlns="http://www.w3.org/1999/xhtml" >
...
</html>
```

Before we dive into the details behind the format of this `*.aspx` file, let's try a test run. First, save your `*.aspx` file to your local hard drive under a folder of your choosing. If you wish to make use of `WebDev.WebServer.exe` manually, open a .NET command prompt and run the `WebDev.WebServer.exe` utility, making sure you specify the path where you saved your `Default.aspx` file, for example:

```
webdev.webserver.exe /port:12345 /path:"C:\CodeTests\SinglePageModel"
```

Now, using your browser of choice, enter the following URL:

```
http://localhost:12345/
```

When the page is served, you will initially see your `Label` and `Button` types. However, when you click the button, a postback occurs to the web server, at which point the web controls render back their corresponding HTML tags.

As a shortcut, you can indirectly launch `WebDev.WebServer.exe` from Visual Studio 2005. Simply right-click the page you wish to browse and select the View In Browser menu option. In either case, Figure 25-10 shows the output.

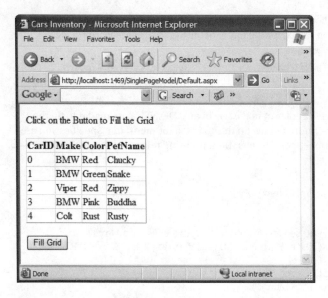

Figure 25-10. *Web-based data access*

That was simple, yes? Of course, as they say, the devil is in the details, so let's dig a bit deeper into the composition of this *.aspx file, beginning by examining the role of the *page directive*.

The <%@Page%> Directive

The first thing to be aware of is that a given *.aspx file will typically open with a set of directives. ASP.NET directives are always denoted with <%@ XXX %> markers and may be qualified with various attributes to inform the ASP.NET runtime how to process the attribute in question.

Every *.aspx file must have at minimum a <%@Page%> directive that is used to define the managed language used within the page (via the language attribute). Also, the <%@Page%> directive may define the name of the related code-behind file (if any), enable tracing support, and so forth. Table 25-2 documents some of the more interesting <%@Page%>-centric attributes.

Table 25-2. *Select Attributes of the* <%@Page%> *Directive*

Attribute	Meaning in Life
CompilerOptions	Allows you to define any command-line flags (represented as a single string) passed into the compiler when this page is processed
CodePage	Specifies the name of the related code-behind file
EnableTheming	Establishes whether the controls on the *.aspx page support ASP.NET 2.0 themes
EnableViewState	Indicates whether view state is maintained across page requests (more details on this property in Chapter 27)
Inherits	Defines a class in the code-behind page the *.aspx file derives from, which can be any class derived from System.Web.UI.Page
MasterPageFile	Sets the master page used in conjunction with the current *.aspx page
Trace	Indicates whether tracing is enabled

The <%Import%> Directive

In addition to the <%@Page%> directive, a given *.aspx file may specify various <%@Import%> directives to explicitly state the namespaces required by the current page. Here, you specified you were making use of the types within the System.Data.SqlClient namespace. As you would guess, if you need to make use of additional .NET namespaces, you simply specify multiple <%@Import%> directives.

■**Note** The <%@Import%> directive is not necessary if you are making use of the code-behind page model described next. When you do make use of code-behind, you will specify external namespaces using the VB 2005 Imports keyword.

Given your current knowledge of .NET, you may wonder how this *.aspx file avoided specifying the System namespace in order to gain access to the System.Object and System.EventHandler types (among others). The reason is that all *.aspx pages automatically have access to a set of key namespaces that are defined within the machine.config file under your installation path of the .NET 2.0 platform. Within this XML-based file you would find the following auto-imported namespaces:

```
<pages>
  <namespaces>
    <add namespace="System"/>
    <add namespace="System.Collections"/>
    <add namespace="System.Collections.Specialized"/>
    <add namespace="System.Configuration"/>
    <add namespace="System.Text"/>
    <add namespace="System.Text.RegularExpressions"/>
    <add namespace="System.Web"/>
    <add namespace="System.Web.Caching"/>
    <add namespace="System.Web.SessionState"/>
    <add namespace="System.Web.Security"/>
    <add namespace="System.Web.Profile"/>
    <add namespace="System.Web.UI"/>
    <add namespace="System.Web.UI.WebControls"/>
    <add namespace="System.Web.UI.WebControls.WebParts"/>
    <add namespace="System.Web.UI.HtmlControls"/>
  </namespaces>
</pages>
```

When you wish to access types within any other namespaces beyond the set shown here, you will be required to make use of the <%Import%> directive, or if you are making use of the code-behind model, the VB 2005 Imports keyword (as you have been doing throughout this text).

To be sure, ASP.NET does define a number of other directives that may appear in an *.aspx file above and beyond <%@Page%> and <%@Import%>; however, I'll reserve commenting on those for the time being.

The "Script" Block

Under the single-file page model, an `*.aspx` file may contain server-side scripting logic that executes on the web server. Given this, it is *critical* that all of your server-side code blocks are defined to execute at the server, using the `runat="server"` attribute. If the `runat="server"` attribute is not supplied, the runtime assumes you have authored a block of *client-side* script to be emitted into the outgoing HTTP response:

```
<script runat="server">
  Protected Sub btnFillData_Click(ByVal sender As Object, ByVal e As EventArgs)
  End Sub
</script>
```

The signature of this helper method should look strangely familiar. Recall from our examination of Windows Forms that a given event handler must match the pattern defined by a related .NET delegate. And, just like Windows Forms, when you wish to handle a server-side button click, the delegate in question is `System.EventHandler` which, as you recall, can only call methods that take a `System.Object` as the first parameter and a `System.EventArgs` as the second.

The ASP.NET Widget Declarations

The final point of interest is the declaration of the `Button`, `Label`, and `GridView` Web Form controls. Like classic ASP and raw HTML, ASP.NET web widgets are scoped within `<form>` elements. This time, however, the opening `<form>` element is marked with the `runat="server"` attribute. This again is critical, as this tag informs the ASP.NET runtime that before the HTML is emitted into the response stream, the contained ASP.NET widgets have a chance to render their HTML appearance:

```
<form id="form1" runat="server">
...
</form>
```

ASP.NET web controls are declared with `<asp>` and `</asp>` tags, and they are also marked with the `runat="server"` attribute. Within the opening tag, you will specify the name of the Web Form control and any number of name/value pairs that will be used at runtime to render the correct HTML.

■**Source Code** The SinglePageModel example is included under the Chapter 25 subdirectory.

Working with the Code-behind Page Model

To illustrate the code-behind page model, let's re-create the previous example using the Visual Studio 2005 Web Site template. (Do know that Visual Studio 2005 is not required to build pages using code-behind; however, this is the out-of-the-box behavior for new websites.) Activate the File ➤ New ➤ Web Site menu option, and select the ASP.NET Web Site template, as shown in Figure 25-11.

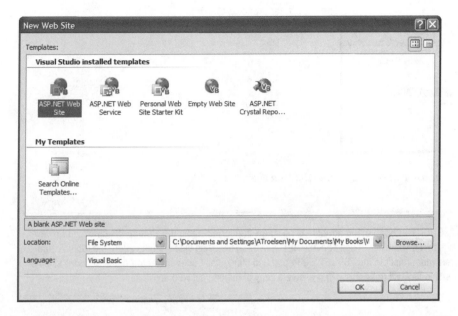

Figure 25-11. *The Visual Studio 2005 ASP.NET Web Site template*

Notice in Figure 25-11 that you are able to select the location of your new site. If you select File System, your content files will be placed within a local directory and pages will be served via WebDev.WebServer.exe. If you select FTP or HTTP, your site will be hosted within a virtual directory maintained by IIS. For this example, it makes no difference which option you select, but for simplicity I'd suggest the File System option.

■**Note** When you wish to open an existing website into Visual Studio 2005, select the File ➤ Open ➤ Web Site menu option and select the folder (or IIS virtual directory) containing the web content.

Once again, make use of the designer to build a UI consisting of a Label, Button, and GridView, and make use of the Properties window to build a UI of your liking. Now, click the Source button at the bottom of your code window, and you will see the expected <asp> and </asp> tags. Also note that the <%@Page%> directive has been updated with a few new attributes:

```
<%@ Page Language="VB" AutoEventWireup="true"
CodeFile="Default.aspx.vb" Inherits="_Default" %>
```

The CodeFile attribute is used to specify the related external file that contains this page's coding logic. By default, these code-behind files are named by suffixing .vb to the name of the *.aspx file (Default.aspx.vb in this example). If you examine the Solution Explorer, you will see this code-behind file is visible via a subnode on the Web Form icon (see Figure 25-12).

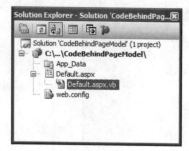

Figure 25-12. *The associated code-behind file for a given* *.aspx *file*

■**Note** The ASP.NET 1.*x* Codebehind attribute is no longer supported within the <%@Page%> directive! However, the good news is that if you were to open an ASP.NET 1.*x* *.sln file using Visual Studio 2005, the IDE will automatically convert your project to the ASP.NET 2.0 format and change all Codebehind attributes to CodeFile. As well, this conversion tool will prompt you to preserve a copy of the original web application.

If you were to open your code-behind file, you would find a partial class deriving from System.Web.UI.Page. Notice that the name of this class (Default) is identical to the Inherits attribute within the <%@Page%> directive:

```
Partial Class _Default
  Inherits System.Web.UI.Page
End Class
```

Handle the Click event for the Button type (again, just like you would for a Windows Forms application). As before, the Button definition has been updated with an OnClick attribute. However, the server-side event handler is no longer placed within a <script> scope of the *.aspx file, but as a method of the _Default class type. To complete this example, add an Imports statement for System.Data.SqlClient inside your code-behind file and implement the handler using the previous ADO.NET logic:

```
Imports System.Data.SqlClient

Partial Class _Default
  Inherits System.Web.UI.Page

  Protected Sub btnFillGrid_Click(ByVal sender As Object, _
    ByVal e As System.EventArgs) Handles btnFillGrid.Click
  Dim sqlConn As New _
    SqlConnection("Data Source=.;Initial Catalog=Cars;UID=sa;PWD=")
  sqlConn.Open()
  Dim cmd As New SqlCommand("Select * From Inventory", sqlConn)
  carsGridView.DataSource = cmd.ExecuteReader()
  carsGridView.DataBind()
  sqlConn.Close()
  End Sub
End Class
```

If you selected the File System option, WebDev.WebServer.exe starts up automatically when you run your web application (if you selected IIS, this obviously does not occur). In either case, the default browser should now display the page's content.

Debugging and Tracing ASP.NET Pages

By and large, when you are building ASP.NET web projects, you can use the same debugging techniques as you would with any other sort of Visual Studio 2005 project type. Thus, you can set breakpoints in your code-behind file (as well as embedded "script" blocks in an *.aspx file), start a debug session (the F5 key; by default), and step through your code.

However, to debug your ASP.NET web applications, your site must contain a properly configured web.config file. The conclusion of this chapter will examine various details behind web.config files, but in a nutshell these XML files provide the same general purpose as an executable assembly's app.config file. By default, all Visual Studio 2005 web applications created with the Visual Basic 2005 programming language will automatically have a web.config file. However, debugging support is initially disabled (as this will degrade performance). When you start a debugging session, the IDE will prompt you for permissions to enable debugging. Once you have opted to do so, the <compilation> element of the web.config file is updated like so:

```
<compilation debug="true" strict="false" explicit="true"/>
```

On a related note, you are also able to enable *tracing support* for an *.aspx file by setting the Trace attribute to true within the <%@Page%> directive (it is also possible to enable tracing for your entire site by modifying the web.config file):

```
<%@ Page Language="VB" AutoEventWireup="true"
CodeFile="Default.aspx.vb" Inherits="_Default" Trace="true" %>
```

Once you do, the emitted HTML now contains numerous details regarding the previous HTTP request/response (server variables, session and application variables, request/response, etc.). To insert your own trace messages into the mix, you can use the Trace property of the System.Web.UI.Page type. Any time you wish to log a custom message (from a script block or VB 2005 source code file), simply call the Write() method:

```
Protected Sub btnFillGrid_Click(ByVal sender As Object, _
  ByVal e As System.EventArgs) Handles btnFillGrid.Click
  ' Emit a custom trace message.
  Trace.Write("My Category", "Filling the grid!")
...
End Sub
```

If you run your project once again and post back to the web server, you will find your custom category and custom message are present and accounted for. In Figure 25-13, take note of the highlighted message, which displays your trace information.

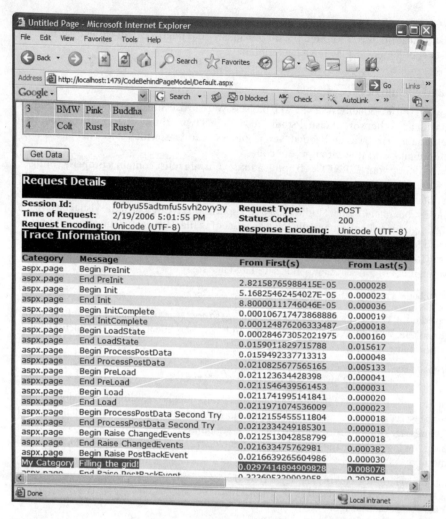

Figure 25-13. *Logging custom trace messages*

Source Code   The CodeBehindPageModel example is included under the Chapter 25 subdirectory.

Details of an ASP.NET Website Directory Structure

If you have created web applications using ASP.NET 1.*x*, you may be quite surprised to see that some familiar files (such as Global.asax) are not included when creating a new website. Furthermore, the Web Site template contains a folder named App_Data and does not appear to have References folder within Solution Explorer.

First of all, do know that *.asax files are most certainly supported under ASP.NET 2.0, but you will need to explicitly add them to your project using the Web Site ➤ Add New Item menu option. Chapter 27 will examine the role of Global.asax, so don't sweat the details for now. Next, be aware that your websites are still able to add references to any number of external .NET assemblies via the Web Site ➤ Add Reference menu option (the end result is a bit different, however, as you will soon see).

Another significant difference is that under Visual Studio 2005, websites may contain any number of specifically named subdirectories, each of which has a special meaning to the ASP.NET runtime. Table 25-3 documents these "special subdirectories."

Table 25-3. *Special ASP.NET 2.0 Subdirectories*

Subfolder	Meaning in Life
App_Browsers	Folder for browser definition files that are used to identify individual browsers and determine their capabilities.
App_Code	Folder for source code for components or classes that you want to compile as part of your application. ASP.NET compiles the code in this folder when pages are requested. Code in the App_Code folder is automatically accessible by your application.
App_Data	Folder for storing Access *.mdb files, SQL Express *.mdf files, XML files, or other data stores.
App_GlobalResources	Folder for *.resx files that are accessed programmatically from application code.
App_LocalResources	Folder for *.resx files that are bound to a specific page.
App_Themes	Folder that contains a collection of files that define the appearance of ASP.NET web pages and controls.
App_WebReferences	Folder for proxy classes, schemas, and other files associated with using a web service in your application.
Bin	Folder for compiled private assemblies (*.dll files). Assemblies in the Bin folder are automatically referenced by your application.

If you are interested in adding any of these known subfolders to your current web application, you may do so explicitly using the Web Site ➤ Add Folder menu option. However, in many cases, the IDE will automatically do so as you "naturally" insert related files into your site (e.g., inserting a new VB 2005 class file into your project will automatically add an App_Code folder to your directory structure if one does not currently exist).

Assembly References and the Bin Folder

As described in a few pages, ASP.NET web pages are eventually compiled into a .NET assembly. Given this, it should come as no surprise that your websites can reference any number of private or shared assemblies. Under ASP.NET 2.0, the manner in which your site's externally required assemblies are recorded is quite different from ASP.NET 1.*x*. The reason for this fundamental shift is that Visual Studio 2005 now treats websites in a *projectless manner*.

Although the Web Site template does generate a *.sln file to load your *.aspx files into the IDE, there is no longer a related *.vbproj file. As you may know, ASP.NET 1.*x* Web Application projects recorded all external assemblies within *.vbproj. This fact brings up the obvious question, Where are the external assemblies recorded under ASP.NET 2.0?

When you reference a private assembly, Visual Studio 2005 will automatically create a Bin directory within your directory structure to store a local copy of the binary. When your code base makes use of types within these code libraries, they are automatically loaded on demand. By way of a simple test, if you activate the Web Site ➤ Add Reference menu option and select any of the previous (non–strongly named) *.dlls you created over the course of this text, you will find a Bin folder is displayed within Solution Explorer, as shown in Figure 25-14.

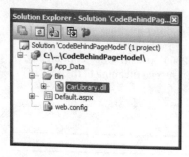

Figure 25-14. *The Bin folder contains copies of all referenced private assemblies.*

If you reference a shared assembly, Visual Studio 2005 will automatically insert a web.config file into your current web solution (if one is not currently in place) and record the external reference within the <assemblies> element. For example, if you again activate the Web Site ➤ Add Reference menu option and this time select a shared assembly (such as System.Data.OracleClient.dll), you will find that your web.config file has been updated as follows:

```
<assemblies>
  <add assembly="System.Data.OracleClient, Version=2.0.0.0,
  Culture=neutral, PublicKeyToken=B77A5C561934E089"/>
</assemblies>
```

As you can see, each assembly is described using the same information required for a dynamic load via the Assembly.Load() method (see Chapter 14).

The Role of the App_Code Folder

The App_Code folder is used to place source code files that are not directly tied to a specific web page (such as a code-behind file) but are to be compiled for use by your website. Code within the App_Code folder will be automatically compiled on the fly on an as-needed basis. After this point, the assembly is accessible to any other code in the website. To this end, the App_Code folder is much like the Bin folder, except that you can store source code in it instead of compiled code. The major benefit of this approach is that it is possible to define custom types for your web application without having to compile them independently.

A single App_Code folder can contain code files from multiple languages. At runtime, the appropriate compiler kicks in to generate the assembly in question. If you would rather partition your code, however, you can define multiple subdirectories that are used to hold any number of managed code files (*.vb, *.cs [for C#], etc.).

For example, assume you have added an App_Code folder to the root directory of a website application that has two subfolders (MyCSharpCode and MyVbNetCode) that contain language-specific files. Once you do, you are able to update your web.config file to specify these subdirectories using a <codeSubDirectories> element nested within the <configuration> element:

```
<compilation debug="true" strict="false" explicit="true">
  <codeSubDirectories>
    <add directoryName="MyVbNetCode" />
    <add directoryName="MyCSharpCode" />
  </codeSubDirectories>
</compilation>
```

Note The App_Code directory will also be used to contain files that are not language files, but are useful nonetheless (*.xsd files, *.wsdl files, etc.).

Beyond Bin and App_Code, the App_Data and App_Themes folders are two additional "special subdirectories" that you should be familiar with, both of which will be detailed in the next two chapters. As always, consult the .NET Framework 2.0 SDK documentation for full details of the remaining ASP.NET subdirectories if you require further information.

The ASP.NET 2.0 Page Compilation Cycle

Regardless of which page model you make use of (single-file or code-behind), your *.aspx files (and any related code-behind file) are compiled on the fly into a valid .NET assembly. This assembly is then hosted by the ASP.NET worker process (aspnet_wp.exe) within its own application domain boundary (see Chapter 14 for details on AppDomains). The manner in which your website's assembly is compiled under ASP.NET 2.0, however, is quite different.

Compilation Cycle for Single-file Pages

If you are making use of the single-file page model, the HTML markup, <script> blocks, and web control definitions are dynamically compiled into a class type deriving from System.Web.UI.Page. The name of this class is based on the name of the *.aspx file and takes an _aspx suffix (e.g., a page named MyPage.aspx becomes a class type named MyPage_aspx). Figure 25-15 illustrates the basic process.

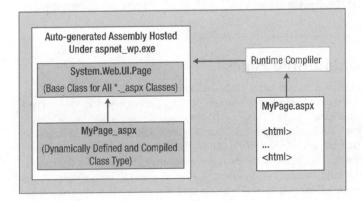

Figure 25-15. *The compilation model for single-file pages*

This dynamically compiled assembly is deployed to a runtime-defined subdirectory under the C:\WINDOWS\Microsoft.NET\Framework\v2.0.50727\Temporary ASP.NET Files root directory. The path beneath this root will differ based on a number of factors (hash codes, etc.), but eventually you will find the *.dll (and supporting files) in question. Figure 25-16 shows the generated assembly for the SinglePageModel example shown earlier in this chapter.

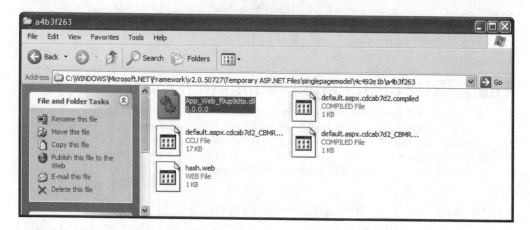

Figure 25-16. *The ASP.NET autogenerated assembly*

■**Note** Because these autogenerated assemblies are true-blue .NET binaries, if you were to open your web applications–related *.dll using ildasm.exe, you would indeed find CIL code, metadata, and an assembly-level manifest.

Compilation Cycle for Multifile Pages

The compilation process of a page making use of the code-behind model is similar to that of the single-file model. However, the type deriving from System.Web.UI.Page is composed from three (yes, *three*) files rather than the expected *two*.

Looking back at the previous CodeBehindPageModel example, recall that the Default.aspx file was connected to a partial class named _Default within the code-behind file. If you have a background in ASP.NET 1.*x*, you may wonder what happened to the member variable declarations for the various web controls as well as the code within InitializeComponent(), such as event handling logic. Under ASP.NET 2.0, these details are accounted for by a third "file" generated in memory. In reality, of course, this is not a literal file, but an in-memory representation of the partial class. Consider Figure 25-17.

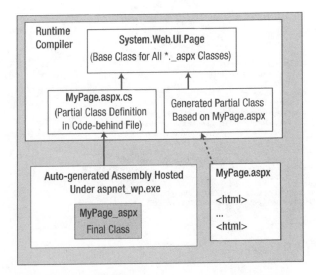

Figure 25-17. *The compilation model for multifile pages*

In this model, the web controls declared in the *.aspx file are used to build the additional partial class that defines each UI member variable and the configuration logic that used to be found within the InitializeComponent() method of ASP.NET 1.*x* (we just never directly see it). This partial class is combined at compile time with the code-behind file to result in the *base class* of the generated _aspx class type (in the single-file page compilation model, the generated _aspx file derived directly from System.Web.UI.Page).

In either case, once the assembly has been created upon the initial HTTP request, it will be reused for all subsequent requests, and thus will not have to be recompiled. Understanding this factoid should help explain why the first request of an *.aspx page takes the longest, and subsequent hits to the same page are extremely efficient.

■**Note** Under ASP.NET 2.0, it is now possible to precompile all pages (or a subset of pages) of a website using a command-line tool named aspnet_compiler.exe. Check out the .NET Framework 2.0 SDK documentation for details.

The Inheritance Chain of the Page Type

As you have just seen, the final generated class that represents your *.aspx file eventually derives from System.Web.UI.Page. Like any base class, this type provides a polymorphic interface to all derived types. However, the Page type is not the only member in your inheritance hierarchy. If you were to locate the Page type (within the System.Web.dll assembly) using the Visual Studio 2005 object browser, you would find that Page "is-a" TemplateControl, which "is-a" Control, which "is-a" Object (see Figure 25-18).

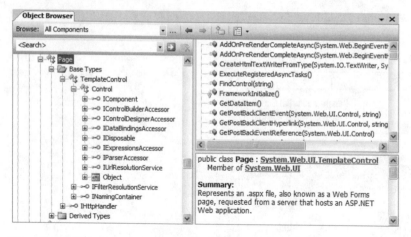

Figure 25-18. *The derivation of an ASP.NET page*

As you would guess, each of these base classes brings a good deal of functionality to each and every *.aspx file. For the majority of your projects, you will make use of the members defined within the Page and Control parent classes. By and large, the functionality gained from the System.Web.UI.TemplateControl class is only of interest to you if you are building custom Web Form controls or interacting with the rendering process. This being said, let's get to know the overall role of the Page type.

The System.Web.UI.Page Type

The first parent class of interest is Page itself. Here you will find numerous properties that enable you to interact with various web primitives such as application and session variables, the HTTP request/response, theme support, and so forth. Table 25-4 describes some (but by no means all) of the core properties.

Table 25-4. *Properties of the Page Type*

Property	Meaning in Life
Application	Allows you to interact with application variables for the current website
Cache	Allows you to interact with the cache object for the current website
ClientTarget	Allows you to specify how this page should render itself based on the requesting browser
IsPostBack	Gets a value indicating whether the page is being loaded in response to a client postback or whether it is being loaded and accessed for the first time
MasterPageFile	Establishes the master page for the current page
Request	Provides access to the current HTTP request
Response	Allows you to interact with the outgoing HTTP response
Server	Provides access to the HttpServerUtility object, which contains various server-side helper functions
Session	Allows you to interact with the session data for the current caller
Theme	Gets or sets the name of the theme used for the current page
Trace	Provides access to a TraceContext object, which allows you to log custom messages during debugging sessions

Interacting with the Incoming HTTP Request

As you saw earlier in this chapter, the basic flow of a web session begins with a client logging on to a site, filling in user information, and clicking a Submit button to post back the HTML form data to a given web page for processing. In most cases, the opening tag of the form statement specifies an action attribute and a method attribute that indicates the file on the web server that will be sent the data in the various HTML widgets, as well as the method of sending this data (GET or POST):

```
<form name="defaultPage" id="defaultPage"
 action="http://localhost/Cars/ClassicAspPage.asp" method = "GET">
...
</form>
```

Unlike classic ASP, ASP.NET does not support an object named Request. However, all ASP.NET pages do inherit the System.Web.UI.Page.Request *property*, which provides access to an instance of the HttpRequest class type. Table 25-5 lists some core members that, not surprisingly, mimic the same members found within the legacy classic ASP Request object.

Table 25-5. *Members of the* HttpRequest *Type*

Member	Meaning in Life
ApplicationPath	Gets the ASP.NET application's virtual application root path on the server
Browser	Provides information about the capabilities of the client browser
Cookies	Gets a collection of cookies sent by the client browser
FilePath	Indicates the virtual path of the current request
Form	Gets a collection of Form variables
Headers	Gets a collection of HTTP headers
HttpMethod	Indicates the HTTP data transfer method used by the client (GET, POST)
IsSecureConnection	Indicates whether the HTTP connection is secure (i.e., HTTPS)
QueryString	Gets the collection of HTTP query string variables
RawUrl	Gets the current request's raw URL
RequestType	Indicates the HTTP data transfer method used by the client (GET, POST)
ServerVariables	Gets a collection of web server variables
UserHostAddress	Gets the IP host address of the remote client
UserHostName	Gets the DNS name of the remote client

In addition to these properties, the HttpRequest type has a number of useful methods, including the following:

- MapPath(): Maps the virtual path in the requested URL to a physical path on the server for the current request.
- SaveAs(): Saves details of the current HTTP request to a file on the web server (which can prove helpful for debugging purposes).
- ValidateInput(): If the validation feature is enabled via the Validate attribute of the page directive, this method can be called to check all user input data (including cookie data) against a predefined list of potentially dangerous input data.

Obtaining Brower Statistics

The first interesting aspect of the HttpRequest type is the Browser property, which provides access to an underlying HttpBrowserCapabilities object. HttpBrowserCapabilities in turn exposes numerous members that allow you to programmatically investigate statistics regarding the browser that sent the incoming HTTP request.

Create a new ASP.NET website named FunWithPageMembers. Your first task is to build a UI that allows users to click a Button web control to view various statistics about the calling browser. These statistics will be generated dynamically and attached to a Label type (named lblOutput). The Button Click event handler is as follows:

```
Protected Sub btnGetBrowserStats_Click(ByVal sender As Object, _
ByVal e As System.EventArgs) Handles btnGetBrowserStats.Click
  Dim theInfo As String = ""
  theInfo &= String.Format("<li>Is the client AOL? {0}</li>", _
    Request.Browser.AOL)
  theInfo &= _
    String.Format("<li>Does the client support ActiveX? {0}</li>", _
    Request.Browser.ActiveXControls)
  theInfo &= String.Format("<li>Is the client a Beta? {0}</li>", _
    Request.Browser.Beta)
  theInfo &= _
    String.Format("<li>Does the client support Java Applets? {0}</li>", _
    Request.Browser.JavaApplets)
  theInfo &= _
    String.Format("<li>Does the client support Cookies? {0}</li>", _
    Request.Browser.Cookies)
  theInfo &= _
    String.Format("<li>Does the client support VBScript? {0}</li>", _
    Request.Browser.VBScript)
  lblOutput.Text = theInfo
End Sub
```

Here you are testing for a number of browser capabilities. As you would guess, it is (very) helpful to discover a browser's support for ActiveX controls, Java applets, and client-side VBScript code. If the calling browser does not support a given web technology, your *.aspx page would be able to take an alternative course of action.

Access to Incoming Form Data

Other aspects of the HttpResponse type are the Form and QueryString properties. These two properties allow you to examine the incoming form data using name/value pairs, and they function identically to classic ASP. Recall from our earlier discussion of classic ASP that if the data is submitted using HTTP GET, the form data is accessed using the QueryString property, whereas data submitted via HTTP POST is obtained using the Form property.

While you could most certainly make use of the HttpRequest.Form and HttpRequest.QueryString properties to access client-supplied form data on the web server, these old-school techniques are (for the most part) unnecessary. Given that ASP.NET supplies you with server-side web controls, you are able to treat HTML UI elements as true objects. Therefore, rather than obtaining the value within a text box as follows:

```
Protected Sub btnGetFormData_Click(ByVal sender As Object, _
ByVal e As System.EventArgs) Handles btnGetFormData.Click
  ' Get value for a widget with ID txtFirstName.
  Dim firstName As String = Request.Form("txtFirstName")
```

```
' Use this value in your page...
End Sub
```

you can simply ask the server-side widget directly via the Text property for use in your program:

```
Protected Sub btnGetFormData_Click(ByVal sender As Object, _
ByVal e As System.EventArgs) Handles btnGetFormData.Click
  ' Get value for a widget with ID txtFirstName.
  Dim firstName As String = txtFirstName.Text

  ' Use this value in your page...
End Sub
```

Not only does this approach lend itself to solid OO principles, but also you do not need to concern yourself with how the form data was submitted (GET or POST) before obtaining the values. Furthermore, working with the widget directly is much more type-safe, given that typing errors are discovered at compile time rather than runtime. Of course, this is not to say that you will *never* need to make use of the Form or QueryString property in ASP.NET; rather, the need to do so has greatly diminished and is usually optional.

The IsPostBack Property

Another very important member of HttpRequest is the IsPostBack property. Recall that "postback" refers to the act of returning to a particular web page while still in session with the server. Given this definition, understand that the IsPostBack property will return true if the current HTTP request has been sent by a currently logged on user and false if this is the user's first interaction with the page.

Typically, the need to determine whether the current HTTP request is indeed a postback is most helpful when you wish to perform a block of code only the first time the user accesses a given page. For example, you may wish to populate an ADO.NET DataSet when the user first accesses an *.aspx file and cache the object for later use. When the caller returns to the page, you can avoid the need to hit the database unnecessarily (of course, some pages may require that the DataSet always be updated upon each request, but that is another issue). Assuming your *.aspx file has handled the page's Load event (described in detail later in this chapter), you could programmatically test for postback conditions as follows:

```
Protected Sub Page_Load(ByVal sender As Object, _
ByVal e As System.EventArgs) Handles Me.Load
  ' Only fill DataSet the very first time
  ' the user comes to this page.
  If Not IsPostBack Then
    ' Populate DataSet and cache it!
  End If
  ' Use cached DataSet.
End Sub
```

Interacting with the Outgoing HTTP Response

Now that you have a better understanding how the Page type allows you to interact with the incoming HTTP request, the next step is to see how to interact with the outgoing HTTP response. In ASP.NET, the Response property of the Page class provides access to an instance of the HttpResponse type. This type defines a number of properties that allow you to format the HTTP response sent back to the client browser. Table 25-6 lists some core properties.

Table 25-6. *Properties of the HttpResponse Type*

Property	Meaning in Life
Cache	Returns the caching semantics of the web page (e.g., expiration time, privacy, vary clauses)
ContentEncoding	Gets or sets the HTTP character set of the output stream
ContentType	Gets or sets the HTTP MIME type of the output stream
Cookies	Gets the HttpCookie collection sent by the current request
IsClientConnected	Gets a value indicating whether the client is still connected to the server
Output	Enables custom output to the outgoing HTTP content body
OutputStream	Enables binary output to the outgoing HTTP content body
StatusCode	Gets or sets the HTTP status code of output returned to the client
StatusDescription	Gets or sets the HTTP status string of output returned to the client
SuppressContent	Gets or sets a value indicating that HTTP content will not be sent to the client

Also, consider the partial list of methods supported by the HttpResponse type described in Table 25-7.

Table 25-7. *Methods of the HttpResponse Type*

Method	Meaning in Life
AddCacheDependency()	Adds an object to the application catch (see Chapter 27)
Clear()	Clears all headers and content output from the buffer stream
End()	Sends all currently buffered output to the client, and then closes the socket connection
Flush()	Sends all currently buffered output to the client
Redirect()	Redirects a client to a new URL
Write()	Writes values to an HTTP output content stream
WriteFile()	Writes a file directly to an HTTP content output stream

Emitting HTML Content

Perhaps the most well-known aspect of the HttpResponse type is the ability to write content directly to the HTTP output stream. The HttpResponse.Write() method allows you to pass in any HTML tags and/or text literals. The HttpResponse.WriteFile() method takes this functionality one step further, in that you can specify the name of a physical file on the web server whose contents should be rendered to the output stream (this is quite helpful to quickly emit the contents of an existing *.htm file).

To illustrate, assume you have added another Button type to your current *.aspx file that implements the server-side Click event handler like so:

```
Protected Sub btnHttpResponse_Click(ByVal sender As Object, _
ByVal e As System.EventArgs) Handles btnHttpResponse.Click
  Response.Write("<b>My name is:</b><br>")
  Response.Write(Me.ToString())
  Response.Write("<br><br><b>Here was your last request:</b><br>")
  ' This assumes that you have a file of this name
  ' in your web directory!
  Response.WriteFile("MyHTMLPage.htm")
End Sub
```

The role of this helper function (which you can assume is called by some server-side event handler) is quite simple. The only point of interest is the fact that the HttpResponse.WriteFile() method is now emitting the contents of a server-side *.htm file within the root directory of the website.

Again, while you can always take this old-school approach and render HTML tags and content using the Write() method, this approach is far less common under ASP.NET than with classic ASP. The reason is (once again) due to the advent of server-side web controls. Thus, if you wish to render a block of textual data to the browser, your task is as simple as assigning a string to the Text property of a Label widget.

Redirecting Users

Another aspect of the HttpResponse type is the ability to redirect the user to a new URL:

```
Protected Sub btnSomeTraining_Click(ByVal sender As Object, _
ByVal e As System.EventArgs) Handles btnSomeTraining.Click
  Response.Redirect("http://www.IntertechTraining.com")
End Sub
```

If this event handler was invoked via a client-side postback, the user will automatically be redirected to the specified URL.

■**Note** The HttpResponse.Redirect() method will always entail a trip back to the client browser. If you simply wish to transfer control to an *.aspx file in the same virtual directory, the HttpServerUtility.Transfer() method (accessed via the inherited Server property) will be more efficient.

So much for investigating the functionality of System.Web.UI.Page. We will examine the role of the System.Web.UI.Control base class in the next chapter. Next up, let's examine the life and times of a Page-derived object.

■**Source Code** The FunWithPageMembers files are included under the Chapter 25 subdirectory.

The Life Cycle of an ASP.NET Web Page

Every ASP.NET web page has a fixed life cycle. When the ASP.NET runtime receives an incoming request for a given *.aspx file, the associated System.Web.UI.Page-derived type is allocated into memory using the type's default constructor. After this point, the framework will automatically fire a series of events. By default, Visual Basic 2005 web pages do not handle any events for a Page-derived type; however, when you wish to do so, simply select Page Events from the left-hand drop-down listbox of your *.vb code file and select the specific event you wish to handle from the right-hand drop-down listbox (see Figure 25-19).

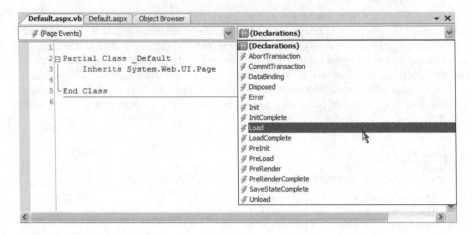

Figure 25-19. *Handling page-level events*

For example, if you select the Load event, the Visual Studio 2005 IDE generates a proper event handler to which you can add your custom code:

```
Partial Class _Default
  Inherits System.Web.UI.Page

  Protected Sub Page_Load(ByVal sender As Object, _
    ByVal e As System.EventArgs) Handles Me.Load
    ' Perform load logic here...
  End Sub
End Class
```

Again, much like a Windows Forms application, notice that the Handles keyword is used to associate the event that is responsible for handling the event in question. If you were to run this page, you would find the message "In Load Event!" is emitted back into the requesting browser.

Beyond the Load event, a given Page is able to intercept any of the core events in Table 25-8, which are listed in the order in which they are encountered (consult the .NET Framework 2.0 SDK documentation for details on all possible events that may fire during a page's lifetime).

Table 25-8. *Select Events of the Page Type*

Event	Meaning in Life
PreInit	The framework uses this event to allocate any web controls, apply themes, establish the master page, and set user profiles. You may intercept this event to customize the process.
Init	The framework uses this event to set the properties of web controls to their previous values via postback or view state data.
Load	When this event fires, the page and its controls are fully initialized, and their previous values are restored. At this point, it is safe to interact with each web widget.
"Event that triggered the postback"	There is of course, no event of this name. This "event" simply refers to whichever event caused the browser to perform the postback to the web server (such as a Button click).
PreRender	All control data binding and UI configuration has occurred and the controls are ready to render their data into the outbound HTTP response.

Event	Meaning in Life
Unload	The page and its controls have finished the rendering process, and the page object is about to be destroyed. At this point, it is a runtime error to interact with the outgoing HTTP response. You may, however, capture this event to perform any page-level cleanup (close file or database connections, perform any form of logging activity, dispose of objects, etc.).

Note Each event of the Page type works in conjunction with the System.EventHandler delegate, and therefore the subroutines that handle these events always take an Object as the first parameter and an EventArgs as the second.

The Role of the AutoEventWireup Attribute

When you wish to handle events for your page, you will need to update your <script> block or code-behind file with an appropriate event handler. As you have just seen, by default VB 2005 pages make use of the Handles keyword for this purpose. However, if you examine the <%@Page%> directive, you will notice a specific attribute named AutoEventWireUp, which by default is set to false:

```
<%@ Page Language="VB" AutoEventWireup="false"
CodeFile="Default.aspx.vb" Inherits="_Default" %>
```

With this default behavior, each page-level event handler must make use of the Handles keyword to inform the runtime you are interested in capturing the event in question. By way of a simple test, if you were to comment out the Handles clause of your Load event as follows:

```
Protected Sub Page_Load(ByVal sender As Object, _
    ByVal e As System.EventArgs) ' Handles Me.Load
        ' Perform load logic here...
End Sub
```

you would now find that the page no longer emits the "In Load Event!" message. However, if you were to enable AutoPageWireUp by setting this attribute to true:

```
<%@ Page Language="VB" AutoEventWireup="true"
CodeFile="Default.aspx.vb" Inherits="_Default" %>
```

the Load event handler is still invoked, even though the Handles keyword has been omitted. As its name suggests, this attribute (when enabled) will generate the necessary event riggings within the autogenerated partial class described in earlier in this chapter. By and large, you will seldom (if ever) need to enable the AutoEventWireup attribute, as the IDE will always add the necessary Handles clause to your page-level events.

The Error Event

Another event that may occur during your page's life cycle is Error, which also works in conjunction with the System.EventHandler delegate. This event will be fired if a method on the Page-derived type triggered an exception that was not explicitly handled. Assume that you have handled the Click event for a given Button on your page, and within the event handler (which I named btnGetFile_Click), you attempt to write out the contents of a local file to the HTTP response.

Also assume you have *failed* to test for the presence of this file via standard structured exception handling. If you have rigged up the page's Error event, you have one final chance to deal with the problem on this page before the end user finds an ugly error. Consider the following code:

```
Partial Class _Default
  Inherits System.Web.UI.Page

  Protected Sub Page_Load(ByVal sender As Object, _
  ByVal e As System.EventArgs) Handles Me.Load
    ' Perform load logic here...
  End Sub

  Protected Sub Page_Error(ByVal sender As Object, _
  ByVal e As System.EventArgs) Handles Me.Error
    ' Gut the current response, issue an error,
    ' and tell the runtime the error has been processed.
    Response.Clear()
    Response.Write("I am sorry...I can't find a required file.")
    Server.ClearError()
  End Sub

  Protected Sub btnPostback_Click(ByVal sender As Object, _
  ByVal e As System.EventArgs) Handles btnPostback.Click
    ' This is just here to allow a postback.
  End Sub

  Protected Sub btnTriggerError_Click(ByVal sender As Object, _
  ByVal e As System.EventArgs) Handles btnTriggerError.Click
    ' Try to open a nonexistent file on the web server.
    ' This will fire the Error event for this page.
    System.IO.File.ReadAllText("C:\IDontExist.txt")
  End Sub
End Class
```

Notice that your Error event handler begins by clearing out any content currently within the HTTP response and emits a generic error message. If you wish to gain access to the specific System.Exception object, you may do so using the HttpServerUtility.GetLastError() method exposed by the inherited Server property:

```
Protected Sub Page_Error(ByVal sender As Object, _
  ByVal e As System.EventArgs) Handles Me.Error
  Response.Clear()
  Response.Write(String.Format("The error was: <b>{0}</b>", _
  Server.GetLastError().Message))
  Server.ClearError()
End Sub
```

Finally, note that before exiting this generic error handler, you are explicitly calling the HttpServerUtility.ClearError() method via the Server property. This is required, as it informs the runtime that you have dealt with the issue at hand and require no further processing. If you forget to do so, you the end user will be presented with the runtime's error page. Figure 25-20 shows the result of this error-trapping logic.

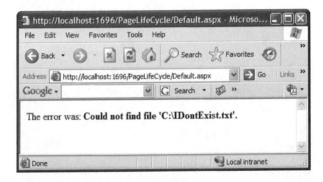

Figure 25-20. *Page-level error handling*

At this point, you should hopefully feel confident with the composition of an ASP.NET Page type. Now that you have such a foundation, you can turn your attention to the role of ASP.NET web controls, themes, and master pages, all of which are the subject of the next chapter. To wrap up this chapter, however, let's examine the role of the web.config file.

■**Source Code** The PageLifeCycle files are included under the Chapter 25 subdirectory.

The Role of the web.config File

By default, all ASP.NET web applications created with Visual Basic 2005 are automatically provided with a web.config file. This is not the case with other .NET languages, however. Thus, if you ever needed to manually insert a web.config file to your site (for example, when you are working with the single-page model and have not created a web solution), you may do so using the using the Web Site ➤ Add New Item menu option. In either case, within this scope of a web.config file you are able to add settings that control how your web application will function at runtime.

■**Note** It is not mandatory for your web applications to include a web.config file. If you do not have such a file, your website will be granted the web-centric settings recorded in the machine.config file for your .NET installation.

Recall during your examination of .NET assemblies (in Chapter 13) that you learned client applications can leverage a XML-based configuration file to instruct the CLR how it should handle binding requests, assembly probing, and other runtime details. The same holds true for ASP.NET web applications, with the notable exception that web-centric configuration files are always named web.config (unlike *.exe configuration files, which are named based on the related client executable). The default structure of a web.config file looks something like the following (various comments removed for clarity):

```
<?xml version="1.0"?>
<configuration>
  <appSettings/>
  <connectionStrings/>
  <system.web>
    <compilation debug="false" strict="false" explicit="true" />
    <pages>
      <namespaces>
        <clear />
        <add namespace="System" />
        <add namespace="System.Collections" />
        <add namespace="System.Collections.Specialized" />
        <add namespace="System.Configuration" />
        <add namespace="System.Text" />
        <add namespace="System.Text.RegularExpressions" />
        <add namespace="System.Web" />
        <add namespace="System.Web.Caching" />
        <add namespace="System.Web.SessionState" />
        <add namespace="System.Web.Security" />
        <add namespace="System.Web.Profile" />
        <add namespace="System.Web.UI" />
        <add namespace="System.Web.UI.WebControls" />
        <add namespace="System.Web.UI.WebControls.WebParts" />
        <add namespace="System.Web.UI.HtmlControls" />
      </namespaces>
    </pages>
    <authentication mode="Windows" />
    <!--
      The <customErrors> section enables configuration
      of what to do if/when an unhandled error occurs
      during the execution of a request. Specifically,
      it enables developers to configure html error pages
      to be displayed in place of a error stack trace.

    <customErrors mode="RemoteOnly" defaultRedirect="GenericErrorPage.htm">
      <error statusCode="403" redirect="NoAccess.htm" />
      <error statusCode="404" redirect="FileNotFound.htm" />
    </customErrors>
    -->
  </system.web>
</configuration>
```

Like any *.config file, web.config defines the root-level <configuration> element. Nested within the root is the <system.web> element, which can contain numerous subelements used to control how your web application should behave at runtime. Under ASP.NET, the web.config file can be modified using any text editor. Table 25-9 outlines some of the more interesting subelements that can be found within a web.config file.

Table 25-9. *Select Elements of a* web.config *File*

Element	Meaning in Life
`<appSettings>`	This element is used to establish custom name/value pairs that can be programmatically read in memory for use by your pages using the `ConfigurationManager` type.
`<authentication>`	This security-related element is used to define the authentication mode for this web application.
`<authorization>`	This is another security-centric element used to define which users can access which resources on the web server.
`<compilation>`	This element is used to enable (or disable) debugging as well the VB-centric `Option Strict` and `Option Explicit` settings.
`<connectionStrings>`	This element is used to hold external connection strings used within this website.
`<customErrors>`	This element is used to tell the runtime exactly how to display errors that occur during the functioning of the web application.
`<globalization>`	This element is used to configure the globalization settings for this web application.
`<namespaces>`	This element documents all of the namespaces to include if your web application has been precompiled using the new `aspnet_compiler.exe` command-line tool.
`<sessionState>`	This element is used to control how and where session state data will be stored by the .NET runtime.
`<trace>`	This element is used to enable (or disable) tracing support for this web application.

A web.config file may contain additional subelements above and beyond the set presented in Table 25-9. The vast majority of these items are security related, while the remaining items are useful only during advanced ASP.NET scenarios such as creating with custom HTTP headers or custom HTTP modules (topics that are not covered here). If you wish to see the complete set of elements (and the related attributes) that can appear in a web.config file, you may do so using the .NET 2.0 Framework SDK documentation. Simply navigate to .NET Development ➤ General Reference ➤ ASP.NET Reference ➤ Configuration File Syntax, as shown in Figure 25-21, and dive in.

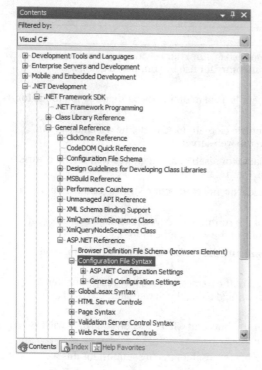

Figure 25-21. *Page-level error handling*

You will come to know various aspects of the web.config over the remainder of this text.

Configuration File Inheritance

One interesting aspect of ASP.NET is that it is possible for a single website to contain multiple copies of a web.config file, provided that they are all within a unique subdirectory of the main root. Recall that a web application can be defined as the set of all files contained within a root directory and any optional subdirectories. In addition to the "special" subdirectories recognized by ASP.NET (App_Data, App_Themes, Bin, and so forth), large-scale web applications tend to define numerous subdirectories off the root, each of which contains some set of related files. Like a traditional desktop application, this is typically done for the benefit of us mere humans, as a hierarchical structure can make a massive set of files more understandable.

When you have an ASP.NET web application that consists of optional subdirectories off the root, you may be surprised to discover that *each* subdirectory may have its own web.config file. By doing so, you allow each subdirectory to effectively override the settings of a parent directory. If the subdirectory in question does not supply a custom web.config file, it will inherit the settings of the next available web.config file up the directory structure. Figure 25-22 illustrates the concept.

Of course, although ASP.NET does allow you to define numerous web.config files for a single web application, you are not required to do so. In a great many cases, your web applications function just fine using nothing other than the web.config file located in the root directory of the web application.

Note Recall from Chapter 13 that the machine.config file defines numerous machinewide settings, many of which are ASP.NET-centric. This file is the ultimate parent in the configuration inheritance hierarchy.

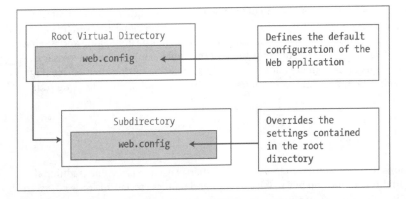

Figure 25-22. *Configuration file inheritance*

The ASP.NET 2.0 Website Administration Utility

Although you are always free to modify the content of a web.config file directly using Visual Studio 2005, ASP.NET 2.0 now provides a handy web-based editor that will allow you to graphically edit numerous elements and attributes of your project's web.config file. To launch this tool, shown in Figure 25-23, simply activate the Web Site ➤ ASP.NET Configuration menu option.

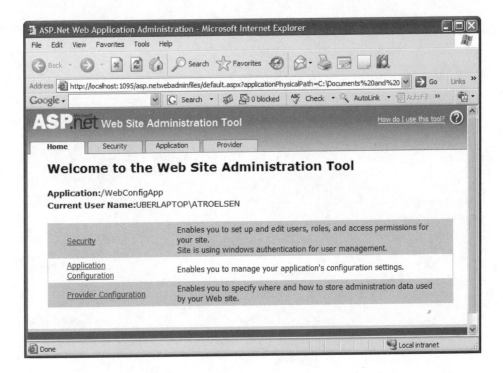

Figure 25-23. *The ASP.NET Web Site Administration tool*

If you were to click the tabs located on the top of the page, you would quickly notice that most of this tool's functionality is used to establish security settings for your website. However, this tool also makes it possible to add settings to your `<appSettings>` element, define debugging and tracing settings, and establish a default error page. You'll see more of this tool in action where necessary; however, do be aware that this utility will *not* allow you to add all possible settings to a `web.config` file. There will most certainly be times when you will need to manually update this file using your text editor of choice.

Summary

Building web applications requires a different frame of mind than is used to assemble traditional desktop applications. In this chapter, you began with a quick and painless review of some core web atoms, including HTML, HTTP, the role of client-side scripting, and server-side scripts using classic ASP. The bulk of this chapter was spent examining the architecture of an ASP.NET page. As you have seen, each `*.aspx` file in your project has an associated `System.Web.UI.Page`-derived class. Using this OO approach, ASP.NET allows you to build more reusable and OO-aware systems. After examining some of the core functionality of a page's inheritance chain, this chapter then discussed how your pages are ultimately compiled into a valid .NET assembly. We wrapped up by exploring the role of the `web.config` file and overviewing the ASP.NET 2.0 Web Site Administration tool.

■ ■ ■

ASP.NET 2.0 Web Controls, Themes, and Master Pages

The previous chapter concentrated on the composition and behavior of ASP.NET 2.0 page objects. This chapter will dive into the details of the "web controls" that make up a page's user interface. After examining the overall nature of an ASP.NET web control, you will come to understand how to make use of several UI elements including the validation controls and data-centric controls.

The later half of this chapter will examine the role of "master pages" and see how they provide a simplified manner to define a common UI skeleton that will be replicated across the pages in your website. I wrap up by showing you how to apply "themes" to your pages, in order to define a consistent look and feel for your page's controls. As you will see, the ASP.NET theme engine provides a server-side alternative to client-side style sheets.

Understanding the Nature of Web Controls

Perhaps the major benefit of ASP.NET is the ability to assemble the UI of your pages using the types defined in the System.Web.UI.WebControls namespace. As you have seen, these controls (which go by the names *server controls*, *web controls*, or *Web Form controls*) are *extremely* helpful in that they automatically generate the necessary HTML for the requesting browser and expose a set of events that may be processed on the web server. Furthermore, because each ASP.NET control has a corresponding class in the System.Web.UI.WebControls namespace, it can be manipulated in an OO manner from your *.aspx file (within a <script> block) as well as within the associated class defined in the code-behind file.

As you have seen, when you configure the properties of a web control using the Visual Studio 2005 Properties window, your edits are recorded in the open declaration of a given widget in the *.aspx file as a series of name/value pairs. Thus, if you add a new TextBox to the designer of a given *.aspx file and change the ID, BorderStyle, BorderWidth, BackColor, Text, and BorderColor properties using the IDE, the opening <asp:TextBox> tag is modified as follows:

```
<asp:TextBox ID="txtNameTextBox" runat="server"
BackColor="#C0FFC0" BorderStyle="Dotted"BorderWidth="5px">
Enter Your Name
</asp:TextBox>
```

Given that the HTML declaration of a web control eventually becomes a member variable from the System.Web.UI.WebControls namespace (via the dynamic compilation cycle), you are able to interact with the members of this type within a server-side <script> block or the page's code-behind file. For example, if you handled the Click event for a given Button type, you could change the background color of the TextBox as follows:

```
Partial Class _Default
  Inherits System.Web.UI.Page

  Protected Sub btnChangeTextBoxColor_Click(ByVal sender As Object, _
    ByVal e As System.EventArgs) Handles btnChangeTextBoxColor.Click
    Me.txtNameTextBox.BackColor = Drawing.Color.DarkBlue
  End Sub
End Class
```

All ASP.NET web controls ultimately derive from a common base class named `System.Web.UI.WebControls.WebControl`. `WebControl` in turn derives from `System.Web.UI.Control` (which derives from `System.Object`). `Control` and `WebControl` each define a number of properties common to all server-side controls. Before we examine the inherited functionality, let's formalize what it means to handle a server-side event.

Qualifying Server-side Event Handling

Given the current state of the World Wide Web, it is impossible to avoid the fundamental nature of browser/web server interaction. Whenever these two entities communicate, there is always an underlying, stateless, HTTP request-and-response cycle. While ASP.NET server controls do a great deal to shield you from the details of the raw HTTP protocol, always remember that treating the Web as an event-driven entity is just a magnificent smoke-and-mirrors show provided by the CLR, and it is not identical to the event-driven model of a Windows-based UI.

Thus, although the `System.Windows.Forms` and `System.Web.UI.WebControls` namespaces define types with the same simple names (Button, TextBox, Calendar, Label, and so on), they do not expose an identical set of events. For example, there is no way to handle a server-side `MouseMove` event when the user moves the cursor over a Web Form `Button` type. Obviously, this is a good thing. (Who wants to post back to the server each time the mouse moves?)

The bottom line is that a given ASP.NET web control will expose a limited set of events, all of which ultimately result in a postback to the web server. Any necessary client-side event processing will require you to author blurbs of *client-side* JavaScript/VBScript script code to be processed by the requesting browser's scripting engine. Given that ASP.NET is primarily a server-side technology, I will not be addressing the topic of authoring client-side scripts in this text.

Note Handling an event for a given web control using Visual Studio 2005 can be done in an identical manner to a Windows Forms control. Simply select the widget from the designer and click the lightening bolt icon on the Properties window.

The AutoPostBack Property

It is also worth pointing out that many of the ASP.NET web controls support a property named `AutoPostBack` (most notably, the `CheckBox`, `RadioButton`, and `TextBox` controls, as well as any widget that derives from the abstract `ListControl` type). By default, this property is set to `False`, which disables the automatic processing of server-side events (even if you have indeed rigged up the event in the code-behind file). In many cases, this is the exact behavior you require, given that UI elements such as check boxes typically don't require postback functionality (as the page object can obtain the state of the widget within a more natural `Button Click` event handler).

However, if you wish to cause any of these widgets to post back to a server-side event handler, simply set the value of `AutoPostBack` to `True`. This technique can be helpful if you wish to have the state of one widget automatically populate another value within another widget on the same page. To illustrate, create a tester website that contains a single `TextBox` (named `txtAutoPostback`) and a single `ListBox` control (named `lstTextBoxData`). Here is the relevant markup generated by the designer:

```
<form id="form1" runat="server">
  <asp:TextBox ID="txtAutoPostback" runat="server"></asp:TextBox>
  <br/>
  <asp:ListBox ID="lstTextBoxData" runat="server"></asp:ListBox>
</form>
```

Now, handle the TextChanged event of the TextBox, and within the server-side event handler, populate the ListBox with the current value in the TextBox:

```
Partial Class _Default
  Inherits System.Web.UI.Page

  Protected Sub txtAutoPostback_TextChanged(ByVal sender As Object, _
  ByVal e As System.EventArgs) Handles txtAutoPostback.TextChanged
    lstTextBoxData.Items.Add(txtAutoPostback.Text)
  End Sub
End Class
```

If you run the application as is, you will find that as you type in the TextBox, nothing happens. Furthermore, if you type in the TextBox and tab to the next control, nothing happens. The reason is that the AutoPostBack property of the TextBox is set to False by default. However, if you set this property to True:

```
<asp:TextBox ID="txtAutoPostback"
runat="server" AutoPostBack="True">
</asp:TextBox>
```

you will find that when you tab off the TextBox (or press the Enter key), the ListBox is automatically populated with the current value in the TextBox. To be sure, beyond the need to populate the items of one widget based on the value of another widget, you will typically not need to alter the state of a widget's AutoPostBack property.

The System.Web.UI.Control Type

The System.Web.UI.Control base class defines various properties, methods, and events that allow the ability to interact with core (typically non-GUI) aspects of a web control. Table 26-1 documents some, but not all, members of interest.

Table 26-1. *Select Members of* System.Web.UI.Control

Member	Meaning in Life
Controls	This property gets a ControlCollection object that represents the child controls within the current control.
DataBind()	This method binds a data source to the invoked server control and all its child controls.
EnableThemeing	This property establishes whether the control supports theme functionality.
HasControls()	This method determines whether the server control contains any child controls.
ID	This property gets or sets the programmatic identifier assigned to the server control.
Page	This property gets a reference to the Page instance that contains the server control.
Parent	This property gets a reference to the server control's parent control in the page control hierarchy.
SkinID	This property gets or sets the "skin" to apply to the control. Under ASP.NET 2.0, it is now possible to establish a control's overall look and feel on the fly via skins.
Visible	This property gets or sets a value that indicates whether a server control is rendered as UI element on the page.

Enumerating Contained Controls

The first aspect of System.Web.UI.Control we will examine is the fact that all web controls (including Page itself) inherit a custom controls collection (accessed via the Controls property). Much like in a Windows Forms application, the Controls property provides access to a strongly typed collection of WebControl-derived types. Like any .NET collection, you have the ability to add, insert, and remove items dynamically at runtime.

While it is technically possible to directly add web controls directly to a Page-derived type, it is easier (and a wee bit safer) to make use of a Panel widget. The System.Web.UI.WebControls.Panel class represents a container of widgets that may or may not be visible to the end user (based on the value of its Visible and BorderStyle properties).

To illustrate, create a new website named DynamicCtrls. Using the Visual Studio 2005 page designer, add a Panel type (named myPanel) that contains a TextBox, Button, and HyperLink widget named whatever you choose (be aware that the designer requires that you drag internal items within the UI of the Panel type). Once you have done so, the <form> element of your *.aspx file will have been updated as follows:

```
<asp:Panel ID="myPanel" runat="server" Height="50px" Width="125px">
  <asp:TextBox ID="TextBox1" runat="server"></asp:TextBox><br/>
  <asp:Button ID="Button1" runat="server" Text="Button"/><br/>
  <asp:HyperLink ID="HyperLink1" runat="server">HyperLink
  </asp:HyperLink>
</asp:Panel>
```

Next, place a Label widget outside the scope of the Panel (named lblControlInfo) to hold the rendered output. Assume in the Page_Load() event you wish to obtain a list of all the controls contained within the Panel and assign the results to the Label type (named lblControlInfo):

```
Partial Class _Default
  Inherits System.Web.UI.Page

  Private Sub ListControlsInPanel()
    Dim theInfo As String
    theInfo = String.Format("Has controls? {0} <br/>", myPanel.HasControls())
    For Each c As Control In myPanel.Controls
      If c.GetType() IsNot GetType(System.Web.UI.LiteralControl) Then
        theInfo += "***************************<br/>"
        theInfo += String.Format("Control Name? {0} <br/>", c.ToString())
        theInfo += String.Format("ID? {0} <br>", c.ID)
        theInfo += String.Format("Control Visible? {0} <br/>", c.Visible)
        theInfo += String.Format("ViewState? {0} <br/>", c.EnableViewState)
      End If
    Next
    lblControlInfo.Text = theInfo
  End Sub

  Protected Sub Page_Load(ByVal sender As Object, _
  ByVal e As System.EventArgs) Handles Me.Load
    ListControlsInPanel()
  End Sub
End Class
```

Here, you iterate over each WebControl maintained on the Panel and perform a check to see whether the current type is of type System.Web.UI.LiteralControl. This type is used to represent literal HTML tags and content (such as <br>, text literals, etc.). If you do not do this sanity check, you might be surprised to find a total of seven types in the scope of the Panel (given the *.aspx declaration seen previously). Assuming the type is not literal HTML content, you then print out some various statistics about the widget. Figure 26-1 shows the output.

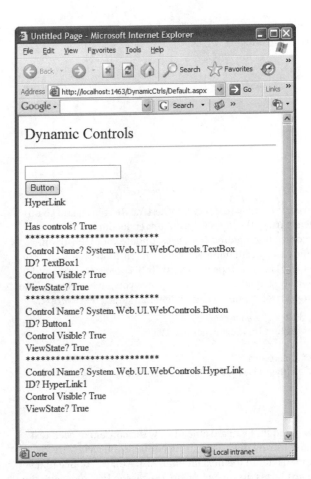

Figure 26-1. *Enumerating contained widgets*

Dynamically Adding (and Removing) Controls

Now, what if you wish to modify the contents of a Panel at runtime? The process should look very familiar to you, given your work with Windows Forms earlier in this text. Let's update the current page to support an additional Button (named btnAddWidgets) that dynamically adds five new TextBox types to the Panel, and another Button (named btnRemovePanelItems) that clears the Panel widget of all controls. The Click event handlers for each are shown here:

```
Protected Sub btnRemovePanelItems_Click(ByVal sender As Object, _
  ByVal e As System.EventArgs) Handles btnRemovePanelItems.Click
    myPanel.Controls.Clear()
    ListControlsInPanel()
End Sub
```

```
Protected Sub btnAddWidgets_Click(ByVal sender As Object, _
   ByVal e As System.EventArgs) Handles btnAddWidgets.Click
   For i As Integer = 0 To 4
      ' Assign a name so we can get
      ' the text value out later
      ' using the HttpRequest.Form()
      ' method.
      Dim t As TextBox = New TextBox()
      t.ID = String.Format("newTextBox{0}", i)
      myPanel.Controls.Add(t)
      ListControlsInPanel()
   Next
End Sub
```

Notice that you assign a unique ID to each TextBox (e.g., newTextBox1, newTextBox2, and so on) to obtain its contained text programmatically using the HttpRequest.Form collection.

To obtain the values within these dynamically generated TextBoxes, update your UI with one additional Button and Label type. Within the Click event handler for the Button, loop over each item contained within the HttpRequest.NameValueCollection type (accessed via HttpRequest.Form) and concatenate the textual information to a locally scoped System.String. Once you have exhausted the collection, assign this string to the Text property of the new Label widget named lblTextBoxText:

```
Protected Sub btnGetTextBoxValues_Click(ByVal sender As Object, _
   ByVal e As System.EventArgs) Handles btnGetTextBoxValues.Click
   Dim textBoxValues As String = ""
   For i As Integer = 0 To Request.Form.Count - 1
      textBoxValues += String.Format("<li>{0}</li><br/>", Request.Form(i))
   Next
   lblTextBoxText.Text = textBoxValues
End Sub
```

When you run the application, you will find that you are able to view the content of each text box, including some rather long (unreadable) string data. This string contains the *view state* for each widget on the page and will be examined later in the next chapter. Also, you will notice that once the request has been processed, the text boxes disappear. Again, the reason has to do with the stateless nature of HTTP. If you wish to maintain these dynamically created TextBoxes between postbacks, you need to persist these objects using ASP.NET state programming techniques (also examined in the next chapter).

■**Source Code** The DynamicCtrls files are included under the Chapter 26 subdirectory.

Key Members of the System.Web.UI.WebControls.WebControl Type

As you can tell, the Control type provides a number of non-GUI-related behaviors (the controls collection, autopostback support, etc.). On the other hand, the WebControl base class provides a graphical polymorphic interface to all web widgets, as suggested in Table 26-2.

Table 26-2. *Properties of the* WebControl *Base Class*

Properties	Meaning in Life
BackColor	Gets or sets the background color of the web control
BorderColor	Gets or sets the border color of the web control
BorderStyle	Gets or sets the border style of the web control
BorderWidth	Gets or sets the border width of the web control
Enabled	Gets or sets a value indicating whether the web control is enabled
CssClass	Allows you to assign a class defined within a Cascading Style Sheet to a web widget
Font	Gets font information for the web control
ForeColor	Gets or sets the foreground color (typically the color of the text) of the web control
Height Width	Get or set the height and width of the web control
TabIndex	Gets or sets the tab index of the web control
ToolTip	Gets or sets the tool tip for the web control to be displayed when the cursor is over the control

I'd bet that almost all of these properties are self-explanatory, so rather than drill through the use of all these properties, let's shift gears a bit and check out a number of ASP.NET Web Form controls in action.

Categories of ASP.NET Web Controls

The types in System.Web.UI.WebControls can be broken down into several broad categories:

- Simple controls
- (Feature) Rich controls
- Data-centric controls
- Input validation controls
- Web part controls
- Login controls

The *simple controls* are so named because they are ASP.NET web controls that map to standard HTML widgets (buttons, lists, hyperlinks, image holders, tables, etc.). Next, we have a small set of controls named the *rich controls* for which there is no direct HTML equivalent (such as the Calendar, TreeView, Menu, Wizard, etc.). The *data-centric controls* are widgets that are typically populated via a given data connection. The best (and most exotic) example of such a control would be the ASP.NET GridView. Other members of this category include "repeater" controls and the lightweight DataList.

The *validation controls* are server-side widgets that automatically emit client-side JavaScript, for the purpose of form field validation. Finally, as of ASP.NET 2.0, the base class libraries ship with a number of security-centric controls. These UI elements completely encapsulate the details of logging into a site, providing password-retrieval services and managing user roles. The full set of ASP.NET web controls can be seen using the Visual Studio 2005 Toolbox. Notice in Figure 26-2, related controls are grouped together under a specific tab.

Figure 26-2. *The ASP.NET web controls*

■**Note** This text will not address the topic of web parts or the ASP.NET security controls. If you are interested in learning about these technologies, I'd recommend obtaining a copy of *Pro ASP.NET 2005* (MacDonald, Apress, 2005) to complete your understanding of ASP.NET.

A Brief Word Regarding System.Web.UI.HtmlControls

Truth be told, there are two distinct web control toolkits that ship with ASP.NET 2.0. In addition to the ASP.NET web controls (within the System.Web.UI.WebControls namespace), the base class libraries also provide the System.Web.UI.HtmlControls widgets.

The HTML controls are a collection of types that allow you to make use of traditional HTML controls on a Web Forms page. However, unlike raw HTML tags, HTML controls are OO entities that can be configured to run on the server and thus support server-side event handling. Unlike ASP.NET web controls, HTML controls are quite simplistic in nature and offer little functionality beyond standard HTML tags (HtmlButton, HtmlInputControl, HtmlTable, etc.). As you would expect, Visual Studio 2005 provides a specific section of the Toolbox to contain the HTML control types (see Figure 26-3).

Figure 26-3. *The HTML controls*

The HTML controls provide a public interface that mimics standard HTML attributes. For example, to obtain the information within an input area, you make use of the Value property, rather than the web control–centric Text property. Given that the HTML controls are not as feature-rich as the ASP.NET web controls, I won't make further mention of them in this text. If you wish to investigate these types, consult the .NET Framework 2.0 SDK documentation for further details.

Note The HTML controls can be useful if your team has a clear division between those who build HTML UIs and .NET developers. HTML folks can make use of their web editor of choice using familiar markup tags and pass the HTML files to the development team. At this point, developers can configure these HTML controls to run as server controls (by right-clicking an HTML widget within Visual Studio 2005). This will allow developers to handle server-side events and work with the HTML widget programmatically.

Building an ASP.NET 2.0 Website

Given that many of the "simple" controls look and feel so close to their Windows Forms counterparts, I won't bother to enumerate the details of the basic widgets (Buttons, Labels, TextBoxes, etc.). Rather, let's build a new website that illustrates working with several of the more exotic controls as well as the new ASP.NET 2.0 master page model and enhanced data binding engine. Specifically, this next example will illustrate the following techniques:

- Working with master pages
- Working with the `Menu` control
- Working with the `GridView` control
- Working with the `Wizard` control

To begin, create a new ASP.NET web application named AspNetCarsSite.

Working with Master Pages

As I am sure you are aware, many websites provide a consistent look and feel across multiple pages (a common menu navigation system, common header and footer content, company logo, etc.). Under ASP.NET 1.*x*, developers made extensive use of `UserControls` and custom web controls to define web content that was to be used across multiple pages. While `UserControls` and custom web controls are still a very valid option under ASP.NET 2.0, we are now provided with the concept of *master pages*, which complements these existing technologies.

Simply put, a master page is little more than an ASP.NET page that takes a `*.master` file extension. On their own, master pages are not viewable from a client-side browser (in fact, the ASP.NET runtime will not serve this flavor of web content). Rather, master pages define a common UI frame shared by all pages (or a subset of pages) in your site.

As well, a `*.master` page will define various content placeholder areas that define a region of UI real estate other `*.aspx` files may plug into. As you will see, `*.aspx` files that plug their content into a master file look and feel a bit different from the `*.aspx` files we have been examining. Specifically, this flavor of an `*.aspx` file is termed a *content page*. Content pages are `*.aspx` files that do not define an HTML `<form>` element (that is the job of the master page).

However, as far as the end user is concerned, a request is made to a given `*.aspx` file. On the web server, the related `*.master` file and any related `*.aspx` content pages are blended into a single unified page. To illustrate the use of master pages and content pages, begin by inserting a new master page into your website via the Web Site ➤ Add New Item menu selection (Figure 26-4 shows the resulting dialog box).

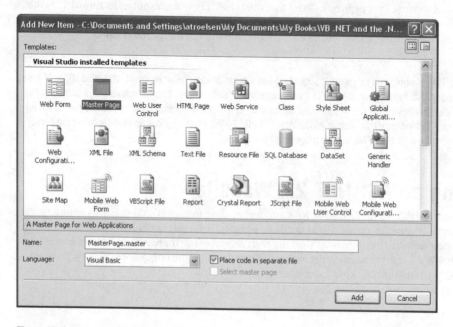

Figure 26-4. *Inserting a new* `*.master` *file*

The initial markup of the `MasterPage.master` file looks like the following:

```
<%@ Master Language="VB" CodeFile="MasterPage.master.vb"
Inherits="MasterPage" %>

<!DOCTYPE html PUBLIC "-//W3C//DTD XHTML 1.0 Transitional//EN"
  "http://www.w3.org/TR/xhtml1/DTD/xhtml1-transitional.dtd">

<html xmlns="http://www.w3.org/1999/xhtml" >
<head runat="server">
    <title>Untitled Page</title>
</head>
<body>
    <form id="form1" runat="server">
    <div>
        <asp:contentplaceholder id="ContentPlaceHolder1" runat="server">
        </asp:contentplaceholder>
    </div>
    </form>
</body>
</html>
```

The first point of interest is the new `<%@Master%>` directive. For the most part, this directive supports the same attributes as the `<%@Page%>` directive described in the previous chapter. For example, notice how by default a master page makes use of a code-behind file (which is technically optional). Like `Page` types, a master page derives from a specific base class, which in this case is `MasterPage`. If you were to open up your related code file, you would find the following class definition:

```
Partial Class MasterPage
  Inherits System.Web.UI.MasterPage
End Class
```

The other point of interest within the markup of the master is the `<asp:contentplaceholder>` type. This region of a master page represents the area of the master that the UI widgets of the related `*.aspx` content file may plug into, not the content defined by the master page itself. If you flip to the designer surface of the `*.master` page, you will find that each `<asp:contentplaceholder>` element is accounted for, as shown in Figure 26-5.

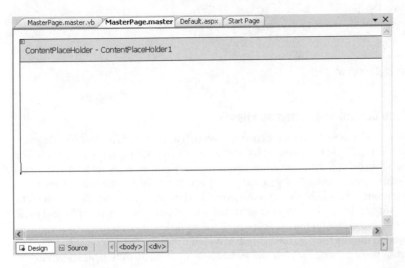

Figure 26-5. *The design-time view of a* `*.master` *file's* `<asp:contentplaceholder>` *tags*

If you do intend to blend an *.aspx file within this region, the scope within the `<asp:contentplaceholder>` and `</asp:contentplaceholder>` tags will be empty. However, if you so choose, you are able to populate this area with various web controls that function as a default UI to use in the event that a given *.aspx file in the site does not supply specific content. For this example, assume that each *.aspx page in your site will indeed supply custom content, and therefore our `<asp:contentplaceholder>` elements will be empty.

Note A *.master page may define as many content placeholders as necessary. As well, a single *.master page may nest additional *.master pages.

As you would hope, you are able to build a common UI of a *.master file using the same Visual Studio 2005 designers used to build *.aspx files. For your site, you will add a descriptive Label (to serve as a common welcome message), an AdRotator control (which will randomly display one of two images), and a Menu control (to allow the user to navigate to other areas of the site). Figure 26-6 shows one possible UI of the master page that we will be constructing (again notice that the content placeholder is empty). Also notice that the AdRotator widget is simply displaying a red "X" right now, as we have not specified an image for it to display.

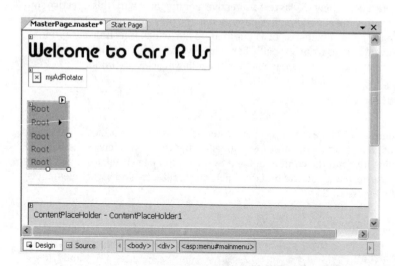

Figure 26-6. *The* *.master *file's shared UI*

Working with the Menu Control and *.sitemap Files

ASP.NET 2.0 ships with several new web controls that allow you to handle site navigation: SiteMapPath, TreeView, and Menu. As you would expect, these web widgets can be configured in multiple ways. For example, each of these controls can dynamically generate its nodes via an external XML file (or an XML-based *.sitemap file), programmatically in code, or through markup using the designers of Visual Studio 2005. Our menu type will be dynamically populated using a *.sitemap file. The benefit of this approach is that we can define the overall structure of our website in an external file, and then bind it to a Menu (or TreeView) widget on the fly. This way, if the navigational structure of our website changes, we simply need to modify the *.sitemap file and reload the page. To begin, insert a new Web.sitemap file into your project using the Web Site ➤ Add New Item menu option, as shown in Figure 26-7.

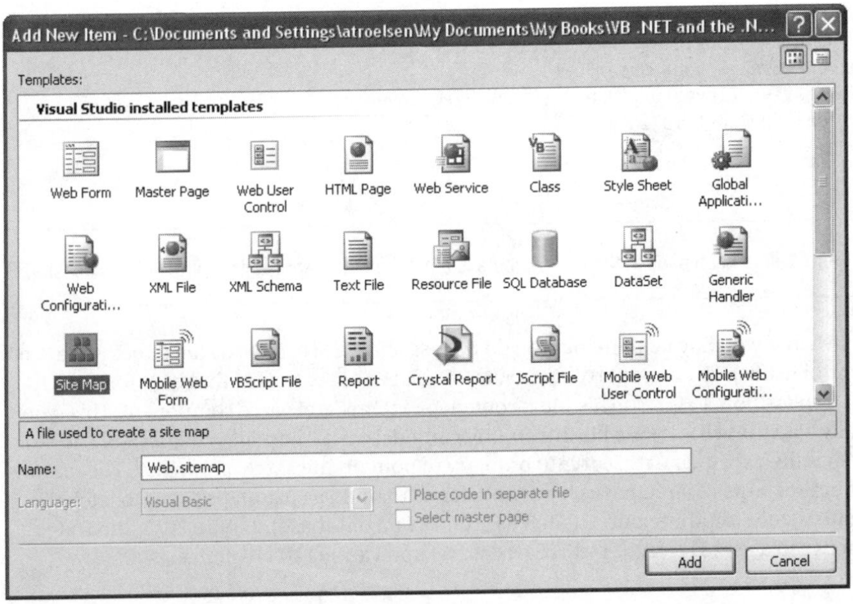

Figure 26-7. *Inserting a new* Web.sitemap *file*

As you can see, the initial Web.sitemap file defines a topmost item with two subnodes:

```
<?xml version="1.0" encoding="utf-8" ?>
<siteMap xmlns="http://schemas.microsoft.com/AspNet/SiteMap-File-1.0" >
  <siteMapNode url="" title=""  description="">
    <siteMapNode url="" title=""  description="" />
    <siteMapNode url="" title=""  description="" />
  </siteMapNode>
</siteMap>
```

If we were to bind this structure to a Menu control (using a SiteMapDataProvider, described in just a moment), we would find a topmost menu item with two submenus. Therefore, when you wish to define subitems, simply define new <siteMapNode> elements within the scope of an existing <siteMapNode>. In any case, the goal is to define the overall structure of your website within a Web.sitemap file using various <siteMapNode> elements. Each one of these elements can define a title and URL attribute. The URL attribute represents which *.aspx file to navigate to when the user clicks a given menu item (or node of a TreeView). Our site contains three subelements, which are set up as follows:

- *Home*: Default.aspx
- *Build a Car*: BuildCar.aspx
- *View Inventory*: Inventory.aspx

Our menu system has a single topmost "Welcome" item with three subelements. Therefore, we can update the Web.sitemap file as follows. (Be aware that each url value must be unique! If not, you receive a runtime error.)

```
<?xml version="1.0" encoding="utf-8" ?>
<siteMap xmlns="http://schemas.microsoft.com/AspNet/SiteMap-File-1.0" >
  <siteMapNode url="" title="Welcome!"  description="">
    <siteMapNode url="~/Default.aspx" title="Home"
```

```
        description="The Home Page" />
      <siteMapNode url="~/BuildCar.aspx" title="Build a car"
        description="Create your dream car" />
      <siteMapNode url="~/Inventory.aspx" title="View Inventory"
        description="See what is in stock" />
    </siteMapNode>
  </siteMap>
```

■**Note** The ~/ prefix before each page in the url attribute is a notation that represents the root of the website.

Now, despite what you may be thinking, you do not associate a Web.sitemap file directly to a Menu or TreeView control using a given property. Rather, the *.master or *.aspx file that contains the UI widget that will display the Web.sitemap file must contain a SiteMapDataSource component. This type will automatically load the Web.sitemap file into its object model when the page is requested. The Menu and TreeView types then set their DataSourceID property to point to the SiteMapProvider. The reason for this level of indirection is that it makes it possible for us to build a custom provider to fetch the website's structure from another source (such as a table in a database). Figure 26-8 illustrates the interplay between a Web.sitemap, SiteMapDataSource, and various UI elements.

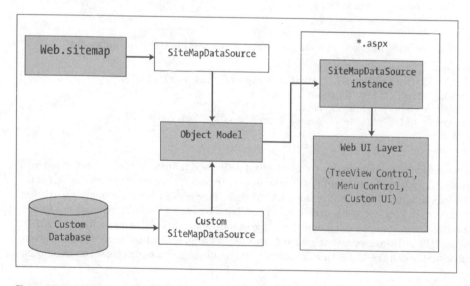

Figure 26-8. *The ASP.NET sitemap navigation model*

To add a new SiteMapDataSource to your *.master file and automatically set the DataSourceID property, you can make use of the Visual Studio 2005 designer. Activate the inline editor of the Menu widget and select New Data Source, as shown in Figure 26-9.

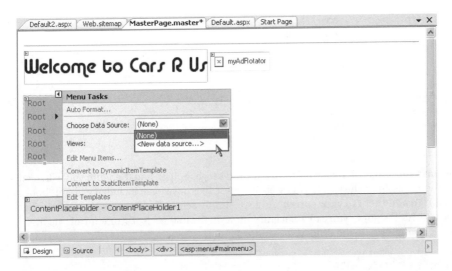

Figure 26-9. *Adding a new* SiteMapProvider

From the resulting dialog box, select the SiteMap icon. This will set the DataSourceID property of the Menu item as well as add a new SiteMapDataSource component to your page. This is all you need to do to configure your Menu widget to navigate to the additional pages on your site. If you wish to perform additional processing when the user selects a given menu item, you may do so by handling the MenuItemClick event. There is no need to do so for this example, but be aware that you are able to determine which menu item was selected using the incoming MenuEventArgs parameter.

Establishing Bread Crumbs with the SiteMapNavigation Type

Before moving on to the AdRotator control, add a SiteMapNavigation type onto your *.master file, beneath the content placeholder element. This widget will automatically adjust its content based on the current selection of the menu system. As you may know, this can provide a helpful visual cue for the end user (formally, this UI technique is termed *bread crumbs*). Once you complete this example, you will notice that when you select the Welcome ➤ Build a Car menu item, the SiteMapNavigation widget updates accordingly automatically.

Working with the AdRotator

The role of the ASP.NET AdRotator widget is to randomly display a given image at some position in the browser. When you first place an AdRotator widget on the designer, it is displayed as an empty placeholder. Functionally, this control cannot do its magic until you assign the AdvertisementFile property to point to the source file that describes each image. For this example, the data source will be a simple XML file named Ads.xml.

Once you have inserted this new XML file to your site, specify a unique <Ad> element for each image you wish to display. At minimum, each <Ad> element specifies the image to display (ImageUrl), the URL to navigate to if the image is selected (TargetUrl), mouseover text (AlternateText), and the weight of the ad (Impressions):

```
<Advertisements>
  <Ad>
    <ImageUrl>SlugBug.jpg</ImageUrl>
```

```
      <TargetUrl>http://www.Cars.com</TargetUrl>
      <AlternateText>Your new Car?</AlternateText>
      <Impressions>80</Impressions>
    </Ad>
    <Ad>
      <ImageUrl>car.gif</ImageUrl>
      <TargetUrl>http://www.CarSuperSite.com</TargetUrl>
      <AlternateText>Like this Car?</AlternateText>
      <Impressions>80</Impressions>
    </Ad>
  </Advertisements>
```

Here you have specified two image files (car.gif and slugbug.jpg), and therefore you will need to ensure that these files are in the root of your website (these files have been included with this book's code download). To add them to your current project, simply select the Web Site ➤ Add Existing Item menu option. At this point, you can associate your XML file to the AdRotator controls via the AdvertisementFile property (in the Properties window):

```
<asp:AdRotator ID="myAdRotator" runat="server"
  AdvertisementFile="~/Ads.xml"/>
```

Later when you run this application and post back to the page, you will be randomly presented with one of two image files. Figure 26-10 illustrates the initial UI of the master page.

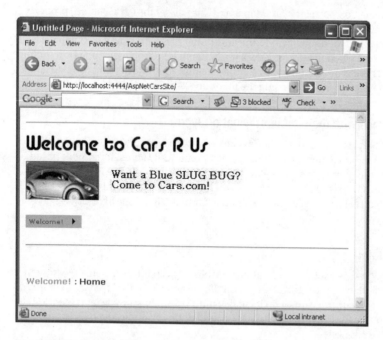

Figure 26-10. *The* AdRotator *control at work*

Defining the Default.aspx Content Page

Now that you have a master page established, you can begin designing the individual *.aspx pages that will define the UI content to merge within the <asp:contentplaceholder> tag of the master page. When you created this new website, Visual Studio 2005 automatically provided you with an initial *.aspx file, but as the file now stands, it cannot be merged within the master page.

The reason is that it is the *.master file that defines the <form> section of the final HTML page. Therefore, the existing <form> area within the *.aspx file will need to be replaced with an <asp:content> scope. While you could update the markup of your initial *.aspx file by hand, go ahead and delete Default.aspx from your project. When you wish to automatically insert a new content page to your project, simply right-click the content placeholder region of the *.master file in the designer and select the Add Content Page menu option. This will generate a new *.aspx file with the following initial markup:

```
<%@ Page Language="VB" MasterPageFile="~/MasterPage.master"
  AutoEventWireup="false" CodeFile="Default.aspx.vb"
  Inherits="_Default" title="Untitled Page" %>
<asp:Content ID="Content1"
  ContentPlaceHolderID="ContentPlaceHolder1" Runat="Server">
</asp:Content>
```

First, notice that the <%@Page%> directive has been updated with a new MasterPageFile attribute that is assigned to your *.master file. Also note that rather than having a <form> element, we have a <asp:Content> scope (currently empty) that has set the ContentPlaceHolderID value identical to the <asp:contentplaceholder> widget in the master file.

Given these associations, you will now find that when you switch back to the design view, the master's UI is now visible. The content area is visible as well, although it is currently empty. There is no need to build a complex UI for your Default.aspx content area, so for this example, simply add some literal text that provides some basic site instructions, as you see in Figure 26-11.

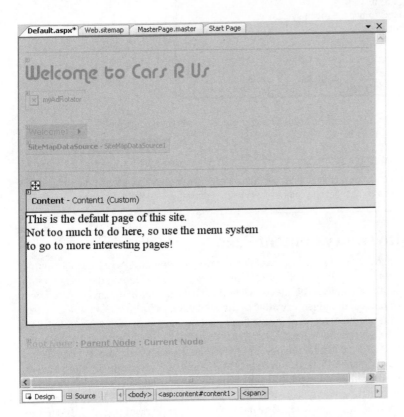

Figure 26-11. *Content pages merge with their master page at design time.*

Now, if you run your project, you will find that the UI content of the *.master and Default.aspx files have been merged into a single stream of HTML. As you can see from Figure 26-12, the end user is unaware that the master page even exists.

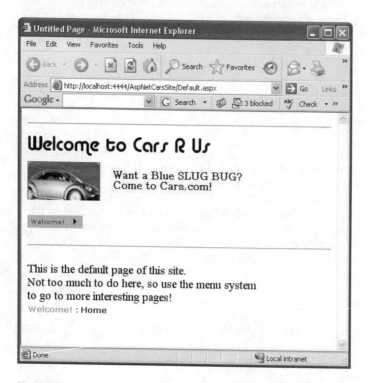

Figure 26-12. *At runtime, master files and content pages render back a single* <form>.

■**Note** Master pages can be assigned programmatically within the PreInit event using the Master property. Furthermore, it is possible for a content page to communicate with its master via the Master property.

Designing the Inventory Content Page

To insert the Inventory.aspx content page into your current project, open the *.master page in the IDE, select Web Site ➤ Add Content Page (if a *.master file is not the active item in the designer, this menu option is not present), and rename this file to Inventory.aspx. The role of the Inventory content page is to display the contents of the Inventory table of the Cars database within a GridView control.

This control is the intended replacement for the legacy DataGrid control used with ASP.NET 1.x. Although this control behaves in many ways identically to the DataGrid, it has support for the new data binding engine of ASP.NET 2.0. Under the new model, it is now possible to represent connection string data and SQL Select, Insert, Update, and Delete statements (or alternatively stored procedures) *in markup*. Therefore, rather than authoring all of the necessary ADO.NET code by hand, you can make use of the new SqlDataSource type. Using the visual designers, you are able to declaratively create the necessary markup, and then assign the DataSourceID property of the GridView to the SqlDataSource component.

■**Note** Despite the name, the `SqlDataSource` provider can be configured to communicate with any ADO.NET data provide (ODBC, Oracle, etc.) that ships with the Microsoft .NET platform, and is not limited to Microsoft SQL server. You may set the underlying DBMS with via the `Provider` property.

With a few simple mouse clicks, you can configure the `GridView` to automatically select, update, and delete records of the underlying data store. While this zero-code mindset greatly simplifies the amount of boilerplate code, understand that this simplicity comes with a loss of control and may not be the best approach for an enterprise-level application. This model can be wonderful for low-trafficked pages, prototyping a website, or smaller in-house applications.

To illustrate how to work with the `GridView` (and the new data binding engine) in a declarative manner, update the `Inventory.aspx` content page with a descriptive label. Next, open the Server Explorer tool (via the View menu) and make sure you have added a data connection to the Cars database created during our examination of ADO.NET (see Chapter 24 for a walkthrough of the process of adding a data connection). Now, select the Inventory icon and drag it onto the content area of the `Inventory.aspx` file. Once you have done so, the IDE responds by performing the following steps:

1. Your `web.config` file was updated with a new `<connectionStrings>` element.

2. A `SqlDataSource` component was configured with the necessary `Select`, `Insert`, `Update`, and `Delete` logic.

3. The `DataSourceID` property of the `GridView` has been set to the new `SqlDataSource` component.

■**Note** As an alternative, you can configure a `GridView` widget using the inline editor. Select New Data Source from the Choose Data Source drop-down box. This will activate a wizard that walks you through a series of steps to connect this component to the required data source.

If you examine the opening declaration of the `GridView` control, you will see that the `DataSourceID` property has been set to the `SqlDataSource` you just defined:

```
<asp:GridView ID="GridView1" runat="server" AutoGenerateColumns="False"
  CellPadding="4" DataKeyNames="CarID" DataSourceID="CarsDataSource"
  ForeColor="#333333" GridLines="None">
...
</asp:GridView>
```

The `SqlDataSource` type is where a majority of the action is taking place. In the markup that follows, notice that this type has recorded the necessary SQL statements (with parameterized queries no less) to interact with the Inventory table of the Cars database. As well, using the new "$" syntax of the `ConnectionString` property, this component will automatically read the `<connectionString>` value from `web.config`:

```
<asp:SqlDataSource ID="SqlDataSource1" runat="server"
 ConnectionString="<%$ ConnectionStrings:CarsConnectionString1 %>"
  DeleteCommand="DELETE FROM [Inventory] WHERE [CarID] = @CarID"
  InsertCommand="INSERT INTO [Inventory] ([CarID], [Make], [Color], [PetName])
    VALUES (@CarID, @Make, @Color, @PetName)"
  ProviderName="<%$ ConnectionStrings:CarsConnectionString1.ProviderName %>"
  SelectCommand="SELECT [CarID], [Make], [Color], [PetName] FROM [Inventory]"
  UpdateCommand="UPDATE [Inventory] SET [Make] = @Make,
    [Color] = @Color, [PetName] = @PetName WHERE [CarID] = @CarID">
  <DeleteParameters>
    <asp:Parameter Name="CarID" Type="Int32" />
```

```
    </DeleteParameters>
    <UpdateParameters>
      <asp:Parameter Name="Make" Type="String" />
      <asp:Parameter Name="Color" Type="String" />
      <asp:Parameter Name="PetName" Type="String" />
      <asp:Parameter Name="CarID" Type="Int32" />
    </UpdateParameters>
    <InsertParameters>
      <asp:Parameter Name="CarID" Type="Int32" />
      <asp:Parameter Name="Make" Type="String" />
      <asp:Parameter Name="Color" Type="String" />
      <asp:Parameter Name="PetName" Type="String" />
    </InsertParameters>
</asp:SqlDataSource>
```

At this point, you are able to run your web program, click the View Inventory menu item, and view your data, as shown in Figure 26-13. Also notice that the "bread crumbs" provided by the SiteMapPath widget have updated automatically.

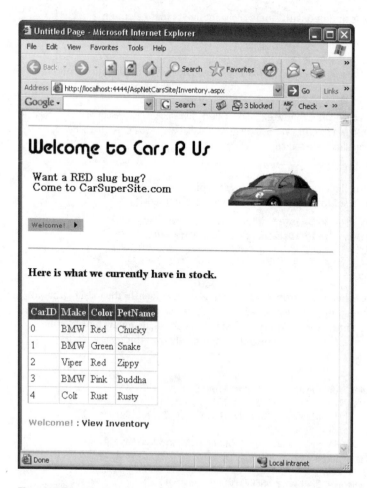

Figure 26-13. *The "zero-code" model of the* SqlDataSource *component*

Enabling Sorting and Paging

The GridView control can easily be configured for sorting (via column name hyperlinks) and paging (via numeric or next/previous hyperlinks). To do so, activate the inline editor and check the appropriate options, as shown in Figure 26-14.

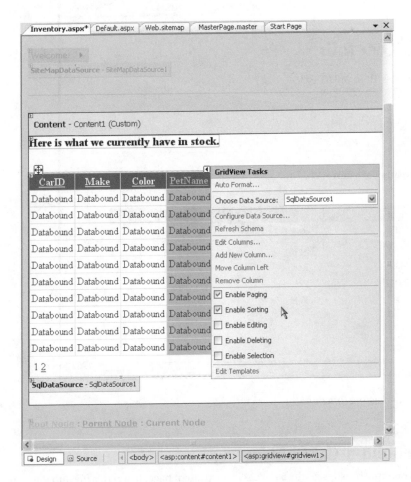

Figure 26-14. *Enabling sorting and paging*

When you run your page again, you will be able to sort your data by clicking the column names and scrolling through your data via the paging links (provided you have enough records in the Inventory table!).

Enabling In-place Editing

The final detail of this page is to enable the GridView control's support for in-place activation. Given that your SqlDataSource already has the necessary Delete and Update logic, all you need to do is check the Enable Deleting and Enable Editing check boxes of the GridView (see Figure 26-14). Sure enough, when you navigate back to the Inventory.aspx page, you are able to edit and delete records, as shown in Figure 26-15, and update the underlying Inventory table of the Cars database.

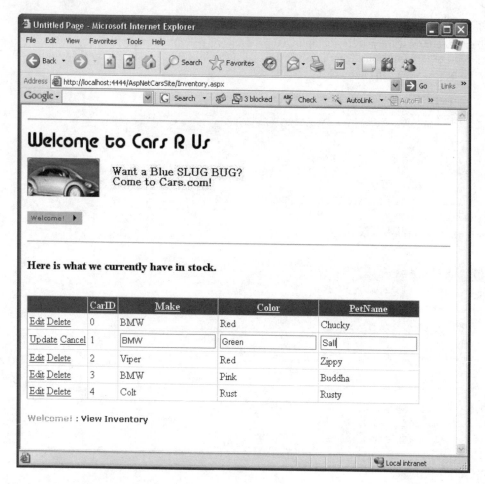

Figure 26-15. *Editing and deleting functionality*

Designing the Build-a-Car Content Page

The final task for this example is to design the BuildCar.aspx content page. Insert this file into the current project (via the Web Site ➤ Add Content Page menu option). This new page will make use of the ASP.NET 2.0 Wizard web control, which provides a simple way to walk the end user through a series of related steps. Here, the steps in question will simulate the act of building an automobile for purchase.

Place a descriptive Label and Wizard control onto the content area. Next, activate the inline editor for the Wizard and click the Add/Remove WizardSteps link. Add a total of four steps, as shown in Figure 26-16.

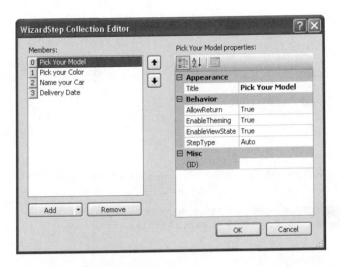

Figure 26-16. *Configurng our wizard*

Once you have defined these steps, you will notice that the Wizard defines an empty content area where you can now drag and drop controls for the currently selected step. For this example, update each step with the following UI elements (be sure to provide a descent ID value for each item using the Properties window):

- *Pick Your Model*: A single TextBox control
- *Pick Your Color*: A single ListBox control
- *Name Your Car*: A single TextBox control
- *Delivery Date*: A Calendar control

The ListBox control is the only UI element of the Wizard that requires additional steps. Select this item on the designer (making sure you first select the Pick Your Color link) and fill this widget with a set of colors using the Items property of the Properties window. Once you do, you will find markup much like the following within the scope of the Wizard definition:

```
<asp:ListBox ID="ListBoxColors" runat="server" Width="237px">
  <asp:ListItem>Purple</asp:ListItem>
  <asp:ListItem>Green</asp:ListItem>
  <asp:ListItem>Red</asp:ListItem>
  <asp:ListItem>Yellow</asp:ListItem>
  <asp:ListItem>Pea Soup Green</asp:ListItem>
  <asp:ListItem>Black</asp:ListItem>
  <asp:ListItem>Lime Green</asp:ListItem>
</asp:ListBox>
```

Now that you have defined each of the steps, you can handle the FinishButtonClick event for the autogenerated Finish button. Within the server-side event handler, obtain the selections from each UI element and build a description string that is assigned to the Text property of an additional Label type named lblOrder:

```
Partial Class _Default
  Inherits System.Web.UI.Page
```

```
Protected Sub carWizard_FinishButtonClick(ByVal sender As Object, _
ByVal e As System.Web.UI.WebControls.WizardNavigationEventArgs) _
Handles carWizard.FinishButtonClick
    ' Get each value.
    Dim order As String = String.Format("{0}, your {1} {2} will arrive on {3}.", _
    txtCarPetName.Text, ListBoxColors.SelectedValue, _
    txtCarModel.Text, carCalendar.SelectedDate.ToShortDateString())
    ' Assign to label
    lblOrder.Text = order
End Sub
End Class
```

At this point your AspNetCarSite is complete! Figure 26-17 shows the Wizard in action.

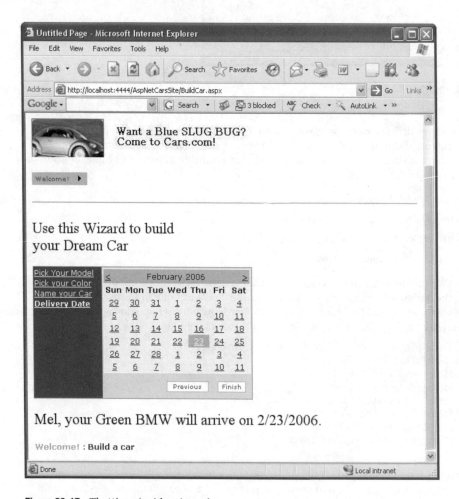

Figure 26-17. *The* Wizard *widget in action*

That wraps up our examination of various core UI web controls. To be sure, there are many other widgets we haven't covered here. You should feel comfortable, though, with the basic programming model and be able to dig into the other widgets on your own terms. Next up, let's look at the validation controls.

■**Source Code** The AspNetCarsSite files are included under the Chapter 26 subdirectory.

The Role of the Validation Controls

The next Web Form controls we will examine are known collectively as *validation controls*. Unlike the other Web Form controls we've examined, validation controls are not used to emit HTML, but are used to emit client-side JavaScript (and possibly server-side operations) for the purpose of form validation. As illustrated at the beginning of this chapter, client-side form validation is quite useful in that you can ensure that various constraints are in place before posting back to the web server, thereby avoiding expensive round-trips. Table 26-3 gives a rundown of the ASP.NET validation controls.

Table 26-3. *ASP.NET Validation Controls*

Control	Meaning in Life
CompareValidator	Validates that the value of an input control is equal to a given value of another input control or a fixed constant.
CustomValidator	Allows you to build a custom validation function that validates a given control.
RangeValidator	Determines that a given value is in a predetermined range.
RegularExpressionValidator	Checks whether the value of the associated input control matches the pattern of a regular expression.
RequiredFieldValidator	Ensures that a given input control contains a value (i.e., is not empty).
ValidationSummary	Displays a summary of all validation errors of a page in a list, bulleted list, or single-paragraph format. The errors can be displayed inline and/or in a pop-up message box.

All of the validation controls ultimately derive from a common base class named System.Web. UI.WebControls.BaseValidator, and therefore they have a set of common features. Table 26-4 documents the key members.

Table 26-4. *Common Properties of the ASP.NET Validators*

Member	Meaning in Life
ControlToValidate	Gets or sets the input control to validate
Display	Gets or sets the display behavior of the error message in a validation control
EnableClientScript	Gets or sets a value indicating whether client-side validation is enabled
ErrorMessage	Gets or sets the text for the error message
ForeColor	Gets or sets the color of the message displayed when validation fails

While we could update the previous example with several validation controls (within the wizard steps, for example), let's create a new Web Site project named ValidatorCtrls. To begin, place four TextBox types (with four corresponding and descriptive Labels) onto your page. Next, place a RequiredFieldValidator, RangeValidator, RegularExpressionValidator, and CompareValidator type adjacent to each respective field. Finally, add a single Button and final Label (see Figure 26-18).

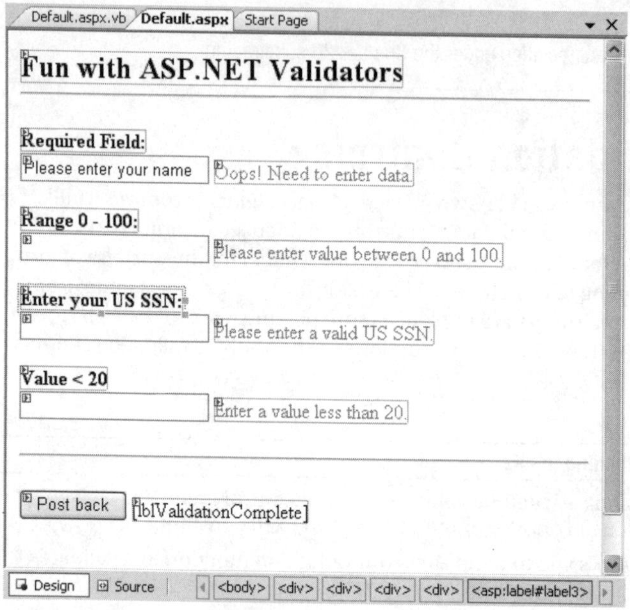

Figure 26-18. *Various validators*

Now that you have a UI, let's walk though the process of configuring each member.

The RequiredFieldValidator

Configuring the RequiredFieldValidator is straightforward. Simply set the ErrorMessage and ControlToValidate properties accordingly using the Visual Studio 2005 Properties window. The resulting *.aspx definition is as follows:

```
<asp:RequiredFieldValidator ID="RequiredFieldValidator1"
  runat="server" ControlToValidate="txtRequiredField"
  ErrorMessage="Oops!  Need to enter data.">
</asp:RequiredFieldValidator>
```

One nice thing about the RequiredFieldValidator is that it supports an InitialValue property. You can use this property to ensure that the user enters any value other than the initial value in the related TextBox. For example, when the user first posts to a page, you may wish to configure a TextBox to contain the value "Please enter your name". Now, if you did not set the InitialValue property of the RequiredFieldValidator, the runtime would assume that the string "Please enter your name" is valid. Thus, to ensure a required TextBox is valid only when the user enters anything other than "Please enter your name", configure your widgets as follows:

```
<asp:RequiredFieldValidator ID="RequiredFieldValidator1"
  runat="server" ControlToValidate="txtRequiredField"
  ErrorMessage="Oops!  Need to enter data."
  InitialValue="Please enter your name">
</asp:RequiredFieldValidator>
```

The RegularExpressionValidator

The RegularExpressionValidator can be used when you wish to apply a pattern against the characters entered within a given input field. To ensure that a given TextBox contains a valid US Social Security number, you could define the widget as follows:

```
<asp:RegularExpressionValidator ID="RegularExpressionValidator1"
  runat="server" ControlToValidate="txtRegExp"
  ErrorMessage="Please enter a valid US SSN."
  ValidationExpression="\d{3}-\d{2}-\d{4}">
</asp:RegularExpressionValidator>
```

Notice how the RegularExpressionValidator defines a ValidationExpression property. If you have never worked with regular expressions before, all you need to be aware of for this example is that they are used to match a given string pattern. Here, the expression "\d{3}-\d{2}\d{4}" is capturing a standard US Social Security number of the form xxx-xx-xxxx (where x is any digit).

This particular regular expression is fairly self-explanatory; however, assume you wish to test for a valid Japanese phone number. The correct expression now becomes much more complex: "(0\d{1,4}-|\(0\d{1,4}\)?)?\d{1,4}-\d{4}". The good news is that when you select the ValidationExpression property using the Properties window, you can pick from a predefined set of common regular expressions by clicking the Ellipse button.

Note If you are interested in regular expressions, you will be happy to know that the .NET platform supplies two namespaces (System.Text.RegularExpressions and System.Web.RegularExpressions) devoted to the programmatic manipulation of such patterns.

The RangeValidator

In addition to a MinimumValue and MaximumValue property, RangeValidators have a property named Type. Because you are interested in testing the user-supplied input against a range of whole numbers, you need to specify Integer (which is *not* the default!):

```
<asp:RangeValidator ID="RangeValidator1"
  runat="server" ControlToValidate="txtRange"
  ErrorMessage="Please enter value between 0 and 100."
  MaximumValue="100" MinimumValue="0" Type="Integer">
</asp:RangeValidator>
```

The RangeValidator can also be used to test whether a given value is between a currency value, date, floating-point number, or string data (the default setting).

The CompareValidator

Finally, notice that the CompareValidator supports an Operator property:

```
<asp:CompareValidator ID="CompareValidator1" runat="server"
  ControlToValidate="txtComparison"
  ErrorMessage="Enter a value less than 20." Operator="LessThan"
  ValueToCompare="20">
</asp:CompareValidator>
```

Given that the role of this validator is to compare the value in the text box against another value using a binary operator, it should be no surprise that the Operator property may be set to values such as LessThan, GreaterThan, Equal, and NotEqual. Also note that the ValueToCompare is used to establish a value to compare against.

Note The CompareValidator can also be configured to compare a value within another Web Form control (rather than a hard-coded value) using the ControlToValidate property.

To finish up the code for this page, handle the Click event for the Button type and inform the user he has succeeded in the validation logic:

```
Partial Class _Default
  Inherits System.Web.UI.Page

  Protected Sub btnPostback_Click(ByVal sender As Object, _
  ByVal e As System.EventArgs) Handles btnPostback.Click
    lblValidationComplete.Text = "You passed validation!"
  End Sub
End Class
```

Now, navigate to this page using your browser of choice. At this point, you should not see any noticeable changes. However, when you attempt to click the Submit button after entering bogus data, your error message is suddenly visible. Once you enter valid data, the error messages are removed and postback occurs.

If you look at the HTML rendered by the browser, you see that the validation controls generate a client-side JavaScript function that makes use of a specific library of JavaScript functions (contained in the WebUIValidation.js file) that is automatically downloaded to the user's machine. Once the validation has occurred, the form data is posted back to the server, where the ASP.NET runtime will perform the *same* validation tests on the web server (just to ensure that no along-the-wire tampering has taken place).

On a related note, if the HTTP request was sent by a browser that does not support client-side JavaScript, all validation will occur on the server. In this way, you can program against the validation controls without being concerned with the target browser; the returned HTML page redirects the error processing back to the web server.

Creating Validation Summaries

The final validation-centric topic we will examine here is the use of the ValidationSummary widget. Currently, each of your validators displays its error message at the exact place in which it was positioned at design time. In many cases, this may be exactly what you are looking for. However, on a complex form with numerous input widgets, you may not want to have random blobs of red text pop up. Using the ValidationSummary type, you can instruct all of your validation types to display their error messages at a specific location on the page.

The first step is to simply place a ValidationSummary on your *.aspx file. You may optionally set the HeaderText property of this type as well as the DisplayMode, which by default will list all error messages as a bulleted list.

```
<asp:ValidationSummary id="ValidationSummary1"
  style="Z-INDEX: 123; LEFT: 152px; POSITION: absolute; TOP: 320px"
  runat="server" Width="353px"
  HeaderText="Here are the things you must correct.">
</asp:ValidationSummary>
```

Next, you need to set the Display property to None for each of the individual validators (e.g., RequiredFieldValidator, RangeValidator, etc.) on the page. This will ensure that you do not see duplicate error messages for a given validation failure (one in the summary pane and another at the validator's location).

Last but not least, if you would rather have the error messages displayed using a client-side MessageBox, set the ShowMessageBox property to True and the ShowSummary property to False.

■**Source Code** The ValidatorCtrls project is included under the Chapter 26 subdirectory.

Working with Themes

At this point, you have had the chance to work with numerous ASP.NET web controls. As you have seen, each control exposes a set of properties (many of which are inherited by System.Web.UI. WebControls.WebControl) that allow you to establish a given UI look and feel (background color, font size, border style, and whatnot). Of course, on a multipaged website it is quite common for the site as a whole to define a common look and feel for various types of widgets. For example, all TextBoxes might be configured to support a given font, all Buttons have a custom image, and all Calendars are light blue.

Obviously it would be very labor intensive (and error prone) to establish the *same* property settings for every widget on *every* page within your website. Even if you were able to manually update the properties of each UI widget on each page, imagine how painful it would be when you now need to change the background color for each TextBox yet again. Clearly there must be a better way to apply sitewide UI settings.

One approach that can be taken to simplify applying a common UI look and feel is to define *style sheets*. If you have a background in web development, you are aware that style sheets define a common set of UI-centric settings that are applied on the browser. As you would hope, ASP.NET web controls can be assigned a given style by assigning the CssStyle property.

However, ASP.NET 2.0 ships with an alternative technology to define a common UI termed *themes*. Unlike a style sheet, themes are applied on the web server (rather than the browser), and can be done so programmatically or declaratively. Given that a theme is applied on the web server, it has access to all the server-side resources on the website. Furthermore, themes are defined by authoring the same markup you would find within any *.aspx file (as you may agree, the syntax of a style sheet is a bit on the terse side).

Recall from Chapter 25 that ASP.NET 2.0 web applications may define any number of "special" subdirectories, one of which is App_Theme. This single subdirectory may be further partitioned with additional subdirectories, each of which represents a possible theme on your site. For example, consider Figure 26-19, which illustrates a single App_Theme folder containing three subdirectories, each of which has a set of files that make up the theme itself.

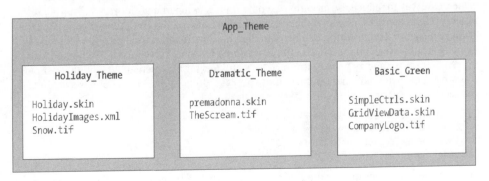

Figure 26-19. *A single App_Theme folder may define numerous themes*

Understanding *.skin Files

The one file that every theme subdirectory is sure to have is a *.skin file. These files define the look and feel for various web controls. To illustrate, create a new website named FunWithThemes. Next, insert a new *.skin file (using the Web Site ➤ Add New Item menu option) named BasicGreen.skin, as shown in Figure 26-20.

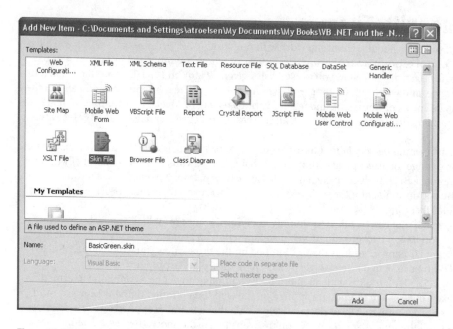

Figure 26-20. *Inserting *.skin files*

Visual Studio 2005 will prompt you to confirm this file can be added into an App_Theme folder (which is exactly what we want). If you were now to look in your Solution Explorer, you will indeed find your App_Theme folder has a subfolder named BasicGreen containing your new BasicGreen.skin file.

Recall that a *.skin file is where you are able to define the look and feel for various widgets using ASP.NET control declaration syntax. Sadly, the IDE does not currently provide designer support for *.skin files. One way to reduce the amount of typing time is to insert a temporary *.aspx file into your program (temp.aspx, for example) that can be used to build up the UI of the widgets using the VS 2005 page designer. The resulting markup can then be copied and pasted into your *.skin file. When you do so, however, you *must* delete the ID attribute for each web control! This should make sense, given that we are not trying to define a UI look and feel for a particular Button (for example) but *all* Buttons. This being said, here is the markup for BasicGreen.skin, which defines a default look and feel for the Button, TextBox and Calendar types:

```
<asp:Label runat="server" Font-Size="XX-Large"/>
<asp:Button runat="server" BackColor="#80FF80"/>
<asp:TextBox runat="server" BackColor="#80FF80"/>
<asp:Calendar runat="server" BackColor="#80FF80"/>
```

Notice that each widget still has the runat="server" attribute (which is mandatory) and none of the widgets have been assigned an ID attribute.

Now, let's define a second theme named CrazyOrange. Using the Solution Explorer, right-click your App_Theme folder and add a new theme named CrazyOrange. This will create a new subdirectory under your site's App_Theme folder. Next, right-click the new CrazyOrange folder within the Solution Explorer and select Add New Item. From the resulting dialog box, add a new *.skin file. Update the CrazyOrange.skin file to define a very obnoxious UI look and feel for the same four web controls. For example:

```
<asp:Button runat="server" BackColor="#FF8000"/>
<asp:TextBox runat="server" BackColor="#FF8000"/>
<asp:Calendar BackColor="White" BorderColor="Black"
  BorderStyle="Solid" CellSpacing="1"
  Font-Names="Verdana" Font-Size="9pt" ForeColor="Black" Height="250px"
  NextPrevFormat="ShortMonth" Width="330px" runat="server">
  <SelectedDayStyle BackColor="#333399" ForeColor="White" />
  <OtherMonthDayStyle ForeColor="#999999" />
  <TodayDayStyle BackColor="#999999" ForeColor="White" />
  <DayStyle BackColor="#CCCCCC" />
  <NextPrevStyle Font-Bold="True" Font-Size="8pt" ForeColor="White" />
  <DayHeaderStyle Font-Bold="True" Font-Size="8pt"
    ForeColor="#333333" Height="8pt" />
  <TitleStyle BackColor="#333399" BorderStyle="Solid"
    Font-Bold="True" Font-Size="12pt"
    ForeColor="White" Height="12pt" />
</asp:Calendar>
```

So now that your site has a few themes defined, the next logic question is how to apply them to your pages. As you might guess, there are many ways to do so.

Applying Sitewide Themes

If you wish to make sure that every page in your site adheres to the same theme, the simplest way to do so is to update your web.config file. Open your current web.config file and locate the <pages> element within the scope of your <system.web> root element. If you add a theme attribute to the <pages> element, this will ensure that every page in your website is assigned the selected theme (which is, of course, the name of one of the subdirectories under App_Theme). Here is the core update:

```
<configuration>
  <system.web>
...
    <pages theme="BasicGreen">
...
    </pages>
  </system.web>
</configuration>
```

If you were to now place various Buttons, Calendars, and TextBoxes onto your Default.aspx file and run the application, you would find each widget has the UI of BasicGreen. If you were to update the theme attribute to CrazyOrange and run the page again, you would find the UI defined by this theme is used instead.

Applying Themes at the Page Level

It is also possible to assign themes on a page-by-page level. This can be helpful in a variety of circumstances. For example, perhaps your web.config file defines a sitewide theme (as described in the previous section); however, you wish to assign a different theme to a specific page. To do so, you can simply update the <%@Page%> directive. If you are using Visual Studio 2005 to do so, you will be happy to find that IntelliSense will display each defined theme within your App_Theme folder (see Figure 26-21).

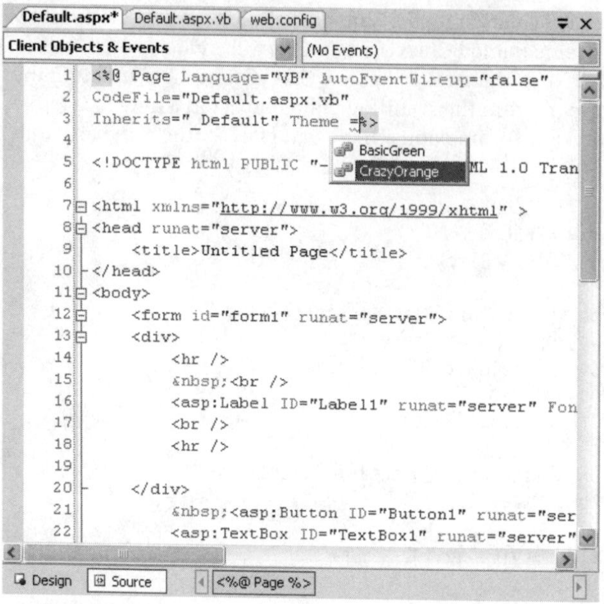

Figure 26-21. *Assigning themes on the page level*

If we did assign the CrazyOrange to this page, but the web.config file specified the BasicGreen theme, then all pages *but this page* will be rendered using BasicGreen.

The SkinID Property

Sometimes you wish to define a set of possible UI look and feels for a single widget. For example, assume you want to define two possible UIs for the Button type within the CrazyOrange theme. When you wish do so, you may differentiate each look and feel using the SkinID property:

```
<asp:Button runat="server" BackColor="#FF8000"/>
<asp:Button runat="server" SkinID = "BigFontButton"
Font-Size="30pt" BackColor="#FF8000"/>
```

Now, if you have a page that makes use of the CrazyOrange theme, each Button will by default be assigned the unnamed Button skin. If you wish to have various buttons within the *.aspx file make use of the BigFontButton skin, simply specific the SkinID property within the markup:

```
<asp:Button ID="Button2" runat="server"
SkinID="BigFontButton" Text="Button" /><br />
```

As an example, Figure 26-22 shows a page that is making use of the CrazyOrange theme. The topmost Button is assigned the unnamed Button skin, while the Button on the bottom of the page has been assigned the SkinID of BigFontButton.

Figure 26-22. *Fun with SkinIDs*

Assigning Themes Programmatically

Last but not least, it is possible to assign a theme in code. This can be helpful when you wish to provide a way for end users to select a theme for their current session. Of course, we have not yet examined how to build stateful web applications, so the current theme selection will be forgotten between postbacks. In a production-level site, you may wish to store the user's current theme selection within a session variable, or persist the theme selection to a database.

Although we really have not examined the use of session variables at this point in the text, to illustrate how to assign a theme programmatically, update the UI of your Default.aspx file with three new Button types as shown in Figure 26-23. Once you have done so, handle the Click event for each Button type.

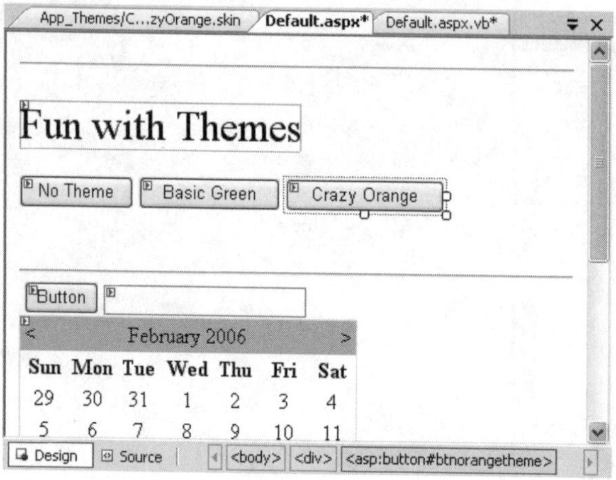

Figure 26-23. *The updated UI*

Now be aware that you can only assign a theme programmatically during specific phases of your page's life cycle. Typically this will be done within the Page_PreInit event. This being said, update your code file as follows:

```
Partial Class _Default
  Inherits System.Web.UI.Page

  Protected Sub btnNoTheme_Click(ByVal sender As Object, _
  ByVal e As System.EventArgs) Handles btnNoTheme.Click
    ' Empty strings result in no theme being applied.
    Session("UserTheme") = ""
    ' Trigger the PreInit event again.
    Server.Transfer(Request.FilePath)
  End Sub

  Protected Sub btnGreenTheme_Click(ByVal sender As Object, _
  ByVal e As System.EventArgs) Handles btnGreenTheme.Click
    Session("UserTheme") = "BasicGreen"
    ' Trigger the PreInit event again.
    Server.Transfer(Request.FilePath)
  End Sub

  Protected Sub btnOrangeTheme_Click(ByVal sender As Object, _
  ByVal e As System.EventArgs) Handles btnOrangeTheme.Click
    Session("UserTheme") = "CrazyOrange"
    ' Trigger the PreInit event again.
    Server.Transfer(Request.FilePath)
  End Sub

  Protected Sub Page_PreInit(ByVal sender As Object, _
  ByVal e As System.EventArgs) Handles Me.PreInit
    Try
      Theme = Session("UserTheme").ToString()
    Catch
      ' Empty strings result in no theme being applied.
      Theme = ""
    End Try
```

```
    End Sub
End Class
```

Without getting too hung up on the notion of a session variable (see Chapter 27 for details), simply notice that we are storing a given theme within a session variable named UserTheme, which is formally assigned within the Page_PreInit() event handler. Also note that when the user clicks a given Button, we programmatically force the PreInit event to fire by calling Server.Transfer() and requesting the current page once again. If you were to run this page, you would now find that you can establish your theme via various Button clicks.

■Source Code The FunWithThemes project is included under the Chapter 26 subdirectory.

Summary

This chapter examined how to make use of various ASP.NET web controls. We began by examining the role of the Control and WebControl base classes, and you came to learn how to dynamically interact with a panel's internal controls collection. Along the way, you were exposed to the new site navigation model (*.sitemap files and the SiteMapDataSource component), the new data binding engine (via the SqlDataSource component and the new GridView type), and various validation controls.

The latter half of this chapter examined the role of master pages and themes. Recall that master pages can be used to define a common frame for a set of pages on your site. Also recall that the *.master file defines any number of "content placeholders" to which content pages plug in their custom UI content. Finally, as you were shown, the ASP.NET theme engine allows you to declaratively or programmatically apply a common UI look and feel to your widgets on the web server.

CHAPTER 27

■■■

ASP.NET 2.0 State Management Techniques

The previous two chapters concentrated on the composition and behavior of ASP.NET pages and the web controls they contain. This chapter builds on that information by examining the role of the Global.asax file and the underlying HttpApplication type. As you will see, the functionality of HttpApplication allows you to intercept numerous events that enable you to treat your web applications as a cohesive unit, rather than a set of stand-alone *.aspx files.

In addition to investigating the HttpApplication type, this chapter also addresses the all-important topic of state management. Here you will learn the role of view state, session and application variables (including the *application cache*) as well as the new ASP.NET 2.0 profiles API. Once you have a solid understanding of the state management techniques offered by the .NET platform, the chapter wraps up with a discussion of the role of the web.config file and shows various configuration-centric techniques.

The Issue of State

At the beginning of the Chapter 25, I pointed out that HTTP on the Web results in a *stateless* wire protocol. This very fact makes web development extremely different from the process of building an executable assembly. For example, when you are building a Windows Forms application, you can rest assured that any member variables defined in the Form-derived class will typically exist in memory until the user explicitly shuts down the executable:

```
Public Class MainWindow
   ' State data!
   Private userFavoriteCar As String
End Class
```

In the world of the World Wide Web, however, you are not afforded the same luxurious assumption. To prove the point, create a new ASP.NET website (named SimpleStateExample). Within the code-behind file of your initial *.aspx file, define a page-level string variable named userFavoriteCar:

```
Partial Class _Default
   Inherits System.Web.UI.Page
   ' State data?
   Private userFavoriteCar As String
End Class
```

Next, construct the web UI as shown in Figure 27-1.

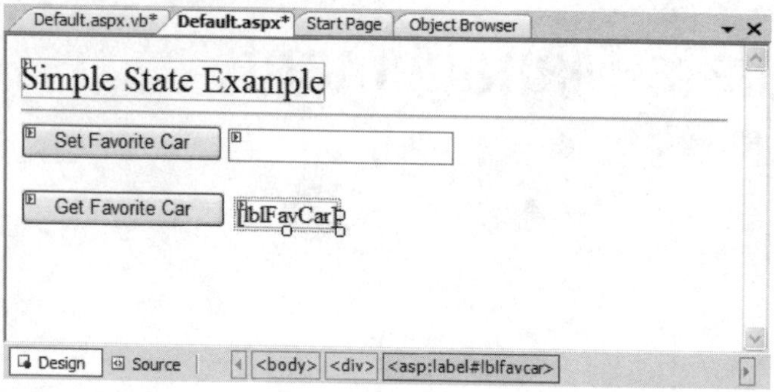

Figure 27-1. *The UI for the simple state page*

The server-side Click event handler for the Set button (named btnSetCar) will allow the user to assign the string member variable to the value within the TextBox (named txtFavCar):

```
Protected Sub btnSetCar_Click(ByVal sender As Object, _
  ByVal e As System.EventArgs) Handles btnSetCar.Click
  ' Store favorite car in member variable.
  userFavoriteCar = txtFavCar.Text
End Sub
```

while the Click event handler for the Get button (btnGetCar) will display the current value of the member variable within the page's Label widget (lblFavCar):

```
Protected Sub btnGetCar_Click(ByVal sender As Object, _
  ByVal e As System.EventArgs) Handles btnGetCar.Click
  ' Set label text to value of member variable.
  lblFavCar.Text = userFavoriteCar
End Sub
```

Now, if you were building a Windows Forms application, you would be right to assume that once the user sets the initial value, it would be remembered throughout the life of the desktop application. Sadly, when you run this web application, you will find that each time you post back to the web server, the value of the userFavoriteCar string variable is set back to the initial empty value; therefore, the Label's text is continuously empty.

Again, given that HTTP has no clue how to automatically remember data once the HTTP response has been sent, it stands to reason that the Page object is destroyed almost instantly. Therefore, when the client posts back to the *.aspx file, a new Page object is constructed that will reset any page-level member variables. This is clearly a major dilemma. Imagine how painful online shopping would be if every time you posted back to the web server, any and all information you previously entered (such as the items you wish to purchase) were discarded. When you wish to remember information regarding the users who are logged on to your site, you need to make use of various state management techniques.

Note This issue is in no way limited to ASP.NET. Java servlets, CGI applications, classic ASP, and PHP applications all must contend with the thorny issue of state management.

To remember the value of the userFavoriteCar string type between postbacks, you are required to store the value of this string type within a *session variable*. You will examine the exact details of session state in the pages that follow. For the sake of completion, however, here are the necessary updates for the current page (note that you are no longer using the private String member variable, therefore feel free to comment out or remove the definition altogether):

```
Partial Class _Default
  Inherits System.Web.UI.Page
  Protected Sub btnSetCar_Click(ByVal sender As Object, _
    ByVal e As System.EventArgs) Handles btnSetCar.Click
    ' Store favorite car in session variable.
    Session("UserFavCar") = txtFavCar.Text
  End Sub

  Protected Sub btnGetCar_Click(ByVal sender As Object, _
    ByVal e As System.EventArgs) Handles btnGetCar.Click
    ' Set label text to value of session variable.
    lblFavCar.Text = CType(Session("UserFavCar"), String)
  End Sub
End Class
```

If you now run the application, the value of your favorite automobile will be preserved across postbacks, thanks to the HttpSessionState object manipulated indirectly by the inherited Session property. Of course, once the user terminates her session with your web application, session data is discarded. If you wish to persist user information beyond the current session, you can roll your own infrastructure to do so, or make use of the ASP.NET 2.0 profiles API (explained at the conclusion of this chapter).

■**Source Code** The SimpleStateExample files are included under the Chapter 27 subdirectory.

ASP.NET State Management Techniques

ASP.NET provides several mechanisms that you can use to maintain stateful information in your web applications. Specifically, you have the following options:

- Make use of ASP.NET view state.
- Make use of ASP.NET control state.
- Define application-level variables.
- Make use of the cache object.
- Define session-level variables.
- Define cookie data.

The one thing each of these approaches has in common is that they each demand that a given user is in session and that the web application is loaded into memory. As soon as a user logs off your site (or your website is shut down), your site is once again stateless. If you wish to persist user data in a permanent manner, ASP.NET 2.0 provides an out-of-the-box profile API. We'll examine the details of each approach in turn, beginning with the topic of ASP.NET view state.

Understanding the Role of ASP.NET View State

The term *view state* has been thrown out numerous times here and in the previous two chapters without a formal definition, so let's demystify this term once and for all. Under classic (COM-based) ASP, web developers were required to manually repopulate the values of the incoming form widgets during the process of constructing the outgoing HTTP response. For example, if the incoming HTTP request contained five text boxes with specific values, the *.asp file required script code to extract the current values (via the Form or QueryString collections of the Request object) and manually place them back into the HTTP response stream (needless to say, this was a drag). If the developer failed to do so, the caller was presented with a set of five empty text boxes!

Under ASP.NET, we are no longer required to manually scrape out and repopulate the values contained within the HTML widgets because the ASP.NET runtime will automatically embed a hidden form field (named __VIEWSTATE), which will flow between the browser and a specific page. The data assigned to this field is a Base64-encoded string that contains a set of name/value pairs that represent the values of each GUI widget on the page at hand.

The System.Web.UI.Page base class's Init event handler is the entity in charge of reading the incoming values found within the __VIEWSTATE field to populate the appropriate member variables in the derived class (which is why it is risky at best to access the state of a web widget within the scope of a page's Init event handler).

Also, just before the outgoing response is emitted back to the requesting browser, the __VIEWSTATE data is used to repopulate the form's widgets, to ensure that the current values of the HTML widgets appear as they did prior to the previous postback.

Clearly, the best thing about this aspect of ASP.NET is that it just happens without any work on your part. Of course, you are always able to interact with, alter, or disable this default functionality if you so choose. To understand how to do this, let's see a concrete view state example.

Demonstrating View State

First, create a new ASP.NET web application called ViewStateApp. On your initial *.aspx page, add a single ASP.NET ListBox web control (named myListBox) and a single Button type (named btnPostback). Handle the Click event for the Button to provide a way for the user to post back to the web server:

```
Partial Class _Default
  Inherits System.Web.UI.Page
  Protected Sub btnPostback_Click(ByVal sender As Object, _
    ByVal e As System.EventArgs) Handles btnPostback.Click
    ' This is just here to allow a postback.
    ' No code required.
  End Sub
End Class
```

Now, using the Visual Studio 2005 Properties window, access the Items property and add four ListItems to the ListBox. The resulting markup looks like this:

```
<asp:ListBox ID="myListBox" runat="server">
    <asp:ListItem>Item One</asp:ListItem>
    <asp:ListItem>Item Two</asp:ListItem>
    <asp:ListItem>Item Three</asp:ListItem>
    <asp:ListItem>Item Four</asp:ListItem>
</asp:ListBox>
```

Note that you are hard-coding the items in the ListBox directly within the *.aspx file. As you already know, all <asp:> definitions found within an HTML form will automatically render back their HTML representation before the final HTTP response (provided they have the runat="server" attribute).

The `<%@Page%>` directive has an optional attribute called `EnableViewState` that by default is set to true. To disable this behavior, simply update the `<%@Page%>` directive as follows:

```
<%@ Page Language="VB" AutoEventWireup="false"
CodeFile="Default.aspx.vb" Inherits="_Default"
EnableViewState ="false" %>
```

So, what exactly does it mean to disable view state? The answer is, it depends. Given the previous definition of the term, you would think that if you disable view state for an `*.aspx` file, the values within your `ListBox` would not be remembered between postbacks to the web server. However, if you were to run this application as is, you might be surprised to find that the information in the `ListBox` is retained regardless of how many times you post back to the page. In fact, if you examine the source HTML returned to the browser, you may be further surprised to see that the hidden `__VIEWSTATE` field is *still present*:

```
<input type="hidden" name="__VIEWSTATE" id="__VIEWSTATE"
 value="/wEPDwUKLTM4MTM2MDM4NGRkqGC6gjEV25JnddkJiRmoIc1OSIA=" />
```

The reason why the view state string is still visible is the fact that the `*.aspx` file has explicitly defined the `ListBox` items within the scope of the HTML `<form>` tags. Thus, the `ListBox` items will be autogenerated each time the web server responds to the client.

However, assume that your `ListBox` is dynamically populated within the code-behind file rather than within the HTML `<form>` definition. First, remove the `<asp:ListItem>` declarations from the current `*.aspx` file:

```
<asp:ListBox ID="myListBox" runat="server">
</asp:ListBox>
```

Next, fill the list items within the `Load` event handler within your code-behind file:

```
Protected Sub Page_Load(ByVal sender As Object, _
   ByVal e As System.EventArgs) Handles Me.Load
   If Not IsPostBack Then
      ' Fill ListBox dynamically!
      myListBox.Items.Add("Item One")
      myListBox.Items.Add("Item Two")
      myListBox.Items.Add("Item Three")
      myListBox.Items.Add("Item Four")
   End If
End Sub
```

If you post to this updated page, you will find that the first time the browser requests the page, the values in the `ListBox` are present and accounted for. However, on postback, the `ListBox` is suddenly empty. The first rule of ASP.NET view state is that its effect is only realized when you have widgets whose values are dynamically generated through code. If you hard-code values within the `*.aspx` file's `<form>` tags, the state of these items is always remembered across postbacks (even when you set `EnableViewState` to `false` for a given page).

Furthermore, view state is most useful when you have a dynamically populated web widget that always needs to be repopulated for each and every postback (such as an ASP.NET `GridView`, which is always filled using a database hit). If you did not disable view state for pages that contain such widgets, the entire state of the grid is represented within the hidden `__VIEWSTATE` field. Given that complex pages may contain numerous ASP.NET web controls, you can imagine how large this string would become. As the payload of the HTTP request/response cycle could become quite heavy, this may become a problem for the dial-up web surfers of the world. In cases such as these, you may find faster throughput if you disable view state for the page.

If the idea of disabling view state for the entire `*.aspx` file seems a bit too aggressive, do know that every descendent of the `System.Web.UI.Control` base class inherits the `EnableViewState` property, which makes it very simple to disable view state on a control-by-control basis:

```
<asp:GridView id="myHugeDynamicallyFilledDataGrid" runat="server"
 EnableViewState="false">
</asp:GridView>
```

■Note ASP.NET pages reserve a small part of the __VIEWSTATE string for internal use. Given this, you will find that the __VIEWSTATE field will still appear in the client-side source even when the entire page (and all the controls) have disabled view state.

Adding Custom View State Data

In addition to the `EnableViewState` property, the `System.Web.UI.Control` base class also provides an inherited property named `ViewState`. Under the hood, this property provides access to a `System.Web.UI.StateBag` type, which represents all the data contained within the __VIEWSTATE field. Using the indexer of the `StateBag` type, you can embed custom information within the hidden __VIEWSTATE form field using a set of name/value pairs. Here's a simple example:

```
Protected Sub btnAddToVS_Click(ByVal sender As Object, _
  ByVal e As System.EventArgs) Handles btnAddToVS.Click
  ViewState("CustomViewStateItem") = "Some user data"
  lblVSValue.Text = CType(ViewState("CustomViewStateItem"), String)
End Sub
```

Because the `System.Web.UI.StateBag` type has been designed to operate on any type-derived `System.Object`, when you wish to access the value of a given key, you should explicitly cast it into the correct underlying data type (in this case, a `System.String`). Be aware, however, that values placed within the __VIEWSTATE field cannot literally be any object. Specifically, the only valid types are `Strings`, `Integers`, `Booleans`, `ArrayLists`, `Hashtables`, or an array of these types.

So, given that `*.aspx` pages may insert custom bits of information into the __VIEWSTATE string, the next logical question is when you would want to do so. Most of the time, custom view state data is best suited for user-specific preferences. For example, you may establish a point of view state data that specifies how a user wishes to view the UI of a `GridView` (such as a sort order). View state data is not well suited for full-blown user data, such as items in a shopping cart, cached `DataSets`, or what-not. When you need to store this sort of complex information, you are required to work with session or application data. Before we get to that point, you need to understand the role of the `Global.asax` file.

■Source Code The ViewStateApp files are included under the Chapter 27 subdirectory.

A Brief Word Regarding Control State

As of ASP.NET 2.0, a control's state data can now be persisted via *control state* rather than view state. This technique is most helpful if you have written a custom ASP.NET web control that must remember data between round-trips. While the `ViewState` property can be used for this purpose, if view state is disabled at a page level, the custom control is effectively broken. For this very reason, web controls now support a `ControlState` property.

Control state works identically to view state; however, it will not be disabled if view state is disabled at the page level. As mentioned, this feature is most useful for those who are developing custom web controls (a topic not covered in this text). Consult the .NET Framework 2.0 SDK documentation for further details.

The Role of the Global.asax File

At this point, an ASP.NET application may seem to be little more than a set of *.aspx files and their respective web controls. While you could build a web application by simply linking a set of related web pages, you will most likely need a way to interact with the web application as a whole. To this end, your ASP.NET web applications may choose to include an optional Global.asax file via the Web Site ➤ Add New Item menu option, as shown in Figure 27-2.

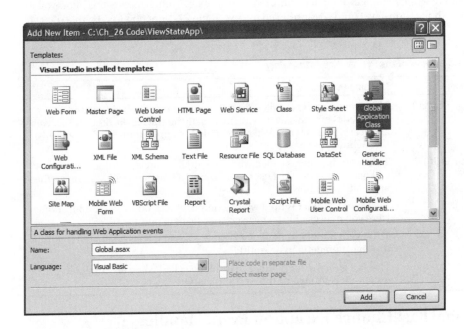

Figure 27-2. *The* Global.asax *file*

Simply put, Global.asax is just about as close to a traditional double-clickable *.exe that we can get in the world of ASP.NET, meaning this type represents the runtime behavior of the website itself. Once you insert a Global.asax file into a web project, you will notice it is little more than a <script> block containing a set of event handlers:

```vb
<%@ Application Language="VB" %>
<script runat="server">
Sub Application_Start(ByVal sender As Object, ByVal e As EventArgs)
End Sub

Sub Application_End(ByVal sender As Object, ByVal e As EventArgs)
End Sub

Sub Application_Error(ByVal sender As Object, ByVal e As EventArgs)
End Sub

Sub Session_Start(ByVal sender As Object, ByVal e As EventArgs)
End Sub
```

```
Sub Session_End(ByVal sender As Object, ByVal e As EventArgs)
End Sub
</script>
```

Looks can be deceiving, however. At runtime, the code within this <script> block is assembled into a class type deriving from System.Web.HttpApplication. If you have a background in ASP.NET 1.*x*, you may recall that the Global.asax code-behind file literally did define a class deriving from HttpApplication.

As mentioned, the members defined inside Global.asax are in event handlers that allow you to interact with application-level (and session-level) events. Table 27-1 documents the role of each member.

Table 27-1. *Core Types of the* System.Web *Namespace*

Event Handler	Meaning in Life
Application_Start()	This event handler is called the very first time the web application is launched. Thus, this event will fire exactly once over the lifetime of a web application. This is an ideal place to define application-level data used throughout your web application.
Application_End()	This event handler is called when the application is shutting down. This will occur when the last user times out or if you manually shut down the application via IIS.
Session_Start()	This event handler is fired when a new user logs on to your application. Here you may establish any user-specific data points.
Session_End()	This event handler is fired when a user's session has terminated (typically through a predefined timeout).
Application_Error()	This is a global error handler that will be called when an unhandled exception is thrown by the web application.

The Global Last Chance Exception Event Handler

First, let me point out the role of the Application_Error() event handler. Recall that a specific page may handle the Error event to process any unhandled exception that occurred within the scope of the page itself. In a similar light, the Application_Error() event handler is the final place to handle an exception that was not handled by a given page. As with the page-level Error event, you are able to access the specific System.Exception using the inherited Server property:

```
Sub Application_Error(ByVal sender As Object, ByVal e As EventArgs)
  ' Obtain the unhandled error.
  Dim ex As Exception = Server.GetLastError()

  ' Process error here...

  ' Clear error when finished.
  Server.ClearError()
End Sub
```

Given that the Application_Error() event handler is the last-chance exception handler for your web application, it is quite common to implement this method in such a way that the user is transferred to a predefined error page on the server. Other common duties may include sending an e-mail to the web administrator (via the types within the System.Web.Mail namespace), writing to an external error log, or what have you.

The HttpApplication Base Class

As mentioned, the Global.asax script is dynamically generated into a class deriving from the System.Web.HttpApplication base class, which supplies the same sort of functionality as the System.Web.UI.Page type. Table 27-2 documents the key members of interest.

Table 27-2. *Key Members Defined by the* System.Web.HttpApplication *Type*

Property	Meaning in Life
Application	This property allows you to interact with application-level variables, using the exposed HttpApplicationState type.
Request	This property allows you to interact with the incoming HTTP request (via HttpRequest).
Response	This property allows you to interact with the incoming HTTP response (via HttpResponse).
Server	This property gets the intrinsic server object for the current request (via HttpServerUtility).
Session	This property allows you to interact with session-level variables, using the exposed HttpSessionState type.

Again, given that the Global.asax file does not explicitly document that HttpApplication is the underlying base class, it is important to remember that all of the rules of the "is-a" relationship do indeed apply. For example, if you were to apply the dot operator to the MyBase keyword within any of the members within Global.asax, you would find you have immediate access to all members of the chain of inheritance, as you see in Figure 27-3.

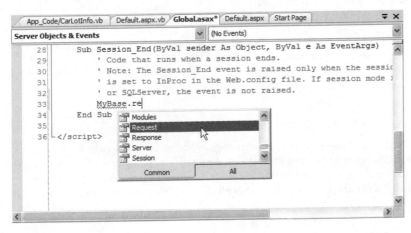

Figure 27-3. *Remember that* HttpApplication *is the parent of the type lurking within* Global.asax.

Understanding the Application/Session Distinction

Under ASP.NET, application state is maintained by an instance of the HttpApplicationState type. This class enables you to share global information across all users (and all pages) who are logged on to your ASP.NET application. Not only can application data be shared by all users on your site, but also if the value of an application-level data point changes, the new value is seen by all users on their next postback.

On the other hand, session state is used to remember information for a specific user (again, such as items in a shopping cart). Physically, a user's session state is represented by the HttpSessionState class type. When a new user logs on to an ASP.NET web application, the runtime will automatically assign that user a new session ID, which by default will expire after 20 minutes of inactivity. Thus, if 20,000 users are logged on to your site, you have 20,000 distinct HttpSessionState objects, each of which is automatically assigned a unique session ID. The relationship between a web application and web sessions is shown in Figure 27-4.

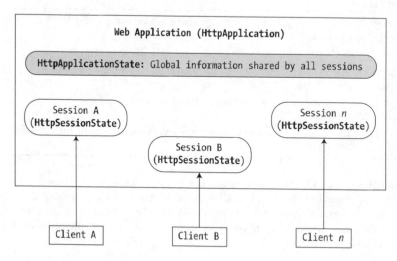

Figure 27-4. *The application/session state distinction*

As you may know, under classic ASP, application-and session-state data is represented using distinct COM objects (e.g., Application and Session). Under ASP.NET, Page-derived types as well as the HttpApplication type make use of identically named properties (i.e., Application and Session), which expose the underlying HttpApplicationState and HttpSessionState types.

Maintaining Application-level State Data

The HttpApplicationState type enables developers to share global information across multiple sessions in an ASP.NET application. For example, you may wish to maintain an application-wide connection string that can be used by all pages, a common DataSet used by multiple pages, or any other piece of data that needs to be accessed on an application-wide scale. Table 27-3 describes some core members of this type.

Table 27-3. *Members of the* HttpApplicationState *Type*

Members	Meaning in Life
AllKeys	This property returns an array of System.String types that represent all the names in the HttpApplicationState type.
Count	This property gets the number of item objects in the HttpApplicationState type.
Add()	This method allows you to add a new name/value pair into the HttpApplicationState type. Do note that this method is typically *not* used in favor of the indexer of the HttpApplicationState class.

Members	Meaning in Life
Clear()	This method deletes all items in the HttpApplicationState type. This is functionally equivalent to the RemoveAll() method.
Lock() Unlock()	These two methods are used when you wish to alter a set of application variables in a thread-safe manner.
RemoveAll() Remove() RemoveAt()	These methods remove a specific item (by string name) within the HttpApplicationState type. RemoveAt() removes the item via a numerical indexer.

To illustrate working with application state, create a new ASP.NET web application named AppState and insert a new Global.asax file. When you create data members that can be shared among all active sessions, you need to establish a set of name/value pairs. In most cases, the most natural place to do so is within the Application_Start() event handler of the HttpApplication-derived type, for example:

```
Sub Application_Start(ByVal sender As Object, ByVal e As EventArgs)
  ' Set up some application variables.
  Application("SalesPersonOfTheMonth") = "Chucky"
  Application("CurrentCarOnSale") = "Colt"
  Application("MostPopularColorOnLot") = "Black"
End Sub
```

During the lifetime of your web application (which is to say, until the web application is manually shut down or until the final user times out), any user (on any page) may access these values as necessary. Assume you have a page that will display the current discount car within a Label via a button Click event handler:

```
Protected Sub btnShowCarOnSale_Click(ByVal sender As Object, _
  ByVal e As System.EventArgs) Handles btnShowCarDiscount.Click
    lblCurrCarOnSale.Text = String.Format("Sale on {0}'s today!", _
    CType(Application("CurrentCarOnSale"), String))
End Sub
```

Like the ViewState property, notice how you should cast the value returned from the HttpApplicationState type into the correct underlying type as the Application property operates on general System.Object types.

Now, given that the HttpApplicationState type can hold any type, it should stand to reason that you can place custom types (or any .NET type) within your site's application state. Assume you would rather maintain the three current application variables within a strongly typed class named CarLotInfo:

```
Public Class CarLotInfo
  Public Sub New(ByVal sPerson As String, _
    ByVal saleCar As String, ByVal popularColor As String)
    salesPersonOfTheMonth = sPerson
    currentCarOnSale = saleCar
    mostPopularColorOnLot = popularColor
  End Sub
  ' Public for easy access.
  Public salesPersonOfTheMonth As String
  Public currentCarOnSale As String
  Public mostPopularColorOnLot As String
End Class
```

With this helper class in place, you could modify the Application_Start() event handler as follows:

```
Sub Application_Start(ByVal sender As Object, ByVal e As EventArgs)
  ' Place a custom object in the application data sector.
  Application("CarSiteInfo") = _
    New CarLotInfo("Chucky", "Colt", "Black")
End Sub
```

and then access the information using the public field data within a server-side `Click` event handler for a `Button` type named `btnShowAppVariables`:

```
Protected Sub btnShowAppVariables_Click(ByVal sender As Object, _
  ByVal e As System.EventArgs) Handles btnShowAppVariables.Click
  ' Get object from application variable.
  Dim appVars As CarLotInfo = _
  CType(Application("CarSiteInfo"), CarLotInfo)

  Dim appState As String = _
  String.Format("<li>Car on sale: {0}</li>", _
  appVars.currentCarOnSale)

  appState &= _
    String.Format("<li>Most popular color: {0}</li>", _
    appVars.mostPopularColorOnLot)
  appState &= _
    String.Format("<li>Big shot SalesPerson: {0}</li>", _
    appVars.salesPersonOfTheMonth)
  lblAppVariables.Text = appState
End Sub
```

Given that the current car-on-sale data is now exposed from a custom class type, your `btnShowCarOnSale` `Click` event handler would also need to be updated like so:

```
Protected Sub btnShowCarOnSale_Click(ByVal sender As Object, _
ByVal e As System.EventArgs) Handles btnShowCarOnSale.Click
  lblCurrCarOnSale.Text = String.Format("Sale on {0}'s today!", _
  CType(Application("CarSiteInfo"), CarLotInfo).currentCarOnSale)
End Sub
```

If you were now to run this page, you would find that a list of each application variable is displayed on the page's `Label` types, as displayed in Figure 27-5.

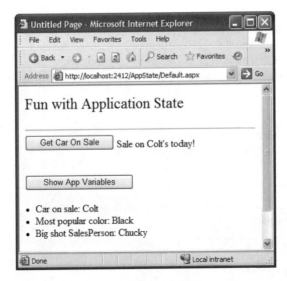

Figure 27-5. *Displaying application data*

Modifying Application Data

You may programmatically update or delete any or all members using members of the
HttpApplicationState type during the execution of your web application. For example, to delete
a specific item, simply call the Remove() method. If you wish to destroy all application-level data,
call RemoveAll():

```
Private Sub CleanAppData()
   ' Remove a single item via string name.
   Application.Remove("SomeItemIDontNeed")

   ' Destroy all application data!
   Application.RemoveAll()
End Sub
```

If you wish to simply change the value of an existing application-level variable, you only need
to make a new assignment to the data item in question. Assume your page now supports a new Button
type that allows your user to change the current hotshot salesperson by reading in a value from
a TextBox named txtNewSP. The Click event handler is as you would expect:

```
Protected Sub btnSetNewSP_Click(ByVal sender As Object, _
   ByVal e As System.EventArgs) Handles btnSetNewSP.Click
   ' Set the new Salesperson.
   CType(Application("CarSiteInfo"), CarLotInfo).salesPersonOfTheMonth _
      = txtNewSP.Text
End Sub
```

If you run the web application, you will find that the application-level variable has been updated.
Furthermore, given that application variables are accessible from all user sessions, if you were to
launch three or four instances of your web browser, you would find that if one instance changes the
current hotshot salesperson, each of the other browsers displays the new value on postback.

Understand that if you have a situation where a set of application-level variables must be updated as a unit, you risk the possibility of data corruption (given that it is technically possible that an application-level data point may be changed while another user is attempting to access it!). While you could take the long road and manually lock down the logic using threading primitives of the System.Threading namespace, the HttpApplicationState type has two methods, Lock() and Unlock(), that automatically ensure thread safety:

```
' Safely access related application data.
Application.Lock()
Application("SalesPersonOfTheMonth") = "Maxine"
Application("CurrentBonusedEmployee") = Application("SalesPersonOfTheMonth")
Application.Unlock()
```

Note Much like the VB 2005 SyncLock statement, if an exception occurs after the call to Lock() but before the call to Unlock(), the lock will automatically be released.

Handling Web Application Shutdown

The HttpApplicationState type is designed to maintain the values of the items it contains until one of two situations occurs: the last user on your site times out (or manually logs out) or someone manually shuts down the website via IIS. In each case, the Application_End() method of the HttpApplication-derived type will automatically be called. Within this event handler, you are able to perform whatever sort of cleanup code is necessary:

```
Sub Application_End(ByVal sender As Object, ByVal e As EventArgs)
    ' Write current application variables
    ' to a database or whatever else you need to do...
End Sub
```

Source Code The AppState files are included under the Chapter 27 subdirectory.

Working with the Application Cache

ASP.NET provides a second and more flexible manner to handle application-wide data. As you recall, the values within the HttpApplicationState object remain in memory as long as your web application is alive and kicking. Sometimes, however, you may wish to maintain a piece of application data only for a specific period of time. For example, you may wish to obtain an ADO.NET DataSet that is valid for only five minutes. After that time, you may want to obtain a fresh DataSet to account for possible database updates. While it is technically possible to build this infrastructure using HttpApplicationState and some sort of handcrafted monitor, your task is greatly simplified using the ASP.NET application cache.

As suggested by its name, the ASP.NET System.Web.Caching.Cache object (which is accessible via the Context.Cache property) allows you to define an object that is accessible by all users (from all pages) for a fixed amount of time. In its simplest form, interacting with the cache looks identical to interacting with the HttpApplicationState type:

```
' Add an item to the cache.
' This item will *not* expire.
Context.Cache("SomeStringItem") = "This is the string item"

' Get item from the cache.
Dim s As String = CType(Context.Cache("SomeStringItem"), String)
```

■Note If you wish to access the `Cache` from within `Global.asax`, you are required to use the `Context` property. However, if you are within the scope of a `System.Web.UI.Page`-derived type, you can make use of the `Cache` object directly.

Now, understand that if you have no interest in automatically updating (or removing) an application-level data point (as seen here), the `Cache` object is of little benefit, as you can directly use the `HttpApplicationState` type. However, when you do wish to have a data point destroyed after a fixed point of time—and optionally be informed when this occurs—the `Cache` type is extremely helpful.

The `System.Web.Caching.Cache` class defines only a small number of members beyond the type's indexer. For example, the `Add()` method can be used to insert a new item into the cache that is not currently defined (if the specified item is already present, `Add()` does nothing). The `Insert()` method will also place a member into the cache. If, however, the item is currently defined, `Insert()` will replace the current item with the new type. Given that this is most often the behavior you will desire, I'll focus on the `Insert()` method exclusively.

Fun with Data Caching

Let's see an example. To begin, create a new ASP.NET web application named `CacheState` and insert a `Global.asax` file. Like an application-level variable maintained by the `HttpApplicationState` type, the `Cache` may hold any `System.Object`-derived type and is often populated within the `Application_Start()` event handler. For this example, the goal is to automatically update the contents of a `DataSet` every 15 seconds. The `DataSet` in question will contain the current set of records from the Inventory table of the Cars database created during our discussion of ADO.NET. Given these stats, update your Global class type like so (code analysis to follow):

```
<%@ Application Language="VB" %>
<%@ Import Namespace = "System.Data.SqlClient" %>
<%@ Import Namespace = "System.Data" %>

<script runat="server">
  ' Define a shared Cache member variable.
  Shared theCache As Cache

  Sub Application_Start(ByVal sender As Object, ByVal e As EventArgs)
    ' First assign the shared 'theCache' variable.
    theCache = Context.Cache

    ' Add a DataSet to the cache via a helper function.
    AddDataSetToCache()
  End Sub

  Shared Sub AddDataSetToCache()
    ' When the application starts up,
    ' read the current records in the
    ' Inventory table of the Cars DB.
    Dim cn As SqlConnection = New SqlConnection _
      ("data source=localhost;initial catalog=Cars; user id ='sa';pwd=''")

    Dim dAdapt As SqlDataAdapter = _
      New SqlDataAdapter("Select * From Inventory", cn)

    Dim theCars As DataSet = New DataSet()
    dAdapt.Fill(theCars, "Inventory")
```

```
    ' Now store DataSet in the cache.
    theCache.Insert("AppDataSet", _
        theCars, Nothing, _
        DateTime.Now.AddSeconds(15), _
        Cache.NoSlidingExpiration, _
        CacheItemPriority.Default, _
        New CacheItemRemovedCallback(AddressOf UpdateCarInventory))
End Sub

' The target for the CacheItemRemovedCallback delegate.
Shared Sub UpdateCarInventory(ByVal key As String, ByVal item As Object, _
    ByVal reason As CacheItemRemovedReason)
    Dim cn As SqlConnection = New SqlConnection _
        ("data source=localhost;initial catalog=Cars; user id ='sa';pwd=''")

    Dim dAdapt As SqlDataAdapter = _
        New SqlDataAdapter("Select * From Inventory", cn)

    Dim theCars As DataSet = New DataSet()
    dAdapt.Fill(theCars, "Inventory")

    ' Now store DataSet in the cache.
    theCache.Insert("AppDataSet", _
        theCars, Nothing, _
        DateTime.Now.AddSeconds(15), _
        Cache.NoSlidingExpiration, _
        CacheItemPriority.Default, _
        New CacheItemRemovedCallback(AddressOf UpdateCarInventory))
End Sub
...
</script>
```

First, notice that the Global type has defined a shared Cache member variable. The reason is that you have defined two shared members (UpdateCarInventory() and AddDataSetToCache()) is that each method needs access the Cache (recall that shared members do not have access to inherited members, therefore you can't use the Context property!).

Inside the Application_Start() event handler, you fill a DataSet and place the object within the application cache. As you would guess, the Context.Cache.Insert() method has been overloaded a number of times. Here, you supply a value for each possible parameter. Consider the following commented call to Add():

```
' Note!  It is a syntax error to have comments after a line
' continuation character, but this is the cleanest way to show each param.
theCache.Add("AppDataSet", _         ' Name used to identify item in the cache.
    theCars, _                       ' Object to put in the cache.
    Nothing, _                       ' Any dependencies for this object?
    DateTime.Now.AddSeconds(15), _   ' How long item will be in cache.
    Cache.NoSlidingExpiration, _     ' Fixed or sliding time?
    CacheItemPriority.Default, _     ' Priority level of cache item.
    ' Delegate for CacheItemRemove event
    New CacheItemRemovedCallback(UpdateCarInventory))
```

The first two parameters simply make up the name/value pair of the item. The third parameter allows you to define a CacheDependency type (which is Nothing in this case, as you do not have any other entities in the cache that are dependent on the DataSet).

> **Note** The ability to define a CacheDependency type is quite interesting. For example, you could establish a dependency between a member and an external file. If the contents of the file were to change, the type can be automatically updated. Check out the .NET Framework 2.0 documentation for further details.

The next three parameters are used to define the amount of time the item will be allowed to remain in the application cache and its level of priority. Here, you specify the read-only Cache. NoSlidingExpiration field, which informs the cache that the specified time limit (15 seconds) is absolute. Finally, and most important for this example, you create a new CacheItemRemovedCallback delegate type, and pass in the name of the method to call when the DataSet is purged. As you can see from the signature of the UpdateCarInventory() method, the CacheItemRemovedCallback delegate can only call methods that match the following signature:

```
Sub UpdateCarInventory(ByVal key As String, ByVal item As Object, _
  ByVal reason As CacheItemRemovedReason)
...
End Sub
```

So, at this point, when the application starts up, the DataSet is populated and cached. Every 15 seconds, the DataSet is purged, updated, and reinserted into the cache. To see the effects of doing this, you need to create a Page that allows for some degree of user interaction.

Modifying the *.aspx File

Update the UI of your initial *.aspx file as shown in Figure 27-6.

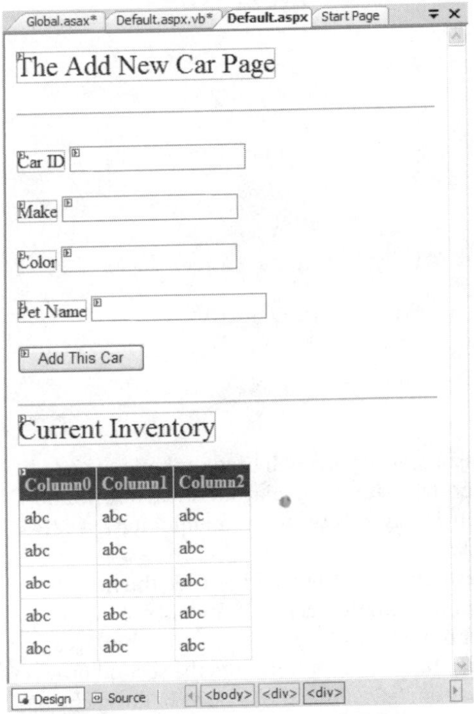

Figure 27-6. *The cache application GUI*

In the page's Load event handler, configure your GridView to display the current contents of the cached DataSet the first time the user posts to the page (be sure to import the System.Data and System.Data.SqlClient namespaces within your *.vb code file):

```
Protected Sub Page_Load(ByVal sender As Object, _
  ByVal e As System.EventArgs) Handles Me.Load
  If Not IsPostBack Then
    carsGridView.DataSource = CType(Cache("AppDataSet"), DataSet)
    carsGridView.DataBind()
  End If
End Sub
```

In the Click event handler of the Add This Car button, insert the new record into the Cars database using an ADO.NET SqlCommand object. Once the record has been inserted, call a helper function named RefreshGrid(), which will update the UI via an ADO.NET SqlDataReader (so don't forget to "use" the System.Data.SqlClient namespace). Here are the methods in question:

```
Protected Sub btnAddCar_Click(ByVal sender As Object, ByVal e As EventArgs)
  ' Update the Inventory table
  ' and call RefreshGrid().
  Dim cn As SqlConnection = New SqlConnection()
  cn.ConnectionString = "User ID=sa;Pwd=;Initial Catalog=Cars;Data Source=(local)"
  cn.Open()
  Dim sql As String
  Dim cmd As SqlCommand
  ' Insert new Car.
  sql = String.Format( _
    "Insert Into Inventory(CarID, Make, Color, PetName) Values" & _
    "('{0}', '{1}', '{2}', '{3}')", _
    txtCarID.Text, txtCarMake.Text, txtCarColor.Text, txtCarPetName.Text)
  cmd = New SqlCommand(sql, cn)
  cmd.ExecuteNonQuery()
  cn.Close()
  RefreshGrid()
End Sub

Private Sub RefreshGrid()
  ' Populate grid.
  Dim cn As SqlConnection = New SqlConnection()
  cn.ConnectionString = "User ID=sa;Pwd=;Initial Catalog=Cars;Data Source=(local)"
  cn.Open()
  Dim cmd As SqlCommand = New SqlCommand("Select * from Inventory", cn)
  carsGridView.DataSource = cmd.ExecuteReader()
  carsGridView.DataBind()
  cn.Close()
End Sub
```

Now, to test the use of the cache, launch two instances of your web browser and navigate to this *.aspx page. At this point, you should see that both DataGrids display identical information. From one instance of the browser, add a new Car. Obviously, this results in an updated GridView viewable from the browser that initiated the postback.

In the second browser instance, click the Refresh button. You should not see the new item, given that the Page_Load event handler is reading directly from the cache. (If you did see the value, the 15 seconds had already expired. Either type faster or increase the amount of time the DataSet will remain in the cache.) Wait a few seconds and click the Refresh button from the second browser instance one more time. Now you should see the new item, given that the DataSet in the cache has expired and the CacheItemRemovedCallback delegate target method has automatically updated the cached DataSet.

As you can see, the major benefit of the Cache type is that you can ensure that when a member is removed, you have a chance to respond. In this example, you certainly could avoid using the Cache and simply have the Page_Load() event handler always read directly from the Cars database. Nevertheless, the point should be clear: the cache allows you to automatically refresh data using the cache mechanism.

■**Note** Unlike the HttpApplicationState type, the Cache class does not support Lock() and Unlock() methods. If you need to update interrelated items, you will need to directly make use of the types within the System.Threading namespace or the VB 2005 lock keyword.

■**Source Code** The CacheState files are included under the Chapter 27 subdirectory.

Maintaining Session Data

So much for our examination of application-level and cached data. Next, let's check out the role of per-user data stores. As mentioned earlier, a *session* is little more than a given user's interaction with a web application, which is represented via a unique HttpSessionState object. To maintain stateful information for a particular user, the HttpApplication-derived type and any System.Web.UI.Page-derived types may access the Session property. The classic example of the need to maintain per-user data would be an online shopping cart. Again, if ten people all log on to an online store, each individual will maintain a unique set of items that she (may) intend to purchase.

When a new user logs on to your web application, the .NET runtime will automatically assign the user a unique session ID, which is used to identify the user in question. Each session ID is assigned a custom instance of the HttpSessionState type to hold on to user-specific data. Inserting or retrieving session data is syntactically identical to manipulating application data, for example:

```vb
' Add/retrieve a session variable for current user.
Session("DesiredCarColor") = "Green"
Dim color As String = CType(Session("DesiredCarColor"), String)
```

The HttpApplication-derived type allows you to intercept the beginning and end of a session via the Session_Start() and Session_End() event handlers. Within Session_Start(), you can freely create any per-user data items, while Session_End() allows you to perform any work you may need to do when the user's session has terminated:

```vb
<%@ Application Language="VB" %>
<script runat="server">
...
  Sub Session_Start(ByVal sender As Object, ByVal e As EventArgs)
    ' Code that runs when a new session is started
  End Sub

  Sub Session_End(ByVal sender As Object, ByVal e As EventArgs)
    ' Code that runs when a session ends.
    ' Note: The Session_End event is raised
    ' only when the sessionstate mode
    ' is set to InProc in the Web.config file.
    ' If session mode is set to StateServer
    ' or SQLServer, the event is not raised.
  End Sub
</script>
```

■**Note** The code comments that are placed within the `Session_End()` event handler will make much more sense when we examine the role of the ASP.NET session state server later in this chapter.

Like the `HttpApplicationState` type, the `HttpSessionState` may hold any `System.Object`-derived type, including your custom classes. For example, assume you have a new web application (SessionState) that defines a class named `UserShoppingCart`:

```
Public Class UserShoppingCart
  Public desiredCar As String
  Public desiredCarColor As String
  Public downPayment As Single
  Public isLeasing As Boolean
  Public dateOfPickUp As DateTime

  Public Overrides Function ToString() As String
    Return String.Format("Car: {0}<br>Color: {1}<br>" & _
      "$ Down: {2}<br>Lease: {3} <br>Pick-up Date: {4}", _
      desiredCar, desiredCarColor, downPayment, _
      isLeasing, dateOfPickUp.ToShortDateString())
  End Function
End Class
```

Within the `Session_Start()` event handler, you can now assign each user a new instance of the `UserShoppingCart` class:

```
Sub Session_Start(ByVal sender As Object, ByVal e As EventArgs)
  Session("UserShoppingCartInfo") = New UserShoppingCart()
End Sub
```

As the user traverses your web pages, you are able to pluck out the `UserShoppingCart` instance and fill the fields with user-specific data. For example, assume you have a simple `*.aspx` page that defines a set of input widgets that correspond to each field of the `UserShoppingCart` type and a `Button` used to set the values and two `Labels` that will be used to display the user's session ID and session information (see Figure 27-7).

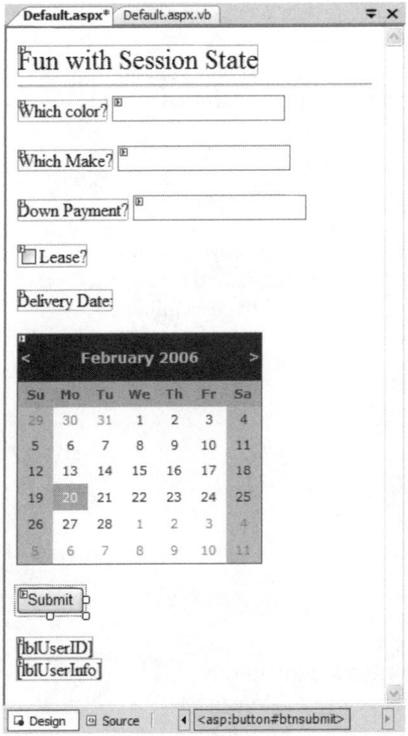

Figure 27-7. *The session application GUI*

The server-side `Click` event handler is straightforward (scrape out values from `TextBox`es and display the shopping cart data on a `Label` type):

```
Partial Class _Default
  Inherits System.Web.UI.Page

  Protected Sub btnSubmit_Click(ByVal sender As Object, _
    ByVal e As System.EventArgs) Handles btnSubmit.Click
    ' Set current user prefs.
    Try
      Dim u As UserShoppingCart = _
      CType(Session("UserShoppingCartInfo"), UserShoppingCart)
      u.dateOfPickUp = myCalendar.SelectedDate
      u.desiredCar = txtCarMake.Text
      u.desiredCarColor = txtCarColor.Text
      u.downPayment = Single.Parse(txtDownPayment.Text)
      u.isLeasing = chkIsLeasing.Checked
      lblUserInfo.Text = u.ToString()
      Session("UserShoppingCartInfo") = u
    Catch ex As Exception
      lblUserInfo.Text = ex.Message
    End Try
  End Sub
End Class
```

Within `Session_End()`, you may wish to persist the fields of the `UserShoppingCart` to a database or whatnot (however, as you will see at the conclusion of this chapter, the ASP.NET 2.0 profiles API will do so automatically). In any case, if you were to launch two or three instances of your browser of choice, you would find that each user is able to build a custom shopping cart that maps to his unique instance of `HttpSessionState`.

Additional Members of HttpSessionState

The `HttpSessionState` class defines a number of other members of interest beyond the type indexer. First, the `SessionID` property will return the current user's unique ID. If you wish to view the automatically assigned session ID for this example, handle your `Load` event of your page as follows:

```
Protected Sub Page_Load(ByVal sender As Object, _
  ByVal e As System.EventArgs) Handles Me.Load
  If Not IsPostBack Then
    lblUserID.Text = String.Format("Here is your ID: {0}", _
      Session.SessionID)
  End If
End Sub
```

The `Remove()` and `RemoveAll()` methods may be used to clear items out of the user's instance of `HttpSessionState`:

```
Session.Remove("SomeItemWeDontNeedAnymore")
```

The `HttpSessionState` type also defines a set of members that control the expiration policy of the current session. Again, by default each user has 20 minutes of inactivity before the `HttpSessionState` object is destroyed. Thus, if a user enters your web application (and therefore obtains a unique session ID), but does not return to the site within 20 minutes, the runtime assumes the user is no longer interested and destroys all session data for that user. You are free to change this default 20-minute expiration value on a user-by-user basis using the `Timeout` property. The most common place to do so is within the scope of your `Global.Session_Start()` method:

```
Sub Session_Start(ByVal sender As Object, ByVal e As EventArgs)
  ' Each user has 5 minutes of inactivity.
  Session.Timeout = 5
  Session("UserShoppingCartInfo") _
    = New UserShoppingCart()
End Sub
```

Note If you do not need to tweak each user's `Timeout` value, you are able to alter the 20-minute default for all users via the `Timeout` attribute of the `<sessionState>` element within the `web.config` file (examined at the end of this chapter).

The benefit of the `Timeout` property is that you have the ability to assign specific timeout values discretely for each user. For example, imagine you have created a web application that allows users to pay cash for a given membership level. You may say that Gold members should time out within one hour, while Wood members should get only 30 seconds. This possibility begs the question, how can you remember user-specific information (such as the current membership level) across web visits? One possible answer is through the user of the `HttpCookie` type. (And speaking of cookies . . .)

Source Code   The SessionState files are included under the Chapter 27 subdirectory.

Understanding Cookies

The next state management technique examined here is the act of persisting data within a *cookie*, which is often realized as a text file (or set of files) on the user's machine. When a user logs on to a given site, the browser checks to see whether the user's machine has a cookie file for the URL in question and, if so, appends this data to the HTTP request.

The receiving server-side web page could then read the cookie data to create a GUI that may be based on the current user preferences. I am sure you've noticed that when you visit one of your favorite websites, it somehow "just knows" the sort of content you wish to see. The reason (in part) may have to do with a cookie stored on your computer that contains information relevant to a given website.

The exact location of your cookie files will depend on which browser you happen to be using. For those using Microsoft Internet Explorer, cookies are stored by default under C:\ Documents and Settings\ <loggedOnUser>\Cookies, as shown in Figure 27-8.

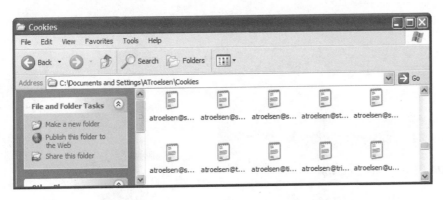

Figure 27-8. *Cookie data as persisted under Microsoft Internet Explorer*

The contents of a given cookie file will obviously vary among URLs, but keep in mind that they are ultimately text files. Thus, cookies are a horrible choice when you wish to maintain sensitive information about the current user (such as a credit card number, password, or whatnot). Even if you take the time to encrypt the data, a crafty hacker could decrypt the value and use it for purely evil pursuits. In any case, cookies do play a role in the development of web applications, so let's check out how ASP.NET handles this particular state management technique.

Creating Cookies

First of all, understand that ASP.NET cookies can be configured to be either persistent or temporary. A *persistent* cookie is typically regarded as the classic definition of cookie data, in that the set of name/ value pairs is physically saved to the user's hard drive. *Temporary* cookies (also termed *session cookies*) contain the same data as a persistent cookie, but the name/value pairs are never saved to the user's machine; rather, they exist *only* within the HTTP header. Once the user logs off your site, all data contained within the session cookie is destroyed.

Note Most browsers support cookies of up to 4,096 bytes. Because of this size limit, cookies are best used to store small amounts of data, such as a user ID that can be used to identify the user and pull details from a database.

The System.Web.HttpCookie type is the class that represents the server side of the cookie data (persistent or temporary). When you wish to create a new cookie, you access the Response.Cookies property. Once the new HttpCookie is inserted into the internal collection, the name/value pairs flow back to the browser within the HTTP header.

To check out cookie behavior firsthand, create a new ASP.NET web application (CookieStateApp) and create the UI displayed in Figure 27-9.

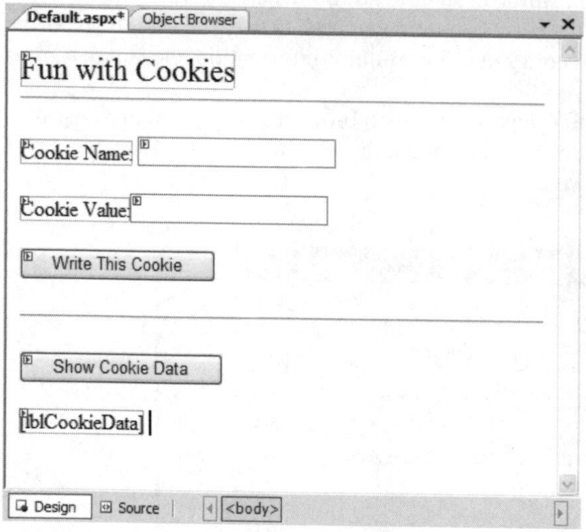

Figure 27-9. *The UI of CookiesStateApp*

Within the Button's Click event handler, build a new HttpCookie and insert it into the Cookie collection exposed from the HttpRequest.Cookies property. Be very aware that the data will not persist itself to the user's hard drive unless you explicitly set an expiration date using the HttpCookie.Expires property. Thus, the following implementation will create a temporary cookie that is destroyed when the user shuts down the browser:

```
Protected Sub btnNewCookie_Click(ByVal sender As Object, _
  ByVal e As System.EventArgs) Handles btnNewCookie.Click
  ' Make a new (temp) cookie.
  Dim theCookie As HttpCookie = _
    New HttpCookie(txtCookieName.Text, _
    txtCookieValue.Text)
  Response.Cookies.Add(theCookie)
End Sub
```

However, the following generates a persistent cookie that will expire on March 26, 2009:

```
Protected Sub btnNewCookie_Click(ByVal sender As Object, _
  ByVal e As System.EventArgs) Handles btnNewCookie.Click
  ' Make a new (persistent) cookie.
  Dim theCookie As HttpCookie = _
    New HttpCookie(txtCookieName.Text, _
    txtCookieValue.Text)
  theCookie.Expires = DateTime.Parse("03/26/2009")
  Response.Cookies.Add(theCookie)
End Sub
```

If you were to run this application and insert some cookie data, the browser automatically persists this data to disk. When you open this text file saved under your cookie folder, you will see something similar to Figure 27-10.

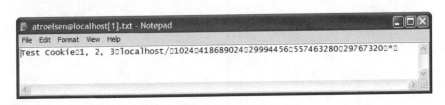

Figure 27-10. *The persistent cookie data*

Reading Incoming Cookie Data

Recall that the browser is the entity in charge of accessing persisted cookies when navigating to a previously visited page. To interact with the incoming cookie data under ASP.NET, access the HttpRequest.Cookies property. To illustrate, if you were to update your current UI with the means to obtain current cookie data via a Button widget, you could iterate over each name/value pair and present the information within a Label widget:

```
Protected Sub btnShowCookie_Click(ByVal sender As Object, _
  ByVal e As System.EventArgs) Handles btnShowCookie.Click
  Dim cookieData As String = ""
  For Each s As String In Request.Cookies
    cookieData += String.Format _
      ("<li><b>Name</b>: {0}, <b>Value</b>: {1}</li>", _
      s, Request.Cookies(s).Value)
  Next
  lblCookieData.Text = cookieData
End Sub
```

If you now run the application and click your new button, you will find that the cookie data has indeed been sent by your browser (see Figure 27-11).

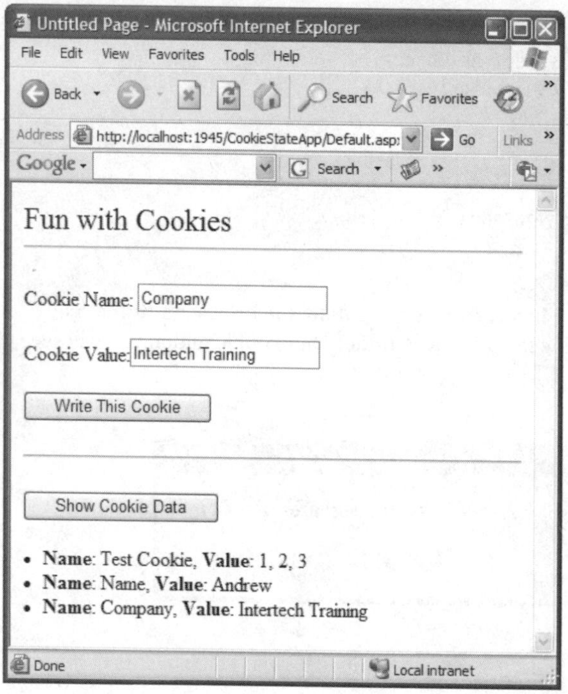

Figure 27-11. *Viewing cookie data*

■**Source Code** The CookieStateApp files are included under the Chapter 27 subdirectory.

The Role of the <sessionState> Element

At this point in the chapter, you have examined numerous ways to remember information about your users. As you have seen, view state and application, cache, session, and cookie data are manipulated in more or less the same way (via a class indexer). As you have also seen, the HttpApplication type is often used to intercept and respond to events that occur during your web application's lifetime.

By default, ASP.NET will store session state using an in-process *.dll hosted by the ASP.NET worker process (aspnet_wp.exe). Like any *.dll, the plus side is that access to the information is as fast as possible. However, the downside is that if this AppDomain crashes (for whatever reason), all of the user's state data is destroyed. Furthermore, when you store state data as an in-process *.dll, you cannot interact with a networked web farm. This default behavior is recorded in the <sessionState> element of your web.config file like so:

```
<sessionState
  mode="InProc"
  stateConnectionString="tcpip=127.0.0.1:42626"
  sqlConnectionString="data source=127.0.0.1;Trusted_Connection=yes"
  cookieless="false"
  timeout="20"
/>
```

This default mode of storage works just fine if your web application is hosted by a single web server. As you might guess, however, this model is not ideal for a farm of web servers, given that session state is "trapped" within a given AppDomain.

Storing Session Data in the ASP.NET Session State Server

Under ASP.NET, you can instruct the runtime to host the session state *.dll in a surrogate process named the ASP.NET session state server (aspnet_state.exe). When you do so, you are able to offload the *.dll from aspnet_wp.exe into a unique *.exe, which can be located on any machine within the web farm. Even if you intend to run the aspnet_state.exe process on the same machine as the web server, you do gain the benefit of partitioning the state data in a unique process (as it is more durable).

To make use of the session state server, the first step in doing so is to start the aspnet_state.exe Windows service on the target machine. To do so at the command line, simply type

```
net start aspnet_state
```

Alternatively, you can start aspnet_state.exe using the Services applet accessed from the Administrative Tools folder of the Control Panel, as shown in Figure 27-12.

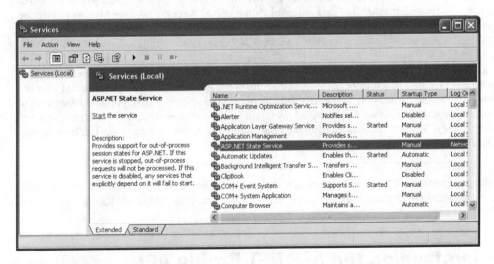

Figure 27-12. *The Services applet*

The key benefit of this approach is that you can configure aspnet_state.exe to start automatically when the machine boots up using the Properties window. In any case, once the session state server is running, alter the <sessionState> element of your Web.config file as follows:

```
<sessionState
  mode="StateServer"
  stateConnectionString="tcpip=127.0.0.1:42626"
  sqlConnectionString="data source=127.0.0.1;Trusted_Connection=yes"
  cookieless="false"
  timeout="20"
/>
```

Here, the mode attribute has been set to StateServer. That's it! At this point, the CLR will host session-centric data within aspnet_state.exe. In this way, if the AppDomain hosting the web application crashes, the session data is preserved. Notice as well that the <sessionState> element can also support a stateConnectionString attribute. The default TCP/IP address value (127.0.0.1) points to the local machine. If you would rather have the .NET runtime use the `aspnet_state.exe` service located on another networked machine (again, think web farms), you are free to update this value.

Storing Session Data in a Dedicated Database

Finally, if you require the highest degree of isolation and durability for your web application, you may choose to have the runtime store all your session state data within Microsoft SQL Server. The appropriate update to the `web.config` file is simple:

```
<sessionState
  mode="SQLServer"
  stateConnectionString="tcpip=127.0.0.1:42626"
  sqlConnectionString="data source=127.0.0.1;Trusted_Connection=yes"
  cookieless="false"
  timeout="20"
/>
```

However, before you attempt to run the associated web application, you need to ensure that the target machine (specified by the `sqlConnectionString` attribute) has been properly configured. When you install the .NET Framework 2.0 SDK (or Visual Studio 2005), you will be provided with two files named `InstallSqlState.sql` and `UninstallSqlState.sql`, located by default under <%windir%>\Microsoft.NET\Framework\<version>. On the target machine, you must run the `InstallSqlState.sql` file using a tool such as the SQL Server Query Analyzer (which ships with Microsoft SQL Server).

Once this SQL script has executed, you will find a new SQL Server database has been created (ASPState) that contains a number of stored procedures called by the ASP.NET runtime and a set of tables used to store the session data itself (also, the tempdb database has been updated with a set of tables for swapping purposes). As you would guess, configuring your web application to store session data within SQL Server is the slowest of all possible options. The benefit is that user data is as durable as possible (even if the web server is rebooted).

■**Note** If you make use of the ASP.NET session state server or SQL Server to store your session data, you must make sure that any custom types placed in the `HttpSessionState` object have been marked with the `<Serializable>` attribute.

Understanding the ASP.NET Profile API

At this point in the chapter, you have examined numerous techniques that allow you to remember user-level and application-level bits of data. However, these techniques suffer from one major limitation: they only exist as long as the user is in session and the web application is running! However, many websites require the ability to persist user information across sessions. For example, perhaps you need to provide the ability for users to build an account on your site. Maybe you need to persist instances of a `ShoppingCart` class across sessions (for an online shopping site). Or perhaps you wish to persist basic user preferences (themes, etc.).

While you most certainly could build a custom database (with several stored procedures) to hold such information, you would then need to build a custom code library to interact with these database atoms. This is not necessarily a complex task, but the bottom line is that *you* are the individual in charge of building this sort of infrastructure. To help simplify matters, ASP.NET 2.0 ships with an out-of-the box user profile management API and database system for this very purpose. In addition to providing the necessary infrastructure, the profile API also allows you to define the data to be persisted directly within your `web.config` file (for purposes of simplification); however, you are also able to persist any `<Serializable>` type. Before we get too far ahead of ourselves, let's check out where the profile API will be storing the specified data.

The ASPNETDB Database

Recall that every ASP.NET 2.0 website built with Visual Studio 2005 automatically provides an App_Data subdirectory. By default, the profile API (as well as other services, such as the ASP.NET role membership provider) is configured to make use of a local SQL Server 2005 database named ASPNETDB.mdf, located within the App_Data folder. This default behavior is due to settings within the machine.config file for the .NET 2.0 installation on your machine. In fact, when your code base makes use of any ASP.NET service requiring the App_Data folder, the ASPNETDB.mdf data file will be automatically created on the fly if a copy does not currently exist.

If you would rather have the ASP.NET runtime communicate with an ASPNETDB.mdf file located on another networked machine, or you would rather install this database on an instance of MS SQL Server 7.0 (or higher), you will need to manually build ASPNETDB.mdf using the aspnet_regsql.exe command-line utility. Like any good command-line tool, aspnet_regsql.exe provides numerous options; however, if you run the tool with no arguments:

```
aspnet_regsql
```

you will launch a GUI-based wizard to help walk you though the process of creating and installing ASPNETDB.mdf on your machine (and version of SQL Server) of choice.

Now, assuming your site is not making use of a local copy of the database under the App_Data folder, the final step is to update your web.config file to point to the unique location of your ASPNETDB.mdf. Assume you have installed ASPNETDB.mdf on a machine named ProductionServer. The following (partial) web.config file (for a website named ShoppingCart) could be used to instruct the profile API where to find the necessary database items:

```
<configuration>
  <connectionStrings>
    <add name="SqlServices"
         connectionString ="Data Source=ProductionServer;Integrated
         Security=SSPI;Initial Catalog=aspnetdb;"
         providerName="System.Data.SqlClient"/>
  </connectionStrings>
  <system.web>
    <profile defaultProvider ="SqlProvider">
      <providers>
        <clear/>
        <add name="AspNetSqlProfileProvider"
             connectionStringName="LocalSqlServer"
             applicationName="ShoppingCart"
             type="System.Web.Profile.SqlProfileProvider, System.Web,
              Version=2.0.0.0,
              Culture=neutral, PublicKeyToken=b03f5f7f11d50a3a" />
      </providers>
    </profile>
  </system.web>
</configuration>
```

Like most *.config files, this is much worse than it looks. Basically we are defining a <connectionString> element with the necessary data, followed by a named instance of the SqlProfileProvider (this is the default provider used regardless of physical location of the ASPNETDB.mdf). If you require further information regarding this configuration syntax, be sure to check out the .NET Framework 2.0 SDK documentation.

■**Note** For simplicity, I will be assuming that you will simply make use of the autogenerated ASPNETDB.mdf database located under your web application's App_Data subdirectory.

Defining a User Profile Within web.config

As mentioned, a user profile is defined within a `web.config` file. The really nifty aspect of this approach is that you can interact with this profile in a strongly typed manner using the inherited `Profile` property. To illustrate this, create a new website named FunWithProfiles and open your `web.config` file for editing. Our goal is to make a profile that models the home address of the users who are in session as well as the total number of times they have posted to this site. Not surprisingly, profile data is defined within a `<profile>` element using a set of name/data type pairs. Consider the following profile, which is created within the scope of the `<system.web>` element:

```
<profile>
  <properties>
    <add name="StreetAddress" type="System.String" />
    <add name="City" type="System.String" />
    <add name="State" type="System.String" />
    <add name="TotalPost" type="System.Int32" />
  </properties>
</profile>
```

Here, we have specified a name and CLR data type for each item in the profile (of course, we could add additional items for ZIP code, name, and so forth, but I am sure you get the idea). Strictly speaking, the type attribute is optional; however, the default is a `System.String`. As you would guess, there are many other attributes that can be specified in a profile entry to further qualify how this information should be persisted in `ASPNETDB.mdf`. Table 27-4 illustrates some of the core attributes.

Table 27-4. *Select Attributes of Profile Data*

Attribute	Example Values	Meaning in Life
Name	String	A unique identifier for this property.
Type	*Primitive | User-defined type*	A .NET primitive type or class. Class names must be fully qualified (e.g., MyApp.UserData.ColorPrefs).
serializeAs	String | XML | Binary	Format of value when persisting in data store.
allowAnonymous	True | False	Restricts or allows anonymous access to this value. If set to false, anonymous users won't have access to this profile value.
Provider	String	The provider used to manage this value. Overrides the defaultProvider setting in web.config or machine.config.
defaultValue	String	Value to return if property has not been explicitly set.
readOnly	True | False	Restricts or allows write access.

We will see some of these attributes in action as we modify the current profile. For now, let's see how to access this data programmatically from within our pages.

Accessing Profile Data Programmatically

Recall that the whole purpose of the ASP.NET profile API is to automate the process of writing data to (and reading data from) a dedicated database. To test this out for yourself, update the UI of your `default.aspx` file with a set of `TextBoxes` (and descriptive `Labels`) to gather the street address, city, and state of the user. As well, add a `Button` type (named btnSubmit) and a final `Label` (named lblUserData) that will be used to display the persisted data, as shown in Figure 27-13.

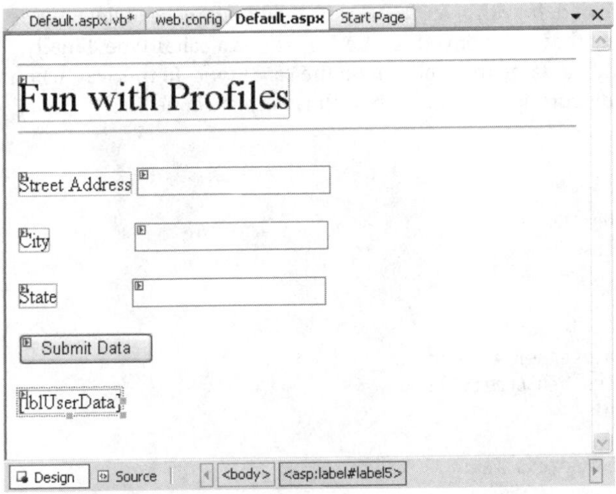

Figure 27-13. *The UI of the FunWithState* default.aspx *page*

Now, within the Click event hander of the button, make use of the inherited Profile property to persist each point of profile data based on what the user has entered in the related TextBox. As you can see from Figure 27-14, Visual Studio 2005 will expose each bit of profile data as a strongly typed property. In effect, the web.config file has been used to define a custom structure!

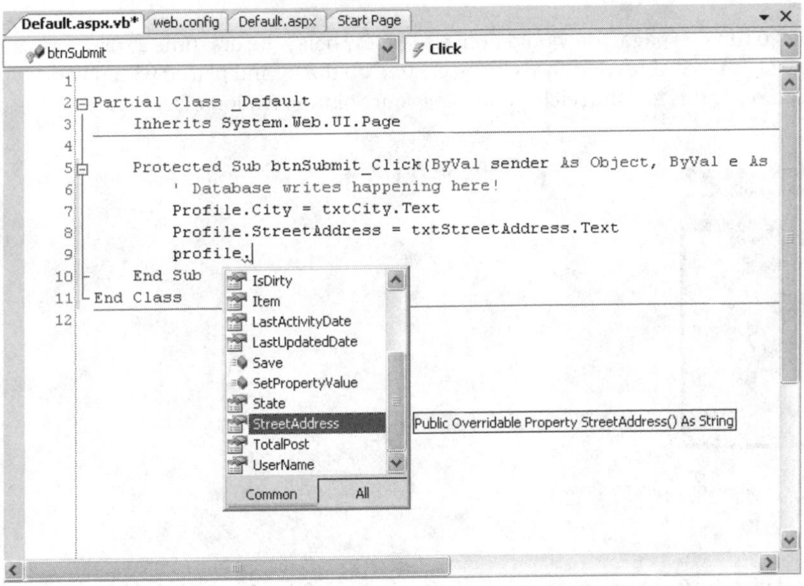

Figure 27-14. *Profile data is strongly typed*

Once you have persisted each piece of data within ASPNETDB.mdf, read each piece of data out of the database, and format it into a String that is displayed on the lblUserData Label type. Finally, handle the page's Load event, and display the same information on the Label type. In this way, when users come to the page, they can see their current settings. Here is the complete code file:

```
Partial Class _Default
  Inherits System.Web.UI.Page

  Protected Sub Page_Load(ByVal sender As Object, _
  ByVal e As System.EventArgs) Handles Me.Load
    GetUserAddress()
  End Sub

  Protected Sub btnSubmit_Click(ByVal sender As Object, _
  ByVal e As System.EventArgs) Handles btnSubmit.Click
    ' Database writes happening here!
    Profile.City = txtCity.Text
    Profile.StreetAddress = txtStreetAddress.Text
    Profile.State = txtState.Text

    ' Get settings from database.
    GetUserAddress()
  End Sub

  Private Sub GetUserAddress()
    ' Database reads happening here!
    lblUserData.Text = String.Format("You live here: {0}, {1}, {2}", _
        Profile.StreetAddress, Profile.City, Profile.State)
  End Sub
End Class
```

Now, if you were to run this page, you would notice a lengthy delay the first time default.aspx is requested. The reason: the ASPNETDB.mdf file is being created on the fly and placed within your App_Data file. You can verify this for yourself by refreshing your Solution Explorer (see Figure 27-15).

Figure 27-15. *Behold!* ASPNETDB.mdf

You will also find that the first time you come to this page, the lblUserData Label does not display any profile data, as you have not yet entered your data into the correct table of ASPNETDB.mdf. Once you enter values in the TextBox controls and post back to the server, you will find this Label is formatted with the persisted data, as shown in Figure 27-16.

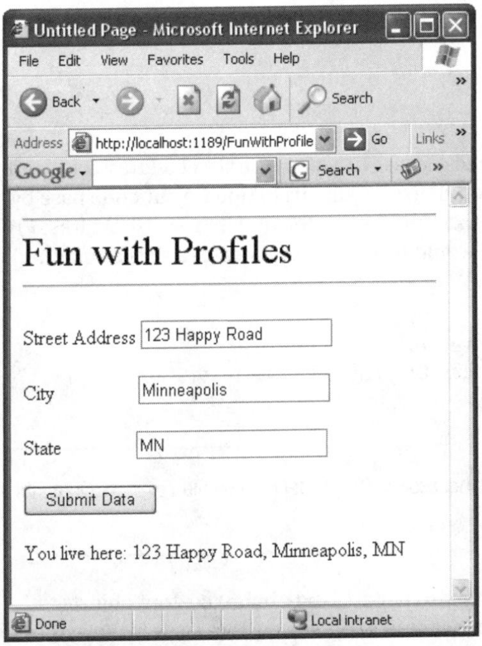

Figure 27-16. *Our persisted user data*

Now, for the really interesting aspect of this technology. If you were to shut down your browser and rerun your website, you will find that your previously entered profile data has indeed been persisted, as the Label displays the correct information. This begs the following obvious question: How were you remembered?

For this example, the profile API made use of your Windows network identity, which was obtained by your current login credentials. However, when you are building public websites (where the users are not part of a given domain), rest assured that the profile API integrates with the Forms-based authentication model of ASP.NET and also supports the notion of "anonymous profiles," which allow you to persist profile data for users who do not currently have an active identity on your site.

■**Note** This text does not cover the details of ASP.NET security, so consult the .NET 2.0 Framework SDK documentation for further details.

Grouping Profile Data and Persisting Custom Objects

To wrap up this chapter, allow me to make a few additional comments on how profile data may be defined within a web.config file. The current profile simply defined four pieces of data that were exposed directly from the profile type. When you build more complex profiles, it can be helpful to group related pieces of data under a unique name. Consider the following update:

```
<profile>
  <properties>
    <group name ="Address">
      <add name="StreetAddress" type="String" />
      <add name="City" type="String" />
```

```
          <add name="State" type="String" />
      </group>
      <add name="TotalPost" type="Integer" />
  </properties>
</profile>
```

This time we have defined a custom group named Address to expose the street address, city, and state of our user. To access this data in our pages would now require us to update our code base by specifying Profile.Address to get each subitem. For example, here is the updated GetUserAddress() method (the Click event hander for the Button type would need to be updated in a similar manner):

```
Private Sub GetUserAddress()
  ' Database reads happening here!
  lblUserData.Text = String.Format("You live here: {0}, {1}, {2}", _
    Profile.Address.StreetAddress, Profile.Address.City, Profile.Address.State)
End Sub
```

Note A profile can contain as many groups as you feel is necessary. Simply define multiple <group> elements within your <properties> scope.

Finally, it is worth pointing out that a profile may also persist (and obtain) custom objects to and from ASPNETDB.mdf. To illustrate, assume that you wanted to build a custom class (or structure) that will represent the user's address data. The only requirement expected by the profile API is that the type be marked with the <Serializable> attribute. For example:

```
<Serializable()> _
Public Class UserAddress
  Public street As String
  Public city As String
  Public state As String
End Class
```

With this class in place, our profile definition can now be updated as follows (notice I removed the custom group, although this is not mandatory):

```
<profile>
  <properties>
    <add name="AddressInfo" type="UserAddress"  serializeAs ="Binary"/>
    <add name="TotalPost" type="Integer" />
  </properties>
</profile>
```

Notice that when you are adding <Serializable> types to a profile, the type attribute is the fully qualified named of the type being persisted. Thus, if you were adding an ArrayList to a profile, type would be set to System.Collections.ArrayList. As well, you can control how this state data should be persisted into ASPNETDB.mdf using the serializeAs attribute. As you will see from the Visual Studio 2005 IntelliSense, your core choices are binary, XML, or string data.

Now that we are capturing street address information as a custom class type, we would (once again) need to update our code base. For example:

```
Private Sub GetUserAddress()
  ' Database reads happening here!
  lblUserData.Text = String.Format("You live here: {0}, {1}, {2}", _
    Profile.AddressInfo.street, Profile.AddressInfo.city, _
    Profile.AddressInfo.state)
End Sub
```

To wrap things up for this chapter, it is worth pointing out that there is much more to the profile API than I have had space to cover here. For example, the Profile property actually encapsulates a type named ProfileCommon. Using this type, you are able to programmatically obtain all information for a given user, delete (or add) profiles to ASPNETDB.mdf, update aspects of a profile, and so forth.

As well, the profile API has numerous points of extensibility that can allow you to optimize how the profile manager accesses the tables of the ASPNETDB.mdf database. As you would expect, there are numerous ways to decrease the number of "hits" this database takes. I'll assume interested readers will consult the .NET Framework 2.0 SDK documentation for further details.

Summary

In this chapter, you rounded out your knowledge of ASP.NET by examining how to leverage the HttpApplication type. As you have seen, this type provides a number of default event handlers that allow you to intercept various application- and session-level events. The bulk of this chapter was spent examining a number of state management techniques. Recall that view state is used to automatically repopulate the values of HTML widgets between postbacks to a specific page. Next, you checked out the distinction of application-and session-level data, cookie management, and the ASP.NET application cache.

The remainder of this chapter exposed you to the ASP.NET profile API. As you have seen, this technology provides an out-of-the-box solution to the issue of persisting user data across sessions. Using your website's web.config file, you are able to define any number of profile items (including groups of items and <Seralizable> types) that will automatically be persisted into ASPNETDB.mdf.

CHAPTER 28

■■■

Understanding XML Web Services

Chapter 20 introduced you to the .NET remoting layer. As you have seen, this technology allows any number of .NET-savvy computers to exchange information across process and machine boundaries. While this is all well and good, one possible limitation of the .NET remoting layer is the fact that each machine involved in the exchange must have the .NET Framework installed, must understand the CTS, and must speak the same wire format (such as TCP).

XML web services offer a more flexible alternative to distributed application development. Simply put, an *XML web service* is a unit of code hosted by a web server that can be accessed using industry standards such as HTTP and XML. As you would guess, using neutral technologies, XML web services offer an unprecedented level of operating system, platform, and language interoperability.

In this final chapter, you will learn how to build XML web services using the .NET platform. Along the way, you will examine a number of related topics, such as discovery services (UDDI and DISCO), the Web Service Description Language (WSDL), and the Simple Object Access Protocol (SOAP). Once you understand how to build an XML web service, you will examine various approaches to generate client-side proxies that are capable of invoking "web methods" in a synchronous and asynchronous fashion.

The Role of XML Web Services

From the highest level, you can define an XML web service as a unit of code that can be invoked via HTTP requests. Unlike a traditional web application, however, XML web services are not (necessarily) used to emit HTML back to a browser for display purposes. Rather, an XML web service often exposes the same sort of functionality found in a standard .NET code library (e.g., crunch some numbers, fetch a DataSet, return stock quotes, etc.).

Benefits of XML Web Services

At first glance, XML web services may seem to be little more than just another remoting technology. While this is true, there is more to the story. Historically speaking, accessing remote objects required platform-specific (and often language-specific) protocols (DCOM, Java RMI, etc.). The problem with this approach is not the underlying technology, but the fact that each is locked into a specific (often proprietary) wire format. Thus, if you are attempting to build a distributed system that involves numerous operating systems, each machine must agree upon the packet format, transmission protocol, and so forth. To simplify matters, XML web services allow you to invoke members of a remote object using standard HTTP requests. To be sure, of all the protocols in existence today, HTTP is the one specific wire protocol that all platforms can agree on (after all, HTTP is the backbone of the World Wide Web).

Another fundamental problem with proprietary remoting architectures is that they require the sender and receiver to understand the same underlying type system. However, as I am sure you can agree, a Java arrayList has little to do with a .NET ArrayList, which has nothing to do with a C++ array. XML web services provide a way for unrelated platforms, operating systems, and programming languages to exchange information in harmony. Rather than forcing the caller to understand a specific type system, information is passed between systems via XML data representation (which is little more than a well-formatted string). The short answer is, if your operating system can go online and parse character data, it can interact with an XML web service.

■Note A production-level Microsoft .NET XML web service is typically hosted under IIS using a unique virtual directory. As explained in Chapter 25, however, as of .NET 2.0 it is now possible to load web content from a local directory (for development and testing purposes) using WebDev.WebServer.exe.

Defining an XML Web Service Client

One aspect of XML web services that might not be readily understood from the onset is the fact that an XML web service consumer is not limited to a web page. Console-based and Windows Forms–based clients (as well as a *.dll code library for that matter) can use a web service just as easily. In each case, the XML web service consumer indirectly interacts with the distant XML web service through an intervening proxy type.

An XML web service proxy looks and feels like the actual remote object and exposes the same set of members of the actual web service. Under the hood, however, the proxy's implementation code forwards requests to the XML web service using standard HTTP. The proxy also maps the incoming stream of XML back into .NET-specific data types (or whatever type system is required by the consumer application). Figure 28-1 illustrates the fundamental nature of XML web services.

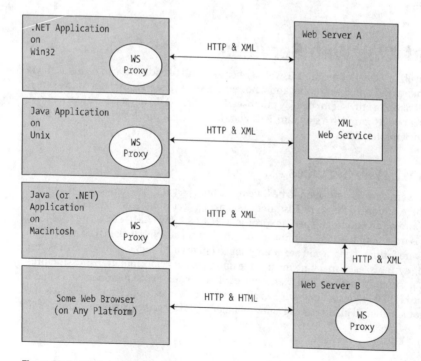

Figure 28-1. *XML web services in action*

The Building Blocks of an XML Web Service

In addition to the managed code library that constitutes the exposed functionality, an XML web service requires some supporting infrastructure. Specifically, an XML web service involves the following core technologies:

- A discovery service (so clients can resolve the location of the XML web service)
- A description service (so clients know what the XML web service can do)
- A transport protocol (to pass the information between the client and the XML web service)

We'll examine details behind each piece of infrastructure throughout this chapter. However, to get into the proper frame of mind, here is a brief overview of each supporting technology.

Previewing XML Web Service Discovery

Before a client can invoke the functionality of a web service, it must first know of its existence and location. Now, if you are the individual (or company) who is building the client and XML web service, the discovery phase is quite simple given that you already know the location of the web service in question. However, what if you wish to share the functionality of your web service with the world at large?

To do this, you have the option of registering your XML web service with a Universal Description, Discovery, and Integration (UDDI) server. Clients may submit requests to a UDDI catalog to find a list of all web services that match some search criteria (e.g., "Find me all web services having to do real-time weather updates"). Once you have identified a specific web server from the list returned via the UDDI query, you are then able to investigate its overall functionality. If you like, consider UDDI to be the yellow pages for XML web services.

In addition to UDDI discovery, an XML web service built using .NET can be located using DISCO, which is a somewhat forced acronym standing for *Discovery of Web Services*. Using static discovery (via a *.disco file) or dynamic discovery (via a *.vsdisco file), you are able to advertise the set of XML web services that are located at a specific URL. Potential web service clients can navigate to a web server's *.disco file to see links to all the published XML web services.

Understand, however, that dynamic discovery is disabled by default, given the potential security risk of allowing IIS to expose the set of all XML web services to any interested individual. Given this, I will not comment on DISCO services for the remainder of this text.

Previewing XML Web Service Description

Once a client knows the location of a given XML web service, the client in question must fully understand the exposed functionality. For example, the client must know that there is a method named GetWeatherReport() that takes some set of parameters and sends back a given return value before the client can invoke the method. As you may be thinking, this is a job for a platform-, language-, and operating system–neutral metalanguage. Specifically speaking, the XML-based metadata used to describe a XML web service is termed the *Web Service Description Language* (*WSDL*).

In a good number of cases, the WSDL description of an XML web service will be automatically generated by Microsoft IIS when the incoming request has a ?wsdl suffix appended to the URL. As you will see, the primary consumers of WSDL contracts are proxy generation tools. For example, the wsdl.exe command-line utility (explained in detail later in this chapter) will generate a client-side proxy class from a WSDL document.

For more complex cases (typically for the purposes of interoperability), many developers take a "WSDL first" approach and begin building their web services by defining the WSDL document manually. As luck would have it, the wsdl.exe command-line tool is also able to generate interface descriptions for an XML web service based on a WSDL definition.

Previewing the Transport Protocol

Once the client has created a proxy type to communicate with the XML web service, it is able to invoke the exposed web methods. As mentioned, HTTP is the wire protocol that transmits this data. Specifically, however, you can use HTTP GET, HTTP POST, or HTTP SOAP to move information between consumers and web services.

By and large, SOAP will be your first choice, for as you will see, SOAP messages can contain XML descriptions of complex types (including your custom types as well as types within the .NET base class libraries). On the other hand, if you make use of the HTTP GET or HTTP POST protocols, you are restricted to a more limited set of core data XML schema types.

The .NET XML Web Service Namespaces

Now that you have a basic understanding of XML web services, we can get down to the business of building such a creature using the .NET platform. As you would imagine, the base class libraries define a number of namespaces that allow you to interact with each web service technology (see Table 28-1).

Table 28-1. *XML Web Service–centric Namespaces*

Namespace	Meaning in Life
System.Web.Services	This namespace contains the core types needed to build an XML web service (including the all-important `<WebMethod>` attribute).
System.Web.Services.Configuration	These types allow you to configure the runtime behavior of a .NET XML web service.
System.Web.Services.Description	These types allow you to programmatically interact with the WSDL document that describes a given web service.
System.Web.Services.Discovery	These types allow a web consumer to programmatically discover the web services installed on a given machine.
System.Web.Services.Protocols	This namespace defines a number of types that represent the atoms of the various XML web service wire protocols (HTTP GET, HTTP POST, and SOAP).

■**Note** All XML web service–centric namespaces are contained within the System.Web.Services.dll assembly.

Examining the System.Web.Services Namespace

Despite the rich functionality provided by the .NET XML web service namespaces, the vast majority of your applications will only require you to directly interact with the types defined in System.Web.Services. As you can see from Table 28-2, the number of types is quite small (which is a good thing).

Table 28-2. *Members of the* System.Web.Services *Namespace*

Type	Meaning in Life
WebMethodAttribute	Adding the <WebMethod> attribute to a method or property in a web service class type marks the member as invokable via HTTP and serializable as XML.
WebService	This is an optional base class for XML web services built using .NET. If you choose to derive from this base type, your XML web service will have the ability to retain stateful information (e.g., session and application variables).
WebServiceAttribute	The <WebService> attribute may be used to add information to a web service, such as a string describing its functionality and underlying XML namespace.
WebServiceBindingAttribute	This attribute (new to .NET 2.0) declares the binding protocol a given web service method is implementing (HTTP GET, HTTP POST, or SOAP) and advertises the level of web services interoperability (WSI) conformity.
WsiProfiles	This enumeration (new to .NET 2.0) is used to describe the WSI specification to which a web service claims to conform.

The remaining namespaces shown in Table 28-1 are typically only of direct interest to you if you are interested in manually interacting with a WSDL document, discovery services, or the underlying wire protocols. Consult the .NET Framework 2.0 SDK documentation for further details.

Building an XML Web Service by Hand

Like any .NET application, XML web services can be developed manually, without the use of an IDE such as Visual Studio 2005. In an effort to demystify XML web services, let's build a simple XML web service by hand. Using your text editor of choice, create a new file named HelloWorldWebService.asmx (by convention, *.asmx is the extension used to mark .NET web service files). Save it to a convenient location on your hard drive (e.g., C:\HelloWebService) and enter the following type definition:

```
<%@ WebService Language="vb" Class="HelloService" %>
Imports System
Imports System.Web.Services

Public Class HelloService
  <WebMethod()> _
  Public Function HelloWorld() As String
    Return "Hello!"
  End Function
End Class
```

For the most part, this *.asmx file looks like any other VB 2005 class definition. The first noticeable difference is the use of the <%@WebService%> directive, which at minimum must specify the name of the managed language used to build the contained class definition and the fully qualified name of the class. In addition to the Language and Class attributes, the <%@WebService%> directive may also take a Debug attribute (to inform the ASP.NET compiler to emit debugging symbols) and an optional CodeBehind value that identifies the associated code file within the optional App_Code directory (see Chapter 25 for details regarding App_Code). In this example, you have avoided the use of a code-behind file and embedded all required logic directly within a single *.asmx file.

Beyond the use of the `<%@WebService%>` directive, the only other distinguishing characteristic of this *.asmx file is the use of the `<WebMethod>` attribute, which informs the ASP.NET runtime that this method is reachable via incoming HTTP requests and should serialize any return value as XML.

Note Only public members that are adorned with `<WebMethod>` are reachable by HTTP. Members not marked with the `<WebMethod>` attribute cannot be called by the client-side proxy.

Testing Your XML Web Service Using WebDev.WebServer.exe

Recall (again, from Chapter 25) that `WebDev.WebServer.exe` is a development ASP.NET web server that ships with the .NET platform 2.0 SDK. While `WebDev.WebServer.exe` would never be used to host a production-level XML web service, this tool does allow you to run web content directly from a local directory. To test your service using this tool, open a Visual Studio 2005 command prompt and specify an unused port number and physical path to the directory containing your *.asmx file:

```
WebDev.WebServer /port:1928 /path:"C:\HelloWebService"
```

Once the web server has started, open your browser of choice and specify the name of your *.asmx file exposed from the specified port:

```
http://localhost:1928/HelloWorldWebService.asmx
```

At this point, you are presented with a list of all web methods exposed from this URL, as shown in Figure 28-2.

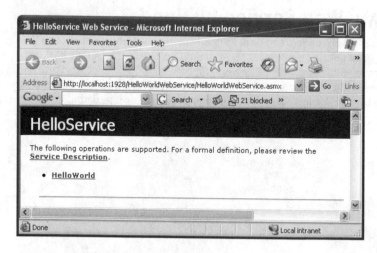

Figure 28-2. *Testing the XML web service*

If you click the HelloWorld link, you will be passed to another page that allows you to invoke the `<WebMethod>` you just selected. Once you invoke `HelloWorld()`, you will be returned not a literal .NET-centric `System.String`, but rather the XML data representation of the textual data returned from the `HelloWorld()` web method:

```
<?xml version="1.0" encoding="utf-8" ?>
<string xmlns="http://tempuri.org/">Hello!</string>
```

Testing Your Web Service Using IIS

Now that you have tested your XML web service using WebDev.WebServer.exe, you'll transfer your *.asmx file into an IIS virtual directory. Using the information presented in Chapter 25, create a new virtual directory named HelloWS that maps to the physical folder containing the HelloWorldWebService.asmx file. Once you do, you are able to test your web service by entering the following URL in your web browser:

```
http://localhost/HelloWS/HelloWorldWebService.asmx
```

Viewing the WSDL Contract

As mentioned, WSDL is a metalanguage that describes numerous characteristics of the web methods at a particular URL. Notice that when you test an XML web service, the autogenerated test page supplies a link named "Service Description." Clicking this link will append the token ?wsdl to the current request. When the ASP.NET runtime receives a request for an *.asmx file tagged with this suffix, it will automatically return the underlying WSDL that describes each web method.

At this point, don't be alarmed with the verbose nature of WSDL or concern yourself with the format of a WSDL document. For the time being, just understand that WSDL describes how web methods can be invoked using each of the current XML web service wire protocols.

The Autogenerated Test Page

As you have just witnessed, XML web services can be tested within a web browser using an autogenerated HTML page. When an HTTP request comes in that maps to a given *.asmx file, the ASP.NET runtime makes use of a file named DefaultWsdlHelpGenerator.aspx to create an HTML display that allows you to invoke the web methods at a given URL. You can find this *.aspx file under the following directory (substitute <version> with your current version of the .NET Framework, of course):

```
C:\Windows\Microsoft.NET\Framework\<version>\CONFIG
```

Providing a Custom Test Page

If you wish to instruct the ASP.NET runtime to make use of a custom *.aspx file for the purposes of testing your XML web services, you are free to customize this page with additional information (add your company logo, additional descriptions of the service, links to a help document, etc.). To simplify matters, most developers copy the existing DefaultWsdlHelpGenerator.aspx to their current project as a starting point and modify the original markup.

As a simple test, copy the DefaultWsdlHelpGenerator.aspx file into the directory containing HelloWorldWebService.asmx (e.g., C:\HelloWebService). Rename this copy to MyCustomWsdlHelpGenerator.aspx and update some aspect of the HTML, such as the <title> tag. For example, change this existing markup:

```
<title><%#ServiceName + " " + GetLocalizedText("WebService")%></title>
```

to the following:

```
<title>My Rocking <%#ServiceName + " " + GetLocalizedText("WebService")%></title>
```

Once you have modified the HTML content, create a web.config file and save it to your current directory. The following XML elements instruct the runtime to make use of your custom *.aspx file, rather than DefaultWsdlhelpGenerator.aspx:

```
<!-- Here you are specifying a custom *.aspx file -->
<configuration>
  <system.web>
    <webServices>
      <wsdlHelpGenerator href="MyCustomWsdlHelpGenerator.aspx" />
    </webServices>
  </system.web>
</configuration>
```

When you request your web service, you should see that the browser's title has been updated with your custom content. On a related note, if you wish to disable help page generation for a given web service, you can do so using the following <remove> element within the web.config file:

```
<!-- Disable help page generation -->
<configuration>
  <system.web>
    <webServices>
      <protocols>
        <!-- This element also disables WSDL generation -->
        <remove name="Documentation"/>
      </protocols>
    </webServices>
  </system.web>
</configuration>
```

Source Code The HelloWorldWebService files are included under the Chapter 28 subdirectory.

Building an XML Web Service Using Visual Studio 2005

Now that you have created an XML web service by hand, let's see how Visual Studio 2005 helps get you up and running. Using the File ➤ New ➤ Web Site menu option, create a new VB 2005 XML web service project named MagicEightBallWebService and save it to your local file system, as shown in Figure 28-3.

Once you click the OK button, Visual Studio 2005 responds by generating a Service.asmx file that defines the following <%@WebService%> directive:

```
<%@ WebService Language="vb"
CodeBehind="~/App_Code/Service.vb" Class="Service" %>
```

Note that the CodeBehind attribute is used to specify the name of the VB 2005 code file (placed by default in your project's App_Code directory) that defines the related class type. By default, Service.vb is defined as follows:

```
Imports System.Web
Imports System.Web.Services
Imports System.Web.Services.Protocols


<WebService(Namespace:="http://tempuri.org/")> _
<WebServiceBinding(ConformsTo:=WsiProfiles.BasicProfile1_1)> _
<Global.Microsoft.VisualBasic.CompilerServices.DesignerGenerated()> _
Public Class Service
  Inherits System.Web.Services.WebService
```

```
<WebMethod()> _
Public Function HelloWorld() As String
   Return "Hello World"
End Function
End Class
```

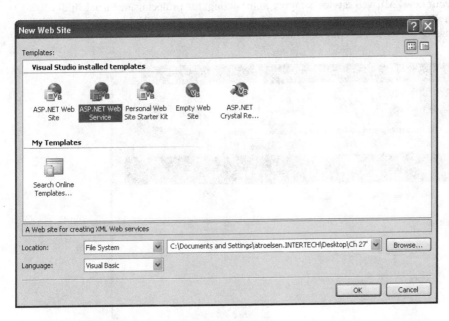

Figure 28-3. *Visual Studio 2005 XML Web Service project*

Unlike the previous HelloWorldWebService example, notice that the Service class now derives from the System.Web.Services.WebService base class. You'll examine the members defined by this type in just a moment, but know for now that deriving from this base class is entirely optional.

Also notice that the Service class is adorned with two (also optional) attributes named <WebService> and <WebServiceBinding>. Again, you'll examine the role of these attributes a bit later in this chapter.

■**Note** The <DesignerGenerated> attribute has nothing to do with your XML web service or how the CLR handles your *.asmx file. Rather, this attribute is used internally by the runtime compiler and can be safely deleted if you so choose.

Implementing the TellFortune() Web Method

Your MagicEightBall XML web service will mimic the classic fortune-telling toy. To do so, add the following new method to your Service class (feel free to delete the existing HelloWorld() web method):

```
<WebMethod> _
Public Function TellFortune(ByVal userQuestion As String) As String
  Dim answers As String() = {"Future Uncertain", "Yes", _
    "No", "Hazy", "Ask again later", "Definitely"}
```

```
' Return a random response to the question.
Dim r As Random = New Random
Return String.Format("{0}? {1}", _
    userQuestion, answers(r.Next(answers.Length)))
End Function
```

To test your new XML web service, simply run (or debug) the project using Visual Studio 2005. Given that the TellFortune() method requires a single input parameter, the autogenerated HTML test page provides the required input field (see Figure 28-4).

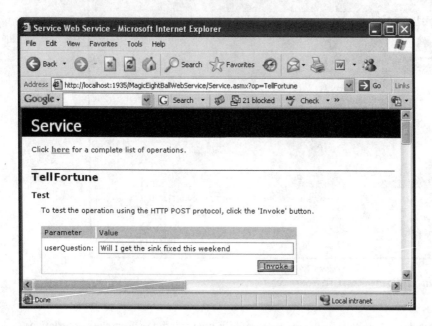

Figure 28-4. *Invoking the* TellFortune() *web method*

Here is a possible response to the question "Will I get the sink fixed this weekend":

```
<?xml version="1.0" encoding="utf-8" ?>
<string xmlns="http://tempuri.org/">
Will I get the sink fixed this weekend? Hazy
</string>
```

So, at this point you have created two simple XML web services: one by hand and the other using Visual Studio 2005. Now that you know the basics, we can dig into the specifics, beginning with the role of the WebService base class.

───

■**Source Code** The MagicEightBallWebService files are included under the Chapter 28 subdirectory.

───

The Role of the WebService Base Class

As you saw during the development of the HelloWorldWebService service, a web service can derive directly from System.Object. However, by default, web services developed using Visual Studio 2005 automatically derive from the System.Web.Service.WebService base class. Table 28-3 documents the core members of this class type.

Table 28-3. *Key Members of the* System.Web.Services.WebService *Type*

Property	Meaning in Life
Application	Provides access to the HttpApplicationState object for the current HTTP request
Context	Provides access to the HttpContext type that encapsulates all HTTP-specific context used by the HTTP server to process web requests
Server	Provides access to the HttpServerUtility object for the current request
Session	Provides access to the HttpSessionState type for the current request
SoapVersion	Retrieves the version of the SOAP protocol used to make the SOAP request to the XML web service; new to .NET 2.0

As you may be able to gather, if you wish to build a *stateful* web service using application and session variables (see Chapter 27), you are required to derive from WebService, given that this type defines the Application and Session properties. On the other hand, if you are building an XML web service that does not require the ability to "remember" information about the external users, extending WebService is not required. We will revisit the process of building stateful XML web services during our examination of the EnableSession property of the <WebMethod> attribute.

Understanding the <WebService> Attribute

An XML web service class may optionally be qualified using the <WebService> attribute (not to be confused with the WebService base class). This attribute supports a few named properties, the first of which is Namespace. This property can be used to establish the name of the XML namespace to use within the WSDL document.

As you may already know, XML namespaces are used to scope custom XML elements within a specific group (just like .NET namespaces). By default, the ASP.NET runtime will assign a dummy XML namespace of http://tempuri.org for a given *.asmx file. As well, Visual Studio 2005 assigns the Namespace value to http://tempuri.org by default via the <WebService> attribute.

Assume you have created a new XML web service project with Visual Studio 2005 named CalculatorService that defines the following two web methods, named Add() and Subtract():

```
<WebService(Namespace:="http://tempuri.org/")> _
<WebServiceBinding(ConformsTo:=WsiProfiles.BasicProfile1_1)> _
<Global.Microsoft.VisualBasic.CompilerServices.DesignerGenerated()> _
Public Class Service
  Inherits System.Web.Services.WebService
  <WebMethod()> _
  Public Function Add(ByVal a As Integer, ByVal b As Integer) As Integer
    Return a + b
  End Function
  <WebMethod()> _
  Public Function Subtract(ByVal a As Integer, ByVal b As Integer) As Integer
    Return a - b
  End Function
End Class
```

Before you publish your XML web service to the world at large, you should supply a proper namespace that reflects the point of origin, which is typically the URL of the site hosting the XML web service. In the following code update, note that the <WebService> attribute also allows you to set a named property termed Description that describes the overall nature of your web service:

```
<WebService(Namespace:="http://IntertechTraining.com/", _
    Description:="The Amazing Calculator Web Service")> _
<WebServiceBinding(ConformsTo:=WsiProfiles.BasicProfile1_1)> _
<Global.Microsoft.VisualBasic.CompilerServices.DesignerGenerated()> _
Public Class Service
...
End Class
```

The Effect of the Namespace and Description Properties

If you run the project, you will find that the warning to replace http://tempuri.org is no longer displayed in the autogenerated test page. Furthermore, if you click the Service Description link to view the underlying WSDL, you will find that the TargetNamespace attribute has now been updated with your custom XML namespace. Finally, the WSDL file now contains a <documentation> element that is based on your Description value:

```
<wsdl:documentation xmlns:wsdl="http://schemas.xmlsoap.org/wsdl/">
    The Amazing Calculator Web Service
</wsdl:documentation>
```

The Name Property

The final property of the WebServiceAttribute type is Name, which is used to establish the name of the XML web service exposed to the outside world. By default, the external name of a web service is identical to the name of the class type itself (Service by default). However, if you wish to decouple the .NET class name from the underlying WSDL name, you can update the <WebService> attribute as follows:

```
<WebService(Namespace:="http://IntertechTraining.com/", _
    Description:="The Amazing Calculator Web Service", _
    Name:="CalculatorWebService")> _
<WebServiceBinding(ConformsTo:=WsiProfiles.BasicProfile1_1)> _
<Global.Microsoft.VisualBasic.CompilerServices.DesignerGenerated()> _
Public Class Service
...
End Class
```

Figure 28-5 shows the test page generated by DefaultWsdlHelpGenerator.aspx based on the <WebService> attribute.

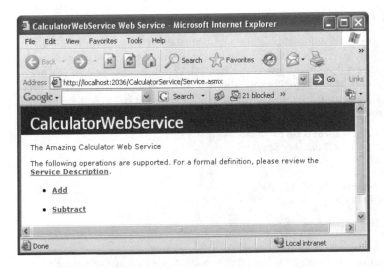

Figure 28-5. *The CalculatorWebService*

Understanding the <WebServiceBinding> Attribute

As of .NET 2.0, an XML web service can be attributed with <WebServiceBinding>. Among other things, this new attribute is used to specify whether the XML web service conforms to "Web services interoperability (WSI) basic profile 1.1." So, what exactly does that mean? Well, if you have been actively working with XML web services, you may know firsthand that one of the frustrating aspects of this technology is that early on, WSDL was an evolving specification. Given this fact, it was not uncommon for the same WSDL element (or attribute) to be interpreted in different manners across development tools (Visual Studio, WSAD), web servers (IIS, Apache), and architectures (.NET, J2EE).

Clearly this is problematic for an XML web service, as one of the motivating factors is to simplify the way in which information can be processed in a multiplatform, multi-architecture, and multilanguage universe. To rectify the problem, the WSI initiative offers a nonproprietary web services specification to promote the interoperability of web services across platforms. Under .NET 2.0, the ConformsTo property of <WebServiceBinding> can be set to any value of the WsiProfiles enumeration:

```
Public Enum WsiProfiles
  ' The web service makes no conformance claims.
  None
  ' The web service claims to conform to the
  ' WSI Basic Profile version 1.1.
  BasicProfile1_1
End Enum
```

By default, XML web services generated using Visual Studio 2005 are assumed to conform to the WSI basic profile 1.1 (BP 1.1). Of course, simply setting the ConformsTo named property to WsiProfiles. BasicProfile1_1 does not guarantee each web method is truly compliant. For example, one rule of BP 1.1 states that every method in a WSDL document must have a unique name (overloading of exposed web methods is not permitted under BP 1.1). The good news is that the ASP.NET runtime is able to determine various BP 1.1 validations and will report the issue at runtime.

Ignoring BP 1.1 Conformance Verification

As of .NET 2.0, XML web services are automatically checked against the WSI basic profile (BP) 1.1. In most cases, this is a good thing, given that you are able to build software that has the greatest reach possible. In some cases, however, you may wish to ignore BP 1.1 conformance (e.g., if you are building in-house XML web services where interoperability is not much of an issue). To instruct the runtime to ignore BP 1.1 violations, set the ConformsTo property to WsiProfiles.None and the EmitConformanceClaims property to False:

```
<WebService(Namespace:="http://IntertechTraining.com/", _
 Description:="The Amazing Calculator Web Service", _
 Name:="CalculatorWebService")> _
<Global.Microsoft.VisualBasic.CompilerServices.DesignerGenerated()> _
<WebServiceBinding(ConformsTo:=WsiProfiles.None, _
 EmitConformanceClaims:= False)> _
Public Class Service
...
End Class
```

As you might suspect, the value assigned to EmitConformanceClaims controls whether the conformance claims expressed by the ConformsTo property are provided when a WSDL description of the web service is published. With this, BP 1.1 violations will be permitted, although the autogenerated test page will still display warnings.

Disabling BP 1.1 Conformance Verification

If you wish to completely disable BP 1.1 verification for your XML web service, you may do so by defining the following <conformanceWarnings> element within a proper web.config file:

```
<configuration>
  <system.web>
    <webServices>
      <conformanceWarnings>
        <remove name='BasicProfile1_1'/>
      </conformanceWarnings>
    </webServices>
  </system.web>
</configuration>
```

Note The <WebServiceBinding> attribute can also be used to define the intended binding for specific methods via the Name property. Consult the .NET Framework 2.0 SDK documentation for further details.

Understanding the <WebMethod> Attribute

The <WebMethod> attribute must be applied to each method you wish to expose from an XML web service. Like most attributes, the WebMethodAttribute type may take a number of optional named properties. Let's walk through each possibility in turn.

Documenting a Web Method via the Description Property

Like the <WebService> attribute, the Description property of the <WebMethod> attribute allows you to describe the functionality of a particular web method:

```
Public Class Service
  Inherits System.Web.Services.WebService

  <WebMethod(Description:="Adds two integers.")> _
  Public Function Add(ByVal a As Integer, ByVal b As Integer) As Integer
    Return a + b
  End Function
  <WebMethod(Description:="Subtracts two integers.")> _
  Public Function Subtract(ByVal a As Integer, ByVal b As Integer) As Integer
    Return a - b
  End Function
End Class
```

Under the hood, when you specify the Description property within a <WebMethod> attribute, the WSDL contract is updated with a new <documentation> element scoped at the method name level:

```
<wsdl:operation name="Add">
  <wsdl:documentation xmlns:wsdl="http://schemas.xmlsoap.org/wsdl/">
    Adds two integers.
  </wsdl:documentation>
  <wsdl:input message="tns:AddSoapIn" />
  <wsdl:output message="tns:AddSoapOut" />
</wsdl:operation>
```

Avoiding WSDL Name Clashes via the MessageName Property

One of the rules of WSI BP 1.1 is that each method within a WSDL document must be unique. Therefore, if you wish your XML web services to conform to BP 1.1, you should not overload public methods adorned with the <WebMethod> attribute in your implementation logic. For the sake of argument, however, assume that you have overloaded the Add() method so that the caller can pass two Integer or Double data types. You would find the following runtime error:

```
Both Single Add(Single, Single) and Int32 Add(Int32, Int32)
use the message name 'Add'. Use the MessageName property
attribute to specify unique of the WebMethod
custom message names for the methods.
```

Again, the best approach is to simply not overload the Add() method in the first place. If you must do so, the MessageName property of the <WebMethod> attribute can be used to resolve name clashes in your WSDL documents:

```
Public Class Service
  Inherits System.Web.Services.WebService

  <WebMethod(Description:="Adds two doubles.", MessageName:="AddDoubles")> _
  Public Function Add(ByVal a As Double, ByVal b As Double) As Double
    Return a + b
  End Function

  <WebMethod(Description:="Adds two integers.", MessageName:="AddInts")> _
  Public Function Add(ByVal a As Integer, ByVal b As Integer) As Integer
    Return a + b
  End Function
...
End Class
```

Once you have done so, the generated WSDL document will internally refer to each overloaded version of Add() uniquely (AddDoubles and AddInts). As far as the client-side proxy code is concerned, however, there is only a single overloaded Add() method.

Building Stateful Web Services via the EnableSession Property

As you may recall from Chapter 27, the Application and Session properties allow an ASP.NET web application to maintain stateful data. XML web services gain the exact same functionality via the System.Web.Services.WebService base class. For example, assume your CalculatorService maintains an application-level variable (and is thus available to each session) that holds the value of PI, as shown here:

```
' This web method provides access to an app-level variable
' named SimplePI.
<WebMethod(Description:="Get the simple value of PI.")> _
Public Function GetSimplePI() As Double
  Return CType(Application("SimplePI"), Double)
End Function
```

The initial value of the SimplePI application variable could be established with the Application_Start() event handler defined in the Global.asax file. Insert a new global application class to your project (by right-clicking your project icon within Solution Explorer and selecting Add New Item) and implement Application_Start() as follows:

```
<%@ Application Language="VB" %>
<script runat="server">
  Sub Application_Start(ByVal sender As Object, ByVal e As EventArgs)
    Application("SimplePI") = 3.14
  End Sub
...
</script>
```

In addition to maintaining application-wide variables, you may also make use of Session to maintain session-centric information. For the sake of illustration, implement the Session_Start() method in your Global.asax to assign a random number to each user who is logged on:

```
<%@ Application Language="VB" %>
<script runat="server">
...
  Sub Session_Start(ByVal sender As Object, ByVal e As EventArgs)
    ' To prove session state data is available from a web service,
    ' simply assign a random number to each user.
    Dim r As New Random()
    Session("SessionRandomNumber") = r.Next(1000)
  End Sub
...
</script>
```

For testing purposes, create a new web method in your Service class that returns the user's randomly assigned value:

```
<WebMethod(EnableSession:=True, _
 Description:="Get your random number!")> _
Public Function GetMyRandomNumber() As Integer
  Return CType(Session("SessionRandomNumber"), Integer)
End Function
```

Note that the `<WebMethod>` attribute has explicitly set the `EnableSession` property to `True`. This step is not optional, given that by default each web method has session state *disabled*. If you were now to launch two or three browsers (to generate a set of session IDs), you would find that each logged-on user is returned a unique numerical token. For example, the first caller may receive the following XML:

```
<?xml version="1.0" encoding="utf-8" ?>
<int xmlns="http://www.IntertechTraining.com/WebServers">931</int>
```

while the second caller may find her value is 472:

```
<?xml version="1.0" encoding="utf-8" ?>
<int xmlns="http://www.IntertechTraining.com/WebServers">472</int>
```

Configuring Session State via Web.config

Finally, recall from Chapter 25 that a `web.config` file may be updated to specify where state should be stored for the XML web service using the `<sessionState>` element.

```
<sessionState
   mode="InProc"
   stateConnectionString="tcpip=127.0.0.1:42424"
   sqlConnectionString="data source=127.0.0.1;Trusted_Connection=yes"
   cookieless="false"
   timeout="20"
/>
```

■Source Code The CalculatorService files are included under the Chapter 28 subdirectory.

Exploring the Web Service Description Language (WSDL)

Over the last several examples, you have been exposed to partial WSDL snippets. Recall that WSDL is an XML-based grammar that describes how external clients can interact with the web methods at a given URL, using each of the supported wire protocols. In many ways, a WSDL document can be viewed as a contract between the web service client and the web service itself. To this end, it is yet another metalanguage. Specifically, WSDL is used to describe the following characteristics for each exposed web method:

- The name of the XML web methods
- The number of, type of, and ordering of parameters (if any)
- The type of return value (if any)
- The HTTP GET, HTTP POST, and SOAP calling conventions

In most cases, WSDL documents are generated automatically by the hosting web server. Recall that when you append the `?wsdl` suffix to a URL that points to an `*.asmx` file, the hosting web server will emit the WSDL document for the specified XML web service:

```
http://localhost/SomeWS/theWS.asmx?wsdl
```

Given that IIS will automatically generate WSDL for a given XML web service, you may wonder if you are required to deeply understand the syntax of the generated WSDL data. The answer typically depends on how your service is to be consumed by external applications. For in-house XML web services, the WSDL generated by your web server will be sufficient most of the time.

However, it is also possible to begin an XML web service project by authoring the WSDL document by hand (as mentioned earlier, this is termed the *WSDL first* approach). The biggest selling point for WSDL first has to do with interoperability concerns. Recall that prior to the WSI specification, it was not uncommon for various web service tools to generate incompatible WSDL descriptions. If you take a WSDL first approach, you can craft the document as required.

As you might imagine, taking a WSDL first approach would require you to have a very intimate view of the WSDL grammar, which is beyond the scope of this chapter. Nevertheless, let's get to know the basic structure of a valid WSDL document. Once you understand the basics, you'll better understand the usefulness of the wsdl.exe command-line utility.

Note To see the most recent information on WSDL, visit http://www.w3.org/tr/wsdl.

Defining a WSDL Document

A valid WSDL document is opened and closed using the root <definitions> element. The opening tag typically defines various xmlns attributes. These qualify the XML namespaces that define various subelements. At a minimum, the <definitions> element will specify the namespace where the WSDL elements themselves are defined (http://schemas.xmlsoap.org/wsdl). To be useful, the opening <definitions> tag will also specify numerous XML namespaces that define simple data WSDL types, XML schema types, SOAP elements, and the target namespace. For example, here is the <definitions> section for CalculatorService:

```
<?xml version="1.0" encoding="utf-8"?>
<wsdl:definitions xmlns:soap="http://schemas.xmlsoap.org/wsdl/soap/"
xmlns:tm="http://microsoft.com/wsdl/mime/textMatching/"
xmlns:soapenc="http://schemas.xmlsoap.org/soap/encoding/"
xmlns:mime="http://schemas.xmlsoap.org/wsdl/mime/"
xmlns:tns="http://www.IntertechTraining.com/"
xmlns:s="http://www.w3.org/2001/XMLSchema"
xmlns:soap12="http://schemas.xmlsoap.org/wsdl/soap12/"
xmlns:http="http://schemas.xmlsoap.org/wsdl/http/"
targetNamespace="http://www.IntertechTraining.com/"
xmlns:wsdl="http://schemas.xmlsoap.org/wsdl/">
...
</wsdl:definitions>
```

Within the scope of the root element, you will find five possible subelements. Thus, a bare-bones WSDL document would look something like the following:

```
<?xml version="1.0" encoding="utf-8"?>
<wsdl:definitions ...>
  <wsdl:types>
    <!-- List of types exposed from WS ->
  <wsdl:/types>
  <wsdl:message>
    <!-- Format of the messages ->
  <wsdl:/message>
  <wsdl:portType>
    <!-- Port information ->
  <wsdl:/portType>
  <wsdl:binding>
    <!-- Binding information ->
```

```
<wsdl:/binding>
<wsdl:service>
  <!-- Information about the XML web service itself ->
<wsdl:/service>
< wsdl:/definitions>
```

As you would guess, each of these subelements will contain additional elements and attributes to further describe the intended functionality. Let's check out the key nodes in turn.

The <types> Element

First, we have the <types> element, which contains descriptions of any and all data types exposed from the web service. As you may know, XML itself defines a number of "core" data types, all of which are defined within the XML namespace: http://www.w3.org/2001/XMLSchema (which appears in your <definitions> root element). For example, recall the Subtract() method of CalculatorService took two Integer parameters. In terms of WSDL, the CLR System.Int32 is described within a <complexType> element:

```
<s:element name="Subtract">
  <s:complexType>
    <s:sequence>
      <s:element minOccurs="1" maxOccurs="1" name="x" type="s:int" />
      <s:element minOccurs="1" maxOccurs="1" name="y" type="s:int" />
    </s:sequence>
  </s:complexType>
</s:element>
```

The Integer that is returned from the Subtract() method is also described within the <types> element:

```
<s:element name="SubtractResponse">
  <s:complexType>
    <s:sequence>
      <s:element minOccurs="1" maxOccurs="1" name="SubtractResult" type="s:int" />
    </s:sequence>
  </s:complexType>
</s:element>
```

If you have a web method that returns or receives custom data types, they will also appear within a <complexType> element. You will see the details of how to expose custom .NET data types via a given web method a bit later in this chapter. For the sake of illustration, assume you have defined a web method that returns a structure named Point:

```
Public Structure Point
  Public x As Integer
  Public y As Integer
  Public pointName As String
End Structure
```

The WSDL description of this "complex type" would look like the following:

```
<s:complexType name="Point">
  <s:sequence>
    <s:element minOccurs="1" maxOccurs="1" name="x" type="s:int" />
    <s:element minOccurs="1" maxOccurs="1" name="y" type="s:int" />
    <s:element minOccurs="0" maxOccurs="1" name="pointName" type="s:string" />
  </s:sequence>
</s:complexType>
```

The <message> Element

The <message> element is used to define the format of the request and response exchange for a given web method. Given that a single web service allows multiple messages to be transmitted between the sender and receiver, it is permissible for a single WSDL document to define multiple <message> elements. Typically, these message definitions use the types defined in the <types> element.

Regardless of how many <message> elements are defined within a WSDL document, they tend to occur in pairs. The first definition represents the input-centric format of the message, while the second defines the output-centric format of the same message. For example, the Subtract() method of CalculatorService is defined by the following <message> element:

```
<wsdl:message name="SubtractSoapIn">
  <wsdl:part name="parameters" element="tns:Subtract" />
</wsdl:message>
<wsdl:message name="SubtractSoapOut">
  <wsdl:part name="parameters" element="tns:SubtractResponse" />
</wsdl:message>
```

Here, you are only viewing the SOAP binding of the service. As you may recall from the beginning of this chapter, XML web services can be invoked via SOAP, HTTP GET, and HTTP POST. Thus, if you were to enable HTTP POST bindings (explained later), the generated WSDL would also show the following <message> data:

```
<wsdl:message name="SubtractHttpPostIn">
  <part name="n1" type="s:string" />
  <part name="n2" type="s:string" />
<wsdl:/message>
<wsdl:message name="SubtractHttpPostOut">
  <part name="Body" element="s0:int" />
<wsdl:/message>
```

In reality, <message> elements are not all that useful in and of themselves. However, these message definitions are referenced by other aspects of a WSDL document.

Note Not all web methods require both a request and response. If a web method is a one-way method, then only a request <message> element is necessary. You can mark a web method as a one-way method by applying the <SoapDocumentMethod> attribute.

The <portType> Element

The <portType> element defines the characteristics of the various correspondences that can occur between the client and server, each of which is represented by an <operation> subelement. As you might guess, the most common operations would be SOAP, HTTP GET, and HTTP POST. Additional operations do exist, however. For example, the one-way operation allows a client to send a message to a given web server but does not receive a response (sort of a fire-and-forget method invocation). The solicit/response operation allows the server to issue a request while the client responds (which is the exact opposite of the request/response operation).

To illustrate the format of a possible <operation> subelement, here is the WSDL definition for the Subtract() method:

```
<wsdl:portType name="CalculatorWebServiceSoap">
  <wsdl:operation name="Subtract">
    <wsdl:input message="tns:SubtractSoapIn" />
    <wsdl:output message="tns:SubtractSoapOut" />
  </wsdl:operation>
<wsdl:/portType>
```

Note how the `<input>` and `<output>` elements make reference to the related message name defined within the `<message>` element. If HTTP POST were enabled for the `Subtract()` method, you would find the following additional `<operation>` element:

```
<wsdl:portType name="CalculatorWebServiceHttpPost">
  <wsdl:operation name="Subtract">
    <wsdl:input message="s0:SubtractHttpPostIn" />
    <wsdl:output message="s0:SubtractHttpPostOut" />
  <wsdl:/operation>
<wsdl:/portType>
```

Finally, be aware that if a given web method has been described using the `Description` property, the `<operation>` element will contain an embedded `<documentation>` element.

The `<binding>` Element

This element specifies the exact format of the HTTP GET, HTTP POST, and SOAP exchanges. By far and away, this is the most verbose of all the subelements contained in the `<definition>` root. For example, here is the `<binding>` element definition that describes how a caller may interact with the `MyMethod()` web method using SOAP:

```
<wsdl:binding name="CalculatorWebServiceSoap12"
  type="tns:CalculatorWebServiceSoap">
  <soap12:binding transport="http://schemas.xmlsoap.org/soap/http" />
  <wsdl:operation name="Subtract">
    <soap12:operation soapAction="http://www.IntertechTraining.com/Subtract"
      style="document" />
    <wsdl:input>
      <soap12:body use="literal" />
    </wsdl:input>
    <wsdl:output>
      <soap12:body use="literal" />
    </wsdl:output>
  </wsdl:operation>
</wsdl:binding>
```

The `<service>` Element

Finally we have the `<service>` element, which specifies the characteristics of the web service itself (such as its URL). The chief duty of this element is to describe the set of ports exposed from a given web server. To do so, the `<services>` element makes use of any number of `<port>` subelements (not to be confused with the `<portType>` element). Here is the `<service>` element for CalculatorService:

```
<wsdl:service name="CalculatorWebService">
  <wsdl:documentation xmlns:wsdl="http://schemas.xmlsoap.org/wsdl/">
    The Amazing Calculator Web Service
  </wsdl:documentation>
  <wsdl:port name="CalculatorWebServiceSoap"
    binding="tns:CalculatorWebServiceSoap">
    <soap:address location="http://localhost:1109/CalculatorService/Service.asmx" />
  </wsdl:port>
  <wsdl:port name="CalculatorWebServiceSoap12"
    binding="tns:CalculatorWebServiceSoap12">
    <soap12:address location=
      "http://localhost:1109/CalculatorService/Service.asmx" />
  </wsdl:port>
</wsdl:service>
```

So, as you can see, the WSDL automatically returned by IIS is not rocket science, but given that WSDL is an XML-based grammar, it is a bit on the verbose side. Nevertheless, now that you have a better understanding of WSDL's place in the world, let's dig a bit deeper into the XML web service wire protocols.

■Note Recall that the `System.Web.Services.Description` namespace contains a plethora of types that allow you to programmatically manipulate raw WSDL (so check it out if you are so interested).

Revisiting the XML Web Service Wire Protocols

Technically, XML web services can use any RPC protocol to facilitate communication (such as DCOM or CORBA). However, most web servers bundle this data into the body of an HTTP request and transmit it to the consumer using one of three core bindings (see Table 28-4).

Table 28-4. *XML Web Service Bindings*

Transmission Binding	Meaning in Life
HTTP GET	GET submissions append parameters to the query string of the URL.
HTTP POST	POST transmissions embed the data points into the header of the HTTP message rather than append them to the query string.
SOAP	SOAP is a wire protocol that specifies how to submit data and invoke methods across the wire using XML.

While each approach leads to the same result (invoking a web method), your choice of wire protocol determines the types of parameters (and return types) that can be sent between each interested party. The SOAP protocol offers you the greatest flexibility, given that SOAP messages allow you to pass complex data types (as well as binary files) between the caller and XML web service. However, for completeness, let's check out the role of standard HTTP GET and POST.

HTTP GET and HTTP POST Bindings

Although GET and POST verbs may be familiar constructs, you must be aware that this method of transportation is not rich enough to represent such complex items as structures or classes. When you use GET and POST verbs, you can interact with web methods using only the types listed in Table 28-5.

Table 28-5. *Supported POST and GET Data Types*

Data Types	Meaning in Life
Enumerations	GET and POST verbs support the transmission of .NET `System.Enum` types, given that these types are represented as a static constant string.
Simple arrays	You can construct arrays of any primitive type.
Strings	GET and POST transmit all numerical data as a string token. *String* really refers to the string representation of CLR primitives such as `Int16`, `Int32`, `Int64`, `Boolean`, `Single`, `Double`, `Decimal`, and so forth.

By default, HTTP GET and HTTP POST bindings are not enabled for remote XML web service invocation. However, HTTP POST is enabled to allow a machine to invoke local web services (in fact, this is exactly what the autogenerated help page is leveraging behind the scenes). These settings are established in the machine.config file (see Chapter 13) using the <protocols> element. Here is a partial snapshot:

```
<!--  In the machine.config file! -->
<webServices>
  <protocols>
    <add name="HttpSoap1.2" />
    <add name="HttpSoap" />
    <add name="Documentation" />
    <!-- HTTP GET/POST disabled! -->
    <!-- <add name="HttpPost"/> -->
    <!-- <add name="HttpGet"/> -->
    <!-- Used by the web service test page -->
    <add name="HttpPostLocalhost" />
  </protocols>
</webServices>
```

To re-enable HTTP GET or HTTP POST for a given web service, explicitly add in the HttpPost and HttpGet names within a local web.config file:

```
<configuration>
  <system.web>
    <webServices>
      <protocols>
        <add name="HttpPost"/>
        <add name="HttpGet"/>
      </protocols>
    </webServices>
  </system.web>
</configuration>
```

Again, recall that if you make use of standard HTTP GET or HTTP POST, you are not able to build web methods that take complex types as parameters or return values (e.g., an ADO.NET DataSet or custom structure type). For simple web services, this limitation may be acceptable. However, if you make use of SOAP bindings, you are able to build much more elaborate XML web services.

SOAP Bindings

Although a complete examination of SOAP is beyond the scope of this text, understand that SOAP itself does not define a specific protocol and can thus be used with any number of existing Internet protocols (HTTP, SMTP, and others). The general role of SOAP, however, remains the same: provide a mechanism to invoke methods using complex types in a language- and platform-neutral manner. To do so, SOAP encodes each complex method with a SOAP message.

A SOAP message defines two core sections. First, we have the SOAP envelope, which can be understood as the conceptual container for the relevant information. Second, we have the rules that are used to describe the information in said message (placed into the SOAP body). An optional third section (the SOAP header) may be used to specify general information regarding the message itself, such as security or transactional information.

```
<soap:Envelope xmlns:xsi="http://www.w3.org/2001/XMLSchema-instance"
xmlns:xsd="http://www.w3.org/2001/XMLSchema"
xmlns:soap="http://schemas.xmlsoap.org/soap/envelope/">
  <soap:Header>
    <!-- Optional header information -->
  </soap:Header>
  <soap:Body>
    <!-- Method invocation information -->
  </soap:Body>
</soap:Envelope>
```

Viewing a SOAP Message

Although you are not required to understand the gory details of SOAP to build XML web services
with the .NET platform, you are able to view the format of the SOAP message for each exposed web
method using the autogenerated test page. For example, if you were to click the link for the Add()
method of CalculatorService, you would find the following SOAP 1.1 request:

```
<soap:Envelope xmlns:xsi="http://www.w3.org/2001/XMLSchema-instance"
xmlns:xsd="http://www.w3.org/2001/XMLSchema"
xmlns:soap="http://schemas.xmlsoap.org/soap/envelope/">
  <soap:Body>
    <Add xmlns="http://www.IntertechTraining.com ">
      <x>int</x>
      <y>int</y>
    </Add>
  </soap:Body>
</soap:Envelope>
```

The corresponding SOAP 1.1 response looks like this:

```
<soap:Envelope xmlns:xsi="http://www.w3.org/2001/XMLSchema-instance"
xmlns:xsd="http://www.w3.org/2001/XMLSchema"
xmlns:soap="http://schemas.xmlsoap.org/soap/envelope/">
  <soap:Body>
    <AddResponse xmlns="http://www.IntertechTraining.com ">
      <AddResult>int</AddResult>
    </AddResponse>
  </soap:Body>
</soap:Envelope>
```

The wsdl.exe Command-Line Utility

Now that you've completed a primer on WSDL and SOAP, let's begin to examine how to build client
programs that communicate with remote XML web services using the wsdl.exe command-line tool.
In a nutshell, wsdl.exe performs two major tasks:

- Generates a server-side file that functions as the skeleton for implementing an XML web
  service
- Generates a client-side file that functions as the proxy to a remote XML web service

wsdl.exe supports a number of command-line flags, all of which can be viewed at the command
prompt by specifying the -? option. Table 28-6 points out some of the more common arguments.

Table 28-6. *Select Options of* wsdl.exe

Command-Line Flag	Meaning in Life
/appsettingurlkey	Instructs wsdl.exe to build a proxy that does not make use of hard-coded URLs. Instead, the proxy class will be configured to read the URL from a client-side *.config file.
/language	Specifies the language to use for the generated proxy class: CS (C#; default), VB (Visual Basic 2005), JS (JScript), or VJS (Visual J#).
/namespace	Specifies the namespace for the generated proxy or template. By default, your type will not be defined within a namespace definition.
/out	Specifies the file in which to save the generated proxy code. If the file is not specified, the file name is based on the XML web service name.
/protocol	Specifies the protocol to use within the proxy code; SOAP is the default. However, you can also specify HttpGet or HttpPost to create a proxy that communicates using simple HTTP GET or POST verbs.
/serverInterface	Generates server-side interface bindings for an XML web service based on the WSDL document.

■**Note** The /server flag of wsdl.exe has been deprecated under .NET 2.0. /serverInterface is now the preferred method to generate server-side skeleton code.

Transforming WSDL into a Server-Side XML Web Service Skeleton

One interesting use of the wsdl.exe utility is to generate server-side skeleton code (via the /serverInterface option) based on a WSDL document. Clearly, if you are interested in taking a WSDL-first approach to building XML web services, this would be a very important option. Once this source code file has been generated, you have a solid starting point to provide the actual implementation of each web method.

Assume you have created a valid WSDL document (CarBizObject.wsdl) that describes a single subroutine named DeleteCar() that takes a single Integer as input. This method is exposed from an XML web service named CarBizObject, which can be invoked using SOAP bindings.

To generate a server-side VB 2005 code file from this WSDL document, open a .NET-aware command window and specify the /language and /serverInterface flags, followed by the name of the WSDL document you wish to process. Note that the WDSL document may be contained in a local *.wsdl file:

```
wsdl /serverInterface /language:VB CarBizObject.wsdl
```

or it can be obtained dynamically from a given URL via the ?wsdl suffix:

```
wsdl /serverInterface /language:VB http://localhost/CarService/CarBizObject.asmx?wsdl
```

Once wsdl.exe has processed the XML elements, you are presented with interface descriptions for each web method. Here is a partial code snippet:

```
Public Interface ICarBizObjectSoap
...
  Sub RemoveCar(ByVal carID As Integer)
End Interface
```

Using these interfaces, you can define a class that implements the various methods of the XML web service.

Source Code The `CarBizObject.wsdl` file is included under the Chapter 28 subdirectory.

Transforming WSDL into a Client-Side Proxy

Although undesirable, it is completely possible to construct a client-side code base that manually opens an HTTP connection, builds the SOAP message, invokes the web method via late binding, and translates the incoming stream of XML back into CTS data types. A much-preferred approach is to leverage `wsdl.exe` to generate a proxy class that maps to the web methods defined by a given `*.asmx` file.

To do so, you will specify (at a minimum) the name and implementation language of the proxy file to be generated (via the /out and /language flags) and the location of the WSDL document. You should also be aware that by default, `wsdl.exe` generates a proxy that communicates with the remote XML web service using SOAP bindings. If you wish to build a proxy that leverages straight HTTP GET or HTTP POST, you may make use of the /protocol flag.

Another important point to be made regarding generating proxy code via `wsdl.exe` is that this tool truly needs the *WSDL* of the XML web service, not simply the name of the `*.asmx` file. Given this, understand that if you make use of `WebDev.WebServer.exe` to develop and test your services, you will most likely want to copy your project's content to an IIS virtual directory before generating a client-side proxy.

For the sake of illustration, assume that you have created a new IIS virtual directory (CalcService), which contains the content for the CalculatorService project developed earlier in this chapter. Once you have done so, you can generate the client proxy code like so:

```
wsdl /out:proxy.vb /language:VB http://localhost/CalcService/Service.asmx?wsdl
```

As a side note, be aware that `wsdl.exe` will not define a .NET namespace to wrap the generated VB 2005 types unless you specify the /n flag at the command prompt:

```
wsdl /out:proxy.vb /language:VB /n:CalculatorClient
  http://localhost/CalcService/Service.asmx?wsdl
```

Examining the Proxy Code

If you open up the generated proxy file, you'll find a type that derives from `System.Web.Services.Protocols.SoapHttpClientProtocol` (unless, of course, you specified an alternative binding via the /protocols option):

```
Public Partial Class CalculatorWebService
  Inherits System.Web.Services.Protocols.SoapHttpClientProtocol
...
End Class
```

This base class defines a number of members leveraged within the implementation of the proxy type. Table 28-7 describes some (but not all) of these members.

Table 28-7. *Core Members of the* SoapHttpClientProtocol *Type*

Inherited Members	Meaning in Life
BeginInvoke()	This method starts an asynchronous invocation of the web method.
CancelAsync()	This method (new to .NET 2.0) cancels an asynchronous call to an XML web service method, unless the call has already completed.

Inherited Members	Meaning in Life
EndInvoke()	This method ends an asynchronous invocation of the web method.
Invoke()	This method synchronously invokes a method of the web service.
InvokeAsync()	This method (new to .NET 2.0) is the preferred way to synchronously invoke a method of the web service.
Proxy	This property gets or sets proxy information for making a web service request through a firewall.
Timeout	This property gets or sets the timeout (in milliseconds) used for synchronous calls.
Url	This property gets or sets the base URL to the server to use for requests.
UserAgent	This property gets or sets the value for the user agent header sent with each request.

The Default Constructor

The default constructor of the proxy hard-codes the URL of the remote web service and stores it in the inherited Url property:

```
Public Sub New()
  MyBase.New
  Me.Url = "http://localhost/CalcService/Service.asmx"
End Sub
```

The obvious drawback to this situation is that if the XML web service is renamed or relocated, the proxy class must be updated and recompiled. To build a more flexible proxy type, wsdl.exe provides the /appsettingurlkey flag (which may be abbreviated to /urlkey). When you specify this flag at the command line, the proxy's constructor will contain logic that reads the URL using a key contained within a client-side *.config file.

```
wsdl /out:proxy.vb /language:VB /n:CalcClient /urlkey:CalcUrl
  http://localhost/CalcService/Service.asmx?wsdl
```

If you now check out the default constructor of the proxy, you will find the following logic (note that if the correct key cannot be found, the hard-coded URL will be used as a backup):

```
Public Sub New()
  Dim urlSetting As String = _
    System.Configuration.ConfigurationManager.AppSettings("CalcUrl")
  If (Not (urlSetting Is Nothing)) Then
    Me.Url = urlSetting
  Else
    Me.Url = "http://localhost/CalcService/Service.asmx"
  End If
End Sub
```

The corresponding client-side app.config file will look like this:

```
<?xml version="1.0" encoding="utf-8" ?>
<configuration>
  <appSettings>
    <add key="CalcUrl" value="http://localhost/CalcService/Service.asmx"/>
  </appSettings>
</configuration>
```

Synchronous Invocation Support

The generated proxy also defines synchronous support for each web method. For example, the synchronous implementation of the Subtract() method is implemented as follows:

```
Public Function Subtract(ByVal x As Integer, ByVal y As Integer) As Integer
  Dim results As Object() = Me.Invoke("Subtract", New Object() {x, y})
  Return CType((results(0)), Integer)
End Function
```

Notice that the caller passes in two Integer parameters that are packaged as an array of System.Objects. Using late binding, the Invoke() method will pass these arguments to the Subtract method located at the established URL. Once this (blocking) call completes, the incoming XML is processed, and the result is cast back to the caller as Integer.

Asynchronous Invocation Support

Support for invoking a given web method asynchronously has changed quite a bit from .NET 1.*x*. As you might recall from previous experience, .NET 1.1 proxies made use of BeginXXX()/EndXXX() methods to invoke a web method on a secondary thread of execution. For example, consider the following BeginSubtract() and EndSubtract() methods:

```
Public Function BeginSubtract(ByVal x As Integer, ByVal y As Integer, _
  ByVal callback As System.AsyncCallback, _
  ByVal asyncState As Object) As System.IAsyncResult
  Return Me.BeginInvoke("Subtract", New Object() {x, y}, callback, asyncState)
End Function

Public Function EndSubtract(ByVal asyncResult As System.IAsyncResult) As Integer
  Dim results As Object() = Me.EndInvoke(asyncResult)
  Return CType((results(0)), Integer)
End Function
```

While wsdl.exe still generates these familiar Begin/End methods, under .NET 2.0 they have been deprecated and are replaced by the new XXXAsync() methods:

```
Public Sub SubtractAsync(ByVal x As Integer, ByVal y As Integer)
  Me.SubtractAsync(x, y, Nothing)
End Sub
```

These new XXXAsync() methods (as well as a related CancelAsync() method) work in conjunction with an autogenerated helper method (being an overloaded version of a specific XXXAsync() method) which handles the asynchronous operation using VB 2005 event syntax. If you examine the proxy code, you will see that wsdl.exe has generated (for each web method) a custom delegate, custom event, and custom "event args" class to obtain the result.

Building the Client Application

Now that you better understand the internal composition of the generated proxy, let's put it to use. Create a new console application named CalculatorClient, insert your proxy.vb file into the project using Project ➤ Add Existing Item, and add a reference to the System.Web.Services.dll assembly. Next, update your Main() method as follows:

```
Module Program
  Sub Main(ByVal args As String())
    Console.WriteLine("***** Fun with WS Proxies *****")
    Console.WriteLine()

    ' Make the proxy.
    Dim ws As CalculatorWebService = New CalculatorWebService()

    ' Call the Add() method synchronously.
    Console.WriteLine("10 + 10 = {0}", ws.Add(10, 10))

    ' Call the Subtract method asynchronously
    ' using the new .NET 2.0 event approach.
    AddHandler ws.SubtractCompleted, AddressOf ws_SubtractCompleted
    ws.SubtractAsync(50, 45)
    Console.ReadLine()
  End Sub

  Sub ws_SubtractCompleted(ByVal sender As Object, _
    ByVal e As SubtractCompletedEventArgs)
    Console.WriteLine("Your answer is: {0}", e.Result)
  End Sub
End Module
```

Notice that the new .NET 2.0 asynchronous invocation logic does indeed directly map to the VB 2005 event syntax, which as you might agree is cleaner than needing to work with BeginXXX()/EndXXX() method calls, the IAsyncResult interface, and the AsyncCallback delegate.

■**Source Code** The CalculatorClient project can be found under the Chapter 28 subdirectory.

Generating Proxy Code Using Visual Studio 2005

Although wsdl.exe provides a number of command-line arguments that give you ultimate control over how a proxy class will be generated, Visual Studio 2005 also allows you to quickly generate a proxy file using the Add Web Reference dialog box (which you can activate from the Project menu). As you can see from Figure 28-6, you are able to obtain references to existing XML web services located in a variety of places.

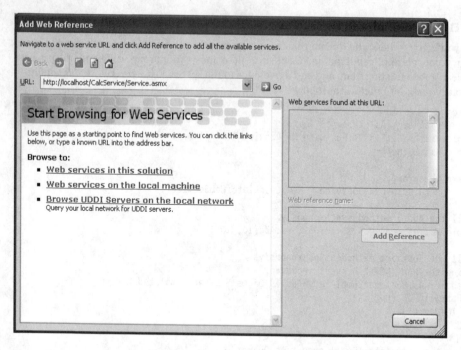

Figure 28-6. *The Add Web Reference dialog box*

Note The Add Web Reference dialog box cannot reference XML web services hosted with WebDev.WebServer.exe. This tool demands the web service be exposed from an IIS virtual directory.

Notice that not only are you able to obtain a list of XML web services on your local development machine, but you may also query various UDDI catalogs (which you'll do at the end of this chapter). In any case, once you type a valid URL that points to a given *.wsdl or *.asmx file, your project will contain a new proxy class. Do note that the proxy's namespace (which is based on the URL of origin) will be nested within your client's .NET namespace. Thus, if you have a client named MyClientApp that added a reference to a web service on your local machine, you would need to specify the following VB 2005 using directive:

```
Imports MyClientApp.localhost
```

Note As of Visual Studio 2005, the Add Web Reference dialog box automatically adds an app.config file to your project that contains the URL of the referenced XML web service or updates an existing app.config file.

Exposing Custom Types from Web Methods

In the final example of this chapter, you'll examine how to build web services that expose custom types as well as more exotic types from the .NET base class libraries. To illustrate this, you'll create a new XML web service that is capable of processing arrays, custom types, and ADO.NET DataSets. To begin, create a new XML web service named CarSalesInfoWS that is hosted under an IIS virtual directory (e.g., http://localhost/CarSalesInfoWS).

> **Note** Read that last sentence one more time. For this example, be sure to host your web service under IIS, given that this will allow us to use the VS 2005 proxy generator. See Chapter 25 for details on creating an IIS virtual directory.

Exposing Arrays

Update your Service class with a web method named GetSalesTagLines(), which returns an array of strings that represent the current specials for various automobiles, and another named SortCarMakes(), which allows the caller to pass in an array of unsorted strings and obtain a new array of sorted strings:

```
<WebMethod(Description:="Get current discount blurbs")> _
Public Function GetSalesTagLines() As String()
  Dim currentDeals As String() = {"Colt prices slashed 50%!", _
    "All BMWs come with standard 8-track", _
    "Free Pink Caravans...just ask me!"}
  Return currentDeals
End Function

<WebMethod(Description:="Sorts a list of car makes")> _
Public Function SortCarMakes(ByVal theCarsToSort As String()) As String()
  Array.Sort(theCarsToSort)
  Return theCarsToSort
End Function
```

> **Note** The default test page generated by DefaultWsdlHelpGenerator.aspx cannot invoke methods that take arrays of types as parameters.

Exposing Structures

The SOAP protocol is also able to transport XML representations of custom data types (both classes and structures). XML web services make use of the XmlSerializer type to encode the type as XML (see Chapter 19 for details). Recall that the XmlSerializer

- Cannot serialize private data. It serializes only public fields and properties.
- Requires that each serialized class provide a default constructor.
- Does not require the use of the <Serializable> attribute.

This being said, our next web method will return an array of SalesInfoDetails structures, defined like so:

```
' A custom type.
Public Structure SalesInfoDetails
  Public info As String
  Public dateExpired As DateTime
  Public Url As String
End Structure
```

Another point of interest regarding the XmlSerializer is the fact that it allows you to have fine-grained control over how the type is represented. By default, the SalesInfoDetails structure is serialized by encoding each piece of field data as a unique XML element:

```
<SalesInfoDetails>
  <info>Colt prices slashed 50%!</info>
  <dateExpired>2004-12-02T00:00:00.0000000-06:00</dateExpired>
  <Url>http://www.CarsRUs.com</Url>
</SalesInfoDetails>
```

If you wish to change this default behavior, you can adorn your type definitions using attributes found within the System.Xml.Serialization namespace (again, see Chapter 19 for full details):

```
Public Structure SalesInfoDetails
  Public info As String
  <XmlAttribute()> _
  Public dateExpired As DateTime
  Public Url As String
End Structure
```

This yields the following XML data representation:

```
<SalesInfoDetails dateExpired="2004-12-02T00:00:00">
  <info>Colt prices slashed 50%!</info>
  <Url>http://www.CarsRUs.com</Url>
</SalesInfoDetails>
```

The implementation of GetSalesInfoDetails() returns a populated array of this custom structure as follows:

```
<WebMethod(Description:="Get details of current sales")> _
Public Function GetSalesInfoDetails() As SalesInfoDetails()
  Dim theInfo(2) As SalesInfoDetails
  theInfo(0).info = "Colt prices slashed 50%!"
  theInfo(0).dateExpired = DateTime.Parse("12/02/04")
  theInfo(0).Url = "http://www.CarsRUs.com"
  theInfo(1).info = "All BMWs come with standard 8-track"
  theInfo(1).dateExpired = DateTime.Parse("8/11/03")
  theInfo(1).Url = "http://www.Bmws4U.com"
  theInfo(2).info = "Free Pink Caravans...just ask me!"
  theInfo(2).dateExpired = DateTime.Parse("12/01/09")
  theInfo(2).Url = "http://www.AllPinkVans.com"
  Return theInfo
End Function
```

Exposing ADO.NET DataSets

To wrap up your XML web service, here is one final web method that returns a DataSet populated with the Inventory table of the Cars database you created during our examination of ADO.NET in Chapter 24:

```
' Return all cars in inventory table.
<WebMethod(Description:= _
  "Returns all autos in the Inventory table of the Cars database")> _
Public Function GetCurrentInventory() As DataSet
  Dim sqlConn As SqlConnection = New SqlConnection
  sqlConn.ConnectionString = _
    "data source=localhost; initial catalog=Cars; uid=sa; pwd="
  Dim myDA As SqlDataAdapter = _
    New SqlDataAdapter("Select * from Inventory", sqlConn)
  Dim ds As DataSet = New DataSet
  myDA.Fill(ds, "Inventory")
  Return ds
End Function
```

■**Source Code** The CarsSalesInfoWS files can be found under the Chapter 28 subdirectory.

A Windows Forms Client

To test your new XML web service, create a Windows Forms application and reference CarsSalesInfoWS using the Visual Studio 2005 Add Web References dialog box shown in Figure 28-7.

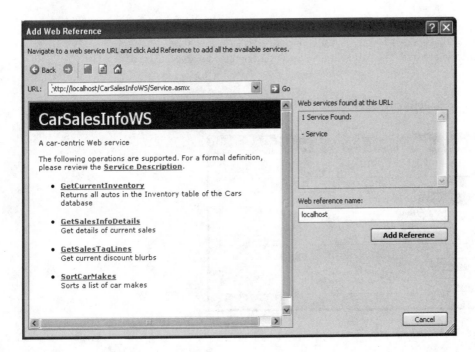

Figure 28-7. *Referencing CarsSalesInfoWS*

At this point, simply make use of the generated proxy to invoke the exposed web methods. Here is one possible Form implementation:

```
Imports CarSalesInfoClient.localhost

Public Class MainWindow
  Private ws As New CarSalesInfoWS

  Private Sub btnGetTagLines_Click(ByVal sender As System.Object, _
    ByVal e As System.EventArgs) Handles btnGetTagLines.Click
    Dim tagLines As String() = ws.GetSalesTagLines()
    For Each tag As String In tagLines
      listBoxTags.Items.Add(tag)
    Next
  End Sub
End Class
```

```
Private Sub btnGetAllDetails_Click(ByVal sender As System.Object, _
  ByVal e As System.EventArgs) Handles btnGetAllDetails.Click
  Dim theSkinny As SalesInfoDetails() = ws.GetSalesInfoDetails()
  For Each s As SalesInfoDetails In theSkinny
    Dim d As String = _
      String.Format("Info: {0} URL:{1} Expiration Date:{2} ", _
    s.info, s.Url, s.dateExpired)
    MessageBox.Show(d, "Details")
  Next
End Sub

Private Sub MainWindow_Load(ByVal sender As System.Object, _
  ByVal e As System.EventArgs) Handles MyBase.Load
  inventoryDataGridView.DataSource = ws.GetCurrentInventory.Tables(0)
End Sub
End Class
```

Figure 28-8 shows a possible test run.

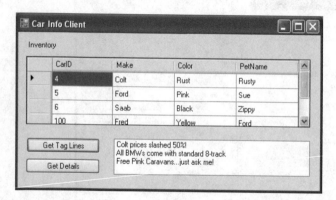

Figure 28-8. *The CarsSalesInfo client*

Client-Side Type Representation

When clients set a reference to a web service that exposes custom types, the proxy class file also contains language definitions for each custom public type. Thus, if you were to examine the client-side representation of SalesInfoDetails (within the generated Reference.vb file), you would see that each field has been encapsulated by a strongly typed property (also note that this type is now defined as a *class* rather than a structure):

```
Partial Public Class SalesInfoDetails
  Private infoField As String
  Private urlField As String
  Private dateExpiredField As Date

  Public Property info() As String
    Get
      Return Me.infoField
    End Get
    Set
      Me.infoField = value
    End Set
End Property
```

```
Public Property Url() As String
   Get
      Return Me.urlField
   End Get
   Set
      Me.urlField = value
   End Set
End Property

<System.Xml.Serialization.XmlAttributeAttribute()>  _
Public Property dateExpired() As Date
   Get
      Return Me.dateExpiredField
   End Get
   Set
      Me.dateExpiredField = value
   End Set
End Property
End Class
```

Now, understand, of course, that like .NET remoting, types that are serialized across the wire as XML do not retain implementation logic. Thus, if the SalesInfoDetails structure supported a set of public methods, the proxy generator will fail to account for them (as they are not expressed in the WSDL document in the first place!). However, if you were to distribute a client-side assembly that contained the implementation code of the client-side type, you would be able to leverage the type-specific logic. Doing so would require a .NET-aware machine, of course.

Source Code The CarSalesInfoClient projects can be found under the Chapter 28 subdirectory.

Understanding the Discovery Service Protocol (UDDI)

It is a bit ironic that the typical first step taken by a client to chat with a remote web service is the final topic of this chapter. The reason for such an oddball flow is the fact that the process of identifying whether or not a given web service exists using UDDI is not only optional, but also unnecessary in a vast majority of cases.

Until XML web services becomes the de facto standard of distributed computing, most web services will be leveraged by companies tightly coupled with a given vendor. Given this, the company and vendor at large already know about each other, and therefore have no need to query a UDDI server to see whether the web service in question exists. However, if the creator of an XML web service wishes to allow the world at large to access the exposed functionality to any number of external developers, the web service may be posted to a UDDI catalog.

UDDI is an initiative that allows web service developers to post a commercial web service to a well-known repository. Despite what you might be thinking, UDDI is not a Microsoft-specific technology. In fact, IBM and Sun Microsystems have an equal interest in the success of the UDDI initiative. As you would expect, numerous vendors host UDDI catalogs. For example, Microsoft's official UDDI website can be found at http://uddi.microsoft.com. The official website of UDDI (http://www.uddi.org) provides numerous white papers and SDKs that allow you to build internal UDDI servers.

Interacting with UDDI via Visual Studio 2005

Recall that the Add Web Reference dialog box allows you not only to obtain a list of all XML web services located on your current development machine (as well as a well-known URL), but also to submit queries to UDDI servers. Basically, you have the following options:

- Browse for a UDDI server on your company intranet.
- Browse the Microsoft-sponsored UDDI production server.
- Browse the Microsoft-sponsored UDDI test server.

Assume that you are building an application that needs to discover the current weather forecast on a per–zip code basis. Your first step would be to query a UDDI catalog with the following question:

- "Do you know of any web services that pertain to weather data?"

If it is the case that the UDDI server has a list of weather-aware web services, you are returned a list of all registered URLs that export the functionality of your query. Referencing this list, you are able to pick the specific web service you wish to communicate with and eventually obtain the WSDL document that describes the functionality of the weather-centric functionality.

As a quick example, create a brand-new console application project and activate the Add Web Reference dialog box. Next, select the Test Microsoft UDDI Directory link, which will bring you to the Microsoft UDDI test server. At this point, enter weather as a search criterion. Once the UDDI catalog has been queried, you will receive a list of all relevant XML web services. When you find an XML web service you are interested in programming against, add a reference to your current project. As you would expect, the raw WSDL will be parsed by the tool to provide you with a VB 2005 proxy.

Note Understand that the UDDI test center is just that: a test center. Don't be too surprised if you find a number of broken links. When you query production-level UDDI servers, URLs tend to be much more reliable, given that companies typically need to pay some sort of fee to be listed.

Summary

This chapter exposed you to the core building blocks of .NET web services. The chapter began by examining the core namespaces (and core types in these namespaces) used during web service development. As you learned, web services developed using the .NET platform require little more than applying the <WebMethod> attribute to each member you wish to expose from the XML web service type. Optionally, your types may derive from System.Web.Services.WebService to obtain access to the Application and Session properties (among other things). This chapter also examined three key related technologies: a lookup mechanism (UDDI), a description language (WSDL), and a wire protocol (GET, POST, or SOAP).

Once you have created any number of <WebMethod>-enabled members, you can interact with a web service through an intervening proxy. The wsdl.exe utility generates such a proxy, which can be used by the client like any other VB 2005 type. As an alternative to the wsdl.exe command-line tool, Visual Studio 2005 offers similar functionality via the Add Web Reference dialog box.

Index